Women's Lives

Multicultural Perspectives

Sixth Edition

Gwyn Kirk

Margo Okazawa-Rey

Mc
Graw
Hill

Connect
Learn
Succeed™

WOMEN'S LIVES: MULTICULTURAL PERSPECTIVES, SIXTH EDITION

Published by McGraw-Hill, a business unit of The McGraw-Hill Companies, Inc., 1221 Avenue of the Americas, New York, NY, 10020. Copyright © 2013 by The McGraw-Hill Companies, Inc. All rights reserved. Printed in the United States of America. Previous editions © 2010, 2007, and 2004. No part of this publication may be reproduced or distributed in any form or by any means, or stored in a database or retrieval system, without the prior written consent of The McGraw-Hill Companies, Inc., including, but not limited to, in any network or other electronic storage or transmission, or broadcast for distance learning.

Some ancillaries, including electronic and print components, may not be available to customers outside the United States.

This book is printed on acid-free paper.

2 3 4 5 6 7 8 9 0 QFR/QFR 1 0 9 8 7 6 5 4 3

ISBN 978-0-07-351234-1
MHID 0-07-351234-6

Senior Vice President, Products & Markets: *Kurt L. Strand*
Vice President, General Manager: *Michael Ryan*
Vice President, Content Production & Technology Services: *Kimberly Meriwether David*
Executive Director of Development: *Lisa Pinto*
Managing Director: *Gina Boedeker*
Marketing Specialist: *Alexandra Schultz*
Managing Development Editor: *Amy Mittelman*
Director, Content Production: *Terri Schiesl*
Project Manager: *Erin Melloy*
Buyer: *Nicole Baumgartner*
Media Project Manager: *Sridevi Palani*
Cover Designer: *Studio Montage, St. Louis, MO.*
Cover Image: *Courtesy of Steve Pitkin and Souls Grown Deep Foundation*
Typeface: *9/11 Palatino*
Compositor: *Cenveo Publisher Services*
Printer: *Quad/Graphics*

All credits appearing on page or at the end of the book are considered to be an extension of the copyright page.

Library of Congress Cataloging-in-Publication Data

Kirk, Gwyn, author.
  Women's lives: multicultural perspectives / Gwyn Kirk, Margo Okazawa-Rey. — Sixth Edition.
    pages cm
  ISBN 978-0-07-351234-1 (alk. paper)
  ISBN 0-07-351234-6 (alk. paper)
  1. Women—United States—Social conditions. 2. Women—United States—Economic conditions. 3. Feminism—United States. I. Okazawa-Rey, Margo, author. II. Title.
HQ1421.K573 2012
305.40973—dc23   2012034639

The Internet addresses listed in the text were accurate at the time of publication. The inclusion of a website does not indicate an endorsement by the authors or McGraw-Hill, and McGraw-Hill does not guarantee the accuracy of the information presented at these sites.

www.mhhe.com

To those who connect us to the past,
our mothers,
who birthed us, raised us,
taught us, inspired us, and took no nonsense from us
Edwina Davies, Kazuko Okazawa, Willa Mae Wells
and Eiko Matsuoka, our Bay Area mother.
To Aunty Yoko Lee who nurtures us now.
To those who connect us to the future
Jeju Daisy Ahn Miles
Charlotte Elizabeth Andrews-Briscoe
Irys Philippa Ewuraba Casey
Zion Neil Akyedzi Casey
Gabrielle Raya Clancy-Humphrey
Jesse Simon Cool
Issac Kana Fukumura-White
Akani Kazuo Ai Lee James
Ayize Kimani Ming Lee James
Hansoo Lim
Uma Talpade Mohanty
Camille Celestina Stovall-Ceja
Aya Sato Venet

Brief Contents

Contents

READINGS

CHAPTER TWO

◆◆◆

Theories and Theorizing: Integrative Frameworks for Understanding   51

READINGS

CHAPTER THREE

◆◆◆

Identities and Social Locations: Who Am I? Who Are My People? 101

◆ PART TWO ◆

OUR BODIES, OURSELVES

CHAPTER FOUR

◆◆◆

Women's Sexuality 173

CHAPTER FIVE

◆◆◆

Women's Bodies, Women's Health   209

CHAPTER SIX

◆◆◆

Violence Against Women   259

◆ PART THREE ◆

WOMEN'S PLACES: HOME AND WORK IN
A GLOBALIZING WORLD

CHAPTER SEVEN

◆◆◆

Making a Home, Making a Living   307

CHAPTER EIGHT

◆◆◆

Living in a Globalizing World   363

◆ **PART FOUR** ◆
SECURITY AND SUSTAINABILITY

CHAPTER NINE

◆◆◆

Women, Crime, and Criminalization   417

CHAPTER TEN

◆◆◆

Women and the Military, War, and Peace   465

CHAPTER ELEVEN

◆◆◆

Women and the Environment   503

◆ PART FIVE ◆
ACTIVISM AND CHANGE

CHAPTER TWELVE

◆◆◆

Creating Change: Theory, Vision, and Action 561

Preface

An introductory course is perhaps the most challenging women's and gender studies course to conceptualize and teach. Depending on their overall goals for the course, instructors must make difficult choices about what to include and what to leave out. Students come into the course for a variety of reasons and with a range of expectations and prior knowledge, and most will not major in women's studies. The course may fulfill a distribution requirement for them, or it may be a way of taking one course during their undergraduate education out of a personal interest in women's lives. For women's and gender studies majors and minors, the course plays a very different role, offering a foundation for their area of study.

Women's and gender studies programs continue to build their reputations in terms of academic rigor and scholarly standards. Women's and gender studies scholarship is on the cutting edge of many academic disciplines, especially in the arts, humanities, and social sciences. At the same time, it occupies a marginal position within academia, challenging male-dominated knowledge and pedagogy, with all the tensions that entails. Women's and gender studies faculty and our allies live with these tensions personally and professionally. Outside the academy, government policies and economic changes have made many women's lives more difficult in the United States—a loss of factory and office work as jobs continue to be moved overseas or become automated; government failure to introduce adequate health care and child care systems; cuts in welfare programs and funding for education; greater restriction of government support to immigrants and their families; a dramatic increase in the number of women now incarcerated compared with thirty years ago; and vast expenditures on war and preparations for war.

In the past decade, the political climate for women's and gender studies on campuses and in the wider society has become more challenging as conservative viewpoints have gained ground through political rhetoric, and the narrow range of public discourse. In addition, a questioning of academic freedom on campuses has made many teachers' lives more difficult. Moreover, the inequalities women in the United States still face, borne out by the data presented in this book, mean that teachers are often in the position of bearing "bad news."

This text started out as two separate readers that we used in our classes at Antioch College (Gwyn Kirk) and San Francisco State University (Margo Okazawa-Rey) in the mid-1990s. Since then, we have learned a lot about teaching an introductory women's studies course, and the book has grown and developed as a result.

What We Want in an Introductory Women's and Gender Studies Book

As teachers, we want to present a broad range of women's and trans people's experiences to our students in terms of class, race, culture, national origin, disability, age, and sexuality. We want teaching materials that do justice to the diversity of women's lives in this country. We also want materials that address the location of the United States in a globalizing world. In our introductory courses, we included some discussion of theory because a basic understanding of theoretical frameworks is a powerful tool not only for women's studies courses but also for other courses students take. We also emphasized women's activism. As women's and gender studies studies has become more established and professionalized, it has tended to grow away from its roots in women's liberation movements, a trend that troubled us. Our own activism has provided us with vital communities in which to learn, grow, and make a contribution to issues we care about. There are many women's activist and advocacy projects across the country, but students often do not know about them. Much of the information that students learn in women's and gender studies concerning the difficulties of women's and trans people's lives may be discouraging, but knowing about their activism can be empowering, even in the face of sometimes daunting realities. This knowledge reinforces the idea that current inequalities and problems are not fixed but have the potential to be changed.

Linking Individual Experiences to National and Transnational Trends and Issues

We are both trained in sociology. We noted that students coming into our classes were much more familiar with psychological explanations for behaviors and experiences than they were with structural explanations. They invariably enjoyed first-person accounts of experiences, but a series of stories—even wonderfully insightful stories—are not enough to understand the complex circumstances and forces that women face and that shape our lives. Accordingly, we provide a broader context for the selected readings in the overview essays that open each chapter.

We recognize that many women in the United States—especially those in higher socioeconomic groups—have greater opportunities for self-expression, for earning a living, and for engagement in the wider world compared with the past. However, we are concerned about the serious challenges facing women and men in the twenty-first century: challenges regarding work and livelihood, personal and family relationships, violence on many levels, and the mounting pressures on the fragile physical environment. These issues raise major questions about personal and societal values, the distribution of resources, and what constitutes everyday security and sustainability. How is our society going to provide for its people in the years to come? What are the effects of the increasing polarization between rich and poor in the United States

and between richer and poorer nations? These themes of security and sustainability provide the wider framework for this book.

As teachers we have been concerned with students' knowledge and understanding, and beyond that, with their aspirations, hopes, and values. One of our goals for this book is to provide a series of lenses that will help students understand their own lives and the lives of others. A second goal is that, through this understanding, they will be able to participate in some way in the creation of a genuinely secure and sustainable future.

New to the Sixth Edition

This sixth edition of *Women's Lives* relies on the analyses, principles, and style of earlier editions, but with substantial changes to take account of recent scholarship:

- A revised first chapter, "Untangling the "F"–word," provides a sampling of feminist thinking from different historical periods to highlight the diversity, breadth, richness, and dynamism of feminist ideas.

- An expanded chapter, "Identities and Social Locations," includes new readings on Arab American feminist experience, representations of mixed-race Asian Pacific Americans, and stronger emphasis on transgender identity.

- A revised chapter, "Women's Sexuality," includes a discussion of sexual freedom and new readings on "raunch" culture, dyke femininity, and the appeal of "bad boys."

- A revised chapter, "Women, Crime, and Criminalization," takes account of recent scholarship on mass incarceration, criminalization, and prison resistance, with new readings on women's experiences of incarceration and immigration detention.

- A revised chapter, "Women and the Environment," features new readings on environmental racism, and the politics of food, gender, and climate change.

- Other new readings concern cultural relativism and U.S. attitudes to Afghan women; men working against gender violence; violence against women in the U.S.-Mexico border region; the privileging of marriage; the transformation of young rural women in China into industrial workers in electronics factories; military rape in the Philippines; working on U.S. electoral campaigns; and transnational feminist organizing.

- Updated statistics are included throughout, with updated information on activist organizations, a revised glossary, and new photos.

- In our overview essays we cluster references on particular topics, often spanning a twenty-year period of feminist scholarship. As well as supporting the arguments we make, these also serve as suggestions for further reading.

- A revised and updated password-protected Instructor's Manual—including alternative Tables of Contents for flexible use of the book—is available on our companion Web site at www.mhhe.com/kirk6.

A number of considerations, sometimes competing or contradictory, have influenced the decisions we made to ensure this edition meets our goals. Since the beginning, we have been committed to including the work of established scholars and lesser-known writers from a range of backgrounds. As in previous editions, we have looked for writers who, implicitly or explicitly, integrate several levels of analysis (micro, meso, macro, and global) in their work. Students we have talked with, including those in our own classes, love first-person accounts because this kind of writing helps to draw them into more theoretical discussions. Teachers invariably want more theory, more history, and more research-based pieces. As we searched for materials, we have found much more theoretical work by white women than by women of color. We assume this is because there are fewer women of color in the academy, because white women scholars and writers have greater access to publishers, and because prevailing ideas about what theory is and what form it should take tend to exclude work by women of color. This can give the misleading impression that, aside from a few notable exceptions, women of color are not theorists. This raises the question of what theory is and who can theorize, which we take up in the second chapter. We have tried hard not to reproduce this bias in our selection, but we note this structural problem here to make this aspect of our process visible. We include personal essays and narratives that make theoretical points, what scholar

and writer Gloria Anzaldúa called "autohistoria-teoria"—a genre of writing about one's personal and collective history that may use fictive elements and that also theorizes. In a similar vein, people living in the United States have limited access to writings by and about women from countries of the global South, whether personal accounts, academic research, journalists' reports, policy recommendations, or critiques of policies imposed by countries of the North. A few scholars and fiction writers, working in English, are published widely. Again, structural limitations of the politics of knowledge affect who has access to book publishers or Web sites and whose work may be translated for English-language readers.

This new edition represents our best effort to balance these considerations as we sought to provide information, analysis, and inspiration concerning the myriad daily experiences, opportunities, limitations, oppressions, hopes, joys, and satisfactions that make up women's and trans people's lives. As before, our focus is on women in the United States, but also, in each chapter, we have a broader reach and give attention to the many ways that they are tied to and part of a globalizing world.

Acknowledgments

Many people—especially our students, teachers, colleagues, and friends—made it possible for us to complete the first edition of this book fifteen years ago. We are grateful to everyone at Mayfield Publishing who worked to put our original manuscript between covers: Franklin Graham, our editor, whose confidence in our ideas never wavered and whose light hand on the steering wheel and clear sense of direction got us into print; also Julianna Scott Fein, production editor; the production team; and Jamie Fuller, copyeditor extraordinaire. For the second edition we were fortunate to have the support of Hamilton College as Jane Watson Irwin Co-Chairs in Women's Studies (1999–2001). Women's studies colleagues, other faculty members, and librarians supported us, as did the Mayfield team: Serina Beauparlant, our editor; Julianna Scott Fein, production editor; the production team; and Margaret Moore, a wonderful copyeditor.

McGraw-Hill published the third edition. We benefited from support of the Women's Leadership

Institute at Mills College and the DataCenter, an Oakland-based nonprofit, providing research and training to grassroots social justice organizations across the country. Thanks to our editors Beth Kaufman and Sherith Pankratz and to Jean Mailander, Jen Mills, Karyn Morrison, Amy Shaffer, and April Wells-Hayes. For edition four, our editors were Kate Scheinman and Sherith Pankratz, with Cathy Iammartino, Jason Huls, Alex Ambrose, and Laurie Entringer on the production team. Editors Kate Scheinman and Gina Boedeker worked on the fifth edition, with Alison Meier, Allister Fein, Brian Pecko, and Tandra Jorgensen.

As before, this sixth edition builds on the accumulated work, help, and support of many people. Particular thanks go to Judith Arcana, Lina Hoshino, Debbie Lee, Albie Miles, Penny Rosenwasser, and Barbara Whitten for providing new material, information, and insights. We especially acknowledge Rickie Solinger for her invaluable insights and assistance in re-conceptualizing the Women, Crime, and Criminalization chapter, and suggesting important new materials. We thank the feminist scholars and activists whose work we have reprinted and all those whose research and writing not only have informed our work but have shaped the field of women's and gender studies. We appreciate the independent bookstores and small presses that keep going thanks to dedicated staff and loyal readers. We also rely on other feminist "institutions": the *Women's Review of Books, Ms.*, scholarly journals, and WMST-L. We have benefited enormously from discussions on this list and suggestions for readings and classroom activities generously shared by teachers.

We acknowledge the encouragement, enthusiasm, and skills of our managing editor, Gina Boedeker, and the work of the entire book team: Alexandra Schultz, Amy Mittelman, Sara Jaeger, Erin Melloy, Karyn Morrison, Nicole Baumgartner and Anupriya Tyagi. Once again we benefited from the insights and advice of reviewers:

Jeanne Gillespie- University of Southern Mississippi

Rachel Hallum-Montes- University of Florida

Mazie Hough-University of Maine

Sheila Katz-Sonoma State University

Alissa R. King-Iowa Central Community College

Anne E. Lacsamana-Hamilton College

Beverly R. Lomer-Florida Atlantic University

Katy Strzepek-St. Ambrose University

The world continues to gain brilliant young feminist writers, teachers, organizers, and artists—some of whose work is included here. We also acknowledge the groundbreaking contributions made by an older generation of feminists who are passing on. Particularly, we honor and remember internationally acclaimed poet Adrienne Rich (1929–2012) who died while this manuscript was in preparation. Her towering contribution to feminist thinking changed many people's lives, including ours. Among the huge compass of her work we note three pivotal essays: *Compulsory Heterosexuality and Lesbian Existence, The Politics of Location,* and *Women and Honor: Some Notes on Lying.*

We want to say a special thank you to Deep South Magazine, Steve Pitkin, and Souls Grown Deep Foundation for allowing us to use their photo of Lola Pettway's quilt from Gee's Bend, Alabama on the cover. Deep South Magazine was instrumental in acquiring this photo and we are grateful for their help. To find out more about Gee's Bend, Alabama, read Deep South Magazine's Article "The Future of Gee's Bend" at http://deepsouthmag.com/2012/04/the-future-of-gees-bend/.

Lastly, we acknowledge our friendship over nearly twenty years, which has provided a deep foundation for our shared understandings and our work together. We continue to be inspired by the "sociological imagination"—C. Wright Mills's concept—that draws on the need for complex social analysis in order to make change.

To everyone, very many thanks.

—Gwyn Kirk and Margo Okazawa-Rey

We have chosen each other
and the edge of each other's battles
the war is the same
if we lose
someday women's blood will congeal
upon a dead planet
if we win
there is no telling
we seek beyond history
for a new and more possible meeting.

—AUDRE LORDE

1

◆◆◆

Untangling the "F"-word

Whether or not you consider yourself a feminist as a matter of personal identity, in women's and gender studies courses you will study feminist perspectives because these seek to understand and explain inequalities based on gender. In a nutshell, feminism concerns the liberation of women and girls from gender-based discrimination. For some this means securing equal rights within existing institutions—such as marriage and the family, law, government policy, and the economy. For others it means fundamentally changing these institutions. For many, feminism has offered exciting ways to understand their lives, and feminist campaigns and projects have mobilized millions of people in this country for more than a century. Although gender inequalities remain, feminist thinking and activism have achieved significant gains.

In the last one hundred years, women in the United States have won the right to speak out on public issues, to vote, to own property in their own names, to divorce, and to have custody of their children; women's access has been expanded in higher education, the professions, and skilled manual trades. Developments in birth control have allowed women to choose to have fewer children; as a

result, family size is much smaller than it was in the early years of the twentieth century. Improved health care and better working conditions mean that women now live longer than ever before. We are freer to choose whether or not to marry and how to express our gender and sexuality. Women's wage rates are inching closer to men's. Domestic violence, rape, and sexual harassment are now public matters. Overall, women in the United States are more independent—economically and socially—than ever before.

Although public opinion about appropriate roles for women has shifted considerably over time, the term *feminism* carries a lot of baggage. For some, it is positive and empowering. For others, it conjures up negative images of women who do not wear makeup or shave their legs or underarms, white women, or women who are said to be lesbians or man-haters or both. Feminist ideas and goals have been consistently distorted, trivialized, and ridiculed by opponents in much media reporting. In the late nineteenth century, suffragists who campaigned for legal rights for women, including the right to vote, were caricatured as "mannish," "castrators," and "home-wreckers." A century later,

Time magazine published no less than 119 negative articles on feminism between the early 1970s and the mid-1990s (Jong 1998). TV evangelist Pat Robertson claimed that feminism "encourages women to leave their husbands, kill their children, and practice witchcraft." Rush Limbaugh commented, "Feminism was established to allow unattractive women easier access to the mainstream of society" (quoted in Douglas 2010, p. 17). Misogynist perspectives, justified as religious and moral beliefs, were a key part of the 2012 Republican primary race, as candidates denounced women's sexuality and rights to reproductive health.

Antifeminist ideas are a staple of right-wing talk shows. When women speak of gender-based violence—battering, incest, rape, sexual abuse, and harassment—or racism or living in poverty or aging without health insurance, detractors may describe them as "victim feminists" or "feminazis"— caricatured as antisex, no fun, whining critics who cannot take a joke and who are out to destroy men and the male establishment. In our society, women are socialized to care for men and to spare their feelings, but recognizing and discussing institutional inequalities between women as a group (even with all our diversity) and men as a group, are very different from "man-bashing."

Some opposition to feminist goals is very direct, such as aggressive picketing outside women's health centers, harassment of women using the centers' services, and the murder of doctors known to perform abortions. State and federal government policies concerning welfare, reproductive rights, budget priorities, and criminalization have eroded gains made for and by women. Feminist ideals have been co-opted by government, as when former President George W. Bush justified attacking Afghanistan and Iraq supposedly to save Muslim women. Some corporate decisions have had serious impacts on women's lives, such as selling subprime mortgages and creating high levels of unemployment. Sylvia Walby (2011, p. 25) describes a spiraling process: "as soon as some feminist goals are achieved, then there is new opposition," whether direct or subtle.

The claim that we are now living in a post-feminist era is part of this opposition. It involves a complex maneuver that recognizes the need for feminism in the past, but declares that this is now over because it has been successful. Nowadays, media critic Susan Douglas notes, "women's achievements, or their desire for achievement, are simply part of the cultural landscape" (2010, p. 9). However, she argues that many media images of women are

> images of imagined power that mask, even erase, how much still remains to be done for girls and women, images that make sexism seem fine, even fun, and insist that feminism is now utterly pointless—even bad for you. *(p. 6)*

Media makers and advertisers have taken "grrl power" or young women's desires for sexual agency, for example, and turned them into the notion that "[t]rue power comes from shopping, having the right logos and being 'hot'" (Douglas 2010, p. 6). The claim that the election of President Obama ushered in a postracial era in the United States rests on similar faulty reasoning and masks the reality of continued racial discrimination.

This book is concerned with the rich diversity of U.S. women's lives. In this chapter we introduce a sampling of women's efforts to understand and explain their very different realities. We have chosen readings from different historical periods to highlight the diversity, breadth, richness, and dynamism of feminist ideas. We hope these articles will also help to stimulate your thinking about how you define feminism and what it means to you.

Feminist Movements and Frameworks

Many historians and commentators have divided U.S. feminist movements into distinctive periods, described as waves. In this formulation, "first wave" denotes efforts to gain legal rights for women, including the right to vote, from the 1840s to 1920. "Second wave" refers to feminist organizing that flourished in the 1960s and '70s. In the 1990s, a younger generation of feminists described themselves as "third wave." Some challenged or rejected what they knew of the feminism associated with their mothers' generation; others emphasized continuities with earlier feminist work.

Defining historical periods is a highly selective process, focusing attention on certain events or perspectives and masking or erasing others. The wave metaphor suggests both continuity and discontinuity with the past as women have shaped theoretical understandings for their generation, circumstances, and time in history. This approach makes multifaceted movements—with their tensions, contradictions, and overlapping and divergent activities and theoretical strands—seem much neater, more unitary, and more static than they really are. This metaphor focuses on the activities and perspectives of white, middle-class feminists, which have come to dominate popular accounts of U.S. feminist history, repeated in media reports as accurate portrayals of much more complex movements. Historian Kathleen Laughlin notes: "The waves metaphor entrenches the perception of a 'singular' feminism in which gender is the predominate category of analysis" (Laughlin et al. 2010, p. 77). It leaves out large areas of women's activism, such as the nineteenth-century movements of women workers in the New England textile mills, Black[1] women's opposition to slavery and lynching, and work for economic improvement (see, e.g., Sacks 1976). Feminist historians have documented histories of women's activism for labor rights, civil rights, welfare rights, and immigrant rights, where gender is "tied to racial, class, religious, sexual, and other identities" (Boris 2010, p. 93).

Native American Antecedents

Among many possible paths into U.S. feminist thought, we chose Paula Gunn Allen's article about the "red roots of white feminism," which she grounded in centuries-old practices that gave Native American women policy-making power in the Iroquois Confederation, especially the power to decide matters of peace and war (Reading 1). She itemizes several traditional Native American principles that overlap with feminist ideals: the central place of women in society, an egalitarian distribution of goods and power, respect for elders, diverse ideas about beauty, cooperation among peoples,

[1]When referring to people we use Black rather than black. Black is an identity forged in the context of a struggle for self-respect. It replaced "negro" in a particular moment of self-assertion and carries that history with it. Capitalized, it's a proper noun, a name. Lower case, it's just an adjective. White does not carry the same connotations, except in the case of White racist organizations. Thus, because of the history of racism and race relations in this country, white and black are not equivalents.

and respect for the earth. She emphasizes the importance in her community of knowing one's ancestry and argues that "feminists must be aware of our history on this continent."

Campaigning for Legal Equality for Women

In the early decades of the nineteenth century women involved in the antislavery movement began to articulate parallels between systems of inequality based on race and gender. In 1840, Lucretia Mott and Elizabeth Cady Stanton—two white middle-class women from the United States—met at the World Anti-Slavery Convention in London. Both were passionately opposed to slavery and were shocked to find that women delegates were excluded from speaking at the convention (Schneir 1994). The irony of working against the system that enslaved people of African descent while experiencing discrimination as women gave them the impetus to work for women's rights. In 1848, they called a Women's Rights Convention at Seneca Falls, New York, where Stanton lived. Mott and Stanton led a small group in drafting the *Declaration of Sentiments and Resolutions* (Reading 2), modeled after the nation's foundational *Declaration of Independence*. This document, which was read out and adopted at the convention, rallied women and men to the cause of legal equality for women, and the issue was fiercely debated in newspaper articles and editorials, public meetings, churches, women's organizations, and at dinner tables nationwide.

Following the Civil War, three constitutional amendments—the thirteenth, fourteenth, and fifteenth amendments—allowed all men the right to vote but still permitted states to deny the vote to women. Suffragists split over whether to support the fifteenth amendment, which enfranchised Black men. The newly formed American Woman Suffrage Association, supported the fifteenth amendment, and campaigned for women's suffrage state by state. Wyoming was the first territory to give women the right to vote in 1869. Elizabeth Cady Stanton and Susan B. Anthony formed the National Woman Suffrage Association and worked for a constitutional amendment granting votes for women. In 1920, seventy-two years after the Seneca Falls convention, the nineteenth amendment to the U.S. Constitution barred states from denying women the right to vote. This ended a campaign that spanned the lives of generations of leaders and activists and included public education, lobbying, mass demonstrations, civil disobedience actions, arrests, and hunger strikes.

This campaign for legal equality grew out of **liberalism,** a theory about individual rights, freedom, choice, and privacy, with roots in seventeenth-century European political ideas (e.g., the writings of political philosopher John Locke). Liberalism has been central to U.S. political thinking since the founding of the nation, although political and legal rights were originally limited to white men who owned land and property. Achieving greater equality among people in this country has been a long, uneven process—marked by hard work, gains, and setbacks. Far from complete, this process continues to this day. Some key milestones are detailed in the box starting on page 10.

Liberal feminism is part of this liberal tradition and explains the oppression of women in terms of unequal access to political, economic, and social institutions (e.g., Eisenstein 1981; Friedan 1963; Steinem 1983). Much feminist organizing in the United States—including campaigns for women's right to vote, to own property, to divorce, to run for political office, and to enter universities and professions—has been based on this view. Many people hold liberal feminist opinions though they may not realize it. Despite the disclaimer, "I'm not a feminist . . ." the comment "but I *do* believe in equal pay" is a liberal feminist position. Liberal feminism may be criticized because it accepts existing institutions as they are, only seeking access for women within them. However, as the decades-long campaign for women's legal rights shows, this objective should not be underestimated, given the strength of **patriarchy,** or male dominance, as a system of power.

Resisting Interlocking Systems of Oppression

The Combahee River Collective, a group of Black feminists active in the Boston area in the 1970s, offered a very different view of feminism from their experiences of interlocking systems of oppression based on race, class, gender, and sexuality (Reading 3). As Black feminists and lesbians, collective members found many white feminists too focused on male domination at the expense of oppressions based on race and class. They also saw lesbian **separatism,** advocated by some white lesbians, as too limiting theoretically and in practice. Group members did not advocate equal rights for women within current institutions but saw the transformation of the political and economic system as fundamental to women's liberation. They defined themselves as **socialists** and believed that "work must be organized for the collective benefit of those who do the work and create the products, and not for the profit of the bosses," as expounded by German philosophers Frederick Engels and Karl Marx during the 1840s (shortly before the Seneca Falls Convention). Collective members offered a strong critique of **capitalism** and **imperialism,** and stood in solidarity with national liberation struggles then being waged in formerly colonized nations of Africa, Asia, and Central America.

Socialist feminism sees the oppression of women in terms of two interconnected and reinforcing systems, patriarchy and capitalism (see, e.g., Eisenstein 1979; Hartmann 1981; Hennessy and Ingraham 1997; Radical Women 2001; Roberts and Mizuta 1993; S. Smith 2005). Although the long cold war rivalry between the West and the (then) Soviet Union led to systematic discrediting socialist thinking in this country, a transnational feminist politics is both relevant and necessary today to understand the gendered effects of the world economic system, a point we take up in later chapters.

Theoretical perspectives that integrate gender with other systems of inequality have become known by the shorthand term, **intersectionality.** For African American women this idea has a long history. From the 1830s onward, Black speakers and writers like Frances E. W. Harper, Maria Stewart, and Sojourner Truth explicitly linked oppressions based on race and gender (Guy-Sheftall 1995). Writing in 1892, Anna Julia Cooper commented:

> The colored woman of today occupies . . . a unique position in this country. . . . She is confronted by both a woman question and a race problem, and is as yet an unknown or unacknowledged factor in both.
>
> *(quoted in Guy-Sheftall 1995, p. 45)*

A century later, organizer and writer Linda Burnham noted that

> Black women's experience as women is indivisible from their experiences as African Americans. They are always "both/and," so analyses that claim to examine gender while neglecting a critical stance towards race and class inevitably do so at the expense of African American women's experiences. *(2001, p. 1)*

Although acknowledging the "invaluable work of university-based theorists," Burnham noted that too many people "assume that the core concepts of Black feminism were born in the academy" (p. 1). She showed the importance of "struggle for social transformation as a powerful generator of theoretical insight," highlighting "the emergence of gender consciousness among Black women activists in the Student Non-Violence Coordinating Committee (SNCC)" through to organizations such as the Third World Women's Alliance and the Combahee River Collective (p. 4).

An integrative perspective that emphasizes intersectionality is not solely the prerogative of women of color. Since the writings of Aphra Behn in the early 1600s, some white women have been concerned with race and class as well as gender. White feminists worked against slavery in the nineteenth century; they organized against lynching and the activities of the Ku Klux Klan in the 1920s and '30s; and they participated in labor movements, the welfare rights movement, and the civil rights movements of the 1950s and 1960s (see, e.g., Bush 2004; Frankenberg 1993; Pratt 1984; Rich 1986c; Segrest 1994; Spelman 1988).

In Reading 4, sociologist Becky Thompson offers a nuanced history of "second-wave" feminism that includes alliances across lines of race and class. This is a much-needed counterbalance to the more limited accounts that focus on the perspectives and activities of white, middle-class feminists in the media spotlight such as Betty Friedan and Gloria Steinem (also see Baxandall and Gordon 2000; Laughlin et al. 2010; Moraga and Anzaldúa 1981; Roth 2003; Springer 2005). This article shows the inaccuracy of many media accounts of second-wave feminism that still circulate among students and younger activists, as well as among antifeminist reporters and commentators.

Radical Heterosexuality

Becky Thompson discusses the concept "radical"—concerned with roots or fundamentals—and suggests many ways that women in the United States have challenged the fundamentals of sexism, classism, racism, and imperialism. In Reading 5, Naomi Wolf uses this term to discuss intimate feminist relationships. She notes: "all over the country, millions of feminists have a secret indulgence. By day they fight gender injustice; by night they sleep with men. . . ." She asks, "Is sleeping with a man, 'sleeping with the enemy'?"

Many feminist thinkers have addressed the issue of sexuality as part of women's liberation. In 1873, Victoria Woodhull advocated "absolute and entire freedom" of sexuality for women (in Kolmar and Bartowski, 2010, p. 88). Margaret Sanger (1920) urged women to take responsibility for birth control as a way to personal freedom. Anne Koedt (1973) dismissed Freud's contention that vaginal orgasm is inherently superior and more mature than clitoral orgasm and noted: "The clitoris has no other function than that of sexual pleasure" (in Kolmar and Bartowski, 2010, p. 187). Such writers made personal matters, often considered private, even taboo, into public issues.

Feminists have engaged in heated debates about women's sexuality and the possibility of genuine sexual agency for women in patriarchal cultures, where sexuality is a site of both pleasure and danger (Vance 1984). Philosopher Marilyn Frye (1992) noted that

> the word *virgin* did not originally mean a woman whose vagina was untouched by any penis, but a free woman, one not betrothed, not married, not bound to, not possessed by any man. It meant a female who is sexually and hence socially her own person.   *(p. 133)*

Frye argued that radical feminist lesbians created ways of living out this kind of virginity, and asked whether this is also possible for heterosexual women. As she put it, "Can you fuck without losing your virginity?" (p. 136). Frye concluded that this is unlikely but conceded it may be possible if women are willing to be wild and undomesticated—sexually, socially, and politically. Naomi Wolf advocated what she called radical heterosexuality, recognizing that for this to be possible women would need financial independence; marriage would have to be very different; and both women and men would have to give up their "gender benefits."

Am I a Feminist?

In Reading 6, Mathangi Subramanian, whose parents emigrated to the United States from the south of India, asks, "What does feminism have to do with me?" In college she was exposed to several ideas about feminism but did not adopt this label until she found a feminism that resonated with her life and concerns, and the life of her family. Having assumed that feminism is a white, Western thing, incompatible with her South Asian identity, she was excited to discover the work of South Asian feminists like Chandra Talpade Mohanty (see Reading 10) that focused on "families and religion and food and history." Subramanian commented, "this feminism fit."

The six readings in this chapter provide a tiny sampling of the richness and complexity of feminist thought as a way to start the conversation about U.S. women's lives. We return to the issues they raise in subsequent chapters of this book.

The Focus and Challenge of Women's Studies

The early 1970s saw the start of many women's studies programs across the United States, building on the insights, energies, and activist commitments of the vibrant women's liberation movements of the times. Early courses had titles like "Women's Liberation," "The Power of Patriarchy," or "Sexist Oppression and Women's Empowerment." Texts often included mimeographed articles from feminist newsletters and pamphlets because there was so little appropriate material in books. By contrast, women's studies—more recently renamed gender studies in some colleges and universities—is now an established academic field with extensive bodies of literature and hundreds of programs in the United States and around the world, including master's and PhD programs. Women's studies graduates are employed in business, community organizing, education, electoral politics, feminist advocacy projects, filmmaking, health, international policy, journalism, law, library work, publishing, and social and human services (Luebke and Reilly 1995; Stewart 2007). Students have reported that women's and gender studies courses are informative and empowering; they provide a perspective on one's own life and on other college courses in ways that are often life changing.

Women's studies seeks new ways of understanding—more comprehensive than those offered by traditional academic disciplines. It started as a critique of scholarship that ignored women's lives or treated women in stereotypical ways. Women's studies sought to provide missing information, new theoretical perspectives, and new ways of teaching. Most women's studies teachers do not use what Brazilian educator Paulo Freire called the "banking method" of education, common in many fields, where students are like banks and teachers deposit information—historical facts, dates, definitions—and withdraw it in quizzes and exams. Regardless of its relevance for other subjects, this method is not appropriate for women's studies where students come into class with life experience, opinions, and insights into many of the topics discussed. Students are familiar with perspectives on issues that are circulating in the media, for example. They know where their spiritual community stands on matters they care about. In a women's studies class, students are encouraged to share and reflect on their experiences and to relate the readings and discussions to their own lives. Women's studies focuses on critical reading and critical thinking, which is a new way of learning for many students. It requires us to synthesize information and integrate diverse points of view, which are significant academic and workplace skills.

Women's studies courses provide data that are often absent in the rest of the curriculum. Students may be challenged to rethink some of their assumptions and experiences as well as their views on complex issues. This kind of study can evoke strong emotional reactions because students may be deeply affected by topics under discussion. Women's studies sometimes generates anger in students at the many forms of women's oppression, at other students' ignorance or lack of concern, at being female in a male-dominated world, and at the daunting nature of the issues and problems that women face (Boxer 1998; Howe 2000). These aspects of women's studies have given rise to criticisms that the discipline is too "touchy-feely" or that it is an extended gripe session against men, and we consider these criticisms below.

For several generations, the goals that dominated U.S. women's education concerned equality: to study alongside men, to have access to the same curriculum, and to be admitted to male professions. Beyond this, women's studies has called into question the gendered nature of knowledge itself, with its focus on white, male, middle-class perspectives that are deemed to be universal, as we discuss in the following chapter. Women's studies programs continue to build their reputation in terms of scholarly work and academic rigor. They occupy a contradictory position within academia, challenging male-dominated knowledge and pedagogy. Women's studies scholars are under pressure from the university system to undertake research and writing that meets "scholarly standards." This has meant that much published work is overly abstract and inaccessible to many readers. As women's studies has become more established and professionalized, it has tended to grow away from its movement roots. At the same time, women's studies remains marginalized and still under attack, as universities move closer to corporate goals, organizational styles, and funding priorities. As suggested earlier, many myths and misunderstandings about feminism and women's studies circulate on campuses and in the wider society. We consider three of these myths here.

Myth 1: Women's Studies Is Ideological

Some people assume that women's studies is not "real" scholarship but feminist propaganda.

Yet feminist inquiry, analysis, and activism have arisen from real problems experienced by real women, from well-researched inequalities and discrimination. For instance, data recorded for more than one hundred years show that, on average, U.S. women's wages for full-time year-round work have never risen above 77 percent of what men earn on average. Women earn 77 cents for every dollar earned by men. For African American women this is 62 cents and for Latinas 53 cents compared to white men.

Women's studies arose out of feminist thinking and activism and values scholarly work that is relevant to activist concerns. Women's studies courses and projects seek to link intellectual, experiential, and emotional forms of knowing with the goal of improving women's lives. Women's studies is a rigorous endeavor but its conception of rigor differs from that of much traditional scholarship, which values abstract, in-depth knowledge, narrowly defined, as discussed in Chapter 2. By contrast, women's studies scholarship places a high value on breadth and connectedness. This kind of rigor requires broad understandings grounded in diverse experiences and the ability to make connections between knowledge and insights from different perspectives and fields of study. Knowledge is never neutral, and in women's studies this is made explicit.

To some students and scholars, feminism is something to believe in because it provides perspectives that make sense of the world and is personally empowering. But students who blithely blame everything on "rich white men" or "the patriarchy" without taking the trouble to read and think critically are anti-intellectual; they limit their own understanding and inadvertently reinforce the notion that women's studies is anti-intellectual.

Myth 2: Women's Studies Is Narrowly Concerned with Women's Issues

Women's studies seeks to understand and explain women's diverse experiences and the significance of gender in the ordering of society, but we do not see this as narrow. On the contrary, feminist analyses provide a series of lenses to examine many topics and academic disciplines, including anthropology, cultural studies, economics, environmental studies, ethnic studies, film and media studies, health

Milestones in U.S. History: Institutionalizing and Challenging Social Inequalities

1565	Spanish settlers established the first European colony in what is now the state of Florida and called it St. Augustine.
1584	Walter Raleigh founded Virginia, an English colony, at Roanoke Island.
1605	A Spanish settlement was established at what is now Santa Fe, New Mexico.
1607	Captain Christopher Newport of the London Company established an English colony at Jamestown, Virginia.
1619	A Dutch "man of war" sailed into Jamestown harbor with 20 Africans on board; the captain sold his human cargo to the colonists.
1691	The first legal ban on interracial marriages was passed in Virginia. Subsequently, other states prohibited whites from marrying Blacks; marriages between whites and Native Americans, Filipinos, Asians, and Indians were forbidden specifically.
1776	The Second Continental Congress adopted the *Declaration of Independence*, written mostly by Thomas Jefferson, and asserting: "all men are created equal."
1787	The Constitution of the United States was sent to the states for ratification. Slaves were to be counted as 3/5 of a person in determining population and allocating numbers of representatives to Congress for each state; Indians were not to be counted or taxed; limitation on the slave trade was prohibited until 1808.
1820	Missouri entered the Union as the twelfth slave state "balanced" by Maine as the twelfth free state. Slavery was banned in the Louisiana Territory (purchased from France in 1803 for approximately $15 million).
1830	Congress passed a law moving all Indian tribes from the southeastern United States to land west of the Mississippi River and granting them rights to these new lands "in perpetuity."
1834	The Department of Indian Affairs was established within the War Department to monitor the creation of reservations for Indian tribes. The Department was later transferred to the Department of the Interior as the Bureau of Indian Affairs.

sciences, history, human biology, law, literature, national income accounting, philosophies of science, political science, psychology, and sociology. Feminist scholarship is on the cutting edge of many of these fields and raises crucial questions about teaching and learning, research design and methodologies, and theories of knowledge. Far from narrow, women's studies is concerned with thinking critically about the world in all its complexity.

Myth 3: Women's Studies is a White, Middle-Class, Western Thing

Many notable scholars, writers, and activists of color identify as feminists, among them Julia Alvarez,

Gloria Anzaldúa, Sandra Cisneros, Patricia Hill Collins, bell hooks, Aurora Levins Morales, Audre Lorde, Chandra Talpade Mohanty, and others included in this anthology. Their approach to feminism links analyses of gender with race, class, and other systems of power and inequality, as mentioned earlier. Two groundbreaking anthologies published in the early 1980s, *This Bridge Called My Back* (Moraga and Anzaldúa 1981) and *Home Girls* (B. Smith 1983), continue to be widely read alongside more recent feminist work by women of color (see, e.g., Arredondo et al. 2003; Green 2007, chs. 5 and 11; Rojas 2009; A. White 2010). African American writer and cultural critic bell hooks (2000) argued: "there should be billboards; ads in magazines; ads

1848   The Treaty of Guadalupe Hidalgo ended the Mexican-American War (begun in 1846). It established the Rio Grande as the international boundary; ceded Texas to the United States together with Arizona, California, Nevada, and New Mexico; and guaranteed existing residents their land, language, culture, and U.S. citizenship.

The first Women's Rights Convention was held in Seneca Falls, New York. Delegates issued a *Declaration of Sentiments,* listing inequities faced by women and urging that women be given the right to vote (see Reading 2).

1857   In *Dred Scott v. Sandford,* the Supreme Court argued that, as an enslaved man, Dred Scott was not a citizen, and therefore had no standing to sue his master for his freedom although he had been living in free territory for four years. To grant Scott's petition, the Court argued, would deprive his owner of property without compensation, violating the Fifth Amendment. This invalidated states' rights to determine whether slavery should be banned.

1863   Abraham Lincoln issued the Emancipation Proclamation freeing slaves in Alabama, Arkansas, Florida, Georgia, Louisiana, Mississippi, North Carolina, South Carolina, Tennessee, Texas, and Virginia.

1864   U.S. military forces terrorized Indian nations. Navajo people endured the "long walk" to imprisonment at Fort Sumner (New Mexico Territory). U.S. troops massacred Cheyenne warriors (supported by Kiowa, Apache, Comanche, and Arapahoe warriors) at Sand Creek (see Readings 12 and 34).

1865   Following the assassination of Abraham Lincoln, the Civil War was ended after four years. Congress established the Freedmen's Bureau, responsible for relief to former slaves and those made destitute by the war. The Thirteenth Amendment to the Constitution officially ended slavery and involuntary servitude.

on buses, subways, trains; television commercials spreading the word, letting the world know more about feminism" because "feminism is for everybody" (p. x).

Men Doing Feminism

It is important to acknowledge that women's studies students include a growing number of men. We are mindful that our readership includes male students and in places we pose questions and offer specific suggestions to them. Men can contribute to and support wider opportunities for women in many ways—as sons, brothers, fathers, partners, friends, coworkers, supervisors, labor organizers, spiritual leaders, teachers, doctors, lawyers, police officers, judges, and legislators. Sociologist Michael Kimmel calls for profeminist men to be cheerleaders, allies, and foot soldiers; "and we must be so in front of other men, risking our own fears of rejection, our own membership in the club of masculinity, confronting our own fears of other men" (in Kimmel and Messner 1998, p. 68). There is a long history of men's support for women's rights in the United States (see, e.g., Digby 1998; Kauffman and Kimmel 2011; Kimmel and Mosmiller 1992; Movement for a New Society 1983; Tarrant 2007), and training in women's studies can provide a powerful basis for this. In Chapter 6, readings by Jonathan Grove and Mimi Kim give examples of men refusing to be bystanders to acts of violence against women. Women cannot achieve the changes we discuss in this book without male allies.

Because masculinity is socially constructed and highly constrained in our society, we assume that there is something for men in feminism beyond being allies to women (see, e.g., Johnson 2005; Tarrant 2007). Those in dominant positions on any social dimension (gender, race, class, age, ability, and so forth) have obvious benefits and are also

1869	The first transcontinental railroad was completed. Chinese workers, allowed into the country to work on the railroad, experienced increased discrimination and "anti-Oriental" hysteria.
1870	Congress ratified the Fifteenth Amendment, which enfranchised Black men but permitted states to deny the vote to all women.
	Julia Ward Howe issued a *Mother's Day Proclamation* for peace (Reading 60).
1877	Ordered off their land in Oregon, the Nez Percé tribe attempted to flee to Canada, a trek of 1,600 miles, to avoid war with U.S. troops. They were forced to surrender 40 miles short of the border and sent to Oklahoma, where many died.
1887	Congress passed the Dawes Severalty Act, providing for the dissolution of Indian tribes and division of tribal holdings among the members. Over the next fifty years, white settlers took nearly two-thirds of Indian land holdings by deceit and intimidation (Reading 12).
1896	In *Plessy v. Ferguson*, the Supreme Court validated a Louisiana law requiring Blacks and whites to ride in separate railroad cars. The law had been challenged as a violation of the Fourteenth Amendment's right of equal protection, but the majority opinion held that "separate but equal" satisfied the constitutional requirement. This decision led to a spate of segregation laws in southern states. From 1870–1900, twenty-two Black men served in Congress. With the introduction of literacy tests, poll taxes, grandfather clauses, and white primaries, none were left by 1901.
1898	The United States declared war on Spain and acquired former Spanish colonial territories: the Philippines, Guam, Puerto Rico, and Cuba, including a military base at Guantanamo Bay, Cuba. Congress also approved U.S. annexation of the Hawaiian Islands.
1919	Suffragists were arrested in Washington, D.C. for blocking sidewalks

limited by these structures of power and inequality. Privilege separates people and makes us ignorant of important truths. To be able to look others in the eye openly and completely, to join together to create a secure and sustainable future for everyone, we have to work to end systems of inequality. This repudiation of privilege, we believe, is not a sacrifice but rather the possibility of entering into genuine community where we can all be more truly human.

The Framework for This Book: Collective Action for a Sustainable Future

There has been a spectacular groundswell of writing and publishing in the past forty years, as well as a proliferation of popular and scholarly books and journals on issues of interest to students of women's studies. When opinion polls, academic studies, government data, public debates, and grassroots research, available in print and through electronic media, are added, it is easy to be swamped with information and opposing viewpoints. In making our selections, as writers and editors, we have filtered this wealth of material according to four main principles—our particular road map.

1. A Matrix of Oppression, Privilege, and Resistance

Underlying our analysis is the concept of oppression, which we see as a group phenomenon, regardless of whether individuals in a group think they are oppressed or want to be in dominant positions. Men, as a group, are advantaged by sexism, whereas women, as a group, are disadvantaged. Every form of oppression—such as **sexism, racism, classism,** during a demonstration in support of women's right to vote.

Fifteen thousand Black people marched silently down New York's Fifth Avenue, protesting lynching and discrimination against Blacks.

The Jones Act granted full U.S. citizenship to Puerto Ricans and the right to travel freely to the continental United States.

1920   The Women's Suffrage Amendment (nineteenth) barred states from denying women the right to vote.

1924   The Indian Citizenship Act extended citizenship to Native Americans, previously defined as wards of the U.S. government. As late as 1952, some states still denied Indians voting rights.

1935   The National Labor Relations Act protected the right of workers to organize into unions.

The Social Security Act established entitlements to government assistance in the form of pensions and health benefit programs.

1941   U.S. Congress declared war on Japan, Italy, and Germany.

1942   President Roosevelt issued Executive Order 9066 permitting military authorities to evacuate 110,000 people of Japanese ancestry from west coast states (mostly U.S. citizens) and incarcerate them in isolated locations.

The Bracero Program permitted Mexican citizens to work in agricultural areas in the United States on a temporary basis and at lower wages than U.S. workers.

1945   World War II ended after the United States dropped atomic bombs on the Japanese cities of Hiroshima and Nagasaki.

heterosexism, anti-Arabism, anti-Semitism, able-bodyism**—is rooted in social institutions: the family, education, religion, government, law, and media. Oppression is systemic and it is systematic. It is used consistently by those who are dominant in this society to rule, control, and exploit (to varying degrees) another group—those who are subordinate—for the benefit of the dominant group.

Oppression works through systems of power and inequality, including the dominance of certain values, beliefs, and assumptions about people and how society should be organized. Members of dominant groups generally have built-in economic, political, and cultural power and benefits regardless of whether they are aware of, or even want, these advantages. This process of accruing benefits is often referred to as privilege. Those most privileged may be least likely to be aware of it or to recognize it (McIntosh 1988).

Oppression involves **prejudice,** which we define as unreasonable, unfair, and hostile attitudes toward people; and **discrimination,** differential treatment favoring those who are in positions of dominance. But oppression reaches beyond individual behavior; it is promoted by every social institution we encounter and are part of; and it cannot be fully changed without fundamental changes in institutional practices and **ideologies**—the ideas, attitudes, and values that institutions embody and perpetuate. Our definition of oppression assumes that everyone is socialized to participate in oppressive practices, thereby helping to maintain them. People may be involved as direct perpetrators or passive beneficiaries, or they may direct **internalized oppression** at members of their own group. Oppression results in appropriation and the loss—both voluntary and involuntary—of voice, identity, and agency of oppressed peoples.

It is important to think about oppression as an intricate system, at times blatantly obvious and at others subtly nuanced, rather than an either-or dichotomy of privileged/disadvantaged or oppressor/oppressed. People may be privileged in some respects (race or gender, for example) and disadvantaged in others (class or sexual orientation, for example). Allan Johnson discusses this in relation to the system of patriarchy in Reading 8. We use the term **matrix of oppression, privilege, and resistance**

1954	In *Brown v. Board of Education*, the Supreme Court reversed its *Plessy v. Ferguson* decision and declared that segregated schools were inherently unequal. In 1955 it ordered the desegregation of schools "with all deliberate speed."	1973	The Rehabilitation Act (Section 504) prohibited discrimination against people with disabilities in programs that receive federal financial assistance.
1963	The Equal Pay Act mandated that men and women doing the same work must receive the same pay. 250,000 people participated in a March on Washington to gain public support for a comprehensive civil rights law.	1975	The Individuals with Disabilities Education Act guaranteed children with disabilities a free, appropriate public education.
1964	Congress passed the most comprehensive Civil Rights Act in the history of the nation. Under Title VII, employment discrimination was prohibited on the basis of race, color, religion, sex, or national origin.	1982	The Equal Rights Amendment failed. It was ratified by 35 states, rather than the required minimum of 38 states. Subsequent efforts to revive this campaign have not been successful.
1965	The Voting Rights Act ended the use of literacy tests as a prerequisite for voting.	1990	The Americans with Disabilities Act prohibited discrimination on the basis of disability by employers, public accommodations, state and local governments, public and private transportation, and in telecommunications.
1972	Congress passed the Equal Rights Amendment and sent it to the states for ratification. It had been introduced in every session since 1923.	1994	The Violent Crime Control and Law Enforcement Act legislated mandatory life imprisonment for persons convicted in federal court of a "serious violent felony" and who had two or more prior convictions in federal or

to describe the interrelatedness of various forms of oppression; the fact that people may have privilege on certain dimensions and be disadvantaged on others; and to recognize both oppression and privilege as potentially powerful sources of resistance and change.

2. Linking the Personal and the Global

Throughout this book we use the terms **micro level** (personal or individual), **meso level** (community, neighborhood, or school), **macro level** (national or institutional), and **global level.** To understand people's experiences or the complexity of a particular issue, it is necessary to look at all these levels and how they interconnect. For instance, a personal relationship might be thought to operate on a micro level. However, both partners bring all of themselves to the relationship. Thus, in addition to individual factors such as looks, generosity, or

determination not to repeat the mistakes of our parents' relationships, there are meso-level factors—such as discrimination and segregation in housing, jobs, and social settings—and macro-level factors—such as the obvious or hidden ways in which men or white people are privileged in this society. As editors we have made connections between these levels of analysis in our overview essays and selected readings that also make these links.

We recognize the racial and ethnic diversity of this country and we argue that people in the United States need to understand the significance of this country's preeminence in the world. This is evident culturally through the dominance of the English language and in the widespread distribution of U.S. movies, news media, TV shows, music, books, magazines, and Web sites. It manifests economically through the power of the dollar as an international currency and the impact of U.S.-based corporations abroad.

state courts, at least one of which was a "serious violent felony" (the "three strikes" law). The other prior offense may be a "serious drug offense." States adopted similar laws.

1996   The Personal Responsibility and Work Opportunity Reconciliation Act replaced families' entitlement to government assistance with Temporary Assistance for Needy Families, a time-limited work-based program.

The Defense of Marriage Act forbade the federal government from recognizing same-sex or polygamous marriages under any circumstances and stipulated that no state, city, or county is required to recognize a marriage between persons of the same sex even if the marriage is recognized in another state.

2001   Uniting and Strengthening America by Providing Appropriate Tools Required to Intercept and Obstruct Terrorism

Act (USA Patriot Act) greatly increased law enforcement agencies' powers of detention, search, and surveillance. It permitted

- detention of non-citizens believed to endanger national security;
- definition of domestic groups as terrorist organizations;
- interception of "wire, oral, and electronic communications relating to terrorism";
- easier FBI access to records about a person that are maintained by a business;
- expanded use of secret searches;
- financial institutions to monitor daily transactions and academic institutions to share information about students.

Primary source: Aileen Hernandez (1975, 2002).
Also see A Timeline of Key U.S. Immigration Law and Policy (Chapter 3).

It is also apparent through the global reach of U.S. foreign policy, troops, and military bases. People in the United States need to understand the significance of the globalization of the economy and how it affects us as well as people of other nations. Although this is not a book about global feminism, we examine the global context within which the United States exercises power culturally, economically, politically, and militarily. We consider the consequences of U.S. policies on people in other nations: the flow of people, jobs, capital, and popular culture across national borders and the factors that facilitate, require, or prohibit such movements. We explore what it means in terms of identity, culture, family, and community to live in a globalizing world.

3. Linking the Head, Heart, and Hands

Women and men worldwide face a range of serious problems in the years ahead if we are to sustain our lives, the lives of our children, our children's

children, and the environment that supports all life forms. Although some women in the United States have benefited from greater opportunities for education and wage earning, many are now working harder or working longer hours than their mothers did, under pressure to keep a job and to juggle waged work with family responsibilities. Over the past forty years, various economic changes and government policies have made many women's lives more difficult. Examples include a loss of factory and office jobs as work has been moved overseas or become automated; government failure to introduce an adequate system of child care or an affordable health care system that benefits everyone; cuts in welfare programs; restrictions of government support to immigrants and their families; and a dramatic increase in the number of women incarcerated compared with the number from thirty years ago. According to the War Resisters League (2012), a massive 47 percent of federal income taxes is earmarked for military spending in fiscal year 2013. Some states spend more public money on incarceration than on higher education. At the same time, thousands of people are homeless, inner-city schools lack basic resources, and funding for a range of services from preschool programs to the Veteran's Administration has been cut back. Individual women and men are personally affected by such changes and policies as they negotiate personal relationships, raise children, and make a living for themselves and their families.

As these examples show, some of the material we present can be depressing. As a counter to this, in each chapter we mention effective and inspiring projects and organizations to give you a sense of how much activist work is going on that is often not visible in the mainstream media. We suggest that you find out more about these projects and organizations on the Web and also take action yourself. We see collective action for progressive social change as a major goal of scholarly work, and thus, in the face of these economic and political trends, we take a deliberately activist approach in this book. Creating change involves using our heads, hearts, and hands in ways that reinforce one another. Doing something about an issue requires us to have a theory, an explanation about it, together with vision and ideas of a different way of doing things, followed by action. We return to these ideas in the final chapter.

4. A Sustainable and Secure Future

We see sustainability and security as central issues for the twenty-first century, which raises questions about economic development and the distribution of wealth, both within the United States and among richer and poorer countries. Another major concern is the rapid deterioration of the physical environment on our overburdened planet. In many chapters security is an underlying theme. This includes the individual security of knowing who we are; having sturdy family relationships; living free from threats, violence, or coercion; having adequate income or livelihood; and enjoying health and well-being. It also involves security for communities, nations, and the planet, and includes issues such as crime, militarism, and environmental destruction. We see structural inequalities based on race, class, gender, and nation as a major threat to long-term security because they create literal and metaphorical walls, gates, and fences that separate people and maintain hierarchies among us. We argue that creating a more sustainable future means rethinking materialism and consumerism and finding new ways to distribute wealth so that everyone has the basics of life. These issues affect not only women, of course, and are not solely women's responsibility, but women are actively involved in community organizing and movements for economic and environmental justice in the United States and many other countries, often in greater numbers than men.

Throughout our discussion we emphasize the diversity of women's experiences. These differences have often divided women. We assume no easy "sisterhood" across lines of race, class, nation, age, or sexuality, but we do believe that alliances built on the recognition and understanding of such differences can make effective collective action possible.

The Scope of This Book

This book is concerned with theorizing about the oppressive conditions facing women today and the long-term work of transforming those conditions. In Part 1 (Chapters 1–3), we introduce examples of feminist thought in the United States; we argue for a theoretical framework that allows people to understand the significance of gender and the diversity of women's lives; and we discuss the role of identity and social location as standpoints for generating knowledge and understanding. Part 2 (Chapters 4–6) explores women's experiences of our bodies, sexuality, health, and gender-based violence. In Part 3 (Chapters 7–8), we look at what is involved in making a home and making a living, and how women's opportunities and experiences are shaped by global factors. In Part 4 (Chapters 9–11), we discuss U.S. women's experiences of crime and criminalization, militarism, and the impacts of environment degradation on women. In Part 5 (Chapter 12), we examine the importance of theories, visions, and actions for creating change.

In each chapter, we present data and theoretical perspectives, and also draw from personal narratives, government reports, journalists' accounts, and the work of nonprofit research and advocacy organizations. Our goal is to provide some his-torical and contemporary context for the read-ings, which have been selected to exemplify key points. Our overall argument is that improving the lives of women in the United States also means directing ourselves, our communities, this society, and the wider world toward a more sustainable future.

◆◆◆

Questions for Reflection

As you read and discuss the readings in this chapter, think about these questions:

1. What is your ancestry—biologically, culturally, and intellectually? How would you answer Paula Gunn Allen's question: Who is your mother?

2. How can you learn more about the history of women's lives and women's move-ments? Who will be your teachers? Your sources?

3. What does feminism mean to you? Keep your answer and return to this question at the end of the course.

4. What feminist viewpoints and representations do you see in the media? What antifeminist viewpoints and representations do you see?

◆◆◆

Finding Out More on the Web

1. In Reading 1, Paula Gunn Allen mentions Lysistrata. Who was she?

2. In Reading 3, the writers mention Dr. Kenneth Edelin, Joan Little, and Inéz Garcia. Who were these people? Why were they significant?

3. In Reading 4, Becky Thompson mentions Hijas de Cuauhtemoc, Women of All Red Nations, and the National Black Feminist Organization. Find out more about their perspectives, strategies, and activities.

4. How many Black men held seats in the U.S. Congress in 2000 compared to 1900?

5. Look at how blogs such as feministing or quirkyblackgirls discuss current feminist issues.

◆◆◆

Taking Action

1. Talk with older people in your family or community about their involvement in women's movements or movements for workers' rights, civil rights of people of color, LGBT rights, immigrant rights, and so forth.

2. Interview professors or staff of your campus women's center to learn about the beginnings of women's studies at your college or university.

3. Join a women's organization or support a campaign on an issue you care about.

4. Find quotes or slogans about feminism that resonate for you.

5. Find a feminist blog whose perspective you appreciate and read it regularly.

ONE

◆◆◆

Who Is Your Mother? Red Roots of White Feminism (1986)

Paula Gunn Allen

Paula Gunn Allen (1939–2008) was a poet, novelist, essayist, and literary critic of Laguna, Sioux, Lebanese, and Scottish ancestry who grew up on the Laguna Pueblo (New Mexico). She taught literature, creative writing, and Native American Studies. Among many awards, she received a Pulitzer Prize nomination for *Pocahontas: Medicine Woman, Spy, Entrepreneur, Diplomat* (2004), a Lifetime Achievement Award from the Native Writer's Circle of the Americas (2001), and the American Book Award from the Before Columbus Foundation for *Spider Woman's Granddaughters: Traditional Tales and Contemporary* Writing (1990).

At Laguna Pueblo in New Mexico, "Who is your mother?" is an important question. At Laguna, one of several of the ancient Keres gynocratic societies of the region, your mother's identity is the key to your own identity. Among the Keres, every individual has a place within the universe—human and nonhuman—and that place is defined by clan membership. In turn, clan membership is dependent on matrilineal descent. Of course, your mother is not only that woman whose womb formed and released you—the term refers in every individual case to an entire generation of women whose psychic, and consequently physical, "shape" made the psychic existence of the following generation possible. But naming your own mother (or her equivalent) enables people to place you precisely within the universal web of your life, in each of its dimensions: cultural, spiritual, personal, and historical.

Among the Keres, "context" and "matrix" are equivalent terms, and both refer to approximately the same thing as knowing your derivation and place. Failure to know your mother, that is, your position and its attendant traditions, history, and place in the scheme of things, is failure to remember your significance, your reality, your right relationship to earth and society. It is the same as being lost—isolated, abandoned, self-estranged, and alienated from your own life. This importance of tradition in the life of every member of the community is not confined to Keres Indians; all American Indian Nations place great value on traditionalism.

The Native American sense of the importance of continuity with one's cultural origins runs counter to contemporary American ideas: in many instances, the immigrants to America have been eager to cast off cultural ties, often seeing their antecedents as backward, restrictive, even shameful. Rejection of tradition constitutes one of the major features of American life, an attitude that reaches far back into American colonial history and that now is validated by virtually every cultural institution in the country. Feminist practice, at least in the cultural artifacts the community values most, follows this cultural trend as well.

The American idea that the best and the brightest should willingly reject and repudiate their origins leads to an allied idea—that history, like everything in the past, is of little value and should be forgotten as quickly as possible. This all too often causes us to reinvent the wheel continually. We find ourselves discovering our collective pasts over and over, having to retake ground already covered by women in the preceding decades and centuries. The Native American view, which highly values maintenance of traditional customs, values, and perspectives, might result in slower societal change and in quite a bit less social upheaval, but it has the advantage of providing a solid sense of identity and lowered levels of psychological and interpersonal conflict.

Contemporary Indian communities value individual members who are deeply connected to the traditional ways of their people, even after centuries of concerted and brutal effort on the part of the American government, the churches, and the corporate system to break the connections between individuals and their tribal world. In fact, in the view of the traditionals, rejection of one's culture—one's traditions, language, people—is the result of colonial oppression and is hardly to be applauded. They believe that the roots of oppression are to be found in the loss of tradition and memory because that loss is always accompanied by a loss of a positive sense of self. In short, Indians think it is important to remember, while Americans believe it is important to forget.

The traditional Indians' view can have a significant impact if it is expanded to mean that the sources of social, political, and philosophical thought in the Americas not only should be recognized and honored by Native Americans but should be embraced by American society. If American society judiciously modeled the traditions of the various Native Nations, the place of women in society would become central, the distribution of goods and power would be egalitarian, the elderly would be respected, honored, and protected as a primary social and cultural resource, the ideals of physical beauty would be considerably enlarged (to include "fat," strong-featured women, gray-haired, and wrinkled individuals, and others who in contemporary American culture are viewed as "ugly"). Additionally, the destruction of the biota, the life sphere, and the natural resources of the planet would be curtailed, and the spiritual nature of human and nonhuman life would become a primary organizing principle of human society. And if the traditional tribal systems that are emulated included pacifist ones, war would cease to be a major method of human problem solving.

Re-membering Connections and Histories

The belief that rejection of tradition and of history is a useful response to life is reflected in America's amazing loss of memory concerning its origins in the matrix and context of Native America. America does not seem to remember that it derived its wealth, its values, its food, much of its medicine, and a large part of its "dream" from Native America. It is ignorant of the genesis of its culture in this Native American land, and that ignorance helps to perpetuate the longstanding European and Middle Eastern monotheistic, hierarchical, patriarchal cultures' oppression of women, gays, and lesbians, people of color, working class, unemployed people, and the elderly. Hardly anyone in America speculates that the constitutional system of government might be as much a product of American Indian ideas and practices as of colonial American and Anglo-European revolutionary fervor.

Even though Indians are officially and informally ignored as intellectual movers and shapers in the United States, Britain, and Europe, they are peoples with ancient tenure on this soil. During the ages when tribal societies existed in the Americas largely untouched by patriarchal oppression, they developed elaborate systems of thought that included science, philosophy, and government based on a belief in the central importance of female energies, autonomy of individuals, cooperation, human dignity, human freedom, and egalitarian distribution of status, goods, and services. Respect for others, reverence for life and, as a by-product, pacifism as a way of life; importance of kinship ties in the customary ordering of social interaction; a sense of the sacredness and mystery of existence; balance and harmony in relationships both sacred and secular were all features of life among the tribal confederacies and nations. And in those that lived by the largest number of these principles, gynarchy [government by women] was the norm rather than the exception. Those systems are as yet unmatched in any contemporary industrial, agrarian, or postindustrial society on earth.

. . . there are many female gods recognized and honored by the tribes and Nations. Femaleness was highly valued, both respected and feared, and all social institutions reflected this attitude. Even modern sayings, such as the Cheyenne statement that a people is not conquered until the hearts of the women are on the ground, express the Indians' understanding that without the power of woman the people will not live, but with it, they will endure and prosper.

Indians did not confine this belief in the central importance of female energy to matters of worship. Among many of the tribes (perhaps as many as 70 percent of them in North America alone), this belief was reflected in all of their social institutions. The Iroquois Constitution or White Roots of Peace, also called the Great Law of the Iroquois, codified the Matrons' decision-making and economic power:

> The lineal descent of the people of the Five Fires [the Iroquois Nations] shall run in the female line. Women shall be considered the progenitors of the Nation. They shall own the land and the soil. Men and women shall follow the status of their mothers. (Article 44)
>
> The women heirs of the chieftainship titles of the League shall be called Oiner or Otinner [Noble] for all time to come. (Article 45)

If a disobedient chief persists in his disobedience after three warnings [by his female relatives, by his male relatives, and by one of his fellow council members, in that order], the matter shall go to the council of War Chiefs. The Chiefs shall then take away the title of the erring chief *by order of the women in whom the title is vested.* When the chief is deposed, the women shall notify the chiefs of the League . . . and the chiefs of the League shall sanction the act. The women will then select another of their sons as a candidate and the chiefs shall elect him. (Article 19) (Emphasis mine)[1]

The Matrons held so much policy-making power traditionally that once, when their position was threatened they demanded its return, and consequently the power of women was fundamental in shaping the Iroquois Confederation sometime in the sixteenth or early seventeenth century. It was women

who fought what may have been the first successful feminist rebellion in the New World. The year was 1600, or thereabouts, when these tribal feminists decided that they had had enough of unregulated warfare by their men. Lysistratas among the Indian women proclaimed a boycott on lovemaking and childbearing. Until the men conceded to them the power to decide upon war and peace, there would be no more warriors. Since the men believed that the women alone knew the secret of childbirth, the rebellion was instantly successful.

In the Constitution of Deganawidah the founder of the Iroquois Confederation of Nations had said: "He caused the body of our mother, the woman, to be of great worth and honor. He purposed that she shall be endowed and entrusted with the birth and upbringing of men, and that she shall have the care of all that is planted by which life is sustained and supported and the power to breathe is fortified: *and moreover that the warriors shall be her assistants.*"

The footnote of history was curiously supplied when Susan B. Anthony began her "Votes for Women" movement two and a half centuries later. Unknowingly the feminists chose to hold their founding convention of latter-day suffragettes in the town of Seneca [Falls], New York. The site was just a stone's throw from the old council house where the

Iroquois women had plotted their feminist rebellion. (Emphasis mine)[2]

Beliefs, attitudes, and laws such as these became part of the vision of American feminists and of other human liberation movements around the world. Yet feminists too often believe that no one has ever experienced the kind of society that empowered women and made that empowerment the basis of its rules of civilization. The price the feminist community must pay because it is not aware of the recent presence of gynarchical societies on this continent is unnecessary confusion, division, and much lost time.

The Root of Oppression Is Loss of Memory

An odd thing occurs in the minds of Americans when Indian civilization is mentioned: little or nothing. As I write this, I am aware of how far removed my version of the roots of American feminism must seem to those steeped in either mainstream or radical versions of feminism's history. I am keenly aware of the lack of image Americans have about our continent's recent past. I am intensely conscious of popular notions of Indian women as beasts of burden, squaws, traitors, or, at best, vanished denizens of a long-lost wilderness. How odd, then, must my contention seem that the gynocratic tribes of the American continent provided the basis for all the dreams of liberation that characterize the modern world.

We as feminists must be aware of our history on this continent. We need to recognize that the same forces that devastated the gynarchies of Britain and the Continent also devastated the ancient African civilizations, and we must know that those same materialistic, antispiritual forces are presently engaged in wiping out the same gynarchical values, along with the peoples who adhere to them, in Latin America. I am convinced that those wars were and continue to be about the imposition of patriarchal civilization over the holistic, pacifist, and spirit-based gynarchies they supplant. To that end the wars of imperial conquest have not been solely or even mostly waged over the land and its resources, but they have been fought within the bodies, minds, and hearts of the people of the earth for dominion over them. I think this is the reason traditionals say we must remember our origins, our cultures, our histories, our mothers and grandmothers, for without that memory, which implies continuance rather than nostalgia, we are doomed to engulf-ment by a paradigm that is fundamentally inimical to the vitality, autonomy, and self-empowerment essential for satisfying, high-quality life.

The vision that impels feminists to action was the vision of the Grandmothers' society, the society that was captured in the words of the sixteenth-century explorer Peter Martyr nearly five hundred years ago. It is the same vision repeated over and over by radical thinkers of Europe and America, from François Villon to John Locke, from William Shakespeare to Thomas Jefferson, from Karl Marx to Friedrich Engels, from Benito Juarez to Martin Luther King, from Elizabeth Cady Stanton to Judy Grahn, from Harriet Tubman to Audre Lorde, from Emma Goldman to Bella Abzug, from Malinalli to Cherrie Moraga, and from Iyatiku to me. That vision as Martyr told it is of a country where there are "no soldiers, no gendarmes or po-lice, no nobles, kings, regents, prefects, or judges, no prisons, no lawsuits . . . All are equal and free," or so Friedrich Engels recounts Martyr's words.[3]

Columbus wrote:

> Nor have I been able to learn whether they [the inhabitants of the islands he visited on his first journey to the New World] held personal property, for it seemed to me that whatever one had, they all took shares of . . . They are so ingenuous and free with all they have, that no one would believe it who has not seen it; of anything that they possess, if it be asked of them, they never say no; on the contrary, they invite you to share it and show as much love as if their hearts went with it.[4]

At least that's how the Native Caribbean people acted when the whites first came among them; American Indians are the despair of social workers, bosses, and missionaries even now because of their deeply ingrained tendency to spend all they have, mostly on others. In any case, as the historian William Brandon notes,

> the Indian *seemed* free, to European eyes, gloriously free, to the European soul shaped by centuries of toil and tyranny, and this impression operated profoundly on the process of history and the development of America. Something in the peculiar character of the Indian world gave an impression of

classlessness, of propertylessness, and that in turn led to an impression, as H. H. Bancroft put it, of "humanity unrestrained . . . in the exercise of liberty absolute."[5]

A Feminist Heroine

Early in the women's suffrage movement, Eva Emery Dye, an Oregon suffragette, went looking for a heroine to embody her vision of feminism. She wanted a historical figure whose life would symbol-ize the strengthened power of women. She found Sacagawea (or Sacajawea) buried in the journals of Lewis and Clark. The Shoshoni teenager had trav-eled with the Lewis and Clark expedition, carrying her infant son, and on a small number of occasions acted as translator.[6]

Dye declared that Sacagawea, whose name is thought to mean Bird Woman, had been the guide to the historic expedition, and through Dye's work Sacagawea became enshrined in American memory as a moving force and friend of the whites, leading them in the settlement of western North America.[7]

But Native American roots of white feminism reach back beyond Sacagawea. The earliest white women on this continent were well acquainted with tribal women. They were neighbors to a num-ber of tribes and often shared food, information, child care, and health care. Of course little is made of these encounters in official histories of colonial America, the period from the Revolution to the Civil War, or on the ever-moving frontier. Nor, to my knowledge, has either the significance or inci-dence of intermarriage between Indian and white or between Indian and Black been explored. By and large, the study of Indian-white relations has been focused on government and treaty relations, warfare, missionization, and education. It has been almost entirely documented in terms of formal white Christian patriarchal impacts and assaults on Native Americans, though they are not often char-acterized as assaults but as "civilizing the savages." Particularly in organs of popular culture and mis-education, the focus has been on what whites imag-ine to be degradation of Indian women ("squaws"), their equally imagined love of white government and white conquest ("princesses"), and the horri-fyingly misleading, fanciful tales of "bloodthirsty, backward primitives" assaulting white Christian settlers who were looking for life, liberty, and happiness in their chosen land.

But, regardless of official versions of relations between Indians and whites or other segments of the American population, the fact remains that great numbers of apparently "white" or "Black" Americans carry notable degrees of Indian blood. With that blood has come the culture of the Indian, informing the lifestyles, attitudes, and values of their descendents. . . . Among these must be included "permissive" child-rearing practices, for . . . imprisoning, torturing, caning, strapping, starving, or verbally abusing children was considered outrageous behavior. Native Americans did not believe that physical or psychological abuse of children would result in their edification. They did not believe that children are born in sin, are congenitally predisposed to evil, or that a good parent who wishes the child to gain salvation, achieve success, or earn the respect of her or his fellows can be helped to those ends by physical or emotional torture.

The early Americans saw the strongly protective attitude of the Indian people as a mark of their "savagery"—as they saw the Indian's habit of bathing frequently, their sexual openness, their liking for scant clothing, their raucous laughter at most things, their suspicion and derision of authoritarian structures, their quick pride, their genuine courtesy, their willingness to share what they had with others less fortunate than they, their egalitarianism, their ability to act as if various lifestyles were a normal part of living, and their granting that women were of equal or, in individual cases, of greater value than men.

Yet the very qualities that marked Indian life in the sixteenth century have, over the centuries since contact between the two worlds occurred, come to mark much of contemporary American life. . . .

Contemporary Americans find themselves more and more likely to adopt a "live and let live" attitude in matters of personal sexual and social styles. Two-thirds of their diet and a large share of their medications and medical treatments mirror or are directly derived from Native American sources. Indianization is not a simple concept, to be sure, and it is one that Americans often find themselves resisting; but it is a process that has taken place, regardless of American resistance to recognizing the source of many if not most of American's vaunted freedoms in our personal, family, social, and political arenas.

This is not to say that Americans have become Indian in every attitude, value, or social institution.

Unfortunately, Americans have a way to go in learning how to live in the world in ways that improve the quality of life for each individual while doing minimal damage to the biota, but they have adapted certain basic qualities of perception and certain attitudes that are moving them in that direction.

An Indian-Focused Version of American History

American colonial ideas of self-government came as much from the colonists' observations of tribal governments as from their Protestant or Greco-Roman heritage. Neither Greece nor Rome had the kind of pluralistic democracy as that concept has been understood in the United States since Andrew Jackson, but the tribes, particularly the gynarchical tribal confederacies, did. It is true that the *oligarchic* form of government that colonial Americans established was originally based on Greco-Roman systems in a number of important ways, such as its restriction of citizenship to propertied white males over twenty-one years of age, but it was never a form that Americans as a whole have been entirely comfortable with. Politics and government in the United States during the Federalist period also reflected the English common law system as it had evolved under patriarchal feudalism and monarchy—hence the United States' retention of slavery and restriction of citizenship to propertied white males.

The Federalists did make one notable change in the feudal system from which their political system derived on its Anglo side. They rejected blooded aristocracy and monarchy. This idea came from the Protestant Revolt to be sure, but it was at least reinforced by colonial America's proximity to American Indian nonfeudal confederacies and their concourse with those confederacies over the two hundred years of the colonial era. It was this proximity and concourse that enabled the revolutionary theorists to "dream up" a system in which all local polities would contribute to and be protected by a central governing body responsible for implementing policies that bore on the common interest of all. It should also be noted that the Reformation followed Columbus's contact with the Americas and that his and Martyr's reports concerning Native Americans' free and easy egalitarianism were in circulation by the time the Reformation took hold.

The Iroquois federal system, like that of several in the vicinity of the American colonies, is remarkably similar to the organization of the federal system of the United States. It was made up of local, "state," and federal bodies composed of executive, legislative, and judicial branches. The Council of Matrons was the executive: it instituted and determined general policy. The village, tribal (several villages), and Confederate councils determined and implemented policies when they did not conflict with the broader Council's decisions or with theological precepts that ultimately determined policy at all levels. The judicial was composed of the men's councils and the Matron's council, who sat together to make decisions. Because the matrons were the ceremonial center of the system, they were also the prime policymakers.

Obviously, there are major differences between the structure of the contemporary American government and that of the Iroquois. Two of those differences were and are crucial to the process of just government. The Iroquois system is spirit-based, while that of the United States is secular, and the Iroquois Clan Matrons formed the executive. The female executive function was directly tied to the ritual nature of the Iroquois politic, for the executive was lodged in the hands of the Matrons of particular clans across village, tribe, and national lines. The executive office was hereditary, and only sons of eligible clans could serve, at the behest of the Matrons of their clans, on the councils at the three levels. Certain daughters inherited the office of Clan Matron through their clan affiliations. No one could impeach or disempower a Matron, though her violation of certain laws could result in her ineligibility for the Matron's council. For example, a woman who married *and took her husband's name* could not hold the title Matron.

American ideas of social justice came into sharp focus through the commentaries of Iroquois observers who traveled in France in the colonial period. These observers expressed horror at the great gap between the lifestyles of the wealthy and the poor, remarking to the French philosopher Montaigne, who would heavily influence the radical communities of Europe, England, and America, that "they had noticed that in Europe there seemed to be two moities, consisting of the rich 'full gorged' with wealth, and the poor, starving 'and bare with need and povertie.' The Indian tourists not only marveled at the division, but marveled that the poor endured 'such an injustice, and that they took not

the others by the throte, or set fire on their house.'"[8] It must be noted that the urban poor eventually did just that in the French Revolution. The writings of Montaigne and of those he influenced provided the theoretical framework and the vision that propelled the struggle for liberty, justice, and equality on the Continent and later throughout the British empire.

The feminist idea of power as it ideally accrues to women stems from tribal sources. The central importance of the clan Matrons in the formulation and determination of domestic and foreign policy as well as in their primary role in the ritual and ceremonial life of their respective Nations was the single most important attribute of the Iroquois, as of the Cherokee and Muskogee, who traditionally inhabited the southern Atlantic region. The latter peoples were removed to what is now Oklahoma during the Jackson administration, but prior to the American Revolution they had regular and frequent communication with and impact on both the British colonizers and later the American people, including the African peoples brought here as slaves.

Ethnographer Lewis Henry Morgan wrote an account of Iroquoian matriarchal culture, published in 1877,[9] that heavily influenced Marx and the development of communism, particularly lending it the idea of the liberation of women from patriarchal dominance. The early socialists in Europe, especially in Russia, saw women's liberation as a central aspect of the socialist revolution. Indeed, the basic ideas of socialism, the egalitarian distribution of goods and power, the peaceful ordering of society, and the right of every member of society to participate in the work and benefits of that society, are ideas that pervade American Indian political thought and action. And it is through various channels—the informal but deeply effective Indianization of Europeans, and christianizing Africans, the social and political theory of the confederacies feuding and then intertwining with European dreams of liberty and justice, and, more recently, the work of Morgan and the writings of Marx and Engels—that the age-old gynarchical systems of egalitarian government found their way into contemporary feminist theory.

When Eva Emery Dye discovered Sacagawea and honored her as the guiding spirit of American womanhood, she may have been wrong in bare historical fact, but she was quite accurate in terms of deeper truth. The statues that have been erected depicting Sacagawea as a Matron in her prime signify an understanding in the American mind, however unconscious, that the source of just government, of right ordering of social relationships, the dream of "liberty and justice for all" can be gained only by following the Indian Matrons' guidance. For, as Dr. Anna Howard Shaw said of Sacagawea at the National American Woman's Suffrage Association in 1905:

> Forerunner of civilization, great leader of men, patient and motherly woman, we bow our hearts to do you honor! . . . May we the daughters of an alien race . . . learn the lessons of calm endurance, of patient persistence and unfaltering courage exemplified in your life, in our efforts to lead men through the Pass of justice, which goes over the mountains of prejudice and conservatism to the broad land of the perfect freedom of a true republic; one in which men and women together shall in perfect equality solve the problems of a nation that knows no caste, no race, no sex in opportunity, in responsibility or in justice! May 'the eternal womanly' ever lead us on![10]

NOTES

1. The White Roots of Peace, cited in *The Third Woman: Minority Women Writers of the United States*, ed. Dexter Fisher (Boston: Houghton Mifflin, 1980), p. 577.

2. Stan Steiner, *The New Indians* (New York: Dell, 1968), pp. 219–220.

3. William Brandon, *The Last Americans: The Indian in American Culture* (New York: McGraw-Hill, 1974), p. 294.

4. Brandon, *Last Americans*, p. 6.

5. Brandon, *Last Americans*, pp. 7–8. The entire chapter "American Indians and American History" (pp. 1–23) is pertinent to the discussion.

6. Ella E. Clark and Margot Evans, *Sacagawea of the Lewis and Clark Expedition* (Berkeley: University of California Press, 1979), pp. 93–98.

7. The implications of this maneuver did not go unnoticed by either whites or Indians, for the statues of the idealized Shoshoni woman, the Native American matron Sacagawea, suggest that American tenure on American land, indeed, the right to be on this land, is given to whites by her. While that implication is not overt, it certainly is suggested in the image of her that the sculptor chose: a tall, heavy woman, standing erect, nobly pointing the way westward with upraised hand. The impression is furthered by the habit of media and scholar of referring to her as "the guide." Largely because of the popularization of the circumstances of Sacagawea's participation in the famed Lewis and Clark expedition, Indian people have viewed her as a traitor to her people, likening her to Malinalli (La Malinche, who acted as interpreter for Cortés and bore him a son) and Pocahontas, that unhappy girl who married John Rolfe (not John Smith) and died in England after bearing him a son. Actually none of these women engaged in traitorous behavior. Sacagawea led a long life, was called Porivo (Chief Woman) by the Commanches, among whom she lived for more than twenty years, and in her old age engaged her considerable skill at speaking and manipulating white bureaucracy to help in assuring her Shoshoni people decent reservation holdings.

8. Brandon, *Last Americans*, p. 6.

9. Lewis Henry Morgan, *Ancient Society or Researches in the Lines of Human Progress from Savagery Through Barbarism to Civilization* (New York, 1877).

10. Clark and Evans, *Sacagawea*, p. 96.

T W O

◆◆◆

Declaration of Sentiments and Resolutions, Seneca Falls (1848)

The Seneca Falls *Declaration of Sentiments and Resolutions* was adopted at a founding convention of nineteenth-century suffragists, called to consider the "social, civil, and religious conditions and rights of woman," held at the Wesleyan Chapel, Seneca Falls, New York, on July 19, 1848 (Schneir 1994, p. 76). Elizabeth Cady Stanton, Lucretia Mott, and others drafted this document, using the *Declaration of Independence* as a model.

When, in the course of human events, it becomes necessary for one portion of the family of man to assume among the people of the earth a position different from that which they have hitherto occupied, but one to which the laws of nature and of nature's God entitle them, a decent respect to the opinions of mankind requires that they should declare the causes that impel them to such a course.

We hold these truths to be self-evident: that all men and women are created equal; that they are endowed by their Creator with certain inalienable rights; that among these are life, liberty, and the pursuit of happiness; that to secure these rights governments are instituted, deriving their just powers from the consent of the governed. Whenever any form of government becomes destructive of these ends, it is the right of those who suffer from it to refuse allegiance to it, and to insist upon the institution of a new government, laying its foundation on such principles, and organizing its powers in such form, as to them shall seem most likely to effect their safety and happiness. Prudence, indeed, will dictate that governments long established should not be changed for light and transient causes; and accordingly all experience hath shown that mankind are more disposed to suffer, while evils are sufferable, than to right themselves by abolishing the forms to which they were accustomed. But when a long train of abuses and usurpations, pursuing invariably the same object evinces a design to reduce them under absolute despotism, it is their duty to throw off such government, and to provide new guards for their future security. Such has been the patient sufferance of the women under this government, and such is now the necessity which constrains them to demand the equal station to which they are entitled.

The history of mankind is a history of repeated injuries and usurpations on the part of man toward woman, having in direct object the establishment of an absolute tyranny over her. To prove this, let facts be submitted to a candid world.

He has never permitted her to exercise her inalienable right to the elective franchise.

He has compelled her to submit to laws, in the formation of which she had no voice.

He has withheld from her rights which are given to the most ignorant and degraded men—both natives and foreigners.

Having deprived her of this first right of a citizen, the elective franchise, thereby leaving her without representation in the halls of legislation, he has oppressed her on all sides.

He has made her, if married, in the eye of the law, civilly dead.

He has taken from her all right in property, even to the wages she earns.

He has made her, morally, an irresponsible being, as she can commit many crimes with impunity, provided they be done in the presence of her husband. In the covenant of marriage, she is compelled to promise obedience to her husband, he becoming, to all intents and purposes, her master—the law giving him power to deprive her of her liberty, and to administer chastisement.

He has so framed the laws of divorce, as to what shall be the proper causes, and in case of separation, to whom the guardianship of the children shall be given, as to be wholly regardless of the happiness of women—the law, in all cases, going upon a false supposition of the supremacy of man, and giving all power into his hands.

After depriving her of all rights as a married woman, if single, and the owner of property, he has taxed her to support a government which recognizes her only when her property can be made profitable to it.

He has monopolized nearly all the profitable employments, and from those she is permitted to follow, she receives but a scanty remuneration. He closes against her all the avenues to wealth and distinction which he considers most honorable to himself. As a teacher of theology, medicine, or law, she is not known.

He has denied her the facilities for obtaining a thorough education, all colleges being closed against her.

He allows her in Church, as well as State, but a subordinate position, claiming Apolstolic authority for her exclusion from the ministry, and, with some exceptions, from any public participation in the affairs of the Church.

He has created a false public sentiment by giving to the world a different code of morals for men and women, by which moral delinquencies which exclude women from society, are not only tolerated, but deemed of little account in man.

He has usurped the prerogative of Jehovah himself, claiming it as his right to assign for her a sphere of action, when that belongs to her conscience and to her God.

He has endeavored, in every way that he could, to destroy her confidence in her own powers, to lessen her self-respect, and to make her willing to lead a dependent and abject life.

Now, in view of this entire disfranchisement of one-half the people of this country, their social and religious degradation—in view of the unjust laws above mentioned, and because women do feel themselves aggrieved, oppressed, and fraudulently deprived of their most sacred rights, we insist that they have immediate admission to all the rights and privileges which belong to them as citizens of the United States.

In entering upon the great work before us, we anticipate no small amount of misconception, misrepresentation, and ridicule; but we shall use every instrumentality within our power to effect our object. We shall employ agents, circulate tracts, petition the State and National legislatures, and endeavor to enlist the pulpit and the press in our behalf. We hope this Convention will be followed by a series of Conventions embracing every part of the country.

Resolutions

WHEREAS, The great precept of nature is conceded to be, that "man shall pursue his own true and substantial happiness." Blackstone in his Commentaries remarks, that this law of Nature being coeval with mankind, and dictated by God himself, is of course superior in obligation to any other. It is binding over all the globe, in all countries and at all times; no human laws are of any validity if contrary to this, and such of them as are valid, derive all their force, and all their validity, and all their authority, mediately and immediately, from this original; therefore,

Resolved, That such laws as conflict, in any way, with the true and substantial happiness of woman, are contrary to the great precept of nature and of no validity, for this is "superior in obligation to any other."

Resolved, That all laws which prevent woman from occupying such a station in society as her conscience shall dictate, or which place her in a position inferior to that of man, are contrary to the great precept of nature, and therefore of no force or authority.

Resolved, That woman is man's equal—was intended to be so by the Creator, and the highest good of the race demands that she should be recognized as such.

Resolved, That the women of this country ought to be enlightened in regard to the laws under which they live, that they may no longer publish their degradation by declaring themselves satisfied with their present position, nor their ignorance, by asserting that they have all the rights they want.

Resolved, That inasmuch as man, while claiming for himself intellectual superiority, does accord to woman moral superiority, it is pre-eminently his duty to encourage her to speak and teach, as she has an opportunity, in all religious assemblies.

Resolved, That the same amount of virtue, delicacy, and refinement of behavior that is required of woman in the social state, should also be required of man, and the same transgressions should be visited with equal severity on both man and woman.

Resolved, That the objection of indelicacy and impropriety, which is so often brought against woman when she addresses a public audience, comes with a very ill-grace from those who encourage, by their attendance, her appearance on the stage, in the concert, or in feats of the circus.

Resolved, That woman has too long rested satisfied in the circumscribed limits which corrupt customs and a perverted application of the Scriptures have marked out for her, and that it is time she should move in the enlarged sphere which her great Creator has assigned her.

Resolved, That it is the duty of the women of this country to secure to themselves their sacred right to the elective franchise.

Resolved, That the equality of human rights results necessarily from the fact of the identity of the race in capabilities and responsibilities.

Resolved, therefore, That, being invested by the Creator with the same capabilities, and the same consciousness of responsibility for their exercise, it is demonstrably the right and duty of woman, equally with man, to promote every righteous cause by every righteous means; and especially in regard to the great subjects of morals and religion, it is self-evidently her right to participate with her brother in teaching them, both in private and in public, by writing and by speaking, by any instrumentalities proper to be used, and in any assemblies proper to be held; and this being a self-evident truth growing out of the divinely implanted principles of human nature, any custom or authority adverse to it, whether modern or wearing the hoary sanction of antiquity, is to be regarded as a self-evident falsehood, and at war with mankind.

[At the last session Lucretia Mott offered and spoke to the following resolution:]

Resolved, That the speedy success of our cause depends upon the zealous and untiring efforts of both men and women, for the overthrow of the monopoly of the pulpit, and for the securing to woman an equal participation with men in the various trades, professions, and commerce.

THREE

◆◆◆

A Black Feminist Statement (1977)

Combahee River Collective

Active in the mid to late seventies, the **Combahee River Collective** was a Black feminist group in Boston whose name came from the guerrilla action led by **Harriet Tubman** that freed more than 750 slaves and is the only military campaign in U.S. history planned and led by a woman.

We are a collective of Black feminists who have been meeting together since 1974. During that time we have been involved in the process of defining and clarifying our politics, while at the same time doing political work within our own group and in coalition with other progressive organizations and movements. The most general statement of our politics at the present time would be that we are actively committed to struggling against racial, sexual, heterosexual, and class oppression and see as our particular task the development of integrated analysis and practice based upon the fact that the major systems of oppression are interlocking. The synthesis of these oppressions creates the conditions of our lives. As Black women we see Black feminism as the logical political movement to combat the manifold and simultaneous oppressions that all women of color face.

We will discuss four major topics in the paper that follows: (1) the genesis of contemporary Black feminism; (2) what we believe, i.e., the specific province of our politics; (3) the problems in organizing Black feminists, including a brief herstory of our collective; and (4) Black feminist issues and practice.

1. The Genesis of Contemporary Black Feminism

Before looking at the recent development of Black feminism we would like to affirm that we find our origins in the historical reality of Afro-American women's continuous life-and-death struggle for survival and liberation. Black women's extremely

negative relationship to the American political system (a system of white male rule) has always been determined by our membership in two oppressed racial and sexual castes. As Angela Davis points out in "Reflections on the Black Woman's Role in the Community of Slaves," Black women have always embodied, if only in their physical manifestation, an adversary stance to white male rule and have actively resisted its inroads upon them and their communities in both dramatic and subtle ways. There have always been Black women activists—some known, like Sojourner Truth, Harriet Tubman, Frances E. W. Harper, Ida B. Wells Barnett, and Mary Church Terrell, and thousands upon thousands unknown—who had a shared awareness of how their sexual identity combined with their racial identity to make their whole life situation and the focus of their political struggles unique. Contemporary Black feminism is the outgrowth of countless generations of personal sacrifice, militancy, and work by our mothers and sisters.

A Black feminist presence has evolved most obviously in connection with the second wave of the American women's movement beginning in the late 1960s. Black, other Third World, and working women have been involved in the feminist movement from its start, but both outside reactionary forces and racism and elitism within the movement itself have served to obscure our participation. In 1973 Black feminists, primarily located in New York, felt the necessity of forming a separate Black feminist group. This became the National Black Feminist Organization (NBFO).

Black feminist politics also have an obvious connection to movements for Black liberation, particularly those of the 1960s and 1970s. Many of us were active in those movements (civil rights, Black nationalism, the Black Panthers), and all of our lives were greatly affected and changed by their ideology, their goals, and the tactics used to achieve their goals. It was our experience and disillusionment within these liberation movements,

March to Protest the Murders of Black Women
Boston, 1979

©1979 Tia Cross

as well as experience on the periphery of the white male left, that led to the need to develop a politics that was antiracist, unlike those of white women, and antisexist, unlike those of Black and white men.

There is also undeniably a personal genesis for Black feminism, that is, the political realization that comes from the seemingly personal experiences of individual Black women's lives. Black feminists and many more Black women who do not define themselves as feminists have all experienced sexual oppression as a constant factor in our day-to-day existence. As children we realized that we were different from boys and that we were treated differently. For example, we were told in the same breath to be quiet both for the sake of being "lady-like" and to make us less objectionable in the eyes of white people. As we grew older we became aware of the threat of physical and sexual abuse by men. However, we had no way of conceptualizing what

was so apparent to us, what we *knew* was really happening.

Black feminists often talk about their feelings of craziness before becoming conscious of the concepts of sexual politics, patriarchal rule, and most importantly, feminism, the political analysis and practice that we women use to struggle against our oppression. The fact that racial politics and indeed racism are pervasive factors in our lives did not allow us, and still does not allow most Black women, to look more deeply into our own experiences and, from that sharing and growing consciousness, to build a politics that will change our lives and inevitably end our oppression. Our development must also be tied to the contemporary economic and political position of Black people. The post–World War II generation of Black youth was the first to be able to minimally partake of certain educational and employment options, previously closed completely to Black people. Although our economic position is still at the very bottom of the American capitalistic economy, a handful of us have been able to gain certain tools as a result of tokenism in education and employment which potentially enable us to more effectively fight our oppression.

A combined antiracist and antisexist position drew us together initially, and as we developed politically we addressed ourselves to heterosexism and economic oppression under capitalism.

2. What We Believe

Above all else, our politics initially sprang from the shared belief that Black women are inherently valuable, that our liberation is a necessity not as an adjunct to somebody else's but because of our need as human persons for autonomy. This may seem so obvious as to sound simplistic, but it is apparent that no other ostensibly progressive movement has ever considered our specific oppression as a priority or worked seriously for the ending of that oppression. Merely naming the pejorative stereotypes attributed to Black women (e.g., mammy, matriarch, Sapphire, whore, bulldagger), let alone cataloguing the cruel, often murderous, treatment we receive, indicates how little value has been placed upon our lives during four centuries of bondage in the Western Hemisphere. We realize that the only people who care enough about us to work consistently for our liberation are us. Our politics evolve from a healthy love for ourselves, our sisters and our community which allows us to continue our struggle and work.

This focusing upon our own oppression is embodied in the concept of identity politics. We believe that the most profound and potentially the most radical politics come directly out of our own identity, as opposed to working to end somebody else's oppression. In the case of Black women this is a particularly repugnant, dangerous, threatening, and therefore revolutionary concept because it is obvious from looking at all the political movements that have preceded us that anyone is more worthy of liberation than ourselves. We reject pedestals, queenhood, and walking ten paces behind. To be recognized as human, levelly human, is enough.

We believe that sexual politics under patriarchy is as pervasive in Black women's lives as are the politics of class and race. We also often find it difficult to separate race from class from sex oppression because in our lives they are most often experienced simultaneously. We know that there is such a thing as racial-sexual oppression which is neither solely racial nor solely sexual, e.g., the history of rape of Black women by white men as a weapon of political repression.

Although we are feminists and lesbians, we feel solidarity with progressive Black men and do not advocate the fractionalization that white women who are separatists demand. Our situation as Black people necessitates that we have solidarity around the fact of race, which white women of course do not need to have with white men, unless it is their negative solidarity as racial oppressors. We struggle together with Black men against racism, while we also struggle with Black men about sexism.

We realize that the liberation of all oppressed peoples necessitates the destruction of the political-economic systems of capitalism and imperialism as well as patriarchy. We are socialists because we believe the work must be organized for the collective benefit of those who do the work and create the products, and not for the profit of the bosses. Material resources must be equally distributed among those who create these resources. We are not convinced, however, that a socialist revolution that is not also a feminist and antiracist revolution will guarantee our liberation. We have arrived at the necessity for developing an understanding of class relationships that takes into account the specific class position of Black women who are generally marginal in the labor force, while at this particular time some of us are temporarily viewed as doubly desirable tokens at white-collar and professional levels. We need to articulate the real class situation of persons who are not merely raceless, sexless workers, but for whom racial and sexual oppression are significant determinants in their working/ economic lives. . . .

A political contribution which we feel we have already made is the expansion of the feminist principle that the personal is political. In our consciousness-raising sessions, for example, we have in many ways gone beyond white women's revelations because we are dealing with the implications of race and class as well as sex. Even our Black women's style of talking/testifying in Black language about what we have experienced has a resonance that is both cultural and political. We have spent a great deal of energy delving into the cultural and experiential nature of our oppression out of necessity because none of these matters has ever been looked at before. No one before has ever examined the multilayered texture of Black women's lives. An example of this kind of revelation/conceptualization occurred at a meeting as we discussed the ways in which our early intellectual interests had been attacked by our peers, particularly Black males. We discovered that all of us, because we were "smart" had also been considered "ugly," i.e., "smart-ugly." "Smart-ugly" crystallized the way in which most of us had been forced to develop our intellects at great cost to our "social" lives. The sanctions in the Black and white communities against Black women thinkers are comparatively much higher than for white women, particularly ones from the educated middle and upper classes.

As we have already stated, we reject the stance of lesbian separatism because it is not a viable political analysis or strategy for us. It leaves out far too much and far too many people, particularly Black men, women, and children. We have a great deal of criticism and loathing for what men have been socialized to be in this society: what they support, how they act, and how they oppress. But we do not have the misguided notion that it is their maleness, per se—i.e., their biological maleness—that makes them what they are. As Black women we find any type of biological determinism a particularly dangerous and reactionary basis upon which to build a politic. We must also question whether lesbian separatism is an adequate and progressive political analysis and strategy, even for those who practice it, since it so completely denies any but the sexual sources of women's oppression, negating the facts of class and race.

3. Problems in Organizing Black Feminists

During our years together as a Black feminist collective we have experienced success and defeat, joy and pain, victory and failure. We have found that it is very difficult to organize around Black feminist issues, difficult even to announce in certain contexts

that we *are* Black feminists. We have tried to think about the reasons for our difficulties, particularly since the white women's movement continues to be strong and to grow in many directions. In this section we will discuss some of the general reasons for the organizing problems we face and also talk specifically about the stages in organizing our own collective.

The major source of difficulty in our political work is that we are not just trying to fight oppression on one front or even two, but instead to address a whole range of oppressions. We do not have racial, sexual, heterosexual, or class privilege to rely upon, nor do we have even the minimal access to resources and power that groups who possess any one of these types of privilege have.

The psychological toll of being a Black woman and the difficulties this presents in reaching political consciousness and doing political work can never be underestimated. There is a very low value placed upon Black women's psyches in this society, which is both racist and sexist. As an early group member once said, "We are all damaged people merely by virtue of being Black women." We are dispossessed psychologically and on every other level, and yet we feel the necessity to struggle to change the condition of all Black women. In "A Black Feminist's Search for Sisterhood," Michele Wallace arrives at this conclusion:

> We exist as women who are Black who are feminists, each stranded for the moment, working independently because there is not yet an environment in this society remotely congenial to our struggle—because, being on the bottom, we would have to do what no one else has done: we would have to fight the world.[1]

Wallace is pessimistic but realistic in her assessment of Black feminists' position, particularly in her allusion to the nearly classic isolation most of us face. We might use our position at the bottom, however, to make a clear leap into revolutionary action. If Black women were free, it would mean that everyone else would have to be free since our freedom would necessitate the destruction of all the systems of oppression.

Feminism is, nevertheless, very threatening to the majority of Black people because it calls into question some of the most basic assumptions about our existence, i.e., that sex should be a determinant of power relationships. Here is the way male and female voices were defined in a Black nationalist pamphlet from the early 1970s.

> We understand that it is and has been traditional that the man is the head of the house. He is the leader of the house/nation because his knowledge of the world is broader, his awareness is greater, his understanding is fuller and his application of this information is wiser . . . After all, it is only reasonable that the man be the head of the house because he is able to defend and protect the development of his home . . . Women cannot do the same things as men—they are made by nature to function differently. Equality of men and women is something that cannot happen even in the abstract world. Men are not equal to other men, i.e., ability, experience or even understanding. The value of men and women can be seen as in the value of gold and silver—they are not equal but both have great value. We must realize that men and women are a complement to each other because there is no house/family without a man and his wife. Both are essential to the development of any life.[2]

The material conditions of most Black women would hardly lead them to upset both economic and sexual arrangements that seem to represent some stability in their lives. Many Black women have a good understanding of both sexism and racism, but because of the everyday constrictions of their lives cannot risk struggling against them both.

The reaction of Black men to feminism has been notoriously negative. They are, of course, even more threatened than Black women by the possibility that Black feminists might organize around our own needs. They realize that they might not only lose valuable and hard-working allies in their struggles but that they might also be forced to change their habitually sexist ways of interacting with and oppressing Black women. Accusations that Black feminism divides the Black struggle are powerful deterrents to the growth of an autonomous Black women's movement.

Still, hundreds of women have been active at different times during the three-year existence of our group. And every Black woman who came, came out of a strongly-felt need for some level of possibility that did not previously exist in her life.

When we first started meeting early in 1974 after the NBFO first eastern regional conference, we did not have a strategy for organizing, or even a focus. We just wanted to see what we had. After a period of months of not meeting, we began to meet again late in the year and started doing an intense variety of consciousness-raising. The overwhelming feeling that we had is that after years and years we had finally found each other. Although we were not doing political work as a group, individuals continued their involvement in Lesbian politics, sterilization abuse and abortion rights work, Third World Women's International Women's Day activities, and support activity for the trials of Dr. Kenneth Edelin, Joan Little, and Inéz García. During our first summer, when membership had dropped off considerably, those of us remaining devoted serious discussion to the possibility of opening a refuge for battered women in a Black community. (There was no refuge in Boston at that time.) We also decided around that time to become an independent collective since we had serious disagreements with NBFO's bourgeois-feminist stance and their lack of a clear political focus.

We also were contacted at that time by socialist feminists, with whom we had worked on abortion rights activities, who wanted to encourage us to attend the National Socialist Feminist Conference in Yellow Springs. One of our members did attend and despite the narrowness of the ideology that was promoted at that particular conference, we became more aware of the need for us to understand our own economic situation and to make our own economic analysis.

In the fall, when some members returned, we experienced several months of comparative inactivity and internal disagreements which were first conceptualized as a Lesbian-straight split but which were also the result of class and political differences. During the summer those of us who were still meeting had determined the need to do political work and to move beyond consciousness-raising and serving exclusively as an emotional support group. At the beginning of 1976, when some of the women who had not wanted to do political work and who also had voiced disagreements stopped attending of their own accord, we again looked for a focus. We decided at that time, with the addition of new members, to become a study group. We had always shared our reading with each other, and some of us had written papers on Black feminism for group discussion a few months before this decision was made. We began functioning as a study group and also began discussing the possibility of starting a Black feminist publication. We had a retreat in the late spring which provided a time for both political discussion and working out interpersonal issues. Currently we are planning to gather together a collection of Black feminist writing. We feel that it is absolutely essential to demonstrate the reality of our politics to other Black women and believe that we can do this through writing and distributing our work. The fact that individual Black feminists are living in isolation all over the country, that our own numbers are small, and that we have some skills in writing, printing, and publishing makes us want to carry out these kinds of projects as a means of organizing Black feminists as we continue to do political work in coalition with other groups.

4. Black Feminist Issues and Projects

During our time together we have identified and worked on many issues of particular relevance to Black women. The inclusiveness of our politics makes us concerned with any situation that impinges upon the lives of women, Third World and working people. We are of course particularly committed to working on those struggles in which race, sex, and class are simultaneous factors in oppression. We might, for example, become involved in workplace organizing at a factory that employs Third World women or picket a hospital that is cutting back on already inadequate health care to a Third World community, or set up a rape crisis center in a Black neighborhood. Organizing around welfare and daycare concerns might also be a focus. The work to be done and the countless issues that this work represents merely reflect the pervasiveness of our oppression.

Issues and projects that collective members have already worked on are sterilization abuse, abortion rights, battered women, rape and health care. We have also done many workshops and educationals on Black feminism on college campuses, at women's conferences, and most recently for high school women.

One issue that is of major concern to us and that we have begun to publicly address is racism in the white women's movement. As Black feminists we are made constantly and painfully aware of how little effort white women have made to understand and combat their racism, which requires among other things that they have a more than superficial comprehension of race, color, and Black history and culture. Eliminating racism in the white women's movement is by definition work for white women to do, but we will continue to speak to and demand accountability on this issue.

In the practice of our politics we do not believe that the end always justifies the means. Many reactionary and destructive acts have been done in the name of achieving "correct" political goals. As feminists we do not want to mess over people in the name of politics. We believe in collective process and a nonhierarchical distribution of power within our own group and in our vision of a revolutionary society. We are committed to a continual examination of our politics as they develop through criticism and self-criticism as an essential aspect of our practice. In her introduction to *Sisterhood Is Powerful,* Robin Morgan writes:

> I haven't the faintest notion what possible revolutionary role white heterosexual men could fulfill, since they are the very embodiment of reactionary-vested-interest-power.

As Black feminists and Lesbians we know that we have a very definite revolutionary task to perform and we are ready for the lifetime of work and struggle before us.

NOTES

1. Michele Wallace, "A Black Feminist's Search for Sisterhood," *The Village Voice,* 28 July 1975, pp. 6–7.
2. Mumininas of Committee for Unified Newark, *Mwanamke Mwananchi (The Nationalist Woman),* Newark, N.J., © 1971, pp. 4–5.

FOUR

◆◆◆

Multiracial Feminism
Recasting the Chronology of Second Wave Feminism (2002)

Becky Thompson

Becky Thompson is the author of several books, including *When the Center is on Fire: Passionate Social Theory for Our Times* (co-author, Diane Harriford) and *A Promise and A Way of Life: White Antiracist Activism.* She co-edited *Fingernails Across the Chalkboard: Poetry and Prose on HIV from the Black Diaspora*, an anthology adapted into a play that premiered in New York City in 2008. She teaches sociology and African American Studies at Simmons College in Boston.

In the last several years, a number of histories have been published that chronicle the emergence and contributions of Second Wave feminism.[1] Although initially eager to read and teach from these histories, I have found myself increasingly concerned about the extent to which they provide a version of Second Wave history that Chela Sandoval refers to as "hegemonic feminism."[2] This feminism is white led, marginalizes the activism and world views of women of color, focuses mainly on the United States, and treats sexism as the ultimate oppression. Hegemonic feminism deemphasizes or ignores a class and race analysis, generally sees equality with men as the goal of feminism, and has an individual rights-based, rather than justice-based vision for social change.

Although rarely named as hegemonic feminism, this history typically resorts to an old litany of the women's movement that includes three or four branches of feminism: liberal, socialist, radical, and sometimes cultural feminism.[3] The most significant problem with this litany is that it does not recognize the centrality of the feminism of women of color in Second Wave history. Missing, too, from normative accounts is the story of white antiracist feminism which, from its emergence, has been intertwined with, and fueled by the development of, feminism among women of color.[4]

Telling the history of Second Wave feminism from the point of view of women of color and white antiracist women illuminates the rise of multiracial

feminism—the liberation movement spearheaded by women of color in the United States in the 1970s that was characterized by its international perspective, its attention to interlocking oppressions, and its support of coalition politics.[5] Bernice Johnson Reagon's naming of "coalition politics"; Patricia Hill Collins's understanding of women of color as "outsiders within"; Barbara Smith's concept of "the simultaneity of oppressions"; Cherríe Moraga and Gloria Anzaldúa's "theory in the flesh"; Chandra Talpade Mohanty's critique of "imperialist feminism"; Paula Gunn Allen's "red roots of white feminism"; Adrienne Rich's "politics of location"; and Patricia Williams's analysis of "spirit murder" are all theoretical guideposts for multiracial feminism.[6] Tracing the rise of multiracial feminism raises many questions about common assumptions made in normative versions of Second Wave history. Constructing a multiracial feminist movement time line and juxtaposing it with the normative time line reveals competing visions of what constitutes liberation and illuminates schisms in feminist consciousness that are still with us today.

The Rise of Multiracial Feminism

Normative accounts of the Second Wave feminist movement often reach back to the publication of Betty Friedan's *The Feminine Mystique* in 1963, the founding of the National Organization for Women in 1966, and the emergence of women's consciousness-raising (CR) groups in the late 1960s. All signaled a rising number of white, middle-class women unwilling to be treated like second-class citizens in the boardroom, in education, or in bed. Many of the early protests waged by this sector of the feminist movement picked up on the courage and forthrightness of 1960s' struggles—a willingness to stop traffic, break existing laws to provide safe and accessible abortions, and contradict the older generation. For younger women, the leadership women had demonstrated in 1960s' activism belied the sex roles that had traditionally defined domestic, economic, and political relations and opened new possibilities for action.

This version of the origins of Second Wave history is not sufficient in telling the story of multiracial feminism. Although there were Black women involved with NOW from the outset and Black and Latina women who participated in CR groups, the feminist work of women of color also extended beyond women-only spaces. In fact, during the 1970s, women of color were involved on three fronts— working with white-dominated feminist groups; forming women's caucuses in existing mixed-gender organizations; and developing autonomous Black, Latina, Native American, and Asian feminist organizations.[7]

This three-pronged approach contrasts sharply with the common notion that women of color feminists emerged in reaction to (and therefore later than) white feminism. In her critique of "model making" in Second Wave historiography, which has "all but ignored the feminist activism of women of color," Benita Roth "challenges the idea that Black feminist organizing was a later variant of so-called mainstream white feminism."[8] Roth's assertion—that the timing of Black feminist organizing is roughly equivalent to the timing of white feminist activism—is true about feminist activism by Latinas, Native Americans, and Asian Americans as well.

One of the earliest feminist organizations of the Second Wave was a Chicana group—Hijas de Cuauhtemoc (1971)—named after a Mexican women's underground newspaper that was published during the 1910 Mexican Revolution. Chicanas who formed this *femenista* group and published a newspaper named after the early-twentieth-century Mexican women's revolutionary group, were initially involved in the United Mexican American Student Organization which was part of the Chicano/a student movement.[9] Many of the founders of Hijas de Cuauhtemoc were later involved in launching the first national Chicana studies journal, *Encuentro Feminil.*

An early Asian American women's group, Asian Sisters, focused on drug abuse intervention for young women in Los Angeles. It emerged in 1971 out of the Asian American Political Alliance, a broad-based, grassroots organization largely fueled by the consciousness of first-generation Asian

American college students. Networking between Asian American and other women during this period also included participation by a contingent of 150 Third World and white women from North America at the historic Vancouver Indochinese Women's Conference (1971) to work with Indochinese women against U.S. imperialism.[10] Asian American women provided services for battered women, worked as advocates for refugees and recent immigrants, produced events spotlighting Asian women's cultural and political diversity, and organized with other women of color.[11]

The best-known Native American women's organization of the 1970s was Women of All Red Nations (WARN). WARN was initiated in 1974 by women, many of whom were also members of the American Indian Movement, which was founded in 1968 by Dennis Banks, George Mitchell, and Mary Jane Wilson, an Anishinabe activist.[12] WARN's activism included fighting sterilization in public health service hospitals, suing the U.S. government for attempts to sell Pine Ridge water in South Dakota to corporations, and networking with indigenous people in Guatemala and Nicaragua.[13] WARN reflected a whole generation of Native American women activists who had been leaders in the takeover of Wounded Knee in South Dakota in 1973, on the Pine Ridge reservation (1973–76), and elsewhere. WARN, like Asian Sisters and Hijas de Cuauhtemoc, grew out of—and often worked with—mixed-gender nationalist organizations.

The autonomous feminist organizations that Black, Latina, Asian, and Native American women were forming during the early 1970s drew on nationalist traditions through their recognition of the need for people of color–led, independent organizations.[14] At the same time, unlike earlier nationalist organizations that included women and men, these were organizations specifically for women.

Among Black women, one early Black feminist organization was the Third World Women's Alliance which emerged in 1968 out of the Student Nonviolent Coordinating Committee (SNCC) chapters on the East Coast and focused on racism, sexism, and imperialism.[15] The foremost autonomous feminist organization of the early 1970s was the National Black Feminist Organization (NBFO). Founded in 1973 by Florynce Kennedy, Margaret Sloan, and Doris Wright, it included many other well-known Black women including Faith Ringgold, Michelle

Wallace, Alice Walker, and Barbara Smith. According to Deborah Gray White, NBFO "more than any organization in the century . . . launched a frontal assault on sexism and racism."[16] Its first conference in New York was attended by 400 women from a range of class backgrounds.

Although the NBFO was a short-lived organization nationally (1973–75), chapters in major cities remained together for years, including one in Chicago that survived until 1981. The contents of the CR sessions were decidedly Black women's issues—stereotypes of Black women in the media, discrimination in the workplace, myths about Black women as matriarchs, Black women's beauty, and self-esteem.[17] The NBFO also helped to inspire the founding of the Combahee River Collective in 1974, a Boston-based organization named after a river in South Carolina where Harriet Tubman led an insurgent action that freed 750 slaves. The Combahee River Collective not only led the way for crucial antiracist activism in Boston through the decade, but it also provided a blueprint for Black feminism that still stands a quarter of a century later.[18] From Combahee member Barbara Smith came a definition of feminism so expansive that it remains a model today. Smith writes that "feminism is the political theory and practice to free *all* women: women of color, working-class women, poor women, physically challenged women, lesbians, old women, as well as white economically privileged heterosexual women. Anything less than this is not feminism, but merely female self-aggrandizement."[19]

These and other groups in the early and mid-1970s provided the foundation for the most far-reaching and expansive organizing by women of color in U.S. history. These organizations also fueled a veritable explosion of writing by women of color, including Toni Cade's pioneering *The Black Woman: An Anthology* in 1970, Maxine Hong Kingston's *The Woman Warrior* in 1977, and in 1981 and 1983, respectively, the foundational *This Bridge Called My Back: Writings by Radical Women of Color and Home Girls: A Black Feminist Anthology*.[20] While chronicling the dynamism and complexity of a multidimensional vision for women of color, these books also traced for white women what is required to be allies to women of color.

By the late 1970s, the progress made possible by autonomous and independent Asian, Latina, and Black feminist organizations opened a space for women of color to work in coalition across organizations with each other. During this period, two cohorts of white women became involved in multiracial feminism. One group had, in the late 1960s and early 1970s, chosen to work in anti-imperialist, antiracist militant organizations in connection with Black Power groups—the Black Panther Party, the Black Liberation Army—and other solidarity and nationalist organizations associated with the American Indian, Puerto Rican Independence, and Chicano Movements of the late 1960s and early 1970s. These women chose to work with these solidarity organizations rather than work in overwhelmingly white feminist contexts. None of the white antiracist feminists I interviewed (for a social history of antiracism in the United States) who were politically active during the civil rights and Black Power movements had an interest in organizations that had a single focus on gender or that did not have antiracism at the center of their agendas.

Militant women of color and white women took stands against white supremacy and imperialism (both internal and external colonialism); envisioned revolution as a necessary outcome of political struggle; and saw armed propaganda (armed attacks against corporate and military targets along with public education about state crime) as a possible tactic in revolutionary struggle. Although some of these women avoided or rejected the term "feminist" because of its association with hegemonic feminism, these women still confronted sexism both within solidarity and nationalist organizations and within their own communities. In her autobiographical account of her late-1960s' politics, Black liberation movement leader Assata Shakur writes: "To me, the revolutionary struggle of Black people had to be against racism, classism, imperialism and sexism for real freedom under a socialist government."[21] During this period, Angela Davis was also linking anticapitalist struggle with the fight against race and gender oppression.[22] Similarly, white militant activist Marilyn Buck, who was among the first women to confront Students for a Democratic Society (SDS) around issues of sexism, also spoke up for women's rights as an ally of the Black Liberation Army.

Rarely, however, have their stories—and those of other militant antiracist women—been considered part of the Second Wave history. In her critique of this dominant narrative, historian Nancy

MacLean writes: "Recent accounts of the rise of modern feminism depart little from the story line first advanced two decades ago and since enshrined as orthodoxy. That story stars white middle-class women triangulated between the pulls of liberal, radical/cultural, and socialist feminism. Working-class women and women of color assume walk-on parts late in the plot, after tendencies and allegiances are already in place. The problem with this script is not simply that it has grown stale from repeated retelling. It is not accurate...."[23]

The omission of militant white women and women of color from Second Wave history partly reflects a common notion that the women's movement followed and drew upon the early civil rights movement and the New Left, a trajectory that skips entirely the profound impact that the Black Power movement had on many women's activism. Omitting militant women activists from historical reference also reflects a number of ideological assumptions made during the late 1960s and early 1970s—that "real" feminists were those who worked primarily or exclusively with other women; that "women's ways of knowing" were more collaborative, less hierarchical, and more peace loving than men's; and that women's liberation would come from women's deepening understanding that "sisterhood is powerful."

These politics were upheld by both liberal and radical white feminists. These politics did not, however, sit well with many militant women of color and white women who refused to consider sexism the primary, or most destructive, oppression and recognized the limits of gaining equality in a system that, as Malcolm X had explained, was already on fire. The women of color and white militant women who supported a race, class, and gender analysis in the late 1960s and 1970s often found themselves trying to explain their politics in mixed-gender settings (at home, at work, and in their activism), sometimes alienated from the men (and some women) who did not get it, while simultaneously alienated from white feminists whose politics they considered narrow at best and frivolous at worst.

By the late 1970s, the militant women who wanted little to do with white feminism of the late 1960s and 1970s became deeply involved in multiracial feminism. By that point, the decade of organizing among women of color in autonomous Black, Latina, and Asian feminist organizations led militant antiracist white women to immerse themselves in multiracial feminism. Meanwhile, a younger cohort of white women, who were first politicized in the late 1970s, saw feminism from a whole different vantage point than did the older, white, antiracist women. For the younger group, exposure to multiracial feminism led by women of color meant an early lesson that race, class, and gender were inextricably linked. They also gained vital experience in multiple organizations—battered women's shelters, conferences, and health organizations—where women were, with much struggle, attempting to uphold this politic.

From this organizing came the emergence of a small but important group of white women determined to understand how white privilege had historically blocked cross-race alliances among women, and what they, as white women, needed to do to work closely with women of color. Not surprisingly, Jewish women and lesbians often led the way among white women in articulating a politic that accounted for white women's position as both oppressed and oppressor—as both women and white.[24] Both groups knew what it meant to be marginalized from a women's movement that was, nevertheless, still homophobic and Christian biased. Both groups knew that "there is no place like home"—among other Jews and/or lesbians—and the limits of that home if for Jews it was male dominated or if for lesbians it was exclusively white. The paradoxes of "home" for these groups paralleled many of the situations experienced by women of color who, over and over again, found themselves to be the bridges that everyone assumed would be on their backs.

As the straight Black women interacted with the Black lesbians, the first-generation Chinese women talked with the Native American activists, and the Latina women talked with the Black and white women about the walls that go up when people cannot speak Spanish, white women attempting to understand race knew they had a lot of listening to do. They also had a lot of truth telling to reckon with, and a lot of networking to do, among other white women and with women of color as well.

Radicals, Heydays, and Hot Spots

The story of Second Wave feminism, if told from the vantage point of multiracial feminism, also encourages us to rethink key assumptions about periodization....

Coinciding with the frequent assumption that 1969 to 1974 was the height of "radical feminism," many feminist historians consider 1972 to 1982 as the period of mass mobilization and 1983 to 1991 as a period of feminist abeyance.[25] Ironically, the years that sociologists Verta Taylor and Nancy Whittier consider the period of mass mobilization for feminists (1972–82) are the years that Chela Sandoval identifies as the period when "ideological differences divided and helped to dissipate the movement from within."[26] For antiracist women (both white and of color), the best days of feminism were yet to come when, as Barbara Smith explains, "Those issues that had divided many of the movement's constituencies—such as racism, anti-Semitism, ableism, ageism, and classism—were put on the table."[27]

Ironically, the very period that white feminist historians typically treat as a period of decline within the movement is the period of mass mobilization among antiracist women—both straight and lesbian. The very year that Taylor and Whittier consider the end of mass mobilization because the ERA failed to be ratified, 1982, is the year that [Sherna Berger] Gluck rightfully cites as the beginning of a feminism far more expansive than had previously existed. She writes: "By 1982, on the heels of difficult political struggle waged by activist scholars of color, ground-breaking essays and anthologies by and about women of color opened a new chapter in U.S. feminism. The future of the women's movement in the U.S. was reshaped irrevocably by the introduction of the expansive notion of feminisms."[28] Angela Davis concurs, citing 1981, with the publication of *This Bridge Called My Back*, as the year when women of color had developed as a "new political subject," due to substantial work done in multiple arenas.[29]

In fact, periodization of the women's movement from the point of view of multiracial feminism would treat the late 1960s and early 1970s as its origin and the mid-1970s, 1980s, and 1990s as a height. A time line of that period shows a flourishing multiracial feminist movement. In 1977, the Combahee River Collective Statement was first published; in 1979, *Conditions: Five,* the Black women's issue, was published, the First National Third World Lesbian Conference was held, and Assata Shakur escaped from prison in New Jersey with the help of prison activists.[30] In 1981, Byllye Avery founded the National Black Women's Health Project in Atlanta;

Bernice Johnson Reagon gave her now-classic speech on coalition politics at the West Coast Women's Music Festival in Yosemite; and the National Women's Studies Association held its first conference to deal with racism as a central theme, in Storrs, Connecticut, where there were multiple animated interventions against racism and anti-Semitism in the women's movement and from which emerged Adrienne Rich's exquisite essay, "Disobedience and Women's Studies."[31] Then, 1984 was the year of the New York Women against Rape Conference, a multiracial, multiethnic conference that confronted multiple challenges facing women organizing against violence against women—by partners, police, social service agencies, and poverty. In 1985, the United Nations Decade for Women conference in Nairobi, Kenya, took place; that same year, Wilma Mankiller was named the first principal chief of the Cherokee Nation. In 1986, the National Women's Studies Association conference was held at Spelman College. The next year, 1987, the Supreme Court ruled that the Immigration and Naturalization Service must interpret the 1980s' Refugee Act more broadly to recognize refugees from Central America, a ruling that reflected the work on the part of thousands of activists, many of whom were feminists, to end U.S. intervention in Central America.

In 1991, Elsa Barkely Brown, Barbara Ransby, and Deborah King launched the campaign called African American Women in Defense of Ourselves, within minutes of Anita Hill's testimony regarding the nomination of Clarence Thomas to the Supreme Court. Their organizing included an advertisement in the *New York Times* and six Black newspapers which included the names of 1,603 Black women. The 1982 defeat of the ERA did not signal a period of abeyance for multiracial feminism. In fact, multiracial feminism flourished in the 1980s, despite the country's turn to the Right.

Understanding Second Wave feminism from the vantage point of the Black Power movement and multiracial feminism also shows the limit of the frequent assignment of the term "radical" only to the white antipatriarchal feminists of the late 1960s and early 1970s. Many feminist historians link the development of radical feminism to the creation of several antipatriarchy organizations—the Redstockings, Radicalesbians, WITCH, and other CR groups. How the term "radical" is used by feminist historians does not square, however, with how women of color and white antiracists used that term from the 1960s through the 1980s. What does it mean when feminist historians apply the term "radical" to white, antipatriarchy women but not to antiracist white women and women of color (including Angela Davis, Kathleen Cleaver, Marilyn Buck, Anna Mae Aquash, Susan Saxe, Vicki Gabriner, and Laura Whitehorn) of the same era whose "radicalism" included attention to race, gender, and imperialism and a belief that revolution might require literally laying their lives on the line? These radical women include political prisoners—Black, Puerto Rican, and white—some of whom are still in prison for their antiracist activism in the 1960s and 1970s. Many of these women openly identify as feminists and/or lesbians but are rarely included in histories of Second Wave feminism.

What does it mean when the term "radical" is only assigned to white, antipatriarchy women when the subtitle to Cherríe Moraga and Gloria Anzaldúa's foundational book, *This Bridge Called My Back,* was "Writings by *Radical* Women of Color"?[32] To my mind, a nuanced and accurate telling of Second Wave feminism is one that shows why and how the term "radical" was itself contested. . . . An expansive history would emphasize that Second Wave feminism drew on the civil rights movement, the New Left, *and* the Black Power movement which, together, helped to produce three groups of "radical" women.

Principles of a Movement

. . . what most interests me about comparing normative feminist history with multiracial feminism are the contestations in philosophy embedded in these coexisting frameworks. Both popular and scholarly interpretations of Second Wave feminism typically link two well-known principles to the movement—"Sisterhood Is Powerful" and the "Personal Is Political." From the point of view of multiracial feminism, both principles are a good start but, in themselves, are not enough.

Conversations and struggles between women of color and white women encouraged white women to think about the limits of the popular feminist slogan "Sisterhood Is Powerful." There were many reasons why the editors of *This Bridge Called My Back* titled one of the sections of the book,

"And When You Leave, Take Your Pictures with You: Racism in the Women's Movement." Lorraine Bethel's poem, "What Chou Mean *We,* White Girl? or the Cullud Lesbian Feminist Declaration of Independence" ("Dedicated to the proposition that all women are not equal, i.e., identical/ly oppressed"), clarifies that "we" between white and Black is provisional, at best.[33] . . .

Cross-racial struggle made clear the work that white women needed to do in order for cross-racial sisterhood to *really* be powerful. Among the directives were the following: Don't expect women of color to be your educators, to do all the bridge work. White women need to be the bridge—a lot of the time. Do not lump African American, Latina, Asian American, and Native American women into one category. History, culture, imperialism, language, class, region, and sexuality make the concept of a monolithic "women of color" indefensible. Listen to women of color's anger. It is informed by centuries of struggle, erasure, and experience. White women, look to your own history for signs of heresy and rebellion. Do not take on the histories of Black, Latina, or American Indian women as your own. They are not and never were yours.

A second principle associated with liberal and radical feminism is captured in the slogan "The Personal Is Political," first used by civil rights and New Left activists and then articulated with more depth and consistency by feminist activists. The idea behind the slogan is that many issues that historically have been deemed "personal"—abortion, battery, unemployment, birth, death, and illness—are actually deeply political issues.

Multiracial feminism requires women to add another level of awareness—to stretch the adage from "The Personal Is Political" to, in the words of antiracist activist Anne Braden, "The Personal Is Political and the Political Is Personal."[34] Many issues that have been relegated to the private sphere are, in fact, deeply political. At the same time, many political issues need to be personally committed to—whether you have been victimized by those issues or not. In other words, you don't have to be part of a subordinated group to know an injustice is wrong and to stand against it. White women need not be victims of racism to recognize it is wrong and stand up against it. Unless that is done, white women will never understand how they support racism. If the only issues that feminists deem political are those they have experienced personally, their frame of reference is destined to be narrowly defined by their own lived experience.

The increasing number of antiracist white women who moved into mixed-gender, multi-issue organizations in the 1980s and 1990s after having helped to build women's cultural institutions in the 1970s and 1980s may be one of the best examples of an attempt to uphold this politic. Mab Segrest, perhaps the most prolific writer among lesbian antiracist organizers, provides the quintessential example of this transition in her move from working on the lesbian feminist journal, *Feminary,* in the late 1970s and early 1980s, to becoming the director of North Carolinians against Racist and Religious Violence in the 1980s. A self-reflective writer, Segrest herself notes this transition in the preface to her first book, *My Mama's Dead Squirrel: Lesbian Essays on Southern Culture.* . . . In Segrest's view, by 1983, her work in building lesbian culture—through editing *Feminary* and her own writing—"no longer seemed enough, it seemed too literary." Segrest found herself both "inspired by and frustrated with the lesbian feminist movement." Segrest recalls that she

> had sat in many rooms and participated in many conversations between lesbians about painful differences in race and class, about anti-Semitism and ageism and ablebodiedism. They had been hard discussions, but they had given me some glimpse of the possibility of spinning a wider lesbian movement, a women's movement that truly incorporates diversity as its strength. But in all those discussions, difficult as they were, we had never been out to kill each other. In the faces of Klan and Nazi men—and women—in North Carolina I saw people who would kill us all. I felt I needed to shift from perfecting consciousness to putting consciousness to the continual test of action. I wanted to answer a question that had resonated through the lesbian writing I had taken most to heart: "What will you undertake?"[35]

This, I believe, remains a dogged and crucial question before us and one that requires us to move beyond litanies ultimately based on only a narrow group's survival.

The tremendous strength of autonomous feminist institutions—the festivals, conferences, bookstores, women's studies departments, women's health centers—were the artistic, political, and social contributions activists helped to generate. All of these cultural institutions required women to ask of themselves and others a pivotal question Audre Lorde had posited: Are you doing your work? And yet, by the mid-1980s, the resurgence of the radical Right in the United States that fueled a monumental backlash against gays and lesbians, people of color, and women across the races led multiracial feminists to ask again: Where and with whom are you doing your work? Many antiracist feminists who had helped to build the largely women-led cultural institutions that left a paper trail of multiracial feminism moved on, into mixed-gender, multiracial grassroots organizations, working against the Klan, in support of affirmative action and immigrant rights, and against police brutality and the prison industry. It is in these institutions that much of the hard work continues—in recognizing that "sisterhood is powerful" only when it is worked for and not assumed and that the "personal is political" only to the extent that one's politics go way beyond the confines of one's own individual experience.

Blueprints for Feminist Activism

There are multiple strategies for social justice embedded in multiracial feminism: a belief in building coalitions that are based on a respect for identity-based groups; attention to both process and product but little tolerance for "all-talk" groups; racial parity at every level of an organization (not added on later but initiated from the start); a recognition that race can not be seen in binary terms; a recognition that racism exists in your backyard as well as in the countries the United States is bombing or inhabiting economically; and a recognition of the limits of pacifism when people in struggle are up against the most powerful state in the world. Multiracial feminism is not just another brand of feminism that can be taught alongside liberal, radical, and socialist feminism. Multiracial feminism is the heart of an inclusive women's liberation struggle. The race-class-gender-sexuality-nationality framework through which multiracial feminism operates encompasses and goes way beyond liberal, radical, and socialist feminist priorities—and it always has. Teaching Second Wave feminist history requires chronicling how hegemonic feminism came to be written about as "the" feminism and the limits of that model. Teaching Second Wave history by chronicling the rise of multiracial feminism challenges limited categories because it puts social justice and antiracism at the center of attention. This does not mean that the work done within hegemonic feminism did not exist or was not useful. It does mean that it was limited in its goals and effectiveness.

Although the strategies for multiracial feminism were firmly established in the 1970s and 1980s, I contend that these principles remain a blueprint for progressive, feminist, antiracist struggle in this millennium. . . .

Because written histories of social movements are typically one generation behind the movements themselves, it makes sense that the histories of the feminist movement are just now emerging. That timing means that now is the time to interrupt normative accounts before they begin to repeat themselves, each time, sounding more like "the truth" simply because of the repetition of the retelling. This interruption is necessary with regard to Second Wave feminism as well as earlier movements.

. . .

. . . I want young women to know the rich, complicated, contentious, and visionary history of multiracial feminism and to know the nuanced controversies within Second Wave feminism. I want them to know that Shirley Chisholm ran for president in 1972; that Celestine Ware wrote a Black radical feminist text in the 1970s which offered an inspiring conception of revolution with a deep sense of humanity; that before Mab Segrest went to work for an organization against the Klan in North Carolina, she and others published an independent lesbian journal in the 1970s that included some of the most important and compelling race-conscious writing by white women and women of color to date.[36] I want people to know that there are antiracist feminist women currently in prison for their antiracist activism in the 1960s and since.[37] Among them is Marilyn Buck, a poet, political prisoner and, in her words, "a feminist with a small 'f,'" who is serving an eighty-year sentence in California.[38] Her poems, including "To the Woman Standing Behind Me in Line Who Asks Me How Long This Black History Month Is Going to Last," eloquently capture why Buck must be included in tellings of multiracial feminism.[39] She writes:

the whole month
even if it is the shortest month
a good time in this prison life

you stare at me
and ask why I think February is so damned fine

I take a breath
prisoners fight for February
African voices cross razor wire
cut through the flim-flam
of Amerikkan history
call its cruelties out
confirm the genius of survival
creation and
plain ole enduring

a celebration!

***

The woman drops her gaze
looks away and wishes
she had not asked
confused that white skin did not guarantee
a conversation she wanted to have
she hasn't spoken to me since
I think I'll try to stand
in line with her
again

Marilyn Buck's poems and the work of other multiracial feminist activists help show that the struggle against racism is hardly linear, that the consolidation of white-biased feminism was clearly costly to early Second Wave feminism, and that we must dig deep to represent the feminist movement that does justice to an antiracist vision.

NOTES

The author thanks several people for their generous help on this article, especially Monisha Das Gupta, Diane Harriford, and two *Feminist Studies* anonymous reviewers.

1. For examples of histories that focus on white feminism, see Sheila Tobias, *Faces of Feminism: An Activist's Reflections on the Women's Movement* (Boulder: Westview Press, 1997); Barbara Ryan, *Feminism and the Women's Movement: Dynamics of Change in Social Movement Ideology and Activism* (New York: Routledge, 1992); Alice Echols, *Daring to Be Bad: Radical Feminism in America, 1967–1975,* (Minneapolis: University of Minnesota Press, 1989).

2. Chela Sandoval, *Methodology of the Oppressed* (Minneapolis: University of Minnesota Press, 2000), 41–42.

3. Of these branches of feminism (liberal, socialist, and radical), socialist feminism, which treats sexism and classism as interrelated forms of oppression, may have made the most concerted effort to develop an antiracist agenda in the 1970s. For example, "The Combahee River Collective Statement" was first published in Zillah Eisenstein's *Capitalist Patriarchy and the Case for Socialist Feminism* (New York: Monthly Review Press, 1979), 362–72, before it was published in Barbara Smith's *Home Girls: A Black Feminist Anthology* (New York: Kitchen Table, Women of Color Press, 1983). *Radical America,* a journal founded in 1967 and whose contributors and editors include many social feminists, consistently published articles that examined the relationship between race, class, and gender. The 1970s' socialist feminist organization, the Chicago Women's Liberation Union, which considered quality public education, redistribution of wealth, and accessible child care key to a feminist agenda, also made room for a race analysis by not privileging sexism over other forms of oppression. However, the fact that socialist feminist organizations were typically white dominated and were largely confined to academic and/or middle-class circles limited their effectiveness and visibility as an antiracist presence in early Second Wave feminism. For early socialist feminist documents, see Rosalyn Baxandall and Linda Gordon, eds., *Dear Sisters: Dispatches from the Women's Liberation Movement* (New York: Basic Books, 2000).

4. For an expanded discussion of the contributions and limitations of white antiracism from the 1950s to the present, see Becky Thompson, *A Promise and a Way of Life: White Antiracist Activism* (Minneapolis: University of Minnesota Press, 2001).

5. For a discussion of the term "multiracial feminism," see Maxine Baca Zinn and Bonnie Thornton Dill, "Theorizing Difference from Multiracial Feminism," *Feminist Studies* 22 (summer 1996): 321–31.

6. Bernice Johnson Reagon, "Coalition Politics: Turning the Century," in *Home Girls,* 356–69; Patricia Hill Collins, *Black Feminist Thought: Knowledge, Consciousness, and the Politics of Empowerment* (Boston: Unwin Hyman, 1990), 11; Barbara Smith, introduction, *Home Girls,* xxxii; Cherríe Moraga and Gloria Anzaldúa, eds., *This Bridge Called My Back: Writings by Radical Women of Color* (New York: Kitchen Table, Women of Color Press, 1981); Chandra Talpade Mohanty, "Under Western Eyes: Feminist Scholarship and Colonial Discourses," in *Third World Women and the Politics of Feminism,* eds., Chandra Talpade Mohanty, Ann Russo, and Lourdes Torres (Bloomington: Indiana University Press, 1991), 51–80; Paula Gunn Allen, "Who Is Your Mother? Red Roots of White Feminism," in her *The Sacred Hoop: Recovering the Feminine in American Indian Traditions* (Boston: Beacon Press, 1986), 209–21; Adrienne Rich, *Blood, Bread, and Poetry* (New York: Norton, 1986); Patricia Williams, *The Alchemy of Race and Rights* (Cambridge: Harvard University Press, 1991).

7. Here I am using the term "feminist" to describe collective action designed to confront interlocking race, class, gender, and sexual oppressions (and other systemic discrimination). Although many women in these organizations explicitly referred to themselves as "feminist" from their earliest political work, others have used such terms as "womanist," "radical women of color," "revolutionary," and "social activist." Hesitation among women of color about the use of the term "feminist" often signaled an unwillingness to be associated with white-led feminism, but this wariness did not mean they were not doing gender-conscious, justice work. The tendency not to include gender-conscious activism by women of color in dominant versions of Second Wave history unless the women used the term "feminist" fails to account for the multiple terms women of color have historically used to designate activism that keeps women at the center of analysis and attends to interlocking oppressions. Although the formation of a women's group—an Asian women's friendship group, a Black women's church group, or a Native American women's arts council—is not inherently a feminist group, those organizations that confront gender, race, sexual, and class oppression, whether named as "feminist" or not, need to be considered as integral to multiracial feminism.

8. Benita Roth, "The Making of the Vanguard Center: Black Feminist Emergence in the 1960s and 1970s," in *Still Lifting, Still Climbing: African American Women's Contemporary Activism,* ed., Kimberly Springer (New York: New York University Press, 1999), 71.

9. Sherna Berger Gluck, "Whose Feminism, Whose History? Reflections on Excavating the History of (the) U.S. Women's Movement(s)," in *Community Activism and Feminist Politics: Organizing across Race, Class, and Gender,* ed., Nancy A. Naples (New York: Routledge, 1998), 38–39.

10. Miya Iwataki, "The Asian Women's Movement: A Retrospective," *East Wind* (spring/summer 1983): 35–41; Gluck, 39–41.

11. Sonia Shah, "Presenting the Blue Goddess: Toward a National Pan-Asian Feminist Agenda," in *The State of Asian America: Activism and Resistance in the 1990s,* ed., Karin Aguilar-San Juan (Boston: South End Press, 1994), 147–58.

12. M. Annette Jaimes with Theresa Halsey, "American Indian Women: At the Center of Indigenous Resistance in Contemporary North America," in *The State of Native America: Genocide, Colonization, and Resistance,* ed., M. Annette Jaimes (Boston: South End Press, 1992), 329.

13. Stephanie Autumn, ". . . This Air, This Land, This Water—If We Don't Start Organizing Now, We'll Lose It," *Big Mama Rag* 11 (April 1983): 4, 5.

14. For an insightful analysis of the multidimensionality of Black nationalism of the late 1960s and early 1970s, see Angela Davis, "Black Nationalism: The Sixties and the Nineties," in *The Angela Davis Reader,* ed., Joy James (Malden, Mass: Blackwell, 1998), 289–96.

15. Ibid., 15, 314.

16. Deborah Gray White, *Too Heavy a Load; Black Women in Defense of Themselves* (New York: Norton, 1999), 242.

17. Ibid., 242–53.

18. Combahee River Collective, "The Combahee River Collective Statement," in *Home Girls*, 272–82.

19. See Moraga and Anzaldúa.

20. Toni Cade, ed., *The Black Woman: An Anthology* (New York: Signet, 1970); Maxine Hong Kingston, *The Woman Warrior* (New York: Vintage Books, 1977); Moraga and Anzaldúa; Smith.

21. Assata Shakur, *Assata: An Autobiography* (Chicago: Lawrence Hill Books, 1987), 197.

22. Angela Davis, *Angela Davis: An Autobiography* (New York: Random House, 1974).

23. Nancy MacLean, "The Hidden History of Affirmative Action: Working Women's Struggles in the 1970s and the Gender of Class," *Feminist Studies* 25 (spring 1999): 47.

24. Several key Jewish feminist texts that addressed how to take racism and anti-Semitism seriously in feminist activism were published during this period and included Evelyn Torton Beck, ed., *Nice Jewish Girls: A Lesbian Anthology* (Trumansburg, N.Y.: Crossing Press, 1982); Melanie Kaye/Kantrowitz and Irena Klepfisz, eds., *The Tribe of Dina: A Jewish Women's Anthology* (Boston: Beacon Press, 1989), first published as a special issue of *Sinister Wisdom*, nos. 29/30 (1986); Melanie Kaye/Kantrowitz, *The Issue Is Power: Essays on Women, Jews, Violence, and Resistance* (San Francisco: Aunt Lute, 1992); Irena Klepfisz., *Periods of Stress* (Brooklyn, N.Y.: Out & Out Books, 1977); and *Keeper of Accounts* (Watertown, Mass: Persephone Press, 1982).

For key antiracist lesbian texts, see Adrienne Rich, *On Lies, Secrets, and Silence: Selected Prose, 1966–1978* (New York: Norton, 1979); Joan Gibbs and Sara Bennett, *Top Ranking: A Collection of Articles on Racism and Classism in the Lesbian Community* (New York: Come! Unity Press, 1980); Mab Segrest, *My Mama's Dead Squirrel: Lesbian Essays on Southern Culture* (Ithaca, N.Y.: Firebrand Books, 1985); Elly Bulkin, Minnie Bruce Pratt, and Barbara Smith, *Yours in Struggle: Three Feminist Perspectives on Anti-Semitism and Racism* (Brooklyn, N.Y.: Long Haul Press, 1984).

25. Verta Taylor and Nancy Whittier, "The New Feminist Movement," in *Feminist Frontiers IV*, eds., Laurel Richardson, Verta Taylor, and Nancy Whittier (New York: McGraw-Hill, 1997), 544–45.

26. Chela Sandoval, "Feminism and Racism: A Report on the 1981 National Women's Studies Association Conference," in *Making Face, Making Soul: Haciendo Caras: Creative and Critical Perspectives by Women of Color*, eds., Gloria Anzaldúa (San Francisco: Aunt Lute, 1990), 55.

27. Smith, "'Feisty Characters,'" 470–80.

28. Gluck, 32.

29. James, 313.

30. Activists who helped Assata Shakur escape include political prisoners Marilyn Buck, Sylvia Baraldini, Susan Rosenberg, and Black male revolutionaries.

31. Adrienne Rich, "Disobedience and Women's Studies," *Blood, Bread, and Poetry* (New York: Norton, 1986), 76–84.

32. Moraga and Anzaldúa.

33. Lorraine Bethel, "What Chou Mean *We*, White Girl?" in *Conditions: Five* (1979): 86.

34. Thompson. See also Anne Braden, *The Wall Between* (Knoxville: University of Tennessee Press, 1999); Anne Braden, "A Second Open Letter to Southern White Women," *Southern Exposure* 6 (winter 1977): 50.

35. Mab Segrest, "Fear to Joy: Fighting the Klan," *Sojourner: The Women's Forum* 13 (November 1987): 20.

36. See *Feminary: A Feminist Journal for the South Emphasizing Lesbian Visions*.

37. Marilyn Buck, Linda Evans, Laura Whitehorn, and Kathy Boudin are among the white political prisoners who are either currently in prison or, in the case of Laura Whitehorn and Linda Evans, recently released, serving sentences whose length and severity can only be understood as retaliation for their principled, antiracist politics.

38. Marilyn Buck is in a federal prison in Dublin, California, for alleged conspiracies to free political prisoners, to protest government policies through the use of violence, and to raise funds for Black liberation organizations. [She was released in July 2010, a month before her death from cancer, aged 62.—Eds.]

39. Marilyn Buck's poem, "To the Woman Standing Behind Me in Line Who Asks Me How Long This Black History Month Is Going to Last," is reprinted with written permission from the author.

F I V E

♦♦♦

Radical Heterosexuality (1992)

Naomi Wolf

Naomi Wolf is a writer and social critic whose international bestseller, *The Beauty Myth*, challenged the marketing of unrealistic beauty standards. Other titles include *Fire with Fire, Promiscuities, Misconceptions,* and *The End of America: A letter of warning to a young patriot.* Wolf is cofounder of the Woodhull Institute for Ethical Leadership and the American Freedom Campaign.

All over the country, millions of feminists have a secret indulgence. By day they fight gender injustice; by night they sleep with men. Is this a dual life? A core contradiction? Is sleeping with a man "sleeping with the enemy"? And is razor burn from kissing inherently oppressive?

It's time to say you *can* hate sexism and love men. As the feminist movement grows more mature and our understanding of our enemies more nuanced, three terms assumed to be in contradiction—radical feminist heterosexuality—can and must be brought together.

Rules of the Relationship

But how? Andrea Dworkin and Catharine MacKinnon have pointed out that sexism limits women to such a degree that it's questionable whether the decision to live with a man can ever truly be free. If you want to use their sound, if depressing, reasoning to a brighter end, turn the thesis around: radical heterosexuality demands substituting choice for dependency.

Radical heterosexuality requires that the woman be able to support herself. This is not to belittle women who must depend financially on men; it is to recognize that when our daughters are raised with the skills that would let them leave abusers, they need not call financial dependence love.

Radical heterosexuality needs alternative institutions. As the child of a good lifetime union, I believe in them. But when I think of pledging my heart and body to a man—even the best and kindest man—within the existing institution of marriage, I feel faint. The more you learn about its legal structure, the less likely you are to call the caterers.

In the nineteenth century, when a judge ruled that a husband could not imprison and rape his wife, the London *Times* bemoaned, "One fine morning last month, marriage in England was suddenly abolished." The phrase "rule of thumb" descends from English common law that said a man could legally beat his wife with a switch "no thicker than his thumb."

If these nightmarish echoes were confined to history, I might feel more nuptial; but look at our own time. Do I want the blessing of an institution that doesn't provide adequate protection from marital rape? That gives a woman less protection from assault by her husband than by a stranger? That assigns men 70 percent of contested child custodies?

Of course I do not fear any such brutality from the man I want to marry (no bride does). But marriage means that his respectful treatment of me and our children becomes, despite our intentions, a kindness rather than a legally grounded right.

We need a heterosexual version of the marriages that gay and lesbian activists are seeking: a commitment untainted by centuries of inequality; a ritual that invites the community to rejoice in the making of a new freely chosen family.

The radical heterosexual man must yield the automatic benefits conferred by gender. I had a lover once who did not want to give up playing sports in a club that had a separate door for women. It must be tempting to imagine you can have both—great squash courts *and* the bed of a liberated woman—but in the mess hall of gender relations, there is *no such thing as a free lunch.*

Radical heterosexual women too must give up gender benefits (such as they are). I know scores of women—independent, autonomous—who avoid assuming any of the risk for a romantic or sexual approach.

I have watched myself stand complacently by while my partner wrestles with a stuck window, an intractable computer printer, maps, or locks. Sisters, I am not proud of this, and I'm working on it. But people are lazy—or at least I am—and it's easy to *rationalize* that the person with the penis is the one who should get out of a warm bed to fix the snow on the TV screen. After all, it's the very least owed to me *personally* in compensation for centuries of virtual enslavement.

Radical heterosexuals must try to stay conscious—at all times, I'm afraid—of their gender imprinting, and how it plays out in their erotic melodramas. My own psyche is a flagrant *son et lumière* of political incorrectness. Three of my boyfriends had motorcycles; I am easy pickings for the silent and dysfunctional. My roving eye is so taken by the oil-stained persona of the labor organizer that myopic intellectuals have gained access to my favors merely by sporting a Trotsky button.

We feminists are hard on each other for admitting to weakness. Gloria Steinem caught flak . . . for acknowledging in *Revolution from Within* that she was drawn to a man because he could do the things with money and power that we are taught men must do. And some were appalled when Simone de Beauvoir's letters revealed how she coddled Sartre.

But the antifeminist erotic template is *in* us. We would not be citizens of this culture if swooning damsels and abandoned vixens had not been beamed at us from our first solid food to our first vote. We can't fight it until we admit to it. And we can't identify it until we drag it, its taffeta billowing and its bosom heaving, into the light of day.

I have done embarrassing, reactionary, abject deeds out of love and sexual passion. . . . Only when we reveal our conditioning can we tell how much of our self-abasement is neurotic femininity, and how much is the flawed but impressive human apparatus of love.

In the Bedroom

Those are the conditions for the radical heterosexual couple. What might this new creation look like in bed? It will look like something we have no words or images for—the eroticization of consent, the equal primacy of female and male desire.

We will need to tell some secrets—to map our desire for the male body and admit to our fascination with the rhythms and forces of male arousal, its uncanny counterintuitive spell.

We will also need to face our creature qualities. Animality has for so long been used against us—bitch, fox, *Penthouse* pet—that we struggle for the merit badges of higher rationality, ambivalent about our animal nature.

The truth is that heterosexual women believe that men, on some level, are animals; as they believe that we are animals. But what does "animal" mean?

Racism and sexism have long used animal metaphors to distance and degrade the Other. Let us redefine "animal" to make room for that otherness between the genders, an otherness fierce and worthy of respect. Let us define animal as an inchoate kinship, a comradeship, that finds a language beyond our species.

I want the love of two unlikes: the look of astonishment a woman has at the sight of a male back bending. These manifestations of difference confirm in heterosexuals the beauty that similarity confirms in the lesbian or gay imagination. Difference and animality do not have to mean hierarchy.

Men We Love

What must the men be like? Obviously, they're not going to be just anyone. *Esquire* runs infantile disquisitions on "Women We Love" (suggesting, Lucky Girls!). Well, I think that the men who are loved by feminists are lucky. Here's how they qualify to join this fortunate club.

Men We Love understand that, no matter how similar our backgrounds, we are engaged in a cross-cultural . . . relationship. They know that we know much about their world and they but little of ours. They accept what white people must accept in relationships with people of other ethnicities: to know that they do not know.

Men We Love don't hold a baby as if it is a still-squirming, unidentifiable catch from the sea.

Men We Love don't tell women what to feel about sexism. . . . They do not presume that there is a line in the sand called "enlightened male," and that all they need is a paperback copy of Djuna Barnes and good digital technique. They understand that unlearning gender oppressiveness means untying the very core of how we become female and male. They know this pursuit takes a lifetime at the minimum.

Sadly, men in our lives sometimes come through on personal feminism but balk at it intellectually. A year ago, I had a bruising debate with my father and brother about the patriarchal nature of traditional religious and literary canons. I almost seized them by their collars, howling "Read Mary Daly! Read Toni Morrison! Take Feminism 101. *No, I can't* explain it to you between the entrée and dessert!"

By spring, my dad, bless his heart, had asked for a bibliography, and last week my brother sent me *Standing Again at Sinai*, a Jewish-feminist classic. Men We Love are willing, sooner or later, to read the Books We Love.

Men We Love accept that successful training in manhood makes them blind to phenomena that are fact to women. Recently, I walked down a New York City avenue with a woman friend, X, and a man friend, Y. I pointed out to Y the leers, hisses, and invitations to sit on faces. Each woman saw clearly what the other woman saw, but Y was baffled. Sexual harassers have superb timing. A passerby makes kissy-noises with his tongue while Y is scrutinizing the menu of the nearest bistro. "There, there! Look! Listen!" we cried. "What? Where? Who?" wailed poor Y, valiantly, uselessly spinning.

What if, hard as they try to see, they cannot hear? Once I was at lunch with a renowned male crusader for the First Amendment. Another Alpha male was present, and the venue was the Supreme Court lunchroom—two power factors that automatically press the "mute" button on the male ability to detect a female voice on the audioscope. The two men began to rev their motors; soon they were off and racing in a policy-wonk grand prix. I tried, once or twice, to ask questions. But the free-speech champions couldn't hear me over the testosterone roar.

Men We Love undertake half the care and cost of contraception. They realize that it's not fair to wallow in the fun without sharing the responsibility. When stocking up for long weekends, they brave the amused glances when they ask, "Do you have this in unscented?"

Men We Love know that just because we can be irrational doesn't mean we're insane. When we burst into premenstrual tears—having just realized the cosmic fragility of creation—they comfort us. Not until we feel better do they dare remind us gently that we had this same revelation exactly 28 days ago.

Men We Love must make a leap of imagination to believe in the female experience. They do not call

women nags or paranoid when we embark on the arduous, often boring, nonnegotiable daily chore of drawing attention to sexism. They treat it like adults taking driving lessons: if irked in the short term at being treated like babies, they're grateful in the long term that someone is willing to teach them patiently how to move through the world without harming the pedestrians. Men We Love don't drive without their gender glasses on.

A Place for Them

It's not simple gender that pits Us against Them. In the fight against sexism, it's those who are for us versus those who are against us—of either gender. . . .

It is time to direct our anger more acutely at the Men We Hate—like George Bush—and give the Men We Love something useful to do. Not to take over meetings, or to set agendas; not to whine, "Why can't feminists teach us how to be free?" but to add their bodies, their hearts, and their numbers, to support us.

I meet many young men who are brought to feminism by love for a woman who has been raped, or by watching their single mothers struggle against great odds, or by simple common sense. Their most frequent question is "What can I do to help?"

Imagine a rear battalion of committed "Men Against Violence Against Women" (or Men for Choice, or what have you)—of all races, ages, and classes. Wouldn't that be a fine sight to fix in the eyes of a five-year-old boy?

Finally, the place to make room for radical feminist heterosexuality is within our heads. If the movement that I dearly love has a flaw, it is a tendency toward orthodoxies about other women's pleasures and needs. This impulse is historically understandable: in the past, we needed to define ourselves against men if we were to define ourselves at all. But today, the most revolutionary choice we can make is to affirm other women's choices, whether lesbian or straight, bisexual or celibate.

NOW President Patricia Ireland speaks for me even though our sexual lives are not identical. Simone de Beauvoir speaks for me even though our sexual lives are not identical. Audre Lorde speaks for me even though our sexual lives are not identical. Is it the chromosomes of your lovers that establish you as a feminist? Or is it the life you make out of the love you make?

SIX

◆◆◆

The Brown Girl's Guide to Labels (2010)

Mathangi Subramanian

Mathangi Subramanian is an Indian American writer and educator. She is a senior policy analyst with New York City Council, where she covers education and social service issues. She has published scholarly work in *PENN GSE Perspectives on Urban Education, Current Issues in Comparative Education,* and the *Encyclopedia of Women and Islamic Cultures.* Her children's fiction has appeared in *Kahani* magazine.

1998

When they heard that I had been accepted at Brown University, friends from my suburban high school filled my yearbook with dire warnings and heartfelt advice about the cosmetic consequences of my potential liberalization.

"Don't forget to shave your armpits," was a popular one.

"Don't let me see you burning your bra on CNN next year," was another.

When I got to Brown, I was told that getting a degree was important, but that the real reason we were in college was to find ourselves.

I soon discovered that the most common way to find oneself was to adopt a label. Among my white girlfriends, the most popular of these labels was *feminist.*

"I'm not saying that men and women shouldn't be different," they told me. "I'm just saying they should be equal."

This sounded about right to me, so I decided to investigate. In between my highly practical science classes, I listened in on spirited conversations about the need to move away from the image of bra-burning, pierced harridans with hairy armpits (this sounded familiar) and toward embracing and celebrating our desire to wear lipstick and short skirts without judgment. Other than a modicum of knowledge I had gained in seventh grade, which is the year I spent wearing foundation and designer skirts in a desperate attempt to cover up my acne

and naiveté, I didn't know much about fashion. Then there was the whole battle to reclaim the word *sexy,* a battle I couldn't join simply because I couldn't bring myself to invest in reclaiming a word I had never claimed in the first place, and probably never would. White girls were sexy. Bespectacled Indian girls who took AP physics and ran for president of the debate team were not.

Of course, the whole Indian thing presented another option: Released from the white-washed suburbs, I discovered a contingent of South Asian Americans who embraced their ethnic identities by labeling themselves either as *desi* or *brown.* I occasionally ate lunch with them before lab or spent late nights with them working on problem sets. The girls ironed their hair, wore huge earrings, and lusted after South Asian boys who shortened their names to "Jay" or "Ace" and wore too much cologne.

"Oh my god, did you hear Deepti likes Jay?" went a typical conversation.

"Seriously. You know she's just trying to snag a husband," it continued.

"Um, gross. Wait, I totally saw the perfect wedding sari online yesterday, wanna see?" it usually ended.

Well, clearly this wasn't going to work. It wasn't until years later that I discovered that these girls were the minority, and that there was a whole subset of desi women who fantasized about political activism and artistic fame, rather than elaborate weddings. At the time, though, I thought that brown was not the label for me.

By the end of my freshman year, I had picked out several potential majors, and no potential labels.

1999

The summer I turned nineteen, I went to India for the second time in my life and hated every minute. I spent half the time sitting silently on display before a parade of relatives who discussed me in Tamil as if I weren't there. The other half I spent cursing my weak stomach: If I wasn't throwing up, I was popping Pepto Bismol.

One morning, while I was sitting on the balcony attempting to catch the weak excuse for a breeze, my mother came out and patted my sweaty hair.

"How you doing?" she asked, flopping into a chair next to me.

"Ugh," I said, wiping the sweat pooled around my temples.

My mother's mother wandered out onto the balcony, wiping her brow with her sari. My *patthi* is impossibly intelligent, able to rattle off everything from the symptoms associated with rare diseases to the color of the heroine's sari in every Tamil movie ever made. In later years, when I visited, we would watch Tamil serials together, and she would provide a running commentary that confirmed my theory that facility with sarcasm is a genetic trait. That summer, though, we did not yet know how much we had in common. To me, she was still a quirky, vacant woman prone to non sequiturs.

"Mathangi, when are you getting married?" she asked me in Tamil.

"Amma!" my mom yelled. "She's only nineteen. Leave her alone."

"She should start thinking now," my grandmother said. "She must get married before she's too old."

"She doesn't have to get married at all," my mom said, stroking my hair, but staring defiantly at my grandmother. "I've always told her and her brother that they should be independent. There's no reason for her to get married if she's not in love."

"Not for love," my grandmother said, unexpectedly switching into her choppy Indian English. "Just to have someone to take care of you."

"She can take care of herself," my mother said firmly, her hands raking through my hair with increasingly violent strokes.

I wandered inside and found my brother huddled beneath the ceiling fan, reading the paper.

"What are you doing?" I asked him.

"Finding you a husband," he said without looking up.

"Seriously?" I said.

"Yeah," he said, pushing his glasses up on his nose. "But you're doomed." He said *doomed* the way my family always said that word to each other: with a thick Indian accent, rolling our tongues

around the d's. "Basically, they all want someone to cook them curry."

"What?" I said. "I make damn good curry."

"It's not about how good the curry is," he said. "It's about focusing your skill set. As in, only being able to make curry. In this market, autonomy and independent thought seem to be discouraged. But hey, if you drop out of college, you might still make the cut. If you finish, you'll be overqualified."

My grandmother slid up beside me and placed her gnarled hand on my shoulder. Her wrinkled brown skin always reminded me of walnuts.

"Mathangi," she said, "men are useless. Your mother is right. Don't get married."

"Oh," I said. "Okay. Um, thanks."

"Good," she said. She nodded, adjusted the *pallu* of her sari, and walked resolutely into the kitchen.

My brother tapped the paper excitedly. "Hey, this guy wants someone with a master's degree. I bet he'd settle for someone with a bachelor's," he said. "This is it! This is your man!"

"Be still my beating heart," I said.

2002

After I graduated from college, I prepared to move to the border of Mexico, where I had landed my first job: teaching chemistry at a public high school. My family was pleased, but my girlfriends were not.

"But don't you want to go to India?" they asked. "I mean, women there are *so* oppressed. Don't you want to help people where you're from?"

I didn't want to go to India and suffer through a year or two of mosquito bites the size of quarters and frequent trips to pit toilets in the middle of nowhere. I wanted to live in the United States and eat whatever I chose and sleep without a mosquito net and cross the street without fear of death-by-autorickshaw. And if it came down to where I was from, I was from America. American girls were failing out of school and living in poverty and raising babies when they were still in their teens. It seemed like I could really make a difference here, at home.

Besides, I wasn't sure what feminism had to do with it. It's not like any Indian women I knew wore makeup, other than a little bit of eyeliner now and then, and why wear a short skirt when you could wear a sari?

2003

"Mmmff, hello?"

"Honey? Did I wake you?"

I forced myself to sit up, blinking in the South Texas sunlight that seeped through the slats of the blinds on my windows.

"Mom, is that you?" I asked, fumbling for my glasses. "What time is it?"

"It's eight o'clock," she said. "Do you want me to call back? Were you sleeping in?"

"No, no," I said, yawning. "Is everything okay?"

"I have big news," she said. I could hear the rhythm of a knife on a cutting board in the background, and I knew that, as she often did, she was cooking as she spoke to me.

"Oh?" I said, getting out of bed and padding across the carpet into my own kitchen, fully stocked with small Tupperware containers of spices my mother gave me when I left home.

"I told you I read that book you gave me, the book about men and makeup?" she said.

"The Beauty Myth," I said. She had stopped buying makeup after she read it.

"Yes, that one! Well, I just read that other book you got me. *Sex and Power?"*

"Right," I said. I hadn't read it at the time, but my mom had just gotten a hard won promotion, so I thought it was appropriate.

"I related to every single page!" she said. "It was like reading my life. There were all these stories about women taking care of their family and working full-time, and how they can't put in the same hours as men because they have to go home and cook dinner, which, you know, I used to do." My mom had taught my father to cook when she went back to school for her associate's degree in computer science and couldn't work, study, and run the house by herself anymore. "And then there was a whole part about how women get passed over for promotions," she continued. What she didn't mention is that, when she figured out her boss had passed her over the last time for yet another white male, she had marched into his office and declared loudly with the door open, "I can be a lot of things, but I can't be white!" *She* got the promotion two weeks later.

"So then I realized something," she said. I could hear the crackle of mustard seeds in hot oil, and my stomach began to rumble.

"Tell me," I said, pushing aside a stack of my students' ungraded chemistry tests to make room on the counter for a box of cereal.

"I'm a feminist!" she said, exhaling all at once.

"Wow, Mom, that's great," I said, weakly.

"Isn't that wonderful? I have been all this time, and we just didn't have a word for it," she said. I heard a splatter and she said, "Oh, hold on, I'm just adding some potatoes to the oil. Just a second."

As I chewed on my cereal, I wondered how everyone in the world seemed to be okay with the label feminist when I wasn't. Lately, I had been working my way through the collection of books about India in the local public library, particularly the ones about Indian women, which I noticed seemed to be mostly written by non-Indian women. If these books were to be believed then Indian women were submissive, abused, mouselike creatures draped in bright colors and regrets. No matter where I looked, the message was clear: You could be Indian, and you could be a feminist, but you couldn't be both.

And yet, here was my mother, who grew up in a village in the South of India, declaring herself a feminist. If she was a feminist, was I?

2006

During my second semester of graduate school, it was time, yet again, to pick a label.

"Don't forget that one of the key parts of writing the methodology section of any ethnography is to discuss your positionality," my professor said. "You should also describe what kind of researcher you are. You might be postmodern for example, or a positivist, or a feminist."

Groan, that word again.

"I'm passing out a couple of articles that may help you decide what you are," she said, passing out a thick packet of reading.

I began reading the packet on the subway the next day. I flipped through the essays and scanned the titles and the authors' names. Then, suddenly, I stopped.

"Chandra Mohanty?" I said out loud, feeling the familiar taste of an Indian name on my tongue. I began to read. And read. And read. And I missed my stop and ended up in Brooklyn. I got out of the train, crossed the platform, and began to read again.

Mohanty called herself a third world feminist. She talked about how Western feminists fought for the right to work, while third world feminists acknowledged that women did most of the world's work, and were therefore fighting for the right to rest. She talked about how third world women fought their battles in the home, defying their family's rules about gender roles. She celebrated daily acts of defiance, like rejecting the necessity of marriage or insisting that men contribute to household chores, and said they required just as much sacrifice and courage as attending any rally in the streets. The stories she told were those of my aunts and my mother and my grandmothers, and, of course, myself.

Now this feminism fit. I wrapped it around me and snuggled in it, the yards of words like the soft fabric of my grandmother's saris.

2008

One morning, before the SAT class I started teaching at a community center in Queens, one of my Indian American students came to class with delicate swirls of henna all over her hands.

"What's with the *mendhi?*" I asked her. "Did someone get married?"

"It's Karwa Chauth," she said, holding out her hands so I could admire them. "Wives are supposed to fast for their husband's health. Are you fasting, miss?"

"No," I said, touching the tips of her fingers approvingly. "I don't have a husband, and I hate fasting. Did your mom do it?"

"Yes," she said. "And so do I."

"Who do you fast for?" I asked.

"My husband," she said. Then, seeing the look on my face, she added, "I mean, my future husband."

"Why?" I asked. "You have plenty of time to worry about being married! Worry about your career and your education now, not your marriage. Besides, it's not like your future husband is fasting for you."

"Actually," she said, "my boyfriend did fast for me."

"Really?" I asked. "Is that common?"

"Well, no," she said. "And especially not him. He's Bangladeshi and Muslim. But I told him I was doing it, and so we agreed that it was only fair if he did it, too. So he is."

"Wow," I said, truly impressed. I was about to tell her that she was quite the young feminist, but I stopped myself. I had dropped the word on the center before, and the girls usually rolled their eyes and told me, "That word's for white ladies."

How could I correct them? Two years before, I had agreed with them. I suppose I could've explained how after reading Chandra Mohanty, I had discovered Uma Narayan and Kumari Jayawardena. I could describe how I had read essay after essay about families and religion and food and history, and how I had discovered a strand of feminism that resonated with me and didn't require me to compromise myself or my past or my future. I could share my realization that every Indian woman I have ever met is a feminist, and every Bangladeshi and Sri Lankan and Pakistani woman, too, because the only place I have ever met submissive desi women is between the pages of books written by women who do not live in our community.

But what was the point? Labeled or unlabeled, brown women everywhere are struggling for each other. No matter what people call them—or, I should say, no matter what people call us—what matters the most is what we call ourselves.

2

Theories and Theorizing:
Integrative Frameworks
for Understanding

People have sought to understand themselves, their home environments, and the wider world since the beginning of time. Using skills of observation, reasoning, and trial-and-error experimentation, women have contributed significant knowledge and insight to the care of infants and children, selective breeding of wild grains, the domestication of animals, production of handicrafts, knowledge of the medicinal properties of plants, and theories of health and illness. With literacy, women observed and analyzed their social worlds in poetry, novels, and essays that conveyed their understandings, feelings, and beliefs.

Some asked feminist questions: Why are women in a subordinate position in our society? What are the origins of this subordination, and how is it perpetuated? How can it be changed?

Why are girls in the United States generally better at creative writing than at math? Why don't U.S. girls do as well in math and science as their international peers? Is rape about sexuality? Power? Both? Or neither? How did rape become a weapon of war? What is pornography? Is it the same as erotica? Why do so many heterosexual marriages in the United States end in divorce? Why are so many children in the world brought up in poverty? Why are more women incarcerated than ever before?

In this chapter we examine theory and theory-making in general terms and continue the discussion of feminist theoretical frameworks we started in Chapter 1. As preparation for understanding the material presented in the rest of the book, we explore various ways in which knowledge is created and validated. People often say that facts speak for themselves. On the contrary, we argue that facts are always open to interpretation and are influenced by one's perspective and beliefs. We use the example of poverty to illustrate some general ideas about theory making. Interestingly, public discourse rarely addresses poverty, which serves to mask its existence. In short, how you think about women's situations and experiences affects what you see and what you understand by what you see.

What Is a Theory?

Consider the following assertion about poverty that many people in our society make: Poor people are poor because they are lazy. Think about the following questions:

1. What is the purpose of this statement?

2. What are the underlying assumptions on which it is based?

3. Who came up with this idea, under what circumstances, and when?

4. How did this idea become popular?

5. If the statement were true, what would it imply about action that should be taken? If the statement were not true, what ideological purpose might it serve?

6. What would you need to know to decide whether this statement is really true?

The preceding statement is a theory. It is one explanation of poverty. It is built on a set of assumptions, or certain factors taken for granted. For example, this theory assumes there are well-paying jobs for all who want to work and that everyone meets the necessary requirements for those jobs, such as education, skills, or a means of providing for child care. These factors are proposed as facts or truths. This explanation of poverty takes a moral perspective. A psychological explanation of poverty may argue that people are poor because they have low self-esteem, lack self-confidence, and take on self-defeating behaviors. A sociological explanation might conclude that structures in our society, such as the educational and economic systems, are organized to exclude certain groups from being able to live above the poverty line. Each theory explicitly or implicitly suggests how to address the problem, which could then lead to appropriate action. If the problem is defined in terms of laziness, a step to ending poverty might be to punish people who are poor; if it is defined in psychological terms, assertiveness training or counseling might be suggested; and if it is defined in terms of structural inequality, ending discrimination or creating more jobs would be the answer.

Theories may also have ideological purposes. The term **ideology** refers to an organized collection of ideas applied to public issues. Dominant ideologies—the ideas that represent the foundational values of a particular society—often appear neutral, whereas alternative ideologies are seen as radical, regardless of their content. Putting forward particular ideologies is a fundamental part of politics, including the role of government, political organizations, lobbyists, and media reporting. Societal institutions, such as education and criminal justice, help to support and perpetuate dominant ideologies. People in both advantaged groups and disadvantaged groups may accept dominant ideologies although these may not be in their best interests. Even for scientists, who advance knowledge by challenging existing beliefs, the power of dominant ways of thinking may block new theories (Kuhn 1962).

Creating Knowledge: Epistemologies, Values, and Methods

Feminist philosopher Sandra Harding (1987) identified three elements that are basic to the process of creating knowledge:

1. *Epistemology*—a theory about knowledge, who can know, and under what circumstances.

2. *Methodology*—the researcher's values and choices about how to carry out research. Researchers can pose questions, collect evidence, and analyze information in different ways based on assumptions about what knowledge is and how the process of creating it is best undertaken.

3. *Method*—or techniques for gathering and analyzing information, whether from observation, listening to personal stories, conducting interviews, reading documents, undertaking media analysis, statistical analysis, and so on.

Virtually everyone thinks up explanations for their experiences; that is, they create theory. For instance, we analyze the causes of poverty, unemployment, anorexia, or obesity in our communities; the impact of immigration on the state we live in; or the experience of rape. Theories generated by ordinary people, however, are usually not regarded as worthy of consideration beyond their own spheres of influence, among friends or coworkers, for example. Historically, Western, university-educated men from the upper classes and their theories, which are

In Attempting to Understand
Any Theoretical Perspective,
Ask Yourself:

1. What does the theory seek to explain?

2. How does it do this? What are the basic arguments and assumptions?

3. What does the theory focus on? What does it ignore?

4. What is the cultural and historical context giving rise to the theory?

5. Do you find this perspective useful? If so, why?

6. Are you convinced by the arguments? Why or why not?

7. What kinds of research questions does this perspective generate?

8. What kinds of actions and projects follow from this perspective?

scientists, rests on the presumption of **objectivity,** "an attitude, philosophy, or claim . . . independent of the individual mind [through emotional detachment and social distance] . . . verified by a socially agreed-upon procedure such as those developed in science, mathematics, or history" (Kohl 1992, p. 84). Objectivity is seen as both a place to begin the process of theorizing and the outcome of that process. It has been long argued that "if done properly, [science] is the epitome of objectivity" (Tuana 1989, p. xi). Therefore, theories developed correctly using the scientific method are held out as value-free and neutral. The method is also empirical. That is, for something to be a fact, it must be physically observable, countable, or measurable. This proposition is extended to include the notion that something is either true or not true, fact or not fact. Last, the experimental method, commonly used in science, "attempts to understand a whole by examining its parts, asking how something works rather than why it works, and derives abstract formulas to predict future results" (Duff 1993, p. 51). In summary, these elements add up to research methods that

> generally require a distancing of the researcher from her or his subjects of study; . . . absence of emotions from the research process; ethics and values are deemed inappropriate in the research process, either as the reason for scientific inquiry or as part of the research process itself; . . . adversarial debates, whether written or oral, become the preferred method of ascertaining truth: the arguments that can withstand the greatest assault and survive intact become the strongest truth.   *(P. H. Collins 1990, p. 205)*

supported by societal institutions such as education and government, have had the greatest impact on how human beings and social phenomena are explained and understood. In the following sections, we discuss how certain kinds of theories have been legitimized in this society and suggest another way of theorizing and developing knowledge.

Dominant Perspectives

From the perspective of the **dominant culture**—the values, symbols, means of expression, language, and interests of the people in power in this society—only certain types of theories have authority. Generally, the authoritativeness of a theory about human beings and society is evaluated along two dimensions. One is its degree of formality, which is determined according to how closely its development followed a particular way of theorizing, the so-called scientific method, the basics of which most of us learned in high school science classes. The second is the scope and generality of the theory.

Although in practice there are several variations of the scientific method, key elements must be present for a theory to fit in this category. The scientific method, originally devised by natural

The scientific method was adopted by scholars in the social sciences as a way to validate and legitimate social scientific knowledge beginning in the late nineteenth century, as disciplines such as psychology and sociology were being developed. Indeed, French philosopher Auguste Comte, credited with coining the term *sociology*, put forward a version of empirical science, which he called **positivism,** to be applied to social as well as physical phenomena. In Comte's view, the only authentic knowledge is scientific knowledge, and such knowledge can only come from positive affirmation of theories through strict scientific method. Since that time, academic disciplines including education, nursing, and social work have also adopted the scientific method as the primary way through which to develop new knowledge in their fields, furthering the dominance or **hegemony** of this approach.

The second dimension for evaluating and judging theory is concerned with its scope and generality. The range is from the most specific explanation with the narrowest scope and most limited generality to the other end of the continuum, the general theory, which is the most abstract and is assumed to have the most general application. Many general theories have been promoted and accepted as being universally applicable. One of them, **biological determinism,** holds that a group's biological or genetic makeup shapes its social, political, and economic destiny. In mainstream society, biology is often assumed to be the basis of women's and men's different roles, especially women's ability to bear children. Most social scientists and feminist theorists see behavior as socially constructed and learned through childhood socialization, everyday experience, education, and the media, as argued by sociologist Judith Lorber (Reading 7). They explain differences in women's and men's roles in these terms and argue that variations in **gender roles** from one society to another provide strong evidence for **social constructionism.**

Critiques of Dominant Perspectives

Evaluating and judging theories according to the scientific method has come under heavy criticism from feminist theorists who have exposed fallacies, biases, and harmful outcomes of that way of creating knowledge (e.g., Bleier 1984; P. H. Collins 1990; Duran 1998; and Shiva 1988). The primary criticisms are that knowledge created by the scientific method is not value-free, neutral, or generalizable to the extent it is claimed to be. Science, as with other academic disciplines, is "a cultural institution and as such is structured by the political, social, and economic values of the culture within which it is practiced" (Tuana 1989, p. xi). As biologist Ruth Hubbard (1989) argued

> To be believed, scientific facts must fit the worldview of the times. Therefore, at times of tension and upheaval . . . some researchers always try to prove that differences in the social, political, and economic status of women and men, blacks and whites, poor people and rich people, are inevitable because they are the

> results of people's inborn qualities and traits. Such scientists have tried to "prove" that blacks are innately less intelligent than whites, or that women are innately weaker, more nurturing, less good at math than men.   *(p. 121)*

Rather than being neutral, all knowledge is value-laden and biased and reflects and serves the interests of the culture that produced it, in this case the dominant culture.

The problem is not that theories are value-laden but that the values and biases of many theories are hidden under the cloak of "scientific objectivity." Moreover, there is the assumption that "if the science is 'good,' in a professional sense [following closely the rules of scientific method], it will also be good for society" (Hubbard 1989, p. 121). Sociologists Margaret Andersen and Patricia Hill Collins (1998) argued that much of what has passed for social knowledge in the United States has been based on exclusionary thinking. By contrast, inclusive thinking "shifts our perspective from the white, male-centered forms of thinking that have characterized much of Western thought, helping us better understand the intersections of race, class, and gender in the experiences of all groups, including those with privilege and power" (p. 13).

Many theories are applied by scholars, policy makers, and commentators not only to the United States but also to the rest of the world, often without acknowledgment that they primarily serve the interests of the dominant group in the United States. They use these theories to justify the inequalities in our society as well as differences and inequalities between the United States and other countries. An example of this can be found in theories of modernization, which assume that the economic development of Western Europe and North America is the path that all other nations should and will follow.

We argue that theorizing is a political project, regardless of whether this is acknowledged. Social theories—explaining the behavior of human beings and society—may serve to support the existing social order or can be used to challenge it. For those who are interested in progressive social change, the work of theorizing is to generate knowledge that challenges conventional wisdom and those formal theories that do not explain the experiences of marginalized people, provide satisfactory solutions to their difficulties, or lead to their liberation.

The Role of Values

Former director of the Center for Women's Global Leadership, Rutgers University, Charlotte Bunch (1987) recommended an effective four-step way to think about theory: describing what exists, analyzing why that reality exists, determining what should exist, and hypothesizing how to change what is to what should be.

"Determining what should exist," the third part of this model, is clearly a matter of values and beliefs. It involves being able to envision (if only vaguely) another way of organizing society, free from discrimination and oppression. Feminism is concerned with values by definition: the liberation of women and girls from discrimination based on gender, race, class, sexuality, nationality, and so on. Values do not come from facts or from the analysis of a situation but rather from people's beliefs in principles like fairness, equality, or justice. We may learn such principles from our families and communities, or through organized religion or a more personal sense of spirituality. We may think of them in terms of fundamental human rights (e.g., Agosín 2001; Bunch and Carillo 1991; Bunch and Reilly 1994; Kerr 1993). Whatever the source, feminist work invariably involves values whether stated explicitly or implied. Notice the value positions in the readings throughout this book. At the individual and community level, spirituality is a source of comfort, connection, inspiration, and meaning for many women who play a key role in teaching their children spiritual beliefs and practices and are respected for this in their families and communities. The world's major religions are all patriarchal, although this plays out in different ways in different traditions. Sacred texts are often open to divergent interpretations and are sometimes much more supportive of women than organized religious practice. At the institutional level, organized religions have a mixed record, at best, in supporting women's agency, empowerment, and human rights.

Socially Lived Theorizing

We argue that theorizing is not the sole domain of elites. Feminist legal scholar Catharine MacKinnon (1991) wrote about the importance of "articulating the theory of women's practice—resistance, visions, consciousness, injuries, notions of community, experiences of inequality. By practic[e], I mean socially lived" (p. 20).

In the 1960s and 1970s, feminists popularized the slogan "the personal is political" to validate individual women's experiences as a starting point for recognizing and understanding discrimination against women as a group. This promoted the practice of "starting from one's own experience" as a legitimate way to theorize and create new knowledge. This practice was also useful in counteracting the dominant view of theorizing that personal experience, along with emotions and values, contaminates the "purity" of the scientific method.

We argue for a theoretical framework that allows us to see the diversity of women's lives and the structures of power, inequality, and opportunity that shape our experiences. Judith Lorber (Reading 7) contends that gender differences are not natural or biological but learned from infancy. Gender differences are maintained by key social institutions such as education, marriage, popular culture, news media, organized religion, government, and law. The implication of her argument is that gender arrangements are not fixed or inevitable but can be changed.

Sociologist Jackie Stacey (1993) noted that the concept of **patriarchy**, meaning "the systematic organization of male supremacy" (p. 53), is one that many feminist theorists have found useful. In Reading 8, sociologist Allan Johnson argues that patriarchy is not just a collection of individuals but a system whose core values are control and domination. Everyone is involved and implicated in this system, but we can choose *how* we participate. This emphasis on a wider system is crucial. Without it, as Johnson shows, our thinking and discussion get reduced to the personal level and bogged down in accusations, defensiveness, and hurt feelings.

First-person stories are compelling ways to learn about others, and we include several articles by writers who reflect on their experience in order to examine social processes and institutions, that is, to open a window onto a wider world. Abra Fortune Chernik (Reading 68) discusses her struggle with an eating disorder and the process of overcoming it. Moving beyond her own experience, she asked "why society would reward my starvation and encourage my vanishing"? She examined psychological, sociological, and feminist theories for answers to this question. In Reading 38, Ann Filemyr uses her standpoint as a white lesbian to reflect on the insights she gained when she "crossed the color line" to live with her partner, Essie. She learned about racism by talking with Essie's grandmother and co-parenting Essie's son. She came to see how much she had taken for granted earlier, including her friendships and family relationships.

Different social and historical situations give rise to different experiences and theories about those experiences, hence the importance of **situated knowledge** (see, e.g., Belenky, Clinchy, Goldberger, and Tarule 1997; P. H. Collins 1990) and **standpoint theory** (Harding 2004; Hartsock 1983) for understanding women's lives.

Standpoint Theory

Sandra Harding (1998) identified four elements that contribute to constructing a standpoint as a place to generate knowledge:

1. *Physical location*—including geographical location, bodily experiences, gendered activities, and the effects of race/ethnicity, class, and nation that "place" people differently.

2. *Interests*—different locations generate different interests.

3. *Access to discourses* that provide tools for making sense of specific experiences.

4. *Social organization of knowledge production*—being situated in a university, working for a women's nonprofit organization, or talking informally with friends and coworkers all facilitate the creation of some kinds of knowledge and obstruct others.

By definition, standpoints are grounded and limited. Our discussion of intersectionality in Chapter 1 provides an example. Many academics cite a groundbreaking paper by critical legal scholar Kimberlé Crenshaw (1993) as the source of this concept. Organizer and writer Linda Burnham (2001) argued that Black women in organizations such as the Combahee River Collective and the Third World Women's Alliance wrote about this idea some twenty years earlier. Beverley Guy-Sheftall (1995, p. 45), a women's studies scholar dedicated to African American women's issues and writings, pointed out

that Black women in the United States were talking publicly about the intersection of race and gender as early as the 1830s, though not using this term. Each of these formulations utilizes a different standpoint, which offers different resources for making sense of the intertwining of race and gender in the lives of African American women—indeed, all women. Poet, writer, and teacher Minnie Bruce Pratt (1984) wrote about the process of becoming aware of her advantaged position and her fear of losing it as she became more conscious of her privilege based on race. She noted the positive side of widening her standpoint:

> I learn a way of looking at the world that is more accurate, complex, multi-layered, multi-dimensional, more truthful. . . . I've learned that what is presented to me as an accurate view of the world is frequently a lie. . . . So I gain truth when I expand my constricted eye, an eye that has only let in what I have been taught to see.   *(p. 17)*

Sociologist Dorothy Smith saw a standpoint "as a strategic choice in doing research—a place from which to start" (Sprague 2005, p. 67). We chose to open this book on U.S. women's lives with Paula Gunn Allen's essay on the "red roots of white feminism" rather than with feminist writings generated in Europe. Allen's standpoint opens up a different history and a more critical view of first-wave feminism.

Many scholars assume that a standpoint is a point of view, something that individuals or groups think or say, often based on their identity or personal experience. Some argue that this means there is no basis for choosing among competing explanations of any social phenomenon. Others "privilege accounts offered by members of oppressed groups" (Sprague 2005, p. 57) on the grounds that people in dominant positions are taken in by their own ideologies, and those in less powerful positions have no interest in supporting ideologies that justify their oppression.

Sociologist Joey Sprague argues that a standpoint should not be read in terms of subjectivity. Patricia Hill Collins also maintained that standpoint is not about individual experiences but about "historically shared, group-based experiences" (1997, p. 375). As a sociology professor raised in an African American community, Collins draws on these two very different standpoints in her discussion of Black feminist thought (Reading 9). She argues that traditional creators of Black feminist thought were not recognized as theorists by university-based Eurocentric masculinist epistemologies. Such thinkers included "blues singers, poets, autobiographers, storytellers, and orators validated by everyday Black women as experts on a Black woman's standpoint." As African American women have gained advanced degrees and academic positions some have chosen to "make creative use of their outsider-within status" in resisting the hegemonic nature of white male patterns of thinking and theorizing. Because Black women's standpoint exists in a context of domination, Collins refers to Black women's thought as **subjugated knowledge.**

Many of us may have sat in class listening to a teacher or other students and have kept quiet when we knew what was being said did not match our experience. The fact that some women's experiences are not included in texts or class discussions is a result of partial standpoints used to explain or generalize. Sprague (2005) notes that knowledge produced in U.S. universities has changed as more women, men of color, and LGBTQ scholars have gained academic positions. She is quick to point out that it is not their identity that is responsible for this but their standpoints. Typically, academic researchers work in settings that separate them from most other people. They have socioeconomic privilege, access to libraries and labs, and opportunities to discuss their work with students and colleagues. They may receive research grants from the university, private foundations, corporations, or government agencies. The priorities of their universities and academic disciplines affect their interests and what is considered legitimate research. Not all women scholars are interested in contributing to feminist theorizing; conversely, some white male scholars are producing new understandings of race and gender. To see beyond the standpoint of their professional location, Sprague (2005) suggests that feminist researchers can "work to compensate for the limitations by actively working to cross boundaries" (p. 73). Scholars who have access to standpoints that are marginalized by the academy, like Patricia Hill Collins, may cross such boundaries on a daily basis.

In Reading 10, feminist educator and scholar Chandra Talpade Mohanty lays out aspects of her genealogy—her standpoint as a South Asian in the United States and a nonresident Indian.

She notes that this telling is "interested, partial, and deliberate" and comments: "The stories I recall, the ones I retell and claim as my own, determine the choices and decisions I make in the present and the future." As a South Asian woman studying in the United States, one of these choices was to anchor herself here through the analytic and political lenses of racism and sexism. She made a significant shift in her sense of self, her interests, and the alliances she wanted to forge when she began to think of herself as a student of color rather than a foreign student. These new understandings also challenged her to rethink her place in Indian society. Mohanty draws on a **postcolonial feminism,** extending analysis of gender, race, and class to include nation and the complex long-term effects of Western colonialism; "the 'post' in post colonialism does not indicate that colonialism is over, but rather that colonial legacies continue to exist" (Mack-Canty 2004, p. 164; also see Alexander and Mohanty 1997; Cooper and Stoler 1997; McClintock 1995; Spivak 1988).

Anthropologist Lila Abu-Lughod examines the ideas deployed to justify U.S. military intervention in Afghanistan on the grounds that this would liberate, or save, Afghan women (Reading 11). Instead of this savior discourse, she argues for a serious appreciation of differences among women in the world—as products of different histories, expressions of different circumstances, and manifestations of differently structured desires—and suggests alternative ways to support Afghan women.

Challenges to Situated Knowledge and Standpoint Epistemology

Critiques of situated knowledge and standpoint epistemology emphasize the self-centeredness of **subjectivity,** "in which knowledge and meaning [are] lodged in oneself and one's own experiences" (Maher and Tétreault 1994, p. 94). This leads to comments such as "I can only know my own experience," "I can only speak for myself," or "What does all this have to do with *me?*"

Historian Joan Scott (1993) examined the authority of personal experience in creating theory. She acknowledged the value of theorizing from experience, especially if this has been ignored, denied, or silenced in dominant systems of knowledge-production, but noted that, in much writing of history, experience has been taken as "the bedrock of evidence on which explanation is built" (p. 399). Yet, as mentioned earlier, facts do not simply speak for themselves; historians construct an interpretation of their material, "a selective ordering of information" (p. 404), as shown by Becky Thompson in her account of second-wave feminism (Reading 4). Scott (1993) warned that assuming experience to be an authoritative source of knowledge may preclude questions about the constructed nature of experience, how one's vision is also structured, as noted earlier by Minnie Bruce Pratt. Scott argued that different experiences may be taken as "evidence for the fact of difference, rather than a way of exploring how difference is established, how it operates, how and in what ways it constitutes subjects who see and act in the world" (pp. 399–400). Scott concluded that experience should not be "the origin of our explanation, but that which we want to explain" (p. 412).

A second critique of situated knowledge involves **relativism.** Situated knowledge is taken as authoritative because it is someone's or some group's real experience. From a relativist perspective, each group's thought is equally valid, and "anything goes." As a result, others may think they have no basis on which to question or challenge it and no right to do so. Thus, the White Supremacist views of Ku Klux Klan members might be considered equally as valid as those held by antiracist activists, or a New York judge could invoke "cultural difference" to justify sentencing a Chinese immigrant man who killed his wife to a mere five years' probation (Yen 1989). In Reading 11, Lila Abu-Lughod examines the limits of cultural relativism in Western thinking about women in Afghanistan, especially the many meanings of veiling in the Muslim world. Rather than seeking to "save" Muslim women, she asks how people in the United States "might contribute to making the world a more just place." This point is echoed by Afghan women's rights advocate Malalai Joya (Reading 59).

Patricia Hill Collins argues that Black feminist thought offers a specific and partial perspective on domination that "allows African American women to bring a Black women's standpoint to larger epistemological dialogues concerning the nature of the matrix of domination." The ideas that are validated by other oppressed groups based on their own

distinctive, but overlapping, standpoints become the most "objective" truths.

For students of women's studies, it is important to take a stand on complex issues after thinking carefully about them and drawing on many standpoints. This is not the same as universalizing from one's own experience or telling other people what to think, what to know, or what to do. Many people's experiences and agency have been excluded or erased by dominant theoretical perspectives, and we do not want to replicate that way of knowing. We argue that standpoint methodology allows students and researchers to build bridges among overlapping standpoints, which can provide a solid place to stand on contentious issues. This generates shared truths that form the basis of what Chandra Talpade Mohanty (2003) has called a "common context of struggle" where people of diverse situations and standpoints can combine their perspectives and use these overlapping understandings to work together.

Purposes of Socially Lived Theorizing

We argue that knowledge should be used for the purposes of helping to transform the current social and economic structures of power and inequality into a sustainable world for all. As Catharine MacKinnon (1991) remarked, "It is common to say that something is good in theory but not in practice. I always want to say, then it is not such a good theory, is it?" (p. 1).

Margaret Andersen and Patricia Hill Collins (1998) argued for inclusive theorizing by putting "at the center of our thinking the experiences of groups who have formerly been excluded" (p. 12). They noted that partial knowledge "leads to the formation of bad social policy . . . that then reproduces, rather than solves, social problems" (p. 13).

For Chandra Talpade Mohanty, the wider goal is **transnational feminism,** or feminism without borders. Like Collins, Mohanty argues that the creation of knowledge must avoid false universalisms and should involve ethical and caring dialogue across differences, divisions, and conflicts, to generate more broad-based understandings. Such dialogues should strive to be "noncolonized" and anchored in equality and respect to avoid reproducing power dynamics and inequalities among feminists that parallel those inherent in colonization (see Reading 72).

You've missed the main points: WHO is her husband? WHAT does he do? WHERE would she be without him, and WHY isn't she at home looking after the kids?

Wheelchair Woman climbs Everest

FEATURES

Socially lived theorizing requires what Brazilian educator Paulo Freire (1989) calls **conscientization,** or gaining a critical consciousness, "learning to perceive social, political, and economic contradictions . . . and to take action against oppressive elements of this reality" (p. 19). This is challenging, as most of us have had little opportunity to engage in honest dialogue with others—both people like ourselves and those from different backgrounds—about important issues. Honest, thoughtful dialogue and asking critical questions move us beyond excessive subjectivity because we are compelled to see and understand many different sides of the same subject. Creating theory for social change—something that will advance human development and create a better world for all—gives us a basis for evaluating facts and experiences. This in turn provides a framework for deciding where to draw the line on cultural relativism. Through ongoing, detailed discussion and conscientious listening to others, we can generate a carefully thought-out set of principles that lead to greater understanding of issues and of acceptable actions in a given situation.

In writing about the Holocaust—the mass murder primarily of Jewish people but also of Roma people, people with disabilities, and gay people in Europe during World War II—philosopher Alan Rosenberg (1988) made an important distinction between knowing and understanding something. According to Rosenberg, knowing is having the facts about a particular event or condition.

We know the Holocaust happened: Eight million people were murdered, and countless others were tortured, raped, and otherwise devastated; the Nazis, under the leadership of Adolf Hitler, were the perpetrators; some people inside and outside Germany tried to resist these atrocities; others, both inside and outside Germany, including the United States initially, were unable or refused to help; the result was the slaughter of six million Jewish people. Traditional educational practices, epitomized by the scientific method, teach us primarily to know. For Rosenberg, knowing is the first step to understanding, a much deeper process that, in the case of the Holocaust, involves not only comprehending its significance and longer-term effects but also trying to discover how to prevent similar injustices in the future.

> Knowing . . . refers to factual information or the process by which it is gathered. Understanding refers to systematically grasping the significance of an event in such a way that it becomes integrated into one's moral and intellectual life. Facts can be absorbed without their having any impact on the way we understand ourselves or the world we live in; facts in themselves do not make a difference. It is the understanding of them that makes a difference.   (Rosenberg 1988, p. 382)

Many assume that the scientific method involves authoritativeness and rigor. We believe the alternative way of theorizing described in this chapter redefines rigor by demanding the engagement of our intellectual, emotional, and spiritual selves. It compels us to think systematically and critically, requires us to face the challenges of talking about our differences, and obligates us to consider the real implications and consequences of our theories. Knowledge created in this way helps us "to systematically grasp . . . the significance of an event in such a way that it becomes integrated into [our] moral and intellectual life," also a form of rigor (Rosenberg 1988, p. 382).

Media Representations and the Creation of Knowledge

A major source of our understanding of our own lives is our ability to reflect on our experiences and to compare them to the experiences of others. We learn about people from other groups through our often limited interactions with them and through many kinds of media representations.

We opened this chapter with a brief discussion of theorizing about poverty. We chose this topic because it has dropped out of mainstream discourse in the United States even though inequalities of wealth and income are becoming more marked in this country as well as in others. Worldwide, approximately one billion people live on the equivalent of $1 a day, and another billion live on the equivalent of $2 a day. Many people in the United States are struggling financially, yet relatively few elected representatives, academics, journalists, or nonprofit organizations concern themselves with poverty. This fact is an example of the political nature of knowledge, discussed earlier. Political interests backed by media reporting influence what people pay attention to.

It is a truism to say that we live in a media-saturated culture with constant access to the Internet, TV and radio stations broadcasting 24 hours a day, daily newspapers, weekly magazines, new movies coming out all the time, and so on. This list shows the plurality of media sources. From opinion polls to academic research, media studies evaluate the role of media in creating opinions, attitudes, and knowledge. Onnesha Roychouduri (2007) argued

> The daily news is composed of articles by writers who string together the handful of facts they have obtained in their research. They call it a "story" for good reason. Every day they are expected to produce a cohesive article on an issue. There are bound to be mistakes and oversights. But we rarely stop to consider this because the end product is so seductively authoritative.   *(Roychouduri 2007, p. 58)*

The line between information and entertainment is blurred as TV shows take up serious issues and U.S. news reporting often focuses on the flip, titillating, and controversial. The repetition of facts and images also shapes our view of events and of history (Morrow 1999). The mainstream media are owned and controlled by mega-corporations like Disney/ABC and Time Warner/Turner. One of the media's main functions is to round up an audience for advertisers, and advertisers exert considerable influence concerning media content, especially in television. From time to time they threaten to pull advertising if they think the content of a show will "turn off" their intended audience, and editors and directors are usually forced to toe the line.

Mainstream media reporters, writers, editors, and corporate sponsors are all involved in the creation of knowledge. They employ their own theories of who is a credible "authority" on an issue and their methodologies are shaped by their values and assumptions regarding what constitutes a "good story" and what "the public wants to hear." Thus, media outlets have their own standpoints: their physical and social locations, interests, and access to particular discourses; they are in powerful positions in the social organization of knowledge production.

Media scholars, critics, and some leading journalists are increasingly concerned about the "unasked" and "unanswered" questions in much contemporary journalism (e.g., Alterman 2003; Borjesson 2002; Cohen 2005; Hamilton 2004), and often attribute this to corporate media ownership, characterized by Robert McChesney (2004) as "hyper-commercialism."

As consumers of media, we develop sophisticated skills in "reading" media texts, whether they are ads, sitcoms, or documentaries. Media audiences bring their experiences, values, and beliefs—their standpoints—to what they watch, read, and hear, just as students bring their standpoints into the classroom. The more we know about particular people, the more we are able to judge the accuracy of media representations and to notice whether they reproduce myths and stereotypes, and romanticize or exoticize people (Carilli and Campbell 2005).

Women have been marginalized in the news media, as have people of color and working-class people. Women on television, for example, are still mainly shown in the context of entertainment, home, and personal relationships. Media representations serve to reinforce ideological notions of women's roles, women's bodies, and sexuality, while also

Principles of Media Literacy

1. **All media messages are "constructed."** Media messages involve many decisions about what to include or exclude and how to present "reality." Knowing this enables readers to challenge the power of media to present transparent messages. Semiotics, the science of signs and how meanings are socially produced, has contributed greatly to media literacy. It aims to challenge the apparent naturalness of a message, the "what-goes-without-saying."

   Question: Who created this message?

2. **Media messages are constructed using a creative language with its own rules.** Students of media literacy analyze the dual meanings of signs: the *signifier*, the more literal reference to content; and the *signified*, the more subjective significations of a message. As you read an article or watch a film or TV show, try to separate what you see or hear from what you think or feel.

   Question: What creative techniques are used to attract my attention?

3. **Different people experience the same media message differently.** Cultural studies professor Stuart Hall distinguished between the encoding of media texts by producers and the decoding by consumers. This distinction highlights the ability of audiences to produce their own readings and meanings and to decode texts in "deviant" or oppositional ways, as well as "preferred" ways in line with the dominant ideology. One's gender, race, class, sexuality, or national origin may produce different readings, and "one's grasp of a media text is enriched by . . . different

   audience perspectives" (Kellner and Share 2005, p. 376).

   Question: How might different people understand this message differently?

4. **Media have embedded values and points of view.** Analyzing the content of media messages is a key approach in cultural studies in order to question and expose ideology, bias, and the connotations explicit and implicit in media representations. Commenting on the TV series *Buffy, the Vampire Slayer*, Kellner and Share (2005) note that the monsters "can be read as signifying the dangers of drugs, rampant sexuality, or gangs producing destructive violence. Content is often highly symbolic and thus requires a wide range of theoretical approaches to grasp the multidimensional social, political, moral, and sometimes philosophical meanings of a cultural text" (p. 376).

   Question: What values, lifestyles, and points of view are represented in, or omitted from, this message?

5. **Most media messages are organized to gain profit or power.** Mainstream media messages are generated in an industry dominated by a handful of mega-corporations. Their purpose is not simply to entertain or inform. Knowing which corporation owns a particular news outlet or what system of production dominates given media forms will help in interpreting the viewpoints embedded in media texts.

   Questions: Why is this message being sent? Why is it being sent at this time?

   Sources: Center for Media Literacy: www.medialit.org; Kellner and Share (2005).

giving complex and sometimes contradictory messages. A study undertaken by the Project for Excellence in Journalism (2005) found that "despite rising numbers of women in the workforce and in journalism schools, the news . . . still largely comes from a male perspective." Women are more likely to be included if the reporter is female, or in "lifestyle" pieces as opposed to "hard" news, business, or sports. Women are least likely to be quoted in stories about foreign affairs, giving the impression that there are no women with expertise in this area. *The Nation* columnist Katha Pollitt noted that white men's voices are assumed to be authoritative and neutral: "a woman's opinion about Iraq or the budget is seen as a woman's opinion. The same for a black person" (quoted in Zimmerman 2003, p. 5). Moreover, the faculty and administrators "who run the nation's journalism and mass communication schools are overwhelmingly white, and two-thirds of them are male," even though about two-thirds of their students are women (University of Maryland 2007).

In the previous chapter we mentioned that feminist ideas and goals have often been distorted, trivialized, and undermined in media reports. Journalist Caryl Rivers (2007) has argued that the news media "sell anxiety to women the way that advertising sells insecurity about their faces, bodies, and sex appeal" (p. 1). Based on more than thirty years of media watching, she identified several stories, repeated from one media outlet to another, that undercut women's advances in business, medicine, law, and academia. Despite these achievements, news reports continue to emphasize:

- Miserable career women who don't have children
- Miserable career women who have lousy sex
- Day care kids who become bullies
- Children of divorced women who face lifelong problems
- Women who get too much education and can't get a man
- Selfish mothers who neglect their children

Ariel Dougherty, cofounder of Women Make Movies, mentioned a 1970s radical feminist comment "No women's media; no women's progress"

(Donna Allen and Dana Densmore 1977, quoted in Dougherty 2007, p. 25). We note the significance of alternative media of many kinds, disseminated through magazines, newsletters, and electronically (see, e.g., Breitbart and Nogueira 2004; Pozner 2006). This includes alternative and critical sources of news (e.g., www.womensenews.org; www.alternet.org; www.dollarsandsense.org), girls' media production (see Bleyer 2004; Kearney 2006), as well as feminist blogs (www.barnard.edu/sfonline/blogs; Friedman and Calixte 2009) and materials posted on YouTube.

International women's groups and networks also distribute information through Web sites, newsletters, radio shows, and community theater (Allen, Rush, and Kaufman 1996; Byerly and Ross 2006). Examples include Arab Women's Solidarity Association, Asia Pacific Forum on Women, Law, and Development, Development Alternatives with Women for a New-Era (DAWN), Federation of African Media Women, Feminist International Radio Endeavor (www.fire.or.cr/indexeng.htm), FEMPRESS (Chile), International Women's Media Foundation, ISIS International-Manila (www.isiswomen.org), Women's Feature Service (India), and feminist organizations and networks we cite in other chapters.

To summarize, in this chapter we argue that facts are always open to interpretation and that everyone makes theory in trying to understand their experiences. Feminist theories that seek to explain women's lives involve clear value positions and constitute a critique of the dominant view that sees theory as "objective" or "value-free." Socially lived theorizing requires collective dialogue, careful listening to other people's theories, and sophisticated skills in "reading" media texts so that we do not draw stereotypical notions of others into our theory making. Socially lived theorizing is essential for women's studies. It creates knowledge that reflects the points of view and interests of a broad range of people. It is visionary and can lead to social change.

This chapter may seem abstract in the beginning, and you may want to return to it as you work with the material in this book. It is also a good idea to review it at the end of your course. Or, you can study this chapter after you have read some of the thematic chapters that follow.

Questions for Reflection

As you read and discuss the readings in this chapter, think about these questions:

1. How do *you* explain poverty? In the United States? Worldwide? How are these linked?

2. How do you explain inequality between women and men in this country? Between white people and people of color in this country?

3. What does it take for a member of a dominant group (e.g., a white man) to be willing to learn from and value the experiences of someone from another group (e.g., a Native American woman)?

4. What standpoints help to give full and cogent explanations of issues such as obesity and global warming?

5. Consider people and events that have affected the development of your thinking. How did this happen?

6. Have spiritual beliefs and religious institutions influenced your values and perspectives? If so, how?

7. How do you know what you know? How is this connected to your genealogy and standpoint?

◆◆◆

Finding Out More on the Web

1. Explore the Web site of a women's organization. What can you learn about the organization's theoretical framework? How does this inform its activities? Here are some examples to get you started:

   Center for Women's Global Leadership: **www.cwgl.rutgers.edu**

   Development Alternatives with Women for a New-Era (DAWN): **www.dawnnet.org**

   Fund for a Feminist Majority: **http://feminist.org**

   Global Fund for Women: **www.globalfundforwomen.org**

   Global Women's Strike: **www.globalwomenstrike.net**

   International Community of Women Living with HIV/AIDS: **www.icw.org**

   National Organization for Women: **www.now.org**

   Revolutionary Association for Women in Afghanistan: **www.rawa.org**

   Third Wave Foundation: **www.thirdwavefoundation.org**

   Women Living Under Muslim Laws: **www.wluml.org/English**

2. Compare editorial perspectives and news coverage of an issue you care about in progressive magazines, Web logs, foreign newspapers online, or WomenseNews (**www.womensenews.org**) with those of mainstream U.S. reporting.

   Examples of feminist blogs:

   www.blogher.com

   http://combaheesurvival.wordpress.com

   http://feministing.com

www.msmagazine.com/blog

http://newmodelminority.com

http://quirkyblackgirls.blogspot.com

3. Find out about the work of international women's media organizations cited in this chapter, also:

Global Media Monitoring Project: www.whomakesthenews.org
International Women's Media Foundation: www.iwmf.org

Taking Action

1. Analyze what happens when you get into an argument with a friend, classmate, or teacher about an issue that matters to you. Are you both using the same assumptions? Do you understand the other person's argument? Do you have compatible understandings of the issue? Can you explain your position more clearly, or do you need to rethink it? Are facts enough to convince someone who is skeptical of your views? Use what you have learned from this chapter to express your opinions.

2. Pay attention to the theoretical ideas incorporated into TV news reports. When the presenter says, "Now for the stories behind the headlines," whose stories are these? Who is telling them? What, if anything, is missing from these accounts? What else do you need to know in order to have a full explanation? How can you incorporate the ideas from this chapter into your "readings" of mass media?

3. Look critically at media representations of people like you and people in other groups. How are they portrayed? What is left out of these representations? What stereotypes do they reinforce?

4. Read a novel like Gerd Brantenberg's *Egalia's Daughters* or Marge Piercy's *Woman on the Edge of Time* that redefines gender roles and stereotypes. What do you learn about your assumptions?

S E V E N

The Social Construction of Gender (1991)

Judith Lorber

Judith Lorber is Professor Emerita of Sociology and Women's Studies at Brooklyn College and The Graduate School, City University of New York, and the author of numerous books and articles on gender, feminism, and women's health. In 1996 she received the American Sociological Association Jessie Bernard Career Award for her contribution to feminist scholarship.

Talking about gender for most people is the equivalent of fish talking about water. Gender is so much the routine ground of everyday activities that questioning its taken-for-granted assumptions and presuppositions is like thinking about whether the sun will come up. Gender is so pervasive that in our society we assume it is bred into our genes. Most people find it hard to believe that gender is constantly created and re-created out of human interaction, out of social life, and is the texture and order of that social life. Yet gender, like culture, is a human production that depends on everyone constantly "doing gender" (West and Zimmerman 1987).

And everyone "does gender" without thinking about it. Today, on the subway, I saw a well-dressed man with a year-old child in a stroller. Yesterday, on a bus, I saw a man with a tiny baby in a carrier on his chest. Seeing men taking care of small children in public is increasingly common—at least in New York City. But both men were quite obviously stared at—and smiled at, approvingly. Everyone was doing gender—the men who were changing the role of fathers and the other passengers, who were applauding them silently. But there was more gendering going on that probably fewer people noticed. The baby was wearing a white crocheted cap and white clothes. You couldn't tell if it was a boy or a girl. The child in the stroller was wearing a dark blue T-shirt and dark print pants. As they started to leave the train, the father put a Yankee baseball cap on the child's head. Ah, a boy, I thought. Then I noticed the gleam of tiny earrings in the child's ears, and as they got off, I saw the little flowered sneakers and lace-trimmed socks. Not a boy after all. Gender done.

Gender is such a familiar part of daily life that it usually takes a deliberate disruption of our expectations of how women and men are supposed to act to pay attention to how it is produced. Gender signs and signals are so ubiquitous that we usually fail to note them—unless they are missing or ambiguous. Then we are uncomfortable until we have successfully placed the other person in a gender status; otherwise, we feel socially dislocated. In our society, in addition to man and woman, the status can be *transvestite* (a person who dresses in opposite-gender clothes) and *transsexual* (a person who has had sex-change surgery). Transvestites and transsexuals construct their gender status by dressing, speaking, walking, gesturing in the ways prescribed for women or men—whichever they want to be taken for—and so does any "normal" person.

For the individual, gender construction starts with assignment to a sex category on the basis of what the genitalia look like at birth. Then babies are dressed or adorned in a way that displays the category because parents don't want to be constantly asked whether their baby is a girl or a boy. A sex category becomes a gender status through naming, dress, and the use of other gender markers. Once a child's gender is evident, others treat those in one gender differently from those in the other, and the children respond to the different treatment by feeling different and behaving differently. As soon as they can talk, they start to refer to themselves as members of their gender. Sex doesn't come into play again until puberty, but by that time, sexual feelings and desires and practices have been shaped by gendered norms and expectations. Adolescent boys and girls approach and avoid each other in an elaborately scripted and gendered mating dance. Parenting is gendered, with different expectations for mothers and for fathers, and people of different genders work at different kinds of jobs. The work adults do as mothers and fathers and as low-level workers and high-level bosses, shapes women's and men's life experiences, and these experiences produce different feelings, consciousness, relationships, skills—ways of being that we call feminine or masculine. All of these processes constitute the social construction of gender.

Gendered roles change—today fathers are taking care of little children, girls and boys are wearing unisex clothing and getting the same education, women and men are working at the same jobs. Although many traditional social groups are quite strict about maintaining gender differences, in other social groups they seem to be blurring. Then why the one-year-old's earrings? Why is it still so important to mark a child as a girl or a boy, to make sure she is not taken for a boy or he for a girl? What would happen if they were? They would, quite literally, have changed places in their social world.

To explain why gendering is done from birth, constantly and by everyone, we have to look not only at the way individuals experience gender but at gender as a social institution. As a social institution, gender is one of the major ways that human beings organize their lives. Human society depends on a predictable division of labor, a designated allocation of scarce goods, assigned responsibility for children and others who cannot care for themselves, common values and their systematic transmission to new members, legitimate leadership, music, art, stories, games, and other symbolic productions. One way of choosing people for the different tasks of society is on the basis of their talents, motivations, and competence—their demonstrated achievements. The other way is on the basis of gender, race, ethnicity—ascribed membership in a category of people. Although societies vary in the extent to which they use one or the other of these ways of allocating people to work and to carry out other responsibilities, every society uses gender and age grades. Every society classifies people as "girl and boy children," "girls and boys ready to be married," and "fully adult women and men," constructs similarities among them and differences between them, and assigns them to different roles and responsibilities. Personality characteristics, feelings, motivations, and ambitions flow from these different life experiences so that the members of these different groups become different kinds of people. The process of gendering and its outcome are legitimated by religion, law, science, and the society's entire set of values.

Gender as Process, Stratification, and Structure

As a social institution, gender is a process of creating distinguishable social statuses for the assignment of rights and responsibilities. As part of a stratification system that ranks these statuses unequally, gender is a major building block in the social structures built on these unequal statuses.

As a *process*, gender creates the social differences that define "woman" and "man." In social interaction throughout their lives, individuals learn what is expected, see what is expected, act and react in expected ways, and thus simultaneously construct and maintain the gender order: "The very injunction to be a given gender takes place through discursive routes: to be a good mother, to be a heterosexually desirable object, to be a fit worker, in sum, to signify a multiplicity of guarantees in response to a variety of different demands all at once" (J. Butler 1990, 145). Members of a social group neither make up gender as they go along nor exactly replicate in rote fashion what was done before. In almost every encounter, human beings produce gender, behaving in the ways they learned were appropriate for their gender status, or resisting or rebelling against these norms. Resistance and rebellion have altered gender norms, but so far they have rarely eroded the statuses.

Gendered patterns of interaction acquire additional layers of gendered sexuality, parenting, and work behaviors in childhood, adolescence, and adulthood. Gendered norms and expectations are enforced through informal sanctions of gender-inappropriate behavior by peers and by formal punishment or threat of punishment by those in authority should behavior deviate too far from socially imposed standards for women and men.

Everyday gendered interactions build gender into the family, the work process, and other organizations and institutions, which in turn reinforce gender expectations for individuals. Because gender is a process, there is room not only for modification and variation by individuals and small groups but also for institutionalized change (J. W. Scott 1988, 7).

As part of a *stratification* system, gender ranks men above women of the same race and class. Women and men could be different but equal. In practice, the process of creating difference depends to a great extent on differential evaluation. As Nancy Jay (1981) says: "That which is defined, separated out, isolated from all else is A and pure. Not-A is necessarily impure, a random catchall, to which nothing is external except A and the principle of order that separates it from Not-A" (45). From the individual's point of view, whichever gender is A, the other is Not-A; gender boundaries tell the individual who is like him or her, and all the rest are unlike. From society's point of view, however, one gender is usually the touchstone, the normal, the dominant, and the other is different, deviant, and subordinate. In Western society, "man" is A, "woman" is Not-A. (Consider what a society would be like where woman was A and man Not-A.)

The further dichotomization by race and class constructs the gradations of a heterogeneous society's stratification scheme. Thus, in the United States, white is A, African American is Not-A; middle class is A, working class is Not-A, and "African American women occupy a position whereby the inferior half of a series of these dichotomies converge" (P. H. Collins 1989, 70). The dominant categories are the hegemonic ideals, taken so for granted as the way things should be that white is not ordinarily thought of as a race, middle class as a class, or men as a gender. The characteristics of these categories define the Other as that which lacks the valuable qualities the dominants exhibit.

In a gender-stratified society, what men do is usually valued more highly than what women do because men do it, even when their activities are very similar or the same. In different regions of southern India, for example, harvesting rice is men's work, shared work, or women's work: "Wherever a task is done by women it is considered easy, and where it is done by [men] it is considered difficult" (Mencher 1988, 104). . . . Conversely, because they are the superior group, white men do not have to do the "dirty work," such as housework; the most inferior group does it, usually poor women of color (Palmer 1989). . . .

Societies vary in the extent of the inequality in social status of their women and men members, but where there is inequality, the status "woman" (and its attendant behavior and role allocations) is usually held in lesser esteem than the status "man." Since gender is also intertwined with a society's other constructed statuses of differential evaluation—race, religion, occupation, class, country of origin, and so on—men and women members of the favored groups command more power, more prestige, and more property than the members of the disfavored groups. Within many social groups, however, men are advantaged over women. The more economic resources, such as education and job opportunities, are available to a group, the more they tend to be monopolized by men. In poorer groups that have few resources (such as working-class African Americans in the United States), women and men are more nearly equal, and the women may even outstrip the men in education and occupational status (Almquist 1987).

As a *structure*, gender divides work in the home and in economic production, legitimates those in authority, and organizes sexuality and emotional life (Connell 1987, 91–142). As primary parents, women significantly influence children's psychological development and emotional attachments, in the process reproducing gender. Emergent sexuality is shaped by heterosexual, homosexual, bisexual, and sadomasochistic patterns that are gendered—different for girls and boys, and for women and men—so that sexual statuses reflect gender statuses.

When gender is a major component of structured inequality, the devalued genders have less power, prestige, and economic rewards than the valued genders. In countries that discourage gender discrimination, many major roles are still gendered; women still do most of the domestic labor and child rearing, even while doing full-time paid work; women and men are segregated on the job and each does work considered "appropriate"; women's work is usually paid less than men's work. Men dominate the positions of authority and leadership in government, the military, and the law; cultural productions, religions, and sports reflect men's interests. . . .

Gender inequality—the devaluation of "women" and the social domination of "men"—has social functions and social history. It is not the result of sex, procreation, physiology, anatomy, hormones, or genetic predispositions. It is produced and maintained by identifiable social processes and built into the general social structure and individual identities deliberately and purposefully. The social order as we know it in Western societies is organized around racial, ethnic, class, and gender inequality. I contend, therefore, that the continuing purpose of gender as a modern social institution is to construct women as a group to be the subordinates of men as a group.

The Paradox of Human Nature

To say that sex, sexuality, and gender are all socially constructed is not to minimize their social power. These categorical imperatives govern our lives in the most profound and pervasive ways, through the social experiences and social practices of what Dorothy Smith calls the "everday/evernight world" (1990, 31–57). The paradox of human nature is that it is *always* a manifestation of cultural meanings, social relationships, and power politics; "not biology, but culture, becomes destiny" (J. Butler 1990, 8). Gendered people emerge not from physiology or sexual orientation but from the exigencies of the social order, mostly, from the need for a reliable division of the work of food production and the social (not physical) reproduction of new members. The moral imperatives of religion and cultural representations guard the boundary lines among genders and ensure that what is demanded, what is permitted, and what is tabooed for the people in each gender is well known and followed by most (C. Davies 1982). Political power, control of scarce resources, and, if necessary, violence uphold the gendered social order in the face of resistance and rebellion. Most people, however, voluntarily go along with their society's prescriptions for those of their gender status, because the norms and expectations get built into their sense of worth and identity as . . . [the way we] think, the way we see and hear and speak, the way we fantasy, and the way we feel.

There is no core or bedrock in human nature below these endlessly looping processes of the social production of sex and gender, self and other, identity and psyche, each of which is a "complex cultural construction" (J. Butler 1990, 36). *For humans, the social is the natural.* Therefore, "in its feminist senses, gender cannot mean simply the cultural appropriation of biological sexual difference. Sexual difference is itself a fundamental—and scientifically contested—construction. Both 'sex' and 'gender' are woven of multiple, asymmetrical strands of difference, charged with multifaceted dramatic narratives of domination and struggle" (Haraway 1990, 140).

REFERENCES

Almquist, Elizabeth M. 1987. "Labor market gendered inequality in minority groups," *Gender & Society* 1:400–14.

Butler, Judith. 1990. *Gender Trouble: Feminism and the Subversion of Identity.* New York and London: Routledge.

Collins, Patricia Hill. 1989. "The social construction of black feminist thought," *Signs* 14:745–73.

Connell, R. [Robert] W. 1987. *Gender and Power: Society, the Person, and Sexual Politics.* Stanford, Calif.: Stanford University Press.

Davies, Christie. 1982. "Sexual taboos and social boundaries," *American Journal of Sociology* 87:1032–63.

Haraway, Donna. 1990. "Investment strategies for the evolving portfolio of primate female," in Jacobus, Mary, Evelyn Fox Keller, and Sally Shuttleworth (eds.). *Body/politics: Women and the Discourse of Science.* New York and London: Routledge.

Jay, Nancy. 1981. "Gender and dichotomy," *Feminist Studies* 7:38–56.

Mencher, Joan. 1988. "Women's work and poverty: Women's contribution to household maintenance in South India," in Daisy Dwyer and Judith Bruce (eds.). *A Home Divided: Women and Income in the Third World.* Stanford, Calif.: Stanford University Press.

Palmer, Phyllis. 1989. *Domesticity and Dirt: Housewives and Domestic Servants in the United States, 1920–1945.* Philadelphia: Temple University Press.

Scott, Joan Wallach. 1988. *Gender and the Politics of History.* New York: Columbia University Press.

Smith, Dorothy E. 1990. *The Conceptual Practices of Power: A Feminist Sociology of Knowledge.* Toronto: University of Toronto Press.

West, Candace, and Don Zimmerman. 1987. "Doing gender," *Gender & Society* 1:125–51.

EIGHT

◆◆◆

Patriarchy, the System (1997)
An It, Not a He, a Them, or an Us

Allan G. Johnson

Allan G. Johnson is a sociologist, author, and public speaker with thirty years of teaching experience exploring the issues of privilege, oppression, and social inequality. His books include *The Forest and the Trees: Sociology as Life, Practice, and Promise,* and *The Gender Knot: Unraveling Our Patriarchal Legacy.* http://www.agjohnson.us.

"When you say patriarchy," a man complained from the rear of the audience, "I know what you

really mean—me!" A lot of people hear "men" whenever someone says "patriarchy," so that criticism of male privilege and the oppression of women is taken to mean that all men—each and every one of them—are oppressive people. It's enough to prompt many men to take it personally, bristling at what they often see as a way to make them feel guilty. And some women feel free to blame individual men for patriarchy simply because they're men. Some of the time, men feel defensive because they identify with patriarchy and its values and don't want to face the consequences these produce or the prospect of giving up male privilege. But defensiveness can also reflect a common confusion about the difference between patriarchy as a kind of society and the people who participate in it. If we're ever going to work toward real change, it's a confusion we'll have to clear up.

To do this, we have to realize that we're stuck in a model of social life that views everything as beginning and ending with individuals. Looking at things in this way, the tendency is to think that if bad things happen in the world, it's only because there are bad people who have entered into some kind of conspiracy. Racism exists, then, because white people are racist bigots who hate members of racial and ethnic minorities and want to do them harm. The oppression of women happens because men want and like to dominate women and act out hostility toward them. There is poverty and class oppression because people in the upper classes are greedy, heartless, and cruel. The flip side of this individualistic model of guilt and blame is that race, gender, and class oppression are actually not oppression at all, but merely the sum of individual failings on the part of Blacks, women, and the poor, who lack the right stuff to compete successfully with whites, men, and others who know how to make something of themselves.

What this kind of thinking ignores is that we are all participating in something larger than ourselves or any collection of us. On some level, most people are familiar with the idea that social life involves us in something larger than ourselves, but few seem to know what to do with that idea. Blaming everything on "the system" strikes a deep chord in many people. But it also touches on a basic misunderstanding of social life, because blaming "the system" (presumably society) for our problems, doesn't take the next step to understanding what that might mean. What exactly *is* a system, for example, and how could it run our lives? Do *we* have anything to do with shaping *it*, and if so, how? How, for example, do we participate in patriarchy, and how does that link us to the consequences? How is what we think of as "normal" life related to male privilege, women's oppression, and the hierarchical, control-obsessed world in which everyone's lives are embedded?

Without asking such questions, we can't understand gender fully and we avoid taking responsibility either for ourselves or for patriarchy. Instead,

"the system" serves as a vague, unarticulated catchall, a dumping ground for social problems, a scapegoat that can never be held to account and that, for all the power we think it has, can't talk back or actually *do* anything.

. . . But we can't have it both ways. If society is a powerful force in social life, as it surely is, then we have to understand it and how we are connected to it. To do this, we have to change how we think about it, because how we think affects the kinds of questions we ask. The questions we ask in turn shape the kinds of answers and solutions we'll come up with.

If we see patriarchy as nothing more than men's and women's individual personalities, motivations, and behavior, for example, then it probably won't even occur to us to ask about larger contexts—such as institutions like the family, religion, and the economy—and how people's lives are shaped in relation to them. From this kind of individualistic perspective, we might ask why a particular man raped, harassed, or beat a woman. We wouldn't ask, however, what kind of society would promote persistent *patterns* of such behavior in everyday life, from wife-beating jokes to the routine inclusion of sexual coercion and violence in mainstream movies. We'd be quick to explain rape and battery as the acts of sick or angry men, but we'd rarely take seriously the question of what kind of society would produce so much male anger and pathology or direct it toward sexual violence rather than something else. We'd rarely ask how gender violence might serve other more "normalized" ends such as male control and domination. We might ask why a man would like pornography that objectifies, exploits, and promotes violence against women, or debate whether the Constitution protects an individual's right to produce and distribute it. But it'd be hard to stir up interest in asking what kind of society would give violent and degrading visions of women's bodies and human sexuality such a prominent and pervasive place in its culture to begin with.

. . . We need to see and deal with the social roots that generate and nurture the social problems that are reflected in and manifested through the behavior of individuals. We can't do this without realizing that we all participate in something larger than ourselves, something we didn't create but that we have the power to affect through the choices we make about *how* to participate.

Some readers have objected to "participate" as a way to describe women's relation to patriarchy. This is based on the idea that participation is something voluntary, freely chosen, entered into as equals, and it therefore makes little sense to suggest that women can participate in their own oppression. But that is not my meaning here, nor is it a necessary interpretation of the word. To *participate* is simply to have a *part* in what goes on, to do something (or *not*) and to have the choice affect the consequences, regardless of whether it is conscious or unconscious, coerced or not. Of course, the *terms* of women's participation differ dramatically from those that shape men's, but it is participation, nonetheless.

This concept is similar to the participation of workers in the system of capitalism. They do not participate as equals to the capitalists who employ them or on terms they would choose if they could. Nevertheless, without them, capitalism cannot function as a system that oppresses them.

The importance of participation can be seen in the great variety of ways that women and working-class people respond to oppression—all the forms that fighting back or giving in can take. To argue that women or workers do not participate is to render them powerless and irrelevant to patriarchy's and capitalism's past and future, for it is only as participants that people can affect anything. . . .

The something larger we all participate in is patriarchy, which is more than a collection of individuals (such as "men"). It is a system, which means it can't be reduced to the people who participate in it. If you go to work in a corporation, for example, you know the minute you walk in the door that you've entered "something" that shapes your experience and behavior, something that isn't just you and the other people you work with. You can feel yourself stepping into a set of relationships and shared understandings about who's who and what's supposed to happen and why, and all of this limits you in many ways. And when you leave at the end of the day you can feel yourself released from the constraints imposed by your participation in that system. You can feel the expectations drop away and your focus shift to other systems such as family or a neighborhood bar that shape your experience in different ways.

To understand a system like a corporation, we have to look at more than people like you, because all of you aren't the corporation, even though you make it run. If the corporation were just a collection of people, then whatever happened to the corporation would by definition also happen to them, and vice versa. But clearly this isn't so. A corporation can go bankrupt or cease to exist altogether without any of the people who work there going bankrupt or disappearing. Or everyone who works for a corporation could quit, but that wouldn't necessarily mean the end of the corporation, only the arrival of a new set of participants. We can't understand a system, then, just by looking at the people who participate in it, for it is something larger and has to be understood as such.

Even more so, we cannot understand the world and our lives in it without looking at the dynamic relationship between individual people and social systems. Nor can we understand the countless details—from sexual violence to patterns of conversation to unequal distributions of power—that make up the reality of male privilege and the oppression of women.

As the accompanying figure shows, this relationship has two parts. The arrow on the right side represents the idea that as we participate in social systems, we are shaped as individuals. Through the process of *socialization*, we learn how to participate in social life—from families, schools, religion, and the mass media, through the examples set by parents, peers, coaches, teachers, and public figures—a continuing stream of ideas and images of people and the world and who we are in relation to them.

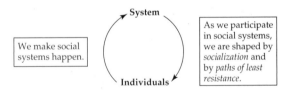

Through all of this, we develop a sense of personal identity—including gender—and how this positions us in relation to other people, especially in terms of inequalities of power. As I grew up watching movies and television, for example, the message was clear that men are the most important people on the planet because they're the ones who supposedly do the most important things as defined by patriarchal culture. They're the strong ones who build, the heroes who fight the good fight, the geniuses, writers and artists, the bold leaders, and even the evil—but always interesting—villains. Even God is gendered male.

Among the many consequences of such messages is to encourage in men a sense of entitlement in relation to women—to be tended to and taken care of, deferred to and supported no matter how badly they behave. In the typical episode of the television sitcom, *Everybody Loves Raymond,* for example, Ray Barone routinely behaves toward his wife, Debra, in ways that are insensitive, sexist, adolescent, and downright stupid, but by the end of each half hour we always find out why she puts up with it year after year—for some reason that's never made clear, she just loves the guy. This sends the message that it's reasonable for a heterosexual man to expect to "have" an intelligent and beautiful woman who will love him and stay with him in spite of his behaving badly toward her a great deal of the time.

Invariably, some of what we learn through socialization turns out not to be true and then we may have to deal with that. I say "may" because powerful forces encourage us to keep ourselves in a state of denial, to rationalize what we've learned in order to keep it safe from scrutiny, if only to protect our sense of who we are and ensure our being accepted by other people, including family and friends. In the end, the default is to adopt the dominant version of reality and act as though it's the only one there is.

In addition to socialization, participation in social systems shapes our behavior through *paths of least resistance,* a concept that refers to the conscious and unconscious choices we make from one moment to the next. When a man hears other men tell sexist jokes, for example, there are many things he *could* do, but they vary in how much social resistance they're likely to provoke. He could laugh along with them, for example, or remain silent or ignore them or object. And, of course, there are millions of other things he could do—sing, dance, go to sleep, scratch his nose, and so on. Most of these possibilities won't even occur to him, which is one of the ways that social systems limit our options. But of those that do occur to him, usually one will risk less resistance than all the rest. The path of least resistance is to go along, and unless he's willing to deal with greater resistance, that's the choice he's most likely to make.

Our daily lives consist of an endless stream of such choices as we navigate among various possibilities in relation to the path of least resistance in each social situation. Most of the time, we make choices unconsciously without realizing what we're doing. It's just what seems most comfortable to us, most familiar, and safest. The more aware we are of what's going on, however, the more likely it is that we can make conscious, informed choices, and therein lies our potential to make a difference.

This brings us to the arrow on the left side of the figure, which represents the fact that human beings are the ones who make social systems happen. . . . Because people make systems happen, then people can also make systems happen differently. And when systems happen differently, the consequences are different as well. In other words, when people step off the path of least resistance, they have the potential not simply to change other people, but to alter the way the system itself happens. Given that systems shape people's behavior, this kind of change has enormous potential. When a man objects to a sexist joke, for example, it can shake other men's perception of what's socially acceptable and what's not so that the next time they're in this kind of situation, their perception of the social environment itself—not just of other people as individuals, whom they may or may not know personally—may shift in a new direction that makes old paths (such as telling sexist jokes) more difficult to choose because of the increased risk of social resistance.

The model in the figure represents a basic sociological view of the world at every level of human experience, from the global capitalist economy to sexual relationships. Patriarchy fits this model as a social system in which women and men participate. As such, it is more than a collection of women and men and can't be understood simply by understanding *them.* We are not patriarchy, no more than people who believe in Allah *are* Islam or Canadians *are* Canada. Patriarchy is a kind of society organized around certain kinds of social relationships and ideas that shape paths of least resistance. As individuals, we participate in it. Paradoxically, our participation both shapes our lives and gives us the opportunity to be part of changing or perpetuating it. But *we are not it,* which means patriarchy can exist without men having "oppressive personalities" or actively conspiring with one another to defend male privilege.

To demonstrate that gender privilege and oppression exist, we don't have to show that men are villains, that women are good-hearted victims, that women don't participate in their own oppression, or that men never oppose it. If a society is oppressive, then people who grow up and live in it will tend to accept, identify with, and participate in it as "normal" and unremarkable life. That's the path of least resistance in any system. It's hard not to follow it, given how we depend on society and its rewards and punishments that hinge on going along with the status quo. When privilege and oppression are woven into the fabric of everyday life, we don't need to go out of our way to be overtly oppressive for a system of privilege to produce oppressive consequences, for, as Edmund Burke tells us, evil requires only that good people do nothing.

"The System"

. . .

The crucial thing to understand about patriarchy or any other social system is that it's something people participate in. It's an arrangement of shared understandings and relationships that connect people to one another and something larger than themselves. In some ways, we're like players who participate in a game. Monopoly, for example, consists of a set of ideas about things such as the meaning of property and rent, the value of competition and accumulating wealth, and various rules about rolling dice, moving around a board, buying, selling, and developing property, collecting rents, winning, and losing. It has positions—player, banker, and so on—that people occupy. It has material elements such as the board, houses and hotels, dice, property deeds, money, and "pieces" that represent each player's movements on the board. As such, the game is something we can think of as a social system whose elements cohere with a unity and wholeness that distinguish it from other games and from nongames.[1] Most important, we can describe it as a system without ever talking about the personal characteristics or motivations of the individual people who actually play it at any given moment.

If we watch people play Monopoly, we notice certain routine patterns of feeling and behavior that reflect paths of least resistance inherent in the game itself. If someone lands on a property I own,

for example, I collect the rent (if I happen to notice); and if they can't pay, I take their assets and force them from the game. The game encourages me to feel good about this, not necessarily because *I'm* greedy and merciless, but because the game is about winning, and this is what winning consists of in Monopoly. Since everyone else is also trying to win by driving me out of the game, each step I take toward winning protects me and alleviates some anxiety about landing on a property whose rent *I* can't pay.

Because these patterns are shaped by the game far more than by the individual players, we can find ourselves behaving in ways that might seem disturbing in other situations. When I'm not playing Monopoly, I behave quite differently, even though I'm still the same person. This is why I don't play Monopoly anymore—I don't like the way it encourages me to feel and behave in the name of "fun," especially toward people I care about. The reason we behave differently outside the game doesn't lie in our personalities but in the *game's* paths of least resistance, which define certain behavior and values as appropriate and expected. When we see ourselves as Monopoly players, we feel limited by the rules and goals the game defines, and experience it as something external to us and beyond our control.

It's important to note how rarely it occurs to people to simply change the rules. The relationships, terms, and goals that organize the game aren't presented to us as ours to judge or alter. The more attached we feel to the game and the more closely we identify ourselves as players, the more likely we are to feel helpless in relation to it. If you're about to drive someone into bankruptcy, you can excuse yourself by saying, "I've got to take your money, those are the rules," but only if you ignore the fact that you could choose not to play or could suggest a change in the rules. Then again, if you can't imagine life without the game, you won't see many alternatives to doing what's expected.

If we try to explain patterns of social behavior only in terms of individual people's personalities and motives—people do greedy things, for example, because they *are* greedy—then we ignore how behavior is shaped by paths of least resistance found in the systems people participate in. The "profit motive" associated with capitalism, for example, is typically seen as a psychological motive that explains capitalism as a system: Capitalism exists because there are people who want to make a profit. But this puts the cart before the horse by avoiding the question of where wanting to make a profit comes from in the first place. We need to ask what kind of world makes such wants possible and encourages people to organize their lives around them, for although we may pursue profit as we play Monopoly or participate in real-world capitalism, the psychological profit motive doesn't originate with us. We aren't born with it. It doesn't exist in many cultures and was unknown for most of human history. The profit motive is a historically developed aspect of market systems in general and capitalism in particular that shapes the values, behavior, and personal motives of those who participate in it.

To argue that managers lay off workers, for example, simply because managers are heartless or cruel ignores the fact that success under capitalism often depends on this kind of competitive, profit-maximizing, "heartless" behavior. Most managers probably know in their hearts that the practice of routinely discarding people in the name of profit and expedience is hurtful and unfair. This is why they feel so bad about having to be the ones to carry it out, and protect their feelings by inventing euphemisms such as "downsizing" and "outplacement." And yet they participate in a system that produces these cruel results anyway, not because of cruel personalities or malice toward workers, but because a capitalist system makes this a path of least resistance and exacts real costs from those who stray from it.

To use the game analogy, it's a mistake to assume that we can understand players' behavior without paying attention to the game they're playing. We create even more trouble by thinking we can understand the *game* without ever looking at it as something more than what goes on inside the people who play it. One way to see this is to realize that systems often work in ways that don't reflect people's experience and motivations. . . .

In spite of all the good reasons to not use individual models to explain social life, doing so constitutes a path of least resistance because personal experience and motivation are what we know best. As a result, we tend to see something like patriarchy as the result of poor socialization through which men learn to act dominant and masculine and women learn to act subordinate and feminine. While there is certainly some truth to this, it doesn't work as

an explanation of patterns like privilege and oppression. It's no better than trying to explain war as simply the result of training men to be warlike, without looking at economic systems that equip armies at huge profits and political systems that organize and hurl armies at one another. It's like trying to understand what happens during Monopoly games without ever talking about the game itself and the kind of society in which it would exist. Of course, soldiers and Monopoly players do what they do because they've learned the rules, but this doesn't tell us much about the rules themselves and why they exist to be learned in the first place. Socialization is merely a process, a mechanism for training people to participate in social systems. Although it tells us how people learn to participate, it doesn't illuminate the systems themselves. As such, it can tell us something about the *how* of a system like patriarchy, but very little about the *what* and the *why*.

. . .

We can't find a way out of patriarchy or imagine something different without a clear sense of what patriarchy is and what it's got to do with us. . . .

We need to see more clearly what patriarchy is about as a system. This includes cultural ideas about men and women, the web of relationships that structure social life, and the unequal distribution of power, rewards and resources that underlies privilege and oppression. We need to see new ways to participate by forging alternative paths of least resistance; for the system doesn't simply "run us" like hapless puppets. It may be larger than us, it may not *be* us, but it doesn't happen except *through* us. And that's where we have power to do something about it and about ourselves in relation to it.

Patriarchy

. . .

Patriarchy's defining elements are its male-dominated, male-identified, male-centered, and control-obsessed character, but this is just the beginning. At its core, patriarchy is based in part on a set of symbols and ideas that make up a culture embodied by everything from the content of everyday conversation to literature and film. Patriarchal culture includes ideas about the nature of things, including women, men, and humanity, with manhood and masculinity most closely associated with being human and womanhood and femininity relegated to the marginal position of "other." It's about how social life is and how it's supposed to be, about what's expected of people and about how they feel. It's about standards of feminine beauty and masculine toughness, images of feminine vulnerability and masculine protectiveness, of older men coupled with younger women, of elderly women alone. It's about defining women and men as opposites, about the "naturalness" of male aggression, competition, and dominance and of female caring, cooperation, and subordination. It's about the valuing of masculinity and maleness and the devaluing of femininity and femaleness. It's about the primary importance of a husband's career and the secondary status of a wife's, about child care as a priority in women's lives and its secondary importance in men's. It's about the social acceptability of anger, rage, and toughness in men but not in women, and of caring, tenderness, and vulnerability in women but not in men.

Above all, patriarchal culture is about the core value of control and domination in almost every area of human existence. From the expression of emotion to economics to the natural environment, gaining and exercising control is a continuing goal. Because of this, the concept of power takes on a narrow definition in terms of "power over"—the ability to control others, events, resources, or one's self in spite of resistance—rather than alternatives such as the ability to cooperate, to give freely of oneself, or to feel and act in harmony with nature. To have power over and to be prepared to use it are culturally defined as good and desirable (and characteristically "masculine"), and to lack such power or to be reluctant to use it is seen as weak if not contemptible (and characteristically "feminine"). This is a major reason that patriarchies with the means to do so are often so quick to go to war. Studies of the (mostly) men who formulate U.S. military strategy, for example, show that it is almost impossible to lose standing by advocating an excessive use of force in international relations (such as the U.S. response to terrorism and the 2003 invasion of Iraq). But anyone—especially a man—who advocates restraint in the use of force, runs the serious risk of being perceived as less than manly and, therefore, lacking credibility.

The main use of any culture is to provide symbols and ideas out of which to construct a sense of what is real. As such, language mirrors social reality in sometimes startling ways. In contemporary usage, for example, the words *crone, witch, bitch,* and *virgin* describe women as threatening, evil, or heterosexually inexperienced and thus incomplete. In prepatriarchal times, however, these words evoked far different images. The crone was the old woman whose life experience gave her insight, wisdom, respect, and the power to enrich people's lives. The witch was the wise-woman healer, the knower of herbs, the midwife, the link joining body, spirit, and Earth. The bitch was Artemis-Diana, goddess of the hunt, most often associated with the dogs who accompanied her. And the virgin was merely a woman who was unattached, unclaimed, and unowned by any man and therefore independent and autonomous. Notice how each word has been transformed from a positive cultural image of female power, independence, and dignity to an insult or a shadow of its former self so that few words remain to identify women in ways both positive and powerful.

Going deeper into patriarchal culture, we find a complex web of ideas that define reality and what's considered good and desirable. To see the world through patriarchal eyes is to believe that women and men are profoundly different in their basic natures, that hierarchy is the only alternative to chaos, and that men were made in the image of a masculine God with whom they enjoy a special relationship. It is to take as obvious the idea that there are two and only two distinct genders; that patriarchal heterosexuality is "natural" and same-sex attraction is not; that because men neither bear nor breast-feed children, they cannot feel a compelling bodily connection to them; that on some level every woman, whether heterosexual or lesbian, wants a "real man" who knows how to "take charge of things," including her; that females can't be trusted, especially when they're menstruating or accusing men of sexual abuse. In spite of all the media hype to the contrary, to embrace patriarchy still is to believe that mothers should stay home and that fathers should work outside the home, regardless of men's and women's actual abilities or needs. It is to buy into the notion that women are weak and men are strong, that women and children need men to support and protect them, all in spite of the fact that in many ways men are not the physically stronger sex, that women perform a huge share of hard physical labor in many societies (often larger than men's), that women's physical endurance tends to be greater than men's over the long haul, that women tend to be more capable of enduring pain and emotional stress.[2] And yet, as Elizabeth Janeway notes, such evidence means little in the face of a patriarchal culture that dictates how things *ought* to be and, like all cultural mythology, "will not be argued down by facts. It may seem to be making straightforward statements, but actually these conceal another mood, the imperative. Myth exists in a state of tension. It is not really describing a situation, but trying by means of this description *to bring about* what it declares to exist."[3]

To live in a patriarchal culture is to learn what's expected of men and women—to learn the rules that regulate punishment and reward based on how individuals behave and appear. These rules range from laws that require men to fight in wars not of their own choosing to customary expectations that mothers will provide child care. Or that when a woman shows sexual interest in a man or merely smiles or acts friendly, she gives up her right to say no and to control her own body. And to live under patriarchy is to take into ourselves ways of feeling—the hostile contempt for femaleness that forms the core of misogyny and presumptions of male superiority, the ridicule men direct at other men who show signs of vulnerability or weakness, or the fear and insecurity that every woman must deal with when she exercises the right to move freely in the world, especially at night and by herself in public places.

Such ideas make up the symbolic sea we swim in and the air we breathe. They are the primary well from which springs how we think about ourselves, other people, and the world. As such, they provide a taken-for-granted everyday reality, the setting for our interactions with other people that continually fashion and refashion a sense of what the world is about and who we are in relation to it. This doesn't mean that the ideas underlying patriarchy determine what we think, feel, and do, but it does mean they define what we'll have to deal with as we participate in it.

The prominent place of misogyny in patriarchal culture, for example, doesn't mean that every man and woman consciously hates all things female. But it does mean that to the extent that we don't feel such hatred, it's *in spite of* paths of least resistance

contained in our culture. Complete freedom from such feelings and judgments is all but impossible. It is certainly possible for heterosexual men to love women without mentally fragmenting them into breasts, buttocks, genitals, and other variously desirable parts. It is possible for women to feel good about their bodies, to not judge themselves as being too fat, to not abuse themselves to one degree or another in pursuit of impossible male-identified standards of beauty and sexual attractiveness. All of this is possible, but to live in patriarchy is to breathe in misogynist images of women as objectified sexual property valued primarily for their usefulness to men. This finds its way into everyone who grows up breathing and swimming in it, and once inside of us it remains, however unaware of it we may be. So, when we hear or express sexist jokes and other forms of misogyny, we may not recognize it, and even if we do, we may say nothing rather than risk other people thinking we're "too sensitive" or, especially in the case of men, "not one of the guys." In either case, we are involved, if only by our silence.

The symbols and ideas that make up patriarchal culture are important to understand because they have such powerful effects on the structure of social life. By *structure,* I mean the ways privilege and oppression are organized through social relationships and unequal distributions of power, rewards, opportunities, and resources. This appears in countless patterns of everyday life in family and work, religion and politics, community and education. It is found in family divisions of labor that exempt fathers from most domestic work even when both parents work outside the home and in the concentration of women in lower-level pink-collar jobs and male predominance almost everywhere else. It is in the unequal distribution of income and all that goes with it, from access to health care to the availability of leisure time. It is in patterns of male violence and harassment that can turn a simple walk in the park or a typical day at work or a lovers' quarrel into a life-threatening nightmare. More than anything, the structure of patriarchy is found in the unequal distribution of power that makes male privilege possible, in patterns of male dominance in every facet of human life, from everyday conversation to global politics. By its nature, patriarchy puts issues of power, dominance, and control at the center of human existence, not only in relationships between men and women, but among men as they compete and struggle to gain status, maintain control, and protect themselves from what other men might do to them. . . .

The System in Us in the System

One way to see how people connect with systems is to think of us as occupying social positions that locate us in relation to people in other positions. We connect to families, for example, through positions such as "mother," "daughter," and "cousin"; to economic systems through positions such as "vice president," "secretary," or "unemployed"; to political systems through positions such as "citizen," "registered voter," and "mayor"; to religious systems through positions such as "believer" and "clergy." How we perceive the people who occupy such positions and what we expect of them depend on cultural ideas—such as the belief that mothers are naturally better than fathers at child care. Such ideas are powerful because we use them to construct a sense of who we and other people are. When a woman marries, for example, how people (including her) perceive and think about her changes as cultural ideas about what it means to be a wife come into play—ideas about how wives feel about their husbands, what's most important to wives, what's expected of them, and what they may expect of others.

From this perspective, *who* we and other people think we are has a lot to do with *where* we are in relation to social systems and all the positions we occupy in them. We wouldn't exist as social beings if it weren't for our participation in one social system or another. It's hard to imagine just who we'd be and what our existence would consist of if we took away all our connections to the symbols, ideas, and relationships that make up social systems. Take away language and all that it allows us to imagine and think, starting with our names. Take away all the positions that we occupy and the roles that go with them—from daughter and son to occupation and nationality—and with these all the complex ways our lives are connected to other people. Not much would be left over that we'd recognize as ourselves.

We can think of a society as a network of interconnected systems within systems, each made up of social positions and their relations to one another.

To say, then, that I'm white, male, college educated, nondisabled, and a writer, sociologist, U.S. citizen, heterosexual, middle-aged, husband, father, grandfather, brother, and son identifies me in relation to positions which are themselves related to positions in various social systems, from the entire world to the family of my birth. In another sense, the day-to-day reality of a society only exists through what people actually do as they participate in it. Patriarchal culture, for example, places a high value on control and maleness. By themselves, these are just abstractions. But when men and women actually talk and men interrupt women more than women interrupt men, or men ignore topics introduced by women in favor of their own or in other ways control conversation, or when men use their authority to harass women in the workplace, then the reality of patriarchy as a kind of society and people's sense of themselves as female and male within it actually happen in a concrete way.

In this sense, like all social systems, patriarchy exists only through people's lives. . . . This has two important implications for how we understand patriarchy. First, to some extent people experience patriarchy as external to them. But this doesn't mean that it's a distinct and separate thing, like a house in which we live. Instead, by participating in patriarchy we are *of* patriarchy and it is *of* us. Both exist *through* the other and neither can exist without the other. Second, patriarchy isn't static. It's an ongoing *process* that's continuously shaped and reshaped. Since the thing we're participating in is patriarchal, we tend to behave in ways that create a patriarchal world from one moment to the next. But we have some freedom to break the rules and construct everyday life in different ways, which means that the paths we choose to follow can do as much to change patriarchy as they can to perpetuate it.

We're involved in patriarchy and its consequences because we occupy social positions in it, which is all it takes. Because patriarchy is, by definition, a system of inequality organized around gender categories, we can no more avoid being involved in it than we can avoid being female or male. *All* men and *all* women are therefore involved in this oppressive system, and none us can control *whether* we participate, only *how*. As Harry Brod argues, this is especially important in relation to men and male privilege:

We need to be clear that there is no such thing as giving up one's privilege to be "outside" the system. One is always in the system. The only question is whether one is part of the system in a way which challenges or strengthens the status quo. Privilege is not something I take and which I therefore have the option of not taking. It is something that society gives me, and unless I change the institutions which give it to me, they will continue to give it, and I will continue to have it, however noble and egalitarian my intentions.[4]

NOTES

1. Although the game analogy is useful, social systems are quite unlike a game in important ways. The rules and other understandings on which social life is based are far more complex, ambiguous, and contradictory than those of a typical game and much more open to negotiation and "making it up" as we go along.

2. See, for example, Rosalyn Baxandall, Linda Gordon, and Susan Reverby, eds., *America's Working Women: A Documentary History—1600 to the Present* (New York: Vintage Press, 1976); Ashley Montagu, *The Natural Superiority of Women* (New York: Collier, 1974); Robin Morgan, ed., *Sisterhood Is Global* (New York: Feminist Press, 1996); and Marilyn Waring, *If Women Counted: A New Feminist Economics* (San Francisco: HarperCollins, 1990).

3. Elizabeth Janeway, *Man's World, Woman's Place: A Study in Social Mythology* (New York: Dell, 1971), 37.

4. Harry Brod, "Work Clothes and Leisure Suits: The Class Basis and Bias of the Men's Movement," in *Men's Lives*, edited by Michael S. Kimmel and Michael A. Messner (New York: Macmillan, 1989), 280.

NINE

◆◆◆

Black Feminist Thought: Knowledge, Consciousness, and the Politics of Empowerment (1990)—Excerpt

Patricia Hill Collins

Patricia Hill Collins is an award-winning writer and social theorist. Her books include *Black Feminist Thought: Knowledge, Consciousness and the Politics of Empowerment,* and *Black Sexual Politics: African Americans, Gender, and the New Racism.* She has held editorial positions with professional journals and acted as a consultant for community organizations. She is Distinguished University Professor of Sociology at the University of Maryland–College Park, and former president of the American Sociological Association Council.

Knowledge, Consciousness, and the Politics of Empowerment

Black feminist thought demonstrates Black women's emerging power as agents of knowledge. By portraying African-American women as self-defined, self-reliant individuals confronting race, gender, and class oppression, Afrocentric feminist thought speaks to the importance that knowledge plays in empowering oppressed people. One distinguishing feature of Black feminist thought is its insistence that both the changed consciousness of individuals and the social transformation of political and economic institutions constitute essential ingredients for social change. New knowledge is important for both dimensions of change. . . .

Epistemological Shifts: Dialogue, Empathy, and Truth

Black Women as Agents of Knowledge Living life as an African-American woman is a necessary prerequisite for producing Black feminist thought because within Black women's communities thought is validated and produced with reference to a particular set of historical, material, and epistemological conditions. African-American women who adhere to the idea that claims about Black women must be substantiated by Black women's sense of our own experiences and who anchor our knowledge claims in an Afrocentric epistemology have produced a rich tradition of Black feminist thought.

Traditionally such women were blues singers, poets, autobiographers, storytellers, and orators validated by everyday Black women as experts on a Black women's standpoint. Only a few unusual African-American feminist scholars have been able to defy Eurocentric masculinist epistemologies and explicitly embrace an Afrocentric feminist epistemology. Consider Alice Walker's description of Zora Neale Hurston:

> In my mind, Zora Neale Hurston, Billie Holiday, and Bessie Smith form a sort of unholy trinity. Zora *belongs* in the tradition of black women singers, rather than among "the literati." . . . Like Billie and Bessie she followed her own road, believed in her own gods, pursued her own dreams, and refused to separate herself from "common" people. (Walker 1977, xvii–xviii)

Zora Neale Hurston is an exception for prior to 1950, few African-American women earned advanced degrees and most of those who did complied with Eurocentric masculinist epistemologies. Although these women worked on behalf of Black women, they did so within the confines of pervasive race and gender oppression. Black women scholars were in a position to see the exclusion of African-American women from scholarly discourse, and the thematic content of their work often reflected their interest in examining a Black women's standpoint. However, their tenuous status in academic institutions led them to adhere to Eurocentric masculinist epistemologies so that their work would be accepted as scholarly. As a result, while they produced Black feminist thought, those African-American women most likely to gain academic credentials were often least likely to produce Black feminist thought that used an Afrocentric feminist epistemology.

An ongoing tension exists for Black women as agents of knowledge, a tension rooted in the sometimes conflicting demands of Afrocentricity and feminism. Those Black women who are feminists are critical of how Black culture and many of its traditions oppress women. For example, the strong pronatal beliefs in African-American communities that foster early motherhood among adolescent girls, the lack of self-actualization that can accompany the double-day of paid employment and work in the home, and the emotional and physical abuse that many Black women experience from their fathers, lovers, and husbands all reflect practices opposed by African-American women who are feminists. But these same women may have a parallel desire as members of an oppressed racial group to affirm the value of that same culture and traditions (Narayan 1989). Thus strong Black mothers appear in Black women's literature, Black women's economic contributions to families is lauded, and a curious silence exists concerning domestic abuse.

As more African-American women earn advanced degrees, the range of Black feminist scholarship is expanding. Increasing numbers of African-American women scholars are explicitly choosing to ground their work in Black women's experiences, and, by doing so, they implicitly adhere to an Afrocentric feminist epistemology. Rather than being restrained by their both/and status of marginality, these women make creative use of their outsider-within status and produce innovative Afrocentric feminist thought. The difficulties these women face lie less in demonstrating that they have mastered white male epistemologies than in resisting the hegemonic nature of these patterns of thought in order to see, value, and use existing alternative Afrocentric feminist ways of knowing.

In establishing the legitimacy of their knowledge claims, Black women scholars who want to develop Afrocentric feminist thought may encounter the often conflicting standards of three key groups. First, Black feminist thought must be validated by ordinary African-American women who, in the words of Hannah Nelson, grow to womanhood "in a world where the saner you are, the madder you are made to appear" (Gwaltney 1980, 7). To be credible in the eyes of this group, scholars must be personal advocates for their material, be accountable for the consequences of their work, have lived or experienced their material in some fashion, and be willing to engage in dialogues about their findings with ordinary, everyday people. Second, Black feminist thought also must be accepted by the community of Black women scholars. These scholars place varying amounts of importance on rearticulating a Black women's standpoint using an Afrocentric feminist epistemology. Third, Afrocentric feminist thought within academia must be prepared to confront Eurocentric masculinist political and epistemological requirements.

The dilemma facing Black women scholars engaged in creating Black feminist thought is that a knowledge claim that meets the criteria of adequacy for one group and thus is judged to be an acceptable knowledge claim may not be translatable into the terms of a different group. Using the example of Black English, June Jordan illustrates the difficulty of moving among epistemologies:

> You cannot "translate" instances of Standard English preoccupied with abstraction or with nothing/nobody evidently alive into Black English. That would warp the language into uses antithetical to the guiding perspective of its community of users. Rather you must first change those Standard English sentences, themselves, into ideas consistent with the person-centered assumptions of Black English. (Jordan 1985, 130)

Although both worldviews share a common vocabulary, the ideas themselves defy direct translation.

For Black women who are agents of knowledge, the marginality that accompanies outsider-within status can be the source of both frustration and creativity. In an attempt to minimize the differences between the cultural context of African-American communities and the expectations of social institutions, some women dichotomize their behavior and become two different people. Over time, the strain of doing this can be enormous. Others reject their cultural context and work against their own best interests by enforcing the dominant group's specialized thought. Still others manage to inhabit both contexts but do so critically, using their outsider-within perspectives as a source of insights and ideas. But while outsiders within can make substantial contributions as agents of knowledge, they rarely do so without substantial personal cost. "Eventually it comes to you," observes Lorraine Hansberry, "the thing that makes you exceptional, if you are at all, is inevitably that which must also make you lonely" (1969, 148).

Once Black feminist scholars face the notion that, on certain dimensions of a Black women's standpoint, it may be fruitless to try and translate ideas from an Afrocentric feminist epistemology into a Eurocentric masculinist framework, then other choices emerge. Rather than trying to uncover universal knowledge claims that can withstand the translation from one epistemology to another

(initially, at least), Black women intellectuals might find efforts to rearticulate a Black women's standpoint especially fruitful. Rearticulating a Black women's standpoint refashions the concrete and reveals the more universal human dimensions of Black women's everyday lives. "I date all my work," notes Nikki Giovanni, "because I think poetry, or any writing, is but a reflection of the moment. The universal comes from the particular" (1988, 57). bell hooks maintains, "my goal as a feminist thinker and theorist is to take that abstraction and articulate it in a language that renders it accessible—not less complex or rigorous—but simply more accessible" (1989, 39). The complexity exists; interpreting it remains the unfulfilled challenge for Black women intellectuals.

Situated Knowledge, Subjugated Knowledge, and Partial Perspectives   "My life seems to be an increasing revelation of the intimate face of universal struggle," claims June Jordan:

> You begin with your family and the kids on the block, and next you open your eyes to what you call your people and that leads you into land reform into Black English into Angola leads you back to your own bed where you lie by yourself, wondering if you deserve to be peaceful, or trusted or desired or left to the freedom of your own unfaltering heart. And the scale shrinks to the size of a skull: your own interior cage. (Jordan 1981, xi)

Lorraine Hansberry expresses a similar idea: "I believe that one of the most sound ideas in dramatic writing is that in order to create the universal, you must pay very great attention to the specific. Universality, I think, emerges from the truthful identity of what is" (1969, 128). Jordan and Hansberry's insights that universal struggle and truth may wear a particularistic, intimate face suggest a new epistemological stance concerning how we negotiate competing knowledge claims and identify "truth."

The context in which African-American women's ideas are nurtured or suppressed matters. Understanding the content and epistemology of Black women's ideas as specialized knowledge requires attending to the context from which those ideas emerge. While produced by individuals, Black feminist thought as situated knowledge is embedded in the communities in which African-American women find ourselves (Haraway 1988).

A Black women's standpoint and those of other oppressed groups is not only embedded in a context but exists in a situation characterized by domination. Because Black women's ideas have been suppressed, this suppression has stimulated African-American women to create knowledge that empowers people to resist domination. Thus Afrocentric feminist thought represents a subjugated knowledge (Foucault 1980). A Black women's standpoint may provide a preferred stance from which to view the matrix of domination because, in principle, Black feminist thought as specialized thought is less likely than the specialized knowledge produced by dominant groups to deny the connection between ideas and the vested interests of their creators. However, Black feminist thought as subjugated knowledge is not exempt from critical analysis, because subjugation is not grounds for an epistemology (Haraway 1988).

Despite African-American women's potential power to reveal new insights about the matrix of domination, a Black women's standpoint is only one angle of vision. Thus Black feminist thought represents a partial perspective. The overarching matrix of domination houses multiple groups, each with varying experiences with penalty and privilege that produce corresponding partial perspectives, situated knowledges, and, for clearly identifiable subordinate groups, subjugated knowledges. No one group has a clear angle of vision. No one group possesses the theory of methodology that allows it to discover the absolute "truth" or, worse yet, proclaim its theories and methodologies as the universal norm evaluating other groups' experiences. Given that groups are unequal in power in making themselves heard, dominant groups have a vested interest in suppressing the knowledge produced by subordinate groups. Given the existence of multiple and competing knowledge claims to "truth" produced by groups with partial perspectives, what epistemological approach offers the most promise?

Dialogue and Empathy   Western social and political thought contains two alternative approaches to ascertaining "truth." The first, reflected in positivist science, has long claimed that absolute truths exist and that the task of scholarship is to develop objective, unbiased tools of science to measure these truths. But Afrocentric, feminist, and other bodies of critical

theory have unmasked the concepts and epistemology of this version of science as representing the vested interests of elite white men and therefore as being less valid when applied to experiences of other groups and, more recently, to white male recounting of their own exploits. Earlier versions of standpoint theories, themselves rooted in a Marxist positivism, essentially reversed positivist science's assumptions concerning whose truth would prevail. These approaches suggest that the oppressed allegedly have a clearer view of "truth" than their oppressors because they lack the blinders created by the dominant group's ideology. But this version of standpoint theory basically duplicates the positivist belief in one "true" interpretation of reality and, like positivist science, comes with its own set of problems.

Relativism, the second approach, has been forwarded as the antithesis of and inevitable outcome of rejecting a positivist science. From a relativist perspective all groups produce specialized thought and each group's thought is equally valid. No group can claim to have a better interpretation of the "truth" than another. In a sense, relativism represents the opposite of scientific ideologies of objectivity. As epistemological stances, both positivist science and relativism minimize the importance of specific location in influencing a group's knowledge claims, the power inequities among groups that produce subjugated knowledges, and the strengths and limitations of partial perspective (Haraway 1988).

The existence of Black feminist thought suggests another alternative to the ostensibly objective norms of science and to relativism's claims that groups with competing knowledge claims are equal. In this volume I placed Black women's subjectivity in the center of analysis and examined the interdependence of the everyday, taken-for-granted knowledge shared by African-American women as a group, the more specialized knowledge produced by Black women intellectuals, and the social conditions shaping both types of thought. This approach allowed me to describe the creative tension linking how sociological conditions influenced a Black women's standpoint and how the power of the ideas themselves gave many African-American women the strength to shape those same sociological conditions. I approached Afrocentric feminist thought as situated in a context of domination and not as a system of ideas divorced from political and economic reality. Moreover, I presented Black feminist thought as subjugated knowledge in that African-American women have long struggled to find alternative locations and techniques for articulating our own standpoint. In brief, I examined the situated, subjugated standpoint of African-American women in order to understand Black feminist thought as a partial perspective on domination.

This approach to Afrocentric feminist thought allows African-American women to bring a Black women's standpoint to larger epistemological dialogues concerning the nature of the matrix of domination. Eventually such dialogues may get us to a point at which, claims Elsa Barkley Brown, "all people can learn to center in another experience, validate it, and judge it by its own standards without need of comparison or need to adopt that framework as their own" (1989, 922). In such dialogues, "one has no need to 'decenter' anyone in order to center someone else; one has only to constantly, appropriately, 'pivot the center'" (p. 922).

Those ideas that are validated as true by African-American women, African-American men, Latina lesbians, Asian-American women, Puerto Rican men, and other groups with distinctive standpoints, with each group using the epistemological approaches growing from its unique standpoint, thus become the most "objective" truths. Each group speaks from its own standpoint and shares its own partial, situated knowledge. But because each group perceives its own truth as partial, its knowledge is unfinished. Each group becomes better able to consider other groups' standpoints without relinquishing the uniqueness of its own standpoint or suppressing other groups' partial perspectives. "What is always needed in the appreciation of art, or life," maintains Alice Walker, "is the larger perspective. Connections made, or at least attempted, where none existed before, the straining to encompass in one's glance at the varied world the common thread, the unifying theme through immense diversity" (1983, 5). Partiality and not universality is the condition of being heard; individuals and groups forwarding knowledge claims without owning their position are deemed less credible than those who do.

Dialogue is critical to the success of this epistemological approach, the type of dialogue long extant in the Afrocentric call-and-response tradition whereby power dynamics are fluid, everyone has a voice, but everyone must listen and respond to other voices in order to be allowed to remain in the community.

Sharing a common cause fosters dialogue and encourages groups to transcend their differences.

Existing power inequities among groups must be addressed before an alternative epistemology such as that described by Elsa Barkley Brown or Alice Walker can be utilized. The presence of subjugated knowledges means that groups are not equal in making their standpoints known to themselves and others. "Decentering" the dominant group is essential, and relinquishing privilege of this magnitude is unlikely to occur without struggle. But still the vision exists, one encompassing "coming to believe in the possibility of a variety of experiences, a variety of ways of understanding the world, a variety of frameworks of operation, without imposing consciously or unconsciously a notion of the norm" (Brown 1989, 921).

REFERENCES

Brown, Elsa Barkely. 1986. *Hearing Our Mothers' Lives.* Atlanta: Fifteenth Anniversary of African-American and African Studies, Emory University. (unpublished)

——. 1989. "African-American Women's Quilting: A Framework for Conceptualizing and Teaching African-American Women's History." *Signs* 14(4): 921–29.

Foucault, Michel. 1980. *Power/Knowledge: Selected Interviews and Other Writings 1972–1977,* edited by Colin Gordon. New York: Pantheon.

Giovanni, Nikki. 1988. *Sacred Cows . . . and Other Edibles.* New York: Quill/William Morrow.

Gwaltney, John Langston. 1980. *Drylongso, A Self-Portrait of Black America.* New York: Vintage.

Hansberry, Lorraine. 1969. *To Be Young, Gifted and Black.* New York: Signet.

Haraway, Donna. 1988. "Situated Knowledges: The Science Question in Feminism and the Privilege of Partial Perspective." *Feminist Studies* 14(3): 575–99.

hooks, bell. 1989. *Talking Back: Thinking Feminist, Thinking Black.* Boston: South End Press.

Jordan, June. 1985. *On Call.* Boston: South End Press.

Narayan, Uma. 1989. "The Project of Feminist Epistemology: Perspectives from a Nonwestern Feminist." In *Gender/Body/Knowledge: Feminist Reconstructions of Being and Knowing,* edited by Alison M. Jaggar and Susan R. Bordo, 256–69. New Brunswick, NJ: Rutgers University Press.

Walker, Alice. 1977. "Zora Neale Hurston: A Cautionary Tale and a Partisan View." Foreword to *Zora Neale Hurston: A Literary Biography,* by Robert Hemenway, xi–xviii. Urbana: University of Illinois Press.

——. 1983. *In Search of Our Mothers' Gardens.* New York: Harcourt Brace Jovanovich.

TEN

◆◆◆

Genealogies of Community, Home, and Nation (1993/2003)

Chandra Talpade Mohanty

Chandra Talpade Mohanty is a professor of women's studies at Syracuse University. Her widely acclaimed scholarly work includes *Feminism Without Borders: Decolonizing Theory, Practicing Solidarity* and focuses on transnational feminist theory, studies of colonialism, imperialism, and culture, and antiracist education.

. . . At a time when globalization (and monoculturalism) is the primary economic and cultural practice to capture and hold hostage the material resources and economic and political choices of vast numbers of the world's population, what are the concrete challenges for feminists of varied genealogies working together? Within the context of the history of feminist struggle in the United States, the 1980s were a period of euphoria and hope for feminists of color, gay and lesbian, and antiracist, white feminists. Excavating subjugated knowledges and histories in order to craft decolonized, oppositional racial and sexual identities and political strategies that posed direct challenges to the gender, class, race, and sexual regimes of the capitalist U.S. nation-state anchored the practice of antiracist, multicultural feminisms.

At the start of this century, however, I believe the challenges are somewhat different. Globalization, or the unfettered mobility of capital and the accompanying erosion and reconstitution of local and national economic and political resources and of democratic processes, the post–cold war U.S. imperialist state, and the trajectories of identity-based social movements in the 1980s and 1990s constitute the ground for transnational feminist engagement in the twenty-first century. Multicultural feminism that is radical, antiracist, and nonheterosexist thus needs to take on a hegemonic capitalist regime and conceive of itself as also crossing national and regional borders. Questions of "home," "belonging," "nation," and "community" thus become profoundly complicated.

One concrete task that feminist educators, artists, scholars, and activists face is that of historicizing and denaturalizing the ideas, beliefs, and values of global capital such that underlying exploitative social relations and structures are made visible. This means being attentive not only to the grand narrative or "myth" of capitalism as "democracy" but also to the mythologies that feminists of various races, nations, classes, and sexualities have inherited about one another. I believe one of the greatest challenges we (feminists) face is this task of recognizing and undoing the ways in which we colonize and objectify our different histories and cultures, thus colluding with hegemonic processes of domination and rule. Dialogue across differences is thus fraught with tension, competitiveness, and pain. Just as radical or critical multiculturalism cannot be the mere sum or coexistence of different cultures in a profoundly unequal, colonized world, multicultural feminism cannot assume the existence of a dialogue among feminists from different communities without specifying a just and ethical basis for such a dialogue.

Undoing ingrained racial and sexual mythologies within feminist communities requires, in Jacqui Alexander's words, that we "become fluent in each other's histories." It also requires seeking "unlikely coalitions" (Davis 1998, 299)[1] and, I would add, clarifying the ethics and meaning of dialogue. What are the conditions, the knowledges, and the attitudes that make a noncolonized dialogue possible? How can we craft a dialogue anchored in equality, respect, and dignity for all peoples? In other words, I want to suggest that one of the most crucial challenges for a critical multicultural feminism is working out how to engage in ethical and caring dialogues (and revolutionary struggles) across the divisions, conflicts, and individualist identity formations that interweave feminist communities in the United States. Defining genealogies is one crucial element in creating such a dialogue.

Just as the very meaning and basis for dialogue across difference and power needs to be analyzed and carefully crafted, the way we define genealogies also poses a challenge. Genealogies that not only specify and illuminate historical and cultural differences but also envision and enact common political and intellectual projects across these differences constitute a crucial element of the work of building critical multicultural feminism.

To this end I offer a personal, anecdotal meditation on the politics of gender and race in the construction of South Asian identity in North America. My location in the United States is symptomatic of large numbers of migrants, nomads, immigrants, workers across the globe for whom notions of home, identity, geography, and history are infinitely complicated in the twenty-first century. . . .

Emotional and Political Geographies of Belonging

On a TWA flight on my way back to the United States from a conference in the Netherlands, the white professional man sitting next to me asks which school I go to and when I plan to go home—all in the same breath. I put on my most professorial demeanor (somewhat hard in crumpled blue jeans and cotton T-shirt) and inform him that I teach at a small liberal arts college in upstate New York and that I have lived in the United States for over twenty years. At this point, my work is in the United States, not in India. (This is no longer entirely true—my work is also with feminists and grassroots activists in India, but he doesn't need to know this.) Being "mistaken" for a graduate student seems endemic to my existence in this country: few Third World women are granted professional (i.e., adult) and/or permanent (one is always a student) status in the United States, even if we exhibit clear characteristics of adulthood such as gray hair and facial lines. The man ventures a further question: what do I teach? On hearing "women's studies," he becomes quiet and we spend the next eight hours in polite silence. He has decided that I do not fit into any of his categories, but what can you expect from a feminist (an Asian one) anyway? I feel vindicated and a little superior, even though I know he doesn't really feel "put in his place." Why should he? He claims a number of advantages in this situation: white

skin, maleness, and citizenship privileges. Judging by his enthusiasm for expensive "ethnic food" in Amsterdam, and his J. Crew clothes, I figured class difference (economic or cultural) wasn't exactly a concern in our interaction. We both appeared to have similar social access as "professionals."

I have been asked the "home" question (when are you going home?) periodically for twenty years now. Leaving aside the subtly racist implications of the question (go home, you don't belong), I am still not satisfied with my response. What is home? The place I was born? Where I grew up? Where my parents live? Where I live and work as an adult? Where I locate my community, my people? Who are "my people"? Is home a geographical space, a historical space, an emotional, sensory space? Home is always so crucial to immigrants and migrants— I even write about it in scholarly texts (perhaps to avoid addressing it, as an issue that is also very personal?). What interests me is the meaning of home for immigrants and migrants. I am convinced that this question—how one understands and defines home—is a profoundly political one.

Since settled notions of territory, community, geography, and history don't work for us, what does it really mean to be "South Asian" in the United States? Obviously, I was not South Asian in India: I was Indian. What else could one be but "Indian" at a time when a successful national independence struggle had given birth to a socialist democratic nation-state? This was the beginning of the decolonization of the Third World. Regional geography (South Asia) appeared less relevant as a mark of identification than citizenship in a postcolonial independent nation on the cusp of economic and political autonomy. However, in North America, identification as South Asian (in addition to Indian, in my case) takes on its own logic. "South Asian" refers to folks of Indian, Pakistani, Sri Lankan, Bangladeshi, Kashmiri, and Burmese origin. Identifying as South Asian rather than Indian adds numbers and hence power within the U.S. state. Besides, regional differences among those from different South Asian countries are often less relevant than the commonalities based on our experiences and histories of immigration, treatment, and location in the United States.

Let me reflect a bit on the way I identify myself, and the way the U.S. state and its institutions categorize me. Perhaps thinking through the various labels will lead me to the question of home and identity. In 1977, I arrived in the United States on an F1 visa (a student visa). At that time, my definition of myself—a graduate student in education at the University of Illinois—and the "official" definition of me (a student allowed into the country on an F1 visa) obviously coincided. Then I was called a "foreign student" and expected to go "home" (to India, even though my parents were in Nigeria at the time) after getting my Ph.D. This is the assumed trajectory for a number of Indians, especially the postindependence (my) generation, who come to the United States for graduate study.

However, this was not to be my trajectory. I quickly discovered that being a foreign student, and a woman at that, meant being either dismissed as irrelevant (the quiet Asian woman stereotype), or treated in racist ways (my teachers asked if I understood English and if they should speak slower and louder so that I could keep up—this in spite of my inheritance of the Queen's English and British colonialism) or celebrated and exoticized ("You are so smart! Your accent is even better than that of Americans"—a little Anglophilia at work here, even though all my Indian colleagues insist we speak English the Indian way).

The most significant transition I made at that time was the one from "foreign student" to "student of color." Once I was able to "read" my experiences in terms of race, and to read race and racism as they are written into the social and political fabric of the United States, practices of racism and sexism became the analytic and political lenses through which I was able to anchor myself here. Of course, none of this happened in isolation: friends, colleagues, comrades, classes, books, films, arguments, and dialogues were constitutive of my political education as a woman of color in the United States.

In the late 1970s and early 1980s feminism was gaining momentum on American campuses: it was in the air, in the classrooms, on the streets. However, what attracted me wasn't feminism as the mainstream media and white women's studies departments defined it. Instead, it was a very specific kind of feminism, the feminism of U.S. women of color and Third World women, that spoke to me. In thinking through the links among gender, race, and class in their U.S. manifestations, I was for the first time able to think through my own gendered, classed, postcolonial history. In the early 1980s,

reading Audre Lorde, Nawal el Sadaawi, Angela Davis, Cherríe Moraga, bell hooks, Gloria Joseph, Paula Gunn Allen, Barbara Smith, Merle Woo, and Mitsuye Yamada, among others, generated a sort of recognition that was intangible but very inspiring. A number of actions, decisions, and organizing efforts at that time led me to a sense of home and community in relation to women of color in the United States: home, not as a comfortable, stable, inherited, and familiar space but instead as an imaginative, politically charged space in which the familiarity and sense of affection and commitment lay in shared collective analysis of social injustice, as well as a vision of radical transformation. Political solidarity and a sense of family could be melded together imaginatively to create a strategic space I could call "home." Politically, intellectually, and emotionally I owe an enormous debt to feminists of color—especially to the sisters who have sustained me over the years. . . .

For me, engagement as a feminist of color in the United States made possible an intellectual and political genealogy of being Indian that was radically challenging as well as profoundly activist. Notions of home and community began to be located within a deeply political space where racialization and gender and class relations and histories became the prism through which I understood, however partially, what it could mean to be South Asian in North America. Interestingly, this recognition also forced me to reexamine the meanings attached to home and community in India.

What I chose to claim, and continue to claim, is a history of anticolonialist, feminist struggle in India. The stories I recall, the ones that I retell and claim as my own, determine the choices and decisions I make in the present and the future. I did not want to accept a history of Hindu chauvinist (bourgeois) upward mobility (even though this characterizes a section of my extended family). We all choose partial, interested stories/histories—perhaps not as deliberately as I am making it sound here, but, consciously or unconsciously, these choices about our past(s) often determine the logic of our present.

Having always kept my distance from conservative, upwardly mobile Indian immigrants, to whom the South Asian world in the United States was divided into green card holders and non–green card holders, the only South Asian links I allowed and cultivated were with South Asians with whom

I shared a political vision. This considerably limited my community. Racist and sexist experiences in graduate school and after made it imperative that I understand the United States in terms of its history of racism, imperialism, and patriarchal relations, specifically in relation to Third World immigrants. After all, we were then into the Reagan-Bush years, when the neoconservative backlash made it impossible to ignore the rise of racist, antifeminist, and homophobic attitudes, practices, and institutions. Any purely culturalist or nostalgic sentimental definition of being "Indian" or "South Asian" was inadequate. Such a definition fueled the "model minority" myth. And this subsequently constituted us as "outsiders/foreigners" or as interest groups that sought or had obtained the American dream.

In the 1980s, the labels changed: I went from being a "foreign student" to being a "resident alien." I have always thought that this designation was a stroke of inspiration on the part of the U.S. state, since it accurately names the experience and status of immigrants, especially immigrants of color. The flip side of "resident alien" is "illegal alien," another inspired designation. One can be either a resident or illegal immigrant, but one is always an alien. There is no confusion here, no melting pot ideology or narratives of assimilation: one's status as an "alien" is primary. Being legal requires identity papers. . . .

One must be stamped as legitimate (that is, not gay or lesbian and not communist) by the Immigration and Naturalization Service. The INS is one of the central disciplinary arms of the U.S. government. It polices the borders and controls all border crossings, especially those into the United States. In fact, the INS is also one of the primary forces that institutionalizes race differences in the public arena, thus regulating notions of home, legitimacy, and economic access to the "American dream" for many of us. For instance, carrying a green card documenting resident alien status in the United States is clearly very different from carrying an American passport, which is proof of U.S. citizenship. The former allows one to enter the United States with few hassles; the latter often allows one to breeze through the borders and ports of entry of other countries, especially countries that happen to be trading partners (much of Western Europe and Japan, among others) or in an unequal relationship with the United States (much of the noncommunist

Third World). At a time when notions of a capitalist free-market economy is seen (falsely) as synonymous with the values attached to democracy, an American passport can open many doors. However, just carrying an American passport is no insurance against racism and unequal and unjust treatment within the United States.

A comparison of the racialization of South Asian immigrants to second-generation South Asian Americans suggests one significant difference between these two generations: experiencing racism as a phenomenon specific to the United States, versus growing up in the ever-present shadow of racism in the case of South Asians born in the United States. This difference in experience would suggest that the psychic effects of racism would also be different for these two constituencies. In addition, questions of home, identity, and history take on very different meanings for South Asians born in North America. But this comparison requires a whole other reflection that is beyond the scope of this chapter.

Home/Nation/Community: The Politics of Being NRI (Nonresident Indian)

Rather obstinately, I refused to give up my Indian passport and chose to remain a resident alien in the United States for many years.[2] This leads me to reflect on the complicated meanings attached to holding Indian citizenship while making a life for myself in the United States. In India, what does it mean to have a green card or U.S. passport, to be an expatriate? What does it mean to visit Mumbai (Bombay) every two to four years and still call it home? Why does speaking in Marathi (my mother tongue) become a measure and confirmation of home? What are the politics of being a part of the majority and the "absent elite" in India, while being a minority and a racialized "other" in the United States? And do feminist politics, or advocating feminism, have the same meanings and urgencies in these different geographical and political contexts?

Some of these questions hit me smack in the face during a visit to India in December 1992, after the infamous destruction of the Babri Masjid in Ayodhya by Hindu fundamentalists on 6 December 1992. (Horrifically, these deadly clashes between Hindus and Muslims took a new turn in March 2002, with Muslims burning a train full of Hindus returning from Ayodhya, inaugurating yet another continuing bloodbath.) In my earlier, rather infrequent visits (once every four or five years was all I could afford), my green card designated me as an object of envy, privilege, and status within my extended family. Of course, the same green card has always been viewed with suspicion by leftist and feminist friends, who (quite understandably) demand evidence of my ongoing commitment to a socialist and democratic India. During my 1992 visit, however, with emotions running high within my family, my green card marked me as an outsider who couldn't possibly understand the "Muslim problem" in India. I was made aware of being an "outsider" in two profoundly troubling shouting matches with my uncles, who voiced the most hostile sentiments against Muslims. Arguing that India was created as a secular state and that democracy had everything to do with equality for all groups (majority and minority) got me nowhere. The very fundamentals of democratic citizenship in India were/are being undermined and redefined as "Hindu."

Mumbai was one of the cities hardest hit with waves of communal violence following the events of Ayodhya. The mobilization of Hindu fundamentalists, even paramilitary organizations, over the last century and especially since the mid-1940s, had brought Mumbai to a juncture at which the most violently racist discourse about Muslims seemed to be woven into the fabric of acceptable daily life. Racism was normalized in the popular imagination such that it became almost impossible to raise questions in public about the ethics or injustice of racial/ethnic/religious discrimination. I could not assume a distanced posture toward religion anymore. Too many injustices were being committed in my name.

Although born into a Hindu family, I have always considered myself a nonpracticing Hindu—religion had always felt rather repressive when I was growing up. I enjoyed the rituals but resisted the authoritarian hierarchies of organized Hinduism. However, the Hinduism touted by fundamentalist organizations like the RSS (Rashtriya Swayamsevak Sangh, a paramilitary Hindu fundamentalist organization founded in the 1930s) and the Shiv Sena (a Maharashtrian chauvinist, fundamentalist, fascist political organization that has amassed a significant

voice in Mumbai politics and government) was one that even I, in my ignorance, recognized as reactionary and distorted. But this discourse was real—hate-filled rhetoric against Muslims appeared to be the mark of a "loyal Hindu." It was heart-wrenching to see my hometown become a war zone, with streets set on fire and a daily death count to rival any major territorial border war. The smells and textures of my beloved Mumbai, of home, which had always comforted and nurtured me, were violently disrupted. The scent of fish drying on the lines at the fishing village in Danda was submerged in the smell of burning straw and grass as whole *bastis* (*chawls*) were burned to the ground. The very topography, language, and relationships that constituted "home" were exploding. What does community mean in this context?

December 1992 both clarified as well as complicated for me the meanings attached to being an Indian citizen, a Hindu, an educated woman feminist, and a permanent resident in the United States in ways that I have yet to resolve. After all, it is often moments of crisis that make us pay careful attention to questions of identity. Sharp polarizations force one to make choices (not in order to take sides, but in order to accept responsibility) and to clarify one's own analytic, political, and emotional topographies.

I learned that combating the rise of Hindu fundamentalism was a necessary ethical imperative for all socialists, feminists, and Hindus of conscience. Secularism, if it meant absence of religion, was no longer a viable position. From a feminist perspective, it became clear that the battle for women's minds and hearts was very much center stage in the Hindu fundamentalist rhetoric and social position of women. (Two journals, the *Economic and Political Weekly of India* and *Manushi,* are good sources for this work.)

Religious fundamentalist constructions of women embody the nexus of morality, sexuality, and nation—a nexus of great importance for feminists. As in Christian, Islamic, and Jewish fundamentalist discourses, the construction of femininity and masculinity, especially in relation to the idea of the nation, are central to Hindu fundamentalist rhetoric and mobilizations. Women are not only mobilized in the "service" of the nation, but they also become the ground on which discourses of morality and nationalism are written. For instance, the

RSS mobilizes primarily middle-class women in the name of a family-oriented Hindu nation, much as the Christian Right does in the United States. But discourses of morality and nation are also embodied in the normative policing of women's sexuality (witness the surveillance and control of women's dress in the name of morality by the contemporary Iranian state and Taliban-ruled Afghanistan). Thus, one of the central challenges Indian feminists face at this time is how to rethink the relationship of nationalism and feminism in the context of religious identities. In addition to the fundamentalist mobilization that is tearing the country apart, the recent incursions of the International Monetary Fund and the World Bank, with their structural adjustment programs that are supposed to "discipline" the Indian economy, are redefining the meaning of postcoloniality and of democracy in India. Categories such as gender, race, caste/class are profoundly and visibly unstable at such times of crisis. These categories must thus be analyzed in relation to contemporary reconstructions of womanhood and manhood in a *global* arena increasingly dominated by religious fundamentalist movements, the IMF, the World Bank, and the relentless economic and ideological colonization of much of the world by multinationals based in the United States, Japan, and Europe. In all these global economic and cultural/ideological processes, women occupy a crucial position.

In India, unlike most countries, the sex ratio has declined since the early 1900s. According to the 1991 census, the ratio was 929 women to 1,000 men, one of the lowest sex ratios in the world. Women produce 70 to 80 percent of all the food in India and have always been the hardest hit by environmental degradation and poverty. The contradictions between civil law and Hindu and Muslim personal laws affect women but rarely men. Horrific stories about the deliberate genocide of female infants as a result of sex determination procedures such as amniocentesis and recent incidents of *sati* (self-immolation by women on the funeral pyres of their husbands) have even hit the mainstream American media. Gender and religious (racial) discrimination are thus urgent, life-threatening issues for women in India. Over the last decade or so, a politically conscious Indian citizenship has necessitated taking such fundamentally feminist issues seriously. In fact, these are the very same issues South Asian feminists in the

United States need to address. My responsibility to combat and organize against the regressive and violent repercussions of Hindu fundamentalist mobilizations in India extends to my life in North America. After all, much of the money that sustains the fundamentalist movement is raised and funneled through organizations in the United States.

On Race, Color, and Politics: Being South Asian in North America

It is a number of years since I wrote the bulk of this chapter,[3] and as I reread it, I am struck by the presence of the journeys and border-crossings that weave into and anchor my thinking about genealogies. The very crossing of regional, national, cultural, and geographical borders seems to enable me to reflect on questions of identity, community, and politics. In the past years I have journeyed to and lived among peoples in San Diego, California; Albuquerque, New Mexico; London, England; and Cuttack, India. My appearance as a brown woman with short, dark, graying hair remained the same, but in each of these living spaces I learned something slightly different about being South Asian in North America; about being a brown woman in the midst of other brown women with different histories and genealogies.

I want to conclude with a brief reflection on my journeys to California and New Mexico since they complicate further the question of being South Asian in North America. A rather obvious fact, which had not been experientially visible to me earlier, is that the color line differs depending on one's geographical location in the United States. Having lived on the East Coast for many years, my designation as "brown," "Asian," "South Asian," "Third World," and "immigrant" has everything to do with definitions of "blackness" (understood specifically as African American). However, San Diego, with its histories of immigration and racial struggle, its shared border with Mexico, its predominantly brown (Chicano and Asian-American) color line, and its virulent anti-immigrant culture unsettled my East Coast definitions of race and racialization. I could pass as Latina until I spoke my "Indian" English, and then being South Asian became a question of (in)visibility and foreignness. Being South Asian here was synonymous with being alien, non-American.

Similarly, in New Mexico, where the normative meanings of race and color find expression in the relations between Native American, Chicano, and Anglo communities, being South Asian was a matter of being simultaneously visible and invisible as a brown woman. Here, too, my brownness and facial structure marked me visibly as sometimes Latina, sometimes Native American (evidenced by being hailed numerous times in the street as both). Even being Asian, as in being from a part of the world called "Asia," had less meaning in New Mexico, especially since "Asian" was synonymous with "East Asian": the "South" always fell out. Thus, while I could share some experiences with Latinas and Native American women, for instance, the experience of being an "alien"—an outsider within, a woman outside the purview of normalized U.S. citizenship—my South Asian genealogy also set me apart. Shifting the color line by crossing the geography and history of the American West and Southwest thus foregrounded questions about being South Asian in a space where, first, my brownness was not read against blackness, and second, Asian was already definitively cast as East Asian. In this context, what is the relation of South Asian to Asian American (read: East Asian American)? And why does it continue to feel more appropriate, experientially and strategically, to call myself a woman of color or Third World woman? Geographies have never coincided with the politics of race. And claiming racial identities based on history, social location, and experience is always a matter of collective analysis and politics. Thus, while geographical spaces provide historical and cultural anchors (Marathi, Mumbai, and India are fundamental to my sense of myself), it is the deeper values and strategic approach to questions of economic and social justice and collective anticapitalist struggle that constitute my feminism. Perhaps this is why journeys across the borders of regions and nations always provoke reflections of home, identity, and politics for me: there is no clear or obvious fit between geography, race, and politics for someone like me. I am always called on to define and redefine these relationships—"race," "Asianness," and "brownness" are not embedded in me, whereas histories of colonialism, racism, sexism, and nationalism, as well as of privilege (class and status) are involved in my relation to white people and people of color in the United States.

Let me now circle back to the place I began: defining genealogies as a crucial aspect of crafting critical multicultural feminist practice and the meanings I have come to give to home, community, and identity. By exploring the relationship between being a South Asian immigrant in America and an expatriate Indian citizen (NRI) in India, I have tried, however partially and anecdotally, to clarify the complexities of home and community for this particular feminist of color/South Asian in North America. The genealogy I have created for myself here is partial and deliberate. It is a genealogy that I find emotionally and politically enabling—it is part of the genealogy that underlies my self-identification as an educator involved in a pedagogy of liberation. Of course, my history and experiences are in fact messier and not at all as linear as this narrative makes them sound. But then the very process of constructing a narrative for oneself—of telling a story—imposes a certain linearity and coherence that is never entirely there. That is the lesson, perhaps, especially for us immigrants and migrants: that home, community, and identity all fit somewhere between the histories and experiences we inherit and the political choices we make through alliances, solidarities, and friendships.

One very concrete effect of my creating this particular space for myself has been my involvement in two grassroots organizations, one in India and the other in the United States. The former, an organization called Awareness, is based in Orissa and works to empower the rural poor. The group's focus is political education (similar to Paolo Friere's notion of "conscientization"), and its members have also begun very consciously to organize rural women. The U.S. organization I worked with is Grassroots Leadership of North Carolina. It is a multiracial group of organizers (largely African American and white) working to build a poor and working people's movement in the American South. While the geographical, historical, and political contexts are different in the case of these two organizations, my involvement in them is very similar, as is my sense that there are clear connections to be made between the work of the two organizations. In addition, I think that the issues, analyses, and strategies for organizing for social justice are also quite similar. This particular commitment to work with grassroots organizers in the two places I call home is not accidental. It is very much the result of the genealogy I have traced here. After all, it took me over a decade to make these commitments to grassroots work in both spaces. In part, I have defined what it means to be South Asian by educating myself about, and reflecting on, the histories and experiences of African American, Latina, West Indian, African, European American, and other constituencies in North America. Such definitions and understandings do provide a genealogy, but a genealogy that is always relational and fluid as well as urgent and necessary.

NOTES

1. Davis, Angela, and Elizabeth Martinez. 1998. "Coalition Building Among People of Color: A Discussion with

Angela Davis and Elizabeth Martinez." In *The Angela Davis Reader*, edited by Joy James. Boston: Blackwell.

2. I became a U.S. citizen in 1998, in order to adopt my daughter Uma Talpade Mohanty from Mumbai. Now I no longer hold an Indian passport, although of course my designation as NRI (Nonresident Indian) remains the same.

3. An earlier version of this chapter, entitled "Defining Genealogies: Feminist Reflections on Being South Asian in North America," was published in *Women of South Asian Descent Collective* (1993). This chapter is dedicated to the memory of Lanubai and Gauribai Vijaykar, my maternal grandaunts, who were single, educated, financially independent, and tall (over six feet), at a time when it was against the grain to be any one of these things; and to Audre Lorde, teacher, sister, friend, whose words and presence continue to challenge me.

◆◆◆

ELEVEN

Do Muslim Women Really Need Saving? Anthropological Reflections on Cultural Relativism and Its Others (2002)

Lila Abu-Lughod

Lila Abu-Lughod is a professor of anthropology at Columbia University. Her seven books, often based on long-term ethnographic research, include *Veiled Sentiments: Honor and Poetry in a Bedouin Society, Writing Women's Worlds: Bedouin Stories, Remaking Women: Feminism and Modernity in the Middle East* (ed.), *Media Worlds: Anthropology on New Terrain* (ed.), and *Nakba: Palestine, 1948, and the Claims of Memory* (co-author).

What are the ethics of the current "War on Terrorism," a war that justifies itself by purporting to liberate, or save, Afghan women? Does anthropology have anything to offer in our search for a viable position to take regarding this rationale for war?

I was led to pose the question of my title in part because of the way I personally experienced the response to the U.S. war in Afghanistan. Like many colleagues whose work has focused on women and gender in the Middle East, I was deluged with invitations to speak—not just on news programs but also to various departments at colleges and universities, especially women's studies programs.

Why did this not please me, a scholar who has devoted more than 20 years of her life to this subject and who has some complicated personal connection to this identity? Here was an opportunity to spread the word, disseminate my knowledge, and correct misunderstandings. The urgent search for knowledge about our sister "women of cover" (as President George Bush so marvelously called them) is laudable and when it comes from women's studies programs where "transnational feminism" is now being taken seriously, it has a certain integrity (see Safire 2001).

My discomfort led me to reflect on why, as feminists in or from the West, or simply as people who have concerns about women's lives, we need to be wary of this response to the events and aftermath of September 11, 2001. 1 want to point out the minefields—a metaphor that is sadly too apt for a country like Afghanistan, with the world's highest number of mines per capita—of this obsession with the plight of Muslim women. I hope to show some way through them using insights from anthropology, the discipline whose charge has been to understand

Afghan women participate in a women's conference convened by the United Nations and the Afghan Women's Association.

and manage cultural difference. At the same time, I want to remain critical of anthropology's complicity in the reification of cultural difference.

Cultural Explanations and the Mobilization of Women

It is easier to see why one should be skeptical about the focus on the "Muslim woman" if one begins with the U.S. public response. I will analyze two manifestations of this response: some conversations I had with a reporter from the PBS *NewsHour with Jim Lehrer* and First Lady Laura Bush's radio address to the nation on November 17, 2001. The presenter from the *NewsHour* show first contacted me in October to see if I was willing to give some background for a segment on Women and Islam. I mischievously asked whether she had done segments on the

women of Guatemala, Ireland, Palestine, or Bosnia when the show covered wars in those regions; but I finally agreed to look at the questions she was going to pose to panelists. The questions were hopelessly general. Do Muslim women believe "x"? Are Muslim women "y"? Does Islam allow "z" for women? I asked her: If you were to substitute Christian or Jewish wherever you have Muslim, would these questions make sense? I did not imagine she would call me back. But she did, twice, once with an idea for a segment on the meaning of Ramadan and another time on Muslim women in politics. . . .

What is striking about these . . . ideas for news programs is that there was a consistent resort to the cultural, as if knowing something about women and Islam or the meaning of a religious ritual would help one understand the tragic attack on New York's World Trade Center and the U.S. Pentagon, or how Afghanistan had come to be ruled by the Taliban, or what interests might have fueled U.S. and other interventions in the region over the past 25 years, or what the history of American support for conservative groups funded to undermine the Soviets might have been, or why the caves and bunkers out of which Bin Laden was to be smoked "dead or alive" as President Bush announced on television, were paid for and built by the CIA.

In other words, the question is why knowing about the "culture" of the region, and particularly its religious beliefs and treatment of women, was more urgent than exploring the history of the development of repressive regimes in the region and the U.S. role in this history. Such cultural framing, it seemed to me, prevented the serious exploration of the roots and nature of human suffering in this part of the world. Instead of political and historical explanations, experts were being asked to give religio-cultural ones. Instead of questions that might lead to the exploration of global interconnections, we were offered ones that worked to artificially divide the world into separate spheres—recreating an imaginative geography of West versus East, us versus Muslims, cultures in which First Ladies give speeches versus others where women shuffle around silently in burqas.

Most pressing for me was why the Muslim woman in general, and the Afghan woman in particular, were so crucial to this cultural mode of explanation, which ignored the complex entanglements in which we are all implicated, in sometimes surprising alignments. Why were these female symbols being mobilized in this "War against Terrorism" in a way they were not in other conflicts? Laura Bush's radio address on November 17 reveals the political work such mobilization accomplishes. On the one hand, her address collapsed important distinctions that should have been maintained. There was a constant slippage between the Taliban and the terrorists, so that they became almost one word—a kind of hyphenated monster identity: the Taliban-and-the-terrorists. Then there was the blurring of the very separate causes in Afghanistan of women's continuing malnutrition, poverty, and ill health, and their more recent exclusion under the Taliban from employment, schooling, and the joys of wearing nail polish. On the other hand, her speech reinforced chasmic divides, primarily between the "civilized people throughout the world" whose hearts break for the women and children

of Afghanistan and the Taliban-and-the-terrorists, the cultural monsters who want to, as she put it, "impose their world on the rest of us."

Most revealingly, the speech enlisted women to justify American bombing and intervention in Afghanistan and to make a case for the "War on Terrorism" of which it was allegedly a part. As Laura Bush said, "Because of our recent military gains in much of Afghanistan, women are no longer imprisoned in their homes. They can listen to music and teach their daughters without fear of punishment. The fight against terrorism is also a fight for the rights and dignity of women" (U.S. Government 2002).

These words have haunting resonances for anyone who has studied colonial history. Many who have worked on British colonialism in South Asia have noted the use of the woman question in colonial policies where intervention into sati (the practice of widows immolating themselves on their husbands' funeral pyres), child marriage, and other practices was used to justify rule. As Gayatri Chakravorty Spivak (1988) has cynically put it: white men saving brown women from brown men. The historical record is full of similar cases, including in the Middle East. In Turn of the Century Egypt, what Leila Ahmed (1992) has called "colonial feminism" was hard at work. This was a selective concern about the plight of Egyptian women that focused on the veil as a sign of oppression but gave no support to women's education and was professed loudly by the same Englishman, Lord Cromer, who opposed women's suffrage back home.

Sociologist Marnia Lazreg (1994) has offered some vivid examples of how French colonialism enlisted women to its cause in Algeria. She writes.

> Perhaps the most spectacular example of the colonial appropriation of women's voices, and the silencing of those among them who had begun to take women revolutionaries . . . as role models by not donning the veil, was the event of May 16, 1958 [just four years before Algeria finally gained its independence from France after a long bloody struggle and 130 years of French control— LA.]. On that day a demonstration was organized by rebellious French generals in Algiers to show their determination to keep Algeria French. To give the government of France evidence that Algerians were

in agreement with them, the generals had a few thousand native men bused in from nearby villages, along with a few women who were solemnly unveiled by French women . . . Rounding up Algerians and bringing them to demonstrations of loyalty to France was not in itself an unusual act during the colonial era. But to unveil women at a well-choreographed ceremony added to the event a symbolic dimension that dramatized the one constant feature of the Algerian occupation by France: its obsession with women. [Lazreg 1994:135]

. . .

Politics of the Veil

I want now to look more closely at those Afghan women Laura Bush claimed were "rejoicing" at their liberation by the Americans. This necessitates a discussion of the veil, or the burqa, because it is so central to contemporary concerns about Muslim women. This will set the stage for a discussion of how anthropologists, feminist anthropologists in particular, contend with the problem of difference in a global world. In the conclusion, I will return to the rhetoric of saving Muslim women and offer an alternative.

It is common popular knowledge that the ultimate sign of the oppression of Afghan women under the Taliban-and-the-terrorists is that they were forced to wear the burqa. Liberals sometimes confess their surprise that even though Afghanistan has been liberated from the Taliban, women do not seem to be throwing off their burqas. Someone who has worked in Muslim regions must ask why this is so surprising. . . .

First, it should be recalled that the Taliban did not invent the burqa. It was the local form of covering that Pashtun women in one region wore when they went out. The Pashtun are one of several ethnic groups in Afghanistan and the burqa was one of many forms of covering in the subcontinent and Southwest Asia that has developed as a convention for symbolizing women's modesty or respectability. The burqa, like some other forms of "cover" has, in many settings, marked the symbolic separation of men's and women's spheres, as part of the general association of women with family and home, not with public space where strangers mingled.

Twenty years ago the anthropologist Hanna Papanek (1982), who worked in Pakistan, described the burqa as "portable seclusion." She noted that many saw it as a liberating invention because it enabled women to move out of segregated living spaces while still observing the basic moral requirements of separating and protecting women from unrelated men. Ever since I came across her phrase "portable seclusion," I have thought of these enveloping robes as "mobile homes." Everywhere, such veiling signifies belonging to a particular community and participating in a moral way of life in which families are paramount in the organization of communities and the home is associated with the sanctity of women.

The obvious question that follows is this: If this were the case, why would women suddenly become immodest? Why would they suddenly throw off the markers of their respectability, markers, whether burqas or other forms of cover, which were supposed to assure their protection in the public sphere from the harassment of strange men by symbolically signaling to all that they were still in the inviolable space of their homes, even though moving in the public realm? Especially when these are forms of dress that had become so conventional that most women gave little thought to their meaning.

To draw some analogies, none of them perfect, why are we surprised that Afghan women do not throw off their burqas when we know perfectly well that it would not be appropriate to wear shorts to the opera? At the time these discussions of Afghan women's burqas were raging, a friend of mine was chided by her husband for suggesting she wanted to wear a pantsuit to a fancy wedding: "You know you don't wear pants to a WASP wedding," he reminded her. New Yorkers know that the beautifully coiffed Hasidic women, who look so fashionable next to their dour husbands in black coats and hats, are wearing wigs. This is because religious belief and community standards of propriety require the covering of the hair. They also alter boutique fashions to include high necks and long sleeves. As anthropologists know perfectly well, people wear the appropriate form of dress for their social communities and are guided by socially shared standards, religious beliefs, and moral ideals, unless they deliberately transgress to make a point or are unable to afford proper cover. If we think that U.S. women live in a world of choice regarding clothing, all we need to do is remind ourselves of the expression, "the tyranny of fashion."

What had happened in Afghanistan under the Taliban is that one regional style of covering or veiling, associated with a certain respectable but not elite class, was imposed on everyone as "religiously" appropriate, even though previously there had been many different styles, popular or traditional with different groups and classes—different ways to mark women's propriety, or, in more recent times, religious piety. Although I am not an expert on Afghanistan, I imagine that the majority of women left in Afghanistan by the time the Taliban took control were the rural or less educated, from nonelite families, since they were the only ones who could not emigrate to escape the hardship and violence that has marked Afghanistan's recent history. If liberated from the enforced wearing of burqas, most of these women would choose some other form of modest headcovering, like all those living nearby who were not under the Taliban— their rural Hindu counterparts in the North of India (who cover their heads and veil their faces . . .) or their Muslim sisters in Pakistan.

Even *The New York Times* carried an article about Afghan women refugees in Pakistan that attempted to educate readers about this local variety (Fremson 2001). The article describes and pictures everything from the now-iconic burqa with the embroidered eyeholes, which a Pashtun woman explains is the proper dress for her community, to large scarves they call chadors, to the new Islamic modest dress that wearers refer to as *hijab*. Those in the new Islamic dress are characteristically students heading for professional careers, especially in medicine, just like their counterparts from Egypt to Malaysia. One wearing the large scarf was a school principal; the other was a poor street vendor. The telling quote from the young street vendor is, "If I did [wear the burqa] the refugees would tease me because the burqa is for 'good women' who stay inside the home" (Fremson 2001:14). Here you can see the local status associated with the burqa—it is for good respectable women from strong families who are not forced to make a living selling on the street.

The British newspaper *The Guardian* published an interview in January 2002 with Dr. Suheila Siddiqi, a respected surgeon in Afghanistan who holds the rank of lieutenant general in the Afghan medical corps (Goldenberg 2002). A woman in her sixties, she comes from an elite family and, like her sisters, was educated. Unlike most women of her class, she chose not to go into exile. She is presented in the article as "the woman who stood up to the Taliban" because she refused to wear the burqa. She had made it a condition of returning to her post as head of a major hospital when the Taliban came begging in 1996, just eight months after firing her along with other women. Siddiqi is described as thin, glamorous, and confident. But further into the article it is noted that her graying bouffant hair is covered in a gauzy veil. This is a reminder that though she refused the burqa, she had no question about wearing the chador or scarf.

Finally, I need to make a crucial point about veiling. Not only are there many forms of covering, which themselves have different meanings in the communities in which they are used, but also veiling itself must not be confused with, or made to stand for, lack of agency. As I have argued in my ethnography of a Bedouin community in Egypt in the late 1970s and 1980s (1986), pulling the black head cloth over the face in front of older respected men is considered a voluntary act by women who are deeply committed to being moral and have a sense of honor tied to family. One of the ways they show their standing is by covering their faces in certain contexts. They decide for whom they feel it is appropriate to veil.

To take a very different case, the modern Islamic modest dress that many educated women across the Muslim world have taken on since the mid-1970s now both publicly marks piety and can be read as a sign of educated urban sophistication, a sort of modernity (e.g., Abu-Lughod 1995, 1998; Brenner 1996; El Guindi 1999; MacLeod 1991; Ong 1990). As Saba Mahmood (2001) has so brilliantly shown in her ethnography of women in the mosque movement in Egypt, this new form of dress is also perceived by many of the women who adopt it as part of a bodily means to cultivate virtue, the outcome of their professed desire to be close to God.

Two points emerge from this fairly basic discussion of the meanings of veiling in the contemporary Muslim world. First, we need to work against the reductive interpretation of veiling as the quintessential sign of women's unfreedom, even if we object to state imposition of this form, as in Iran or with the Taliban. (It must be recalled that the modernizing states of Turkey and Iran had earlier in the century banned veiling and required men, except religious clerics, to adopt Western dress.) What does freedom mean if we accept the fundamental premise that humans are social beings, always raised in certain social and historical contexts and belonging to particular communities that shape their desires and understandings of the world? Is it not a gross violation of women's own understandings of what they are doing to simply denounce the burqa as a medieval imposition? Second, we must take care not to reduce the diverse situations and attitudes of millions of Muslim women to a single item of clothing. Perhaps it is time to give up the Western obsession with the veil and focus on some serious issues with which feminists and others should indeed be concerned.

Ultimately, the significant political-ethical problem the burqa raises is how to deal with cultural "others." How are we to deal with difference without accepting the passivity implied by the cultural relativism for which anthropologists are justly famous—a relativism that says it's their culture and it's not my business to judge or interfere, only to try to understand. Cultural relativism is certainly an improvement on ethnocentrism and the racism, cultural imperialism, and imperiousness that underlie it; the problem is that it is too late not to interfere, The forms of lives we find around the world are already products of long histories of interactions.

I want to explore the issues of women, cultural relativism, and the problems of "difference" from three angles. First, I want to consider what feminist anthropologists . . . are to do with strange political bedfellows. I used to feel torn when I received the e-mail petitions circulating for the last few years in defense of Afghan women under the Taliban. I was not sympathetic to the dogmatism of the Taliban; I do not support the oppression of women. But the provenance of the campaign worried me. I do not usually find myself in political company with the likes of Hollywood celebrities (see Hirschkind and Mahmood 2002). I had never received a petition from such women defending the right of Palestinian women to safety from Israeli bombing or daily harassment at checkpoints, asking the United States to reconsider its support for a government that had dispossessed them, closed them out from work and citizenship rights, refused them the most basic freedoms. Maybe some of these same people might be signing petitions to save African women

from genital cutting, or Indian women from dowry deaths. However, I do not think that it would be as easy to mobilize so many of these American and European women if it were not a case of Muslim men oppressing Muslim women—women of cover for whom they can feel sorry and in relation to whom they can feel smugly superior. Would television diva Oprah Winfrey host the Women in Black, the women's peace group from Israel, as she did RAWA, the Revolutionary Association of Women of Afghanistan, who were also granted the *Glamour Magazine* Women of the Year Award? What are we to make of post-Taliban "Reality Tours" such as the one advertised on the internet by Global Exchange for March 2002 under the title "Courage and Tenacity: A Women's Delegation to Afghanistan"? The rationale for the $1,400 tour is that "with the removal of the Taliban government, Afghan women, for the first time in the past decade, have the opportunity to reclaim their basic human rights and establish their role as equal citizens by participating in the rebuilding of their nation." The tour's objective, to celebrate International Women's Week, is "to develop awareness of the concerns and issues the Afghan women are facing as well as to witness the changing political, economic, and social conditions which have created new opportunities for the women of Afghanistan" (Global Exchange 2002).

To be critical of this celebration of women's rights in Afghanistan is not to pass judgment on any local women's organizations, such as RAWA, whose members have courageously worked since 1977 for a democratic secular Afghanistan in which women's human rights are respected, against Soviet-backed regimes or U.S.-, Saudi-, and Pakistani-supported conservatives. Their documentation of abuse and their work through clinics and schools have been enormously important.

It is also not to fault the campaigns that exposed the dreadful conditions under which the Taliban placed women. The Feminist Majority campaign helped put a stop to a secret oil pipeline deal between the Taliban and the U.S. multinational Unocal that was going forward with U.S. administration support. Western feminist campaigns must not be confused with the hypocrisies of the new colonial feminism of a Republican president who was not elected for his progressive stance on feminist issues or of administrations that played down the terrible record of violations of women by the United State's allies in the Northern Alliance, as documented by Human Rights Watch and Amnesty International, among others. Rapes and assaults were widespread in the period of infighting that devastated Afghanistan before the Taliban came in to restore order.

It is, however, to suggest that we need to look closely at what we are supporting (and what we are not) and to think carefully about why. How should we manage the complicated politics and ethics of finding ourselves in agreement with those with whom we normally disagree? I do not know how many feminists who felt good about saving Afghan women from the Taliban are also asking for a global redistribution of wealth or contemplating sacrificing their own consumption radically so that African or Afghan women could have some chance of having what I do believe should be a universal human right—the right to freedom from the structural violence of global inequality and from the ravages of war, the everyday rights of having enough to eat, having homes for their families in which to live and thrive, having ways to make decent livings so their children can grow, and having the strength and security to work out, within their communities and with whatever alliances they want, how to live a good life, which might very well include changing the ways those communities are organized.

Suspicion about bedfellows is only a first step; it will not give us a way to think more positively about what to do or where to stand. For that, we need to confront two more big issues. First is the acceptance of the possibility of difference. Can we only free Afghan women to be like us or might we have to recognize that even after "liberation" from the Taliban, they might want different things than we would want for them? What do we do about that? Second, we need to be vigilant about the rhetoric of saving people because of what it implies about our attitudes.

Again, when I talk about accepting difference, I am not implying that we should resign ourselves to being cultural relativists who respect whatever goes on elsewhere as "just their culture." I have already discussed the dangers of "cultural" explanations; "their" cultures are just as much part of history and an interconnected world as ours are. What I am advocating is the hard work involved in recognizing and respecting differences—precisely as products of different histories, as expressions of

different circumstances, and as manifestations of differently structured desires. We may want justice for women, but can we accept that there might be different ideas about justice and that different women might want, or choose, different futures from what we envision as best (see Ong 1988)? We must consider that they might be called to personhood, so to speak, in a different language.

Reports from the Bonn peace conference held in late November [2001] to discuss the rebuilding of Afghanistan revealed significant differences among the few Afghan women feminists and activists present. RAWA's position was to reject any conciliatory approach to Islamic governance. According to one report I read, most women activists, especially those based in Afghanistan who are aware of the realities on the ground, agreed that Islam had to be the starting point for reform. Fatima Gailani, a U.S.-based advisor to one of the delegations, is quoted as saying, "If I go to Afghanistan today and ask women for votes on the promise to bring them secularism, they are going to tell me to go to hell." Instead, according to one report, most of these women looked for inspiration on how to fight for equality to a place that might seem surprising. They looked to Iran as a country in which they saw women making significant gains within an Islamic framework—in part through an Islamically oriented feminist movement that is challenging injustices and reinterpreting the religious tradition.

The situation in Iran is itself the subject of heated debate within feminist circles, especially among Iranian feminists in the West (e.g., Mir-Hosseini 1999; Moghissi 1999, Najmabadi 1998, 2000). It is not clear whether and in what ways women have made gains and whether the great increases in literacy, decreases in birthrates, presence of women in the professions and government, and a feminist flourishing in cultural fields like writing and filmmaking are because of or despite the establishment of a so-called Islamic Republic. The concept of an Islamic feminism itself is also controversial. Is it an oxymoron or does it refer to a viable movement forged by brave women who want a third way?

One of the things we have to be most careful about in thinking about Third World feminisms, and feminism in different parts of the Muslim world, is how not to fall into polarizations that place feminism on the side of the West. I have written about the dilemmas faced by Arab feminists when Western feminists initiate campaigns that make them vulnerable to local denunciations by conservatives of various sorts, whether Islamist or nationalist, of being traitors (Abu-Lughod 2001). As some like Afsaneh Najmabadi are now arguing, not only is it wrong to see history simplistically in terms of a putative opposition between Islam and the West (as is happening in the United States now and has happened in parallel in the Muslim world), but it is also strategically dangerous to accept this cultural opposition between Islam and the West, between fundamentalism and feminism, because those many people within Muslim countries who are trying to find alternatives to present injustices, those who might want to refuse the divide and take from different histories and cultures, who do not accept that being feminist means being Western, will be under pressure to choose, just as we are: Are you with us or against us?

My point is to remind us to be aware of differences, respectful of other paths toward social change that might give women better lives. Can there be a liberation that is Islamic? And, beyond this, is liberation even a goal for which all women or people strive? Are emancipation, equality, and rights part of a universal language we must use? To quote Saba Mahmood, writing about the women in Egypt who are seeking to become pious Muslims, "The desire for freedom and liberation is a historically situated desire whose motivational force cannot be assumed a priori, but needs to be reconsidered in light of other desires, aspirations, and capacities that inhere in a culturally and historically located subject" (2001:223). In other words, might other desires be more meaningful for different groups of people? Living in close families? Living in a godly way? Living without war? I have done fieldwork in Egypt over more than 20 years and I cannot think of a single woman I know, from the poorest rural to the most educated cosmopolitan, who has ever expressed envy of U.S. women, women they tend to perceive as bereft of community, vulnerable to sexual violence and social anomie, driven by individual success rather than morality, or strangely disrespectful of God.

Mahmood (2001) has pointed out a disturbing thing that happens when one argues for a respect for other traditions. She notes that there seems to be a difference in the political demands made on those who work on or are trying to understand Muslims and Islamists and those who work on secular-humanist projects. . . . But there never seems to be a parallel demand for those who study secular humanism and its projects, despite the terrible violences that have been associated with it over the last couple of centuries, from world wars to colonialism, from genocides to slavery. We need to have as little dogmatic faith in secular humanism as in Islamism, and as open a mind to the complex possibilities of human projects undertaken in one tradition as the other.

Beyond the Rhetoric of Salvation

Let us return, finally, to my title, "Do Muslim Women Need Saving?" The discussion of culture, veiling, and how one can navigate the shoals of cultural difference should put Laura Bush's self-congratulation about the rejoicing of Afghan women liberated by American troops in a different light. It is deeply problematic to construct the Afghan woman as someone in need of saving. When you save someone, you imply that you are saving her from something. You are also saving her *to* something. What violences are entailed in this transformation, and what presumptions are being made about the superiority of that to which you are saving her? Projects of saving other women depend on and reinforce a sense of superiority by Westerners, a form of arrogance that deserves to be challenged. All one needs to do to appreciate the patronizing quality of the rhetoric of saving women is to imagine using it today in the United States about disadvantaged groups such as African American women or working-class women. We now understand them as suffering from structural violence. We have become politicized about race and class, but not culture.

As anthropologists, feminists, or concerned citizens, we should be wary of taking on the mantles of those 19th-century Christian missionary women who devoted their lives to saving their Muslim sisters. One of my favorite documents from that period is a collection called *Our Moslem Sisters*, the proceedings of a conference of women missionaries held in Cairo in 1906 (Van Sommer and Zwemer 1907). The subtitle of the book is *A Cry of Need from the Lands of Darkness Interpreted by Those Who Heard It*. Speaking of the ignorance, seclusion, polygamy, and veiling that blighted women's lives across the Muslim world, the missionary women spoke of their responsibility to make these women's voices heard. As the introduction states, "They will never cry for themselves, for they are down under the yoke of centuries of oppression" (Van Sommer and Zwemer 1907:15). "This book," it begins, "with its sad, reiterated story of wrong and oppression is an indictment and an appeal. It is an appeal to Christian womanhood to right these wrongs and enlighten this darkness by sacrifice and service" (Van Sommer and Zwemer 1907:5).

One can hear uncanny echoes of their virtuous goals today, even though the language is secular, the appeals not to Jesus but to human rights or the liberal West. The continuing currency of such imagery and sentiments can be seen in their deployment for perfectly good humanitarian causes. In February 2002, I received an invitation to a reception honoring an international medical humanitarian network called Medecins du Monde/Doctors of the World (MdM). Under the sponsorship of the French Ambassador to the United States, the Head of the delegation of the European Commission to the United Nations, and a member of the European Parliament, the cocktail reception was to feature an exhibition of photographs under the clichéd title "Afghan Women: Behind the Veil."

The invitation was remarkable not just for the colorful photograph of women in flowing burqas walking across the barren mountains of Afghanistan but also for the text, a portion of which I quote:

> For 20 years MdM has been ceaselessly struggling to help those who are most vulnerable. But increasingly, thick veils cover the victims of the war. When the Taliban came to power in 1996, Afghan Women became faceless. To unveil one's face while receiving medical care was to achieve a sort of intimacy, find a brief space for secret freedom and recover a little of one's dignity. In a country where women had no access to basic medical care because they did not have the right to appear in public, where women had no right to practice medicine, MdM's program stood as a stubborn reminder of human rights. . . . Please join us in helping to lift the veil.

Although I cannot take up here the fantasies of intimacy associated with unveiling, fantasies reminiscent of the French colonial obsessions so brilliantly unmasked by Alloula in *The Colonial Harem* (1986), I can ask why humanitarian projects and human rights discourse in the 21st century need rely on such constructions of Muslim women.

Could we not leave veils and vocations of saving others behind and instead train our sights on ways to make the world a more just place? The reason respect for difference should not be confused with cultural relativism is that it does not preclude asking how we, living in this privileged and powerful part of the world, might examine our own responsibilities for the situations in which others in distant places have found themselves. We do not stand outside the world, looking out over this sea of poor benighted people, living under the shadow— or veil—of oppressive cultures; we are part of that world. Islamic movements themselves have arisen in a world shaped by the intense engagements of Western powers in Middle Eastern lives.

A more productive approach, it seems to me, is to ask how we might contribute to making the world a more just place. A world not organized around strategic military and economic demands; a place where certain kinds of forces and values that we may still consider important could have an appeal and where there is the peace necessary for discussions, debates, and transformations to occur within communities. We need to ask ourselves what kinds of world conditions we could contribute to making such that popular desires will not be overdetermined by an overwhelming sense of helplessness in the face of forms of global injustice. Where we seek to be active in the affairs of distant places, can we do so in the spirit of support for those within those communities whose goals are to make women's (and men's) lives better. . . . Can we use a more egalitarian language of alliances, coalitions, and solidarity, instead of salvation?

Even RAWA, the now celebrated Revolutionary Association of the Women of Afghanistan, which was so instrumental in bringing to U.S. women's attention the excesses of the Taliban, has opposed the U.S. bombing from the beginning. They do not see in it Afghan women's salvation but increased hardship and loss. They have long called for disarmament and for peacekeeping forces. Spokespersons point out the dangers of confusing governments with people, the Taliban with innocent Afghans who will be most harmed. They consistently remind audiences to take a close look at the ways policies are being organized around oil interests, the arms industry, and the international drug trade. They are not obsessed with the veil, even though they are the most radical feminists working for a secular democratic Afghanistan. Unfortunately, only their messages about the excesses of the Taliban have been heard, even though their criticisms of those in power in Afghanistan have included previous regimes. A first step in hearing their wider message is to break with the language of alien cultures, whether to understand or eliminate them. Missionary work and colonial feminism belong in the past. Our task is to critically explore what we might do to help create a world in which those poor Afghan women, for whom "the hearts of those in the civilized world break," can have safety and decent lives.

Acknowledgments. I want to thank Page Jackson, Fran Mascia-Lees, Tim Mitchell, Rosalind Morris, Anupama Rao, and members of the audience at the symposium "Responding to War," sponsored by Columbia University's Institute for Research on Women and Gender (where I presented an earlier version), for helpful comments, references, clippings, and encouragement.

REFERENCES

Abu-Lughod, Lila. 1986. Veiled Sentiments: Honor and Poetry in a Bedouin Society. Berkeley: University of California Press.

Abu-Lughod, Lila. 1995. Movie Stars and Islamic Moralism in Egypt. Social Text 42:53–67.

Abu-Lughod, Lila. 1998. Remaking Women: Feminism and Modernity in the Middle East. Princeton: Princeton University Press.

Abu-Lughod, Lila. 2001. Orientalism and Middle East Feminist Studies. Feminist Studies 27(1): 101–113.

Ahmed, Leila. 1992. Women and Gender in Islam. New Haven, CT: Yale University Press.

Alloula, Malek. 1986. The Colonial Harem. Minneapolis: University of Minnesota Press.

Brenner, Suzanne. 1996. Reconstructing Self and Society: Javanese Muslim Womenand "the Veil." American Ethnologist 23(4):673–697.

El Guindi, Fadwa. 1999. Veil: Modesty, Privacy and Resistance. Oxford: Berg.

Fremson, Ruth. 2001. Allure Must Be Covered. Individuality Peeks Through. New York Times, November 4: 14.

Global Exchange. 2002. Courage and Tenacity: A Women's Delegation to Afghanistan. Electronic document, http://www.globalexchange.org/tours/auto/2002-03-05_CourageandTenacityAWomensDeIe. html. Accessed February 11.

Goldenberg, Suzanne. 2002. The Woman Who Stood Up to the Taliban. The Guardian, January 24. Electronic document, http://222.guardian.co.uk/afghanistan/story/0,1284,63840.

Hirschkind, Charles, and Saba Mahmood. 2002. Feminism, the Taliban, and the Politics of Counter-Insurgency. Anthropological Quarterly, Volume 75(2): 107–122.

Lazreg, Marnia. 1994. The Eloquence of Silence: Algerian Women in Question. New York: Routledge.

MacLeod, Arlene. 1991. Accommodating Protest. New York: Columbia University Press.

Mahmood, Saba. 2001. Feminist Theory, Embodiment, and the Docile Agent: Some Reflections on the Egyptian Islamic Revival. Cultural Anthropology 16(2):202–235.

Mir-Hosseini, Ziba. 1999. Islam and Gender: The Religious Debate in Contemporary Iran. Princeton: Princeton University Press.

Moghissi, Haideh. 1999. Feminism and Islamic Fundamentalism, London: Zed Books.

Najmabadi, Afsaneh. 1998. Feminism in an Islamic Republic. In Islam, Gender and Social Change. Yvonne Haddad and John Esposito, eds. Pp. 59–84. New York: Oxford University Press.

Najmabadi, Afsaneh. 2000. (Un)Veiling Feminism. Social Text 64:29–45.

Ong, Aihwa. 1988. Colonialism and Modernity: Feminist Re-Presentations of Women in Non-Western Societies. Inscriptions 3-4:79–93.

Ong, Aihwa. 1990. State Versus Islam: Malay Families, Women's Bodies, and the Body Politic in Malaysia. American Ethnologist 17(2):258–276.

Papanek, Hanna. 1982. Purdah in Pakistan: Seclusion and Modem Occupations for Women. In Separate Worlds. Hanna Papanek and Gail Minault, eds. Pp. 190–216. Columbus, MO: South Asia Books.

Safire, William. 2001. "On Language." New York Times Magazine, October 28: 22.

Spivak, Gayatri Chakravorty. 1988. Can the Subaltern Speak? In Marxism and the Interpretation of Culture. Cary Nelson and Lawrence Grossberg, eds. Pp. 271–313. Urbana: University of Illinois Press.

U.S. Government. 1907. Our Moslem Sisters: A Cry of Need from Lands of Darkness Interpreted by Those Who Heard It. New York: Fleming H. Revell Co.

U.S. Government. 2002. Electronic document, http://www.whitehouse.gov/news/releases/2001/11/20011117. Accessed January 10.

3

◆◆◆

Identities and Social Locations:
Who Am I? Who Are My People?

Discovering and claiming our unique identity is a process of growth, change, and renewal throughout our lifetime. One's identity may seem tangible and fixed at any given point. Over the life span, however, identity is more fluid. For example, an able-bodied woman who suddenly finds herself confined to a wheelchair after an automobile accident, an assimilated Jewish woman who begins the journey of recovering her Jewish heritage, an immigrant woman from a traditional Guatemalan family "coming out" as a lesbian in the United States, or a young, middle-class college student, away from her sheltered home environment for the first time and becoming politicized by an environmental justice organization on campus, will probably find herself redefining who she is, what she values, and what "home" and "community" mean to her.

Identity formation is the result of a complex interplay among a range of factors: individual decisions and choices, particular life events, community recognition and expectations, societal categorization, socialization, and key national or international incidents. It is an ongoing process that involves several key questions:

Who am I? Who do I want to be?

Who do others think I am and want me to be?

Who and what do societal and community institutions, such as schools, religious institutions, the media, and the law, say I am?

Where/what/who are my "home" and "community"?

Which social group(s) do I want to affiliate with?

Who decides the answers to these questions, and on what basis?

The *American Heritage Dictionary* (1993) defines *identity* as

> the collective aspect of the set of characteristics by which a thing is definitely known or recognizable;
>
> a set of behavioral or personal characteristics by which an individual is recognizable as a member of a group;
>
> the distinct personality of an individual regarded as a persisting entity;
>
> individuality.

The same dictionary defines *to identify* as "to associate or affiliate (oneself) closely with a person or group; to establish an identification with another or others."

These definitions point to the connections between us as individuals and how we are perceived by other people and classified by societal institutions. They also involve a sense of individual agency and choice regarding affiliations with others. Gender, race, ethnicity, class, nationality, sexuality, age, religion, dis/ability, culture, and language are all significant social categories by which people are recognized by others. Indeed, on the basis of these categories alone, others often think they know who we are and how we should behave. Personal decisions about our affiliations, culture, and loyalties to specific groups are also shaped by these categories. For example, in communities of color, women may struggle over the question of race versus gender. Is race a more important factor than gender in shaping their lives? If a Latina speaks out publicly about sexism within the Latino community, is she betraying her people? This separation of categories tends to set up false dichotomies in which people often feel that they have to choose one aspect of their identity over another. It also presents particular difficulties for mixed-race, bisexual, or transgender people who do not fit neatly into such narrow categories, and reinforces the need for an intersectional framework as we argued in Chapter 1.

In order to understand the complexity and richness of women's experiences, we must examine them from the micro, meso, macro, and global levels of social relations (see Fig. 3.1). Each level involves the standards—beliefs, behaviors, customs, and worldview—that people value. But it is important to emphasize that in a society marked by serious social and economic inequality, such as the United States, people in subordinate positions rarely see their values reflected in the dominant culture. Indeed, this absence is an important aspect of their oppression. For example, writing about her family, whom she describes as "the ungrateful poor," Dorothy Allison (Reading 13) states: "My family's lives were not on television, not in books, not even comic books. There was a myth of the poor in this country; but it did not include us, no matter how hard I tried to squeeze us in."

Critically analyzing the issue of identity at all these levels will allow us to see that identity is much more than an individual decision or choice about who we are in the world. Rather, it is a set of complex and often contradictory and conflicting psychological, physical, geographical, political, cultural, historical, and spiritual factors.

Being Myself: The Micro Level

At the micro level, individuals usually feel the most comfortable as themselves. Here one can say, for example, "I am a woman, heterosexual, middle class, African American, Buddhist, with a movement disability; but I am also much more than those categories." At this level we define ourselves and structure our daily activities according to our needs and preferences. At the micro level we can best feel and experience the process of identity formation, which includes naming specific forces and events that shape our identities. At this level we also seem to have more control of the process, although there are always interconnections between events and experiences at this level and the other levels.

Critical life events, such as entering kindergarten, losing a parent through death or divorce, or the onset of puberty, may all serve as catalysts for a shift in how we think about ourselves. A five-year-old Vietnamese American child of immigrants may experience the first challenge to her sense of identity when her kindergarten teacher admonishes her to speak only in English. A white, middle-class professional woman who thinks of herself as "a person" and a "competent attorney" may begin to give more weight to the significance of gender if she witnesses younger, less experienced male colleagues in her law office passing her by for promotions. A woman who has been raped who attends her first meeting of a women's campus support group feels the power of connection with other rape survivors and their allies. An eighty-year-old woman, whose partner of fifty years has just died, must face the loss of her lifetime companion, friend, and lover. Such experiences shape each person's ongoing formulation of self, whether or not the process is conscious, deliberate, reflective, or even voluntary.

Identity formation is a lifelong process that includes discovery of the new; recovery of the old, forgotten, or appropriated; and synthesis of the new and old, as illustrated by several writers in this chapter who reflect on how their sense of identity has developed over the course of their lives. At especially important junctures during the process, individuals mark an identity change in tangible ways. An African American woman may change her name from the anglicized Susan to Aisha, with roots in Islamic and African cultures. A Chinese immigrant woman, on the other hand, may adopt an anglicized name, exchanging Nu Lu for Yvonne Lu as part of becoming a U.S. citizen. Another way of marking and effecting a shift in identity is by altering your physical appearance: changing your wardrobe or makeup; cutting your hair very short, wearing it natural rather than permed or pressed, dyeing it purple, or letting the gray show after years of using hair coloring. More permanent changes might include having a tattoo, having your body pierced, having a face lift or tummy tuck, or, for Asian American women, having eye surgery to "Europeanize" your eyes. Transsexuals—female to male and male to female—have surgery to make their physical appearance congruent with their sense of self. Other markers of a change in identity include setting up home for the first time, or relocating to another neighborhood, another city, or another part of the country or the world in search of a new home.

For many people, home is where we grow up until we become independent, by going to college, for example, or getting married; where our parents, siblings, and maybe grandparents are; where our needs for safety, security, and material comfort are met. In reality, what we think of as home may be a complicated and contradictory place where some things we need are present and others are not. Some people's homes are comfortable and secure in a material sense but are also places of emotional or physical violence and cruelty. Some children grow up in homes that provide emotional comfort and a sense of belonging, but as they grow older and their values diverge from those of their parents, home may become a source of discomfort and alienation. Children who have been adopted across lines of race, culture, and nation may never feel very comfortable in their adoptive homes. An important step in integrating the different parts of their identities may be to find their birth mothers, to trace their biological ancestry, or to gain the support and friendship of other transracial adoptees (see Simon and Roorda 2000; Trenka, Oparah, and Shin 2006).

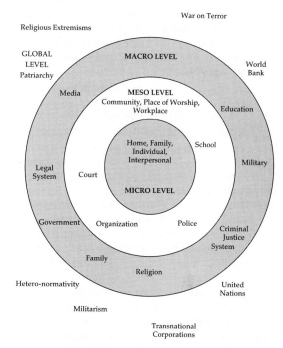

FIGURE 3.1 Levels of Analysis and Interaction
(*Source:* Margo Okazawa-Rey)

Regardless of such experiences, or perhaps because of them, most people continue to seek places of comfort and solace and others with whom they feel they belong and with whom they share common values and interests. Home may be a geographic, social, emotional, and spiritual space where we hope to find safety, security, familiarity, continuity, acceptance, love, and understanding, and where we can feel and be our best, whole selves. Home may be in several places at once or in different places at different times of our lives. Some women may have a difficult time finding a home, a place that feels comfortable and familiar, even if they know what it is. Finally, this process may involve not only searching outside ourselves but also piecing together in some coherent way the scattered parts of our identities—an inward as well as an outward journey.

In the readings that follow, women offer us a view of their identities. An emphasis on the micro level helps us to understand them, to empathize, and to see their humanity, an important corrective to the distorted representations and stereotyping often found in the mainstream media. Also crucial, these articles are not only about individual experiences but go beyond the micro level to include insights regarding the author's community and the macro-level factors that shape community history and experience.

Community Recognition, Expectations, and Interactions: The Meso Level

It is at the meso level—at school, in the workplace, in the neighborhood, or on the street—that people most frequently ask "Who are you?" or "Where are you from?" in an attempt to categorize us and determine their relationship to us. Moreover, it is here that people experience the complexities, conflicts, and contradictions of multiple identities, which we consider later.

The single most visible signifier of identity is physical appearance. How we look to others affects their perceptions, judgments, and treatment of us. Questions such as "Where do you come from?" and questioning behaviors, such as feeling the texture of your hair or asking if you speak a particular language, are commonly used to interrogate people whose physical appearances or behaviors do not match the characteristics designated as belonging to established categories. At root, we are being asked, "Are you one of us or not?" These questioners usually expect simple and straightforward answers, assuming that everyone will fit existing social categories, which are conceived of as undifferentiated and unambiguous. Among people with disabilities, for example, people wanting to identify each other may expect to hear details of another's disability rather than the fact that the person being questioned also identifies equally strongly as, say, a woman who is white, working class, and bisexual.

Community, like home, may be geographic and emotional, or both, and provides a way for people to express group affiliations. "Where are you from?" is a commonplace question in the United States among strangers, a way to break the ice and start a conversation, expecting answers like "I'm from Tallahassee, Florida," or "I'm from the Bronx." Community might also be an organized group like Alcoholics Anonymous, a religious group, or a political organization like the African American civil rights organization, the National Association for the Advancement of Colored People (NAACP). Community may be cultural or religious as discussed by Melanie Kaye/Kantrowitz (Reading 14), Patti Duncan (Reading 16), Julia Alvarez (Reading 17), and Nadine Naber (Reading 18), or something more abstract, as in "the women's community" or "the queer community," where there is presumed to be an identifiable group. Increasingly these communities may be virtual as the Internet links people worldwide. In these examples there is an assumption of shared values, interests, culture, or language sometimes thought of as essential qualities that define group membership and belonging. This can lead to **essentialism,** where complex identities get reduced to specific qualities deemed to be essential for membership of a particular group: being Muslim or gay, for example.

At the community level, individual identities and needs meet group standards, expectations, obligations, responsibilities, and demands. You compare yourself with others and are subtly compared. Others size up your clothing, accent, personal style, and knowledge of the group's history and culture. You may be challenged directly, "You say you're Latina. How come you don't speak Spanish?" "You say you're working class. What are you doing in a professional job?" These experiences may both affirm our identities and create or highlight inconsistencies and contradictions in who we believe we are, how we are viewed by others, our role and status in the community, and our sense of belonging. In Reading 17, writer Julia Alvarez examines the significance of the quinceañera coming-of-age ceremony for Latina girls, their families, and communities as a way of affirming cultural identities and traditions that are, paradoxically, made—and remade—in the United States. This formerly upper-class celebration has become a rite of passage for U.S.-born daughters of immigrant families with very modest incomes. It incorporates traditions from Mexico, Central America, and the Caribbean, enlarged by U.S. consumerism. Also, these North American ways of celebrating the quinceañera, Alvarez notes, are being exported "back home."

Some individuals experience **marginality** if they can move in two or more worlds and, in part, be accepted as insiders (Stonequist 1961). Examples include bisexuals, mixed-race people, and immigrants, who all live in at least two cultures. Tracey, a white, working-class woman, for instance, leaves her friends behind after high school graduation as she goes off to an elite university. Though excited and eager to be in a new setting, she often feels alienated at college because her culture, upbringing, and level of economic security differ from those of the many upper-middle-class and upper-class students. During the winter break, she returns to her hometown where she discovers a gulf between herself and her old friends who remained at home and took jobs or attended community colllege. She notices that she is now speaking a slightly different language from them and that her interests and preoccupations are different from theirs. Tracey has a foot in both worlds. She has become sufficiently acculturated at college to begin to know that community as an insider, and she has retained her old community of friends, but she is not entirely at ease or wholly accepted by either community. Her identity is complex, composed of several parts.

Dorothy Allison (Reading 13) describes her experience of marginality in high school and college. First-generation immigrants invariably experience marginality, as described by Chandra Talpade Mohanty (Reading 10), Patti Duncan (Reading 16), Julia Alvarez (Reading 17), Nadine Naber (Reading 18), and Shailja Patel (Reading 45). The positive effect of marginality—also mentioned by writers in this chapter—is the ability to see both cultures more clearly than people who are embedded in only one context. This gives bicultural people a broader range of vision, a broader standpoint, and allows them to see the complexity and contradictions of both cultural settings. It also helps them to be cultural interpreters and bridge builders, especially at the micro and meso levels (Chiawei O'Hearn 1998; Kich 1992; Okazawa-Rey 1994; Root 1996; Walker 2001).

Social Categories, Classifications, and Structural Inequality: Macro and Global Levels

Classifying and labeling human beings, often according to real or assumed physical, biological, or genetic differences, is a way to distinguish who is included and who is excluded from a group, to ascribe particular characteristics, to prescribe social roles, and to assign status, power, and privilege. People are to know their places. Thus social categories

such as gender, race, and class are used to establish and maintain a particular kind of social order. The classifications and their specific features, meanings, and significance are socially constructed through history, politics, and culture. The specific meanings and significance were often imputed to justify the conquest, colonization, domination, and exploitation of entire groups of people, and although the specifics may have changed over time, this system of categorizing and classifying remains intact. For example, Native American people were described as brutal, uncivilized, and ungovernable savages in the writings of early colonizers on this continent. This justified the near-genocide of Native Americans by white settlers, public officials, and the U.S. military, as well as the breaking of treaties between the U.S. government and Native American tribes (Zinn 1995). Today, Native Americans are no longer called savages but are often thought of as a vanishing species, or a nonexistent people already wiped out, thereby rationalizing their neglect by the dominant culture and erasing their long-standing and continuing resistance. Frederica Y. Daly speaks to the oppression of Native American people, as well as their success in retaining traditional values and the cultural revival they have undertaken (Reading 12). Paula Gunn Allen (Reading 1) and Andy Smith (Reading 33) also provide perspectives on Native American history and contemporary life that are pertinent here. Dorothy Allison points out that a "horror of class stratification, racism, and prejudice is that some people begin to believe that the security of their families and community depends on the oppression of others, that for some to have good lives others must have lives that are mean and horrible" (Reading 13).

These social categories are the foundation of the structural inequalities present in our society. Those in dominant positions are deemed superior and legitimate and those relegated—whether explicitly or implicitly—to subordinate positions are deemed inferior and illegitimate. Of course, individuals are not simply in dominant or subordinate positions. A college-educated, Arab American, heterosexual man has privilege in terms of gender, class, and sexuality, but is considered subordinate in terms of race and culture. Depending on context, these aspects of his identity will contribute to his experience of privilege or disadvantage. Self-awareness involves recognizing and understanding the significance of our identities. For white people descended from European immigrants to this country, the advantages of being white are not always fully recognized or acknowledged. In Reading 15, Mary C. Waters describes how, at the macro level, this country's racial hierarchy benefits European Americans who can choose to claim an ethnic identity as, for example, Irish Americans or Italian Americans. These symbolic identities are individualistic, she argues, and do not have serious social costs for the individual compared with racial and ethnic identities of people of color in the United States. As a result, white people in the United States tend to think of all identities as equal: "I'm Italian American, you're Polish American. I'm Irish American, you're African American." This assumed equivalence ignores the very big differences between an individualist symbolic identity and a socially enforced and imposed racial identity. Note that all Europeans were not considered equal when they immigrated to the United States in the nineteenth and early twentieth centuries. Germans, English, Scots, Irish, French, Italian, Polish, and Russian Jewish people, for example, were differentiated in a hierarchy based on skin color, culture, language, and their histories in Europe. In Reading 14, Melanie Kaye/Kantrowitz writes about the complex social location of Jews in the United States, and her conviction that privilege can and should be deployed to bring about equality and justice.

Maintaining Systems of Structural Inequality

Maintaining systems of inequality requires ongoing objectification and dehumanization of subordinated peoples. Appropriating their identities is a particularly effective method of doing this, for it defines who the subordinated group/person is or ought to be. This happens in several ways:

Using the values, characteristics, features of the dominant group as the supposedly neutral standard against which all others should be evaluated. For example, men of a particular racial/ethnic group are generally physically larger and stronger than women of that group. Many of the clinical trials for new pharmaceutical drugs have been conducted using men's bodies and activities as the standard. The results, however, have been applied equally to both men and women. Women are often prescribed the same dosage of a medication as men are even though their physical makeup is not the same. Thus women, as a distinct group, do not exist in this research.

Using terms that distinguish the subordinate from the dominant group. Terms such as "non-white" and "minority" connote a relationship to another group, white in the former case and majority in the latter. A non-white person is the negative of the white person; a minority person is less than a majority person. Neither has an identity on her or his own terms.

Stereotyping. Stereotyping involves making a simple generalization about a group and claiming that all members of the group conform to it. Stereotypes are behavioral and psychological attributes; they are commonly held beliefs about groups rather than individual beliefs about individuals; and they persist in spite of contradictory evidence. Lesbians hate men. Latinas are dominated by macho Latinos. Women with physical disabilities are asexual. Fat women are good-humored but not healthy. As philosopher Judith Andre (1988) asserted, "A 'stereotype' is pejorative; there is always something objectionable in the beliefs and images to which the word refers" (p. 260).

Exoticizing and romanticizing. These two forms of appropriation are particularly insidious because on the surface there is an appearance of appreciation. For example, Asian American women may be described as personifying the "mysterious Orient," Native American women as "earth mothers" and the epitome of spirituality, and Black women as perpetual towers of strength. In all three cases, seemingly positive traits and cultural practices are identified and exalted. This "positive" stereotyping prevents people from seeing the truth and complexity of who these women are.

Another aspect of romanticization may be **cultural appropriation,** where, for example, white people wear nose studs or dreadlocks, have their hands decorated with henna, or claim to have been Native American in a former life (Smith 1991). Fashion is always seeking something new. Typically, consumers do not think too much about the culture or history of the people who created the styles that are now commodified and sold in the global market place. Thus, objects and styles are lifted out of their original cultural context and become "cool stuff" for other people to buy. Joanna Kadi (1996) argued that cultural appropriation reinforces imperialist

attitudes and constitutes a form of cultural genocide. She urged people to think carefully about their
right to wear "exotic" clothing or to play musical
instruments from other cultures. Our intentions,
our knowledge of those cultures, and developing
authentic connections with people from different
groups are all part of moving from cultural appropriation to what Kadi called "ethical cultural connections."

Images that are circulated and popularized
about a group may also contribute to their "exotici-
zation" or romanticization. How are various groups
of women typically depicted in this society? The four
processes of identity appropriation described above
are used to project images of women that demean,
dehumanize, denigrate, and otherwise violate their
humanity. In Chapter 2, we noted the importance of
independent media with reports and images produced by a diversity of women who speak the truths
of their own lives.

In the face of structural inequalities, the issue of
identity and representation can literally and meta-
phorically be a matter of life and death for members of subordinated groups for several reasons.
They are reduced to the position of the "other"—
that is, fundamentally unlike "us"—made invisible, misunderstood, misrepresented, sometimes
demonized, and often feared. Equally significant,
designating a group as "other" justifies its exploitation, its exclusion from whatever benefits the society may offer, and the violence and, in extreme
cases, genocide committed against it. Therefore,
at the macro and global levels, identity is a matter
of collective well-being and survival. Individual
members of subordinate groups tend to be judged
by those in dominant positions according to negative stereotypes. If any young African American
women, for example, are poor single mothers, they
merely reinforce the stereotype the dominant group
holds about them. When young African American
women hold college degrees and are economically
well off, they are regarded as exceptional by those
in the dominant group, who rarely let disconfirm-
ing evidence push them to rethink their stereotypes.

Given the significance of identity appropriation
as an aspect of oppression, it is not surprising that
many liberation struggles have included projects
and efforts aimed at changing identities and taking
control of the process of positive identity formation
and representation. Oppressed people often use the
same terminology to name themselves as the dominant group uses to label them. One crucial aspect of
liberation struggles is to get rid of pejorative labels
and use names that express, in their own terms, who
they are in all their humanity. Thus, groups may
change the name they use to refer to themselves
to fit their evolving consciousness. As with individual identity, naming ourselves collectively is an
important act of empowerment. One example of
this is the evolution of the names African Americans
have used to identify themselves, moving from
Colored to Negro to Black to Afro-American, and
African American. Similarly, Chinese Americans
gradually rejected the derogatory label "Chink"
preferring to be called Orientals and now Chinese
Americans or Asian Americans. These terms are
used unevenly, perhaps according to the age and
political orientation of the person or the geographic
region, where one usage may be more popular than
another. Among the very diverse group of people
connected historically, culturally, and linguistically
to Spain, Portugal, and their former colonies (parts
of the United States, Mexico, the Caribbean, and
Central and South America), some use more inclusive terms such as Latino or Hispanic; others prefer
more specific names such as Chicano, Puerto Rican,
Nicaraguan, Cuban, and so on. Also, many transgendered people now use the broad term "trans"
rather than medical terminology developed by doctors and psychotherapists that suggests abnormal-
ity and pathology.

Colonization, Immigration, and the U.S. Landscape of Race and Class

Global-level factors affecting people's identities include colonization and immigration. Popular folklore would have us believe that the United States
has welcomed "the tired, huddled masses yearning
to breathe free" (Young 1997). This ideology that
the United States is "a land of immigrants" obscures
several important issues excluded from much
mainstream debate about immigration: Not all
Americans came to this country voluntarily. Native
American peoples and Mexicans were already
here on this continent, but the former experienced
near-genocide and the latter were made foreigners
in their own land. African peoples were captured,
enslaved, imported to this country, and forced to
labor and bear children. All were brutally exploited

Young Latinas at a rally for immigration rights.

and violated—physically, psychologically, culturally, and spiritually—to serve the interests of those in power. The relationships between these groups and this nation and their experiences in the United States are fundamentally different from the experiences of those who chose to immigrate here, though this is not to negate the hardships the latter may have faced. These differences profoundly shaped the social, cultural, political, and economic realities faced by these groups throughout U.S. history and continue to do so today.

Robert Blauner (1972) makes a useful analytical distinction between colonized minorities, whose original presence in this nation was involuntary, and all of whom are people of color, and immigrant minorities, whose presence was voluntary. According to Blauner, colonized minorities faced insurmountable structural inequalities, based primarily on race, that have prevented their full participation in social, economic, political, and cultural arenas of U.S. life. Early in the history of this country, for example, the Naturalization Law of 1790 (which was only repealed in 1952) prohibited peoples of color from becoming U.S. citizens, and the Slave Codes

restricted every aspect of life for enslaved African peoples. These laws made race into an indelible line that separated "insiders" from "outsiders." White people were designated insiders and granted many privileges while all others were confined to systematic disadvantage. (See *A Timeline of Key U.S. Immigration Laws and Policies* on page 110.) As Mary C. Waters points out in Reading 15, the stories that European Americans learn of how their grandparents and great-grandparents triumphed in the United States "are usually told in terms of their individual efforts." The role of labor unions, community organizations, and political parties, as well as the crucial importance of racism, is usually left out of these accounts, which emphasize individual effort and hard work.

Studies of U.S. immigration "reveal discrimination and unequal positioning of different ethnic groups" (Yans-McLaughlin 1990, p. 6), challenging the myth of equal opportunity for all. According to political scientist Lawrence Fuchs (1990), "Freedom and opportunity for poor immigrant whites in the seventeenth and eighteenth centuries were connected fundamentally with the spread of slavery" (p. 294). It was then that diverse groups of European immigrants, such as Irish, Polish, and Italian people, ranked according to a European hierarchy began to learn to be white (Roediger 1991). Whiteness in the United States was constructed in relation to blackness (Morrison 1992). Acclaimed novelist and essayist James Baldwin (1984) commented: "no one was white before he/she came to America" and "it took generations, and a vast amount of coercion, before this became a white country." Thus the common belief among descendants of European immigrants that the successful **assimilation** of their foremothers and forefathers against great odds is evidence that everyone can "pull themselves up by the bootstraps" if they work hard enough does not take into account the racialization of immigration that favored white people. In Reading 14, Melanie Kaye/Kantrowitz discusses Jewish assimilation in the United States, and notes that despite its benefits, this process has been accompanied by extreme cultural loss—of language, history, literature, music, cultural diversity, and experience of rich Jewish traditions.

On coming to the United States, immigrants are drawn into the racial landscape of this country. In media debates and official statistics, this is still dominated by a Black/white polarization, with the addition of "Hispanics" as a non-white third category. Demographically, the U.S. population is much more diverse but often characterized in binary terms: people of color or white people. Immigrants generally identify themselves according to nationality—for example, as Cambodian or Guatemalan. Once in the United States, they may adopt the term *people of color* as an aspect of their identity here. Chandra Talpade Mohanty notes her transition from "foreign student" to "student of color" in the United States. "Racist and sexist experiences in graduate school and after made it imperative that I understand the U.S. in terms of its history of racism, imperialism, and patriarchal relations, specifically in relation to Third World immigrants" (Reading 10).

This emphasis on race tends to mask differences based on class, an important distinction among immigrant groups. For example, the Chinese and Japanese people who came in the nineteenth century and early twentieth century to work on plantations in Hawaii, as loggers in Oregon, or building roads and railroads in several western states were poor and from rural areas of China and Japan.

The 1965 immigration law made way for "the second wave" of Asian immigration (Takaki 1987). It set preferences for professionals, highly skilled workers, and members of the middle and upper-middle classes. The first wave of Vietnamese refugees who immigrated between the mid-1970s and 1980 were the middle and upper classes, including many professionals; by contrast, the second wave of immigrants from Vietnam was composed of poor and rural people. The class backgrounds of immigrants affect not only their sense of themselves and their expectations but also how they can succeed as strangers in a foreign land. For example, a poor woman who arrives with no literacy skills in her own language will have a more difficult time learning to become literate in English than one who has formal schooling in her country of origin that may have included basic English. Some immigrants retain strong ties to their country of origin and may travel back and forth regularly, maintaining family and community connections in more than one place, as described by Julia Alvarez (Reading 17). In Chapter 8, we discuss patterns of migration, geographical and cultural displacement, and increasing cultural standardization related to economic globalization.

Challenging the Gender Binary

Legally, everyone in the United States must identify as female or male. To obtain a driver's license or passport or to buy a plane ticket one must check the M/F box and have the appropriate gender ID. In most states and at the federal level, marriage is defined in law as the union of a man and a woman. Language is gendered, especially pronouns; clothing, children's games, and most public bathrooms are gendered.

Gender regimes are fundamental to patriarchal societies, with social roles attributed accordingly. A gendered division of labor is central, as in the United States, where most care work, whether paid or unpaid, is done by women (see Chapter 7). In families, schools, and community settings, children are taught gender conformity despite some tolerance for tomboyish girls and young boys playing with dolls (see Reading 7). A daily barrage of media images illustrates appropriate gender behavior. Feelings of unhappiness or distress about one's gender identity are defined as a mental illness—gender

A Timeline of Key U.S. Immigration Laws and Policies*

U.S. immigration laws and policies seek to balance a concern for national security with the fact that immigrants contribute greatly to the U.S. economy. Tens of millions of newcomers have made their way to the United States throughout the nation's history, and the United States has resettled more refugees on a permanent basis than any other industrialized country. Immigration law changes in response to economic shifts, political concerns, and perceived threats to national security.

1790   The Naturalization Law of 1790, which was not repealed until 1952, limited naturalization to "free white persons" who had resided in the United States for at least two years. Slave Codes restricted every aspect of life for enslaved African peoples.

1875   The Immigration Act of 1875 denied admission to individuals considered "undesirable," including revolutionaries, prostitutes, and those carrying "loathsome or dangerous contagious diseases."

_____
* Thanks to Wendy A. Young for providing material.

1882   The Chinese Exclusion Act, one of the most racist immigration laws in U.S. history, was adopted; variations were enforced until 1943. The act was a response to fear of the large numbers of Chinese laborers brought to the United States to lay railroads and work in mines.

1917   Congress banned immigration from Asia except Japan and the Philippines.

1921   The Immigration Act of 1921 set an overall cap on the number of immigrants admitted each year and established a nationalities quota system that strongly favored northern Europeans at the expense of immigrants from southern and eastern Europe and Asia.

1924   The Immigration Act of 1924 based immigration quotas on the ethnic composition of the U.S. population in 1920; it also prohibited Japanese immigration.

1945   President Harry Truman issued a directive after World War II allowing for the admission of 40,000 refugees.

---

identity disorder—and included in the *Diagnostic and Statistical Manual of Mental Disorders.*

At the micro level, individuals may change their sex/gender—the terms have often been used interchangeably—through some combination of surgery, hormone therapy, and the ways they choose to dress, talk, and move through the world (see, e.g., Bornstein 1995; Bornstein and Bergman 2010; Girshick 2008; Serano 2007; Stryker 2008; Wilchins 1997). They may opt to live in the "other" gender or emphasize their desire for the personal freedom to live without, or beyond, gender. In Reading 19, Leslie Feinberg writes:

I am a human being who unnerves some people. As they look at me, they see a kaleidoscope of characteristics they associate with both males and females. I appear to be a tangled knot of gender contradictions. . . . I'm a female who is more masculine than those prominently portrayed in mass culture. . . . My life only comes into focus when the word transgender is added to the equation.

Philosopher and queer theorist Judith Butler (1990) considered the gender binary to be a "regulatory fiction" that consolidates and naturalizes the power of masculine and heterosexist oppression (p. 33). Her much-cited conception of gender as performative allows and requires us to think of it more fluidly than two rigid categories permit. The idea of gender fluidity opens up the possibility that, under less limiting circumstances, people would have a wider repertoire of gender behaviors than

1946	The War Brides Act permitted 120,000 foreign wives and children to join their husbands in the United States.		of Asian immigrants, especially middle-class and upper-middle-class people.
1948	The Displaced Persons Act of 1948 permitted entry to an additional 400,000 refugees and displaced persons as a result of World War II.	1980	The Refugee Act of 1980 codified into U.S. law the 1951 United Nations Convention Relating to the Status of Refugees and its 1967 Protocol; it defines a refugee as a person outside her or his country of citizenship who has a well-founded fear of persecution on account of race, religion, nationality, political opinion, or membership in a particular ethnic or social group.
1952	The Immigration and Nationality Act of 1952 was a response to U.S. fear of communism and barred the admission of anyone who might engage in acts "prejudicial to the public interest, or that endanger the welfare or safety of the United States." It allowed immigration for all nationalities, however, and established family connections as a criterion for immigrant eligibility.	1986	The Immigration Reform and Control Act of 1986 was intended to control the growth of illegal immigrants through an "amnesty" program to legalize undocumented people resident in the United States before January 1, 1982, and imposing sanctions against employers who knowingly employ undocumented workers.
1953	The Refugee Relief Act of 1953 admitted 200,000 people, including Hungarians fleeing communism and Chinese emigrating after the Chinese revolution.	1990	The Immigration Act of 1990 affirmed family reunification as the basis for most immigration cases; redefined employment-based immigration; created a new system to diversify the nationalities immigrating
1965	The Immigration Act of 1965 established an annual quota of 120,000 immigrants from the Eastern Hemisphere, which increased the number		

most currently do. At the same time, Butler noted that people "who fail to do their gender right" by standards held to be appropriate in specific contexts, may be punished for it, through name calling, discrimination, hate, and outright violence (p. 140). Using gender-neutral pronouns, Feinberg describes an occasion when a doctor refused to treat hir in a hospital emergency room due to his anger and disgust over hir gender expression.

Most feminists argue that gender is socially constructed though some have supported what Feinberg calls "the cramped compartments of gender" by limiting access to "women-only" spaces such as battered women's shelters or cultural events like the Michigan Womyn's Music Festival. York University researcher Krista Scott-Dixon (2006) has argued for common ground between feminism and transgender activism. In *The Trans-feminist Manifesto*, Emi Koyama (2003) urged trans women—"individuals who identify, present, or live more or less as women despite their sex assignment at birth"—to speak out about their lives (p. 245).

Transsexuals who change sex/gender through hormones and surgery may appear to support the gender binary. Transgendered people make up a broader category, including "masculine females and feminine males, cross-dressers, transsexual men and women, intersexuals born on the anatomical sweep between female and male, gender-blenders, many other sex and gender-variant people, and our significant others," defined by Leslie Feinberg as "transgender warriors" (Reading 19).The fact that surgery is more available and that transgender communities exist, especially in large U.S. cities, means to the United States, ostensibly to compensate for the domination of Asian and Latin American immigration since 1965; and created new mechanisms to provide refuge to those fleeing civil strife, environmental disasters, or political upheaval in their homelands.

1996   The Illegal Immigration Reform and Immigrant Responsibility Act provided for increased border controls and penalties for document fraud; changes in employer sanctions; restrictions on immigrant eligibility for public benefits; and drastic streamlining of the asylum system.

The Personal Responsibility and Work Opportunity Reconciliation Act mainly dealt with changes in the welfare system and made legal immigrants ineligible for various kinds of federal assistance. In 1997, Congress restored benefits for some immigrants already in the country when this law took effect. There is a five-year waiting period before noncitizens can receive Medicaid or Temporary Assistance for Needy Families.

2001   The Uniting and Strengthening America by Providing Appropriate Tools Required to Obstruct Terrorism Act (USA Patriot Act) was signed into law following the attacks on the World Trade Center and the Pentagon on September 11. It significantly enhances the government's powers of detention, search, and surveillance. See "Milestones in U.S. History" (Chapter 1).

2001-12   Various bills were introduced into Congress to benefit children of undocumented immigrants who came to this country with their parents, but none passed into law. In 2012, President Obama issued a policy directive, effective for two years, that allows some 800,000 children of undocumented immigrants to stay here without fear of deportation.

The "pull" factors drawing immigrants to the United States include the possibility of better-paying jobs, better education—especially for children—and greater personal freedom. "Push" factors include poverty, wars, political upheaval, authoritarian regimes, and fewer personal freedoms in the countries they have left. Immigration will continue to be a thorny issue in the United States as the goals of global economic restructuring, filling the country's need for workers, and providing opportunities for family members to live together are set against the fears of those who see continued immigration as a threat to the country's prosperity and security and to the dominance of European Americans.

Airport security has been tightened nationwide. The U.S.–Mexico border has become increasingly militarized. Immigration and Customs Enforcement (ICE) has stepped up raids on homes, schools, and workplaces in many towns and cities (see Reading 54). At the same time, immigrant communities have asserted their presence by taking to the streets in huge demonstrations.

that more people these days may define themselves as trans or consider having surgery or taking hormones (Stryker 2008). In response to the view that trans people are born into the wrong body, Riki Anne Wilchins (1997) argued, "No one is trapped in the wrong body, though many of us are trapped in the wrong culture" (p. 230).

According to historian Susan Stryker (2008), in 1990 only three U.S. cities (Minneapolis, MN; Harrisburg, PA; and Seattle, WA) had legal protection for transgendered people, a number that is slowly rising. In 2007, the first piece of federal legislation to address transgender issues, a hate crimes bill, passed both the U.S. Senate and House of

Representatives. She comments:

> Since the terrorist attacks of September 11, 2001, heightened border surveillance, increased attention to travel documents, and more stringent standards for obtaining state-issued identification all have made life more complicated for many transgender people. (p. 150)

As a result, she argues that transgendered people have a lot in common with immigrants, refugees, and undocumented workers and urges transgender activists to join campaigns "that might seem at first to have little to do with gender identity or expression—but everything to do with how the state polices those who differ from social norms" (p. 150).

Multiple Identities, Social Location, and Contradictions

The social features of one's identity incorporate individual, community, societal, and global factors. **Social location** is a concept used to express the core of a person's existence in the social and political world. It places us in particular relationships to others, to the dominant culture of the United States, and to the rest of the world. It determines the kinds of power and privilege we have access to and can exercise, as well as situations in which we have less power and privilege.

Because social location is where all the aspects of one's identity meet, our experience of our own complex identities is both enriching and contradictory, and pushes us to confront questions of loyalty to individuals and groups. It is through the complexity of social location that we are forced to differentiate our inclinations, behaviors, self-definition, and politics from how we are classified by larger societal institutions. An inclination toward bisexuality, for example, does not mean that one will necessarily act on that inclination. Defining oneself as working class does not necessarily lead to activity in progressive politics based on a class consciousness.

Social location is where we meet others socially and politically. Who are we in relation to people who are both like us and different from us? How do we negotiate the inequalities in power and privilege? How do we both accept and appreciate who we and others are and grow and change to meet the challenges of a multicultural world? In the readings that follow, the writers note significant changes in the way they think about themselves over time. Some mention difficulties in coming to terms with who they are and the complexities of their contradictory positions. They also write about the empowerment that comes from a deepening understanding of identity, enabling them to claim their place in the world.

The concept of social location overlaps with three concepts we introduced in Chapter 2 in our discussion of theory-making: intersectionality, standpoint, and subjugated knowledge. Paula Gunn Allen (Reading 1), Chandra Talpade Mohanty (Reading 10), and Melanie Kaye/Kantrowitz

(Reading 14) address the importance of knowing one's genealogy, which they define broadly to include family, culture, and history. An ability to reflect on one's social location contributes to the generation of knowledge. Remember that Patricia Hill Collins argues that standpoint is not about individual experiences or identities but about "historically shared, group-based experiences" (1997, p. 375), the meso- and macro-aspects of identity. In the readings that follow, notice how the writers use their particular standpoints to locate their families and communities in the wider society. Note, too, that some writers' standpoints represent subjugated knowledges, deriving from their domination by other groups.

◆◆◆

Questions for Reflection

As you read and discuss the readings in this chapter, think about these questions:

1. Who are you? How do you figure out your identity? Has your identity changed? If so, when and how did it change?

2. Which parts of your identity do you emphasize? Which do you underplay? Why? How does a particular context shape your identity?

3. Who are your "people"? Where or what are your "home" and "community"?

4. How many generations have your family members been in the United States? Under what conditions did they become a part of the United States?

5. What do you know of your family's culture and history before it became a part of the United States?

6. What is your social location?

7. Which of the social dimensions of your identity provide power and privilege? Which provide less power and disadvantage?

8. How do people with privilege contribute to eliminating the systems of privilege that benefit them? Why might they want to do this?

◆◆◆

Finding Out More on the Web

1. Find out about women who are very different from you (in terms of culture, class, race/ethnicity, nationality, or religion) and how they think about their identities.

2. Research identity-based organizations. Why did they form? Who are their members? What are their purposes and goals? Did/do they have a vision of justice and equality?

3. Frederica Y. Daly mentioned the "trail of tears." What was it? Why is it famous?

4. Mary C. Waters mentions the "one drop rule." What is it? Why is it significant?

Taking Action

1. Take some action to affirm an aspect of your identity.

2. Talk to your parents or grandparents about your family history. How have they constructed their cultural and racial/ethnic identities?

TWELVE

Perspectives of Native American Women on Race and Gender (1994)

Frederica Y. Daly

Frederica Y. Daly was a psychologist and educator. She taught psychology at Howard University, the State University of New York, and the University of New Mexico. In retirement she writes poetry and is engaged in genealogical research into her African and Indian ancestries.

. . . Native Americans constitute well over five hundred recognized tribes, which speak more than two hundred (mostly living) languages. Their variety and vital cultures notwithstanding, the official U.S. policy unreflectively, and simply, transforms them from Indians to "Americans" (Wilkinson 1987). Some consideration will be given to their unifying traditions, not the least of which are their common history of surviving genocide and their strong, shared commitment to their heritage.

Any discussion of Indian people requires a brief review of the history of the violent decimation of their populations as well as the massive expropriation of their land and water holdings, accomplished with rare exception with the approval of American governments at every level. To ignore these experiences prevents us from understanding the basis for their radical and profound desire for self-determination, a condition they enjoyed fully before the European incursions began. . . .

Historical Overview

Indian history, since the European invasion in the early sixteenth century, is replete with incidents of exploitation, land swindle, enslavement, and murder by the European settlers. The narration includes well-documented, government-initiated, biological warfare, which included giving Indians clothing infected with smallpox, diphtheria, and other diseases to which Indians were vulnerable. Starvation strategies were employed, with forced removal from their lands and the consequent loss of access to basic natural resources, [for] example, the Cherokee and Choctaw experiences in the famous "trail of tears."

Wilkinson as well as Deloria and Lytle (1983) assert that Indian history is best understood when presented within a historical framework established by four major, somewhat overlapping, periods. The events dominate federal policy about Indians, subsequent Indian law, and many of the formational forces described in Indian sociology, anthropology, and culture.

Period 1: 1532–1828

This period is described by Europeans as one of "discovery" and is characterized by the conquest of Indians and the making of treaties. The early settlers did not have laws or policies governing their relationships with the indigenous tribes until the sixteenth-century theologian Francisco de Vitorio advised the king of Spain in 1532 that the tribes should be recognized "as legitimate entities capable of dealing with the European nations by treaty." As a result, writes Deloria, treaty making became a "feasible method of gaining a foothold on the continent without alarming the natives" (1970, 3). Deloria explains further that inherent in this decision was the fact that it encouraged respect for the tribes as societies of people and, thus, became the workable tool for defining intergroup relationships. By 1778 the U.S. government entered into its first treaty, with the Delaware Indians, at which point the tribe became, and remains, the basic unit in federal Indian law. . . .

Period 2: 1828–87

The second period, beginning . . . a few decades before the Civil War, witnessed massive removal of Indians from their ancestral lands and subsequent relocation, primarily because of their resistance to mainstream assimilation and the "missionary efforts" of the various Christian sects.

Early in his presidency Andrew Jackson proposed voluntary removal of the Indians. When none of the tribes responded, the Indian Removal Act of 1830 was passed. The act resulted in the removal of the tribes from the Ohio and Mississippi valleys to the plains of the West. "Nearly sixteen thousand Cherokees walked from Georgia to Eastern Oklahoma . . . the Choctaws surrendered more than ten million acres and moved west" (Deloria and Lytle 1983, 7). Soldiers, teachers, and missionaries were sent to reservations for policing and proselytizing purposes, activities by no means mutually exclusive and which represented the full benefit of the act as far as the tribes were concerned. Meanwhile, discovery of gold (especially "strikes" on or near Indian land) in the West, coupled with the extension of the railroad, once again raised the "Indian Problem." But at this point, with nowhere else to be moved, Indian tribes were even more in jeopardy, setting the basis for the third significant period.

Period 3: 1887–1928

During the final years of the nineteenth century, offering land allotments seemed to provide a workable technique for assimilating Indian families into the mainstream. The Dawes Act of 1887 proposed the formula for allotment. "A period of twenty-five years was established during which the Indian owner [of a specified, allotted piece of reservation property] was expected to learn proper methods of self-sufficiency, e.g., business or farming. At the end of that period, the land, free of restrictions against sale, was to be delivered to the allottee" (Deloria and Lytle 1983, 9). At the same time, the Indian received title to the land and citizenship in the state.

The Dawes Act and its aftermath constitute one of the most sordid narratives in American history involving tribal peoples. Through assimilation, swindling, and other forms of exploitation, more than ninety million acres of allotted land were transferred to non-Indian owners. Furthermore, much of the original land that remained for the Indians was in the "Great American Desert," unsuitable for farming and unattractive for any other kind of development. During this same period, off-reservation boarding schools began to be instituted, some in former army barracks, to assist in the overall program of assimilation, and the Dawes Act also made parcels of reservation land available to whites for settlement. The plan to assimilate the Indian and thereby eradicate the internal tribal nations caused immense misery and enormous economic loss. But as we know, it failed. Phyllis Old Dog Cross, a nurse of the North Dakota Mandan Tribe, mordantly puts it, "We are not vanishing" (1987, 29).

Period 4: 1928–Present

The fourth period is identified by Wilkinson especially as beginning just before the Depression in 1928. It is characterized by reestablishment of tribes as separate "sovereignties" involving moves toward formalized self-government and self-determination, and cessation, during World War II, of federal assistance to the tribes.

Prucha (1985) reminds us that, with the increased belief in the sciences in the 1920s and the accompanying beliefs that the sciences could solve human problems, attitudes toward Indians hardened. At this point the professional anthropologist began to be sent and be seen on the reservations to study and live with the people, alongside the missionaries. The changing attitudes continued into the 1930s with the

Roosevelt administration. It was during this period that John Collier became commissioner of Indian Affairs, and the reforms of the Indian Reorganization Act of 1934 invalidated the land allotment policies of the Dawes Act, effectively halting the transfer of Indian land to non-Indians. As Deloria indicates, the Reorganization Act provided immense benefits, including the establishment and reorganization of tribal councils and tribal courts.

After about a decade of progress, the budgetary demands of World War II resulted in deep reductions in domestic programs, including assistance to the tribes. John Collier resigned in 1945 under attack from critics and amid growing demands in Washington to cancel federal support for Indians. . . .

Deloria writes that Senator Watkins of Utah was "firmly convinced that if the Indians were freed from federal restrictions, they would soon prosper by learning in the school of life those lessons that a cynical federal bureaucracy had not been able to instill in them" (1970, 18). He was able to implement his convictions during the Eisenhower administration into the infamous Termination Act of 1953, in consequence of which several tribes in at least five states were eliminated. In effect, as far as the government was concerned, the tribes no longer existed and could make no claims on the government. Contrary to its original intent as a means of releasing the tribes from their status as federal wards under BIA [Bureau of Indian Affairs] control, the Termination Act did just the opposite, causing more loss of land, further erosion of tribal power, and literally terrorizing most of the tribes with intimidation, uncertainty, and, worst of all, fear of the loss of tribal standing.

Deloria quotes HR Doc. 363 in which, in 1970, President Nixon asserted, "Because termination is morally and legally unacceptable, because it produces bad practical results, and because the mere threat of termination tends to discourage greater self-sufficiency among Indian groups, I am asking the Congress to pass a new concurrent resolution which would expressly renounce, repudiate, and repeal the termination policy" (1970, 20). This firm repudiation by Nixon of the termination policy earned him the esteem of many Indian people, in much the same way that presidents Kennedy and Johnson are esteemed by many African Americans for establishing programs designed to improve their socioeconomic conditions.

From the Nixon administration through the Carter administration, tribal affairs were marked by strong federal support and a variety of programs aimed at encouraging tribal self-determination. The Indian Child Welfare Act of 1978, which gave preference to Indians in adoptions involving Indian children and authorized establishment of social services on and near reservations, was one of the major accomplishments of this period.

Prucha believes that the tribes' continued need for federal programs is an obstacle to their sovereignty . . . (1985, 97). Deloria insists that Indians are citizens and residents of the United States and of the individual states in which they live and, as such, "are entitled to the full benefits and privileges that are offered to all citizens" (246). . . .

Contemporary Native American Women and Sexism

I have just presented a very abbreviated statement of the general, post-European influx historical experiences of Indians in America, drawing from the research and insights of lawyers and social scientists. Without this introduction it would be difficult to understand Native American women and their contemporary experiences of sexism and racism.

Although many tribes were matrilineal, Indian women were seldom mentioned prominently in the personal journals or formal records of the early settlers or in the narratives of the westward movement. They were excluded from treaty-making sessions with federal government agents, and later ethnologists and anthropologists who reported on Indian women frequently presented distorted accounts of their lives, usually based on interviews with Christianized women, who said what they believed would be compatible with the European worldview. Helen Carr, in her essay in Brodzki and Schenck's *Life-Lines: Theorizing Women's Autobiographies*, offers some caveats about the authenticity of contemporary autobiographies of Indian women, when they are written in the Euro-American autobiographical tradition. She cautions that, in reading the autobiographies collected by early anthropologists, we need to be "aware that they have been structured, consciously or unconsciously, to serve particular 'white' purposes and to give credence to particular white views" (1988, 132).

Ruby Leavitt, writing in Gornick and Moran's *Women in Sexist Society,* states: "Certainly the status of women is higher in the matrilineal than the patrilineal societies. Where women own property and pass it on to their daughters or sisters, they are far more influential and secure. Where their economic role is important and well defined . . . they are not nearly so subject to male domination, and they have much more freedom of movement and action" (1972, 397).

We do not learn from social scientists observing Indian communities that women also were the traders in many tribes. With this history of matrilinealism and economic responsibilities, it is not surprising that some Indian women deny the existence of an oppressed, nonparticipatory tribal female role. Yet just as other North American women, they are concerned with child care needs, access to abortion, violence against women, and the effects of alcoholism on the family, all symptomatic of sexism experiences. They are also aware of these symptoms as prevalent throughout our society in the United States; they do not view them as specifically Indian related.

Bea Medicine, Lakota activist, anthropologist, and poet, as quoted in the preface of *American Indian Women—Telling Their Lives,* states "Indian women do not need liberation, they have always been liberated within their tribal structure" (1984, viii). Her view is the more common one I have encountered in my readings and in conversations with Native American women. In the middle 1970s, Native American women who were in New York City to protest a U.S. treaty violation, in a meeting to which they had invited non-Indian women, were adamant that they did not need the "luxury of feminism." Their focus, along with that of Indian men, concerned the more primary needs of survival.

The poet Carol Sanchez writes in *A Gathering of Spirit,* "We still have Women's societies, and there are at least thirty active woman-centered Mother rite cultures existing and practicing their everyday life in that manner on this continent" (1984, 164). These groups are characterized by their "keeping of the culture" activities.

Medicine and Sanchez concur about the deemphasis of the importance of gender roles in some tribes as reflected in the "Gia" concept. *Gia* is the word in the Pueblo Tewa language which signifies the earth. It is also used to connote nurturance and biological motherhood. The tribal core welfare role, which can be assumed by a male or a female, is defined by the tribe in this Gia context. To be a nurturing male is to be the object of much respect and esteem, although one does not act nurturing to gain group approval. Swentzell and Naranjo, educational consultant and sociologist, respectively, and coauthors, write, "The male in the gia role is a person who guides, advises, cares, and universally loves and encompasses all." The authors describe the role, saying, "The core gia was a strong, stable individual who served as the central focus for a large number of the pueblo's members . . . [for example], 'she' coordinated large group activities such as marriages, feast days, gathering and preparing of food products, even house building and plastering" (1986, 37). With increasing tribal governmental concerns the role of core group Gia has lessened, "so that children are no longer raised by the core group members" (39). Interestingly, the Gia concept is being used currently by social ecologists. For them it parallels the notion of Mother Earth and corresponds with the increasingly widespread understanding of the earth as a living organism.

Charles Lange, in *Cochiti—A New Mexico Pueblo, Past and Present,* says: "Among the Cochiti, the woman is boss; the high offices are held by men, but in the households and in the councils of the clans, woman is supreme. . . . She has been arbiter of destinies of the tribe for centuries" (1959, 367). The important role performed by the "Women's Society," Lange continues, includes "the ceremonial grinding of corn to make prayer meal" (283). Compatible with women's having spiritual role assignments is the fact that in some tribes the gods are women—for example, in the matrifocal Cherokee and Pueblo nations, Corn Mother is a sacred figure.

A Cheyenne saying reflects the tribe's profound regard for women: "A nation is not conquered until the hearts of its women are on the ground. Then it is done, no matter how brave its warriors, nor how strong its weapons" (Kutz 1988, 143–58). Historically, in some tribes women were warriors and participated in raiding parties. The Apache medicine woman and warrior Lozen lived such a role and was the last of the women warriors (Kutz 1988, 143–58). Paula Gunn Allen, in *The Sacred Hoop* (1986), notes that "traditional tribal lifestyles are more often gynocratic . . . women are not merely doomed victims of Western progress; they are also the carriers of the dream. . . . Since the first attempts at colonization . . .

the invaders have exerted every effort to remove Indian women from every position of authority, to obliterate all records pertaining to gynocratic social systems and to ensure that no Americans . . . would remember that gynocracy was the primary social order of Indian America" (2–3). Later she alludes to the regeneration of these earlier roles: "Women migrating to the cities are regaining self-sufficiency and positions of influence they had held in earlier centuries" (31). "Women's traditions," she says, "are about continuity and men's are about change, life maintenance/risk, death and transformation" (82).

When Indian women deny having experienced sexism they seem mainly to be referring to their continuing historical roles within their tribes, in which they are seen as *the keepers of the culture.* There exists a general consensus that the powerful role of tribal women, both traditionally and contemporarily, is not paralleled in the non-Indian society. Additionally, they allude to the women serving in various tribes as council members, and they point to such prominent, well-known leaders as Wilma Mankiller, [former] chief of the Oklahoma Cherokee Nation; Verna Williamson, former governor of Isleta Pueblo; and Virginia Klinekole, former president of the Mescalero Apache Tribal Council.

Contemporary Native American Women and Racism

The relentless system of racism, in both its overt and covert manifestations, impacts the lives of Indian women; most are very clear about their experiences of it, and they recognize it for what it is. Although many are reticent about discussing these experiences, a growing number of Native American women writers are giving voice to their encounters with racism.

Elizabeth Cook-Lynn, a poet and teacher with combined Crow, Creek, and Sioux heritage, writes about an editor who questioned her about why Native American poetry is so incredibly sad. Cook-Lynn describes her reaction . . . : "Now I recognize it as a tactless question asked out of astonishing ignorance. It reflects the general attitude that American Indians should have been happy to have been robbed of their land and murdered" (1987, 60–61).

In the same anthology Linda Hogan, from the Chickasaw Tribe in Oklahoma, writes with concern about the absence of information about Native American people throughout the curricula in our educational systems: "The closest I came to learning what I needed was a course in Labor Literature, and the lesson there was in knowing there were writers who lived similar lives to ours. . . . This is one of the ways that higher education perpetuates racism and classism. By ignoring our lives and work, by creating standards for only their own work" (1987, 243). Earlier she had written that "the significance of intermarriage between Indian and white or between Indian and black [has not] been explored . . . but the fact remains that great numbers of apparently white or black Americans carry notable degrees of Indian blood" (216). And in Brant's *A Gathering of Spirit* Carol Sanchez says, "To be Indian is to be considered 'colorful,' spiritual, connected to the earth, simplistic, and disappointing if not dressed in buckskin and feathers" (1984, 163).

These Indian women talk openly about symptoms of these social pathologies, [for] example, experiencing academic elitism or the demeaning attitudes of employees in federal and private, nonprofit Indian agencies. Or they tell of being accepted in U.S. society in proportion to the lightness of skin color. The few who deny having had experiences with racism mention the equality bestowed upon them through the tribal sovereignty of the Indian nations. In reality the tribes are not sovereign. They are controlled nearly completely by the U.S. Department of Interior, the federal agency that, ironically, also oversees animal life on public lands.

Rayna Green, a member of the Cherokee nation, in her book *That's What She Said* (1984), makes a strong, clear statement about racism and sexism: "The desperate lives of Indian women are worn by poverty, the abuse of men, the silence and blindness of whites. . . . The root of their problem appears attributable to the callousness and sexism of the Indian men and white society equally. They are tightly bound indeed in the double bind of race and gender. Wasted lives and battered women are part of the Indian turf" (10). It is not surprising to find some Indian men reflecting the attitudes of the white majority in relating to Indian women. This is the psychological phenomenon found in oppressed people, labeled as identification with the oppressor.

Mary Tallmountain, the Native Alaskan poet, writes in *I Tell You Now* (1987) that she refused to attend school in Oregon because her schoolmates mocked her "Indianness": "But, I know who I am. Marginal person, misfit, mutant; nevertheless, I am of this country, these people" (12). Linda Hogan describes the same experience, saying, "Those who are privileged would like for us to believe that we are in some way defective, that we are not smart enough, not good enough" (237). She recalls an experience with her former employer, an orthodontist, whom she says, "believed I was inferior because I worked for less than his wife's clothing budget or their liquor bill . . . and who, when I received money to attend night school and was proud, accused me of being a welfare leech and said I should be ashamed" (242). In her poem "Those Who Thunder," Linda translated the experience into verse:

> *Those who are timid are sagging in the soul,*
> *And those poor who will inherit the earth*
> *already work it*
> *So take shelter you*
> *because we are thundering and beating on floors*
> *And this is how walls have fallen in other cities.*
> (242)

In the United States we do not know one another, except from the stereotypes presented in the media. As a result, there is the tendency to view people of a differing group vicariously, through the eyes of media interpreters.

Louise Erdrich and Michael Dorris, both Indian and both university professors and eminent writers, reported in Bill Moyers's *World of Ideas* (1989): "We had one guy come to dinner, and we cleaned our house and made a nice dinner, and he looks and says, kind of depressed, 'Do you always eat on the table?'" (465). They used the example to demonstrate how people "imagine" (as distinguished from "know") Indians on the basis of movie portrayals, usually as figures partially dressed or dressed in the fashion of the nineteenth century and typically eating while seated on the ground. It is difficult to form accurate perceptions of the people and worldview of another group. Carol Sanchez seems to challenge us to do just that when she asks us not to dismiss Native Americans and then asks, "How many Indians do you know?" (163). . . .

Sanchez charges non-Indians with the wish to have Indians act like whites, so they will be more acceptable to whites, another example of accommodation, assimilation. She is describing the attitude cited by the young child care worker who said to me,

"They like our food, our drum music, our jewelry, why don't they like us!?" Activist Winona La Duke, of the Ojibwa Tribe and by profession an economist, asserts in her offering in *A Gathering of Spirit:* "As far as the crises of water contamination, radiation, and death to the natural world and her children are concerned, respectable racism is as alive today as it was a century ago . . . a certain level of racism and ignorance has gained acceptance . . . in fact respectability . . . we either pick your bananas or act as a mascot for your football team . . . in this way, enlightened people are racist. They are arrogant toward all of nature, arrogant toward the children of nature, and ultimately arrogant toward all of life" (65–66). . . .

Continuing Tensions

That since the sixteenth century the history of Native Americans is one of racist oppression has become an integral part of contemporary historical understanding. Indian women are speaking with increasing frequency and force about their experiences of the double jeopardy of racism and sexism. I wish now to consider three factors that continue to contribute to serious tensions within the tribes and between the tribes and the so-called dominant culture. . . .

Tensions Within the Indian Community

Indian people who wish to retain their identity and culture by continuing reservation life have constantly to struggle with choices regarding adaptation to the dominant culture. They realize that extremism in either direction will result in destruction of their ways of life. Those who resist any adaptation will be made to do so involuntarily, and those who accept "white men's ways" completely and without modification by that very fact forgo their heritage. For well over a century, governmental policy favored assimilation and the concomitant dissolution of Indian tribal existence. Real estate value and greed for precious natural resources were crucial motivating factors throughout the period. Indians simply were in the way of the invaders' efforts to amass money. . . .

At the Flathead reservation in Montana, attempts are under way to "revive the traditional Salish culture and preserve the rugged land from development" (Shaffer 1990, 54). Attempts to protect the

Indian land for future generations are buttressed by the traditional, nearly universal Indian belief that we do not own the land, that we are simply caretakers of it and will pass it on to future generations. Thus, how the land is used can become an issue of deep tension between strict traditionalists and those who want to assimilate contemporary economic development thinking into tribal life and institutions. Likewise, nearly universally held precepts include the prevailing rights of the tribe over individual rights and the discouragement of aggression and competitiveness, which are seen as threats to tribal harmony and survival. Phyllis Old Dog Cross, a Sioux and a nurse, speaking at a health conference in Denver in 1987, stated: "The need not to appear aggressive and competitive within the group is still seen among contemporary Indians . . . even quite acculturated Indians tend to be very unobtrusive. . . . [If not,] they receive strong criticism . . . also anything that would seem to precipitate anger, resentment, jealousy was . . . discouraged, for it is believed that tribal group harmony is threatened" (1987, 20).

Acknowledging their need for self-sufficiency as reductions in federal funding continue, the tribes are searching intensively for economic solutions. Some have introduced organized gambling onto the reservations and the leasing of land to business corporations; others are considering storage on reservation land of toxic wastes from federal facilities. Many of these measures are resisted, especially by traditionalists within the tribes, who see them as culturally destructive.

Erosion of Tribal Life: Cultural Marginality

Cultural marginality is increasingly experienced by Indian people because of the confusion resulting from ambiguities about what defines Indian identity, individually and tribally. The questions "Who is an Indian?" and "What is a tribe?" no longer permit neat unequivocal answers.

Different tribes have different attitudes toward people of mixed heritage. In some a person with white blood may be accepted, while a person with some African-American blood may or may not be identified as Indian. Indian women, if they marry non-Indians, may or may not be identified within their tribes as Indians. To be a member of a tribe, a person must meet that tribe's requirements. Many tribes require proof of a person's being one-sixteenth

or one-quarter or more of Indian descent to receive tribal affiliation. . . .

A group or an individual may qualify as an Indian for some federal purposes but not for others. A June 1977 statement by the U.S. Department of Labor on American Indian Women reads: "For their 1970 Census, the Bureau included in their questionnaire the category 'American Indian,' persons who indicated their race as Indian. . . . In the Eastern U.S., there are certain groups with mixed white, Negro, and Indian ancestry. In U.S. censuses prior to 1950, these groups had been variously classified by the enumerators, sometimes as Negro and sometimes as Indian, regardless of the respondent's preferred racial identity." LeAnne Howe, writing in Paula Gunn Allen's *Spider Woman's Granddaughters,* says, "Half-breeds live on the edge of both races . . . you're torn between wanting to kill everyone in the room or buying them all another round of drinks" (1989, 220).

Paula Gunn Allen, of the Laguna Pueblo tribe and a professor of literature, in her essay in *I Tell You Now,* writes: "Of course I always knew I was an Indian. I was told over and over, 'Never forget that you're an Indian.' My mother said it. Nor did she say, 'Remember you're part Indian'" (1987, 144).

Conflicts Between Tribal and Other Governmental Laws

The Bureau of Indian Affairs, which has specific oversight responsibilities for the reservations, has played, at best, an ambivalent role, according to its very numerous critics. There have been many rumors of mishandled funds, especially of failure of funds to reach the reservations. It is the source of endless satire by Indian humorists, who, at their kindest, refer to it as the "Boss the Indian Around" department. By federal mandate the BIA is charged with coordinating the federal programs for the reservations. Originally, it was a section of the War Department, but for the last century and a half it has operated as part of the Department of the Interior.

Continuing skirmishes occur over violations of reservation land and water rights. Consequently, the tribes continue to appeal to the Supreme Court and to the United Nations for assistance in redressing federal treaty violations. When these cases are made public, they become fodder for those who continue to push for the assimilation of Indians into the dominant society as well as for the ever-present cadre of racial bigots.

Federal law and policy have too often been paternalistic, detrimental, and contrary to the best interests of the Indian people. Further, the federal dollar dominance of the tribes has a controlling interest on Indian life. Levitan and Johnston conclude that "for Indians, far more than for any other group, socioeconomic status is a federal responsibility, and the success or failure of federal programs determines the quality of Indian lives" (1975, 10).

To receive eligibility for government services requires that the person live on or near a reservation, trust, or restricted land or be a member of a tribe recognized by the federal government. To be an Indian in America can mean living under tribal laws and traditions, under state law, and under federal laws. The situation can become extremely complex and irksome, for example, when taxes are considered. The maze and snarl of legalese over such questions as whether the Navajo tribe can tax reservation mineral developments without losing its "trust status" and accompanying federal benefits would defeat, and does, the most ardent experts of jurisprudence. And the whole question of income tax for the Indian person living on a reservation and working in a nearby community requires expertise that borders on the ridiculous.

University of New Mexico law professor Fred Ragsdale, describing the relationship of reservation Indians with the federal government, compares it to playing blackjack: "Indians play with their own money. They can't get up and walk away. And the house gets to change the rules any time it wants" (1985, 1).

The outlawing of certain Indian religious practices occurred without challenge until the 1920s, when the laws and policies prohibiting dancing and ceremonies were viewed as cultural attacks. With the passage of the Indian Civil Rights Act in 1964, Indians have been able to present court challenges to discrimination based on their religious practices. Members of the North American Church use peyote, a psychoactive drug, in their ceremonies. Many consider their religion threatened by the . . . Supreme Court ruling that removes First Amendment protection of traditional worship practiced by Native Americans.

The negative impact of the 1966 Bennett freeze, a federally attempted solution to the bitter Navajo-Hopi land dispute, continues to cause pain to the Hopi, who use this 1.5-million-acre land mass for grazing, and to the Navajo, many of whom have resided on this land for generations. Sue Ann Presley, a *Washington Post* reporter, describes the area as being among the poorest in the nation and notes that the people living there are prohibited by law from participating in federal antipoverty programs. She reports that 90 percent of the homes have neither electricity nor indoor plumbing, and home repairs are not permitted. She quotes Navajo chair, Peterson Zah: "There are many Navajos who want to live in what we call the traditional way. But that does not mean they want to live with inadequate sewers, unpaved roads, no running water or electricity and under the watchful eye of the Hopi Tribe" (1993, B1). The forced removal of some of the Navajos from this area to border town housing caused a tremendous increase in the number of people who sought mental health treatment for depression and other disorders, according to the clinical observations of Tuba City, Arizona, psychologist Martin Topper. . . .

Conclusions

. . . Studies showing the impact of the privileged culture and dominant race on the development of Native Americans deserve continued exposure and extended development. We need medical research that investigates the health conditions and illnesses of minorities, including Native American women, whose general health status has to be among the worst in America. . . .

The development of new theories must include appropriate, representative definitions of the total population, free of gender bias and not derived disproportionately from the observation of middle-class white men and women. Curriculum offerings with accurate and comprehensive historical data about gender-specific Native American experiences are needed. . . .

As a country, we have failed to acknowledge our despicable treatment of the Indians. . . . It is hoped that the Indian quest for self-determination and proper respect will be realized, and with it will come our healing as a nation as well. There exists a tremendous need to help the U.S. public begin to understand the real significance of Indian history. . . .

REFERENCES

Allen, P. G. 1986. *The Sacred Hoop.* Boston: Beacon Press.

———. 1987. "The Autobiography of a Confluence." In *I Tell You Now,* ed. B. Swann and A. Krupat. Lincoln: University of Nebraska Press, 141–54.

———. ed. 1989. *Spider Woman's Granddaughters.* Boston: Beacon Press.

Bataille, G., and K. Sands. 1984. *American Indian Women—Telling Their Lives.* Lincoln: University of Nebraska Press.

Bergman, R. 1971. "Navajo Peyote Use: Its Apparent Safety." *American Journal of Psychiatry* 128:6.

Canby, W. C. 1981. *American Indian Law.* St. Paul, Minn.: West Publishing.

Carr, H. 1988. "In Other Words: Native American Women's Autobiography." In *Life-Lines: Theorizing Women's Autobiographies,* ed. Bella Brodzki and Celeste Schenck. Ithaca, N.Y.: Cornell University Press, 131–53.

Cook-Lynn, E. 1987. "You May Consider Speaking about Your Art." In *I Tell You Now,* ed. B. Swann and A. Krupat. Lincoln: University of Nebraska Press, 55–63.

Deloria, V. 1970. *We Talk, You Listen.* New York: Dell Publishing.

Deloria, V., and C. Lytle. 1983. *American Indians, American Justice.* Austin: University of Texas Press.

Erdrich, L., and M. Dorris. 1989. "Interview." In *Bill Moyers: A World of Ideas,* ed. B. S. Flowers. New York: Doubleday, 460–69.

Gornick, V., and B. Moran, eds. 1972. *Women in Sexist Society.* New York: Signet.

Green, R. 1984. *That's What She Said.* Bloomington: University of Indiana Press.

Hogan, L. 1987. "The Two Lives." In *I Tell You Now,* ed. B. Swann and A. Krupat. Lincoln: University of Nebraska Press, 231–49.

Howe, L. 1989. "An American in New York." In *Spider Woman's Granddaughters,* ed. P. G. Allen. Boston: Beacon Press, 212–20.

Kutz, J. 1988. *Mysteries and Miracles of New Mexico.* Corrales, N.M.: Rhombus Publishing.

La Duke, W. 1988. "They Always Come Back." In *A Gathering of Spirit,* ed. B. Brant. Ithaca, N.Y.: Firebrand Books, 62–67.

Lange, C. 1959. *Cochiti—A New Mexico Pueblo, Past and Present.* Austin: University of Texas Press.

Levitan, S., and W. Johnston. 1975. *Indian Giving.* Baltimore: Johns Hopkins University Press.

Old Dog Cross, P. 1987. "What Would You Want a Caregiver to Know about You?" *The Value of Many Voices Conference Proceedings,* 29–32.

Presley, S. 18 July 1993. "Restrictions Force Deprivations on Navajos." *The Washington Post,* G1–G2.

Prucha, F. 1985. *The Indians in American Society.* Berkeley: University of California Press.

Ragsdale, F. 1985. Quoted in Sherry Robinson's "Indian Laws Complicate Development." *Albuquerque Journal,* 1.

Sanchez, Carol. 1984. "Sex, Class and Race Intersections: Visions of Women of Color." In *A Gathering of Spirit,* ed. B. Brant. Ithaca, N.Y.: Firebrand Books.

Shaffer, P. January/February 1990. "A Tree Grows in Montana." *Utne Reader,* 54–63.

Swentzell, R., and T. Naranjo. 1986. "Nurturing the Gia." *El Palacio* (Summer–Fall): 35–39.

Tallmountain, M. 1987. "You Can Go Home Again: A Sequence." In *I Tell You Now,* ed. B. Swann and A. Krupat. Lincoln: University of Nebraska Press, 1–13.

Wilkinson, C. 1987. *American Indians, Time, and the Law.* New Haven, Conn.: Yale University Press.

T H I R T E E N

◆◆◆

A Question of Class (1993)

Dorothy Allison

Dorothy Allison authored the critically acclaimed novel, *Bastard Out of Carolina*, a finalist for the 1992 National Book Award, which became an award-winning movie. Other titles include *Trash; Skin: Talking About Sex, Class and Literature;* and *Cavedweller.* She has won many awards, including the 2007 Robert Penn Warren Award for Fiction. She describes herself as a feminist, a working-class storyteller, a Southern expatriate, a sometime poet, and a happily born-again Californian.

. . . My people were not remarkable. We were ordinary, but even so we were mythical. We were the *they* everyone talks about, the ungrateful poor. I grew up trying to run away from the fate that destroyed so many of the people I loved, and having learned the habit of hiding, I found that I also had learned to hide from myself. I did not know who I was, only that I did not want to be *they*, the ones who are destroyed or dismissed to make the real people, the important people, feel safer. By the time I understood that I was queer, that habit of hiding was deeply set in me, so deeply that it was not a choice but an instinct. Hide, hide to survive, I thought, knowing that if I told the truth about my life, my family, my sexual desire, my real history, then I would move over into that unknown territory, the land of *they,* would never have the chance to name my own life, to understand it or claim it.

Why are you so afraid? my lovers and friends have asked me the many times when I have suddenly seemed to become a stranger, someone who would not speak to them, would not do the things they believed I should do, simple things like applying for a job, or a grant, or some award they were sure I could acquire easily. Entitlement, I have told them, is a matter of feeling like *we,* not *they.* But it has been hard for me to explain, to make them understand. You think you have a right to things, a place in the world, I try to say. You have a sense of entitlement I don't have, a sense of your own importance. I have explained what I know over and over again, in every possible way I can, but I have never been able to make clear the degree of my fear, the extent to which I feel myself denied, not only that I am queer in a world that hates queers but that I was born poor into a world that despises the poor. The need to explain is part of why I write fiction. I know that some things must be felt to be understood, that despair can never be adequately analyzed; it must be lived. . . .

I have known I was a lesbian since I was a teenager, and I have spent a good twenty years making peace with the effects of incest and physical abuse. But what may be the central fact of my life is that I was born in 1949 in Greenville, South Carolina, the bastard daughter of a poor white woman from a desperately poor family, a girl who had left the seventh grade the year before, who worked as a waitress and was just a month past fifteen when she had me. That fact, the inescapable impact of being born in a condition of poverty that this society finds shameful, contemptible, and somehow deserved, has dominated me to such an extent that I have spent my life trying to overcome or deny it. I have learned with great difficulty that the vast majority of people pretend that poverty is a voluntary condition, that the poor are different, less than fully human, or at least less sensitive to hopelessness, despair, and suffering.

The first time I read [Jewish writer] Melanie Kaye/Kantrowitz's poems, I experienced a frisson of recognition. It was not that my people had been "burned off the map" or murdered as hers had. No, we had been erased, encouraged to destroy ourselves, made invisible because we did not fit the myths of the middle class. Even now, past forty and stubbornly proud of my family, I feel the draw of that mythology, that romanticized, edited version of the poor. I find myself looking back and wondering what was real, what true. Within my family, so much was lied about, joked about, denied or told with deliberate indirection, an undercurrent of humiliation, or a brief pursed grimace that belies everything that has been said—everything, the very nature of truth and lies, reality and myth. What was real? The poverty depicted in books and movies was romantic, a kind of backdrop for the story of how it was escaped. The reality of self-hatred and violence was either absent or caricatured. The poverty I knew was dreary, deadening, shameful. My family was ashamed of being poor, of feeling hopeless. What was there to work for, to save money for, to fight for or struggle against? We had generations before us to teach us that nothing ever changed, and that those who did try to escape failed.

My mama had eleven brothers and sisters, of whom I can name only six. No one is left alive to tell me the names of the others. It was my grandmother who told me about my real daddy, a shiftless pretty man who was supposed to have married, had six children, and sold cut-rate life insurance to colored people out in the country. My mama married when I was a year old, but her husband died just after my little sister was born a year later. When I was five, Mama married the man she lived with until she died. Within the first year of their marriage Mama miscarried, and while we waited out in the hospital parking lot, my stepfather molested me for the first time, something he continued to do until I was past thirteen. When I was eight or so, Mama took us away to a motel after my stepfather beat me so badly it caused a family scandal, but we returned after two weeks. Mama told me that she really had no choice; she could not support us alone. When I was eleven I told one of my cousins that my stepfather was molesting me. Mama packed up my sisters and me and took us away for a few days, but again, my stepfather swore he would stop, and again we went back after a few weeks. I stopped talking for a while, and I have only vague memories of the next two years.

My stepfather worked as a route salesman, my mama as a waitress, laundry worker, cook, or fruit packer. I could never understand how, since they both worked so hard and such long hours, we never had enough money, but it was a fact that was true also of my mama's brothers and sisters, who worked in the mills or the furnace industry. In fact, my parents did better than anyone else in the family, but eventually my stepfather was fired and we hit bottom—nightmarish months of marshals at the door, repossessed furniture, and rubber checks. My parents worked out a scheme so that it appeared my stepfather had abandoned us, but instead he went down to Florida, got a new job, and rented us a house. In the dead of night, he returned with a U-Haul trailer, packed us up, and moved us south.

The night we left South Carolina for Florida, my mama leaned over the back seat of her old Pontiac and promised us girls, "It'll be better there." I don't know if we believed her, but I remember crossing Georgia in the early morning, watching the red clay hills and swaying gray blankets of moss recede through the back window. I kept looking back at the trailer behind us, ridiculously small to contain everything we owned. Mama had, after all, packed nothing that wasn't fully paid off, which meant she had only two things of worth, her washing and sewing machines, both of them tied securely to the trailer walls. Through the whole trip, I fantasized an accident that would burst that trailer, scattering old clothes and cracked dishes on the tarmac.

I was only thirteen. I wanted us to start over completely, to begin again as new people with nothing of the past left over. I wanted to run away completely from who we had been seen to be, who we had been. That desire is one I have seen in other members of my family, to run away. It is the first thing I think of when trouble comes, the geographic solution. Change your name, leave town, disappear, and make yourself over. What hides behind that solution is the conviction that the life you have lived, the person you are, are valueless, better off abandoned, that running away is easier than trying to change anything, that change itself is not possible, that death is easier than this life. Sometimes I think it is that conviction—more seductive than alcoholism or violence and more subtle than sexual hatred or gender injustice—that has dominated my life, and made real change so painful and difficult.

Moving to central Florida did not fix our lives. It did not stop my stepfather's violence, heal my shame, or make my mother happy. Once there our lives became dominated by my mother's illness and medical bills. She had a hysterectomy when I was about eight and endured a series of hospitalizations for ulcers and a chronic back problem. Through most of my adolescence she superstitiously refused to allow anyone to mention the word cancer. (Years later when she called me to tell me that she was recovering from an emergency mastectomy, there was bitter fatalism in her voice. The second mastectomy followed five years after the first, and five years after that there was a brief bout with cancer of the lymph system which went into remission after prolonged chemotherapy. She died at the age of fifty-six with liver, lung, and brain cancer.) When she was not sick, Mama, and my stepfather, went on working, struggling to pay off what seemed an insurmountable load of debts.

By the time I was fourteen, my sisters and I had found ways to discourage most of our stepfather's sexual advances. We were not close but we united against our stepfather. Our efforts were helped along when he was referred to a psychotherapist after losing his temper at work, and was prescribed psychotropic drugs that made him sullen but less violent. We were growing up quickly, my sisters moving toward dropping out of school, while I got good grades and took every scholarship exam I could find. I was the first person in my family to graduate from high school, and the fact that I went on to college was nothing short of astonishing.

Everyone imagines her life is normal, and I did not know my life was not everyone's. It was not until I was an adolescent in central Florida that I began to realize just how different we were. The people we met there had not been shaped by the rigid class structure that dominated the South Carolina Piedmont. The first time I looked around my junior high classroom and realized that I did not know who those people were—not only as individuals but as categories, who their people were and how they saw themselves—I realized also that they did not know me. In Greenville, everyone knew my family, knew we were trash, and that meant we were supposed to be poor, supposed to have grim low-paid jobs, have babies in our teens, and never finish school. But central Florida in the 1960s was full of runaways and immigrants, and our mostly white working-class suburban school sorted us out, not by income and family background, but by intelligence and aptitude tests. Suddenly I was boosted into the college-bound track, and while there was plenty of contempt for my inept social skills, pitiful wardrobe, and slow drawling accent, there was also something I had never experienced before, a protective anonymity, and a kind of grudging respect and curiosity about who I might become. Because they did not see poverty and hopelessness as a foregone conclusion for my life, I could begin to imagine other futures for myself.

Moving into that new world and meeting those new people meant that I began to see my family from a new vantage point. I also experienced a new level of fear, a fear of losing what before had never been imaginable. My family's lives were not on television, not in books, not even comic books. There was a myth of the poor in this country, but it did not include us, no matter how hard I tried to squeeze us in. There was an idea of the good poor— hard-working, ragged but clean, and intrinsically noble. I understood that we were the bad poor, the ungrateful: men who drank and couldn't keep a job; women, invariably pregnant before marriage, who quickly became worn, fat, and old from working too many hours and bearing too many children; and children with runny noses, watery eyes, and bad attitudes. My cousins quit school, stole cars, used drugs, and took dead-end jobs pumping gas or waiting tables. We were not noble, not grateful, not even hopeful. We knew ourselves despised.

But in that new country, we were unknown. The myth settled over us and glamorized us. I saw it in the eyes of my teachers, the Lions' Club representative who paid for my new glasses, and the lady from the Junior League who told me about the scholarship I had won. Better, far better, to be one of the mythical poor than to be part of the *they* I had known before. *Don't let me lose this chance*, I prayed, and lived in fear that I might suddenly be seen again as what I knew I really was.

As an adolescent, I thought that the way my family escaped South Carolina was like a bad movie. We fled like runaway serfs and the sheriff who would have arrested my stepfather seemed like a border guard. Even now, I am certain that if we had remained in South Carolina, I would have been trapped by my family's heritage of poverty,

jail, and illegitimate children—that even being smart, stubborn, and a lesbian would have made no difference. My grandmother died when I was twenty and after Mama went home for the funeral, I had a series of dreams in which we still lived up in Greenville, just down the road from where Granny had died. In the dreams I had two children and only one eye, lived in a trailer, and worked at the textile mill. Most of my time was taken up with deciding when I would finally kill my children and myself. The dreams were so vivid, I became convinced they were about the life I was meant to have had, and I began to work even harder to put as much distance as I could between my family and me. I copied the dress, mannerisms, attitudes, and ambitions of the girls I met in college, changing or hiding my own tastes, interests, and desires. I kept my lesbianism a secret, forming a relationship with an effeminate male friend that served to shelter and disguise us both. I explained to friends that I went home so rarely because my stepfather and I fought too much for me to be comfortable in his house. But that was only part of the reason I avoided home, the easiest reason. The truth was that I feared the person I might become in my mama's house.

It is hard to explain how deliberately and thoroughly I ran away from my own life. I did not forget where I came from, but I gritted my teeth and hid it. When I could not get enough scholarship money to pay for graduate school, I spent a year of blind rage working as a salad girl, substitute teacher, and maid. I finally managed to get a job by agreeing to take any city assignment where the Social Security Administration needed a clerk. Once I had a job and my own place far away from anyone in my family, I became sexually and politically active, joining the Women's Center support staff and falling in love with a series of middle-class women who thought my accent and stories thoroughly charming. The stories I told about my family, about South Carolina, about being poor itself, were all lies, carefully edited to seem droll or funny. I knew damn well that no one would want to hear the truth about poverty, the hopelessness and fear, the feeling that nothing you do will make any difference, and the raging resentment that burns beneath the jokes. Even when my lovers and I formed an alternative lesbian family, sharing all our resources, I kept the truth about my background and who I knew myself to be a carefully obscured mystery. I worked as hard as I could to make myself a new person, an emotionally healthy radical lesbian activist, and I believed completely that by remaking myself I was helping to remake the world.

For a decade, I did not go home for more than a few days at a time.

It is sometimes hard to make clear how much I have loved my family, that every impulse to hold them in contempt has sparked in me a countersurge of stubborn pride. . . . I have had to fight broad generalizations from every possible theoretical viewpoint. Traditional feminist theory has had a limited understanding of class differences or of how sexuality and self are shaped by both desire and denial. The ideology implies that we are all sisters who should turn our anger and suspicion only on the world outside the lesbian community. It is so simple to say the patriarchy did it, that poverty and social contempt are products of the world of the fathers. How often I felt a need to collapse my sexual history into what I was willing to share of my class background, to pretend that both my life as a lesbian and my life as a working-class escapee were constructed by the patriarchy. The difficulty is that I can't ascribe everything that has been problematic or difficult about my life simply and easily to the patriarchy, or even to the invisible and much-denied class structure of our society. . . .

One of the things I am trying to understand is how we internalize the myths of our society even as we hate and resist them. Perhaps this will be more understandable if I discuss specifically how some of these myths have shaped my life and how I have been able to talk about and change my own understanding of my family. I have felt a powerful temptation to write about my family as a kind of moral tale with us as the heroes and the middle and upper classes as the villains. It would be within the romantic myth, for example, to pretend that we were the kind of noble Southern whites portrayed in the movies, mill workers for generations until driven out of the mills by alcoholism and a family propensity to rebellion and union talk. But that would be a lie. The truth is that no one in my family ever joined a union. Taken as far as it can go, the myth of the poor would make my family over into union organizers or people broken by the failure of the unions. The reality of my family is far more complicated and lacks the cardboard nobility of the myth.

As far as my family was concerned, union organizers, like preachers, were of a different class, suspect and hated as much as they might be admired for what they were supposed to be trying to achieve. Serious belief in anything—any political ideology, any religious system, or any theory of life's meaning and purpose—was seen as unrealistic. It was an attitude that bothered me a lot when I started reading the socially conscious novels I found in the paperback racks when I was eleven or so. I particularly loved Sinclair Lewis's novels and wanted to imagine my own family as part of the working man's struggle. But it didn't seem to be that simple.

"We were not joiners," my Aunt Dot told me with a grin when I asked her about the union. My cousin Butch laughed at that, told me the union charged dues and said, "Hell, we can't even be persuaded to toss money in the collection plate. Ain't gonna give it to no fat union man." It shamed me that the only thing my family wholeheartedly believed in was luck, and the waywardness of fate. They held the dogged conviction that the admirable and wise thing to do was to try and keep a sense of humor, not to whine or cower, and to trust that luck might someday turn as good as it had been bad—and with just as much reason. Becoming a political activist with an almost religious fervor was the thing I did that most outraged my family and the Southern working-class community they were part of.

Similarly, it was not my sexuality, my lesbianism, that was seen by my family as most rebellious; for most of my life, no one but my mama took my sexual preference very seriously. It was the way I thought about work, ambition, and self-respect that seemed incomprehensible to my aunts and cousins. They were waitresses, laundry workers, and counter girls. I was the one who went to work as a maid, something I never told any of them. They would have been angry if they had known, though the fact that some work was contemptible was itself a difficult notion. They believed that work was just work, necessary, that you did what you had to do to survive. They did not believe so much in taking pride in doing your job as they did in stubbornly enduring hard work and hard times when you really didn't have much choice about what work you did. But at the same time they did believe that there were some forms of work, including maid's work, that were only for black people, not white, and while I did not share that belief, I knew how intrinsic it was to how my family saw the world. Sometimes I felt as if I straddled cultures and belonged on neither side. I would grind my teeth at what I knew was my family's unquestioning racism but still take pride in their pragmatic endurance, but more and more as I grew older what I truly felt was a deep estrangement from the way they saw the world, and gradually a sense of shame that would have been completely incomprehensible to them.

"Long as there's lunch counters, you can always find work," I was told by both my mother and my aunts, and they'd add, "I can always get me a little extra with a smile." It was obvious that there was supposed to be nothing shameful about it, that needy smile across a lunch counter, that rueful grin when you didn't have rent, or the half-provocative, half-begging way my mama could cajole the man at the store to give her a little credit. But I hated it, hated the need for it and the shame that would follow every time I did it myself. It was begging as far as I was concerned, a quasi-prostitution that I despised even while I continued to use it (after all, I needed the money). But my mother, aunts, and cousins had not been ashamed, and my shame and resentment pushed me even further away from them.

"Just use that smile," my girl cousins used to joke, and I hated what I knew they meant. After college, when I began to support myself and study feminist theory, I did not become more understanding of the women of my family but more contemptuous. I told myself that prostitution is a skilled profession and my cousins were never more than amateurs. There was a certain truth in this, though like all cruel judgments made from the outside, it ignored the conditions that made it true. The women in my family, my mother included, had sugar daddies, not johns, men who slipped them money because they needed it so badly. From their point of view they were nice to those men because the men were nice to them, and it was never so direct or crass an arrangement that they would set a price on their favors. They would never have described what they did as prostitution, and nothing made them angrier than the suggestion that the men who helped them out did it just for their favors. They worked for a living, they swore, but this was different.

I always wondered if my mother had hated her sugar daddy, or if not *him* then her need for what he offered her, but it did not seem to me in memory that she had. Her sugar daddy had been an old man, half-crippled, hesitant and needy, and he treated my mama with enormous consideration and, yes, respect. The relationship between them was painful because it was based on the fact that she and my stepfather could not make enough money to support the family. Mama could not refuse her sugar daddy's money, but at the same time he made no assumptions about that money buying anything she was not already offering. The truth was, I think, that she genuinely liked him, and only partly because he treated her so well.

Even now, I am not sure whether or not there was a sexual exchange between them. Mama was a pretty woman and she was kind to him, a kindness he obviously did not get from anyone else in his life, and he took extreme care not to cause her any problems with my stepfather. As a teenager with an adolescent's contempt for moral failings and sexual complexity of any kind, I had been convinced that Mama's relationship with that old man was contemptible and also that I would never do such a thing. The first time a lover of mine gave me money, and I took it, everything in my head shifted. The amount she gave me was not much to her, but it was a lot to me and I needed it. I could not refuse it, but I hated myself for taking it and I hated her for giving it to me. Worse, she had much less grace about my need than my mama's sugar daddy had displayed toward her. All that bitter contempt I had felt for my needy cousins and aunts raged through me and burned out the love I had felt. I ended the relationship quickly, unable to forgive myself for *selling* what I believed should only be offered freely—not sex but love itself.

When the women in my family talked about how hard they worked, the men would spit to the side and shake their heads. Men took real jobs—hard, dangerous, physically daunting work. They went to jail, not just the hard-eyed, careless boys who scared me with their brutal hands and cold eyes, but their gentler, softer brothers. It was another family thing, what people expected of my mama's family, my people. "His daddy's that one was sent off to jail in Georgia, and his uncle's another. Like as not, he's just the same," you'd hear people say of boys so young they still had their milk teeth. We were always driving down to the county farm to see somebody, some uncle, cousin, or nameless male relation. Shaven-headed, sullen, and stunned, they wept on Mama's shoulder or begged my aunts to help. "I didn't do nothing, Mama," they'd say and it might have been true, but if even we didn't believe them, who would? No one told the truth, not even about how their lives were destroyed. . . .

By 1975, I was earning a meager living as a photographer's assistant in Tallahassee, Florida, but the real work of my life was my lesbian feminist activism, the work I did with the local Women's Center and the committee to found a Feminist Studies Department at Florida State University. Part of my role as I saw it was to be a kind of evangelical lesbian feminist, and to help develop a political analysis of this woman-hating society. I did not talk about class, more than by giving lip service to how we all needed to think about it, the same way I thought we all needed to think about racism. I was a serious and determined person, living in a lesbian collective, studying each new book that purported to address feminist issues and completely driven by what I saw as a need to revolutionize the world. . . .

The idea of writing fiction or essays seemed frivolous when there was so much work to be done, but everything changed when I found myself confronting emotions and ideas that could not be explained away or postponed for a feminist holiday. The way it happened was simple and completely unexpected. One week I was asked to speak to two completely divergent groups: an Episcopalian Sunday School class and a juvenile detention center. The Episcopalians were all white, well-dressed, highly articulate, nominally polite, and obsessed with getting me to tell them (without their having to ask directly) just what it was that two women did together in bed. The delinquents were all women, eighty percent black and Hispanic, dressed in green uniform dresses or blue jeans and work shirts, profane, rude, fearless, witty, and just as determined to get me to talk about what it was that two women did together in bed.

I tried to have fun with the Episcopalians, teasing them about their fears and insecurities, and being as bluntly honest as I could about my sexual practices. The Sunday School teacher, a man who had assured me of his liberal inclinations, kept blushing and stammering as the questions about my growing up and coming out became more detailed.

When the meeting was over, I stepped out into the sunshine angry at the contemptuous attitude implied by all their questions, and though I did not know why, also so deeply depressed that I couldn't even cry. The delinquents were different. Shameless, they had me blushing within the first few minutes, yelling out questions that were partly curious and partly a way of boasting about what they already knew.

"You butch or femme?" "You ever fuck boys?" "You ever want to?" "You want to have children?" "What's your girlfriend like?" I finally broke up when one very tall confident girl leaned way over and called out, "Hey girlfriend! I'm getting out of here next weekend. What you doing that night?" I laughed so hard I almost choked. I laughed until we were all howling and giggling together. Even getting frisked as I left didn't ruin my mood. I was still grinning when I climbed into the waterbed with my lover that night, grinning right up to the moment when she wrapped her arms around me and I burst into tears.

It is hard to describe the way I felt that night, the shock of recognition and the painful way my thoughts turned. That night I understood suddenly everything that happened to my cousins and me, understood it from a wholly new and agonizing perspective, one that made clear how brutal I had been to both my family and myself. I understood all over again how we had been robbed and dismissed, and why I had worked so hard not to think about it. I had learned as a child that what could not be changed had to go unspoken, and worse, that those who cannot change their own lives have every reason to be ashamed of that fact and to hide it. I had accepted that shame and believed in it, but why? What had I or my cousins really done to deserve the contempt directed at us? Why had I always believed us contemptible by nature? I wanted to talk to someone about all the things I was thinking that night, but I could not. Among the women I knew there was no one who would have understood what I was thinking, no other working-class women in the women's collective where I was living. I began to suspect that we shared no common language to speak those bitter truths.

In the days after that I found myself . . . thrown back into my childhood, into all the fears and convictions I had tried to escape. Once again I felt myself at the mercy of the important people who knew how to dress and talk, and would always be given the benefit of the doubt while I and my family would not.

I felt as if I was at the mercy of an outrage so old I could not have traced all the ways it shaped my life. I understood again that some are given no quarter, no chance, that all their courage, humor, and love for each other is just a joke to the ones who make the rules, and I hated the rule makers. Finally I also realized that part of my grief came from the fact that I no longer knew who I was or where I belonged. I had run away from my family, refused to go home to visit, and tried in every way to make myself a new person. How could I be working-class with a college degree? As a lesbian activist? I thought about the guards at the detention center, and the way they had looked at me. They had not stared at me with the same picture-window emptiness they turned on the girls who came to hear me, girls who were closer to the life I had been meant to live than I could bear to examine. The contempt in their eyes was contempt for me as a lesbian, different and the same, but still contempt. . . .

In the late 1970s, the compartmentalized life I had created burst open. It began when I started to write and work out what I really thought about my family. . . . I went home again. I went home to my mother and my sisters, to visit, talk, argue, and begin to understand.

Once home I saw that, as far as my family was concerned, lesbians were lesbians whether they wore suitcoats or leather jackets. Moreover, in all that time when I had not made peace with myself, my family had managed to make a kind of peace with me. My girlfriends were treated like slightly odd versions of my sisters' husbands, while I was simply the daughter who had always been difficult but was still a part of their lives. The result was that I started trying to confront what had made me unable to really talk to my sisters for so many years. I discovered that they no longer knew who I was either, and it took time and lots of listening to each other to rediscover my sense of family, and my love for them.

It is only as the child of my class and my unique family background that I have been able to put together what is for me a meaningful politics, gained a sense of why I believe in activism, why self-revelation is so important for lesbians, reexamining the way we are seen and the way we see ourselves. There is no all-purpose feminist analysis that explains away all the complicated ways our sexuality and core identity are shaped, the way we see ourselves as parts of both our birth families and the extended family of friends and lovers we invariably create within the lesbian community. For me the bottom line has simply become the need to resist that omnipresent fear, that urge to hide and disappear, to disguise my life, my desires, and the truth about how little any of us understand—even as we try to make the world a more just and human place for us all. Most of all I have tried to understand the politics of *they*, why human beings fear and stigmatize the different while secretly dreading that they might be one of the different themselves. Class, race, sexuality, gender, all the categories by which we categorize and dismiss each other need to be examined from the inside.

The horror of class stratification, racism, and prejudice is that some people begin to believe that the security of their families and community depends on the oppression of others, that for some to have good lives others must have lives that are mean and horrible. It is a belief that dominates this culture; it is what made the poor whites of the South so determinedly racist and the middle class so contemptuous of the poor. It is a myth that allows some to imagine that they build their lives on the ruin of others, a secret core of shame for the middle class, a goad and a spur to the marginal working class, and cause enough for the homeless and poor to feel no constraints on hatred or violence. The power of the myth is made even more apparent when we examine how within the lesbian and feminist communities, where so much attention has been paid to the politics of marginalization, there is still so much exclusion and fear, so many of us who do not feel safe even within our chosen communities.

I grew up poor, hated, the victim of physical, emotional, and sexual violence, and I know that suffering does not ennoble. It destroys. To resist destruction, self-hatred, or lifelong hopelessness, we have to throw off the conditioning of being despised, the fear of becoming that *they* that is talked about so dismissively, to refuse lying myths and easy moralities, to see ourselves as human, flawed and extraordinary. All of us—extraordinary.

◆◆◆

Jews in the U.S. (1994/5755)
The Rising Costs of Whiteness

Melanie Kaye/Kantrowitz

Melanie Kaye/Kantrowitz has taught literature, Women's Studies, and Jewish Studies. She is also a long-time activist for social justice, was founding director of Jews for Economic and Racial Justice, and former Director of Queens College/CUNY Worker Education Extension Center. Her published work includes *The Issue Is Power: Essays on Women, Jews, Violence, and Resistance* and *The Colors of Jews: Racial Politics and Radical Diasporism.* After her father's death she reclaimed her Jewish name, Kantrowitz, which "pressured by the exigencies of being a Jew in the forties" he had changed to Kaye.

Before America No One Was White

In 1990 I had returned to New York City to do antiracist work with other Jews, when a friend sent me an essay by James Baldwin. "No one was white before he/she came to America," Baldwin had written:

> It took generations, and a vast amount of coercion, before this became a white country. . . . It is probable that it is the Jewish community—or more accurately, perhaps, its remnants—that in America has paid the highest and most extraordinary price for becoming white. For the Jews came here from countries where they were not white, and they came here in part because they were not white, and incontestably—in the eyes of the Black American (and not only in those eyes) American Jews have opted to become white. . . .[1]

Everything I think about Jews, whiteness, racism, and contemporary U.S. society begins with this passage. What does it mean: *Jews opted to become white.* Did we opt? Did it work? Was it an illusion? Could we have opted otherwise? Can we still?

. . .

Where is *Jewish* in the race/class/gender grid? . . .

Race or Religion?

"Race or religion?" is how the question is usually posed, as though this doublet exhausts the possibilities. Christians—religiously observant or not—usually operate from the common self-definition of Christianity, a religion any individual can embrace through belief, detached from race, peoplehood, and culture.

But I have come to understand this detachment as false. Do white Christians feel kinship with African American Christians? White slaveowners, for example, with their slaves? White Klansmen with their black neighbors? Do white Christians feel akin to Christians converted by colonialists all over the globe? Doesn't Christianity really, for most white Christians, imply *white*? And for those white Christians, does *white* really include *Jewish*? Think of the massive Christian evasion of a simple fact: Jesus Christ was not, was never, a Christian. He was a Jew. What did he look like, Jesus of Nazareth, 2000 years ago? Blond, blue-eyed?

Of course Jewish is not a race,[2] for Jews come in all races. Though white-identified Jews may skirt the issue, Jews are a multiracial people. There are Ethiopian, Indian, Chinese Jews. And there are people of every race who choose Judaism, were adopted, or born into it from mixed parents. The dominant conception of "Jewish"—European, Yiddish-speaking—is in fact a subset, Ashkenazi. Estimated at 85–97% of Jews in the U.S. today, Ashkenazi Jews are those whose religious practice and diaspora path can be traced through Germany.[3] The huge wave of Jewish immigration from Eastern Europe was Ashkenazi (as was the earlier, much smaller, highly assimilated community of German Jews, who looked with dread upon the arrival of—from their perspective—an impoverished, Yiddish-babbling, superstitious horde).

Ashkenazi Jews also migrated to the far points of the globe—to South America, Australia, Africa, Asia. They may be very fair or very dark.

Sephardic Jews are those whose mother tongue is/was Ladino (Judeo-Español) and whose religious practice and diaspora path can be traced at some point through the Iberian Peninsula (Spain and Portugal), where they flourished, unghettoized, contributing along with Muslims to Spanish culture, until the Inquisition (read, *torture*) forced conversion or expulsion from Spain of all non-Christians. Sephardim migrated to, and lived for generations and even centuries, in Holland, Germany, Italy, France, Greece, the Middle East, and the Americas. The first Jews in the New World were Sephardim: 1492 marks not only Columbus's voyage but also the expulsion of the Jews from Spain. Some Sephardi consider themselves the aristocrats of the Jews, and look with contempt upon the Ashkenazi history of ghettoization and persecution. They may also be quite fair or quite dark.

Mizrachi Jews are those who lived in the Arab world and Turkey (basically, what was once the Ottoman Empire), as minorities in Muslim rather than Christian culture. Their mother tongue often is/was Judeo-Arabic. *Mizrachi* means "Eastern," commonly translated as "Oriental," and is used by and about Israelis, often interchangeably with *Sephardi.* Spanish Sephardim sometimes resent the blurring of distinctions between themselves and Mizrachim, reacting with pride in their history and with Eurocentric bias against non-Europeans, referring to themselves as "true" or "pure" Sephardim.[4] The confusion between the categories is only partly due to Ashkenazi ignorance/arrogance, lumping all non-Ashkenazi together. Partly it's the result of Jewish history: some Jews never left the Middle East, and some returned after the expulsion from Spain, including to Palestine. Some kept Ladino, some did not. I imagine there was intermarriage. Mizrachim, though they may also range from fair to dark, are usually defined as people of color.

The point is, categories of white and color don't correspond neatly to Jewish reality. (What does correspond is Ashkenazi cultural hegemony: in the U.S., where they are dominant by numbers, and in Israel, where Sephardi/Mizrachi Jews make up about two-thirds of the Jewish population and strongly contest this hegemony.) Jewish wanderings have created a people whose experience eludes conventional categories of race, nationality, ethnicity, geography, language—even religion. Cataclysm and assimilation have depleted our store of common knowledge.

No, Jews are not a single race. Yet there is confusion here, and subtext. Confusion because we have so often been racialized, hated *as if* we were a race. Ethnic studies scholars have labored to document the process of racialization, the fact that race is not biological, but a socio-historically specific phenomenon. . . .

Confusion, too, because to say someone *looks Jewish* is to say something both absurd (Jews look a million different ways) and commonsense communicative.

When I was growing up in Flatbush (in Brooklyn, NY), every girl with a certain kind of nose—sometimes named explicitly as a Jewish nose, sometimes only as "too big"—wanted a nose job, and if her parents could pay for it, often she got one. I want to be graphic about the euphemism "nose job." A nose job breaks the nose, bruises the face and eye area like a grotesque beating. It hurts. It takes weeks to heal.

What was wrong with the original nose, the Jewish one? Noses were discussed ardently in Flatbush, this or that friend looking forward to her day of transformation.[5] My aunts lavished on me the following exquisite praise: *look at her, a nose like a shiksa* (gentile woman). This hurt my feelings. Before I knew what a *shiksa* was, I knew I wasn't it, and, with that fabulous integrity of children, I wanted to look like who I was. But later I learned my nose's value, and would tell gentiles this story so they'd notice my nose.

A Jewish nose, I conclude, identifies its owner as a Jew. Nose jobs are performed so that a Jewish woman does not look like a Jew.

Tell me again Jewish is just a religion.

Yet Nazi racial definitions have an "only a religion" response. Even earlier, the lure of emancipation (in Europe) and assimilation (in the U.S.) led Jews to define Judaism as narrowly as possible, as religion only: "a Jew at home, a man in the streets,"[6] a private matter, taken care of behind closed doors, like bathing.

Judaism, the religion, does provide continuity and connection to Jews around the globe. There is something powerful even for atheists about entering a synagogue across the continent or the ocean, and hearing the familiar service.

But to be a Jew, one need not follow religious practice; one need not believe in god—not even to become a rabbi, an element of Judaism of which I am especially fond.[7] Religion is only one strand of being Jewish. It is ironic that it is precisely this century's depletion of Jews and of Jewish identity, with profound linguistic and cultural losses—continuing as Yiddish[8] and Ladino speakers age and die— that makes imaginable a Jewishness that is *only a religion*—only now, when so much else has been lost. But to reduce *Jewishness* to *Judaism* is to forget the complex indivisible swirl of religion/culture/ language/history that *was* Jewishness until, in the 18th century, Emancipation began to offer some Jews the possibility of escaping from a linguistically/ culturally/economically isolated ghetto into the European "Enlightenment." To equate Jewishness with religion is to forget how even the contemporary, often attenuated version of this Jewish cultural swirl is passed down *in the family*, almost like genetic code.

Confusion and subtext. *Jewish* is often trivialized as something you choose, a preference, like tea over coffee. In contrast with visible racial identity, presumptions of choice—as with gayness—are seen as minimizing one's claim to attention, sympathy, and remedy. As a counter to bigotry, *I was born like this* strategically asserts a kind of victim status, modeled on race, gender, and disability: if you can't help yourself, maybe you're entitled to some help from others. . . .

What happens if, instead, I assert my right to choose and not suffer for it. To say, *I choose*: my lesbianism and my Jewishness.[9] Choose to come out, be visible, embrace both. I could live loveless or sexless or in the closet. I could have kept the name *Kaye*, and never once at Christmas—in response to the interminable "what are you doing for . . .? have you finished your shopping?"—never once answer, "I don't celebrate Christmas. I'm a Jew." I could lie about my lover's gender. I could wear skirts uncomfortably. I could bleach my hair again, as I did when I was fifteen. I could monitor my speech, weeding out the offensive accent, as I was taught at City College, along with all the other first and second generation immigrants' children in the four speech classes required for graduation, to teach us not to sound like ourselves. I could remain silent when queer or anti-Semitic jokes are told, when someone says "you know how *they* are." I could

endure the pain in the gut, the hot shame. I could scrunch up much, much smaller.

In the U.S., *Christian*, like *white*, is an unmarked category in need of marking.[10] Christianness, a majority, dominant culture, is not only about religious practice and belief, any more than Jewishness is. As *racism* names the system that normalizes, honors, and rewards whiteness, we need a word for what normalizes, honors and rewards Christianity. Jews designate the assumption of Christianity-as-norm, the erasure of Jews, as "anti-Semitic." In fact, the erasure and marginalization of non-Christians is not just denigrating to Jews. We need a catchier term than *Christian hegemony*, to help make visible the cultural war against all non-Christians.

Christianism? Awkward, stark, and kind of crude. . . . *Sexism* once sounded stark and kind of crude. Such a term would help contextualize Jewish experience as an experience of marginality shared with other non-Christians. Especially in this time of rising Christian fundamentalism, . . . this contextualization is critical for progressive Jews, compelling us to seek allies among Muslims and other religious minorities.

I also want to contextualize Jews in a theoretical framework outside the usual bipolar frame of black/white—to go beyond dualism; to distinguish race from class, and both from culture; to understand "whiteness" as the gleaming conferral of normality, success, even survival; to acknowledge who owns what in whose neighborhood; to witness how money does and does not "whiten."

. . .

The Cost of Whiteness

Aryan ideology aside, Jews are often defined as white, though this wipes out the many Jews who are by anyone's definition people of color, and neglects the role of context: many Jews who look white in New York City look quite the opposite in the South and Midwest. Radicals often exclude the category *Jewish* from discussion, or subsume us into *white*, unless we are by *their* definition also people of color, in which case they subsume us as *people of color*.

The truth is, Jews complicate things. *Jewish* is both a distinct category and an overlapping one. Just as homophobia is distinct from sexism yet has everything to do with sexism, anti-Semitism in this country is distinct from racism yet has everything to do with racism. It's not that a Jew like myself should "count" as a person of color, though I think sometimes Jews do argue this because the alternative seems to be erasure. But that means we need another alternative. The problem is a polarization of white and color that excludes us. We need a more complex vision of the structure of racism, one that attends to the sick logic of white supremacists. We need a more complex understanding of the process of "whitening."

> It is probable that it is the Jewish community—
> or more accurately, perhaps, its remnants—
> that in America has paid the highest and more
> extraordinary price for becoming white.

Every time I read this passage, at the word "remnants," my hand moves to the hollow at the base of my throat, to help me breathe. *Remnants.*

What have we paid?

How many of us speak or read Yiddish or Ladino or Hebrew? How many of us have studied Jewish history or literature, recognize the terms that describe Jewish experience, are familiar with the Jewish calendar, can sing more than three or four Jewish songs, know *something* beyond matzoh balls or stuffed grape leaves? Many . . . of us have lost our culture, our sense of community. Only anti-Semitism reminds us who we are, and we have nothing to fight back with—no pride and no knowledge—only a feeble, embarrassed sense that hatred and bigotry are wrong. I have even heard Jews, especially, "progressives," justify anti-Semitism: maybe we really are "like that," rich and greedy, taking over, too loud, too pushy, snatching up more than our share, ugly and parasitical, Jewish American Princesses, Jewish landlords, Jewish bosses, emphasis on *Jewish.* Maybe we really deserve to be hated. . . .

Do we even know the history of which we, Jewish radicals, are a part? As Trotsky's master biographer Isaac Deutscher explained "the non-Jewish Jew" to the World Jewish Congress in 1958:

> The Jewish heretic who transcends Jewry belongs to a Jewish tradition. . . . Spinoza, Heine, Marx, Rosa Luxemburg, Trotsky, and Freud . . . all went beyond the boundaries of Jewry. They all found Jewry too narrow, too archaic, and

too constricting. . . . Yet I think that in some ways they were very Jewish indeed. . . . as Jews they dwelt on the borderlines of various civilizations, religions, and national cultures.[11]

. . . It is frustrating that those Jews best equipped to grasp what it means to choose *not to be white*—not to blend, pass, or mute one's differences—are the Hasidim (ultra-orthodox).[12] But because they are also separatist, and by ideology and theology do not value encounters with diversity, the Hasidim have rarely forged alliances around diversity and against bigotry. Instead, they tend to protect their individual communities and to blame urban chaos on their neighbors, often people of color, with law-and-order rhetoric and actions both racist and quintessentially American.[13]

The response of other Jews toward the Hasidim is instructive. Embarrassment, exposure, shame, rage; *why do they have to be so blatant?*—including *so blatantly Jewish* and *so blatantly racist*—as opposed to the discreet liberal norm of moving out of the neighborhood or sending the kids to private schools faintly integrated by race but starkly segregated by class. And somewhere, for Jews who care about Jewish identity, the Hasidim also represent a kind of courage: they dare to walk around looking Jewish.

Progressive Jews need to reconstruct an authentically American progressive Jewish identity, choosing from the vast storehouse of history/culture/religion which pieces we want to reclaim, which will enable us to be out as Jews with our own brand of Jewish courage. It's not that most Jews in the U.S. will endure the same unsheddable visual vulnerability as most people of color, though buttons and t-shirts, the *kipah* (skullcap worn by observant men) and the *magen david* (Star of David—"Jewish star") may draw us into street visibility. But Jews, like all other people, make political choices. With whose interests will we identify and stake our future? With the dominant and privileged few—white, Christian, and rich, ensuring that poverty remains part of the American landscape, leaving bigotry unchallenged, to feed on the local minority of choice?

. . . Many Jews who work against racism and on various progressive issues do this work as progressives, as women, as workers, as queers, as whites, as people of color. We are invisible *as Jews,* while Jewish political conservatives are highly visible.

We relinquish to the Jewish right wing the claim to represent the Jewish community, though the sheer number of Jews involved with progressive politics is stunning. We abandon Jewish culture to the religious orthodox: we think they are the "real Jews" and we are not. We neglect the powerful tradition of Jewish radicalism, a potential source of instruction, inspiration, and courage. Committed as progressives to the survival of people's culture, we stand, unseeing and uncaring, at the edge of a chasm opened by assimilation and infinitely deepened by the Holocaust. We facilitate the dwindling of the Jewish community—*to remnants.*

Is It Coming Again?

. . .

I am writing this at Rosh Hashonah, the Jewish New Year opening year 5755 of the Jewish calendar. We call the ten days following Rosh Hashonah *Yamim Noraim,* the Days of Awe, the most solemn time of our year, culminating in Yom Kippur, the Day of Atonement. If a Jew steps foot inside a synagogue once a year, Yom Kippur is the day. I am thinking about the danger, in this time of increased attacks on Jews, of stepping inside visibly Jewish spaces packed with Jews. At this time of heightened danger I feel intensely, paradoxically, the need to be among Jews in a Jewish space.

Elsewhere I have written, "to be a Jew is to tangle with history."[14] In the U.S. people tend to be both ahistorical and insulated from the impact of international events. From this tunnel perspective, Jews have it good. What are we worried about? And we *do* have it good. And we do worry. Jews have a history of nearly 6000 recorded years of repeated cycles of calm, then chaos: periods of relative safety and prosperity disrupted by persecution, brutal oppression, murder, and expulsion or exile for the surviving remnant to a strange land where the cycle begins again. Grace Paley reports her immigrant mother's succinct comment on Hitler's rise to power: "It's coming again."[15]

In the U.S. much of the bias against Jews has been mitigated by the development of some institutionalized Jewish power. This should be a cause for celebration. Instead it makes us nervous. Jewish success is often used against us, as evidence of our excessive control, power, and greed, evidence which could at any moment topple us from the calm and, for many Jews, prosperous phase of the cycle into danger and chaos.

Besides, Jewish success—like any other U.S. success—has been achieved inside a severe class structure, and Jews, like many other ethnic and racial minorities, have benefitted in concrete ways from racism against African Americans. Karen Sacks' brilliant investigation, "How Did Jews Become White Folks?" describes how "federal programs which were themselves designed to assist demobilized GIs and young families systematically discriminated against African Americans," and functioned as "affirmative action . . . [which] aimed at and disproportionately helped male, Euro-origin GIs."[16] Thus she convincingly explains post-World War II Jewish upward mobility.

. . .

To Discover Water

. . .

My grandparents immigrated from Russia and Poland early in this century. My father, a teenager in Brownsville (a poor Jewish ghetto in Brooklyn) during the Depression, joined the Young Communist League; as an adult his major hero remained his friend Aaron, a communist who had spoken on street corners and died fighting in the second World War. My mother had circulated petitions against the Korean War, walking up to people on the streets of Flatbush during peak McCarthy period, and she had been spat on.

. . . This was my Jewish upbringing, as much as the candles we lit for Hanukkah, or the seders where bread and matzoh shared the table. My father had been raised observant, my mother, not. But to us breaking religious observance was progressive, the opposite of superstitious. When we ate on Yom Kippur, it never occurred to me that this was unJewish. I knew I was a Jew. I knew Hitler had been evil. I knew Negroes—we said then—had been slaves and that was evil too. I knew prejudice was wrong, stupid. I knew Jews believed in freedom and justice. . . .

That this set of principles was Jewish never occurred to me. Around me was Flatbush, a swirling Jewish ghetto/community of first and second generation immigrants, including Holocaust survivors;

. . . there were clerks, trade unionists, salespeople, plumbers, small business people, radio and TV repairmen, people like my parents (small shopkeepers) "in the middle," apartment dwellers where the kids shared a room, and fathers worked 60–70 hours a week; and people poorer than us, who lived in apartments where kitchen smells lingered on the stairs, someone slept in the living room, and summers the kids swam in underwear instead of bathing suits. There were teachers and even doctors who were rich and lived in what we called "private houses" in the outreaches of the neighborhood at the point where not everyone was Jewish.

But where I lived, everyone was, or almost. Jewish was the air I breathed, nothing I articulated, everything I took for granted.

. . .

. . . Not until the early seventies when I moved to Oregon and encountered white Christian anti-Semites, did I even understand that to them I was not white: I was a Jew.

In 1972, I had just moved to Portland, Oregon, and was attending a feminist conference, talking with a woman while we waited for the elevator. I have forgotten the context for what she said: that she did not like Jews. Jews were loud and pushy and aggressive. This was the first time I had heard someone say this outright. I was stunned, didn't know what to say—"no, they're not?"—and I couldn't believe she didn't know that I was Jewish. My voice came out loud and flat: "I'm Jewish." To this day I can't remember how she responded or what I did next.

. . .

That first year in Portland, I read Hannah Arendt's *Eichmann in Jerusalem,* and realized something I had somehow up to this point managed not to notice: I would have been killed. My family, everyone I grew up around, practically, would have been killed. Random family tidbits clicked into place: my grandparents' families *had* been killed. . . .

What is clear is this: the more outside of a Jewish ambience I was, the more conscious I became of Jewishness. Like Marshall McLuhan's perhaps apocryphal remark: *I don't know who discovered water, but I'm sure it wasn't a fish.* Inside a Jewish environment, where I could take for granted a somewhat shared culture, an expectation about Jewish survival, where my body type and appearance were familiar, my voice ordinary, my laughter not too loud but hearty and normal, above all, normal . . . in this environ-

ment, I did not know what it meant to be a Jew, only what it meant to be a *mentsh.* I did not know that *mentsh* was a Jewish word in a Jewish language.

To Create Solidarity

The more conscious I became, the more I thought and talked and came to write about it and act visibly and politically as a Jew, the more I encountered both blankness and kinship, anti-Semitism and solidarity. . . .

. . .

On the evening of Election Day, 1992, I was driving down from Seattle to Portland, Oregon, where Measure 9, the most vitriolic of the homophobic hate measures, was on the ballot. Measure 9 would have sanctioned discrimination explicitly and violence implicitly; would have banned from public libraries and schools books that deal positively with gay and lesbian experience; would have blocked funding of any public institutions that aided gays and lesbians—for example, AIDS counselling.

. . . As I pulled into my friend's neighborhood, Northeast Portland, a neighborhood mixed by income and by race—not especially gay—I saw signs on every lawn—NO ON 9. I started to cry, and I realized I had no concept of allies. Even though the friend I was going to stay with was heterosexual, and I knew she'd been working very hard on this issue, I had still somewhere assumed that no one would stand with us—that we would be fighting alone. And I knew this came from my history as a Jew.

I had heard about the escalation of violence against Oregon lesbians and gays. But I still was not prepared for what I found. I saw antigay propaganda that copied actual Nazi cartoons which showed Jews controlling the economy, substituting gays instead. Powell's Bookstore, which had been featuring displays of books endangered by 9, had received bomb threats, as had individuals working against 9. House and car windows had been smashed, cars tampered with. Physical attacks on lesbians and gays had skyrocketed, and in Salem a black lesbian and a white gay man had been murdered. . . .

I heard bits and pieces of this struggle: how some people in Portland or Salem didn't want to bother organizing rurally, how some white people did not understand the need to build coalitions with communities of color. Yet despite some reluctance and ignorance, a vast broad coalition was created. People told me not about the ease of creating this coalition but about the clarity and desperation and drive. . . . Out of something ugly and outrageous has come something astonishing and inspiring, a model for the rest of the country, for the continued struggle against hatred—for survival.

A model for Jews as well. Oregon's Jews stood unanimously against Measure 9: every synagogue, every community organization and institution, every rabbi. . . . Here is an excerpt from the Oregon Jews' statement, deeply informed by Jewish history, and by Jewish recognition of the intolerably high cost and inevitable slippage of any safety based on "whiteness":

> [The Holocaust] began with laws exactly like Ballot Measure 9. Those laws first declared groups of people to be sub-human, then legalized and finally mandated discrimination against them. Comparisons to the Holocaust must be limited. But clearly, this is the start of hatred and persecution that must stop now.

At the victory rally the night after the election, all the coalition partners spoke to celebrate, warn, rage, and comfort. There were representatives from the Jewish community, African American community, Native American community, labor. . . . Two voices especially stand out in my memory. One was a Chicano organizer from the Farmworkers Union, who said, "In this, we were there for you. Now we're organizing our strike, and I need to ask you to be there for us." The other voice was a white lesbian activist, who answered the farmworker: *"Su lucha es mi lucha." Your struggle is my struggle.*

I may be secular, but I know holiness when I hear it. One of its names is solidarity, the opposite of "whiteness." The more you claim it, honor it, and fight for it, the less it costs.

NOTES

I thank Esther Kaplan, Roni Natov, and Nancy Ordover for substantial critical feedback. Sections of this essay are drawn from earlier writings published in *The Issue Is Power: Essays on Women, Jews, Violence and Resistance* (San Francisco: Aunt Lute, 1992).

1. "On Being 'White'. . . and Other Lies," *Essence* (April, 1984).

2. On the other hand, Karen Sacks, "How Did Jews Become White Folks?" in *Race,* eds., Steven Gregory and Roger Sanjek (New Brunswick: Rutgers University Press, 1994), points to "a 1987 Supreme Court ruling that Jews and Arabs could use civil rights laws to gain redress for discrimination against them . . . on the grounds that they are not racial whites."

3. *Ashkenazi* comes from the word for Germany; *Sephardi,* from Spain.

4. For Sephardi in the former Ottoman Empire, see Interview with Chaya Shalom in *The Tribe of Dina: A Jewish Women's Anthology,* eds., Melanie Kaye/Kantrowitz and Irena Klepfisz (Boston: Beacon Press, 1989): pp. 214–226.

5. See Aisha Berger's poem, "Nose is a country . . . I am the second generation," in *The Tribe of Dina.* pp. 134–138. One of Berger's many illuminating images: "this unruly semitic landmass on my face." The era of Jewish nose jobs is not over, though Barbra Streisand broke the spell that mirrored Jewish noses as inherently ugly.

6. First expressed by Moses Mendelssohn (1729–86), the central figure in the German Jewish *Haskalah* (Enlightenment), as the ideal of Jewish assimilation.

7. One is, however, hard put to be a Jew without Jewish community. Even in religious practice, the unit of prayer is not the individual but the *minyan,* at least ten adult Jews, the Jewish quorum—in Orthodox Judaism, ten men.

8. There is painful irony in the fact that Yiddish, the beloved *mame-losbn* of Jewish socialists, is dwindling to a living language only for the ultra-orthodox Hasidim.

9. In this discussion I am indebted to Nancy Ordover, "Visibility, Alliance, and the Practice of Memory." *Socialist Review.* 25, no. 1 (1995): 119–134.

10. Ruth Frankenberg's *White Women/Race Matters* (Minneapolis: University of Minnesota, 1993) offers useful insight on whiteness as an unmarked racial category. But Frankenberg misses opportunities to note the significance of *Jewish* as a category, although she and a disproportionate number of the white anti-racist activists she interviewed are Jews.

11. Isaac Deutscher, "The Non-Jewish Jew," in *The Non-Jewish Jew and Other Essays* (London: Oxford University Press, 1968). pp. 26–27.

12. In appearance, immediately identifiable as Jews because of distinct dress (black hats and coats for the men, arms and legs fully covered for the women) and hair (*peyes*—unshorn sideburns—for the men; hair cropped and covered by a *sheytl*—wig—or headscarf for the women), the Hasidim are magnets for anti-Semitism. Similarly, anti-Semitic graffiti, vandalism, and bombing of synagogues demonstrate that identifiable Jewish places are also vulnerable.

13. Though the Hasidim are vulnerable as individuals to acts of bigotry and violence, in New York City the

Hasidic communities (Lubovitcher, in Crown Heights, and Satmar, in Williamsburg) wield influence. This is not a function of numbers; the Hasidim comprise a tiny percent of the world's Jews. Nor is it a function of wealth; indeed, a great many families in the Hasidic communities are poor, partly due to family size (as in all fundamentalist religions, the use of birth control is prohibited). Hasidic influence is a function of social organization: Hasidic leaders can deliver votes in an election and bodies in a demonstration. . . . Here is a lesson for progressive Jews about the need for *progressive* Jewish visibility and organization.

14. In "The Issue Is Power: Some Notes on Jewish Women and Therapy," *The Issue Is Power: Essays on Women, Jews, Violence and Resistance* (San Francisco: Aunt Lute, 1992).

15. Grace Paley, "Now and Then." *Tikkun* (May/June 1989), p. 76. In particular, European medieval and Renaissance history from a Jewish perspective reads like a disaster chronicle: expelled from here, massacred there, forced conversions someplace else. Occasionally there is a bright spot: "Jews return to Worms" (from which they had been expelled the year before); "Jews allowed to settle in England" (from which they had been expelled some centuries earlier). The late nineteenth and early twentieth century, especially in Eastern Europe, presents a similar wave of persecution, dwarfed only by the magnitude of what followed. Grievous official and unofficial oppression of Jews was a common feature of modern pre-Holocaust Europe.

16. Karen Sacks, in *Race,* eds. Steven Gregory and Roger Sanjek.

FIFTEEN

❖❖❖

Optional Ethnicities (1996)
For Whites Only?

Mary C. Waters

Mary C. Waters is the M.E. Zukerman Professor of Sociology at Harvard University who specializes in the study of immigration, intergroup relations, the formation of racial and ethnic identity among the children of immigrants, and the challenges of measuring race and ethnicity. Her many books include *Black Identities: West Indian Immigrant Dreams and American Realities; Inheriting the City: The Second Generation Comes of Age* (co-author); *The New Americans: A Guide to Immigration Since 1965* (co-author); and *The Next Generation: The Children of Immigrants in Europe and North America* (co-edited with Richard Alba).

. . . What does it mean to talk about ethnicity as an option for an individual? To argue that an individual has some degree of choice in their ethnic identity flies in the face of the commonsense notion of ethnicity many of us believe in—that one's ethnic identity is a fixed characteristic, reflective of blood ties and given at birth. However, social scientists who study ethnicity have long concluded that while ethnicity is based in a *belief* in a common ancestry, ethnicity is primarily a *social* phenomenon, not a biological one (Alba 1985, 1990; Barth 1969; Weber [1921] 1968, p. 389).

The belief that members of an ethnic group have that they share a common ancestry may not be a fact. There is a great deal of change in ethnic identities across generations through intermarriage, changing allegiances, and changing social categories. There is also a much larger amount of change in the identities of individuals over their life than is commonly believed. While most people are aware of the phenomenon known as "passing"—people raised as one race who change at some point and claim a different race as their identity—there are similar life course changes in ethnicity that happen all the time and are not given the same degree of attention as "racial passing."

White Americans of European ancestry can be described as having a great deal of choice in terms of their ethnic identities. The two major types of options White Americans can exercise are (1) the option of whether to claim any specific ancestry, or to just be "White" or American (Lieberson [1985] called these people "unhyphenated Whites"), and (2) the choice of which of their European ancestries to choose to include in their description of their own identities. In both cases, the option of choosing how to present yourself on surveys and in everyday social interactions exists for Whites because of social changes and societal conditions that have created a great deal of social mobility, immigrant assimilation, and political and economic power for Whites in the United States. Specifically, the option of being able to not claim any ethnic identity exists for Whites of European background in the United States because they are the majority group—in terms of holding political and social power, as well as being a numerical majority. The option of choosing among different ethnicities in their family backgrounds exists because the degree of discrimination and social distance attached to specific European backgrounds has diminished over time.

The Ethnic Miracle

When European immigration to the United States was sharply curtailed in the late 1920s, a process was set in motion whereby the European ethnic groups already in the United States were for all intents and purposes cut off from any new arrivals. As a result, the composition of the ethnic groups began to age generationally. The proportion of each ethnic group made up of immigrants or the first generation began to gradually decline, and the proportion made up of the children, grandchildren, and eventually great-grandchildren began to increase. Consequently, by 1990 most European-origin ethnic groups in the United States were composed of a very small number of immigrants, and a very large proportion of people whose link to their ethnic origins in Europe was increasingly remote.

This generational change was accompanied by unprecedented social and economic changes. The very success of the assimilation process these groups experienced makes it difficult to imagine how much the question of the immigrants' eventual assimilation was an open one at the turn of the century. At the peak of immigration from southern and central Europe, there was widespread discrimination and hostility against the newcomers by established Americans. Italians, Poles, Greeks, and Jews were called derogatory names, attacked by nativist mobs, and derided in the press. Intermarriage across ethnic lines was very uncommon—castelike in the words of some sociologists (Pagnini and Morgan 1990). The immigrants and their children were residentially segregated, occupationally specialized, and generally poor.

After several generations in the United States, the situation has changed a great deal. The success and social mobility of the grandchildren and great-grandchildren of that massive wave of immigrants from Europe has been called "The Ethnic Miracle" (Greeley 1976). These Whites have moved away from the inner-city ethnic ghettos to White middle-class suburban homes. They are doctors, lawyers, entertainers, academics, governors, and Supreme Court justices. But contrary to what some social science theorists and some politicians predicted or hoped for, these middle-class Americans have not completely given up ethnic identity. Instead, they have maintained some connection with their immigrant ancestors' identities—becoming Irish American doctors, Italian American Supreme Court justices, and Greek American presidential candidates. In the tradition of cultural pluralism, successful middle-class Americans . . . maintain some degree of identity with their ethnic backgrounds. They have remained "hyphenated Americans." So, while social mobility and declining discrimination have created the option of not identifying with any European ancestry, most White Americans continue to report some ethnic background.

With the growth in intermarriage among people of European ethnic origins, increasingly these people are of mixed ethnic ancestry. This gives them the option of which ethnicity to identify with. The U.S. census has asked a question on ethnic ancestry in the 1980 and 1990 censuses. In 1980, 52 percent of the American public responded with a single ethnic ancestry, 31 percent gave multiple ethnic origins (up to three were coded, but some individuals wrote in more than three), and only 6 percent said they were American only, while the remaining 11 percent gave no response. In 1990 about 90 percent of the population gave some response to the ancestry question, with only 5 percent giving American as a response and only 1.4 percent reporting an uncodeable response such as "don't know" (McKenney and Cresce 1992; U.S. Bureau of the Census 1992).

Several researchers have examined the pattern of responses of people to the census ancestry question. These analyses have shown a pattern of flux and inconsistency in ethnic ancestry reporting.

For instance, Lieberson and Waters (1986, 1988, p. 93) have found that parents simplify children's ancestries when reporting them to the census. For instance, among the offspring in situations where one parent reports a specific single White ethnic origin and the other parent reports a different single White origin, about 40 percent of the children are not described as the logical combination of the parents' ancestries. For example, only about 60 percent of the children of English-German marriages are labeled as English-German or German-English. About 15 percent of the children of these parents are simplified to just English, and another 15 percent are reported as just German. The remainder of the children are either not given an ancestry or are described as American (Lieberson and Waters 1986, 1993).

In addition to these intergenerational changes, researchers have found changes in reporting ancestry that occur at the time of marriage or upon leaving home. At the ages of eighteen to twenty-two, when many young Americans leave home for the first time, the number of people reporting a single as opposed to a multiple ancestry goes up. Thus while parents simplify children's ancestries when they leave home, children themselves tend to report less complexity in their ancestries when they leave their parents' homes and begin reporting their ancestries themselves (Lieberson and Waters 1986, 1988; Waters 1990).

These individual changes are reflected in variability over time in the aggregate numbers of groups determined by the census and surveys. Farley (1991) compared the consistency of the overall counts of different ancestry groups in the 1979 Current Population Survey, the 1980 census, and the 1986 National Content Test (a pretest for the 1990 census). He found much less consistency in the numbers for northern European ancestry groups whose immigration peaks were early in the nineteenth century—the English, Dutch, Germans, and other northern European groups. In other words, each of these different surveys and the census yielded a different estimate of the number of people having this ancestry. The 1990 census also showed a great deal of flux and inconsistency in some ancestry groups. The number of people reporting English as an ancestry went down considerably from 1980, while the number reporting German ancestry went up. The number of Cajuns grew dramatically. This has led officials at the Census Bureau to assume that

the examples used in the instructions strongly influence the responses people give. (Cajun was one of the examples of an ancestry given in 1990 but not in 1980, and German was the first example given. English was an example in the 1980 instructions, but not in 1990.)

All of these studies point to the socially variable nature of ethnic identity—and the lack of equivalence between ethnic ancestry and identity. If merely adding a category to the instructions to the question increases the number of people claiming that ancestry, what does that mean about the level of importance of that identity for people answering the census? Clearly, identity and ancestry for Whites in the United States, who increasingly are from mixed backgrounds, involve some change and choice.

Symbolic Ethnicities for White Americans

What do these ethnic identities mean to people, and why do they cling to them rather than just abandoning the tie and calling themselves American? My own field research with suburban Whites in California and Pennsylvania found that later-generation descendants of European origin maintain what are called "symbolic ethnicities." Symbolic ethnicity is a term coined by Herbert Gans (1979) to refer to ethnicity that is individualistic in nature and without real social cost for the individual. These symbolic identifications are essentially leisure-time activities, rooted in nuclear family traditions and reinforced by the voluntary enjoyable aspects of being ethnic (Waters 1990). Richard Alba (1990) also found later-generation Whites in Albany, New York, who chose to keep a tie with an ethnic identity because of the enjoyable and voluntary aspects to those identities, along with the feelings of specialness they entailed. An example of symbolic ethnicity is individuals who identify as Irish, for example, on occasions such as Saint Patrick's Day, on family holidays, or for vacations. They do not usually belong to Irish American organizations, live in Irish neighborhoods, work in Irish jobs, or marry other Irish people. The symbolic meaning of being Irish American can be constructed by individuals from mass media images, family traditions, or other intermittent social activities. In other words, for later-generation White ethnics, ethnicity is not something that influences their lives unless they want it to. In the world of work and school and neighborhood, individuals do not have to admit to being ethnic unless they choose to. And for an increasing number of European-origin individuals whose parents and grandparents have intermarried, the ethnicity they claim is largely a matter of personal choice as they sort through all of the possible combinations of groups in their genealogies.

Individuals can choose those aspects of being Italian, for instance, that appeal to them, and discard those that do not. Or a person whose father is Italian, and mother part Polish and part French, might choose among the three ethnicities and present herself as a Polish American. For instance, a nineteen-year-old college student, interviewed in California in 1986, told me he would have answered Irish on the 1980 census form that asked about ethnic ancestry. These are his reasons:

Q: Why would you have answered that?
A: Well, my Dad's name is Kerrigan and my mom's name is O'Leary, and I do have some German in me, but if you figure it out, I am about 75 percent Irish, so I usually say I am Irish.
Q: You usually don't say German when people ask?
A: No, no, I never say I am German. My dad just likes being Irish. . . . I don't know I just never think of myself as being German.
Q: So your dad's father is the one who immigrated?
A: Yes. On his side is Irish for generations. And then my grandmother's name is Dubois, which is French, partly German, partly French, and then the rest of the family is all Irish. So it is only the maternal grandmother who messes up the line.
(Waters 1990, p. 10)

Thus in the course of a few questions, this man labeled himself Irish, admitted to being part German but not identifying with it, and then as an afterthought added that he was also part French. This is not an unusual case. With just a little probing, many people will describe a variety of ancestries in their family background, but do not consider these ancestries to be a salient part of their own identities. Thus the 1990 census ancestry question, which estimated that 30 percent of the population is of mixed ancestry, most surely underestimates the degree of mixing among the population. . . .

But note that this freedom to include or exclude ancestries in your identification to yourself and others would not be the same for those defined racially in our society. They are constrained to identify with the part of their ancestry that has been socially defined as the "essential" part. African Americans, for example, have been highly socially constrained to identify as Blacks, without other options available to them, even when they know that their forebears included many people of American Indian or European background. Up until the mid-twentieth century, many state governments had specific laws defining one as Black if as little as one-thirty-second of one's ancestors were defined as Black (Davis 1991; Dominguez 1986; Spickard 1989). Even now when the one drop rule has been dropped from our legal codes, there are still strong societal pressures on African Americans to identify in a particular way. Certain ancestries take precedence over others in the societal rules on descent and ancestry reckoning. If one believes one is part English and part German and identifies in a survey as German, one is not in danger of being accused of trying to "pass" as non-English and of being "redefined" English by the interviewer. But if one were part African and part German, one's self identification as German would be highly suspect and probably not accepted if one "looked" Black according to the prevailing social norms.

. . .

. . . [T]he comparative latitude that White respondents have does not mean that Whites pick and choose ethnicities out of thin air. For the most part, people choose an identity that corresponds with some element of their family tree. However, there are many anecdotal instances of people adopting ethnicities when they marry or move to a strongly identified neighborhood or community. For instance, Micaela di Leonardo (1984) reported instances of non-Italian women who married into Italian American families and "became Italian." Karen Leonard (1992) describes a community of Mexican American women who married Punjabi immigrants in California. Some of the Punjabi immigrants and their descendants were said to have "become Mexican" when they joined their wives' kin group and social worlds. Alternatively she describes the community acknowledging that Mexican women made the best curry, as they adapted to life with Indian-origin men.

But what do these identities mean to individuals? Surely an identity that is optional in a number of ways—not legally defined on a passport or birth certificate, not socially consequential in terms of societal discrimination in terms of housing or job access, and not economically limiting in terms of blocking opportunities for social mobility—cannot be the same as an identity that results from and is nurtured by societal exclusion and rejection. The choice to have a symbolic ethnicity is an attractive and widespread one despite its lack of demonstrable content, because having a symbolic ethnicity combines individuality with feelings of community. People reported to me that they liked having an ethnic identity because it gave them a uniqueness and feeling of being special. They often contrasted their own specialness by virtue of their ethnic identities with "bland" Americanness. Being ethnic makes people feel unique and special and not just "vanilla" as one of my respondents put it. For instance, one woman describes the benefits she feels from being Czech American:

> I work in an office and a lot of people in there always talk about their background. It's weird because it is a big office and people are of all different backgrounds. People are this or that. It is interesting I think to find out. Especially when it is something you do not hear a lot about. Something that is not common like Lithuania or something. That's the good part about being Czech. People think it is something different.   *(Waters 1990, p. 154)*

Because "American" is largely understood by Americans to be a political identity and allegiance, and not an ethnic one, the idea of being "American" does not give people the same sense of belonging that their hyphenated American identity does. When I asked people about their dual identities—American and Irish or Italian or whatever—they usually responded in a way that showed how they conceived of the relationship between the two identities. Being an American was their primary identity; but it was so primary that they rarely, if ever, thought about it—most commonly only when they left the country. Being Irish American, on the other hand, was a way they had of differentiating themselves from others whom they interacted with from day to day—in many cases from spouses or in-laws. Certain of their traits—being emotional, having a sense of humor, talking with their hands—were understood as stemming from their ethnicity. Yet when asked about their identity as Americans, that identity was both removed from their day-to-day consciousness and understood in terms of loyalty and patriotism. Although they may not think they behave or think in a certain way because they are American, being American is something they are both proud of and committed to.

Symbolic ethnicity is the best of all worlds for these respondents. These White ethnics can claim to be unique and special, while simultaneously finding the community and conformity with others that they also crave. But that "community" is of a type that will not interfere with a person's individuality. It is not as if these people belong to ethnic voluntary organizations or gather as a group in churches or neighborhoods or union halls. They work and reside within the mainstream of American middle-class life, yet they retain the interesting benefits—the "specialness"—of ethnic allegiance, without any of its drawbacks.

It has been suggested by several researchers that this positive value attached to ethnic ancestry, which became popular in the ethnic revival of the 1970s, is the result of assimilation having proceeded to an advanced stage for descendants of White Europeans (Alba 1985; Crispino 1980; Steinberg 1981). Ironically, people celebrate and embrace their ethnic backgrounds precisely because assimilation has proceeded to the point where such identification does not have that much influence on their day-to-day life. Rather than choosing the "least ethnic" and most bland ethnicities, Whites desire the "most ethnic" ones, like the once-stigmatized "Italian," because it is perceived as bringing the most psychic benefits. For instance, when an Italian father is married to an English or a Scottish or a German mother, the likelihood is that the child will be reported to the census with the father's Italian ancestry, rather than the northern European ancestries, which would have been predicted to have a higher social status. Italian is a good ancestry to have, people told me, because they have good food and a warm family life. This change in the social meaning of being Italian American is quite dramatic, given that Italians were subject to discrimination, exclusion, and extreme negative stereotyping in the early part of the twentieth century.

Race Relations and Symbolic Ethnicity

However much symbolic ethnicity is without cost for the individual, there is a cost associated with symbolic ethnicity for the society. That is because symbolic ethnicities of the type described here are confined to White Americans of European origin. Black Americans, Hispanic Americans, Asian Americans, and American Indians do not have the option of a symbolic ethnicity at present in the United States. For all of the ways in which ethnicity does not matter for White Americans, it does matter for non-Whites. Who your ancestors are does affect your choice of spouse, where you live, what job you have, who your friends are, and what your chances are for success in American society, if those ancestors happen not to be from Europe. The reality is that White ethnics have a lot more choice and room to maneuver than they themselves think they do. The situation is very different for members of racial minorities, whose lives are strongly influenced by their race or national origin regardless of how much they may choose not to identify themselves in terms of their ancestries.

When White Americans learn the stories of how their grandparents and great-grandparents triumphed in the United States over adversity, they are usually told in terms of their individual efforts and triumphs. The important role of labor unions and other organized political and economic actors in their social and economic successes are left out of the story in favor of a generational story of individual Americans rising up against communitarian, Old World intolerance and New World resistance. As a result, the "individualized" voluntary, cultural view of ethnicity for Whites is what is remembered.

One important implication of these identities is that they tend to be very individualistic. There is a tendency to view valuing diversity in a pluralist environment as equating all groups. The symbolic ethnic tends to think that all groups are equal; everyone has a background that is their right to celebrate and pass on to their children. This leads to the conclusion that all identities are equal and all identities in some sense are interchangeable— "I'm Italian American, you're Polish American. I'm Irish American, you're African American."

The important thing is to treat people as individuals and all equally. However, this assumption ignores the very big difference between an individualistic symbolic ethnic identity and a socially enforced and imposed racial identity.

My favorite example of how this type of thinking can lead to some severe misunderstandings between people of different backgrounds is from the *Dear Abby* advice column. A few years back a person wrote in who had asked an acquaintance of Asian background where his family was from. His acquaintance answered that this was a rude question and he would not reply. The bewildered White asked Abby why it was rude, since he thought it was a sign of respect to wonder where people were from, and he certainly would not mind anyone asking HIM about where his family was from. Abby asked her readers to write in to say whether it was rude to ask about a person's ethnic background. She reported that she got a large response, that most non-Whites thought it was a sign of disrespect, and Whites thought it was flattering:

Dear Abby,
I am 100 percent American and because I am of Asian ancestry I am often asked "What are you?" It's not the personal nature of this question that bothers me, it's the question itself. This query seems to question my very humanity. "What am I? Why I am a person like everyone else!"
Signed, A REAL AMERICAN

Dear Abby,
Why do people resent being asked what they are? The Irish are so proud of being Irish, they tell you before you even ask. Tip O'Neill has never tried to hide his Irish ancestry.
Signed, JIMMY

In this exchange, JIMMY cannot understand why Asians are not as happy to be asked about their ethnicity as he is, because he understands his ethnicity and theirs to be separate but equal. Everyone has to come from somewhere—his family from Ireland, another's family from Asia—each has a history and each should be proud of it. But the reason he cannot understand the perspective of the Asian American is that all ethnicities are not equal; all are not symbolic, costless, and voluntary. When White Americans equate their own symbolic ethnicities with the socially enforced identities of non-White Americans, they obscure the fact that the experiences of Whites and non-Whites have been qualitatively different in the United States and that the current identities of individuals partly reflect that unequal history. . . .

Institutional Responses

Our society asks a lot of young people [on college campuses]. We ask young people to do something that no one else does as successfully on such a wide scale—that is to live together with people from very different backgrounds, to respect one another, to appreciate one another, and to enjoy and learn from one another. The successes that occur every day in this endeavor are many, and they are too often overlooked. However, the problems and tensions are also real, and they will not vanish on their own. We tend to see pluralism working in the United States in much the same way some people expect capitalism to work. If you put together people with various interests and abilities and resources, the "invisible hand" of capitalism is supposed to make all the parts work together in an economy for the common good.

. . . There is a lot to be said for the idea that bringing people who belong to different ethnic or racial groups together in institutions with no interference will have good consequences. Students from different backgrounds will make friends if they share a dorm room or corridor, and there is no need for the institution to do any more than provide the locale. But like capitalism, the invisible hand of pluralism does not do well when power relations and externalities are ignored. When you bring together individuals from groups that are differently valued in the wider society and provide no guidance, there will be problems. In these cases the "invisible hand" of pluralist relations does not work, and tensions and disagreements can arise without any particular individual or group of individuals being "to blame." On college campuses . . . some of the tensions between students are of this sort. They arise from honest misunderstandings, lack of a common background, and very different experiences of what race and ethnicity mean to the individual.

The implications of symbolic ethnicities for thinking about race relations are subtle but consequential. If your understanding of your own ethnicity and its relationship to society and politics is one of individual choice, it becomes harder to understand the need for programs like affirmative action, which recognize the ongoing need for group struggle and group recognition, in order to bring about social change. It also is hard for a White college student to understand the need that minority students feel to band together against discrimination. It also is easy, on the individual level, to expect everyone else to be able to turn their ethnicity on and off at will, the way you are able to, without understanding that ongoing discrimination and societal attention to minority status makes that impossible for individuals from minority groups to do. The paradox of symbolic ethnicity is that it depends upon the ultimate goal of a pluralist society, and at the same time makes it more difficult to achieve that ultimate goal. It is dependent upon the concept that all ethnicities mean the same thing, that enjoying the traditions of one's heritage is an option available to a group or an individual, but that such a heritage should not have any social costs associated with it.

As the Asian Americans who wrote to *Dear Abby* make clear, there are many societal issues and involuntary ascriptions associated with non-White identities. The developments necessary for this to change are not individual but societal in nature. Social mobility and declining racial and ethnic sensitivity are closely associated. The legacy and the present reality of discrimination on the basis of race or ethnicity must be overcome before the ideal of the pluralist society, where all heritages are treated equally and are equally available for individuals to choose or discard at will, is realized.

REFERENCES

Alba, Richard D. 1985. *Italian Americans: Into the Twilight of Ethnicity.* Englewood Cliffs, NJ: Prentice-Hall.

———. 1990. *Ethnic Identity: The Transformation of White America.* New Haven, CT: Yale University Press.

Barth, Frederik. 1969. *Ethnic Groups and Boundaries.* Boston: Little, Brown.

Crispino, James. 1980. *The Assimilation of Ethnic Groups: The Italian Case.* Staten Island, NY: Center for Migration Studies.

Davis, Floyd James. 1991. *Who Is Black? One Nation's Definition.* University Park: Pennsylvania State University Press.

di Leonardo, Micaela. 1984. *The Varieties of Ethnic Experience: Kinship, Class and Gender among Italian Americans.* Ithaca, NY: Cornell University Press.

Dominguez, Virginia. 1986. *White by Definition: Social Classification in Creole Louisiana.* New Brunswick, NJ: Rutgers University Press.

Farley, Reynolds. 1991. "The New Census Question about Ancestry: What Did It Tell Us?" *Demography* 28:411–29.

Gans, Herbert. 1979. "Symbolic Ethnicity: The Future of Ethnic Groups and Cultures in America." *Ethnic and Racial Studies* 2:1–20.

Greeley, Andrew M. 1976. "The Ethnic Miracle." *Public Interest* 45 (Fall): 20–36.

Leonard, Karen. 1992. *Making Ethnic Choices: California's Punjabi Mexican Americans.* Philadelphia: Temple University Press.

Lieberson, Stanley. 1985. "Unhyphenated Whites in the United States." *Ethnic and Racial Studies* 8:159–80.

Lieberson, Stanley, and Mary Waters. 1986. "Ethnic Groups in Flux: The Changing Ethnic Responses of American Whites." *Annals of the American Academy of Political and Social Science* 487:79–91.

———. 1988. *From Many Strands: Ethnic and Racial Groups in Contemporary America.* New York: Russell Sage.

———. 1993. "The Ethnic Responses of Whites: What Causes Their Instability, Simplification, and Inconsistency?" *Social Forces* 72(2): 421–50.

McKenney, Nampeo R., and Arthur R. Cresce. 1992. "Measurement of Ethnicity in the United States: Experiences of the U.S. Census Bureau." Paper presented at the Joint Canada–United States Conference on the Measurement of Ethnicity, Ottawa, Canada, April 1–3.

Pagnini, Deanna L., and S. Philip Morgan. 1990. "Intermarriage and Social Distance among U.S. Immigrants at the Turn of the Century." *American Journal of Sociology* 96(2): 405–32.

Spickard, Paul R. 1989. *Mixed Blood.* Madison: University of Wisconsin Press.

Steinberg, Stephen. 1981. *The Ethnic Myth: Race, Ethnicity, and Class in America.* Boston: Beacon Press.

U.S. Bureau of the Census. 1992. *Census of Population and Housing, 1990: Detailed Ancestry Groups for States.* Supplementary Reports CP-S-1-2. Washington, DC: U.S. Government Printing Office.

Waters, Mary C. 1990. *Ethnic Options: Choosing Identities in America.* Berkeley and Los Angeles: University of California Press.

Weber, Max. 1921. *Economy and Society: An Outline of Interpretive Sociology,* edited by Guenther Roth and Claus Wittich, translated by Ephraim Fischoff. New York: Bedminster Press.

SIXTEEN

◆◆◆

In Search of Other "Others": Exploring Representations of Mixed Race Asian Pacific Americans (2012)

Patti Duncan

Patti Duncan is Associate Professor of Women's Studies at Oregon State University. She specializes in transnational feminist theories and movements, women of color studies, and Asian Pacific American women's writings. She is author of *Tell This Silence: Asian American Women Writers and the Politics of Speech* (2004) and co-produced/directed *Finding Face* (2009), a documentary about acid violence as a form of gendered violence in Cambodia.

"There is nothing I want from you, except for you to know that I exist."

—*Left By the Ship*

Growing up mixed race in America meant being interrogated on a regular basis about my racial and ethnic heritage: *"Where are you from?"* or *"What are you?"* When my childhood responses didn't satisfy, the questions became more aggressive: *"Well, how did your parents meet?"* *"What's your nationality?"* or *"Can I guess your background?"* Growing up mixed race meant enduring the constant scrutiny of the non-mixed, who never tried to hide their feelings of superiority, illustrated by comments like, *"It must be so hard to be mixed,"* or *"You must feel caught between two worlds,"* and other, more insidious remarks: *"Mixed race people are so exotic,"* or *"Mixed race people are so beautiful."* I learned to live with ambiguity as I was frequently subjected to such contradictory statements and assumptions.

Growing up mixed race meant feeling invisible, always having to justify my existence and my identity. It meant apologizing to one community or another, for never being *enough.* Sometimes it meant passing, or being passed over by those who needed to categorize or quantify my racial identity for their own comfort. It meant feeling different, other, *wrong.* At other times, I was accused of "selling out" one race or the other. Frequently, it was implied that I was not "Asian enough." When I was very young, my (Asian) mother was occasionally mistaken for my nanny. When people found out my (white) father had served in the U.S. military, stationed in South Korea, they sometimes asked if my mother had been a prostitute. Always, growing up mixed race meant constant assumptions about who I am, who my parents are, and what my experiences must be.

Today, mixed-race people are the fastest growing racial "group" according to the U.S. census, which only began to include the designation "two or more races" and allow individuals to self identify regarding race as recently as 2000. With mixed race sports figures like Tiger Woods, celebrities like Halle Berry and Keanu Reeves, and even President Obama, some might argue that being mixed race is becoming the norm in the United States. In 2011, more than 4.2 million young people identified themselves as multiracial.[1] However, because mixed race people were compelled to choose only one racial category in the past, and due to the "one drop rule" that defined individuals with "one drop of Black blood" as Black, there were actually many more multiracial people in this country than previously recorded.

Within the Asian Pacific American communities of my childhood, mixed race individuals were associated with Asian women who had children with U.S. soldiers during and after war or armed conflict. The U.S. military presence in South Korea, Vietnam, Okinawa (Japan), and the Philippines, for example, has produced the conditions that led to the birth of large numbers of mixed race children. For local populations, U.S. militarism has involved poverty, violence, and the creation of a sex economy characterized by unequal power relations, economic disparities, and language and cultural barriers between U.S. troops and local women. Also, these gendered, racialized, and sexualized encounters have resulted in the stigmatization of mixed race children, assumed to be associated with both prostitution and U.S. occupation of the homeland.

Born the daughter of a Korean immigrant woman and a U.S. serviceman, I grew up very aware of how my mother and I were perceived. I witnessed the discrimination she faced within U.S. society, but the disparagement from other Koreans was more painful and difficult to comprehend—the contemptuous looks, ridicule, avoidance, and rejection from various Korean community gatherings and organizations. As her mixed race daughter, I experienced it too, in the form of constant reminders that neither she nor I could ever be Korean enough to fully belong in the Korean community of my hometown.

But I grew up dreaming of Korea. I imagined it as the answer to all my questions and problems, the mysteries of growing up in a mixed race military household, where my mother's alienation and displacement was a constant theme of my childhood. As a child, I spoke only a smattering of Korean; I was encouraged to speak "English only" at school and in other public places. I ate *bulgogi* and *kimchi* in private with my mother, knowing that most of my U.S. friends would not appreciate her Korean cooking. I outgrew the *hanbok* (the Korean traditional dress) my mother brought for me from Korea, and I assimilated as much as I could into a typical (white) American adolescence. But I was constantly questioned about my race, a persistent reminder of my lack of belonging. I witnessed my mother's encounters with American racism and anti-Asian sentiments, and I saw other Koreans ignore her. I know she made friends with other women like herself who had married U.S. soldiers and had mixed race children in the United States. But when my mother talked about "home" she always meant Korea, and I, too, began to imagine Korea as my home and my birthright, the place where all my questions would find answers.

During the fall of 2004, I traveled to Korea for the first time. With a research sabbatical from my university and a courtesy appointment at a university in Seoul—and having run out of excuses—it was finally time to go. During my time there, I encountered a large community of Korean American activists attempting to make their lives in Korea, and trying to understand what it means to be Korean today. I researched the experiences of *kijich'on* women, working alongside the many U.S. bases that still flourish in South Korea.[2] I studied the language and tried to learn my way around the city. I learned about the oppression of mixed race people—"Amerasians"—in Korea.[3] I attempted to understand the complex and unequal relationship between Korea and the United States. And I slowly began to define and explore my own relationship to a country that had existed primarily in my imagination until this trip.

While my experience in Korea was overwhelmingly positive and I learned a great deal about my family and my own identity, I also learned some difficult truths. I learned that Amerasians are regarded as the dregs of Korean society, and that our mothers—often referred to as "war brides" or "military brides"—continue to be viewed in extremely negative ways.[4] Although not all Korean women who marry American men worked in prostitution, many Korean women have worked in the sex or service industry around U.S. bases. It is important to remember that this system is condoned and bolstered by both governments. The Status of Forces Agreement signed by South Korea and the United States in 1966 gave the U.S. military wide latitude in Korea, including the free use of land for military activities and the shared assumption that there would be areas for "rest and relaxation" alongside the bases.[5]

Due to poverty, the death of one or both parents during and after the Korean War, divorce, sexual abuse or rape (and subsequent rejection by one's family), human trafficking, and a host of other factors, it is estimated that over one million Korean women have worked in military prostitution since the end of the Korean War (1953).[6] According to Katharine Moon, "The fact that they have mingled flesh and blood with foreigners . . . in a society that has been racially and culturally homogeneous for thousands of years makes them pariahs, a disgrace to themselves and their people, Korean by birth but no longer Korean in body and spirit."[7] Even second-generation Korean Americans often ignore or look down upon them. Moon suggests another reason why these women have been rendered invisible and nearly written out of Korean and Korean American history: "Koreans have not wanted reminders of the war lurking around them and the insecurity that their newfound wealth and international power have been built on."[8] Women like my mother are living symbols of the devastation of the Korean War, the forced partition of the nation, and the subsequent dependence of South Korea on the United States. Korean women who married

Americans, and their children—mixed race people like me—signify the unequal neo-imperialist relationship between the U.S. and South Korea.

The film, *Camp Arirang* (Dir. Diana S. Lee and Grace Yoon-Kung Lee, 1995), a powerful documentary about military camptowns in South Korea, portrays Amerasian children who attend the True Love Mission, an alternative educational center run by Yon Ja Kim, who previously worked in military prostitution. When asked, "Which is better, Korea or America?" they respond in unison, "America! America!" These children are unable to attend public schools because of the discrimination against mixed race people in South Korea. Attempting to counter this, Ms. Kim decided to open the True Love Mission in her modest home. Here, the children learned English from student volunteers, spent the night when their mothers worked late at the clubs, and were taught that, although born and raised in South Korea, they belonged in the U.S. with their birth fathers, many of whom abandoned the children and their mothers. This portrayal of these mixed race children demonstrates the ways in which they are literally caught between two worlds—in effect, stateless within Korea and without access to the United States, which they are taught is superior.

U.S. militarization and its corollary, militarized prostitution, have a long history in the Asia Pacific region. As many as fifteen thousand mixed race children fathered by U.S. soldiers were left after the Vietnam War, where they have been subjected to discrimination and extreme hardship.[9] Similarly, in the Philippines most Amerasians experience poverty, severe harassment and intimidation from peers, and very few opportunities for education. Mixed race people in each of these settings are constant physical reminders of U.S. domination, whether through war or colonization. Also, they are gendered and sexualized in particular ways. Since, according to Fiona Ngo, Amerasians in Vietnam are presumed to be the product of a sexual encounter between an American man (read: serviceman) and a Vietnamese woman (read: prostitute), the "progeny of this illicit pairing bears the marks of the mother's supposed immorality, particularly if the child is a woman."[10] Mixed race girls and women are stigmatized and sexualized in accordance with Orientalist stereotypes that exoticize and fetishize Asia and people of Asian descent as part of a system and strategy of imperialist conquest. This is also true for mixed race boys and men. Furthermore, the conditions associated with the production of large mixed race communities are also racialized, gendered, and sexualized. Stereotypes and controlling images contribute to the sexual exploitation of Asian women by U.S. military forces.

The Beautiful Country (Dir. Hans Petter Moland, 2004) is a narrative feature film that relates the story of Binh, a young mixed race Vietnamese man born to a Vietnamese woman and an unknown (white) U.S. soldier. Referred to as *bui doi,* a term that literally translates to "less than dust," he is verbally abused on a regular basis, ridiculed and stigmatized for having "the face of the enemy." Forced to eat outside and perform the dirtiest work for his aunt's family, he finally leaves his home village for Ho Chi Minh City in search of his mother. He finds her working as a maid for a wealthy family, and living in poverty with his young half-brother, Tam, a child born due to rape by her employer's adult son. Binh fears that his presence brings her shame, but she claims that she is proud of him. Although Vietnamese Amerasian children of Binh's generation are presumed to be the children of prostitutes, she tells him that she was married to his father, and this becomes a point of pride for them both. Binh's mother persuades her employer to allow Binh to help her with the cleaning, and he is forced to witness the sexual harassment she endures on a regular basis. When an accident results in the death of her employer, Binh and his mother flee the scene, knowing that they will be blamed. She tells him that his father is living in Houston, Texas, and gives him all her money, urging him to go and find his father. She also asks him to take his younger brother with him. In the next poignant scene we see her sobbing as she loses another child. This scene highlights what has often remained invisible in the discourse about Amerasians—the grief experienced by mothers compelled to either give up their children or to witness their suffering.

Binh and Tam escape by sea, but their ship is diverted by a storm and they end up in a crowded refugee camp in Malaysia. The two brothers endure hard labor but find an unlikely friend in a young Chinese woman named Ling, who trades sexual favors for survival. She manages to earn enough money to buy passage for the three of them on a British ship bound for America, as "trafficked persons." On the ship, all three experience near-starvation, dehydration, abuse, and fear of what will happen to them. Their rations are taken by gamblers whose competition revolves around shouting out American brand names and sports teams, highlighting both the neoliberal capitalism underlying their passage as well as a desire for the "American dream" and the consumer culture that goes with it. Tragically, little Tam succumbs to illness, and Binh and Ling are forced to bury him at sea. This journey is all the more tragic when Binh later learns that, as a Vietnamese Amerasian, he could have flown to the United States for free, under the terms of the Amerasian Immigration Act.

Later, Binh and Ling find themselves in New York in low-wage jobs; Binh works as a dishwasher in a Chinese restaurant and Ling performs in a nightclub and continues to work in the sex industry. She eventually finds a U.S. businessman to support her, and Binh, alone, and still outraged over his brother's death, resolves to go to Houston in search of his father. What he finds—a man broken by the long-term consequences of war—helps Binh to understand why his father never came back to Vietnam. This film, while bolstering the stereotype of Amerasians as tragic, lost figures, also offers a critique of the social and political conditions underlying the experiences of mixed race Vietnamese people. It is never made explicit, for example, which country is "the beautiful country" of its title. Binh experiences poverty and discrimination in both Vietnam and the United States. However, the film also depicts scenes of grace and beauty in each setting—the love he shares with his mother in Ho Chi Minh City, and the scenic journey he makes in search of his father in Texas.

Daughter from Danang (Dir. Gail Dolgin and Vicente Franco, 2002) also revolves around mixed race Asian Pacific American experience, featuring Heidi Bub who lives in Pulaski, Tennessee. Born Mai Thi Hiep in Danang, Vietnam in 1968, Heidi/Hiep is the daughter of a Vietnamese woman and U.S. serviceman. At seven, she was sent to the U.S. through Operation Babylift, a 1975 government program authorized by President Gerald Ford, which resulted in the transfer of more than four thousand children to the U.S., Canada, Europe, and Australia for adoption. At least half of these children were believed to be Amerasian; their mothers reportedly gave them up for adoption because they feared for the children's safety in Vietnam. Hiep was adopted by Ann Neville, a single white mother, who renamed her Heidi, and forbade her from disclosing her Vietnamese heritage. Hiep became Heidi, and apparently assimilated successfully into white American culture. The film's narrative revolves around her decision to return to Vietnam to be reunited with her birth mother and siblings. The reunion, though deeply emotional, is also intensely problematic, as Hiep feels stifled by her birth mother's desire for close physical affection and she misunderstands her Vietnamese family's request for financial support. This request underscores her relative economic privilege, particularly when compared to other mixed race subjects such as Binh and the Amerasian children depicted in *Camp Arirang*. Her status as a mixed race American reveals both her sense of displacement and her elevated social and economic status.

Gregory Paul Choy and Catherine Ceniza Choy discuss this film in the context of a growing body of literature about international and transracial adoption. As they argue, the film's narrative "shifts away from discussions of the collective history of international adoption (a history greatly informed by U.S. military interests but popularly framed as humanitarian rescue) and instead foregrounds an *individual* West-meets-East story of culture clash, facilitated by Heidi Bub's 'ugly American' naivete."[11] The result, they suggest, obscures the long-term effects of war and militarism, focusing instead on Heidi's very individualized emotional breakdown. This representation, I would add, individualizes the sociopolitical context not only for transnational adoption but also for mixed race experience, as Heidi/Hiep's identity as a mixed race person is not adequately addressed in the film. The social, political, and economic systems that shaped Heidi's displacement and removal are peripheral to the film's narrative. There is a brief mention of her mother's presumed sexual transgression or victimization during the war, but the ways in which U.S. militarism structured—and continues to structure—Heidi's life as a mixed race transnationally adopted woman remain open questions within this representation.

Finally, a more recent portrayal of mixed race Asian Pacific American experience is found in *Left By the Ship* (Dir. Emma Rossi-Landi and Alberto Vendemmiati, 2010). This film follows four Filipino Amerasians over the course of two years as they search for information about their birth fathers and struggle to come to terms with their identities. Robert, an Amerasian journalist, narrates the film in the form of a letter to his unknown father. He seeks out others like him, explaining, "[t]hrough the accident of my birth, I'm inextricably linked to all these other lives." Later he states, "We are not so different from other Filipinos . . . but inside us is a secret burden, a weight we all share," of being Amerasian in the Philippines.

Two other subjects of the film—JR and Charlene—are, like Robert, the children of Filipina sex workers and U.S. servicemen stationed at the former Subic Bay Naval Base, which was the largest navy base outside the continental United States. Margarita, a thirteen-year-old girl, is a second-generation Amerasian, surviving on the streets with her mixed race father. The narratives included in *Left By the Ship* concern extreme poverty and stigma, bullying, and encounters with multiple systems of oppression. JR, for example, abandoned by his father and abused by his stepfather, has joined a gang and is incarcerated for a time before returning to his mother's home province. Robert helps him locate his birth father in the U.S., but after one brief phone conversation he never hears from his father again. Charlene, who was excluded from participation in school events because she is a Black Amerasian, decides to enter a beauty contest, "a chance to prove who I really am," she says. She is booed by a member of the audience, illustrating the discrimination she encounters on a regular basis. Later, before completing school, she becomes pregnant and decides to keep her baby. These narratives highlight the fact that Amerasian experience in the Philippines is inextricably linked to the sex industry, and to systematic and structural forms of gender and economic oppression. The subjects' mothers explain the social conditions that led to their entry into the sex industry, some of them as teenagers, and the rejection they faced from their own families for having Amerasian children.

Margarita, who collects bottles and picks through garbage on the street as a way to survive, states, "I am ugly." Homeless at thirteen, she has internalized Philippine society's attitudes toward Amerasians. Her perception of herself parallels Charlene's treatment in the beauty contest, as both young women encounter socially constructed standards of beauty that denigrate mixed race—particularly Black Amerasian—women. "There is no place to hide when you are an Amerasian," Robert narrates, suggesting a sense of extreme visibility in which mixed race subjects embody the consequences of the U.S. military occupation of the Philippines. An estimated 52,000 Amerasians live in the Philippines, and the film stresses this point at the end by including images of many more mixed race Filipinos, which provides a counterpoint to the negative forms of mixed race visibility. Instead, these subjects seem to demand their visibility—to be acknowledged and recognized. "There is nothing I want from you," states Robert, presumably to his unknown father, "except for you to know that I exist." His words go against the common expectation that Amerasians yearn for their fathers and for America. Rather, Robert implies, he simply desires that his father acknowledge his existence.

The film's conclusion resonates with a book of portraits created by Kip Fulbeck, *Part Asian, 100% Hapa*.[12] The Hawaiian term *hapa*, a slang word for mixed racial heritage with some Asian/Pacific Islander ancestry, has been claimed by mixed race Asian Pacific American activists and artists. It also signifies histories and cultures that include oppression, colonialism, war, and conflict. The book presents photographs of self-identified *hapas* of various ages and backgrounds. Each image is juxtaposed with a quotation from the subject, some providing context, some explaining racial and ethnic heritage, and others offering no explanation at all. The photographs are striking in that each subject looks directly into the camera, creating a sense of confrontation and even challenge. When I interviewed Fulbeck about this work, he discussed the importance of locating community among those of us who identify as *hapa*. Doing so, he suggested, can break down the isolation so many of us feel growing up mixed race. He also suggested that we do not necessarily have anything in common as mixed race Asian Pacific Americans. "What's interesting is ambiguity," he writes in his introduction to the book:

> What's interesting is the haziness, the blurrings, the undefinables, the space and tension between people, the area between the margins that pushes us to stop, to question. Hapas know the question inside out. *What are you?* And we know we can't answer it any

more than we can choose one body part over another. We love the question. We hate the question. And we know many times people aren't satisfied with our answers.[13]

Fulbeck's portraits contrast with the images of (primarily) tragic mixed race people in *Camp Arirang, The Beautiful Country, Daughter from Danang,* and *Left By the Ship*. By contextualizing and critiquing the common portrayals of mixed race subjects, I hope to intervene in a discourse that suggests our lives are always already tragic, yet somehow exotic, and to understand the social locales in which these representations are produced, as well as the social, political, and economic conditions that enable such constructions. I believe it is critical to interrogate the gendered racialization of these images and of mixed race Asian Pacific Americans in general, in order to explore the ways in which systems of oppression intersect and interact.

Now I have a son, and he's also mixed race. His father is white. I wonder how he will experience his racial identity. What does it mean to "look white" or "look Asian"? What are the politics of visibility and visuality for Asian Pacific Americans and other people of color, particularly those of us who are mixed race? As I consider my son's future, I take inspiration from Maria P. P. Root's "Bill of Rights for Racially Mixed People."[14] "I have the right," she asserts, "not to justify my existence in this world . . ."[15] This is what I hope for my son: that he will grow up with a sense of community and belonging, taking pride in all the parts of who he is, and that he will know that we are whole—just as we are—and that we never need to apologize for or justify our mixed race identities.

NOTES

1. U.S. Bureau of Census, 2012.
2. There is no compact word for *kijich'on* in English. It is often translated as "camptown," meaning the town or village that grew up around a U.S. military base—such as Camp Casey, Camp Humphreys, or Camp Stanley—starting in the 1950s after the Korean War. It is also a coded way of referring to the sex trade around these bases. Packed into this small word are pity, condemnation, disgust, stigma, taboo, fascination, and patriarchal distinctions between so-called "good" women and "bad" women.
3. "Amerasian," a term coined by Pearl S. Buck, refers to the biracial offspring of Asian women and American (usually military) men, is still widely used in Korea today.

4. According to Katharine H.S. Moon, these women are called highly derogatory names *yanggalbo* (western whore) and *yanggongju* (western princess). See *Sex Among Allies: Military Prostitution in U.S.-Korea Relations* (New York: Columbia University Press, 1997). Korean women who had liaisons with African American and Latino soldiers are viewed even more negatively than those who entered relationships with white soldiers. Subsequently, the children of such pairings are stigmatized even more than Amerasians with white fathers.

5. See Ji-Yeon Yuh, *Beyond the Shadow of Camptown: Korean Military Brides in American.* New York: New York University Press, 2002. See also Margo Okazawa-Rey, "Amerasian Children of GI Town: A Legacy of U.S. Militarism in South Korea," *Asian Journal of Women's Studies,* 3, no.1, 1997: 71–102.

6. Moon, 1, citing *The Women Outside,* a film directed by J.T. Takagi and Hye Hung Park, 1996 (aired on PBS, July 16, 1996).

7. Moon, p. 3.

8. Ibid. p. 8.

9. Linda Trinh Vo, "Managing Survival: Economic Realities for Vietnamese American Women," in *Asian/Pacific Islander American Women: A Historical Anthology,* ed. Shirley Hune and Gail M. Nomura (New York: New York University Press, 2003), 237–52.

10. Fiona I.B. Ngo, "A Chameleon's Fate: Transnational Mixed-Race Vietnamese Identities," *Amerasia Journal,* 31, no. 2 (2005): 57.

11. Gregory Paul Choy and Catherine Ceniza Choy, "What Lies Beneath: Reframing *Daughter from Danang.*" In *Outsiders Within: Writing on Transracial Adoption,* ed. Jane Jeong Trenka, Julia Chinyere Oparah, and Sun Yung Shin (Cambridge, MA: South End Press, 2006), p. 223.

12. Fulbeck, *Part Asian, 100% Hapa* (SF: Chronicle Books, 2006).

13. Fulbeck, p. 13.

14. "A Bill of Rights for Racially Mixed People," in *The Multiracial Experience: Racial Borders as the New Frontier,* ed. Maria P. P. Root (Thousand Oaks, CA: Sage Publications, 1996): 3–14.

15. Root, p. 7.

S E V E N T E E N

◆◆◆

Once Upon a Quinceañera (2007)—Excerpt
Coming of Age in the U.S.A.

Julia Alvarez

Born in New York City and raised in the Dominican Republic, **Julia Alvarez** has published essays, collections of poetry, books for children, and five books of fiction, including *How the García Girls Lost Their Accents.* Her work has earned numerous awards, including the 2009 F. Scott Fitzgerald Award for Excellence in American Literature. With her husband she founded Alta Gracia, a sustainable farm in the Dominican Republic that produces organic coffee and serves as a literacy center. She is a writer in residence at Middlebury College, Vermont.

You are dressed in a long, pale pink gown, not sleek and diva-ish, but princessy, with a puffy skirt of tulle and lace that makes you look like you're floating on air when you appear at the top of the stairs. Your court of fourteen couples has preceded you, and now they line up on the dance floor, forming a walkway through which you will pass to sit on a swing with garlanded ropes, cradling your last doll in your arms. Your mami will crown you with a tiara recessed in a cascade of curls the hairstylist spent most of the afternoon sculpting on your head. Then your papi will replace the flats you are wearing with a pair of silver heels and lead you out to the dance floor, where you will dance a waltz together.

No, you are not Miss America or a princess or an actress playing Cinderella in a Disney movie. In fact, you are not exceptionally beautiful or svelte and tall, model material. Your name is María or Xiomara or Maritza or Chantal, and your grandparents came from Mexico or Nicaragua or Cuba or the Dominican Republic. Your family is probably not rich; in fact, your mami and papi have been saving since you were a little girl or they've mortgaged the house or lined up forty godparents to help sponsor this celebration, as big as a wedding. If challenged about spending upward of five thousand dollars— the average budget—on a one-night celebration instead of investing in your college education or putting aside the money for their own mortgage payments, your parents will shake their heads knowingly because you do not understand: this happens only once.

What is going on?

You are having your quinceañera . . .

A "quinceañera" (the term is used interchangeably for the girl and her party) celebrates a girl's passage into womanhood with an elaborate, ritualized fiesta on her fifteenth birthday. (Quince años, thus quinceañera, pronounced: *keen-seah-gneer-ah.*) In the old countries, this was a marker birthday: after she turned fifteen, a girl could attend adult parties; she was allowed to tweeze her eyebrows, use makeup, shave her legs, wear jewelry and heels. In short, she was ready for marriage. . . . Even humble families marked a girl's fifteenth birthday as special, perhaps with a cake, certainly with a gathering of family and friends at which the quinceañera could now socialize and dance with young men. Upper-class families, of course, threw more elaborate parties at which girls dressed up in long, formal gowns and danced waltzes with their fathers.

Somewhere along the way these fancier parties became highly ritualized. In one or another of our Latin American countries, the quinceañera was crowned with a tiara; her flat shoes were changed by her father to heels; she was accompanied by a court of fourteen damas escorted by fourteen chambelanes, who represented her first fourteen years; she received a last doll, marking both the end of childhood and her symbolic readiness to bear her own child. And because our countries were at least nominally Catholic, the actual party was often preceded by a Mass or a blessing in church or, at the very least, a priest was invited to give spiritual heft to the fiesta. These celebrations were covered in the newspapers, lavish spreads of photos I remember poring over as a little girl in the Dominican Republic, reassured by this proof that the desire to be a princess did not have to be shed at the beginning of adulthood, but could in fact be played out happily to the tune of hundreds upon thousands of Papi's pesos.

In the late sixties, when many of our poor headed to el Norte's land of opportunity, they brought this tradition along, and with growing economic power, the no-longer-so-poor could emulate the rich back home. The spin-offs grew (quinceañera cruises, quinceañera resort packages, quinceañera videos and photo shoots); . . . further elaborations were added (Disney themes, special entrances, staged dance routines à la Broadway musicals); and in our Pan-Hispanic mixing stateside, the U.S. quinceañera adopted all the little touches of specific countries to become a much more elaborate (and expensive) ceremony, exported back to our home countries. But rock-bottom, the U.S. quinceañera is powered by that age-old immigrant dream of giving the children what their parents had never been able to afford back where they came from.

In fact, . . . many of us older, first-generation Latinas never had a quinceañera. There was no money back when we were fifteen, or we had recently arrived in the United States and didn't want anything that would make us stand out as other than all-American. Or we looked down our noses at such girly-girl fuss and said we didn't want a quince because we didn't understand that this was not just about us.

These cultural celebrations are also about building community in a new land. Lifted out of the context of our home cultures, traditions like the quinceañera become malleable; they mix with the traditions of other cultures that we encounter here; they become exquisite performances of our ethnicities within the larger host culture while at the same time reaffirming that we are not "them" by connecting us if only in spirit to our root cultures. In other words, this tradition tells a larger story of our transformation into Latinos, a Pan-Hispanic group made in the USA, now being touted as the "new Americans."

It's that story which intrigues me. Why, when I was invited by an editor to write a book about quinceañeras, I welcomed the opportunity to follow the tradition wherever it might lead me. . . .

. . . I traveled to various Latino communities in the United States: Dominican-Americans in Lawrence, Massachusetts, and Queens, New York; Cuban Americans in Miami; Mexican Americans in San Antonio and Los Angeles. . . .

I also spoke with dozens of girls and their families and members of their courts, with events providers and photographers, with parish priests and youth ministers and choreographers. I talked to Latinas my age and older, Latinas in academia and in businesses catering to the quinceañera market, who observed that the quinceañera has become an even bigger deal stateside than it had ever been back home.

With that elaboration and expense, a certain entitlement has set in. Many of the Latina girls I interviewed who responded in writing often termed

Concluslo—

the celebration "my right of passage." Given that spell-check would not have picked up this transposition, this was an understandable orthographical mistake, but it also seemed an apt description of what happens to traditions in the United States. Rites become rights. New generations feel entitled to what older first generations struggled to obtain for them.

By the same token, this entitlement ethic does not seem to shield our young Latina population from failure. As I read the research, I was alarmed by how our teen Latinas are topping the charts for all sorts of at-risk behaviors: from teen pregnancy to substance abuse to dropping out of high school. What is going on? We are crowning them princesses, and meanwhile the statistics are showing a large number of our young girls headed for poverty and failure! Are these the same girls, I wonder?

So, what began as the study of a tradition became a journey of exploration rife with questions and misgivings. I admit that the disjunction between this grand Latina debut and the reality of their lives, the enormous cost of the celebration to struggling families, made me initially skeptical about the tradition. And yet, time and time again as I attended these celebrations I felt deeply moved by something at the heart of the tradition, a desire to empower our young women, a need to ritually mark their passage into adulthood, remind them of their community and its past, and by doing so give them and ourselves hope. Who could argue with that?

. . . Our exported tradiciones mix and combine with those of other Latin American and Caribbean countries stateside and become more elaborate, more expensive, more traditional than they ever were back home.

In fact, to have a full-blown traditional quinceañera in our Pan-Hispanic United States is to have adopted every other Latino group's little traditions and then some. So that now, Cuban quinceañeras in Miami are hiring Mexican mariachis to sing the traditional "Las Mañanitas." The full court of fourteen damas and chambelanes, "each couple representing a year of the quinceañera's life," a mostly Mexican practice, is now a traditional must. As is the changing of the shoes to heels, which seems to originally have been a Puerto Rican embellishment. From the Puerto Ricans as well, though some say from the Mexicans, came the tradition of la última muñeca, a "last doll" dressed exactly like the quinceañera, which the girl cradles to symbolize the "end of her childhood" or "the child that she herself will be having in the not-too-distant future" (both explanations given to me by different events planners). The quinceañera might keep this last doll as a keepsake or give it away to a younger member of the family. In one celebration, perhaps inspired by the wedding bouquet, the quinceañera threw her last doll over her shoulder to be caught by a screaming group of little girls, anticipating their own future quinceañeras.

This symbol of bygone childhood is also mirrored in a Central American or Puerto Rican custom (I've heard both) of having a very little girl dress up in a minuscule version of the quinceañera's dress and be "the symbol of innocence." Sometimes she is accompanied by a little escort, though the tradition has now been further elaborated so that "the symbol of innocence" as well as a little prince and princess (slightly older) are part of a full traditional court.

There is also always some sort of photo session to commemorate the event . . . there are whole albums of the young lady in different outfits, in different locations, a practice that seems to have started with the Cuban community in Miami, where girls sometimes just have the photo shoot and forego the party. Many girls also have videos made, recounting their lives since birth, with still shots and footage of themselves at different ages and credits rolling as if this were a real movie with the quinceañera playing the lead and her parents starring as "padre" and "madre" and Julio Iglesias's "De Niña a Mujer" as the score, of course. . . .

The tradition of crowning the young girl is often ascribed to the Mexicans, who seem to be the group that has most ritualized the ceremony. But here in America, every quinceañera gets her tiara. The bouquet the quinceañera carries to put at the Virgin Mary's statue at the Mass is also part of the Mexican and Central American tradition, as is the Mass, which our more hedonistic Caribbean party-cultures dispensed with back home. But now the Mass and the Virgin's bouquet have become part of our Dominican and Puerto Rican and Cuban "tradition" in the United States. . . .

"Today, it's all about supersizing," Nina Diaz, the executive producer of *My Super Sweet 16*, told *U.S. News & World Report*. (The price tag for a recent quince party featured in one of the episodes was $180,000.) One quince site I happened upon in cruising the Web for Q-lore—just Google "quinceañera" and you will get 8,230,000 hits (if you put the tilde over the "n") or 4,220,000 hits (if you dispense with the tilde)—urged providers to register with their site. "The Hispanic population's buying power is expected to reach $300 billion by 2006. Timing is prime to begin your Sweet 16 and Quinceanera advertising campaign. The demand for more vendors that cater to Latinos is of epic proportions." . . .

At Disneyland, Denny Nicholas, manager of corporate and wedding sales, says he has seen anything from a modest $5,000 to $50,000 for a quinceañera, the average nowadays being about $12,000 to $15,000. When I ask Denny if he doesn't find this *average* shocking given that the poverty threshold for a family of three is $15,277, he laughs. "By the time families come to me, they've already made the decision that this is what they want. All I do is provide the elements they need to make their dreams come to life." . . .

Trying to track down the origins of the quinceañera tradition is a little like playing that old party game, telephone. A whispers some news in B's ear, B then recounts the news to C, all the way around the circle. By the time the news has come back to A, and is pronounced out loud, it has morphed into a skewed version of whatever it was that A claims to have originally said.

Many books, articles, and Web sites state that the roots of the quinceañera tradition lie in an ancient Aztec rite. Sometimes the origin is given as Mayan as well as Aztec, and sometimes more generally described as "indigenous." I don't know if it's because the phrase "an ancient Aztec tradition" has a phony ring to it—an alliterative angling for authenticity in ancientness. But when I repeatedly read this claim in too many articles, I begin to search the bibliographies (in the few cases where one is provided) to see what I can find.

Most folks quote as their source Michele Salcedo's *Quinceañera!*, an informative, well-written guide, the best in its genre. Through a series of e-mails, I finally track down Michele Salcedo at the *South Florida Sun-Sentinel,* where she is assistant city editor. She tells me how about a decade ago, she took a year off from her reporting job to study the quinceañera tradition and write a planner-slash-background book. She is gracious and generous with her time but understandably cannot cite chapter and verse for the

source of a detail in a book she wrote more than fifteen years ago. She does recall getting some of her material on origins from "a nun's book." This has to be one of Sister Angela's many manuals where I, too, have read about this ancient Aztec and Mayan tradition.

And so I e-mail Sister Angela trying not to sound like the doubting Thomas I am, and she sends me to some books—Sylvanus Morley's *The Ancient Maya* and Victor Von Hagen's *Los Aztecas: Hombre y Tribu.* I end up inside the compendious *Florentine Codex,* which was assembled back in the 1560s by a Spanish priest, Fray Bernardino de Sahagún, from testimonies given forty years earlier to a mission of Franciscan monks by twelve high priests of the Aztec empire about their traditions. (Think again of the telephone game: a conquered nation as understood by Catholic priests interviewed four decades later by another Franciscan.) Whatever "facts" we know about the Aztecs are several critical removes from a true and living practice.

But Sister Angela is absolutely right that our indigenous American ancestors did indeed acknowledge the passage of young girls into womanhood. What is uncertain is the age at which the ritual took place. We do know that the Aztec maiden was ready for marriage at the age of fifteen. Presumably at an earlier juncture there was a ceremony of some sort. The *Codex* cites long ceremonial speeches in which fathers and mothers publicly admonished their daughters, probably as part of some ritual. The speeches themselves are quite moving to read. The tenderness is palpable. The father describes his daughter's coming-of-age in heart-tugging words:

> It is as if thou wert an herb, a plant which hath propagated, sprouted, blossomed. It is also as if thou hadst been asleep and hadst awakened.

Meanwhile, the mother warns "my dove, my little one, my child, my daughter" that life is dangerous and she must be careful. (So my own mami's dire warnings were not so off the mark. It seems a traditional task of mothers to terrify their daughters into good behavior.) "Behold the road thou art to follow," the mother advises:

> On earth we live, we travel along a mountain peak. Over here there is an abyss, over there is an abyss. If thou goest over here, or if thou

goest over there, thou wilt fall in. Only in the middle doth one go, doth one live. Place this word, my daughter, dove, little one, well within the chambers of thy heart. Guard it well.

This is a far cry from Mami crowning her daughter with a rhinestone tiara or Papi dancing with her as Julio Iglesias sings "De Niña a Mujer." But in both cases there is a transmission going on, an acknowledgment that womanhood is upon her and a life of perils and possibilities is about to begin.

Mayans, too, celebrated the onset of puberty with an elaborate ceremony. Again, the age given by sources varies. Part of the female ceremony involved the mother cutting off a red shell that had been tied around her daughter's waist as a child. Presumably the girl was now considered ripe for marriage and childbearing. We can, of course, stretch the comparison and find in the cutting off of the red shell of virginity a parallel to the casting off of the last doll of childhood. But why belabor the point? Down through the generations the human family has celebrated passages in our mortal lives with rites that use the symbols and signs of our moment in time. We don't have to prove the legitimacy of these rites. They are what they are, part of our human legacy.

This push to legitimize the quinceañera by connecting it with an indigenous past is a fairly recent thing. Back in our home countries in the fifties, elite families would have blanched at any suggestion that their presentation parties had any connection at all to an "Indian" rite. "Indigenous heritage was played down in favor of European and North American culture," writes Valentina Napolitano in *Migration, Mujercitas, and Medicine Men.* Instead, "the fifteenth-birthday celebration used the symbology of European culture (for example, waltzes, performances of classical music, maids of honor, and pages)." It was only with the democratizing of the tradition stateside that the supposed Aztec connection began to be talked about. The desire for native credentials demonstrates both a yearning to reconnect with something forever lost as well as what Renato Rosaldo calls in *Culture & Truth* "imperialist nostalgia," a nostalgia for a culture you have dominated, a people you have destroyed.

More traceable are the courtly elements of the quinceañera tradition. "The first elaborate quinceañeras were balls staged by families of means who liked to pride themselves on their Spanish ancestry and manners," writes Maricel Presilla in an article in the *Miami Herald.* Michele Salcedo cites that its origin might have come from a practice of the Duchess of Alba in eighteenth-century Spain in which she would "invite girls on the cusp of womanhood to the palace, where she would dress them and make them up as adults for the first time." The Empress Carlotta of Mexico, a century later, also "invited the daughters of members of her court to be presented as young ladies eligible for marriage." Interestingly, though its origin might have been these courtly presentations, the quinceañera is unknown in Spain . . . the quinceañera has changed from a celebration for daughters of the elite to a fiesta for all classes. "When I was your age, only rich girls had quinceañeras," Estrella's mother tells her in *Estrella's Quinceañera,* one of the young adult novels . . . that centers on this tradition.

Most historians trace this shift to the 1960s and the beginning of vast migrations to el Norte's land of opportunity; the tradition soon became an option for middle and lower classes, both here in the USA and back home. Cross-fertilization knows no borders, and influences travel without visa or green card. In fact, even in present-day Cuba, the quinceañera is seeing a revival, as Cuban girls dream of parties like their Cuban-American cousins enjoy in Miami. Many stateside families send their old quinceañera gowns and tiaras along with dollars and medicines to their needy relatives.

Certainly the quinceañera found welcome soil in the American consumer culture, where businesses stood to gain from the expensive elaborations of the ceremony. In fact, when the Los Angeles archdiocese issued guidelines back in January 1990 to try to curtail the growing commercialization and expense of quinceañeras, the outcry came not from the parishioners but from Grupo Latino Por Nuestras Tradiciones, which despite its name was made up of many small-business owners. The group's president, Luis Yanez, declared that "for the church, quinceañeras are not important, but for us they are one of the few traditions we have left," and in the same breath he complained that his shop, which supplies everything from the dresses to the headpieces and artificial bouquets and monogrammed cups, had seen a drastic decline from fifty quinceañeras to five since the guidelines were issued.

And so, while the quinceañera is touted as a marker of ethnicity, it is in many ways an ethnicity with a label that reads MADE IN THE USA (or "Remade in the USA," if you will). Even as the younger generations assimilate in every other way to a mainstream culture, they are holding on to this old-country tradition, which is actually being created here. Odd. Or is it?

In fact, this creation of a past that never was turns out to be a common enough social phenomenon. In his book *The Invention of Tradition*, Eric Hobsbawm coins the term "invented traditions" to describe both traditions actually invented from whole cloth (Kwanzaa, the Bat Mitzvah, just to mention a couple) as well as traditions that "emerge in a less easily traceable manner within a brief and datable period, establishing themselves with great rapidity." These invented traditions are likely to appear when a group is undergoing transformation, and they serve as a way to legitimize and galvanize its members by establishing continuity with a past that may be largely fictitious.

This is not to dismiss them as bogus, Hobsbawm is quick to point out. Instead, they are interesting hot spots in a group's evolution where adaptation and self-creation and legitimization are in progress, as well as moving testimonies toward cohesion just as the winds of dispersal are blowing us hither and yon. . . .

And so, it makes perfect sense for Mr. Ramos to want his daughter to hold on to her roots by doing something that comes to him from a past that never was—at least not for his working-class family prior to 1960. As his daughters grow up in the USA, speaking spotty Spanish and celebrating their quinces at sixteen, this is the one thing he can give them that might remind them of who they are. *One of the few traditions we have left.* A last Latin spin with his little girl because who knows where she'll end up?

"It used to be that you could give your daughter a wedding. But you don't know anymore if she's going to get married or if she's going to live with her boyfriend first like they do here, or if she's going to get divorced and get remarried several times," Mr. Ramos explained to me, a sentiment echoed by many parents. . . .

Twenty-five-year-old Maurice Mompoint, . . . based in Miami, represents a younger generation of quinceañera business entrepreneurs. His Web site, yourquinces.com, is allied with his mother's Happy Holidays Travel Agency, which does a large volume of the crucero business.

. . . "I give it ten years," he says cryptically, and for a moment I think he's talking about how long he can last at his job. But he says that in ten years, quinces will be a thing of the past. "The next generation growing up, their parents will all have been born and raised here. A lot of them won't even speak Spanish that well. There isn't going to be that grandparent or parent from the old country pushing for the quinceañera." Is he worried about this? Not really. "In ten years, a lot of these girls are going to be getting married. I've been building my database, and with a couple of switches, I can turn yourquinces.com into a wedding site."

I wondered about Maurice's prognosis. Are quinceañeras on a culturally endangered list? Higinio Muñoz, who is part of the Muñoz dynasty of photographers that for three generations has been snapping quinces in Cuba and now in south Florida, does not think so at all. "For the last forty years of this business, you think, oh, the tradition is going to end with the next generation, but I've now got second- and third-generation girls, and the tradition is not waning. In fact, it's growing. I have Haitian quinceañeras and African American quinceañeras and American girls wanting quinceañeras." He has a point. At www.quinceañera.us.com, where you can register your quinceañera, there are mothers registering little girls who will be turning fifteen in 2015!

But history would seem to be on Maurice's side. After all, generations of immigrants have trod the assimilation path in America, shedding most of their ethnic past, with maybe only a parade left to commemorate those roots, a green cardigan on St. Patrick's Day, a polka night at the Polish-American club. . . .

On the other hand, America is now seeing a new kind of immigrant whose ties to a homeland are never completely severed. In his rousing and passionate book *Living in Spanglish: The Search for Latino Identity in America,* Ed Morales explains that the old idea of "Americanization" involved the loss of contact with people from the old country. "But the continuing migration of Latinos to the north has the effect of reinforcing the Latin culture that we would otherwise have lost."

And the travel is not just north but back and forth. In fact, the whole concept of nation-states with set borders you cross and leave behind is not the way the world really works anymore, according to Michael Dear, head of the Geography Department at the University of Southern California. In "Postborder Cities/Postborder World?" he notes how people, money, communication, and culture are all moving in new currents and combinations. Globalization is creating a new kind of mobile and mutating world citizenry. . . .

Quinces definitely have the potential of introducing a new story into the imagination of the next generation, one that might indeed help them live happier, more productive lives.

Why else would companies like Maggi and Kern's Nectar choose the quinceañera as the target tradition at which to aim their public relations campaigns? They know a powerful cultural icon when they see one.

But others are drawn to the tradition not as an advertising tool but as an opportunity to truly empower young people to believe that their dreams for their lives can come true.

Enter the fairy godmothers.

Isabella Martínez Wall . . . dispensing advice from her Web site, bellaquinceanera.com, and committed to making each girl feel like the queen of her life; Priscilla Mora, organizing expos to educate Latinas on financially responsible and culturally meaningful quinceañeras; Sister Angela, using the tradition as a teachable moment for Catholic youth, boys and girls, Latino or not. A fourth fairy godmother, Ana Maria Schachtell, founded the Stay-in-School Quinceañera Program, which could well become a model for such programs elsewhere. In Idaho, of all places. . . .

. . . "We start in January, twice a week, one school night and then one Saturday, thirty to forty fourteen-year-old girls and boys," Ana Maria explains. "We have them until the end of school in June. Most of them have just started high school or are going to start in the fall." She figures she has a small window in which to make a difference about how their lives are going to go. "Most of these kids come from poor migrant families. Their parents haven't had much education. They need to hear it can be done. So, we bring in teachers from the high school to talk about what to expect there. We bring in community leaders to encourage them to think about their future and make them proud of their past, their roots, their traditions. Judge Gutierrez, our only Hispanic judge in Idaho, has come to talk to them, and this last year we brought in Loretta Sanchez!" This is obviously a big fish, and I'm embarrassed not to know who she is. Later I Google her and find out she is a congresswoman from California. . . .

According to Ana Maria, the kids have a lot of fun—"or they wouldn't keep coming back, week after week." Much of that fun comes from doing things that affirm their sense of pride in their culture. "They learn old cerámica techniques. We brought in an eighty-nine-year-old woman to teach the girls how to make their traditional coronas out of wax flowers, a Mexican handiwork that is being lost because of the cheap plastic crowns around. And for the boys, we bring in a charro, that's the original American cowboy. A lot of people don't know that. The charro tradition represents the best of machismo, how to be a real hombre, responsible to your familia and community. The boys eat it up."

I bet they do. How could they not, with Ana Maria cheering them on? The whole program culminates in a gala night, a fundraiser for the Hispanic Cultural Center. The center has a stock of thirty gowns for the girls, and it rents tuxedos for the boys. The governor comes, the senators, the mayor. (The Hispanic population of the state is growing at four times the rate of the non-Hispanic population. No doubt, these elected officials have done the numbers.)

What is inspiring about Ana Maria's program, which is now in its eighth year, is that it takes the tradition of the quinceañera, acknowledging its power as a coming-of-age ceremony, but recasts it with new content, including a strong emphasis on education. What does it mean to be a man, un hombre, un charro, in this new country? What does it mean to be una mujer who knows her tradiciones, can make the old-country wax flowers for a corona but can also run for Congress? In other words, the Stay-in-School program takes the occasion of the quinceañera to revise the limited narrative the rite has traditionally endorsed. . . .

But the fact that these old restrictive narratives about womanhood persist in our young Latina girls speaks to the need for retooling. And the quinceañera tradition—as a number of fairy godmothers have discovered—can provide that amazing learning opportunity. . . .

◆◆◆

EIGHTEEN

Decolonizing Culture
Beyond Orientalist and Anti-Orientalist Feminisms (2010)

Nadine Naber

Nadine Naber is associate professor of American Culture and Women's Studies at the University of Michigan. Her scholarly articles focus on family, gender, and sexuality among Arab Americans in the context of homeland wars. Her books include *Articulating Arabness: Gender and Cultural Identity in the Diaspora*, and *Arab and Arab American Feminisms* (co-editor). She is cofounder of the Arab Women's Solidarity Association, North America (cyber AWSA); the Arab Movement of Women Arising for Justice (AMWAJ), the Arab Women's Activist Network (AWAN), and involved in INCITE! Women of Color against Violence.

I was born in San Francisco, three years after my parents arrived from Al Salt, Jordan. Over the next twenty years, my parents moved a dozen times across the Bay Area, creating for me a childhood and a sense of community that was both rigidly structured and ever changing. Throughout my childhood, "culture" was a tool, an abstract, ephemeral notion of what we do and what we believe, of who belongs and who does not. Culture was the way that my parents exercised their control over me and my siblings. The same fight, I knew from my aggrieved conversations with friends and relatives, was playing out in the homes of countless other Arab families. The typical generational war— about whether we teenagers could stay out late at night, or whether we could spend the night at our friends' slumber parties—was amplified into a grand cultural struggle. The banalities of adolescent rebellion became a battle between two stereotypes, between rigid versions of "Arab" and "American" values. To discipline us, our parents' generation invoked the royal "we," as in: "No, you can't go to the school dance because we don't do that." Here, "we" meant "Arabs."

I hated these words. I hated these declarations of what "we" did and didn't do. Yet, they worked. Sort of. Sometimes, I actually listened. Or, more

often as time went on, I simply tried to hide these parts of my life from my parents. Because even worse than disobeying my parents was the threat— always tangible in my house and in our community centers—that I might be disobeying *my people*— a term that signified anyone from the Naber family, to everyone in Jordan, to all Arab Christians, to *al Arab*. Transgressing my parents' rules was not merely adolescent rebellion, but was a form of cultural loss, of cultural betrayal. And even worse, each moment of transgression meant the loss of Arab culture to *al Amerikan*, that awesome and awful world that encompassed everything from the American people to the American government to the American way of life (at least as my parents seemed to imagine it).

Our Arab community, like so many immigrant networks, was wildly diverse, comprising Muslim and Christian, Jordanian, Lebanese, Palestinian, and Syrian families. Yet we all seemed to have a remarkably similar idea of what "American" and "Arab" meant. We seemed to share a tacit knowledge that *al Amerika* was the trash culture, degenerate, morally bankrupt, and sexually depraved. In contrast, *al Arab* (Arabs) were morally respectable—we valued marriage, family, and close relationships. It was not only our parents who put this pressure on us. What we learned at school and from the U.S. media reinforced this dichotomy.

As with all products of human belief, there were caveats, and shades of gray, and matters of proportion. Our immigrant parents' generation disproportionately pressured girls to uphold idealized demands of Arab culture. Girls' behavior seemed to symbolize the respectability of our fathers and our families, as well as no less than the continuation of Arab culture in America. Particularly as my girlfriends, cousins, and I hit puberty, the pressure seemed to intensify. I couldn't wear my trendy jeans with the tear down the side for fear that my relatives and parents' friends would curse my sloppy clothes and my bare skin. By the time my friends and I graduated from college, young women's bodies and behaviors seemed to be the key signifiers in the stereotyped distinction between Arabs and Americans.

Compounding matters, our parents raised us in predominantly white suburbs and encouraged us—in certain ways—to assimilate. They encouraged us to befriend the "American kids" and dress up for colonial days at school. And many of us watched our fathers change their names from Yacoub, Mohammed, and Bishara to Jack, Mo, and Bob when they arrived at their grocery and convenience stores as the sun rose. It was only later that I came to understand that many men of my parents' generation changed their names after being called "dirty Arab" or "Palestinian terrorist," or after customers refused to shop at their stores.

Despite this, and despite the fact that our parents were encouraging us to adopt the values of middle-class America, the fundamental message in our family and community remained: *we* were Arab and *they* were American. It felt like we were living between two worlds, one within the confines of our modest suburban homes and the Arabic church, the other at the mall and in the unfettered streets of San Francisco. With each passing year, it seemed more and more impossible to live in such a bifurcated way. I fought with my parents all the time, and because I started to doubt which "side" of me was really me, the demands from both sides just made me want to rebel against everything.[1]

Even as I yelled at them, I knew that my parents wanted only the best for me. Because of my adolescent myopia, I had only the faintest sense of the difficulties of their lives and the concurrent struggle of their immigrant generation to simultaneously foster cultural continuity and be Arab in America. Just like I was with my ripped jeans, they too were trying to articulate who they were. It would be years before I grasped how each day they confronted not only the pressures of assimilation but also the realities of an expanding U.S. imperialist war in the Arab region and intensifying anti-Arab Orientalist and racist discourses in their new home.

More than thirty years ago, Edward Said argued that "Orientalism" is a European fabrication of "the East," that "the Orient" is shaped by European imperialist attitudes and assumes that Eastern or Oriental people can be defined in terms of cultural or religious essences that are invulnerable to historical change. Orientalism, he explained, configures the "East" in irreducible attributes such as religiosity or femininity. This political vision, he contended, has promoted the idea of insurmountable differences between the familiar (Europe, West, "us") and the strange (the Orient, the East, "them"). Like Said, critics of Orientalism have long argued that essentialist representations of Islam are crucial to Orientalist thought. In Orientalist thought, Muslims, Arabs, and other "Orientals" are hopelessly mired in a host of social ills, the cause of which is an unchanging tradition that exists outside of history and is incompatible with civilization.[2] Feminist scholars such as Rabab Abdulhadi have in turn argued that this strand of Orientalist thought has constructed our contemporary visions of Arab and Muslim societies as either completely decadent, immoral, and permissive or strict and oppressive to women.[3] This new Orientalism relies on representations of culture (Arab) and religion (Islam) as a justification for post-cold war imperial expansion in the Middle East and the targeting of people perceived to fit the racial profile of a potential terrorist living in the United States—Arabs, Middle Easterners, Muslims.[4] New Orientalist discourses have birthed a variety of widely accepted ideas: of Arab and Muslim queers oppressed by a homophobic culture and religion, of hyperoppressed shrouded Arab and Muslim women who need to be saved by American heroes, of a culture of Arab Muslim sexual savagery that needs to be disciplined—and in the process, modernized—through U.S. military violence.[5]

The impact of Orientalism, I began to see, was everywhere. Our Arab community had a plethora of cultural and political organizations to put on music concerts, festivals, and banquets and a range of political organizations that focused on civil rights issues and homeland politics. Yet there were no resources for dealing with the difficult issues within our families. As in many immigrant families, ours opted to avoid bringing attention to personal matters, particularly in public space and particularly among other Arabs. Throughout high school especially, many of my Arab American peers were devastated by the conflicting feelings of love, pain, and guilt toward our parents and the ideas about Arab culture that we learned from our parents and U.S. society. We joked about fleeing our community altogether. We swore to each other that we would never marry an Arab. It was clear that these problems were pushing Arabs away from each other. In addition, on my trips to Jordan to visit relatives, I learned that many of my neighbors in the Bay Area had more socially conservative understandings of religion, family, gender, and sexuality than their counterparts in Jordan. I was baffled: why were the stakes of family respectability so high in America?

Articulating Arabness

After I survived the dual gauntlet of high school and my parents' expectations, and after I moved out of their home, I began listening more carefully to the stories of our immigrant parents. I began asking why they came to the United States, what they experienced when they arrived, and what they dreamed of and worked for in America. Not surprisingly, our parents' commitments to cultural continuity were much more complicated than what I had understood them to be. As the twentieth century became the twenty-first, I spent several years researching these cultural ideas and exploring how they operated as a major site of struggle for middle-class second-generation Arab Americans then growing up in the San Francisco Bay Area. I worked with community-based organizations and did ethnographic research with eighty-six men and women, ages eighteen to twenty-eight, whose families had immigrated to the United States, primarily from Jordan, Lebanon, Palestine, and Syria. I interviewed fifteen immigrants from their parents' generation, immigrants who came to the Bay Area between the 1950s and 1970s, an era characterized by increased Arab migration to the United States, the expansion of American empire in the Arab region, and the intensification of racism and xenophobia in California.[6]

. . .

For several years, as I conducted in-depth interviews with teens and twentysomethings, we shared stories about the norms and expectations of our immigrant communities. Orientalism was at the heart of this struggle. The dominant middle-class Arab immigrants' articulation of Arabness through rigid, binary categories (good Arab girls versus bad American girls, for example) was based on a similar framework that guided Orientalist discourses

about Arabs. My parents and their peers simply reversed Orientalism and used its binary categories (liberated Americans versus oppressed Arab women, bad Arabs versus good Americans) differently and for different purposes. Articulating immigrant cultural identity through rigid binaries is not an unfamiliar resolution to immigrant and people of color's struggles in a society structured by a pressure for assimilation and racism.[7] As Vijay Prashad argues, this dynamic, while a reaction to political and historical conditions, is an attempt to depoliticize the immigrant experience where culture is articulated not as living, changing social relations but a set of timeless traits.[8] In many ways, I found that in the San Francisco Bay Area, articulations of Arabness in America have been haunted by culture or, more precisely, by Orientalist definitions of culture.

The uninterrogated naturalization of a dichotomy between Arab and American culture among Arab Americans—usually associated as it is with essentialist understandings of religion, family, gender, and sexuality among Arab communities—allows Orientalist thought to be left intact and activated. Consigned to the "cultural," aspects of dynamic, lived experience come to be seen as frozen in time—essentialist Arab traditions that exist outside of history—which is the same conceptualization that operates as the basis for the demonization of Arab communities in the discourses of U.S. empire.

Within the dominant middle-class Arab immigrant discourse that circulated in my interlocutors' homes and community networks, gender and sexuality were among the most powerful symbols consolidating an imagined difference between "Arabs" and "Americans." . . .

> JUMANA: My parents thought that being American was spending the night at a friend's house, wearing shorts, the guy-girl thing, wearing make-up, reading teen magazines, having pictures of guys in my room. My parents used to tell me, "If you go to an American's house, they're smoking, drinking . . . they offer you this and that. But if you go to an Arab house, you don't see as much of that. *Bi hafzu ala al banat* [They watch over their daughters]."
>
> TONY: There was a pressure to marry an Arab woman because the idea was that "She will stand by her family, she will cook and clean, and have no career. She'll have kids,

raise kids, and take care of her kids, night and day. She will do anything for her husband." My mom always says, "You're not going to find an American woman who stands by her family like that. . . . American women leave their families."

In the quotes above, concepts of "good Arab girls" operate as a marker of community boundaries and the notion of a morally superior "Arab culture" in comparison to concepts of "American girls" and "American culture." Idealized concepts of femininity are connected to idealized notions of family and an idealized concept of heterosexual marriage. These ideals underpin a generalized pressure for monogamy—and more specifically, for no sex before marriage—and for compulsory heterosexuality. Some interlocutors recalled their parents' reaction to what they perceived to be signs of homosexuality. Here is how Ramsy said his Palestinian mother reacted to photographs of him in drag: "My mom took one look at the pictures and said, 'My God! What are we doing in this country! Oh, look what this country did to us!' They definitely see it as an American thing. They don't know that there are a lot of gay people back home." Among the middle-class Arab immigrant communities I worked with, dominant articulations of Arabness were structured by a strict division between an inner Arab domain and an outer American domain, a division that is built upon the figure of the woman as the upholder of values and an ideal of family, heterosexuality, and, most important, heterosexual marriage.

This jumble of ideals about Arabness and Americanness was the buoy that guided and girded —but also threatened to drown—the middle-class Arab diasporas in the Bay Area. These ideals created a fundamental split between a gendered and sexualized notion of an inner-familial-communal (Arab) domain and an external-public (American) domain— a split that both provided a sense of empowerment and belonging and also constrained the lives of many of my interlocutors. This split was terribly familiar to me and, at the same time, largely undiscussed both in my own life and in the larger Arab American community. I have spent nearly a decade trying to decipher the divide within the Arab community between the internal and the external, the private and public, and figuring out how we find meaning and formulate a life within this imagined split.

As my research progressed, I began interpreting the predicament of growing up in new ways. Both my parents and the parents of my interlocutors constantly referred to Arab culture—as the thing that rooted us, and often, it seemed, ruled us. This amorphous entity shaped our calendar and our thoughts, what our goals were and who our friends were. But the more I searched, the harder it became to find this culture. All I could find, instead, was an amalgam of influences. The concepts of "Arab culture" my parents' generation relentlessly invoked are indeed historically grounded in long-standing Arab histories, yet they were just as much shaped by the immigrant journey of displacement and diaspora and the pressures of middle-class assimilation in the United States. Concepts of Arabness among my parents' generation, and through them my peers' and my interlocutors', have ultimately been shaped not by a ceaseless and unchanging Arab tradition but by a collision of historically contingent realities and varying modes of diasporic living in the American empire—of running a grocery store, of traveling to the Arab world, of the travel of news and stories through the Internet and satellite television, by past and present Arab responses to European colonialism and U.S. empire, and by the words of the corporate media.

By interrogating the process by which middle-class Arab diasporas come to herald particular ideals as markers of an authentic, essential, true, or real Arab culture, I have learned that these ideals are best understood as cultural sensibilities that have permeated the Arab region for centuries and have become entangled in concepts of Arabness and Americanness that circulate in the United States. Even with regards to the Arab region, essentialist cultural frameworks cannot explain concepts and practices of family, marriage, gender, and sexuality, as these are very much entangled in European and U.S. discourses and are constantly changing in light of socioeconomic transformations.[9] Consider, for instance, that modernist nationalist concepts of gender and sexuality became dominant in the Arab region as European involvement in the region introduced certain new ideas about gender and sexuality.[10] These new European-influenced concepts replaced a much more varied structure of gender and ambiguous, fluid sexual attitudes that were common during centuries of Islamic rule.[11]

To a certain extent, I interpret dominant middle-class Arab American concepts of "Arab culture" as an immigrant survival strategy for replacing U.S. colonialist and Orientalist discourses about Arabs, Muslims, and the Middle East with seemingly positive or empowering concepts of cultural identity, a strategy that reverses the binary structure of bad, misogynist Arabs versus good, modern Americans and instead advances good Arab girls versus bad American(ized) girls. Specifically, the dominant middle-class Arab American discourse presented Arab cultural identity and community through the ideal of the good Arab family, good Arab girls, and compulsory heterosexuality, all of which was in opposition to an imagined America and its apparent sexual promiscuity, broken families, and bad women. Yet I also contend that this dominant middle-class Arab American discourse is shaped by the liberal logic of U.S. multiculturalism, a logic for imagining and performing cultural identity that becomes available to Arab diasporas upon their arrival in the United States. Liberal U.S. multiculturalism requires immigrants, people of color, and indigenous people to craft concepts of culture that are depoliticized and ahistorical. Vijay Prashad contends, "Whereas assimilation demands that each inhabitant of the United States be transformed into the norm, U.S. multiculturalism asks that each immigrant group preserve its own heritage. . . . The heritage, or 'culture,' is not treated as a living set of social relations but as a timeless trait.[12] Conjoining masculinist nationalist binaries (good Arab girls versus bad American girls) with the logics of liberal U.S. multiculturalism, dominant middle-class Arab American discourses posit an essentialist, authentic Arab identity that exists outside of history. Furthermore, while the dominant middle-class Arab American discourse idealizes family and heterosexual marriage as *Arab,* and not American, in fact, patriarchy and idealized concepts of "family values" and compulsory heterosexuality are fundamental to the demands of white U.S. middle-class acceptability. This small sampling from my research calls for a broader analysis of sensationalized issues such as "Arab" and "Muslim" patriarchy and homophobia. At the least, it points to an urgent need to transcend essentialist frameworks that explain structures of patriarchy among Arab families and communities as simply "cultural" matters. I believe that a diasporic Arab feminist theory, a theory that locates "Arab" patriarchy and homophobia at the interplay among long-standing

cultural sensibilities, Orientalism and imperial formations, and the pressures of immigration and assimilation, opens up such possibilities.

Social Movements and "Arab Culture"

Working within various Arab and Arab American activist movements, I learned that it was not only conventional middle-class Arab American discourses that conceptualized family, gender, and sexuality as characteristics of an inner-communal-"cultural" domain. . . . In leftist Arab American political movements focused on Palestine and Iraq, for instance, many Arab and Arab American feminists have been working to liberate issues of gender and sexuality from a seemingly internal-cultural domain. In nearly every Arab and Arab American organization where I have worked, political actions were focused externally—on ending war and racism, on raising awareness about the links between sexual violence and U.S. and Israeli militarism, and on liberating Arab land from colonization. In 2002, I participated in a community-based organization that led a campaign to end U.S. sanctions on Iraq and launched a divest-from-Israel movement modeled after the South African anti-Apartheid movement. This leftist Arab movement operated according to a collective consciousness that Israel was killing and displacing Palestinians en masse, that the U.S. war in Iraq was looking more and more like genocide, and that U.S. tax dollars were paying for it. Mobilized by daily images circulating in alternative media sources of dead Palestinian and Iraqi children, activists operated as a community in crisis.

Crisis mode meant that certain issues were privileged over others. This point was most clearly evident in moments when people raised critiques of sexism or homophobia within our movement. These critiques were met with an official movement logic that contended that the issue of sexism was secondary to the fact that "our people are dying back home." Alternately, it positioned discussions of homophobia as entirely irrelevant or outside the boundaries of acceptability. . . .

Not only were gender and sexuality barely discussed, but the official movement discourse insisted that discussing these internal issues in public could actually endanger the goals activists were fighting for. Many members of this movement shared the belief that U.S. Orientalist representations of Arabs and Muslims, specifically images of hyperoppressed Arab and Muslim women and Arab Muslim sexual savagery, were among the most common images Americans saw—especially from the news media and Hollywood. In their analysis, Orientalist representations were a key reason so many Americans supported U.S. military interventions in the Middle East and why many Americans, particularly liberals, expressed profound empathy for Arab and Muslim women—perceived to be victims of their culture and religion—but little concern over the impact of U.S. policies on Arab and Muslim communities.[13]

In response, many activists feared that discussing sexism and compulsory heterosexuality within Arab communities would reinforce Orientalism. Activists advocated an anti-Orientalist politics that reinforced the relegation of gender and sexuality to the margins. Activists feared that speaking out about sexism and homophobia could reinforce stereotypes of Arabs and strengthen the very violence they were fighting to eliminate. The tacit belief was that activists who publicly critiqued sexism or homophobia within Arab and Arab American communities were no better than traitors to their people. The result—of yet another binary structure—was that attempts to develop feminist or queer critiques were often confined between two extremes: untenable silence, on the one hand, and the reification of Orientalist representations, on the other.

The fear of washing our dirty laundry in public has haunted my own experiences working on various Arab and Arab American feminist issues in the United States. Since 1993, I have been involved in a range of projects that presented various Arab and Arab American feminist perspectives at UN international conferences (the Durban conference on racism, the Cairo conference on population and development, and the Beijing conferences on women), various U.S. feminist conferences, and a range of U.S.-national political demonstrations and protests in support of Palestinian and Iraqi people.[14] All of these projects were anchored in a sort of anti-Orientalist feminism that disregarded issues internal to our communities because we were either cautious about the ways such issues could be used

against us or because we felt that other matters such as war and occupation were the more pressing issues of our times. These efforts focused on deconstructing the proliferation of Orientalist U.S. discourses that represent Arab culture through images of oppressed Arab women, explaining the magnitude of these discourses to the legitimization of U.S. and Israeli militarism and war, and calling liberal U.S. feminists to task for reinforcing Orientalist feminisms and ignoring critiques of U.S. empire and its gendered and sexualized underpinnings.

In 2002, I joined the Arab Movement of Women Arising for Justice (AMWAJ), a new group of Arab and Arab American feminists, some of whom had been active in the previous projects but were tired of the privileging of "external" problems of racism and war among Arab feminist activists in the United States. Many of us were also tired of the silence surrounding forms of sexism and homophobia that take place among our families and communities. Yet we recognized that there were few spaces to talk about "internal" issues—particularly since we felt that most U.S. feminist spaces, as well as some Arab American feminist spaces—were dominated by Orientalist perspectives about Arab women. . . . [M]any AMWAJ members felt that "internal" issues were crucial to the range of issues that shaped our lives as Arab feminists, queers, and transgender people living in the United States. We also . . . conceptualized gender and sexuality not within an isolated internal-cultural-familial domain but as interconnected to race and racism, class, empire, and so on. A shared desire for a space to discuss the range of issues that impact our lives—including the issues that we confront among our families and Arab communities—inspired us to organize a gathering for Arab women, queer, and transgender people living in the United States in Chicago in 2005. . . . We were very clear that the project of addressing "internal" Arab community-based matters was fraught in the United States, but we were committed to going beyond Orientalism and anti-Orientalism. We strategically used the idea of "internal" and "external" domains for organizing our initial gathering. We began by fostering a space where people could speak openly about "internal" matters—since many of us rarely had this opportunity beforehand—beyond the intimate spaces of friendship and loved ones. . . .

AMWAJ activists modeled our gathering after the "I Am Your Sister" conference honoring Audre

Lorde. Harnessing the wisdom of other "third-world" and women-of-color feminist collectives that have come before them, AMWAJ activists created new possibilities for transcending dominant masculinist and colonialist concepts of what can and what cannot be discussed or fought for. We were contributing to the emergence of a diasporic Arab feminist politics, a multi-issued, feminist politics that seeks to dismantle sexism, homophobia, imperialism, and racism and refuses to be silent on the ways these power structures operate within Arab families and communities. Yet while we maintained these commitments, we could not escape the predicament that has circumscribed antiracist, anti-imperialist Arab feminisms: how can we speak frankly about our experiences in ways that neither reinscribe Arab bashing nor engage in Orientalism?

Decolonizing Arabness

Collective projects such as AMWAJ have fostered new visions for social justice that are aiming to transcend bifurcated and simplistic options represented by the "cultural" self and the "political" self that force activists to choose between speaking about internal issues or working on externally focused causes such as war and racism. The overt ways that anti-Arab racism operates—with and through the themes of family, gender, and sexuality—elucidate that these categories of oppression are linked and cannot be dismantled separately. During the Israeli siege on Gaza in January 2009, I heard a guest on National Public Radio claim that Israel will continue to have the right to attack Palestinians as long as "Arabs love their guns more than they love their children." While this statement is loaded with assumptions about Palestinian culture and Palestinian mothers, it also reflects a dominant U.S. and Israeli discourse that justifies violence and occupation. A fuller analysis of empire takes seriously the gendered and sexualized logics through which empire works. Yet we also need to take heed of critiques of U.S. empire that focus only on the center of power and turn a blind eye to the range of issues that matter in the everyday lives of the people who are targeted by the empire, thereby subsuming Arabs, Muslims, and South Asians, for instance, into scholarly and political discussions as but targets of the war, and contributing to their disappearance

as human subjects and agents. I believe we need to broaden our analysis of the empire. How are Arab diasporas, for instance, articulating who they are, determining their community boundaries and who is included and excluded against the invasive and shifting relations of power central to U.S. imperial formations? I believe we need to struggle beyond crisis mode, create alternatives to the sense that the external attacks are so profound that "we can't take anything else on right now." What are the historical conditions and power structures through which anti-imperialist social movements detetmine what constitutes violence or what forms of violence are worth ending? How will we define the fragility of life and what forms of life are worth fighting for? Arab diasporas live life on multiple tracks—our days are built upon the divide between the internal and the external, "the communal" and "the political." Sometimes these tracks seem to exist side by side, and sometimes the gulf between the two seems impossible to bridge. Navigating the multiplicity can be maddening, yet, I believe, it can also be liberating. By unlocking the rigid back-and-forth between Orientalism and anti-Orientalism, we can respond to imperialism and Orientalism and we can also transcend the reliance upon the figure of the "woman" or compulsory heterosexuality to determine the survival of "Arabs" in "America."

This essay is an excerpt from my book, *Articulating Arabness: Gender and Cultural Identity in the Diaspora.* I am grateful to Rabab Abdulhadi, Evelyn Alsultany, Lara Deeb, and Andrea Smith for their invaluable feedback on this essay. My deepest appreciation goes to all of the people who participated in my research. There are not enough words to thank them for their contribution.

NOTES

1. To some extent, working-class Arab kids we knew from church or school faced similar struggles. Yet the stakes seemed to be different among middle-class immigrant families, as the reputation of one's father's family name was very much tied up in socioeconomic class status.

2. Anouar Majid, *Unveiling Traditions: Postcolonial Islam in a Polycentric World* (Durham: Duke Univ. Press, 2000), 7; Minoo Moallem, *Between Warrior Brother and Veiled Sister: Islamic Fundamentalism and the Politics of Patriarchy in Iran* (Berkeley and Los Angeles: Univ. of California Press, 2005); Ella Shohat and Robert Stam,

Unthinking Eurocentrism. Multiculturalism and the Media (New York: Routledge, 1994).

3. Rabab Abdulhadi, "Sexualities and the Social Order in Arab and Muslim Communities," in *Islam and Homosexuality*, ed. Samar Habib (Santa Barbara: Praeger, 2010), 470.

4. This also includes South Asians and others perceived to be any of these categories (Sunaina Maira, *Missing: Youth, Citizenship, and Empire after 9/11* [Durham: Duke Univ. Press, 2009]).

5. Jasbir K. Puar, *Terrorist Assemblages: Homonationalism in Queer Times*, Next Wave (Durham: Duke Univ. Press, 2007); Lila Abu-Lughod, "Do Muslim Women Really Need Saving? Anthropological Reflections on Cultural Relativism and Its Others," *American Anthropologist* 104, no. 3 (2002). Feminist scholars like Robin L. Riley, Chandra Talpade Mohanty, and Minnie Bruce Pratt ("Feminism and U.S. Wars: Mapping the Ground," introduction to *Feminism and War: Confronting U.S. Imperialism* [London: Zed, 2008], 1-19), Andrea Smith ("Heteropatriarchy and the Three Pillars of White Supremacy: Rethinking Women of Color Organizing," in *Color of Violene: The IN-CITE! Anthology*, ed. Incite! Women of Color Against Violence [Boston: South End Press, 2006], 66–73), Sherene H. Razack (*Casting Out: The Eviction of Muslims from Western Law and Politics* [Toronto: Univ. of Toronto Press, 2008]), and Chandra Talpade Mohanty ("U.S. Empire and the Project of Women's Studies: Stories of Citizenship, Complicity, and Dissent," *Gender, Place, and Culture* 13, no. 1 [2006]: 7-20) have contributed an invaluable assessment of how the new Orientalism operates in relationship to imperial feminisms. Queer-studies scholars like Jasbir Puar have theorized the logic of homonationalism, thus contributing an analysis of how the idea of a "failed heterosexuality" serves as a crucial justification for violence and war (see Puar; and Puar and Amit S. Rai, "Monster, Terrorist, Fag: The War on Terrorism and the Production of Docile Patriots," *Social Text* 20, no. 3 [2002]: 117-48).

6. For analyses of intensified xenophobia and racism in California, see Jewelle Taylor Gibbs and Teiahsha Bankhead, *Preserving Privilege: California Politics, Propositions, and People of Color* (Westport, Conn.: Praeger, 2001); and Tomas Almaguer, *Racial Fault Lines: The Historical Origins of White Supremacy in California* (Berkeley and Los Angeles: Univ. of California Press, 1994). Engseng Ho ("Empire Through Diasporic Eyes: A View from the Other Boat," *Comparative Studies in Society and History* 46, no. 2 [2004]: 210-46) provides a useful analysis of the United States as an empire. He argues that U.S. empire is a mode of imperial domination that has global reach and disavows administration on the ground. He argues that the logic of U.S. empire purports that nations are free to choose their destinies and friends and that the United States epitomizes religious, political, social, and sexual liberation. Yet at the same time, the United States has a devastating mode

of domination that forces local governments to make appalling choices. Generally, the theorization of U.S. empire contends that U.S. empire works through covert and overt mechanisms and through economic, military, and cultural hegemony, which continue to take on new forms in different historical contexts inside and outside the United States.

7. Vijay Prashad, *The Karma of Brown Folk* (Minneapolis: Univ. of Minnesota Press, 2000); Yen Le Espiritu, *Home Bound: Filipino American Lives Across Cultures, Communities, and Countries* (Berkeley and Los Angeles: Univ. of California Press, 2003); Cathy J. Cohen, *The Boundaries of Blackness: AIDS and the Breakdown of Black Politics* (Chicago: Univ. of Chicago Press, 1999); Kevin Gaines, *Uplifting the Race: Black Leadership, Politics, and Culture in the Twentieth Century* (Chapel Hill: Univ. of North Carolina Press, 1996).

8. Prashad, 150.

9. Lila Abu-Lughod, "The Marriage of Feminism and Islamism in Egypt: Selective Repudiation as a Dynamic of Postcolonial Cultural Politics," in *Remaking Women: Feminism and Modernity in the Middle East*, ed. Lila Abu-Lughod (Princeton: Princeton Univ. Press, 1998), 243-69; Homa Hoodfar, *Between Marriage and the Market: Intimate Politics and Survival in Cairo*, Comparative Studies on Muslim Societies, vol. 24 (Berkeley and Los Angeles: Univ. of California Press, 1997).

10. Afsaneh Najmabadi, *Women with Mustaches and Men Without Beards: Gender and Sexual Anxieties of Iranian Modernity* (Berkeley and Los Angeles: Univ. of California Press, 2005); Abdul-hadi, "Sexualities and Social Order"; Leila Ahmed, *Women and Gender in Islam: Historical Roots of a Modern Debate* (New Haven: Yale Univ. Press, 1992).

11. Abdulhadi, "Sexualities and Social Order"; Joseph Andoni Massad, *Desiring Arabs* (Chicago: Univ. of Chicago Press, 2007); Najmabadi; Samar Habib, ed., *Islam and Homosexuality* (Santa Barbara: Praeger, 2010).

12. Prashad, 112.

13. For further analysis of the deployment of images of women in discourses of war, see Amira Jarmakani, *Imagining Arab Womanhood: The Cultural Mythology of Veils, Harems, and Belly Dancers in the U.S.* (New York: Palgrave Macmillan, 2008); Abu-Lughod, "Do Muslim Women Really Need Saving?"; and Sherene H. Razack, "Geopolitics, Culture Clash, and Gender after September 11," *Social Justice* 32, no. 4 (2005).

14. Various chapters of the Arab Women's Solidarity Association organized these conference delegations and presentations. See, for example, Nadine Naber, Eman Desouky, and Lina Baroudi, "The Forgotten '-Ism': Arab American Perspectives on Zionism, Racism, and Sexism" in *Time to Rise* by the Women of Color Resource Center. This essay was presented and distributed at the United Nations World Conference Against Racism in Durban, South Africa.

NINETEEN

We Are All Works in Progress (1998)

Leslie Feinberg

Leslie Feinberg is a novelist, historian, and activist. Hir award-winning titles include *Stone Butch Blues; Transliberation: Beyond Pink or Blue; Transgender Liberation: A Movement Whose Time Has Come;* and *Drag King Dreams.* For many years sie wrote a regular column, "Lavender and Red," in *Worker's World,* a socialist weekly newspaper.

The sight of pink-blue gender-coded infant outfits may grate on your nerves. Or you may be a woman or a man who feels at home in those categories. Trans liberation defends you both.

Each person should have the right to *choose* between pink or blue tinted gender categories, as well as all the other hues of the palette. At this moment in time, that right is denied to us. But together, we could make it a reality. . . .

I am a human being who would rather not be addressed as Ms. or Mr., ma'am or sir. I prefer to use gender-neutral pronouns like *sie* (pronounced like *"see"*) and *hir* (pronounced like *"here"*) to describe myself. I am a person who faces almost insurmountable difficulty when instructed to check off an "ꜰ" or an "ᴍ" box on identification papers.

I'm not at odds with the fact that I was born female-bodied. Nor do I identify as an intermediate sex. I simply do not fit the prevalent Western concepts of what a woman or man "should" look like. And that reality has dramatically directed the course of my life.

I'll give you a graphic example. From December 1995 to December 1996, I was dying of endocarditis—a bacterial infection that lodges and proliferates in the valves of the heart. A simple blood culture would have immediately exposed the root cause of my raging fevers. Eight weeks of 'round-the-clock intravenous antibiotic drips would have eradicated every last seedling of bacterium in the canals of my heart. Yet I experienced such hatred from some health practitioners that I very nearly died.

I remember late one night in December my lover and I arrived at a hospital emergency room during a snowstorm. My fever was 104 degrees and rising. My blood pressure was pounding dangerously high. The staff immediately hooked me up to monitors and worked to bring down my fever. The doctor in charge began physically examining me. When he determined that my anatomy was female, he flashed me a mean-spirited smirk. While keeping his eyes fixed on me, he approached one of the nurses, seated at a desk, and began rubbing her neck and shoulders. He talked to her about sex for a few minutes. After his pointed demonstration of "normal sexuality," he told me to get dressed and then he stormed out of the room. Still delirious, I struggled to put on my clothes and make sense of what was happening.

The doctor returned after I was dressed. He ordered me to leave the hospital and never return. I refused. I told him I wouldn't leave until he could tell me why my fever was so high. He said, "You have a fever because you are a very troubled person."

This doctor's prejudices, directed at me during a moment of catastrophic illness, could have killed me. The death certificate would have read: Endocarditis. By all rights it should have read: Bigotry.

As my partner and I sat bundled up in a cold car outside the emergency room, still reverberating from the doctor's hatred, I thought about how many people have been turned away from medical care when they were desperately ill—some because an apartheid "whites only" sign hung over the emergency room entrance, or some because their visible Kaposi's sarcoma lesions kept personnel far from their beds. I remembered how a blemish that wouldn't heal drove my mother to visit her doctor repeatedly during the 1950s. I recalled the doctor finally wrote a prescription for Valium because he decided she was a hysterical woman. When my mother finally got to specialists, they told her the cancer had already reached her brain.

Bigotry exacts its toll in flesh and blood. And left unchecked and unchallenged, prejudices create a poisonous climate for us all. Each of us has a stake in the demand that every human being has a right to a job, to shelter, to health care, to dignity, to respect.

I am very grateful to have this chance to open up a conversation with you about why it is so vital to also defend the right of individuals to express and define their sex and gender, and to control their own bodies. For me, it's a life-and-death question. But I also believe that this discussion will have great meaning for you. All your life you've heard such dogma about what it means to be a "real" woman or a "real" man. And chances are you've choked on some of it. You've balked at the idea that being a woman means having to be thin as a rail, emotionally nurturing, and an airhead when it comes to balancing her checkbook. You know in your guts that being a man has nothing to do with rippling muscles, innate courage, or knowing how to handle a chain saw. These are really caricatures. Yet these images have been drilled into us through popular culture and education over the years. And subtler, equally insidious messages lurk in the interstices of these grosser concepts. These ideas of what a "real" woman or man should be straightjacket the freedom of individual self-expression. These gender messages play on and on in a continuous loop in our brains, like commercials that can't be muted.

But in my lifetime I've also seen social upheavals challenge this sex and gender doctrine. As a child who grew up during the McCarthyite, Father-Knows-Best 1950s, and who came of age during the second wave of women's liberation in the United States, I've seen transformations in the ways people think and talk about what it means to be a woman or a man.

Today the gains of the 1970s women's liberation movement are under siege by right-wing propagandists. But many today who are too young to remember what life was like before the women's movement need to know that this was a tremendously progressive development that won significant economic and social reforms. And this struggle by women and their allies swung human consciousness forward like a pendulum.

The movement replaced the common usage of vulgar and diminutive words to describe females with the word *woman* and infused that word with strength and pride. Women, many of them formerly isolated, were drawn together into consciousness-raising groups. Their discussions—about the root of women's oppression and how to eradicate it—resonated far beyond the rooms in which they took place. The women's liberation movement sparked a mass conversation about the systematic degradation, violence, and discrimination that women faced in this society. And this consciousness-raising changed many of the ways women and men thought about themselves and their relation to each other. In retrospect, however, we must not forget that these widespread discussions were not just organized to *talk* about oppression. They were a giant dialogue about how to take action to fight institutionalized anti-woman attitudes, rape and battering, the illegality of abortion, employment and education discrimination, and other ways women were socially and economically devalued.

This was a big step forward for humanity. And even the period of political reaction that followed has not been able to overturn all the gains made by that important social movement.

Now another movement is sweeping onto the stage of history: Trans liberation. We are again raising questions about the societal treatment of people based on their sex and gender expression. This discussion will make new contributions to human consciousness. And trans communities, like the women's movement, are carrying out these mass conversations with the goal of creating a movement capable of fighting for justice—of righting the wrongs.

We are a movement of masculine females and feminine males, cross-dressers, transsexual men and women, intersexuals born on the anatomical sweep between female and male, gender-blenders, many other sex and gender-variant people, and our significant others. All told, we expand understanding of how many ways there are to be a human being.

Our lives are proof that sex and gender are much more complex than a delivery room doctor's glance at genitals can determine, more variegated than pink or blue birth caps. We are oppressed for not fitting those narrow social norms. We are fighting back.

Our struggle will also help expose some of the harmful myths about what it means to be a woman or a man that have compartmentalized and distorted your life, as well as mine. Trans liberation has meaning for you—no matter how you define or express your sex or your gender.

If you are a trans person, you face horrendous social punishments—from institutionalization to gang rape, from beatings to denial of child visitation. This oppression is faced, in varying degrees, by all who march under the banner of trans liberation. This brutalization and degradation strips us of what we could achieve with our individual lifetimes.

And if you do not identify as transgender or transsexual or intersexual, your life is diminished by our oppression as well. Your own choices as a man or a woman are sharply curtailed. Your individual journey to express yourself is shunted into one of two deeply carved ruts, and the social baggage you are handed is already packed.

So the defense of each individual's right to control their own body, and to explore the path of self-expression, enhances your own freedom to discover more about yourself and your potentialities. This movement will give you more room to breathe—to be yourself. To discover on a deeper level what it means to be your self.

Together, I believe we can forge a coalition that can fight on behalf of your oppression as well as mine. Together, we can raise each other's grievances and win the kind of significant change we all long for. But the foundation of unity is understanding. So let me begin by telling you a little bit about myself.

I am a human being who unnerves some people. As they look at me, they see a kaleidoscope of characteristics they associate with both males and females. I appear to be a tangled knot of gender contradictions. So they feverishly press the question on me: woman or man? Those are the only two words most people have as tools to shape their question.

"Which sex are you?" I understand their question. It sounds so simple. And I'd like to offer them a simple resolution. But merely answering woman or man will not bring relief to the questioner. As long as people try to bring me into focus using only those two lenses, I will always appear to be an enigma.

The truth is I'm no mystery. I'm a female who is more masculine than those prominently portrayed in mass culture. Millions of females and millions of males in this country do not fit the cramped compartments of gender that we have been taught are "natural" and "normal." For many of us, the words *woman* or *man*, *ma'am* or *sir*, *she* or *he*—in and of

themselves—do not total up the sum of our identities or of our oppressions. Speaking for myself, my life only comes into focus when the word *transgender* is added to the equation.

Simply answering whether I was born female or male will not solve the conundrum. Before I can even begin to respond to the question of my own birth sex, I feel it's important to challenge the assumptions that the answer is always as simple as either-or. I believe we need to take a critical look at the assumption that is built into the seemingly innocent question: "What a beautiful baby—is it a boy or a girl?"

The human anatomical spectrum can't be understood, let alone appreciated, as long as female or male are considered to be all that exists. "Is it a boy or a girl?" Those are the only two categories allowed on birth certificates.

But this either-or leaves no room for intersexual people, born between the poles of female and male. Human anatomy continues to burst the confines of the contemporary concept that nature delivers all babies on two unrelated conveyor belts. So, are the birth certificates changed to reflect human anatomy? No, the U.S. medical establishment hormonally molds and shapes and surgically hacks away at the exquisite complexities of intersexual infants until they neatly fit one category or the other.

A surgeon decides whether a clitoris is "too large" or a penis is "too small." That's a highly subjective decision for anyone to make about another person's body. Especially when the person making the arbitrary decision is scrubbed up for surgery! And what is the criterion for a penis being "too small"? Too small for successful heterosexual intercourse. Intersexual infants are already being tailored for their sexuality, as well as their sex. The infants have no say over what happens to their bodies. Clearly the struggle against genital mutilation must begin here, within the borders of the United States.

But the question asked of all new parents: "Is it a boy or a girl?" is not such a simple question when transsexuality is taken into account, either. Legions of out-and-proud transsexual men and women demonstrate that individuals have a deep, developed, and valid sense of their own sex that does not always correspond to the cursory decision made by a delivery-room obstetrician. Nor is transsexuality a recent phenomenon. People have undergone social sex reassignment and surgical and hormonal sex changes throughout the breadth of oral and recorded human history.

Having offered this view of the complexities and limitations of birth classification, I have no hesitancy in saying I was born female. But that answer doesn't clear up the confusion that drives some people to ask me, "Are you a man or a woman?" The problem is that they are trying to understand my gender expression by determining my sex—and therein lies the rub! Just as most of us grew up with only the concepts of *woman* and *man,* the terms *feminine* and *masculine* are the only two tools most people have to talk about the complexities of gender expression.

That pink-blue dogma assumes that biology steers our social destiny. We have been taught that being born female or male will determine how we will dress and walk, whether we will prefer our hair shortly cropped or long and flowing, whether we will be emotionally nurturing or repressed. According to this way of thinking, masculine females are trying to look "like men," and feminine males are trying to act "like women."

But those of us who transgress those gender assumptions also shatter their inflexibility.

So, why do I sometimes describe myself as a masculine female? Isn't each of those concepts very limiting? Yes. But placing the two words together is incendiary, exploding the belief that gender expression is linked to birth sex like horse and carriage. It is the social contradiction missing from Dick-and-Jane textbook education.

I actually chafe at describing myself as masculine. For one thing, masculinity is such an expansive territory, encompassing boundaries of nationality, race, and class. Most importantly, individuals blaze their own trails across this landscape.

And it's hard for me to label the intricate matrix of my gender as simply masculine. To me, branding individual self-expression as simply feminine or masculine is like asking poets: Do you write in English or Spanish? The question leaves out the possibilities that the poetry is woven in Cantonese or Ladino, Swahili or Arabic. The question deals only with the system of language that the poet has been taught. It ignores the words each writer hauls up, hand over hand, from a common well. The music words make when finding themselves next to each other for the first time. The silences echoing in the space between ideas. The powerful winds of passion and belief that move the poet to write.

That is why I do not hold the view that gender is simply a social construct—one of two languages that we learn by rote from early age. To me, gender is the poetry each of us makes out of the language we are taught. When I walk through the anthology of the world, I see individuals express their gender in exquisitely complex and ever-changing ways, despite the laws of pentameter.

So how can gender expression be mandated by edict and enforced by law? Isn't that like trying to handcuff a pool of mercury? It's true that human self-expression is diverse and is often expressed in ambiguous or contradictory ways. And what degree of gender expression is considered "acceptable" can depend on your social situation, your race and nationality, your class, and whether you live in an urban or rural environment.

But no one can deny that rigid gender education begins early on in life—from pink and blue color-coding of infant outfits to gender-labeling toys and games. And those who overstep these arbitrary borders are punished. Severely. When the steel handcuffs tighten, it is human bones that crack. No one knows how many trans lives have been lost to police brutality and street-corner bashing. The lives of trans people are so depreciated in this society that many murders go unreported. And those of us who have survived are deeply scarred by daily run-ins with hate, discrimination, and violence.

Trans people are still literally social outlaws. And that's why I am willing at times, publicly, to reduce the totality of my self-expression to descriptions like masculine female, butch, bulldagger, drag king, cross-dresser. These terms describe outlaw status. And I hold my head up proudly in that police lineup. The word *outlaw* is not hyperbolic. I have been locked up in jail by cops because I was wearing a suit and tie. Was my clothing really a crime? Is it a "man's" suit if I am wearing it? At what point—from field to rack—is fiber assigned a sex?

The reality of why I was arrested was as cold as the cell's cement floor: I am considered a masculine female. That's a *gender* violation. My feminine drag queen sisters were in nearby cells, busted for wearing "women's" clothing. The cells that we were thrown into had the same design of bars and concrete. But when we—gay drag kings and drag queens—were thrown into them, the cops referred to the cells as bull's tanks and queen's tanks. The cells were named after our crimes: gender transgression. Actual statutes against cross-dressing and cross-gendered behavior still exist in written laws today. But even where the laws are not written down, police, judges, and prison guards are empowered to carry out merciless punishment for sex and gender "difference."

I believe we need to sharpen our view of how repression by the police, courts, and prisons, as well as all forms of racism and bigotry, operates as gears in the machinery of the economic and social system that governs our lives. As all those who have the least to lose from changing this system get together and examine these social questions, we can separate the wheat of truths from the chaff of old lies. Historic tasks are revealed that beckon us to take a stand and to take action.

That moment is now. And so this conversation with you takes place with the momentum of struggle behind it.

What will it take to put a halt to "legal" and extralegal violence against trans people? How can we strike the unjust and absurd laws mandating dress and behavior for females and males from the books? How can we weed out all the forms of transphobic and gender-phobic discrimination?

Where does the struggle for sex and gender liberation fit in relation to other movements for economic and social equality? How can we reach a point where we appreciate each other's differences, not just tolerate them? How can we tear down the electrified barbed wire that has been placed between us to keep us separated, fearful, and pitted against each other? How can we forge a movement that can bring about profound and lasting change—a movement capable of transforming society?

These questions can only be answered when we begin to organize together, ready to struggle on each other's behalf. Understanding each other will compel us as honest, caring people to fight each other's oppression as though it was our own.

4

♦♦♦

Women's Sexuality

Sexual attitudes and behaviors vary considerably from society to society and across historical time periods (Caplan 1987; Lancaster and di Leonardo 1997; Weeks 2010). Sexuality is both instinctive and also learned from our families, our peers, sex education in school, media and popular culture, negotiations with partners, and listening to our own bodies. At the same time, there is a need for accurate information about women's sexuality, and there are many constraints on it. Over the course of our lives, sexuality may take different forms and take on different degrees of significance.

This chapter focuses on women's experiences of sexuality, the meso- and macro-level forces that shape our personal experiences, and the ways that women are defining sexuality for themselves. As you read this chapter, think also about the social construction of male sexuality.

The Erotic as Power

Black lesbian poet, teacher, and activist Audre Lorde discussed the power of the erotic in the broadest way in her now classic essay (Reading 20). She described the erotic "as our most profoundly creative source," noting that women have been "taught to separate the erotic . . . from most vital areas of our lives other than sex." By contrast, she wrote: "When I speak of the erotic . . . I speak of it as an assertion of the life-force of women: of that creative energy empowered, the knowledge and use of which we are now reclaiming in our language, our history, our dancing, our loving, our work, our lives." Lorde saw the distortion and suppression of the erotic as one of the ways that women are oppressed under patriarchal institutions and cultures, and concluded: "Recognizing the power of the erotic in our lives can give us the energy to pursue genuine change within our world."

As Audre Lorde argued, dominant U.S. culture takes a limited view of the erotic, reducing it to sexuality, and restricted notions of sexuality at that. By foregrounding her perspective in this chapter we make this explicit. Also, we recognize that sexuality can be a source of restriction and vulnerability for women as well as a source of power, affirmation, and self-definition. Many women are claiming the right to sexual pleasure on their own terms, despite the distortions, contradictions, and double standards of patriarchal cultures regarding women's sexuality.

What Does Sexuality Mean to You?

Sexuality is one of the few recognized ways in our society for people to make intimate connections, especially for men, who typically are not socialized to express emotions easily. Historian Jeffrey Weeks (2010) notes that sexuality is

> a transmission belt for a wide variety of needs and desires: for love and anger, tenderness and aggression, intimacy and adventure, romance and predatoriness, pleasure and pain, empathy and power. We experience the erotic very subjectively and in a host of often contradictory ways. (p. 2)

Shere Hite (1994) conducted extensive surveys of men's and women's sexual experiences and preferences. In her groundbreaking research into women's and men's attitudes about sexuality and love, she found that, for male respondents, dating and marriage were primarily about sex, and they often shopped around for varied sexual experiences. For the female respondents, expressing emotion through sexual intimacy and setting up a home were usually more important than they were for men. Hite attributed much of the frustration in heterosexual relationships to these very different approaches. Also, she saw women as "revolutionary agents of change" in relationships, working with men to renegotiate this intimate part of their lives. The following questions, from one of Hite's surveys, were written for women, but they are also relevant for men:

> Is sex important to you? What part does it play in your life?
>
> Who sets the pace and style of sex—you or your partner or both? Who decides when it's over?
>
> Do you think your genital area and vagina are ugly or beautiful?
>
> If you are sexually active, do you ever fake orgasms? Why?
>
> What are your best sex experiences? What would you like to try that you never have?
>
> What is it about sex that gives you the greatest pleasure? Displeasure?
>
> Have you chosen to be celibate at any point? What was/is that like for you?

> In the best of all possible worlds, what would sexuality be like?
>
> Do you know as much as you'd like to know, about your own body? Orgasm? Conception and pregnancy? Safe sex?
>
> Do your partners know about your sexual desires and your body? If not, do you ask for it or act yourself to get it?
>
> *(Hite 1994, pp. 17–22)*

To discover what is sexually empowering for us, ideally women need a safe place and freedom from worries about being attractive and the risk of pregnancy or sexually transmitted infections. In addition, we need information on safer sex, access to reliable contraception, and open discussion with sexual partners.

For many teens, sex is a "rite of passage," an essential part of growing up. How "sex" is defined can vary; for example, many sexually active heterosexual teens do not count oral sex as sex. Magazine editor Susannah Indigo (2000) interviewed girls about their experience with sex play including masturbation, phone sex, and oral sex, which they jokingly referred to as "outercourse," as opposed to "real sex" or intercourse. Some young people pledge virginity before marriage but do not necessarily rule out sex play. Lee Che Leong (2004, p. 37), director of the Teen Health Initiative at the New York Civil Liberties Union, commented that "[t]he ranks of those 'saving themselves' by being blowjob queens are increasing as oral sex is on the rise" among teens of all racial groups. Similarly, only 20 percent of university students participating in a 2007 survey agreed that oral-genital contact constituted sex (Hans, Gillen, and Akande 2010). Freelance writer and blogger Cara Kulwicki (2008) argues that sex education means teaching about sex: "that sex is more than heterosexual intercourse and should be consensual *and pleasurable* for all participants" (p. 305).

Psychologist Lynne Segal (1994) and sociologist Pepper Schwartz (1994) described how some heterosexual couples negotiate sex to make it more egalitarian. Schwartz commented that in U.S. culture there is a commonly held belief that "male leadership and control is inherently erotic," that role differences between women and men and "the mystery of not knowing each other" make for a more exciting sex life (p. 70). But only some men,

Schwartz wrote, "perhaps those with strong mothers, or with a great respect for competence and intelligence, find equality compelling and sexy" (p. 78). And not all women "refuse to be an instrument in male orchestration" (p. 78). She commented that sexual passion is a Western ideal for marriage, although research shows that passion decreases over the length of a relationship. A long-term peer marriage that is intentionally egalitarian, she noted, may be better at providing romance and respect than providing passion as currently defined.

Cultural Messages about Women's Sexuality

Girls and women are barraged by a range of messages about sexuality. How do we decide what is true or right for us? What are the wider forces that shape these messages? The questions we raised in Chapter 2 about evaluating media messages are useful here.

Stereotypes, Contradictions, and Double Standards

In advertising images and popular culture, sexuality is the prerogative of the young, slender, and able-bodied. Many of these images portray white women. Melba Wilson (1993) noted that racism and sexism converge in mainstream stereotypes of women of color as "exotic creatures of passion" (p. 66). Asian and Asian American women are stereotyped as "exotic flowers," overly promiscuous and at the same time submissive, sexually accommodating and focused on serving men. A 1957 novel, *The World of Suzie Wong,* also adapted for stage, film, and ballet, reinforced racist and sexist stereotypes of Asian women in its portrayal of a bar girl working in a hotel catering to British and U.S. sailors. Suzie Wong also personified another stereotype: the hooker with a heart of gold. The films *Slaying the Dragon* (1988) and *Slaying the Dragon: Reloaded* (2011) provide an excellent critique of such stereotypes. Sociologist Patricia Hill Collins (2004, p. 30) argued that ideas of pure white womanhood, developed as part of European national identity, "required a corresponding set of ideas about hot-blooded Latinas, exotic Suzy Wongs, wanton jezebels." She continued:

Civilized nation-states required uncivilized and backward colonies for their national identity to have meaning, and the status of women in both places was central to this endeavor. In this context, Black women became icons of hypersexuality.

These powerful stereotypes continue to be reinforced in media representations.

By contrast, women with disabilities and older women of all racial groups are stereotyped as sexless. According to the late Barbara Waxman Fiduccia, an advocate for people with disabilities, and Marsha Saxton, a teacher of disability studies, women with disabilities have been socially isolated and discouraged from expressing their sexuality. In their *Disability Feminism: A Manifesto* (1997), they wrote: "We want our sexuality accepted and supported with accurate information" (p. 60). Among other disability activists, Lillian Gonzales Brown, of the Institute on Disability Culture (Honolulu, Hawaii), has conducted workshops on sexuality for women with disabilities, urging participants to explore their sexuality and to see themselves as sexual beings (see also Kaufman, Silverberg, and Odette 2003; Smith and Hutchison 2004; Wilkerson 2011).

Ads that use women's bodies to sell products also sell ideas of sexuality, especially heterosexuality. As sex objects, women are commonly portrayed as child-like or doll-like playthings. These images flow from and reinforce macro-level patriarchal constructions of gender and sexuality based on the following assumptions: Heterosexuality is prescribed or natural for women and men, men are the initiators in heterosexual encounters, and men's sexuality is assertive and in need of regular release. In such scenarios a woman's role is to be modest and virtuous, to look beautiful, and, simultaneously, to lure men and to fend them off. Traditionally, a woman has been expected to remain a virgin until marriage, untouched except by her husband, and this attitude is still strong in some communities in the United States and around the world. Men's sexual activity is assumed and accepted; after all, "Boys will be boys." Girls may easily get a "bad reputation" and be condemned as "sluts." Writers Leonora Tanenbaum (2000) and Emily White (2002) found many reasons that girls are labeled this way: they may be early developers, victims of rape, outsiders to the community, or targets of revenge. Some may be sexually active, but many are not.

This fundamental contradiction between encouraging men's sexuality and expecting women to be chaste has resulted in the construction of two categories of women: "good" women and "bad" women, virgins and whores. This double standard controls women's sexuality and autonomy and serves to divide women from each other. Growing up in a Mexican American community, Sandra Cisneros (Reading 21) writes that *la Virgen de Guadalupe* was the model held up to girls. The boys "were fornicating like rabbits," she writes, "while the Church ignored them and pointed us women towards our destiny— marriage and motherhood. The other alternative was *puta*hood," being defined a whore. Writer and literature professor Gloria Wade-Gayles (1993) learned the same double standard, but women in her Memphis neighborhood also divided men into two categories: good men who cared for their wives and families, and "dogs" who "only want one thing." This latter category included white men who cruised through the neighborhood "in search of Black women who, they assumed, were naturally sensuous, sexually superior, and easy" (p. 84).

Julia Serano describes a predator/prey mind-set in which men are viewed as sexual aggressors and women as sexual objects (Reading 22). As well as the virgin/whore bind for women, she notes a similar double bind for men: "assholes" are men who fulfill the sexual aggressor stereotype; "nice guys" are those who refuse it. She argues that some men become "assholes" to get attention from women and asks why women are attracted to the bad-boy stereotype, and why "nice guys" are seen as desexualized and unmanly. She concludes: "A movement that refuses to render invisible and desexualize men who are not predators . . . would excite and attract many male allies."

Traditional cultural limitations on women's sexuality and sexual expression can divide younger women and older women in immigrant communities, as described by Nadine Naber in the context of Arab American communities (Chapter 3) and by human rights activist Surina A. Khan who struggled for many years to reconcile her queer and Pakistani identities (Reading 25). Mother and daughter, psychologist Shamita das Dasgupta and pediatrician Sayantani DasGupta, wrote:

As Asian women of two different generations, we attest to the politically divisive and psychologically unbearable situation in which we have been placed. As daughters, we are faced with the choice of rejecting our community and culture or destroying our sexual selves. As mothers, we can be exiled as destroyers of community culture or be our daughters' prison guards.   *(1996, p. 240)*

They understand the South Asian communities' control of women's sexuality as an attempt to resist cultural erasure in the United States and as a response to the racism of this society, as well as a result of patriarchal control within their own communities. They endorse Indian women's activism (against violence against women, and for gay, lesbian, and bisexual rights) as a way of creating a progressive South Asian space to "define our private selves as public and discover our collective power" (p. 241).

It is important to note that many girls and women experience sexual coercion and abuse—in childhood, as adults, or both (see Chapter 6). Some women struggle for many years with the devastating effects of sexual abuse on their confidence, trust, sexuality, and sense of themselves in the world. In Reading 34, Aurora Levins Morales refers to her childhood experience of sexual abuse and her path toward reclaiming "the wounded erotic." At the core of that process, she writes, is "blazing and untarnished aliveness."

Sexual Freedom, Hooking Up, Raunch Culture

In the 1960s and 1970s there was much talk of a sexual revolution in the United States, partly made possible by the availability of contraceptive pills for the first time. Women "on the pill" could be sexually active with men without the same fear of pregnancy as in the past. In practice, many feminists argued that this "revolution" was on men's terms (e.g., Segal 1994). Over the years there has been increasing discussion of women's own sexual needs and preferences (see, e.g., Boston Women's Health Book Collective 2005; Cox 1999; Ehrenreich, Hess, and Jacobs 1986; Ensler 1998; hooks 1993; Johnson 2002; Muscio 1999; Rose 2003). Women's health advocate Rebecca Chalker (1995) described this

THOUGHT FREQUENCY AS PIE CHARTS

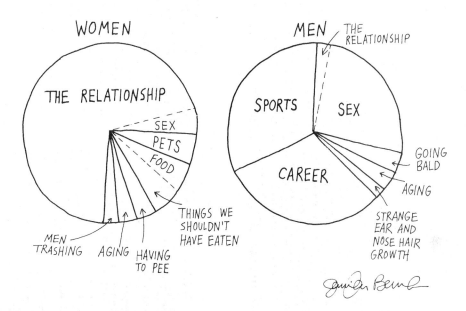

process as a "real woman-friendly sexual revolution in progress" (p. 52). Women's magazines and women's erotica have provided a forum for this discourse (e.g., Blank 2001; Bright 2000; Bruce 2001; Slugocki and Wilson 2000), as well as stars like Beyonce and Britney Spears who revel in their sexuality in public. In contrast to the double standard mentioned earlier, some women have reclaimed "slut" as a positive identification that emphasizes independence and sexual agency, and others have written of their own sexual experimentation (see, e.g., Johnson 2002; Walker 1995b; Wolf 1997).

Filmmakers and TV producers are also promoting ideas of women's sexual freedom, as in MTV's *Spring Break*, Comedy Central's *The Man Show*, or the video series, *Girls Gone Wild*, which features young women on spring break in vacation resorts or nightclubs who agree to show their bodies on camera in exchange for *Girls Gone Wild*–branded paraphernalia. These shows create a space to push the boundaries of what is acceptable.

Sociologist Gail Markle (2008) analyzed the "sexual scripts" embedded in the comedy series *Sex and the City,* an instant hit internationally, which broke new ground in its explicit discussion of women's sexuality. She argued that it is important to examine media representations of women as a key site through which gender and sexual identities are constructed. In her analysis of the four characters' sexual encounters, she draws on sexual script theory, which argues that sexuality is not innate but learned through cultural messages. As successful thirty-something single women in Manhattan, their goal was to have sex like a man, characterized as "without feeling, for pleasure only, and with no commitment." Despite the fact that their many sexual encounters were much more likely to be recreational than relational, by the end of the six-year series all four were involved in committed relationships.

Markle noted that the sexual scripts in *Sex and the City* differed significantly from behavior women actually reported about their sex lives. Nevertheless, young women generally are much more sexually active than in the past. Journalist Paula Kamen (2000) saw young women choosing to be in sexual relationships—or not—very much on their own terms. Psychologist Lynn Phillips (2000) argued that young women are "flirting with danger" and struggling to negotiate and make sense of power differences around sexuality, and in some cases, sexual abuse and violation. For those who choose to have sex with men, attitudes about condoms and women's ability to influence their partners to use them are important aspects of safer sex practices. New Zealand psychologists Nicola Gavey, Kathryn McPhillips, and Marion Doherty (2001) found that power dynamics between women and men, women's assumptions about assertiveness and what it means to be a "good lover," together with their ideals of giving and sharing, may be in conflict with their desire for safer sex.

Sociologist Kathleen Bogle (2008) interviewed mostly white heterosexual college students about sexual behavior and "hooking up." She noted that each person must decide how far to take things sexually, and that there is a wide range both in participation and in sexual activity, from kissing to oral sex to intercourse. Bogle's work raised the question of sexual agency. Is sex play and "hooking up" empowering for girls and women? Are women valued only for their sexual skills and availability? Are they allowing themselves to be used by boys and men, or is the issue more complicated? Young people make decisions about sexual activity with reference to their perceptions of what *everybody* is doing and what they believe is normal—ideas shaped by peer culture in the "campus sexual arena" (meso-level factors) and popular culture (macro-level factors). Bogle concluded that women have much more sexual freedom these days but that unwritten rules continue to limit their options. Both women and men reported a double standard in hooking up: women were much more likely to want a sexual encounter to develop into a relationship, and they were much more likely to get a bad reputation if they hooked up with too many guys.

As this discussion suggests, our individual behaviors are shaped by the wider social context. Many women want to throw off the "nice girl" image. They say, "We should be able to wear what we like and go where we like." Ideally, this should be the case, but individual behavior must be seen in relation to how boys and men are socialized to see women's sexuality in a sexist and sex-saturated culture. Journalist Ariel Levy (2005) examined the trend toward "raunch culture"—from women wearing skimpy outfits, T-shirts with a Playboy Bunny logo or PORN STAR across the chest, to lap dancing, pole dancing, "stripper aerobics" classes, and going to strip clubs and commercial sex parties (see Reading 23). She notes that women describe

these activities as fun, tongue-in-cheek, sexy, and empowering.

Levy discusses the overlap between sexuality and commercialism. In interviews she conducted, film producers, magazine editors, and club owners and managers argued that raunch culture is a sign that feminist goals have been met, that women have come so far we do not need to worry about objectification or misogyny, as mentioned in Chapter 1. They argued that "it was time for us to join the frat party of popular culture where men had been enjoying themselves all along" (p. 4). Levy questions whether "equal opportunity" sexual freedom in a sexist society is liberating for women and argues that "raunchy" and "liberated" are not the same. Women in the United States have far less political and economic power than men. Levy quotes Erica Jong, author of the 1973 novel, *Fear of Flying*, made famous by her idea that women may desire a consequence-free sexual encounter—the zipless fuck—who contends: "Sexual freedom can be a smokescreen for how far we *haven't* come" (p. 195).

Challenging Sex/Gender Binaries

As discussed in Chapter 3, U.S. society constructs sex and gender as binary categories: male/masculine as opposed to female/feminine. Often, the terms sex and gender have been used interchangeably, which makes for considerable confusion in discussion. Many feminists have differentiated biological sex from socially constructed gender, though the experiences of transsexual, transgendered, and intersex people show that reality is more complex than this neat distinction suggests.

According to Jonathan Katz (1995), a historian of sexuality, the concept of heterosexuality developed in parallel with the concept of homosexuality, and both date from the end of the nineteenth century. The word *heterosexuality* was first used in the 1890s, an obscure medical term applied to non-procreative sex—that is, sex for pleasure. At the time, this was considered a deviant idea, showing "abnormal or perverted appetite toward the opposite sex" (p. 86). Webster's dictionary did not include the word *heterosexuality* until 1934, and it gradually came into common usage in the United States as a "stable sign of normal sex" (p. 40). The binary is built in: heterosexuality involves desire for the "opposite" sex. Heterosexuality is so taken-for-granted that is it rarely questioned. As with other dominant dimensions of systems of power such as whiteness, wealth, and masculinity, heterosexuality has been much less scrutinized than homosexuality. Sociologist Chrys Ingraham (2004) argued that heterosexuality is a dominant institution that is much broader than sexuality. Many aspects of everyday life--marriage, family arrangements, work, income, and law—are organized along heterosexual lines.

Lesbians and gay men have long challenged the legitimacy and "normalcy" of heterosexuality (see, e.g., Allen 1986; Boswell 1994; Cavin 1985; Duberman, Vicinus, and Chauncey 1989; Faderman 1981; Grahn 1984; History Project 1998). Bisexual people express and argue for greater fluidity in sexual desire and behaviors, what Kathleen Bennett (1992) called "a both/and option for an either/or world" (see also Anderlini-D'Onofrio 2003; Hutchins and Ka'ahumanu 1991; Ochs and Rowley 2005; Storr 1999; Weise 1992). Lisa Orlando (1991) noted that stereotypes about bisexuality have grown out of the fact that bisexuals are poised between what "appear as two mutually exclusive sexual cultures" and from a common assumption "that homosexual and heterosexual desires exclude each other." On the basis of research into the sexual lives of nearly 100 young women over a ten-year period, psychologist Lisa Diamond (2008) came to see women's sexuality as a dynamic process characterized by fluidity, openness to variation, and a capacity to act on varying attractions and desires. The late June Jordan, poet, essayist, and scholar, urged bisexuality and sexual freedom as part of a wider struggle for freedom and justice. She wrote

> If you are free, you are not predictable and you are not controllable. To my mind, that is the keenly positive, politicizing significance of bisexual affirmation: . . . to insist upon the equal validity of all the components of social/sexual complexity.   *(1992, p. 193)*

Trans people complicate this even further. Riki Anne Wilchins (1997) pointed out the limited notion of the erotic entailed in hetero-homo dualism: "an entire Geography of the Absent—body parts that aren't named, acts one mustn't do, genders one can't perform—because they are outside the binary box" (p. 167). Those who refuse to tailor their looks and actions to conventional categories—for example, butch lesbians, cross-dressers, drag kings and queens, and queers—are involved in something profoundly challenging and transgressive. Leslie Feinberg explains why she is proud to claim this identity (Reading 19). In this chapter, Wendy Somerson examines her experience as a queer dyke, noting that femininity tends to be treated as less valid, the "unspoken and unacknowledged Other of 'gender transgression'" (Reading 24).

During the 1980s and 1990s, younger people reclaimed the word *queer,* which for many older lesbians and gay men was a hateful and oppressive term (Bernstein and Silberman 1996). This is a broader definition of queerness, with an emphasis on experimentation and playfulness, and can include all who challenge **heteronormativity** (Gage, Richards, and Wilmot 2002; Nestle, Howell, and Wilchins 2002; Rodríguez 2003). What was defined forty years ago as a gay/lesbian movement has grown enormously in size, complexity, and visibility. The most inclusive current term may be LGBTQQI—lesbian, gay, bisexual, transgender, queer, questioning, and intersex. Leslie Feinberg (1998), Kate Bornstein (1995, 1998),

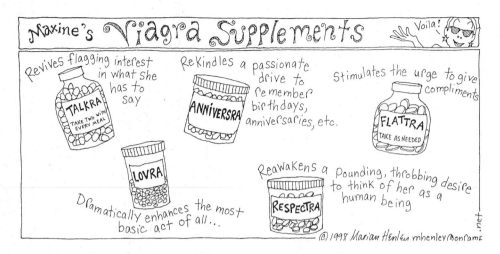

and Riki Anne Wilchins (1997) have argued that transgendered people are creating a broader space for everyone to express diverse genders and sexualities (see also Boylan 2003; Halberstam 1998, 2005). In the past fifteen years or so, TV shows featuring LGBTQQ people such as *Will and Grace*, *Queer as Folk*, *The L Word*, and *Queer Eye for the Straight Guy* have attracted significant audiences. Diane Raymond (2003), professor of philosophy and women's studies, has argued that there are many ways to "read" these shows depending on viewers' own perspectives, and that, ironically, these queer representations may reinforce the "normalcy" of heterosexism. By contrast, Amy Jo Goddard describes the work of three New-York based performance artists—Imani Henry, Susana Cook, and Diyaa MilDred Gerestant—who address sexuality, gender, ethnic, and class identities in shows that are entertaining, challenging, and educational (Reading 70).

Theorizing Sexuality

Medical anthropologist Carole Vance (1984) summed up the contradictions of sexuality for women:

> Sexuality is simultaneously a domain of restriction, repression, and danger as well as a domain of exploration, pleasure, and agency. To focus only on pleasure and gratification ignores the patriarchal structure in which women act, yet to speak only of sexual violence and oppression ignores women's experience with sexual agency and choice.   *(p. 1)*

As mentioned in Chapter 1, feminists have engaged in heated argument about women's sexuality and the possibility of genuine sexual agency in patriarchal cultures (see, e.g., Jaggar 1994; Snitow, Stansell, and Thompson 1983; Vance 1984). Marilyn Frye (1992) was skeptical that genuine sexual autonomy is possible for heterosexual women unless they are willing to be wild and undomesticated. Naomi Wolf advocated what she called "radical heterosexuality," recognizing that women would need financial independence, marriage would have to be very different, and both women and men would have to give up their "gender benefits" (Reading 5).

Gayle Rubin (1984) noted two strains of feminist thought concerning sexuality: one criticizing "restrictions on women's sexual behavior," denouncing "the high costs imposed on women for being sexually active," and calling for "a sexual liberation that would work for women as well as for men"; the other considering "sexual liberation to be inherently a mere extension of male privilege" (p. 301). Feminist debate about sexuality, power, and violence has continued for many years, especially with regard to issues such as prostitution/sex work and pornography (see, e.g., Califia 2000; Cornell 2000; Dines 2010; Douglas 2010; Dworkin 1993; Feminist Anti-Censorship Task Force 1992; Jeffreys 1997; Johnson 2002; Kempadoo and Doezema 1998; Levy 2005; Nagel 1997; Queen 2002; Russell 1993; Stan 1995; Strossen 2000; Whisnant and Stark 2004).

Many feminists have focused on sexual violence—both theoretically and through active participation in rape crisis centers and shelters for battered women—and understand that sexuality

can be a source of profound vulnerability for women (see Chapter 6). The late writer and activist Andrea Dworkin (1987), for example, argued that intercourse is inherently repressive for women, partly for anatomical reasons, but more because of unequal power relations between women and men. As a way of repudiating the eroticization of inequality, some feminists have argued that women's sexuality should be based on sexual acts that are safe, loving, and intimate, in the context of a caring, monogamous relationship. Others have seen this as a new restriction on women's freedom of expression (see, e.g., Duggan and Hunter 1995; Jaggar 1994; Johnson 2002; Leidholdt and Raymond 1990).

In her now-classic essay, award-winning poet and writer Adrienne Rich (1986a) discussed how social institutions like law, religion, philosophy, official kinship, and popular culture support what she termed "compulsory heterosexuality." She argued that patriarchy demands heterosexuality to keep women serving masculinist interests. For Rich, what needs to be explained is not why women identify as lesbians, but how and why so many women are heterosexual, because typically we first experience the intimacy of emotional caring and physical nurture with women—our mothers or other female caregivers. In many cultural settings, women and girls spend time together, care for, and depend on one another, and enjoy each other's friendship—often passionately. Rich asks: Why would women ever redirect that search?

Lisa Orlando (1991) noted that the very notion of sexual identity is specific to our culture and time in history. Historian John D'Emilio (1984) argued that economic and social trends like the growth of cities, decreasing family size, the development of the contraceptive pill, and other reproductive technologies have created conditions "that allow some men and women to organize a personal life around their erotic/emotional attraction to their own sex" (p. 104). They have "made possible the formation of urban communities of lesbians and gay men, and more recently, of a politics based on a sexual identity" (p. 104). On this analysis, sexual identity has a basis in macro-level circumstances as much as personal factors (D'Emilio and Freedman 1997), although cultural acceptance of lesbians and gay men has not always followed (see, e.g., Anzaldúa 1987;

Eng and Hom 1998; Leong 1996; Rodríguez 2003; B. Smith 1998; Trujillo 1991). Like many other writers, D'Emilio (1984) accepted that there have been same-sex partnerships for generations. However, he complicated this claim by differentiating homosexual behavior from homosexual identity and argued that only under certain economic conditions are homosexual identity and community possible. In her discussion of Northampton (Mass.) and San Francisco as cities with strong LGBTQQI communities, Clare Hemmings (2002) noted that such communities both generate and require supportive locations to survive and flourish.

This links to the experience of Surina A. Khan (Reading 25). Despite the fact that images of same-sex couples have been part of South Asian history and culture for hundreds of years, she notes that most people from South Asia do not have words for homosexuality and regard it as a Western phenomenon. This apparent paradox is what D'Emilio's distinction between behavior and identity helps to explain. Further, it may be useful to think of four categories: inclination, behavior, identity, and politics. One may have sexual inclinations but may decide not to act on them. One may engage in certain sexual behaviors but not adopt LGBTQQI identity. One may identify as a lesbian or transgendered woman but not act on that identity in a political way.

Activism and Sexuality

Over the past decade or so, the internet has opened up spaces for "erotic excitement, enticement and entanglement at the click of a button" with sex chat rooms, news groups, bulletin boards, social networks, virtual sex and more (Weeks 2010, p. 107).

A number of online educational and activist organizations provide information for young people about sexuality and health (e.g., Go Ask Alice, Scarleteen, Teenwire, and Youth Resource). Many informal networks, local groups, and national organizations support and advocate for lesbians, bisexuals, transgender people, and gay men, especially in urban areas. Some are primarily social groups; others are support groups that provide information and social connections. Still others focus on particular issues like sexual health, HIV/AIDS, parenting, police violence, religious oppression, or the situation of gays in the military. Others run journals, magazines, newsletters, bookstores, presses, churches, bars, coffeehouses, bands, sports teams, and theater companies; support political candidates for local, state, or national office; oppose city and state ordinances designed to limit LGBTQQI rights; or raise funds for LGBTQQI organizations. These various networks and organizations span a broad political spectrum. Some are overtly feminist; others are more closely aligned with queer politics. Examples include BiNet USA (Arlington, VA), Bi Women Boston, Old Lesbians Organizing for Change (Athens, Ohio), Trikone: Lesbian, Gay, Bisexual, and Transgendered South Asians (San Francisco), Gender Equity Resource Center (Berkeley), New York Association for Gender Rights Advocacy, the National Center for Transgender Equality (Washington, D.C.) the National Gay and Lesbian Taskforce (Washington, D.C.), Unid@s: the National Latino/a LGBT Human Rights Organization (Washington, D.C.), Gender Education and Advocacy (www.gender.org), and the International Gay and Lesbian Human Rights Commission (New York, Buenos Aires, and Johnnesburg). In addition, women who identify as lesbian, bisexual, queer, or transgender are active in antiracist organizing, rape crisis centers, shelters for battered women, labor unions, antimilitarist organizations, and women's studies programs where they link their knowledge and experiences of oppression based on sexuality with other oppressions.

◆◆◆

Questions for Reflection

1. As you read and discuss the readings that follow, consider the questions raised by Shere Hite, listed on p. 174.

2. What are "the societal forces that wrench women's emotional and erotic energies away from themselves and other women" (Rich 1986a, p. 35), and which seek to teach us to see men as appropriate partners?

3. What advice would you give to high school students about sexuality?

◆◆◆

Finding Out More on the Web

1. Review the information about sexuality and health given on one of the online sites mentioned in this chapter.

2. The World Wide Web is a significant new tool in the commodification of women. Type "Philippine women" or "Asian women" into your search engine and see what comes up.

3. Research an organization mentioned in this chapter. What are its goals, strategies, and activities?

4. Research the history of transgender experience in the United States. The following site has a useful glossary of terms: www.thefword.org.uk/features/2008/03/trans_101

◆◆◆

Taking Action

1. Write in your journal or have a candid conversation with a friend about your ideas regarding sexuality. How do you recognize the power of the erotic as Audre Lorde describes it?

2. Analyze the way women's magazines and men's magazines discuss women's sexuality.

3. Look critically at the way women's sexuality is portrayed in movies, on TV, and in ads. What is being represented?

4. However you define your sexuality, participate in campus or community events to commemorate National Coming-Out Day (usually in October) or Gay Pride (usually in June).

TWENTY

Uses of the Erotic (1984)

The Erotic as Power

Audre Lorde

Audre Lorde (1934–1992) was an acclaimed writer and educator whose books included *Sister Outsider, The Cancer Journals,* and *Zami: A New Spelling of My Name.* She held many teaching positions and toured the world as a lecturer, founding a sisterhood in South Africa and the St. Croix Women's Coalition. She published ten volumes of poetry, numerous essays, and won awards and honors, including being named New York State's Poet Laureate. She co-founded Kitchen Table: Women of Color Press.

There are many kinds of power, used and unused, acknowledged or otherwise. The erotic is a resource within each of us that lies in a deeply female and spiritual plane, firmly rooted in the power of our unexpressed or unrecognized feeling. In order to perpetuate itself, every oppression must corrupt or distort those various sources of power within the culture of the oppressed that can provide energy for change. For women, this has meant a suppression of the erotic as a considered source of power and information within our lives.

We have been taught to suspect this resource, vilified, abused, and devalued within western society. On the one hand, the superficially erotic has been encouraged as a sign of female inferiority; on the other hand, women have been made to suffer and to feel both contemptible and suspect by virtue of its existence.

It is a short step from there to the false belief that only by the suppression of the erotic within our lives and consciousness can women be truly strong. But that strength is illusory, for it is fashioned within the context of male models of power.

As women, we have come to distrust that power which rises from our deepest and nonrational knowledge. We have been warned against it all our lives by the male world, which values this depth of feeling enough to keep women around in order to exercise it in the service of men, but which fears this same depth too much to examine the possibilities of it within themselves. So women are maintained at a distant/inferior position to be psychically milked, much the same way ants maintain colonies of aphids to provide a life-giving substance for their masters.

But the erotic offers a well of replenishing and provocative force to the woman who does not fear its revelation, nor succumb to the belief that sensation is enough.

The erotic has often been misnamed by men and used against women. It has been made into the confused, the trivial, the psychotic, the plasticized sensation. For this reason, we have often turned away from the exploration and consideration of the erotic as a source of power and information, confusing it with its opposite, the pornographic. But pornography is a direct denial of the power of the erotic, for it represents the suppression of true feeling. Pornography emphasizes sensation without feeling.

The erotic is a measure between the beginnings of our sense of self and the chaos of our strongest feelings. It is an internal sense of satisfaction to which, once we have experienced it, we know we can aspire. For having experienced the fullness of this depth of feeling and recognizing its power, in honor and self-respect we can require no less of ourselves.

It is never easy to demand the most from ourselves, from our lives, from our work. To encourage excellence is to go beyond the encouraged mediocrity of our society. To go beyond the encouraged mediocrity of our society is to encourage excellence. But giving in to the fear of feeling and working to capacity is a luxury only the unintentional can afford, and the unintentional are those who do not wish to guide their own destinies.

This internal requirement toward excellence which we learn from the erotic must not be misconstrued as demanding the impossible from ourselves nor from others. Such a demand incapacitates everyone in the process. For the erotic is not a question only of what we do; it is a question of how acutely and fully we can feel in the doing. Once we know the extent to which we are capable of feeling that sense of satisfaction and completion, we can then observe which of our various life endeavors bring us closest to that fullness.

The aim of each thing that we do is to make our lives and the lives of our children richer and more possible. Within the celebration of the erotic in all our endeavors, my work becomes a conscious decision—a longed-for bed, which I enter gratefully and from which I rise up empowered.

Of course, women so empowered are dangerous. So we are taught to separate the erotic demand from most vital areas of our lives other than sex. And the lack of concern for the erotic root and satisfactions of our work is felt in our disaffection from so much of what we do. For instance, how often do we truly love our work even at its most difficult?

The principal horror of any system that defines the good in terms of profit rather than in terms of human need or that defines human need to the exclusion of the psychic and emotional components of that need—the principal horror of such a system is that it robs our work of its erotic value, its erotic power and life appeal and fulfillment. Such a system reduces work to a travesty of necessities, a duty by which we earn bread or oblivion for ourselves and those we love. But this is tantamount to blinding a painter and then telling her to improve her work and to enjoy the act of painting. It is not only next to impossible; it is also profoundly cruel.

As women, we need to examine the ways in which our world can be truly different. I am speaking here of the necessity for reassessing the quality of all the aspects of our lives and of our work and of how we move toward and through them.

The very word *erotic* comes from the Greek word *eros*, the personification of love in all its aspects—born of Chaos and personifying creative power and harmony. When I speak of the erotic, then, I speak of it as an assertion of the lifeforce of women, of that creative energy empowered, the knowledge and use of which we are now reclaiming in our language, our history, our dancing, our loving, our work, our lives.

There are frequent attempts to equate pornography and eroticism, two diametrically opposed uses of the sexual. Because of these attempts, it has become fashionable to separate the spiritual (psychic and emotional) from the political, to see them as contradictory or antithetical. "What do you mean, a poetic revolutionary, a meditating gunrunner?" In the same way, we have attempted to separate the spiritual and the erotic, thereby reducing the spiritual to a world of flattened affect, a world of the ascetic who aspires to feel nothing. But nothing is farther from the truth. For the ascetic position is one of the highest fear, the gravest immobility. The severe abstinence of the ascetic becomes the ruling obsession. And it is one not of self-discipline but of self-abnegation.

The dichotomy between the spiritual and the political is also false, resulting from an incomplete attention to our erotic knowledge. For the bridge which connects them is formed by the erotic—the sensual—those physical, emotional, and psychic expressions of what is deepest and strongest and richest within each of us, being shared: the passions of love in its deepest meanings.

Beyond the superficial, the considered phrase, "It feels right to me," acknowledges the strength of the erotic into a true knowledge, for what that means is the first and most powerful guiding light toward any understanding. And understanding is a handmaiden, which can only wait upon, or clarify, that knowledge, deeply born. The erotic is the nurturer or nursemaid of all our deepest knowledge.

The erotic functions for me in several ways, and the first is in providing the power that comes from sharing deeply any pursuit with another person. The sharing of joy, whether physical, emotional, psychic, or intellectual, forms a bridge between the sharers, which can be the basis for understanding much of what is not shared between them and lessens the threat of their difference.

Another important way in which the erotic connection functions is the open and fearless underlining of my capacity for joy. In the way my body stretches to music and opens into response, hearkening to its deepest rhythms, so every level upon which I sense also opens to the erotically satisfying experience, whether it is dancing, building a bookcase, writing a poem, examining an idea.

That self-connection shared is a measure of the joy that I know myself to be capable of feeling, a reminder of my capacity for feeling. And that deep and irreplaceable knowledge of my capacity for joy comes to demand from all of my life that it be lived within the knowledge that such satisfaction is possible and does not have to be called *marriage*, nor *god*, nor *an afterlife*.

This is one reason why the erotic is so feared and so often relegated to the bedroom alone when it is recognized at all. For once we begin to feel deeply all the aspects of our lives, we begin to demand from ourselves and from our life-pursuits that they feel in accordance with that joy that we know ourselves to be capable of. Our erotic knowledge empowers us, becomes a lens through which we scrutinize all aspects of our existence, forcing us to evaluate those aspects honestly in terms of their relative meaning within our lives. And this is a grave responsibility, projected from within each of us, not to settle for the convenient, the shoddy, the conventionally expected, nor the merely safe.

During World War II, we bought sealed plastic packets of white, uncolored margarine, with a tiny, intense pellet of yellow coloring perched like a topaz just inside the clear skin of the bag. We would leave the margarine out for a while to soften, and then we would pinch the little pellet to break it inside the bag, releasing the rich yellowness into the soft pale mass of margarine. Then taking it carefully between our fingers, we would knead it gently back and forth, over and over, until the color had spread throughout the whole pound bag of margarine, thoroughly coloring it.

I find the erotic such a kernel within myself. When released from its intense and constrained pellet, it flows through and colors my life with a kind of energy that heightens and sensitizes and strengthens all my experience.

We have been raised to fear the *yes* within ourselves, our deepest cravings. But, once recognized, those which do not enhance our future lose their power and can be altered. The fear of our desires keeps them suspect and indiscriminately powerful, for to suppress any truth is to give it strength beyond endurance. The fear that we cannot grow beyond whatever distortions we may find within ourselves keeps us docile and loyal and obedient, externally defined, and leads us to accept many facets of our oppression as women.

When we live outside ourselves, and by that I mean on external directives only rather than from our internal knowledge and needs, when we live away from those erotic guides from within ourselves, then our lives are limited by external and alien forms, and we conform to the needs of a structure that is not based on human need, let alone an individual's. But when we begin to live from within outward, in touch with the power of the erotic within ourselves, and allowing that power to inform and illuminate our actions upon the world around us, then we begin to be responsible to ourselves in the deepest sense. For as we begin to recognize our deepest feelings, we begin to give up, of necessity, being satisfied with suffering and self-negation and with the numbness which so often seems like their only alternative in our society. Our acts against oppression become integral with self, motivated and empowered from within.

In touch with the erotic, I become less willing to accept powerlessness or those other supplied states of being which are not native to me, such as resignation, despair, self-effacement, depression, self-denial.

And yes, there is a hierarchy. There is a difference between painting a back fence and writing a poem, but only one of quantity. And there is, for me, no difference between writing a good poem and moving into sunlight against the body of a woman I love.

This brings me to the last consideration of the erotic. To share the power of each other's feelings is different from using another's feelings as we would use a kleenex. When we look the other way from our experience, erotic or otherwise, we use rather than share the feelings of those others who participate in the experience with us. And use without consent of the used is abuse.

In order to be utilized, our erotic feelings must be recognized. The need for sharing deep feeling is a human need. But within the European-American tradition, this need is satisfied by certain proscribed erotic comings-together. These occasions are almost always characterized by a simultaneous looking away, a pretense of calling them something else, whether a religion, a fit, mob violence, or even playing doctor. And this misnaming of the need and the deed gives rise to that distortion which results in pornography and obscenity—the abuse of feeling.

When we look away from the importance of the erotic in the development and sustenance of our power, or when we look away from ourselves as we satisfy our erotic needs in concert with others, we use each other as objects of satisfaction rather than share our joy in the satisfying, rather than make connection with our similarities and our differences. To refuse to be conscious of what we are feeling at any time, however comfortable that might seem, is to deny a large part of the experience and to allow ourselves to be reduced to the pornographic, the abused, and the absurd.

The erotic cannot be felt secondhand. As a Black lesbian feminist, I have a particular feeling, knowledge, and understanding for those sisters with whom I have danced hard, played, or even fought. This deep participation has often been the forerunner for joint concerted actions not possible before.

But this erotic charge is not easily shared by women who continue to operate under an exclusively European-American male tradition. I know it was not available to me when I was trying to adapt my consciousness to this mode of living and sensation.

Only now, I find more and more women-identified women brave enough to risk sharing the erotic's electrical charge without having to look away and without distorting the enormously powerful and creative nature of that exchange. Recognizing the power of the erotic within our lives can give us the energy to pursue genuine change within our world rather than merely settling for a shift of characters in the same weary drama.

For not only do we touch our most profoundly creative source, but we do that which is female and self-affirming in the face of a racist, patriarchal, and anti-erotic society.

◆◆◆

TWENTY-ONE

Guadalupe the Sex Goddess (1996)

Sandra Cisneros

Sandra Cisneros is an award-winning fiction and poetry writer whose first book, *House on Mango Street,* sold
over 2 million copies. Her writing has earned her numerous honors, including the prestigious MacArthur
Foundation Fellowship. She is the president and
founder of the Macondo Foundation, an association
of socially engaged writers working to advance creativity, and Writer-in-Residence at Our Lady of the Lake
University in San Antonio (Texas).

In high school I marveled at how white women
strutted around the locker room, nude as pearls, as
unashamed of their brilliant bodies as the Nike of
Samothrace. Maybe they were hiding terrible secrets
like bulimia or anorexia, but, to my naive eye then, I
thought of them as women comfortable in their skin.

You could always tell us Latinas. We hid when
we undressed, modestly facing a wall, or, in my case,
dressing in a bathroom stall. We were the ones who
still used bulky sanitary pads instead of tampons,
thinking ourselves morally superior to our white
classmates. *My mama said you can't use tampons till
after you're married.* All Latina mamas said this, yet
how come none of us thought to ask our mothers
why they didn't use tampons *after* getting married?

Womanhood was full of mysteries. I was as
ignorant about my own body as any female ancestor who hid behind a sheet with a hole in the center when husband or doctor called. Religion and our
culture, our culture and religion, helped to create that
blur, a vagueness about what went on "down there."
So ashamed was I about my own "down there" that
until I was an adult I had no idea I had another orifice
called the vagina; I thought my period would arrive
via the urethra or perhaps through the walls of my skin.

No wonder, then, it was too terrible to think
about a doctor—a man!—looking at you down
there when you could never bring yourself to look
yourself. *¡Ay, nunca!* How could I acknowledge my
sexuality, let alone enjoy sex, with so much guilt?
In the guise of modesty my culture locked me in

a double chastity belt of ignorance and *vergüenza,*
shame.

I had never seen my mother nude. I had never
taken a good look at myself either. Privacy for self-
exploration belonged to the wealthy. In my home a
private space was practically impossible; aside from
the doors that opened to the street, the only room
with a lock was the bathroom, and how could anyone who shared a bathroom with eight other people
stay in there for more than a few minutes? Before
college, no one in my family had a room of their
own except me, a narrow closet just big enough for
my twin bed and an oversized blond dresser we'd
bought in the bargain basement of *el Sears.* The
dresser was as long as a coffin and blocked the door
from shutting completely. I had my own room, but I
never had the luxury of shutting the door.

I didn't even see my own sex until a nurse at the
Emma Goldman Clinic showed it to me—*Would you
like to see your cervix? Your os is dilating. You must be
ovulating. Here's a mirror; take a look.* When had anyone
ever suggested I take a look or allowed me a specu-
lum to take home and investigate myself at leisure!

I'd only been to one other birth control facility
prior to the Emma Goldman Clinic, the university
medical center in grad school. I was 21 in a strange
town far from home for the first time. I was afraid
and I was ashamed to seek out a gynecologist, but
I was more afraid of becoming pregnant. Still, I
agonized about going for weeks. Perhaps the anonymity and distance from my family allowed me
finally to take control of my life. I remember wanting to be fearless like the white women around me,
to be able to have sex when I wanted, but I was too
afraid to explain to a would-be lover how I'd only
had one other man in my life and we'd practiced
withdrawal. Would he laugh at me? How could I
look anyone in the face and explain why I couldn't
go see a gynecologist?

One night, a classmate I liked too much took
me home with him. I meant all along to say something about how I wasn't on anything, but I never
quite found my voice, never the right moment to

cry out—*Stop, this is dangerous to my brilliant career!* Too afraid to sound stupid, afraid to ask him to take responsibility too, I said nothing, and I let him take me like that with nothing protecting me from motherhood but luck. The days that followed were torture, but fortunately on Mother's Day my period arrived, and I celebrated my nonmaternity by making an appointment with the family planning center.

When I see pregnant teens, I can't help but think that could've been me. In high school I would've thrown myself into love the way some warriors throw themselves into fighting. I was ready to sacrifice everything in the name of love, to do anything, even risk my own life, but thankfully there were no takers. I was enrolled at an all-girls' school. I think if I had met a boy who would have me, I would've had sex in a minute, convinced this was love. I have always had enough imagination to fall in love all by myself, then and now.

I tell you this story because I am overwhelmed by the silence regarding Latinas and our bodies. If I, as a graduate student, was shy about talking to anyone about my body and sex, imagine how difficult it must be for a young girl in middle school or high school living in a home with no lock on the bedroom door, perhaps with no door, or maybe with no bedroom, no information other than misinformation from the girlfriends and the boyfriend. So much guilt, so much silence, and such a yearning to be loved; no wonder young women find themselves having sex while they are still children, having sex without sexual protection, too ashamed to confide their feelings and fears to anyone.

What a culture of denial. Don't get pregnant! But no one tells you how not to. This is why I was angry for so many years every time I saw a *la Virgen de Guadalupe*, my culture's role model for brown women like me. She was damn dangerous, an ideal so lofty and unrealistic it was laughable. Did boys have to aspire to be Jesus? I never saw any evidence of it. They were fornicating like rabbits while the Church ignored them and pointed us women toward our destiny—marriage and motherhood. The other alternative was *puta*hood.

In my neighborhood I knew only real women, neither saints nor whores, naive and vulnerable *huerquitas* like me who wanted desperately to fall in love, with the heart and soul. And yes, with the *panocha* too.

As far as I could see, *la Lupe* was nothing but a Goody Two-Shoes meant to doom me to a life of unhappiness. Thanks, but no thanks. Motherhood and/or marriage were anathema to my career. But being a bad girl, that was something I could use as a writer, a Molotov cocktail to toss at my papa and *el Papa*, who had their own plans for me.

Discovering sex was like discovering writing. It was powerful in a way I couldn't explain. Like writing, you had to go beyond the guilt and shame to get to anything good. Like writing, it could take you to deep and mysterious subterranean levels. With each new depth I found out things about myself I didn't know I knew. And, like writing, for a slip of a moment it could be spiritual, the cosmos pivoting on a pin, could empty and fill you all at once like a Ganges, a Piazzolla tango, a tulip bending in the wind. I was no one, I was nothing, and I was everything in the universe little and large—twig, cloud, sky. How had this incredible energy been denied me!

When I look at *la Virgen de Guadalupe* now, she is not the Lupe of my childhood, no longer the one in my grandparents' house in Tepeyac, nor is she the one of the Roman Catholic Church, the one I bolted the door against in my teens and twenties. Like every woman who matters to me, I have had to search for her in the rubble of history. And I have found her. She is Guadalupe the sex goddess, a goddess who makes me feel good about my sexual power, my sexual energy, who reminds me that I must, as Clarissa Pinkola Estés so aptly put it, "[speak] from the vulva . . . speak the most basic, honest truth," and write from my *panocha*.

In my research of Guadalupe's pre-Columbian antecedents, the she before the Church desexed her, I found Tonantzin, and inside Tonantzin a pantheon of other mother goddesses. I discovered Tlazolteotl, the goddess of fertility and sex, also referred to as Totzin. Our Beginnings, or Tzinteotl, goddess of the rump. *Putas*, nymphos, and other loose women were known as "women of the sex goddess." Tlazolteotl was the patron of sexual passion, and though she had the power to stir you to sin, she could also forgive you and cleanse you of your sexual transgressions via her priests who heard confession. In this aspect of confessor Tlazolteotl was known as Tlaelcuani, the filth eater. Maybe you've seen her; she's the one whose image is sold in the tourist markets even now, a statue of a woman squatting in childbirth, her face grimacing in pain. Tlazolteotl, then, is a duality of maternity *and* sexuality. In other words, she is a sexy mama.

To me, *la Virgen de Guadalupe* is also Coatlicue, the creative/destructive goddess. When I think of the Coatlicue statue in the National Museum of Anthropology in Mexico City, so terrible it was unearthed and then reburied because it was too frightening to look at, I think of a woman enraged, a woman as tempest, a woman *bien berrinchuda,* and I like that. *La Lupe as cabrona.* Not silent and passive, but silently gathering force.

Most days, I too feel like the creative/destructive goddess Coatlicue, especially the days I'm writing, capable of fabricating pretty tales with pretty words, as well as doing demolition work with a volley of *palabrotas* if I want to. I am the Coatlicue-Lupe whose square column of a body I see in so many Indian women, in my mother, and in myself each time I check out my thick-waisted, flat-assed torso in the mirror.

Coatlicue, Tlazolteotl, Tonantzin, *la Virgen de Guadalupe.* They are each telescoped one into the other, into who I am. And this is where *la Lupe* intrigues me—not the Lupe of 1531 who appeared to Juan Diego, but the one of the 1990s who has shaped who we are as Chicanas/*mexicanas* today, the one inside each Chicana and *mexicana.* Perhaps it's the Tlazolteotl-Lupe in me whose *malcriada* spirit inspires me to leap into the swimming pool naked or dance on a table with a skirt on my head. Maybe it's my Coatlicue-Lupe attitude that makes it possible for my mother to tell me, "No wonder men can't stand you." Who knows? What I do know is this: I am obsessed with becoming a woman comfortable in her skin.

I can't attribute my religious conversion to a flash of lightning on the road to Laredo or anything like that. Instead, there have been several lessons learned subtly over a period of time. A grave depression and near suicide in my thirty-third year and its subsequent retrospection. Vietnamese Buddhist monk Thich Nhat Hanh's writing that has brought out the Buddha-Lupe in me. My weekly peace vigil for my friend Jasna in Sarajevo. The writings of Gloria Anzaldúa. A crucial trip back to Tepeyac in 1985 with Cherríe Moraga and Norma Alarcón. Drives across Texas, talking with other Chicanas. And research for stories that would force me back inside the Church from where I'd fled.

My *Virgin de Guadalupe* is not the mother of God. She is God. She is a face for a god without a face, an *indigena* for a god without ethnicity, a female deity for a god who is genderless, but I also understand that for her to approach me, for me to finally open the door and accept her, she had to be a woman like me.

Once watching a porn film, I saw a sight that terrified me. It was the film star's *panocha*—a tidy, elliptical opening, pink and shiny like a rabbit's ear. To make matters worse, it was shaved and looked especially childlike and unsexual. I think what startled me most was the realization that my own sex has no resemblance to this woman's. My sex, dark as an orchid, rubbery and blue-purple as *pulpo,* an octopus, does not look nice and tidy, but otherworldly. I do not have little rosette nipples. My nipples are big and brown like the Mexican coins of my childhood.

When I see *la Virgen de Guadalupe* I want to lift her dress as I did my dolls, and look to see if she comes with *chones* and does her *panocha* look like mine, and does she have dark nipples too? Yes, I am certain she does. She is not neuter like Barbie. She gave birth. She has a womb. *Blessed art thou and blessed is the fruit of thy womb. . . .* Blessed art thou, Lupe, and, therefore, blessed am I.

T W E N T Y - T W O

◆◆◆

Why Nice Guys Finish Last (2008)

Julia Serano

Julia Serano is a writer, spoken-word artist, trans activist, and the author of *Whipping Girl: A Transsexual Woman on Sexism and the Scapegoating of Femininity.* Other writings have appeared in *BITCHfest: Ten Years of Cultural Criticism from the Pages of Bitch Magazine; Desire:* *Women Writing about Wanting; Word Warriors: 30 Leaders in the Women's Spoken Word Movement; Yes Means Yes: Visions of Female Sexual Power and a World Without Rape;* and magazines such as *Out, Clamor, Kitchen Sink, make/shift, other, LiP,* and *Transgender Tapestry.*

Sexualization and intimidation haunt all of us who move through the world as women. I have had men talk over me, speak down to me, and shout angrily at me when I've tried to deflect their unwanted passes. Strange men have hurled catcalls and sexual innuendos at me, and have graphically described what they'd like to do with me as I pass by them on city streets. I've also survived an attempted date rape. And frankly, I consider myself lucky that nothing more serious than that has happened to me. Needless to say, like all women, I have a great interest in bringing an end to rape culture.

Having said that, being transsexual—having had the experience of navigating my way through the world as male prior to my transition to female—has given me a somewhat different take on rape culture than the view that is often taken for granted among many cisgender (i.e., non-transgender) women. From my perspective, much of the existing rhetoric used to describe and theorize sexual harassment, abuse, and rape is, unfortunately, mired in the concept of "unilateral sexism"—that is, the belief that men are the oppressors and women are the oppressed, end of story.

Some of those who buy into unilateral sexism believe that men are inherently oppressive, dominating, and violent. Others believe that the problem is rooted in patriarchy and male socialization conspiring to condition men to become sexual predators. While there is certainly some truth to the idea that men are socialized to be sexually aggressive, even predatory, this is not the only force at work in their lives. Male children and teenagers are also regularly and explicitly reminded that they should be respectful of girls and women, and are often punished severely for picking on, or "playing rough" with, their female peers. Further, the men-are-just-socialized-that-way argument fails to explain the countless men who never sexually abuse or harass women in their lifetime.

The truth is that rape culture is a mindset that affects each and every one of us, shaping how we view and respond to the world, and creating double binds for both women and men. I call this phenomenon the predator/prey mindset, and within it, men can only ever be viewed as sexual aggressors and women as sexual objects.

The predator/prey mindset creates many of the double standards that exist in how we view female versus male sexuality. For example, on numerous occasions I've heard heterosexual female friends of mine ogle some man and make comments about how he has a nice ass. While one could certainly make the case that such discussions are "objectifying" or "sexualizing," what strikes me is that they don't *feel* that way. But if I were to overhear a group of men make the exact same comments about a woman, they would *feel* very different. They would *feel* sexualizing.

Similarly, if a male high school teacher were to have sex with one of his female teenage students, we would all be appalled. The incident would clearly *feel* like statutory rape to us. However, when the roles are reversed—when the adult teacher is female and the teenage student is male—it generally *feels* like a completely different thing to us. While it still fits the definition of statutory rape, we often have problems mustering up the *feeling* that the boy has been violated or abused. In fact, after one recent high-profile case, comedian Bill Maher joked that such teenage boys are "lucky," and the audience broke into laughter.

What these anecdotes reveal is that the predator/prey mindset essentially ensures that men cannot be viewed as legitimate sexual objects, nor can women be viewed as legitimate sexual aggressors. This has the effect of rendering invisible instances of man-on-man and woman-on-woman sexual harassment and abuse, and it makes the idea of woman-on-man rape utterly inconceivable. It's also why women cannot simply "turn the tables" and begin sexualizing men. After all, if a woman were to shout catcalls at a man, or were to pinch a guy's ass as he walked by, her actions wouldn't mean the same thing as they would if the roles were reversed. Her actions would likely be seen as suggestive and slutty, rather than intimidating and predatory.

Because of the predator/prey mindset, when a woman does act in a sexually active or aggressive way, she is generally not viewed as a sexual aggressor, but rather as opening herself up to being sexually objectified by others. This is why rape trials have historically dwelled on whether the woman in question was dressed in a revealing or provocative fashion, or whether she met with the man privately, and so on. If she did any of these things, others are likely to view her as inviting her own sexualization, as "asking for it." The underlying assumption is that women should simply know better—they should recognize that they are prey and men are predators, and they should act "appropriately."

What should be becoming increasingly clear is that the predator/prey mindset enables the virgin/whore double bind that feminists have long been rallying against. Women, as prey, are expected to play down their sexuality—to hide or repress it. Good girls, after all, are supposed to be "virgins." Women who do not downplay or repress their sexualities—that is, who do not act like prey—are viewed stereotypically as "whores." As stereotypes, both "virgin" and "whore" are disempowering, because they both frame female sexuality in terms of the predator/prey mindset. This is why reclaiming their sexuality has been such a double-edged sword for women. If a woman embraces her sexuality, it may be personally empowering for her, but she still has to deal with the fact that others will project the "whore" stereotype onto her and assume that she's inviting male sexualization. In other words, a woman may be personally empowered, but she is not seen as being sexually powerful and autonomous in the culture at large. In order for that to happen, we as individuals must begin to challenge our own (as well as other people's) perceptions and interpretations of gender. We must all move beyond viewing the world through the predator/prey mindset.

To do that, we must examine an issue that has traditionally received far less attention: the ways in which the predator/prey mindset complicates the lives of men. Trans perspectives (those of trans women, trans men, and other transgender-spectrum people) can be really vital in this regard, as many of us have had the experience of moving through the world as both women and men at different points in our lives, and thus can consider the male position without undermining or dismissing female perspectives (and vice versa). In thinking about these issues, I draw heavily on my own experiences being raised as a boy, and as a young adult who was viewed by others as a heterosexual man (as I am primarily attracted to women). It is not my intention to speak on behalf of all men, both because I never fully identified as male at the time, and also because I had a very specific and privileged male existence (for example, I am white and middle-class). It will take the experiences of other trans folks and cisgender men to fill in the whole picture.

Just as it is difficult for women to navigate their way through the world, given the fact that they are nonconsensually viewed as prey, it is often difficult for men to move through a world in which they are nonconsensually viewed as predators. When I was male-bodied, it was not uncommon for women to cross the street if I was walking behind them at night, or to have female strangers misinterpret innocent things that I said as unsolicited sexual advances. It is telling, I think, that I had to deal with the predator stereotype despite the fact that my appearance was about as unthreatening as it gets: I was a very small and unmasculine/androgynous man. Bigger and more masculine-appearing men have to deal with this stereotype much more than I ever did. Perhaps no issue exacerbates the male predator stereotype more than race. I have heard several trans men of color say that they feel that the male privilege they have gained since transitioning has been very much offset by the increased visibility and the societal stereotypes of black men as predators that others are constantly projecting onto them.

. . .

Obviously, men make up the overwhelming majority of sexual predators. But that does not mean that *all* men are necessarily sexual predators. It is important for us to keep in mind that the men-as-predator stereotype is exactly that—a stereotype—and it creates obstacles that all men must navigate, whether they are predators or not. This is especially true for those men who are additionally marginalized with regard to race and class. Given how destructive and injuring sexual abuse and violence are to those who experience them, I wouldn't dare suggest that it is the (potential or actual) victim's fault for propagating these stereotypes. At the same time, the truth is that we cannot begin to have an honest discussion about how to dismantle rape culture unless we are willing to acknowledge the negative impact that this stereotype has on those men who are not predatory.

The predator stereotype also complicates and constrains male sexuality. While many feminists have discussed how the sexual object/prey stereotype creates a double bind for women in which they can only ever be viewed as either "virgins" or "whores," not enough have considered how the sexual aggressor/predator stereotype might create a similar double bind for men. Having experienced this dilemma myself firsthand, I have come to refer to it (for reasons that will be clear in a moment) as the assholes/nice guys double bind. "Assholes" are men who fulfill the men-as-sexual-aggressors stereotype; "nice guys" are the ones who refuse or eschew it.

Just as women receive mixed messages in our culture—some encouraging them to be "virgins," others encouraging them to be "whores"—men receive similar mixed messages. As I alluded to earlier, male children often receive lots of explicit encouragement to be respectful of women. Even in adulthood, men who make blatantly sexist comments, or who suggest (in mixed company, at least) that women are "only good for one thing" will often be looked down upon or taken to task for it. So when it comes to their formal socialization, boys/men receive plenty of encouragement to be "nice guys."

The problem is that boys/men receive conflicting messages from society at large. This informal socialization comes mostly from the meanings and expectations that are regularly projected onto women and men, especially in the media and within the context of heterosexual relationships. Just as women are expected to fulfill the stereotype of being sexual objects in order to gain male attention, men are expected to fulfill the sexual aggressor stereotype in order to gain female attention. In other words, they have to act like "assholes." Granted, this isn't true in *all* situations. For example, in the progressive, artsy, and/or queer circles I inhabit nowadays, men who act like "assholes" don't get very far. But in the heterosexual mainstream culture, men who unapologetically act like "assholes" tend to thrive.

This really confused me in my late teens and young adulthood. I had lots of close female friends back then, and it always used to bum me out when they would completely fall for a guy doing the "asshole" routine: acting confident to the point of being cocky, being sexually forward if not downright pushy, and relentlessly teasing girls in a junior high school–esque way with the expectation that they would smile and giggle in response. It always seemed really contrived to me. I suppose I was privy to insider information: I had the experience of interacting regularly with many of those same men *as a man* (not a woman), and in those situations they did not act nearly as cocky or presumptive or dismissive toward me as they did around women they were interested in.

Anyway, time and time again, my female friends would fall for an "asshole" and then be crushed because he never called her the next day, as he'd promised, or because he started bragging to his guy friends about his "sexual conquest," or because he tried to push things along faster and farther sexually than she was willing to go. Sometimes after being hurt by some "asshole," my female friends would come to me for advice or to be consoled. They came to me because I was a "nice guy." In their eyes, I was safe. Respectful. Harmless. Sometimes during these post-"asshole" conversations, my friends would go on a tirade about how all men are jerks and cannot be trusted, or they'd ask, "Why can't I find a guy who will treat me with respect?" Whenever they did this, I would point out that there are lots of guys who are not jerks, who are respectful of women. I'd even name a few. Upon hearing the names I suggested, my friends would invariably say something like "I don't find him attractive" or "I think of him more as a friend."

Just as women who refuse to play the role of sexual object often fail to attract male attention, "nice guys" who refuse to play the role of sexual aggressor typically fail to attract female attention. (Note that I'm not speaking here of the type of man referred to in the feminist blogosphere as a Nice Guy, who is the sort of man who argues that being a "nice guy" entitles him to sex with whomever he wants, thus revealing himself to be merely a closeted "asshole.") In high school and college, I had several male friends who, apparently concerned with the lack of action I was getting, literally told me that women like it when guys act like "assholes." For them, it was just something one did to attract women. And as much as I hate to admit it, it generally seemed to be true. During my college years, I watched a number of "nice guys" transform into "assholes." And when they did, women suddenly became interested in them. The most stunning transformation I witnessed was in this guy who lived in my dorm, whom I'll call Eric. Freshman and sophomore years, he was a super-sweet and respectful guy. Despite the fact that he was fairly good-looking, women were not generally interested in him. Somewhere around junior year, he suddenly began acting like an "asshole" (around women, at least). Instead of engaging women in conversations (as he used to), he would instead relentlessly tease them. The things he would say sounded really dismissive to me, but often the intended recipient would just giggle in response. Suddenly he was picking women up at parties, and

I'd occasionally overhear women who never knew Eric back when he was a "nice guy" discussing how cute they thought he was.

The last time I saw Eric was about two years after college. We had both moved to New York City, and a mutual friend came up to visit and suggested that we all go out together. The bar that we went to was really crowded, and at one point, Eric started talking about how in situations like this, he would sometimes fold his arms across his chest and subtly grope women as they walked by. Between the fact that the bar was so crowded and the way he held his arms to obscure his hands, women weren't able to figure out that it was Eric. Upon hearing this, I walked out of the bar, appalled.

The reason I tell this story is that it complicates many of the existing presumptions regarding the origins of rape culture. Some have suggested that men are biologically programmed to be sexual predators. The existence of Eric (and others like him) challenges that argument because, after all, he was a "nice guy" for most of his life until about the age of twenty—well after his sex drive kicked in. Eric challenges overly simplistic men-are-socialized-to-be-that-way arguments for the same reason: He made it to early adulthood—well beyond his formative childhood and teenage years—before becoming an "asshole." It would be really hard to make the case that Eric became a sexual predator because he was influenced by media imagery or pornography, or because his male peers egged him on. Like I said, I lived in the same dorm as he did, and I never once saw any guys teasing him for being a "nice guy" or coercing him into being an "asshole." I would argue that the primary reason Eric became sexually aggressive was that he was interested in attracting women. And, as with many men, once Eric began disrespecting women on a regular basis, the lines between flirting and harassment, between sex and violation, between consensual and nonconsensual, became blurred or unimportant to him.

Not to sound corny, but we all want the same things in life: to gain other people's attention, to be adored, to be sexually desired, to be intimate with people we find attractive, and to have great sex. In a culture where women are generally viewed as sexual objects, some women will take on that role in order to gain attention and to feel desirable. By the same token, in a world where men are only ever viewed as sexual aggressors, some men will take on that role in order to gain attention and to feel desirable. So long as the predator/prey mindset predominates and a demand remains for women and men to fulfill those stereotypes, a large percentage of people will continue to gravitate toward them.

This is why single-tact solutions to abolish rape culture will always fail. For instance, many people in both the political/religious Right, as well as many anti-pornography feminists, seem to take what I call the "virgin" approach. Their line of reasoning goes something like this: Because men are predators, we should desexualize women in the culture by, for example, banning pornography and discouraging representations of women (whether media imagery or actual women) that others can interpret as sexually arousing or objectifying. This approach not only is sexually repressive and disempowering for many women, but it also reinforces the idea that men are predators and women are prey. In other words, it reaffirms the very system that it hopes to dismantle.

I also get frustrated by people who think that it's simply up to male allies to call out those men who are sexist or disrespectful of women. While this approach can have some positive effect, I believe that many cisgender women overestimate its potential. First off, it essentially makes the "nice guys" responsible for policing the "assholes." This overlooks the fact that in the heterosexual mainstream, "assholes" are seen as being higher up in the social pecking order than "nice guys." As a result, a "nice guy" calling out an "asshole" about how he needs to be more respectful of women tends to have as much societal clout as if the geeky girl in class were to lecture the cheerleaders about how they shouldn't play dumb and giggle at every joke that the popular boys make.

Such comments, when they are made, are often ignored or outright dismissed. Furthermore, I've experienced a number of situations in my life (e.g., high school locker rooms) where I honestly did not feel safe enough to protest the sexist comments that some boys and men make. After all, one of the ways in which the hierarchical status quo is maintained in male circles is through the threat of physical intimidation and violence.

Any attempts to critique men for being sexually aggressive, or to critique women for fulfilling the role of sexual object, will have a very limited effect. These tactics, after all, fail to address the crucial issue of demand. So long as heterosexual women are attracted to men who act like aggressors, and heterosexual men are attracted to women who act like objects, people will continue to fulfill those roles. In contrast, critiques that challenge why individuals desire stereotypical "sex objects" and "sexual aggressors" seem to me to get closer to the root of the problem.

I have heard many feminists critique men who prefer women that fulfill the sexual object stereotype. Many of these critiques (rightfully, I think) suggest that the man in question must be somewhat shallow or insecure if he's willing to settle for someone whom he does not view as his intellectual and emotional equal. What I have seen far less of are critiques of women who are attracted to sexually aggressive men. Perhaps this stems in part from the belief that such comments might be misinterpreted as blaming women for enabling the sexual abuse they receive at the hands of men. While I can understand this reluctance, I nevertheless feel that it is a mistake to ignore this issue, given the fact that many men become sexual aggressors primarily, if not solely, to attract the attention of women. In fact, if heterosexual women suddenly decided en masse that "nice guys" are far sexier than "assholes," it would create a huge shift in the predator/prey dynamic. While I wouldn't suggest that such a change would completely eliminate rape or sexual abuse (because there are clearly other societal forces at work here), I do believe that it would greatly reduce the number of men who harass and disrespect women on a daily basis.

Those feminists who have critiqued the tendency of women to be attracted to sexually aggressive men often refer to the phenomenon as "internalized misogyny." In other words, they presume that because women have been socialized to take shit from men, they have become conditioned to continually seek out men who will treat them like shit. Personally, I find this explanation unsatisfying. I don't think that women are attracted to sexual aggressors because they believe that those men will treat them like shit. Rather, they tend to be attracted to other aspects of sexual aggressors, and only later become disappointed by the way they are treated.

This phenomenon is more accurately viewed as a form of "externalized misogyny." There are a lot of subliminal meanings built into the predator/prey mindset: that men are aggressive and women are passive, that men are strong and women are weak, that men are rebellious and women are harmless,

and so on. It is no accident that the meanings associated with women are typically viewed as inferior to . . . those associated with men. Given this context, I would argue that "nice guys" are generally read as emasculated or effeminized men in our culture. In a world where calling a man "sensitive" is viewed as a pejorative, the very act of showing respect for women often disqualifies a male from being seen as a "real man." I believe that this is a major reason why many heterosexual women are not sexually interested in "nice guys."

I think that women who are attracted to sexual aggressors are primarily drawn to the rebellious, bad-boy image they project—an image that is essentially built into our cultural ideal of maleness. The odd thing is that for many men, fulfilling the aggressor role represents the path of least resistance. How rebellious can it be to fulfill a stereotype? "Nice guys," on the other hand, *are* rebellious, at least in one sense: They buck the system and refuse to reduce themselves to the predator stereotype. It is time that we begin to recognize and celebrate this rebellion.

Lots of women I know want to create a world in which women are allowed and encouraged to be sexual without having to be nonconsensually sexualized. This is a laudable goal. But having been on the other side of the gender divide, I would argue that for this to happen, we will also have to work to simultaneously ensure that men can be respectful of women without being *desexualized*. One cannot happen without the other. I think that a lot of men would be eager to work with women to create such a world. A movement that refuses to render invisible and desexualize men who are not predators, and that attempts to debunk both the virgin/whore *and* the asshole/nice guy double binds, would excite and attract many male allies.

Perhaps most important, understanding the predator/prey mindset can help us to recognize that rape culture is reinforced both by people's actions *and* by their perceptions. The system will not be dismantled until all (or at least most) of us learn not to project the predator stereotype onto men and the prey stereotype onto women. Just as we must learn to debunk the many racist, sexist, classist, homophobic, and ageist cultural stereotypes we've absorbed over the course of a lifetime, we must also learn to move beyond predator/prey stereotypes. Honestly, I find this the most personally challenging aspect of this work. Moving through the world as a woman, and having to deal with being harassed by men on a regular basis, makes me wary of letting my guard down in any way. Viewing all men as predators is a convenient self-defense mechanism, but it ignores the countless men who are respectful of women. I am not suggesting that we, as women, ignore the important issue of safety—to do so at this moment in time would be beyond unwise. What I am suggesting is that we won't get to where we want to be until the men-as-predator/sexual aggressor assumption no longer dominates our thinking. It's difficult to imagine getting there from here, but we're going to have to try.

TWENTY-THREE

Women and the Rise of Raunch Culture—Excerpt (2005)

Ariel Levy

Ariel Levy is a staff writer at *The New Yorker* magazine and author of *Female Chauvinist Pigs: Women and the Rise of Raunch Culture.* Her work has also appeared in *the Washington Post, Vogue, Slate,* and the *New York Times.* In 2009, she was named one of the "Forty Under 40" most influential *out* individuals by *The Advocate.*

On the Web site for the group CAKE, it says "The new sexual revolution is where sexual equality and feminism finally meet." CAKE throws monthly parties in New York City and London at which women can "explore female sexuality" and experience "feminism in action." They lament, "Back in the day, because fighting sexual abuse was the priority, mainstream feminism tended to treat sexuality like a dark horse." CAKE wants to fix all that. Founders Emily Kramer and Melinda Gallagher cite Hugh Hefner as a hero.

CAKE parties are so prominent they were featured on an episode of *Law & Order* in 2004—renamed Tart parties, which actually seems like a more apt moniker when you think about it. (In an interview with ABC's *20/20,* Kramer and Gallagher said that they chose "cake" as their name because it is a slang term for female genitalia, and connotes something "gooey, sweet, yummy, sexy, sticky.") They have 35,000 online subscribers, a book deal, a Web boutique through which they sell tank tops and vibrators, and a Showtime reality pilot in the works.

CAKE is also a sort of hypersexual sorority. You have to pledge to get in, which involves writing an essay and paying a hundred dollars. Then, if you are accepted, you get regular e-mails from CAKE's founders called "CAKE Bytes," with commentary on everything from the Bush Administration's war of attrition on abortion rights to the perceived weaknesses of *Sex and the City.* Kramer and Gallagher engage in a certain amount of old-school grassroots organizing— they arranged for a bus to take women from Manhattan to Washington, D.C., for the April 25, 2004, March for Women's Lives, for example—but their parties are what have put them on the map.

Themes have ranged from "Striptease-a-thons" to porn parties, and the events are thrown at upscale venues like the W hotels and velvet-rope clubs throughout Manhattan and London. CAKE made the front page of the *New York Post* with one of their early parties in 2001, at which two guests, the adult film actors Marie Silva and Jack Bravo, had intercourse and oral sex inside CAKE's designated "Freak Box," a steel closet with a camera inside offering everyone outside live streaming video of the shagging-in-action projected onto huge screens throughout the party.

In the fall of 2003, they threw an event called "CAKE Underground" at a club called B'lo in Manhattan. On the e-vite, they said it was an opportunity to "witness the REAL LIFE ACTUALIZATION of women's sexual desires."

They had hired a dwarf to work the elevator. The words "exhibitionism" and "voyeurism" and the letters XXX were projected onto the club walls. *The hos they wanna fuck,* 50 Cent boomed over the sound system. I was presented with a sticker of a woman's hip to knee region clad in garters and fishnets above the words, "ASK ME: If I know where my G-spot is." (I am strangely shy about discussing the topography of my vagina with strangers, so I declined to wear the sticker as instructed by the woman in pigtails at the door.)

Gallagher, a stunning thirty-year-old with long chestnut hair and the physique of a short model, and Kramer, who wore punky clothes and a wary expression as she surveyed her party, have adopted the women's movement's early policy on admissions to anti-rape speak-outs: Men pay double and have to be accompanied by a woman. That did not seem to hurt the male attendance at B'lo. The room was packed with women wearing extremely revealing clothing or just lingerie, and young men in jeans and button-down shirts who couldn't believe their luck.

A blonde in a white fur jacket over a pink lace bra sucked a lollipop while she waited for her $11 vodka tonic at the bar. A fellow in his early thirties wearing a suit with no tie asked her, "Have you ever had a threesome?"

"What?" she said. Then she realized that he was only reading off the ASK ME sticker she had plastered on her right breast. "Sorry," she said. "Yeah, I've had like four."

At around eleven, a troop of CAKE dancers got on the stage in the center of the huge room. They wore thigh-high patent leather boots, fishnets, and satin bra and panty sets the colors of cotton candy and clear skies.

At first, they shimmied onstage like garden variety lusty club-goers. But then a visiting crew from Showtime turned on their cameras and when the lights hit the dancers they started humping each other as if possessed. A blonde woman with improbably large breasts immediately bent over and a dancer with a souped-up Mohawk got behind her and started grinding her crotch against the other woman's rear end.

Many, many men formed a pack around the stage and most pumped their fists in the air to the beat of the music and the humping.

"The girls are much hotter here than at the last party," a mousy young woman in a gray skirt-suit told her friend, who was in similar straight-from-work attire.

"You think? Look at that one," she said, pointing at Mohawk. "She's basically flat!"

A twenty-five-year-old assistant with lovely green eyes and an upswept ponytail was looking back and forth between the dancers onstage and her ex-boyfriend, who was having a smile-filled conversation with a sleek woman in a black bra. "What should I do?" she said. "Should I go over there? Should I go home?"

The next day, I called her at her office at around one o'clock. (She was so hung over I could almost smell the alcohol through the phone.) "He went home

with that girl," she said. "I ended up staying really late. My friend and I were in the back room and we got really drunk and kind of hooked up with like seven people. Mostly girls. The guys just watched. Uck."

Many of the conflicts between the women's liberation movement and the sexual revolution and within the women's movement itself were left unresolved thirty years ago. What we are seeing today is the residue of that confusion. CAKE is an example of the strange way people are ignoring the contradictions of the past, pretending they never existed, and putting various, conflicting ideologies together to form one incoherent brand of raunch feminism.

Some of this is motivated by a kind of generational rebellion. Embracing raunch so casually is a way for young women to thumb our noses at the intense fervor of second-wave feminists (which both Kramer and Gallagher's mothers were). Nobody wants to turn into their mother. Certainly, this generation can afford to be less militant than Susan Brownmiller's compatriots because the world is now a different place. In their book *Manifesta: Young Women, Feminism, and the Future* (2000), Jennifer Baumgardner and Gloria Steinem's former assistant Amy Richards tell us they are different from their "serious sisters of the sixties and seventies" because they live in a time when the "feminist movement has such a firm and organic toehold in women's lives."

But raunch feminism is not *only* a rebellion. It is also a garbled attempt at continuing the work of the women's movement. "Whether its volunteering at a women's shelter, attending an all women's college or a speak-out for Take Back the Night, or dancing at a strip club," write Baumgardner and Richards, "whenever women are gathered together there is great potential for individual women, and even the location itself, to become radicalized." They don't explain what "radicalized" means to them, so we are left to wonder if it is their way of saying "enlightened" or "sexually charged" or if to them those are the same things. In this new formulation of raunch feminism, stripping is as valuable to elevating womankind as gaining an education or supporting rape victims. Throwing a party where women grind against each other in their underwear while fully-clothed men watch them is suddenly part of the same project as marching on Washington for reproductive rights. According to Baumgardner and Richards, "watching TV shows *(Xena! Buffy!)* can . . . contain feminism in action"—just as CAKE bills their parties as "feminism in action." Based on these examples, it would seem raunch feminism in action is pretty easy to achieve: The basic requirements are hot girls and small garments.

I had occasion to talk to Erica Jong, one of the most famous sex-positive feminists—"one of the most interviewed people in the world," as she's put it—on the thirtieth anniversary of her novel *Fear of Flying*. "I was standing in the shower the other day, picking up my shampoo," she said. "It's called 'Dumb Blonde.' I thought, *Thirty years ago you could not have sold this.* I think we have lost consciousness of the way our culture demeans women." She was quick to tell me that she "wouldn't pass a law against the product or call the PC police." But, she said, "let's not kid ourselves that this is liberation. The women who buy the idea that flaunting your breasts in sequins is power—I mean, I'm for all that stuff—but let's not get so into the tits and ass that we don't notice how far we haven't come. Let's not confuse that with real power. I don't like to see women fooled."

Nouvelle raunch feminists are not concocting this illogic all by themselves. Some of it they learned in school. A fervid interest in raunchy representations of sex and a particular brand of women's studies are both faddish in academia now, and the two are frequently presented side by side, as if they formed a seamless, comprehensible totality.

. . .

When I met . . . [Kramer], she was not long out of Columbia University, where she majored in gender studies and wrote her thesis on "how the power dynamics of sexuality should ideally allow for both men and women to explore, express and define sexuality for themselves." In an e-mail, she told me she started CAKE with Gallagher because she felt the "mainstream messaging related to sexuality either pitted female sexuality *in terms of* male sexuality —like articles in popular women's magazines on how to please your man—or defined sexuality as dominated by men . . . like critical feminist texts." (Kramer's writing here has echoes of Shere Hite, who wrote in the preface to the original *Hite Report*, published in 1976, "female sexuality has been seen essentially as a response to male sexuality and intercourse. There has rarely been any acknowledgment that female sexuality might have a complex nature of its own which would be more than just the logical counterpart of [what we think of as] male sexuality") Kramer was edging in on a solution. "I thought there should be another option for women, and began to

formulate a theory behind what that option should be." She wouldn't spell her theory out for me, but presumably CAKE parties are its embodiment.

Despite Kramer and Gallagher's magniloquence on "mainstream messaging" and "feminism in action," I was reminded of CAKE parties a few months later when I attended an event in a giant parking lot in Los Angeles for *Maxim* magazine's "Hot 100," their annual assessment of the hundred hottest famous women. People were lined up in scantily clad droves on Vine Street, waiting to get rejected when their names were mysteriously found missing from the phone book–sized list at the door. Past the gatekeepers, there was an orange Jeep and two hired girls in bikini tops and black cowboy boots who spent the evening smiling, arching their backs, and buffing the vehicle with bandannas.

This was a high-profile party with press coverage and celebrities (Denzel Washington, Christian Slater, the model Amber Valletta, the singer Macy Gray, and of course, Paris Hilton). Somehow, a pair of inordinately geeky-looking guys who were actually wearing backpacks got in. One turned to the other and said, "See that black girl in front of you? Look at her face. She's so fine." The dance floor was a sea of naked legs perched on high-heeled sandals.

The party extended into an adjacent warehouse, where a smoke machine kept the air gauzy, and in the center, there was a large bed on a raised dais on which two girls, one Asian, one blonde, both in lingerie and pigtails, had an extended pillow fight. Behind the bar, tall females in white feathered tops danced on poles, their faces set in masks of lascivious contempt. Keith Blanchard, then *Maxim's* editor-in-chief, told me, "It's a sexy night!"

To me, "sexy" is based on the inexplicable overlap of character and chemicals that happens between people . . . the odd sense that you have something primal in common with another person whom you may love, or you may barely even like, that can only be expressed through the physical and psychological exchange that is sex. When I'm in the plastic "erotic" world of high, hard tits and long nails and incessant pole dancing—whether I'm at a CAKE party, walking past a billboard of Jenna Jameson in Times Square, or dodging pillows at the Maxim Hot 100—I don't feel titillated or liberated or aroused. I feel bored, and kind of tense.

In defense of CAKE parties, Gallagher told a reporter from *Elle* magazine, "*you* try getting 800 people to behave in a feminist way!" To be sure, that's no small project. But we have to wonder how displaying hot chicks onstage in exactly the same kind of miniature outfits they've always been in moves things in the right direction. If CAKE is promoting *female* sexual culture, I can't believe there aren't other ways to excite women. I even believe there are other ways to excite men.

Kramer said, "CAKE's mission is to change public perceptions about female sexuality," and their Web site claims they seek to "redefine the cur-

rent boundaries [of] female sexuality." If the whole point is change and redefinition, then I wonder why the CAKE imagery—from the porn movies they project on the walls at their parties to the insignia they use on their Web site, a sexy cartoon silhouette of a lean, curvy lady with wind-swept hair and her hand on her hip—looks so utterly of a piece with every other bimbo pictorial I've seen in my life. Why is this the "new feminism" and not what it looks like: the old objectification?

◆◆◆

On the Complications of Negotiating Dyke Femininity (2004)

Wendy Somerson

Wendy Somerson is a writer, artist, and activist. Her work has appeared in *Bitch, Tikkun,* and other publications. She helped to found the Seattle chapter of Jewish Voice for Peace, which "supports the aspirations of Israelis and Palestinians for security and self-determination" and calls for "an end to the Israeli occupation of the West Bank, the Gaza Strip, and East Jerusalem." In 2011, she was one of the women Seattle NOW honored "for their dedication to the people in our community."

When I was in the third grade, my best friend Lauren and I proclaimed that we were boys. I can't remember the day it happened or the particular reason, but it was based on the specious logic that girls were "dumb" and boys were "cool." We simply called ourselves boys and stopped wearing skirts or dresses, and when we encountered gender divisions in the classroom, we joined the boys. We thought by declaring our gender, we simply made it so. Wouldn't it be ideal if gender were such a simple matter of choice for all of us? It actually didn't go too badly for us as third-graders in the 1970s. Our teacher, Ms. (emphasis on the *Ms.)* Elam, was mostly tolerant of our joining the boys' groups. . . . But the boys themselves were not so welcoming and taunted us with threats to pull down our pants to prove our "real" gender. That never made sense to me; even back then, I didn't understand why genitalia determined gender.

I remember dealing with the gender contradictions fairly gracefully as a third-grader, without giving them too much thought. When I had to wear my Girl Scout tunic to school, I didn't worry about the group affiliation; I simply wore pants under it and called it a long shirt. Our reassigning of our gender wasn't the only thing or probably even the most important thing going on that year in our lives. Our new gender allowed us to shoot marbles obsessively at recess, play kickball, wear scrappy (preferably muddy) clothes, and disdain "girl" games on the playground. Since we refused to hang out with other "silly" girls, and we weren't really accepted by the boys, we did everything together in a wonderful childhood world of two. In our own little universe, we affirmed each other's gender choices without a lot of discussion and got on with the important business of collecting marbles, playing four square, and jumping off the roof of the tree house (until Lauren broke her wrist). The next year, when we were separated into different classes, we left behind our boy identifications. I don't remember making any conscious decision about it.

Lots of girls spend time in their childhood as "tomboys," and I think this childhood gender choice links to ways that I continue to negotiate gender as a feminine-identified dyke. Masculine or nontraditional ways of being feminine are still part and parcel of my identity, but as a committed feminist, I am now determined to question whether I'm basing my gender choices on denigrating more traditional aspects of femininity. While I may raise more questions than answers in this essay, my intention is to generate more complicated feminist discussions and perceptions of femininity within dyke communities. First, I will look at how femininity has been presented and positioned in a few gender panels and discussions that have taken place in Seattle in the past few years. I will then consider how I negotiate my particular brand of femininity and how feminine-identified dykes engage in complicated gender interactions all the time. My aim is to shine a spotlight on queer femininity, which does not often get discussed on its own but more often as a counterpart to butch, or as the unspoken and unacknowledged Other of "gender transgression." . . .

Female Femininity

There has been a recent celebration of female masculinity within dyke communities: a proliferation of drag king shows, butch erotica shows, FTM/butch/transgender panels, and discussions of gender transgression or "transcendence." While I do not want to disparage this trend or disdain female masculinity, I do want to consider what happens to female femininity within this debate and to suggest that we need to be careful not to reproduce and reinforce traditional gender hierarchies within queer communities. Several immediate questions come to mind in light of some of these public performances: Why don't we often explicitly talk about femininity? Do we assume that we already know or understand it? Is there an underlying paradigm in these discussions that as we move farther away from our assigned gender, the more transgressive our gender enactments will become? Many of these panels, including one that I organized for a queer film festival, had no feminine or self-identified femme dykes on them at all, and most of them did not specifically address femininity as an issue of concern or interest for our communities.

A local panel on transcending gender in 2000 brought together two FTMs (female-to-male transgendered people), two dykes who identified as butch, and one dyke who identified as a femme partner FTM. Only one of these five panelists was introduced with a comment on her looks. While the FTM organizer described the other panelists based on their accomplishments, he described the femme panelist as "beautiful." When it came time for her own explanation of her relationship to the issue

of transcending gender, she commented that after giving it much thought, she decided that she had "only" one gender and thus was "just a girl." While she did a great job moderating the panel, this apologetic comment lingered in my mind, and it disturbs me still. It suggests that her feminine identity is not as complicated or interesting as FTM or butch identities because she stuck with the gender she was seemingly assigned at birth. The more genders, the more transgressive? Does stockpiling or altering genders confer prestige? Throughout the discussion, several butch women in the audience referred to the femme panelist in order to claim that their girlfriends looked "just like" her in order (presumably) to indicate that their girlfriends were visibly feminine. Unless she really did have a bunch of identical twins running around, this phenomenon indicates the assumption that we know exactly what "femme" looks like, and it often looks the same. It also suggests that gender transgressors sometimes rely on naturalizing feminine identity in order to measure their own departure from a norm. Although queer femininity may appear less constructed than female masculinity, I insist that it is just as constructed, whether consciously or unconsciously.

In a 1998 butch/FTM borderlands panel that I organized in conjunction with the documentary *The Brandon Teena Story* for the Seattle Lesbian and Gay Film Festival, the panel (of two butches and two FTMs) and the audience struggled to address the socioeconomic issues that the film raised. In the contentious discussion, panelists and audience members alike offended each other with questionable remarks about class, which often stereotyped and scapegoated the working class as "White trash." While class discussions in the United States are consistently fraught, I think that an obsessive focus on female masculinity or gender crossing can stabilize and naturalize other aspects of identity—in this case, class—that may not appear as obvious on a visual level. One of the panelists suggested that Brandon's rape and murder and the 1998 murder of Matthew Shepard in Wyoming could only happen in a small town. While obviously homophobic and transphobic violence occurs everywhere, this comment exemplifies a displacement of these phobias onto rural areas. As the documentary makes clear, Falls City, Nebraska, where Brandon lived for the last few months of his life, became an increasingly

Hilary Swank plays Brandon Teena in *Boys Don't Cry* (1999)

discussion, one panelist described Brandon's last girlfriend, Lana, as a "manipulative girl who didn't try to better herself." Meanwhile, both panelists and audience members often described Brandon as a hero for choosing to live his life so bravely. Marked as an individual gender transgressor in this discussion, Brandon was often able to escape the class-biased descriptions that were applied to Nebraska and Nebraskans. Brandon seemingly transcended his location in contrast with the other citizens of these small Nebraska towns, who were marked as homophobic bigots in order for city dwellers to feel better about themselves. While the issues of class, gender, and sexuality in Brandon Teena's situation deserve their own discussion, other identity attributes—in this case, class and femininity—get stabilized, naturalized, and simplified when our focus is purely on visual gender subversion.

Psychic Complexity

At another local gender event, an acquaintance dismissed the possibility of a femme drag show by suggesting, "That seems to be pushing it." Why? Because femininity is not seen as a performance as such? Is femininity seen as performative only when it is done in excess? (Think drag queens.) Roles can work on other levels aside from the visual, and we need to start talking about complexity in gender roles and how other factors, including race, class, ethnicity, and nationality, contribute to and produce various gender roles. There isn't one standard of femininity or masculinity for every race, ethnic group, class, or nation. In addition, someone may present one gender expression in a given context, but that same appearance can indicate something else in a different cultural context. For instance, I might appear more traditionally feminine at a dyke event, but when I work out in the university gym, I don't appear particularly feminine with my un-shaved legs and short hair. I'm not sure that the larger culture always recognizes some distinctions we make between butch and femme.

dangerous and violent place to live in the 1990s, at least partially because of economic underdevelopment and its corresponding effect on unemployment. One audience member also wondered why Brandon didn't just move to New York City. This shows no acknowledgment that he may not have had access to resources or a desire to move to a big city or that he may have encountered the same kind of violence in a big city.

Another audience participant remarked that she couldn't distinguish among Brandon Teena's girlfriends because they all had "big hair." Marked as "White trash," these women were dismissed because of their classed feminine appearances. Like the femme panelist on the transcending gender panel, these women were lumped together as indistinguishable representatives of femininity. After the

We also have complicated psychic identifications, which cannot be determined on a strictly visual level. At another panel I organized on questioning traditional models of masculinity, one of the FTM panelists made an extremely interesting point about attempting to maintain what he sees as a specifically femme and feminist psychology in his FTM body. That identification isn't something that we can necessarily identify visually; it complicates the notion that we can always understand how someone negotiates gender based solely upon visual appearance. Unfortunately, this continual focus on visually subversive gender roles marginalizes many identities, including femme and feminine ones.

Sexuality is one arena in which complicated psychic identifications occur. For example, in some sexual contexts, I feel the most feminine—sometimes in contrast with butch energy—but that can also shift midscene. With some of my butch lovers, I often started out in what felt like a feminine role of seduction, but as we moved deeper sexually, I imagined myself as a man in my fantasies, while my butch lover became my fantasy woman. At the beginning of my most recent relationship, this mental shifting really upset my butch lover. She could sense some of my male energy, but she didn't know how to act or what persona to take in relation to my shifts and fantasies. After we negotiated these fantasies for a couple years, we became more comfortable playing with these roles and switching genders. In this case, our psychic realities didn't always correspond with our physical coupling. I don't want to dwell . . . on my sexual personae, but this is an arena in which queer gender roles often get enacted and exaggerated. Butch–femme roles are useful in providing a difference around which desire can mobilize, but even that desire can be more complicated than visual cues might indicate. At one gender panel discussion, a panelist claimed that gender identities are based on where we obtain power. She claimed that butches feel empowered by a masculine-identified role and disempowered by a feminine role, and femmes feel the opposite. But why can't we gain power from more than one place? Just because I'm feminine, why should that mean that I can imagine myself only in a feminine role in both fantasies and sexual acts?

My Body as Text

In addition to complex psychic identifications, feminine-identified dykes can also have complicated visual appearances, which may include masculine elements. While I am arguing that we need to stop limiting our gender definitions to the realm

of the visual, even in this realm, many of us who identify as femme or feminine still have to negotiate femininity with care. I certainly don't feel as if my appearance completely explains or covers my fraught feminine identification, but at various moments in my life, it has highlighted some of these contradictions. An assumption exists that if you identify as a feminine dyke, you "pass" as straight (along with all that implies). We need to disrupt this assumption. Identifying as feminine or femme does not always mean sporting long hair and makeup, and these visual attributes do not necessarily add up to passing in all circumstances. Femininity presents conflicts in any dyke's life because rejecting compulsory heterosexuality in and of itself challenges traditional notions of femininity.

I sometimes identify as feminine; I generally and currently identify as dyke and queer. But my appearance has caused "trouble" for quite some time. When I turned seventeen in the 1980s I identified as a punk rocker and rejected the traditional white middle-class standards of femininity. I shaved the sides of my head, stopped shaving my legs, got my nose pierced, and generally appeared as a "freak," especially because I was living in Columbus, Ohio. While my days as a rocker are long gone, I still have very short hair, never wear skirts or dresses in public, don't shave, and don't feel as though I appear particularly feminine. My clothing and shoes come from both men's and women's departments. I don't think my style is very feminine, but that obviously depends on the definition. Maybe I should be redefining femininity instead of separating myself from the category. I still wonder if my choices are partially based on internalized misogyny. Does that make them less valid? Perhaps they hark back to my childhood belief that skirts were "silly," or perhaps I just don't feel comfortable in them.

When I get my hair cut every six weeks, I get it clippered down to a style one-quarter-inch short of bald. My scalp shows for a week, but I always leave a few slight curls around my face. More than one (butch) girlfriend has pointed to these curls as a difference between us and something that marks me as feminine. And this may be right; these curls feel feminine, and I like them. But at the same time, I challenge enough traditional elements of femininity that when I taught a freshman college class on the boundaries of identity, my body immediately became a text: students identified my appearance as blurring the lines between traditional masculine and feminine attributes. They pointed to my short hair, lack of makeup, and "masculine" clothes. I am sometimes mistaken for a man (for some bizarre reason this generally occurs at my local Safeway), but because of my features, this occurrence is fairly rare. But I recently realized that I don't know how to talk about this experience. I don't know how to join in the discussions when butches talk about being mistaken for men because the consequences of their gender transgressions often seem more dangerous or violent. I rarely fear actual violence (except when I lived in Columbus, Ohio). I worry that if I bring up my experiences, I will be scoffed at because I identify as feminine but never as butch. I rarely, if ever, hear stories about other femmes or feminine-identified dykes getting mistaken for men.

Suitable Gender

A few years ago, in preparation for an academic conference where I was interviewing for a position as a professor, I embarked upon the adventure of buying a suit. Having credit at Ann Taylor (for returning one of my mom's unfathomable gifts), I began with the goal of buying a suit that would look professional enough for me to interview in without feeling too uncomfortable or too uncomfortably feminine. Having dressed up in my more traditionally feminine attire even to shop for the suit, I arrived at the store, feeling like an imposter on various levels. I felt as if I was performing as more traditionally female than I really was—as someone who actually gets paid enough to live on (not a graduate student who couldn't afford to pay her rent without the benefit of student loans), as a respectable "adult" (that ephemeral category that seems perpetually beyond my grasp). Being a proper adult seems to be linked in my mind with performing the proper gender.

I picked out the simplest, most tailored black suit (jacket and pants) that I could find and successfully avoided getting help from the sales clerks before slinking into the dressing room to try it on. Looking at myself in the mirror under the glaring white lights, I looked like a kid playing dress-up. I didn't know what to think; the waist seemed too high, the shoulders too padded, and my whole look incongruous. When I finally succumbed to creeping

out of the stall to look at myself in the three-way mirror and get some help, a saleswoman rushed over and immediately insisted that I had chosen a suit that was two sizes too big. Mortified by my error (which I feared exposed me as an imposter), I agreed to try on another size, but I asked that she bring me just one size smaller than the twelve. She arrived with a size eight, and suggested that I "at least try it on," while I asked her again for a ten, this time with a note of pleading in my voice. Temporarily deferring to her expertise, I squeezed myself into the size eight, but I couldn't stand feeling so constricted or the sight of myself in its form-fitting darts and pinching waist. I felt so exposed. I never wear anything that accentuates my waist or emphasizes my breasts.

Later I wondered, am I simply uncomfortable with my femininity? (I've heard feminine women who don't identify as femme accused of this, while few dykes would accuse a butch of something similar. Isn't that part of a butch's appeal?) Is this a butch feeling? a dyke feeling? a nontraditional woman feeling? a former punk feeling? just my feeling? a discomfort with my body? Why did I have to highlight my body in this way? The saleswoman and I compromised on the size ten, although it still felt a little snug (by this time, I felt transported back to negotiating the endless costume drama of adolescence with my mother). As I stared at myself in the mirror, trying to become accustomed to my appearance in a suit, the saleswoman returned with the dreaded "accessories"—a pearl necklace and knee-highs—which she suggested that I try on with some pumps. Aghast, I mumbled, "Ummmm, no thanks," with a tight smile, and retreated to the dressing room. As I pulled on my jeans, sweater, and clunky shoes, I felt anxious, as if I had failed in my quest to perform my act properly.

. . .

After having escaped the store, shaken but intact, I wondered about how I was making those decisions. How was I choosing to participate in one custom of femininity without another? How was I *constructing* my identity . . . in relation to what gendered norms and images? Was this a valid gendered decision, as worthy of support as it would be if I were describing the experience of buying a men's suit? While I do tell the story to a few of my friends for sympathy and laughs, I never consider it important enough to retell in light of gender panels or discussions. At a party after a gender panel, a couple of butch women were describing their experiences of buying men's suits, and I shared my suit-buying story. While I did feel support and interest, I also felt vaguely uneasy and slightly ashamed. I felt like another kind of imposter; who was I to tell this story when it wasn't as dramatic or transgressive as buying or wearing a man's suit?—now there's a real transgendered experience; there's real oppression for you. But I questioned my own reactions and their link to which gender experiences are validated within queer communities. These are the kinds of stories we need to start hearing and discussing if we want to generate more complicated discussions and perceptions of femininity.

I'm not using this example because it's dramatic, unique, or interesting, but for the very fact that it is actually mundane and fairly commonplace. This is often the realm in which we negotiate femininity. I also realize that layers of privilege exist in this story; I am aspiring to an elite, classed standard of belonging in which femininity can encompass having a career, as long as you appear a certain way. I am not so far outside the standard that I can't shop at Ann Taylor at all. Was the saleswoman really the representative of gender norms, and didn't I have some power over her by virtue of being a customer? I feel that I am distorting the story if I don't include the fact that the other saleswoman—a woman with short hair behind the counter—was clearly sympathetic to my plight. While ringing up my purchase, she gently gave me some tips on how to get the most out of wearing my suit for every possible interview and occasion. I worry about what gets left out when this story is based on my visible identification with some aspects of femininity.

In fact, if I stop here at the realm of visual implications about gender, then I think it is very easy to ignore and thus stabilize other aspects of identity, such as race and class. I believe that a middle-class standard of white femininity was being upheld as the standard in this shopping scenario, as it is in many gender discussions, while other racialized and classed representations of femininity exist and complicate this model. These other standards of femininity all but get erased in many discussions. When we assume we know what feminine is, I think we are often assuming a model of traditional White femininity. Whiteness and femininity might be linked together in our collective imagination. To

consider what remains invisible in my shopping experience is obviously important because invisibility is at the heart of privilege. My discomfort in shopping for a suit might have been multiplied exponentially if I weren't White and middle-class. If I didn't fit these standards, I would likely be treated differently, especially in terms of what kind of womanhood I might be expected to present and uphold. Would a saleswoman still insist that I wear pearls? Would she help me at all?

Feminist Feminine

I've been told at various times that I "secretly" want to be butch! What does that mean? That I don't have the nerve or the right stuff to do it all the way? Should that be my ultimate goal? Why would it be secret? Masculine expression doesn't have to be about my desire to be butch; it can be part of femme or feminine identity. I've also heard that feminine dykes "never look more feminine than when they are wearing men's clothes." I think these comments function to protect butchness or female masculinity as if it were a scarce commodity by asserting and naturalizing a difference between butches and feminine dykes, so that the lines can never possibly blur. Our definitions need not to be so rigid. We are replicating traditional gender dynamics when we don't allow for more fluidity in expression and classification.

I also worry that this desire to complicate the classifications of butch/feminine will somehow make me seem dull, unsexy, and/or an advocate for strict androgyny. I will become the dreaded spectacle of a "1970s lesbian feminist." I sometimes want to single-handedly reclaim that category! Androgyny, or borrowing from both traditionally masculine and feminine roles, no longer necessarily equates to the stereotype of dykes all wearing the same uniform of flannel shirts and hiking boots. I certainly don't want to suggest that we discard butch/femme roles or that the roles themselves are suspect. I also don't subscribe to the notion that we should all appear butch one day and then feminine the next just to mix things up into a hip, postmodern jumble. But I do want to bring more flux into our tentative gender definitions and fewer rigid assumptions about what defines queer gender roles.

When I got in touch with my childhood friend Lauren on email a couple of years ago after having lost contact with her for at least ten years, I asked if she remembered "the year we were boys." While we exchanged several nostalgic correspondences about our memories as childhood best friends, she never responded to that particular question or made mention of that year. I wonder if it disturbed her (she grew up to be straight) because I had also come out on email. Perhaps she felt implicated in a homoerotic childhood dynamic that she would rather forget. The different paths that Lauren and I took suggest that we should be wary of forcing our childhood memories to correspond in any simple way to our adult identities. As adults, we still pick and choose (with varying degrees of choice, aware-

ness, outside influence, coercion, rewards, and punishments) how we present our gender. This story of my year as a boy doesn't fit in with a seamless feminine or feminine childhood of playing dress-up or with Barbies, but it doesn't exclude that history either. As feminists, it's time to reclaim some of the lessons of lesbian feminism to examine and expand our notions of femininity itself. I believe that we can acknowledge gender extremes within the community at the same time that we acknowledge roles that don't fit into those models. If we insist upon the constructed aspect of all gender roles, then we have more room to negotiate gender and more freedom to alter the definitions of gender itself.

T W E N T Y - F I V E

◆◆◆

The All-American Queer Pakistani Girl (1997)

Surina A. Khan

Surina Khan was born in Pakistan and came to the United States as a child. A writer, researcher, and advocate, she served as Executive Director of the International Gay and Lesbian Human Rights Commission for several years. Currently, Ms. Khan is a program officer at the Ford Foundation and responsible for its LGBT initiative. She serves on boards and advisory committees of nonprofit organizations working on gender, LGBT, and human rights issues.

As a kid, I remember being constantly reminded that I was different—by my accent, my brown skin color, my mother's traditional clothing, and the smell of the food we ate. And so I consciously Americanized myself. I spent my early childhood perfecting my American accent, my adolescence affirming my American identity to others, and my late teens rejecting my Pakistani heritage. Now, at the age of twenty-seven, I'm feeling the void I created for myself.

Sometimes I think of what my life would be like if my parents hadn't moved to Connecticut in 1973, when I was five. Most of my family has since moved back to Pakistan, and up until seven years ago, when I came out, I went back somewhat regularly. But I never liked going back. It made me feel stifled, constrained. People were always talking about getting married. First it was, "You're almost old enough to start thinking about finding a nice husband," then, "When are you getting married?" Now I imagine they'd say, with disappointment, "You'll be an old maid."

I don't know if my grandmother is dead or alive. I can't remember the last time I saw her—it must have been at least ten years ago, when I was in Pakistan for a visit. She was my only living grandparent, and her health was beginning to fail. Every once in a while, I think she's probably dead and no one bothered to tell me.

I'm completely out of touch with my Pakistani life. I can hardly speak Urdu, my first language; I certainly can't read or write it. I have no idea how many cousins I have. I know my father comes from a large family—eleven brothers and sisters—but I don't know all their names. I've never read the Koran, and I don't have faith in Islam.

My family is more liberal than most of Pakistani society. By American standards that translates into conservative (my mother raised money for George Bush). But I was brought up in a family that valued education, independence, integrity, and love. I never had to worry about getting pressured into an arranged marriage, even though several of my first cousins were—sometimes to each other. Once I went to a wedding in which the bride and groom saw each other for the first time when someone passed them a mirror after their wedding ceremony and they both looked into it at once. That's when I started thinking my family was "modern."

Unfortunately they live in a fundamentalist culture that won't tolerate me. I can't even bring myself to visit Pakistan. The last time I went back was seven years ago, for my father's funeral, and sometimes I wonder if the next time will be for my mother's funeral. She asks me to come visit every time I talk to her. I used to tell her I was too busy, that I couldn't get away. But three years ago I finally answered her truthfully. I told her that I didn't like the idea of traveling to a country that lashed lesbians one hundred times in public. More important, I didn't feel comfortable visiting when she and I had not talked about anything important in my life since I had come out to her.

Pakistan has always been my parents' answer to everything. When they found out my sisters were smoking pot in the late 1970s, they shipped all of us back. "You need to get in touch with the Pakistani culture," my mother would say. When my oldest sister got hooked on transcendental meditation and started walking around the house in a trance, my father packed her up and put her on a plane back to the homeland. She's been there ever since. Being the youngest of six, I wised up quickly. I waited to drop my bomb until after I had moved out of the house and was financially independent. If I had come out while I was still living in my parents' home, you can bet I'd have been on the next flight to Islamabad.

When I came out to my mother, she suggested I go back to Pakistan for a few months. "Just get away from it all," she begged. "You need some time. Clear your head." But I knew better. And when I insisted that I was queer and was going to move to Washington, D.C., to live with my girlfriend, Robin (now my ex-girlfriend, much to my mother's delight), she tried another scare tactic: "You and your lover better watch out. There's a large Pakistani community in D.C., and they'll find out about you. They'll break your legs, mutilate your face." That pretty much did it for me. My mother had just validated all my fears associated with Pakistan. I cut

all ties with the community, including my family. *Pakistan* became synonymous with *homophobia*.

My mother disowned me when I didn't heed her advice. But a year later, when Robin and I broke up, my mother came back into my life. It was partly motivated by wishful thinking on her part. I do give her credit, though, not only for nurturing the strength in me to live by my convictions with integrity and honesty but also for eventually trying to understand me. I'll never forget the day I took her to see a lawyer friend of mine. She was on the verge of settling a lawsuit started by my father before he died and was unhappy with her lawyer. I took her to see Maggie Cassella, a lawyer/comedian based in Hartford, Connecticut, where I was again living. "I presume this woman's a lesbian," my mother said in the car on the way to Maggie's office. "Yes, she is," I replied, thinking, *Oh, no, here it comes again.* But my mother took me by surprise. "Well, the men aren't helping me; I might as well go to the dykes." I didn't think she even knew the word *dyke.* Now, *that* was a moment.

Her changing attitude about my lesbian identity was instilling in me a desire to reclaim my Pakistani identity. The best way to do this, I decided, would be to seek out other Pakistani lesbians. I barely knew any Pakistanis aside from my family, and I sure as hell didn't know, or even know of, any Pakistani lesbians. I was just naive enough to think I was the only one.

It wasn't easy for me even to arrive at the concept of a Pakistani lesbian. Having rejected my culture from a young age, I identified only as a lesbian when I came out, and in my zeal to be all-American, I threw myself into the American queer liberation movement. I did not realize that there is an active South Asian gay and lesbian community in the United States— and that many of us are here precisely because we're able to be queer and out in the Western world.

South Asian culture is rampant with homophobia—so much so that most people in South Asia literally don't have words for homosexuality, which is viewed as a Western phenomenon despite the fact that images of gays and lesbians have been a part of the subcontinent's history for thousands of years. In the temples of Khajuraho and Konarak in India, there are images of same-gender couples—male and female—in intimate positions. One temple carving depicts two women caressing each other, while another shows four women engaged in sexual play.

There are also references to homosexuality in the *Kāma-sūtra*, the ancient Indian text on the diversities of sex. Babar, the founder of the Mughal dynasty in India, is said to have been gay, as was Abu Nawas, a famous Islamic poet. The fact is that homosexuality is as native to South Asia as is heterosexuality. But since the culture pressures South Asian women to reject our sexual identity, many South Asian queers living in the United States reject South Asian culture in turn. As a result, we are often isolated from one another.

Despite the odds, I started my search for queer people from South Asia—and I found them, all across America, Canada, and England. Connecting with this network and talking with other queer South Asians has begun to fill the void I've been feeling. But just as it took me years to reject my Pakistani heritage, it will likely take me as long, if not longer, to reintegrate my culture into my life as it is now.

I'm not ready to go back to Pakistan. But I am ready to start examining the hostility I feel toward a part of myself I thought I had discarded long ago.

5

◆◆◆

Women's Bodies, Women's Health

Our bodies grow and develop from the first moments of life. Through them we experience sexuality, pain, healing, and the complex physical, hormonal, neurological, and emotional changes that come with menstruation and menopause, pregnancy, and aging. Many of us develop strength, agility, concentration, and coordination through exercise, dance, sports, martial arts, yoga, or outdoor activities. We show dexterity in handling tools, from kitchen knives to wrenches, hammers, and saws. Pregnancy and childbirth provide intense understanding of our bodies' elasticity and stamina, and the wonder of being able to sustain another body developing inside us. We have an awareness of our bodily rhythms throughout the day or through the menstrual cycle—the ups and downs of mental and physical energy, tiredness, stiffness, and cramps.

Although there are physiological, financial, and technological limits to how much we can shape them, up to a point our bodies are malleable. We may diet or exercise, use skin-lightening creams or tanning lotions, have a nose job or a tummy tuck, and adopt particular postures and body language. We may have surgeries to counteract disabilities; our bodies may be altered by mastectomy due to breast cancer; we may need to use reading glasses, wheelchairs, or hearing aids. We may take hormones or have surgery to make our physical appearance congruent with our internal sense of self.

Describing the variability in human bodies, biologist Anne Fausto-Sterling (1993) proposed that there should be at least five sexes. She pointed out that experts "have distinguished between sex at the genetic level and at the cellular level (sex-specific gene expression, X and Y chromosomes); at the hormonal level (in the fetus, during childhood and after puberty); and at the anatomical level (genitals and secondary sexual characteristics)" (Fausto-Sterling 2000). She argued that "one can find levels of masculinity and femininity in almost every possible permutation" and that male and female "cannot be parsed as some kind of continuum" but "are best conceptualized as points in a multidimensional space." Leslie Feinberg refers to "masculine females and feminine males" who challenge Western culture's deep commitment to a sex/gender binary (Reading 19).

The question "Who is a woman?" was at the root of the controversy over Caster Semenya, an athlete from South Africa who won the women's 800-meter race at the World Championships in Berlin in 2009 (Levy 2009). Semenya, who was raised female and is apparently intersex, was subjected to "highly publicized gender verification testing" and withdrawn from competition until the International Association of Athletics Federations (IAAF) cleared her to compete as a woman (Hall 2011, p. 2).

This chapter discusses body issues and wellness; reproductive health; and the effects of age, race, and class on women's health. We see health as a complex mix of physical, mental, emotional, and spiritual well-being, though these connected aspects tend to be separated into distinctive specializations with different practitioners in Western societies.

Women's Bodies and the Beauty Ideal

Rosemarie Garland-Thompson argues that, within Western thought, female bodies and disabled bodies are viewed as "deviant and inferior" (Reading 27). She grounds this association of femaleness and disability in Aristotle's discourse on the "normal and the abnormal," where he differentiated "the generic type" (read male) from "monstrosities," or deviations from this type (read female and disabled). Hierarchical thinking also separates body and mind, and considers organic, bodily processes (associated with femaleness) inferior to the mind (associated with maleness). She shows connections between feminist theorizing and disability discourse and argues that each can gain from perspectives of the other (also see Clare 2009; Fine and Asch 1988; Hall 2011; Linton 1999; Mairs 1996; Rousso 2001; Smith and Hutchison 2004; Wendell 1996).

Dominant U.S. culture often reduces women to bodies, valuing us only as sex objects or as bearers of children. The advertising industry uses women's bodies to sell shampoo, soft drinks, beer, tires, cars, fax machines, chain saws, and gun holsters, as well as concepts of womanliness, manliness, and heteronormativity. The **objectification** and **commodification** of women in advertising pave the way for women's dismemberment (literal and figurative) in pornography.

A key part of liberation movements for women, LGBTQQI people, people of color, and people with disabilities has been the reclaiming of our bodies as strong and beautiful, with calls for ethnic pride, LGBTQQI pride, and disability pride. Many people with disabilities argue that they are more handicapped by the mental limitations of nondisabled people than by their own minds and bodies. From some cultural perspectives, disability is considered an act of God; other cultures blame women who

birth children with disabilities. Garland-Thompson suggests that it is not meaningful to insist on a clear-cut boundary between the categories "disabled" and "nondisabled." Ynestra King (1993a) also emphasized the contingent nature of bodily experience due to illness, injury, and also the effects of aging:

> The common ground for the person—the human body—is a place of shifting sand that can fail us at any time. It can change shape and properties without warning; this is an essential truth of embodied existence. Of all the ways of becoming "other" in our society, disability is the only one that can happen to anyone in an instant, transforming that person's life and identity forever. *(p. 75)*

Beauty "Ideals" Can Make You Sick

Everyone needs nourishing food, clean drinking water, and adequate exercise in order to maintain health and vitality. The appropriate balance of food and exercise is somewhat subjective, depending on age, physical ability, personal tastes, and cultural preferences. Two examples of serious imbalance are eating disorders like anorexia and bulimia, often with a punishing exercise regime, and overeating, typically accompanied by too little exercise.

Much research, commentary, and concern has focused on the damaging health effects of obsessive dieting, which mainly affects young white middle-class women, exemplified by Abra Fortune Chernik who describes her experience with anorexia in Reading 68. Feminist scholars have analyzed the oppressive nature of ads and media representations that bombard women and girls with an ideal of beauty defined as thin, lean, tall, young, white, and heterosexual, with flawless skin and well-groomed hair (see, e.g., Bordo 1993; Brumberg 1997; Hesse-Biber 1996; Kilbourne 1999; Martin 2007; Wolf 1991). Where women of color are used, they are often light-skinned and conform to this same body type. This beauty standard is backed by a multi-billion-dollar beauty industry that sees women's bodies as a series of problems in need of correction. The aim is to promote insecurity, self-hatred, and distorted perceptions of size, appetite, and attractiveness, so that we will consume the countless products, diet plans, and cosmetic surgeries marketed to remedy our alleged deficiencies. Realty TV shows like *Extreme*

Makeover and *America's Next Top Model* normalize this goal. Writer Courtney Martin (2007) discusses what she calls the "frightening new normalcy of hating your body." To the extent that women internalize ideal beauty standards, what Kim Chernin (1994) called "the tyranny of slenderness," we set ourselves up to pursue a goal that is largely unattainable. Even the elite corps of full-time fashion models, "deployed in a way that keeps 150 million women in line" (Wolf 1991, p. 41), have their photos airbrushed and digitally enhanced (see, e.g., Collins 2008; Reaves et al. 2004). Jean Kilbourne (1999; *Killing Us Softly 4; Slim Hopes*) described the "toxic cultural environment" surrounding U.S. girls and shows how advertising images can severely undermine girls' self-confidence and sense of agency, which can lead to serious physical and emotional health problems.

Kilbourne notes how women's bodies and body parts are objectified as commodities, as things, especially in advertising. We learn to see ourselves as disconnected parts—thighs, hips, bottoms, breasts, noses, and chins—all in need of improvement.

A particularly egregious example concerns enslaved African women, whose body parts were divided from each other:

> Her back and muscle were pressed into field labour where she was forced to work with men and work like men. Her hands were demanded to nurse and nurture the white man and his family. . . . Her vagina, used for his sexual pleasure, was the gateway to the womb, which was his place of capital investment—the capital investment being the sex act and the resulting child the accumulated surplus, worth money on the slave market. *(Omolade 1983, p. 354)*

Resisting Beauty Stereotypes

Ideal beauty standards are ableist, ageist, heterosexist, and racist, and many women and girls do their best to resist them by not using makeup, for example, or by wearing practical shoes and clothes. Some breast cancer survivors who have had one or both breasts removed have chosen to go without artificial breasts or have had their mastectomy scars tattooed. Beauty standards are always cultural constructs and vary among different groups, hence the importance of meso-level analysis. Extreme thinness may be associated with poverty, malnutrition, or illnesses such as cancer or AIDS, which eat away the body from the inside.

Women in their fifties, sixties, or older often feel that they have newfound confidence and purpose as they age (Bird 1995; Brice 2003). These years may be a time of self-definition and autonomy when they can resist earlier pressures to conform to dominant beauty standards. Writer Meridel Le Sueur (1982) used the word "ripening" to describe the development of her work over five decades and her satisfaction with her fulfilling life—a positive way of thinking about aging with an emphasis on "generativity, rather than decline" (Browne 1998, p. 68).

Noting that mainstream culture equates beauty and power for women, Silva Tenenbein (1998) reversed the beauty-power equation for lesbians:

> For dykes it's not beauty which makes us powerful but power that makes us beautiful . . . our passion, our strength, and our courage to choose to be the "other" . . . our adamant refusal to be deflected from what we want.
> *(pp. 159, 160)*

Samantha Kwan (2010, p. 146) has argued that, like "structures that privilege whiteness, cultural and social structures privilege the thin . . . body." Large women of all racial/ethnic groups challenge weight-loss industry stereotypes and mainstream assumptions that they are sloppy, irresponsible, undisciplined, depressed, sexless, unwanted, or unhealthy (see, e.g., Lamm 1995; Rothblum and Solovay 2009; Wann 1998; and Sirena Riley, Reading 26). American Jewish culture has the word *zaftig*, a positive term for women who are fleshy, voluptuous, and thought to embody strength, sexiness, comfort, and nurturance (St. Paige 1999). Judith Ortiz Cofer (1993) noted that, "a fuller figure" was admired in her Puerto Rican community. Many African American women say, "I don't want to be no skinny minny!" Queen T'isha wrote:

> Racism and sexism as practiced in America includes body hostilities. I didn't grow up with the belief that fat women were to be despised. The women in my family were fat, smart, sexy, employed, wanted, married, and the rulers of their households.
> *(Quoted in Edison and Notkin 1994, p. 106)*

Italian fashion designer Valentino and two supermodels who helped make his collection a success.

And Elise Matthesen argued,

> We have a right to take up space. We have a right to stretch out, to be big, to be "too much to handle." To challenge the rest of the world to grow up, get on with it, and become big enough to "handle" us. . . .
> *(Quoted in Edison and Notkin 1994, p. 107)*

Dora Dewey-McCracken confounded common assumptions about fatness with regard to health:

> I've been diabetic since I was nineteen. . . . All my life I gained and lost at least sixty pounds each year. . . . I tried all diets, eating disorders, and fasts, only to gain the fat back, and more each time. I'm the fattest I've ever been, and yet my diabetic blood work is the best it's ever been. My doctor once told me, "As long as your disease is controlled and your blood chemistry is good, your fat is just a social issue." I'm extremely lucky to have this doctor;

with most doctors, fat phobia is the rule, not the exception. They see the fat and their brains turn off.
> *(Quoted in Edison and Notkin 1994, p. 104)*

Size Acceptance, Obesity, and Health

In response to discrimination and stigma experienced by women who are considered overweight, some feminists have welcomed the notion of "size acceptance" and view "fat as an aesthetic . . . issue" (Yancey, Leslie, and Abel 2006, p. 425), seeing obesity as a social construction. A growing number of organizations are working to counter fat oppression including Boston Area Fat Liberation (Cambridge, Mass.), the Council on Size and Weight Discrimination (Mount Marion, N.Y.), Largesse—the Network for Size Esteem (New Haven, Conn.) and the National Association to Advance Fat Acceptance (Sacramento, Calif.). Photographers have also undertaken "full body" projects that celebrate women

Overweight and Obesity:
Social and Economic Factors

- *Access to nutritious food.* Eating well takes greater effort in low-income neighborhoods, which tend to have a preponderance of liquor and convenience stores rather than full-service supermarkets that carry fresh fruits and vegetables. Fast food restaurants are more prevalent in poorer neighborhoods than in middle-class areas; fast food is offered at a lower price relative to more healthy options (Agyeman and Alkon 2011; Azuma 2007; Gottlieb and Joshi 2010; Guthman 2011; Morland et al. 2002).

- *Industrialized food processing* has made "energy-dense" snacks and desserts (with a high proportion of fat and sugar) extremely inexpensive (Brownell and Horgen 2004).

- *Costs for foods* such as milk, eggs, bread, vegetables, chicken, and beef have risen, mainly because of increased oil prices and the growing demand for food crops, such as corn and soybeans for alternative fuels like ethanol and biodiesel.

- *Time.* Women juggling responsibilities of waged-work and caring for their families may have difficulty finding time to shop for food, cook meals at home, or exercise.

- *Exercise.* Most people in the United States lead sedentary lives. Fewer girls than boys take up sports; many adult women have no regular exercise practice. Larger women feel self-conscious in gyms that mainly cater to young, thin women. Women do not want to walk—or allow their children to hang out—in unsafe neighborhoods (Yancey, Leslie, and Abel 2006).

- *Culture of self-care.* Many women have been socialized to take care of others in their families and communities rather than themselves (Beauboeuf-Lafontant 2009). They may prioritize their outward appearance and pay for clothes, hair-care, and nails rather than exercise programs or fitness classes.

- *Overeating.* Eating can be a significant source of comfort and pleasure; it is socially acceptable for women and a safer way to buffer pain than drugs or alcohol. Women may overeat as a way to cope with frustration, anger, anxiety, and sadness; physical, emotional, or sexual abuse; and the daily pain of sexism, racism, classism, and heterosexism (Gold 2011; Morrone 2009; Skover 2012; Thompson 1994).

of all shapes and sizes (e.g., Edison and Notkin 1994; Nimoy 2007; Olson 2008).

Public health researchers Antronette Yancey, Joanne Leslie, and Emily Abel (2006) argued that women's studies teachers and scholars have tended to downplay the "accumulating data about the health consequences of the obesity epidemic," which they found "surprising and troubling" (p. 425). These writers endorsed government definitions of overweight as having a body mass index of 25 to 29.9, and obesity as an index of 30 or more. On this standard, 68 percent of U.S. adults are overweight or obese, and 34 percent are obese (Centers for Disease Control and Prevention 2008a). More women are overweight than men; 50 percent of Black women are defined as overweight compared with 32 percent of white women.

Scholars and advocates concerned with the health of women of color have underlined the links between obesity and illness, especially heart disease, diabetes, strokes, and joint problems (see, e.g., Avery 1990; hooks 1993; Lovejoy 2001; Thompson 1994; White 1991). Yancey, Leslie, and Abel (2006) argue that public health practitioners generally view obesity in terms of social and economic factors that contribute to an obesity-causing environment, which particularly affects low-income people of color (see Box). They advocate prevention policies and programs that address underlying causes as much more effective than urging individuals to lose weight.

The discourse of fat acceptance is in marked contrast with many health practitioners' views on obesity, which raises significant questions of where to draw the line in the interests of physical, emotional, and spiritual health. A range of micro- and meso-level factors are involved in being able to care for ourselves, as shown in this chapter. Also, attention to macro-level factors provides an understanding of the health disparities among women based on race, class, culture, sexuality, and national origin.

Reproductive Health

The ability to become pregnant and have a baby is a profound experience, usually with far-reaching consequences for the mother. A woman becomes pregnant for many reasons: she wants to have a child; she wants to experience pregnancy and childbirth; she wants to be recognized as a grown woman; she believes it will make her a "real" woman; she's not sure what to do with her life; she hopes it will keep her relationship together or make her partner happy. Some women plan to be pregnant; others get pregnant by accident; still others as a result of being raped. This deeply personal experience is also a public issue. For some women—especially teenagers, lesbians, and mothers receiving welfare—there may be a serious tension between the personal event of pregnancy and societal attitudes to it. African American women have consistently tried to be self-determining in their reproductive lives despite having been used as breeders by slaveholders and despite subsequent systematic state interventions to control their fertility (Darling and Tyson 1999; Dula 1996; Hill Collins 2004; Roberts 1997; Ross 1993; Silliman et al. 2004; Taylor 1997). These include state-sponsored sterilization programs, chemical contraceptives like Depo-Provera and Norplant, and the chemical sterilizing agent, Quinacrine. Law professor and legal scholar Dorothy Roberts (1997) has referred to this phenomenon as nothing less than "killing the black body."

Controlling Fertility

Women's reproductive years span roughly half our lifetimes, from our teens to our forties. Many women in the United States want to control their fertility—to limit the number of children they have, to postpone pregnancy until they are older, to avoid pregnancy with a particular partner, or to avoid it altogether. Women also want the freedom to bear children. To do this we need sex education that is accurate and culturally appropriate; affordable and reliable birth control; safe, legal, affordable abortion; prenatal care and care through childbirth; health care for infants and children; and alternative insemination. In addition we need an adequate income, good general health care, and widespread cultural acceptance that we have a right to control our lives in this way. As argued by Rosemarie Garland-Thompson (Reading 27), women with disabilities must also fight for the right to have children in the face of a dominant view that they are nonsexual beings who could not cope with being mothers (see also Finger 1990; Prilleltensky 2003; Saxton 1995; Wilkerson 2002).

Birth Control   Barrier methods like condoms and diaphragms have been used for many years. In the 1960s the intrauterine device (IUD), often called the coil, was introduced despite severe unwanted side effects for some women, such as heavy bleeding, pain, and cramps. The pill, introduced around the same time—and the most popular form of contraception today for women under 30—was the first chemical contraceptive to be taken every day. It affects the whole body continuously, as do newer methods like Depo-Provera (an injectable contraceptive that is effective for three months) and Implanon (implanted under the skin and effective for up to three years). Low-income African American and Native American women and Latinas are much more likely than white women to be encouraged to use these long-acting contraceptives. Official policy seeks to limit their pregnancies and assumes that these women would be unreliable using other methods, thereby continuing the long connection between birth control and **eugenics,** or selective breeding, often linked to racism and ableism, supposedly to create healthier and more intelligent people, to save resources, and to lessen human suffering (Roberts 1997; Ross 1993; Smith 2002). The Black Women's Health Network, the National Latina Health Organization, and other women's health advocates have called for the withdrawal of Depo-Provera as unsafe and also called attention to the fact that many women using implants had difficulty getting them removed. These methods compound many of the health problems that affect poor women of color, including hypertension, diabetes, and stress.

NON SEQUITOR

Other birth-control methods include the female condom, a loosely fitting, polyurethane (not latex) pouch with a semiflexible plastic ring at each end that lines the vagina and fits over the vulva. It provides protection from sexually transmitted infections (STIs) as well as pregnancy, but is not as effective as the male condom. A popular over-the-counter contraceptive, the Today Sponge, came back on the market in 2003 but does not offer the same degree of protection as oral contraceptives. Emergency contraception that prevents fertilization is available over the counter to women and men 17 years and over, under the trade names Plan B One Step or Next Choice. They can be used in the event of unprotected sex or if another form of contraception fails. This is a chemical method that involves taking oral contraceptives up to five days after unprotected sex, the sooner the better.

Pharmaceutical companies have all but abandoned the field of contraceptive research in this country because of a decline in funding from the government, international sources, and private foundations, as well as political opposition.

Abortion Attitudes toward abortion have varied greatly over time and from one society to another. Historically, the Catholic Church held the view that the soul did not enter the fetus for at least forty days after conception and allowed abortion up to that point. In 1869, however, Pope Pius IX declared that life begins at conception, and thus all abortion became murder in the eyes of the Church. In the United States up until the mid-nineteenth century, women were allowed to seek an abortion in the early part of pregnancy before they felt the fetus moving, a subjectively determined time, referred to as the quickening. After the Civil War more restrictive abortion laws were passed, partly to increase population and partly to shift authority over women's reproductive lives to the developing medical profession. By 1900 the only legal ground for an abortion was to save the life of the mother. Many women were forced to bring unwanted pregnancies to term in poverty, illness, or appalling personal circumstances. Thousands died trying to abort themselves or at the hands of "backstreet" abortionists. Some upper- and middle-class women found doctors to perform safe abortions for a high price; some doctors did abortions for poor women. The women and the doctors risked prosecution if they were found out, as described by Grace Paley (1998) in her short article, "The Illegal Days" (also see Joffe 1995; Miller 1993; Reagan 1997; Solinger 1994, 2000). Women with knowledge of herbs, massage, or medicine helped other women. The Janes organized a clandestine feminist abortion service in the Chicago area in the early 1970s (Arcana 2005; Kamen 2000; Kaplan 1995).

In 1973 the landmark case *Roe v. Wade* made abortion legal. It defined freedom of choice as a right to privacy, protected by the U.S. Constitution. It recognized that no one except the woman herself has the right to decide whether to have an abortion. Ever since this legislation was enacted, it has been contested. This began in 1977 with the Hyde Amendment that withdrew state funding for abortion for poor women. Subsequent measures have included rules requiring waiting periods, parental consent for teens, bans on late-term abortions, and being required to hear about risks and alternatives as a condition of getting an abortion. Anti-choice organizations have staged violent protests at abortion clinics, bombed clinics, harassed patients, and killed doctors known to perform abortions as part of their practice (Baird-Windle and Bader 2001; Jaggar 1994; Jeffferis 2011; Robb 2010). Women's health advocates have struggled to keep clinics open and lobbied for the Freedom of Access to Clinic Entrances Act 1994, which reduced harassment outside clinics. These legal restrictions, together with severe, ongoing harassment, have reduced the number of abortion providers; in 2009, 87 percent of U.S. counties and 98 percent of rural counties had no abortion provider (Harding 2009). Fewer doctors are being trained to carry out the procedure, and many have stopped performing abortions because of the risks to themselves and their families (Joffe 2009).

In 2008, 19 out of every 1,000 women aged 15 to 44 had abortions, the lowest rate since 1975 (Guttmacher Institute 2011). Factors assumed to be responsible for this decline include increased willingness to use contraception, reduced access to abortion, and negative attitudes toward abortion. Most women who had an abortion in 2008 were 25 or younger, white, and unmarried; 62 percent of the procedures were done in the first eight weeks of pregnancy, and 88 percent in the first twelve weeks. Proportionate to their numbers in the overall population, Black women and Latinas were more likely to have an abortion than white women. In 2000, the Food and Drug Administration approved RU-486 (the "abortion pill," also called mifespristone). An increasing number of providers now offer medication abortions; in 2008 these accounted for 25 percent of all abortions before nine weeks and 17 percent of all abortions (Guttmacher Institute 2011). Reasons women gave for terminating an unwanted pregnancy included their responsibility toward other people (74 percent); they could not afford a baby (73 percent); a baby would interfere with their commitments to schooling, employment, or caring for other dependents (69 percent); and not wanting to be single parents (48 percent) (Guttmacher Institute 2011).

Women's thoughts and feelings about abortion, about the profound responsibility of choosing to end a life, have been downplayed by pro-abortion activists as they focused on keeping abortion legal. Judith Arcana (1994) argued that abortion is a motherhood issue, a decision a woman makes because she believes it is the best for herself and her baby. Like anti-choice activists, she called a fetus a baby. Unlike them, she passionately defends a woman's right to abortion. She argued that the semantics of *"fetus or embryo"* used by pro-choice organizers skirts the central moral issue and has cost them potential support (also see Halva-Neubauer and Zeigler 2010). It has conceded the space for anti-choice activists to excoriate women who have abortions as heartless and irresponsible monsters. Arcana called for women to speak about our abortions "in open recognition of our joy or sadness, our regret or relief—in conscious acceptance of the responsibility for our choice" (see also Arcana 2005; Jacob 2002).

White feminists made abortion the centerpiece of reproductive rights activism in the 1980s and 1990s. By contrast, women of color have generally seen abortion as only one part of a wider reproductive-health agenda that includes health care for women and children and the freedom to have children (see, e.g., Nelson 2003; Ross et al. 2002; Silliman et al. 2004). Abortion advocates originally campaigned for women's *right* to abortion but have moved to a "softer" pro-choice framework. Rights apply to everyone; choice is only meaningful for those with resources. Thus, a pro-choice framework creates a hierarchy among women based on resources. Some women of color health advocates have developed the concept of **reproductive justice** that relates health and reproductive rights to broader issues of social and economic justice, as elaborated by Asian Communities for Reproductive Justice (Reading 30; Silliman et al. 2004; Smith 2005a). This offers a way of thinking about wellness for individuals, communities, and the wider society in terms of the eradication of systems of oppression and injustice. Historian Rickie Solinger (2005) argued that this is a long way off in the United States where male elites have always sought to control women's fertility through laws, attitudes, and social pressure. She cites ongoing restrictions on abortion, beliefs that value the fetus over the mother, women prisoners' lack of reproductive control, and inadequate sex education as evidence that this continues.

Meanwhile, more than one generation of women has grown up, taking abortion rights for granted despite the wide and growing gap between legality and access. In April 2004, more than one million people from all walks of life, many of them young women, participated in the March for Women's Lives, in Washington, D.C., the largest protest march in U.S. history. Their main demand was for broad reproductive freedoms. According to a 2011 Gallup poll on attitudes to abortion, 50 percent of respondents polled nationwide favored keeping abortion legal under certain circumstances; 27 percent said that abortion should be legal in all cases; 22 percent wanted it illegal in all cases (Saad 2011).

For nearly forty years, well-funded anti-abortion groups have worked strategically to undermine and overturn the right to abortion. They have used public education, mainstream media, protests, and direct action—including attacks on clinics and their staffs as mentioned earlier. They have financed and elected anti-choice political candidates at state and congressional levels. Republican congresspersons have introduced bills session after session to whittle away at the legality of abortion and elevate the unborn child, even as a "nonviable fetus," to the status of "personhood" with rights equal to or greater than those of the mother. If the Supreme Court overturns *Roe v. Wade,* legal jurisdiction will revert to the states, many of which are poised to ban abortion or to re-criminalize it (Guttmacher Institute 2012). This issue is central to women's autonomy and will continue to be highly contentious (see, e.g., Feldt 2004; Nelson 2003; Petchesky 1990; Silliman et al. 2004; Smith 2005a; Solinger 1998, 2005).

Sterilization Sterilization abuse, rather than the right to abortion, has been a concern of low-income women, especially women of color, for many years. Sterilization, without women's full knowledge or under duress, has been a common practice in the United States for poor Latina, African American, and Native American women. By the early 1980s, 24 percent of African American women, 35 percent of Puerto Rican women, and 42 percent of Native American women had been sterilized, compared with 15 percent of white women (Black Women's Health Project 1995; also see Davis 1983a; Jaimes and Halsey 1986; Lopez 1997; Nelson 2003; Silliman et al. 2004; Smith 2002). Currently, sterilization is federally funded under the Medicaid program and is free on demand to low-income women.

Teen Pregnancy Babies born to teens present a tremendous responsibility for young mothers and their families, and the U.S. has the highest rate of teen pregnancy of all industrialized countries. Analyzed by race and ethnicity, teen birthrates are highest for Latinas, African Americans, and Asian or Pacific Island teens. Government and community organizations have made major efforts to reduce the number of teen births from an all-time high of 62 births per 1,000 girls in 1991. In 2009, the rate was 39 births per 1,000 girls aged 15–19 (Centers for Disease Control and Prevention 2009). The reduction in teen births is due to increased use of condoms or injectable and implant contraceptives (Hamilton, Martin, and Ventura 2007). Many people advocate comprehensive sex education for teens (see, e.g., Kulwicki 2008). However, for eight years under President George W. Bush, federal funding was only available for abstinence-only sex education programs, which made up 35 percent of sex education programs in 2007. Heather Boonstra (2007), a researcher with the Alan Guttmacher Institute, reviewed compelling evidence that abstinence-only programs did not stop—or even delay—teen sex. Given that teen pregnancy rates are higher for Latinas and African Americans, the SisterSong Women of Color Reproductive Justice Collective has organized "Let's Talk About Sex" conferences to discuss this vital issue.

Sexually Transmitted Infections (STIs) About 19 million new cases of sexually transmitted infections are thought to occur each year, almost half of them to young people aged 15–24 (Office on Women's Health 2009). The term STI refers to more than twenty-five diseases, including herpes, genital warts, pubic lice ("crabs"), chlamydia, gonorrhea, syphilis, and HIV. With the exception of syphilis, all STIs are increasing at an alarming rate. For women, STIs may not be noticeable or may be difficult to diagnose as women often do not have any symptoms or, if they do, the symptoms are mistaken for something else. Sexually transmitted infection can affect how a woman feels about her body and her partner and can lead to pelvic inflammatory disease or infertility. Knowing about safer sexual practices is important in reducing the risk of sexually transmitted infections, including HIV/AIDS. It is important to note that condoms (male or female) are the only form of birth control that also give some protection against sexually transmitted infections. However, psychologists Nicola Gavey, Kathryn McPhillips, and Marion Doherty (2001) noted several factors that limit women's ability to influence their partners to use condoms. These include the power dynamics between women and men, women's assumptions about what it means to be a "good lover," and their ideals of giving and sharing. In Reading 31, Emma Bell and Luisa Orza, staff members of the International Community of Women Living with HIV/AIDS, discuss challenges faced by women diagnosed as HIV-positive, including stigma, intimate partnerships, and family relationships.

Medicalization of Reproductive Life

Childbirth Before there were male gynecologists, midwives helped women through pregnancy and childbirth (Ehrenreich and English 2010). As medicine became professionalized in the nineteenth century, gynecology and obstetrics developed as an area of medical specialization. Doctors eroded the position of midwives and ignored or scorned their knowledge as "old wives' tales." Largely for the convenience of the doctor, women began to give birth lying on their backs, perhaps the hardest position in which to deliver a baby. Forceps and various painkilling medications were widely used. From the 1950s onward cesarean sections (C-sections) became more common, often for the doctors' convenience or from fear of malpractice suits. In 2010, 32 percent of births in the United States were C-sections, one of the highest rates in the world (Hamilton, Martin, and Ventura 2011). The past forty years have seen a further extension of this medicalization process as doctors monitor pregnancy from the earliest stages with a battery of techniques such as amniocentesis, sonograms, and ultrasound. Although this technology allows medical practitioners, and through them, pregnant women, to know details about the health and condition of the fetus, as well as its sex, it also changes women's experiences of pregnancy and childbirth and may erode their knowledge of and confidence in their bodily processes. In Reading 28, Joy Harjo describes experiences of childbirth over three generations—her mother, her self, and her daughter. These included variations in their life circumstances, medical technology, and their treatment by hospital staff as Native American women. She notes the routine way she was offered the option of being sterilized and told that "the moment of birth was the best time to do it."

Reproductive Technologies Technologies such as in vitro fertilization (IVF), in which a woman's eggs are fertilized by sperm outside her body and the fertilized embryo is then implanted into her womb, are an important development. They push the medicalization of pregnancy and childbirth one step further and hold out the hope that infertile couples or postmenopausal women will be able to have children. Bearing a child as a surrogate mother under contract to an infertile couple is one way a young woman can earn an estimated $15,000–20,000 plus medical expenses for nine months' "work." Ads specify attributes sought in the birth mother, including race, age, IQ, etc. Fertility clinics also need ovum donors and seek to harvest the eggs of young, college-educated women from a range of specified racial and ethnic groups, as discussed by Elizabeth Reis (Reading 30). Infertility treatments have had a notably low success rate so far and are very expensive. They are aimed at middle- and upper-middle-class women as a way of widening individual choice. Infertility may stem from a range of causes such as sexually transmitted infections, the effects of IUDs, delayed childbearing, and occupational and environmental factors. Infertility rates were lower in the 1990s than in previous decades, but this issue has a higher profile nowadays because of technological developments.

These reproductive technologies open up an array of economic, legal, and moral questions (see, e.g., Davis 2009; Donchin and Purdy 1999; Ginsburg and Rapp 1995; Hubbard 1990; Ragone and Twine 2000; Teays and Purdy 2001). Are they liberating for women? For which women? And, at what costs? Some feminists have argued that women's biology and the ability to reproduce have been used to justify their social and economic subordination. In her now classic radical feminist text, Shulamith Firestone (1970), for example, was convinced that women's liberation required freedom from biological reproduction and looked forward to developments in reproductive technology that would make it possible for a fetus to develop outside the womb.

This is in stark contrast to sociologist Barbara Katz Rothman (1986) and the myriad women who believe that, if women lose their ability to reproduce, we lose a "quintessential female experience" (p. 111). Other feminist critics of reproductive technologies have focused on their invasiveness and consumers' lack of power over and knowledge about these methods, as compared with that of medical experts or "medocrats" (Corea 1985, 1987; Deech and Smajdor 2007; Lublin 1998; Mamo 2007; Morgan and Michaels 1999; Mundy 2007; Petchesky 1997).

Menopause This natural life process is increasingly treated as a disease rather than as a series of bodily and emotional changes. Many middle-aged women have been advised to take hormone-replacement therapy (HRT) to control the symptoms of menopause such as hot flashes, insomnia, and vaginal dryness. A major study of 46,355 women conducted by the National Cancer Institute confirmed that long-term use of hormone replacement after menopause can increase the risk of breast cancer (Grady 2000).

Executive Director of National Women's Health Network, Cindy Pearson, "uses science to challenge science," opposing the biomedical "definition of older women's bodies as deficient" and proving that what is "lost" through menopause "does not need to be replaced in order for a woman to live out the rest of her life healthfully" (*NWSAction* 2004, p. 39; also see Worcester 2004).

Women and Illness

There is a rich and growing literature on women's experiences of illness, healing, and recovery, particularly in relation to breast cancer, chronic fatigue immune deficiency syndrome (CFIDS), and multiple sclerosis (e.g., Duff 1993; Griffin 1999; Lorde 1996; Mairs 1996; Rosenblum 1997; Sigler, Love, and Yood 1999). Counselor and writer Kat Duff (1993) noted that our society's "concepts of physical and psychological health have become one-sidedly identified with the heroic qualities most valued in our culture: youth, activity, productivity, independence, strength, confidence, and optimism" (p. 37). Illness challenges us to rethink our definition of self, our value and worth, in this ableist society, as these authors attest.

The World's Deadliest Disease Is Poverty

- In 2010, worldwide, 7.6 million children died before their fifth birthday, mainly from malnutrition, malaria, acute respiratory infections, diarrhea, and HIV/AIDS.

- Most of these conditions can be prevented or cured with improvements in sanitation, clean water supply, better housing, an adequate food supply, and general hygiene. The majority of deaths from infectious diseases can be prevented with existing, cost-effective measures including childhood vaccinations, bed nets and other malaria prevention treatments, oral rehydration therapy, and antibiotics.

- Poor nutrition and underweight puts children under 5 at increased risk for infections like diarrhea and pneumonia. Underweight remains a pervasive problem in developing countries where poverty is a strong underlying determinant, contributing to household food insecurity, mothers' inadequate nutrition, unhealthy environments, and poor health care.

- Diseases linked to high blood pressure, cholesterol, tobacco, alcohol, and obesity have been most common in industrialized countries. They are now becoming more prevalent in countries of the global South, reflecting changes in living patterns, including diet, physical activity, the availability of tobacco and alcohol, and cultural upheavals.

Sources: UNICEF 2007; U.N. Interagency Group on Child Mortality Estimation 2011.

Health Disparities: Race, Class, and Gender

A growing literature evidences marked disparities in health among different groups in the United States (see, e.g., Barr 2008; Braveman 2006; Kawachi, Daniels, and Robinson 2005; LaVeist 2005; Schultz and Mullings 2005). This disparity is attributable to a mix of overlapping factors including income level, educational attainment, occupation, access to health services, neighborhood and work conditions, and so forth—factors linked to both race and class. In the United States, most government statistics are analyzed according to race/ethnicity in three undifferentiated categories: white, Black, and Hispanic—which includes Puerto Ricans, Cubans, Mexican Americans, and people from Central and South America. Some reports give details for Native Americans and Native Alaskans, or for Asians and Pacific Islanders—another very heterogeneous group. Data on many social issues are rarely analyzed according to socio-economic class. Bear this in mind during this discussion, which suffers from limitations of the data available. Also note that some racial/ethnic and gender disparities in health persist even after controlling for the beneficial effects of education and economic well-being.

Taken as a whole, the health of white women and Asian American women is significantly better than that of African American women, Native American women, and Latinas (Ross et al. 2002). However, middle-class, educated women of all races are more likely than low-income women to know about mammograms as a screening procedure for the early detection of breast cancer and that they are recommended for women over 40. They are more likely to have insurance to cover mammograms and to be registered with a doctor who encourages having them. Late diagnosis of breast cancer is directly related to higher mortality rates. Breast cancer affects one woman in nine nationwide, though there are much higher incidences in certain geographic areas. Several researchers have argued that environmental contamination is a cause of breast cancer (see, e.g., Arditti and Schreiber 1998; McCormick 2010). Race and class are relevant here as low-income women, especially women of color, often live in areas with poor physical environment.

Tuberculosis, an infectious disease associated with poverty and poor living conditions, was prevalent in the late nineteenth century and all but eradicated in the United States during the twentieth century. Compared with the general population, Native Americans are four times as likely to have tuberculosis. Frederica Daly (Reading 12) gives detailed historical, legal, and economic background for her brief discussion of Native American health, which is among the worst in the country.

Hypertension, a major risk factor for heart disease and stroke, is much more prevalent among African American women than it is among white women. Public health researchers have attributed this difference, in part, to stress related to racism and poverty. More African American women die in their twenties compared to white women due to drug use, HIV/AIDS, homicide, and maternal mortality.

Another indicator of health disparities is found in data on infant mortality, the number of infants who die before their first birthday. Infant mortality for babies born in 2005, for example, showed the typical pattern in the United States. Asian and Pacific Islanders have the lowest rate (4.9 deaths per 1,000 live births), followed by white (5.7), Puerto Rican (8.3), American Indian (8.1), and African American infants (13.6) (MacDorman and Mathews 2008). The United States ranked twenty-ninth in the world for infant mortality, tied with Poland and Slovakia. Infant mortality rates have steadily decreased over the past seventy years, but Black infants continue to die at more than twice the rate of white infants. Infant mortality rates are linked to personal factors such as smoking during pregnancy and macro-level factors like poverty. Mortality rates were higher for infants whose mothers did not have prenatal care in the first trimester, more common among Native American, Mexican American, and African American women, compared with Asian American women and white women. Biologist Sandra Steingraber (2001) discussed the complex process of fetal development and linked fetal and infant health to external environmental factors like contamination due to lead, chemical weed-killers, and other hazardous substances (Reading 62).

Gender has also been a significant factor in diagnosing women with HIV/AIDS. Women have not been diagnosed as early as men because their symptoms are not so clear-cut and doctors were less likely to look for symptoms of HIV/AIDS in women. Also, because there were fewer women in clinical research trials, they did not receive the better treatment received by men who participated in such trials. Primary care internist Barbara Ogur (1996) pointed out that negative stereotypes of HIV-positive women (as drug users and women with multiple sex partners) have affected their visibility and care. Of the women in the United States who were living with HIV/AIDS in 2009, 64 percent were Black, 15 percent were white, 18 percent were Latina, 1 percent were Asian or Pacific Islander, and less than 1 percent were American Indian or Native Alaskan (Kaiser Family Foundation 2012.). Far more women than men contract HIV through heterosexual contact. The International Community of Women Living with HIV/AIDS, a nonprofit organization founded in 1992, is the only international network of HIV-positive women. In Reading 31, Emma Bell and Luisa Orza discuss the policy framework established in various countries to support women with HIV/AIDS, and argue for improvements in services and changes in attitudes on the part of medical professionals and policy makers, especially regarding women's sexuality, pregnancy, and mothering.

Toxic workplaces are a serious health hazard, especially for women of color. Some companies have kept women out of the most hazardous work—often the highest paid among blue-collar jobs—or required that they be sterilized first, to avoid being sued if these workers later give birth to babies with disabilities. Women working in computer manufacturing, nursing, housecleaning, chicken processing, and the dairy industry are all exposed to chemicals as part of their work, as are manicurists and farm workers. We take up this issue of environmental contamination and health again in Chapter 11.

Women of all race and class groups who are beaten by their partners or suffer emotional violence or sexual abuse are subject to a significant health hazard (see Chapter 6).

Mental and Emotional Health

Many more women are classified as having some sort of mental illness compared to men, especially depression, and the proportion of women seeking help for personal or emotional problems is twice as high as it is for men. However, one cannot infer from this that everyone who "seeks help" does so voluntarily; sometimes seeing a counselor or therapist is required by a social service agency or is a condition of probation. Voluntarily seeking help for emotional problems is linked to one's ability to pay, finding a suitable therapist, and cultural attitudes toward this kind of treatment. Also, it is more socially acceptable for women to seek help for mental health concerns compared to men. Patients in mental hospitals represent a relatively small proportion of those who are suffering mentally and emotionally. In general, women are admitted to mental hospitals as inpatients in roughly the same numbers as men.

Many people of all classes and racial groups attempt to deal with the pain and difficulty of their lives through drugs and alcohol. Frederica Daly noted that rates of alcoholism, homicide, and suicide among Native Americans are significantly higher than the national rates (Reading 12). In the United States, drug addiction is often thought of as a crime rather than as a health issue. We discuss it further under the topic of crime and criminalization in Chapter 9, but we also see it as a symptom of stress brought on by the pressures of life, often caused by social and economic inequality. There are far fewer drug-treatment programs than required, and fewer for women than for men.

A number of feminist writers have argued that contemporary approaches to mental distress, as illness, can be harmful to women (see, e.g., Chesler 1972; Ehrenreich and English 2005; Lerman 1996; Russell 1995; Showalter 1987; Ussher 1991). Philosopher Denise Russell (1995) traced the history of definitions of madness from medieval Europe, where it was thought of as a combination of error and sin. During the seventeenth century, economic crises and rising unemployment in Europe prompted local officials to build houses of confinement for beggars, drunks, vagabonds, and other poor people and petty criminals, as well as for those who were thought mad. Through the eighteenth and nineteenth centuries, psychiatry gradually developed as a medical specialty and asylums in Europe and the United States were headed by doctors, who theorized that much mental distress experienced by women was due to their reproductive capacities and sexuality. Hysteria, thought to be due to a disturbance of the womb, became a catchall category to describe women's mental illness. (The English word *hysterical* comes from the Greek word *hysterikos*, meaning "of the womb.") Writer/literary critic Elaine Showalter (1987) and psychologist/ psychotherapist Phyllis Chesler (1972) showed how definitions of madness were used to suppress women's agency, creativity, education, and political involvement. Nineteenth-century white upper- and middle-class women who wanted to write, paint, travel, or speak out in public on issues of the day were assumed by their

husbands—and by psychiatrists—to be insane. Charlotte Perkins Gilman's powerful fictional work *The Yellow Wallpaper,* for example, describes this experience and was written as a result of having lived through it. More recently, depression and premenstrual syndrome (PMS) have replaced "hysteria" as stock phrases used in describing mental illness in women.

Feminist writers offer scathing critiques of the alleged objectivity of much contemporary mental health theorizing and of the value judgments and blatant sexism involved in many diagnostic categories like depression, behavioral disorders, and personality disorders that affect women more than men. Symptoms for these disorders are often very general, vague, and overlapping, and, according to Russell (1995), there is little agreement among practitioners as to what conditions are indicated by the symptoms. The American Psychological Association did not drop homosexuality from its list of mental disorders until 1973. Lesbianism was thought to be caused by dominant mothers and weak fathers or, conversely, by girls having exclusively male role models. Those who "came out" in the 1950s and 1960s risked being sent to psychiatrists or mental institutions for a "cure." Since the 1980s, women who do not conform to traditional gender roles may be diagnosed with "gender identity disorder" (Chapter 3; Scholinski 1997; Stryker and Whittle 2006).

Russell questioned the assumption that there is a biological or neurological basis for mental distress and argued that drug therapies based on this assumption have had very mixed results in practice. Rather, she pointed to many external factors affecting women's mental equilibrium, including childhood sexual abuse, rape, domestic violence, restricted educational or economic opportunities, racism, and pressure to look beautiful, to be thin, to be compliant wives and long-suffering mothers, any of which could reasonably make women depressed or "crazy." Hopelessness and anger at such circumstances are not irrational reactions. Women's symptoms may seem vague to doctors, who may not really try to find out what is troubling them. Even when understood by doctors, such traumas and problems are not easy to cure.

Women have written powerful fiction and autobiographical accounts of mental illness and medical treatments (e.g., Danquah 1998; Kaysen 1994; Millet 1990; Plath 1971; Shannonhouse 2003; Slater 1998). In Reading 32, cultural critic bell hooks shows the serious long-term effects of racism and internalized oppression on African Americans' mental and spiritual health. She notes that slave narratives often emphasized the importance of Black people's capacity to repress feelings as a key to survival, and that this ingrained habit has been passed on through family experiences for several generations. As a result, she argues, "many black females have learned to deny our inner needs while we develop the capacity to cope and confront in public life." Sociologist Tamara Beauboeuf-Lafontant (2007, 2009) confirms this in her study of Black women and depression. She argues that "being strong" may be taken as a sign of emotional health for white women. However, "being strong" is a "culturally specific expectation placed on Black women," which "normalizes struggle, selflessness, and internalization strategies" that compromise Black women's health (2007, p. 46; see also Parks 2010).

Health and Aging

Women's average life expectancy in the United States is 80 years, compared to 75 years for men. On average, African American women die younger than white women (at age 76) but live longer than African American men, who have a life expectancy of 70 years (Arias 2011). Typically, Asian American women and men live longer than white people. Like men, U.S. women are most likely to die from heart disease or cancer, followed by strokes, diabetes, respiratory diseases, pneumonia, and accidents. Older women suffer higher rates of disabling diseases such as arthritis, Alzheimer's, cataracts, diabetes, deafness, broken bones, digestive conditions, and osteoporosis than do men. Women under 45 mostly use reproductive heath services. Women over 45 use hospitals less than men do, reflecting a basic health difference between the sexes: Men are more likely to have fatal diseases, whereas women have chronic conditions that worsen with age.

The health of women in middle age and later life is partly linked to how healthy they were when they were younger. The effects of stress, poor nutrition, smoking, or not getting enough exercise build up over time. Exposure to toxic chemicals, the physical and emotional toll of pregnancies, accidents, injuries, and caring for others all affect our health as we grow older.

Older women have to face their changed looks, physical limitations, and the loss of independence and loved ones, which calls on their emotional and spiritual resources, including patience, forbearance, courage, optimism, and religious faith (see, e.g., Doress-Worters and Siegal 1994). In 2008, nearly ten million adult children over age 50 provided basic care for an aging parent: 17 percent of men and 28 percent of women. This included help with dressing, feeding, bathing, and other personal care, as well as grocery shopping, driving parents to appointments, and helping them with financial matters (MetLife 2011). This caretaking of elders may go on for as much as fifteen years and often overlaps with women's other responsibilities: paid work, taking care of growing children, and managing homes. This regimen can be very trying; it involves physical and emotional stress and added expense and can seriously affect the quality of life and health for women in their middle years, who may have to give up opportunities for education,

professional development, social life, or leisuretime activities. Such women may be reluctant and resentful at times but accept their situation as part of what it means to be a good wife or daughter. It is important to recognize that women who care for others need support and respite themselves.

Shevy Healey (1997) argued that confronting ageism in society, as well as individual women's negative feelings about aging, is a must for women's mental health. Women's studies researchers Margaret Morganroth Gullette (2004; 2011) and Margaret Cruickshank (2003; 2008) both emphasized the social construction of aging. Cruickshank (2003) argued that "aging in America is shaped more by . . . beliefs, customs, and traditions than by bodily changes" and that "awareness of social constructions and resistance to them is crucial for women's comfortable aging" (p. ix). She critiqued the field of gerontology for the acceptance of a medical model of aging and proposed a new approach, gerastology, that emphasizes longevity, life changes, older women's needs, and research conducted by older women. Collette Browne (1998) faulted feminist theorists who, typically, have not focused on older women or the process of aging. She urged "a feminist age analysis that can document the strengths of older women, who . . . are trivialized and ignored by patriarchal society" (p. 109). Calasanti and Slevin (2006) also countered the cultural insistence on "successful aging" (p. 3) and the ways "the anti-aging industry operates to reinscribe gendered, ageist stereotypes onto the body" (quoted in Winterich 2007, p. 784).

Health as Wellness

Limits of the U.S. Medical Industry

The Western medical model focuses on illness and disease rather than on the wholeness of people's lives, often treating symptoms rather than causes. For example, though stressors generated by racism are a strong influence in the hypertension that disproportionately affects African Americans, the medical response is to treat the symptoms with medication, rather than to involve doctors, patients, and the wider society in combating racism. Similarly, many women are prescribed antidepressants rather than being empowered and supported in changing their life circumstances. This medical model also contributes to fantasies of immortality to be achieved by life-prolonging surgeries and drug treatments, as well as expensive cosmetic surgeries.

Because medical care is provided on a fee-paying basis in the United States, the medical industry has many of the characteristics of any business venture (see Chapter 8). The emphasis is on high-tech treatments, particularly drug therapies and surgery, as these are the most profitable for drug companies and manufacturers of medical equipment. Most people have benefited from vaccines and antibiotics, and the use of drugs and surgery may improve the lives of cancer patients, give relief from arthritic pain, or restore good vision to people with cataracts. However, this overall emphasis has severely skewed the range of treatments available. It has led to an overproduction of intensive care equipment, for example, while some people have little access to the most rudimentary medical services. This emphasis has also shaped public policy through the testing and use of new drugs, the routine use of mammograms in breast cancer screening, sonograms and amniocentesis in pregnancy, and the prevalence of hysterectomies and births by cesarean section.

The United States is the only industrialized country without a comprehensive national health care system. Provisions comprise a patchwork of government programs for those who are eligible with employment-based insurance for some workers. Many children, students, people with disabilities, immigrants, self-employed, and unemployed people have fallen through the cracks.

In March 2010, President Obama signed the Patient Protection and Affordable Care Act, a health insurance reform law that would include 32 million people previously not covered by health insurance. The changes are being phased in between 2010 and 2014 (see www.healthcare.gov/law/timeline/index.html). Although this is not the sweeping health care reform that many people wanted, it includes important gains for women (Stites 2010).

Insurers must now provide maternity coverage; about 80 percent of individual insurance policies had not included this coverage previously. Fewer African American women and Latinas had prenatal care in the first trimester of pregnancy, at least in part because they lacked insurance coverage. Screening procedures such as PAP smears and mammograms must be provided without co-pays. Charging women more than men for health insurance, a common practice that in effect made being female a "preexisting condition," has been eliminated. Also, health plans must cover contraception, which is considered a preventive service. This provision was hotly debated in Congress in the spring of 2012, with high-profile Republicans and the United States Conference of Catholic Bishops opposing this rule as a violation of religious liberty (Goodstein 2012). The U.S. Supreme Court upheld the constitutionality of this law in June 2012.

Twenty-five percent of people are covered by Medicaid or Medicare insurance. More women than men are covered this way, reflecting Medicaid eligibility criteria that focus on mothers and children, and the greater numbers of women among the elderly who rely on Medicare. However, cuts in Medicaid and Medicare over the past ten to fifteen years have meant that some people have lost medical coverage in part or altogether.

Aside from the availability and cost of medical insurance, other barriers to people's use of medical services include fear of treatment, transportation difficulties, long waiting times, not being able to take time off work or losing pay for doing so, child care responsibilities, language and cultural differences, and residential segregation, which may mean that there are few medical facilities in some communities. Most inner cities have large teaching hospitals that treat local people, predominantly people of color, in their emergency rooms, but this treatment may be slanted toward the educational needs of the hospital's medical students rather than to the health needs of patients. A growing number of doctors, nurses, elected officials, labor organizers, and community members continue to campaign for universal health care (e.g., www.healthcareforall.org; www.healthcare-now.org; www.pnhp.org).

A More Holistic Health System

The United Nations World Health Organization defined health very broadly as "a state of complete physical, mental, and social well-being and not merely the absence of disease or infirmity" (WHO 1946). Health requires clean water and air, access to nutritious food, adequate housing, safety, healthy working conditions, emotional and material supports, as well as culturally appropriate and affordable health care services. The many newspaper and magazine articles that focus on individual lifestyle factors—diet, cigarette smoking, weight, exercise, and a positive attitude to coping with stress—urge us to take more personal responsibility for our health. Although this is valuable advice, lifestyle is only part of the story, as suggested by the data we presented earlier. Living in damp housing or near a busy freeway or polluted industrial area, working in hazardous factories and mines, being exposed to toxic pesticides in agricultural work, doing repetitive tasks all day, and sitting in the same position for long periods of time are all aspects of daily life that can compromise one's health.

Women's health has been a central concern for feminists for the past forty-five years (see, e.g., Avery 1990; Morgen 2002; Norsigian 1996; Nowrojee and Silliman 1997; Ross et al. 2002; Silliman et al. 2004; White 1990). Because many women's health needs are not met under the current system, feminist health practitioners and advocates urge a fundamental shift in emphasis toward a more holistic system of health care that recognizes that physical, emotional, and mental health are intimately connected.

Self-Education and Preventive Care   One way that women can support their health is to eat healthy food, with an emphasis on fruit and vegetables. Countering the stereotype that this is "white, hippy" food, Black vegan writers Breeze Harper (2010) and Tracey Lynn McQuirter (2010) advocate a plant-based diet to African American women on health grounds (also Reading 64). Preventing illness through self-education has had low priority in the United States, and beyond basic dietary guidelines, immunization for infants, and minimal sex education for teens, it has generally been left to interested practitioners, organizations like the American Cancer Society, or community health care projects. It involves learning to listen to our bodies and becoming more conscious of what they can tell us; learning to eat well and to heal common ailments with home remedies; taking regular exercise; getting enough sleep; quitting smoking; doing breast self-exams; and practicing safer sex. Self-education and preventive care also include various types of self-help programs. Many of these, like Alcoholics Anonymous, Al-Anon, Narcotics Anonymous, Workaholics Anonymous, and other twelve-step programs, have been successful in helping people change negative habits and attitudes, though they usually do not address macro-level factors like institutionalized racism, sexism, and heterosexism. A self-help approach also means taking a greater degree of personal responsibility for one's health and being able to make informed decisions about possible remedies and treatments, rather than simply consuming services. Finally, preventive care encompasses creative activities, like dancing, music, poetry, sports, yoga, crafts, and homemaking, that give us joy and make us feel alive.

Complementary and Alternative Therapies   Therapies such as acupuncture, homeopathy, chiropractic care, and massage may be highly beneficial for a range of complaints. They are considered "alternative" from the perspective of contemporary Western medicine with its emphasis on drugs and surgery but are rooted in much older systems of knowledge. Acupuncture, ayurvedic care, and Shiatsu massage, for example, are available in Asian American communities. Native American, Latino, Caribbean, and African American communities also include practitioners who know the medicinal properties of plants and long-standing traditions of herbal medicines. Many alternative therapies have been scorned as "unscientific" and "unproven" by the U.S. medical establishment but are being used more widely, sometimes in conjunction with Western medicine. Many are not covered by medical insurance.

Feminist Health Projects   Such projects have been active since the early 1970s. Examples include courses in women's health; informal self-health groups like the Bloomington Women's Health Collective (Bloomington, Ind.); women's health centers (e.g., Concord Feminist Health Center, N.H.); campaigns for reproductive rights (e.g., NARAL Pro-Choice America and regional affiliates) or for public funding for breast cancer research and treatment (e.g., Women's Community Cancer Project, Cambridge, Mass.); community health campaigns (e.g., GLBT Health Access Project); and national organizations like Black Women's Health Imperative (Washington, D.C.), Lesbian Health Fund (San Francisco), the National Asian Women's Health Organization (San Francisco), the National Latina Health Organization (Oakland, Calif.), the National Women's Health Network (Washington, D.C.), and the Native American Women's Health and Education Resource Center (Lake Andes, S. Dak.). The Boston Women's Health Book Collective's groundbreaking book *Our Bodies, Ourselves* first started as mimeographed notes for a course in women's health and was later developed for publication. It has become an essential resource on women's health and sexuality for women of all ages and has been translated and adapted for use in many countries (Davis 2007).

◆◆◆

Questions for Reflection

As you read and discuss this chapter, consider these questions:

1. How do you feel about your own body? What makes you feel good about your body? How do you know when you're healthy? Sick?

2. What are the main body and health issues for women in your family, your community, or on your campus?

3. What theoretical frameworks and activist projects are associated with reproductive rights and reproductive justice? What are the strengths and weaknesses of these approaches?

4. Who should pay for health care? How? Why?

5. How much did you eat while reading this section? How much exercise did you do?

◆◆◆

Finding Out More on the Web

1. Mobility International USA is involved with disability rights activists internationally (www.miusa.org). How are they improving the lives of women with disabilities?

2. Several governments, including Australia, Britain, Italy, and Spain, have introduced regulations that ban very thin models from participating in fashion shows, and ban companies from using overly photoshopped advertising images. The governments are urging fashion designers to present a healthy image of women's bodies. Use your search engine to find out the effects of such initiatives.

3. Visit www.genderads.com to analyze media images used in print advertising, and the following websites to see how fashion photos are retouched:

   http://demo.fb.se/e/girlpower/retouch/

   http://www.newyorker.com/reporting/2008/05/12/080512fa_fact_collins

4. Find out about the history of *Roe v. Wade*. How and why did this piece of legislation gain support? What was the cultural and historical context? Who were some of the key players who helped to make it happen? What is its status now?

5. Find out more about the positions, arguments, and activities of anti-choice organizations (e.g., the Army of God, the Christian Coalition, Focus on the Family, Operation Rescue) and pro-choice organizations (e.g., Choice USA, Fund for a Feminist Majority, Planned Parenthood, NARAL Pro-Choice America). What did you learn from this?

◆◆◆

Taking Action

1. Make it your daily practice to affirm your body. List all the steps you take to care for yourself and any additional ones you could take.

2. Write to a TV station or magazine that shows positive (or negative) images of women and let them know what you think. Send examples of sexist ads to *Bitch* magazine or *Ms.* Magazine's "No Comment" section; participate in the Third Wave Foundation's "I Spy Sexism" campaign or Mind on the Media's "GirlCaught" campaign.

3. Find out more about your body by, for example, reading *Our Bodies, Ourselves* (2011 edn.).

4. Organize an activity on your campus or in your home community to draw attention to body issues for women and to challenge common stereotypes.

5. Find out more about what your family and community consider effective self-care practices. Where can women go to keep healthy or to get quality health care in your community?

TWENTY-SIX

◆◆◆

The Black Beauty Myth (2002)

Sirena J. Riley

Sirena J. Riley is a writer who graduated in Women's Studies from the University of Maryland–College Park. She has been a campus organizer for the Feminist Majority Foundation.

For those of you well versed in the study of body image, I don't need to tell you that negative body image is an all too common phenomenon. The issue of young women's and girls' dissatisfaction with their bodies in the United States has slowly garnered national attention and has made its way into the public discourse. Unfortunately, the most visible discussions surrounding body image have focused on white women. As a result, we presume that women of color don't have any issues when it comes to weight and move on. As a black woman, I would love to believe that as a whole we are completely secure with our bodies. But that would completely miss the racism, sexism and classism that affect the specific ways in which black women's beauty ideals and experiences of body dissatisfaction are often different from those of white women.

To our credit, black women have often been praised for our positive relationships with our bodies. As a teenager, I remember watching a newsmagazine piece on a survey comparing black and white women's body satisfaction. When asked to describe the "perfect woman," white women said she'd be about five foot ten, less than 120 pounds, blond and so on. Black women described this ideal woman as intelligent, independent and self-confident, never mentioning her looks. After the survey results were revealed to the group of both black and white twentysomethings, the white women stood, embarrassed and humiliated that they could be so petty and shallow. They told stories of starving themselves before dates and even before sex. The black women were aghast! What the hell were these white women talking about?!

I was so proud. I went around telling everyone about the survey results. I couldn't believe it. Black women being praised on national television! There they were telling the whole country that their black men loved the "extra meat on their bones." Unfortunately, my pride also had a twinge of envy.

In my own experience, I couldn't quite identify with either the black women or the white women.

In my black middle-class suburban family, we were definitely expected to be smart. My family didn't work so hard so that we could be cute and dumb. I'd expressed interest in medical school and I got nothing but support in my academics. Raised by a single mother, independence was basically in my blood. But in a neighborhood of successful, often bourgeois black families, it was obvious that the "perfect woman" was smart, pretty and certainly not overweight. As a child, no one loved the "extra meat" on my bones. I was eight years old when I first started exercising to Jane Fonda and the cadre of other leotard-clad fitness gurus. I knew how to grapevine and box step as well as I knew my multiplication tables. I now have a sister around that age, and when I look at her and realize how young that is, it breaks my heart that I was so concerned about weight back then.

Still, I consider myself lucky. I had an even temper. That made me no fun to tease, since I wouldn't give the perpetrator any satisfaction by reacting. Plus, I had good friends who would be there to have my back. But despite this support, I was a very self-conscious middle-school girl. And that's where I gained the most weight, sixty pounds in the course of three years. Because hindsight is twenty-twenty, it is easy to understand why I put on so much weight then. My mom got married when I was ten years old. The next year she had my first little sister, and then another sister was added when I turned fourteen. I love them, but that's a lot of stress for a little kid. My single-parent, only-child home had turned into a pseudo-nuclear family almost overnight. My grades started slipping and the scale started climbing.

Enter my first year of high school. Being an overweight teenager, I don't need to describe the hell that was gym class. To my relief, I only had to take one year of gym and then never had to do it again. Plus, in high school I had options. In addition to regular gym, there was an aerobic dance class and something called "physical training." Now, considering that Jane Fonda and I were well acquainted, I wanted to take the aerobics class. But when I went to register, the class was full. I guess I wasn't the only one who'd had it with the kickball scene. I was left with either regular gym or this physical training class. I decided that I'd played my last game of flag football and opted for the latter.

Physical training turned out to be running and lifting weights. And when I say weights, I mean *real* weights. None of those wimpy three-pound dumbbells. We were lifting heavy weights and learning professional weight-lifting moves. Well, it worked. By sophomore year I'd lost over forty pounds. The thing is, I didn't even know it. Remember, I had only enrolled in the class to get out of regular gym. I'd thought it might have been nice to lose some weight, but that wasn't what I was concentrating on. After all, I'd been doing exercise videos since I was a kid and I'd only managed to gain weight.

How did I not notice that I'd lost weight? Well, I was completely out of touch with my body. I didn't want to live there. I don't even think I really considered it a part of *me*. No one ever said anything good about it, so I just pretended it didn't exist. I basically swept my body under the rug. All I was wearing back then were big baggy jeans and sweatshirts, so most of my clothes still fit despite the weight loss. People had been asking me for several months if I'd lost weight before I noticed. They were also asking me how I did it, as if I knew. While back-to-school shopping before my sophomore year, I decided to just see if I could fit into size 10 jeans. Not only did those fit me, I could even squeeze into a size 8.

Ironically, it wasn't being overweight that really screwed up my body image and self-esteem, it was *losing* weight. All of a sudden I was pretty. No one had ever really told me that I was pretty before. So if I was pretty now, then I must have been ugly then. My perception of myself before my weight loss was forever warped. I ripped up pictures of myself from middle school. I never wanted to be fat again! Boys had never really been interested in me before, but now guys were coming out of the woodwork. Family I hadn't seen in years just couldn't believe it was *me*. Some even told me that they always knew I'd grow out of my "baby fat" to become a beautiful woman. At fifteen, this was my introduction to womanhood. I had dates now. I could go shopping and actually fit into cool clothes. I was planning for college and looking forward to my new life as a pretty, smart, successful, independent black superwoman.

For a few years I actually did eat and exercise at what I'd consider a comfortable rate. But after that year of intense exercising, it was impossible to completely maintain my significant weight loss. I just didn't have the time, since it wasn't built into my schedule anymore. I settled in at around a size 12, although at the time I still wanted to be a "perfect" size 8. This actually was the most confusing time for me. I kept telling everyone that I still wanted to lose twenty pounds. Even my family was divided on this one. My grandmother told me that I was fine the way I was now, that I shouldn't gain any weight, but I didn't need to lose any more. She didn't want me to be fat but thought it was good that I was curvy. Meanwhile, my grandfather told me that if I lost twenty more pounds, he'd give me one thousand dollars to go shopping for new clothes. And my mom thought that my skirts were too short and my tops too low cut, even though as a child she prompted me to lose weight by saying that if I stayed fat, I wouldn't be able to wear pretty clothes when I grew up. What the hell did these people want from me?

I wasn't overeating and my self-esteem had improved but for all of the wrong reasons. I thought I was happier because I was thinner. In reality, I still hadn't made peace with myself or my body. Over the years I gained the weight back, but not before dabbling in some well-known eating disorders. I had a stint with bulimia during my second semester of my first year away at college. But I never got to the clinical stage. I pretty much only did it when something bad happened, not on a daily basis. I didn't binge on huge amounts of food. I'd eat two bowls of Lucky Charms and the next thing you know, I'd be sticking the spoon down my throat. This was not at all like the bulimics I saw on those after-school specials. They were eating sheets of cake, loaves of bread, sticks of butter, anything and everything they could get their hands on. That wasn't me.

Then I started compulsively exercising. I mean I couldn't think straight if I hadn't been to the gym that morning. And even after I went to the gym, all I could think about was how great it was going to be to work out tomorrow. I was also planning my whole day around my food. It wasn't necessarily that I was dieting, but I was always aware of when I was going to eat, how much and how long it would be until I ate again. I was completely obsessed.

Around my junior year in college, I finally realized that something was wrong. I just couldn't take it anymore, so I started seeing a counselor on campus. At first I didn't tell her about my encounters with bulimia, but any trained therapist could see right through me. One day she asked me point blank if I'd ever had an eating disorder, so I told her everything. I realized then that what I had been doing was considered disordered eating. I also realized that inherently I knew it wasn't right, since this was the first time I had breathed a word about it to anyone. I had never even tried to articulate it. I decided not to exercise or worry about what I ate until I got through therapy.

Throughout my course of therapy, I was in three body image and eating disorder therapy groups with other young women on my campus. I was always the only black woman. The memory of that television news survey I had seen as a teen comparing body image issues for black and white women stayed with me over the years. Looking at the other women in my therapy groups, I had to wonder if I was an anomaly. I had read one or two stories in black women's magazines about black women with eating disorders, but it was still treated like a phenomenon that was only newsworthy because of its rarity.

As a women's studies major in college, body image was something we discussed almost ad nauseam. It was really cathartic because we embraced the personal as political and felt safe telling our stories to our sister feminists. Whenever body image was researched and discussed as a project, however, black women were barely a footnote. Again, many white feminists had failed to step out of their reality and see beyond their own experiences to understand the different ways in which women of color experience sexism and the unattainable beauty ideals that society sets for women.

Discussions of body image that bother to include black women recognize that there are different cultural aesthetics for black and white women. Black women scholars and activists have attacked the dominance of whiteness in the media and illuminated black women's tumultuous history with hair and skin color. The ascension of black folks into the middle class has positioned them in a unique and often difficult position, trying to hold onto cultural ties while also trying to be a part of what the white bourgeois has created as the American Dream. This not only permeates into capitalist material goals, but body image as well, creating a distinctive increase in black women's body dissatisfaction.

White women may dominate pop culture images of women, but black women aren't completely absent. While self-deprecating racism is still a factor in the way black women view themselves, white women give themselves too much credit when they assume that black women still want to look like them. Unfortunately, black women have their own beauty ideals to perpetually fall short of. The representation of black women in Hollywood is sparse, but among the most famous loom such beauties as Halle Berry, Jada Pinkett Smith, Nia Long, Iman and Angela Bassett. In the music scene there are the young women of Destiny's Child, Lauryn Hill and Janet Jackson. Then, of course, there is model Naomi Campbell and everyone's favorite cover girl, Tyra Banks. Granted, these women don't necessarily represent the waif look or heroin chic that plagues the pages of predominately white fashion and entertainment magazines, but come on. They are still a hard act to follow.

In addition to the pressure of unrealistic body images in the media, another force on women's body image can be men's perspectives. In this category black men's affinity for big butts always comes up. Now, I'm not saying that this is a completely false idea—just about every black guy I know has a thing for the ass. I've heard both black guys and white guys say, "Damn, she's got a big ass"—the former with gleeful anticipation and the latter with loathsome disgust. Of course, dwelling on what men find attractive begs the question, why the hell do we care so much what they think anyway, especially when not all women are romantically involved with men?

Indeed, many songs have been written paying homage, however objectifying, to the black behind. "Baby Got Back," "Da Butt" and "Rumpshaker" are by now old standards. There's a whole new crop of ass songs like "Shake Ya Ass," "Wobble Wobble" and everyone's favorite, "The Thong Song." But did anyone actually notice what the girls in the accompanying videos look like? Most of those women are models, dancers and aspiring actresses whose full-time job it is to make sure they look unattainably beautiful. So what if they're slightly curvier?

Now that rap music is all over MTV, the rock videos of the eighties and early nineties featuring white women in leather and lace have been replaced with black and Latino models in haute couture and designer thongs. Rappers of the "ghetto-fabulous" genre are selling platinum several times over. Every day, their videos are requested on MTV's teen-driven Total Request Live (TRL) by mostly white, suburban kids—the largest group of consumers of hip-hop culture. It is the latest mainstream forum for objectifying women of color, because almost all of the ghetto-fabulous black male rappers have the obligatory video girls parading around everywhere from luxury liner cruise ships to mansions in the Hamptons. If this doesn't speak to the distinctive race/class twist that these images add to the body image discussion, I don't know what does.

The old mantra "You can never be too rich or too thin" may have been associated with the excessive eighties, but some of that ideal still holds true today. Obesity is associated with poverty and in our society, poverty is not pretty. Being ghetto-fabulous is all about going from rags to riches. It includes having the money, house(s), car(s), clothes and throngs of high-maintenance women at your disposal. An ironic twist to the American Dream, considering many of these rappers claim to have attained their wealth not with a Puritan work ethic but through illegal activity.

Overweight women of color aren't included in these videos because they aren't seen as ghetto-fabulous, just ghetto (Not that I'm waiting for the day when *all* women can wash rappers' cars in cut-offs with twelve of their girlfriends, but you get the picture). Talented comedienne Mo'nique, star of UPN's *The Parkers*, is representative of this idea. She is a full-figured woman whose character, Nikki, has a crush on a black, upwardly mobile college professor who lives in her apartment building. Through his eyes she's seen as uncouth and out of control. For the audience her sexual advances are funny because she's loud, overweight and can't take a hint. He squirms away from her at every turn and into the arms of some slim model-type.

The professor in *The Parkers* views Nikki the same way that many middle-class people view overweight people, greedy and out of control. Instead, we get to see it through a black lens—ghetto women with no class, talking loud, wearing bright colors and tight clothes. I'm sure in true sitcom fashion, the professor and Nikki will eventually get together, but well after we've had our fun at Nikki's expense.

For the past few years a popular black R&B radio station in Washington, D.C, has a contest where they give away free plastic surgery every summer. You know, to get ready for thong season. Needless to say, the average contestant is a woman. At first it was just breast implants and reductions, but now they've expanded to liposuction and even pectoral implants for the men. That hasn't had much impact on the demographics of the participants. Despite the expanded offerings, the contestant pool remains overwhelmingly female. In order to win the "prize" you have to send in a letter, basically pouring out all of your insecurities to get the DJs to see why you need the surgery more than the other contestants do. Sick, isn't it? Anyone who thinks that black women are oblivious to body insecurities needs to listen to some of these letters, which by the way pour in by the thousands. The one thing they have in common is that all the women really want to "feel better about themselves." Even in this black middle-class metropolis, somewhere these women got the idea that plastic surgery is the way to go. Clearly, it is not just white America telling them this.

Sexism has played a starring role in every facet of popular culture, with men by and large determining what shows up on TV and in the movies, and the fact is that they've fallen for it, too. I have male friends and relatives who buy into these unrealistic beauty ideals and feel no shame in letting me know where they think I stack up, so to speak. Just yesterday, for example, my grandfather decided to make it his business to know how much weight I had gained in the past few months. Now I'm old enough and secure enough to know that his and other men's comments have nothing to do with me, with who I am. But growing up, these comments shaped the way I saw myself.

I've consciously decided to treat my body better by not being obsessed with diet and exercise and not comparing myself to anyone (including my former self). When I'm eating well and exercising regularly, I'm usually in the size 12 to 14 range.

This is OK with me, but I know for a fact that this is another place where many white women and I don't connect. As much as we get praised for loving our full bodies, many young white women would rather be dead than wear a size 14. They nod their heads and say how great it is that we black women can embrace our curves, but they don't want to look like us. They don't adopt our presumably more generous beauty ideals. White women have even told me how lucky black women are that our men love and accept our bodies the way they are. I've never heard a white woman say that she's going to take her cue from black women and gain a few pounds, however. In a way it is patronizing, because they're basically saying, "It's OK for you to be fat, but not me. You're black. You're different."

In this society we have completely demonized fat. How many times have you had to tell a friend of yours that she isn't fat? How many times has she had to tell you the same thing? Obviously, when people have unrealistic perceptions of themselves it should not go unnoticed, but in this act, while we are reassuring our friends, we put down every woman who is overweight. The demonization of fat and the ease of associating black women with fat exposes yet another opportunity for racism.

If we really want to start talking more honestly about all women's relationships with our bodies, we need to start asking the right questions. Just because women of color aren't expressing their body dissatisfaction in the same way as heterosexual, middle-class white women, it doesn't mean that everything is hunky-dory and we should just move on. If we are so sure that images of rail-thin fashion models, actresses and video chicks have contributed to white girls' poor body image, why aren't we addressing the half-naked black female bodies that have replaced the half-naked white female bodies on MTV? Even though young black women slip through the cracks from time to time, I still believe that feminism is about understanding the intersections of all forms of oppression. It only works when we all speak up and make sure that our voices are heard. I don't plan to wait any longer to include young women of color in a larger discussion of body image.

◆◆◆

TWENTY-SEVEN

Feminist Theory, the Body, and the Disabled Figure (1997)

Rosemarie Garland-Thomson

Rosemarie Garland-Thomson is professor of Women's Studies at Emory University where she teaches feminist theory, American literature, and disability studies. Author of *Staring: How We Look* and *Extraordinary Bodies: Figuring Physical Disability in American Literature and Culture*, she is devoted to developing the field of disability studies within women's studies and the humanities.

The Female Body and the Disabled Body

Many parallels exist between the social meanings attributed to female bodies and those assigned to disabled bodies. Both the female and the disabled body are cast within cultural discourse as deviant and inferior; both are excluded from full participation in public as well as economic life; both are defined in opposition to a valued norm which is assumed to possess natural corporeal superiority. Indeed, the discursive equation of femaleness with disability is common, sometimes in the service of denigrating women and sometimes with the goal of defending them. Examples abound, from Freud's understanding femaleness in terms of castration to late nineteenth-century physicians' defining menstruation as a disabling and restricting "eternal wound" to Thorstein Veblen's describing women in 1900 as literally disabled by feminine roles and costuming. Feminists today even often invoke negative images of disability to describe the oppression of women, as does Jane Flax—to cite a common example—in her assertion that women are "mutilated and deformed" by sexist ideology and practices.[1]

Perhaps, however, the founding association of femaleness with disability occurs in the fourth book of *Generation of Animals*, Aristotle's inaugural discourse of the normal and the abnormal. . . . "[A]nyone who does not take after his parents," Aristotle asserts, "is really in a way a monstrosity,

since in these cases Nature has in a way strayed from the generic type. The first beginning of this deviation is when a female is formed instead of a male." Here the philosopher whom we might consider the founding father of Western taxonomy projects idealism onto corporeality to produce a definitive, seemingly neutral "generic type" along with its particularized antithesis, the "monstrosity," whose departure from such a "type" constitutes a profound "deviation." . . . Aristotle's choreography of bodies thus conjoins the "monstrosity"—whom we would today term "congenitally disabled"—and the female on a course leading away from the definitive norm. In Book Two, Aristotle also affirms his connection of disabled and female bodies by stating that "the female is as it were a deformed male" or—as it appears in other translations—"a mutilated male."[2]

More significant than his simple conflation of disability and femaleness is that Aristotle reveals here the source from which all otherness arises: the concept of a normative, "generic type" against which all corporeal variation is measured and found to be different, derivative, inferior, and insufficient. Not only does this definition of the female as a "mutilated male" inform later versions of woman as a diminished man, but it arranges somatic diversity into a hierarchy of value that assigns plenitude to some bodies and lack to others based on their configurations. Furthermore, by focusing on defining femaleness as deviant rather than the maleness he assumes to be essential, Aristotle also initiates the discursive practice of marking what is deemed aberrant while concealing the position of privilege by asserting its normativeness. Thus we witness perhaps the originary operation of the logic which has become so familiar in discussions of gender, race, or disability: male, white, or able-bodied superiority is naturalized, remaining undisputed and obscured by the ostensible problem of female, black, or disabled deviance. What this passage makes clearest, however, is that without the monstrous body to demarcate the borders of the generic, without the female body to distinguish the shape of the male, and without the

pathological to give form to the normal, these tax-
onomies of bodily value that underwrite political,
social, and economic arrangements would collapse.

Considering this persistent intertwining of disability with femaleness in Western discourse provides a fruitful context for explorations of social
identity and the body. As Aristotle's pronounce-
ment suggests, the social category of disability turns
upon the significance accorded bodily functioning
and configuration, just as the social category woman
does. Placing disability studies in a feminist context
allows feminist theory's . . . inquiries into gender as
a category, the body's role in identity and selfhood,
and the complexity of social power relations to be
brought to bear on an analysis of disability. Moreover, applying feminist theory to disability analyses
infuses it with feminism's politicized insistence on
the relationship between the meanings attributed
to bodies by cultural representations and the consequences of those meanings in the world. In viewing
disability through a feminist lens, I hope at the same
time to suggest how the category of disability might
be inserted into feminist theory so that the bodily
configurations and functioning we call "disability"
will be included in all feminist examinations of culture and representation. This brief exploration aims
then at beginning the work of altering the terms of
both feminist and disability discourses.

Feminist Theory
and Disability Discourse

. . . I want to extend . . . the association of disability
and femaleness with which I began this essay. Rather
than simply conflating the disabled body with the
female body, however, I want to theorize disability
in the ways that feminism has theorized gender.
Both feminism and the interrogation of disability I
am undertaking challenge existing social relations;
both resist interpretations of certain bodily configurations and functioning as deviant; both question
the ways that particularity or difference is invested
with meaning; both examine the enforcement of
universalizing norms; both interrogate the politics
of appearance; both explore the politics of naming; both participate in positive identity politics.
Nevertheless, feminism has formulated the terms
and probed the logic of these concerns much more
thoroughly than has disability studies, at this point.

Eve Sedgwick's distinction, for example, between a "minoritizing" and a "universalizing"
view of difference can be applied usefully to disability discourse. One minoritizes difference, . . . by
imagining its significance and concerns as limited
to a narrow, specific, relatively fixed population or
arena of inquiry. In contrast, a universalizing view
sees issues surrounding a particularized form of
difference as having "continuing, determinative importance in the lives of people across the spectrum
of [identities].[3] . . . I would advocate for disability
studies to be seen as a universalizing discourse. . . .
Such a conceptualization makes possible, among
other things, recognizing that disability (or gender
or homosexuality) is a category that structures a
wide range of thought, language, and perception
not explicitly articulated as "disability" (or gender
or homosexuality). Universalizing, then, names the
impulse behind the attempt here to show how the
unarticulated concept of disability informs such
national ideologies as American liberal individualism and sentimentalism, as well as explorations
of African-American and lesbian identities. Such
semantics emerging from feminist theory can be
enlisted to dislodge the persistent assumption that
disability is a self-evident condition of bodily inadequacy and private misfortune whose politics concern only a limited minority—just as femaleness so
easily seemed before feminism.

A universalizing disability discourse which
draws on feminism's confrontation with the gender system requires asserting the body as a cultural
text which is interpreted, inscribed with meaning,
indeed *made*, within social relations of power. Such
a perspective advocates political equality by denaturalizing disability's assumed inferiority, casting its configurations and functions as difference
rather than lack. But while this broad constructionist perspective does the vital cultural work of des-
tigmatizing gender or racial differences as well as
the corporeal traits we call disability, it also threatens to obscure the material and historical effects of
those differences and to destabilize the very social
categories we analyze and, in many cases, claim as
significant in our own and others' lives. . . .

. . . The kind of legally mandated access to public
spaces and institutions which began for women in
the nineteenth century and has accelerated since the
1960s was only fully launched for disabled people
by the Americans with Disabilities Act of 1990. . . .

. . . And while race and gender are accepted generally as differences rather than deviances in the political moves toward equality, disability is still most often seen as bodily inadequacy or misfortune to be compensated for through a pity, rather than a civil rights, model. So, on the one hand, it is important to employ the constructionist argument to denaturalize the assumption that disability is bodily insufficiency and to assert instead that disability arises from the interaction of embodied differences with an unaccommodating physical and social environment. But, on the other hand, the particular, historical materiality of the disabled body that demands both accommodation and recognition must be preserved as well. Consequently, the embodied difference that using a wheelchair or being deaf makes should be claimed, but without casting that difference as lack.[4]

Both constructionism and essentialism, then, become theoretical strategies—framings of the body—invoked when useful to achieve specific ends in the political arena, to liberate psychologically subjects whose bodies have been narrated to them as defective, or to facilitate imagined communities from which a positive identity politics can emerge. Thus, a strategic constructionism destigmatizes the disabled body, locates difference relationally, denaturalizes normalcy, and challenges appearance hierarchies. A strategic essentialism, by contrast, validates experience and consciousness, imagines community, authorizes history, and facilitates self-naming. The identity "disabled" operates, then, as a pragmatic narrative, what Susan Bordo calls "a life-enhancing fiction," grounded in the materiality of a particular embodiment and perspective embedded in specific social and historical contexts.

Imagining Feminist Disability Discourse

But if the category "disabled" is a useful fiction, the disabled body set in a world structured for the normative, privileged body is not. Disability, perhaps more than other forms of alterity, demands a reckoning with the messiness of bodily variegation, with literal individuation run amok. Because the embodiment we think of as disability exists not so much as a set of observable predictable traits—like racialized or gendered physical features—but

rather as *any* departure from an unstated corporeal norm, disability foregrounds embodiment's specificity. In other words, the concept of disability unites a highly marked, heterogeneous collection of embodiments whose only commonality is being considered abnormal. As a departure from a norm made neutral by an environment created to accommodate it, disability becomes intense, extravagant, and problematic embodiment. It is the unorthodox made flesh. Occupying the province of the extraordinary, disability refuses to be normalized, neutralized, or homogenized. More important yet, in an era governed by the abstract principle of universal equality, disability signals the body that cannot be universalized. Unified only by exclusion, disability confounds any notion of a generalizable, constant corporeal subject by flaunting the vagaries of an embodiment shaped by history, defined by particularity, and at odds with its environment. The cripple before the stairs, the blind before the printed page, the deaf before the radio, the amputee before the typewriter, and the dwarf before the counter—all testify with their particular bodies to the fact that the myriad structures and practices of material, daily life enforce the cultural expectation of a certain standard, universal subject before whom all others appear inferior.

Indeed, the identity category of disability can pressure feminist theory to acknowledge bodily particularity and history. Perhaps feminism's most useful concept for doing so is standpoint theory, which recognizes the local and complex quality of embodiment. Emphasizing the multiplicity of all women's identities, history, and embodiment, this theory of positionality recognizes that individual material situations structure the subjectivity from which particular women can speak and perceive with authority. . . . Standpoint theory and the feminist practice of explicitly situating oneself when speaking make way for complicating inflections such as disabilities or, more broadly, the category of corporeal configuration—as in such attributions as fat, disfigured, abnormal, ugly, or deformed—to be inserted into our considerations of identity and subjectivity. Such a dismantling of the unitary category woman has enabled feminist theory to encompass—although not without contention—such feminist differentiations as Patricia Hill Collins's "black feminist thought," for instance, or my own explorations of a "feminist disability studies."[5] . . .

I am suggesting, then, that a feminist political praxis for women with disabilities needs strategically to focus at times on the specificity and perhaps the ineluctability of the flesh and to find clarity in the identity it occasions. For example, in one of the inaugural explorations of the politics of self-naming, Nancy Mairs claims the appellation "cripple" because it demands that others acknowledge the singularity of her embodiment. "People . . . wince at the word 'cripple,'" Mairs contends. Even though she retains what has been a derogatory term, she insists on determining its significance herself: "Perhaps I want them to wince. I want them to see me as a tough customer, one to whom the fates/gods/viruses have not been kind, but who can face the brutal truth of her existence squarely. As a cripple, I swagger." Here Mairs is not so much rehabilitating the term of otherness as a celebration or as an attempt to reverse its contemptuous connotation; rather, she wants to call attention less to her oppression and more to the material reality of her crippledness, to her bodily difference, her experience of it. For Mairs, the social constructionist argument risks neutralizing the difference of her pain and her struggle with an environment built for a body other than hers.[6]

The confrontation with bodily difference that disability provokes also places some disabled women at odds with several mainstream feminist assumptions that do not take into account disabled women's material situations. For example, while feminism quite legitimately decries the sexual objectification of women, disabled women often encounter what Harlan Hahn has called "asexual objectification," the assumption that sexuality is inappropriate in disabled people. One woman who uses a wheelchair and is at the same time quite beautiful reports, for example, that people often respond to her as if this combination of traits were a remarkable and lamentable contradiction. The judgment that the disabled woman's body is asexual and unfeminine creates what Michelle Fine and Adrienne Asch term "rolelessness," a kind of social invisibility and cancellation of femininity which sometimes prompts disabled women to claim an essential femininity which the culture denies them. For example, Cheryl Marie Wade insists upon a harmony between her disability and her womanly sexuality in a poem characterizing herself as "The Woman with Juice"[7] [see photo]. As Mairs's exploration of

Cheryl Marie Wade is an award-winning writer performer, poet, and activist, whose videos include *Body Talk* and *Vital Signs: Crip Culture Talks Back*.

self-naming and Wade's assertion of sexuality suggest, a feminist disability politics would uphold the right for women to define their corporeal differences and their relationship to womanhood for themselves rather than acceding to received interpretations of their embodiment.

Wade's poem of self-definition echoes Mairs by maintaining firmly that she is "not one of the physically challenged," but rather she claims, "I'm the Gimp/I'm the Cripple/I'm the Crazy Lady." Affirming her body as at once sexual and different, she asserts, "I'm a French kiss with cleft tongue." Resisting the cultural tendency to erase not only her sexuality but the depreciated materiality of her embodiment, she characterizes herself as "a sock in the eye with gnarled fist." This image of the disabled body as a visual assault, as a shocking spectacle to the normative eye, captures a defining aspect of disabled experience. Whereas feminists claim that women are objects of the male gaze which demarcates their subjectivity, Wade's image of her body as "a sock in the eye" subtly reminds us that the disabled body is the object not of the appropriating gaze but of the stare. If the male gaze informs the normative female self as a sexual spectacle, then the stare sculpts the disabled subject as a grotesque spectacle. The stare is the gaze intensified, framing her body as an icon of deviance. Indeed, as Wade's poem suggests, the stare is the material gesture that creates disability as an oppressive social relationship. And as every person with a visible disability knows intimately, managing, deflecting, resisting, or renouncing that stare is the daily business of life.

In addition to having to prove their sexuality, disabled women must sometimes defend as well against the assessment that their bodies are unfit for motherhood or that they are the infantilized objects upon which others exercise their virtue. Whereas motherhood is often seen as compulsory for women, disabled women are often denied access or discouraged from entrance to the arena of reproduction that some feminist thinkers have found oppressive. The controversial feminist ethic of care also has been criticized by feminist disability scholars as potentially threatening to symmetrical, reciprocal relations among disabled and nondisabled women as well as for suggesting that care is the sole responsibility of women. . . .

Perhaps more problematic yet, feminist abortion rationale seldom questions the prejudicial assumption that "defective" fetuses destined to become disabled people should be eliminated.[8] The concerns of older women, who are often disabled, tend also to be ignored by younger feminists, as well. One of the most pervasive feminist assumptions that undermines some disabled women's struggle is the ideology of autonomy and independence emanating from liberal feminism and the broader impulse toward female empowerment. By tacitly incorporating the liberal premise that levels individual particularities and differences in order to posit an abstract, disembodied subject of democracy, feminist practice often leaves no space for the needs and accommodations that disabled women's bodies require.[9] The angry and disappointed words prominent disability rights activist Judy Heumann

spoke to me reflect an alienation not unlike that between some black women and some white feminists: "When I come into a room full of feminists, all they see is a wheelchair."[10] These conflicts testify that feminists, like everyone else, including disabled people themselves, have been acculturated to stigmatize those whose bodies are deemed aberrant.

Femininity and Disability

So while I want to insist on disabled women's particularity and identity even while questioning its sources and its production, I also want to suggest nevertheless that a firm boundary between "disabled" and "nondisabled" women cannot be meaningfully drawn—just as any absolute distinction between sex and gender must be problematized. Femininity and disability are inextricably entangled in Western culture, as Aristotle's equation of women and disabled men illustrates. Not only has the female body been represented as deviant, but historically the practices of femininity have configured female bodies in ways that duplicate the parameters of disability. Feminizing conventions such as Chinese foot binding, African scarification, clitoridectomy, and Euroamerican corseting were (and are) socially accepted, encouraged, even compulsory, forms of female disablement that ironically constitute feminine social enablement, increasing a woman's value and status as a woman at a given moment in a particular society. Similarly, such conditions as anorexia, hysteria, and agoraphobia are in a sense standard feminine scripts writ large enough to become disabling conditions, blurring the line between normal feminine behavior and pathology.[11]

Feminine beauty's disciplinary regime often obscures the seemingly self-evident categories of the "normal" and the "pathological" as well. For example, the nineteenth-century Euroamerican prescription for upper-class feminine beauty precisely paralleled the symptoms of tuberculosis just as the cult of thinness promoted by the fashion industry approaches the appearance of disease. In another instance, the iconography and language of contemporary cosmetic surgery presented in women's magazines persistently casts the unreconstructed female body as having "abnormalities" that can be "corrected" by surgical procedures which "improve" one's appearance by producing "natural looking" noses, thighs, breasts, chins, and so on. This discourse casts women's unmodified bodies as unnatural and abnormal while the surgically altered bodies become normal and natural. Although cosmetic surgery is in one sense only the logical extension of beauty practices such as make-up, perms, relaxers, skin lighteners, and hair removal, it differs profoundly from these basically decorative forms of self-reconstruction because, like clitoridectomies and scarification, it involves mutilation, pain, and wounding that is definitive of many disabilities.

While all of these practices cannot, of course, be equated, each nevertheless transforms an infinitely plastic body in ways similar to the ways disability alters the body. The difference is that these changes are imagined to be choices that will sculpt the female body so it conforms to a feminine ideal. Disabilities, despite their affinities with beautifiction procedures, are imagined, in contrast, to be random transformations that move the body away from ideal forms. Within the visual economy in which appearance has come to be the primary index of value for women, feminizing practices normalize the female body, while disabilities abnormalize it. Feminization prompts the gaze, while disability prompts the stare. Feminization alterations increase a woman's cultural capital, while disabilities reduce it.

But as Aristotle's equation of femaleness with mutilated males suggests, the normalized female body is abnormal in reference to the universally human male body. The normative female body—the figure of the beautiful woman—is a narrowly prescribed version of what the ideal male figure is not. If he is to be strong, active, hirsute, hard, and so on, then she must be his opposite—weak, passive, hairless, soft, and so on. The normative female body, then, occupies a dual and paradoxical cultural role: it is the negative term opposing the male body, but it is also simultaneously the privileged term in reference to the abnormalized female body.

For example, the nineteenth-century obsession with scientific quantification actually produced a detailed description of absolute beauty, laid out by Havelock Ellis, which posited a Darwinian ranking of beauty, determined entirely by corporeal characteristics and ranging from the "beautiful" European woman to what was considered to be her grotesque opposite, the African woman. Moreover, scientific discourse conceived this anatomical scale of beauty

as simultaneously one of pathology. The further a female body departed from absolute beauty, the more "abnormal" it became as a female body. The markers of this indubitable pathology were traits such as dark skin and physical disability, or behaviors like prostitution, which were often linked to bodily characteristics. Within this scheme, all women are seen as deviant in their femaleness, but some women are imagined as doubly deviant. So the simple dichotomy of objectified feminine body and masculine subject is complicated, then, by other sets of binary oppositions that further clarify the original terms. Indeed, the unfeminine, unbeautiful body mutually constitutes the very shape of the feminine body. This other figure of woman has been identified variously in history and discourse as black, fat, lesbian, sexually appetitive, disabled, ugly, and so on. What is important for this study, however, is that her deviance and subsequent devaluation are always attributed to some visible bodily characteristic—a mark that can operate as an emblem of her difference—just as beauty has always been located in the body of the feminine woman. As one manifestation of the unbeautiful woman, the third term that disrupts a tidy pair of antinomies, the figure of the disabled woman tends to complicate discourses announcing themselves as trafficking in oppositional paradigms.

As this discussion of normalized and abnormalized female bodies suggests, it is the cultural figure of the disabled woman, rather than the actual woman with a disability, that this essay focuses upon. Within the politics of representation I have explored here, the figure of the disabled woman is best apprehended as a product of a conceptual triangulation. She is a cultural third term, a figure constituted by the originary binary pair of the masculine figure and the feminine figure. Thus, the disabled female figure occupies an intragender position; that is, she is not only defined against the masculine figure, but she is imagined as the antithesis of the normative woman as well. . . .

NOTES

1. See Patricia Vertinsky, "Exercise, Physical Capability, and the Eternally Wounded Woman in Late Nineteenth-Century North America," *Journal of Sport History* 14, 1 (1987): 7–27, p. 7; Thorstein Veblen, *The Theory of the Leisure Class* (Boston: Houghton Mifflin, 1973); Jane Flax, *Thinking Fragments: Psychoanalysis, Feminism, and Postmodernism*

in the Contemporary West (Berkeley: University of California Press, 1990), p. 136.

2. Aristotle, *Generation of Animals,* trans. A. L. Peck, (Cambridge: Harvard University Press, 1944) Book IV, 401 and Book II, 175.

3. Eve Kosofsky Sedgwick, *Epistemology of the Closet* (Berkeley: University of California Press, 1990), p. 1.

4. See Joseph Shapiro, *No Pity: People with Disabilities Forging a New Civil Rights Movement* (New York: Times Books/Random House, 1993); Claire Liachowitz, *Disability as a Social Construct*; and Richard Scotch, *From Good Will to Civil Rights.*

5. See Collins, *Black Feminist Thought*, and Rosemarie Garland-Thomson, "Redrawing the Boundaries of Feminist Disability Studies," *Feminist Studies* 20 (Fall 1994): 583–95.

6. Nancy Mairs, "On Being a Cripple," *Plaintext: Essays* (Tucson: University of Arizona Press, 1986), p. 90.

7. Michelle Fine and Adrienne Asch, "Disabled Women: Sexism without the Pedestal," *Women and Disability: The Double Handicap,* eds., Mary Jo Deegan and Nancy A. Brooks (New Brunswick, NJ: Transaction Books, 1985), 6–22, 12. Cheryl Marie Wade, MS II (3): 57.

8. For discussions of disability in relation to abortion and reproductive rights, see Ruth Hubbard, "Who Should and Should Not Inhabit the World," in Ruth Hubbard, ed., *The Politics of Women's Biology* (New Brunswick, NJ: Rutgers University Press, 1990); Marsha Saxton, "Born and Unborn: The Implications of Reproductive Technologies for People with Disabilities," in Rita Arditti, Renate

Duell Klein, and Shelley Minden, eds., *Test-Tube Women: What Future for Motherhood?* (Boston: Pandora, 1984), 298–312; and Anne Finger, "Claiming All of Our Bodies: Reproductive Rights and Disability," in Arditti et al., ed., *Test-Tube Women,* pp. 281–96; Fine and Asch, eds., *Women with Disabilities,* esp. ch. 12 and 13; and Deborah Kaplan, "Disabled Women," in Alison Jaggar, ed., *Living with Contradictions: Controversies in Feminist Social Ethics* (Boulder: Westview Press, 1994).

9. Susan Bordo argues in a similar vein that the feminist search for equality has caused a flight from gender and, hence, from the body, that often masquerades as "professionalism." Disabled women's inability to erase the claims of their bodies or to be able to fit the standardized image of the "professional" often alienates them from feminists who enter the workplace on such terms. See Bordo, *Unbearable Weight: Feminism, Western Culture, and the Body* (Berkeley: University of California Press, 1993), 229–33, for a discussion of this point; also see Fine and Asch, eds., *Women with Disabilities,* 26–31.

10. Personal conversation, Society for Disability Studies Annual Meeting, June, 1991, Denver, CO.

11. The philosopher Iris Marion Young argues for the construction of femininity as disability, for example, by asserting that the cultural objectification of women is manifest in their tendency to be inhibited in using their bodies as unselfconscious agents of physical capability. "Women in a sexist society are physically handicapped," concludes Young in the essay that focuses on the phenomenon of "Throwing Like a Girl" (*Throwing Like a Girl,* 153).

TWENTY-EIGHT

◆◆◆

Three Generations of Native American Women's Birth Experience (1991)

Joy Harjo

Poet, musician, and teacher **Joy Harjo** has published many award-winning poetry collections, most recently *How We Became Human: New and Selected Poems.* Her memoir, *Crazy Brave,* was published in 2012. She is the recipient of numerous fellowships and awards including the American Indian Distinguished Achievement in the Arts Award and the William Carlos Williams Award of the Poetry Society of America. Harjo is also an award-winning saxophone player.

It was still dark when I awakened in the stuffed back room of my mother-in-law's small rented house with what felt like hard cramps. At 17 years of age I had read everything I could from the Tahlequah Public Library about pregnancy and giving birth. But nothing prepared me for what was coming. I awakened my child's father and then ironed him a shirt before we walked the four blocks to the Indian hospital because we had no car and no money for a taxi. He had been working with another Cherokee artist silk-screening signs for specials at the supermarket and making $5 a day, and had to leave me alone at the hospital because he had to go to work. We didn't awaken his mother. She had to get up soon enough to fix breakfast for her daughter and granddaughter before leaving for her job at the nursing home. I knew my life was balanced at the edge of great, precarious change and I felt alone and cheated. Where was the circle of women to acknowledge and honor this birth?

It was still dark as we walked through the cold morning, under oaks that symbolized the stubbornness and endurance of the Cherokee people who had made Tahlequah their capital in the new lands. I looked for handholds in the misty gray sky, for a voice announcing this impending miracle. I wanted to change everything; I wanted to go back to a place before childhood, before our tribe's removal to Oklahoma. What kind of life was I bringing this child into? I was a poor, mixed-blood woman heavy with a child who would suffer the struggle of poverty, the legacy of loss. For the second time in my life I felt the sharp tug of my own birth cord, still connected to my mother. I believe it never pulls away, until death, and even then it becomes a streak in the sky symbolizing that most important warrior road. In my teens I had fought my mother's weaknesses with all my might, and here I was at 17, becoming as my mother, who was in Tulsa, cooking breakfasts and preparing for the lunch shift at a factory cafeteria as I walked to the hospital to give birth. I should be with her; instead, I was far from her house, in the house of a mother-in-law who later would try to use witchcraft to destroy me.

After my son's father left me I was prepped for birth. This meant my pubic area was shaved completely and then I endured the humiliation of an enema, all at the hands of strangers. I was left alone in a room painted government green. An overwhelming antiseptic smell emphasized the sterility of the hospital, a hospital built because of the U.S. government's treaty and responsibility to provide health care to Indian people.

I intellectually understood the stages of labor, the place of transition, of birth—but it was difficult to bear the actuality of it, and to bear it alone. Yet in some ways I wasn't alone, for history surrounded me. It is with the birth of children that history is given form and voice. Birth is one of the most sacred acts we take part in and witness in our lives. But sacredness seemed to be far from my lonely labor room in the Indian hospital. I heard a woman screaming in the next room with her pain, and I wanted to comfort her. The nurse used her as a bad example to the rest of us who were struggling to keep our suffering silent.

The doctor was a military man who had signed on this watch not for the love of healing or out of awe at the miracle of birth, but to fulfill a contract for medical school payments. I was another statistic to him; he touched me as if he were moving equipment from one place to another. During my last visit I was given the option of being sterilized. He explained to me that the moment of birth was the best time to do it. I was handed the form but chose not to sign it, and am amazed now that I didn't think too much of it at the time. Later I would learn that many Indian women who weren't fluent in English signed, thinking it was a form giving consent for the doctor to deliver their babies. Others were sterilized without even the formality of signing. My light skin had probably saved me from such a fate. It wouldn't be the first time in my life.

When my son was finally born I had been deadened with a needle in my spine. He was shown to me—the incredible miracle nothing prepared me for—then taken from me in the name of medical progress. I fell asleep with the weight of chemicals and awoke yearning for the child I had suffered for, had anticipated in the months proceeding from his unexpected genesis when I was still 16 and a student at Indian school. I was not allowed to sit up or walk because of the possibility of paralysis (one of the drug's side effects), and when I finally got to hold him, the nurse stood guard as if I would hurt him. I felt enmeshed in a system in which the wisdom that had carried my people from generation to generation was ignored. In that place I felt ashamed I was an Indian woman. But I was also proud of what my body had accomplished despite the rape by the bureaucracy's machinery, and I got us out of there as soon as possible. My son would flourish on beans and fry bread, and on the dreams and stories we fed him.

My daughter was born four years later, while I was an art student at the University of New Mexico. Since my son's birth I had waitressed, cleaned hospital rooms, filled cars with gas (while wearing a mini-skirt), worked as a nursing assistant, and led dance classes at a health spa. I knew I didn't want to cook and waitress all my life, as my mother had done. I had watched the varicose veins grow branches on her legs, and as they grew, her zest for dancing and sports dissolved into utter tiredness. She had been born with a caul over her face, the sign of a gifted visionary.

My earliest memories are of my mother writing songs on an ancient Underwood typewriter after she had washed and waxed the kitchen floor on her hands and knees. She too had wanted something different for her life. She had left an impoverished existence at age 17, bound for the big city of Tulsa. She was shamed in a time in which to be even part Indian was to be an outcast in the great U.S. system. Half her relatives were Cherokee full-bloods from near Jay, Oklahoma, who for the most part had nothing to do with white people. The other half were musically inclined "white trash" addicted to country-western music and Holy Roller fervor. She thought she could disappear in the city; no one would know her family, where she came from. She had dreams of singing and had once been offered a job singing on the radio but turned it down because she was shy. Later one of her songs would be stolen before she could copyright it and would make someone else rich. She would quit writing songs. She and my father would divorce, and she would be forced to work for money to feed and clothe four children, all born within two years of each other.

As a child growing up in Oklahoma, I liked to be told the story of my birth. I would beg for it while my mother cleaned and ironed. "You almost killed me," she would say. "We almost died." That I could kill my mother filled me with remorse and shame. And I imagined the push-pull of my life, which is a legacy I deal with even now when I am twice as old as my mother was at my birth. I loved to hear the story of my warrior fight for my breath. The way it was told, it had been my decision to live. When I got older, I realized we were both nearly casualties of the system, the same system flourishing in the Indian hospital where later my son Phil would be born.

My parents felt lucky to have insurance, to be able to have their children in the hospital. My father came from a fairly prominent Muscogee Creek family. *His* mother was a full-blood who in the early 1920s got her degree in art. She was a painter. She gave birth to him in a private hospital in Oklahoma City; at least that's what I think he told me before he died at age 53. It was something of which they were proud.

This experience was much different from my mother's own birth. She and five of her six brothers were born at home, with no medical assistance. The only time a doctor was called was when someone was dying. When she was born her mother named her Wynema, a Cherokee name my mother says means beautiful woman, and Jewell, for a can of shortening stored in the room where she was born.

I wanted something different for my life, for my son, and for my daughter, who later was born in a university hospital in Albuquerque. It was a bright summer morning when she was ready to begin her journey. I still had no car, but I had enough money saved for a taxi for a ride to the hospital. She was born "naturally," without drugs. I could look out of the hospital window while I was in labor at the bluest sky in the world. I had support. Her father was present in the delivery room—though after her birth he disappeared on a drinking binge. I understood his despair, but did not agree with the painful means to describe it. A few days later Rainy Dawn was presented to the sun at her father's pueblo and given a name so that she will always be recognized as a part of the people, as a child of the sun.

That's not to say that my experience in the hospital reached perfection. The clang of metal against metal in the delivery room had the effect of a tuning fork reverberating fear in my pelvis. After giving birth I held my daughter, but they took her from me for "processing." I refused to lie down to be wheeled to my room after giving birth; I wanted to walk out of there to find my daughter. We reached a compromise, and I rode in a wheelchair. When we reached the room I stood up and walked to the nursery and demanded my daughter. I knew she needed me. That began my war with the nursery staff, who deemed me unknowledgeable because I was Indian and poor. Once again I felt the brushfire of shame, but I'd learned to put it out much more quickly, and I demanded early release so I could take care of my baby without the judgment of strangers.

I wanted something different for Rainy, and as she grew up I worked hard to prove that I could make "something" of my life. I obtained two degrees as a single mother. I wrote poetry, screenplays, became a professor, and tried to live a life that would be a positive influence for both of my children. My work in this life has to do with reclaiming the memory stolen from our peoples when we were dispossessed from our lands east of the Mississippi; it has to do with restoring us. I am proud of our history, a history so powerful that it both destroyed my father and guarded him. It's a history that claims my mother as she lives not far from the place her mother was born, names her as she cooks in the cafeteria of a small college in Oklahoma.

When my daughter told me she was pregnant, I wasn't surprised. I had known it before she did, or at least before she would admit it to me. I felt despair, as if nothing had changed or ever would. She had run away from Indian school with her boyfriend, and they had been living in the streets of Gallup, a border town notorious for the suicides and deaths of Indian peoples. I brought her and her boyfriend with me because it was the only way I could bring her home. At age 16, she was fighting me just as I had so fiercely fought my mother. She was making the same mistakes. I felt as if everything I had accomplished had been in vain. Yet I felt strangely empowered, too, at this repetition of history, this continuance, by a new possibility of life and love, and I steadfastly stood by my daughter.

I had a university job, so I had insurance that covered my daughter. She saw an obstetrician in town who was reputed to be one of the best. She had the choice of a birthing room. She had the finest care. Despite this, I once again battled with a system in which physicians are taught the art of healing by dissecting cadavers. My daughter went into labor a month early. We both knew intuitively the baby was ready, but how to explain that to a system in

which numbers and statistics provide the base of understanding? My daughter would have her labor interrupted; her blood pressure would rise because of the drug given to her to stop the labor. She would be given an unneeded amniocentesis and would have her labor induced—after having it artificially stopped! I was warned that if I took her out of the hospital so her labor could occur naturally my insurance would cover nothing.

My daughter's induced labor was unnatural and difficult, monitored by machines, not by touch. I was shocked. I felt as if I'd come full circle, as if I were watching my mother's labor and the struggle of my own birth. But I was there in the hospital room with her, as neither my mother had been for me, nor her mother for her. My daughter and I went through the labor and birth together.

And when Krista Rae was born she was born to her family. Her father was there for her, as were both her grandmothers and my friend who had flown in to be with us. Her paternal great-grandparents and aunts and uncles had also arrived from the Navajo Reservation to honor her. Something *had* changed.

Four days later, I took my granddaughter to the Saguaro forest before dawn and gave her the name I had dreamed for her just before her birth. Her name looks like clouds of mist settling around a sacred mountain as it begins to speak. A female ancestor approaches on a horse. We are all together.

TWENTY-NINE

◆◆◆

Young Women's Eggs: Elite and Ordinary (2011)

Elizabeth Reis

A historian, **Elizabeth Reis** is the author of *Bodies in Doubt: An American History of Intersex* (Johns Hopkins University Press, 2009) and associate professor of Women's and Gender Studies at the University of Oregon. Her research interests include the history of sexuality and medical ethics.

My college-age daughter can earn $50,000–$100,000 just for being smart, beautiful, tall, white and a Harvard student.[1] Yes, going to Harvard could actually pay off, even sooner than we might have

imagined. $100,000 would go a long way toward paying her tuition and fees, a fact that she has pointed out to me many times. And all she would have to do is "donate" her eggs to an infertile couple willing to pay.

"Donate" is quite a misnomer. Young women are getting paid handsomely, though there is outrageous discrepancy between what are considered "elite"—currently with high demand for eggs from Chinese, Korean, Indian, and Jewish women—and more ordinary eggs. At the University of Oregon, where I teach, advertisements frequently appear in the student newspaper offering only $5,000 for my students' eggs. Still, many are tempted. I worry that young women are being unfairly lured by these exorbitant sums (even $5,000 is a lot to a college student at a public university) to sign on to something that we can't really be sure is safe in the long run.

One danger is ovarian hyperstimulation syndrome (OHSS), a potentially harmful condition caused by the daily hormone injections taken to produce high numbers of eggs. In some cases OHSS can lead to blood clots, kidney failure, and electrolyte imbalance. And my UO students may run an even higher medical risk than my daughter. Because their eggs aren't worth as much in a world that overvalues so-called "elite" eggs, these women may decide to undergo the egg stimulation and retrieval process multiple times to pay for rent, school, or their living expenses. The more times they go through the procedure, the greater the infusion of hormones and the greater their risk of ovarian hyperstimulation.

Fertility specialists have been performing ovulation induction and oocyte retrieval for roughly thirty years, yet statistics have not been gathered regarding the donors' future fertility prospects or their risks of cancer. If my daughter underwent egg retrieval at twenty years of age, would she be able to get pregnant easily, should she wish to, in another ten years? Is it possible that the risks of ovulation induction might include a decreased ability to ovulate successfully as she ages? Would she be more likely to experience ovarian or uterine cancer years down the road? These are crucial questions that existing studies have not yet answered.

There are other ways to make money from one's eggs. If my daughter wanted to "donate" her eggs to science to satisfy an altruistic impulse, she would also be rewarded, though not nearly as lucratively. New York is the first state to pass a law authorizing compensation for egg donors' time and trouble when they donate directly to cloning techniques used in stem cell research.[2] The legislature allows payments in line with recommendations from the American Society for Reproductive Medicine (ASRM), recognizing that providing one's eggs is much more difficult than providing sperm.[3] After all, women must take hormones to stimulate egg production and then undergo an invasive retrieval process when the eggs are ready. Less than $5,000 seemed like too little to the lawmakers, more than $10,000 too much; they decided that researchers might offer anything in

between. They also ruled that women could repeat the process only three times to diminish the chances of ovarian overstimulation.

I can appreciate the desire to advance medical science. When I was a small girl, I donated my baby teeth to Dr. Louise Reiss, a scientist in St. Louis, Missouri (no relation to me). With her husband, Dr. Eric Reiss, she collected and tested 320,000 children's baby teeth for Strontium 90, a radioactive byproduct of atmospheric nuclear testing, to show that dangerous levels of radioactivity were seeping into the nation's food supply.[4] It was little trouble and quite gratifying to send the researchers my baby teeth, which of course had fallen out naturally, and in exchange I received a pin and certificate announcing my crucial role in the research process.

But donating eggs, even for the laudable goal of assisting stem cell research, is not the same as donating teeth or blood or sperm. Recently *The American Journal of Bioethics* published an article by Brooke Ellison and Jaymie Meliker that emphasized the safety of donating to stem cell research; the authors pointed out that the risks were fewer among women who only gave up their eggs as compared to women who took hormones to stimulate their own eggs in preparation for in-vitro fertilization and pregnancy.[5] The actual steps to stimulate egg production are the same in both groups of women, yet it seems that complications associated with IVF are higher. We don't really know why, as the authors admitted. It could be that the increased chances of ovarian hyperstimulation syndrome are due to issues related to pregnancy itself. Or perhaps the difficulties arise from the very problems that have made that group of women infertile in the first place.

Ellison and Meliker suggest that the medical risks can be eliminated if "proper precautions" are taken. But what if they are not? Hormones are powerful drugs, as anyone who has experienced symptoms from hormonal birth control methods can attest. Taking hormonal birth control is a necessary hazard for many women; taking hormones to advance somatic cell nuclear transfer, not so much. Scientists might instead search harder for ways to utilize stem cells harvested from umbilical cord blood or placentas, rather than to employ a procedure that might well affect our daughters' health years later.

I worry that focusing merely on comparative risk might encourage a false and misplaced confidence, encouraging young women to take the plunge and sell their eggs. If young women come to believe that ovulation induction is harmless, perhaps they will turn repeatedly to this relatively "easy" way to make money. And in the face of financial incentives, why bother wasting one's time and eggs by donating to stem cell research, when one can service the thousands of couples seeking "desirable" eggs, who incidentally also offer huge payouts? If the money is right, and the risks are minimized, young women might discount the relatively meager rewards, financial and otherwise, associated with donating eggs for research and instead sell their eggs to infertile couples, particularly if their eggs are in particular demand.[6]

What is to prevent someone from undergoing the procedure seven, eight, or nine times at different clinics, despite warnings not to act as a repeated donor?[7] It is easy to imagine a dangerous alliance between college students, infertile couples, and clinics willing to soft-pedal potential risks to achieve their goals. If we really care about families, and our

daughters, we need to make the young "donors" our highest priority.

NOTES

This article first appeared in *Biopolitical Times*, the weblog for the Center for Genetics and Society, September 15th, 2011.

1. http://elitedonors.com/index2.html
2. http://www.worldstemcellsummit.com/2010-report-egg-donation-stem-cell-research-how-new-york-state-developed-its-oversight-and-compensat
3. http://www.asrm.org/uploadedFiles/ASRM_Content/News_and_Publications/Ethics_Committee_Reports_and_Statements/financial_incentives.pdf
4. http://www.nytimes.com/2011/01/10/science/10reiss.html?_r=1&emc=eta1
5. http://ajobonline.com/journal/j_articles.php?aid=2629&display=abstract
6. http://www.amazon.com/Confessions-Serial-Donor-Julia-Derek/dp/0974907901
7. http://www.thehastingscenter.org/Publications/HCR/Detail.aspx?id=4549

T H I R T Y

◆◆◆

Reproductive Justice: Vision, Analysis, and Action for a Stronger Movement (2005)

Asian Communities for Reproductive Justice

Founded in 1989, **Asian Communities for Reproductive Justice** (Oakland, California) has been at the forefront of building a reproductive justice movement that places the reproductive health and rights of Asian women and girls within a social justice framework.

We believe reproductive justice is the complete physical, mental, spiritual, political, economic, and social well being of women and girls, and that it will be achieved when women and girls have the economic, social, and political power and resources to make healthy decisions about our bodies, sexuality, and reproduction for ourselves, our families and our communities. For this to become a reality, we need to make change on the individual, community, institutional, and societal levels.

Oppression and Reproduction

The fight for women's emancipation has been inextricably linked to control over reproduction. The reproductive health and reproductive rights agendas have largely focused on individual rights and solutions rather than structural societal changes. Many women at the margins of the movement have championed the need for greater analysis of oppressions in discussions of reproduction. As Dorothy Roberts stated, "Reproduction is not just a matter of individual choice. Reproductive health policy affects the status of entire groups. It reflects which people are valued in our society, who is deemed worthy to bear children and capable of making decisions for themselves. Reproductive decisions are made within a social context, including inequalities of wealth and power."[1] The focus on individualism neglects the broader societal context in which Asian and Pacific Islander (API) women live.

Repeatedly, economic, social, and institutional policies have severely affected women's choice to determine reproduction. The regulation and control of API women and girls' bodies, sexuality, and reproduction have played a key role in colonization and racial oppression, and in controlling API communities in the United States. Historically, the nation's immigrant exclusion laws targeted people from Asia and served as a form of population control. As early as 1870, in an attempt to limit the size of the Asian population in California, the state legislature passed a law that prohibited the immigration of Asian women, and in 1875 the United States Congress passed the Page Law to forbid entry of mostly "Chinese, Japanese and Mongolian" women. Current policies restricting immigration and access to social services also significantly prevent API women from truly being able to make reproductive choices.

In focusing on a narrow abortion agenda or even a broader reproductive health agenda, the mainstream reproductive health and reproductive rights movement typically neglects critical circumstances that many Asian and Pacific Islander women face. For example. API women who are immigrants or those with limited English proficiency have little power to negotiate interactions with reproductive health providers. Many queer API women face homophobia that deters them from accessing reproductive care. Reproductive health programs and service providers often focus on women as individuals and may adopt a paternalistic approach that oppresses and regulates women's reproduction. Although there is, currently, a movement to incorporate "cultural competence" and language access in health services, these interventions usually do not address power differentials in the patient-provider relationship. They do not empower API women to be partners with medical practitioners in making decisions. Also they usually do not incorporate or respect traditional health practices that API women value such as homeopathic medicine, herbal healing, or acupuncture. Moreover, numerous Asian cultures promote societal, community, and family decision-making that is incompatible with an individualistic approach to reproductive rights. API women often have to navigate social taboos and traditions within their cultures in making reproductive decisions, so that "choice" is not necessarily theirs to make.

Creation of the Women of Color Reproductive Justice Movement

In response to the limitations of mainstream frameworks in addressing their reality, women of color . . . have advocated for a broader reproductive justice analysis that addresses race, class, gender, sexuality, ability, generation, and immigration status.

Although some historians have tended to erase the contributions of women of color to the movement, women of color have been actively organizing for reproductive justice for many years. In the past two decades, this race and ethnic-based organizing has gained visibility and increasing success. The National Black Women's Health Project was formed in 1984 as the first women-of-color reproductive health organization, building a foundation for organizations representing the major ethnic groups. The Mother's Milk Project on the Akwesasne Reservation in New York was created in 1985, followed by the National Latina Health Organization in 1986. The Native American Women's Health Education and Resource Center was launched in 1988, and Asian Pacific Islanders for Choice (forerunner to ACRJ) in 1989. Since then, women of color have organized numerous conferences, collaborated with each other, and formed alliances with civil rights and women's rights organizations.

In November 1994, a Black women's caucus first coined the term *reproductive justice,* naming themselves "Women of African Descent for Reproductive Justice" at the Illinois Pro-Choice Alliance Conference. According to Loretta Ross, one of the caucus participants, "We were dissatisfied with the pro-choice language, feeling that it did not adequately encompass our twinned goals: To protect the right to have—and not to have—children. Nor did the language of choice accurately portray the many barriers African American women faced when trying to make reproductive decisions. We began exploring the use of the human rights framework in our reproductive rights activism in the United States, as many grassroots activists do globally. We sought a way to partner reproductive rights to social justice and came up with the term 'reproductive justice'."[2] Later, the SisterSong Women of Color Reproductive Health Collective was formed by 16 women-of-color organizations in 1997, with a focus on grassroots mobilization and public policy. . . .

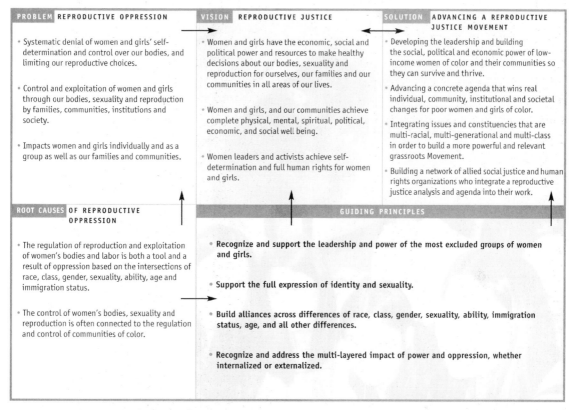

FIGURE 5.1 ACRJ's Reproductive Justice Agenda

Attacking Reproductive Oppression: Asian Communities for Reproductive Justice (ACRJ)

At ACRJ we work towards a vision of the world where Asian women and girls have self-determination, power, and resources to make the decisions they need. Our Reproductive Justice Agenda illustrates our vision, solutions, and values for attacking the root causes of reproductive oppression. In this Agenda we articulate our analysis based on the experiences, issues, and research carried out for and by Asian women and girls to develop a model that is at the nexus of the intersections of gender, race, class, sexuality, ability, generation, and immigration status. In our organizing work, we use popular education and community-based participatory research to develop the leadership of Asian women and girls to plan campaigns for specific and measurable gains at the local and state level. For instance, we worked in collaboration with environmental justice groups to shut down a toxic medical waste incinerator in Oakland, California, and have been working to pass and enforce state legislation that ensures comprehensive sex education in public high schools. And finally, we build and strengthen women of color and mainstream alliances for reproductive justice. We recognize the importance of broader inclusion and leadership of the most excluded groups of women. These include low-income women, queer women, women with disabilities, young women, immigrant and refugee women. Many are women of color; some white women are also excluded on account of their class position, sexuality, language competence, and so on. We believe that organized communities, particularly the most marginalized groups mentioned above, are key agents of change, and we focus on improving social conditions and changing power and access to resources on all levels. Figure 5.1 summarizes our approach.

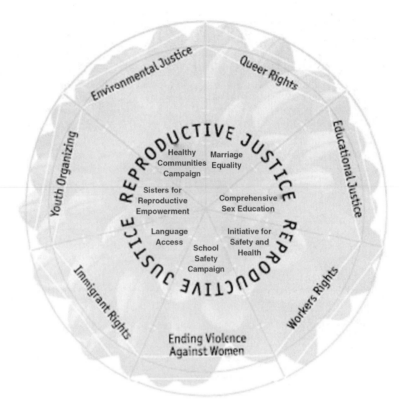

FIGURE 5.2 **Intersectionality of ACRJ's Reproductive Justice Work with Social Justice Issues**

ACRJ's Reproductive Justice Agenda (RJA) places reproductive justice at the center of the most critical social and economic justice issues facing our communities such as domestic safety, labor rights, environmental justice, queer rights, and immigrant rights. For example, under conditions of reproductive justice, we will live in homes free from sexual and physical violence; we will live and work without fear of sexual harassment; we will have safe work and home environments protected from corporate exploitation and environmental toxins; we will be free from hatred due to sexual identity; we will be valued for all the forms of work we do; we will earn equitable and livable wages; we will eat healthy and affordable food; we will have comprehensive health care for ourselves and our families. Moreover, the government and private institutions will support our decisions whether or not to have a child and we will receive the necessary support for our choices. In addition we will receive an education that honors and teaches the contributions of women, people of color, working class communities, and queer communities.

. . .

Translating Vision into Action: ACRJ's Impact

Efforts to advance reproductive justice cannot be achieved by vision and analysis alone. In our work with Asian women and girls, we have translated our vision for reproductive justice into action.

Since 1998, ACRJ has instituted a youth organizing program that involves over 250 low-income Asian young women across California. ACRJ-trained youth leaders have won two campaigns, the School Safety Campaign and the Healthy Communities Campaign, protecting the reproductive health of Asian women. The School Safety Campaign resulted in six school-wide sexual harassment policy changes as well as a district-wide task force on school safety for girls in Long Beach, California. In collaboration with environmental justice groups, the Healthy Communities Campaign increased the visibility of reproductive health issues related to toxic emissions and culminated in victory when one of the most toxic medical waste incinerators in the nation was forced to close in 2002. ACRJ has partnered with the ACLU of Northern California to pass and enforce state legislation that simplifies sex education guidelines and ensures that public school sex education is comprehensive, accurate, and free of bias. Also, in response to the wide body of evidence that shows the health hazards of beauty products, ACRJ has established POLISH, the Participatory Research, Organizing, and Leadership Initiative for Safety and Health. POLISH participants are currently researching the degree to which Asian women and girls and nail salon workers are exposed to toxic chemicals through both personal use and professional occupation. The results will fill major gaps in information, and the project will increase Asian girls' and women's capacity to identify reproductive justice problems and intervene in their community's health. Figure 5.2 illustrates how ACRJ's work fits into a Reproductive Justice Agenda.

The ultimate goal of our work is to build self-determination for individuals and communities. We believe that translating the vision of our Reproductive Justice Agenda into action will yield social change on all levels. For example,

1. An individual woman or girl will acquire skills, leadership ability, and commitment to furthering reproductive justice;

2. A community will change its norms to support women and girls as community leaders;

3. An institution such as a church, school/school district, business/workplace, or legislative body will make changes to stop reproductive oppression and protect reproductive justice for women and girls; and

4. Women and girls will gain complete self-determination.

NOTES

1. Roberts, Dorothy. "Race, Reproduction, and the Meaning of Liberty: Building A Social Justice Vision of Reproductive Freedom." Delivered 18 April 2000 at a Public Forum presented by The Othmer Institute.

2. Ross, Loretta. "Revisions to the ACRJ Reproductive Justice paper." E-mail to the author. 3 August 2005.

THIRTY-ONE

◆◆◆

Understanding Positive Women's Realities (2006)

Emma Bell and Luisa Orza

When they wrote this article, **Emma Bell** and **Luisa Orza** were staff members at the London office of the International Community of Women Living with HIV/AIDS (ICW), a nonprofit organization founded in 1992 and the only international network of HIV-positive women. Emma Bell held the position of Communications and Research Officer, and Luisa Orza, Monitoring and Evaluations Officer.

Despite growing recognition of the right of HIV-positive women to have healthy, fulfilling sexual lives and reproductive choices, there remain myriad factors that make such rights only a dream for most of them. The reasons women have sex and how they have it are influenced by various factors. It is widely known that violence, abandonment, and blame on disclosure can be major problems for positive women as are loss of land, livelihoods, and children. The fear thus created can be an even more pervasive influence on how HIV-positive women live their sexual lives, including whether or not they will talk openly to their partners about their sexual health and needs.

Then there are the very human desires of love, trust, and intimacy that make practicing ABC (Abstinence, Being faithful, Condom use) not as easy or desirable as it sounds. These often go unrecognized in sexual health programs, which tend to render sex sterile and pragmatic, rather than the expression of a complex mix of emotions, identity, and intimacy, which is what many people experience. "Messages are abstract and sterile. We need to bring love back into the whole thing," an International Community of Women Living with HIV/AIDS (ICW) member from Namibia said at a session entitled Love, Sex, and Abstinence at the International AIDS Conference (IAC) in Toronto held in August 2006.

For many women, an HIV diagnosis brings about significant changes in the way they enact their sexuality and how they feel about sexual relationships. There are many reasons why HIV-positive women continue to have sex or not. Some choose abstinence while others feel that abstinence is thrust upon them. For many, a period of time is needed before they discover that sexual relationships can still be a necessary and healing part of their lives. At the session in Toronto an ICW member from Zimbabwe said: "At the time of my diagnosis, I was in a good relationship with someone, and although we had always had protected sex, I could no longer have sex with him. I felt dirty, disgusting, used, defiled, and as far from sexy as humanly possible. The relationship ended, and I spent the next four years celibate." In some cases, HIV-positive women are able to use their status to negotiate safer sex. An ICW member from the United Kingdom said: "I grew to like condoms as there is no mess. And I felt as if I was in control and I wasn't prepared to let anybody have unsafe sex with me and throw it in my face. . . . So in some ways [HIV] has made me more assertive sexually."

Testing and Rights

HIV and sexual and reproductive health programmes and policies generally fail to recognize the complexity of people's lives and the contexts in which their sexual and reproductive choices are situated. Take for example the drive to test as many people as possible for HIV. It is as though programmers equate knowing one's status with being able to act on that knowledge to improve one's well-being and that of one's partners and children. For many, this is not the case, and services are not preparing people for the consequences of a positive result of an HIV test. In many cases, more women than men have access to voluntary counseling and testing services, and though testing is usually framed as voluntary, the power imbalance existing between service providers and service users is often not taken into account as the following testimony shows: "When I was pregnant and went for antenatal care, I was told to have a blood test. They did not tell me what the test was for . . . I realized it was the AIDS test when I received the results" (HIV-positive woman from Thailand).[1]

Testing, along with other HIV services, has to be carried out and projected within a sexual rights framework which takes into account the context of women's and men's daily realities. This should include their sexual realities and the appropriate support services to enable them to manage the complexities of their post-diagnosis lives. Voluntary, informed, confidential testing is the cornerstone of ICW's work in protecting the rights of people living with HIV. An example of good practice in this arena is the Liverpool Voluntary Counselling and Testing Project in Kenya. This project addresses HIV from a perspective of gender-based violence and their training addresses gender inequalities within relationships. Counsellors are trained to discuss women's experience of sexual power relations with clients and to provide them with strategies for sexual negotiation and disclosure.

Understanding Women's Realities

Many HIV-positive women have sexual desires and sexual relationships, and services need to recognize this by providing them with contraceptive advice and services, sexual health check-ups, and comprehensive advice on pre- and post-natal care for mother and child. There is need for service providers to understand that women's relationships impact on their ability to access treatment and other health services. Women's relationships also impact their ability to act on advice given to them by service providers. Partner control can prevent women from accessing treatment and can also impede their ability to adhere to treatment regimes.

A woman from Tanzania said during a treatment mapping meeting organized by ICW: "Most of us women living with HIV and who are using antiretrovirals (ARVs), we face a common problem that our husbands or partners tend to force us to give them our ARV dose while he has not tested for HIV and doesn't know his CD4 count. They do not want to go for testing while they show all HIV symptoms. Even if you refuse he will find out where you keep your medicine and steal them." Too often health care workers fail to recognize such pressures and label patients "difficult to manage" or feel that their advice is ignored.

The Right to Have Sex and Children

More problematic is that health care workers, under pressure themselves, often make harsh judgments concerning HIV-positive women's rights to have sex and children and pressure them into taking certain courses of action. HIV-positive women with children are frequently considered deviant in some way—to have made a mistake. Health care workers, community members, the media, even HIV activists have labeled HIV-positive women who get pregnant as irresponsible. In fact ICW members have reported that access to ARVs can sometimes be offered only to those who are on contraceptives; women in Lesotho and Namibia have reported that access to ARVs has been tied to use of certain types of contraceptives—either hormonal injections or IUDs, in both cases doctor-controlled methods, because it is believed that as HIV-positive women they should not get pregnant.[2] This is not only a violation of their reproductive rights but also places them in danger of re-infection and STIs as safer sex is often negotiated around contraceptive use.

Conversely, others have been denied contraceptives because it is believed that they should not be having sex, as one HIV-positive woman from Thailand learned: "I'd been to hospital and was told to have an IUD fitted. Then, when he checked my medical file and learned that I had HIV, they said 'Oh! This one was infected! The HIV-infected should not use it'."[3] Under such circumstances when HIV-positive women do become pregnant, the emphasis is on saving the life of the child, neglecting the health of the 'undeserving' mother, which not only reverses the impact of prevention of mother to child transmission but also denies women their right to health: "You are only important when you get pregnant;

the baby becomes important; once you are separated you have to see to yourself."[4]

Balancing Fear, Security, and Desires

For many women, the balancing act requires them to manage the fear of abandonment from partners, fear of unwanted disclosure, fear of stigma, discrimination, and violence, and fear of infecting infants and partners, with the need for security, support, and the desire for intimacy, love, and possibly children. This can simply be too much to manage. "If you start using milk powder, everyone will know you must be HIV-positive. If you demand condom use, to stop repeated exposure, he will either hit you or just go off and have sex somewhere else and likely bring back other infections. So you just go on having unprotected sex and breast feeding even though you know you are doing exactly what they tell you you mustn't do. . . ."[5]

Women are often left to research treatment options for themselves, and only those who have access to and confidence in the relevant information are successful in accessing the treatment they require, especially around reproductive choices. "[The Support group] is run by an NGO, but if you get pregnant you have to go to the Federal AIDS Centre and they try to discourage you from having a child. . . . It is very much frowned upon for a woman with HIV to have a child and a sex life . . . at the Federal AIDS Centre you are told to have an abortion. You can get information [about prevention of mother-to-child transmission] from the support group . . . but the doctors will convince you that it's not effective. . . . If a woman does decide and insists on having a child they will help."[6]

Towards More Meaningful Involvement

The complexities of the lives and circumstances of women living with HIV require their involvement in policy and program design in order to effectively address these issues. More often than not, people living with HIV, and especially women, are still excluded from decision-making forums, and when they are invited to participate, it is still someone else who has set the agenda. Such situations can be intimidating and overwhelming, and many ICW members report having felt sidelined once they have delivered a personal testimony on how they became infected. Yet these same policy makers claim to embrace the principle of Greater Involvement of People living with HIV and AIDS. ICW actually prefers the term Meaningful Involvement of People living with HIV and AIDS—including HIV-positive women—in all decision making that affects their lives. This means that policy makers need to ensure that such inclusiveness is developed. At present the onus still lies with the people who are living with HIV to push for their own inclusion.

Challenging Stereotypes and Inequalities

Examples of good practice in the areas described here do not abound, but they do exist. An example is the Mother to Child Transition Plus Initiative in clinics in South Africa operated by Médecins Sans Frontières in Cape Town. The program involves HIV-positive women who have already been through the program to support new mothers and families entering the scheme. The initiative provides long-term follow-up care for HIV-positive mothers, their children, and their partners, fostering caring and healthy families in which the responsibility for childbearing and rearing is shared.

Programs need to be non-stigmatizing and reflect the realities people living with HIV already face rather than burdening them with a host of new ones. They need to challenge existing stereotypes and inequalities and, if possible, be led by women living with HIV. If not, then they need to involve HIV-positive women at every level—from planning

and consultation to development of the budget, implementation, training, monitoring, and evaluation.

ICW's vision is a world where women have the right to make choices concerning their reproductive and sexual lives. This cannot be achieved through top-down calls for abstinence or fidelity or tokenistic, strategically-placed boxes of condoms but by changing the conditions of all women's lives. It also involves challenging the existing power relations between men and women and inequalities that influence these women's reproductive and sexual lives. Only then will HIV-positive women realize their sexual and reproductive rights.

NOTES

This article was produced by International Community of Women living with HIV/AIDS (ICW: www.icw.org) as part of Oxfam's Knowledge Infrastructure with and between Counterparts project (www.oxfamkic.org).

1. Quoted in S. Paxton, A. Welbourn, P. Kousalya, et al., *"Oh! This one is infected!" Women, HIV and Human Rights in the Asia-Pacific Region.* Paper prepared for UNHCHR, March 2004: www.icw.org/tiki-download_file.php?fileId579

2. J. Gatsi, *ICW treatment mapping project report*, Namibia, ICW: www.icw.org/node/218; and M. de Bruyn, 2005. *Reproductive rights for women affected by HIV/AIDS? A project to monitor Millennium Development Goals 5 and 6*, Chapel Hill, N.C.: Ipas, www.icw.org/tiki-download_file.php?fileId5185

3. S. Paxton, A. Welbourn, P. Kousalya, et al., *"Oh! This one is infected!" Women, HIV and Human Rights in the Asia-Pacific Region.*

4. ICW members from South Africa and Swaziland, interviews conducted during a policy development and training project in Durban, South Africa, 2005, report available from ICW.

5. Ibid.

6. ICW member from Russia, interviewed for *ICW News*, Issue 35, 2006: www.icw.org/files/English_35_Web.pdf

---

THIRTY-TWO

◆◆◆

Living to Love (1993)

bell hooks

bell hooks describes herself as a "black woman intellectual" and "revolutionary activist." She is an educator and popular public speaker whose work focuses on gender, race, culture, and media representations. A prolific writer, she has published over thirty books and numerous articles for scholarly and popular audiences.

Love heals. We recover ourselves in the act and art of loving. A favorite passage from the biblical Gospel of John that touches my spirit declares: "Anyone who does not love is still in death."

Many black women feel that we live lives in which there is little or no love. This is one of our private truths that is rarely a subject for public discussion. To name this reality evokes such intense pain that black women can rarely talk about it fully with one another.

It has not been simple for black people living in this culture to know love. Defining love in *The Road Less Traveled* as "the will to extend one's self for the purpose of nurturing one's own or another's personal growth," M. Scott Peck shares the prophetic insight that love is both an "intention and an action." We show love via the union of feeling and action. Using this definition of love, and applying it to black experience, it is easy to see how many black folks historically could only experience themselves as frustrated lovers, since the conditions of slavery and racial apartheid made it extremely difficult to nurture one's own or another's spiritual growth. Notice, that I say, difficult, not impossible. Yet, it does need to be acknowledged that oppression and exploitation pervert, distort, and impede our ability to love.

Given the politics of black life in this white-supremacist society, it makes sense that internalized racism and self-hate stand in the way of love. Systems of domination exploit folks best when they deprive us of our capacity to experience our own agency and alter our ability to care and to love ourselves and others. Black folks have been deeply and profoundly "hurt," as we used to say down home, "hurt to our hearts," and the deep psychological pain we have endured and still endure affects our capacity to feel and therefore our capacity to love. We are a wounded people. Wounded in that part of ourselves that would know love, that would be loving. The choice to love has always been a gesture of resistance for African Americans. And many of us have made that choice only to find ourselves unable to give or to receive love.

Slavery's Impact on Love

Our collective difficulties with the art and act of loving began in the context of slavery. It should not shock us that a people who were forced to witness their young being sold away; their loved ones, companions, and comrades beaten beyond all recognition; a people who knew unrelenting poverty, deprivation, loss, unending grief, and the forced separation of family and kin; would emerge from the context of slavery wary of this thing called love. They knew firsthand that the conditions of slavery distorted and perverted the possibility that they would know love or be able to sustain such knowing.

Though black folks may have emerged from slavery eager to experience intimacy, commitment, and passion outside the realm of bondage, they must also have been in many ways psychologically unprepared to practice fully the art of loving. No wonder then that many black folks established domestic households that mirrored the brutal arrangements they had known in slavery. Using a hierarchical model of family life, they created domestic spaces where there were tensions around power, tensions that often led black men to severely whip black women, to punish them for perceived wrongdoing, that led adults to beat children to assert domination and control. In both cases, black people were using the same harsh and brutal methods against one another that had been used by white slave owners against them when they were enslaved. . . . We know that slavery's end did not mean that black people who were suddenly free to love now knew the way to love one another well.

Slave narratives often emphasize time and time again that black people's survival was often determined by their capacity to repress feelings. In his 1845 narrative, Frederick Douglass recalled that he had been unable to experience grief when hearing of his mother's death since they had been denied sustained contact. Slavery socialized black people to contain and repress a range of emotions. Witnessing one another being daily subjected to all manner of physical abuse, the pain of over-work, the pain of brutal punishment, the pain of near-starvation, enslaved black people could rarely show sympathy or solidarity with one another just at that moment when sympathy and solace was most needed. They rightly feared reprisal. It was only in carefully cultivated spaces of social resistance, that slaves could give vent to repressed feelings. Hence, they learned to check the impulse to give care when it was most needed and learned to wait for a "safe" moment when feelings could be expressed. What form could love take in such a context, in a world where black folks never knew how long they might be together? Practicing love in the slave context could make one vulnerable to unbearable emotional pain. It was often easier for slaves to care for one another while being very mindful of the transitory nature of their intimacies. The social world of slavery encouraged black people to develop notions of intimacy connected to expedient practical reality. A slave who could not repress and contain emotion might not survive.

Repressed Emotions: A Key to Survival

The practice of repressing feelings as a survival strategy continued to be an aspect of black life long after slavery ended. Since white supremacy and racism did not end with the Emancipation Proclamation, black folks felt it was still necessary to keep certain emotional barriers intact. And, in the worldview of many black people, it became a positive attribute to be able to . . . mask, hide, and contain feelings. . . . To show one's emotions was seen as foolish. Traditionally in Southern black homes, children were often taught at an early age that it was important to repress feelings. Often, when children were severely whipped, we were told not to cry. Showing one's emotions could lead to further punishment. Parents would say in the midst of painful punishments: "Don't even let me see a tear." Or if one dared to cry, they threatened further punishment by saying: "If you don't stop that crying, I'll give you something to cry about."

How was this behavior any different from that of the slave owner whipping the slave by denying access to comfort and consolation, denying even a space to express pain? And if many black folks were taught at an early age not only to repress emotions but to see giving expression to feeling as a sign of weakness, then how would they learn to be fully open to love? Many black folks have passed down from generation to generation the assumption that to let one's self go, to fully surrender emotionally, endangers survival. They feel that to love weakens one's capacity to develop a stoic and strong character.

"Did You Ever Love Us?"

When I was growing up, it was apparent to me that outside the context of religion and romance, love was viewed by grown-ups as a luxury. Struggling to survive, to make ends meet, was more important than loving. In that context, the folks who seemed most devoted to the art and act of loving were the old ones, our grandmothers and great grandmothers, our granddaddys and great granddaddys, the Papas and Big Mamas. They gave us acceptance, unconditional care, attention and, most importantly, they affirmed our need to experience pleasure and joy. They were affectionate. They were physically demonstrative. Our parents and their struggling-to-get-ahead generation often behaved as though love was a waste of time, a feeling or an action that got in the way of them dealing with the more meaningful issues of life.

When teaching Toni Morrison's novel *Sula*, I am never surprised to see black female students nodding their heads in recognition when reading a passage where Hannah, a grown black woman, asks her mother, Eva: "Did you ever love us?" Eva responds with hostility and says: "You settin' here with your healthy-ass self and ax me did I love you? Them big old eyes in your head would a been two holes of maggots if I hadn't." Hannah is not satisfied with this answer for she knows that Eva has responded fully to her children's material needs. She wants to know if there was another level of affection, of feeling and action. She says to Eva: "Did you ever, you know, play with us?" Again Eva responds by acting as though the question is completely ridiculous:

> Play? Wasn't nobody playin' in 1895. Just 'cause you got it good now you think it was always this good? 1895 was a killer girl. Things was bad. Niggers was dying like flies. . . . What would I look like leapin' round that little old room playin' with youngins with three beets to my name?

Eva's responses suggest that finding the means for material survival was not only the most important gesture of care, but that it precluded all other gestures. This is a way of thinking that many black people share. It makes care for material well-being synonymous with the practice of loving. The reality is, of course, that even in a context of material privilege, love may be absent. Concurrently, within the context of poverty, where one must struggle to make ends meet, one might keep a spirit of love alive by making a space for playful engagement, the expression of creativity, for individuals to receive care and attention in relation to their emotional well-being, a kind of care that attends to hearts and minds as well as stomachs. As contemporary black people commit ourselves to collective recovery, we must recognize that attending to our emotional well-being is just as important as taking care of our material needs.

It seems appropriate that this dialogue on love in *Sula* takes place between two black women, between mother and daughter, for their interchange symbolizes a legacy that will be passed on through the generations. In fact, Eva does not nurture Hannah's spiritual growth, and Hannah does not nurture the spiritual growth of her daughter, Sula. Yet, Eva does embody a certain model of "strong" black womanhood that is practically deified in black life. It is precisely her capacity to repress emotions and do whatever is needed for the continuation of material life that is depicted as the source of her strength. . . .

If We Would Know Love

Love needs to be present in every black female's life, in all of our houses. It is the absence of love that has made it so difficult for us to . . . live fully. When we love ourselves we want to live fully. Whenever people talk about black women's lives, the emphasis is rarely on transforming society so that we can live fully, it is almost always about applauding how well we have "survived" despite harsh circumstances or how we can survive in the future. When we love ourselves, we know that we must do more than survive. We must have the means to live fully. To live fully, black women can no longer deny our need to know love.

If we would know love, we must first learn how to respond to inner emotional needs. This may mean undoing years of socialization where we have been taught that such needs are unimportant. Let me give an example. In . . . *The Habit of Surviving: Black Women's Strategies for Life,* Kesho Scott opens the book sharing an incident from her life that she feels taught her important survival skills:

Thirteen years tall, I stood in the living room doorway. My clothes were wet. My hair was mangled. I was in tears, in shock, and in need of my mother's warm arms. Slowly, she looked me up and down, stood up from the couch

and walked towards me, her body clenched in criticism. Putting her hands on her hips and planting herself, her shadow falling over my face, she asked in a voice of barely suppressed rage, "What happened?" I flinched as if struck by the unexpected anger and answered, "They put my head in the toilet. They say I can't swim with them." "They" were eight white girls at my high school. I reached out to hold her, but she roughly brushed my hands aside and said, "Like hell! Get your coat. Let's go."

. . . [Kesho] asserts: "My mother taught me a powerful and enduring lesson that day. She taught me that I would have to fight back against racial and sexual injustice." Obviously, this is an important survival strategy for black women. But Kesho was also learning an unhealthy message at the same time. She was made to feel that she did not deserve comfort after a traumatic painful experience, that indeed she was "out-of-line" to even be seeking emotional solace, and that her individual needs were not as important as the collective struggle to resist racism and sexism. Imagine how different this story would read if we were told that as soon as Kesho walked into the room, obviously suffering distress, her mother had comforted her, helped repair the damage to her appearance, and then shared with her the necessity of confronting (maybe not just then, it would depend on her psychological state whether she could emotionally handle a confrontation) the racist white students who had assaulted her. Then Kesho would have known, at age thirteen, that her emotional well-being was just as important as the collective struggle to end racism and sexism—that indeed these two experiences were linked.

Many black females have learned to deny our inner needs while we develop our capacity to cope and confront in public life. This is why we can often appear to be functioning well on jobs but be utterly dysfunctional in private. . . . I see this chaos and disorder as a reflection of the inner psyche, of the absence of well-being. Yet until black females believe, and hopefully learn when we are little girls, that our emotional well-being matters, we cannot attend to our needs. Often we replace recognition of inner emotional needs with the longing to control. When we deny our real needs, we tend to feel fragile, vulnerable, emotionally unstable and untogether. Black females often work hard to cover up these conditions.

Let us return to the mother in Kesho's story. What if the sight of her wounded and hurt daughter called to mind the mother's deep unaddressed inner wounds? What if she was critical, harsh, or just downright mean, because she did not want to break down, cry, and stop being the "strong black woman"? And yet, if she cried, her daughter might have felt her pain was shared, that it was fine to name that you are in pain, that we do not have to keep the hurt bottled up inside us. What the mother did was what many of us have witnessed our mothers doing in similar circumstances—she took control. She was domineering, even her physical posture dominated. Clearly, this mother wanted her black female presence to have more "power" than that of the white girls.

A fictional model of black mothering that shows us a mother able to respond fully to her daughters when they are in pain is depicted in Ntozake Shange's novel *Sassafrass, Cypress and Indigo.* Throughout this novel, Shange's black female characters are strengthened in their capacity to self-actualize by a loving mother. Even though she does not always agree with their choices she respects them and offers them solace. Here is part of a letter she writes to Sassafrass who is "in trouble" and wants to come home. The letter begins with the exclamation: "Of course you can come home! What do you think you could do to yourself that I wouldn't love my girl?" First giving love and acceptance, Hilda later chastises, then expresses love again:

> You and Cypress like to drive me crazy with all this experimental living. You girls need to stop chasing the coon by his tail. And I know you know what I'm talking about . . . Mark my words. You just come on home and we'll straighten out whatever it is that's crooked in your thinking. There's lots to do to keep busy. And nobody around to talk foolish talk or experiment with. Something can't happen every day. You get up. You eat, go to work, come back, eat again, enjoy some leisure, and go back to bed. Now, that's plenty for most folks. I keep asking myself where did I go wrong? Yet I know in my heart I'm not wrong. I'm right. The world's going crazy and trying to take my children with it. Okay. Now I'm through with all that. I love you very much. But you're getting to be a grown woman and

I know that too. You come back to Charleston and find the rest of yourself. Love, Mama.

Loving What We See

The art and practice of loving begins with our capacity to recognize and affirm ourselves. That is why so many self-help books encourage us to look at ourselves in the mirror and talk to the image we see there. Recently, I noticed that what I do with the image I see in the mirror is very unloving. I inspect it. From the moment I get out of bed and look at myself in the mirror, I am evaluating. The point of the evaluation is not to provide self-affirmation but to critique. Now this was a common practice in our household. When the six of us girls made our way downstairs to the world inhabited by father, mother, and brother, we entered the world of "critique." We were looked over and told all that was wrong. Rarely did one hear a positive evaluation.

Replacing negative critique with positive recognition has made me feel more empowered as I go about my day. Affirming ourselves is the first step in the direction of cultivating the practice of being inwardly loving. I choose to use the phrase "inwardly loving" over self-love, because the very notion of "self" is so inextricably bound up with how we are seen by and in relation to others. Within a racist/sexist society, the larger culture will not socialize black women to know and acknowledge that our inner lives are important. Decolonized black women must name that reality in accord with others among us who understand as well that it is vital to nurture the inner life. As we examine our inner life, we get in touch with the world of emotions and feelings. Allowing ourselves to feel, we affirm our right to be inwardly loving. Once I know what I feel, I can also get in touch with those needs I can satisfy or name those needs that can only be satisfied in communion or contact with others.

Where is the love when a black woman looks at herself and says: "I see inside me somebody who is ugly, too dark, too fat, too afraid—somebody nobody would love, 'cause I don't even like what I see;" or maybe: "I see inside me somebody who is so hurt, who is just like a ball of pain and I don't want to look at her 'cause I can't do nothing about that pain." The love is absent. To make it present, the individual has to first choose to see herself, to just look at that inner self without blame or censure. And once she names what she sees, she might think about whether that inner self deserves or needs love.

I have never heard a black woman suggest during confessional moments in a support group that she does not need love. She may be in denial about that need but it doesn't take much self-interrogation to break through this denial. If you ask most black women straight-up if they need love—the answer is likely to be yes. To give love to our inner selves we must first give attention, recognition and acceptance. Having let ourselves know that we will not be punished for acknowledging who we are or what we feel can name the problems we see. I find it helpful to interview myself, and I encourage my sisters to do the same. Sometimes it's hard for me to get immediately in touch with what I feel, but if I ask myself a question, an answer usually emerges.

Sometimes when we look at ourselves, and see our inner turmoil and pain, we do not know how to address it. That's when we need to seek help. I call loved ones sometimes and say, "I have these feelings that I don't understand or know how to address, can you help me?" There are many black females who cannot imagine asking for help, who see this as a sign of weakness. This is another negative debilitating world view we should unlearn. It is a sign of personal power to be able to ask for help when you need it. And we find that asking for what we need when we need it is an experience that enhances rather than diminishes personal power. Try it and see. Often we wait until a crisis situation has happened when we are compelled by circumstances to seek the help of others. Yet, crisis can often be avoided if we seek help when we recognize that we are no longer able to function well in a given situation. For black women who are addicted to being controlling, asking for help can be a loving practice of surrender, reminding us that we do not always have to be in charge. Practicing being inwardly loving, we learn not only what our souls need but we begin to understand better the needs of everyone around us as well.

Black women who are *choosing* for the first time (note the emphasis on choosing) to practice the art and act of loving should devote time and energy showing love to other black people, both people we know and strangers. Within white-supremacist capitalist patriarchy, black people do not get enough love. And it's always exciting for those of us who are undergoing a process of decolonization to see other black people in our midst respond to loving care. Just the other day T. told me that she makes a point of going into a local store and saying warm greetings to an older black man who works there. Recently, he wanted to know her name and then thanked her for the care that she gives to him. A few years ago when she was mired in self-hate, she would not have had the "will" to give him care. Now, she extends to him the level of care that she longs to receive from other black people when she is out in the world.

When I was growing up, I received "unconditional love" from black women who showed me by their actions that love did not have to be earned. They let me know that I deserved love; their care nurtured my spiritual growth.

Many black people, and black women in particular, have become so accustomed to not being loved that we protect ourselves from having to acknowledge the pain such deprivation brings by acting like only white folks or other silly people sit around wanting to be loved. When I told a group of black women that I wanted there to be a world where I can feel love, feel myself giving and receiving love, every time I walk outside my house, they laughed. For such a world to exist, racism and all other forms of domination need to change. To the extent that I commit my life to working to end domination, I help transform the world so that it is that loving place I want it to be.

Love Heals

Nikki Giovanni's "Woman Poem" has always meant a lot to me because it was one of the first pieces of writing that called out black women's self-hatred. Published in the anthology, *The Black Woman*, edited by Toni Cade Bambara, this poem ends with the lines: "face me whose whole life is tied up to unhappiness cause it's the only for real thing i know." Giovanni not only names in this poem that black women are socialized to be caretakers, to deny our inner needs, she also names the extent to which self-hate can make us turn against those who are caring toward us. The black female narrator says: "how dare you care about me—you ain't got no good sense—cause i ain't shit you must be lower than that to care." This poem was written in 1968. Here we are, decades later, and black women are still struggling to break through denial to name the hurt in our lives and find ways to heal. Learning how to love is a way to heal.

I am empowered by the idea of love as the will to extend oneself to nurture one's own or another's spiritual growth because it affirms that love is an action, that it is akin to work. For black people it's an important definition because the focus is not on material well-being. And while we know that material needs must be met, collectively we need to focus our attention on emotional needs as well.

There is that lovely biblical passage in "Proverbs" that reminds us: "Better a dinner of herbs, where love is, than a stalled ox and hatred therewith."

When we as black women experience fully the transformative power of love in our lives, we will bear witness publicly in a way that will fundamentally challenge existing social structures. We will be more fully empowered to address the genocide that daily takes the lives of black people—men, women and children. When we know what love is, when we love, we are able to search our memories and see the past with new eyes; we are able to transform the present and dream the future. Such is love's power. Love heals.

SAN FRANCISCO COMMISSION ON THE STATUS OF WOMEN

The sexiest thing you

can say to a woman is,

"Is this okay with you?"

Make sure she wants you as much as you want her - ask her first. There's a fine line between sexual pressure and sexual violence. And words can be a powerful way to prevent both. To find out more or help end the abuse in a relationship, call (415)647-7273 or (415)864-4722.

RESPECT IS WHAT'S SEXY

6

♦♦♦

Violence Against Women

Gender violence affects women in all socioeconomic classes, all racial/ethnic groups, and it can occur throughout the life cycle (Heise, Pitanguy, and Germain 1994). In the United States, this includes battering, rape, child sexual abuse, stalking, hassles on the street, obscene phone calls, and sexual harassment at school or workplace. Underlying these incidents and experiences are systemic inequalities, also a kind of violence, that maintain women's second-class status—culturally, economically, and politically. This chapter focuses on violence against women in this country and the many efforts to stop it. This is a key issue and we refer to it in other chapters also with regard to relationships, family, and work (Chapter 7), regarding women in prison (Chapter 9), and in connection with the military (Chapter 10). We recognize that this is a tough issue for women and for many men. It may bring up memories or push you to rethink your own experiences. Support yourself by talking to a friend, a professor, members of your campus Women's Center or anti-rape group, or go to your campus counseling center.

What Counts as Violence Against Women?

Most women—heterosexual, queer, lesbian, or transgender—experience a certain amount of what could be defined as sexual violence as part of daily life. We experience hassles on the street, in parks, on public transit, or in cafés and bars. We put up with sexist comments from bosses or coworkers. We sometimes make compromises as part of maintaining intimate relationships, including going along with sex when we do not really want it, or tolerating "joking," put-downs, threats, and inconsiderate behavior. We may define some of these experiences as violence, and others not, and different women may define violence differently.

Researchers and writers use terms like *sexual assault, sexual abuse, battering,* or *domestic violence* but not in a standardized way. Differences of definition and terminology have led to marked discrepancies in reporting and have contributed to considerable confusion and debate about these issues, which should be borne in mind throughout this chapter.

The United Nations Declaration on Violence Against Women (General Assembly resolution 48/104) of December 20, 1993, defined such violence as:

> any act of gender-based violence that results in, or is likely to result in, physical, sexual or psychological harm or suffering to women, including threats of such acts, coercion or arbitrary deprivation of liberty whether occurring in public or private life.
>
> *(quoted in Heise et al. 1994, p. 46)*

This includes physical acts like battering, rape, child sexual abuse, stalking, and inappropriate touching. It includes verbal and psychological violence against intimate partners like yelling, intimidation, and humiliation; inappropriate personal remarks made to coworkers or students; and offensive sexist "jokes." It also includes forced isolation, denial of support, and threats of violence or injury to women in the family (see Figure 6.1). This broad definition implicitly recognizes that men as a group have power over women—the women they are close to and those they encounter in public places. Women may be physically smaller or weaker, they may be economically dependent on their partner, or they may need their boss's support to keep their jobs or to get a promotion or a pay raise. Thus, macro-level inequalities are present in violence at the micro level. An important element of this male power is that it is sexualized.

LGBTQQI people are also victims and perpetrators of intimate partner violence (Girshick 2002; Kaschak 2002; Latty 2006; Renzetti 1992; Ristock 2002, 2009; Wingspan Domestic Violence Project 1998), as well as being subjected to intimidation, physical and verbal abuse, and hate crimes by people outside LGBTQQI communities, as mentioned in Chapter 3.

Many researchers and commentators focus on specific physical acts that can be measured. Emotional violence and the fear of threats are impossible to quantify precisely. It is much easier to bring charges of violence if one can show clear evidence of physical coercion or harm. Indeed, the legal system demands demonstrable damage or there is nothing to claim. The problem with this kind of quantification is that one cannot see the interpersonal dynamics or the structural power relationships within which violence occurs.

Women may be violent as well as men. Women may abuse children, other family members, their peers, and people who work for them. Writer and cultural critic bell hooks (1984b) noted that women "may employ abusive measures to maintain authority in interactions with groups over whom they exercise power" (p. 119). Research shows that, in general, women hit children more than men do, but they also spend much more time with children and often shoulder the major responsibilities for raising children, even in two-parent families. Women may contribute to the dynamic of a violent relationship; they may provoke an argument or hit their partner first. Occasionally women kill abusive partners, seemingly the only way out of situations in which they believe they would be killed if they did not defend themselves (see Rennison 2003; Ritchie 1996). According to Bureau of Justice statistician Shannan Catalano, in 2005, 3 percent of male murder victims were killed by their wives or girlfriends compared to 33 percent of female murder victims who were killed by their husbands or boyfriends (Catalano 2008). Indeed, the vast majority of gender violence is violence against women. The chance of being victimized by an intimate is significantly greater for women (85 percent) than for men (15 percent) (Rennison 2003). We use the term *violence against women* as well as *gender-based violence* because it makes this fact explicit.

The definition of violence against women can also be expanded beyond the United Nations definition quoted earlier. Psychologist Hussein Bulhan (1985), for example, proposed the following:

> Violence is any relation, process, or condition by which an individual or a group violates the physical, social, and/or psychological integrity of another person or group. From this perspective, violence inhibits human growth, negates inherent potential, limits productive living, and causes death.   *(p. 135)*

This would include colonization, poverty, racism, lack of access to education, health care, and negative media representations. These factors affect men as well as women. But women as a group are poorer than men; women's rights may be limited due to cultural factors; and women are systematically objectified and commodified in the media. We argue that such macro-level factors jeopardize

FIGURE 6.1 The Dynamics of Domestic Violence: Power and Control Wheel. (*Source:* Asian Women's Shelter, adapted from Domestic Abuse Intervention Project, Duluth, MN. Used with permission.)

women's security and should be part of the broader discussion of violence.

Andy (Andrea) Smith, Native American scholar and cofounder of Incite! Women of Color Against Violence, shows how sexualized violence was integral to European colonization of North America (Smith 2005b). She gives graphic examples of the dehumanization of Native American women by white settlers and soldiers, a dimension of U.S. history that is rarely taught in U.S. schools and which persists into the present (Reading 33). Indeed, most acts of violence against Native American women are committed by men who are not Native American.

Gender Violence Worldwide, Throughout the Life Cycle

PHASE	TYPE OF VIOLENCE
Prebirth	Inadequate prenatal care due to poverty; battering during pregnancy (emotional and physical effects on the woman; effects on birth outcome); coerced pregnancy (for example, mass rape in war); and sex-selective abortion.
Infancy	Emotional and physical abuse; differential access to food and medical care for girl infants; and female infanticide.
Girlhood	Sexual abuse by family members and strangers; differential access to food and medical care; child prostitution; child marriage; and genital mutilation.
Adolescence	Dating and courtship violence; economically coerced sex; sexual abuse in the workplace; rape; sexual harassment; forced prostitution; trafficking in women.
Reproductive age	Abuse of women by intimate male partners; marital rape; partner homicide; psychological abuse; sexual abuse in the workplace; sexual harassment; rape; abuse of women with disabilities; dowry abuse and murders.
Elderly	Abuse of widows; elder abuse (in the United States, for example, elder abuse affects mostly women).

Source: Heise, Pitanguy, and Germain (1994), p. 5.

The Incidence of Violence Against Women

Domestic violence, rape, sexual abuse, and child sexual abuse are all illegal in the United States. The incidence of such violence is difficult to estimate accurately because of discrepancies in definition and terminology, limited research, and underreporting. We include several estimates, recognizing the limitations of available data.

Intimate Partner Violence

The idealized family is assumed to provide a secure home for its members, what historian Christopher Lasch (1977) called "a haven in a heartless world." For some this is generally true. For many women and children, however, home is not a safe place but one where they experience emotional or physical violence. For purposes of this discussion, intimate partners include current and former spouses, boyfriends, and girlfriends. The narrower term, *domestic violence,* used for many years, still appears in some government reports and academic studies.

According to the Centers for Disease Control and Prevention (2008b), nearly one in four women in the United States reported experiencing violence by a current or former spouse or boyfriend at some point in her life, and U.S. women experience some two million injuries from intimate partner violence each year. Abuse-related injuries include bruises, cuts, burns and scalds, concussion, broken bones, penetrating injuries from knives, miscarriages, permanent injuries such as damage to joints, partial loss of hearing or vision, and physical disfigurement. There are also serious mental health effects of isolation, humiliation, and ongoing threats of violence. As mentioned earlier, some researchers do not take account of psychological and emotional dimensions of intimate partner violence because they are difficult to measure. They define it as physical assault only, which gives the impression that quantifiable acts of violence—kicking, punching, or using a weapon—tell the whole story.

Writing in an anthology of short stories about battering and resistance, Barbara Harman (1996) described how a woman in an abusive relationship is always second-guessing and responding to an abusive partner in her attempts to avoid further violence:

Don't raise your voice. Don't talk back. Don't say no to sex. Like whatever he does. Don't ask him to do anything he has not already done. Get up when he gets up. Go to bed when he goes to bed. Wait. Do what he wants to do. Never contradict him. Laugh at what he thinks is funny. Never ask for his time, attention, his money. Have your own money, but give it to him if he wants it. Never go out alone but do not expect him to go with you. If he is angry in the car, walk home. Be his friend except when he needs an enemy. Defend his family except when he hates them. Understand everything.   *(p. 287)*

According to research published by the National Council on Crime and Delinquency, approximately one in three adolescent girls in the United States is a victim of physical, emotional, or verbal abuse from a dating partner (Davis 2008). June Larkin and Katherine Popaleni's (1997) earlier interviews with young women revealed how young men use criticism, intimidation, surveillance, threats, and force to establish and maintain control over their girlfriends. The popularity of cell phones has increased the ease of informal "surveillance." Young women are vulnerable to abuse because they may feel that involvement in a personal relationship is necessary to fit in; they may be flattered by a dating partner who demands time and attention; and they lack experience negotiating affection and sexual behavior.

Rape and Sexual Assault

The legal definition of rape turns on force and nonconsent. Consent to sexual intercourse is not meaningful if given under the influence of alcohol, drugs, or prescription medication. Consent may be defined as a "Yes" that is freely given when the option of "No" is present and viable. Like domestic violence, rape is not always reported, and the true scope of the problem is difficult to assess. Rates of rape vary widely among studies according to how the crime is defined, who participates in the study, and what methodology is used. Between 1992 and 2000, an estimated 63 percent of completed rapes and 65 percent of attempted rapes were not reported to the police (Rennison 2002). Rape is defined as forced sexual intercourse—vaginal, anal, or oral penetration. Sexual assault includes attacks involving unwanted sexual contact; it may involve force and include grabbing or fondling, also verbal threats. The groups most at risk for rape and sexual assault are 20- to 24-year-olds, then 16- to 19-year-olds (U.S. Department of Justice 2011). In contrast to popular ideas about rape committed by a stranger in a dark alley, 73 percent of women who reported that they had been raped or physically assaulted said that their partner or date committed the assault (Catalano 2008).

In 1991, the FBI's Uniform Crime Report (compiled from over 16,000 law enforcement agencies covering 96 percent of the nation's population) estimated that one in four U.S. college women was a victim of rape or attempted rape, and this estimate is still widely used by academics, activists, and journalists. Skeptics have countered that such figures are highly inflated and that many women who claim to have been raped blame their dates for their own poor judgement in having sex (see, e.g., Paglia 1990; Roiphe 1993). According to the U.S. Bureau of Justice, the most recent and methodologically rigorous studies show that sexual assault still occurs at rates similar to those identified more than twenty years ago when Koss, Giducz, and Wisiewski (1987) found that approximately 27.5 percent of college women reported experiences that met the legal criteria for rape (Office of Justice Programs 2007). Given the continued prevalence of rape, especially for young women, some advocates and commentators describe the United States as having a "rape culture" (see e.g., Buchwald, Fletcher, and Roth 2005). Police consultant Rana Sampson (2002) reported that most rapes of college women are not date rapes, but rapes by acquaintances maybe at a party or while studying together in a dorm room. Ninety percent of college women who are victims of rape or attempted rape know their assailant, usually a classmate, friend, boyfriend, or ex-boyfriend (in that order) (Fisher, Cullen, and Turner 2000). College athletes are disproportionately reported to campus officers for acquaintance rape, and fraternities have been at the center of controversy for rapes and attempted rapes at fraternity house parties. Psychologists Stephen Humphrey and Arnold Kahn (2000) distinguished between fraternities and athletic teams that are high risk and low risk for rape, and found that college women correctly

identified them, based on the type of parties they held. Under the 1990 Student Right-to-Know and Campus Security Act (updated as the 1998 Jeanne Cleau Disclosure of Campus Security Policy and Campus Crime Statistics Act), all colleges and universities that receive federal funding must spell out rape victims' rights and publish information on prevention programs. In Reading 35, Jonathan Grove discusses the Men's Project at Pacific Lutheran University, which seeks to engage a majority of men on campus as allies on this issue.

Female students are most at risk of acquaintance rape in the first few weeks of college. They often do not report a rape because of confusion, guilt, or fear, or because they feel betrayed; they may be ashamed to tell parents or college counselors; and they may not identify the experience as rape. However, the reporting of rape increased significantly on U.S. college campuses during the 1990s. The psychological effects of rape can be traumatic and long-lasting. They include feelings of humiliation, helplessness, anger, self-doubt, self-hate, and fear; and a student may become depressed and withdrawn, lack concentration, sleep badly, and do poorly in school.

Effects of Race, Class, Nation, Sexuality, and Disability

Although these forms of violence occur across the board, women's experiences are complicated by race, class, national origin, sexuality, and disability.

Research   The Bureau of Justice Statistics (1995) noted that domestic violence was consistent across racial and ethnic lines. Jody Raphael and Richard Tolman (1997) found that victims of domestic violence were overrepresented among women on welfare and families with extremely low incomes. Bureau of Justice statistician Callie Marie Rennison (2002) found that, in 1999, African American women aged 20 to 24 experienced more intimate violence than white women of the same age. Official estimates of violence are limited by the fact that many cases are not reported, and research into this issue is limited by the scope of studies undertaken. Children and adolescents, prostituted women, homeless women, women with mental disabilities, institutionalized women, very poor women, and women in neighborhoods with high crime rates are rarely included in surveys. Women and girls with physical and mental disabilities are particularly vulnerable to physical, emotional, and sexual abuse from partners, caregivers, and service providers (Abramson et al. 2000; Young et al. 1997). The few studies that exist suggest that women with disabilities are between four and ten times as likely to be sexually assaulted as other women.

Reporting Although violence between intimate partners is illegal in this country, it is seriously underreported because of confusion, shame, self-blame, loyalty to the abuser, lack of information, or fear of repercussions, including loss of a partner's income. Women may not believe that reporting violence to the police will do any good. Women of color, poor women, and prostituted women often have very negative experiences with the police. Women of color may decide not to report acts of violence or rape to avoid bringing more trouble on husbands, partners, friends, and acquaintances who already suffer discrimination based on race, as mentioned by Andy Smith (Reading 33) and Mimi Kim (Reading 36). In many communities of color the police are perceived not as helpful but, rather, as abusive, harassing, and violent. Women as well as men "bear the brunt of police indifference and abuse" and "men are frequently targeted for false arrest" (M. Smith 1997). Their community may expect women of color to maintain silence about sexual assault, to protect "family honor and community integrity" (Crenshaw 1993, p. 5). Melba Wilson (1993) discussed the conflicting pressures operating here and urged Black women to hold men accountable for sexual abuse of children. African American feminist academics Johnnetta Cole and Beverly Guy-Sheftall (2003) decided to share their personal experiences as part of an extended discussion with other prominent African American thinkers and writers regarding violence against women in African American families and communities. They took this step to show how the dehumanization of racism distorts and limits ideas of manhood and womanhood for many African Americans, and to honor those seeking to transform interpersonal and family relationships. Sociologist Patricia Hill Collins (2004) analyzed the micro-, meso-, and macro-level forces that affect African Americans' experiences of sexuality as well as violence. All three authors commented on the difficulty of "airing dirty linen in public" and the possibility that their work would be used to reinforce racist stereotypes. They decided to take this risk in order to strengthen relationships between African American men and women (also see Reading 32).

Elderly women may not report acts of violence committed by spouses, adult children, caregivers, relatives, and neighbors, because they fear being rejected, losing their caregiver, or losing their home or independent access to money. Immigrant women who are dependent on an abusive partner for their legal status may fear repercussions from ICE (Immigration and Customs Enforcement) if they report violence. Some women have been reluctant to speak about abuse in lesbian or transgender relationships, not wanting to feed negative stereotypes circulating in the wider society (see, e.g., Kaschak 2002; Latty 2006; Renzetti 1992; Ristock 2002, 2009).

Responses of the Police and Medical and Legal Systems The response to reports of violence against women and the provision of services have greatly expanded as this issue has become recognized publicly. Police officers, judges, doctors, nurses, and emergency-room staff may undergo professional training, although much more still needs to be done in this regard.

During slavery times, the rape of Black women in the United States was legal and commonplace. They were chattel, the legal property of their masters, and available for anything and everything. Andy Smith notes that in "patriarchal thinking, only a 'pure' body can really be violated. The rape of bodies that are considered inherently impure simply does not count" (Reading 33). Currently, negative stereotypes about women of color, poor white women, prostituted women, lesbians, and transgender women all perpetuate the idea, in the wider society, that these women are not worthy of respect. They are less likely to be taken seriously if they report acts of violence. Law professor Kimberlé Crenshaw (1993) noted an early-1990s study of sentences given to convicted rapists in Dallas: "The average sentence given to the rapist of a Black woman was two years . . . to the rapist of a Latina . . . five years, and . . . to the rapist of a white woman . . . ten years. Interviews with jurors revealed that the low conviction rate of men accused of raping Black women is based on ongoing sexual stereotypes about Black women" (p. 4) as mentioned in Chapter 4. Law professor Tania Tetlow

(2009) argued that contemporary statistics "show a marked disparity in conviction rates according to the race of the rape victim" (p. 90).

Explanations of Violence Against Women

Most explanations of violence against women are social theories. Before discussing some of these, we note the resurfacing of a biological explanation of rape. Randy Thornhill and Craig Palmer (2000) argued that rape evolved historically as a form of male reproductive behavior. These authors based their claims on studies of animal species from the scorpion fly to primates. As with other sociobiological theories, they make huge leaps between animal behavior and human life, they are not grounded in an analysis of social systems, and their claims are not borne out by the experience of women who have suffered acts of violence.

As in other chapters, we focus on social theories and separate micro- and macro-level explanations.

Micro-Level Explanations

Intimate partner violence, rape, and child sexual abuse are often explained in terms of an individual mental health problem, innate sexual craving, or personal dysfunction on the part of perpetrators. Another micro-level explanation for intimate partner violence is that the partners have an "unhealthy" relationship.

Three psychological syndromes have been advanced to explain violence against women: battered woman syndrome, rape trauma syndrome, and false memory syndrome.

Battered Woman Syndrome   Psychologist Lenore Walker (1979, 1984) noted a pattern of behavior that she termed "learned helplessness," whereby women who are repeatedly battered "learn" it is impossible to escape. After an episode of violence, they are seduced back by the batterer with declarations of love and promises that he will change. These calm, loving episodes alternate with periods of accelerating violence, isolating the woman further and tying her closer to him. Attorneys have used a "battered woman syndrome" defense for women who kill violent partners by arguing that their clients'

judgment was affected "in such a way as to make them honestly believe that they were in imminent danger and that the use of force was their only means of escape" (Gordon 1997, p. 25).

Rape Trauma Syndrome   This term has been used by mental health and legal professionals to refer to women's coping strategies following rape. The focus is on women's reactions and responses rather than on the actions of the perpetrators. Rape trauma syndrome has been used to explain women's supposedly "counterintuitive" reactions—such as not reporting a rape for days or even months, not remembering parts of the assault, appearing too calm, or expressing anger at their treatment by police, hospital staff, or the legal system. Such responses have been defined as pathological (Stefan 1994, p. 1274). Women diagnosed with rape trauma syndrome—who are generally white and middle class—are given psychiatric treatment with the goal of recovery and resolution. Expert testimony concerning rape trauma syndrome in rape trials has improved the chances that a perpetrator would be convicted but at the cost of representing the woman as a pathetic victim.

False Memory Syndrome   Childhood sexual abuse by parents, older siblings, stepparents, and other family members is another aspect of family life that has gradually become a public issue through the efforts of survivors, counselors, and feminist advocates. Many abused children block out memories of what happened to them, and these may not surface again until their adult years, perhaps through flashbacks, nightmares, panic attacks, or pain (Petersen 1991; White 1988). They then gradually piece together fragments of their experience that have been suppressed. Those who have been abused as children often experience confusion, shame, fear, or fear of being crazy. They may spend years thinking they were to blame. They may have feelings of not being worth much, or conversely, they may feel special. The child is invariably told that this special secret must never be spoken about. Healing from the effects of childhood sexual abuse takes time, courage, and support, as described by Aurora Levins Morales (Reading 34), and many families do not want to open up this can of worms (Bass and Davis 1988; Haines 1999; Herman 1992; Petersen 1991; E. C. White 1985; L. White 1988; Wilson 1993).

False memory syndrome (FMS) has been invoked by parents who believe they "have been falsely accused [of incest] as a result of their adult children discovering 'memories' in the course of therapy" (Wasserman 1992, p. 18) and by lawyers acting on their behalf. According to FMS, the incest survivor is someone with impaired cognitive functioning. Memory is complex cognitively, and there are well-regarded psychologists on both sides of this issue.

These syndromes were developed for legal or therapeutic purposes. As explanations of violence against women, they are all inadequate. They pathologize women who experience acts of violence as helpless victims. As legal defenses, they are also highly problematic. A battered-woman-syndrome defense for women who have killed abusive partners represents battered women as impaired, rather than as "rational actors responding to perceived danger" (Gordon 1997, p. 25).

These syndromes all **blame the victim** for her situation. The advice that police departments often give to women for their safety also assumes that we bring assaults on ourselves: Do not go out alone late at night; do not wear "provocative" clothing; always walk purposefully; do not make eye contact with men on the street; park your car in a lighted area; have your keys ready in your hand before you leave the building; look into the back seat before getting in your car, and so on. This advice is well intentioned and may be helpful. However, it assumes that women are responsible for acts of violence against us, either directly "asking for it" by their dress or behavior or indirectly encouraging it by not being sufficiently cautious.

Macro-Level Explanations

Micro-level explanations of violence against women can be compelling if one focuses on specific personal interactions, but by themselves they cannot explain such a universal and systemic phenomenon. It is essential to analyze this issue at the meso and macro levels to understand it fully and to generate effective strategies to stop it. At the same time it is important to remember that all men do not participate in gender-based violence. Julia Serano notes that most boys are taught to be respectful of girls and women, but "nice guys" are not validated in mainstream culture or by some women (Reading 22).

Macro-level explanations focus on the cultural legitimation of male violence and the economic, political, and legal systems that marginalize, discriminate against, and disempower women.

Hussein Bulhan's (1985) very broad definition of violence mentioned earlier emphasized the structural nature of violence and rests on several assumptions:

> Violence is not an isolated physical act or a discrete random event. It is a relation, process, and condition undermining, exploiting, and curtailing the well-being of the victim. . . . Violence in any of the three domains—physical, social, or psychological—has significant repercussions in the other two domains. Violence occurs not only between individuals, but also between groups and societies. Intention is less important than consequence in most forms of violence. Any relation, process, or condition imposed by someone that injures the health and well-being of others is by definition violent. *(p. 135)*

Applying these ideas to violence against women may make it easier to see this violence in terms of inequalities of power under patriarchy, as argued by Allan Johnson (Reading 8). In Reading 33, Andy Smith shows how sexual violence was part of U.S. colonization of Native Americans. Macro-level factors such as sexism, heterosexism, racism, economic opportunities, working conditions, unemployment, poverty, or loss of status and cultural roots that may accompany immigration also affect personal and family relationships from the outside. Lora Jo Foo (2007) mentions the severe cultural and economic disruptions and dislocations experienced by first-generation immigrants, which contribute to the incidence of domestic violence in these communities. Immigrants are often at the bottom of the U.S. job hierarchy; they may not speak or read English; the U.S. legal and political system is unfamiliar; and parents may have to rely on their children to negotiate and interpret the world outside home and family. This is not to excuse those who abuse their partners or children but, rather, to provide a wider context for understanding violence.

The Cultural Legitimation of Male Violence This includes cultural beliefs in male superiority and male control of women's behavior and of the family, which are supported by social institutions such as education, law, religion, and popular culture. War toys, competitive games, violent and aggressive sports, and violence on TV, in video games, and in movies are integral to children's socialization, especially that of boys. Popular culture, news media, and advertising all reinforce these cultural attitudes and contribute to the objectification and commodification of women. The music business, MTV, TV shows, and feature films all contribute to a culture of violence against women. At the meso level too, in various communities, cultural attitudes and religious beliefs support domestic violence as a husband's prerogative to "discipline" his wife. Historically, wives were assumed to agree to sex whenever their husbands wanted it as part of their marriage contract, and rape laws included a marital exemption. In response to pressure from advocacy groups, states criminalized rape in marriage during the 1970s and 1980s; by 1993, marital rape was a crime in all fifty states, though it continues to be underreported and difficult to prosecute. Another example of male control is street harassment, where women may be "touched, harassed, commented upon in a stream of constant small-scale assaults" (Benard and Schlaffer 1997, p. 395). The public street is defined as male space where women without male escorts may be considered "fair game."

The cultural legitimation of male superiority involves patterns of male and female socialization in the family and in schools, and the social construction of masculinity and of male sexuality (see Kimmel 1993; 2000, chap. 11; Kimmel and Messner 1998; Lefkowitz 1997; Messner 1992). In a White Supremacist society, men of color may be attracted to a construction of masculinity that derives from white patriarchal attitudes and behavior. Discussing violence against women in African American communities, bell hooks (1994) commented:

> Black males, utterly disenfranchised in almost every arena of life in the United States, often find that the assertion of sexist domination is their only expressive access to the patriarchal power they are told all men should possess as their gendered birthright.   *(p. 110)*

Finally, armed conflict, war, and threats of war legitimate violence between groups and nations, and contribute to a culture of violence throughout society.

Economic Systems That Disempower Women
Women as a group earn less than men as a group. It may be difficult for a woman to leave a violent marriage or relationship if she is financially dependent on her partner. In the workplace, women may find it difficult to speak up about sexual harassment. Sociologist Michael Kimmel (1993) noted that sexual harassment "fuses two levels of power: the power of employers over employees and the power of men over women. Thus what may be said or intended as a man to a woman is also experienced in the context of superior and subordinate" (p. 130).

Legal Systems That Discriminate Against Women
This includes inadequate laws and practices concerning violence against women, and insensitive treatment of women by police and the courts. Martha Mahoney (1994) emphasized the narrowness of legal categories and procedures in dealing with violence against women. For instance, the "statute of limitations," a limit on the time period allowed for bringing a lawsuit for damages or criminal charges against a perpetrator, stops some women from using the law for redress in cases of rape or childhood sexual abuse. In the latter case, they may be in their twenties, and years past the time limit, before they recognize that they were abused as children and gain the personal strength to confront the perpetrator publicly.

Political Systems That Marginalize Women's Concerns   Women are still a minority in elected office in the United States, especially at the congressional level. Violence against women is often not taken seriously by policy makers or legislators. Compared to male voters, more women are concerned about gender-based violence. More women also favor meaningful gun control, an end to the international trade in arms, reductions in military spending, and disarmament, believing that such changes would greatly increase their security and the well-being of their communities (Ducat 2004; Gallagher 1993). We take up the issue of women in electoral politics in Chapter 12.

The levels of violence mentioned earlier are interconnected and reinforce each other. Debra Borkovitz (1995) argued that it is necessary to transform prevailing ideas of *domination,* whether of racism, imperialism, male violence against women, or same-sex battering. Similarly, bell hooks (1984b) argued against the "notion of hierarchical rule and coercive authority that is the root cause of violence against women, of adult violence against children, of all violence between those who dominate and those who are dominated" (p. 118). She maintained that feminists should oppose all forms of coercive domination rather than concentrating solely on male violence against women.

Ending Violence Against Women

Women have made various efforts to stop gender-based violence. Historian Linda Gordon (1988, 1997) noted that U.S. feminists challenged wife-beating as part of antidrinking campaigns in the late nineteenth century, then again in the 1930s in campaigns for child custody and welfare for single mothers so that they could leave abusive men. Extremely important feminist work in the 1960s and 1970s broke through the prevailing silence on this subject (e.g., Brownmiller 1975; Griffin 1971; Russell 1975). Feminists reframed and politicized the issue of rape, exposing the myth that rape is about sex—a crime of "frustrated attraction, victim provocation, or uncontrollable biological urges, perpetrated only by an aberrant fringe" (Caputi and Russell 1990, p. 34). Rather, rape is about power and control—a "direct expression of sexual politics and an assertion of masculinist norms that reinforce and preserve the gender status quo" (p. 34). Feminist writers and organizers insisted that no woman deserves to be abused, or brings it on herself, or "asks for it." Students, staff, and faculty from hundreds of U.S. colleges and universities have performed Eve Ensler's script, *The Vagina Monologues,* as part of the V-Day College Initiative, a nationwide project to celebrate women and to oppose sexual violence.

The Importance of a Political Movement

Educator and organizer Judith Herman, M.D. (1992) argued that changing public consciousness about violence against women takes a concerted political movement. In her study of trauma and recovery connected to violence, she wrote that perpetrators of violence "ask bystanders to do nothing, simply to ignore the atrocity"; whereas "victims demand action, engagement, and remembering" (pp. 7–8). In Reading 36, Barbara comments that it is important to raise boys not to commit sexual violence, and "it's just as important for them not to be bystanders."

To emphasize women's agency, feminist writers and workers in shelters and rape crisis projects often use the term *survivor* to refer to women who are coping with acts of violence. Herman's use of the term *victim* in the following discussion is perhaps unfortunate, but her comments on the processes of denial and silencing that often surround violence against women are very insightful.

> In order to escape accountability for his crimes, the perpetrator does everything in his power to promote forgetting. Secrecy and silence are the perpetrator's first line of defense. If secrecy fails, the perpetrator attacks the credibility of his victim. If he cannot silence her absolutely, he tries to make sure that no one listens. To this end, he marshals an impressive array of arguments, from the most blatant denial to the most sophisticated . . . rationalization. After every atrocity one can expect to hear the same predictable apologies: it never happened; the victim lies; the victim exaggerates; the victim brought it upon herself; and in any case it is time to forget the past and move on. The more powerful the perpetrator, the greater is his prerogative to name and define reality, and the more completely his arguments prevail. *(1992, p. 8)*

Herman argued that to cut through the power of the perpetrators' arguments "requires a social context that affirms and protects the victim and that joins victim and witness in a common alliance" (p. 9). For the individual victim of violence, relationships with family and friends create this context. For the wider society, "the social context is created by political movements that give voice to the disempowered" (p. 9).

Philosopher Nadya Burton (1998) criticized second-wave feminists for using oversimplistic rhetoric in their attempts to break the silence and to get the issue of violence against women on the public agenda. They also emphasized fear, passivity, and victimhood as ways to call attention to this issue. While acknowledging the damage suffered as a result of violence, it is also important to see women as survivors, people who cope with violation, who are not defined by it and who often go on to thrive despite it. More recently, many feminists have emphasized women's agency—their ability to make decisions and to deal effectively with their circumstances. The underlying issue is respect and dignity for people who have been violated—not pity, disbelief, judgment, do-goodism, or condescension. In wanting to avoid these unhelpful responses, some feminist researchers and advocates have overemphasized women's agency to the point where the real-life effects of trauma and violation are minimized. We argue that women may be both victims of violence and agents who can direct their lives. A person who has been violated can decide what kind of support s/he wants and ask for it; can choose if and when to speak out; can undertake the personal work that is part of healing; can decide to confront the perpetrator directly (with friends, family, or other community support), or press charges, or not deal with the perpetrator at all.

Providing Support for Victims/Survivors

Feminist theorizing about the systemic nature of violence against women under patriarchy led to concerted efforts to provide supports for women who experienced such violence, to educate the wider society on the issue, and to change public policy.

The first shelter for battered women in the United States opened in 1974. Now there are more than 2,500 shelters and service programs nationwide, stretched to capacity. More shelters are needed, and those that exist need to be more accessible—physically and culturally—to women with disabilities, women of color, immigrant women, lesbians, and transgender women. Organizations that emphasize culturally relevant perspectives and services include the Asian Women's Shelter (San Francisco); Ayuda-Hermanas Unidas (Washington, D.C.); Baitul Salaam (Atlanta); Black, Indian, Hispanic and Asian Women in Action—BIHA (Minneapolis); Casa Myrna (Boston); the Farmworker Women's Organizing and Gendered Grassroots Leadership Project (Pomona, Calif.); the Korean American Family Service Center (New York); Sakhi (New York); and Uzuri African Women's Resource Center (Minneapolis). They include an analysis and understanding of cultural factors, religious beliefs, economic issues, and the language and conceptual barriers facing their clients. Organizations formed

to work with LGBTQQI clients include Community United Against Violence (San Francisco) and Forge (Milwaukee).

Similarly, rape crisis centers operate in many cities throughout the country. Volunteers and paid staff answer emergency calls to crisis hotlines, give information, and refer women who have been raped to counseling, medical, and legal services. They may accompany a woman to the police or a doctor or advocate for her in court proceedings. Rape crisis centers often conduct public education and self-defense training for women, and many have peer counselors who are rape survivors. Over the years, some rape crisis projects that mainly served white women have become multicultural by broadening their perspectives to include antiracist work. Other organizations focus their efforts on the needs of women of color, lesbians, bisexuals, and transgender women.

Students and women's organizations continue to organize "Take Back the Night" marches and rallies on campuses and in their neighborhoods where women and men speak out about their experiences of sexual violence, some of them for the first time in a public setting. College women reporting rapes have often been blamed for putting themselves in compromising situations, especially if they have been drinking. In many cases, the men involved have been protected and punished lightly if at all, especially if they are university athletes. Some administrators have been concerned about the effects of alcohol and drug use and the role of fraternity parties in campus rapes. Others seem more concerned to protect their college's reputation. Campus materials and workshops on date rape for incoming students emphasize girls' and boys' different socialization and attitudes toward dating. The work of Students Active for Ending Rape (N.Y.) is notable among the efforts to deal with this issue, as is Antioch College's sexual offense policy, which expected students to talk through a sexual encounter step by step, giving verbal consent at each step (Gold and Villari 2000).

Men's projects that work on violence against women are making a crucial contribution to creating change on this issue. Examples include the National Organization for Men Against Sexism, Emerge (Cambridge, Mass.), Men Can Stop Rape (Washington, D.C.), Men Stopping Violence (Decatur, Ga.), and Moving Forward (San Francisco). Men's campus groups offer educational programs in men-only settings, show films, bring speakers to campus, and participate in campus or community events. Examples include Haverford Men Against Sexism and Rape, Men Educating Men on the Prevention of Sexual Assault (Bowling Green, Ohio), Tulane Men Against Rape, Men Against Rape and Sexual Violence (Yale), Western Men against Violence (Western Washington University), Men Acting for Change (Duke), and the Men's Project (Pacific Lutheran University; Reading 35).

Finally, an organization working with survivors of child sexual abuse is Generation Five (San Francisco), which has the goal of eliminating this devastating problem within five generations. In Reading 34, Aurora Levins Morales describes her journey to reclaim her sexuality and sense of integrity after experiencing sexual abuse as a child.

Public and Professional Education

Compared with a generation ago, there is now considerable public information and awareness about violence against women, including public service announcements, bumper stickers, and ads on billboards, buses, and TV. Increasingly, employers and labor unions recognize that domestic violence can interfere with a woman's ability to get, perform, or keep a job. Some corporations and labor unions have developed education and training programs on domestic violence for managers and workers. Others contribute financially to shelters.

There is a great deal of research as well as theoretical, therapeutic, and political writing on this subject (see, e.g., Bart and O'Brien 1993; Bass and Davis 1988; Bohmer and Parrot 1993; Buchwald, Fletcher, and Roth 2005; Fineman and Mykitiuk 1994; Herman 1992; Jones 1994; Koss et al. 1994; NiCarthy 1987, 2004; Russell 1990; White 1985; Zambrano 1985). Public exhibitions like The Clothesline Project (Yarmouthport Mass.) also make powerful statements. In this project, women express their thoughts, feelings, and experiences of gender violence by decorating a T-shirt, which they hang on a clothesline as testimony to be viewed by others.

Another development has been the growth of professional education on violence against women for doctors, nurses, emergency-room staff, and other health care providers, as well as social workers and teachers. Greater knowledge and understanding are also imperative for police officers, judges, and legislators. National-level organizations like Alianza-National Latino Alliance for the Elimination of Domestic Violence (Albuquerque, N.M.), Futures Without Violence (San Francisco), Incite! Women of Color Against Violence, the National Coalition Against Domestic Violence (Washington, D.C.), National Domestic Violence Hotline (www.ndvh .org), the National Resource Center on Domestic Violence (Harrisburg, Pa.), the Network for Battered Lesbians and Bisexual Women (Boston), Rape Abuse and Incest National Network (Washington, D.C.), and V-Day (New York) provide visibility, public education, research, and expertise to local organizations, the news media, and policy makers at state and federal levels.

Policy and Legislative Initiatives

Forty years ago there were no U.S. laws concerning intimate partner violence. Now there is a growing, if uneven, body of law, mainly at the state level, including protection orders that prohibit the abuser from coming near or contacting the woman and her children. The rape laws have also been reformed because of pressure from feminists and rape survivors. This has been a piecemeal process and also varies from state to state. Nowadays, rape laws no longer require the corroboration of a victim's testimony; women are no longer required to have resisted their attackers; and the sexual histories of rape victims are no longer a subject for cross-examination, unless shown to be relevant.

On the federal level, the Violence Against Women Act (VAWA) was signed into law as part of the Violent Crime and Law Enforcement Act of 1994. It authorized funds for battered women's shelters and community initiatives, training for judges and court personnel, improvements in arrest policies, and legal advocacy programs for victims.

Contradictions in Seeking State Support to End Violence Against Women

An increase in government funding and increasing professionalization of work involving violence against women may be seen as major successes. A negative aspect of this development is the fact that shelters and rape crisis centers have come under closer official scrutiny. Although there is still a vital role for volunteers, many leadership positions require a master's degree in social work (MSW) or a counseling qualification. This is linked to the current emphasis on individual services and therapeutic remedies compared to the more political approach of the 1970s and 1980s. Yet, as hard as women work to help particular individuals, there are always many more—seemingly an endless stream of women needing help.

There is an inherent contradiction in looking to the government—the State—to solve this problem. The State is a patriarchal institution involved in the subordination of women through laws, public policy, judge's decisions, and police treatment. Government employees, U.S. prison guards, and border patrols rape and abuse women (Amnesty International 2000; Falcón 2006; Kurshan 1996; Martinez 1998, Pilkington 2011). U.S. military personnel also commit acts of violence against women, including their colleagues, "enemy" women, and women involved in militarized prostitution (Bonsignore 2011; Enloe 1993, 2000a; Guenter-Schlesinger 1999; Jamall 2010a, 2010b; Morris 1999).

As described by Mimi Kim (Reading 36), participants at the Color of Violence conference, held at the University of California, Santa Cruz in April 2000, called for a re-politicization of work regarding violence against women and set up a new organization, Incite! Women of Color Against Violence. In the opening keynote, activist, writer, and scholar Angela Davis (2001) highlighted a core contradiction in antiviolence work that looks to the State for solutions:

> Given the racist and patriarchal patterns of the state, it is difficult to envision the state as the holder of solutions to the problem of violence against women. However, as the anti-violence movement has been institutionalized and professionalized, the state plays an increasingly dominant role in the way we conceptualize and create strategies to minimize violence against women. One of the major tasks of this conference, and of the anti-violence movement as a whole, is to address this contradiction, especially as it presents itself to poor communities of color.   *(p. 13)*

Mimi Kim notes that increased federal funding for anti-violence organizations under the Violence

Against Women Act is "often tied to collaboration with the police, prosecutors or promotion of pro-arrest policies" (p. 46). Rather, she advocates the development of community-based approaches that address violence against women without increasing State violence against men (Reading 36). In Reading 33, Andy Smith gives examples of "anticolonial responses" currently being pursued in Native American communities in contrast to mainstream antiviolence organizations that are calling for longer prison sentences for batterers and rapists.

Women's Rights as Human Rights

Violence against women has engaged the attention, anger, and activist efforts of scholars, policy makers, and organizers around the world in response to the many forms of gender-based violence in all countries.

In December 1979, the United Nations adopted the Convention on the Elimination of All Forms of Discrimination Against Women (CEDAW), which includes violence against women. One hundred eighty-five countries have ratified CEDAW and adopted it as national policy, though often with many reservations so that implementation has been much more limited. More than thirty years later, U.S. women's organizations are still lobbying for the United States to ratify CEDAW.

Defining violence against women in terms of human rights has been a successful strategy to get this issue onto the international agenda (see, e.g., Agosín 2001; Beasley and Thomas 1994; Bunch and Carillo 1991; Kerr 1993). In June 1993, women from many countries organized the Global Tribunal on Violations of Women's Human Rights to coincide with the Non-Governmental Organization (NGO) Forum of the U.N. World Conference on Human Rights, held in Vienna (Bunch and Reilly 1994). In 1994 the U.N. Commission on Human Rights created a new position—the Special Rapporteur on Violence Against Women, Its Causes and Consequences—based in Geneva, Switzerland. The Center for Women's Global Leadership (Rutgers University) sponsors an annual 16 Days of Activism Against Gender Violence (from Nov. 25, International Day of Violence Against Women, to Dec. 10, International Human Rights Day). Initiated by activists from the global North and South, the campaign emphasizes that all forms of violence, whether in the public or private sphere, are a violation of human rights.

An example of systematic violence against women can be found in the U.S.–Mexico border area, centered on Ciudad Juárez, where hundreds of women and girls have been murdered, tortured, and subjected to sexual violence since the early 1990s. In Reading 37, Brazilian anthropologist Rita Laura Segato attempts to understand the economic, political, and cultural factors that may explain why these killings have been carried out, and why the authorities have done so little to identify the perpetrators, despite outrage and protest from family members, Mexican women's groups, and international human rights organizations. According to Mexican Congresswoman Marcela Lagarde y de los Ríos (2010, p. xiv), "For fifteen years, disinformation, uncertainty, and anxiety have held sway, fostering the exaggeration or downplaying of the facts." Rather than using the term *femicide* (*femicidio* in Spanish, which means the homicide of women), feminist policy makers, lawyers, and organizers have introduced the term *feminicide* (*feminicidio*) to emphasize the collective nature of these violent crimes as genocide against women (Fregoso and Bejarano 2010). Some frame *feminicidio* as a state crime, pointing to "the state's role in fomenting a climate of impunity for the most heinous violations of women's rights," and arguing that "a state's failure to guarantee women's rights to live a life free from violence is itself a human rights violation" (Fregoso and Bejarano 2010, p. 19). Margaret Randall (2011, p. 13) maintains that "it's important to note US complicity in these crimes. The companies who hire these women at $5.50 a day have shown no concern for their murdered workers," who are easily replaced (also see Gaspar de Alba and Guzmán 2010). Segato's research and theorizing contribute to a broader transnational feminist discourse on this issue that is both analytical and deeply engaged at an activist level.

As this chapter makes clear, there is an urgent need for many changes at micro, meso, macro, and global levels for women to be secure from violence including:

- the socialization and education of children and young people to respect and value each other;
- changes in social constructions of femininity and masculinity, and the abolition of cultural attitudes and systems of inequality that support male superiority;
- an end to the objectification and commodification of women;
- changes in women's work and wages, and support for community-based economic development to give women economic security and independence;
- changes in laws, court decisions, police practices, and political systems so that women's human rights are central; and
- continued collaboration among all who are working to end violence, and challenges to those who are not.

◆◆◆

Questions for Reflection

In reading and discussing this chapter, consider these questions:

1. What beliefs about rape are really myths? How would your life be different if rape and the threat of rape did not exist?

2. How do boys in your community learn to respect women? To disrespect women?

3. How has abuse or violence affected your life? Your family? Your community?

4. What kinds of masculinity would help to create personal security for women and for men?

5. What are men's roles and responsibilities in ending violence against women?

6. How do the intersections of gender, race, class, nation, sexuality, and so forth, affect violence against women?

Finding Out More on the Web

1. Research how the Web is used to support and reinforce beliefs about violence against women.

2. Research U.S. and international organizations mentioned in this chapter that are working to end violence against women. What are their goals, strategies, and activities? What theoretical frameworks shape their work? Additional organizations:

   Green Dot: www.livethegreendot.com

   Madre: www.madre.org

   Men Can Stop Rape: www.mencanstoprape.org

   National Organization for Men Against Sexism: www.nomas.org

   Women Against Violence Europe: www.wave-network.org/start.asp?ID=22650

   Women Living Under Muslim Laws: www.wluml.org/english/index.shtml

Taking Action

1. Talk about this issue with your peers, and contribute to public discussion on your campus or in your community. Find out about your college's policy on sexual assault and how it is enforced (or not). Find out about rape crisis centers, shelters, and support groups in your area so that you can offer this information to someone who is coping with sexual assault.

2. Volunteer with a rape crisis project on campus or at a shelter for victims of domestic violence. Men students: Work with other men on this issue.

3. Support a campus or community event concerned with violence against women.

T H I R T Y - T H R E E

Sexual Violence and American Indian Genocide (1999)

Andy Smith

Scholar, writer, and activist **Andrea (Andy) Smith** is cofounder of Incite! Women of Color Against Violence. She is an award-winning teacher and has published widely including *Native Americans and the Christian Right: The Gendered Politics of Unlikely Alliances*, and *Conquest: Sexual Violence and American Indian Genocide*.

I once attended a conference where a speaker stressed the importance of addressing sexual violence within Native communities. When I returned home, I told a friend of mine, who was a rape survivor, about the talk. She replied, "You mean other Indian women have been raped?" When I said yes, she asked, "Well, why don't we ever talk about it?" Indeed, the silence surrounding sexual violence in Native communities—particularly the sexual assault of adult women—is overwhelming. Under Janet Reno, the Department of Justice poured millions of dollars into tribally-based sexual and domestic violence programs. Although domestic violence programs are proliferating, virtually no tribes have developed comprehensive sexual assault programs.

Native survivors of sexual violence often find no support when they seek healing and justice. When they seek help from non-Indian agencies, they are often told to disassociate themselves from their communities, where their abusers are. The underlying philosophy of the white-dominated anti-rape movement is implicit in Susan Brownmiller's statement: "[Rape] is nothing more or less than a conscious process of intimidation by which all men keep all women in a state of fear."[1] The notion that rape is "nothing more or less" than a tool of patriarchal control fails to consider how rape also serves as a tool of racism and colonialism. At the same time, when Native survivors of sexual violence seek healing within their communities, other community members accuse them of undermining Native sovereignty and being divisive by making their abuse public. According to the Mending the Hoop Technical Assistance Project in Minnesota, tribally-based sexual assault advocates believe that a major difficulty in developing comprehensive programs to address sexual assault in tribal communities, particularly sexual violence against adult women, is that many community members believe that sexual violence is "traditional." Historical evidence suggests, however, that sexual violence was rare in Native communities prior to colonization, and that it has served as a primary weapon in the U.S. war against Native nations ever since. . . . Far from being traditional, sexual violence is an attack on Native sovereignty itself. As one elder stated at a conference I attended: "As long as we destroy ourselves from inside, we don't have to worry about anyone on the outside."

The Colonial Context of Sexual Violence

Ann Stoler argues that racism is a permanent part of the social fabric: "[R]acism is not an effect but a tactic in the internal fission of society into binary opposition, a means of creating 'biologized' internal enemies, against whom society must defend itself."[2] She notes that in the modern state, it is the constant purification and elimination of racialized enemies that ensures the growth of the national body. "Racism

does not merely arise in moments of crisis, in sporadic cleansings. It is internal to the biopolitical state, woven into the web of the social body, threaded through its fabric."[3] Similarly, Kate Shanley notes that Native peoples are a permanent "present absence" in the U.S. colonial imagination, an "absence" that reinforces the conviction that Native peoples are vanishing and that the conquest of native lands is justified.[4] . . . This "absence" is effected through the metaphorical transformation of Native bodies into a pollution from which the colonial body must purify itself. In the 1860s, white Californians described Native people as "the dirtiest lot of human beings on earth." They wear "filthy rags, with their persons unwashed, hair uncombed and swarming with vermin."[5] An 1885 Proctor & Gamble ad for Ivory Soap also illustrates this equation between Indian bodies and dirt:

We were once factious, fierce and wild,
In peaceful arts unreconciled
Our blankets smeared with grease and stains
From buffalo meat and settlers' veins.
Through summer's dust and heat content
From moon to moon unwashed we went.
But IVORY SOAP came like a ray
Of light across our darkened way
And now we're civil, kind and good
And keep the laws as people should.
We wear our linen, lawn and lace
As well as folks with paler face
And now I take, where'er we go
This cake of IVORY SOAP to show
What civilized my squaw and me
And made us clean and fair to see.[6]

In the colonial imagination, Native bodies are also polluted with sexual sin. . . . In 1613, Alexander Whitaker, a minister in Virginia, wrote: "They live naked in bodie, as if their shame of their sinne deserved no covering: Their names are as naked as their bodie: They esteem it a virtue to lie, deceive and steale as their master the divell teacheth them."[7] Furthermore, according to Bernardino de Minaya: "Their [the Indians'] marriages are not a sacrament but a sacrilege. They are idolatrous, libidinous, and commit sodomy. Their chief desire is to eat, drink, worship heathen idols, and commit bestial obscenities."[8]

. . .

Because Indian bodies are considered "dirty," they are sexually violable and "rapable." In patriarchal thinking, only a "pure" body can really be violated. The rape of bodies that are considered inherently impure simply does not count. For instance, women in prostitution have an almost impossible time if they are raped because the dominant society considers a prostituted woman as lacking bodily integrity and violable at all times. Similarly, the history of mutilation of Indian bodies, both living and dead, makes it clear to Indian people that they are not considered to have bodily integrity. President Andrew Jackson, for instance, ordered the mutilation of approximately 800 Muscogee Indian corpses, cutting off their noses and slicing long strips of flesh from their bodies to make bridle reins.[9] Tecumseh's skin was flayed and made into razor-straps.[10] A soldier cut off the testicles of White Antelope to make a tobacco pouch. Colonel John Chivington led an attack against the Cheyenne and Arapahoe in which nearly all the victims were scalped, their fingers, arms, and ears amputated to obtain rings, necklaces, and other jewelry, and their private parts were cut out to be exhibited before the public in Denver.[11] Throughout the history of massacres against Indian people, colonizers attempted not only to defeat Indian people but to eradicate their very identity and humanity. They attempted to transform Indian people from human beings into tobacco pouches, bridle reins, or souvenirs—objects for white people's consumption.

As Stoler explains this process of racialized colonization, "[T]he more 'degenerates' and 'abnormals' [in this case, Native peoples] are eliminated, the lives of those who speak will be stronger, more vigorous, and improved. The enemies are not political adversaries, but those identified as external and internal threats to the population. Racism is the condition that makes it acceptable to put [certain people] to death in a society of normalization."[12] She further notes that "the imperial discourses on sexuality cast white women as the bearers of a racist imperial order."[13] By extension, as bearers of a counter-imperial order, Native women pose a supreme threat to the imperial order. Symbolic and literal control over their bodies is important in the war against Native people, as these examples attest:

> When I was in the boat I captured a beautiful Carib woman. . . . I conceived desire to take pleasure. . . . I took a rope and thrashed her well, for which she raised such unheard screams that you would not have believed

your ears. Finally we came to an agreement in such a manner that I can tell you that she seemed to have been brought up in a school of harlots.[14]

> Two of the best looking of the squaws were lying in such a position, and from the appearance of the genital organs and of their wounds, there can be no doubt that they were first ravished and then shot dead. Nearly all of the dead were mutilated.[15]

> One woman, big with child, rushed into the church, clasping the altar and crying for mercy for herself and unborn babe. She was followed, and fell pierced with a dozen lances . . . the child was torn alive from the yet palpitating body of its mother, first plunged into the holy water to be baptized, and immediately its brains were dashed out against a wall.[16]

> The Christians attacked them with buffets and beatings. . . . Then they behaved with such temerity and shamelessness that the most powerful ruler of the island had to see his own wife raped by a Christian officer.[17]

> I heard one man say that he had cut a woman's private parts out, and had them for exhibition on a stick. I heard another man say that he had cut the fingers off of an Indian, to get the rings off his hand. I also heard of numerous instances in which men had cut out the private parts of females, and stretched them over their saddle-bows and some of them over their hats.[18]

Although the era of deliberate, explicit Indian massacres in North America is over, in Latin America the wholesale rape and mutilation of indigenous women's bodies has continued. . . . Many white feminists are correctly outraged by mass rapes in Bosnia, and have organized to instigate a war crimes tribunal against the Serbs. Yet one wonders why the mass rapes of indigenous women in Guatemala, Chiapas, or elsewhere in Latin America have not sparked the same outrage. Feminist legal scholar Catherine MacKinnon argues that in Bosnia, "the world has *never* seen sex used this consciously, this cynically, this elaborately, this openly, this systematically . . . as a means of destroying a whole people."[19] She seems to forget that she only lives on this land because millions of Native people were raped, sexually mutilated and murdered. Is mass rape of European women "genocide," while mass rape of indigenous women is business as usual? Even in the white feminist imagination, are native women's bodies more rapable than white women's bodies?

The colonization of Native women's bodies continues today. In the 1980s, when I served as a nonviolent witness for the Chippewa spearfishers who were being harassed by white racist mobs, one white harasser carried a sign saying "Save a fish; spear a pregnant squaw." During the 1990 Mohawk crisis in Oka [Quebec], a white mob surrounded an ambulance taking a Native woman off the reservation because she was hemorrhaging after giving birth. She was forced to "spread her legs" to prove it. The police at the scene refused to intervene. An Indian man was arrested for "wearing a disguise" (he was wearing jeans), and was brutally beaten, with his testicles crushed. Two women from Chicago WARN (Women of All Red Nations, the organization I belong to) went to Oka to videotape the crisis. They were arrested and held in custody for eleven hours without being charged, and were told that they could not go to the bathroom unless the male police officers could watch. The place they were held was covered with pornographic magazines.

In 1982, this colonial desire to subjugate Indian women's bodies was quite apparent when Stuart Kasten marketed a new video, "Custer's Revenge," in which players get points each time they, in the character of Custer, rape an Indian woman. The slogan of the game is "When you score, you score." He describes the game as "a fun sequence where the woman is enjoying a sexual act willingly." According to the promotional material:

> You are General Custer. Your dander's up, your pistol's wavin'. You've hog-tied a ravishing Indian maiden and have a chance to rewrite history and even up an old score. Now, the Indian maiden's hands may be tied, but she's not about to take it lying down, by George! Help is on the way. If you're to get revenge you'll have to rise to the challenge, dodge a tribe of flying arrows and protect your flanks against some downright mean and prickly cactus. But if you can stand pat and last past the strings and arrows—You can stand last. Remember? Revenge is sweet.[20]

Ironically, while enslaving women's bodies, colonizers argued that they were actually freeing Native women from the "oppression" they supposedly faced in Native nations. Thomas Jefferson, for example, argued that Native women "are submitted to unjust drudgery. This I believe is the case with every barbarous people. It is civilization alone which replaces women in the enjoyment of their equality."[21] The *Mariposa Gazette* similarly noted that when Indian women were safely under the control of white men, they "are neat, and tidy, and industrious, and soon learn to discharge domestic duties properly and creditably."[22] In 1862, a Native man in Conrow Valley was killed and scalped with his head twisted off; his killers said, "You will not kill any more women and children."[23] Apparently, Native women can only be free while under the dominion of white men, and both Native and white women have to be protected from Indian men, rather than from white men. . . .

. . . Although stereotypes of Native women as beasts of burden for their men prevail, prior to colonization Indian societies were not male-dominated for the most part. Women served as spiritual, political, and military leaders. Many societies were matrilineal and matrilocal. Although there was a division of labor between women and men, women's and men's labor was accorded similar status.[24] Thus, the historical record would suggest, as Paula Gunn Allen argues, that the real roots of feminism should be found in Native societies. . . .

Just as, historically, white colonizers who raped Indian women claimed that Indian men were the real rapists, white men who rape and murder Indian women often make this same claim today. In Minneapolis, a white man, Jesse Coulter, raped, murdered and mutilated several Indian women. He claimed to be Indian, adopting the name Jesse Sittingcrow, and emblazoning an AIM tattoo on his arm.[25] Similarly, Roy Martin, a full-blooded Native man, was charged with sexual assault. The survivor identified the rapist as white, about 25 years old, with a shag haircut. Martin was 35 with hair past his shoulders.[26] Although this case was eventually dismissed, the fact that it even made it to trial indicates the extent to which Native men are seen as the rapists of white women.

Of course, Indian men do commit acts of sexual violence. After years of colonialism and boarding-school experiences, violence has been internalized in

Indian communities. However, this view of the Indian man as the "true" rapist serves to obscure who has real power in this racist and patriarchal society. The U.S. is indeed engaged in a "permanent social war" against Native bodies, particularly Native women's bodies, which threaten its legitimacy.[27] Colonizers evidently recognize the wisdom of the Cheyenne saying, "A Nation is not conquered until the hearts of the women [and their bodies as well] are on the ground."

Through this colonization and abuse of their bodies, Indian people have learned to internalize self-hatred. Body image is integrally related to self-esteem. When one's body is not respected, one begins to hate oneself.[28] For example, Anne, a Native boarding-school student, reflects on this process:

> You better not touch yourself. . . . If I looked at somebody . . . lust, sex, and I got scared of those sexual feelings. And I did not know how to handle them. . . . What really confused me was if intercourse was sin, why are people born? . . . It took me a really long time to get over the fact that . . . I've sinned: I had a child.[29]

As her words indicate, when the bodies of Indian people are inherently sinful and dirty, it becomes a sin just to be Indian. Thus, it is not a surprise that Indian people who have survived sexual abuse often say that they no longer wish to be Indian. The Menominee poet Chrystos writes in such a voice in her poem "Old Indian Granny."

You told me about all the Indian women you counsel
who say they don't want to be Indian anymore
because a white man or an Indian one raped them
or killed their brother
or somebody tried to run them over in the street
or insulted them or all of it
our daily bread of hate
Sometimes I don't want to be Indian either
But I've never said so out loud before
Since I'm so proud and political
I have to deny it now
Far more than being hungry
having no place to live or dance
no decent job no home to offer a Granny
It's knowing with each invisible breath
that if you don't make something pretty
they can hang on their walls or wear around their
    necks
you might as well be dead.[30]

The fact that many Native peoples will argue that sexual violence is "traditional" indicates the extent to which our communities have internalized self-hatred. . . . Then, as Michael Taussig notes, Native peoples are portrayed by the dominant culture as inherently violent, self-destructive and dysfunctional. For example, in 1990, Mike Whelan made the following statement at a zoning hearing in South Dakota, calling for the denial of a permit for a shelter to serve Indian women who have been battered:

> Indian Culture as I view it, is presently so mongrelized as to be a mix of dependency on the Federal Government and a primitive society wholly on the outside of the mainstream of western civilization and thought. The Native American Culture as we know it now, not as it formerly existed, is a culture of hopelessness, godlessness, of joblessness, and lawlessness. . . . Alcoholism, social disease, child abuse, and poverty are the hallmarks of this so-called culture that you seek to promote, and I would suggest to you that the brave men of the ghost dance would hang their heads in shame at what you now pass off as that culture. . . . I think that the Indian way of life as you call it, to me means cigarette burns in arms of children, double-checking the locks on my cars, keeping a loaded shotgun by my door, and car bodies and beer cans on the front lawn. . . . This is not a matter of race, it is a matter of keeping our community and neighborhood away from that evil that you and your ideas promote.[31]

Taussig comments on the irony of this logic: "Men are conquered not by invasion but by themselves. It is a strange sentiment, is it not, when faced with so much brutal evidence of invasion."[32]

Completing the destruction of a people involves the destruction of the integrity of their culture and spirituality that forms the matrix of Native women's resistance to sexual colonization. Native counselors generally agree that a strong cultural and spiritual identity is essential if Native people are to heal from abuse. This is because Native women's healing entails healing not only from any personal abuse she has suffered, but also from the patterned history of abuse against her family, her nation, and the environment in which she lives.[33] Because Indian spiritual traditions are holistic, they have the ability to restore survivors of abuse to the community, and to restore their bodies to wholeness. That is why the most effective programs for healing revolve around reviving indigenous spiritual traditions.

. . .

. . . [T]he colonizing religion [of Native peoples], Christianity, which is supposed to "save" Native women from allegedly sexually exploitative traditional practices, has only made them more vulnerable to sexual violence. The large-scale introduction of sexual violence in Native communities is largely a result of the Christian boarding-school system, which began in the 1600s under Jesuit priests along the St. Lawrence River. The system was more formalized in 1870 when Congress set aside funds to erect school facilities to be run by churches and missionary societies.[34] Attendance was mandatory and children were forcibly taken from their homes for the majority of the year. They were forced to practice Christianity (native traditions were prohibited) and speak English only.[35] Children were subjected to constant physical and sexual abuse. Irene Mack Pyawasit, a former boarding-school resident from the Menominee reservation, testifies to her experience, which is typical of many:

> The government employees that they put into the schools had families, but still there were an awful lot of Indian girls turning up pregnant. Because the employees were having a lot of fun, and they would force a girl into a situation, and the girl wouldn't always be believed. Then, because she came up pregnant, she would be sent home in disgrace. Some boy would be blamed for it, never the government employee. He was always scot-free. And no matter what the girl said, she was never believed.[36]

Even when teachers were charged with abuse, boarding schools refused to investigate. In the case of just one teacher, John Boone, at the Hopi school, FBI investigations found that he had sexually abused over 142 children, but the school principal had not investigated any allegations of abuse.[37] Despite the epidemic of sexual abuse in boarding schools, the Bureau of Indian Affairs did not issue a policy on reporting sexual abuse until 1987, and did not issue a policy to strengthen the background checks of potential teachers until 1989.[38]

Although all Native people did not view their boarding-school experiences as negative, it appears that abuse became endemic in Indian families after the establishment of boarding schools in Native communities. Randy Fred, a former boarding-school student, says that children in his school began to mimic the abuse they were experiencing.[39] After Father Harold McIntee from St. Joseph's residential school on the Alkali Lake reserve was convicted of sexual abuse, two of his victims were later convicted of sexual abuse charges.[40]

Anti-Colonial Responses to Sexual Violence

The struggle for Native sovereignty and the struggle against sexual violence cannot be separated. Conceptualizing sexual violence as a tool of genocide and colonialism leads to specific strategies for combatting it. Currently, the rape crisis movement has called for strengthening the criminal justice system as the primary means to end sexual violence. Rape crisis centers receive much state funding, and, consequently, their strategies tend to be state-friendly: hire more police, give longer sentences to rapists, etc. There is a contradiction, however, in relying upon the state to solve the problems it is responsible for creating. Native people *per capita* are the most arrested, most incarcerated, and most victimized by police brutality of any ethnic group in the country.[41] Given the oppression Native people face within the criminal justice system, many communities are developing their own programs for addressing criminal behavior based on traditional ways of regulating their societies. However, as James and Elsie B. Zion note, Native domestic violence advocates are often reluctant to pursue traditional alternatives to incarceration for addressing violence against women.[42] Survivors of domestic and sexual violence programs are often pressured to "forgive and forget" in tribal mediation programs that focus more on maintaining family and tribal unity than on providing justice and safety for women. In his study of traditional approaches for addressing sexual/domestic violence on First Nations reserves in Canada, Rupert Ross notes that these approaches are often very successful in addressing child sexual abuse where communities are less likely to blame the victim for the assault. In such cases, the community makes a pro-active effort in holding perpetrators accountable so that incarceration is often unnecessary. When a crime is reported, the working team that deals with sexual violence talks to the perpetrator and gives him the option of participating in the program. The perpetrator must first confess his guilt and then follow a healing contract, or go to jail. The perpetrator can decline to participate in the program and go through the normal routes in the criminal justice system. Everyone affected by the crime (victim, perpetrator, family, friends, and the working team) is involved in developing the healing contract. Everyone also holds the perpetrator to his contract. One Tlingit man noted that this approach was often more difficult than going to jail.

> First one must deal with the shock and then the dismay on your neighbors' faces. One must live with the daily humiliation, and at the same time seek forgiveness not just from victims, but from the community as a whole. . . . [A prison sentence] removes the offender from the daily accountability, and may not do anything towards rehabilitation, and for many may actually be an easier disposition than staying in the community.[43]

Along similar lines, Elizabeth Barker notes that the problem with the criminal justice system is that it diverts accountability from the community to players in the criminal justice system. Perpetrators are taken away from their community and are further limited from developing ethical relationships within a community context.[44] Ross notes: "In reality, rather than making the community a safer place, the threat of jail places the community more at risk."[45] Since the Hollow Lake reserve adopted this approach, 48 offenders have been identified. Only five chose to go to jail, and only two who entered the program have repeated crimes (one of the re-offenders went through the program again and has not re-offended since). However, Ross notes, these approaches often break down in cases where the victim is an adult woman because community members are more likely to blame her instead of the perpetrator for the assault.[46]

Many Native domestic violence advocates I have interviewed note similar problems in applying traditional methods of justice to cases of sexual assault and domestic violence. One advocate from a tribally-based program in the Plains area contends that traditional approaches are important for addressing violence against women, but they are insufficient. To be effective they must be backed up by the threat of incarceration. She notes that medicine men have come to her program saying, "We have worked with this offender and we have not been successful in changing him. He needs to join your batterers' program." Traditional approaches to justice presume that the community will hold a perpetrator accountable for his crime. However, in cases of violence against adult women, community members often do not regard this violence as a crime and will not hold the offender accountable. Before such approaches can be effective, we must implement community education programs that will change community attitudes about these issues.

Another advocate from a reservation in the Midwest argues that traditional alternatives to incarceration might be more harsh than incarceration. Many Native people presume that traditional modes of justice focused on conflict resolution. In fact, she argues, penalties for societal infractions were not lenient. They included banishment, shaming, reparations, and sometimes death. This advocate was involved in an attempt to revise tribal codes by reincorporating traditional practices, but she found that it was difficult to determine what these practices were and how they could be made useful today. For example, some practices, such as banishment, would not have the same impact today. Prior to colonization, Native communities were so close-knit and interdependent that banishment was often the equivalent of a death sentence. Today, however, Native peoples can simply leave home and join the dominant society. In addition, the elders with whom she consulted admitted that their memories of traditional penal systems were tainted with the experience of being in boarding school. Since incarceration is understood as punishment, this advocate believes that it is the most appropriate way to address sexual violence. She argues that if a Native man rapes someone, he subscribes to white values rather than Native values because rape is not an Indian tradition. If he follows white values, then he should suffer the white way of punishment.

However, there are a number of difficulties in pursuing incarceration as the solution for addressing sexual assault. First, so few rapes are reported that the criminal justice system rarely has the opportunity to address the problem. Among tribal programs I have investigated, an average of about two cases of rape are reported each year. Because rape is a major crime, rape cases are generally handed to the State's Attorney, who then declines the vast majority of cases. By the time tribal law-enforcement programs even see rape cases, a year might have passed since the assault, making it difficult for them to prosecute. Also, because rape is covered by the Major Crimes Act, many tribes have not developed codes to address it as they have for domestic violence. One advocate who conducted a training for southwestern tribes on sexual assault says that the participants said they did not need to develop codes because the "Feds will take care of rape cases." She asked how many rape cases had been federally prosecuted, and the participants discovered that not one case of rape had ever reached the federal courts. In addition, there is inadequate jail space in many tribal communities. When the tribal jail is full, the tribe has to pay the surrounding county to house its prisoners. Given financial constraints, tribes are reluctant to house prisoners for any length of time.

But perhaps most importantly, as sociologist Luana Ross (Salish) notes, incarceration has been largely ineffective in reducing crime rates in the dominant society, much less Native communities. "The white criminal justice system does not work for white people; what makes us think it's going to work for us?" she asks.

. . .

The premise of the justice system is that most people are law-abiding except for "deviants" who do not follow the law. However, given the epidemic rates of sexual and domestic violence . . . , it is clear that most men are implicated in our rape culture. It is not likely that we can send all of these men to jail. As Fay Koop argues, addressing rape through the justice system simply furthers the myth that rape/domestic violence is caused by a few bad men, rather than seeing most men implicated in such violence.[47] Thus, relying upon the criminal justice system to end violence against women may strengthen the colonial apparatus in tribal communities that furthers violence while providing nothing more than the illusion of safety to survivors of sexual and domestic violence. . . .

Sexual violence is a fundamental attack on Indian sovereignty, and both Native and non-Native communities are challenged to develop programs that address sexual violence from an anti-colonial, anti-racist framework so that we don't attempt to eradicate acts of personal violence by strengthening the apparatus of state violence. Nothing less than a holistic approach towards eradicating sexual violence can be successful. As Ines Hernandez-Avila states:

> We must imagine a world without rape. But I cannot imagine a world without rape, a world without misogyny, without imagining a world without racism, classism, sexism, homophobia, ageism, historical amnesia and other forms and manifestations of violence directed against those communities that are seen to be "asking for it." Even the Earth is presumably "asking for it." . . . What do I imagine then? From my own Native American perspective, I see a world where sovereign indigenous peoples continue to plunge our memories to come back to our originality, to live in dignity and carry on our resuscitated and ever-transforming cultures and traditions with liberty. . . . I see a world where native women find strength and continuance in the remembrance of who we really were and are . . . a world where more and more native men find the courage to recognize and honor— that they and the women of their families and communities have the capacity to be profoundly vital and creative human beings.[48]

NOTES

1. Susan Brownmiller, *Against our will* (Toronto: Bantam Books, 1986), p. 5.

2. Ann Stoler, *Race and the education of desire* (Durham, N.C.: Duke University Press, 1997), p. 59.

3. Ibid., p. 59.

4. Lecture, Indigenous Intellectual Sovereignties Conference. UC Davis, April 1998.

5. James Rawls, *Indians of California: The changing image* (Norman: University of Oklahoma Press, 1984), p. 195.

6. Andre Lopez, *Pagans in our midst* (Mohawk Nation: Akwesasne Notes), p. 119.

7. Robert Berkhofer, *The white man's Indian* (New York: Vintage, 1978), p. 19.

8. David Stannard, *American Holocaust: Columbus and the conquest of the New World* (New York: Oxford University Press, 1992), p. 211.

9. Stannard, *American Holocaust*, p. 121.

10. David Wrone and Russell Nelson (eds.), *Who's the savage? A documentary history of the mistreatment of the Native North Americans* (Malabar: Robert Krieger Publishing, 1982), p. 82. Quote William James, *A full and correct account of the military occurrences of the late war*

between Great Britain and the United States of America (2 vols., London: printed by the author, 1818), vol. 1, pp. 293–296.

11. John Terrell, *Land grab: The truth about the "winning of the West"* (New York: Doubleday, 1972), p. 13.

12. Stoler, p. 85.

13. Ibid., p. 35.

14. From Cuneo, an Italian nobleman, quoted in Kirkpatrick Sale, *The conquest of paradise: Christopher Columbus and the Columbian legacy* (New York: Knopf, 1990), p. 140.

15. Wrone and Nelson, *Who's the savage?* p. 123. Cite U.S. Commissioner of Indian Affairs, *Annual Report for 1871* (Washington, D.C.: Government Printing Office, 1871), pp. 487–488.

16. Ibid., p. 97. Cite LeRoy R. Haven (ed.), *Ruxton of the Rockies* (Norman: University of Oklahoma Press, 1950), pp. 46–149.

17. Las Casas, p. 33.

18. *The Sand Creek Massacre: A documentary history,* pp. 129–130. Quotes Lieutenant James D. Cannon from "Report of the Secretary of War," 39th Congress, Second Session, Senate Executive Document 26, Washington, D.C., 1867. New York: Sol Lewis, 1973.

19. Catherine MacKinnon, Turning rape into pornography: Postmodern genocide, in *Ms. Magazine,* 4, no. 1, p. 27 (emphasis added).

20. Undated promotional material from Public Relations: Mahoney/Wasserman and Associates, Los Angeles, Calif.

21. Quoted in Roy Harvey Pearce, *Savagism and civilization* (Baltimore: Johns Hopkins Press, 1965), p. 93.

22. Robert Heizer (ed.), *The destruction of California Indians* (Lincoln: University of Nebraska Press, 1993), p. 284.

23. James Rawls, *Indians of California,* p. 182.

24. See Annette Jaimes and Theresa Halsey, American Indian women: At the center of indigenous resistance in North America, in Annette Jaimes (ed.), *The state of Native America: Genocide, colonization, and resistance* (Boston: South End Press, 1992), pp. 311–344.

25. Mark Brunswick and Paul Klauda, Possible suspect in serial killings jailed in N. Mexico, in *Minneapolis Star and Tribune,* May 28, 1987, p. 1A.

26. Indian man being tried for rape with no evidence, in *Fargo Forum,* January 9, 1995.

27. Stoler, p. 69.

28. For further discussion on the relationship between bodily abuse and self-esteem, see *The courage to heal: A guide for women survivors of child sexual abuse,* edited by Ellen Bass and Laura Davis (New York: Harper & Row, 1988), esp. pp. 207–222; and Bonnie Burstow, *Radical feminist therapy* (London: Sage, 1992), esp. pp. 187–234.

29. Quoted in Celia Haig-Brown, *Resistance and renewal* (Vancouver: Tilacum, 1988), p. 108.

30. Chrystos, *Fugitive colors* (Vancouver: Press Gang, 1995), p. 41.

31. Native American Women's Health and Education Resource Center, *Discrimination and the double whammy* (Lake Andes, S. Dak.: Native American Women's Health and Education Resource Center, 1990), pp. 2–3.

32. Michael Taussig, *Shamanism, colonialism and the wild man* (Chicago: University of Chicago Press, 1987), p. 20.

33. Justine Smith (Cherokee), personal conversation, February 17, 1994.

34. Jorge Noriega, American Indian education in the United States: Indoctrination for subordination to colonialism, in *State of Native America,* p. 380.

35. Frederick Binder and David M. Reimers (eds.), *The way we lived* (Lexington, Mass.: D. C. Heath, 1982), p. 59. Quotes U.S. Bureau of Indian Affairs, "Rules for Schools," Annual Report of the Commissioner of Indian Affairs, 1890, Washington, D.C., pp. cxlvi, cl–clii.

36. Fran Leeper Buss, *Dignity: Lower income women tell of their lives and struggles* (Ann Arbor: University of Michigan Press, 1985), p. 156. For further accounts of the widespread nature of sexual and other abuse in boarding schools, see Native Horizons Treatment Center, *Sexual abuse handbook* (Hagersville, Ont.), pp. 61–68; The end of silence, *Maclean's,* vol. 105, no. 37, September 14, 1992, pp. 14, 16; Jim deNomie, American Indian boarding schools: Elders remember, in *Aging News,* Winter 1990–91, pp. 2–6; David Wrone and Russell Nelson, *Who's the savage?* pp. 152–154, cite U.S. Congress, Senate, Subcommittee on Indian Affairs, *Survey of the conditions of the Indians in the United States,* Hearings before a subcommittee of the Committee on Indian Affairs, Senate, SR 79, 70th Congress, 2d session, 1929, pp. 428–429, 1021–1023, 2833–2835.

37. Goodbye BIA, Hello New Federalism, in *American Eagle,* vol. 2, no. 6, December 1994, p. 19. After the allegations of abuse became public, the BIA merely provided a counselor for the abused children who used his sessions with them to write a book.

38. Child sexual abuse in federal schools, in *The Ojibwe News,* January 17, 1990, p. 8.

39. Celia Haig-Brown, *Resistance and renewal,* pp. 14–15.

40. Native Horizons Treatment Center, *Sexual abuse handbook,* p. 66. Quotes *The Province,* July 19, 1989, and *Vancouver Sun,* March 17, 1990.

41. Troy Armstrong, Michael Guilfoyle, and Ada Pecos Melton, Native American delinquency: An overview of prevalence, causes, and correlates, in Marianne O. Nielsen and Robert A. Silverman (eds.), *Native Americans, crime, and justice* (Boulder, Colo.: Westview Press, 1996), p. 81.

42. James Zion and Elsie Zion, Hazho's Sokee'—Stay together nicely: Domestic violence under Navajo common law, in Nielsen and Silverman (eds.), *Native Americans, crime, and justice,* p. 106.

43. Rupert Ross, *Return to the teachings* (London: Penguin Books, 1997), p. 18.

44. Elizabeth Barker, The paradox of punishment in light of the anticipatory role of abolitionism, in Herman Bianchi and Rene van Swaaningern (eds.), *Abolitionism* (Amsterdam: Free University Press, 1986), p. 91.

45. Ross, *Return to the teachings,* p. 38.

46. Rupert Ross, Leaving our white eyes behind: The sentencing of native accused, in Nielsen and Silverman (eds.), *Native Americans, crime, and justice*, p. 168.

47. Fay Honey Koop, On radical feminism and abolition, in *We who would take no prisoners: Selections from the Fifth International Conference on Penal Abolition* (Vancouver: Collective Press, 1993), p. 592.

48. Ines Hernandez-Avila, In praise of insubordination, or what makes a good woman go bad? In Emilie Buchwald, Pamela R. Fletcher, and Martha Roth (eds.), *Transforming a rape culture* (Minneapolis: Milkweed, 1993), pp. 388–389.

THIRTY-FOUR

◆◆◆

Radical Pleasure (1998)
Sex and the End of Victimhood

Aurora Levins Morales

Aurora Levins Morales is a feminist writer and historian who identifies as Puerto Rican and Jewish. Published work includes poetry, essays, and two books: *Getting Home Alive* and *Remedios*. Now living with chronic illness, she writes and creates visual art about sustainability, community, and connectedness.

eroticism is one that is honored in survivor culture, evidence of blows inflicted and then denied by our abusers. When the skeptical ask us "Where are your scars?" we can point to the unsteady rhythms of fascination and disgust, obsession and revulsion through which we experience sex as evidence of what we know to be true.

1

I am a person who was sexually abused and tortured as a child. I no longer define myself in terms of my survival of this experience, but what I learned from surviving it is central to my political and spiritual practice. The people who abused me consciously and deliberately manipulated me in an attempt to break down my sense of integrity so they could make me into an accomplice to my own torture and that of others. They deliberately and consciously interfered with my sexuality as one method of accomplishing this. We are so vulnerable in our pleasures and desires. The fact they could induce physical pleasure in me against my will allowed them to shame me. It allowed them to persuade me that my sexuality was untrustworthy and belonged to others. It allowed them to persuade me that my desires were dangerous and were one of the causes of my having been abused. My sexuality has stuttered ever since, flaring and subsiding in ways I have not known how to manage, ricocheting from intense excitement to absolute numbness, from reckless trust to impenetrable guardedness. This place of wounded

2

"So why choose to reclaim sex?" This is the final question in a five-hour interview of me by my friend Staci Haines. We have been talking about the seductiveness of the victim role; about the thin satisfactions that come from a permanent attitude of outrage. About how having to resist too much, too young, locks us into rigid stances of resistance that interfere with intimacy, which ultimately requires vulnerability and surrender. About the seductiveness of an identity built on righteous indignation, and how close that stance actually lies to rampant self-pity. So when she asks me "Why reclaim sex?" I answer in layers.

Of course because it is part of aliveness. But among the many topics we've ranged over in our hours of conversation, the one that grabs me now is the need and obligation to leave victimhood behind. Staci and I share a somewhat taboo belief that as survivors we have an obligation to think about the healing of the perpetrators who are, after all, our kin—victims who survived in body but were unable to remain spiritually intact. So what comes to mind is the high price we pay when we settle for being wronged. Victimhood absolves us from having to decide to have good lives. It allows us to stay small and wounded instead of spacious, powerful and whole. We don't have to face up to our own responsibility for taking charge of things, for changing the world and ourselves. We can place our choices about being vulnerable and intimate and effective in the hands of our abusers. We can stay powerless and send them the bill.

But deciding not to heal fully, not to reclaim that place of intimate harm and make it flourish, is also unjust. By making the damage done to us permanent and irreversible, we lock both ourselves and the perpetrators away from any hope of healing. We saddle them with an even bigger spiritual debt than they have already incurred, and sometimes the reason is revenge, as if our full recovery would let them off the hook and we must punish them by seeing to it that our victimhood is never diminished or challenged. But when we refuse healing for the sake of that rage, we are remaking ourselves in the image of those who hurt us, becoming the embodiment of the wound, forsaking both ourselves and the abandoned children who grew up to torment us.

3

The path of reclaiming the wounded erotic is neither placid nor boring. It is full of dizzying precipices, heady moments of release, crushing assaults of shame. But at its core is the real fire we are all after, that blazing and untarnished aliveness that lies within everything of value and spirit that we do. Right here in our bodies, in our defense of our right to experience joy, in the refusal to abandon the place where we have been most completely invaded and colonized, in our determination to make the bombed and defoliated lands flower again and bear fruit, here where we have been most shamed is one of the most radical and sacred places from which to transform the world. To shamelessly insist that our bodies are for our own delight and connection with others clearly defies the predatory appropriations of incestuous relatives and rapists; but it also defies the poisoning of our food and water and air with chemicals that give us cancer and enrich the already obscenely wealthy, the theft of our lives in harsh labor, our bodies used up to fill bank accounts already bloated, the massive abduction of our young people to be hurled at each other as weapons for the defense and expansion of those bank accounts—all the ways in which our deep pleasure in living has been cut off so as not to interfere with the profitability of our bodies. Because the closer I come to that bright, hot center of pleasure and trust, the less I can tolerate its captivity, and the less afraid I am to be powerful, in a world that is in desperate need of unrepentant joy.

THIRTY-FIVE

◆◆◆

Engaging Men Against Violence (2012)

Jonathan Grove

Jonathan Grove coordinates the Men's Project at Pacific Lutheran University Women's Center where he oversees the education, prevention, and male engagement efforts of the Voices Against Violence project. Jonathan has been involved in engaging men in gender violence response and prevention since 2002. He also serves on the YWCA of Pierce County Board of Directors and on the Washington Sexual Violence Prevention College Coalition Steering Committee.

Fighting against the world that we don't want is a critical first step, but fighting for the world that we do want is where liberation truly begins.

—Courtney Martin

This article explores why men have largely been absent from anti-violence efforts and offers strategies to engage men in this work. I contextualize my approach through my own experience. I believe that our lives are the greatest resource we have for understanding each other. Further, our stories offer a point of connection for others to hear us in a profoundly human way.

What is most critical for you to know about me is that my writing this article is an accident. My goal upon enrolling in college was to find a way out of working-class life by becoming an FBI agent. A badge and gun would secure my masculinity and class standing, as well as allow me to help people. What I did not realize then was that it was I who needed the "helping."

Men benefit from patriarchy in a multitude of ways and we do not often think of the price we pay for this power. I felt that any attack on the status quo was an attack on me personally, rather than on a male-dominant system. Traditional masculinity values traits like being tough, unemotional, successful, and dominant (O'Neil 1981), though it is impossible for a human being to always be unemotional or successful. Men inevitably fail to perfectly embody the version of masculinity that is socially valued. As a result, many men experience tremendous insecurity because they fail to be fully valued as men. This is important, given that men exhibit hyper-masculinity in direct proportion to their level of insecurity about their male identity. Rather than challenge the patriarchal system that keeps us from loving ourselves, we re-double our efforts to use sexism and heterosexism to deny the value of others. What I had not realized was that my insecurity about my masculinity had caused me to hurt people. Equally, I had yet to learn to love myself regardless of how well I fit someone else's definition of who I should be.

Luckily, I had mentors who helped me to value my humanity above my masculinity. The first, an insightful professor, challenged me to consider violence *and* gender—specifically my own. She connected me with our campus Women's Center but it took two weeks for this "tough guy" to find the courage to walk in there! The center's director helped me begin to understand how others may experience parts of me in ways that feel marginalizing. More recently, another Women's Center director offered me an opportunity to both teach and continue to learn about gender, violence and privilege. These women built upon the foundation my parents created in my childhood: that boys and men can also be human.

Through this process I came to understand how patriarchy harms everyone, though in different ways. As bell hooks (1984) noted, some suffer far less than others but patriarchy has the potential to make us all comrades in struggle (also hooks 2004). Drawing on this insight and my own experience, my approach to working with men is based on three related ideas:

- *Rates of gender-based violence are high*

  Although only a small percentage of men are perpetrators, levels of assault are high: 1 in 4 college women (Krebs et al. 2007) or 1 in 6 boys (Dube et al. 2005). Many men feel guilty by association. We often excuse the perpetrator by blaming the victims, or we compromise our integrity by remaining silent. Our silence effectively condones the harm done to those we love, as well as those we may never meet. While we are taught to protect patriarchy with a battle-cry of "bros before hoes," this is inconsistent with our love for the women in our lives. Men must end our collective silence about the abuse of those we love at the hands of other men.

- *Restricted ideas of masculinity limit everyone*

  Sexism and heterosexism are used to narrowly define what is considered manly in our culture. This hurts everyone, including heterosexual men, by creating an impossible standard of masculinity that can never be fully achieved. Dominant ideas of manhood deny us meaningful connection to ourselves and to other men. Masculinity is vaguely defined as "not female," which creates huge opportunities for insecurity for men. Lastly, all men are familiar with other men's violence from a young age. Constant competition to not be seen as "queer" or "weak" produces the threat or real experience of bullying and physical assault to ensure that boys learn to negotiate violence.

- *Self-interest motivates us most effectively*

  While this may sound cynical, it offers great hope in understanding what will make people change their behavior. The previous two points (that women and children are victimized at shocking rates, and restrictive masculinity hurts men) can be powerful motivations for men to become critical of patriarchy.

To date, relatively few men have chosen to participate in anti-violence projects and to consciously challenge hegemonic masculinity. Generally, those

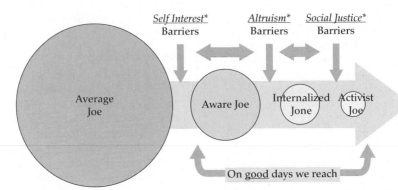

A Framework for Engaging Men

FIGURE **6.2 A Framework for Engaging Men** (*Source: Created by Jonathan Grove, image by Bobbi Hughes, and drawn from the work of Dr. Erin Casey, Rus Funk, Dr. Dorothy Edwards and Dr. Keith Edwards. *Edwards, Keith; Aspiring Social Justice Ally Identity Development: A Conceptual Model.*)

who do this have some pre-existing analysis of oppression and violence, often gained through their own experience around gender, sexuality, race, class, or another subordinated identity. They take Women's Studies classes, attend events like Take Back the Night, or volunteer at a shelter. Though these men certainly are familiar with dominant ideas of masculinity they do not often represent the "Average Joe." The assumption that these men will bring others into this work is false because they have little social capital in the traditional male hierarchy. Given the high cost of gendered violence, there is an immediate need for everyone to help change the culture of violence that affects us all. The overall goal is to engage the majority of men who are needed if we are to do so this.

Speaking to the Majority of Men

Men cannot challenge violence rooted in sexism and heterosexism without challenging hegemonic masculinity because gender-based violence is woven into the very fabric of that identity. Men who are trapped in a hyper-masculine identity are often unable or unwilling to address violence against women and children. Doing so would require them to defy the sexism that defines what is "manly." Understanding how men might come to perceive and challenge the very thing that causes their dominance and their insecurity is critical to their involvement.

I use two theoretical tools in my work: the "Framework for Engaging Men" (Fig. 6.2) and the work of Dr. Keith Edwards (2006), which help us think about how men become allies in the work against violence against women. Edwards' research provides insight into how some men move from believing that they should respond to gender violence only when it impacts someone they love, to becoming involved to protect women in general, to involvement for the sake of everyone's liberation (see Fig. 6.3). Although each man is unique, he is expected to conform to the hegemonic male norm, as mentioned earlier, which provides a commonality of experience among men. The Framework is designed to work with men as a group by speaking to that norm.

The Framework lays out a continuum showing how men in our culture might move from the understandings of an "Average Joe" to become "Activist Joes." Most men have given little thought to gender-based violence and may resist conversations about it. As they realize that some of their friends and loved ones are impacted by it (an "Aware Joe") this results in a desire to protect those they love. This may prompt a man to become concerned for women who are impacted by violence, male privilege, and his own participation in sexism (an "Internalized Joe"). Some may get stuck in a chivalrous approach to anti-violence work. Although this can provide a starting point, it is rooted in the sexism that violence against women supports. "Saving the women" does not address the central problem.

Aspiring Ally Identity Development

(Partial Summary)   Dr Keith Edwards

Aspiring Ally for:	Self-Interest	Altruism	Social Justice
Motivation	Selfish—for people I know and love	Other—I do this for them	Combined Selfishness and Altruism—we do this for us
Ally to...	A person	target group	an issue
Relationship to system	Not Interested in systems—just stopping the bad people	An exception from the system, yet ultimately perpetuates it	Seeks to escape, amend, and/or redefine the system
Privilege	Doesn't see privilege—but wants to maintain status quo	Feels guilty about privilege and tries to distance self from privilege	Sees illumination of privilege as liberating
Power	I'm powerful—protective	Empower them—they need out help	Empower us all
Admitting Mistakes	I don't make mistakes—I'm good, and perpetrators are just bad people	Difficult—struggles with critique or own issues—highly defensive about behavior	Seeks critique and admits mistakes—has accepted own isms and seeks help
Focus of the work	Perpetrators	Other members of the dominant group	My people—doesn't separate self from other agents

FIGURE 6.3 **Ally Identity Development**

Gradually, Joe may come to understand that everyone is harmed by sexism, and begin to understand his participation in this system as both oppressor and repressed.[1] He becomes an "Activist Joe" and begins the hard work necessary for personal and societal change. For male allies on this journey, there must be a community where men can learn, share their struggles, be challenged, get feedback, and refine their views with others engaged in a similar process. If men get involved without wrestling with the costs of patriarchy to themselves—and the generally higher price that others pay within this system—they may inadvertently act from a place of paternalism that can negate their best intentions.

It is easy to believe that the "Average Joe" is somehow unreachable. Examining ourselves, and the messages we received in the past, are critical steps to engaging the majority of men. Assumptions about what other men care about may be incorrect and may keep us from asking them to join our efforts. Initially, I bought into the stereotype that football players on our campus did not care about preventing sexual violence. As a former football player myself, I should have known better, but

at first I denied those men the opportunity to help by stereotyping them.

The Messages Men Hear

A major initial barrier to men's involvement is the belief that gender-based violence is a "women's issue." Men hear messages based in women's experience of rape culture. These often sound like: "Don't Rape." This message is based in an assumption that all men have the potential to rape if they are not told otherwise. However, what men hear is that all men are rapists. Given that this is not true and that no one wants to be called a bad person, it is not surprising that men respond very defensively to the topic when presented like this. Because this perspective does not define any helping role for them, it reinforces the idea that male violence is a women's problem.

Since men's experience of patriarchy is different from women's, effective messages must acknowledge this. While we maintain that male experience is privileged, we must also understand and validate a man's experiences of frustration and struggle with gender roles. This provides an opportunity for him to help, to critique patriarchy, and launch a powerful conversation about how women experience his privilege. The basis for his involvement is who he is, what he values, and how that conflicts with the version of manhood he has been sold.

This focus on how men can help create change (for himself and others) is critical to creating the space for Average Joe to minimize his defensiveness and to become an ally. Discussing masculinity produces insecurity because, while it is easy to list negative "manly" characteristics (being violent, emotion-less, controlling, etc.), it is much more difficult to note positive attributes. Therefore, it is easy for men to only hear negative things about their gender. Since they may have little evidence to challenge these stereotypes, they can feel powerless and defensive in their insecurity. By focusing on men as helpers with a personal stake in change, we offer security and avoid defensiveness.

Similarly, when men model positive masculinity for boys by engaging in prevention activities, they offer an example to emulate. This empowers the men to continue redefining masculinity in ways that promote their identity, and shows others that it can be done. Language, practical examples, and discussions of positive masculinity are very rare among men. I believe we hunger for them, and the sense of security they bring. This approach validates men's own problematic experiences of patriarchy and frees them to critique a culture that sanctions rape, the de-humanization of women, queer-identified people, and men as well. By addressing self-interest, men can be allies from the start.

What does this *look* like?

There are a growing number of examples of all this in practice. One is the *Walk A Mile In Her Shoes* fundraising event, in which men raise money for antiviolence projects by walking a mile in high-heeled shoes. Although there is legitimate concern about the potential for reinforcing homophobia or transphobia, having men participate in large numbers provides an opportunity to start a conversation about these topics. Other examples are *Mentors in Violence Prevention,*[2] *Green Dot,*[3] and *Where Do You Stand?*[4] that build skills and knowledge to prepare whole communities to prevent violence. These bystander engagement models offer a useful first step

because they are intentional about creating a space for men to help.

On the Pacific Lutheran University campus, male leaders from every corner of campus—Diversity Center, Residential Life, Campus Ministry, ROTC, Health Center, men's basketball, football and the Women's Center to name a few—are partners in our Men's Project. I began this coalition by identifying and then meeting with leaders among male groups who had not been involved in anti-violence work. I shared my concern about the lack of positive examples of masculinity and the strengths I believed each of them might share. I asked them to help guide younger men to become better men and community members, and they responded.

This unique collaboration allows us to connect with the whole campus while maintaining accountability to women leaders. The Men's Project has three central goals:

1. To develop ideas and language for positive, healthy, responsible and equitable masculinities, as men often lack terminology to discuss their humanity in positive ways. What does it look like to be an emotionally present, courageous, and nurturing man? If you cannot describe it, living that way is far more difficult.

2. To share this language with others. This not only passes along language developed in privileged spaces, but also requires the "teacher" to fully understand and practice what he claims. Further, grounded in the belief that each person has important truths to share, it opens up a conversation in which the "teacher" may also be the learner.

3. To act out this identity for our communities. Many have few positive examples of what it means to be a man who is fully connected to his humanity. Providing those examples can present a powerful opportunity for hope and change.

An example of how these three goals are put into practice is a men's retreat that explores notions of hegemonic masculinity and the costs of patriarchy in men's lives. Male leaders representing a wide-range of campus groups and identities provide real-life examples of the many ways one can be male, thus challenging dominant norms. Following the retreat, participants host an event for

A basketball player supports Men As Partners Promoting Equality (M.A.P.P.E.) at a Pacific Lutheran University home game.

boys in a domestic violence shelter. After playing ultimate Frisbee, the men lead boys in a conversation about how positive sportsmanship is more fun and draw contrasts between that and bullying behaviors at school. On campus, these men create an event where they share their stories in "Taking Back Our Gender" men's monologues. Hearing about men's struggle to define themselves in authentic ways, rather than accepting the prevailing version of masculinity, is a novel and potentially life changing experience for everyone. Moreover, legitimizing multiple versions of maleness offers permission and a pathway toward healthier manhood.

Other Men's Project events have included men hosting a Mother's Day Brunch for women in a domestic violence shelter, and talking with boys in the shelter about positive expressions of masculinity; also a Celebration of Children put on for kids in the community who may not get much affirmation, or who may have had few positive experiences

with men. Specific examples must meet individual community needs, but the three core goals remain the same.

In all these cases, the event supports violence prevention by challenging sexism and heterosexism, while offering men a point of entry that supports their male identity. What is most important is providing men a welcoming and supportive environment to voice their concerns and struggles in fitting the masculine stereotype they have been taught to project. In order to make it clear that I am such a resource, I regularly meet one on one with men who have social capital on our campus. I talk about my own experience and why it is important to me to be involved in anti-violence and gender related work, with the assumption that they, too, want to be a better friend to women and men, and to reclaim their gender. I say explicitly that these men are often stereotyped as not caring. I offer my perspective on what is at stake for them (safety and support for those they love, and their own liberation), and the fact that involvement in our project can begin to redefine the image of football or basketball players, ROTC cadets, etc. My participation, driven by my own self-interest, becomes a roadmap for their involvement.

While men must maintain accountability to women's leadership in these efforts, this does not mean that we should wait for women to do our work for us. It is imperative that men who are involved in anti-oppression work take a more active role. Feminism's promise of gender equity and intrinsic human value is something I believe men desperately want. Given the high cost in human lives, none of us can allow our fears that our actions are not seen as manly enough to stand in the way. Yes this can be scary, and absolutely requires hard work, courage and leadership—but isn't that what we expect of men already?

NOTES

1. I use repressed here to denote that men's experience under patriarchy is not directly comparable to that of women and gender queer individuals; men retain benefits that others do not.

2. See www.jacksonkatz.com/aboutmvp.html
3. See www.livethegreendot.com
4. See www.mencanstoprape.org

REFERENCES

Dube, S. R., Anda, R. F., Whitfield, C. L., et al. 2005. Long-term consequences of childhood sexual abuse by gender of victim. *American Journal of Preventive Medicine*, 28, 430–438.

Edwards, K. E. 2006. Aspiring social justice ally identity development. *NASPA Journal*, 43(4), 39–60.

hooks, bell. 1984. *Feminist theory: From margin to center*. Cambridge, Mass.: South End Press.

_____. 2004. *The will to change: Men, masculinity and love*. New York: Washington Square Press.

Kaufman, M. 1999. Men, feminism, and men's contradictory experiences of power. In J. A. Kuypers (ed.), *Men and power* (pp. 59–83). Halifax: Fernwood Books.

Kivel, P. 1992. *Men's work: How to stop the violence that tears our lives apart*. Center City, MN: Hazelden.

Krebs, C. P. et al. 2007. *The campus sexual assault study final report*, National Criminal Justice Reference Service (xiii, 5–5). Oct. 2007, available at http://www.ncjrs.gov/pdffiles1/nij/grants/221153.pdf.

O'Neil, J. M. 1981. Patterns of gender role conflict and strain: Sexism and fear of femininity in men's lives. *Personnel and Guidance Journal*, 60 (4), 203–210.

THIRTY-SIX

◆◆◆

Alternative Interventions to Violence: Creative Interventions (2006)

Mimi Kim

Mimi Kim is the Director of Creative Interventions, a nonprofit organization working on family and community solutions to interpersonal violence. She has worked at Asian Women's Center and co-founded Shimtuh: Korean Domestic Violence and Sexual Assault Program. She is a doctoral candidate in the School of Social Welfare at the University of California–Berkeley.

Are the solutions to violence against women and children to be found via state interventions—through the police, prosecution and imprisonment? Or are alternative, grassroots, community-based responses required? These are questions being asked by many women of color in the USA. Creative Interventions is an organization based in Oakland, California, which seeks to empower families and communities to resolve family, intimate partner and other forms of interpersonal violence.[1] It is hoped that this piece will spark conversations about ways of supporting community initiatives to address violence against women. Practitioners and community members working on similar issues in other countries are invited to contribute their ideas and stories.

Anti-Violence Movement in the U.S.

My involvement in exploring creative interventions in relation to violence against women and children has a particular history. It is linked to two pathways—the work of social justice movements in the U.S. that have been led by people of color to address the concerns of our communities, and years of anti-violence work, primarily within Asian American immigrant communities.

These pathways of social justice movements and the anti-violence movement have not always run a parallel course. The anti-violence movement in the U.S. has strayed from the grassroots and radical origins of its nascent years in the 1970s. Indeed, many would say that this can no longer be called a movement but rather a human service sector which has professionalized and legitimized itself into a provider of social service rather than as an agent of social change.

Throughout the 1980s and, particularly, the 1990s, government funding of anti-violence organizations in the U.S. increased significantly. This funding was often tied to collaboration with the police, prosecutors or promotion of pro-arrest policies. This funding trend both reflects and promotes the increasing reliance upon criminal legal interventions for domestic and sexual violence. As a long-time worker in anti-violence organizations, I witnessed this increase in federal and state funding, celebrated the availability of much-needed resources, and also came to recognize the short-term and long-term consequences these developments would have upon the very movement which fostered these gains.

During the ten years I worked within the Asian Women's Shelter with women who had been subjected to interpersonal violence, I embraced three key beliefs/principles of the mainstream anti-violence movement in the U.S.:

- that victims are a class of people distinct from perpetrators;

- that change for perpetrators is unlikely and, more often than not, not worth the effort; and

- that engagement with perpetrators is dangerous and therefore best left to the state.

While I understand the evolution of these beliefs/principles and am all too familiar with the victim-blaming, anti-woman myths from which these were

a welcome departure, I also saw us walk into another sort of trap.

While the anti-violence movement originally challenged patriarchy within the family and the patriarchal state which protected it, successful attempts to lobby for changes to state policies and practices led to a shift towards a collaborative relationship. Furthermore, the anti-violence movement was primarily led by white women (who were becoming increasingly professionalized) who experienced this shift in relationship with the state as beneficial to abused women and children as well as to their organizations which gained legitimacy and, in some cases, increased funding due to this improved relationship. While the positions of women of color with regard to this shift can in no way be described as homogeneous, women of color have been much more likely to challenge this relationship between the anti-violence movement and the state.

In recent years, this challenge has escalated with the alarming rise in rates of incarceration particularly among people of color. Likewise, increasing anti-immigrant sentiment and policies in the U.S. have contributed to concern over the pro-criminalization approach supported by anti-violence advocates and the state. Many of us, already wary of the pro-arrest recommendations often offered to women seeking assistance from our own organizations, were particularly struck by earlier compromises represented in the passage of the Violence Against Women Act (VAWA) in 1994. This important act was the first piece of federal legislation regarding violence against women in the U.S. and the result of years of struggle from anti-violence and immigrant rights advocates. Among other measures, its passage led to significant increases in federal funding available to anti-violence organizations and allowed for critical gains for immigrant women facing domestic violence from their U.S. citizen or legal resident spouses. These were outcomes we all celebrated.

At the same time, however, VAWA was passed as a section of the Violent Crime Control and Law Enforcement Act of 1994 (1994 Crime Bill), the bill backed by President Clinton which significantly increased prison construction and legislated "three strikes you're out"—a mandate for automatic long-term sentencing for anyone convicted of three felony offenses. For many of us, this compromise symbolized the untenable position the mainstream anti-violence movement had reached with regard to the state and its embrace of criminalization as a primary intervention response.

On the ground, women experiencing domestic violence had been encouraged to seek safety through our services. Our help lines often advised women to call the police. When women reached our phone lines after hours, they were told to call 911 (the dial code for the police) in case of emergency. While we were often skeptical of the response they might actually receive and spent time instructing women on how best to manage a police response, we failed to think of an alternative way to protect women and children and engage perpetrators of abuse.

Safety, we believed, was paramount. And safety was defined as devising a plan to leave the abuser and engage the police if necessary. Of course, we knew that women more often than not did not leave the relationships or when they left, they often returned at a later date. This is common for anyone involved in an abusive relationship. But for women in immigrant communities and communities of color there are additional concerns. For instance, the fear of an abusive partner may be matched by fear of the police. Immigrant women want violence to end, but they do not necessarily want their partner arrested, nor to go to a shelter, nor to leave their homes. Those concerned about their immigration status also risk exposure to deportation for themselves, their children, and for their abusive partners.

For those involved in abusive same-gender relationships or for the lesbian/gay/bi-sexual/transgender or queer community, fears in relation to the police or state involvement are heightened by knowledge that most conventional anti-violence programs will fail to understand them and their situations. Few anti-violence advocacy services actively target the queer community or have effective anti-homophobia policies and practices. And police response towards the queer community is known to range from insensitivity to brutal violence.

While advocate-led trainings about domestic violence, and the experience of immigrant communities and queer communities may have mitigated some of the most egregious aspects of police response and positively changed policies and practices within some parts of the criminal legal system, the system remains one based on separation, punishment, state definitions of crimes, and state control. Embedded in a criminal legal system which purports "blind" justice remain deep biases based upon class, race, gender, sexual orientation, immigration status, nationality, religion, and physical and mental ability which permeate the system on all levels. Since 9/11, changes in laws, policies and practices have had devastating effects on already oppressed groups.

Even the most ardent supporters of the current anti-violence intervention approach in the U.S. will admit these limitations. However, many fail to see an alternative. The basic assumptions that the best way to achieve safety is through the survivor leaving an abusive relationship and the best way to engage a perpetrator is through the criminal legal system remain. Other options are deemed too dangerous, too subject to the manipulation of the perpetrator, or simply unimaginable.

In recent years, those raising a critique of state interventions and demanding new alternative responses to challenge intimate violence and state violence have coalesced into a vocal and powerful force. In 2000, an organisation called *Incite! Women of Color Against Violence* was formed during the *Color of Violence* conference in Santa Cruz to name and respond to the complex intersection of forms of oppression facing women of color and communities of color. This organization has continued to articulate a new analysis of violence while creating spaces for alternative responses.

Incite! and *Critical Resistance,* a multi-racial national organization challenging the prison-industrial-complex, created a joint statement which acknowledged the uncharted territory between those trying to address state violence associated with prisons, and those in the anti-violence movement trying to address interpersonal violence against women and children. The preamble to the *Critical Resistance–Incite statement on gender violence and the prison industrial complex* articulates a joint commitment to work together:

> We call social justice movements to develop strategies and analysis that address both state AND interpersonal violence, particularly violence against women. Currently, activists/movements that address state violence (such as anti-prison, anti-police brutality groups) often work in isolation from activists/movements that address domestic and sexual violence. The result is that women of color, who suffer disproportionately from both state and interpersonal violence, have become marginalized

within these movements. It is critical that we develop responses to gender violence that do not depend on a sexist, racist, classist, and homophobic criminal justice system. It is also important that we develop strategies that challenge the criminal justice system and that also provide safety for survivors of sexual and domestic violence. To live violence-free lives, we must develop holistic strategies for addressing violence that speak to the intersection of all forms of oppression. (Incite! Women of Color Against Violence, 2006, p. 223)

Communities as Spaces of Possibility

Many of us within oppressed communities seek safety within the same collective spaces which hold those who perpetrate violence against us. Leaving violent situations may not seem possible because of potential persecution from those around us, not only abusive partners but family, faith communities, friends, community members, and leaders. These are attitudes which many of us in the anti-violence community are challenging in order to make it possible for those who have been subjected to violence to speak out about this, and to be embraced and supported rather than shunned or blamed. Leaving violent contexts may also expose us to new vulnerabilities, some of which may in the long run be less safe than the homes and communities from which we escape, i.e., poverty, racism, exposure to deportation, religious persecution, language barriers, cultural barriers, homophobia, transphobia, and so on. As anti-violence advocates and those committed to wider social justice, we are doing all we can to change these conditions.

However, despite conditions of violence, communities also offer multiple forms of safety: emotional safety; material resources; security of home and family; shared language, culture, history and religion; sense of belonging; and so on. These are important to most human beings. For members of oppressed communities, however, these are particularly scarce resources which may only be accessible within the sacred pockets of our intimate spaces. How can these treasures be salvaged? How can the positive benefits of community be nurtured? And, in situations of intimate violence, how can we rely

upon these very community resources to lead the way towards safety and accountability—and not simply rely upon outside systems to "pull us out of danger" by removing us or those from within our communities who violate us?

The shortcomings of currently available intervention options and the need to develop new models for community-based responses to violence became painfully clear to me as I faced the violence in the relationship of my own long-time friends. When I learned what was happening, my instinct was to gather a collective group of our community together to form a system of response not only to support the survivor but also to engage her abusive partner. My professional training told me that this would be too dangerous. Going to a shelter, seeking refuge at a friend's home, calling the police—these were all familiar suggestions which were rejected outright by my friend. I had worked all these years in the anti-violence movement and, yet, the options we had to offer were so ineffective. This was not because a woman was not ready to make these difficult choices. This was because, for her, these choices were the wrong ones.

Creating Alternative Community-Based Interventions to Violence

Despite a growing critique of the limited intervention approaches available and despite the development of some proposed alternative frameworks (Generation Five, 2006; Incite! Women of Color against Violence 2005; Kim 2002; Mills 2003), on-the-ground implementation of alternative responses to violence in the U.S. has been surprisingly lacking. Restorative justice applications to intimate forms of violence have been attempted in only a few places (Bazemore & Earle 2002; Blagg 2002; Coker 1999, 2002; Kelly 2002; Pennell & Anderson 2005; Pranis 2002; Stubbs 1997, 2002), and most have been closely tied to the criminal legal system. Some anti-violence organizations have prioritized community organizing over a social service model (Asian and Pacific Islander Women & Family Safety Center 2001; Bhattacharjee 1997; Close to Home 2003; Das Dasgupta 2002; Fullwood 2002; Kim 2005; Mitchell-Clark & Autry 2004), but few have engaged the community to take a more active role in actually intervening in violence.

After researching existing programs and participating in local and national discussions confirming the need for alternative options, I decided to form an independent organization from which to nurture these alternative community-based interventions to violence. In 2004, with the support and inspiration of long-time visionaries in the anti-violence movement, I established *Creative Interventions* in Oakland, California. I also knew of a handful of local and national anti-violence organizations which would be willing to work together collaboratively to explore these alternative options but which individually lacked the institutional resources to develop them.[2]

Creative Interventions begins with the assumption that those closest to and most impacted by violence have the greatest motivation to end that violence, i.e., survivors, friends, family and community members. And as these are often the people to whom survivors first turn, they are in a position to offer the most accessible and culturally-appropriate assistance at the earliest stages of violence. It also assumes that the intimate network is often already engaged with the perpetrator and may be in the best position to leverage their authority and connection to demand and support change. Thus the key to community-based interventions is not outside systems, but rather the intimate network. The missing pieces are the framework, knowledge, and resources to equip these intimate networks to offer effective, ethical, and sustainable intervention options.

Creating New Knowledge to Support Alternative Community-Based Interventions

The first project of Creative Interventions is a documentation project called the StoryTelling and Organizing Project which gathers stories from everyday people on successful and not-so-successful community-based interventions to violence. We have become so conditioned to think of our current system of shelters, police, and professional intervention programs for those who are violent, that many of us cannot even imagine what a community-based intervention would look like. Yet, I have found that when any group has discussed the topic, people invariably think of efforts that they or others have carried out.

"Oh yes, I remember that my cousin and his friends helped this girl who was being beaten up by her dad. They went to his house and told him that they knew what was happening and he'd better not do it again." Stories like these contain rich information regarding community-based interventions. What we need to do is to recognize the value of these stories, seek them out, and then rigorously explore these often hidden stories for more information:

- Who decided to start the intervention?
- Why did you do this?
- Why then? What made you know that this was the time to do this?
- How did you decide to move forward?
- What skills were involved in taking this action?
- How did you learn how to do this?
- Who else did you involve?
- What effects did this have?
- Did it reduce or end the violence?
- How?
- What did you learn from this process?
- What advice would you give to others who are in a similar situation?

If these stories of courageous acts of everyday people can be collected in one place, documented, analyzed and then turned back to our communities, what further community interventions will be inspired?

Creative Interventions will also add to community knowledge through a second project, the Community-Based Intervention Project, which seeks to demonstrate ways of creating alternative community-based models of intervention. An alternative model which organizes collective responses to violence including support for survivors, engagement of perpetrators, and education for the community, is currently being developed among partner organizations primarily working within communities of color, immigrant, and queer communities in the San Francisco Bay Area. Upon completion of this pilot project and its evaluation, the model will be documented and disseminated widely.

These are our efforts to create new paradigms and tools to address and prevent violence. This organization and its collaborative projects represent just one of many efforts among women of color in the U.S.

to create alternative responses to intimate forms of violence, while at the same time addressing the very real effects of state violence on our communities.

I will end this piece with Barbara's[3] story collected through the StoryTelling and Organizing Project in order to provide an example of how these stories can inspire and inform.[4]

Barbara's Story

I have three children; the oldest two are boys. I had them when I was still running a rape crisis center and a battered women's program/child sexual abuse program. And I remember panic about having boys: "How in the world am I going to love boys?" 'Cause in my view, men were responsible for much of what was wrong with the culture, and cultures in general, and that aggression and that violence that we were seeing happen in families and in communities. It was deeply life-transforming to *completely* love—love like I've never loved before—these two little boys. And watch them grow up, and shepherding their growth in a really racist, sexist, screwed-up world. And knowing that you could only do as good of a job as you can do.

When my oldest son was a freshman at high school, he was dying to go to these unsupervised parties that were actually being given by seniors when their parents were out of town. The good news is he was deeply honest and said, "I really want to go to these parties." And I'd say, "No, you can't go to these parties." And we had a running debate for half of the year.

He kept saying, "Mom, you know I'm not going to do anything terrible. And you know in yourself that at some point I'm going to experiment, but I'm not going to do more than that. What's the problem?" And I realize, as we talk about it, that the problem was I *knew* that at these parties—at some point—there'd be a young woman who would either have gotten too drunk or too high, or was too confused about the attention . . . of some powerful senior, to not end up upstairs in a bedroom, and that she would be raped. And I *knew*—I had no question—that my son would not be the person to do that. I had not an iota of doubt or worry.

But I couldn't bear the idea that he would be there and not stop it. And that he'd be part of a problem by not being able to stop it. So I said, "You're not going to be the problem. But somebody else is. And I don't know how I could bear you being present. So the only way you can go to this unsupervised party is if you can role-play with me—if you can strategize with me—what you're going to do, because you *have* to be able to stop it. And if that means putting your body in the way, or if it means calling the police and dealing with whatever trouble you might get for calling the authorities on the older boys, or gathering a group of your friends together to stop it in some way . . . you *have* to . . . I have to know that you will not allow it to happen because being on the side and not doing it yourself is not enough. You've got to be an active part of the solution." And we had long talks about this.

We talked through what he would do, how he would feel, what he would do if he had to call the police—how before he did it he'd have to know the address, he'd have to know how to describe it, he'd have to be willing to be there when they came so that they weren't turned away at the door . . . There were a million details that we had to walk through in order for me to feel confident. And in the end, right near the end of freshman year, he convinced me that he would be strong enough. And that whatever it was—if it took getting a posse of his friends together to stand in the way, . . . if it meant grabbing the girl and running off and getting her to safety— that he would do it. That was our agreement.

And then, I think it was a week before his senior graduation, he came to me one day and said, "Mom, do you remember those discussions we had my freshman year?" And I said, "You mean about the parties?" And he said, "Yeah." He said, "Mom, I did it." I said, "What are you saying?" And he said, "There was a party I was at and six guys led a girl upstairs and I watched that. And I ran upstairs and I stood in the doorway. And I grabbed her hand and I ran downstairs with her, and I told those young men they had to get out. And I took her home. And she was okay." And he didn't cry when he told me.

And actually, later that day, a girlfriend of his, and I don't know if she was the girl, or if she just knew the girl . . . she came to me and said, "Barbara, do you know what your son did?" And I said, "You mean at the party?" And she said, "Yes. He saved this girl." And she said, "Barbara, you should be really proud."

. . . So I think it's possible. You can raise boys. And it's important to raise them and know they won't do it. But it's just as important for them not to be bystanders—to raise them to be courageous and to have them understand that their job is far more than that; they have to stop it.

NOTES

1. See www.creative-interventions.org.
2. These include Generation Five, a San Francisco–based national organization committed to ending child sexual abuse through community organizing and leadership development, and local immigrant-specific domestic violence programs, including Shimtuh in the Korean community; Narika, which works in the South Asian community; and Asian Women's Shelter, a pan-Asian battered women's shelter which has been particularly interested in looking at alternatives for the Asian and Pacific Islander queer community. Other affiliated organizations include prison abolitionist organizations in the Bay Area including Critical Resistance and Justice Now, the latter organization advocating for women in prison, and DataCenter, a social justice research center.
3. Barbara gave permission for her first name to be shared publicly.
4. If you want to contribute stories of grassroots community initiatives to address violence, Creative Interventions would be delighted to hear from you. Contact stories@creative-interventions.org

REFERENCES

Asian & Pacific Islander Women & Family Safety Center 2001: *Organizing with passion: Domestic violence organizing strategies.* Seattle: Asian & Pacific Islander Women & Family Safety Center.

Bazemore, G. & Earle, T. H. 2002: 'Balance in the response to family violence: Challenging restorative principles'. In Strang, H. & Braithwaite, J. (eds), *Restorative justice and family violence*, pp. 153–177. Cambridge: Cambridge University Press.

Bhattacharjee, A. 1997: 'A slippery path: Organizing resistance to violence against women'. In Shah, S. (ed), *Dragon ladies*, pp. 29–45. Boston, MA: South End Press.

Blagg, H. 2002: 'Restorative justice and Aboriginal family violence: Opening a space for healing'. In Strang H. & Braithwaite, J. (eds), *Restorative justice and family violence*, pp. 191–205. Cambridge: Cambridge University Press.

Close to Home 2003: *Mobilizing family, friends, & neighbors to prevent domestic violence.* Dorchester, MA: Close to Home.

Coker, D. 1999: 'Enhancing autonomy for battered women: Lessons from Navajo peacemaking', *University of California Los Angeles Law Review*, 47:1.

Coker, D. 2002: 'Anti-subordination processes in domestic violence'. In Strang H. & Braithwaite, J. (eds), *Restorative justice and family violence*, pp. 128–152. Cambridge: Cambridge University Press.

Das Dasgupta, S. 2002: *Organizing communities to challenge violence against women.* Duluth, MN: Praxis International.

Fullwood, P. C. 2002: *Preventing family violence: Community engagement makes the difference.* San Francisco, CA: Family Violence Prevention Fund.

Generation Five 2006: *Transformative justice approaches to child sexual abuse: Challenges, principles, and applications.* San Francisco: Generation Five.

Incite! Women of Color Against Violence 2005: *Gender oppression, abuse, violence: Community accountability within the people of color progressive movement.* Incite: Women of Color Against Violence.

Incite! Women of Color Against Violence 2006: *The Incite! anthology.* Boston: South End Press.

Kelly, L. 2002: 'Using restorative justice principles to address family violence in Aboriginal communities'. In Strang, H. & Braithwaite, J. (eds), *Restorative justice and family violence*, pp. 206–222. Cambridge: Cambridge University Press.

Kim, M. 2002: *Innovative strategies to address domestic violence in Asian and Pacific Islander communities: Examining themes, models, and interventions.* San Francisco: Asian & Pacific Islander Institute on Domestic Violence.

Kim, M. 2005: *The community engagement continuum: Outreach, mobilization, organizing and accountability to address violence against women in Asian and Pacific Islander communities.* San Francisco: Asian & Pacific Islander Institute on Domestic Violence.

Mills, L. 2003: *Insult to injury: Rethinking our responses to intimate abuse.* Princeton: Princeton University Press.

Mitchell-Clark, K. & Autry, A. 2004: *Preventing family violence: Lessons from the Community Engagement Initiative.* San Francisco: Family Violence Prevention Fund with support from the Annie E. Casey Foundation.

Pennell, J. & Anderson, G. (eds). 2005: *Widening the circle: The practice and evaluation of family group conferencing with children, youths, and their families.* Washington, DC: NASW Press.

Pranis, K. 2002: 'Restorative values and confronting family violence'. In Strang H. & Braithwaite, J. (eds), *Restorative justice and family violence*, pp. 23–41. Cambridge: Cambridge University Press.

Stubbs, J. 1997: 'Shame, defiance and violence against women: A critical analysis of "communitarian conferencing"'. In Cook, S. & Bessant, J. (eds): *Women's encounters with violence: Australian experiences.* Thousand Oaks, CA: Sage Publishing.

Stubbs, J. 2002: 'Domestic violence and women's safety: Feminist challenges to restorative justice'. In Strang, H. and Braithwaite, J. (eds): *Restorative justice and family violence*, pp. 42–61. Cambridge: Cambridge University Press.

◆◆◆

THIRTY-SEVEN

Territory, Sovereignty, and Crimes of the Second State
The Writing on the Body of Murdered Women (2010)

Rita Laura Segato

Rita Laura Segato is a professor of anthropology at the Universidad de Brasilia (Brazil), senior researcher at the Consejo Nacional de Investigaciones Científicas, and project director of the NGO, Actions in Gender Citizenship and Development. She is the author of two books and many articles on structures of violence.

. . .

I was invited to go to Ciudad Juárez in July 2004 because in the preceding year two women from the Mexican organizations Epikeia and Nuestras Hijas de Regreso a Casa (Bring Our Daughters Home) had heard me lay out what seemed to me the only plausible hypothesis for the enigmatic crimes that haunted the city: the deaths of women of a similar physical type, which were perpetrated with an excess of cruelty, exhibited evidence of gang rape and torture, and being disproportionately numerous and continuing for more than eleven years, seemed unintelligible.

. . .

It is worth remembering that, in Ciudad Juárez, it appears that there are no coincidences. As I will try to argue, everything works as part of one complex communication machine whose messages are intelligible only to those who, for one reason or another, are able to break the code. Thus, the first problem that the hideous crimes of Ciudad Juárez pose for foreigners and distant audiences is that of intelligibility. And it is precisely in their unintelligibility that the murderers take refuge, as if using a sinister war code, an argot made up entirely of "acting out" behavior. To give only one example of this logic of signification, I turn to one of the journalist Graciela Atencio's articles on the murdered women of Ciudad Juárez. In it she questions whether it was mere coincidence that precisely on August 16, 2003, when her newspaper, the daily *La Jornada* of Mexico City, first published the news of a Federal Bureau of Investigation (FBI) report "describing a possible *modus operandi* in the kidnapping and disappearance of young women" that problems with the mail prevented its distribution in Ciudad Juárez (Atencio 2003).

Unfortunately, this was not the only apparently significant coincidence during my time in the city. On Monday, July 26, after having given my first talk and halfway through our forum—and exactly four months after the discovery of the last corpse—the dead body of the maquiladora worker Alma Brisa Molina Baca appeared. I will spare you the description of the many irregularities committed by investigators and the local press regarding Alma Brisa's remains. It is no exaggeration to say that you had to see it to believe it; you had to witness the inconceivable, the unbelievable. But I will note that the body was found in the same empty lot in the center of the city where another victim had been found the year before. That other victim was the murdered daughter, still a child, of the mother who we had in fact interviewed just the evening before, on July 25, in the bleak neighborhood of Lomas de Poleo, in the barren desert that crosses the border between Chihuahua and the U.S. State of New Mexico.[1] General comments also pointed to the fact that the year before another body had been found during the federal intervention in the Mexican State of Chihuahua ordered by then President Vicente Fox. The cards were on the table. This sinister "dialogue" seemed to confirm that we were inside the code and that the traces we were following led to a destination.

This is the interpretative path I will trace here. . . . It is a path that describes the relationship between the deaths, the illicit results of the ferocious neoliberalism globalized across the borders of the "Great Frontier" after the North America Free Trade Agreement, and the unregulated accumulation that was concentrated in the hands of certain families of Ciudad Juárez. Indeed, what stands out the most when you take the pulse of Ciudad Juárez is the vehemence with which public opinion rejects the names that law enforcement presents as the presumed culprits. It gives the impression that people

want to look in another direction and are waiting for the police to direct their suspicions to the other side—to the city's rich neighborhoods.[2] The illegal traffic to the other side is of every possible type: It includes the commodities produced from the work extorted from the maquiladora workers and the surplus that the value extracted from that work adds, as well as drugs and bodies—in short, all of the considerable capital that these businesses generate south of paradise. This illicit movement is similar to a process of constant repayment to an unfair, voracious, and insatiable tax collector who nevertheless hides his appetite and disengages himself from the seduction he exerts. The border between the misery of excess and the misery of lack is an abyss.

Two things can be said of Ciudad Juárez without risk. They are, in fact, said by everybody: the police, the attorney general, the special prosecutor, the human rights commissioner, the press, and the activists. One is that "the *narcos* (drug traffickers) are responsible for the crimes," sending us to a subject that looks like a thug and reaffirming our fear of the margins of social life. The other is that "these are sexually motivated crimes." On the day after Alma Brisa's body was discovered, the newspaper repeated that this was "yet another sexually motivated crime,"

and the special prosecutor emphasized, "It is very difficult to reduce the number of sexual crimes"— confusing the evidence yet again and sending the public down what I believe is the wrong path. This is how, while pretending to speak in favor of the law and rights, opinion makers and the authorities foster an indiscriminate perception of the misogynist crimes occurring in Ciudad Juárez, as well as in other parts of Mexico, Central America, and the world: crimes of passion, domestic violence, sexual abuse, rape by serial aggressors, crimes related to drug debts, trafficking of women, cyber-pornography crimes, trafficking of organs, and so on. . . .

It is as if concentric circles formed by various forms of aggression are hiding in their center a particular type of crime (not necessarily the most numerous but the most enigmatic, given its precise, almost bureaucratic, characteristics): the kidnapping of young women of a distinct physical type, most of them workers or students, who are held captive for several days and tortured, gang raped . . ., mutilated, and murdered. This is followed by the mixing or loss of clues and evidence by law enforcement, threats and attacks by lawyers and journalists, deliberate pressure by authorities to blame scapegoats who are clearly innocent—and, ultimately, the continuation of these crimes, uninterrupted, from 1993 to the present. The impunity over all these years is terrifying and can be described by three characteristics: (1) the absence of indicted perpetrators who are credible in public opinion; (2) the absence of consistent lines of inquiry; and (3) an endless repetitive cycle of this sort of crime as a consequence.

Two brave investigative journalists—Diana Washington Valdez, the author of *Cosecha de mujeres* (Harvest of women; 2005), and Sergio González Rodríguez, the author of *Huesos en el desierto* (Bones in the desert; 2002)—gathered numerous details that the police had set aside over the years and came up with a long list of places and people that, in one way or another, are linked to the disappearances and murders of women.[3]

I spoke with Diana Washington on two occasions on the other side of the border (the FBI does not let her cross the bridge without an escort), and I read Sergio González's book. What emerges is that people from "good" families—large landholders—are connected to the murders. But a crucial link is missing: What drives these respected, financially successful heads of prestigious families to become involved in gruesome and, as all signs indicate, collectively committed crimes? What could be the plausible link between these men and the kidnappings and gang rapes that would allow them to be identified and formally accused? A reason seems missing. It is precisely here, in the search for this reason, that the overused idea of "sexual motives" is insufficient. New classifications, legal categories, and clearer definitions are needed to be able to understand the specificity of a limited number of deaths in Ciudad Juárez. It is particularly necessary to state what appears obvious: that no crime committed by common outcasts would remain in complete impunity for this long, and no serious police force would speak so lightly of criminal motives, which generally are determined after lengthy investigation. Those basic truths make Ciudad Juárez shudder and become unspeakable.

. . .

. . . I tend not to understand the feminicides of Ciudad Juárez as crimes in which hatred toward the victim is the dominant factor (Radford and Russell 1992). I do not doubt that misogyny, in the strict sense of intense hatred of women, is common in the environment in which the crimes take place and

constitute a precondition for their occurrence. Yet I am convinced that the victim is the waste product of the process, a discardable piece, and that extreme conditions and requirements for being accepted into a group of peers are behind the enigma of Ciudad Juárez. Those who give meaning to the scene are other men, not the victim, whose role is to be consumed to satisfy a group's demands to become and remain cohesive as a group. The privileged interlocutors in this scene are the peers: the members of this mafia fraternity, to guarantee and seal their covenant; its opponents, to exhibit power before their business competitors, local authorities, federal authorities, activists, scholars, and journalists who dare to get mixed up in their sacred domain; or the victims' fathers, brothers, or male friends. These requirements and forms of exhibitionism are characteristics of the patriarchal regime of a mafia order.

The Feminicides of Ciudad Juárez: A Criminological Proposal

I present here a list of several ideas that together paint a possible picture of the feminicides' setting, motives, ends, meanings, and occasions and the conditions that make them possible. My problem is that the analysis can be rendered only in the form of a list. Nevertheless, the issues outlined together paint a picture that makes sense. It is not a linear list of successive items but a meaningful whole: the world of Ciudad Juárez. . . . To speak of causes and effects does not seem adequate to me; to speak of a universe of intertwined meanings and intelligible motivations does.

The Place: The Great Border

As a frontier between excess and lack, North and South, Mars and the Earth, Ciudad Juárez is not a cheerful place. It embraces many tears, many fears.

It is the frontier that money has to cross, virtually and materially, to reach the firm land where capital finds itself finally safe and gives its rewards in prestige, security, comfort and health. It is the frontier beyond which capital gets moralized and reaches worthwhile, sound banks.

It is the frontier to the most patrolled country in the world, with its almost infallible tracking and close-range surveillance. Here, around this line in the desert more than anywhere else, illicit actions must be carried out in the utmost stealth and secrecy by the most cohesive clandestine organization. A rigorous pact of silence is its requisite.

This is the frontier where the great entrepreneurs "work" on one side and live on the other. It is the frontier of the great expansion and fast valorization, where terrain is literally stolen from the desert each day, each time nearer the Río Bravo.

It is the frontier of the world's most lucrative traffic—in drugs; in bodies.

It is the frontier that separates one of the most expensive labor forces from one of the cheapest.

This frontier is the background of the longest-lasting series of attacks on women's bodies with similar modus operandi known in so-called peacetime.

The Purposes

The evidence that the justice system had an extremely long period of inertia around these crimes immediately points our attention to their persistent subtext: The crimes speak of impunity. Impunity is their grand issue, and as such impunity is the way into deciphering them. Although the environment I have just described, characterized by a concentration of economic and political power and, therefore, high levels of privilege and protection for some groups, is the ideal cauldron for brewing the murders, it occurs to me that we are mistaken when we see impunity exclusively as a causal factor.

I propose that the feminicides of Ciudad Juárez can be better understood if we stop thinking of them as a consequence of impunity and imagine them as producers and reproducers of impunity. This was my first hypothesis, and it is also possible that it was the first purpose of perpetrators: to seal, with collectively shared complicity in the hideous torturing and killing of captive and defenseless women, a vow of silence able to guarantee the unbreakable loyalty to mafia brotherhoods operating across the most patrolled border in the world. The feminicides also serve as proof of the capacity for cruelty and power of death required for conducting extremely dangerous business. The sacrificial ritual, violent and macabre, unites the members of the mafia and makes their bond unbreakable. The sacrificial victim, part of a dominated territory, is forced to hand over the tribute of her body for the cohesion and

vitality of the group. The stain of her blood defines the assassins' esoteric belonging to the group. In other words, more than a cause, impunity can be understood as a product, as the result, of these crimes, and the crimes can be seen as a means for producing and reproducing impunity: a blood pact sealed with the victims' blood. There is also another dimension: to give proof of the capacity for the extreme cruelty and unwavering death power that highly dangerous and illicit businesses require.

In this sense, we can point to a fundamental difference between this sort of crime and the gender crimes perpetrated in the intimacy of domestic space against daughters, stepdaughters, nieces, wives, and other victims who belong to the circle of the abuser. If in the shelter of domestic space a man abuses the women who depend on him because he can—that is, because they are part of the territory that he controls—the aggressor who takes possession of the female body in an open, public space does so because he must prove that he can. The first case is a matter of affirming an existing domination; the latter is the exhibition of a capacity for domination that must be restaged with certain regularity and can be associated with the ritual gestures that renew vows of virility. Power here is conditioned on a regularly dramatized public exhibition of a predatory action against a woman's body. But the production and maintenance of impunity through the sealing of a pact of silence in reality cannot be distinguished from what could be described as the exhibition of impunity. The classic strategy that sovereign power uses to reproduce itself as such is to broadcast and even spectacularize the fact that it is above the law and can legislate. We can also understand the crimes of Ciudad Juárez in this way and suggest that they also fulfill the *exemplary function* by means of which sovereign power lets slip the crude reality of its presence in everyday life together with its underworld vitality as a ruling *second state* that is acting and shaping society from beneath the law.

This is so because, in the capacity to kidnap, torture, and kill repeatedly and with impunity, the subject/author of these crimes displays, beyond any doubt, the cohesion, vitality, and territorial control of the corporatist web that he commands and the code of norms at work in it. It is evident that the continuity of this sort of crime over eleven years requires considerable human and material resources, including the command of an extensive web of loyal associates; access to detention and torture sites; vehicles for transporting victims; and access to, influence over, or power to blackmail or intimidate representatives of public order at every level, including the federal level. What is important to note is that, as this powerful network of allies is set in motion for cover-up by those who command the corporatist crimes of Ciudad Juárez, the existence of the web is exhibited in an ostentatious display of a totalitarian domination over the area.

The Meanings

It is precisely when this last function is accomplished that the crimes begin to behave as a communication system. If we listen carefully to the messages that circulate there, we can see the face of the subject speaking through them. Only when we understand what he says, to whom and with what ends, will we be able to locate the position from which he speaks. This is why we must insist that each time the sexual-motive explanation is repeated lightly, before analyzing minutely what is being "said" in these dialogic acts, we lose a chance to follow the trail of he who hides behind the bloody text.

In other words, the feminicides are messages sent by a subject/author who can be identified, located, and profiled only by rigorously "listening" to these crimes as communicative acts. It is within his discourse that we find the subject who speaks; it is within discourse that the reality of this subject is inscribed as identity and subjectivity and therefore becomes traceable and recognizable. Likewise, in its enunciation we can find the interlocutor's trail, his imprint, like a photographic negative. . . .

If the violent act is understood as a message, and the crimes are seen as orchestrated in a clear call-and-response style, we find ourselves in a scene where the acts of violence communicate efflciently with those who "know" the code, the well informed, those who speak the language, *even when they are not taking part directly in the enunciative action.* This is why once a communication system with a violent alphabet is installed it is very difficult to de-install and eliminate it. Violence, constituted and crystallized within a communication system, is transformed into a stable language and comes to behave in the nearly automatic fashion of any language.

To ask in these cases why there are killings in a certain place is similar to asking why a certain language is spoken there—Italian in Italy, Portuguese in Brazil. At some point, each one of these languages was established through historical processes, be they conquest, colonization, migration, or the unification of territories under one national state. In this sense, the reason we speak a certain language is arbitrary and cannot be explained by logic. The processes by which a language is wiped out, eradicated from a territory, are also historical. The problem of violence as a language is even worse if we consider that there are certain languages that, in particular historical conditions, tend to become the lingua franca and spread across the ethnic or national borders that defined their original niche.

And so we ask: Who is speaking here? To whom? What is being said? When? What is the language of feminicide? My bet is that the author of these crimes is a subject who values profit and control of territory above all else, even above his own personal happiness; a subject with an entourage of vassals who in this way makes it absolutely clear that Ciudad Juárez has landlords and that these landlords kill women precisely to show themselves as such. *Sovereign power does not affirm itself unless it is able to spread terror in a way that nobody is safe. . . .*

He, the sovereign, addresses himself to all men in the domain: to those who should have been responsible for the victim and all of the others like her in the domestic space and to those responsible for their protection as representatives of the state. He also speaks to the men of the other, either friendly or hostile fraternities to show the array of resources he has at his disposal and the strength of his support network. To his allies and business partners he confirms that the group communion and loyalty continue unaltered. He tells them that his control over the territory is total; that his web of alliances is cohesive and trustworthy; and that his resources and contacts are unlimited.

He pronounces himself in this way during the consolidation of a brotherhood; when planning a dangerous, illicit business transaction on this patrolled border; when the doors are opened to a new member; when another mafia group challenges his control of the territory; or when there are external inspections, intrusions on his total control of the area.

The language of feminicide uses women's bodies to indicate what can be sacrificed for a higher good, a collective good, such as the constitution of a mafia brotherhood. The woman's body is the supreme index of the position of she who renders tribute, of the victim whose sacrifice and consumption will be most easily absorbed and naturalized by the community. Part of this process of digestion is the usual double victimization of she who is already victim, as well as the double and triple victimization of her family, usually represented by a mourning mother. . . .

Just as it is usual for the convicted to blame their victims for their own fate and loss of freedom, in the same way the community is ever more engulfed in a misogynist cycle that, lacking appropriate support for dealing with the discomfort, leads it to blame the victim herself for the cruelty she faced. We easily choose to reduce our own suffering when confronted with testimony of intolerable injustices, alleging that "there must be a reason." In this way, the women murdered in Ciudad Juárez quickly are transformed into prostitutes, liars, partygoers, drug addicts, and all that which can inoculate us from the responsibility and bitterness of facing the injustice of their fate.

. . .

Gang rape, as in pacts of blood, is the mixing of body substances of all those who take part in it; the act of sharing intimacy in its most ferocious aspect, of exposing what is kept under the greatest of zeal— sex itself, as the leak of the most intimate of all secretions. As the willing cut from where blood flows, rape is the making public of the fantasy, the transgression of a limit, a radically compromising gesture.

In the language of feminicide, the female body also signifies territory, and its etymology is as archaic as its transformations are recent. It has been constitutive of the language of wars, tribal and modern, that the woman's body is annexed as part of the nation that is conquered. The sexuality poured over it expresses the taming act, the taking possession of, when inseminating the woman's body territory. This is how the mark of territorial control by the lords of Ciudad Juárez can be inscribed on the body of the city's women as part of or as an extension of the domain they declare as their own. Rape as sexual domination implies, in conjunction, not only physical control over the victim, but also moral reduction of the victim and its associates. Moral reduction is a requisite for domination to be consummated, and sexuality in the world we know plays a fundamental part in the moral chart.

What, then, does *feminicide* mean in the sense that Ciudad Juárez gives to the term? It is the murder of a generic woman, of a type of woman, simply for being a woman and being of this type, in the same way genocide is a generic and lethal attack on all who belong to the same ethnic, racial, linguistic, religious, or ideological group. Both crimes are directed at a category, not a specific subject. Indeed, this subject is depersonalized as a subject, for the category it belongs to is more relevant than its individual biographical or personality traits.

But it seems to me that there is a difference between these two kinds of crimes that should be further examined and discussed. If in genocide the rhetorical construction of hate toward the other leads to the act of his or her elimination, in feminicide the misogyny that lies behind the act is a feeling more like that of hunters for their trophy: a contempt for that life or the conviction that the only value of that life lies in its availability for appropriation.

. . . Nevertheless, in the more than terrible contemporary postmodern, neoliberal, post-state, post-democratic order, the baron has become capable of controlling his territory in an almost unrestricted way as a consequence of the unruly accumulation characteristic of the frontier's expansion region, exacerbated by globalization of the economy and the loose neoliberal market rules in effect. Its only regulating force is the greed and predatory potency of his competitors, the other barons. . . .

. . .

The Conditions of Possibility: Asymmetry and Siege

The extreme asymmetry that results from local elites' unregulated extraction of wealth is essential to establishing a context of impunity. When the inequality is as extreme as it is in an unrestricted neoliberal regime, there is no real chance to separate legal from illicit business. Inequality becomes so extreme that it allows for absolute territorial control at a sub-state level by certain groups and their webs of support and alliance. These webs establish a true provincial totalitarianism and come to mark and express, without a doubt, the regime of control in force in the region. The torturing and murdering of women in Ciudad Juárez seem to me to be a way to signify this territorial control.

One thing that strongly characterizes totalitarian regimes is enclosure—that is, the representation of totalitarian space as a universe with no outside, encapsulated and self-sufficient, where the siege strategy of the elites hinders inhabitants' access to a different, external, alternative perception of reality. A nationalistic rhetoric that asserts itself in a primordialist construction of national unity (as in the case of "Mexican-ness" in Mexico, . . . benefits those who hold territorial control and monopolize the collective voice.

. . .

Like national totalitarianism, one of the principal strategies of regional totalitarianism is to turn the collective away from any discourse that might be called non-native, not issued and sealed by the commitment to an internal loyalty. "Foreigner" and "outsider in town" are transformed into accusations, and the possibility of speaking "from the outside" is barred. Therefore, the rhetoric is one of a cultural heritage that must be defended above all else and of a loyalty to territory that predominates and excludes other loyalties—for example, those of abiding by the law, of struggling to expand rights, and of activism and international mediation to protect human rights. This is why, if placing a premium on inwardness and using well-disguised techniques of media siege are the totalitarian leaders' sure strategy, the outer side is always the basis for action in the field of human rights. In a totalitarian environment, the value most hammered away at is the "we." The idea of "us" becomes defensive, entrenched, patriotic, and anyone who infringes it is accused of treason. In this kind of patriotism the first victims are the others inside the nation, the region, the locale—always the women, the black people, the First Nations/indigenous people, and the dissidents. These inside others are coerced to sacrifice, and postpone their complaints and the argument of their differences in the name of the sacralized and essentialized unity of the collective.

It is by articulating in public discourse these "patriotic" values (of a provincial totalitarianism) that the media of Ciudad Juárez disqualify, one by one, foreign views of the local cruel practices on women. When we "listen" to the subtext of the discourse of the news media, when we read between the lines, we hear: "Better a local murderer, no matter how cruel, than a foreign avenger, even if he is in the right." This well-known basic propaganda strategy builds up, every day, the totalitarian wall around Ciudad Juárez and has contributed over all these

years to holding back the truth from the people and the neutralization of the law, from the municipal to the federal level, that resist a prosthetic articulation with the local powers that be.

. . .

The feminicides of Ciudad Juárez's are not ordinary gender crimes. They are corporative crimes and, more specifically, crimes of the second state, of a parallel state. As a phenomenon, they are more like the rituals cementing the unity of secret societies and totalitarian regimes. They share an idiosyncratic characteristic of the abuses of political power: They appear to be crimes without a personalized subject carried out against victims who are also not personalized: A secret force abducts a certain type of woman, victimizing her, to reaffirm and renew its capacity for control. Therefore, they are more like state crimes, crimes against humanity, where the parallel state that produces them cannot be classified for lack of efficient legal categories and procedures.

This is why it would take the creation of new juridical categories to make these crimes legally intelligible, classifiable. They are not ordinary crimes—that is, gender crimes with a sexual motivation or resulting from power relationships in the domestic sphere—as law enforcement, authorities, and many activists frivolously argue. They are crimes that we could say are of the second state, or corporative crimes, where the expressive dimension of violence prevails. Here I understand the "corporation" to be the group or web managing resources, rights, and duties of a parallel state, firmly established in the region and with tentacles that reach to the country's top administration.

. . .

Epilogue

. . . As part of my results I have understood that even if the greatest suffering is that of the victims themselves, their mothers and next of kin, the atrocious crimes against Ciudad Juárez's women are the obligatory jurisdiction of all legal codes and an unavoidable concern for all who value justice and collective well-being. This is so in two ways. On the one hand, the theoretical, ethical, and legal issue of the feminicides is similar to the great issue of the Holocaust and its dilemmas. Both crimes are a heritage and a lesson that belong to all of humanity.

Its perpetrators are not beyond the limits of our common humanity; nor are its victims gifted with an idiosyncratic and essential quality that distinguishes them from all other peoples massacred across history. Historical conditions that can transform us into monsters or the accomplices of monsters threaten us all, and the menace of becoming monsters hangs over us all, without exception, as does the threat of becoming victims. All it takes is the creation of a strict and exact frontier between an "us" and a "them" for the process to begin. . . .

But this is not the only reason I say we are facing a problem that concerns us all. As I have argued, in the particular case of the feminicides of Ciudad Juárez, I understand these to be crimes perpetrated against us, addressed to us and for us, the law-abiding citizens. What puts us into dialogue with the perpetrators is deliberate and intentional. I am saying this not in general but in the strict sense that I am convinced that these crimes are directed at us, thrown our way as a declaration of that sovereign power acting in partnership with the state persists and continues in force underneath the statutory surface. They tell us about the permanent reissuing of a second law whose judges and prosecutors act as shadow authorities of the state. In other words, I am not saying that we are involved simply because the crimes affect us, make us suffer, offend us. Rather, I mean that the exhibition of a discretionary power over the life and death of those who live in that limit territory is represented and inscribed on the bodies of women as a document, as an edict, the unappeal-able sanction of a decree, as the staging of a dialogue with all who seek shelter under the law. These murders are aimed at exhibiting *for us* an intense capacity to produce death, an expertise in cruelty, and a sovereign domain over a territory to tell us that this is a matter of an occupied jurisdiction in which we cannot interfere. It is precisely because we disagree with this, because we think that Ciudad Juárez is neither outside Mexico nor outside the world—that we have to resist the submissive position where the murders prevent us from engaging in an active opposition to the regime they impose on us.

What to Do?

. . .

In my heart of hearts I wonder whether, and am afraid that, the tragic nature of human destiny may be the pattern structuring personal lives and histories. If tragedy has one characteristic, among many, it is that it does not shelter the possibility of justice without distorting its nature. What if justice is not possible, but some occasional degree of peace is? Would any peace be enough? Could we resign ourselves to the women's murders of Ciudad Juárez simply stopping one day and slowly transforming into a thing of the past, without justice ever being done?

I ask these questions seriously, honestly. I ask them first of all of myself, in deepest privacy. If we were told that the only way out is an armistice, would I, would you, be able to accept it? And would we be able not to accept it? I am still perplexed by this question . . . A decade of impunity indicates that the crimes of Ciudad Juárez are crimes of power, and therefore it may be that we can only negotiate their decrease and cessation.

NOTES

Translated by Sara Koopman.

1. Alma Brisa's remains were found amid sunflowers on the same plot of land in the center of the city where the body of Brenda Berenice, daughter of Juanita, one of the main collaborators of the Epikeia project, was found.

2. For example, in November 2004 in the main plaza of the neighborhood of Coyoacan, in Mexico City, I witnessed a protest of mothers and relatives of the victims who demanded both an end to impunity for the real murderers of women and the liberation of *"el cerillo,"* a youngster jailed and, according to them, falsely accused of the crimes. The attorney Irene Blanco, whose child suffered an attack, is also well known for her work defending Latif Sharif, who was falsely accused of the crimes, as is the work of the mothers against the jailing of the Los Rebeldes (Rebels) gang, for the same reason.

3. Also published in Spanish in Mexico and Spain, *Harvest of Women* compiles Washington's column for the *El Paso Times* newspaper. González Rodríguez was beaten and left for dead on a street in Mexico City in 2000 while he researched his book. He was hospitalized for a month and lost all his teeth.

REFERENCES

Atencio, Graciela. 2003. "El circuito de la muerte." *Triple Jornada* (monthly feminist supplement to *La Jornada*) September, 61.

Russell, Diana E. H., and Jill Radford. 1992. *Femicide: The politics of woman killing*. New York: Twayne.

7

◆◆◆

Making a Home, Making a Living

Asking for support from family and friends, falling in love, moving in with a roommate, holding your newborn baby for the first time, breaking up with a partner, struggling to understand a teenage son or daughter, or helping your mother die in peace are commonplace events that define the very texture of our personal lives. This chapter explores U.S. women's experiences of home, family, and making a living. We argue that personal and economic security are fundamental to women's well-being and to the security of our families and communities.

The recent economic recession—the worst since the Great Depression of the 1930s—has been disastrous for many people who have lost jobs or homes, or seen the value of their home or pension drop dramatically (Reading 43). Employers have downsized jobs, replacing full-time workers with part-timers at lower wages and without benefits like health insurance. Unemployment rates, poverty, and hunger have increased. According to economist Randy Albelda (2009), women of color were targeted for high-risk home loans and more likely to have had their mortgages foreclosed as banks went under. Individual decisions about home and work are shaped by macro-economic factors that greatly affect economic security.

Relationships, Home, and Family

Personal and family relationships are central to individual development, as noted in Chapter 3. In the family, we learn about socially defined **gender roles:** what it means to be a daughter, brother, wife, or father, and what is expected of us. We learn about our cultural heritage, ideas of right and wrong, practical aspects of life, and how to negotiate the world outside the home. Family resources, including material possessions, emotional bonds, cultural connections, language, and status in the wider community, all contribute to our identity and sense of belonging. How parents and siblings treated us during childhood and our observation of adult relationships provide the early foundation for our own intimate relationships. Friends and family, magazine features, and advice columns coach us on how to catch a man or woman and how to keep him or her happy once we have.

Grandmothers play an important role in passing on family history and cultural traditions.

Marriage and Domestic Partnership

Marriage is often thought to be an essential part of a woman's life, and there is still a stigma attached to being single in many cultural groups if a woman remains unmarried after a certain age. At the micro and meso levels marriage provides recognition, validation, and status. It is the conventional and respected way of publicly affirming one's commitment to a partner and being supported in this commitment by family and friends as well as societal institutions. Also, there are macro-level material benefits in terms of taxes, health insurance, pension rights, ease of inheritance, and immigration status. In 1997, the U.S. General Accounting Office found no less than 1,049 federal laws in which benefits, rights, and privileges were contingent on marital status.

The ideal of a committed partnership seems to hold across sexual orientation—with many women looking for Mr. or Ms. Right—even though fewer U.S. women are marrying these days, and those who do are marrying later. Many women appear to be less interested in what sociologist Judith Stacey (1996) called "the patriarchal bargain." Jaclyn Geller (2001) detailed the history of marriage as the institutionalization of inequalities between women and men. She viewed marriage as the paradigmatic institution that makes heterosexuality appear natural and "normal," and as a heterosexual woman she vehemently opposed it. Some lesbians, bisexual and transgender women, gay men, and heterosexual couples who have chosen not to marry have campaigned for the benefits of "domestic partnership"—to be covered by a partner's health insurance, for example, or to be able to draw the partner's pension if she or he dies. And increasing numbers of state and local governments, academic institutions, and major corporations offer domestic partnerships, though many firms still do not.

Demands for gay marriage in the interest of equal treatment for LGBTQ and heterosexual couples provide an interesting counterweight to feminist critiques of marriage as inherently patriarchal. Advocates argue that mixed-sex marriage laws are discriminatory and unjust, denying same-sex couples the many legal, economic, and social benefits that privilege heterosexual marriages. Paula Ettelbrick (1989) argued that the goals of gay liberation must be much broader than the right to marry. Political science professor Mary Shanley (2004) proposed various arrangements that would offer personal freedoms as well as supports for committed

relationships—gay or straight—such as civil unions, universal care-giving partnerships, "nonconjugal relationships of economic and emotional interdependency," and polyamorous relationships (p. 112). Not all lesbians or gay men want to marry; some critique the institution of marriage and seek alternative family forms, which would provide legal recognition and community support for many families, not only LGBTQ families (Cornell 2004; Polikoff 2008). Other critics have argued against the assimilationist goals of same-sex marriage on the grounds that it involves racially constructed ideas of sexual respectability and citizenship (see, e.g., Bailey, Kandaswamy, and Richardson 2004; Brandzel 2005; Kandaswamy 2008).

The Netherlands first allowed gay marriage in 2001. By 2011, Argentina, Belgium, Canada, Iceland, Norway, Portugal, South Africa, Spain, and Sweden had done the same, while other nations have allowed same-sex civil unions. In 2004, Massachusetts became the first U.S. state to legalize gay marriage (see Gozemba, Kahn, and Humphries 2007). By 2011, Connecticut, Iowa, New Hampshire, New York, Vermont, and Washington, D.C. had followed this example. Twenty-six states have passed laws or constitutional amendments restricting marriage to a union between a man and a woman. In 1996 the U.S. Congress passed the Defense of Marriage Act that excludes same-sex couples from receiving federal protections and rights of marriage. Even if some states

allow gay marriage, the Defense of Marriage Act blocks gay partners from receiving federal benefits.

That same year, Congress also passed the Personal Responsibility and Work Opportunity Reconciliation Act (PRWORA) which declared that "marriage is the foundation of a successful society." Law professor Kaaryn Gustafson points out how marriage has been privileged by various groups seeking to influence national policy (Reading 40). Given that two-parent families have higher incomes than single parents, apparently the framers of PRWORA reasoned that marriage would lift single mothers out of poverty. Accordingly, the federal government provided millions of dollars to states for marriage promotion programs.

The Ideal Nuclear Family

In much public debate, the nuclear family is touted as the centerpiece of American life. This idealized family, immortalized in the 1950s TV show, *Leave It to Beaver,* consists of a heterosexual couple, married for life, with two or three children. The father is the provider while the wife/mother spends her days running the home. This family is regularly portrayed in ads for food, cars, cleaning products, or life insurance, which rely on our recognizing—if not identifying with—this symbol of togetherness and care. Conservative politicians invoke this family in their rhetoric on "traditional family values." Although this mythic family makes up a minority of U.S. families today, the prevalence of this ideal has a strong ideological impact. It serves both to mask and delegitimize the diversity of family forms and gives no hint of family violence or the conflicts inherent in juggling paid work and caring for children. Sociologist Stephanie Coontz (1997) argued that nostalgia for the so-called traditional family is based on myths. Specifically, the post–World War II white, middle-class family was the product of a particular set of circumstances that were short-lived:

> Fewer women remained childless during the 1950s than in any decade since the late nineteenth century. The timing and spacing of children became far more compressed so that young mothers were likely to have two or more children in diapers at once. . . . The result was that family life and gender roles became much more predictable, orderly, and settled in the 1950s than they were either twenty years earlier or would be twenty years later.   *(p. 36)*

This ideal family, with its rigid gender-based division of labor, always applied more to white families than to families of color, and to middle-class families of all racial/ethnic groups. Many women of color and working-class white women have always had to work outside the home. Moreover, families take many forms. Eleanor Palo Stoller and Rose Campbell Gibson (1994) noted that "when children are orphaned, when parents are ill or at work, or biological mothers are too young to care for their children alone, other women take on child care, sometimes temporarily, sometimes permanently" (p. 162). Sociologist Barbara Omolade (1986) described strong female-centered networks linking African American families in which single mothers support one another in creating stable homes for their children. She challenged official characterization of these families as "dysfunctional." Anthropologist Leith Mullings (1997) noted that women-headed households are an international phenomenon, shaped by global as well as local factors like the movement of jobs from former industrialized nations to countries of the global South. An increasing number of families are split between countries through work, migration, or the dislocations of conflict and war (as discussed in Chapter 8).

Pam and Lisa Liberty-Bibbens with McKenzie and Brennan.

Lesbians, gay men, and transgender people have established intimate partnerships and extensive networks of friends who function as families. The Family Equality Council estimates that gay and lesbian parents are raising two million children nationally, as birth parents or adoptive parents. Same-sex couples of color are more likely to be raising children than same-sex white couples (Family Equality Coalition 2011; also see Brettschneider 2006; Drucker 1998; Goss and Strongheart 1997; Howey and Samuels 2000; Moraga 1997). In Reading 38, writer and teacher Ann Filemyr describes "loving across the boundary," as a white woman in partnership with Essie, a woman of color; their family included Essie's son and her grandmother. Filemyr makes insightful connections between their personal experiences; other people's reactions to their caring, multiracial household; and the impacts of racism and heterosexism on their lives.

Defining Women's Work

All women in the world work. They are farmers, artists, craft workers, factory workers, businesswomen, maids, nannies, engineers, secretaries, soldiers, teachers, nurses, sex workers, journalists, bus drivers, lawyers, therapists, waitpersons, prison guards, doctors, cashiers, airline pilots, executives, sales staff, professors, carpenters, dishwashers, filmmakers, mail carriers, dancers, homemakers, mothers, and wives. Many find satisfaction and challenge, even enjoyment in their work; for others it is a necessary drudgery.

Anthropologist Leith Mullings (1997) distinguished four kinds of women's work in the United States: paid work in the formal sector; reproductive work including housework and raising children, as well as paid work taking care of children, elderly people, or those who are sick; work in the informal sector, which may be paid under the table or in favors returned; and transformational work, volunteering in community organizations, professional groups, and clubs of all kinds.

According to dictionary definitions, the English word *economy* comes from two Greek words: *oikos,* meaning "house," and *nemo,* meaning "to manage." Thus, economy can be understood as managing the affairs of the household, and beyond that, the wider society. Modern-day economists make a distinction between "productive" and "unproductive" work, which is not implied in this original definition. So-called productive work is done for money; unpaid work is defined as unproductive to the economy. On this analysis a woman who spends her day making meals for her family, changing diapers, doing laundry, finding schoolbooks and football shoes, packing school lunches, making beds, washing the kitchen floor, waiting for the TV repair person, taking the toddler to the park, walking the dog, meeting older children after school, going to the doctor's office with her mother, planning a celebration for her mother-in-law's birthday, making calls for an upcoming PTA (Parent-Teacher Association) meeting, changing the cat litter, paying bills, or balancing her checkbook is not involved in productive work (Waring 1988).

One effect of the **gendered division of labor** in the home has been a similar distinction between women's and men's waged work. In the past forty-five years, some women have broken into professions and blue-collar jobs that were once the preserve of men, but most women work in day care centers, elder care facilities, garment factories, food processing, retail stores, restaurants, laundries, and other women's homes. Even professional work is gendered: elementary school teachers, social workers, nurses, and health care workers tend to be women. There is an emphasis on caring for and serving others in many women's jobs; some may also require being on display and meeting dominant beauty standards.

Debby Tewa, solar electrician for the Hopi Foundation.

Natasha Josefowitz listed stereotypical ways supervisors and coworkers judge women and men as workers (see Box). More than thirty years later, gendered double standards still apply. According to journalist Lisa Belkin (2007), women senior executives are advised: Take charge but don't get angry; Be nice but not too nice; Speak up but don't talk too much. She reported that women who focus on work relationships and express concern for other people's perspectives are considered less competent. However, if they behave in ways that are seen as more "male"—such as acting assertively, focusing on the task, or displaying ambition— they are seen as "too tough" and "unfeminine." Awareness of such bias is an essential step toward reframing perceptions and evaluations of women's work.

He Works, She Works, but What Different Impressions They Make

The family picture is on HIS desk:
Ah, a solid, responsible family man.

The family picture is on HER desk:
Hmm, her family will come before her career.

HIS desk is cluttered:
He's obviously a hard worker and busy man.

HER desk is cluttered:
She's obviously a disorganized scatterbrain.

HE'S talking with coworkers:
He must be discussing the latest deal.

SHE'S talking with coworkers:
She must be gossiping.

HE'S not at his desk:
He must be at a meeting.

SHE'S not at her desk:
She must be in the ladies' room.

HE'S having lunch with the boss:
He's on his way up.

SHE'S having lunch with the boss:
They must be having an affair.

HE'S getting married.
He'll get more settled.

SHE'S getting married:
She'll get pregnant and leave.

HE'S having a baby:
He'll need a raise.

SHE'S having a baby:
She'll cost the company in maternity benefits.

HE'S leaving for a better job:
He recognizes a good opportunity.

SHE'S leaving for a better job:
Women are undependable.

HE'S aggressive.

SHE'S pushy.

HE'S careful.

SHE'S picky.

HE loses his temper.

SHE'S bitchy.

HE'S depressed.

SHE'S moody.

HE follows through.

SHE doesn't know when to quit.

HE'S firm.

SHE'S stubborn.

HE makes wise judgments.

SHE reveals her prejudices.

HE is a man of the world.

SHE'S been around.

HE isn't afraid to say what he thinks.

SHE'S opinionated.

HE exercises authority.

SHE'S tyrannical.

HE'S discreet.

SHE'S secretive.

HE'S a stern taskmaster.

SHE'S difficult to work for.

Source: Natasha Josefowitz, 1980.

Balancing Home and Work

Despite the influx of relatively inexpensive consumer goods into the United States, especially clothing and electronic items from "global factories" around the world, it has become much harder for many U.S. families to make ends meet. Several factors have made it imperative that more and more women are income earners. Rents and housing payments, medical insurance, and the cost of college tuition, for example, have increased. Much manufacturing, such as car assembly work, which was relatively well paid and largely done by men, has been automated or moved out of the country, and, on average, men's wages have fallen. Almost 50 percent of divorced mothers with custody of their children are employed full time; 30 percent are employed part time. Many fathers (50 percent by some estimates) pay little or no child support (Grail 2009). In 2009, 60 percent of all U.S. working-age women were in the paid workforce (Bureau of Labor Statistics 2011). Juggling the conflicting demands of paid work and family responsibilities is a defining life experience for many women (see, e.g., Albrecht 2004; Barnett and Rivers 1996; Douglas and Michaels 2004; Folbre 2001; Hochschild 1989, 1997; Stone 2007; Williams 2000).

Adrienne Rich (1986b) argued that it is not motherhood itself that is oppressive to women but the way our society constructs motherhood. She advocated thinking of pregnancy and childbirth, a short-term condition, quite separately from child rearing, a much longer term responsibility. Psychologists Nancy Chodorow (1978) and Dorothy Dinnerstein (1976) both advocated shared parenting as essential to undermining rigid gender roles under which many men are cut off, practically and emotionally, from the organic and emotional concerns of children, thus, dissociated from life processes. Two decades later, sociologists Pepper Schwartz (1994) and Barbara Risman (1998) made similar arguments. A contemporary media image of a young mother with immaculate hair and makeup, wearing a chic business suit, briefcase in one hand and toddler in the other, may define an ideal for some young women. But it also sets a standard that is virtually unattainable without causing the mother to come apart at the seams—especially if she does not have a generous budget for convenience foods, restaurant meals, work clothes, dry cleaning, hairdressing, and child care. Despite contradictions and challenges, many women find great joy and affirmation in motherhood (see, e.g., Abbey and O'Reilly 1998; Blakely 1994; Gore and Lavendar 2001; Hays 1996; Jetter, Orlech, and Taylor 1997; Kline 1997; Meyers 2001). In the early 1990s, writer and editor Ariel Gore started the upbeat zine, *Hip Mama,* as her senior project in college; highlights from the first ten years provide hilarious and heart-wrenching essays "from the cutting edge of parenting" (Gore 2004; also see Kinser 2010; O'Reilly 2006, 2010; Sarah 2006). May Friedman and Shana Calixte (2009)

explore mommy blogging as a forum for sharing satisfations and frustrations of mothering (e.g., at www.blogher.com). In Reading 39, Carol Gill and Larry Voss describe their experiences of feminist parenting as people with disabilities.

The Second Shift

Most women employed outside the home still carry major responsibility for housework and raising children, what sociologist Arlie Hochschild (1989) called a **second shift.** Although this is particularly acute for single parents, many women living with men also do more housework and child care than their partners (see Bianchi et al. 2002; Mainardi 1992). Undoubtedly, this pattern varies among couples and perhaps also at different stages in their lives. Suzanne Bianchi and colleagues (2002) reported significant changes in the gender division of household labor since the 1960s, with men taking on more responsibility as a result of wives devoting more time to waged work, and "changed attitudes about what is expected, reasonable and fair for men to contribute to the maintenance of their home" (p. 184). Economists Jooyeoun Suh and Nancy Folbre estimated that, from 2003 to 2007, women spent an average of 4.5 hours a day doing housework and caring for children or elders, compared to men's 2.8 hours (cited in Albelda 2009. p. 36). With so many women in waged work, families rely more on take-out meals; they do less cleaning, and far less ironing than in the past. Affluent households hire other women as cleaners, nannies, maids, and caregivers for elderly relatives—which helps to free upper-middle-class women from much of the stress and time crunch of balancing home and work.

Caring for Children

For many families, child care is a major expense. For some women who want to do waged work, the cost of child care is prohibitive. Federal and state governments, employers, and labor unions offer some assistance in the form of tax credits to parents, grants to child care programs, on-site care, provisions for child care as part of a benefits package, flextime, and leave for family emergencies. Taken overall these provisions are woefully inadequate. It is particularly difficult to obtain child care for the hours before and after school and during

BABY BLUES

school vacations. Head Start programs, for example, which offer preschool education to low-income children, are usually available only for a half day and many children eligible for federal child care assistance do not get this support (Children's Defense Fund 2010).

Overall, 70 percent of U.S. mothers with children under 18 years of age are doing waged work. Black mothers are more likely to be in the paid workforce than white or Latina mothers. In 2010, 19 percent of families were maintained solely by women, with a wide disparity based on race: 45 percent of Black families, 25 percent of Latino families, 14 percent of white families, and 13 percent of Asian families were maintained by women (Bureau of Labor Statistics 2010, Table 2.).

Although parents may struggle to afford child care, child care workers are poorly paid and many have no health insurance or retirement benefits. On average, child care workers earn less than animal caretakers, parking lot attendants, or garbage collectors. Several scholars point to a "crisis of care" in the United States and other wealthy nations. High numbers of women from countries of the global South, such as the Dominican Republic, El Salvador, and the Philippines, are caring for children, elderly people, and sick people in the United States (see Brown 2011; Cancian et al. 2002; Ehrenreich and Hochschild 2003; Hondagneu-Sotelo 2001; Macdonald 2010; Parreñas 2001; Tuominen 2003; Uttal 2002). In Reading 46, Rhacel Salazar Parreñas analyzes the situation of children in the Philippines whose mothers are doing care work overseas.

Flextime, Part-Time Work, Home Working, and the Mommy Track

The labor market is still structured so that the best positions are reserved "for those adults who have someone on call to handle the life needs of an always-available worker" (Withorn 1999, p. 9). Many women need flexible work schedules so that they can look after children or aging parents. This may mean working jobs that allow some flextime, seeking part-time work, or working at home. Ann Withorn (1999), a professor of social policy, noted that part-time work is often a "devil's bargain," with low wages and no benefits. In 2009, 24 percent of employed women (aged 20 and older) worked part time (White House Council on Women and Girls 2011). Home working by telecommuting is touted for professional and corporate workers as a means to greater personal freedom and no stressful commute. For garment workers and child care providers, who account for the majority of home workers, the pay is poor and there are no benefits. Garment workers on piecework rates put in long hours; they are also isolated from one another, which makes it much more difficult to improve their pay through collective bargaining.

Another possible solution, first put forward in the 1980s, was that firms adopt a "mommy track." Professional women who wanted career advancement comparable to that of men either would not have children or would somehow combine family life with working long hours, attending out-of-town meetings, taking little vacation time, and generally doing whatever the job demanded.

Otherwise, they could "opt" for the mommy track and be recompensed accordingly. Law professor and legal scholar Joan Williams (2000) argued that professional women knew full well that this would mean being marginalized in their careers, and all but a few avoided the mommy track like the plague. Journalist and writer Ann Crittenden decided to leave her job at the *New York Times* for parenting and later calculated what this cost her in lost earnings (Reading 41). She estimated that, in her case, this discriminatory "mommy tax" amounted to "between $600,000 and $700,000, not counting the loss of a pension." She argues for new laws and policies to prevent discrimination against people with care-giving responsibilities as a way to improve a mother's lifetime earnings.

Women's Economic Security

The best-paid jobs for U.S. women are as lawyers, physicians, pharmacists, computer software engineers, and managers in many fields, but many more women earn the minimum wage or not much more. According to the Women of Color Policy Network (2011), on average, women who worked full time year round earned 77 cents for every dollar that men earned in 2010. This gap has slowly narrowed since passage of the Equal Pay Act in 1963 when women workers, on average, earned 59 cents for men's dollar. This is partly because women's wages have improved but more because men's wages have fallen. The U.S. Census Bureau reported the following average annual earnings for full-time workers for 2010:

	Earnings ($)	Wage Ratio
All women	36,931	
White women	40,270	77.6
Asian women	41,309	82.3
Black women	32,290	62.3
Latinas	27,992	54.0
All men	47,715	
White men	51,865	100
Asian men	51,838	99.9
Black men	36,803	70.9
Latinos	31,408	60.5

Source: U.S. Census Bureau, *Current Population Survey*, Labor Force Statistics 2010.

Education

The more education a woman has the more likely she is to be employed and the higher her earnings, as emphasized by Veronica Chambers (Reading 42) and Dorothy Allison (Reading 13). Women have made steady gains in educational attainment across all racial and ethnic groups; nowadays more women than men enroll in undergraduate and graduate programs, as well as adult education courses. However, the male-female pay gap persists at all educational levels. One factor in this is that most women graduates earn degrees in the humanities, arts, education, and health and welfare, whereas men are the majority in fields that command higher pay, especially engineering and information sciences (White House Council on Women and Girls 2011).

A lack of educational qualifications is a key obstacle for many women, particularly those on welfare who need greater educational opportunity if they are to acquire meaningful work at sustainable wage levels. Women receiving welfare used to be able to attend college, and many moved out of poverty as a result, including Congresswoman Barbara Lee who graduated from Mills College (Oakland). The 1996 Personal Responsibility and Work Opportunity Reconciliation Act only allows short-term vocational training or "job readiness education" as work activity, not preparation for professional work. Several scholars and activists have advocated for changes in this policy and for more academic institutions, community agencies, and foundations to provide academic, financial, and social support necessary for poor women's education (see, e.g., Adair 2004; Adair and Dahlberg 2003; Martinson and Strawn 2003; Marx 2002).

Women with disabilities generally have lower educational attainment than nondisabled women. They may have missed a lot of school as children or may not have been provided with relevant special education programs. Vocational schools and rehabilitation programs for women who suffer a disability after completing their education tend to channel them into dependent roles within the family or to low-paying "women's work." Researcher Mary Grimely Mason (2004) interviewed thirty women with disabilities. Her respondents spoke of the great satisfaction they experienced by being able to work and live independently, as well as the challenges they faced: the need to make special arrangements for transportation or home care, the prejudices and ignorance of employers and coworkers, and their frustration with having to prove they were capable of doing the job. She noted that women with a disability are likely to work part time, and their earnings are less than those of disabled men and nondisabled women. Lisa Schur (2004), professor of labor studies, argued that high schools and colleges need to assist young women with disabilities in making the transition from school to work; advocates and self-help organizations should offer employment counseling to help women with disabilities find jobs; and women with disabilities need to be actively involved in developing programs to improve their job prospects.

Even with a college education, however, and equivalent work experience and skills, professional women are far less likely than men to get to the top of their professions or corporations. They are halted by unseen structural barriers, such as men's negative attitudes to senior women and perceptions of their leadership abilities and styles, their motivation, training, and skills. This barrier has been called a **glass ceiling.** Women can see what the senior positions in their company look like, but few women reach them (Morrison et al. 1992). In 2010, women were roughly 14 percent of executive officers at Fortune 500 companies (Catalyst 2010). A related term, **sticky floor,** describes the structural limitations for women in low-paid, low-status jobs who cannot move up.

Organized Labor and Collective Action

Workers usually make significant gains in wage levels and working conditions when they are members of a labor union. In 2011, women union members in full-time work earned 26 percent more than non-union women; the differential was 24 percent for Asian women, 23 percent for African Americans, and 33 percent for Latinas (U.S. Department of Labor, Bureau of Labor Statistics 2012). Union workers are also more likely to have health and pension benefits. Currently, women are joining unions at a faster rate than men, particularly hotel workers (HERE), service employees (SEIU), garment workers (UNITE), public employees (AFSCME), and communication workers (CWA) (see Cobble 2007). The United Farm Workers of America, founded by Cesar Chavez and Dolores Huerta, has pressured growers to sign union contracts to improve the pay and working conditions of its members, many of whom are migrant workers and immigrants to the United States.

The majority of women in the U.S. workforce are not union members. This is partly due to the decline of unions nationally in recent decades. Also, many women work in jobs that are hard to unionize, such as retailing or the fast-food business, where they are scattered at separate locations. The nation's largest employer, Wal-Mart, is strongly anti-union. Wal-Mart's stringent cost cutting—of prices, wages, and operating costs—has become legendary and has redefined corporate practice, summed up in the phrase: the "Wal-Mart-ing" of the economy.

Domestic workers—nannies, housekeepers, and caregivers for the elderly—are generally not covered by labor laws and are specifically excluded from the National Labor Relations Act. This mostly female and immigrant domestic workforce is particularly vulnerable due to the isolated nature of their work, which takes place behind closed doors and out of the public eye. For several years the National Domestic Workers Alliance and affiliated groups have been organizing for respect, recognition, and fair labor standards. In 2010, the state of New York introduced the first Domestic Workers Bill of Rights, bringing domestic workers into line with workers in other industries. Under this new law, domestic workers are entitled to minimum wage or more, overtime pay, and meal breaks, regardless of their citizenship or immigration status. This campaign continues in other states with the goal of eliminating discrimination against domestic workers.

Working and Poor

Organized labor calls attention to low wages. Some advocates have campaigned for a "living wage" that reflects regional variations in the cost of living. Others use a "self-sufficiency standard" that "provides a measure of income needed to live at a basic level . . . without public or private assistance" (Women's Foundation 2002). More women than men make up the working poor, and women of color are more than twice as likely to be poor compared with white women. Policy researchers Peiyun She and Gina A. Livermore (2006) found that a majority of those in the working-age population who experience long-term poverty have a disability.

Many employers are reluctant to hire people with disabilities. But more than that, the economic system as a whole discriminates against them. It is constructed around the necessity for people to work, yet work is organized in an inflexible way that cannot accommodate many people with disabilities.

In public debate, poor people are usually assumed to be on welfare, masking the reality of life for many working poor people. Some people with very low incomes are working minimum-wage jobs; others work part time or seasonally. They may be involved in the informal economy as babysitters, or gardeners, for example, doing home work for the garment trade, fixing cars, carrying and selling small amounts of drugs, getting money for sex, selling roses at off ramps. Still others work in sweatshops, discussed in the next chapter, which are also unregulated in terms of wages, hours, and conditions of work.

Pensions, Disability Payments, and Welfare

For women who cannot work because of illness, age, or disability, and for those who are made redundant or who cannot leave their children, there is a complex patchwork of income-support measures and means-tested allowances provided by federal and state governments and private pension plans. Pensions are based on wage levels while the person was working and on the number of years in paid work. Women's pensions are significantly lower than those paid to men because, generally, women earn less than men, are more likely to work part time, and may move in and out of the workforce as they balance paid work with family responsibilities. Sixty-eight percent of women over 65 years of age rely on Social Security for 50 percent of their income or more (Hartmann 2012). For Black women and Latinas, Social Security income, though very modest, is their most common source of income (Institute for Women's Policy Research 2011). Social Security benefits are guaranteed for life, which is important because of women's longer life span. Income support for people with disabilities is designed with the needs of working men in mind. As a result, fewer women with disabilities can claim Social Security Disability Insurance (DI) and must rely on the Supplemental Security Income program (SSI), which is subject to a means test for eligibility and greater bureaucratic scrutiny.

Economic Inequalities

- As of 2007, the richest 1 percent of U.S. households owned 34 percent of the nation's wealth: real estate, bank deposits, stocks and bonds, life insurance, pension plans, mutual funds, equity in businesses, and trust funds. The bottom 80 percent owned 15 percent (Domhoff 2011, Table 1).

- In 2011, the richest 1 percent took home 24 percent of national income, compared to 9 percent in 1976—an increase of nearly 300 percent (Domhoff 2011).

- In 1980, 11.5 million children lived in poverty; in 2008, this had increased to 14.1 million. One in five children are poor; Black and Latino children are more than twice as likely to be poor as white children (Children's Defense Fund 2010, pp. x, xii).

- A federal minimum wage job paying $7.25 an hour for a full-time, year-round worker with two children provides a family income that is two-thirds of the federal poverty level for a four-person family (Children's Defense Fund 2010, p. xiii).

- The United States leads the world in Gross Domestic Product (GDP), billionaires, military technology, defense expenditures, and military exports but ranks highest among industrialized nations in child poverty and in the gap between rich and poor (Children's Defense Fund 2010, p. v).

- In 2008, the highest-paid CEO in the United States took home more than $100 million, an amount equal to the salaries of 2,028 elementary school teachers, or 3,827 Head Start teachers, or 5,275 child care workers. The average CEO of a *Fortune* 500 company earned 319 times as much as the average worker (Children's Defense Fund 2010, p.vi).

- The combined net worth of the 408 U.S. billionaires is $1.3493 trillion—greater than the combined GDP of 134 countries where more than 1 billion people live (Children's Defense Fund 2010, p.vi).

- The richest 20 percent of people worldwide consume 86 percent of everything that is sold for private consumption (Samath 2011).

Social Security and Social Security Disability Insurance allow individuals, considered to be "deserving," to draw from an insurance fund to which they have contributed during their working lives. Welfare payments, by contrast, are based on the concept of public assistance. In 1996, the federal government ended entitlements to assistance dating back to the 1935 Social Security Act and replaced them with grants to states for Temporary Assistance for Needy Families (TANF). TANF is a work-based program with lifetime limits and an emphasis on marriage incentive programs, as mentioned earlier. Women are required to spend up to 40 hours a week in "work experience." States have flexibility to provide other benefits, such as health care, transportation, or child care subsidies to cushion the transition from welfare to work. For employers, TANF has the advantage that—in place of wages—it is paid out of state funds.

Myths about welfare recipients abound in public discourse, stigmatizing those who need to rely on assistance. Women's Studies professor Gwendolyn Mink (2002) argued that single mothers are poor because their family caregiving work is not remunerated. Several welfare-rights organizations have redefined welfare as caregivers' income, including Every Mother Is a Working Mother Network, and Welfare Warriors (Wisconsin) (also see Nadasen 2005; Orleck 2005; Reese 2005).

TANF rates are too low to live on, which means that recipients have to supplement their welfare checks in some way. Not reporting additional income to the welfare office may make women liable for criminal charges for perjury or fraud. No one who is wanted by law enforcement officials for a felony or for violating the terms of parole or probation—which may be as little as missing a meeting—can receive any government benefits. Anyone found guilty of a drug-related felony is banned from receiving benefits for life. States can require drug tests, fingerprints, and photographs for those applying for benefits. Women who give birth to a child while on welfare are denied a financial increase despite the fact that they have another child to care for. Law professor Kaaryn Gustafson (2005) concluded that poor families are penalized through "completely inadequate levels of support, through public shaming, and through intrusive administrative forays into their personal lives that none but the truly needy would tolerate" (p. 2).

It is important to note that many people in this society receive some kind of government support, be it through income-tax deductions for homeowners, medical benefits for those in the military, tax breaks for corporations, agricultural subsidies to farmers, government bailouts to banks, or government funding for high-tech military-related research conducted by universities and private firms. This is often not mentioned in discussions of welfare, but it should be.

Feminist Approaches to Marriage, Family, and Work

Many feminist scholars, policy makers, and activists have argued for shared parental responsibility for child care, payment of child support, and redrawing the terms of divorce so that both post-divorce households would have the same standard of living. Feminists have campaigned for good-quality child care subsidized by government and employers, on-site at big workplaces, and they have organized community child care facilities and informal networks of parents who share child care. Although some of these efforts have been successful, there is still a great deal to be done if women are not to be penalized for having children.

Although policy makers and politicians often declare that children are the nation's future and greatest resource, parents are given little practical help in caring for them (see Box on page 319). Nearly twenty years ago, the editors of *Mothering* magazine pulled no punches when they asked:

> Why is the United States the only industrial democracy in the world that provides no universal pre- or postnatal care, no universal health coverage; . . . has no national standards for child care; makes no provision to encourage at-home care in the early years of life; . . . has no explicit family policies such as child allowances and housing subsidies for all families?
>
> *(Quoted in Brennan, Winklepleck, and MacNee 1994, p. 424)*

Most European countries have instituted family policies. In the United States, family policy is still an unfamiliar term, and the few policies that support families, like welfare, unemployment assistance, and tax relief, are inadequate and uncoordinated.

Pro-Family Policies for the United States

- Provide financial support for full-time child care.

- Create more jobs and stop assuming job-holders have a wife at home.

- Raise wages to a "living wage" level. Mandate equal pay for comparable work.

- Provide financial support to cover housing and health costs—the two major "family budget busters."

- Expand the safety net—through unemployment insurance, temporary disability insurance, or welfare payments.

- Provide affordable and accessible education and training for all.

- Promote community-based economic development.

- Introduce a fairer tax structure that benefits people in the lower tax brackets.

Source: Albelda and Tilly 1997, pp. 147–64.

Feminist researchers and policy analysts have long challenged inequities in pay between women and men. These inequities may be partly explained by differences in education, qualifications, and work experience, but part of this wage gap is simply attributable to gender. This has led to detailed discussion of the **comparable worth** of women's jobs when considered next to men's jobs requiring comparable levels of skill and knowledge. Advocates for comparable worth have urged employers to evaluate employees without regard to gender, race, or class, but in terms of knowledge and skills needed to perform the job, mental demands or decision making involved in the job, accountability or the degree of supervision involved, and working conditions, such as how physically safe the job is. Such calculations reveal many discrepancies in current rates of pay between women's work and men's work.

Also, feminist advocates have encouraged women to return to school to improve their educational qualifications, opposed sexual harassment on the job, exposed the dangers of occupational injury and the health hazards of toxic work environments, and argued for women in senior positions in all fields. Examples of such organizations include the Institute for Women's Policy Research (Washington, D.C.), the National Organization for Women (Washington, D.C.), and 9 to 5 National Organization of Working Women (with chapters in several states). Several organizations have worked to open up opportunities for women to enter well-paying trades such as carpentry and construction, including Hard Hatted Women (Cleveland, Ohio), Women in the Building Trades (Jamaica Plain, Mass.), Minnesota Women in the Trades, and Vermont Works for Women (Winooski Vt.). Many local groups help women to start small businesses, utilizing existing skills. The Women's Bean Project (Denver), Tierra Wools (Los Ojos, N. Mex.), and Four Winds Weavers (Winslow Ariz.) are group projects that promote self-sufficiency.

Feminist researchers have also pointed to the **feminization of poverty** (Abramovitz 1996; Dujon and Withorn 1996; Sidel 1996). The two poorest groups in the United States are women raising children alone and women over sixty-five living alone. *Poverty* is a complex term with economic, emotional, and cultural dimensions. One may be materially well-off but emotionally impoverished, for example, and vice versa. Poverty also needs to be thought about in the context of costs—for housing, food, transportation, health care, child care, and clothes needed to go to work—hence the value of a self-sufficiency standard. Poverty is also linked to social expectations of this materialist culture. Many poor children in the United States clamor for expensive name-brand clothing, for example, in response to high-pressure advertising campaigns.

Understanding Class Inequalities

Class is a key concept in any discussion of work, income, and economic security. For Marxist theorists, a person's class is defined in relation to economic production—whether she or he must work for a living. The vast majority of people in the United States are workers, but most describe themselves as "middle class," a loose term that includes a very wide range of incomes, occupations, life situations, and levels of personal and economic security. In much U.S. public debate, class is more of a psychological concept rather than an economic one. Poverty is often explained as resulting from low self-esteem, laziness, or dysfunctional families, as we pointed out in Chapter 2. In Reading 13, Dorothy Allison notes the power of class stratification, racism, and prejudice whereby

> some people begin to believe that the security of their families and community depends on the oppression of others. . . . It is a belief that dominates this culture: it is what made the poor whites of the South so determinedly racist and the middle class so contemptuous of the poor.

In Reading 42, writer Veronica Chambers reports on the contradictions and challenges Black women professionals face as they balance the benefits of college education and material success with a sense of responsibility to family networks and the wider Black community.

In U.S. public discourse on inequality, race is invariably emphasized at the expense of class. As mentioned in Chapter 5, government studies and census data are analyzed for racial differences, which gives the impression that race is much more significant than class. Intersectional analysis makes class one facet of a person's or group's social location along with many others. In practice, race and class overlap, but greater attention to economic sources of inequality may provide a basis for alliances between people of color and white people along class lines. There is currently no politically accepted way for most people to make a livelihood except by working for it, and in this society work, in addition to being an economic necessity, also carries a strong moral overtone. Note that this principle is not applied to those among the very rich who live on unearned income from corporate profits, investments, trust funds, or rents.

Toward a Redefinition of Home and Work

On the basis of the data we cite in this chapter, we argue that elevating the ideal of the nuclear, two-parent family is a major contradiction in contemporary U.S. society. Regardless of its form, we believe that the family should

> be able to care for family members emotionally and materially;

> promote egalitarian relationships among the adults, who should not abuse their power over children;

> share parenting between women and men so that it is not the province of either gender;

> do away with a gendered division of labor;

> teach children nonsexist, antiracist, and anti-classist attitudes and behavior and the values of caring and connectedness to others; and

> pass on cultural heritage.

Low educational attainment, low wages, having children, and divorce all work against women's economic security, as do macro-level economic trends, discussed in Reading 43. If current trends continue, many young people in the United States—especially young people of color—will never be in regular, full-time employment in their lives. Changes in the economy, which include the continued impact of globalization on the availability of work and wage rates in the United States, force us to confront some fundamental contradictions that affect women's work and the way work is thought about generally:

> What should count as work?

> Does the distinction between "productive" and "unproductive" work make sense?

> How should work be rewarded?

> How should those without paid work be supported?

> How can inequalities between haves and have-nots be justified?

> Is the work ethic useful?

> Is materialism the mark of success?

Years ago, pushed by the impact of the Great Depression, social commentators saw great potential for a much shorter working week promised by (then) new technologies like telephones, Dictaphones, and washing machines. The British philosopher Bertrand Russell (1935), for example, favored such "idleness" as an opportunity to become more fully human, to develop oneself in many dimensions of life. Recognizing that this could not happen if material living standards had to keep rising, he put forth a modest notion of what people "need." He also understood that these kinds of changes would require political imagination and will if people were to be freed from unnecessary work. Three generations later, the pace and scale of production and consumption of goods and services is unprecedented, and time has been redefined in market terms so that "all time and everyone's time is money" (Albrecht 2004, p. 129).

We discuss further implications of this reality in the following chapter, and again in Chapter 11, where we consider the environmental effects of current consumption patterns, and the ecofeminist argument that a sustainable future must be geared to biological rather than market time.

◆◆◆

Questions for Reflection

As you read and discuss this chapter, think about these questions:

1. What do you expect/hope for in an intimate relationship?

2. How do you define family? Whom do you consider your family?

3. What is at stake with regard to same-sex marriage? Where do you stand on this issue? Why?

4. What changes are necessary to involve more men in parenting? Look at the micro, meso, macro, and global levels of analysis.

5. What have you learned through working? About yourself? About other people's lives? About the wider society? How did you learn it? Who were your teachers?

6. What have you wanted to change in your work situations? What would it take to make these changes? What recourse do you have as a worker to improve your conditions of work?

7. How do you justify differences in pay?

◆◆◆

Finding Out More on the Web

1. Find out more about the Defense of Marriage Act (1996). What assumptions is it based on?

2. Find out about family policies in western European countries (especially Denmark, Germany, the Netherlands, and Sweden). Why do you think these countries provide better supports for families than the United States?

3. Consult these Web sites for more information on the wage gap, poverty levels, and family and welfare policies in your state and nationally:

   9 to 5 National Association of Working Women: www.9to5.org

   Children's Defense Fund: www.childrensdefense.org

   Coalition of Labor Union Women: www.cluw.org

   Institute for Women's Policy Research: www.iwpr.org

   Moms Rising: www.momsrising.org

   National Jobs for All Coalition: www.njfac.org

   Economic Success Clearinghouse: www.financeproject.org

4. Find out to what extent women's and men's economic security has changed since the Economic Security Survey undertaken by Jeff Hayes and Heidi Hartmann (Reading 43).

5. Compare the very low amounts the government spends on welfare with other federal expenditures. See:

    National Priorities Project: www.nationalpriorities.org

    War Resisters League: www.warresisters.org/federalpiechart

◆◆◆

Taking Action

1. Talk with your peers about your non-negotiables in a personal relationship. What are you willing to compromise on, if anything? Why?

2. Draw up a detailed budget of your needs, expenses, income, and savings. What did you learn by doing this?

3. Talk with your mother or grandmother (or women of their ages) about their experiences of marriage, parenting, family, and work. What opportunities did they have? What choices did they make? What similarities and differences do you notice between your own life and theirs at the same age?

4. Look critically at how magazines, ads, movies, and TV shows portray women in relationships and family and as workers. What is being promoted through these media?

THIRTY-EIGHT

Loving Across the Boundary (1995)

Ann Filemyr

Writer, teacher, and artist **Ann Filemyr** is the Dean of the Center for Arts and Cultural Studies at the Institute of American Indian Arts in Santa Fe, New Mexico. She publishes essays and poems and has been nominated twice for a Pushcart Prize in Poetry. Her latest collection is *The Healer's Diary.*

Nubian, our puppy, scratches and whines at the bedroom door. Essie sits bolt upright in bed crying out: "What time is it?" Groggy, I squint at the clock, "Almost seven—"

"Granny was supposed to wake us up at six!"

"Maybe she forgot—" I hustle into my bathrobe at the insistent scratching on the door, "I've got to let Nubi out—"

"Granny never forgets to wake us," Essie mutters under her breath as she scrambles out of the tangled sheets.

I race down the stairs, "Granny! GRANNY!"

I find her body on the cold kitchen floor, but she is gone. I can feel her spirit lifting up and out into the golden morning light filtering through the grand old maples that surround the farmhouse. Despite the utter peace in the room, I panic.

"Essie! Essie Carol!" I scream up the stairs to my partner.

Granny's breath is gone, but her body remains. A line from the book *Daughters of Copper Woman* circles through my mind, *"And she left her bag of bones on the beach. . . ."* Sun crowds the kitchen and the golden maple leaves gleam in October light. Essie flies barefoot across cold linoleum, cradling Granny in her arms, the first sob rising in our throats. . . .

Granny had made her bed that morning. She was dressed and ready for her Monday morning walk. But instead of the familiar stroll, Granny had traveled where we could not follow. We shared a long, sad look. Essie's face crumpled in pain. . . .

In the hospital emergency room we wept, our heads bent over Granny's body. Stroking back her wavy black hair (even at 79 her hair had not turned white) we sighed and pleaded. Two years earlier in ICU the doctors had told us she was gone. Her heart would not hold a steady beat. They pointed to the monitor above her unconscious body to show us the erratic yellow line, the uneven blip across the screen. Only the machines kept her breathing. We said no. It was her second heart failure in three months that winter of 1991, but we had plans for our shared lives— Granny, Essie and me. We were anticipating spring. . . .

Granny regained her strength that time. But that was March 1991 and this was October 1993. The doctor nodded to us and spoke with her strong Pakistani accent, "She looks happy. She had a long life. She would die one day." Then she left us alone, but the nurse on duty asked us a million questions about "the body"—about funeral arrangements—about donating organs—about contacting "the family"— we could not respond.

We *are* the family—an elder with her two granddaughters. This is our story of love, though now we are the body of women weeping. Granny was ours to care for, we had taken her into our daily lives because we loved her, and now she is sleeping, and we cannot wake her.

Skin color marked Essie as the one who belonged to Granny. The nurse nodded and smiled at me, "It's so nice of you to stand by your friend at a time like this."

Where else would I be? Granny was my grandmother, too. She loved me like no one else in my life: she loved me fiercely. She knew I had stepped across the line in North America which is drawn across the center of our faces to keep us separate— to keep the great grandchildren of slavekeepers from the great grandchildren of slaves. When she met me as Essie's "friend" twelve years earlier, she had watched me closely, but then she accepted me into her household and into her family. As the elder, her acceptance meant acceptance. She recognized my love for her granddaughter and would say to me, "People talk, but you hold your head up. You walk tall. The Lord sees what you're doing for my granddaughter, how you help her with her son. He sees how you stick together and help each other out." As far as Granny was concerned it was the *quality of our caring* not our sexuality that mattered. In this she was far wiser than most.

For the past three years we had lived together in Yellow Springs, sharing meals and dishes. She would sometimes pull out her old photo albums and tell her stories, laughing at memories of wild times out dancing with her friends in the juke joint or riding horses with her cousin on her father's ranch or traveling cross country in the rig with her husband and his magical black cat when he worked as a truckdriver. Rich, warm memories, and I would sip my coffee and imagine her days and nights. What sustained her? Love—no doubt. Love and greens and cornbread—good food. That's what she craved. And the kitchen was her favorite room next to her bedroom.

She had been raised in the fields and farms of the south. When I was deciding whether or not to take the job in Ohio, Granny was part of the decision-making process. Moving back to the country after four decades in the city felt like coming full circle to her. She said she wanted to come with us. And it was here in Ohio that Granny and I had the luxury of time together to make our own relationship to each other. She would talk to me about "the things white folks do—" how they tend to "put themselves first like they better than other folks—" how foolish they looked on the TV talk shows "tellin' all their business—" or how much she had enjoyed some of the white friends she and her husband once had.

She spoke her mind without embarrassment or apology. I listened. She had survived the jim crow laws of the south. She had survived segregation and desegregation. She kept a gun under her pillow she called "Ole Betsy" in case someone would try to break in or "mess with her." Granny paid attention to details as a matter of survival. She prided herself on the subtle things she observed in watching how people acted and how they treated one another. She would interpret everything: tone of voice, a simple gesture, the hunch of someone's shoulders. She always knew when someone felt sad or tired. You didn't have to say anything. She comforted. She sympathized. She was extremely skilled at making others feel loved, feel noticed, feel good about themselves. But if Essie had not been in my life it is doubtful that I would have ever known this remarkable woman, her namesake, Essie (Granny) Hall.

When I moved in with Essie in 1982, my nomadic tendencies were pulling at me, urging me to convince Essie that it was a perfect time for us to relocate to another city. I had lived in Milwaukee for two and a half years, for me that was long enough. I'd found a new love, an important someone in my life. It seemed like the perfect time to move on with my new partner. But Essie's life was described and defined by different currents. She had roots. She had family. She told me, "I will be here as long as Granny needs me." I was shocked. My feet carried me freely; I fought against family attachments. Was this difference cultural? Personal? Both? But now I have grown to respect and appreciate this way of being, this way of belonging. Is it a middle-class white cultural tendency to break free, to move on, to move up, to move out? Certainly the bonds of family and of commitment were far stronger for Essie than for me. One of the greatest gifts in my life has been that she shared her son and grandmother with me.

I wanted to tell the emergency room nurse all of this. I held Essie Carol in my arms as she cried. I wanted to scream, "Here we are, can't you see us? Lovers and partners holding each other in a time of crisis—What do you need for proof?". . .

Sunday mornings Granny listened to gospel preachers on her old radio, rocking and clapping to the music. When we weren't home, she'd get up and dance through the rooms of the house, tears flowing freely as she sang out loud. We'd catch her and tease her. Once Granny hung a plastic Jesus in the bathroom; he had his hands folded in prayer and flowing blonde locks thrown back over his shoulders. Essie groaned, "A white man on the bathroom wall!" She took it down and tried to explain to Granny everybody did not worship the same way she did.

We were not only a multiracial household, but one that held different spiritual beliefs. Essie followed a path she had first been introduced to by Granny's mother, her great-grandmother, Caroline Kelly Wright, affectionately known as Ma. Ma wore her hair in long braids and had been called "the little Indian" most of her life. She had married a freed African slave, but she herself was Blackfoot. Ma smoked a pipe and prayed to the sun. Essie remembered as a child the whole family would gather in Ma's bedroom facing East. The dawn's pale light would begin to appear through the open window only a few city blocks from the enormous freshwater ocean called Lake Michigan. Everyone listened as Ma prayed aloud over the family, telling all secrets, opening up all stories, praying to Creator to provide answers, to help guide them to find their purpose in life and hold to it, to be strong. Everything was said on these Sunday mornings and tears fell as Ma blew her smoke toward the light of the rising sun.

Ma had delivered Essie during a wild January blizzard. Ma was a midwife, herbalist, neighborhood dream interpreter, the community sage and soothsayer. If the term had been as popular then as it is now, Ma would have been honored as a shaman. Essie remembers the Baptist preacher visiting their house and saying to Ma, "I'll pray for you, Miz Caroline," and Ma responding, "You can't pray for me, but I can pray for you."

At the age of eight after a preacher had singled her out to stand up and read the Bible as a punishment for something she hadn't even done, Essie told her great-grandmother that she did not want to attend church anymore. Ma agreed. So Essie had little patience for Granny's Christianity. She was especially offended by refrains such as the "Good Master" and would try to point out to Granny how Black Christian faith was a result of slavery, the product of an enforced cultural genocide. Essie would try to "educate" Granny about the ways slaves were punished for trying to hold on to older beliefs, such as the care and worship of the ancestors or relating to land and nature as an expression of the Sacred. Of course this didn't work, and I would try to negotiate peace settlements between the two generations, between the two Essies, between the centuries, between the ancestors and the youth. Neither one of them really listened to me. I would take the younger Essie aside and tell her, "Leave Granny alone. You're not going to change her." And the younger Essie would retort, "But she's trying to change me!". . .

[A]t the funeral the man in the black suit did his best. He tried to save us. He opened the doors of the church and urged us to enter. He forgot about the corpse in the casket behind him, and he called the stray flock home. White men and Black men held each other in the back row. White women held Black women in the front row. And in between were all shades of brown and pink, young and old, from four-week-old Jade, the last baby Granny had blessed, to Mrs. Cooper, Granny's phone buddy. They had spoken every day on the phone for a year. Granny adored "Cooper" as she called her, though they had never met in person. Here we sat in rows before an open casket: all colors, ages, sexualities, brought together by a mutual love for an exceptional person. As some of Essie's family members called out urgently, encouraging the preacher with *Amen* and *Yes, Lord* others ignored the eulogy, attending to their own prayers.

At the funeral we sat side by side in the front row in dark blue dresses. Essie's sister and son sat on the other side of her. We wept and held each other's hands. If Granny loved us for who we were, then we weren't going to hide our feelings here. Certainly there were disapproving glances from some family members, but not all. During the decade we lived in Milwaukee, we had shared childcare and holidays, made it through illnesses and the deaths of other beloved family members—what else qualifies someone as family? Yet despite this, I knew there were those who despised my presence for what I represented was the alien. I was the lesbian, and I was white. For some my presence was an inexcusable reminder of Essie's betrayal. She had chosen to be different, and I was the visible reminder of her difference. For some this was a mockery of all they valued, but she did not belong to them so they could control her identity. Granny knew this, and Granny loved her because she had the strength to be herself.

My family is liberal Democrat, yet my mother once said to me that my choice to love other women would make my life more difficult. She wanted to discourage me from considering it. She said, *I would tell you the same thing if you told me you loved a Black man.* I was then nineteen. It struck me as curious that to love someone of the same sex was to violate the same taboo as to love someone across the color line. In the end I chose to do both. Does this make me a rebel? Certainly if my attraction was based initially on the outlaw quality of it, that thrill would not have been enough to sustain the trauma of crossing the color line in order to share love. The rebellious young woman that I may have been could not make sense of the other story, the story of her darker-skinned sister, without a willingness to question everything I had been raised to accept as "normal," without an active analysis of the politics of racial subjugation and institutionalized white male supremacy. And without personal determination, courage, a refusal to be shamed, a sheer stubbornness based on our assumption that our lives held unquestionable worth as women, as women together, as women of different colors together, despite the position of the dominant culture—and even at times the position of the women's community—to diminish and deny us, we would not have been able to make a life together.

I have participated in and been witness to a side of American life that I would never have glimpsed if Essie had not been my partner. The peculiar and systematic practice of racial division in this country has been brought into sharp focus through many painful but revealing experiences. By sharing our lives, our daily survival, our dreams and aspirations, I have been widened and deepened. It has made me much more conscious of the privileges of being white in a society rigidly structured by the artificiality of "race."

One of the first awakenings came near the beginning of our relationship when her son came home with a note from the school librarian that said, "Your overdue books will cost 45 cents in fines. Irresponsible handling of school property can lead to problems later including prison." I was shocked—threatening a nine-year-old boy with prison because of overdue books? I couldn't imagine what that librarian was thinking. Did she send these letters home with little white boys and girls? I wanted to call the school and confront her. Essie stopped me by telling me a number of equally horrifying stories about this school so we agreed to take Michael out.

We decided that Michael, who had been staying with Granny and Daddy Son and attending the school near their home during the week, should move in full-time with us. Essie worked first shift at the hospital, and I was a graduate student at the university. She left for work at 6 A.M., and I caught the North Avenue bus at 9:30. I would be able to help Michael get to school before I left for the day. We decided to enroll Michael in our neighborhood school.

The neighborhood we lived in was one of the few mixed neighborhoods in the city. It formed a border between the rundown urban center and the suburbs on the west side. The neighborhood school was across an invisible boundary, a line I did not see but would grow to understand. Somewhere between our house and this building, a distance of approximately six blocks, was a color line. A whites-only-no-Blacks-need-apply distinctly drawn and doggedly patrolled. We scheduled a visit with the principal, and when both of us appeared the next morning, we observed a curious reaction. Though polite, she was absolutely flustered. She could not determine who to direct her comments to. She looked from Essie's closely cropped black hair to my long loose wavy hair, from cream skin to chocolate skin, and stammered, "Who—who is the mother?"

"I am," said Essie.

"I'm sorry," was the reply. "We have already reached our quota of Black students in this school."

"Quota? We live in this neighborhood," I replied. "This is not a question of bussing a child in. He lives here."

She peered at the form we had filled out with our address on it. Then responded coldly, "We are full."

"That's ridiculous," I objected.

"Are you telling me that my child is not welcome to attend the fourth grade in your school?" Essie asked icily.

"We simply don't have room."

Essie stood up and walked out of the room without another word. I wanted to scream. I wanted to force the principal to change her mind, her politics, her preoccupation with the boundaries defined by color. I sat there staring at her. She refused to meet my eyes. I said slowly, "This will be reported to the Superintendent and to the school board," and walked out following Essie to the car.

We scheduled a meeting at the school administration to register a formal complaint and find Michael another school. I was furious. We were taxpayers. These are public schools. How can he be refused entrance? How can a child be denied because of some quota determined by an administrator somewhere? I was naive in matters of race.

I would have to say all white people are naive about the persistence of the color line. We prefer naiveté—in fact we insist on it. If we, as white people, actually faced the entrenched injustice of our socioeconomic system and our cultural arrogance, we might suffer tears, we might suffer the enormous weight of history, we might face the iceberg of guilt which is the underside of privilege. We might begin to glimpse our losses, our estrangement from others, our intense fear as the result of a social system that places us in the precarious position of the top. We might be moved to call out and protest the cruelty that passes for normal behavior in our daily lives, in our cities, and on our streets. . . .

Nothing in my life, my education, my reading, my upbringing, prepared me to straddle the color-line with Essie under the Reagan years in Milwaukee, a post-industrial city suffering economic decline and social collapse. The rigidly entrenched division of social power by race and the enormously draining limitations we faced on a daily basis began to tear at the fabric of our daily survival. I began to experience a kind of rage that left me feeling as sharp as broken glass. I was in this inner state when we finally arrived in the long quiet corridors of the central administration of Milwaukee Public Schools.

We were ushered into an office with a man in a suit sitting behind a desk. He could have been an insurance salesman, a loan officer, or any other briefcase-carrying decision-making tall white man in a position of power and control. We were two women of small build and modest dress, but we were carrying the larger presence—righteous anger. We sat down. I leaned across his desk and challenged him to explain to us why Michael had been refused admittance into the school of our choice. He back-pedaled. He avoided. He dodged. Essie suddenly said, "I am finished. I am taking my child out of school," and stood up.

I snapped my notebook closed, signaling the end of the conversation. The man had never asked me who I was. Did he assume I was a social worker? a family member? a friend? a lawyer? a journalist? Had it even crossed his mind that he was looking at a pair of lovers, at a family, at the two acting parents of this child? For the first time he looked worried, "I am sure we can find an appropriate school for your son. Tell me his interests. We'll place him in one of our specialty schools."

We hesitated.

"I'll personally handle his registration," he seemed to be pleading with us. He looked from Essie to me wondering who his appeal would reach first.

We settled on a school with a square of wild prairie, the environmental science specialty school. It was a half hour bus ride from our home. Michael liked the school, but we did not feel completely victorious. How could we? Though we had challenged the system, these policies and practices which place undue emphasis on the color of a child's skin had not been changed. The school system simply accommodated us, perhaps fearing our potential to cause widespread dissent by giving voice to the intense dissatisfaction of the African American community with the public school system.

We compromised—perhaps exhausted by the constant fight against feeling invisible and powerless. It was not just that Michael was Black. It was also that his family consisted of a white woman and a Black woman, and regardless of our commitment to him, we were not perceived as a valid family unit though we functioned as a family. . . .

It is heartbreaking to raise an African American boy in the U.S. From an early age he is taught that others fear him. He is taught that he is less than. He is taught that his future is defined by certain streets in certain neighborhoods, or that the only way out is through musical or athletic achievement. Michael played basketball and football. He wrote raps and performed them to the punctuated beat of electronic keyboards and drum machines. When it was fashionable, he would breakdance on the living-room floor. He had a few good years in school, but by and large school did not satisfy his quest for knowledge, nor did it provide him with creative avenues for self-expression. . . .

There were so many things I could not do for Michael. I could not clothe him in transparent skin to prevent him from being prejudged by color-conscious teachers who would label him inferior. I could not surround him with safety on the street corner where he waited for his school bus. One grisly morning in November he came home shaking. He and a small boy had been shot at while waiting on a familiar corner two blocks from the house. It was 7:30 A.M. While he was preparing to attend school, boys his age were shooting guns out of car windows hoping to kill somebody in order to get into a gang so they could make money.

On that gray morning, the capitalist notion of success as the acquisition of material wealth appeared for what it is: an absolute perversion of human dignity. Yet white American culture persists in holding material affluence as the highest symbol of achievement. The way this plays out in the lives of people of color and those who love them can be summed up in one word: cruelty. We suffer for a lack of basic resources because of the hoarding, the feverish consumerism, and the complete lack of concern by people who have more than they will ever possibly need. Fashion crimes, ganking [gang violence targeting rival gang members or other young people], children beating and killing other children to acquire the stingy symbols of status in a society devoid of real meaning—this is what

happens on the city streets of the richest nation in the world.

I could not keep Michael from the bullets. I could not move him out into the suburbs where another kind of violence would confront him daily, those who would question his presence and limit his right to move freely from one house to the next. I could not close his eyes to the terror he would see in his friends when death visited among them. I could not hold him against the rage he held inside. A rage that thundered through the house pulverizing everything in its path, terrifying me, tearing at his mother.

What could we say to him about how to live on the mean streets of a bully nation? We did not live on those same streets even though we lived in the same neighborhood. His experience, my experience, his mother's experience—we walked out of the front door into three separate worlds. Worlds we did not define or control except in how we would respond to them. Michael watched the hours I spent typing, writing, scratching out, rewriting. He watched the transformations his mother carried out with color on canvas, making lumps of cold clay into warm red altar bowls with her naked hands. He saw that we took our pain and rage, our grinding frustration and radiant hope, and made something out of it that gave us strength. Michael is still writing, making music, performing in his own music videos. He sees himself as an artist as we see ourselves; this is the thing that has carried us through.

The Westside where we bought a home had always been a working class neighborhood where people invested in their sturdy brick and wood frame houses planting roses in their green squares of grass. The neighborhood had been built in the teens and twenties by German immigrants who took a certain pride in quality. These homes had fireplaces and stained-glass windows, beautifully crafted built-in bookshelves and beveled mirrors. Only a few generations earlier, there was safety and prosperity here. Waves of immigrants—Greek, Polish, Hasidic Jews, African Americans coming North to work in the factories, shared these streets. I can remember walking into the corner bakery and the Greek woman behind the counter asked Essie and I if we were sisters. It was possible there at that time. Blood was shared. Love between the races happened. We laughed and nodded, "Yes—yes, we're sisters." In these moments we utterly and joyfully belonged together.

My friends who lived on the Eastside of the city rarely came to visit after I moved in with Essie. It was as if I had moved to the other side of the moon. . . . I trusted white women less and less as friends because they could not be counted on when things got tough. They tended to retreat. Race issues are ugly and hard, but if white women who want to fight male supremacy can't stand up to their own fears around the issue of color and simultaneously fight white supremacy, how can they really undertake the work of women's liberation? Certainly without an analysis and willingness to deal with race, there is no depth to the commitment. It is simply a get-ahead strategy for a particular middle class white female minority. Today I feel there is a greater commitment to address issues of racism within the feminist movement, but most of the voices I hear are still women of color. . . .

White women are conditioned to stay put, even rebellious daughters who love other women rarely cross the road that divides the races. Any woman who engages in a serious relationship—as friend or family, as lover, or mother to daughter—with a woman of a different shade of skin will find this relationship demanding a deeper vulnerability than any other as long as race relationships continue to be fraught with tension. But if we settle for a divided nation, we settle for social rigidity and police brutality, we settle for ignorance and stereotypes, we settle for emptiness and fear.

I am still learning how to confront racism when I see it, how to educate my friends without alienating them, how to ask for what I need in terms of support. It has been a rare occurrence, but a joyful one, for us to find other mixed-race lesbian couples. When we begin to talk about how difficult it is, we discover certain patterns and find solace that we are not alone. But why should we suffer for being ourselves and finding ourselves in the borderless culture between races, in the undefined space where wakefulness is necessary for survival, where honest communication and self-reflection must replace the simple recipes of romance. . . .

Few of us born in the Americas can trace our bloodline with impunity. So many of our ancestors have been erased or invented as need be. I know very few family names that have not gone without at least one attempt at revision—to anglicize

it—simplify it—discard the ethnic or cultural baggage of a *ski* or *stein* or other markers of race/ethnic identity. One who is raised as part of an unwanted people will shift the identity to become acceptable. Note the number of Chippewa and Menominee people in Wisconsin with French last names. One Chippewa man explained to me how in every neighborhood his family adopted another identity: Mexican when living on the Southside, French on the Eastside. Only back up on the reservation could they say aloud their true names. . . .

How many of us are of African descent? Slavery was challenged in part because of the enormous outcry against the "white slave children." Children of enslaved African women who were the result of forced sex with slavemasters ended up on the auction block. Some of these children looked just like the "free" children of "free" European-American mothers. Obviously there was a tremendous outcry resulting from the confusion that the rationale for chattel slavery was based on a strict hierarchy of skin color as the basis of privilege. How could they justify selling these children that by all appearances looked white even if the mother was a light-skinned African American slave? White men in the South parented children on both sides of the yard: women they took as wives, and women who worked the fields. The brown and pale children were half-brothers and half-sisters related by blood through the father. This simple truth was denied, and these children were taught to never consider themselves as one family. There is no doubt that many of us have relatives we never considered before. Part of my work has been beginning to claim these unnamed Ancestors as family.

The day after I wrote that paragraph, I visited my parents. It was a week before Christmas, and I was planning to spend the day with my two grandmothers and my parents. . . . While in my parents' home, I asked about an old photo album that I remembered from childhood. My mother commented that it had recently surfaced from the jumble of daily life and brought it into the kitchen. Tintypes and daguerreotypes, family photographs spanning 1850–1900. Fifty years of Walkers, my mother's father's family.

That night, back in the city, stretched across the guest bed at a friend's house, I slowly turned the pages. There are my Ancestors, among the first generation here from the British Isles. Aunt Mary and Uncle Tom Walker. By pulling the photographs out and inspecting the little leather and brass book, I discovered they settled in Clinton and Seaforth, Ontario. I knew these relatives had lived in Canada, but hadn't known they lived between Lakes Huron, Erie and Ontario! All of the faces were unfamiliar, stiff, caught in frozen poses over a century ago. A few of the photographs I remembered from my childhood, especially the sad-faced child in the unusual robe with straight cropped black hair and Asian eyes. For the first time it occurred to me that this could be the face of a native child—not European at all! Who is this child? Then a particularly striking face caught my attention. A young woman gazed confidently, intently, at what? Her hair hung around her wide face and high cheekbones in thick black ringlets, her full lips barely open, her strong chin—this is a woman of African descent. Who is she to me? She wore a gold hoop earring and a checkered bow over a satin dress. With one arm resting against an upholstered pillow, she posed proudly. Why had I never heard of her before?. . .

No one in my family seems to know much about these faces, these people, these lives, and how they relate to us. . . . If I am supposed to be a proud daughter of the colonizing English and the migrating Irish, why can't I also be a proud daughter of the Anishinabeg or Haudenausaunee, two of the indigenous peoples of this Great Lakes region, as well as a proud daughter of the African Diaspora? In America the idea of Europe was created, as if my English Ancestors weren't trying to dominate my Irish Ancestors. Why can't we talk about our truly diverse heritages? Nothing has been passed down in my family of these darker-skinned faces in my family's picture album. Is the refusal to see ourselves as something other than Northern European based in a fearful grasping after shreds of white-skinned privilege? What do we lose if we acknowledge our connection? What do we gain?

Granny kept a photo album. The pictures were important. Some were tattered and worn out, but they mattered. They held the faces of relatives—cousins, aunts, sisters—men in fine hats and women in silk dresses looking into the camera, into the future. In the album is a small square black and white snapshot of two plump white babies seated outdoors on a stuffed armchair. The Kelly boys. Irish. Part of the family. Essie remembers her great-grandmother telling her children, grandchildren and great-grandchildren, "These are your cousins." I bet those white boys don't show the dark faces of their cousins to their kin. . . .

The tight little boxes of identity defined by our society keep the building blocks of political and economic power in place. How can we gender-bend, race-cross, nature-bond, and love ourselves in our plurality enough to rebel against the deadening crush of conformity? Is it a crisis of the imagination which prevents us from extending compassion beyond the boundaries of limited personal experience to listen *and be moved to action* by stories of injustice others suffer. How can we extend the boundaries of our own identities so that they include "the other"? If we have any hope for the future of life, how can we expand our sense of self to include other people as well as beings in nature? The structure of our society is articulated by separation and difference. How do we challenge this by living according to a sense of connection not alienation?

For us, for Essie and I, the greatest challenge has been inventing ourselves as we went along for we could not find a path to follow. Where are our foremothers? Light and Dark women who held each other's hands through childbirth and child-raising? Who stood side by side and loved each other refusing to budge despite everybody's objections? Who pooled their measly resources together to make sure there was food and heat and light enough for everyone's needs? I want to know them. I want to hear their stories. I'll tell them mine. . . .

Despite the absence of role models, we share specific Ancestors, disembodied presences gliding through our lives like a sudden breeze teasing the candle flame on the altar; secret-keepers who come under guard of moonlight, carrying apple baskets full of fresh fruit which they drop into our sleeping; we wake up before dawn with the sweet taste on our lips of good dreams and lucky numbers. We have our shared Ancestors to thank, and we are fortunate to count Granny among them.

◆◆◆

THIRTY-NINE

Shattering Two Molds (1994)
Feminist Parents with Disabilities

Carol J. Gill and Larry A. Voss

A clinical and research psychologist, **Carol J. Gill** is the Director of Graduate Studies in Disabilities and an Associate Professor in the Department of Disability and Human Development at the University of Illinois (Chicago). She also directs the department's Chicago Center for Disability Research. She writes frequently on issues of disability culture, identity, health, and ethics for professional journals and the popular disability press.

Larry A. Voss is a researcher in the Department of Disability and Human Development at the University of Illinois (Chicago), engaged in research, training, and community service projects in the social sciences, emphasizing a disability studies approach.

We are two persons with extensive physical disabilities who have raised a nondisabled son. Countering the stereotype of people with disabilities as childlike, fragile, and suffering, we have nurtured and, we believe, nurtured powerfully. With wonder and relief, we have watched our child's development into a generous, emotionally open, strong, and socially responsible adult. It was not a snap. All three of us waged a long struggle against society's devaluation of human difference to get to this place.

Our war against ableist beliefs began in childhood when we acquired our disabilities in the 1950 polio epidemic. We used braces and wheelchairs and would have had little problem attending our neighborhood school if not for architecture and its real foundation: attitudes. In those days before the disability rights movement, we were barred from mainstream life. No ramps or elevators were installed to ensure our access. Instead, we were bussed miles each day to a "special" school with similarly displaced children.

Undoubtedly, these experiences laid the groundwork for our acceptance of a feminist perspective.

We acquired a deep suspicion of unequal treatment and stereotyping in any form. In high school, we identified with the civil rights struggle. In college, our rejection of sexism took definite shape. For Carol, the conscious decision to participate in the women's movement grew from classroom discussion of the work of Greer, Friedan, and Steinem. For Larry, it grew out of heated ideological debates between men and women in radical student collectives during the antiwar movement.

When Larry married a woman from this movement (his first marriage), he found daily life to be a mixture of new and traditional gender roles. During most of the marriage, his partner, who was not disabled, worked as an intensive care nurse while Larry completed his education. Although they shared household duties according to preferences as well as Larry's disability limitations, it was expected that his partner would cook and perform "housewife" chores after coming home from her job.

The decision to have a baby, on the other hand, was planned to be as joint a venture as possible. Larry remained by his wife's side during her prenatal exams and, long before it was accepted practice, he participated in the birth of his son in the hospital delivery room. He remembers this experience as ecstasy and agony—the incomparable joy of watching his child's birth and his sense of helpless horror as the emerging head made an audible tear in his wife's tissues. That painful moment registered clearly in Larry's consciousness—a factor, perhaps, in his later diligence in shouldering childcare duties.

Larry, in fact, became the primary parent. As is true of most children of disabled parents, Brian had little trouble adapting to his father's wheelchair and unconventional strategies for accomplishing daily tasks. When Larry's marriage foundered, he had no intention of parting with his son, then a toddler. Although it was rare for men to get custody of children in divorces, and even rarer for disabled persons, Larry fought to keep Brian with him and won.

Single parenthood was a rich and difficult time for them. Although Larry's sister and mother helped baby-sit, he experienced the loneliness and weight of responsibility that many single parents face. Additionally, there were unique physical and social difficulties. Unemployed and without child support, Larry could afford neither personal assistance nor adequate accessible housing. Consequently, errands such as grocery shopping became all-day feats of endurance. After driving home from the store, he would be forced to leave his wheelchair at the top of the stairs, crawl down the steps several times to his basement apartment and up again, hauling each bag of groceries followed by the baby, and then drag his wheelchair down the steps so he could get back into it and put groceries away!

Even more exhausting were the social hurdles. Strangers as well as family members challenged Larry's decision to keep his child, citing both gender- and disability-based concerns. Brian's first teachers suggested he was being shortchanged by not having a mother or nondisabled parent. (Brian's biological mother moved out of state and maintained very limited contact with him.) Neighborhood children teased or grilled him about his "wheelchair father" and asked why he had no mother. People who knew nothing about Larry's parenting skills would cluck over Brian's misfortune and tell him that having a "crippled daddy" was his cross to bear.

Although we—Carol and Larry—knew each other superficially while attending the same "special" high school, our paths did not cross again until a mutual friend brought us together at the time of Larry's divorce. After several years of intense and romantic friendship, we married.

At first, Brian was thrilled about Carol joining the family. Even before the wedding, which took place when he was seven, he insisted on calling her "Mom." But once it was official, he was ambivalent. Due both to her disability and her feminism, Brian's "new mother" was anything but the traditional nurturing figure people had told him he needed. She was physically incapable of performing many of the cooking and household chores mothers were supposed to do. She was not conventionally pretty. She was unexpectedly strong in communicating her ideas and affecting household decisions. She was even unwilling to change her name when she got married.

Not that Brian had been raised to be sexist. He had a father who baked cookies, cared for a home, brushed his lover's hair, and became an elementary school teacher. He also knew Larry's fondness for baseball, tools, and macho action movies. Father and son openly shared hugs and kisses between bouts of arm wrestling. Larry's philosophy of child-rearing, like his philosophy of education, stressed openness. He had always been pleased that Brian's early years were fairly non-sex-typed. He had let the toddler's strawberry blond hair grow to shoulder length undaunted by family predictions of gender confusion. He admired Brian's eclectic taste in toy trucks and stuffed animals as well as his drawings of kittens, nudes, Army tanks, Spiderman and posies.

But despite Larry's efforts to raise a child liberated from all the "isms," Brian was exposed to and affected by the sexism and ableism (not to mention racism, ethnocentrism, and heterosexism) of the surrounding culture. Dealing with this in addition to the typical tensions of stepparenting introduced a great deal of struggle into our family life.

It is hard for us to separate where our parenting was guided by feminism or by our experience and values as disabled persons. We believe in both notions of a women's culture and a disabled people's culture. Further, we believe the overlap of cultural values in the two communities is significant. Both feminist analysis and the disability independent living philosophy embrace values of interdependence, cooperative problem-solving, flexibility/adaptability, and the importance of relationships in contrast to traditional male values of autonomy, performance, competition, dominance, and acquisition.

By necessity, a guiding principle of our partnership has always been unfettered cooperation. There has been no "women's work" or "men's work." From the start, we negotiated most tasks of life by deciding who could do it, who was good at it, who wanted to do it, who had time, who needed help, etc. Larry's arm strength meant he had kitchen duty. Carol's greater physical limitations meant she organized the lists and schedules. In our professional jobs, we alternated being the major breadwinner. Everything from lovemaking to getting out of the car was an exercise in cooperation and respect—an orchestration of timing, assistance, and down-to-earth tolerance.

Our parenting was similarly orchestrated. As the only one who could drive, Larry did the carpooling. Carol's math acuity made her the homework authority. Larry did more of the "hands-on" parenting jobs: cuddling, restraining, washing, roughhousing. Carol nurtured by storytelling, instructing, reprimanding, discussing, and watching endlessly ("Mom, watch this!").

We both did an enormous amount of talking. Larry explained and lectured. Carol questioned motivations and articulated feelings. We even entered family counseling during several difficult times to talk some more. Reflecting back on it, we realize one of the central themes of all this talking was nurturance: caring for and being responsible for people, animals, plants, and the environment. Larry encouraged empathy in Brian through questions like "How do you think you would feel if that happened to you?" Carol nudged Brian to write notes and make gifts for family members. We gave him regular chores to do for the family and engaged him in many rescues of abandoned and injured stray animals.

Another major theme was prejudice and unfairness. Disability rights and women's rights were frequent topics in our household. Carol often directed Brian's attention to surrounding events, attitudes, and images that contributed to women's oppression, e.g., *Playboy,* sadistic images in rock videos, crude jokes. Most of the time, Brian would roll his eyes and protest that Carol could find sexism in anything. Larry usually backed her up but sometimes he lightened the tension by joining Brian in teasing Carol about her unwillingness to take her menfolk's last name. This was a family joke that ironically conveyed both affection and respect for Carol and got everyone to smile.

We also did a lot of the standard things most people do to raise a nonsexist son, from respecting his need to cry, to encouraging his interests and talents regardless of their traditional "gender appropriateness." Again, this lent a certain eclecticism to Brian's activities, which included sports, cooking, ceramics, drawing, music, reading, swimming and surfing, collecting, etc. On both feminist and pacifist grounds, we tried to avoid the most destructive "macho" stuff. For example, at his request, we enrolled Brian in a karate class. But when we discovered the instructor tested each boy's mettle by getting the class to take turns punching him in the stomach, Larry pronounced it barbaric and encouraged Brian to drop out, which he did. We also kept Brian out of formal team sports run by zealous competitive coaches and pressured him not to join the military when the gung-ho recruiters tried to nab him in high school.

Although we often held little hope that our battle against the "isms" was making an impact, like other parents, we now see that children do pay attention. Brian is now 22 and spontaneously uses words like "sexism" when critiquing the world. He is also our only relative who consistently uses Carol's proper name in introductions and addressing mail. He is comfortable in the friendship of both men and women. He loves sports and still hugs his childhood stuffed dog when he's sick. He has argued for the rights of women, people with disabilities, and other minorities.

Brian has shared his life for four years with a woman who also has strong goals and opinions. They have found a way to support each other, argue, and give space as needed. Like us, they are lover, companion, and family—equals. Seeing them interact is the great payoff to all our years of struggle. We enjoy watching our son laundering his partner's delicate sweaters or lovingly constructing her sandwiches. We listen to him express the depth of his feelings and respect for her. (Yes, he is a talker like his parents!) They have negotiated their course with cooperation, nurturance, and concern about unfairness. They want to have a family, they want to protect the earth.

When we told Brian about writing this piece, we asked his permission to tell the story of our family. He was enthusiastic and helped us reminisce about the past. One of his recollections confirmed how much he had been affected by the equity in his parents' relationship. He told us that sometimes as a child when he would answer the family telephone, callers would ask to speak to the "head of the house." Brian remembers his natural response to this request was to ask "Which one?" Then he and the caller would have a confusing discussion about which parent was needed on the phone. He said it was always simpler when only one of us was home because then the choice was clear: he would just summon whichever "head of the house" happened to be present!

◆◆◆

FORTY

Why Privilege Marriage? (2012)

Kaaryn Gustafson

Kaaryn Gustafson is a law professor at the University of Connecticut School of Law. Her research and writing focus on law and inequality and on the growing intersection between the welfare system and the criminal justice system.

During the 1970s, the U.S. women's movement sought gender equality in the workplace, the home, and among families—whether male-headed or not. In recent years, however, there has been an increased emphasis on marriage and fatherhood as solutions to concerns about changing gender roles, economic vulnerability, and the role of religion in society. This article examines three contemporary marriage-promotion movements: the religious-based "soft patriarchy" movement; the federally-funded Healthy Marriage and Fatherhood Initiatives; and the grassroots movement for government recognition of same-sex marriage. Despite the diversity of family forms in this country, there is a heavy emphasis on marriage as the legal basis for the family. I argue, however, that marriage promotion may undermine movements for gender and racial equality; reinforce economic inequality among families; and perpetuate the disparate and inferior treatment of individuals whose networks of mutual support do not revolve around state-sanctioned marriage.

A Brief Overview: Marriage, Non-Marriage, and Real Families

In this section I highlight the increasing diversity among U.S. households, despite the fact that notions of family continue to center around marriage.

Marriage and Divorce

In 2011, more than two-thirds of U.S. adults over the age of 15 were married or had been married in the past (U.S. Census Bureau 2011, tbl. A1). The likelihood of divorce or separation has increased over the last century and some conservatives cite the divorce rate as a fundamental justification for public policies promoting marriage. Barbara Whitehead, for example, identified family disruption—separation, divorce, and out-of-wedlock birth—as the "central cause of many of our most vexing social problems," namely "poverty, crime, and declining school performance" (1993, p. 47, 77).

The percentage of marriages that end within ten years varies by age at first marriage. More than 40 percent of women who marry in their teens divorce within ten years, compared to 24 percent of women who marry over the age of twenty-five (Bramlett and Mosher 2002). Karla Hackstaff (1999) argued that several factors have contributed to the rise in divorce rates, including women's increased economic independence. As a result of wider cultural, political, and economic shifts, marriage has become less focused on a contractual, lifelong commitment and more focused on personal aspirations for intimacy and happiness. Although the introduction of "no-fault" laws in the 1970s made divorce more accessible, Hackstaff argues that the statutes simply codified a phenomenon that was already occurring.

In addition, an increasing number of adults are living alone. In 2010, more than 31 million people in the United States (approximately 13 percent of the adult population) lived alone (U.S. Census Bureau 2011, tbl. H1), including a significant number of people over age sixty-five. If this trend continues, the number of adults living alone will increase as the baby boom generation ages.

Living arrangements tend to change throughout the life course. A shift from thinking about marriage as the centerpiece of a person's life to a limited period of a person's life might allow policymakers to address the diverse needs of people in various living arrangements.

Raising Children Within and Without Marriage

The percentage of children born to two-parent, married, heterosexual couples is declining while births to unmarried mothers has risen over the last three decades, with the non-marital birth rate reaching 41 percent in 2009 (Center for Disease Control 2011, pp. 1–2). However, the rise in non-marital childbearing between 1980 and 2000 was not primarily due to births to single mothers, but rather to births to cohabiting but unmarried partners (Bumpass and Lu 2000). This suggests that two-parent families are more common than marriage-centric statistics reflect.

Nonetheless, the percentage of one-parent families has increased greatly during the last thirty years. In the 1960s, social reformers pointed to Black families headed by women as the source of crime, poverty, unemployment, and general unrest in society. A widely cited 1965 U.S. Department of Labor report authored by Daniel Patrick Moynihan described Black mother-headed households as a "tangle of pathology" (U.S. Department of Labor 1965, pp. 29–30). Since then, concerns about Black family structures have remained a central issue for policymakers who have been slow to develop social policies, at least other than marriage promotion, that acknowledge and reflect overall changes in marriage and childbearing.

To view single parents as non-conforming is at odds with data showing the prevalence of single-parent families. However, it is taking a long time for many people to loosen their grip on the idea that children whose biological fathers are not legally married to their biological mothers are "illegitimate." For example, Charles Murray, a conservative social scientist influential in guiding the debates over the welfare reforms of the 1990s, argued that "illegitimacy is the single most important social problem of our time" and stressed the need to stigmatize single parenthood through social policy (1993, p. A14).

In reality, family forms are fluid and diverse, and caretaking roles are not always defined by heterosexual marriage. Children may grow up with a single parent, with cohabiting parents, or with married parents—and those parents may be of different sexes or the same sex. Children may also live with grandparents, or in a household of related kin. Children may grow up with step-parents or step-siblings. And increasingly, children move from one family structure to another during childhood. Those who design law and policy, however, have difficulty accepting this diversity of family forms.

Families Living in the Material World

Family life and engagement with the labor market are deeply intertwined—with waged work commonly influencing which activities are performed in the home, and by whom. Work life in the United States is still largely structured around presumptions that individuals in the workforce either have few caretaking obligations or that they can assign those caretaking functions to others, usually to spouses or caretaking professionals.

These presumptions play out in various ways. For example, many employers who provide health benefits only provide them to full-time, or near-full-time, employees. The Patient Protection and Affordable Health Care Act of 2010 mandates that large employers provide health insurance to full-time employees, leaving part-time employees or employees of smaller business with less protection. While limiting the number of employees who receive employer-provided health care may be in the interests of employers, for whom health insurance is an ever-increasing cost, these policies commonly mean that in a household where there are great caretaking demands (for young children or the elderly, for example), the entire household will go uninsured unless someone works full-time. Rarely do two-adult families have the option of both adults working part-time and sharing the caretaking responsibilities equally.

Many benefits, from employer-provided benefits to government benefits, take account of marital status, despite the variety in household composition and webs of economic interdependence.

Marriage Promotion: Programs and Ideals

Several cultural and political movements have emphasized marriage promotion through social policy and legal reforms. These movements are described briefly below.

The New Patriarchy

Over the last two decades, patriarchy has made an ideological comeback in the United States. During the mid-1990s, psychologists, religious leaders, and scholars declared a "masculinity crisis" (Levant 1997). According to this view, the economic successes of the women's movement had displaced men from their roles as "good providers," while men themselves were resistant to assuming the role of the "good family man." Despite differences among these cultural movements, they all represent efforts to empower men and to re-stabilize notions of masculinity (Newton 2004). They have influenced public debate about women's roles in the family, work, and society, and have similarly influenced social policies and government spending.

There have been several distinct men's movements over the last two decades or so. One effort, led by Robert Bly, included "Wildman Retreats" where men connected with other men to mourn the wildness they lost, as they became civilized men (Bly 2004). Another was marked by the Million Man March on October 17, 1995, when unprecedented numbers of African American men gathered in Washington, D.C. (Hicks 1995).

Some men's movement groups have focused on men's roles as husbands and fathers and have encouraged men to get married and stay married. These efforts are largely informed by the religious Right and by a small group of social scientists (e.g., Blankenhorn 1995; Popenoe 1996; Popenoe, Elshtain, and Blankenhorn 1996). Examples include the Fatherhood Responsibility Movement, epitomized by groups such as the Promise Keepers (Gavanas 2004). For several years the Promise Keepers held rallies in football stadiums where men vowed to eschew sexual promiscuity and intoxicating substances, and to commit themselves to their families (Levant 1997; Hardisty 2008). This Christian-centered men's movement has been recognized as a reaction to the women's movement and an effort by men to reinforce their masculinity and redefine their social and economic roles (Van Leeuwen 1997).

These movements tend to address anxieties about the status of men in U.S. society by fixating on their roles as fathers and husbands within heterosexual marriage. For some men this may be affirming; for others it may be stifling. Rather than interrogating existing gender norms and examining how both men and women might build networks of emotional and material security in a changing world, the men's movements are, for the most part, retreating to something known—patriarchy—and presenting it as something new.

Many religious-based marriage promotion activists specifically advocate patriarchal family structures, where there is a clear gendered division of wage work and household labor, and where men serve as authority figures in the family and women occupy subordinate roles (Wilcox 2004, p. 1). An unequal distribution of labor, however, also means an unequal gender distribution of opportunities should the marriage end.

Sociologist Bradford Wilcox (2004) has described the gender inequalities in conservative Protestant marriages, with an ideological commitment to male authority and men's active and expressive parenting, as "soft patriarchy." However, his study offered some interesting contradictions. He found that women in such marriages worked outside the home at about the same rate as women who held more liberal views (Wilcox 2004, p. 70). In addition, divorce rates were just as high in conservative Protestant marriages as in other families (Wilcox 2004, p. 70). Wilcox concluded that, "patriarchy is moving in the direction of being more symbolic than practical" (2004, p. 143), with the ideology of separate spheres and the belief in lifelong marriage stronger in rhetoric than in practice.

The calls to new patriarchs are often labeled "responsible fatherhood." The federal government, for example, established a website titled "National Responsible Fatherhood Clearinghouse" (www.fatherhood.gov). In many ways, this call for responsibility is a noble one. The Christian marriage movement has promoted therapy for married couples to address relationship problems, and churches make literature and relationship counseling available to their members. The attention many religious organizations are giving to what Wilcox called "emotion work" may be reconstructing old notions of masculinity on the individual level and encouraging men to become more engaged with their children. However, a truly new men's movement might explore responsible personhood and the scope of men's care, concern, and commitment more broadly, beyond a wife and biological children.

Government Sponsored Marriage Promotion and the Fatherhood Initiative

Marriage promotion has not only happened in the religious sphere; it also became a significant focus of federal and state policymaking over the last fifteen years or so, particularly in government aid programs for the poor. The goals of marriage-promotion policies were to encourage heterosexual marriage through financial incentives; to diminish non-marital childbearing and child rearing; to reduce government support to low-income families; and to increase the influence of faith-based organizations.

This marriage initiative was indirectly sparked by feminist efforts to address economic inequality between women and men by opening up the family, once considered the private sphere, to public intervention. Initial demands for women's equality, however, have been transformed into a government-led effort blaming unmarried, low-income parents for poverty. Moreover, the latest social welfare policy reforms have reduced cash resources for low-income women and their children while allocating funds to educate low-income families about the virtues of marriage.

Defining Poverty and Welfare as the Problems, and Marriage as the Cure   During the 1980s, feminist scholars drew attention to high poverty rates for women with children and demanded government action (Sidel 1992; Scott 1994). Some noted that other industrialized Western nations have lower marriage rates and higher divorce rates than the United States, yet lower rates of child poverty (Coontz and Folbre 2002; Smeeding 2004). Identifying and remedying the systemic causes of economic disadvantage is a difficult task that has been largely abandoned in this country. President Ronald Reagan quipped that we fought the war on poverty and "poverty won" (DeParle 1993, p. 3). Policymakers under President George H. W. Bush saw poverty as an insoluble problem and called for a withdrawal of government efforts to solve it. Poverty was no longer the problem; instead, out-of-control federal spending, the non-working poor, and "the fractured family" were the problems.

Marriage promotion began as a welfare program in Wisconsin in 1994, popularly known as Bridefare. Under this program, teenage welfare recipients who married were offered an increase in cash welfare benefits. Marriage became a centerpiece of federal welfare reforms during the Clinton Administration. The Personal Responsibility and Work Opportunity Reconciliation Act of 1996 listed the following Congressional findings as the first two findings of fact:

- Marriage is the foundation of a successful society.

- Marriage is an essential institution of a successful society which promotes the interests of children.

Although given the highest priority, these findings are not findings of proven fact. The first mention of poverty comes only in Finding (9), which highlights the lower rates of poverty among married couples with children compared to female-headed households with children. Rather than highlighting the high poverty rates for children—almost 20 percent of U.S. children lived in poverty at the time the bill was signed—or stressing the need to improve the economic circumstances for these children, legislators chose to focus on marriage and identify it as the way to address poverty.

The Personal Responsibility and Work Opportunity Reconciliation Act (PRWORA) amended the Social Security Act's provisions for Aid to Families with Dependent Children, a federal statute providing aid to needy families, most often single-parent families headed by women. PRWORA established Temporary Assistance for Needy Families (TANF), a new cash assistance program. TANF left the use and distribution of federal monies to state discretion, and established a multitude of requirements—and penalties for non-compliance—for low-income parents in need of government assistance.

Healthy Marriage and Fatherhood Initiatives   Marriage promotion became a priority under President George W. Bush, who appointed Wisconsin's Bridefare creator, Tommy Thompson, as U.S. Secretary of Health and Human Services. Wade Horn, one of the staunchest and most vocal government supporters of federally funded marriage formation policies, became Assistant Secretary at the Department of Health and Human Services (D.H.H.S.). Horn's position on these issues was not surprising given his service as a founding board member of Marriage Savers, a pro-marriage organization that advocated for increased government attention to marriage, and as founder and president of the National Fatherhood Initiative. Horn's nomination was opposed by women's organizations that objected to (among other things) his failure to support no-fault divorce and his statements that daughters raised by single mothers were more apt to be sexually promiscuous at a younger age (Taylor 2001). Also, conservative think tanks like the Brookings Institute and the Heritage Foundation were influential in shaping pro-marriage policies (e.g., Fagan 2001; McLanahan, Garfinkel, and Mincy 2001).

In 2000, the D.H.H.S. allocated $10 million to reward the ten states with the greatest increase in the proportion of children living in homes headed by a married couple. Wade Horn spent several years traveling around the country encouraging states to use their TANF dollars to promote marriage. Marriage promotion picked up steam in 2002–2003 when the D.H.H.S. devoted $90 million to marriage-related research and demonstration projects. In 2004, when George W. Bush was running for re-election, marriage promotion took center stage, where it not only appealed to conservative supporters who viewed the initiatives as a commitment to family values and faith-based funding, but also served as a counter to debates over same-sex marriage (Pear and Kirkpatrick 2004).

The Personal Responsibility and Work Opportunity Reconciliation Act requires periodic reauthorization by Congress. In 2006, Congress reauthorized the federal welfare reform legislation of 1996, and also appropriated an annual $150 million in federal money for five years to marriage promotion efforts. In 2010, Congress approved another $150 million per year for the next five years aimed at promoting marriage and responsible fatherhood.

Programs vary from state to state under these federal initiatives but all are designed to encourage heterosexual marriage and childbearing within marriage. Many are described as providing "marriage enhancement and marriage skills training." Much of the federal grant money allocated through the Healthy Marriage and Fatherhood Initiative has gone to faith-based organizations such as Catholic Charities, the Hebrew Immigrant Aid Society, the Lutheran Immigration Refugee Service, and Bethany Christian Services. The Healthy Marriage Initiative also targeted particular ethnic groups, specifically Asian and Pacific Islanders, African Americans, Hispanics, and Native Americans.

Some of the organizations that have received federal marriage promotion funding have also pushed for state legislative reforms. For example, Marriage Savers has promoted what it calls a "Community Marriage Policy," where local churches commit to provide pre-marital counseling, marital counseling, and step-family counseling in their communities. Marriage Savers has also sought to abolish no-fault divorce laws and replace them with mutual consent divorce in cases involving children. These reforms would not permit divorce unless both parties agree and would mandate joint custody of children.

Concerns About Government-Sponsored Marriage Promotion The federal marriage promotion programs serve a number of interests, but addressing poverty does not appear to be the central one. The Healthy Marriage and Fatherhood Initiatives have served as opportunities for the government to expand faith-based funding and for community service organizations, both faith-based and secular, to expand their funding streams. This has drawn criticism regarding the influence of religion in the development of pro-marriage policies and the fuzzy boundary between religion and politics when it comes to federal marriage-promotion funding (e.g., Hardisty 2008).

A surge of popular and academic publications has assumed causality between marriage and various family conditions and outcomes (e.g., Bennett 2001; Doherty et al. 2002; Gallagher and Waite 2000). Barbara Whitehead commented: "Family diversity in the form of increasing numbers of single-parent and stepparent families does not strengthen the social fabric. It weakens and undermines society, placing new burdens on schools, courts, prisons, and the welfare system" (1993, pp. 77–78). However, a number of scholars have questioned the arguments that single parenting is the cause of poverty and other poor outcomes for children. Martha Fineman has argued, "The problem with society is not that marriage is in trouble. The real crisis is that we expect marriage to be able to compensate for the inequality created by our other institutions" (2000, p. 554).

Indeed, research has shown that the relationship between poverty and family structure is complicated (Handler and Hasenfeld 2007). Some have found that people may choose to delay marriage based on individual circumstances, but not necessarily because they do not value commitment (Edin and Kefalas 2007). Advocates of the Healthy Marriage Initiative portray the issues as straightforward, if simplistic: introduce financial incentives for marriage and more poor people will marry and stay married; the more married families, the less poverty. But marrying is not always a simple choice or the best choice. And living in poverty is rarely a choice at all.

The Forgotten Issue of Family Poverty Marriage alone will not move women (or men) out of poverty. Pro-marriage proposals ignore the fact that the twenty-first century economy usually requires both parents in a two-parent family to be in waged work. The "family wage"—the pay that a man used to receive to support an entire family—is not available to many workers in today's service economy, particularly those with low levels of education.

While more households now include two wage earners than in decades past, even these families are struggling. According to the U.S. Census Bureau, nearly 3.6 million married-couple households lived in poverty in 2010 (DeNavas-Walt, Proctor, and Smith 2011, p. 16, tbl. 4). Parents receiving welfare, who tend to have lower than average levels of education and work experience, are, if they marry at all, likely to marry partners who are also low wage earners. If policymakers are concerned about family economic wellbeing, then they should ensure livable wages or public benefits, family leave, and health insurance for all individuals. Households with low-income workers, even those with two workers, are economically insecure.

It is not anti-family to propose a change in outlook, to revamp notions of family so that they align with the realities of family life. An estimated half of all U.S. children will grow up in a single-parent household for at least a portion of their childhoods (Clarke-Stewart et al. 2000). The majority of these children will reside with their mothers. The welfare reforms of 1996 brought dramatic reductions in the availability of cash assistance to families who are most economically vulnerable and established time limits on receipt of aid. Channeling government money away from cash assistance and supportive services, such as childcare, in favor of marriage promotion programs ignores the day-to-day challenges that most poor families with children face.

The Same-Sex Marriage Movement

At first glance it might seem strange to group the movement for same-sex marriage with the two movements described above. Indeed, many marriage promoters and soft patriarchy advocates are staunchly opposed to same-sex marriage. Their efforts to promote heterosexual marriage as "healthy" marriage are intended to insinuate that same-sex marriages are anything but healthy.

While demanding equality between heterosexual unions and same-sex unions, advocates of same-sex marriage have commonly been uncritical about some of their movement's goals and rhetoric. Note this idealized argument for same-sex marriage: "Marriage promotes stability for adults and children

and helps them all lead happier and more productive lives" (Strasser 2003, p. 33). One might think this means that the unmarried are unhappy and unproductive. This lack of critical engagement with the complex issues of family structure and social justice is not, of course, a universal approach by same-sex marriage promoters. Holmes Hummel, for example, connects the Defense of Marriage Act and welfare-based marriage promotion policies—both passed in 1996— as dual efforts to "reinforce the myth that the only valid family is one with a powerful man and a dependent wife and children" (in Shenker 2004). Yet, many activists have not openly acknowledged that the movement for same-sex marriage reinforces rather than dismantles the legal, social, and material reality that marriage is a privileged and exclusive institution.

The movement for same-sex marriages has had successes and failures. Massachusetts, Connecticut, Iowa, Vermont, New Hampshire, New York, Washington, and the District of Columbia have legalized same-sex marriage. In California, the courts are still analyzing the Constitutionality of Proposition 8, a voter referendum that amended the California constitution to recognize only unions between a man and a woman as marriage. Several states have recognized domestic partnerships among same-sex couples and afford these partnerships some or all of the rights of marriage. At the same time, more than half the states have passed statutes or amended their constitutions to define marriage as a partnership between a man and a woman.

Advocates for same-sex marriage have attempted to dismantle the divide between heterosexual unions and same-sex unions. They have danced an interesting tango with marriage-promotion advocates, following their lead in marriage promotion language. They have also reinforced the privileged status of marriage and the stigmatization of other family constructs. The Massachusetts Supreme Court decision legalizing same-sex marriage did not offer language valuing diverse family types, but instead reinforced the idea that marriage is sacrosanct. Chief Justice Margaret Marshall's opinion in the Massachusetts decision stated:

> Extending civil marriage to same-sex couples reinforces the importance of marriage to individuals and communities. That same-sex couples are willing to embrace marriage's solemn obligations of exclusivity, mutual support, and

commitment to one another is a testament to the enduring place of marriage in our laws and in the human spirit.

(Goodridge, 798 N.E.2d at 963*)*

From their own experiences, families with lesbian, gay, bisexual, or transgender (LGBT) members could be well placed to fight for the recognition of all families rather than just the recognition of marriage. LGBT families have commonly constructed families that transgress and transform notions of family and have often had to push the boundaries of legal categories and social norms to have their families recognized (Richman 2002). LGBT families may also dislodge assumptions about "natural" hierarchies within families and about bonds between children and non-biological versus biological parents. Surveying family research, for example, Stacey and Biblartz (2001) found non-biological lesbian parents to be more involved and skilled parents than stepfathers. Yet, much of the LGBT rights movement has been focused on marriage in the last few years, reinforcing conventional notions of family rather than envisioning alternatives.

Renewing Vows of Equality outside the Realm of Marriage

Should those who are concerned with meaningful equality be engaged in debates about marriage rights? The answer is not straightforward.

Some have argued that the government should not play a role in governing consensual relationships. Tamara Metz, for example, argues that the goals of care and equality "would be better served if the state withdrew from its current role of defining and conferring marital status" (2004, pp. 99–100). The alternative to marriage, she writes, would be civil unions and close attention to caregiving. Martha Fineman (1995) has argued that nuclear families are neither natural, nor private, nor economically independent, but are instead constructed and heavily subsidized by the state. She contends that a more just system would recognize families as relationships between caretaker(s) and dependent(s). This would protect the most vulnerable members of society rather than privileging heterosexual adults in intimate relationships. Government programs would then direct resources to promoting secure families rather than stable

marriages. Nancy Polikoff (2008) argues that if the legal status of marriage remains on the books, then it should be extended to same-sex partners; but she argues more broadly that the law should value all families equally—heterosexual and same-sex, married and un-married, with children and without. Laura Rosenbury (2007) has suggested that even Polikoff's view is too narrow. Rosenbury notes that marriage and parentage are recognized under the law, but that friendship, an increasingly salient form of interdependence, goes unrecognized by law. Further, Melissa Murray (2008) has highlighted the practical importance, and legal non-recognition, of kinship networks in U.S. families.

Those concerned about equality, economic justice, and the security and well-being of families should engage in the debates about marriage in ways that broaden the focus, challenge assumptions, and re-orient policies toward a renewed commitment to egalitarianism. Some modest steps toward this are described below.

Highlight the problems inherent in law's privileging of marriage

The 1967 majority opinion in *Loving v. Virginia,* concerning the right to interracial marriage, states: "Under our Constitution, the freedom to marry, or not marry, a person of another race resides with the individual and cannot be infringed by the State" (381 U.S. at 12). More recently, advocates have cited this statement frequently in arguments for same-sex marriage.

Supreme Court cases regarding marriage address situations where the government has attempted to place restrictions on persons trying to marry. The Court has not spoken directly to a person's desire *not* to enter into marriage. In other words, the desire to be a "libertine" has not been addressed as a liberty interest. In fact, the desire not to marry and yet to be treated with equal respect, dignity, and benefits under the law receives little credence under marriage promotion policies, particularly for low-income persons.

In many ways, marriage promotion does not square with widely shared and fundamental values of individual liberty, equality, privacy, economic security, and the pursuit of happiness. Pro-marriage initiatives suggest that public policy should guide very private choices. Such policies reinforce the notion that unmarried adults and single-parent families are inherently harmful to society, and that heterosexual two-parent families are superior. They perpetuate notions that the state should legitimately favor some families over others.

Put the focus on economic security

The marriage-promotion movements foster economic inequality in various ways. They not only distract attention from the larger issue of poverty but also divert government resources from programs that serve low-income families of all types. Second, the marriage promotion movements do little or nothing to address the rising number of married adults who live in poverty. Third, some marriage promotion efforts are part of a conservative effort to privatize economic vulnerability. Finally, marriage promotion fosters a divide between the married "haves" and the unmarried "have nots."

If this society were truly concerned about children, we would do more to support their material wellbeing, no matter the structures of their families. However, broad social commitment to children has been limited in this country. The United States is one of the few industrialized nations that do not provide parents with a government-sponsored child allowance. There are a number of reasons for this: the central place of the market in U.S. economic policy, historical distrust of government redistribution of wealth, a distrust of "others," and a fear that some parents would fail to spend government monies in ways that would directly benefit their children. Another fear is that government provision for children would undermine what is considered an already precarious role for fathers in modern family life. The United States does have an Earned Income Tax Credit designed to provide some government funding to low-income wage earners without providing the stigma of public assistance (Batchelder 2003). This tax credit, though, provides little help to the non-working poor or to families whose earnings fluctuate significantly from year to year.

Children's wellbeing is generally tied to the stability of their family circumstances. They tend to fare well in married households because two-parent, married families tend to be more economically stable than other types of families. And heterosexual married families are more economically stable, in part, because they hold a privileged position under the law.

Redefine the role of the state

Marriage promotion policies highlight several contentious and unresolved debates in political philosophy (Bernstein 2003). These include the separation of church and state, the role of government in private life, the acceptance or exclusion of "non-traditional" families, and the balance of state and federal power where federal efforts to regulate marriage contravene a long-standing tradition that issues of marriage are properly left to the states.

While conservatives have urged deregulation in the economic sphere, they have urged increased regulation of the private sphere. The current period of economic crisis is due in large part to unregulated financial risk among businesses. Jacob Hacker (2006) has illustrated how the privatization of economic risk has produced both economic insecurity for families and increasing inequality among families. The economic turbulence of the moment may offer an opportunity to introduce fresh ideas, especially as the government safety net has become increasingly threadbare.

Pro-marriage reformers repeatedly declare that marriage is the foundation of society. But as Andrew Cherlin (2004) has argued, marriage is becoming de-institutionalized in both the United States and other Western countries: it is becoming less prevalent; it is losing its normative force; and it is changing in both meaning and practice. It is time for those of us concerned about equality among families to release ourselves from the distracting and suffocating embrace of marriage and focus on deeper issues of equality.

NOTE

A longer version of this article appeared under the title "Breaking Vows" in the *Stanford Journal of Civil Rights & Civil Liberties*, October 2009. Thanks to Linda Burnham, Aimee Durfee, and Jean Hardisty who greatly influenced the content of that article. Thanks to Tovah Ross and Leslie Shanley for research assistance and to Jill Anderson, Mario Barnes, Jill Davies, and Melissa Murray for their thoughts and suggestions.

REFERENCES

Batchelder, Lily. 2003. Taxing the Poor: Income Averaging Reconsidered, 40 *Harv. J. on Legis.*

Bennett, William J. 2001.*The Broken Hearth.*

Bernstein, Anita. 2003. For and Against Marriage: A Revision, 102 *Mich. L. Rev.*

Blankenhorn, David. 1995. *Fatherless America.*

Bly, Robert. 2004. *Iron John.*

Bramlett, Matthew D. and William D. Mosher. 2002. *Vital Health Statistics. 23–22, Cohabitation, Marriage, Divorce, and Remarriage in the United States* 10 tbl. B. Department of Health and Human Services.

Bumpass, Larry and Hsien-Hen Lu, 2000. Trends in Cohabitation and Implications for Children's Family Contexts in the United States, 54 *Population Studies* 29, 35.

Centers for Disease Control and Prevention 2011. Births: Final Data for 2009. 60(1) National Vital Data Statistics Reports. Nov.

Clarke-Stewart, K. Alison, et al. 2000. Effects of parental separation and divorce on very young children, 14 *J. Fam. Psych.* 304, 305–308.

Cherlin, Andrew J. 2004. The Deinstitutionalization of American Marriage, 66 *J. Marriage & Fam.*

Coontz, Stephanie and Nancy Folbre. 2002. Marriage, Poverty, and Public Policy, *Am. Prospect Online*, Mar. 19. (www.prospect.org/cs/articles?article=marriage_poverty_and_public_policy#47)

DeNavas-Walt, Carmen, Bernadette D. Proctor, and Jessica C. Smith. 2011. Income, Poverty, and Health Insurance Coverage in the United States: 2010. U.S. Census Bureau, Current Population Rep.

DeParle, Jason. 1993. The Nation: Debris of Past Failures Impedes Poverty Policy, *N.Y. Times*, Nov. 7, B4, p. 3.

Doherty, William J., et al. 2002. *Why Marriage Matters: Twenty-one Conclusions from the Social Sciences.*

Edin, Kathryn and Maria Kefalas. 2007. *Promises I Can Keep: Why Poor Women Put Motherhood Before Marriage.*

Fagan, Patrick F. 2001. *Encouraging Marriage and Discouraging Divorce*, The Heritage Foundation Backgrounder, March 26.

Fineman, Martha. 1995. *The Neutered Mothers, the Sexual Family and Other Twentieth Century Tragedies.*

_____. 2000. The Family in Civil Society, 75 *Chi.-Kent L. Rev.*

_____. 2004. Why Marriage? in *Just Marriage*, edited by Mary Lyndon Shanley.

Gallagher, Maggie and Linda J. Waite. 2002. *The Case for Marriage: Why Married People Are Happier, Healthier, and Better Off Financially.*

Gavanas, Anna. 2004. *Fatherhood Politics in the United States: Masculinity, Sexuality, Race, and Marriage.*

Goodwin, Paula Y., William D. Mosher, and Anajani Chandra. 2010. Marriage and Cohabitation in the United States: A Statistical Portrait Based on Cycle 6 (2002) of the National Survey of Family Growth. U.S. Dept. of Health and Human Services. Feb.

Hacker, Jacob S. 2006. *The Great Risk Shift: The Assault on American Jobs, Families, Health Care and Retirement and How You Can Fight Back.*

Hackstaff, Karla B. 1999. *Marriage in a Culture of Divorce.*

Handler, Joel F., and Yeheskel Hasenfeld. 2007. *Blame Welfare, Ignore Poverty and Inequality.*

Hardisty, Jean. 2008. *Pushed to the Altar: The Right Wing Roots of Marriage Promotion.* Pol. Res. Assocs. & Women of Color Resource Ctr.

Hicks, Jonathan P. 1995. Answering the March's Call: More Community Involvement by Black Men, *N.Y. Times*, Dec. 29, at B1.

Levant, Ronald F. 1997. The Masculinity Crisis, 5 *J. Men's Stud.* 221.

McLanahan, Sara, Irwin Garfinkel, and Ronald B. Mincy, 2001. *Fragile Families, Welfare Reform, and Marriage, Welfare Reform & Beyond*, Brookings Inst., Policy Brief No. 10.

Metz, Tamara. 2004. Why We Should Disestablish Marriage, in *Just Marriage* edited by Mary Lyndon Shanley.

Murray, Charles. 1993. The Coming White Underclass, *Wall St. J.*, Oct. 29, at A14.

Murray, Melissa. 2008. Networked Family: Reframing the Legal Understanding of Caregiving and Caregivers, 94 *Va. L. Rev.*

Newton, Judith. 2004. *From Panthers to Promise Keepers.*

Pear, Robert and David D. Kirkpatrick. 2004. Bush Plans $1.5 Billion Drive for Promotion of Marriage, *N.Y. Times*, Jan. 14, at A1.

Polikoff, Nancy D. 2008. *Beyond (Straight and Gay) Marriage: Valuing All Families Under the Law.*

Popenoe, David. 1996. *Life Without Father.*

Popenoe, David, Jean Elshtain, and David Blankenhorn.1996. *Promises to Keep: Decline and Renewal of Marriage in America.*

Richman, Kimberly. 2002. Lovers, Legal Strangers, and Parents: Negotiating Parental and Sexual Identity in Family Law, 36 *L. & Soc'y Rev.*

Rosenbury, Laura A. 2007. Friends with Benefits? 106 *Mich. L. Rev.*

Scott, Hilda. 1984. *Working Your Way to the Bottom: The Feminization of Poverty.*

Shenker, Jill. 2004. Untying the Knots: Marriage Equality and the Struggle for Civil Rights, *Clamor*, Communique #49.

Sidel, Ruth. 1992. *Women and Children Last: The Plight of Poor Women in Affluent America.*

Smeeding, Timothy M. 2004. Twenty Years of Research on Income Inequality, Poverty, and Redistribution in the Developed World: Introduction and Overview, 2 *Socio-Economic Rev.*

Stacey, Judith and Timothy J. Biblarz. 2001. (How) Does the Sexual Orientation of Parents Matter? 66 *Am. Soc. Rev.*

Strasser, Mark. 2003. The State Interests in Recognizing Same-Sex Marriage, in *Marriage and Same-Sex Unions: A Debate* edited by Lynn D. Wardle et al.

Taylor, Sarah Stewart. 2001. Wade Horn Says in Senate Hearing He Was Wrong, *Women's eNews*, June 22 (www.womensenews.org/article.cfm/dyn/aid/590).

U.S. Census Bureau. 2011. America's Families and Living Arrangements: 2011 at http://www.census.gov/population/www/socdemo/hh-fam/cps2011.html

U.S. Census Bureau. 2009. *Statistical Abstract of the United States* 51 tbl.57 at http://www.census.gov/compendia/statab/2009edition.html

U.S. Department of Labor. 1965. *The Negro Family: The Case for National Action.* Office of Policy Planning and Research.

Van Leeuwen, Mary Stewart. 1997. Servanthood or Soft Patriarchy? A Christian Feminist Looks at the Promise Keepers Movement, 5 *J. Men's Stud.* 233.

Whitehead, Barbara Dafoe. 1993. Dan Quayle Was Right, *The Atlantic*, Apr.

Wilcox, W. Bradford. 2004. *Soft Patriarchs, New Men: How Christianity Shapes Fathers and Husbands.*

FORTY-ONE

The Mommy Tax (2001)

Ann Crittenden

Ann Crittenden was an economics reporter for the *New York Times* for eight years and nominated for a Pulitzer Prize. She also reported on economic issues for *Fortune* magazine and *Newsweek*. Her recent books include *The Price of Motherhood* and *If You've Raised Kids, You Can Manage Anything.*

On April 7, 1999, the Independent Women's Forum, a conservative antifeminist organization, held a news conference at the National Press Club in Washington, D.C. Displayed in the corner of the room was a large green "check," made out to feminists, for ninety-eight cents. The point being made was that American women now make ninety-eight cents to a man's dollar and have therefore achieved complete equality in the workplace.

The sheer nerve of this little exercise in misinformation was astonishing. Upon closer examination, it turned out that the women who earn almost as much as men are a rather narrow group: those who are between the ages of twenty-seven and thirty-three and who have never had children.[1] The Independent Women's Forum was comparing young childless women to men and declaring victory for all women, glossing over the real news: that mothers are the most disadvantaged people in the workplace. One could even say that motherhood is now the single greatest obstacle left in the path to economic equality for women.

For most companies, the ideal worker is "unencumbered," that is, free of all ties other than those to his job. Anyone who can't devote all his or her

What is the Value of Unpaid Labor?

1. Decide which non-market activities are work, e.g., cooking, cleaning, childcare, yard work, and repairs. If someone else could do these tasks they count as work.

2. Record how much time is spent on these activities.

3. Calculate the money value of that time.

   • Estimate what it would cost to hire someone to do all the jobs performed by a wife and mother—the "housekeeper wage" approach.

   • Estimate the cost of hiring different specialists for the various services, e.g., cleaners, cooks, childcare workers, etc.—the "specialist wage" approach.

   Both these methods underestimate the value of women's unpaid labor because they are based on the low wage rates for work traditionally done by women rather than the level of a middle manager or social worker.

   • Estimate the homemakers' "opportunity costs"—or the amount she would expect to earn outside the home. This gives much higher valuations for women who can command high rates of pay in the workforce.

Source: Crittenden (2001) pp. 79–80.

energies to paid work is barred from the best jobs and has a permanently lower lifetime income. Not coincidentally, almost all the people in that category happen to be mothers.

The reduced earnings of mothers are, in effect, a heavy personal tax levied on people who care for children, or for any other dependent family members. This levy, a "mommy tax," is easily greater than $1 million in the case of a college-educated woman.[2] For working-class women, there is increasing evidence both in the United States and worldwide that mothers' differential responsibility for children . . . is the most important factor disposing women to poverty.

. . . The much-publicized earnings gap between men and women narrowed dramatically in the 1980s and early 1990s. All a girl had to do was stay young and unencumbered. The sexual egalitarianism evident in so many television sit-coms, from *Friends* to *Seinfeld* to *Ally McBeal,* is rooted

in economic reality. Young women don't need a man to pay their bills or take them out, any more than men need a woman to iron their shirts or cook their dinner. Many childless women under the age of thirty-five firmly believe that all of the feminist battles have been won, and as far as they're concerned, they're largely right.

But once a woman has a baby, the egalitarian office party is over. I ought to know.

Million-Dollar Babies

After my son was born in 1982, I decided to leave the *New York Times* in order to have more time to be a mother. I recently calculated what that decision cost me financially.

I had worked full-time for approximately twenty years, eight of those at the *Times.* When I left, I had a yearly salary of roughly $50,000, augmented by speaking fees, freelance income, and journalism awards. Had I not had a child, I probably would have worked at least another fifteen years, maybe taking early retirement to pursue other interests. Under this scenario, I would have earned a pension, which I lost by leaving the paper before I had worked the requisite ten years to become vested. (The law has since changed to allow vesting after five years with one employer.)

My annual income after leaving the paper has averaged roughly $15,000, from part-time freelance writing. Very conservatively, I lost between $600,000 and $700,000, not counting the loss of a pension. Without quite realizing what I was doing, I took what I thought would be a relatively short break, assuming it would be easy to get back into journalism after a few years, or to earn a decent income from books and other projects. I was wrong. As it turned out, I sacrificed more than half of my expected lifetime earnings. And in the boom years of the stock market, that money invested in equities would have multiplied like kudzu. As a conservative estimate, it could have generated $50,000 or $60,000 a year in income for my old age.

At the time, I never sat down and made these economic calculations. I never even thought about money in connection with motherhood, or if I did, I assumed my husband would provide all we needed. And had I been asked to weigh my son's childhood against ten or fifteen more years at the *Times,*

So then the KNiGHT slew the drAGoN AND MArrieD the beAutiFuL princess AND they botH went to work For A MAJor LAW Firm AnD iN Addition to Her Job sHe HAD priMAry responsibility for the Housework, AND wHen the KiDs were Home sick sHe . . .

Does this story HAVe A HAPPY enDinG?

I doubt whether the monetary loss would have tipped the scales. But still, this seems a high price to pay for doing the right thing.

. . .

Those who care for elderly relatives also discover that their altruism will be heavily penalized. A small survey of individuals who provided informal, unpaid care for family members found that it cost them an average of $659,139 in lost wages, Social Security, and pension benefits over their lifetimes. The subjects reported having to pass up promotions and training opportunities, use up their sick days and vacations, reduce their workload to part-time, and in many cases even quit their paid jobs altogether. This exorbitant "caring tax" is being paid by an increasing number of people, three-quarters of them women.[3]

The mommy tax is obviously highest for well-educated, high-income individuals and lowest for poorly educated people who have less potential income to lose. All else being equal, the younger the mother, and the more children she has, the higher her tax will be, which explains why women are having fewer children, later in life, almost everywhere.

The tax is highest in the Anglo-Saxon countries, where mothers personally bear almost all the costs of caring, and lowest in France and Scandinavia, where paid maternity leaves and public preschools make it easier for mothers to provide care without sacrificing their income.

Most women never think about the mommy tax until they have an encounter with rude reality. Virginia Daley was an interior designer for Aetna Life & Casualty in Hartford, Connecticut. After almost ten years with the company, and consistently good performance reviews, raises, and promotions, Daley was fired in 1993 from her $46,640-a-year job. The dismissal occurred after she had had a baby and then tried to arrange a more flexible work week, in accordance with the company's stated policies.

Not only were her requests for flexibility denied, her workload was actually increased in the wake of a massive corporate downsizing. Already frustrated, Daley was furious to learn in late 1992 that Aetna's chairman Ronald Compton had been awarded a "Good Guy" award from the National Women's Political Caucus for his support of model family-leave programs. (Aetna also consistently made *Working Mother* magazine's annual list of best companies for employed mothers, and in 1992 was touted as one of the *four* "most family-friendly companies" in America by the Families and Work Institute.)

Daley dashed off a memo to Compton, charging that "when it comes to offering flexible family arrangements, Aetna's performance is far from award-winning." The memo concluded that "realistic options for Aetna employees to meet their family obligations without sacrificing their careers are not generally available today. To continue to represent to Aetna employees and the national media that these options are available is unconscionable."

Three months later Daley was terminated, on the grounds of poor performance.

She sued, and the case went to trial in 1997. Aetna maintained that Daley had lost her position because she wasn't able to handle the additional responsibilities that she was assigned after the downsizing (and the baby). The jury essentially agreed with Aetna. It also agreed with the company that Daley was not speaking out on a matter of public concern when she complained that numerous employees were being denied family-friendly schedules. Her memo to Compton was therefore not "protected speech," i.e., an important statement that entitles an employee to protection from retaliation. Daley lost the case, as well as subsequent appeal.

. . .

According to Daley's lawyer, Philip L. Steele, the jury foreman told him after the trial that although the panel was very sympathetic to Daley, its members felt she had probably "overextended" herself. "They believed it was just too hard for a woman to raise little kids and do a good job," Steele told me. "The thinking was, how can a woman do all that, not how could a company do that?"

The decision cost Daley dearly. She calculates that over the next five years following her departure from Aetna, her income as a part-time consultant was from $90,000 to $154,000 lower than if she had stayed at the company. And that doesn't include the loss of Aetna's annual contribution to her 401(K) retirement plan. "I figure that if I'd stayed at Aetna another ten years," Daley told me, "their contribution to my 401(K) alone would have been more than $25,000. That could easily become more than six figures by the time I am retirement age. . . . People need to know that once you have a child you'll definitely be poorer."[4]

The Cost of Being a Mother

A small group of mostly female academic economists has added another twist to the story. Their research reveals that working mothers not only earn less than men, but also less per hour than childless women, even after such differences as education and experience are factored out. . . .

. . .

. . . Jane Waldfogel at Columbia University . . . set out to assess the opportunity cost of motherhood by asking exactly how much of the dramatic wage gains made by women in the 1980s went to women without family responsibilities. How many of the female winners in the 1980s were people like Donna Shalala, Janet Reno, Elizabeth Dole, and Carole Bellamy, the director of UNICEF: childless women whose work patterns were indistinguishable from those of traditional males.

Back in the late 1970s, Waldfogel found, the difference between men's and women's pay was about the same for all women. Nonmothers earned only slightly higher wages. But over the next decade things changed.[5] By 1991, thirty-year-old American women without children were making 90 percent of men's wages, while comparable women with children were making only 70 percent. Even when Waldfogel factored out all the women's differences, the disparity in their incomes remained—something she dubbed the "family wage gap."[6]

Why do working mothers earn so much less than childless women? Academic researchers have worried over this question like a dog over a bone but haven't turned up a single, definitive answer.

Waldfogel argues that the failure of employers to provide paid maternity leaves is one factor that leads to the family wage gap in the United States. This country is one of only six nations in the world that does not require a paid leave. (The others are Australia, New Zealand, Lesotho, Swaziland, and Papua New Guinea.)[7] With no right to a paid leave, many American mothers who want to stay at home with a new baby simply quit their jobs, and this interruption in employment costs them dearly in terms of lost income. Research in Europe reveals that when paid maternity leaves were mandated, the percentage of women remaining employed rose, and women's wages were higher, unless the leaves lasted more than a few months.[8]

In the United States as well, women who are able to take formal paid maternity leave do not suffer the same setback in their wages as comparably placed women who do not have a right to such leaves. . . .

Paid leaves are so valuable because they don't seem to incur the same penalties that employers impose on even the briefest of unpaid career interruptions. A good example is the experience of the 1974 female graduates of the University of Michigan Law School. During their first fifteen years after law school, these women spent an average of only 3.3 months out of the workplace, compared with virtually no time out for their male classmates. More than one-quarter of the women had worked part-time, for an average of 10.1 months over the fifteen years, compared with virtually no part-time work among the men. While working full-time, the women put in only 10 percent fewer hours than full-time men, again not a dramatic difference.

But the penalties for these slight distinctions between the men's and women's work patterns were strikingly harsh. Fifteen years after graduation, the women's average earnings were not 10 percent lower, or even 20 percent lower, than the men's, but almost 40 percent lower. Fewer than one-fifth of the women in law firms who had worked part-time for more than six months had made partner in their firms, while more than four-fifths of the mothers with little or no part-time work had made partner.[9]

Another survey of almost 200 female M.B.A.s found that those who had taken an average of only 8.8 months out of the job market were less likely to reach upper-middle management and earned 17 percent less than comparable women who had never had a gap in their employment.[10]

Working-class women are also heavily penalized for job interruptions, although these are the very women who allegedly "choose" less demanding occupations that enable them to move in and out of the job market without undue wage penalties. The authors of one study concluded that the negative repercussions of taking a little time out of the labor force were still discernible after twenty years.[11] In blue-collar work, seniority decides who is eligible for better jobs, and who is "bumped" in the event of layoffs. Under current policies, many women lose their seniority forever if they interrupt their employment, as most mothers do.

Training programs, required for advancement, often take place after work, excluding the many mothers who can't find child care.[12]

Mandatory overtime is another handicap placed on blue-collar mothers. Some 45 percent of American workers reported in a recent survey that they had to work overtime with little or no notice.[13] . . . Where does that leave a woman who has to be home in time for dinner with the kids? Out of a promotion and maybe out of a job. Increasingly in today's driven workplace, whether she is blue- or white-collar, a woman who goes home when she is supposed to go home is going to endanger her economic well-being.

The fact that many mothers work part-time also explains some of the difference between mothers' and comparable women's hourly pay. About 65 percent of part-time workers are women, most of whom are mothers.[14] Employers are not required to offer part-time employees equal pay and benefits for equal work. As a result, nonstandard workers earn on average about 40 percent less an hour than full-time workers, and about half of that wage gap persists even for similar workers in similar jobs.

Many bosses privately believe that mothers who work part-time have a "recreational" attitude toward work, as one Maryland businessman assured me. Presumably, this belief makes it easier to justify their exploitation. But the working conditions they face don't sound very much like recreation. A recent survey by Catalyst, a research organization focused on women in business, found that more than half of the people who had switched to part-time jobs and lower pay reported that their workload stayed the same. Ten percent reported an increase in workload after their income had been reduced. Most of these people were mothers.[15]

Another factor in the family wage gap is the disproportionate number of mothers who operate their own small businesses, a route often taken by women who need flexibility during the child-rearing years. . . . In 1999, women owned 38 percent of all U.S. businesses, compared with only 5 percent in 1972, a remarkable increase that is frequently cited as evidence of women's economic success. One new mother noted that conversations at play groups "center as much on software and modems as they do on teething and ear infections."[16]

Less frequently mentioned is the fact that many of these women-owned businesses are little more than Mom-minus-Pop operations: one woman trying to earn some money on the side, or keep her career alive, during the years when her children have priority. Forty-five percent of women-owned businesses are home-based. And the more than one-third of businesses owned by women in 1996 generated only 16 percent of the sales of all U.S. businesses in that year.[17]

In 1997, although women were starting new businesses at twice the rate of men, they received only 2 percent of institutional venture capital, a principal source of financing for businesses with serious prospects for growth. Almost one-quarter of female business owners financed their operations the same way that they did their shopping: with their credit cards.[18]

Some researchers have suggested that mothers earn less than childless women because they are less productive. This may be true for some mothers who work at home and are subject to frequent interruptions, or for those who are exhausted from having to do most of the domestic chores, or distracted by creaky child-care arrangements. But the claim that mothers have lower productivity than other workers is controversial and unproven. . . .

It's Discrimination, Stupid

It is revealing that those occupations requiring nurturing skills, such as child care, social work, and nursing, are the most systematically underpaid, relative to their educational and skill demands.[19] These are also, of course, the occupations with the highest percentage of females. But men who are primary caregivers also pay a heavy price: a "daddy tax," if you will. This suggests that at least part of the huge tax on mothers' earnings is due to work rules and practices and habits of mind that discriminate against anyone, of either sex, who cannot perform like an "unencumbered" worker. In other words, discrimination against all good parents, male or female.

Surveys have found that wives may adore husbands who share the parenting experience, but employers distinctly do not. A majority of managers believe that part-time schedules and even brief parental leaves are inappropriate for men.[20] When Houston Oiler David Williams missed one Sunday game to be with his wife after the birth of their first child, he was docked $111,111.

A survey of 348 male managers at twenty Fortune 500 companies found that fathers from dual-career families put in an average of *two* fewer hours per week—or about 4 percent less—than men whose wives were at home. That was the only difference between the two groups of men. But the fathers with working wives, who presumably had a few more domestic responsibilities, earned almost 20 percent less. There it is again: a 20 percent family wage gap.[21]

"Face time still matters as much or more than productivity in many companies," Charles Rodgers, a management consultant in Boston, said. Rodgers told me about a man in a high-tech company who regularly came to work two hours early so that he could occasionally leave early for Little League games with his son. He was given a poor performance rating.[22]

. . .

How to Lower the Mommy Tax

Until now, narrowing the gender wage gap in the United States has depended almost entirely on what might be called the "be a man" strategy. Women are told to finish school, find a job, acquire skills, develop seniority, get tenure, make partner, and put children off until the very last minute. The longer a woman postpones family responsibilities, and the longer her "preparental" phase lasts, the higher her lifetime earnings will be.

Ambitious women of the baby-boom generation and younger have by and large tried to be a man in this way. A good example is Susan Pedersen, a historian who achieved tenure at Harvard in the mid-1990s. By that time, she was married and in her late thirties, but she had postponed having children until her academic career was secure. Motherhood was something she wanted very much, she commented during an interview, but it posed a serious threat to her professional dreams and had to be delayed.[23]

As Pedersen's success demonstrates, this strategy does work—for the very small number who are able to pull it off. And women who have their children later in life do have higher lifetime earnings and a wider range of opportunities than younger mothers. The advice dished out by writers like Danielle Crittenden—no relation—an antifeminist ideologue who has urged women to marry and

have their babies young, ignores this, along with some other hard truths. Crittenden never tells her readers that young parents tend to separate and divorce much more frequently than older couples, leaving young mothers and children vulnerable to poverty. Large numbers of the women who end up on welfare are there because they have done exactly what she recommends: married and had children young and then been left to support them alone.[24]

But trying to be a man has its own risks. Many baby-boomer women postponed families only to discover that when they wanted to become pregnant, it was too late. . . . And millions of women don't feel that being a man is the way they want to live their lives. . . .

An alternative strategy is followed in countries like France and Sweden, where the government, private employers, and/or husbands share much more of the costs of raising children. This makes it far easier for women to be mothers and to work. In France, for example, families with two preschool-age children receive about $10,000 worth of annual subsidies, including free health care and housing subsidies and excellent free preschools.[25] As a result, child poverty is unusual, and the pay gap between mothers and others is much smaller in France than in the United States. . . .

Whenever Europe is singled out as a model, the usual response is that Americans would never support such generous social policies. But in fact, the United States already does have an extremely generous social welfare state. But unlike the welfare states of western Europe, the American government doesn't protect mothers; it protects soldiers.

Men who postpone or interrupt civilian employment for military service pay a tax on their lifetime earnings that is quite comparable to the mommy tax. White men who were drafted during the Vietnam War, for example, were still earning approximately 15 percent less in the early 1980s than comparable nonveterans.[26] This "warrior wage gap" is strikingly similar to the family wage gap, again indicating that mothers' lower earnings are not entirely attributable to gender discrimination.

But there is unquestionable discrimination in the way the government has responded to the financial sacrifices that soldiers and parents, particularly mothers, make. . . .

To illustrate this double standard, let's look at two men with identical characteristics. One works as a computer technician, is married to a woman in the same occupation, and has two children. He is a conscientious father, making sure to be home for dinner every night, even helping to cook it. He takes his kids to sporting events, attends teacher conferences, and tries to limit his travel and outside commitments.

This man is legitimately worried about what his dedication to family will do to his career. Let's say he does get fewer promotions and over the years earns 15 to 20 percent less than he would have had he not shared the family obligations. We can realistically say that he pays a significant daddy tax.

Now take a man with the same education and imagine that he spends three or four years in military service. He is worried that these years out of his active professional life will affect his economic future, and they might, although his boss believes that his service was good leadership training. But whatever career losses he suffers will be cushioned by the generous thanks that the nation pays to its ex-servicemen. He discovers that his warrior tax is lowered by these benefits, which are available to him even if he never got near a battlefield:

- He can stay in the military for twenty years as a *part-time reservist* and draw half pay for the rest of his life.[27]

- He will get special preference for government jobs. Extra points will be added to whatever civil service exams he may take, and some rules are written so that he will be chosen over closely ranked nonveterans. In government layoffs, he will have extra protection. Unlike mothers or fathers who find that after a few years out of the job market their credentials are downgraded, his are given a major boost by veterans' preferences.

- If he decides to go back to school for more education, he can qualify for thirty-six months of cash payments worth more than $17,000.

- He also qualifies for a government-guaranteed housing loan, financed at interest rates usually half a percentage point below the going market rate.

- He can make use of a hospital system costing the federal government $17 billion a year.

- He will have access to special low auto insurance rates, available only to individuals with

some connection to the military. These come in especially handy when his teenage son begins to drive.

- As long as he remains in the military or works on a military base as a civilian, he can enjoy subsidized child care provided by the best daycare system in the country. For only $37 to $98 a week (in 1997), depending on his income, he can enroll his children in infant and toddler care and preschools staffed by expertly trained and licensed teachers. In the private sector, the fees would be two to four times higher, for often inferior care.

None of these benefits is contingent on service in combat. In 1990, 6.3 million of the 27 million veterans eligible for benefits served only during peacetime. Millions of ex-servicemen, who do not even have a hangnail to show for their harrowing experience in uniform, enjoy the same government largesse that flows to the veterans who were once put in the way of danger.

The benefits paid to military veterans are . . . second only to Social Security in terms of government payments to individuals. And they do an excellent job of reducing the warrior tax. The educational benefits in particular help veterans overcome many of the economic disadvantages they suffer by leaving the workplace for a few years.

A congressional study in the early 1990s concluded that the veterans of World War II who took advantage of the G.I. Bill to earn a college degree enjoyed incomes of up to 10 percent more than they might otherwise have earned. Society was also the beneficiary, for the additional taxes paid by the college-educated veterans during their working lives more than paid for the program.[28]

It hardly needs to be said that there is no G.I. Bill, no health care, no subsidized housing, and no job preferences for mothers. As things now stand, millions of women sacrifice their economic independence and risk economic disaster for the sake of raising a child. This says a lot about family values, the nation's priorities, and free riding.

A third way to reduce the mommy tax would be to expand the antidiscrimination laws to cover parents. Joan Williams, a law professor at American University's Washington College of Law, argues that the design of work around masculine norms can be reconceptualized as discrimination. As an example, Williams suggests that if a woman works full-time, with good job evaluations for a significant period, then switches to part-time because of family responsibilities and is paid less per hour than full-time employees doing similar work, she could claim discrimination under the Equal Pay Act. Williams believes that disparate-action suits could also be filed against employers whose policies (including routine and mandatory overtime, promotion tracks, resistance to part-time work) have a disparate impact on women, producing disproportionate numbers of men in top-level positions.[29]

The essential point is that existing laws, and new laws preventing discrimination against people with caregiving responsibilities, could go a very long way toward improving mothers' lifetime earnings.

The Ultimate Mommy Tax: Childlessness

The cost of children has become so high that many American women are not having children at all. One of the most striking findings of Claudia Goldin's survey of white female college graduates is their high degree of childlessness (28 percent). Now that the baby-boomer generation is middle-aged, it is clear that more than one-quarter of the educated women in that age group will never have children. Indeed, the percentage of all American women who remain childless is also steadily rising, from 8 to 9 percent in the 1950s to 10 percent in 1976 to 17.5 percent in the late 1990s.

Is this rising childlessness by choice? Goldin thinks not. She found that in 1978, while in their twenties, almost half of the college-educated boomers who would remain childless had said that they did want children. Goldin calculated that almost one-fifth of this entire generation (19 percent) of white college graduates was disappointed in not having a child. This is the ultimate price of the "be a man" strategy that has been forced on working women. For women in business, the price is staggering. A recent Catalyst survey of 1,600 M.B.A.s found that only about one-fifth of the women had children, compared with 70 percent of the men.

. . .

Americans have a hard time realizing that such deeply personal choices as when or whether to have a child can be powerfully circumscribed by broader social or economic factors. American women, in particular, are stunningly unaware that their "choices" between a career and a family are much more limited than those of women in many European countries, where policies are much more favorable to mothers and children.

. . .

In sum, an individual woman's decision whether to have a child or not, and whether to stay home or not, is heavily influenced by her country's willingness to help her bear the costs. In . . . the United States, the official message is *caveat mater*, or "mothers beware": you're on your own.

NOTES

1. This calculation was made by economist June O'Neill, using data from the National Longitudinal Survey of Youth. June O'Neill and Solomon Polachek, "Why the Gender Gap in Wages Narrowed in the 1980s," *Journal of Labor Economics* 11 (1993): 205–28.

2. The concept of the mommy tax was inspired by development economist Gita Sen, who has described the extra economic burden borne by women as a "reproduction tax."

3. The National Alliance for Caregivers estimates that the number of employed people who provide care for elderly family members will grow to 11 to 15.6 million in the first decade of the twenty-first century.

4. *Virginia V. Daley et al. v. Aetna Life & Casualty et al.*, August 12, 1994. Virginia Daley, personal communication, May 1996; Philip L. Steele, personal communication, October 2000.

5. Jane Waldfogel, "Women Working for Less: Family Status and Women's Pay in the US and UK," Malcolm Wiener Center for Social Policy Working Paper D-94-1, Harvard University, 1994.

6. Jane Waldfogel, "Understanding the 'Family Gap' in Pay for Women with Children," *Journal of Economic Perspectives* 12, no. 1 (winter 1998): 137–56.

7. Elizabeth Olson, "U.N. Surveys Paid Leave for Mothers," *New York Times*, February 16, 1998.

8. Christopher J. Ruhm, "The Economic Consequences of Parental Leave Mandates: Lessons from Europe," *Quarterly Journal of Economics* CXIII, no. 1 (1998): 285–317.

9. Wood, Corcoran, and Courant, "Pay Differentials," pp. 417–28.

10. This 1993 study was coauthored by Joy Schneer of Rider University's College of Business Administration and Frieda Reitman, professor emeritus at Pace University's Lubin School of Business.

11. Joyce Jacobsen and Arthur Levin, "The Effects of Intermittent Labor Force Attachment on Female Earnings," *Monthly Labor Review* 118, no. 9 (September 1995): 18.

12. For a good discussion of the obstacles to mothers' employment in relatively well-paying blue-collar work, see Williams, *Unbending Gender,* pp. 76–81.

13. This survey of 1,000 workers was conducted by researchers at the University of Connecticut and Rutgers University, and was reported in the *Wall Street Journal,* May 18, 1999.

14. A survey of more than 2,000 people in four large corporations found that 75 percent of the professionals working part-time were women who were doing so because of child-care obligations. Only 11 percent of the male managers surveyed expected to work part-time at some point in their careers, compared with 36 percent of women managers. *A New Approach to Flexibility: Managing the Work/Time Equation* (New York: Catalyst, 1997), pp. 25–26.

15. See Reed Abelson, "Part-Time Work for Some Adds Up to Full-Time Job," *New York Times,* November 2, 1998.

16. Tracy Thompson, "A War Inside Your Head," *Washington Post Magazine,* February 15, 1998, p. 29.

17. Information on women-owned businesses provided by the National Foundation for Women Business Owners in Washington, D.C., September 2000.

18. Noelle Knox, "Women Entrepreneurs Attract New Financing," *New York Times,* July 26, 1998.

19. See Paula England, George Farkas, Barbara Kilbourne, Kurt Beron, and Dorothea Weir, "Returns to Skill, Compensating Differentials, and Gender Bias: Effects of Occupational Characteristics on Wages of White Women and Men," *American Journal of Sociology* 100, no. 3 (November 1994): 689–719.

20. [One] study found that 63 percent of large employers thought it was inappropriate for a man to take *any* parental leave, and another 17 percent thought it unreasonable unless the leave was limited to two weeks or less. Martin H. Malin, "Fathers and Parental Leave," *Texas Law Review* 72 (1994): 1047, 1089; cited in Williams, *Unbending Gender,* p. 100.

21. This study, by Linda Stroh of Loyola University, was reported by Tamar Lewin, "Fathers Whose Wives Stay Home Earn More and Get Ahead, Studies Find," *New York Times,* October 12, 1994.

22. Charles Rodgers, personal communication, October 1993.

23. Susan Pedersen, personal interview, June 1996.

24. Being a young mother obviously worked for Crittenden, who was affluent enough to have purchased a $1.3-million home in Washington, D.C., while still in her midthirties. But not many mothers enjoy such options.

25. Barbara Bergmann, personal conversation, January 4, 1999.

26. Joshua D. Angrist, "Lifetime Earnings and the Vietnam Era Draft Lottery: Evidence from Social Security Administrative Records," *American Economic Review* 80, no. 3 (June 1990): 313–31.

27. The United States is the only country in the world that offers *full* retirement to military reservists. In 1993 the cost to taxpayers was $1.9 billion. See Congressional Budget Office, *Reducing the Deficit: Spending and Revenue Options,* Washington, D.C., 1995, p. 64.

28. David O'Neill, "Voucher Funding of Training Programs: Evidence from the G.I. Bill," *Journal of Human Resources* 12, no. 4 (fall 1977): 425–45; and Joshua D. Angrist, "The Effects of Veterans' Benefits on Education and Earnings," *Industrial and Labor Relations Review* 46, no. 4 (July 1993): 637–57.

29. Williams, *Unbending Gender,* pp. 101–10.

FORTY-TWO

◆◆◆

To Whom Much Is Given, Much Is Expected: Successful Women, Family, and Responsibility (2003)

Veronica Chambers

Former editor and writer at *Newsweek* and *New York Times Magazine,* **Veronica Chambers** is also a children's book author. Much of her work, including her awardwinning memoir *Mama's Girl* (1996), focuses on stories that reflect her African and Latina heritage. Other titles include *Having It All: Black Women and Success* and *Kickboxing Geishas: How Modern Japanese Women Are Changing Their Nation.*

"To whom much is given, much is expected" was both personal and political to young black women in the 1970s. At the time, Walteen Grady-Truely was getting her undergraduate degree at Michigan State University. She remembers two things distinctly: the culture of black nationalism that permeated her campus and the sense of marriage panic that hung over her heart. "As I reflect over the atmosphere of the 70s, my decisions were overlaid by the sense that the revolution was going to happen tomorrow and that you had to choose sides," says Walteen. "If you didn't make the right choice, you could hurt the whole black community. It wasn't like I could have the luxury of finding myself. I had to choose the right side of the battle lines. . . . "

For those women who came of age right after the civil rights movement, life was a mixture of often contradictory rules. You were supposed to say it loud about being black and proud, but to assert your independence with black men was counter-revolutionary. Education was a key component to uplifting the race, but as Stokely Carmichael so famously put it, "the black woman's place in the movement is prone." Black men could, and would, date white women without losing their place in the black power movement. Yet, black women who chose to date white men were nothing more than self-deluded, voluntary chattel, ignorant of 200 years of rape and slavery.

At six-feet tall, with a short salt-and-pepper afro, Walteen is now in her late 40s. At the time of our first conversation she's recruiting mentors for at-risk teens as the Director of the New York Volunteer for Youth Campaign. She radiates a strong, calming presence. As we sit and talk at a Thai restaurant near her New York City office, she is in the process of divorcing her husband of 15 years. Her smooth, dark skin is unlined, but there is a definite furrow across her brow. She has been taking a memoir-writing course, she tells me, and it has helped her as she tries to assess the choices that she has made in her life; there are pieces of her younger self that she misses and that she hopes to recover.

Walteen spent her teenage years traveling with her family; her father was in the military. She lived in Nigeria for four years, attended a Swiss boarding school for another year, then graduated from a high school in Bangkok. One of the memories that her writing course has brought up is that in Thailand, as a high school senior, she asked a white classmate to the Sadie Hawkins dance. Returning to the United States to go to school, she would never have considered such a possibility. "When I went to college, there was such a strong era of nationalism," she remembers. "I felt that I didn't have the right not to marry a black man. I felt I had a responsibility to have a black child."

"I didn't have the right." "I felt I had a responsibility." Those are powerful words to use when discussing one's personal life. How did she end up shouldering so much guilt? "It's guilt and responsibility," Walteen corrects me. "I think the two things are very much entwined. No one ever told me that I could be true to myself and still carry out that sense of responsibility." Yet she is hardly alone in her generation of women, who allowed the politics of the black power movement to dictate who and how she loved.

Guilt was also a factor in how Walteen chose her life's work. "Oh absolutely!" she says emphatically. "I believe it is what drove me in almost all my career choices. I chose to go into education. Before that, I wanted to be a lawyer. It was always with an eye towards creating a world where there would be more people like me, where there would be more people who shared a quality educational background, who had the advantage of having access to the whole world, not just the neighborhood."

This was a powerful notion for Walteen, who felt it was her life's work to bridge the gaps between the blacks who were haves and those who were have-nots. Growing up as a middle-class black girl, Walteen remembers complaining to her parents about her sense of isolation. "I didn't have any friends like me," she says. "I wasn't meeting people. My mother used to say, 'Well, I've been lonely all my life.' I guess she thought that was comforting, but it wasn't." Her mother's comments are clearly a painful memory for Walteen. During our most recent interview, she had moved back home to the Poconos where she's an instructor of education and coordinator for the Learning Support Center at the local Penn State campus. She moved so her son could be near his grandmother and attend better schools, but she worries that while he is now thriving academically, he's also suffering from the same loneliness she once did. "I don't think it's new," she says. "But there's a sense that if you're African American and on the cutting edge economically and educationally, there are not going to be other people like you. There are so few of us. I definitely have that feeling and my son has it, too."

Several years earlier, when she worked in Tribeca, she decided to register her son, Romare, at a nearby school. She knew it would be a marked improvement from the school he attended in their Fort Greene neighborhood. In an effort to ease the transition, she made it a point to continue Romare's play dates with his best friend, Rodney. The boys were both ten when Walteen overhead the following conversation. Rodney asked, "So what's your school like?" Romare said, "Oh, it's a school." Rodney paused, then asked, "Well, do you have gunshot holes in your windows?" It's a painful memory for Walteen, whose face, as she tells the story, displays a mixture of shame and hurt. "It just blew me away," she says. "It was almost as if we had to have a choice between having a community of black people and an environment that was very unsafe or having a safer environment physically and no community. It hurts me to see that repeated over and over again." Even in this day and age, a whole new generation of young people are being offered opportunities that aren't afforded the majority. As far as we have come, there is still a talented tenth—with all the weight of responsibility and guilt that comes along with it.

The Talented Tenth

In 1903, the great scholar W. E. B. DuBois published his masterwork, *The Souls of Black Folk*. DuBois's writing was an intellectual, improvisational pastiche of narrative fiction and social criticism, anthropology and state of the union address—it reads like highly developed literary jazz. In it, he famously declared "the problem of the 20th century is the problem of the color line." DuBois would be hailed as a visionary, again and again. His words resonated throughout almost all of the 20th century's great social struggles and tragedies. Whether it was the Turkish massacres of Armenians, the German slaughter of Jews, or the colonizers' ways with the colonized, it's remarkable how we've been driven again and again into war, massacre and upheaval by the power of racial difference. DuBois, who always meant his quote to address a far greater scale than racial politics in the United States, saw it coming.

DuBois's prophecy was marked not only by the eloquence of his words, but also by the breadth of his scope: what ambitious statesman—black or white—would look a hopeful people in the eye and tell them that racism would last not a decade or two, but 100 years? As bold as it was, his proclamation was hardly a news flash. Even Langston Hughes's fictional colored man on the corner, Jesse B. Semple, could have looked at the masses of sharecropping southerners and northern factory workers addled by poor working conditions and minimum pay and declared "Houston, we have a problem." Any uneducated black man or woman could have told you that Lincoln didn't solve the race problem as they cited the tyranny of hapless, random violence that was a constant threat to their lives. In those fragile years, as former slaves and their children tried to construct a place for themselves within the severe constraints of the northern-mandated freedom, *The Souls of Black Folk* could have been merely a preacher yapping at the choir.

DuBois, however, operated like a jazz musician. For the most part, his book wasn't aimed at black folks at all. Like other great race men and women before him, such as Frederick Douglass and Sojourner Truth, he sweetened the melody for the liberal white audience that he hoped would start swaying in beat to his cause. Yet he knew that blacks were listening and, in order not to lose their attention and support, he would sometimes curve a note in their direction. His theory of the Talented Tenth swung like that. DuBois's Tenth was the segment of the black community who had the wit, social skills and means to uplift the entire race. This Talented Tenth would be the leaders and architects of black achievement in America. Our shining glory.

From the beginning, the theory brewed controversy. At the turn of the century, the problem of entry into the upper echelons of black society was indeed the problem of the color line. Black elites monitored membership in the most prestigious black civic organizations, churches, fraternities and sororities with a paper bag test: anyone darker than a paper bag need not apply. Despite their own intraracism, these people considered themselves sanctioned by birth and skin color to lead the poorer black masses. They beamed with pride at DuBois's notion of the Talented Tenth because surely, they reasoned, he was talking about them.

Conversely, there were those who disagreed vehemently with DuBois. Some of them could care less about the colorism that plagued the black upper classes. These critics simply saw the idea of a Talented Tenth as being inherently divisive and problematic. How could we commit the wealth of our resources and energies to just one-tenth of our community? How could we be sure that once educated and anointed they would uplift our cause? And what happens, generation after generation, to those who are left behind? It's a question that black people struggle with to this day. Cheryl Mills, former deputy White House counsel and current Oxygen Media vice president, put it this way to Lynette Clemetson in a *Newsweek* article: "We're now getting to this place where we have the privilege to decide if we are all going to be on the same bus or whether or not we are going to get off the bus. I think the black community is finding itself now at this crossroads where it has to decide. Are we going to continue to be connected as a community or are the privilege levels and the progress we're seeing going to mean different things for different [people]?"[1]

Take, for example, an anecdote separated from the race issue altogether. Each year, a poor village has ten students that complete the modest lessons taught in its one-room schoolhouse. They pick one young man to continue his education in the big city. They pay for his schooling, his lodging, his expenses—everything, so he can focus on his studies and become a doctor. Obligation, and some might say guilt, would predicate that the young man returns to the village to open a practice, and perhaps one day, a hospital. But who's to say that the young man will? Maybe he will take a job at a research facility; maybe his destiny is not to cure colicky babies and ill farm animals, but to find the cure to some interminable disease. Maybe his aim or intention isn't even as noble as that. Maybe he takes a job with a big city hospital, gets rich and builds himself a big house. What happens to the village then? What good is their investment in the Talented Tenth? Maybe they should have sent two students to college, with partial scholarships each. Maybe they should have truly hedged their bets and sent three.

Shaking Off the Guilt: A Generational Shift

At 31, Angela Kyle feels much less anxious than Walteen Grady-Truely about finding a place in the black community. And she feels none of the guilt.

It's the gift that women of Walteen's generation have given to the women of mine: we have the luxury to find ourselves without worrying that our actions are, as Walteen phrased it, "hurting the whole black community." Angela and I meet at the Bel Age Hotel in Los Angeles; she lives nearby in Beverly Hills. Angela is tall and thin with the kind of All-American freshness of a J. Crew model. Today, she's wearing a close-fitting T-shirt, slacks and has a cardigan tied around her hips. Angela's chestnut-colored skin is flawless, without a hint of makeup, and she wears her shoulder-length hair in a fashionable bob. She's just finished her second day in her new job as senior director of business development at Live Planet—a company often in the news because of its two co-founders, Ben Affleck and Matt Damon. The heartthrobs want to bring together old media (film and television) with new media (the Internet) in intriguing, profitable ways.

It's a high-stakes gambit. Other Internet-related companies led by such visionaries as Steven Spielberg and Ron Howard blew through millions of dollars, then failed. Ben and Matt have Hollywood convinced they'll do better. Angela's an anomaly in the office; the executive suite is largely a good young boys' network from Boston and their early days as struggling actors in L.A. She's an Ivy League graduate, with business degrees from Columbia University and the London School of Economics. She's a young, black woman in a business that could care less about affirmative action or the Talented Tenth or diversity. She's at Live Planet for one reason alone—to make deals and making deals is what she loves.

Angela remembers that growing up, "I lived in a predominantly white neighborhood and went to a predominantly white school. In order to balance the whole white thing, I went to a black church." It's interesting to me that even Angela's language is more flippant, more casual, than Walteen's pained confessions. By the late 1970s and early 1980s, "the whole white thing" was not a big deal at all. "I was really active in church stuff so I had a group of black girls my age," she says. "Then at school, I had white female friends. I never really tried to bridge the two or bring them together, I was comfortable with them being separate."

Later, at Brown University, Angela felt none of the social or political pressures that Walteen experienced at Michigan State. At Brown, she joined a group called OUAP, the Organization of United African Peoples. But this was hardly her social center. "I wanted to be in OUAP," she says. "I wasn't really active, but I was at least present and accounted for." The desire to be simply "present and accounted for" is a seismic shift from Walteen's college years when she felt weighed down by her obligations to the movement. . . . In contrast, Angela describes her experience with black groups at Brown to being similar to the way her Asian friends felt about Asian-American organizations. "We were all aware of what was going on in our respective communities," she says. "But what drove my experience was meeting people that I had things in common with. I was pretty comfortable forging this network of friends that was racially mixed."

Similarly, when Angela talks about her career in business development, race hardly enters the conversation at all. She's not pressured to find a black husband, hasn't even begun to think about kids. "My thought is that right now I can't get married and I can't have kids," she says. "For me, the ultimate success as an adult is career success, getting to the top of something, winning awards. This is the arena in which I feel like I'm making my mark on the world. I know that I can't balance my life with family in any way, shape or form so I haven't really tried."

In Angela's conversation, there are hints of so many things, especially the luxury of young black women today to put career first. . . . There may be so much talk in the public sphere about successful black women and the dearth of highly educated, high-income earning male counterparts, but there seems to be little realization that for women like Angela, marriage and family aren't a priority. She doesn't know or care if there are "enough" black men out there. She's not really looking. It's not that she doesn't value her black girlfriends or that she isn't interested in black men. It's just that right now she's having too much fun and is way too ambitious to worry.

"My friend Suzie was here last weekend," Angela mentions. "She was saying that sometimes it stresses her out to be in a group of all black women. She says that no matter where the conversation starts, be it on the topic of work or family, it always ends on men and how everyone's looking and can't find one. Blah. Blah. Blah. It's not so much that the fantasy of a Prince Charming doesn't apply to me as a black woman. It's more that I'm a workaholic and I have other issues." And on that note, Angela gets up to leave. Her company is throwing a party to announce the winner of a screenplay competition they've been running. It will be one of her first opportunities to get face time with the heads of her company. With a wave, she is off—to gather intelligence, to meet and greet, to make deals.

Even though they live on different sides of the country, I know that Walteen would be proud of Angela. That in some ways, Angela's attitude is something she is striving for herself. Both women represent a vision of DuBois's Talented Tenth, but they embody it in radically different ways. The last time we met, Walteen said that what she has always admired about my generation is that "You've always represented for me the right to have stuff, the right to carve our own space and not just be the banner carrier for the race. You feel a right to be yourself. This is the next level of black liberation: the right to be ourselves, the right to define our own successes. In the '60s, I might have defined success as the right to fight for my people. That was the pinnacle. You are part of a group of women who are enjoying their lives. That's the next frontier."

Who Do We Owe?

If the civil rights act of 1964 was our economic emancipation, the open sesame to access to the education and jobs that would level the playing field, then it is a relatively recent freedom. One of the markers of the black middle class is that, for the most part, its members are still closely tied to those in real poverty. The women I interviewed spoke of their concern for the black community in general. But they could also each point to a sibling or a cousin or other relatives who were struggling.

To a certain extent, the problem of the villager who goes off to medical school and feels an obligation to his community is one these women can relate to easily. On a Saturday afternoon in Hoboken, I got together with a group of 30-something and 40-something women. The walls of Tracie Howard's living room were painted a warn golden hue that brought to mind the faded gilt of Renaissance Italy. The chandelier was a 1920s Art Deco find and framed photos of family and friends graced the surface of her baby grand piano. Paintings by prominent African-American artists hung on most walls, while a lighted breakfront displayed her collection of three-legged teacups from Limoges, Japan and Italy. In complete defiance of the old paper bag rule, the women were a rainbow mix from fair-skinned to very dark-skinned. All of them were members of the upper middle class and had ventured to Tracie's from their homes in New York City, Westchester and Greenwich, Connecticut.

The women talked animatedly about their passion for mentoring and community service. For them, it's more than doing a good deed. They see themselves in the young people that they are helping, they believe that their actions are improving the lot not of "poor black folks" but of "brothers and sisters." There's a big difference in the way these women speak about community service and the language their white society counterparts use. By doing good, they feel they are also "doing the right thing," as Spike Lee so aptly called it. Furthermore, their charitable efforts keep them in touch with a home they don't want to leave behind.

I probe a little deeper, and each woman admits that while community service is fulfilling, trying to meet the needs of poorer family members is almost always a losing battle. The women in their 40s have come to terms with the economic disparities in their own families. "No guilt," says one of the guests, an investment banker on Wall Street. Her simple declaration is followed by so many "Amens," the room is almost transformed into Sunday church. But these are women in their 40s, who've made the tough choices and don't take any mess off anyone. I found that among my peers, women in our 30s, there's not always the same confidence. We're not always sure that we don't owe the village every penny in our pockets.

Though I'm not a banker or Wall Street broker, my "Amen" was right here with the others. As the first person in my immediate family to graduate from college, I basked in the glow of achievement. I lived the dream deferred. A year after graduation, I was making more money than my mother was. My role as the family money store began. Siblings and other more distant relatives began to pull a guilt trip on me: I'd been "lucky" to get a scholarship, "lucky" to meet whites who mentored me and offered me jobs. They'd not been so lucky in life. Where they lived, life was hard—or had I forgotten?

Looking back, I could say that I was young and easily influenced. But I know that it was more than that. Despite the hefty student loan bill that I pay each month, I would not have been able to attend college at all had it not been for the largesse of a W. E. B. DuBois scholarship that handled a sizeable portion of my tuition every year. My school, Simon's Rock College, is in Great Barrington, Massachusetts: birth home of DuBois. My reading of *The Souls of Black Folk* at the age of 16 had a powerful impact on how I viewed race and its obligations. I would never have called myself part of the Talented Tenth, but I certainly took my place among its platoons of strivers.

When my summa cum laude degree was rewarded with one good job after another, I knew I had to give back. And as my family laid it out for me: charity begins at home. Throughout my 20s, I buckled under the guilt and pressure and gave out thousands of dollars in "loans" that could never, would never, be repaid. Even when lending money meant draining my savings account or giving away the next month's rent, I jumped at the desperate calls in the middle of the night and the wailing darkness of "I have nowhere else to turn." Like many professional black women, I'm hardly wealthy by mainstream American standards. But compared to the poverty of those I love so dearly, the fact that I even had next month's rent in the bank meant that I was rich. Absolutely loaded. "We have extended family who think we're Rockefellers," says Robin Nelson Rice, a former pharmaceutical company executive now living in London. "We're not even Rock, forget Rockefeller! But from their viewpoint, it's 'Oh yes. Somebody comes and cleans your house. I need that job. I could be that. You could pay me that money.' They're always calculating. 'Oh, the nanny. Do you hear that? They've got a nanny.'"

For Tarin Washington, a 32-year-old finance executive, earning an MBA roused the jealousy of old friends. As one male friend put it, "You think you're better than me because you're successful and moved out of the hood." It had been a bonanza year for Tarin: she'd recently completed her MBA and purchased a home in Connecticut as well as a used luxury model car. She says, "I realized that his perception of my having reached success was just that, perception. I wasn't anywhere near the success that I have planned for myself. I still have a very long way to go. As a matter of fact, I was still living in the 'hood, just in a new development in a different city!" But like a lot of the women I spoke to, poorer relations and friends thought that the purchase of luxury items, an advanced degree and a healthy income meant that all of your problems were solved, forever and ever.

Soon after I graduated from college I read an article in *Money* magazine that struck a similar chord about the expectations of extended family on young black professionals. The headline of the piece was: "Hunting for the First House." The sub-head read: "Home-buying can be a financial and emotional challenge for any couple. As African Americans looking in Chicago's white suburbs, Trish and Larry Harvey faced special hurdles—but overcame them."[2]

The story went on to introduce us to the Harveys, ages 26 and 29. They were "both MBAs, with fast-track jobs and a combined income close to $100,000 a year." But the article showed this couple to be more than materialistic Buppies. Although childless themselves and still so young, they were raising Trish's 16-year-old niece, Raven. And their "carefully calculated budget" included not only money for rent and insurance, food and a vacation fund, but $500 a month toward assisting relatives. Money that, out of politeness, might be called a loan; but money the Harveys never expected to see again.

Who Is Giving? What Is Expected?

I can't remember the first time I heard the phrase, "to whom much is given, much is expected," though I suspect I was still in diapers. Nor can I tell you how often the phrase was repeated throughout my childhood; the number would have to be in the hundreds, if not the thousands. I heard it every Sunday that I attended church and every Saturday when our family went visiting. I heard it from my teachers when I received high grades and heard it, underlined, when I brought home Cs. The parents of my friends uttered it during pep talks after school and old black ladies murmured it in my ear when I respectfully leaned forward to kiss

their powdery cheeks. Along with the West Indian equivalent of "Walk good" and the also often-repeated "Each one teach one," "to whom much is given, much is expected," was passed down as more than a platitude. It was the knight's code, a secret moral compass that would guide me should I make it through the woods, into the kingdom of higher education and on to the palaces of good fortune beyond.

Though I did not know it then, the reference is biblical. It's in the New Testament, Luke 12:48: "For unto whomsoever much is given, of him shall be much required: and to whom men have committed much, of him they will ask the more." The first sentence of the verse had been passed down in the black community (no doubt by savvy pastors who found their collection plates to be a little light). The second part of the verse may not have been uttered, but was certainly implied. I know that I'm not alone among middle-class women and men who have had to learn that you aren't a traitor to the people when you turn down a relative or a friend for a loan. I also know that as black women continue to outpace black men educationally and financially, more of the burden of helping falls upon us. We pay for our success not only financially, but emotionally as well.

In the work place, the "much is given, much is expected" motto can be a double-edged sword for successful black women. Clearly, our success provides an opportunity for service. "It's about taking ownership," one 30-something programmer . . . told me. "I love going out on recruiting trips and being able to reach out to young black kids. Even if they don't come and work for my company, I can give them the tools and tips they need to get ahead. I feel like I'm helping people."

At the same time, the expectation can be that our success means we should be ever grateful and behave accordingly. We are dealt our daily share of racism and sexism, yet our class—and the means by which we make our living—predicates that we must often bite our tongue or risk being labeled as "angry," "difficult," or even "racist.". . .

At home, the challenge can be equally painful. One need only look at the hit film *Soul Food*, the story of three sisters and their families in Chicago. The most successful one is a lawyer named Terry. As portrayed by Vanessa L. Williams, Terry is brittle, caustic and quick to criticize. The message the filmmakers send is that Terry's ambition has drained her soul. She's on her second marriage and, when husband number two commits adultery, it's Terry's fault for working so hard. Her sister Maxine, in contrast, has no loot but a lot of love: she's been married to her husband for 11 years and the two still flirt shamelessly. Maxine has three beautiful kids, while Terry is trying, but childless. Maxine can also cook huge Sunday dinners, steeped in Southern tradition. Terry has no domestic skills, but a seemingly endless ability to write checks. The film sets her up as a bad guy, but I painfully recognized her plight. Who can blame her for being so cranky when she's the one who's got to pay her mother's hospital bills, fund her youngest sisters' business ventures and bail her brother-in-law out of jail? With not so much as a thank you, mind you. It's little wonder that when Terry explodes, she says, "As far as you know, I'm an ATM. It's always Automatically Terry's Money." My generation is getting better at shaking off the guilt, but for those of us who come from families that were born poor and have stayed poor, balancing the weight of expectation is never easy.

What We Owe Ourselves

As chair of the African-American studies program at Princeton University, Valerie A. Smith is a high-profile figure in a high-pressure job. She is the Woodrow Wilson Professor of Literature and the author of many critically acclaimed books, including *Self-Discovery and Authority in Afro-American Narrative and Representing Blackness: Issues in Film and Video*. Among certain passionate circles of Afro-Bohemia, she is known as the woman who brought Andrea Lee's *Sarah Phillips* back into print, a novel about race, class and identity that is now taught in hundreds of colleges nationwide. She is smart. She is powerful. But what I hear more than anything about Valerie Smith is that she is physically fit. I mean really fit. I begin to hear a rumor that while she was a professor at UCLA, she would only hold student conferences during her daily hour-and-a-half hike up Runyon Canyon. I hear that she is known for urging her black women colleagues, students and friends not to give so much of themselves that they don't take time for themselves.

It's when this last comment drifts back to me that I decide I have to meet her.

We meet for tea, at 4:00 at Sally Lunn's in Princeton, an old-fashioned teashop that looks like a scene out of *Mary Poppins*. I ask Valerie, who is indeed fit and who looks barely old enough to buy alcohol, much less chair a university department, about her fitness journey. "In junior high school and high school, I really wasn't athletic at all," she tells me. "For a variety of reasons. Mostly I was this high-achieving academic kid, who couldn't get into competitive sports. Then I began running in graduate school. There was a group of us who got together and running was a social thing."

. . . I ask her about the student conferences held during grueling canyon hikes and she laughs out loud. "I'm notorious for that," she says, mischievously. "I'd get my grad students to have conferences with me during my 6:30 A.M. hike. I felt like I was sending a message: channel your anxiety into this exercise. I also felt like this was a way for them to have my full attention. They certainly were not going to get an hour and a half of my time while I was busy in my office." Not only did some of her students begin to exercise on their own, but a number of them also quit smoking. "They didn't have enough wind to talk, going up those hills," Valerie says with a smile.

. . .

Smith believes that if we are going to continue to thrive as black women we need to take care of not only our minds and our spirits, but our bodies as well. The week before we meet, thousands of black women had mourned the death of the poet June Jordan. She was 65. For me, as for others, it had echoes of the deaths of Audre Lorde, Virginia Hamilton, Sherley Anne Williams. "We're beginning to see how many of our successful sisters are dying young or suffering from chronic illness," says Smith. "We've got to pay attention to what we eat, what we do physically. We take responsibility for so much. We've got to take responsibility for ourselves."

NOTES

1. Lynette Clemetson and Allison Samuels. "We Have the Power." *Newsweek,* September 18, 2000.

2. Bill Sheeline. "Hunting for the First House." *Money,* December 1993.

FORTY-THREE

◆◆◆

Women and Men Living on the Edge: Economic Insecurity After the Great Recession (2011)

Jeff Hayes and Heidi Hartmann

Heidi Hartmann is the founder and president of the Institute for Women's Policy Research, based in Washington, D.C. She has written extensively on women and economics, frequently testifies before Congress, and is often cited in various media outlets. She received a MacArthur Fellowship Award in 1994.

Jeff Hayes is Senior Research Associate at the Institute for Women's Policy Research.

The Institute for Women's Policy Research/ Rockefeller Survey of Economic Security, like several other recent surveys, finds that the effects of the 2007–2009 recession, known as the Great Recession, are both broad and deep. The IWPR/Rockefeller survey shows that more than one and a half years after the recession came to an official end, and the recovery supposedly began, many women and men report that they are still suffering significant hardships. They are having difficulty paying for basics like food (26 million women and 15 million men), health care (46 million women and 34 million men), rent or mortgage (32 million women and 25 million men), transportation (37 million women and 28 million men), utility bills (41 million women and 27 million men), and they have difficulty saving for the future (65 million women and 53 million men). On almost every measure of insecurity and hardship the survey reveals the Great Recession has visited more hardship on women than it has on men.

Many women and men have seen the value of their assets decline and have had to withdraw funds from their savings or retirement accounts to make ends meet, further depleting them. Many report borrowing more and finding other ways to cope such as doubling up. More than one-third of respondents reported that they and/or someone else in their household was unemployed in the prior two years. That figure rises to almost one-half in

black and Hispanic households and above one-half for single mothers.

In the year prior to the survey, 136 million adults reported cutting back on household spending, 126 million cut back on vacation or entertainment, 81 million failed to pay a bill on time, 50 million did not go to a doctor because of the cost, 45 million did not fill a prescription, 20 million adults qualified for food stamps, and 16 million went hungry because they could not afford food (only about one-third of those who experienced hunger also got food stamps).

The IWPR/Rockefeller Survey of Economic Security interviewed 2,746 adults age 18 years and older, approximately 900 each of non-Hispanic whites, non-Hispanic blacks, and Hispanics in September through November of 2010. Interviews lasted approximately 34 minutes and were conducted in English or Spanish. The results reported have been statistically adjusted so that they reflect the U.S. adult population. The margin of sampling error for the weighted sample is 3.7 percentage points.

In several key areas, the IWPR/Rockefeller survey results can be compared with other surveys administered earlier that asked similar or identical questions. The 2007 Rockefeller American' Worker Survey, for example, was administered in the spring of 2007 before the recession began. Between the spring of 2007 and the fall of 2010 when the IWPR/Rockefeller survey was in the field, the share of women and men who say that different groups, such as older Americans or recent college graduates, have somewhat less or a lot less economic security than they did ten years earlier shifted from a minority opinion to one held by most Americans. For example, in 2007, 38 percent of women responded that they believe young married couples had somewhat or a lot less economic security compared with ten years earlier; by 2010, 77 percent of women thought so. The comparable shares for men's views of the economic security of young married couples are 33 percent in 2007 and 71 percent in 2010. Similarly, for workers with health insurance under age 65, the share of women saying they are worried or fairly worried about losing their health care coverage ratcheted up from 26 percent in 2007 to 43 percent in 2010. For men, the comparable percentages in the two years are 20 percent and 36 percent.

The IWPR/Rockefeller Survey of Economic Security is particularly useful in several additional ways besides the comparability of some of its key questions. All the responses are disaggregated by gender, as well as by the three largest race/ethnic groups in the United States (non-Hispanic whites, non-Hispanic blacks, and Hispanics), age, educational level, and several other variables of interest. The gender analysis reveals that the Great Recession, dubbed the "mancession" because men's job losses were more than twice as large as women's, has increased women's economic vulnerability more than it has men's. For example, among workers, whereas 61 percent of men report having enough savings to cover two months of earnings if they lost their jobs, only 43 percent of women would have that much savings. The share reporting savings adequate to cover two months is lower for black and Hispanic women, young women, women with low levels of education, and single mothers. Women report more hunger, more difficulty paying bills or affording health care, and more inability to meet their children's needs. For example, 39 percent of women report difficulties paying monthly utility bills compared with 26 percent of men. The figures are higher for black women (52 percent) and Hispanic women (48 percent). Women's lower earnings compared with men and their greater likelihood of raising children on their own no doubt contribute to their difficult circumstances. Women seem to have remained in the recession a year and a half after its end, and in the year since the survey was completed, women have failed to share in the small gains afforded by the weak jobs recovery.

Mothers are particularly hard hit, whether single or married: 38 percent of single mothers and 34 percent of married mothers report trouble paying for medical care for self or family in the past year; 80 percent of both single and married mothers have cut back on household spending (compared with 72 percent of all women and 57 percent of all men); 43 percent of single mothers and 42 percent of

married mothers have not bought something their children needed; and 38 percent of single mothers and 42 percent of married mothers stopped or reduced their contributions to retirement savings to meet expenses. In some ways, single mothers clearly fare worse than married mothers: 16 percent of single mothers report going hungry at some time in the prior year because they could not afford to purchase food; whereas, for married mothers, the percentage is lower at 9 percent (the percentage for married women with no minor children is 3 percent). Several results for parents are compared to those from identical questions asked in the 2007 Rockefeller American Workers Survey, and, whether the issue was going hungry, failing to pay a bill, not going to a doctor or filling a prescription, or not taking a child to the doctor when needed, the 2010 results are all markedly worse than those from 2007.

The IWPR/Rockefeller Survey pioneers the use of several innovative measures of hardship, coping, and job quality. To measure the extent to which a household has been affected by unemployment, the survey asks whether the respondent (or another member) was unemployed and looking for work for at least one month at any time during the prior two years, and whether the respondent or the other unemployed person was the household's highest earner when she or he became unemployed. From the responses to these questions, two indicators of the intensity of the unemployment experienced by the household are derived: 1) unemployed high earner, and 2) a scale ranging from no one unemployed, through respondent *or* other member unemployed, to respondent *and* other member unemployed. Not surprisingly, on almost every indicator, the highest rates of hardship are experienced by those in the households with the most intense unemployment. For example, 27 percent of women and 20 percent of men in households with two or more members unemployed for at least one month in the past two years report going hungry in the past year compared with five percent of women and four percent of men in households with no unemployment in the past two years.

Another innovative indicator measures the extent of doubling up as a result of financial pressures by asking respondents how many additional adults they now live with as a result of financial pressures compared with the end of 2007. Overall, 17 percent of women and 11 percent of men reported having doubled up. Younger adults, those with less education, and black and Hispanic adults report higher shares doubling up than older adults, those with more education, or whites; in every category more women report doubling up than do men.

Innovative indicators of job quality include measures of whether workers fear job loss or lesser penalties such as lower raises, fewer promotions, or poor task assignments for absences from work, whether authorized or not, and of the extent to which sharing pay information with co-workers is discouraged or punished. About two-fifths of both female and male workers report that attendance is tracked in such a way at their workplace that they would lose their job if they missed too much time, regardless of the reason, and about half of working women and men report that sharing wage information at their workplace is discouraged or punished. On the positive side of job quality, about three-quarters of both female and male workers report that their supervisors try to accommodate their personal or family needs, about half of women and men can change their starting and quitting times as needed and about one-fifth can do some of their work at home. Single mothers, however, report having substantially less work flexibility than other workers.

When the survey was administered nearly a year ago, respondents' expectations were not rosy. About one-tenth of both women and men thought their employer might go out of business or relocate. Just less than one-fifth feared they might be laid off, and almost one-fourth thought they might be asked to take a pay cut, while about one half thought they might get a raise. About one-fifth expected to withdraw funds from retirement savings, about one-third expected to stop or reduce contributions to retirement savings. Significantly more women than men thought they would have trouble saving money for the future (65 percent of women versus 45 percent of men), would have to cut back on household expenses (70 percent of women versus 47 percent of men), and would have trouble paying bills (44 percent of women versus 30 percent

of men). Parents' expectations were even less rosy. About half of both married and single mothers expected to have trouble paying bills, about three-fourths expected to cut back on household spending, and about three-fourths expected to have trouble saving for the future.

Respondents' support for policies that could improve the quality of their jobs, help balance work and family, and increase economic security—as indicated by their support for candidates who would propose policies in these areas—is strong across the board. Asked to self-identify as Democrats, Republicans or independents, large majorities of each group (except Republican men) support laws that would provide workers with paid sick days, paid vacation, and the right to request a flexible schedule. Even larger shares, including clear majorities of Republican men, support paid leave for family care and childbirth and policies that would improve the quality and affordability of child care. The right to refuse overtime is supported by about 60 percent of women and men, including at least 50 percent of every group. More respondents support higher minimum wages (except Republican men who fall below 50 percent in their support) and challenging discrimination and unfair treatment on the job. The strongest support of all policies goes to ensuring that Social Security benefits are maintained, ranging from a low of 73 percent of men who identify themselves as independent, to a high of 93 percent of Democratic women.

Respondents, suffering economically and seeing little hope for the immediate future, have an answer. They suggest they would support candidates who propose initiatives that can increase their access to high-quality jobs, help them balance work and family, and enhance their economic security.

For millions of American families, the market economy is failing them in the wake of the Great Recession and meaningful recovery is not yet in sight. According to the IWPR/Rockefeller Survey, Americans believe the government is and should be a lifeline, providing economic security in a turbulent economy.

8

◆◆◆

Living in a Globalizing World

To understand the situation of women in the United States, it is important to know something of those of women worldwide and the ways we all participate in, and are affected by, an increasingly integrated global system. This chapter takes this wider angle of view, with nation as an additional analytical category together with gender, race, and class. We discuss personal experiences of home and family that cross national borders, patterns of migration and displacement, cultural diversity and homogenization, the movement of work from one nation to another, and efforts to reduce global inequalities. Throughout this book we refer to the global level of analysis and interaction; in this chapter we emphasize the global and macro-level structures within which people organize their lives.

Locations, Circuits, and Flows

In Chapter 3, we noted that connections to people, communities, and home are important parts of our identities. For many people those connections may be in several places, as with some writers in this collection. Surina Khan, for example, was born in Pakistan and immigrated to the United States as a child. In Reading 25, she comments that, "Pakistan has always been my parents' answer to everything." As a young lesbian she rejected Pakistan as synonymous with homophobia but gradually sought out queer people from South Asia, which led her to examine a part of herself she thought she had discarded. In Reading 17, Julia Alvarez notes that some Latino/a immigrants retain strong ties to their countries of origin and may travel back and forth regularly, maintaining family and community connections in more than one place.

In this chapter, Gloria Anzaldúa traces the original migrations into what is now the United States, and the subsequent conquest and settlement of Mexico and the U.S. by Spanish and British colonizers, respectively. She writes as a mixed race person, a mestiza, located in more than one place, with more than one consciousness, who moves smoothly between two languages and who has learned "to be an Indian in Mexican culture and to be Mexican from an Anglo point of view" (1987, p. 79). The current U.S.–Mexico border was defined in the 1848

Treaty of Guadalupe Hidalgo that established the Rio Grande River as the international boundary and ceded Texas to the United States together with Arizona, California, Nevada, and New Mexico. Referring to this history, Mexican Americans often say: We didn't cross the border; the border crossed us. Anzaldúa describes the 2,000-mile long border between the United States and Mexico as a place where "the Third World grates against the first and bleeds" and considers the challenges, benefits, and losses involved in border-crossing (Reading 44).

In Reading 47, Swiss filmmaker Ursula Biemann describes flows of women crisscrossing the globe in her video essay, *Remotely Sensed,* concerning the trafficking of women for the sex industry. She argues that they travel along ever-changing routes and trajectories shaped by economic hardship, cultures and laws that provide for men's sexual lives, and the immigration policies of receiving countries. We draw on this imagery of circuits and flows to visualize the world in terms of interconnected networks of people, homes, goods, information, work, money, and cultural productions like music and movies. Movement along global pathways is facilitated or impeded by specific conditions, rules, and assumptions about what should be traded, who should travel, and for what reasons. Notice the direction of these flows. Are they reciprocal? Are they mainly one way?

Migrations and Displacements

Migration

The political and economic interests and aspirations of ancient empires, colonial powers, and modern-day states have resulted in huge movements of people, mainly according to the needs and priorities of dominant nations. This includes the transporting of some 12 million enslaved West Africans to the "New World" during the eighteenth and nineteenth centuries, with others taken to the Mediterranean or across the Indian Ocean. After the ending of slavery in the United States, Chinese, Filipino, Indian, and Japanese workers were allowed to enter the country to meet the increasing demand for labor (see *Immigration Timeline* in Chapter 2). Also the rise of the United States as a major industrial power, together with weakening economies and political repression in Europe, led to massive European immigration to the

United States starting in the mid-nineteenth century. More recent immigration has mainly involved people from Asia and Central America. Some are high-tech employees, but most fill the "3D jobs"—dirty, difficult, and dangerous.

According to the International Organization for Migration, migration "is considered one of the defining global issues of the early twenty-first century" (IOM 2008). Consider the following data from 2008:

- There were an estimated 214 million migrants worldwide, up from 150 million in 2000.

- Migrants comprised 3 percent of the global population.

- Women accounted for 49 percent of global migrants.

- If the total number of migrants were a nation, it would be the fifth most populated country in the world (after China, India, the United States, and Indonesia).

The United Nations distinguishes several types of migrants (see Box). Personal dreams and decisions, community expectations and pressures, macro-level immigration policies, or global labor markets all influence who moves, where they move from and to, the conditions under which they relocate, and the situations they face at their destinations. Also, given a combination of opportunity, education, hard work, support, and luck, some people are able to go "offtrack." Shailja Patel describes her parents' struggle to maneuver their daughters from the East African nation of Kenya to Britain and the United States (Reading 45). They confronted a succession of gatekeepers, including school principals, officials who evaluated visa applications, overseas examination boards, and immigration officers, while the exchange rate between Kenyan shillings and British pounds and U.S. dollars spiraled upwards.

Movements of people are facilitated and limited by immigration policies, which shift in response to economic booms and slumps, political concerns like support for refugees, relationships with allied nations, and perceived threats to national security. Overall, tens of millions of people have started new lives in the United States and have contributed greatly to the nation's economy

Categories of Migrants Recognized by the United Nations

Asylum seekers: People who apply for asylum in a country other than their own and who remain in this status until their application is decided.

Contract migrant workers: People working in a country other than their own under contractual arrangements that limit the period of employment and the specific job held.

Diplomats and consular personnel: Foreigners working under diplomatic permits for foreign embassies or consulates in the receiving country.

Domestic employees: Foreigners admitted for the purpose of providing personal services to foreign diplomatic and consular personnel in the country.

Foreign retirees (as settlers): People beyond retirement age who are granted the right to stay over a long period or indefinitely in a State other than their own, provided that they have sufficient independent income and do not become a charge to that State.

Foreign students: People admitted by a country other than their own, usually under special permits or visas, for the purpose of following a particular course of study in an accredited institution of the receiving country.

Foreign tourists: People admitted under tourist visas (if required) for leisure, visits to friends or relatives, health or medical treatment, or religious pilgrimage.

Foreigners admitted for family formation or reunification: Immediate relatives of people residing in the receiving country or the foreign fiance(e)s or adopted children of citizens. Immediate relatives are generally defined as the spouse and minor children of the person concerned.

Internally displaced persons: People forced to flee from their homes as a result of or in order to avoid the effects of armed conflict, situations of generalized violence, violations of human rights, or natural or man-made disasters, and who have not crossed an internationally recognized State border.

Military personnel: Foreign military personnel, officials, and advisers stationed in the country. Dependents and domestic employees may be allowed to accompany them.

Refugees: Foreign persons granted refugee status and entering to be resettled in the receiving country or persons granted refugee status on a group basis.

Stateless persons: People who are not recognized as citizens of any State.

Trafficked persons: People who are illegally recruited, coerced, and/or forcibly moved within national or across national borders.

---

and cultural diversity (see Chapter 3 for key immigration laws and policies).

Immigration is currently a highly contentious issue in the United States and in other receiving countries such as Britain, France, and Germany. The U.S. government has strengthened and militarized the long border with Mexico in an attempt to stop undocumented immigrants from entering that way. Armed guards, infrared night-vision scopes, low-light TV cameras, motion sensors, helicopters, and all-terrain vehicles patrol the border fence day and night. Immigration and Customs Enforcement (ICE) has stepped up raids on homes, schools, and workplaces in many towns and cities. At the same time, immigrant communities have asserted their presence and the contributions they make to this nation by taking to the streets in huge demonstrations. Race and class are significant factors in immigration policies, practices, and enforcement. People who hold Australian, Canadian, European, Japanese, and U.S. passports have relative freedom of travel, especially for short-term trips and vacations. By contrast, people from poorer countries, as well as countries identified by the government as "terrorist" or "hostile," need visas and are subject to greater scrutiny at borders.

Migration Patterns

Migration often originates from a country in the global South with a Northern country as the final destination. A woman may leave her home and family in a rural area, move to a city in her country, then to a neighboring country, and finally to her intended destination. People who migrate voluntarily usually move to places where they have connections based on national, community, or family ties. For example, people from the Middle East, Afghanistan, Bosnia, and Southeast Asia have settled in Dearborn (Michigan), Fremont (California), Utica (New York), and Minneapolis (Minnesota), respectively.

Contemporary migration patterns are unique in two important ways. First, women constitute half the world's migrants, often as the primary breadwinners for their families. In Europe, Latin America, and the Caribbean, more migrants are women than men because of the demand for women as domestic workers, nurses' aides, and home health care workers, as part of what Ehrenreich and Hochschild (2003) called a "global care chain." We noted the crisis of care work in North America and Western Europe in the previous chapter, allowing—and needing—women from impoverished countries like the Philippines, El Salvador, and the Dominican Republic to migrate for such jobs. Conditions in the sending countries are also key factors. The Philippines is a predominantly agrarian country where over half the population subsists on less than the equivalent of $2 per day. Government policies encourage women and men to seek work in Europe, North America, the Middle East, Hong Kong, and Japan. Rhacel Salazar Parreñas discusses the impact of this macro-level policy on Philippine families and communities when mothers undertake care work abroad (Reading 46; see also Boris and Parrenas 2010; Heymann 2006; Yeates 2009; Zimmerman, Litt and Bose 2006). Similarly, Indonesia, the country with the largest Muslim population, exports women to work in Arab states such as Jordan and Lebanon because Muslim employers prefer Muslim household help. Jacquelyn Litt and Mary Zimmerman emphasize that the labor of women from poorer nations "serves as the infrastructure on which **First World** economic expansion depends" (2003, p. 157).

A second feature of contemporary migration patterns is the blurring of boundaries between points of origin, transit, and destination. As a result, according to migration scholar Alejandro Portes, this has created transnational communities that are made up of

> dense networks across political borders created by immigrants in their quest for economic advancement and social recognition. Through these networks, an increasing number of people are able to live dual lives. Participants are often bilingual, move easily between cultures, frequently maintain homes in two countries, and pursue economic, political, and cultural interests that require presence in both. *(1997, p. 812)*

These people include migrant workers who live in the United States and support their families and home communities in El Salvador or the Philippines, for example, by sending regular remittances or sponsoring schools or other community projects. It also includes professionals, corporate executives, hi-tech workers, and academics, whose families and professional lives straddle national borders. Chandra Talpade Mohanty discusses her relationship to "home" in the United States as well as India (Reading 10).

Although our focus here is on those who move, it is important to note that millions of people are prevented from moving or their movements are monitored and curtailed. Within the United States, for example, it is very difficult for working-class and poor young people of color to move out from inner-city communities unless they join the military. Others who are restricted include Arab and Muslim people during this era of "war on terror," Palestinians in the West Bank and Jerusalem, and refugees in war-torn countries.

Transnational Adoptions, Tourism, and Trafficking

We consider three types of movement within and across national borders: transracial/transnational adoption, tourism, and trafficking. Despite major differences, these examples share certain characteristics. They are each structured as industries that include recruiters and procurement agencies, businesses that apply for visas and deal with government bureaucracies, and the organization of transportation, including escorts and guides (see, e.g., Hübinette 2006).

Transracial/Transnational Adoptions Children who are adopted across national boundaries constitute a particular case of migration, as heterosexual couples, single women, and LGBTQ couples in countries of the global North expand their families this way (see Dubinsky 2010; Kim 2010; Marre and Briggs 2009; Simon and Roorda 2000; Trenka, Oparah, and Shin 2006). Angelina Jolie and Madonna, for example, have made headlines as fulfilled adoptive mothers of children born in the global South, exemplifying the consumption aspect of adoption, what Kim Park Nelson (2006) called "shopping for children in the international marketplace." Media images of these celebrity mothers and their adopted children depict an ideal family, with the children on their way to a new and privileged life in the States. These images make transracial/transnational adoption seem unproblematic for the child, for the newly constituted family, and for the child's country of birth. Of course, at the micro level, children need homes, love, and nurturing. Birth mothers decide or are forced to give up their babies depending on their personal circumstances, which are affected by macro-level economic conditions, or policies like China's one child policy and cultural preference for sons (Hoon 2010). Others are sometimes tricked and deceived into surrendering their parental rights. Many transracial/transnational adoptions have involved children from South Korea, Vietnam, Cambodia, Guatemala, and Nicaragua, which were all devastated by wars. Transnational adoption may have been the best option at the time for the birth parents and the babies, but it also represents a loss to these children's home communities.

Adapting to their new home in the United States may not be easy for such children, especially if they are raised by white parents in a predominantly white neighborhood. Establishing a sense of identity and belonging is more difficult across lines of race and culture. These adopted children have been cut off from their ancestry as well as their biological parents. As we noted in Chapter 3, they may need to reconnect with their family and culture of origin in some way as part of the process of resolving their hybrid identity. In the United States, there is also a history of forced removal of Native American children to boarding schools and adoptive homes away from their original communities, with some parallels to transnational adoptions (Trenka, Oparah, and Shin 2006).

Tourism Traveling abroad is something that many people in the United States want to do, whether this is through college programs, volunteering with nonprofit organizations, taking a tour, or enlisting in the military. Travel is fun, a chance to see new places and meet new people, though such "meetings" happen on artificial and unequal terms. By definition, tourists have leisure time and disposable income, which sets us apart from people who live and work in tourist destinations. In her classic essay, *Report from the Bahamas,* the late June Jordan (1985) noted with deep regret the social distance between herself—an African American university professor, poet, and writer—and the Black people staffing the hotel where she stayed. Jamaica Kincaid (1988) gave a caustic account of what tourists see, what they do not see, and how local people view them in the Caribbean island of Antigua. Attorney and activist Mililani Trask (1992) noted the negative effects of tourism on Hawaiian communities and the commodified, exoticized version of Hawaiian culture that is retailed to tourists (also see Haunani-Kay Trask 1999). Although the tourist industry generates jobs, these may be seasonal and usually pay low wages; the most profitable businesses geared toward tourists are national and international chains, such as car rental agencies, hotels, and restaurants, which undercut local businesses. Tourism also competes with other forms of development; consumes scarce resources, including land, water, and food supplies; and generates considerable waste for local communities to absorb.

Trafficking Researchers and advocates Lora Jo Foo, Gabriela Villareal, and Norma Timbang define human trafficking as "the recruitment, harboring, movement, or obtaining of a person by force, fraud, or coercion for the purpose of involuntary servitude, debt bondage, or slavery" (2007, p. 38). Electronic communications, poverty, demand for low-wage labor, and increasingly restrictive immigration laws have all contributed to a rise in human trafficking. Both women and men are trafficked to work in agriculture, domestic service, restaurants, hotels, manufacturing, construction, and the sex industry.

Structural adjustment policies instituted by the World Bank and IMF, and free trade agreements between richer and poorer nations have undermined subsistence economies, eliminated social services, and resulted in job losses and food crises in many poorer nations. Economic upheaval due to

the break-up of the former Soviet Union left many thousands of people unemployed. Religious or political persecution, armed conflict, crop failures, and other hardships are also "push" factors that compel people to risk emigration. Grace Chang and Kathleen Kim note the "coercive nature of most migration" given this reality (2007, p. 327). Despite the difficulties and the possibilities for fraud and deception, when faced with responsibilities for their family's survival, women and men make the decision to travel abroad for work. A person may initially participate on the basis of 'knowledge and consent'; she "may later wish to leave the work or particular employment site, yet be held captive by an employer" (Chang and Kim 2007, p. 327).

Trafficking can happen within a nation or across national borders. Typically, poorer countries are the sending countries. For example, men from Bangladesh are taken to work in sweatshops in South Korea; women from the former Soviet Union end up in Israel; people from China and Central America are brought to the United States; men from Turkey

are taken to France; and women from Thailand are brought into Japan. Traffickers may use complex routes with transit points in a third country. They may change routes and destinations depending on changes in national laws, immigration policies and enforcement, and penalties for getting caught. Recruiters front the money for visas, transportation, guidance, and other services, so their clients are indebted to them from the beginning.

Ursula Biemann comments that women who travel for sex work enter "cross-border circuits, illegal and illicit networks as well as alternative circuits of survival." She notes that they often feel that agents who recruit them are providing a valuable service in helping them to achieve their desire to move to a richer country. She argues that women enter these migration circuits for many reasons and with varying expectations. She asks what meanings women ascribe to their life decisions, how they understand the constraints within which they live, and the opportunities available to them. She questions whether one can call these movements voluntary and, if so, in what sense. In her video, the migrating women appear as data streams, scans, and X-rays portrayed over landscapes passing by. Their anatomical and demographic data are recorded; their routes appear in electronic travel schedules on the screen. They are the embodiment of the abstract financial flows that feed the global economy (Reading 47 and photo).

Trafficking of women always entails the risk of sexual abuse and violation, and trafficking of girls and women into the sex industry is significant, for example, in Thailand, Cambodia, India, and the Philippines (see, e.g., Shih 2007; Tadiar 2003). Sex trafficking into the United States represents a minority of people who are trafficked. Non-governmental organizations and academic researchers estimate that from one-half to two-thirds of trafficking into the United States occurs in non-sex-related industries. For example, the Coalition to Abolish Slavery and Trafficking reported that clients trafficked to Los Angeles are subject to exploitation in many fields, including domestic work (40 percent), factory work (17 percent), sex work (17 percent), restaurant work (13 percent), and servile marriage (13 percent) (cited in Chang and Kim 2007). This is in contrast to the U.S. government's conflation of human trafficking and prostitution, which has resulted in the narrow application of the federal Trafficking Victims Protection Act to sex trafficking cases. Chang and Kim cite a range of advocates and service providers who seek to redefine trafficking as a labor migration issue. Paradoxically, although current U.S. policy seeks to clamp down on trafficking, U.S. economic and immigration policies are major factors causing the conditions that lead to it.

Consumption: Goods, Information, Popular Culture

Material Flows

Supermarkets and stores in countries of the global North source the products they sell from farms and factories worldwide (Figure 8.1). Wal-Mart, the world's biggest retailer, exemplifies this model. In 2012, the company bought products from over 60,000 suppliers worldwide and sold to over 200 million consumers every week through over 10,000 stores in 27 countries (Wal-Mart 2012). Companies at the top of the global supply chains seek flexibility and the freedom to operate wherever it is most beneficial for them. This results in precarious conditions of employment for those at the bottom of the chain—whether in the global South, migrants to countries of the global North, or low-income people in richer countries. Subcontractors in the middle of the chain are pressured for low prices and speedy turnaround. They pass this on to their workers in low wages, stressful quotas, and enforced overtime in the scramble to fill orders.

Information Flows

It is a commonplace to say that we live in an "information age." Spike Peterson (2003) discussed some of the implications of this in her analysis of how power operates in the global economy. Information is at the core of the international financial system and has extended and transformed the speed of cross-border transactions. The information economy compresses both time and space, and redefines geographical distance. In some ways, physical location is immaterial—you can work anywhere as long as you have reliable Internet access. For example, computer support services have been outsourced to India (English speakers) and El Salvador (Spanish speakers). The script readers are "over there," but at the same time they are also "here," their voices coming through the phones in our hands as they talk us through how to fix our computers.

Information workers participate in a fast-paced industry, which demands a high degree of flexibility. Work is organized in short-term contracts; workers are responsible for gaining experience and keeping their skills and networking contacts up to date. Johanna Shih (2006) noted the restructuring of U.S. immigration categories in 1990 that fostered the migration of hi-tech, high-skilled workers, and argued that their transnational ties and cultural know-how are a critical part of the expansion of Silicon Valley through subcontracting agreements, for example, with companies in India or marketing agreements with companies in China.

Information is not just a part of manufacturing or cultural production; increasingly information is what is traded. Although much assembly-line work has been outsourced from former industrial centers of the global North, the design of new products, decisions about style, market positioning, and

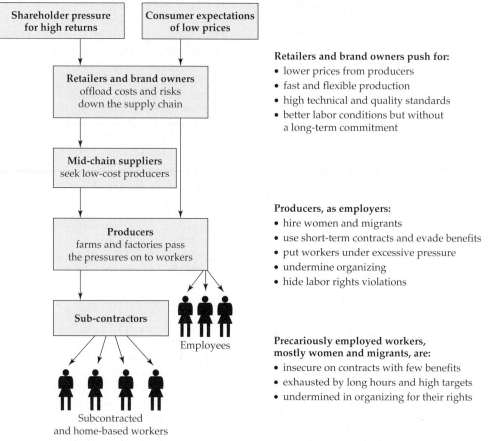

Retailers and brand owners push for:
- lower prices from producers
- fast and flexible production
- high technical and quality standards
- better labor conditions but without a long-term commitment

Producers, as employers:
- hire women and migrants
- use short-term contracts and evade benefits
- put workers under excessive pressure
- undermine organizing
- hide labor rights violations

Precariously employed workers, mostly women and migrants, are:
- insecure on contracts with few benefits
- exhausted by long hours and high targets
- undermined in organizing for their rights

FIGURE 8.1 Supply chain pressures create precarious employment. (*Source:* Oxfam International (2004, p. 5).

finance are retained by company headquarters in the United States or Western Europe, and this work is increasingly centralized. Selling information, Peterson (2003) noted, is very different from selling material goods or services. Information can be sold to multiple buyers and still be retained by the seller; it increases in value the more people are "locked in" to particular products.

Given the rapid, unceasing innovation of the information economy, Peterson underscored the politics of knowledge, a point we introduced in Chapter 2 in our discussion of theories and theorizing. This concerns:

> whose questions are pursued, whose concerns are silenced, . . . whose methods are

authorized, whose paradigm is presumed, whose project is funded, whose findings are publicized, whose intellectual property is protected. (Petersen 2003, p. 139)

She comments that conventional distributions of power are reflected in and tend to be reproduced by the information economy. This economy is both diffused and concentrated in particular groups and locations. Moreover, decision makers in the global information economy are predominantly men.

Cultural Flows

Global cultural flows include mass communications such that U.S. news outlets like CNN and Fox

News, and Britain's BBC, are sources of information worldwide. An example of news flowing "upstream" is the weblog written by Riverbend (2005, 2006), an Iraqi woman in Baghdad, who described her family's experiences of war and occupation, as well as commenting on mainstream news reporting of events. Although nowhere near the scale of CNN and BBC, Al-Jazeera News, based in Doha, Qatar, is another example.

U.S.-produced music, movies, and TV series such as *Friends, Desperate Housewives,* and *Sex in the City;* reality shows like *Survivor* and *American Idol;* and talk shows featuring *Oprah Winfrey* or *Dr. Phil* are distributed worldwide. It is possible to travel to many places around the globe, especially metropolitan areas, and hear the voices of musicians like 50 Cent, Christina Aguilera, Mariah Carey, Michael Jackson, and Garth Brooks—as well as those who were part of earlier U.S. and British popular music scenes, such as the Beatles, the Carpenters, Billy Joel, and "Motown Sound" performers. At the same time, musicians singing in Arabic, Japanese, Korean, and European languages are fusing their respective forms with hip-hop forms that originated in urban, African American youth culture (see, e.g., Condry 2006; Elam and Jackson 2005; Mitchell 2001). You may not understand the words, but you recognize the beat as hip-hop. Some commercialized U.S. hip-hop is misogynist and homophobic, but fundamentally the form has been one of resistance and has been adopted this way outside the United States.

Spike Peterson (2003) discussed the effects of digitization on the commodification of culture. She argued that globalization does not only homogenize cultures; it also "celebrates novelty and the local," but decision-making power over what is selected as valuable is highly concentrated. Some see cultural merging as evidence that "the world has become one." Critics decry the loss of traditional or locally produced cultural forms and loss of cultural diversity. Cultural richness and variation is in danger of becoming flattened into a handful of uniformly recognizable symbols, representations, and icons. Some have referred to this as "McDonaldization," a term coined by sociologist George Ritzer (1993) to mean standardization, whether of french fries, burgers, and Coke, or high-ticket items.

The direction of flow of globalizing processes reflects the power imbalances among nations and regions. Hollywood-made films and U.S. music dominate global markets. How often do you hear Arabic, Japanese, Korean, or French popular music on your local radio station or at your music shop? How often do you see titles of films from Nigeria, China, or Chile displayed on the marquee of your local movie theater? The U.S. music industry differentiates various genres, including "world music." What does this term mean? Why is "classical music" in the United States usually taken to mean European classical composers though all cultures have classical music? Who controls the flow of cultural productions? Who benefits, who are disadvantaged, and in what ways?

Depictions of U.S. life in TV shows, replete with remodeled kitchens, color-coordinated furnishings, lavish meals, and different outfits from scene to scene, also serve to generate desires for consumer goods and an affluent lifestyle. Through popular culture, people are likely to be more aware of disparities in living standards among nations. U.S. movies and TV shows sell the idea of the "America Dream" and notions of U.S. superiority. They promote dominant beauty standards and help to create a demand for hair straighteners and skin-lightening products. The "B" movies made in the United States that are a staple of TV programming in many nations also sell ideas of individualism—hard, blue-eyed, white masculinity, tough Black gangstas, and long-legged, grasping women—in pursuit of greed, money, violence, killing, and sex. How people "read" these media productions depends on their perspectives and values. They may find them appealing or irrelevant, so far removed from local realities and values as to be ridiculous; or they may loathe and despise U.S. popular culture as cultural pollution awash with sleaze, crime, and degradation, what Spike Peterson (2003) called "westoxification."

In order to counter mainstream media stereotypes and to provide alternative representations of women's lives, feminist projects in many countries are creating their own media, as mentioned in Chapter 2. Examples include A Woman's Place, in India, Feminist International Radio Endeavour, FEMPRESS (Chile), ISIS International-Manila, Women's Feature Service (India), and Women's E-news (USA).

Production: The Global Factory

In the past forty years, electronic communications and air transport have made it increasingly possible for corporations to move work to places where they can pay lower wages, or where there are fewer constraints on their operations. Nike, Playtex, Dell, Apple, Mattel, and General Motors (based in the U.S.); East Asian companies like Sony, Panasonic, and Hyundai; and European companies like Nokia, Siemens, and Philips all have much of their manufacturing work done overseas—in, for example, Indonesia, China, Mexico, the Philippines, Guatemala, or Eastern Europe (see, e.g., Collins 2003; Enloe 1995; Greider 1997; Kamel 1990; Kamel and Hoffman 1999; Ross 1997). This organization of work results in inexpensive consumer goods for Australian, European, Japanese, Canadian, and U.S. markets, particularly clothing, toys, household appliances, and electronic equipment. The global assembly line also includes computer-based services done by women in the Caribbean, for example, who make hotel reservations for some U.S. and Canadian hotel chains (Freeman 2000), and computer support, as mentioned earlier. The fact that standards of living and wage rates differ greatly from country to country means that the process of moving work around the world is likely to continue and to become increasingly complex. In the textile industry, in 2008, for example, labor costs ranged from more than $40 per hour in Switzerland, to less than $5 per hour in Poland, Turkey, and Mexico, to less than $1 an hour in several Asian countries (Werner International 2009).

Note the significance of gender in the international division of labor and that this intersects with inequalities based on race, ethnicity, and national origin. Roughly 90 percent of the factory workers in offshore production are young women in their late teens and early twenties. Some countries, like the Philippines and China, have established Export Processing Zones (EPZs), where transnational corporations subcontract work to local companies making products for export. In Mexico, this is done through *maquiladoras*—factories that make goods on contract to a "parent" company. The majority are owned by U.S. interests and located within thirty miles of the border (see, e.g., Fernández-Kelly 1983; Fregoso and Bejarano 2010; Peña 1997; Reading 37).

Even in countries like Mexico, with protective labor and environmental laws, these regulations are often not strongly—if ever—enforced in relation to the operations of transnational corporations. Thus, workers experience oppressive working conditions, suffer stress from trying to make the assigned quotas, and contract illnesses from exposure to glues, solvents, and other toxic chemicals, or lint and dust in the case of textile factories. Women's eyesight deteriorates from hours spent at microscopes. They are subject to sexual harassment by male supervisors and have been required to undergo pregnancy tests as a condition of employment.

When workers complained and organized to protest such dire conditions, they were often threatened that the plants would close and move elsewhere; indeed, this has happened. For example, when women campaigned for better wages and working conditions, Nike moved some of its production from South Korea to Indonesia and China, pitting workers in one country against those in another, in what has been described as "a race to the bottom."

In Reading 48, Pun Ngai examines how young rural women in China are transformed into an industrial workforce through the imposition of factory discipline. Her detailed ethnographic study explores the desires of these women to leave their villages and become wage earners, despite the fact that their work is tedious, repetitive, exhausting, and low-paid. Figure 8.2 shows 2010 production costs and profits for the iPhone, produced in Shenzhen (southern China) by the Taiwan-based Foxconn Technology Group, a subcontractor for Apple. Working practices at Foxconn's huge plants in China came under intense scrutiny in 2010 after a series of suicides among young workers. A *New York Times* investigation into working practices at Apple's supplier plants documented poor health and safety conditions and long working hours (Duhigg and Barboza 2012). In response, Apple contracted the Washington D.C.-based Fair Labor Association (FLA) to monitor conditions at supplier plants. The FLA reported "serious and pressing" concerns over excessive working hours, unpaid overtime, health and safety failings, and management interference in labor unions, practices that break Chinese labor laws (Garside 2012). The FLA's president also said that conditions at

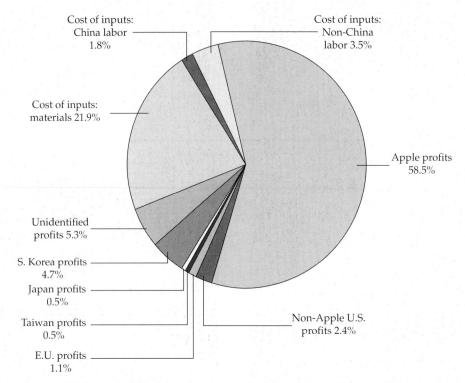

Figure 8.2 iPhone production costs and profits, 2010. (*Source:* Kraemer, Linden, and Dedrick, 2011, p. 5).

Apple supplier plants were better than those at garment factories or other facilities elsewhere in China (Reuters 2012a).

The International Financial System

Corporate activities take place within a wider context of rules and agreements that are part of the international economic system that is based on **neoliberal** policies that call for the freedom of business to operate with minimal interference from governments, international organizations, or labor unions. Basic tenets include the dominance of the market, privatization of government-owned industries, reduction of social welfare spending, and belief in individual responsibility rather than valuing community and the public good.

Major international financial institutions include the World Bank and the International Monetary Fund (IMF), created as part of the Bretton Woods Agreements about ways to rebuild and regulate the international economic system following World War II. The World Trade Organization, established in 1995, adjudicates cases brought by nations regarding restraints on trade due to limiting factors in other nations' laws (see Box: Key International Financial Institutions and Trade Agreements). The World Bank and IMF have required nations applying for loans to make stringent changes to their economies. The aim of such Structural Adjustment Programs is to increase the profitability of corporations on the argument that this will benefit everyone. Required measures include:

- cutting back government spending on social services;
- abolishing price controls, particularly on food, fuel, and public transportation;
- adding new taxes and increasing existing taxes;

Key International Financial Institutions and Trade Agreements

The World Bank

Headquartered in Washington, D.C., the World Bank was set up in 1944 to provide loans for reconstruction after the devastation of World War II and to promote development in countries of the global South, where the bank's emphasis has been on major, capital-intensive projects such as roads, dams, hydroelectric schemes, irrigation systems, and the development of large-scale, chemical-dependent, cash-crop production. The bank's investors are the governments of rich countries that make money on the interest on these loans. Because the World Bank assigns voting power in proportion to the capital provided by its shareholders, its decisions are dominated by the governments of the global North, and its policies are in line with their concerns.

International Monetary Fund (IMF)

Also based in Washington, the IMF is an international body with 187 member countries. It was founded at the same time as the World Bank to promote international trade and monetary cooperation. It makes loans to governments for development projects and in times of severe budget deficits. France, Germany, Japan, Britain, and the United States have 37 percent of the votes, which are allocated according to financial contribution to the fund.

Trade Agreements

The General Agreement on Tariffs and Trade (GATT) was started after World War II to regulate international trade. Starting in 1986, the agreement was changed significantly in response to transnational corporations' demand for fewer tariffs on the goods they move around the world— data, components, finished products, and foods.

The United States entered into specific agreements with Mexico and Canada in 1994 (North American Free Trade Agreement— NAFTA); with Costa Rica, the Dominican Republic, El Salvador, Guatemala, Honduras, and Nicaragua, beginning in 2005 (Central America Free Trade Agreement—CAFTA); and with South Korea, starting in 2007 (KORUS-FTA). These agreements reduce import tariffs on certain goods, eliminate import quotas, and open up local resources to outside ownership and extraction. Proponents contend that additional trade will result in increased prosperity. Labor unions, farmers, environmentalists, community organizers, and fair trade activists argue that such trade agreements involve job losses, damage the environment, and undermine food security because local farmers cannot compete with U.S.-produced corn and rice, which are subsidized through the U.S. farm bill.

World Trade Organization (WTO)

This is an unelected international body over which member nations and their peoples have no democratic control. The WTO allows national governments to challenge each others' laws and regulations as violations of WTO rules against restraints to trade. Cases are decided by a panel of three trade experts. WTO tribunals are secret, binding on member states, and provide no outside appeal or review. Once a WTO ruling is issued, losing countries have a set time to change their laws to conform to WTO requirements, pay compensation to the winning country, or face trade sanctions (Working Group on the WTO 1999, p. 5).

The WTO ruled that the U.S. Endangered Species Act, which requires domestic and foreign fishers to catch shrimp by methods that do not kill sea turtles, violated WTO rules. It ruled against the European Union in a case that challenged European nations' rights to give preference to bananas produced by small-scale farmers in Africa and the Caribbean Other examples include a challenge by the U.S., Canada, and Argentina to European Union restrictions on importing genetically modified foods and a challenge by Canada and Brazil to U.S. farm subsidies.

Ripples from the Epicenter of the Global Economy

What started as a housing-sector crisis in the United States in 2008 turned into a global financial crisis. As the U.S. economy contracted, the consequences were felt all over the world. In countries of the global South:

- Export orders were cancelled. Factories producing textiles and electronics closed.

- Women workers in these industries were laid off. Often employers did not pay back wages or give notice; governments turned a blind eye to these breaches of labor law.

- Tourism and related service industries declined. Women were laid off.

- Workers who kept their jobs faced delays in payment of wages, reduced overtime, reduced facilities such as meals, and extension of probationary periods for new workers.

- Laid-off workers tried to enter the informal economy—for example, by cooking or becoming a street vendor; some took homework on a piecework basis.

- Laid-off migrant workers could not send remittances to their families, which lowered household incomes. Even though women migrants earn less than men, they send more money home to support their children.

- Legal channels for overseas migration decreased, and new migrants faced the reality of being undocumented. Xenophobia rose in some countries, posing a security risk to migrants.

- Families ate cheaper food and less food; women skipped meals in favor of children and men.

- National governments provided stimulus packages to ameliorate hardship for low-income households; they also saved money by cutting services and laying off workers in health and education sectors, many of whom were women.

- Women's time burden increased as domestic responsibilities intensified, for example, having to travel further to find cheap food and spending more time cooking.

- Some families decided to take girls out of school to help at home.

- People's physical and mental health suffered; domestic violence increased under these pressures. Sometimes gender norms changed, at least temporarily, as unemployed men cared for children or cooked the family meal.

_____

Sources: Craviotto 2010; Emmett 2009; King and Sweetman 2010; Sirimanne 2009.

- selling nationalized industries, or at least a majority of the shares, to private corporations, often from outside the country;

- improving profitability for corporations through wage controls, tax breaks, loans, and credit; or by building ports, better roads, or rail transportation; and

- increasing the output of cash crops for export.

Though not required to do so by the World Bank, successive U.S. administrations have adopted similar policies, including, for example, the deregulation of air transport, cuts in welfare and social services, the privatization of public utilities like water and electricity, as well as aspects of the prison industry and military contracting.

One of the roles of nation-states is to provide the social and political conditions that make it possible for business to operate. They may also seek to control corporate activities, though this is limited by shared assumptions about the central role of business in the current economic and political system as well as by their different resources. Governments of some small countries have operating budgets smaller than those of transnational corporations. Exxon-Mobil, General Motors, and Ford have higher revenues than the national budgets of all but seven countries: United States, Germany, Japan, China,

You don't understand; the "econo-me" grew, not the "econo-you."

Italy, Britain, and France. Some companies have more revenue than the budgets of their home governments (e.g., Shell/Netherlands and Daewoo/South Korea). The logic of economic **globalization** entails a borderless world for capital and corporate activities. Indeed, national boundaries have become more porous with regard to capital but not with regard to all workers or people who migrate for other reasons. The increased integration of the global system means that a crisis that starts in one nation may spread to many others. The U.S. housing-sector crisis of 2008 turned into a global financial crisis, with consequences all over the world (see Box).

Assumptions and Ideologies

Countries of the global South are often called developing countries, assuming that they will become industrialized like Canada, the United States, and Western Europe. Constructing a continuum from "undeveloped" to "developed" suggests that this process is both linear and the best way for a nation to progress. This continuum masks the fact that so-called developing countries have great wealth in terms of natural resources and indige-

nous knowledge. Much of the wealth of developed nations has come from poorer ones; indeed this is a key reason for their lack of economic development. Vandana Shiva (1988), a scientist and writer on environment and development policy, used the term "devastated" instead of "undeveloped" economies to emphasize this process.

Economic growth is often conflated with "progress"—a much more complex concept with social, moral, spiritual, and intellectual dimensions. This view of progress often leads people in a highly material society like the United States to value themselves primarily in terms of the money they make and the things they own or consume. At a national level, too, it leads to an emphasis on material success and material security with support for government policies that facilitate profit making regardless of social costs.

People in dominant positions may justify inequalities among and within nations with reference to ideologies of racism, classism, sexism, and national superiority. Others argue that in principle, inequality is unjust. Some people's freedom and comfort should not be bought at the expense of other's people's oppression, degradation, and poverty. More pragmatically, inequality is an ongoing source of tension and conflict. On an international level it is a cause of war; on a community level it can lead to alienation, anger, violence, vandalism, and crime.

Legacies of Colonization

Current disparities among nations are often based on older inequalities resulting from colonization. Former British colonies include India, Ghana, Hong Kong, Kenya, Nigeria, and Pakistan. France had colonial possessions in Algeria, Senegal, Togo, and Vietnam. Although the details varied from one colonial power to another, several factors were central to this process:

- the imposition of legal and political institutions;
- cultural and spiritual devastation and replacement of language;
- changes in social relations, including gender roles and ethnic and class stratification;
- psychological dimensions of ethnocentrism and racism, such as internalized racism and colorism rooted in whiteness and white supremacy; and
- distortions of the economy with dependence on a few agricultural products or raw materials for export.

Colonial powers extracted raw materials—timber, minerals, and cash crops—which were processed into manufactured goods in the colonial centers for consumption there and for export. During the second half of the twentieth century, virtually all colonies gained political independence, but many have remained tied to their colonizers politically, culturally, and linguistically. In terms of inhibiting self-determination, continuing economic ties may be the most devastating. This includes dependence on firms established during colonial times, the activities of transnational corporations, and loans from governments and banks of countries of the global North. These factors have led many commentators to characterize the continuing inequalities between richer and poorer countries as **neocolonialism.** In this connection, Sokari Ekine describes the environmental destruction caused by Shell, Chevron and other transnational corporations that extract oil in the Niger Delta region of Nigeria. She discusses the Nigerian government's support for the oil companies, including vicious repression of local communities who protest their operations (Reading 67).

Toward a Secure and Sustainable Future

As this chapter suggests, the rules and conditions imposed by corporate and government decision makers have resulted in increasing insecurity for many people worldwide. Alternative ways of organizing society and redistributing income and wealth are often marginalized as "unrealistic." In this last section, we explore several changes under way that point toward the possibility of a more secure and sustainable future.

Understanding the Significance of Global Connections

Women in the global North need to learn much more about the effects of "our" corporate and government policies on women in Asia, Africa, Latin America, and the Caribbean and to understand the connections between these women's situations and our own. In countries of the global South, thousands of workers' organizations, environmentalists, feminists, religious groups, and human rights organizations have been campaigning for better pay and working conditions and for economic development that is environmentally sound. Increased consumer awareness and activism in the United States, Canada, and Western Europe has brought about some changes in wages and working conditions for workers making Nike shoes or Apple electronics. In 1997, North Olmsted, Ohio, a working-class suburb of Cleveland, became the first U.S. city to ban municipal purchases of sweatshop-made products. Students from over 100 U.S. colleges called on their institutions to honor strict codes of conduct for overseas factories that make goods bearing college names (Featherstone 2002), and this campaign continues to expand.

To develop our understanding of global connections, in the United States we need much greater access to materials written by and about women in countries of the global South, including academic research, activist concerns, journalists' accounts, policy recommendations, and critiques of policies imposed by countries of the North. A few notable writers are published worldwide, including Vandana Shiva (Reading 49), and the Web opens up additional resources, but those tend to feature U.S.-based NGOs working with women overseas. Our search for materials for this book was affected by these realities.

Fair Trade

Movements for fair trade have arisen in response to the negative effects of so-called free trade on individuals and communities. Fair trade criteria include paying a fair wage in the local context; providing equal opportunities, especially for the most disadvantaged people; engaging in environmentally sustainable practices; providing healthy and safe working conditions; and being open to public accountability.

However, researchers have pointed out that, even with fair trade, producers of export crops like coffee depend on the vagaries of the international coffee market, which makes them vulnerable to fluctuations in price and demand (Smith 2010; Müller 2010).

A number of U.S. nonprofit organizations support fair trade between producers and craftspeople in the global South and consumers in the North. These include Equal Exchange (West Bridgewater, Mass.), Global Exchange (San Francisco Bay Area), Just Coffee (Madison, Wis.), Pachamama (San Rafael, Calif.), Pueblo to People (Houston, Tex.), and Ten Thousand Villages (Akron, Pa.), which all sell through stores and the Internet. Maquiladora Dignidad y Justicia (Dignity and Justice Maquiladora Company), a small worker-owned and operated business, was started by five members of Comite Fronterizo de Obrer@s (Border Committee of Women Workers) in Mexico in 2003. They took this initiative after being laid off when large *maquiladoras* closed down (Hernández and Flory 2005). In 2008, eight women were able to pay themselves double the standard wage in the *maquiladoras* and to determine the terms of their employment. Their product line included organic cotton T-shirts, sweatshirts, and tote bags. Such businesses are small seeds toward a more sustainable economy.

Addressing the issue of consumption, or overconsumption, in countries of the global North goes far beyond fair trade and will take huge changes in consciousness, priorities, and economic organization. We return to this issue in Chapter 11.

Debt Cancellation

For many poor countries, especially in Africa and Latin America, the burden of debt is catastrophic. At times, some nations, including Mexico and Argentina, have refused to repay their debts. Advocacy organizations argue that much of the money borrowed from international financial institutions has benefited only upper-class and professional elites or has gone into armaments, nuclear power plants, or luxuries such as prestige buildings, especially in urban areas. It is an inescapable fact that the world's poorest countries will never be able to pay their international debts. With agreement of the leading industrialized nations, the governing boards of the IMF and World Bank adopted a debt-relief proposal in 1996 for the most heavily indebted nations, mostly in Africa. This was partly in response to major protests against world economic priorities and concerted lobbying by Jubilee 2000, a worldwide alliance of NGOs and religious groups, which urged debt cancellation. Several nations, including Britain, Canada, France, Italy, and Spain, have written off some debts, but much more has been promised than has been delivered. The Global Call to Action against Poverty continues to pressure the governments of richer countries to address global imbalances of wealth and power.

Self-Determination and Democratization

Despite political and economic limits to national and local decision-making processes, many individuals and communities are challenging international financial institutions or government policies that jeopardize their livelihood and security. In Reading 49, Vandana Shiva reports on a successful challenge to corporate plunder of water supplies by the Coca-Cola Company. This was initiated by marginalized women in Kerala (southern India) who mobilized support from community officials, political leaders, notable writers, and internationally

known activists with extensive contacts. This two-year campaign involved protest, scientific research, a lawsuit, lobbying, and actions taken by elected officials. The Kerala High Court argued in favor of protecting water supplies from excessive exploitation and ordered the Coca-Cola Company to stop using underground water. In 2007, the state government of Kerala filed criminal charges against Coca-Cola for damages it has caused in the community of Plachimada.

Thousands of environmentalists, union members, indigenous people, feminists, and people of many faiths participated in workshops on economic and environmental issues as part of a major protest against the World Trade Organization (WTO) at its third ministerial conference, in Seattle in November 1999. This coordinated opposition was successful in stalling the "Seattle round" of talks aimed at further opening up global trade. Massive international protests followed at IMF, World Bank, and WTO meetings on all continents (see, e.g., Prokosch and Raymond 2002; Starhawk 2002). A new form of international gathering, the World Social Forum, started in 2001 when 20,000 people from 117 countries came together in Porto Alegre (Brazil) under the slogan "Another World Is Possible." Such meetings have continued internationally, regionally, and locally and have given rise to new U.S.-based coalition efforts, like Grassroots Global Justice.

Citing historical evidence, activists and writers Mary Zepernick (1998a, 1998b) and Virginia Rasmussen (1998) argued that corporate dominance is not inevitable. In the eighteenth and nineteenth centuries, U.S. city and state governments watched corporations closely and revoked or amended their charters if they harmed the general welfare or exceeded the powers granted to them by government. In 1843, for example, the Pennsylvania Legislature declared: "A corporation in law is just what the incorporation act makes it. It is the creature of the law and may be moulded to any shape or for any purpose the Legislature may deem most conducive for the common good" (quoted in Grossman 1998a). Corporate owners worked hard to change such limiting perspectives. In an 1886 decision, the U.S. Supreme Court declared corporations legal persons. Gradually they were given a long list of civil and political rights, such as free speech, property rights, and the right to define and control investment, production, and the organization of work (Grossman 1998b). This resulted in a gradual reversal of the sovereignty of the people over corporations—originally mere legal entities—and an undermining of democracy, for people who are subordinate to corporations are consumers not citizens. The Program on Corporations, Law, and Democracy (POCLAD) has shown the fundamental contradiction between democracy and corporate control (Ritz 2001). It advocates that city governments, for example, create policies and programs to ensure control over corporations that conduct business with the city as a step toward reclaiming people's power over corporate entities.

Self-determination also has strong cultural elements, as suggested by Gloria Anzaldúa (Reading 44; 1987), who drew on her ancestry and history to forge a visionary mestiza consciousness. In opposition to cultural homogenization of mass media, myriad projects worldwide sustain and celebrate living cultures. In immigrant communities in the United States, too, people speak many languages, play traditional instruments, perform and teach traditional dance, often adapting and reviving aspects of their cultures for current times and consciousness and as part of their resistance to cultural homogenization.

Transnational Alliances

The worldwide mobility of capital calls for transnational labor movements to standardize wages and hold corporations accountable for working conditions. Indeed, the global economic situation has generated new alliances and organizations working across national borders. Examples include STITCH (Support Team International for Textileras), a network of women organizers in the United States and Guatemala, the Central American Network of Women in Solidarity with Maquila Workers (see Mendez 2002), and the Comite Fronterizo de Obrer@s (Border Committee of Women Workers) in Mexico, which works with the American Friends Service Committee.

In the 1960s and 1970s, people active in U.S. social movements made theoretical and practical connections with anti-colonial struggles in such countries as South Africa, Vietnam, Cuba, Angola, and Mozambique. In the twenty-first century, these international linkages are crucial, as scholar and activist Angela Davis (1997) remarked, not merely "as a matter of inspiration or identification, but as a matter of necessity," because of the impacts of globalization—positive and negative—on people's lives. We continue this discussion of security and sustainability in later chapters and also take up the issue of transnational alliances among women in Chapter 12.

◆◆◆

Questions for Reflection

In thinking about the issues raised in this chapter, consider these questions:

1. What do you know about countries outside the United States? What are your sources of information?

2. Why does the globalization of the economy matter to people living in the United States? What does it tell us about structural privilege (which we may not know we have and may not want)? If some of this material is new to you, why do you think you have not learned it before?

3. How does global inequality reinforce sexism, racial prejudice, and institutionalized racism in the United States?

4. How do you define wealth, aside from material possessions? List all the ways you are enriched.

5. How do you think about being an ethical consumer? How are you supported or constrained in this?

6. How do people in elite positions justify the perpetuation of inequalities to others? To themselves? How are the ideologies of nationalism, racial superiority, male superiority, and class superiority useful here?

◆◆◆

Finding Out More on the Web

1. Find examples of the influence of U.S. media abroad, for example, at a movie theater in Zurich, Switzerland: www.kitag.com

2. Study the maps on the following sites that show colonial histories and contemporary disparities among nations:

   www-personal.umich.edu/~mejn/cartograms/

   http://en.wikipedia.org/wiki/Image:World_1898_empires_colonies_territory.png

   http://www.worldmapper.org

3. The following Web sites have information about alternatives to globalization, including fair trade and debt relief:

   CorpWatch: www.corpwatch.org

   Global Exchange: www.globalexchange.org

   Global Women's Strike: www.globalwomenstrike.net

   Jubilee USA Network: www.jubileeusa.org

   Sweatshop Watch: www.change.org/groups/sweatshop_watch

   World Social Forum: www.forumsocialmundial.org.br

4. Use your search engine to research organizations concerned with the global sex trade and trafficking such as:

   Coalition Against Trafficking in Women (CATW)

   Global Alliance Against Traffic in Women (GAATW)

   Women's Education, Development, Productivity and Research Organization (WEDPRO)

5. Find out what has happened in Plachimada since the court ruling against Coca-Cola.

◆◆◆

Taking Action

1. Interview someone who immigrated to the United States to understand why that person left his or her home country and how the person got to where he or she is now.

2. Look at the labels in your clothes and on all the products you buy. Where were they made? Look up these countries on a map if you don't know where they are.

3. Do you need all you currently own? List everything you need to sustain life. Which items do you need to buy? Which might you make yourself, share, or barter with others?

4. Find out who manufactures the clothing that bears your college's name, and whether there are sweatshops in your region.

5. Get involved with a campaign that is tackling the issue of sweatshop production or debt relief.

◆◆◆

The Homeland (1987)
Aztlán / El otro México

Gloria Anzaldúa

> **Gloria Anzaldúa** (1942–2004) was a Chicana lesbian-feminist poet and fiction writer. With Cherríe Moraga, she co-edited the ground-breaking anthology *This Bridge Called My Back: Writings by Radical Women of Color,* winner of the Before Columbus Foundation American Book Award. She taught Chicano Studies, Feminist Studies, and creative writing at various universities. Her other books include *Borderlands: La Frontera—The New Mestiza* and *The Bridge We Call Home: Radical Visions for Transformation* (edited with Analouise Keating).

El otro México que acá hemos construido
el espacio es lo que ha sido
territorio nacional.
Esté el esfuerzo de todos nuestros hermanos
y latinoamericanos que han sabido
progressar.

—Los Tigres del Norte[1]

"The *Aztecas del norte* . . . compose the largest single tribe or nation of Anishinabeg (Indians) found in the United States today. . . . Some call themselves Chicanos and see themselves as people whose true homeland is Aztlán [the U.S. Southwest]."[2]

Wind tugging at my sleeve
feet sinking into the sand
I stand at the edge where earth touches ocean
where the two overlap
a gentle coming together
at other times and places a violent clash.

Across the border in Mexico
  stark silhouette of houses gutted by waves,
    cliffs crumbling into the sea,
      silver waves marbled with spume
        gashing a hole under the border fence.

> *Miro el mar atacar*
>   *la cerca en* Border Field Park
> *con sus buchones de agua,*

an Easter Sunday resurrection
of the brown blood in my veins.

Oigo el llorido del mar, el respiro del aire,
  my heart surges to the beat of the sea.
    In the gray haze of the sun
      the gulls' shrill cry of hunger,
        the tangy smell of the sea seeping into me.

        I walk   through the hole in the fence
          to the other side.
      Under my fingers I feel the gritty wire
        rusted by 139 years
          of the salty breath of the sea.

Beneath the iron sky
Mexican children kick their soccer ball across,
run after it, entering the U.S.

      I press my hand to the steel curtain—
        chainlink fence crowned with rolled barbed wire—
      rippling from the sea where Tijuana touches San Diego
          unrolling over mountains
            and plains
              and deserts,
  this "Tortilla Curtain" turning into *el río Grande*
    flowing down to the flatlands
      of the Magic Valley of South Texas
        its mouth emptying into the Gulf.

1,950 mile-long open wound
      dividing a *pueblo,* a culture,
        running down the length of my body,
          staking fence rods in my flesh,
          splits me   splits me
            me raja me raja

        This is my home
        this thin edge of
          barbwire.

        But the skin of the earth is seamless.
        The sea cannot be fenced,
      el mar does not stop at borders.

To show the white man what she thought of his
arrogance,
Yemaya blew that wire fence down.

This land was Mexican once,
was Indian always
and is.
And   will be again.

*Yo soy un puente tendido
    del mundo gabacho al del mojado,
lo pasado me estirá pa' 'trás
    y lo presente pa' 'delante.
Que la Virgen de Guadalupe me cuide
Ay ay ay, soy mexicana de este lado.*

The U.S.-Mexican border *es una herida abierta*
where the Third World grates against the first and
bleeds. And before a scab forms it hemorrhages
again, the lifeblood of two worlds merging to form
a third country—a border culture. Borders are set
up to define the places that are safe and unsafe, to
distinguish *us* from *them.* A border is a dividing
line, a narrow strip along a steep edge. A border-
land is a vague and undetermined place created by
the emotional residue of an unnatural boundary. It
is in a constant state of transition. The prohibited
and forbidden are its inhabitants. *Los atravesados*
live here: the squint-eyed, the perverse, the queer,
the troublesome, the mongrel, the mulato, the
half-breed, the half dead; in short, those who cross
over, pass over, or go through the confines of the
"normal." Gringos in the U.S. Southwest consider
the inhabitants of the borderlands transgressors, aliens—whether they possess documents or
not, whether they're Chicanos, Indians or Blacks.
Do not enter, trespassers will be raped, maimed,
strangled, gassed, shot. The only "legitimate" inhabitants are those in power, the whites and those
who align themselves with whites. Tension grips
the inhabitants of the borderlands like a virus.
Ambivalence and unrest reside there and death is
no stranger.

In the fields, *la migra.* My aunt saying, *"No cor-
ran,* don't run. They'll think you're *del otro lado."*
In the confusion, Pedro ran, terrified of being
caught. He couldn't speak English, couldn't
tell them he was fifth generation American.
Sin papeles—he did not carry his birth certificate to work in the fields. *La migra* took him
away while we w atched. *Se lo llevaron.* He tried

to smile when he looked back at us, to raise
his fist. But I saw the shame pushing his head
down, I saw the terrible weight of shame
hunch his shoulders. They deported him to
Guadalajara by plane. The furthest he'd ever
been to Mexico was Reynosa, a small border
town opposite Hidalgo, Texas, not far from
McAllen. Pedro walked all the way to the Valley. *Se lo llevaron sin un centavo al pobre. Se vino
andando desde Guadalajara.*

During the original peopling of the Americas, the
first inhabitants migrated across the Bering Straits
and walked south across the continent. The oldest
evidence of humankind in the U.S.—the Chicanos'
ancient Indian ancestors—was found in Texas and
has been dated to 35000 B.C.[3] In the Southwest United
States archeologists have found 20,000-year-old
campsites of the Indians who migrated through, or
permanently occupied, the Southwest, Aztlán—land
of the herons, land of whiteness, the Edenic place of
origin of the Azteca.

In 1000 B.C., descendants of the original Cochise
people migrated into what is now Mexico and Central
America and became the direct ancestors of many
of the Mexican people. (The Cochise culture of the
Southwest is the parent culture of the Aztecs. The Uto-
Aztecan languages stemmed from the language of the
Cochise people.)[4] The Aztecs (the Nahuatl word for
people of Aztlán) left the Southwest in 1168 A.D.

Now let us go.
    Tihueque, tihueque,
Vámonos, vámonos.
        Un pájaro cantó.
*Con sus ocho tribus salieron
        de la "cueva del origen,"
los aztecas siguieron al dios
        Huitzilopochtli.*

Huitzilopochtli, the God of War, guided them to
the place (that later became Mexico City) where an
eagle with a writhing serpent in its beak perched
on a cactus. The eagle symbolizes the spirit (as the
sun, the father); the serpent symbolizes the soul (as
the earth, the mother). Together, they symbolize the
struggle between the spiritual/celestial/male and
the underworld/earth/feminine. The symbolic sacrifice of the serpent to the "higher" masculine powers indicates that the patriarchal order had already
vanquished the feminine and matriarchal order in
pre-Columbian America.

At the beginning of the 16th century, the Spaniards and Hernán Cortés invaded Mexico and, with the help of tribes that the Aztecs had subjugated, conquered it. Before the Conquest, there were twenty-five million Indian people in Mexico and the Yucatán. Immediately after the Conquest, the Indian population had been reduced to under seven million. By 1650, only one-and-a-half-million pure-blooded Indians remained. The *mestizos* who were genetically equipped to survive small pox, measles, and typhus (Old World diseases to which the natives had no immunity), founded a new hybrid race and inherited Central and South America.[5] *En 1521 nació una nueva raza, el mestizo, el mexicano* (people of mixed Indian and Spanish blood), a race that had never existed before. Chicanos, Mexican-Americans, are the offspring of those first matings.

Our Spanish, Indian, and *mestizo* ancestors explored and settled parts of the U.S. Southwest as early as the sixteenth century. For every gold-hungry *conquistador* and soul-hungry missionary who came north from Mexico, ten to twenty Indians and *mestizos* went along as porters or in other capacities.[6] For the Indians, this constituted a return to the place of origin, Aztlán, thus making Chicanos originally and secondarily indigenous to the Southwest. Indians and *mestizos* from central Mexico intermarried with North American Indians. The continual intermarriage between Mexican and American Indians and Spaniards formed an even greater *mestizaje*.

El destierro/The Lost Land

> *Entonces corré la sangre*
> *no sabe el indio que hacer,*
> *le van a quitar su tierra,*
> *la tiene que defender,*
> *el indio se cae muerto,*
> *y el afuerino de pie.*
> *Levántate, Manquilef.*
>
> *Arauco tiene una pena*
> *más negra que su chamal,*
> *ya no son los españoles*
> *los que les hacen llorar,*
> *hoy son los propios chilenos*
> *los que les quitan su pan.*
> *Levántate, Pailahuan.*
> —Violeta Parra, *"Arauco tiene una pena"*[7]

In the 1800s, Anglos migrated illegally into Texas, which was then part of Mexico, in greater and greater numbers and gradually drove the *tejanos* (native Texans of Mexican descent) from their lands, committing all manner of atrocities against them. Their illegal invasion forced Mexico to fight a war to keep its Texas territory. The Battle of the Alamo, in which the Mexican forces vanquished the whites, became, for the whites, the symbol for the cowardly and villainous character of the Mexicans. It became (and still is) a symbol that legitimized the white imperialist takeover. With the capture of Santa Anna later in 1836, Texas became a republic. *Tejanos* lost their land and, overnight, became the foreigners.

> *Ya la mitad del terreno*
> *les vendió el traidor Santa Anna,*
> *con lo que se ha hecho muy rica*
> *la nación americana.*
>
> *¿Qué acaso no se conforman*
> *con el oro de las minas?*
> *Ustedes muy elegantes*
> *y aquí nosotros en ruinas.*
> —from the Mexican corrido,
> *"Del peligro de la Intervención"*[8]

In 1846, the U.S. incited Mexico to war. U.S. troops invaded and occupied Mexico, forcing her to give up almost half of her nation, what is now Texas, New Mexico, Arizona, Colorado and California.

With the victory of the U.S. forces over the Mexican in the U.S.-Mexican War, *los norteamericanos* pushed the Texas border down 100 miles, from *el río Nueces* to *el río Grande*. South Texas ceased to be part of the Mexican state of Tamaulipas. Separated from Mexico, the Native Mexican-Texan no longer looked toward Mexico as home; the Southwest became our homeland once more. The border fence that divides the Mexican people was born on February 2, 1848 with the signing of the Treaty of Guadalupe-Hidalgo. It left 100,000 Mexican citizens on this side, annexed by conquest along with the land. The land established by the treaty as belonging to Mexicans was soon swindled away from its owners. The treaty was never honored and restitution, to this day, has never been made.

> The justice and benevolence of God
> will forbid that . . . Texas should again

become a howling wilderness
trod only by savages, or . . . benighted
by the ignorance and superstition,
the anarchy and rapine of Mexican misrule.
The Anglo-American race are destined
to be forever the proprietors of
this land of promise and fulfillment.
Their laws will govern it,
their learning will enlighten it,
their enterprise will improve it.
Their flocks range its boundless pastures,
for them its fertile lands will yield . . .
luxuriant harvests . . .
The wilderness of Texas has been redeemed
by Anglo-American blood & enterprise.
                          —William H. Wharton[9]

The Gringo, locked into the fiction of white superiority, seized complete political power, stripping Indians and Mexicans of their land while their feet were still rooted in it. *Con el destierro y el exilo fuimos desuñados, destroncados, destripados*—we were jerked out by the roots, truncated, disemboweled, dispossessed, and separated from our identity and our history. Many, under the threat of Anglo terrorism, abandoned homes and ranches and went to Mexico. Some stayed and protested. But as the courts, law enforcement officials, and government officials not only ignored their pleas but penalized them for their efforts, *tejanos* had no other recourse but armed retaliation.

After Mexican-American resisters robbed a train in Brownsville, Texas, on October 18, 1915, Anglo vigilante groups began lynching Chicanos. Texas Rangers would take them into the brush and shoot them. One hundred Chicanos were killed in a matter of months, whole families lynched. Seven thousand fled to Mexico, leaving their small ranches and farms. The Anglos, afraid that the *mexicanos*[10] would seek independence from the U.S., brought in 20,000 army troops to put an end to the social protest movement in South Texas. Race hatred had finally fomented into an all out war.[11]

My grandmother lost all her cattle,
they stole her land.

"Drought hit South Texas," my mother tells me. *"La tierra se puso bien seca y los animales comenzaron a morrirse de se'. Mi papá se murió de un* heart attack *dejando a mamá* pregnant *y con ocho huercos,* with eight kids and one on the way. *Yo fuí la mayor, tenía diez años.* The next year the drought continued *y el ganado* got hoof and mouth. *Se calleron* in droves *en las pastas y el* brushland, *pansas blancas* ballooning to the skies. *El siguiente año* still no rain. *Mi pobre madre viuda perdió* two-thirds of her *ganado.* A smart *gabacho* lawyer took the land away *mamá* hadn't paid taxes. *No hablaba inglés,* she didn't know how to ask for time to raise the money." My father's mother, Mama Locha, also lost her *terreno.* For a while we got $12.50 a year for the "mineral rights" of six acres of cemetery, all that was left of the ancestral lands. Mama Locha had asked that we bury her there beside her husband. *El cemeterio estaba cercado.* But there was a fence around the cemetery, chained and padlocked by the ranch owners of the surrounding land. We couldn't even get in to visit the graves, much less bury her there. Today, it is still padlocked. The sign reads: "Keep out. Trespassers will be shot."

In the 1930s, after Anglo agribusiness corporations cheated the small Chicano landowners of their land, the corporations hired gangs of *mexicanos* to pull out the brush, chaparral and cactus and to irrigate the desert. The land they toiled over had once belonged to many of them or had been used communally by them. Later the Anglos brought in huge machines and root plows and had the Mexicans scrape the land clean of natural vegetation. In my childhood I saw the end of dryland farming. I witnessed the land cleared; saw the huge pipes connected to underwater sources sticking up in the air. As children, we'd go fishing in some of those canals when they were full and hunt for snakes in them when they were dry. In the 1950s I saw the land, cut up into thousands of neat rectangles and squares, constantly being irrigated. In the 340-day growth season, the seeds of any kind of fruit or vegetable had only to be stuck in the ground in order to grow. More big land corporations came in and bought up the remaining land.

To make a living my father became a sharecropper. Rio Farms Incorporated loaned him seed money and living expenses. At harvest time, my father repaid the loan and forked over 40% of the earnings. Sometimes we earned less than we owed, but always the corporations fared well. Some had major holdings in vegetable trucking, livestock auctions and cotton gins. Altogether we lived on three successive Rio farms; the second was adjacent to the King Ranch and included a dairy farm; the third was a chicken farm. I remember the white feathers of three thousand Leghorn chickens blanketing the land for acres around. My sister, mother and I cleaned, weighed and packaged eggs. (For years afterwards I couldn't stomach the sight of an egg.) I remember my mother attending some of the meetings sponsored by well-meaning whites from Rio Farms. They talked about good nutrition, health, and held huge barbeques. The only thing salvaged for my family from those years are modern techniques of food canning and a food-stained book they printed made up of recipes from Rio Farms' Mexican women. How proud my mother was to have her recipe for *enchiladas coloradas* in a book.

El cruzar del mojado/Illegal Crossing

> *"Ahora si ya tengo una tumba para llorar,"*
> *dice Conchita,* upon being reunited with
> her unknown mother just before the
> mother dies.
> —from Ismael Rodriguez' film,
> *Nosotros los pobres*[12]

La crisis. Los gringos had not stopped at the border. By the end of the nineteenth century, powerful landowners in Mexico, in partnership with U.S. colonizing companies, had dispossessed millions of Indians of their lands. Currently, Mexico and her eighty million citizens are almost completely dependent on the U.S. market. The Mexican government and wealthy growers are in partnership with such American conglomerates as American Motors, IT&T and Du Pont which own factories called *maquiladoras.* One-fourth of all Mexicans work at *maquiladoras;* most are young women. Next to oil, *maquiladoras* are Mexico's second greatest source of U.S. dollars. Working eight to twelve hours a day to wire in backup lights of U.S. autos or solder miniscule wires in TV sets is not the Mexican way. While the women are in the *maquiladoras,* the children are left on their own. Many roam the street, become part of *cholo* gangs. The infusion of the values of the white culture, coupled with the exploitation by that culture, is changing the Mexican way of life.

The devaluation of the *peso* and Mexico's dependency on the U.S. have brought on what the Mexicans call *la crisis.* No *hay trabajo.* Half of the Mexican people are unemployed. In the U.S. a man or woman can make eight times what they can in Mexico. By March, 1987, 1,088 pesos were worth one U.S. dollar. I remember when I was growing up in Texas how we'd cross the border at Reynosa or Progreso to buy sugar or medicines when the dollar was worth eight *pesos* and fifty *centavos.*

La travesía. For many *mexicanos del otro lado,* the choice is to stay in Mexico and starve or move north and live. *Dicen que cada mexicano siempre sueña de la conquista en los brazos de cuatro gringas rubias, la conquista del país poderoso del norte, los Estados Unidos. En cada Chicano y mexicano vive el mito del tesoro territorial perdido.* North Americans call this return to the homeland the silent invasion.

> *"A la cueva volverán"*
> —El Puma *en la cancion "Amalia"*

South of the border, called North America's rubbish dump by Chicanos, *mexicanos* congregate in the plazas to talk about the best way to cross. Smugglers, *coyotes, pasadores, enganchadores* approach these people or are sought out by them. *"¿Qué dicen muchachos a echársela de mojado?"*

> "Now among the alien gods with
> weapons of magic am I."
> —Navajo protection song,
> sung when going into battle.[13]

We have a tradition of migration, a tradition of long walks. Today we are witnessing *la migración de los pueblos mexicanos,* the return odyssey to the historical/mythological Aztlán. This time, the traffic is from south to north.

El retorno to the promised land first began with the Indians from the interior of Mexico and the *mestizos* that came with the *conquistadores* in the 1500s. Immigration continued in the next three centuries, and, in this century, it continued with the *braceros* who helped to build our railroads and who picked our fruit. Today thousands of Mexicans are crossing the border legally and illegally; ten million people without documents have returned to the Southwest.

Faceless, nameless, invisible, taunted with "Hey cucaracho" (cockroach). Trembling with fear, yet filled with courage, a courage born of desperation. Barefoot and uneducated, Mexicans with hands like boot soles gather at night by the river where two worlds merge creating what Reagan calls a frontline, a war zone.

The convergence has created a shock culture, a border culture, a third country, a closed country.

Without benefit of bridges, the *"mojados"* (wetbacks) float on inflatable rafts across *el río Grande,* or wade or swim across naked, clutching their clothes over their heads. Holding onto the grass, they pull themselves along the banks with a prayer to *Virgen de Guadalupe* on their lips: *Ay virgencita morena, mimadrecita, dame tu bendición.*

The Border Patrol hides behind the local McDonalds on the outskirts of Brownsville, Texas, or some other border town. They set traps around the river beds beneath the bridge.[14] Hunters in army-green uniforms stalk and track these economic refugees by the powerful nightvision of electronic sensing devices planted in the ground or mounted on Border Patrol vans. Cornered by flashlights, frisked while their arms stretch over their heads, *los mojados* are handcuffed, locked in jeeps, and then kicked back across the border.

One out of every three is caught. Some return to enact their rite of passage as many as three times a day. Some of those who make it across undetected fall prey to Mexican robbers such as those in Smugglers' Canyon on the American side of the border near Tijuana. As refugees in a homeland that does not want them, many find a welcome hand holding out only suffering, pain, and ignoble death.

Those who make it past the checking points of the Border Patrol find themselves in the midst of 150 years of racism in Chicano *barrios* in the Southwest and in big northern cities. Living in a no-man's-borderland, caught between being treated as criminals and being able to eat, between resistance and deportation, the illegal refugees are some of the poorest and the most exploited of any people in the U.S. It is illegal for Mexicans to work without green cards. But big farming combines, farm bosses and smugglers who bring them in make money off the "wetbacks'" labor—they don't have to pay federal minimum wages, or ensure adequate housing or sanitary conditions.

The Mexican woman is especially at risk. Often the *coyote* (smuggler) doesn't feed her for days or let her go to the bathroom. Often he rapes her or sells her into prostitution. She cannot call on county or state health or economic resources because she doesn't know English and she fears deportation. American employers are quick to take advantage of her helplessness. She can't go home. She's sold her house, her furniture, borrowed from friends in order to pay the

coyote who charges her four or five thousand dollars to smuggle her to Chicago. She may work as a live-in maid for white, Chicano or Latino households for as little as $15 a week. Or work in the garment industry, do hotel work. Isolated and worried about her family back home, afraid of getting caught and deported, living with as many as fifteen people in one room, the *mexicana* suffers serious health problems. *Se enferma de los nervios, de alta presión.*[15]

La mojada, la mujer indocumentada, is doubly threatened in this country. Not only does she have to contend with sexual violence, but like all women, she is prey to a sense of physical helplessness. As a refugee, she leaves the familiar and safe homeground to venture into unknown and possibly dangerous terrain.

> This is her home
>   this thin edge of
>   barbwire.

NOTES

1. Los Tigres del Norte is a *conjunto* band.

2. Jack D. Forbes, *Aztecas del Norte: The Chicanos of Aztlán* (Greenwich, CT: Fawcett Publications, Premier Books, 1973), 13, 183; Eric R. Wolf, *Sons of Shaking Earth* (Chicago, IL: University of Chicago Press, Phoenix Books, 1959), 32.

3. John R. Chávez, *The Lost Land: The Chicano Images of the Southwest* (Albuquerque, NM: University of New Mexico Press, 1984), 9.

4. Chávez, 9. Besides the Aztecs, the Ute, Gabrillino of California, Pima of Arizona, some Pueblo of New Mexico, Comanche of Texas, Opata of Sonora, Tarahumara of Sinaloa and Durango, and the Huichol of Jalisco speak Uto-Aztecan languages and are descended from the Cochise people.

5. Reay Tannahill, *Sex in History* (Briarcliff Manor, NY: Stein and Day/Publishers/Scarborough House, 1980), 308.

6. Chávez, 21.

7. Isabel Parra, *El Libro Major de Violeta Parra* (Madrid, España: Ediciones Michay, S.A., 1985), 156–7.

8. From the Mexican *corrido,* "Del peligro de la Intervención." Vicente T. Mendoza, *El Corrido Mexicano* (México. D.F.: Fondo De Cultura Económica, 1954), 42.

9. Arnoldo De León, *They Called Them Greasers: Anglo Attitudes Toward Mexicans in Texas, 1821–1900* (Austin, TX: University of Texas Press, 1983), 2–3.

10. The Plan of San Diego, Texas, drawn up on January 6, 1915, called for the independence and segregation of

the states bordering Mexico: Texas, New Mexico, Arizona, Colorado, and California. Indians would get their land back, Blacks would get six states from the south and form their own independent republic. Chávez, 79.

11. Jesús Mena, "Violence in the Rio Grande Valley," *Nuestro* (Jan/Feb. 1983), 41–42.

12. *Nosotros los pobres* was the first Mexican film that was truly Mexican and not an imitation European film. It stressed the devotion and love that children should have for their mother and how its lack would lead to the

dissipation of their character. This film spawned a generation of mother-devotion/ungrateful-sons films.

13. From the Navajo "Protection Song" (to be sung upon going into battle). George W. Gronyn, ed., *American Indian Poetry: The Standard Anthology of Songs and Chants* (New York, NY: Liveright, 1934), 97.

14. Grace Halsell, *Los ilegales*, trans. Mayo Antonio Sánchez (Editorial Diana Mexica, 1979).

15. Margarita B. Melville, "Mexican Women Adapt to Migration," *International Migration Review*, 1978.

FORTY-FIVE

Shilling Love (2004)

Shailja Patel

Born and raised in Kenya, **Shailja Patel** is an award-winning poet and playwright whose one-woman show, *Migritude*, published by Kaya Press, has been acclaimed by audiences across the United States, Europe, and Africa. www.shailja.com

Editors' note: In the late nineteenth century, British colonial administrators moved men from India to Kenya (East Africa) to build railroads. After the railroads were completed, they were allowed to stay and go into business. They were used as a "buffer group" between the British elite and Kenyan Africans. By the 1970s, when Kenya gained political independence from Britain, many Kenyan Asian families were relatively prosperous. They were highly unpopular in independent Kenya on economic and cultural grounds and ultimately forced to leave, which threw families into personal, economic, and political crisis.

One

They never said / they loved us

Those words were not / in any language / spoken by my parents

I love you honey was the dribbled caramel / of Hollywood movies / Dallas / Dynasty / where hot water gushed / at the touch of gleaming taps / electricity surged / 24 hours aday / through skyscrapers banquets obscene as pornography / were mere backdrops / where emotions had no

consequences words / cost nothing meant nothing would never / have to be redeemed

My parents / didn't speak / that / language

1975 / 15 Kenyan shillings to the British pound / my mother speaks battle

Storms the bastions of Nairobi's / most exclusive prep schools / shoots our cowering / six-year-old bodies like cannonballs / into the all-white classrooms / scales the ramparts of class distinction / around Loreto convent / where the president / sends his daughter / the government ministers, foreign diplomats / send their daughters / because my mother's daughters / will / have world-class educations

She falls / regroups / falls and re-groups / in endless assaults on visa officials / who sneer behind their bulletproof windows / at US and British consulates / my mother the general / arms her daughters / to take on every citadel

1977 / 20 Kenyan shillings to the British pound / my father speaks / stoic endurance / he began at 16 the brutal apprenticeship / of a man who takes care of his own / relinquished dreams of / fighter pilot rally driver for the daily crucifixion / of wringing profit from a small business / my father the foot soldier, bound to an honour / deeper than any currency / *you must / finish what you start you*

*must / march until you drop you must / give
your life for those / you bring into the world*
I try to explain love / in shillings / to those who've
never gauged / who gets to leave who has to
stay / who breaks free and what they pay /
those who've never measured love / by every
rung of the ladder / from survival / to choice

A force as grim and determined / as a boot up the
backside / a spur that draws blood / a moun-
taineer's rope / that yanks / relentlessly / up

My parents never say / they love us / they save
and count / count and save / the shilling falls
against the pound / college fees for overseas
students / rise like flood tides / love is a
luxury / priced in hard currency / ringed by
tariffs / and we devour prospectuses / of ivied
buildings smooth lawns vast / libraries the
way Jehovah's witnesses / gobble visions of
paradise / because we know we'll have to be /
twice as good three times as fast four times as
driven / with angels powers and principalities
on our side just / to get / on / the / plane

Thirty shillings to the pound forty shillings to the
pound / my parents fight over money late in
the night / my father pounds the walls and
yells / *I can't—it's impossible—what do you think
I am?* / My mother propels us through school
tuition exams applications / locks us into rooms
to study / keeps an iron grip on the bank books

1982 / gunfire / in the streets of Nairobi / military
coup leaders / thunder over the radio / Asian
businesses wrecked and looted Asian women
raped / after / the government / regains
control / we whisper what the coup leaders
planned

Round up all the Asians at gunpoint / in the national stadium / strip them of whatever / they
carry / march them 30 miles / elders in wheelchairs / babies in arms / march them 30 miles
to the airport / pack them onto any planes / of
any foreign airline / tell the pilots / down the
rifle barrels / *leave / we don't care where you take
them / leave*

I learn like a stone in my gut that / third-generation
Asian Kenyan will never / be Kenyan
enough / all my patriotic fervor / will never

turn my skin black / as yet another western
country / drops a portcullis / of immigration
spikes / my mother straps my shoulders back
with a belt / to teach me / to stand up straight

50 Kenyan shillings to the pound / we cry from
meltdown pressure / of exam after exam where
second place is never good enough / they
snap / faces taut with fear / *you can't be soft /
you have to fight / or the world will eat you up*

75 Kenyan shillings to the pound / they hug us /
tearless stoic at airports / as we board planes
for icy alien England / cram instructions into
our pockets like talismans / *Eat proper meals so
you don't get sick / cover your ears against the
cold / avoid those muffathias / the students without purpose or values / learn and study / succeed /
learn and study / suceed / remember remember
remember the cost of your life*

they never say / they love us

Two

I watch how I love / I admonish exhort / like a
Himalayan guide I / rope my chosen ones /
yank them remorselessly up / when they don't
even want to be / on the frigging mountain

like a vigilante squad I / scan dark streets for
threats I / strategize for war and famine I /
slide steel down spines

I watch heat / steam off my skin / when Westerners
drop / *I love you's* into conversation / like blue-
berries hitting / soft / muffin / dough /
I convert it to shillings / and I wince

December 2000 / 120 shillings to the British
pound / 90 Kenyan shillings to the US dollar /
my sister Sneha and I / wait for our parents /
at SFO's international terminal /

Four hours after / their plane landed / they have
not emerged

And we know with the hopeless rage / of third-
world citizens / African passport holders /
that the sum of their lives and labour / dreams
and sacrifice / was measured sifted weighted
found / wanting / by the INS

Somewhere deep in the airport's underbelly / in a room rank with fear and despair / my parents / who have travelled / 27 hours / across three continents / to see their children / are interrogated / by immigration officials

My father the footsoldier / numb with exhaustion / is throwing away / all the years / with reckless resolve / telling them / *take the passports / take them / stamp them / no readmission EVER / just let me out to see my daughters*

My mother the general / dizzy with desperation / cuts him off shouts him down / demands *listen to me I'm the one / who filled in the visa forms* / in her mind her lip curls she thinks / *these Americans / call themselves so advanced so / modern but still / in the year 2000 / they think it must be the husband in charge / they won't let the wife speak*

On her face a lifetime / of battle-honed skill and charm / turns like a heat lamp / onto the INS man until he / stretches / yawns / relents / he's tired / it's late / he wants his dinner / and my parents / trained from birth / to offer Indian / hospitality / open their bags and give their sandwiches / to this man / who would have sent them back / without a thought

Sneha and I / in the darkened lobby / watch the empty exit way / our whole American /

dream-bought-with-their-lives / hisses mockery around our rigid bodies / we swallow sobs because / they raised us to be tough / they raised us to be fighters and into that / clenched haze / of not / crying

here they come

hunched / over their luggage carts our tiny / fierce / fragile / dogged / indomitable parents

Hugged tight they stink / of 31 hours in transit / hugged tighter we all stink / with the bravado of all the years / pain bitten down on gargantuan hopes / holding on through near-disasters / never ever / giving in / to softness

The stench rises off us / unbearable / of what / was never said

Something / is bursting the walls of my arteries something / is pounding its way up my throat like a volcano / rising / finally / I understand / why I'm a poet

Because I was born to a law / that states / before you claim a word you steep it / in terror and shit / in hope and joy and grief / in labour endurance vision costed out / in decades of your life / you have to sweat and curse it / pray and keen it / crawl and bleed it / with the very marrow / of your bones / you have to earn / its / meaning

---

◆◆◆

The Care Crisis in the Philippines (2003)
Children and Transnational Families in the New Global Economy

Rhacel Salazar Parreñas

Rhacel Salazar Parreñas is a professor of sociology at the University of Southern California. She is the author of *Children of Global Migration: Transnational Families and Gendered Woes; Engendering Globalization: Essays on Women, Migration and the Philippines;* and *Servants of Globalization: Women, Migration, and Domestic Work.* Her latest book is the co-edited volume *Intimate Labors: Cultures, Technologies and the Politics of Care.*

A growing crisis of care troubles the world's most developed nations. Even as demand for care has increased, its supply has dwindled. The result is a care deficit,[1] to which women from the Philippines have responded in force. Roughly two-thirds[2] of Filipino migrant workers are women, and their exodus, usually to fill domestic jobs,[3] has generated tremendous social change in the Philippines. When female migrants are mothers, they leave behind their own children, usually in the care of other women. Many Filipino children now grow up in divided households, where geographic separation places children under serious emotional strain. And yet it is impossible to overlook the significance of migrant labor to the Philippine economy. Some 34 to 54 percent of the Filipino population is sustained by remittances from migrant workers.[4]

Women in the Philippines, just like their counterparts in postindustrial nations, suffer from a "stalled revolution." Local gender ideology remains a few steps behind the economic reality, which has produced numerous female-headed, transnational households.[5] Consequently, a far greater degree of anxiety attends the quality of family life for the dependents of migrant mothers than for those of migrant fathers. The dominant gender ideology, after all, holds that a woman's rightful place is in the home, and the households of migrant mothers present a challenge to this view. In response, government officials and journalists denounce migrating mothers, claiming that they have caused the Filipino family to deteriorate, children to be abandoned, and a crisis of care to take root in the Philippines. To end this crisis, critics admonish, these mothers must return. . . .

The Philippine media reinforce this position by consistently publishing sensationalist reports on the suffering of children in transnational families. These reports tend to vilify migrant mothers, suggesting that their children face more profound problems than do those of migrant fathers; and despite the fact that most of the children in question are left with relatives, journalists tend to refer to them as having been "abandoned." One article reports, "A child's sense of loss appears to be greater when it is the mother who leaves to work abroad."[6] Others link the emigration of mothers to the inadequate child care and unstable family life that eventually lead such children to "drugs, gambling, and drinking."[7] Writes one columnist, "Incest and rapes within blood relatives are alarmingly on the rise not only within Metro Manila but also in the provinces. There are some indications that the absence of mothers who have become OCWs [overseas contract workers] has something to do with the situation."[8] The same columnist elsewhere expresses the popular view that the children of migrants become a burden on the larger society: "Guidance counselors and social welfare agencies can show grim statistics

on how many children have turned into liabilities to our society because of absentee parents."[9]

From January to July 2000, I conducted sixty-nine in-depth interviews with young adults who grew up in transnational households in the Philippines. Almost none of these children have yet reunited with their migrant parents. I interviewed thirty children with migrant mothers, twenty-six with migrant fathers, and thirteen with two migrant parents. The children I spoke to certainly had endured emotional hardships; but contrary to the media's dark presentation, they did not all experience their mothers' migration as abandonment. The hardships in their lives were frequently diminished when they received support from extended families and communities, when they enjoyed open communication with their migrant parents, and when they clearly understood the limited financial options that led their parents to migrate in the first place.

To call for the return of migrant mothers is to ignore the fact that the Philippines has grown increasingly dependent on their remittances. To acknowledge this reality could lead the Philippines toward a more egalitarian gender ideology. Casting blame on migrant mothers, however, serves only to divert the society's attention away from these children's needs, finally aggravating their difficulties by stigmatizing their family's choices.

The Philippine media has certainly sensationalized the issue of child welfare in migrating families, but that should not obscure the fact that the Philippines faces a genuine care crisis. Care is now the country's primary export. Remittances—mostly from migrant domestic workers—constitute the economy's largest source of foreign currency, . . . With limited choices in the Philippines, women migrate to help sustain their families financially, but the price is very high. Both mothers and children suffer from family separation, even under the best of circumstances.

Migrant mothers who work as nannies often face the painful prospect of caring for other people's children while being unable to tend to their own. One such mother in Rome, Rosemarie Samaniego,[10] describes this predicament:

> When the girl that I take care of calls her mother "Mama," my heart jumps all the time because my children also call me "Mama."

I feel the gap caused by our physical separation especially in the morning, when I pack [her] lunch, because that's what I used to do for my children. . . . I begin thinking that at this hour I should be taking care of my very own children and not someone else's, someone who is not related to me in any way, shape, or form. . . . The work that I do here is done for my family, but the problem is they are not close to me but are far away in the Philippines. Sometimes, you feel the separation and you start to cry. Some days, I just start crying while I am sweeping the floor because I am thinking about my children in the Philippines. Sometimes, when I receive a letter from my children telling me that they are sick, I look up out the window and ask the Lord to look after them and make sure they get better even without me around to care after them. [*Starts crying.*] If I had wings, I would fly home to my children. Just for a moment, to see my children and take care of their needs, help them, then fly back over here to continue my work.

The children of migrant workers also suffer an incalculable loss when a parent disappears overseas. As Ellen Seneriches,[11] a twenty-one-year-old daughter of a domestic worker in New York, says:

There are times when you want to talk to her, but she is not there. That is really hard, very difficult. . . . There are times when I want to call her, speak to her, cry to her, and I cannot. It is difficult. The only thing that I can do is write to her. And I cannot cry through the e-mails and sometimes I just want to cry on her shoulder.

Children like Ellen, who was only ten years old when her mother left for New York, often repress their longings to reunite with their mothers. Knowing that their families have few financial options, they are left with no choice but to put their emotional needs aside. Often, they do so knowing that their mothers' care and attention have been diverted to other children. When I asked her how she felt about her mother's wards in New York, Ellen responded:

Very jealous. I am very, very jealous. There was even a time when she told the children she was caring for that they are very lucky that she was taking care of them, while her

children back in the Philippines don't even have a mom to take care of them. It's pathetic, but it's true. We were left alone by ourselves and we had to be responsible at a very young age without a mother. Can you imagine?

Children like Ellen do experience emotional stress when they grow up in transnational households. But it is worth emphasizing that many migrant mothers attempt to sustain ties with their children, and their children often recognize and appreciate these efforts. Although her mother, undocumented in the United States, has not returned once to the Philippines in twelve years, Ellen does not doubt that she has struggled to remain close to her children despite the distance. In fact, although Ellen lives only three hours away from her father, she feels closer to and communicates more frequently with her mother. Says Ellen:

I realize that my mother loves us very much. Even if she is far away, she would send us her love. She would make us feel like she really loved us. She would do this by always being there. She would just assure us that whenever we have problems to just call her and tell her. [*Pauses.*] And so I know that it has been more difficult for her than other mothers. She has had to do extra work because she is so far away from us.

Like Ellen's mother, who managed to "be there" despite a vast distance, other migrant mothers do not necessarily "abandon" their traditional duty of nurturing their families. Rather, they provide emotional care and guidance from afar.[12] Ellen even credits her mother for her success in school. Now a second-year medical school student, Ellen graduated at the top of her class in both high school and college. She says that the constant, open communication she shares with her mother provided the key to her success. She reflects:

We communicate as often as we can, like twice or thrice a week through e-mails. Then she would call us every week. And it is very expensive, I know. . . . My mother and I have a very open relationship. We are like best friends. She would give me advice whenever I had problems. . . . . She understands why I would act this or that way. She knows me really well. And she is also transparent to me. She always knows when I have problems, and likewise I know when she does. I am closer to her than to my father.

Ellen is clearly not the abandoned child or social liability the Philippine media describe. She not only benefits from sufficient parental support—from both her geographically distant mother and her nearby father—but also exceeds the bar of excellence in schooling. Her story indicates that children of migrant parents can overcome the emotional strains of transnational family life, and that they can enjoy sufficient family support, even from their geographically distant parent.

Of course, her good fortune is not universal. But it does raise questions about how children withstand such geographical strains; whether and how they maintain solid ties with their distant parents; and what circumstances lead some children to feel that those ties have weakened or given out. The Philippine media tend to equate the absence of a child's biological mother with abandonment, which leads to the assumption that all such children, lacking familial support, will become social liabilities. But I found that positive surrogate parental figures and open communication with the migrant parent, along with acknowledgment of the migrant parent's contribution to the collective mobility of the family, allay many of the emotional insecurities that arise from transnational household arrangements. Children who lack these resources have greater difficulty adjusting.

Extensive research bears out this observation. The Scalabrini Migration Center, a nongovernmental organization for migration research in the Philippines, surveyed 709 elementary-school-age Filipino children in 2000, comparing the experiences of those with a father absent, a mother absent, both parents absent, and both parents present. While the researchers observed that parental absence does prompt feelings of abandonment and loneliness among children, they concluded that "it does not necessarily become an occasion for laziness and unruliness." Rather, if the extended family supports the child and makes him or her aware of the material benefits migration brings, the child may actually be spurred toward greater self-reliance and ambition, despite continued longings for family unity.

Jeek Pereno's life has been defined by those longings. At twenty-five, he is a merchandiser for a large department store in the Philippines. His mother more than adequately provided for her children, managing with her meager wages first as a domestic worker and then as a nurse's aide, to send them $200 a month and even to purchase a house in a fairly exclusive neighborhood in the city center. But Jeek still feels abandoned and insecure in his mother's affection, he believes that growing up without his parents robbed him of the discipline he needed. Like other children of migrant workers, Jeek does not feel that his faraway mother's financial support has been enough. Instead, he wishes she had offered him more guidance, concern, and emotional care.

Jeek was eight years old when his parents relocated to New York and left him, along with his three brothers, in the care of their aunt. Eight years later, Jeek's father passed away, and two of his brothers (the oldest and youngest) joined their mother in New York. Visa complications have prevented Jeek and his other brother from following—but their mother has not once returned to visit them in the Philippines. When I expressed surprise at this, Jeek solemnly replied: "Never. It will cost too much, she said."

Years of separation breed unfamiliarity among family members, and Jeek does not have the emotional security of knowing that his mother has genuinely tried to lessen that estrangement. For Jeek, only a visit could shore up this security after seventeen years of separation. His mother's weekly phone calls do not suffice. And because he experiences his mother's absence as indifference, he does not feel comfortable communicating with her openly about his unmet needs. The result is repression, which in turn aggravates the resentment he feels. Jeek told me:

> I talk to my mother once in a while. But what happens, whenever she asks how I am doing, I just say okay. It's not like I am really going to tell her that I have problems here. . . . It's not like she can do anything about my problems if I told her about them. Financial problems, yes she can help. But not the other problems, like emotional problems. . . . She will try to give advice, but I am not very interested to talk to her about things like that. . . . Of course, you are still young, you don't really know what is going to happen in the future. Before you

realize that your parents left you, you can't do anything about it anymore. You are not in a position to tell them not to leave you. They should have not left us. (*Sobs.*)

I asked Jeek if his mother knew he felt this way. "No," he said, "she doesn't know." Asked if he received emotional support from anyone, Jeek replied, "As much as possible, if I can handle it, I try not to get emotional support from anyone. I just keep everything inside me."

Jeek feels that his mother not only abandoned him but failed to leave him with an adequate surrogate. His aunt had a family and children of her own. Jeek recalled, "While I do know that my aunt loves me and she took care of us to the best of her ability, I am not convinced that it was enough. . . . Because we were not disciplined enough. She let us do whatever we wanted to do." Jeek feels that his education suffered from this lack of discipline, and he greatly regrets not having concentrated on his studies. Having completed only a two-year vocational program in electronics, he doubts his competency to pursue a college degree. At twenty-five, he feels stuck, with only the limited option of turning from one low-paying job to another.

Children who, unlike Jeek, received good surrogate parenting managed to concentrate on their studies and in the end to fare much better. Rudy Montoya, a nineteen-year-old whose mother has done domestic work in Hong Kong for more than twelve years, credits his mother's brother for helping him succeed in high school:

My uncle is the most influential person in my life. Well, he is in Saudi Arabia now. . . . He would tell me that my mother loves me and not to resent her, and that whatever happens, I should write her. He would encourage me and he would tell me to trust the Lord. And then, I remember in high school, he would push me to study. I learned a lot from him in high school. Showing his love for me, he would help me with my schoolwork. . . . The time that I spent with my uncle was short, but he is the person who helped me grow up to be a better person.

Unlike Jeek's aunt, Rudy's uncle did not have a family of his own. He was able to devote more time to Rudy, instilling discipline in his young charge as

well as reassuring him that his mother, who is the sole income provider for her family, did not abandon him. Although his mother has returned to visit him only twice—once when he was in the fourth grade and again two years later—Rudy, who is now a college student, sees his mother as a "good provider" who has made tremendous sacrifices for his sake. This knowledge offers him emotional security, as well as a strong feeling of gratitude. When I asked him about the importance of education, he replied, "I haven't given anything back to my mother for the sacrifices that she has made for me. The least I could do for her is graduate, so that I can find a good job, so that eventually I will be able to help her out, too."

Many children resolve the emotional insecurity of being left by their parents the way that Rudy has: by viewing migration as a sacrifice to be repaid by adult children. Children who believe that their migrant mothers are struggling for the sake of the family's collective mobility, rather than leaving to live the "good life," are less likely to feel abandoned and more likely to accept their mothers' efforts to sustain close relationships from a distance. One such child is Theresa Bascara, an eighteen-year-old college student whose mother has worked as a domestic in Hong Kong since 1984. As she puts it, "[My inspiration is] my mother, because she is the one suffering over there. So the least I can give back to her is doing well in school."

For Ellen Seneriches, the image of her suffering mother compels her to reciprocate. She explained:

Especially after my mother left, I became more motivated to study harder. I did because my mother was sacrificing a lot and I had to compensate for how hard it is to be away from your children and then crying a lot at night, not knowing what we are doing. She would tell us in voice tapes. She would send us voice tapes every month, twice a month, and we would hear her cry in these tapes.

Having witnessed her mother's suffering even from a distance, Ellen can acknowledge the sacrifices her mother has made and the hardships she has endured in order to be a "good provider" for her family. This knowledge assuaged the resentment Ellen frequently felt when her mother first migrated.

Many of the children I interviewed harbored images of their mothers as martyrs, and they often found comfort in their mother's grief over not being able to nurture them directly. The expectation among such children that they will continue to receive a significant part of their nurturing from their mothers, despite the distance, points to the conservative gender ideology most of them maintain.[13] But whether or not they see their mothers as martyrs, children of migrant women feel best cared for when their mothers make consistent efforts to show parental concern from a distance. As Jeek's and Ellen's stories indicate, open communication with the migrant parent soothes feelings of abandonment; those who enjoy such open channels fare much better than those who lack them. Not only does communication ease children's emotional difficulties; it also fosters a sense of family unity, and it promotes the view that migration is a survival strategy that requires sacrifices from both children and parents for the good of the family.

For daughters of migrant mothers, such sacrifices commonly take the form of assuming some of their absent mothers' responsibilities, including the care of younger siblings. As Ellen told me:

> It was a strategy, and all of us had to sacrifice for it. . . . We all had to adjust, every day of our lives. . . . Imagine waking up without a mother calling you for breakfast. Then there would be no one to prepare the clothes for my brothers. We are all going to school. . . . I had to wake up earlier. I had to prepare their clothes. I had to wake them up and help them prepare for school. Then I also had to help them with their homework at night. I had to tutor them.

Asked if she resented this extra work, Ellen replied, "No. I saw it as training, a training that helped me become a leader. It makes you more of a leader doing that every day. I guess that is an advantage to me, and to my siblings as well."

Ellen's effort to assist in the household's daily maintenance was another way she reciprocated for her mother's emotional and financial support. Viewing her added work as a positive life lesson, Ellen believes that these responsibilities enabled her to develop leadership skills. Notably, her high school selected her as its first ever female commander for its government-mandated military training corps.

Unlike Jeek, Ellen is secure in her mother's love. She feels that her mother has struggled to "be there"; Jeek feels that his has not. Hence, Ellen has managed to successfully adjust to her household arrangement, while Jeek has not. The continual open communication between Ellen and her mother has had ramifications for their entire family: in return for her mother's sacrifices, Ellen assumed the role of second mother to her younger siblings, visiting them every weekend during her college years in order to spend quality time with them.

In general, eldest daughters of migrant mothers assume substantial familial responsibilities, often becoming substitute mothers for their siblings. Similarly, eldest sons stand in for migrant fathers. Armando Martinez, a twenty-nine-year-old entrepreneur whose father worked in Dubai for six months while he was in high school, related his experiences:

> I became a father during those six months. It was like, ugghhh, I made the rules. . . . I was able to see that it was hard if your family is not complete, you feel that there is something missing. . . . It's because the major decisions, sometimes, I was not old enough for them. I was only a teenager, and I was not that strong in my convictions when it came to making decisions. It was like work that I should not have been responsible for. I still wanted to play. So it was an added burden on my side.

Even when there is a parent left behind, children of migrant workers tend to assume added familial responsibilities, and these responsibilities vary along gender lines. Nonetheless, the weight tends to fall most heavily on children of migrant mothers, who are often left to struggle with the lack of male responsibility for care work in the Philippines. While a great number of children with migrant fathers receive full-time care from stay-at-home mothers, those with migrant mothers do not receive the same amount of care. Their fathers are likely to hold full-time jobs, and they rarely have the time to assume the role of primary caregiver. Of thirty children of migrant mothers I interviewed, only four had stay-at-home fathers. Most fathers passed the caregiving responsibilities on to other relatives, many of whom, like Jeek's aunt, already had families of their own to care for and regarded the children of migrant relatives as an extra burden. Families of migrant fathers are less likely to rely on the care work of extended kin.[14] Among my interviewees, thirteen of twenty-six children with migrant fathers lived with and were cared for primarily by their stay-at-home mothers.

Children of migrant mothers, unlike those of migrant fathers, have the added burden of accepting nontraditional gender roles in their families. The Scalabrini Migration Center reports that these children "tend to be more angry, confused, apathetic, and more afraid than other children."[15] They are caught within an "ideological stall" in the societal acceptance of female-headed transnational households. Because her family does not fit the traditional nuclear household model, Theresa Bascara sees her family as "broken," even though she describes her relationship to her mother as "very close." She says, "A family, I can say, is only whole if your father is the one working and your mother is only staying at home. It's okay if your mother works too, but somewhere close to you."

Some children in transnational families adjust to their household arrangements with greater success than others do. Those who feel that their mothers strive to nurture them as well as to be good providers are more likely to be accepting. The support of extended kin, or perhaps a sense of public accountability for their welfare, also helps children combat feelings of abandonment. Likewise, a more gender-egalitarian value system enables children to appreciate their mothers as good providers, which in turn allows them to see their mothers' migrations as demonstrations of love.

Even if they are well-adjusted, however, children in transnational families still suffer the loss of family intimacy. They are often forced to compensate by accepting commodities, rather than affection, as the most tangible reassurance of their parents' love. By putting family intimacy on hold, children can only wait for the opportunity to spend quality time with their migrant parents. Even when that time comes, it can be painful. As Theresa related:

> When my mother is home, I just sit next to her. I stare at her face, to see the changes in her face, to see how she aged during the years that she was away from us. But when she is about to go back to Hong Kong, it's like my heart is going to burst. I would just cry and cry. I really can't explain the feeling. Sometimes, when my mother is home, preparing to leave for Hong Kong,

> I would just start crying, because I already start missing her. I ask myself, how many more years will it be until we see each other again?
>
> . . . Telephone calls. That's not enough. You can't hug her, kiss her, feel her, everything. You can't feel her presence. It's just words that you have. What I want is to have my mother close to me, to see her grow older, and when she is sick, you are the one taking care of her and when you are sick, she is the one taking care of you.

Not surprisingly, when asked if they would leave their own children to take jobs as migrant workers, almost all of my respondents answered, "Never." When I asked why not, most said that they would never want their children to go through what they had gone through, or to be denied what they were denied, in their childhoods. Armando Martinez best summed up what children in transnational families lose when he said:

> You just cannot buy the times when your family is together. Isn't that right? . . . . The first time your baby speaks, you are not there. Other people would experience that joy. And when your child graduates with honors, you are also not there. . . . Is that right? When your child wins a basketball game, no one will be there to ask him how his game went, how many points he made. Is that right? Your family loses, don't you think?

Children of transnational families repeatedly stress that they lack the pleasure and comfort of daily interaction with their parents. Nonetheless, these children do not necessarily become "delinquent," nor are their families necessarily broken, in the manner the Philippine media depicts. Armando mirrored the opinion of most of the children in my study when he defended transnational families: "Even if [parents] are far away, they are still there. I get that from basketball, specifically zone defense." [He laughed.] "If someone is not there, you just have to adjust. It's like a slight hindrance that you just have to adjust to. Then when they come back, you get a chance to recover. It's like that."

Recognizing that the family is an adaptive unit that responds to external forces, many children make do, even if doing so requires tremendous sacrifices. They give up intimacy and familiarity with their parents. Often, they attempt to make up for their migrant parents' hardships by maintaining close bonds across great distances, even though most of them feel that such bonds could never possibly draw their distant parent close enough. But their efforts are frequently sustained by the belief that such emotional sacrifices are not without meaning—that they are ultimately for the greater good of their families and their future. Jason Halili's mother provided care for elderly persons in Los Angeles for fifteen years. Jason, now twenty-one, reasons, "If she did not leave, I would not be here right now. So it was the hardest route to take, but at the same time, the best route to take."

Transnational families were not always equated with "broken homes" in the Philippine public discourse. Nor did labor migration emerge as a perceived threat to family life before the late 1980s, when the number of migrant women significantly increased. This suggests that changes to the gendered division of family labor may have as much as anything else to do with the Philippine care crisis.

The Philippine public simply assumes that the proliferation of female-headed transnational households will wreak havoc on the lives of children. The Scalabrini Migration Center explains that children of migrant mothers suffer more than those of migrant fathers because child rearing is "a role women are more adept at, are better prepared for, and pay more attention to."[16] The center's study, like the Philippine media, recommends that mothers be kept from migrating. The researchers suggest that "economic programs should be targeted particularly toward the absorption of the female labor force, to facilitate the possibility for mothers to remain in the family."[17] Yet the return migration of mothers is neither a plausible nor a desirable solution. Rather, it implicitly accepts gender inequities in the family, even as it ignores the economic pressures generated by globalization.

As national discourse on the care crisis in the Philippines vilifies migrant women, it also downplays the contributions these women make to the country's economy. Such hand-wringing merely offers the public an opportunity to discipline women morally and to resist reconstituting family life in a manner that reflects the country's increasing dependence on women's foreign remittances. This pattern is not exclusive to the Philippines. As Arjun Appadurai observes, globalization has commonly led to "ideas

about gender and modernity that create large female work forces at the same time that cross-national ideologies of 'culture,' 'authenticity,' and national honor put increasing pressure on various communities to morally discipline working women."[18]

The moral disciplining of women, however, hurts those who most need protection. It pathologizes the children of migrants, and it downplays the emotional difficulties that mothers like Rosemarie Samaniego face. Moreover, it ignores the struggles of migrant mothers who attempt to nurture their children from a distance. Vilifying migrant women as bad mothers promotes the view that the return to the nuclear family is the only viable solution to the emotional difficulties of children in transnational families. In so doing, it directs attention away from the special needs of children in transnational families—for instance, the need for community projects that would improve communication among far-flung family members, or for special school programs, the like of which did not exist at my field research site. It's also a strategy that sidelines the agency and adaptability of the children themselves.

To say that children are perfectly capable of adjusting to nontraditional households is not to say that they don't suffer hardships. But the overwhelming public support for keeping migrant mothers at home does have a negative impact on these children's adjustment. Implicit in such views is a rejection of the division of labor in families with migrant mothers, and the message such children receive is that their household arrangements are simply wrong. Moreover, calling for the return migration of women does not necessarily solve the problems plaguing families in the Philippines. Domestic violence and male infidelity, for instance—two social problems the government has never adequately addressed—would still threaten the well-being of children.

Without a doubt, the children of migrant Filipina domestic workers suffer from the extraction of care from the global south to the global north. The plight of these children is a timely and necessary concern for nongovernmental, governmental, and academic groups in the Philippines. Blaming migrant mothers, however, has not helped, and has even hurt, those whose relationships suffer most from the movement of care in the global economy. Advocates for children in transnational families should focus their attention not on calling for a return to the nuclear family but on trying to meet the special needs transnational families possess. One of those needs is for a reconstituted gender ideology in the Philippines; another is for the elimination of legislation that penalizes migrant families in the nations where they work.

If we want to secure quality care for the children of transnational families, gender egalitarian views of child rearing are essential. Such views can be fostered by recognizing the economic contributions women make to their families and by redefining motherhood to include providing for one's family. Gender should be recognized as a fluid social category, and masculinity should be redefined, as the larger society questions the biologically based assumption that only women have an aptitude to provide care. Government officials and the media could then stop vilifying migrant women, redirecting their attention, instead, to men. They could question the lack of male accountability for care work, and they could demand that men, including migrant fathers, take more responsibility for the emotional welfare of their children.

The host societies of migrant Filipina domestic workers should also be held more accountable for their welfare and for that of their families. These women's work allows First World women to enter the paid labor force. As one Dutch employer states, "There are people who would look after children, but other things are more fun. Carers from other countries, if we can use their surplus carers, that's a solution."[19]

Yet, as we've seen, one cannot simply assume that the care leaving disadvantaged nations is surplus care. What is a solution for rich nations creates a problem in poor nations. Mothers like Rosemarie Samaniego and children like Ellen Seneriches and Jeek Pereno bear the brunt of this problem, while the receiving countries and the employing families benefit.

Most receiving countries have yet to recognize the contributions of their migrant care workers. They have consistently ignored these workers' rights and limited their full incorporation into society. The wages of migrant workers are so low that they cannot afford to bring their own families to join them, or to regularly visit their children in the Philippines; relegated to the status of guest workers, they are restricted to the low-wage employment sector, and with very few exceptions, the migration of their spouses and children is also restricted.[20] These arrangements work to the benefit of employers, since migrant care workers can give the best possible care for their employers' families when they are free of care-giving responsibilities to their own families. But there is a dire need to lobby for more inclusive policies, and for employers to develop a sense of accountability for their workers' children. After all, migrant workers significantly help their employers to reduce *their* families' care deficit.

NOTES

1. Arlie Hochschild, "The Culture of Politics: Traditional, Post-modern, Cold Modern, Warm Modern Ideals of Care," *Social Politics*, vol. 2, no. 3 (1995): pp. 331–46.

2. IBON Facts and Figures, "Filipinos as Global Slaves," vol. 22, nos. 5–6 (March 15–31, 1999), p. 6.

3. Notably, Filipino women. . . also alleviate the care crisis plaguing hospitals and hospices in more developed nations by providing services as professional nurses. At the expense of the quality of professional care in the Philippines, nurses have sought the better wages available outside the country.

4. Gina Mission, "The Breadwinners: Female Migrant Workers," *WIN: Women's International Net Issue* (November 1998): p. 15A.

5. Hochschild and Machung, 1989. By "stalled revolution," Hochschild refers to the fact that the economic contributions of women to the family have not been met with a corresponding increase in male responsibility for household work.

6. Perfecto G. Caparas, "OCWs Children: Bearing the Burden of Separation," *Manila Times* (September 30, n.d.), pp. 1–2.

7. Susan Fernandez, "Pamilya ng OFWs maraming hirap" (Many hardships in the families of OFWs), *Abante* (January 27, 1997), p. 5.

8. Lorie Toledo, "Child Sexual Abuse Awareness," *People's Journal* (February 19, 1996), p. 4. Although incest is a social problem in the Philippines, its direct correlation to the emigration of mothers is an unproven speculation.

9. Lorie Toledo, "Overseas job vs. family stability," *People's Journal* (December 15, 1993), p. 4.

10. Rosemarie Samaniego is a pseudonym. This excerpt is drawn from Rhacel Salazar Parreñas, *Servants of Globalization: Women, Migration, and Domestic Work* (Stanford, Calif.: Stanford University Press, 2001).

11. Ellen Seneriches and the names of the other children whom I quote in this article are all pseudonyms.

12. Pierrette Hondagneu-Sotelo and Ernestine Avila, "'I'm Here, but I'm There': The Meanings of Latina Transnational Motherhood," *Gender and Society*, vol. 11, no. 5 (1997), pp. 548–71.

13. Similarly, I found that children use the corollary image of the struggling "breadwinner" father to negotiate the emotional strains of their transnational household arrangement.

14. Scalabrini Migration Center (SMC), *Impact of Labor Migration on the Children Left Behind* (Quezon City, Philippines: Scalabrini Migration Center, 2000).

15. SMC, 2000, p. 65.

16. SMC, 2000, p. 57.

17. SMC, 2000, p. 65.

18. Arjun Appadurai, "Globalization and the Research Imagination," *International Social Science Journal,* vol. 160 (June 1999), p. 231.

19. Marije Meerman, "The Care Chain," episode 42 of *The New World* (Netherlands: VPRO-TV); www.dnv.vpro.nl/carechain.

20. Policies in various receiving countries restrict the migration of workers' families. Such restrictions can be found both in countries, such as Singapore and Taiwan, that have illiberal policies and in those, like Canada, with liberal policies.

FORTY-SEVEN

♦♦♦

Remotely Sensed (2002)
A Topography of the Global Sex Trade

Ursula Biemann

Ursula Biemann is a researcher at the Institute for Theory of Art and Design in Zurich. Her art, writings, and curatorial work focus on media, geography, migration, and gender relations in the economy. Her award-winning video essays and installations have been widely shown at international exhibitions and museums including the Museum of Modern Art (MOMA) in New York.

. . . Globalization is a very gendered process: an evergrowing proportion of migrant people looking for work are female. However, beyond a simple feminization of migration we notice that women's labour is being sexualized, that is to say, global processes actually address women directly in their sexuality. The worldwide migration of women into the sex industry or more specifically the burgeoning trafficking in women can be read as a structural part of pancapitalism. . . . I am using the theoretical framework of geography because it allows for an examination of female migrancy, mobility and routing in relation to specific sites, while at the same time permitting an integration of their psychological and material experience. In other words, I am interested in the practice of linking geo-politics to an understanding of how subjects are produced.

Geography is understood as a visual culture in this context. Satellite media and other geographic information systems are generating profuse quantities of topographic images to be interpreted for scientific, social and military use. Increasingly they make their way into our daily lives, inform the way we think about the world and code our concept of globality. I make it my project to explore how these satellite visions of globality are producing a sexual economy in which it has become thinkable to reorganize women geographically on a global scale.

Countergeographies

Spiralling down from an orbital view the video essay *Remote Sensing* takes an earthly perspective on the topography of the global sex trade. It is a project of countergeography that engages in migration and cross-border circuits, illegal and illicit networks as well as alternative circuits of survival, where women have emerged as key actors. The digital documents generated for the video essay trace the routes and reasons of women who travel across the globe to enter this gigantic Fordism [production line] of service that is the sex industry.

Trafficking hinges on the displacement of women, their costly transportation across topographies from one cultural arrangement to another, from one spatial organization to another, from one abandoned economy to a place of greater accumulations. It is the route that counts. The agents charge money for the vehicle and for the escort who knows the path and the border geography, the contacts and the bribes. Female bodies are the new cargo in these transactions across boundaries that generate massive amounts of footloose capital, abstract global capital that is nevertheless so physical for some. The travel money will go back into bonding women to do unpaid sex work for the trafficking ring. It is a common practice of debt-bondage that places women in the contexts of the historical spaces of the brothel and the colony.

There are numerous structural and political reasons why women move, and are being moved, into the global sex industry. The Mekong region [South East Asia] has traditionally been a burgeoning basin for the trafficking of women who criss-cross borders in all directions. . . . Thailand is no longer just a sending country, but has also become a country of transit and destination. While Thai women migrated in the 1970s to Europe and North America or have been promoted to the higher echelons of the sex industry catering to foreign tourists, there is a need to supply new women and girls to the lower class brothels in Thailand. This market segment draws on the young rural female population in neighbouring countries like Burma, Laos, and Vietnam. China goes through a different predicament. The prolonged period under the one-child policy has caused a major gender disparity in the present generation. Many Chinese men who do not find wives will acquire them abroad. In Taiwan, on the other hand, women prefer a modern life in the city and male farmers have a hard time attracting a wife who wants to live a hardworking rural lifestyle. They also have to import females from the Philippines by the tens of thousands for unpaid agricultural labour and every year 100,000 South East Asian women are shipped into the Japanese entertainment industry, which equals Japan's defence budget in volume.

The commodification and displacement of female bodies in South East Asia generates impressive figures, but my work does not situate itself in the production of factual information. The questions I have to ask myself as an artist and video maker are: How can I dislocate and recontextualize a much belaboured question such as the

marketability of women and the objectification of female sexuality? How can a video, rather than simply arguing against capitalism and affirming rigid gender identities, reflect and produce the expansion of the very space in which we write and speak of the feminine? There is a need to investigate the interplay between the symbolization of the feminine and the economic and material reality of women. To reproduce closed, privatized and restricted images of women is confining the feminine further. Some women take the route into sex work voluntarily, others not, it is true, but there is a large grey zone in between these two conditions, a vast field of negotiation, on which I focus my attention. The process of re-signification, which I undertake in my video practice, then, is not only an incessant struggle against the effacement of the diversification and differentiation of the feminine, it is also an analysis of the gendered dynamic inscribed in social and material landscapes. Of course I would like to see the space in which we write our lives, our bodies and sexuality as a heterogeneous one but in the course of creating this space, I am bound to look at the existing technologies and networks of knowledge that operate in delimiting and formalizing it.

Bandana Pattanaik *(Global Alliance Against Traffic in Women, GAATW):* I think seeing them as victims creates a lot of sympathy and therefore people find it easier to accept. If I'll say that I have been forced into prostitution, people say, oh poor thing, let's help her, she is in a really bad situation. But if somebody says I chose to become a prostitute that's very difficult to accept or to understand. Why would you choose to be a prostitute? So many times it's framed in this either/or debate. Either you are a victim or you are an agent. Either you have chosen to be a sex worker or you have been forced into prostitution. And I think there are such large grey areas in between.

While all of my videos to date elaborate on the relations of gender, technology and transnational capitalism, *Remote Sensing* engages maybe most explicitly in a critique of visualizing technologies, particularly the orbital omniscient view of satellite imagery. Taking up a feminist critique that has claimed the importance of the viewing structures and apparatuses for the power relations established by the gaze, there is a need to displace and interrogate the images and to reintroduce a situated way of seeing and knowing. Geographic information systems (GIS) propose an abstract and highly accurate view of the world from the top down. GIS are criticized by feminist scientists for applying binary and mutually exclusive categories that are unable to hold and interpret a great variety of conflicting information. They are also completely unable to think in relational terms and reveal the gendered meaning of data. Cartography is insufficient, then, to map the subjective path of people on the move.

A major objective of *Remote Sensing* is to propose a mode of representation that traces the trajectory of people in a pancapitalist world order wherein the space between departure and arrival is understood as a transnational one, i.e., a potentially subversive space which does not adhere to national rules, but nevertheless a complex material and social space that is formed by economic relations. All this is from a gendered perspective. Remotely gazed at from the orbital perspective, transnational sexuality comes into full sight. In this topography of the global sex trade, the female bodies get sensed and identified, evaluated and re-routed according to their assigned function. The moving women appear as data streams in the video, scans and X-rays portrayed over landscapes passing by, their anatomical and demographic data are recorded, their routes appear in electronic travel schedules on the screen. They are the embodiment of the abstract financial flows that feed the global economy.

Remote Sensing visualizes the multilayered meaning of geography where the mobilization and the sexualization of women is linked to the implementation of new technologies, often in contradictory ways. While the Internet facilitates the migration flow, particularly for women via the bride market, border reinforcement technologies on the other hand hinder and push it into the illegal sector.

Heat and movement sensors, infra-red and roentgen cameras, digital and genetic control mechanisms are developed and put to use along the . . . borders. Parallel to this, European migration politics are quite explicit in their practice of directing migrant women straight into the sex industry without giving them any future option to switch to another trade. For non-European female applicants, the Swiss government only issues "dancers' visas" which hinge on cabaret contracts. The automatic channelling of migrant women into sex work is an index of their status under national rule, but it also speaks of the place of sex in that national space where laws protect the flourishing sexual life of male citizens as a privilege and source of power. Two-thirds of the 500,000 women entering Europe's entertainment industry every year are from Eastern post-socialist countries. The social change in these sending countries since the 1990s and the migration politics of the receiving countries both impact the flow of women into the sex trade. Even though the official policy is to fight human trafficking and to help women getting out of the sex trade, the fact is that the number of trafficked women is steadily increasing. Technologies of marginalization always affect women, and particularly economically disadvantaged women, in their sexuality because powerful players like states, scientific complexes, and military institutions tend to create a sexuality that eroticizes hierarchies.

Aida Santos (*Women's Education, Development, Productivity and Research Organization, WEDPRO*): The history of the American involvement in prostitution and trafficking should not be missed. . . . In the 40s the Americans came and established their bases in the Philippines. The presence of the U.S. Army and Navy contributed dramatically to the rise in prostitution and trafficking, in the sense that when you have an institution like twenty-one military bases scattered all over the country in a situation of poverty and where women's status is very low, families are willing to send off their kids to work, and the elder daughters are bound by tradition to help their families and send their siblings to school, you've got very rich soil for exploitation. And that's what happened in the former U.S. baselands. The Marines are still coming here for training and when the big carriers dock in the harbour, 10,000 servicemen go on shore. In the small town near the Subic base of Olongapo, there are 6000 women registered [to work] in bars.

Since the infrastructure for the entertainment industry was already in place, many of the Rest and Recreation areas created for the U.S. soldiers during the war in Vietnam and Korea have been turned into sites of prostitution and sex tourism. Most of the women who came to the baselands expected to find restaurant jobs, but as it turns out, waitresses do not have a regular salary but work on a commission basis only. Unless they go out with the customers and provide personal entertainment and sexual services, they will not earn a living. Some of the former bases have been transformed into assembly plants for outsourced production paying wages that do not cover their living costs so that many women are bound to gain a complementary income by prostituting. Whether [through] . . . an offspring of military camps or a by-product of Western off-shore operations, women are displaced and drawn into the global economy through sexual labor. Sexual difference becomes a primary structural factor in understanding a migration-bound economy.

Another reason for the trafficking of women is that movements of exile, migration, and international business have created the need to supply "familiar" services abroad. So Filipinas are routed to Lagos in Nigeria to cater to Chinese businessmen; Thai women are trafficked to Paris to serve French-born Chinese and Cambodian immigrants; and girls from Nicaragua are dispatched to Southern California to supply camps of Mexican agricultural workers while others are kept in mobile trailer brothels that circulate in the Chicano suburbs of Los Angeles. The clandestine becomes an obscure form of living the locality of culture, a location that remains suspended and transitory. There is no arrival. The existence of these women is marked by a constant mobility, their time is scheduled, their space is confined, civil rights and sexual governance are suspended. The non-status of their existence speaks of a geographic ambivalence, and it is not surprising that these bodies are usually suspended from the cartographic discourse even though they have become an important part of illicit border transactions and underground economic circuits and increasingly represent a major source of foreign currency for national households. The video makes an effort to track and register the movement of these women and to infuse meaning into the mapping of their trajectories. Why is it so important to trace their paths through space? I think because these very bodies are in fact the site of numerous conflicts. Clearly, they represent a phantasmatic femininity that has been ruled out from Western consciousness but continues to thrive in the a-national space in which the fleeing temporality of their presence and their non-adherence to a national program are major criteria. Their service needs to be secured materially but denied in the official ideology. While their civil status is suspended, their figurative representation reveals another phantasm deeply rooted in the bourgeois projections onto permanently seductive postcolonial places. Silk dresses and an Asian gentleness mask the drastic economic imbalance in which the hard bargain between the sexes takes place in capitalist society.

While the powerful players certainly lay the foundation for the global trafficking of women, we have to recognize that most trafficking operations are not conducted by mighty syndicates. They work in small units, relatives or acquaintances who recruit girls in slum neighbourhoods; frequently there are bi-national couples who have good contacts to the source country. Women often feel that these agents are not exploiting them but actually providing a valuable service in their desire to move to richer countries or to the cities for a modern and more exciting life, helping them to trade a slum existence for the glamour of a Bunny Club. And even if they feel lonely and exhausted, they are still able to send money home, not only supporting their family but generating hard cash for their governments.

Siriporn Skrobanek: We respect these women because many are illiterate, cannot speak a word of English but still have a strong will and encounter the whole world. And many of them can survive and struggle in their own way.

The video, *Remotely Sensing*, is available from Women Make Movies (www.wmm.com). A Web site includes images and text: www.geobodies.org/video/sensing/sensing.html

◆◆◆

Made in China (excerpt) (2005)

Pun Ngai

Pun Ngai is Associate Professor of Social Science at Hong Kong University of Science and Technology. She was the first Asian scholar to win the prestigious C. Wright Mills Award, for *Made in China: Women Factory Workers in a Global Workplace* (2005), which has been described as a "passionate, engaged ethnography." Her research interests include labor and gender, globalization, and relations between mainland China and Hong Kong.

. . . Turning a young and rural body into an industrialized and productive laborer, a seemingly universal project of disciplining labor, is the primary task of transnational production when it meets migrant labor in urban China. . .

Chinese Workers, Socialist Bodies

. . .

An often-repeated story in the [Meteor]workplace, made up by Hong Kong businessmen, managers, and technical persons, was that mainland Chinese workers—socialist and rural bodies—were unfit for capitalist production[1]. Making working bodies thus involved a delicate politics of value and assessment that made use of such reified images as the "socialist" worker and the urban-rural disparity in China. Because Hong Kong businessmen were very distrustful of mainland workers, rural migrant workers were portrayed as uneducated, "uncivilized," and thus undisciplined in the workplace. There was a general belief that these working bodies were ready to spit on the floor, to leave their work position at will, and even worse, to destroy the production machinery.

. . . Thus the first task of capital was to transform individual undesirable migrants into useful workers, which involved projects of culture and power, both covertly and overtly, that worked on bodies and minds, behaviors and beliefs, gestures and habits, and attitudes and aptitudes.

. . . Everywhere in the Meteor plant, there were complaints of *suzhi*, that the quality and nature of labor was unreasonably poor and unacceptable. . . .

I often heard managers from various departments fussing that the workers lacked *jingzheng yishi*, the sense of competition and struggle that was the basic principle of survival in a capitalist society.

. . .

The Art of Spacing: Positioning on the Line

. . . With twenty to twenty-five workers on assembly lines and fifteen to twenty on quality control (QC) lines, there was a total of ten production assembly lines and four QC lines on the shop floor. Placing a body on the line was the first technique of the disciplinary machine to work on the worker. A cog in a machine, the body was pinned down to its own specific position, functional and productive. . . .

A coworker, Meifang, sat directly across from me on the production line. We had a particular relationship that would not have developed in another place or with other people. My presence as an ethnographer in that particular work position and the demands of production jointly shaped our relationship. Meifang was a fresh hand, hired two days after I arrived. With her rounded face she still looked rustic, and she was timid in expressing herself. At age eighteen she was a fresh junior secondary school graduate from a village in Hunan Province. . . .

We were both placed on the screwing positions on a production line of twenty-two workers. We had one foreman, one line leader, and one line assistant. The model produced on the line was an MB201 route-finder, a kind of electronic road map for drivers, produced for a big-name car company in Europe. The product came to our line at nearly the final stage of the production process. We assembled the main board, the liquid crystal display (LCD), and the plastic case around the whole product. With work divided into twelve processes, normally there were two or three people with responsibility for one process. My process was performed by three people: myself, Meifang, and Chinghua. To this day

I still believe that Meifang was hired to accelerate the pace on the line because of my slow speed.

. . . Workers were trained as specialists in just one process; only the workers who had been working on the line for more than a year had the opportunity to learn more than one work process. The work process was seldom changed unless a new model required a new arrangement of work positions. In front of every seat there was a layout hung on the shelf that demonstrated meticulously with pictures and graphics each step the worker should follow. The work was minute, specified, and systematic: what the individual could and should do was to follow it with precision, and if one were attentive and disciplined enough, one needed only to mechanically repeat specific bodily movements.

. . .

But what the disciplinary machine actually wanted was to produce a body without mind, a mindless body. "I don't need to use my mind anymore. I've been doing the same thing for two years. Things come and go, repeating every second and minute. I can do it with my eyes closed," Damei told me. And because the body was mindless, it was replaceable. Thus the strategy of the production machine, in order to safeguard its power and prevent any possibility of the producing body taking charge, was to ensure that every body be trained to be a mindless body. The Chinese migrant workers, as stated earlier, were always seen as untrustworthy workers who would leave the factory any time they liked. This situation was often exaggerated, but the turnover rate was particularly high during the Chinese New Year period. At Meteor, management estimated that every year at this time more than 20 percent of the workforce would leave for good and never come back. Thus for the producing body to be changeable, it was necessary that it be further individualized. One only took responsibility for one's own duty and only became an expert in one's own position. Everybody was useful, but not crucial; no one individual could know and affect the operation of the whole work.

. . .

A Technique of Power: The Assembly Line

If we say the disciplinary spacing of the body results in the individuation and fragmentation of labor power, the assembly line devised in modern industry is a technique of power reuniting individualized bodies in a concerted action. All ten assembly lines at Meteor were equipped with moving conveyor belts. The moving of the belt was, simply, the movement of power. Like a chain, it coupled an individualized body with a specific position, but at the same time it linked the individuals to form a collective social body devoted to the singular aim of maximizing production.

The operation of the moving belt was not only cooperative and productive but also symbolic. The flashing light set at the head of the belt signaled and dictated the actions of each body and combined individual energies into a collective labor force, thus showing its power to control. The light acted like a conductor directing an orchestra, and each individual act formed part of a symphony. It flashed once every two to two and a half minutes, telling workers on the lines that a new set was being run. It controlled speed, time, and bodily movement. The working body was thus individualized, yet paradoxically not one of the bodies could be individualistic, idiosyncratic, or different. Ultimately it was the collective labor and cooperation of the line that mattered. . . .

. . .

Besides the staff in the personnel section, those whom the workers disliked most in the company were the time analysts—all of whom were men. Again and again they came out from the engineering department holding a timing calculator and stood behind the backs of the women workers to measure their time. Male power and female subordination were vividly contrasted. The analysts made suggestions and sent orders, and female bodies would need to catch up to the pace again. The time analysts studied not only the amount of time the work required but also the workers' bodily actions—the gestures and the gaps between bodily movements. No time was wasted; every bodily action had to be accurate and correct. The distance between each body, the distance between the body and the conveyor belt, the height of the chair, and the table and the shelf were all carefully measured and planned. Time and space were all to be used economically; there was to be no waste of surplus bodily actions and no waste of surplus labor force. This was, at least, the dream of the production machine.

On line B, the work of assembling the ROF, the final processing product, was divided into twelve processes. Once a new lot arrived on the line, the time analysts would again measure the work pace. The data they collected would be analyzed by computer to calculate the target for daily production, the speed of the conveyor belt, and the work pace of each individual body. Work speed was reviewed on a weekly basis, which put pressure not only on individuals but also on the line as a whole. Comparisons were made between the lines, and if the gap were too large Mr. Yeung, the chief of the timing analysts section, would personally issue a warning to the workers. The foreperson and the line leader, who were responsible for keeping the line operating, would also share the same pressure. They were assigned to train the workers, keep discipline, and arrange work positions and raw materials. But they also had to keep the line working smoothly by eliminating or controlling human factors such as slow down, sickness, temporary leave to use the washroom, and whatever unpredictable human elements might escape the dictates of the moving line (Cavendish 1982; Glucksman 1990).

We complained every day about the work speed and the unequal arrangement of jobs and time. Although every work process was "scientifically" studied and carefully measured, the simultaneous ordering of a multitude of individualized bodies was not an easy task. Despite the fact that each job was dissected minutely, it was still impossible to keep each work process within a similar amount of time. Some were forced to work faster than others, and some were required to perform more difficult work than others. However, the assembly line simply sped on its way, indifferent to the nature of the work and human differences. Individual bodies were required to accommodate to the line, rather than the line to individual bodies.

Time and time again it was impossible to avoid the units piling up in front of our table. Shutong, who was nicknamed "Fatso" because of her boyish character, sat in front of Meifang and shared the same work process with us. One day she complained: "People can't work at this sort of killing speed. The line should not run so fast. You ought to know that our task requires more time. I am already killing my body." Bailan, our line leader, quickly came and hushed her. "Don't shout. The line is not under our control." This was true; the running of the line had nothing to do with the workers, not even the line leader or the foreman. As a technique of power, the assembly line was completely autocratic; the movement of the belt had a will of its own once the line was set up by the engineering department.

. . .

Speed, Control, and Defiance

Where there was power, there was room for escape, defiance, and transgression. . . . The moving line was set to homogenize the work pace, but the work itself was heterogeneous and variable. . . . Rush orders and frequent changes in production models were characteristic of Meteor because it was a subcontracting factory. So the management had to rely on workers' cooperation and their willingness not only to work overtime but also to finish the work on time. The working women thus held a certain power, albeit interstitial rather than formal, to negotiate their work situation (Knights and Wilmott 1986). . . .

Tactics of defiance often targeted work speed. The production machine tried in manifold ways to turn the human body into a working machine, and the dagongmei on the line learned very quickly that the moving line was an electric despot, binding their bodies to work as fast as possible for the least amount of money.[2] Fu-hui, the worker stationed in front of me, talked to me one drowsy afternoon: "I dream about the line suddenly stopping for a while. I simply can't take a breath. It drags us to work faster and faster. But the more we work, the more the boss earns. They give the workers a little more, yet they make big money." Class-consciousness was articulated thus in the workplace from time to time, although typically in an individual and passing way. The pressures of the assembly line and the work tensions it produced led the women each day to confront their own exploitation in a very immediate way.

Although the work speed was predetermined, the women nevertheless could exert a certain influence on the pace at certain moments. Sometimes, especially at night, when the work speed was unbearable to overstressed bodies, or when a new speed was set for new products and the workers had not yet gotten used to it, all of the women on the line would suddenly slow down at the same time, demonstrating a silent collective resistance to the line leader and the foreman. Nobody would utter a word but simply let the jobs pile up like hills while someone else was left with empty hands. Thus they let the line alone to run itself, making it like a "paper tiger" (a powerless despot). In response the foreman would say a lot of "good words" to persuade the women to be tolerant and catch up on the work. He would say, "Girls, the more you work, the more bonus you get. So why don't you catch up?" Or, "Have some patience, you are all girls. The more you work, the more you can handle it." But if these "good words" were not heeded and the slowdown persisted, the foreman's only recourse was to report to the supervisor and have the time analysts readjust the pace.

Needless to say, the women would view these moments as victories. They knew the rush seasons were the most appropriate moments to exert their bodily power by simply letting their bodies relax and earn time to breathe. Rush period were the times that the new pace of work and amount of the bonus were often bargained over and fought for [Westwood 1984; Rosen 1987]. Sometimes other working and living conditions were challenged as well. However, once the busy period was over the women's bargaining power was dramatically weakened. The workers knew too well that their bargaining power, although recurrent, was ephemeral. They had to seize the right moment or it would be gone.

Controlling pace was an effective strategy for resisting the overwhelming domination of disciplinary power in the workplace. At Meteor, nonassembly line workers, such as in the bonding room or functional testing room, had more power to "hustle and idle" the work speed according to their own interests. As Hua, foreman of the bonding room, told me one day: "If there is a moody hour, the girls will assemble the components slowly and then pass the work to the next girl slowly. They work as slowly as tortoises. If you force them to do it quicker, they can sometimes make it all wrong and you need to redo it. Or they can all pretend to be ill."

Collective illness was common if the speed were set too fast and the bonus rate was too harsh. The bonus rate was an incentive mechanism that supplemented the fixed hourly rate paid to all of the shop floor workers. Every worker in the workplace knew that the bonus system was designed to induce him or her to work as fast as possible. So when the rate of pay was good, they worked faster; if not, they simply slowed down. . . .

Programming the Work Habit: The Daily Timetable

. . .

. . . The usual working day was eleven or twelve hours. If there were a rush order, however, workers were required to stay until 11:00 P.M. or 12 A.M. The nightshift workers started work at 8:00 P.M. and finished at 8:00 A.M. with one rest hour between 3:00 A.M. and 4:00 A.M. Overtime work was considered part of normal working hours, directly violating the Labor Law of 1995 and the Regulation of Labor Contract of Shenzhen Special Economic Zone (1995). These regulating documents address overtime as follows:

1. The working hours of the worker should not be over eight hours per day; the weekly average working hours should not be over forty-four hours.

2. The worker should have one rest day per week.

3. The normal overtime work should not be extended over one hour; for some special reason and with consideration of the worker health condition, the prolonging of working hours should not be over three hours each day.

4. The total overtime work per month should not be over thirty-six hours (Shenzhen Labor Bureau 1995).

No factory in Shenzhen took these regulations seriously, Meteor included. During my time there, half of every month we would be working at night for over three hours. Moreover, although it was called overtime work, the company planned it as normal production.

Daily life was rigorously regulated by the timetable and everybody struggled to live up to the strict schedule. . . . The section following is from my field notes—one of my many attempts to capture a day in the workplace and how the workers struggled to meet the work schedule.

The Sense of Time: 19 January 1995

It was a cold and windy winter day. The sun was still sleeping and the sky was dark, but we had to wake up. The alarms of clocks in my room sounded at 6:30 A.M., some a few seconds faster or slower. Six people, six clocks, and I was definitely sure that with only my own alarm I could never have gotten up. Yunling, Fang, Yue, Huahong, and Mei were my roommates. Yunling slept above me on the upper bunk; she was usually the last one to get up. She murmured in a sleepy voice: "Gosh! What kind of life is this! Wake up at half past six. In winter I thought I'd never experience this kind of bitterness. Only my mum in the village would do it. She's great, getting up to feed us and the pigs." We all laughed and told her it was better to act than talk.

After waking up, we rushed for the toilet, brushed our teeth, washed our faces, and changed our clothes. We had to take turns because there was only one toilet and one washroom. "Hurry up, hurry up"; there was shouting everywhere in the room, but none of the arguing that often occurred in other rooms, especially when someone lost their temper. In our room, the situation was still bearable because we had all learned to keep our patience with one another. Time was pressing and we could not afford to waste a minute, so while someone was using the toilet, others would wash themselves in the washroom, while still others would change their overalls or comb their hair on the bed. Turns were arranged silently and we lived on consent rather than written orders. To make life easier, self-disciplining was nurtured from the moment we woke up.

About 6:45 to 7:00 A.M. we began to leave the dormitory. We could reserve fifteen minutes for breakfast if we could make it to the factory in less than twenty minutes. I often walked with Yunling and Mei, two Cantonese girls from rural Guangdong. Yunling complained of the harsh life in the workplace: "At home, I got up when the sun rose and it was time to be hungry for breakfast. But here, we are all forced to wake up to the alarms." I asked her, "Don't you need to help your mum cook or feed pigs in the morning?" "Sometimes," she replied, "but I was not the one supposed to do so." Yunling had two elder sisters and one sister-in-law who helped the family do domestic chores and farm work. She was the free hand at home, which was why she was able to do factory work in Shenzhen.

. . .

At 7:50 A.M. we had to queue up, enter the factory gate, and punch our timecards. Security guards stood at the big gate carefully checking company permits, which had to be pinned to the chest pocket of one's overalls. Those who forgot to bring the permit would not be allowed in, even if recognized as a company worker by the security guards. There was then no recourse but to go back to the dormitory and find the permit, which would make one late for work and result in a fine and condemnation: five minutes late would be counted as one hour late and wages would be deducted for two hours. . . . Such serious punishment reflected the saying that every minute of labor was crucial to the functioning of the entire production machine.

"Time is money" was the new disciplinary discourse prevailing in the rapidly developed industrialized areas. It was much highlighted in post-socialist China with the rapid growth of global production and the attempts to articulate a global consciousness of speed and money. Work quicker and work harder was the secret to producing wealth and the primary ideology of global capitalism. Losing time was losing one's money along with the company profit. Workers were thus self-technologized with this time/money sense that money was assigned to time and labor in their production process. It was felt not only that the disciplinary techniques would induce them to work, but more fundamentally that money and wealth inspired them to work harder and longer. . . .

With our overalls, caps, and gloves in place and our work tools and materials prepared, the factory clock bell rang at exactly 8:00. The day would start with a ten-minute meeting reporting the output performance and commenting on each line's productivity and quality. After the workers returned to their positions, the light flashed, the line started running, and our morning work began. Music—popular Cantonese songs—was played for fifteen minutes to freshen our minds to work more efficiently. It was said that the workers could work faster in the morning with their energy refreshed by a few hours of sleep, so discipline in the morning was often strict and it was difficult to find a chance to talk or joke. There was a common understanding on the line that the higher management was in a mood to keep things straight in the morning hours. Talk and laughter caught by the foreman or supervisor often was not tolerated. Silence, fast-moving lines, and the speed of time out of control—this was the feel of morning work.

Five minutes before lunch at noon the line would stop and we started to finish up our jobs.

Talk immediately mounted and all kinds of noises filled the silence. We had kept quiet for the whole morning, and it seemed that everyone had to talk at once. We were not permitted to leave the shop floor at the same time. Each line took turns to leave because there was only one staircase for all of the shop floor workers. Rushing to eat lunch in fifteen minutes, we would then come back to our seats to take a nap. All of the lights were switched off and the bright workshop turned to a dark world. Because we were exhausted every day, all of us would fall asleep. . . .

At 12:50 P.M., the lights were turned on and we awoke to punch our time cards. At 1:00 the clock bell rang, music was turned on, and the line ran again. Work was repetitive and never-ending. The closed environment, with all of the windows sealed and covered by a plastic curtain, kept the workers from being distracted by the outside world. We could not judge the time by seeing the rising and setting of the sun, nor could we breathe natural air. The workplace air was regulated twenty-four hours a day by the central air conditioning. The temperature was kept at 68° F throughout the year, which was low enough not only to cool the electronic parts but also to wake up drowsy eyes. Talking, gossiping, joking, and secret snacks were sometimes allowed in the afternoon on the condition that they not affect the speed and running of the line. And it seemed that noise and laughter also served as an effective way to keep the workers awake.

What the girls complained about most was not the low wage or harsh workload, but lack of adequate sleep sustained over months and years. An eighteen-year-old worker, Li Peng, told me, "Everyday I can only sleep for five or six hours. It doesn't drive me mad, but makes me like a sleeping pig. Whenever there's a chance, I fall asleep. I can't help but be drowsy." What the girls could do was making an effort to cheer themselves up. Every chance to have fun and share snacks was taken, each little moment was important to keeping up spirits. Another way of killing drowsiness was to take a short break by going to the washroom. But workers could not leave their work seats unless granted an out-of-position permit by the assistant line leader, and five minutes was the maximum allowed. Workers often complained about the time limit, especially when they were menstruating. Drowsiness was the contagious virus that the disciplinary machine found most difficult to deal with: work pace would slow down

and the jobs piled up on the line, and some workers would slip and get hurt by the soldering gun or the molding machine. Small accidents such as hurting a finger often occurred in late afternoon or at night, when workers did not have enough concentration. When somebody suffered more significant bodily pain and was sent to the hospital, the others on the shop floor would suddenly wake up to their work.

By 5:00 P.M. we could all hear our stomachs rumbling and we were hungry for dinner. Work started again at 6:00 P.M. and the time card was punched again. We were then told what time we could end our work that night. If it was at 9:00 we thought we had a lucky day. Normally we stopped work at 10:00, and sometimes the shift extended to 11:00 or 12:00 for a rush production order. Night work was comparatively more relaxed, and the radio was turned on for the duration. The workers listened to the Hong Kong channels, which they found more interesting than the Shenzhen or Guangzhou channels. Chatting about popular film stars and favorite singers helped to pass time quickly; dreaming of the romance provoked by the love songs or stories from the radio helped to kill time in the extreme exhaustion and boredom of night work.

Inspections by the personnel department or higher management in the production department seldom occurred at night. As Fatso explained to me on the line, "The white-collar staff members, with their good fate, need more time to take care of their bodies; they don't have time to inspect us." At 9:00 or 10:00 we stopped for the day and dashed back to the dormitory, queuing up for hot water to bathe. After bathing, we still needed to wash our clothes, and someone with a free hand would cook some snacks because we all felt hungry after working three or four hours after dinner. Eating and talking took another hour. After midnight we all went to bed. . . .

. . .

Institutionalizing Everyday Life: The Factory Codes

If the timetable was the heart of the disciplinary power regulating factory life, then the factory regulations were the heart of the timetable. A strict timetable needed a severe prosecutor to enforce it. The modality of power itself was extremely despotic, but it was justified by the nature and massive number of the workers that had to be governed. There were over five hundred workers, and all were from diverese places of origin, spoke different dialects, and had different habits of life and codes of behavior and standards. To order these heterogeneous migrants into one standardized set of behaviors, and mold the confused mind into a well-disciplined psyche, the disciplinary machine needed ingrained techniques of power. It also needed an impartial and equitable legislator machine to set unbiased codes and state clearly how to punish and reward. . . .

New workers were asked to read the factory regulation handbook before they could start work on the shop floor. . . . On the staircase landings and in the canteen, important factory regulations were framed under glass on the wall. . . .

At the landing of the second-floor staircase, every day we could see the following:

PRODUCTION REGULATIONS

1. Workers should do all preparations such as wearing work cap, electronic-prevention belt, gloves, and so forth five minutes before the on-work time. To prevent any dirt on the products, no one is allowed to comb their hair or do anything that may cause dust or dirt. Each violation is fined 2 yuan.

2. All workers should obey the production arrangements of the higher authorities. If anyone has a different opinion, complete the job first before seeking out the authorities.

3. Workers are not allowed to leave work positions or change work position during work time unless approved by the supervisors. If leaving the work position for personal reasons such as going to toilet the worker must apply for a *out-of-position permit*. Each violation is fined 2 yuan.

4. No one will be allowed to leave the factory unless there is a *company exit permit* signed by the affiliated department manager and the personnel department, and examined by the security guard before leaving the factory. Leaving the factory without permission will be seriously punished and each violation is fined 50 yuan.

5. Punching a timecard for others or asking another person to punch a timecard for you is prohibited. The first time of violation will be given serious warning and fined 20 yuan; the second time will be fined 100 yuan and the worker will be dismissed at once.

6. All workers must arrive at work on time. Arriving over five minutes late will be counted as late for one hour, while wages will be deducted at two hours rate.

At the third floor and in the canteen, the following framed rules were on the wall:

DAILY BEHAVIOR REGULATIONS

1. No talking, eating, playing, chasing, or fighting is allowed on the shop floor.

2. No dumping waste and no spitting. Each violation is fined 5 yuan.

3. Receiving or making personal phone calls is not allowed. If discovered, no matter how long the call, the worker will be immediately dismissed and all wages deducted.

4. For stealing factory property the worker will be dismissed at once and fined 50 to 500 yuan. If the case is serious, the offender will be sent to the Public Security Bureau.

5. The normal period of wear for an overall is one year. If one requires a new overall, there should be a reasonable explanation; otherwise, 50 yuan will be deducted from the wage.

6. The normal period of wear for a pair of work shoes is eight months. If there is unreasonable damage, 12 yuan will be deducted from the wage.

. . .

These framed codes, of course, did not have a dramatic effect on factory life. We felt their existence only when we were on the verge of violating them or actually violating them. It was possible to find ways around these codes, as there is with any law. No talking, eating, or playing in the workplace was one of the primary regulations. But as I have described above, talking, eating snacks, making jokes, and teasing were all done openly in the late afternoon and on night work. Workers simply could not help but violate the regulation if they were to kill the boredom and drowsiness. Individual defiance like deliberately not performing the job, speaking loudly, making fun of others, or leaving the work seat without waiting for a permit happened from time to time as well. Passing jokes on the line, sometimes overtly, sometimes covertly, could be seen as resistance to the extreme work conditions and as a chance to refresh an empty mind. Sexual innuendoes directed at the male technicians or supervisors were the funniest type of joke on the line. Who forgot to close the zipper of his trousers, or who had a new haircut or wore new clothes were all fodder for assembling jokes. Foremen and line leaders tended to ignore such behavior because they knew that the daily operation of the line could never be guided by factory regulations that were too adamant and relentless. . . . As Bailan, the leader of my line, told me, "It's no use being too harsh. We need to understand the workers' situation and individual problems. I would prefer to ask the worker to leave her seat to wash her face with cold water than to see her yawning all the time. . . . Sometimes I don't prevent them from talking or daydreaming, you know, it is the only way to keep the work moving." Even to the foremen, stringent disciplinary techniques seemed despotic, external, and impractical in regulating the human world of action, agency, and limitation.

There were also other clever tactics, often invisible and unrecorded, that workers in the workplace developed to cope with the work pressure and to humanize the harsh conditions (Kondo 1990). While some preferred daydreaming, others passed around sweets and snacks, and still others listened to tapes and radio broadcasts. Some women workers also brought photos of loved ones or pictures of favorite stars and placed them on their work desks. . . .

Although there was no strict code against listening to the radio during work time, the practice was that music was played only for fifteen minutes at the start of work each morning and afternoon. For overtime work at night, the radio was often on for the whole session; but it was a common consensus and expectation rather than a rule. Indeed, the workers had to struggle to keep it as an expectation. The radio was crucial in alleviating the harshness of working life, and despite the fact that indulging in music was an individual strategy to cope with everyday work pressure and tension, any opposition to this individual act could develop into some sort of united defiance. Defiance in this vein is a good example to show that workplace transgression is not always oriented toward economic interests. It is not always about bread and dignity but pleasure and work as well.

. . .

. . . The residence and living regulations were posted on the wall on each floor of the dormitory. Again: no spitting, no fighting, no gambling, no drinking, no faction gangs, no change of beds, no talking, laughing, or visiting after midnight, no visitors staying overnight, no use of cooker, heater, personal fan, and many other codes regulating daily behavior, with fines ranging from 5 yuan to 500. Nevertheless, there were more violations of regulations in the dormitory than in the workplace.

Workers frequently changed beds to form kin and ethnic clusters because they found it easier to cope with each other. Moreover, it was impossible to stop cooking in the room because all workers were hungry at night after overtime work. Visitors from the same villages often stayed overnight until they could find jobs elsewhere. Sometimes, even, a man was found in a woman's bed; if reported, the worker would be dismissed at once. Gambling and drinking, albeit less of an issue in the women's rooms, were common in men's dorms. Daily life transgressions were innumerable and in general were tolerated if the acts did not seriously threaten the order of dormitory life.

The Electronic Eye

. . .

At Meteor an electronic eye was installed at the corner of the wall on each floor. But none of the workers could see it actually work and no one knew when it was on or off. Although some workers completely ignored it, others were highly sensitive to the electronic eye, worrying that their behaviors in the workplace would be recorded in detail through the camera. One day Fatso told me, thinking that I did not know of its existence, "There's an electronic eye hanging on the wall, always checking our behavior. The director doesn't need to keep a watch on the line. He just sits there but he can watch every one of us. The pictures are flowing before his eyes and he can control the computer and have the picture focused on anyone." She kept her voice as low as possible, but it seemed that the eye was gazing at her. . . .

. . . The production line workers sometimes would point to the electronic eye to remind adjacent workers if they worked too slow or sneaked away to take a rest, as if upper management was watching them. There were also rumors that once the director noticed who was talking or laughing on the shop floor, he or she would be dismissed immediately without warning. I also heard it said by some line leaders that it would be more difficult for workers to steal production materials in those workplaces where an electronic eye was installed. "It is expensive, perhaps. But it is worth it," said Bailan, the line leader. The power of the eye as the symbol of supreme power was actualized in the way that it helped to induce self-discipline and mutual control in the workplace.

With the eye poking through the wall, workers were forced to think that they were all continuously under supervision. . . .

Sometimes the workers would totally forget about it, but other times they kept on telling each other that it was there. . . .

EDITORS' NOTES

1. Pun Ngai chose the name Meteor Electronics Company as a pseudonym for the factory where she did her ethnographic research.

2. The young women working in China's economic processing zones are called *dagongmei*—a new term for a new social identity. Pun Ngai explains that *dagong* "means 'working for the boss' or 'selling labor,' thereby connoting commodification and capitalist exchange of labor for wages" (*Made in China*, p. 120). *Mei* means younger sister: unmarried, female, and signifying a lower status.

She contrasts dagong with the term "worker," which carried the highest status during the Maoist period. "The new word dagong signifies a lesser identity—that of a hired hand—in a new context shaped by the rise of market factors in labor relations" (*Made in China*, p. 111).

REFERENCES

Cavendish, R. 1982. *Women on the line*. London: Routledge and Kegan Paul.
Gluckman, M. 1990. *Women assemble*. London: Routledge.
Knights, D. and H. Wilmott (eds.) 1986. *Gender and the labor process*. London: Gower.
Rosen, E. I. 1987. *Bitter choices: Blue-collar women in and out of work*. Chicago: Chicago University Press.
Shenzhen Labor Bureau. 1995. *Regulation of labor contract of Shenzhen Special Economic Zone*. Shenzhen: Shenzhen Labor Bureau.
Westwood, S. 1984. *All day, every day: Factory and family in the making of women's lives*. London: Pluto.

F O R T Y - N I N E

◆◆◆

Building Water Democracy (2004)
People's Victory Against Coca-Cola in Plachimada
Vandana Shiva

> **Vandana Shiva** directs the Research Foundation for Science, Technology and Natural Resource Policy in India, where she is also involved in Naydanya, a movement for biodiversity conservation and farmers' rights. She is a recipient of the Right Livelihood Award (an alternative to the Nobel Prize). Her many books include *Staying Alive: Women, Ecology and Development; Water Wars: Privatization, Pollution, and Profit;* and *Earth Democracy: Justice, Sustainability and Peace.*

Two years ago, adivasi[1] women in a small hamlet, Plachimada, in Palghat, Kerala, started a movement against Coca-Cola. Today, the Coca-Cola plant in Plachimada has been shut down. The victory of the Plachimada movement is a major step in reversing corporate hijacking of our precious water resources. It provides both inspiration and lessons for building water democracy in other parts of India and in the rest of the world.

The Coca-Cola plant in Plachimada was commissioned in March 2000 to produce 1,224,000 bottles of Coca-Cola, Fanta, Sprite, Limca, Thums Up, Kinley Soda, and Maaza. The Panchayat[2] was issued a conditional license for installing a motor for drawing water. However, the company started to illegally extract millions of litres of clean water from more than 6 bore wells installed by it using electric pumps in order to manufacture millions of bottles of soft drink.

According to the local people, Coca-Cola was extracting 1.5 million litres per day. The water level started to fall, going from 150 feet to 500 feet. Not only did Coca-Cola "steal" the water of the local community, it also polluted what was left. The company is also pumping wastewater into dry bore wells within the company premises for disposing of solid waste.

Earlier it was depositing the waste material outside the company premises, and during the rainy season it spread into paddy fields, canals, and wells, causing serious health hazards.

As a result of this, 260 bore wells which were provided by public authorities for drinking water

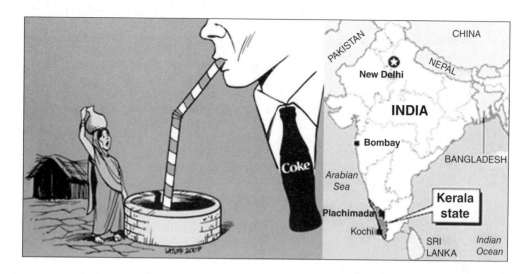

and agriculture facilities have become dry. Complaints were also being received from tribals and farmers that storage of water and sources of water were being adversely affected by indiscriminate installation of bore wells for tapping ground water, leading to serious consequences for crop cultivation in the area on which residents of the Panchayat depend for their living: e.g., maintenance of traditional drinking water sources, preservation of ponds and water tanks, maintenance of waterways and canals, and shortage of drinking water. When the Panchayat asked for details, the company failed to comply.

The Panchayat therefore served a show cause notice and cancelled the license. Coca-Cola tried to bribe the Panchayat President A. Krishnan with Rs. 300 million, but he refused to be corrupted and coopted. In 2003, the district medical officer informed the people of Plachimada their water was unfit for drinking.

The women already knew their water was toxic. Instead of drawing water from the wells in their homes they had to walk miles. Coca-Cola had created a water scarcity in a water abundant region. And the women of Plachimada were not going to allow this "hydropiracy." They started a "dharna" (sit-in) at the gates of Coca-Cola. On Earth Day 2003, they invited me to celebrate one year of their agitation.

On 21st September, 2003, a huge rally was organized to give an ultimatum to Coca-Cola. On 21st and 22nd of January, 2004 a World Water Conference brought global activists like Jose Bove and Maude Barlow to Plachimada to support the local activists.

A movement started by local adivasi women had unleashed a national and global wave of people's energy in their support. On 17th February, 2004, the Kerala Chief Minister, under pressure of the growing movement and the aggravation of the water crisis because of a drought, ordered closure of the Coke plant. The victory of the movement in Plachimada was the result of creating broad alliances and using multiple strategies.

The rainbow alliances, beginning with the local women and activists like Veloor Swaminthan, Convenor of the anti Coca-Cola task force in Plachimada, grew to include the local Gram Panchayat and its members Girija Devi, Geetha Mohandas, Sheeba Radhakrishnan, Aruchamy K, Sivakam, Subbayyan, MK Arumugham, K Varathara, A Krishnan, President, K Parthan, Presitha Mohandas, M Shanmugham, G Ponnukkuttam, N Chellankutty, C Murughan.

The local Panchayat used its constitutional rights to serve notice to Coca-Cola. The Perumatty Panchayat also filed a public interest litigation in the Kerala High Court against Coca-Cola.

The courts supported the women's demands. In an order given on 16th December, 2003, Justice Balakrishnana Nair ordered Coca-Cola to stop pirating Plachimada's water. As the Honorable Justice stated:

The Public Trust Doctrine primarily rests on the principle that certain resources like air, sea waters and the forests have such a great importance to the people as a whole that it would be wholly unjustified to make them a subject of private ownership. The said resources being a gift of nature, they should be made freely available to everyone irrespective of the status in life. The doctrine enjoins upon the government to protect the resources for the enjoyment of the general public rather than to permit their use for private ownership or commercial purpose. . . .

Our legal system—based on English common law—includes the public trust doctrine as part of its jurisprudence. The State is the trustee of all natural resources, which are by nature meant for public use and enjoyment. Public at large is the beneficiary of the seashore, running waters, airs, forests and ecologically fragile lands. The State as a trustee is under a legal duty to protect the natural resources. These resources meant for public use cannot be converted into private ownership. . . .

In view of the above authoritative statement of the Honourable Supreme Court, it can be safely concluded that underground water belongs to the public. The State and its instrumentalities should act as trustees of this great wealth. The State has got a duty to protect ground water against excessive exploitation and the inaction of the State in this regard is tantamount to infringement of the right to life of the people, guaranteed under Article 21 of the Constitution of India.

The Apex Court has repeatedly held that the right to clean air and unpolluted water forms part of the right to life under Article 21 of the Constitution. So, even in the absence of any law governing ground water, I am of the view that the Panchayat and the State are bound to protect ground water from excessive exploitation. In other words, the ground water, under the land of the 2nd respondent, does not belong to it.

Even assuming the experts' opinion that the present level of consumption by the 2nd respondent is harmless, the same should not be permitted for the following reasons:

The underground water belongs to the general public and the 2nd respondent has no right to claim a huge share of it and the Government have no power to allow a private party to extract such a huge quantity of ground water, which is a property, held by it in trust.

If the 2nd respondent is permitted to draw such a huge quantity of ground water, then similar claims of the other landowners will also have to be allowed. The same will result in drying up of the underground aqua-reservoirs.

Accordingly, the following directions are issued:

The 2nd respondent shall stop ground water for its use after one month from today.

The Panchayat and the State shall ensure that the 2nd respondent does not extract any ground water after the said time limit. This time is granted to enable the 2nd respondent to find out alternative sources of water.

The alliance grew to include people like Veerandra Kumar of Mathrubhumi and me. And we mobilized our networks to offer our full support to the local movement. The January conference was co-organised with the local Panchayat. It brought on one platform every political party, and the leader of the opposition V.S. Achuthanandan who kept up the pressure in the Kerala Assembly to translate the Court decision into Executive action.

The literary movement provided leadership through Dr. Sukumar Azhikode. And global support came in the presence of Jose Bove, Maude Barlow, European Parliamentarians and activists from across the world. The women's protest, the heart and soul of the movement, got support through legal action, parliamentary action and scientific research. This pluralism and diversity in support of local action was the secret of the victory of people against Coke in Plachimada.

This is the strength of our multiplicities and complementarities; we have to mobilize in other parts of India where Coke and Pepsi are mining and stealing people's water resources. The Plachimada Declaration issued at the World Water conference of 21st–23rd January, 2004 states:

Plachimada Declaration

Water is the basis of life; it is the gift of nature; it belongs to all living beings on earth.

Water is not a private property. It is a common resource for the sustenance of all.

Water is the fundamental right of man. It has to be conserved. Protected and managed. It is our fundamental obligation to prevent water scarcity and pollution and to preserve it for generations.

Water is not a commodity. We should resist all criminal attempts to marketise, privatize and corporatise water. Only through these means we can ensure the fundamental and inalienable right to water for the people all over the world.

The Water Policy should be formulated on the basis of this outlook.

The right to conserve, use and manage water is fully vested with the local community. This is the very basis of water democracy. Any attempt to reduce or deny this right is a crime.

The production and marketing of the poisonous products of the Coca-Cola, Pepsi Cola corporates lead to total destruction and pollution and it also endangers the very existence of local communities.

The resistance that has come up in Plachimada, Pududdery and in various parts of the world is the symbol of our valiant struggle against the devilish corporate gangs who pirate our water.

We, who are in the battlefield in full solidarity with the Adivasis who have put up resistance against the tortures of the horrid commercial forces in Plachimada, exhort the people all over the world to boycott the products of Coca-Cola and Pepsi Cola.

Coca-Cola—Pepsi Cola: "Quit India".

EDITORS' NOTES

1. *Adivasi* means "original inhabitants" in Sanskrit, or indigenous people, who have a distinct identity and culture. They have been marginalized within India, often brutally, starting with the British colonial administration, which opened up Adivasi areas for timber and developed these lands as estates. Adivasis continue to struggle for autonomy, control over resources, and restoration of traditional rights. Access to land is a major issue for Adivasis of Kerala.

2. *Panchayat* is the local community in tribal areas, recognized under the 1996 Provision of the Panchayats Act as the highest form of authority in matters of culture, resources, and conflict resolution. Village communities retained the power to approve or reject development plans and programs (Shiva 2002).

9

♦♦♦

Women, Crime, and Criminalization

The number of women who are serving time in U.S. jails and prisons, on probation, or otherwise caught up in the "correctional" system has increased dramatically in the past thirty years. Criminalization is one of the most dramatic ways in which gender, race, and class position shape women's lives, and it is essential for students of women's studies to understand the processes whereby women become defined as criminals. Many of us are shielded from this reality because incarcerated women are literally locked away, behind bars, and out of sight.

The societal assumptions that justify and reinforce this separation between "inside" and "outside" are that these are bad women, perhaps foolishly involved with criminal men, maybe crazy from drink, drugs, or the pain of their lives, but that they must have done something *very wrong* to end up in prison. This chapter examines the experiences of

incarcerated women, processes of criminalization, and theoretical frameworks for understanding the increase in women's imprisonment.

The National Context: "Get Tough on Crime"

The **criminalization** of U.S. women, a process whereby certain behaviors are defined as crimes, must be understood in the context of national penal policy and the dramatic expansion of the criminal justice system over the past three decades. Political scientist Marie Gottschalk (2006) argued that the United States has "built a carceral state that is unprecedented among Western countries and in U.S. history" with three defining characteristics: the large size of the prison and jail population; reliance on harsh degrading punishment; and the persistence of the death penalty (p. 1). *New York Times* correspondent Adam Liptak (2008) reported that

---

Thanks to Barbara Bloom, MSW, PhD who drafted this chapter for the first edition.

the United States leads the world "in producing prisoners"; it has less than 5 percent of the world's population but almost 25 percent of the world's prisoners. In December 2010, 7.1 million people, or 1 in 33 adults, were under the supervision of U.S. correctional authorities. This included 1.6 million people in state and federal prisons and nearly 4.9 million people on probation or parole (Guerino, Harrison, and Sabol 2011). The huge growth in incarceration by states has slowed somewhat since 2006 as many states have large budget deficits, partly due to the economic recession and the high costs of incarceration (Justice Policy Institute 2011).

Law professor Michelle Alexander (2012) has argued that mass incarceration has become normalized in this country, with more "African American adults . . . under correctional control today . . . than were enslaved in 1850, a decade before the Civil War began" (p. 180; also Herivel and Wright 2003). African American women are affected by this in two ways: they are trying to hold their families and communities together while so many men of color are incarcerated, and increasingly they are incarcerated themselves. On their release, formerly incarcerated people have few resources and the stigma of a criminal record. Legal discrimination follows them for the rest of their lives. They are denied public housing and welfare benefits, and a large number of jobs exclude potential employees with felony records. Moreover, in the state of Florida, a felony conviction means the loss of civil rights including voting, serving on juries, and running for public office (Bousquet and Edds 2012).

Alexander (2012) considered various arguments to explain this phenomenon: increased crime rates, Black culture, bad schools, unraveling morals, and a lack of thrift and perseverance among Black youth. But she identified economic changes and loss of jobs as the more fundamental factor:

> In 1954, black and white youth unemployment rates in America were equal. . . . By 1984, however, the black unemployment rate had nearly quadrupled, while the white rate had increased only marginally. This was *not* due to a major change in black values, behavior, or culture; this dramatic shift was the result of deindustrialization, globalization, and technological advancement. Urban factories shut down as our nation transitioned to a service economy.

> Suddenly African Americans were trapped in jobless ghettos.   *(p. 218)*

She argued that the nation could have responded to the economic collapse of inner-city communities in several ways, including a new War on Poverty, economic stimulus packages, resources for education, job training, public transportation, and relocation assistance to help people access jobs in other areas. Such interventions would have helped all blue-collar workers, Alexander noted, not only African Americans. "All this could have happened, but it didn't. Instead we declared a War on Drugs" (p. 218).

The War on Drugs

The "war on drugs," initiated in the 1980s under the Reagan administration, has been largely responsible for the vast increase in incarceration in this country. Proponents argued that massive government intervention was necessary to quell the drug epidemic, gang violence, and "narco-terrorism." Alexander (2012) noted that in the early years of the war on drugs politicians "competed with each other to prove who could be tougher on crime by passing ever harsher drug laws" (p. 191). This resulted in federal and state funding for additional police officers on the streets, more federal law enforcement officers, and construction of new jails and prisons, rather than funding for education, job training, drug prevention, or rehabilitation. Mandatory sentencing laws introduced in 1986 forced judges to send first-time offenders to prison. Moreover, "three-strikes-you're-out" laws enacted by various states require a life sentence (often without parole) for three-time felons. The war on drugs allows the police to stop, interrogate, and search anyone for drug investigations, and many commentators have noted the racial bias in patterns of arrest and sentencing (Reading 55; also Alexander 2012; Gottschalk 2006; Johnson 2002). These policies have been pursued aggressively in low-income African American and Latino neighborhoods despite the fact that white people are the majority of U.S. drug users and sellers (Alexander 2012). The Children's Defense Fund (2010) reported that "[a] cradle to prison pipeline, driven by poverty and racial disparities, is becoming the new American apartheid threatening to undermine the hard earned racial and social progress of the last half century" (p. vii). Michelle Alexander called the racial profiling and incarceration policies that have created a permanent racial under-caste "the new Jim Crow."

The United States has also pursued the drug war internationally, especially in countries of the global South such as Colombia, Guatemala, and Mexico (Boyd 2004). Ethnic studies professor Julia Sudbury takes up this issue in her analysis of economic globalization and the criminalization of women of color (Reading 55). South American leaders have challenged U.S. drug policy, which has entailed widespread spraying of herbicides to destroy coca crops and cost "hundreds of millions of dollars and tens of thousands of drug-related murders" (Meckler and Crowe 2012). Moreover, mandatory minimum prison sentences appear to have had negligible effect on the drug trade in the United States.

A related issue is the criminalization of pregnancy, especially in states that grant the fetus "legal personhood." Criminologist Susan Boyd (2004) found that since the 1980s "over two hundred women have been arrested for suspicious behavior during their pregnancies," mostly based on suspicions of illegal drug use (p. 87). Women who have miscarried or experienced stillbirth have been arrested for trafficking to the fetus, manslaughter, assault with a deadly weapon, or homicide. Boyd noted that legal substances such as alcohol, tobacco, or prescription drugs may also affect fetal development, and that the focus on illegal drugs is a political decision. She argued that medical research into the harm caused by a mother's drug use in pregnancy is uneven and contradictory and does not screen out other possible causes. Macro-level factors such as access to affordable health care, drug treatment programs, social and economic supports, and nutritious food all affect maternal health, as we argued in Chapter 5. Women who use illegal drugs come from diverse backgrounds, but poor women are less protected from state intervention than middle-class and wealthy women. Black women "are ten times more likely to be reported for substance abuse during pregnancy than women of other races" (Warner, 2011, p. 231).

Prison Industrial Complex

The increase in incarceration is big business. The construction and servicing of prisons and jails provide income for prison staff estimated at 700,000 people (Alexander 2012, p. 230), and it generates profits for architecture firms designing prisons, security companies supplying equipment, food distribution companies providing food services, and other companies that provide medical services (Reading 52), or benefit from prison labor (Herivel and Wright 2007). For example, TWA and Best Western (the international motel chain) have used prisoners to take calls from customers during peak times. Boeing, Microsoft, Nintendo, Starbucks, and Victoria's Secret have used prison labor, and prison-generated products ended up attached to well-known labels like No Fear, Lee Jeans, and Trinidad Tees (Barnett 2002; Levister 2006). Chris Levister (2006) reported that, after deductions, many prisoners "earn about $60 for an entire month of nine-hour days" (p. 1). Prisoners are the ultimate flexible and dependable workforce; they do not have to be paid minimum wage, provided with health benefits or vacation time, or covered by workers' compensation (a tax employers must pay for regular employees), and they cannot unionize. Telephone companies also profit from incarceration because family members are not allowed to call prisoners directly; prisoners are allowed only to call collect, the most expensive way to make calls. Corporations are, thus, "deeply interested in expanding the market—increasing the supply of prisoners . . . who can be held captive for a profit" (Alexander 2012, p. 230). The Corrections Corporation of America manages many prisons and immigration detention centers in this country and lobbies state and federal politicians to keep laws harsh (Herivel and Wright 2007). Borrowing from the term "military industrial complex," coined by President Dwight Eisenhower, the "prison industrial complex" refers to a similar mesh of interconnected relationships among private corporations, the public prison system, public investment, and public interests (Reading 55; also see Barnett 2002; Browne 1996; Davis 1997; Parenti 1999; Walker 1996).

White-Collar Crime

Although conservative politicians and media reports have focused on the incidence of street crime—burglary, auto theft, mugging, murder, and rape committed by strangers—as a key national issue, crime has been decreasing for more than a decade. The FBI Crime Report (2009) showed that crime rates continued to drop across all categories. Furthermore, the greatest economic losses from crime have never happened on the street. "Society's losses from 'white collar crime' far exceed the economic impact of all burglaries, robberies, larcenies, and auto thefts combined" (Lichtenstein and Kroll 1996, p. 20). Nonetheless, high-income criminals who commit fraud and embezzlement, for example, are less likely to be incarcerated and are less likely to be considered hardened criminals; rather, they are described as people who used bad judgment or went "off track" (Sherrill 1997). Dozens of corporate executives, financial analysts, regulators, and politicians are criticized for conflicts of interest and the possibility of fraud. Some are investigated; few are convicted. Negligence, disregard of rules governing financial institutions, and other crimes committed by bankers, mortgage lenders, and hedge fund managers triggered the worldwide economic recession which started in the U.S. housing market in 2008 (see Chapter 8). Some U.S. banks collapsed, and the government bailed out others to prevent a complete collapse of the financial system. The Bank Bailout Bill allocated $700 billion of public money to corporate banks (Amadeo 2012), far overshadowing support to homeowners, and taking money away from other social needs.

Women in the Criminal Justice System

I stood with my forehead pressed as close as possible to the dark, tinted window of my jail cell. The window was long and narrow, the foot-deep wall that framed it made it impossible to stand close. The thick glass blurred everything outside. I squinted and focused, and I concentrated all my attention on the area where my mother said the family would stand and wave. . . . It would be good to see my grandparents and my mother, but it was my daughter I really wanted to see. My daughter who would be two years old in two months.

A couple of minutes passed, and in that small space of time, I rethought my entire life and how it had come to this absurd moment, when I became a twenty-one-year-old girl in

jail on a drug charge, a mother who had to wait for someone to bring my own daughter to glimpse me. I could not rub my hands across her fat, brown cheeks, or plait her curly hair the way I like it.   *(Gaines 1994, p. 1)*

In 2010, more than 200,000 women were being held in U.S. jails and prisons, comprising 7 percent of the state and federal prison population, or 112,822 prisoners (Guerino, Harrison, and Sabol, 2011, table 1) and 12 percent of local jail populations (92,368 women) (Minton 2011, table 6). Another 815,458 women were on probation or parole (Glaze and Bonczar 2011). Historically, researchers and media reporters paid little attention to women offenders because their numbers were small in comparison with those of men. During the 1990s, however, the rate of growth in women's imprisonment far outstripped that of men's, and a growing literature of firsthand accounts began to document women's experiences of incarceration (see, e.g., Díaz-Cotto 2006; Gaines 1994; Johnson 2002; Lamb and the Women of York Correctional Facility 2003, 2007; Lawston and Lucas 2011; Rathbone 2006; Richie 1996; Rierden 1997; Solinger et al. 2010; Watterson 1996). The late Marilyn Buck (2004) discussed how incarcerated women cope with idle time—literally "doing time"—and prison work, which is a means of punishment as well as the only way to earn "a pittance . . . to buy items of personal hygiene, a candy bar . . . any material we might want to use for our own human productivity . . . as well as for telephone calls to our families, children, and friends with whom we desperately seek to maintain some level of attachment" (p. 454).

The majority of female arrests are for small-scale drug offenses, such as possession and dealing, and crimes committed to support a drug habit, particularly shoplifting and prostitution. In 2009, 26 percent of women in state prisons had been convicted for drug offenses, 30 percent for property offenses, and 36 percent for violent crimes (Guerino, Harrison, and Sabol, 2011, app. table 17B). When women commit acts of violence, these are often against abusive spouses or partners (see, e.g., Dermody 2002; Jacobsen 2008; Jones 1980; Rennison 2003; Richie 1996; Stark 2007).

Contemporary gender-neutral prison policies mean that female and male prisoners are treated alike, based on the male prisoner model. There is no physical contact on prison visits, for example, so women are not allowed to hug, kiss, or even touch their children. Male guards may be assigned to women's housing units, thus "subjecting women prisoners to twenty-four-hour male supervision—while showering, dressing, and performing basic bodily functions" (Labelle and Kubiak 2004, p. 419). Another effect of the "equal treatment" approach has been in the types of facilities women are sentenced to. For example, boot camps, based on a military model, have been popular with prison authorities as an alternative to prison. This includes uniforms, shorn hair, "in your face" tactics, and humiliation for behaviors considered to be disrespectful of staff (National Institute of Justice 2003). A Phoenix, Arizona, sheriff proudly boasted, "I don't believe in discrimination in my jail system," after he established the first female chain gang in the United States in 1996, where women, whose work boots are chained together, pick up trash in downtown Phoenix and other cities (In Phoenix chain gangs for women 1996; also see Allen 2011).

Women's accounts of incarceration often mention the degradation and harshness of prison conditions, and their feelings of guilt, anger, depression, and despair, as described by Andrea James (Reading 51). In Reading 50, Marilyn Buck discusses the difficulty of having to "negotiate the unfamiliar minefield" of prison life "where your every word and action is subject to censorship, control, punishment, and even possible torture by guards hired to watch and secure you." Over her decades-long imprisonment she developed certain routines and habits of mind that helped in this, as well as inner resources of patience and forbearance. She comments that women may refuse to cooperate with guards as a "personal act of rebellion" and a way to retain "some modicum" of their own power. Stormy Ogden (2006), a member of the Tule River Yokuts, Kashaya Pomo, and Lake County Pomo nations in northern California, noted that medicating incarcerated women was a routine practice that made it easier for prison authorities to manage them. She was given Elavil (an antidepressant) and Mellaril (an antipsychotic) while in county jail awaiting sentencing; in prison she was given Thorazine (an antipsychotic) and chlorohydrate (a sedative), which made her into "one of the 'walking zombies'" (p. 168). Although Native American women are overrepresented in the prison system,

they are absent from much information about incarcerated women because prisons classify people as white, Black, Hispanic, or "other." Every morning she would replace "other" with "AI" (American Indian) on the name card outside her cell door. Each afternoon she returned to find that prison staff had replaced "AI" with "other." She kept correcting her name card and was punished for this infraction of prison discipline by losing 60 days of good behavior. She remarked, "it was well worth it" (p. 169).

Victoria Law (2009) has documented instances of incarcerated women's resistance to prison conditions. These may be small acts of support and kindness that break the dehumanization and alienation of prison life, as well as sharing information, or setting up educational resources that have a wider effect. A major problem for incarcerated women is access to medical care. Inadequate staffing leads to long delays in obtaining medical attention, disrupted and poor quality treatment, and overmedication of prisoners with psychotropic drugs rather than mental health care. Services such as mammograms and Pap smears often entail a long wait. Treatable diseases like asthma, diabetes, sickle cell anemia, and cancer may lead to death or permanent injury due to neglect. In Reading 52, Law gives examples of women's activism in challenging barriers to basic health care in prison. Juanita Díaz-Cotto (2006) reported women's efforts to improve their conditions. This included using the prison grievance procedure, filing a lawsuit, refusing to return to their cells when ordered, or going on hunger strikes.

Characteristics of Incarcerated Women

Women in prison have a host of medical, psychological, educational, and financial needs. Poverty, unemployment, physical and mental illness, substance abuse, homelessness, police harassment, and a history of physical and sexual abuse often propel them into a revolving cycle of life inside and outside jails and prisons.

Some women come to prison pregnant; others become pregnant in prison. Few receive prenatal care, and pregnant prisoners suffer a high rate of miscarriage as a result. Congress has banned the use of federal funds for abortion in prison; women who can pay for an abortion themselves may be able to get one at a clinic, but they need to convince prison authorities to transport them there. Women who

Sexual Abuse of Women Inmates and Detainees

- Sexual abuse of women inmates by male staff is common. This includes insults, harassment, rape, voyeurism in showers and during physical exams, and touching women's breasts and genitals during pat-downs and strip searches (Amnesty International 2000; Phifer 2011; Ritchie 2006). Some women are coerced into sex for favors like extra food or personal hygiene products, or to avoid punishment (Amnesty International n.d.).

- Many incarcerated women have histories of physical and sexual abuse, which makes them more vulnerable to abuse by guards and other prison staff.

- A prisoner's sexuality (perceived or actual) or their gender expression make them a likely target for sexual abuse or for retaliation if they report it (Heidenreich 2011; Just Detention 2012).

- The Prison Rape Elimination Act became federal law in 2003. It provided for data collection and policy recommendations, and required the National Institute of Corrections to train officials at all levels to prevent sexual abuse in prisons and to punish offenders, whether inmates or guards. However, the first nationwide study "focused solely on prisoner-on-prisoner assaults in male prisons" with no recognition of sexual abuse of incarcerated women (Law 2009, p. 69).

- The American Civil Liberties Union obtained details of 185 complaints of sexual abuse against Immigration and Customs Enforcement since 2007 (Pilkington 2011; Rentz 2011).

- The United States is a party to international laws that require governments to protect incarcerated women from violence, including the Convention Against Torture and Other Cruel, Inhuman or Degrading Treatment or Punishment and the Declaration on the Elimination of Violence Against Women.

carry their pregnancies to term are often treated inhumanely, denied prompt medical attention, and may be forced to undergo labor and childbirth in shackles (Law 2009; Liptak 2006).

Most women in prisons are mothers; many of them single heads of households. Sixty-two percent have children under the age of 18, and this figure is higher (81 percent) for women aged 25–34 (Glaze and Maruschak 2008, table 5). Public school teacher and administrator Cynthia Martone (2005) estimated that 2.3 million children had a parent in prison. Black children are seven times as likely as white children to have a parent in prison (Children's Defense Fund 2010, p. H-12). Public policy analysts Erika Kates and Paige Ransford (2005) emphasized the criminal justice system's lack of recognition of women's role as mothers and the impacts of incarceration on parenting and family life. They identified a range of factors that prevent regular contact between incarcerated mothers and their children. These include isolated prison locations served by poor or nonexistent public transport; restrictive policies governing visits and phone calls; the removal of infants born to women in prison; speedy termination of child custody for incarcerated women; restrictive welfare policies that make it difficult for families to be reunited; and some women's repeated periods in custody. The majority of such children live with relatives, primarily grandparents, and approximately 10 percent of them are in foster care, a group home, or other social service agency (Glaze and Maruschak 2008, table 8). Despite the enormous difficulties, some mothers try a variety of means to mother their children from prison, and children are often the key motivating factor for women to get their lives back on track (Reading 51; also Enos 2001; Golden 2005; Solinger et al. 2010).

Race and Class Disparities

Disparities in incarceration based on race and class have been a consistent trend in U.S. law enforcement,

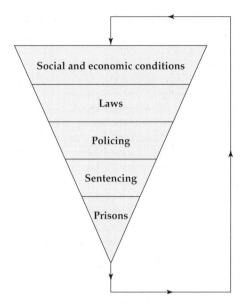

FIGURE 9.1 The Funnel of Injustice
(*Source*: Honderich 2003, p. 10.)

as argued above (also Boyd 2004; Kurshan 1996). In 2010, for sentenced prisoners under state and federal jurisdiction, the incarceration rate for white women was 47 per 100,000 population, compared to 133 for Black women, and 77 for Latinas (Guerino, Harrison and Sabol 2011, table 14). White women are more likely to be placed on probation than women of color. Many crimes committed on Native American reservations are classified as federal offenses, which means people must serve their sentences in federal prisons, usually in remote places long distances from home and hard to get to by public transportation (Ogden 2006).

Racial bias is a consistent factor in arrests, pretrial treatment, and differential sentencing of women. The few studies that report race-specific differences indicate more punitive treatment of women of color. Economist Kiaran Honderich (2003) described this channeling of poor women of color into the criminal justice system as a "funnel of injustice" (see Figure 9.1). Differential sentencing for possession of cocaine is a case in point. Currently, possession of any amount of crack cocaine, mainly used by low-income people of color, carries a mandatory minimum sentence of five years, the same sentence as for possession of 500 grams of powder cocaine,

mainly used by middle- and upper-middle-class white people (Alexander 2012, p. 112).

Girls in the Criminal Justice System

When people think of juvenile crime they often think of boys, but the number of girls in juvenile detention centers surged in the 1990s, and by 2004 girls accounted for 30 percent of juvenile arrests (Zahn et al. 2008). Researchers have questioned whether this increase is because girls have become more unruly or whether policy changes and greater media attention are responsible for it. The Girl's Study Group, initiated by the Office of Juvenile Justice and Delinquency Prevention, confirmed the latter view, reporting that "a change in how the juvenile justice system is responding to girls' behavior is largely responsible for the increased number of girls entering the system" (Zahn et al. 2008, p. 7). In some areas, running away from home, truancy, scuffling with family members, or repeated discipline problems have been reclassified as criminal offenses. Also, zero-tolerance policies in schools have turned relatively minor offenses that used to be addressed informally into crimes.

African American girls are much more likely to be held in detention than white girls or Latinas. Also, middle-class girls with similar behavior are likely to end up in therapy, treatment programs, boarding schools, or private hospitals, rather than becoming criminalized. Many girls in the juvenile justice system have been abused physically, emotionally, or sexually, often from a young age (see, e.g., Chesney-Lind and Pasko 2003, 2004; Chesney-Lind and Irwin 2008). In some cases their parents are absent due to death, drug use, or incarceration. Sociologist Juanita Díaz-Cotto (2006) found that many Chicanas who ended up in prison were first arrested as juveniles. As girls they had become "more and more alienated from their parents and other adults as a result of abuse and neglect" (p. 53). In response, they "confronted their parents angrily at home, cut school, bullied other children, ran away from home, experimented with alcohol and illegal drugs, and /or joined barrio youth gangs" (p. 7). In a study of 112 girls in shelter care, juvenile detention, and state correctional facilities, girls reported that they got into the most trouble for drugs, boyfriends, and sex (Garcia and Lane 2009). They were mostly arrested for drug and alcohol use and possession, hitting their parents or grandparents, or running away from home and from custodial placements. Assessing various programs they had experienced, they said they found programs that helped them understand their thinking and their anger to be the most helpful, as well as counseling for grief and loss, and for sexual abuse. They wanted to have a voice in what happened to them and play an active role in their cases, to work with caring staff and probation officers, and to learn practical life skills that would help them live independently.

There are fewer rehabilitation and housing placements available for girls compared to boys, so girls spend more time in detention awaiting placement. Criminologist Stacy Mallicoat (2012) noted that juvenile facilities are often very poorly equipped to address girls' emotional needs, or their physical and mental health. Moreover, punishment in detention is not appropriate for girls who run away to escape their abusers.

Women Political Prisoners

Despite constitutional guarantees of free speech and freedom to organize, political activists many risk arrest and imprisonment. Suffragists were jailed in the early 1900s for peacefully picketing the White House as part of the decades-long campaign for votes for women. In January 1917, for example, mainly white, middle-class women organized pickets around the clock. At first the police ignored them. By June they began to be arrested, and in August some received thirty-day and sixty-day sentences for obstructing traffic. A number of those who were jailed went on hunger strike; they were forcibly fed and threatened with transfer to an insane asylum. These women received disproportionately long sentences and harsh treatment, clearly intended to discourage determined opposition to government policy. They were released the following year by order of President Wilson, and the Washington, D.C. Court of Appeals later ruled that their arrests, convictions, and imprisonment were illegal (Gluck 1976).

A small but significant group of women activists were incarcerated in the 1970s and 1980s, including members of the Puerto Rican Socialist Party, supporters of Native American sovereignty movements, and participants in Black revolutionary movements in the United States and abroad.

Angela Davis, for example, was imprisoned for two years on murder, conspiracy, and kidnapping charges—but later acquitted. Silvia Baraldini, an Italian citizen, was given a forty-year sentence for conspiracy charges arising out of her activities in solidarity with national liberation movements, including assisting in the escape of Black activist Assata Shakur. Like Marilyn Buck, Susan Rosenberg, and Laura Whitehorn, Baraldini was active in the women's movement and the anti-Vietnam War movement. From 1986 to 1988, Silvia Baraldini and Susan Rosenberg were held in the "High Security Unit," a specially built sixteen-bed underground prison for political prisoners in Lexington, Kentucky, which became the center of intense scrutiny by national and international human rights organizations. As a result of sustained pressure from activists and the Italian government, Silvia Baraldini was released to Italian authorities in 1999 because of serious complications associated with cancer. Susan Rosenberg and Laura Whitehorn were released in 1999, having served sixteen- and fourteen-year sentences, respectively. In Reading 52, Victoria Law notes that Whitehorn set up peer-education programs for women with AIDS "in every federal prison where she was housed." Marilyn Buck received an eighty-year sentence. She was released in 2010, less than a month before her death from cancer at age 62. In her account of her daily life, she shows how prisoners are deprived of autonomy (Reading 50). She worried about becoming "inured to the casual cruelty that prevails. It lures us into becoming the very creatures the prison system advertises us to be. . . . I worry about succumbing, losing my will to resist dehumanization, and ultimately, losing my own sense of who I am as a human being."

Criminalization as a Political Process

Criminalization is a political process whereby people who do not fit dominant societal norms are labeled as criminals, and their circumstances and behaviors are defined as crimes, as we noted regarding the criminalization of girls and drug users. Other examples include gender nonconforming people, homeless people, immigrants, and people from "enemy" nations. Ideologies of nationalism, patriotism, racism, sexism, and heterosexism are all deployed to justify criminalization. Policy shifts occur in response to a range of factors, including national disasters, economic expansion or downturn, the prevailing political climate, and public opinion on social issues in favor of greater tolerance or restrictiveness. These factors overlap, making for a multilayered context in which criminalization happens. Because crime is politically constructed, in a sense all incarcerated people are political prisoners.

On one hand, behaviors that were criminalized in the past may be decriminalized. For example, miscegenation laws banning interracial marriages in this country have been repealed. Homosexuality has been decriminalized. Abortion was made legal (Chapter 5). On the other hand, feminists have been successful in getting rape and domestic violence recognized as crimes, which has inadvertently strengthened the power of law enforcement, as argued in Chapter 6 (Readings 33 and 36; also Gottschalk 2006).

The government has the power to criminalize people from "enemy" groups, as with Marilyn Buck and other political prisoners previously mentioned. National disasters often provide the pretext. The internment of about 110,000 men, women, and children of Japanese ancestry following the bombing of Pearl Harbor by the Japanese military in 1941 was justified on nationalist and racist grounds. Most were U.S. citizens living in west coast states. They were forced to leave their homes, farms, and businesses and incarcerated in remote prison camps until the end of World War II (see, e.g., Daniels, Taylor, and Kitano 1991; Iwamura 2007; Tateishi 1984; Yoo 2000). Constitutional guarantees to "due process of law" were suspended, "and the Government was able to implement this massive program with few questions asked," though there was no evidence that these Japanese Americans were in any way "disloyal" to the United States (Takahashi 1998 p. 362).

In a similar move, authorities arrested some 1,200 men, mostly Arabs, after the attacks on the World Trade Center and the Pentagon on September 11, 2001, and President Bush's declaration of a "war on terrorism" (Reading 53). In November 2002, a "Special Registration" program required males over sixteen years of age, from twenty-five mainly Arab and Muslim countries, to be fingerprinted, photographed, and questioned about terrorism. This program lasted eighteen months with devastating impacts on affected communities (Nguyen 2005). Several thousand men were detained and an unknown number deported though few, if any, of

Samar Kaukab with her ACLU lawyer

those arrested were found to have any connection to terrorism. Officials and private citizens committed acts of violence against Arab Americans, South Asians, and "people who look like Muslims." In one instance, Samar Kaukab, a U.S. woman of Pakistani descent, was detained at Chicago's O'Hare International Airport in November 2001 and subjected to an unjustified, illegal, and degrading search by airport security personnel (see photo). Negative media coverage of Arabs and Arab Americans has contributed to a climate of opinion whereby racial profiling, preemptive arrests and detentions, abuse and humiliation of those detained, and suspension of constitutional rights can be justified in the name of "national security." Anthropologist Suad Joseph initiated the Media Project to analyze the representation of Arabs, Muslims, Arab Americans, and Muslim Americans in major print news publications, a project that began as a classroom assignment (see Reading 53; also Nacos and Torres-Reyna 2007). Articles by Lila Abu Lughod (Reading 11) and Nadine Naber (Reading 18) also provide material for this discussion.

Congress increased the government's powers of investigation in the Uniting and Strengthening America by Providing Appropriate Tools Required to Intercept and Obstruct Terrorism Act (USA PATRIOT Act), which became law on October 26, 2001. It includes measures that

- allow for indefinite detention of noncitizens who are not terrorists on minor visa violations;
- minimize judicial supervision of federal telephone and Internet surveillance by authorities;
- expand the government's powers to conduct secret searches;
- give the Attorney General and the Secretary of State the power to designate domestic groups as terrorist organizations and deport any noncitizens who belong to them;
- give the FBI access to business records about individuals without having to show evidence of a crime;
- lead to large-scale investigation of U.S. citizens for "intelligence" purposes.

(American Civil Liberties Union 2002)

The Homeland Security Act, signed into law on November 25, 2002, involved the creation of a new Department of Homeland Security, which includes the functions of the former Immigration and Naturalization Service (INS), now Immigration and Customs Enforcement (ICE). Among its sweeping provisions, the act authorizes the collection of data on individuals and groups from databases that combine personal, governmental, and corporate records, including e-mails and Web sites viewed. Again, this was justified in terms of the "war on terrorism," but it allows for much broader surveillance and targeting of any individual or group.

Latino communities have been increasingly targeted for investigation, especially "people who look undocumented" and those without official documentation. Whole communities have become the targets of ICE raids on workplaces, homes, and schools. In the first decade of this century the number of people held in ICE detention nearly doubled, from 209,000 in 2001 to 392,000 in 2010 (Detention Watch Network 2011). Law professor Nina Rabin

(2011) noted that "[c]ontrary to popular perception, living in the United States without authorization is not a crime in and of itself. The act of crossing the border without proper documentation is a crime, as is re-entering the country without permission after a deportation order . . . many undocumented immigrants enter the country legally but then overstay their visa or violate its terms" (p. 19). She argued:

> . . . [d]espite the fact that only a small fraction of immigrants apprehended by immigration enforcement are actually prosecuted for any crime, the current immigration enforcement regime criminalizes all immigrants, even those who are not criminal offenders. This shapes public perceptions of immigrants in ways that have insidious effects far beyond the simple threat of actual immigration enforcement measures.
> *(pp. 19–20)*

Reading 54 provides a summary of research conducted by Rabin and colleagues at the University of Arizona on the impacts of immigration enforcement on parents who are separated from their children, some of whom are U.S. citizens.

According to the National Immigration Forum (2011), the problems of isolation, inhumane conditions, and lack of access to health care or legal counsel that characterize immigration detention are particularly problematic for women. This includes medical conditions for pregnant and nursing mothers, sexual assault, separation from children, and lack of treatment for abuse and trauma (see box on Immigration Detention). In the 1990s, a time of economic expansion, the federal government authorized an amnesty for undocumented migrants from many nations, recognizing their contribution to the U.S. economy (see Chapter 3). Due to economic recession, shifts in sentiments against immigrants, and the introduction of harsher federal and state policies against immigrant communities, legal channels for immigration have decreased. At the same time, economic globalization continues to generate great pressures on people from poorer nations to migrate for work (see Chapter 8; Reading 55).

The dominant discourse on immigration glosses over the fact that western states—Arizona, California, New Mexico, Texas and parts of Colorado, Nevada, and Utah—were Spanish territories ceded to the

Immigration Detention

- Immigration and Customs Enforcement (ICE) can detain up to 33,400 people at a time, at a cost of $166 per person per day (National Immigration Forum 2011). The average length of an immigrant's detention is thirty days but may last years in some cases, often in remote facilities far from family and legal counsel (Human Rights Watch 2011).

- People in ICE custody are housed in some three hundred detention facilities, including centers operated by ICE, detention facilities managed by private companies, state and county jails under contract with ICE, or facilities run by the Federal Bureau of Prisons (Human Rights Watch 2011).

- A total of 121 detainees died in ICE custody between 2003 and 2011, many from health issues that required timely treatment. The focus is on short-term, emergency care, even though many detainees suffer from chronic health problems like diabetes, hypertension,

or tuberculosis. Mental health issues also go untreated (National Immigration Forum 2011).

- In a January 2012 open letter to the Director of ICE, more than sixty-five immigrant, civil rights, and faith-based organizations argued that immigrant families require educational, medical, and legal support, and that detention in closed facilities is both inappropriate and unnecessarily costly. They urged ICE to prioritize alternatives to detention for families awaiting asylum or immigration hearings (Shah 2012).

- Approximately 5.5 million children live with at least one undocumented parent. Three million of these children are U.S. citizens. Arrest, detention, and deportation set off a series of events that undermine parents' ability to make decisions about their children's care, complicate family reunification, and can lead to the termination of parental rights (Women's Refugee Commission 2010).

United States in 1848 under the Treaty of Guadalupe Hidalgo after the Mexican-American War (De Leon and Griswold del Castillo 2006). Thus, people of Mexican ancestry may say, "We didn't cross the border. The border crossed us." Gloria Anzaldúa discusses this history in Reading 44.

Criminalization is used to assert heteronormativity, for example, through police harassment and targeting of transgender or genderqueer people (Heidenreich 2011; Sudbury 2011), or by bans on gay teachers in public schools, limiting what they can say to students, and banning books said "to promote homosexuality" from school and public libraries. Criminalization can be used to impose cultural, religious, or moral beliefs as with limitations on legal access to abortion in many states (see Chapter 5). Law professor Kaaryn Gustafson (2005) noted that welfare rules have become more punitive with explicit links to law enforcement (see Chapter 7). Law enforcement officials may access

information in welfare files. Women wanted by law enforcement officials for a felony or for violating the terms of parole or probation—which may be as little as missing a meeting—cannot receive government benefits. In addition, states can require drug tests, fingerprints, and photographs for those applying for benefits. Poor and homeless women—many of them mothers—have become subject to criminalization as many cities have passed ordinances that prohibit begging and sleeping in public places.

As these examples show, criminalization is a way of punishing certain groups, and the targets may change over time. However, the criminalization of African Americans has been a consistent reality (Alexander 2012; Golden 2005). Slavery and Jim Crow segregation are now illegal, but African Americans, who are increasingly marginal to the needs of employers, are controlled and warehoused through mass incarceration.

Theories of Women, Crime, and Incarceration

Until recently there had been little research on women in conflict with the law, in part because far fewer women than men were incarcerated and because it is difficult for researchers to obtain access to women in prison. Official data collected by the Bureau of Justice are limited and often date back several years by the time they are published, a drawback of the data cited in this chapter.

Early theories of women's criminality attempted to explain it in individual terms or used theories developed to explain male criminality and applied them to women. Theories that emphasized individual behavior applied stereotypical assumptions about the "female psyche" that were blatantly sexist and without much evidence to support them. An increase in crime committed by women in the 1970s prompted theories attributing female criminality and girls in gangs to the women's liberation movement (Chesney-Lind and Pasko 2004; Chesney-Lind and Shelden 1992). Sociologist Freda Adler (1975) suggested that the women's movement had created a liberated, tougher class of women who were committing more violent crimes. Criminologist Rita Simon (1975) argued that a rise in women's involvement in property crimes, such as theft, embezzlement, and fraud, was due to women entering previously male occupations, like banking and business, which gave them greater opportunity for crimes that were previously the preserve of men. Neither of these theses was supported by much empirical evidence. Others argued that it was the absence, rather than the availability, of job opportunities for women that led to an increase in crime (Giordano, Kerbel, and Dudley 1981; Naffine 1987). Proponents argued that women mostly committed petty property crimes such as shoplifting, a rational response to poverty and economic insecurity (Rafter 1990). They noted that the feminization of poverty rather than women's liberation was the social trend more relevant to female criminality.

Some feminist criminologists saw the origins of women's crime in male supremacy and men's efforts to control women. They argued that the physical and sexual victimization of girls caused some to run away from home or to begin using drugs, which often led to criminal activity (Chesney-Lind 1995; Owen and Bloom 1995). Others argued that women commit fewer crimes than men because capitalism renders women relatively powerless in the home and in the economic arena (Connell 1990; Messerschmidt 1986). They have fewer opportunities to engage in crime, and any crimes they commit tend to be nonviolent, self-destructive crimes such as theft, drug possession, and prostitution. Moreover, women's relative powerlessness also increases the likelihood that they will be the targets of violent acts, usually by men. Yet other feminist scholars foregrounded institutionalized racism in explaining the disproportionately high incarceration rates for women of color (e.g., Davis 1998; Silliman and Bhattacharjee 2002; Smith 2005). They focused on women's struggles to keep their families and communities intact in the face of arrests, harassment, and raids by the police.

In Reading 55, Julia Sudbury takes an intersectional approach to explain the upsurge in women's incarceration. Instead of focusing on women's behavior she asks: "Who benefits when more women are imprisoned? What are the processes by which certain actions are labeled criminal and others are not, and how are women channeled into these actions and thus into conflict with the criminal justice system?" Sudbury explores three macro- and global-level factors to account for increases in women's imprisonment: the effects of globalization on national economies, the expansion of the prison industry as a profit-making business, and the "war on drugs." She critiques feminist criminology on two counts: first, for focusing on women's behavior to explain their incarceration rather than government actions that seek to control poor communities. Second, she argues that feminist criminologists have focused on gender at the expense of race and class. Advocates, policy makers, and theorists who seek to understand and explain the criminal justice system must, as she puts it, "engage meaningfully with the significance of race."

More recently, Sudbury (2011) has argued that much research and writing on women in prison, including her own, has not taken account of gender fluidity among incarcerated people. Rather, it has inadvertently reinforced the gender binary and legitimized the "state's power to determine and police the gender identification of those it imprisons" (p. 171). The criminal justice system only recognizes two genders and differentiates people according to their genitalia not self-identity.

It allocates butches, bois, and FtMs to "women's correctional facilities," while MtFs and transsexuals are defined as "male offenders." This "neat division . . . is achieved at the expense of transgender and nonconforming prisoners who are policed and punished because of the threat they pose to the gendered order of the penal system" (p. 177). Sudbury argued that the experiences of transwomen make visible how the state polices gender for all women (also, e.g., Heidenreich 2011; Ritchie 2006).

Inside/Outside Connections

Formerly incarcerated women have been key to establishing supports and services for women in jails and prisons, and organizing with advocates and allies outside the law enforcement system (Law 2009; Lawston and Lucas 2011; Solinger et al. 2010; Women's Prison Association 2009). A growing number of organizations support women in prison and formerly incarcerated women including Aid to Inmate Mothers (Montgomery, Ala.), Alabama Women's Resource Network/Long-Timers (Montgomery, Ala.), California Coalition for Women Prisoners (San Francisco), Chicago Legal Advocacy for Incarcerated Mothers, Families for Justice as Healing (Boston, Mass.), Just Detention International (Los Angeles), Justice Now (Oakland), JusticeWorks Community (Brooklyn), Legal Services for Prisoners with Children (Oakland), Let's Start (St. Louis, Mo.), Michigan Women's Justice and Clemency Project (Ann Arbor), National Women's Prison Project (Baltimore), A New Way of Life Reentry Project (Los Angeles), Portia Project (Eugene, Ore.), Power Inside (Baltimore), Women Evolving (Plainfield, Vt.), Women on the Rise Telling HerStory-WORTH (New York), and Women's Re-entry Network (Tucson, Ariz.). *Women and Prisons: A Site for Resistance* is a Web space for prisoners, those previously incarcerated, activists, students, and teachers that makes visible women's experiences in the criminal justice system (http://womenandprison.org).

Women on the outside are working with women prisoners in literacy classes, creative writing, and art projects, providing books (e.g., Books Through Bars, New York; Women's Prison Book Project, Minneapolis), and undertaking theater productions with incarcerated women (e.g., The Medea Project, San Francisco) (see Davis 2011; Fraden 2001; Hernandez 2011; Troustine 2001; Warner 2011). Independent filmmakers have made films about women who killed abusive partners, such as *Defending Our Lives*, which tells the story of Battered Women Fighting Back!, in Framingham Correctional Institution (Mass.). *From One Prison . . .* was produced by the Michigan Women's Justice and Clemency Project in collaboration with women at a Michigan prison who are serving life or long-term sentences for killing their batterers.

Prison Reform, Decriminalization, Decarceration, or Abolition

Given the overwhelmingly punitive approach of the law enforcement system and harsh conditions of incarceration, many legal scholars, researchers, and advocacy organizations argue for substantial changes to help women. Susan Tucker and Eric Cadora (2003) noted the failures of what they called "prison fundamentalism." They challenged the logic of current policy that expects people released from prison with no new skills or resources to return to the same impoverished communities and make a go of their lives. Advocates are pressing for health care, drug treatment, and educational, therapeutic, and life-skills programs for incarcerated women. However, since most state budgets are in deficit as a result of economic recession and changes in federal allocations to states, many have cut back severely on such programs. The enormous costs of mandatory minimum sentences and three-strikes laws have caused some states to reassess these policies and to expand parole and early release, and develop alternative sentencing programs (Falk 2003; Miller 2005). Moreover, the colossal investment in new jails and prisons has eaten up a growing portion of states' resources nationwide, in direct competition with other investments like education (see box on Comparable Costs for details).

Some advocate for measures that will help women return to their communities after incarceration. Especially needed are safe affordable housing, transitional income, and employment (see, e.g., Sentencing Project 2007; Women's Prison Association 2009). Tucker and Cadora (2003) argued for "justice reinvestment" in poor communities for

Comparable Costs: Education, Drug Treatment, and Imprisonment

- Education is necessary to compete in today's workforce and to secure jobs that pay decent wages and benefits. Many people in prison or on probation do not have high school or an equivalent level of educational achievement.

- Prisons and education compete for budget dollars from a state's General Fund. In 2011, Georgia spent $18,000 to house a prisoner and about one-third of that amount to put a child through public school. Figures for the state of New York were $56,000 per inmate and $16,000 per school student; Michigan spent $34,000 per prisoner and $11,000 per school student (Prann 2011).

- Throughout the 1980s and 1990s, state spending on prisons, on average, grew at six times the rate of spending on higher education. A college student costs the state of California $8,667 per year; a prisoner costs it $45,006 a year (Zakaria 2012). The cost for a year at Princeton is $37,000, and the state of New Jersey spends $44,000 to hold a prisoner for a year (Resnick 2011).

- Research on the Drug Treatment Alternative-to-Prison Program, started in Brooklyn (NY) in the 1990s, has shown that participants in this program had lower rearrest and reconviction rates compared to those who were incarcerated for similar offenses. Two years after leaving the program, 92 percent of graduates were employed; graduates were 67 percent less likely to be reconvicted than a comparison group who went to prison. These results were achieved at half the average cost of incarceration (Swern 2008).

- Close to a million people incarcerated in the United States are African American (Alexander 2012, p. 179). Between 1980 and 2000, thirty-eight states and all federal prisons added more African American men to prison populations than to enrollment in state colleges and universities (Justice Policy Institute 2002, table 6). Most African American students in public schools do not read or do math at grade level (Children's Defense Fund 2010, p. G-6). Students in two thousand high schools identified as "dropout factories" account for 46 percent of the nation's Black students and 39 percent of Latino students (p. G-12).

education, health care, job creation, and job training. Another approach would be to decriminalize various behaviors, especially drug use. The nonprofit Justice Policy Institute has argued for repealing mandatory sentencing, reforming drug laws to direct offenders into treatment programs, restructuring sentencing guidelines, and reforming parole practices—where high numbers of parolees currently are returned to custody not for committing new crimes but for technical violations of their parole orders. Twenty-five years ago, criminologist Pat Carlen (1989) advocated the supervision of women in noncustodial settings in their communities, where they could remain connected with their children and families and benefit from programs that address their emotional and economic needs. In reviewing ten years of research on correctional boot camps, the government's National Institute of Justice (2003) noted that women need a very different environment that takes account of their role as mothers, their likely history of physical or sexual abuse, and that uses "nonaggressive program management styles" (p. 3).

Many professional organizations oppose prosecution of pregnant women who use illegal drugs, including the American Academy of Pediatrics, the American College of Obstetricians and Gynecologists, the Association of Maternal and Child Health, the American Medical Association, and the American Nurses Association. Boyd (2004) argued that if women are offered "non-judgemental prenatal and infant care, economic and social support," then prenatal outcomes improve (p. 123). Beyond this, she advocated legalization of drug use.

Many researchers and advocates challenge the idea that prisons can solve social problems rooted in racism, poverty, and inequality. They seek to halt prison expansion and redirect resources toward the development of alternative sentencing, prevention, and treatment programs, as does the nationwide Critical Resistance network (Critical Resistance 2005; Magnani and Wray 2006). Julia Sudbury argues that prison abolitionists see prison as "a fundamentally unjust institution that, like slavery, cannot be reformed" and notes: "Prison abolition challenges the belief that prison works" (Reading 55). Although prison abolition does not offer an immediate solution, it provides "a critical framework within which proposed legislation, campaigns, and activism can be assessed."

Criminalization is a major source of insecurity for many women and their families, especially African Americans and Latinas. There is a considerable gap between organizations working on behalf of women caught up in the criminal justice system and the broader U.S. women's movement. Data presented in this chapter give grounds for more effective efforts across lines of race, class, and sexuality to address the needs of formerly incarcerated women and those currently in custody.

◆◆◆

Questions for Reflection

As you read and discuss this chapter, consider these questions:

1. How do you define crime?

2. Where is the prison nearest to where you live? Are men, women, or both incarcerated there? Who are they in terms of class, race, and age?

3. Note the official language of "corrections" or the "correctional system." What is being corrected? Why? How? And corrected to what?

4. How do you define security and for whom? How does women's incarceration contribute to security—at micro, meso, macro, and global levels? Does it undermine security? If so, how and for whom?

◆◆◆

Finding Out More on the Web

1. Research the work of organizations cited in this chapter. How are they working to support women in the criminal justice system? Try to find organizations that are active in your city or state.

2. Find out the financial and human costs each year of white-collar crime in the United States. How do those compare to the cost of street crimes?

3. What is the relationship between state spending on the criminal justice system and spending on higher education in your state?

◆◆◆

Taking Action

1. Analyze the way the news media report crime, or analyze the portrayal of criminals in movies and TV shows. How are women who have committed crimes portrayed? Pay particular attention to issues of race, class, and sexuality. Contact media outlets to express your views on the representation of women caught up in the law enforcement system.

2. Find out about the daily conditions for women in the jail or prison nearest to you.

3. Find out about activist groups in your area that support incarcerated women. What can you do on behalf of women in prison?

4. The USA PATRIOT Act allows law enforcement agencies access to information on students and to student records. Find out what steps your college or university has taken to provide information under the terms of this act.

F I F T Y

Prison Life: A Day (2004)

Marilyn Buck

Marilyn Buck (1947–2010) described herself as a political prisoner, activist, poet, and artist. Arrested in 1985, she received an eighty-year sentence, but was released in 2010 three weeks before her death from cancer. She completed her bachelors degree in psychology from prison, as well as becoming an accomplished potter. Recipient of the 2001 PEN Prison Writing Program poetry prize, she was involved in cultural and educational activities for women prisoners.

Don't let your throat tighten with fear. Take sips of breath all day and night. Before death closes your mouth.—Jalaluddin Rumi

The seemingly normal routine life behind the walls is more than sufficiently punishing and corrosive. When I awake, I do not shudder with fear to face another day of extreme measures; instead, I worry more about becoming more inured to the casual cruelty that prevails. It lures us into becoming the very creatures the prison system advertises us to be and robs us of our humanity. I worry about succumbing, losing my will to resist dehumanization, and ultimately, losing my own sense of who I am as a human being.

What is normal and routine about this world would be a nightmare to one who has not had to experience such indignity and lack of control over one's self. Prison is a parallel world to the "outside." Only if one has lived in a Black community,

under martial law in Puerto Rico (or in other parts of the world), survived military invasions, or been held as a virtual hostage in an abusive, battering relationship, might one have an idea of what it is like to live in conditions where your every word and action is subject to censorship, control, punishment, and even possible torture by guards hired to watch and secure you. Most new prisoners walk around in a state of shock, fear, and uncertainty. The new prisoner is alternatively on the verge of tears or filled with rage at the way she is treated by the guards and "administrators." She cannot believe that she has so few rights and that there is no due process when a guard tells her that she must do as he or she says or suffer the consequences. Even to be transferred to another prison causes a similar, though less intense, response. One must learn to negotiate the unfamiliar minefield—the personalities and boundaries of the prison guards as well as those of the prisoners, each of whom is arduously negotiating each day.

At 5:30 I rise, still tired from being awakened during the night by flashlights in my eyes during three "morning-shift" counts. After the 5:00 count, I finally stumble out of bed into the cold dankness of the cell, three steps to the toilet. I move to the sink to wash my face, trying to open the metal locker without great screeching (so as not to wake my cellmates), both women younger than my own children would be. One moans at the sound of the flushing toilet, the creaking locker, and the water dripping into the sink. Already I feel anxiety, knowing that I am disrupting her sleep and that she will jump up in a moment exasperated and frustrated. I know how it feels not to be able to sleep because of constant intrusions—loud voices, metal doors clanging, and cellmates who live on a different schedule.

I am fortunate that both my cellmates are considerate; we all get along in this space built for one prisoner. But the constant attention to consideration creates a tension—an artificial politeness—as well as the vigilance of constantly moving out of each other's way, predicting the next move, like playing in a championship tennis tournament and trying to determine where the ball will land.

At 6:00 AM the officer begins screeching over the loudspeaker. Names and commands blare out. My ears strain to hear whether my name is being called. I am on constant alert; I feel like Pavlov's dog waiting for a bell—or an electrical shock. Even though I am aware of the phenomenon and resist it, I am subject to it. Every interaction— conversation, reading, even thinking—is subject to this harsh intrusion. Concentration flees. The act of being on alert—hypervigilant—almost 24 hours per day wreaks havoc on my nervous system.

I make a phone call. The person on the line stops, aware that I am distracted—the guards are calling out names. I have to ask my caller to speak louder so that I can hear over the constant din of voices and background noise. Morning is the quietest time; I have managed to work in the afternoons and evenings in order to have some moments of relative quiet in which I might concentrate and read or write.

Thinking is a luxury. Most of my thought processes have retreated below the conscious level. Someone is hollering that the iron is dirty, and who is the trifling @#%^* who messed it up? Oh, to be like Buddha beneath the tree becoming enlightened. But he did not have to function in this world. He had the choice to get up at any moment.

I sit down to write; I look for what I need in a pile of papers. There is no place to store materials or books. We are permitted by policy to have five books. An hour of intermittent silence; the loud speaker intrudes only once. The fire alarm goes off at 9:05 am. I sigh and hurriedly grab a book, water, and jacket. Is this one more false alarm set off by someone smoking, or is it to be a unit shakedown in which we will be exiled to the yard for hours and

hours? (I'm glad I am dressed, a habit of mine to be prepared, not to be caught off guard.) The guard announces, "Clear the unit!" Another comes banging on doors, "Everyone outdoors! Now!"

Women file out doors opened only in emergencies. Many are still in their nightclothes. They are among those who have contrived to sleep their days away. Most are very young, 20–25 years old. We stand outside in the chill wind. The alarm continues to blare, raking my eardrums. The smokers light up. I move further away from the crowd to avoid the press of bodies. Lieutenants stride purposefully through the crowd into the building.

Ten minutes pass. No order to leave the area. Relief. Today will not be a shakedown. Today I will not have to spend hours reorganizing my pitiful few possessions. I might still get something accomplished before work.

The Lieutenant walks out the door screaming, "You must stand behind the yellow line!" Two sisters who are deaf and mute remain standing where they were along with several others who do not understand English and have not been here long enough to know that until everyone moves across the plain yellow line we will be forced to remain standing. Another woman, closer to the "offenders" goes and pulls them gently across the line. I am irritated at the whole show. I also realize that I'm irritated at those women who don't move. I am irritated at myself for being exasperated at the other women even though I understand that some have not moved as their own personal act of rebellion. I, too, have done that and may do so in some other situation in order to retain some modicum of my own power. Six more minutes pass. Everyone is now behind the line. The Lieutenant strides out through the crowd, ignoring us. Resentment hovers over us. Finally, a guard walks out to say, "You can return now."

At 10:45 AM women come speed walking by from UNICOR, on their way to lunch.[1] By 11:30– 11:45, my unit is released to lunch. We are "out last" this week because we were ranked last in the sanitation and safety inspection. One of the orderlies/ workers did not have her steel-toed boots on when cleaning labels off plastic bottles with a toothbrush and bucket of water. A collective punishment for a petty procedural offense.

I have stood waiting at the front door to get out of the unit among the first in order not to stand long in the line. Even so, as I stand in line, ten women come racing by to cut. I say something to the woman who cuts in front of me. She swings her hair and moves in front of her friend, looking back at me, a challenge in her eyes. It's not worth the energy—but I am exasperated. I never get used to such lack of regard among the women. The lines are long, but we're all anxious not to spend one minute longer than necessary in any given line.

Once inside, before I can get into the line there, the Lieutenant stops me, "Button your shirt! Take off your sunglasses!" I button my shirt perturbed by the ridiculousness of the rule. But it is a direct order. After all, I am wearing a tee shirt beneath my uniform shirt. I do not look provocative. . . I do not remove my sunglasses, telling the Lieutenant that they are prescription lenses. He already knows that, but says, "Let me see your eyes!" I sigh; do I really want to eat? I have made it this far.

I get my tray. Before me is a scene not unlike Times Square at rush hour. Too many people in too little space. The women on the serving line are all ill humored by this time; the vegetables are steamed beyond recognition, and the cantaloupe is gone. Only apples, the ever present last year's apples. I look out on the floor. Against a low wall stand a number of the suited administrators: warden, bureaucrats, and department heads. Their policy is to be available to the prisoner population to listen to requests, problems. Most carry a small notebook into which they may write the prisoner's name, then smile and say, "We'll look into it." I move into the fray. There is a line to get water, a line to get soup, a free-for-all to get a few wilted salad greens already picked over. If one waits for the salad bar to clear out, one will never get anything. She who gets there first gets the tomato or the potato salad. I move off to find a place to sit, jockeying with my tray in order not to end up with it in my chest or on someone else. There are 300–400 women in this area. Some have left, thank goodness. Others could not face the dining room today.

I eat then juggle my way out carefully. I avoid getting pat searched—a daily gauntlet to run, which is done ostensibly to prevent women from taking even a slice of bread from the dining room. I do not have any "contraband," but recoil at being patted down—felt up—by some female or even male guard. Eighteen years in prison has not inured

me to the invasive violations of hands that assert the right to paw on my body.

Now I must hurry back to the unit to pick up my work materials and a bottle of water, which is, I hope, less toxic than that in the tap. Off to work. The loudspeaker sounds, "The yard is closed. Return to your work site." We have ten minutes on the half hour to move from one area to another. A Lieutenant is yelling at some woman across the yard to turn around and return to wherever she came from. The woman is pleading her case. I hurry and make it across without an encounter. The Education Department is a relatively safe place to work unless the "suits" or a guard brings a tour through—new guard recruits, visiting prison officials (like the officials from the People's Republic of China who were escorted through proudly a few years ago by higher-ranking U.S. Bureau of Prison officials). We go about our business. We are not anxious to engage in conversation with tour-types. We are not saleswomen for the criminal justice system.

I work as the correspondence clerk in the Vocational Training area (where computer training is given). I work with those few women who are able to pay for college correspondence courses, or other distance-learning courses and take care of the "paperwork" involved in documenting prisoner activities for my supervisor. Both the supervisors in VT are interested in women gaining skills in order to get work that will sustain them economically once they are released. That interest is rare inside prison walls. One can feel nearly like an efficacious human being here, except of course for the endemic male supremacy. A main perk of working here is that, as in the rest of the Education Department, the loudspeaker does not penetrate. It is usually quiet.

At 3:30 PM, we wait for the last students to leave so that we, the prisoner clerks may also return to the units for the nationwide, official 4:00 PM standing count.[2] Back to the unit. The guard is yelling on the loudspeaker, "Clear the unit, go to your rooms." I try to get a cup of hot water for coffee before the unit is cleared. Success. I exhale and whisper-chat with one cellmate; the other is lying down. A few minutes later the loudspeaker blares, "Stand up for the count." We strain to hear which unit they will count first. If we can't discern the distorted sounds clearly, we sit tensely, waiting to leap up at the sound of approaching keys, or we stand, waiting for 15–20 minutes.

After the count, there is a visible lessening of tension. Most of the "suits" are gone. Even the evening shift guards are somewhat less tense. The loudspeaker continues to invade, haranguing someone to go somewhere—all evening long, incessantly. "Mail call" is the one welcome announcement. Since we are "out last," we must wait nearly an hour before being released from the unit to pursue evening duties, activities, and have dinner. It is our unit's day to go to commissary. At last the door does open, and the mad rush begins. "No running!" Women stop running to walk fast. Do I have time to eat before my number is called? Yes, I rush to the dining hall, get through the line relatively quickly, and gulp down my food. I do not want to miss my number. I need soap and tea. I rush out to find my number hasn't been called yet. Relief. Now, how much longer? I have to go back to work, so I'm feeling pressed. Finally I shop and hurry back to my unit to drop off my commissary, hoping no one decides to come into my cell and make off with my bag. I don't have time to put it away. Off to work. At 8:30 VT closes.

I rush back to the unit to sign up for laundry—it's our tier's evening to sign up for the next day, an improvement from years of dashing at 5:30 AM to try to get a space. I get a wash time when I can actually wash. Now I dash to try to get a shower before the 9:15 PM call for count. Fortunately, only one woman stands in line before me. On my way back to my cell from the shower, I check to see whether a phone call will be possible. No, a line there too.

Once we are locked in for the count, I do not leave the cell again. I lay down to read the news from several days earlier. I try to relax and go to sleep. Hopefully, after 10:00 PM, the loudspeaker will fall silent. Barring a fire alarm or a guard waking me to give a urine sample, I will get a full night's rest.

NOTES

1. UNICOR is the acronym for Federal Prison Industries. It is a highly profitable set of factories from data processing to furniture-making, military supplies, etc. Prisoners are paid "third-world" wages, $1.10/hour is the highest wage. Women compete to work there, as it is the only source of income for most prisoners. With this small wage, they can sustain themselves and perhaps send some money home to their families.

2. Every prisoner must be standing upright at this count unless one has the proper medical approval not to do so.

FIFTY-ONE

◆◆◆

A Mother's Love (2012)

Andrea C. James

Andrea C. James worked in the criminal justice system for over twenty-five years from youth worker to criminal defense attorney. In 2009 she was convicted of wire fraud, disbarred as an attorney, and sentenced to two years in federal prison. She founded Families for Justice as Healing (Boston, Mass.) to fulfill the promise she made to women who remain in prison: to speak their truth, to advocate for an end to the war on drugs, and to promote alternatives to incarceration. She is the author of *Upper Bunkies Unite: And Other Thoughts on the Politics of Mass Incarceration* and *My Grandparents Are Polar Bears*, a children's book.

The pain is overflowing in the women.
Ever brimming, spilling over the edge.
At moments, in the classroom. On our bunks.
Cleaning toilets. Mowing lawns.
Our heavy hearts overflow. Sagging.
A child leaves the visiting room pleading with his
*   mother.*
How much longer? How much longer?
The love of a mother fills up sagging like the magnolias
heavy, waiting for their love to be carried further.

Many incarcerated women have children. The women are in prison, but still are mothers who love their children deeply. They do their best to mother from prison. Standing at the crowded telephones trying to still be a wife and mother myself, I often heard conversations about things going on with the children of the women in Danbury. Talking to your children from a telephone in prison, every conversation is a clipped verbal dance of concern, love, anger, discipline and inquisition. Missed weddings, anniversaries, graduations and funerals. A young boy's hamster died. A daughter's details of abuse in the hands of her caregivers. Requests for pictures for lockers full of childhood histories over the years, as they've grown while their mothers were warehoused in prison.

For women in prison, every request made to the outside regarding the care of their children is a cause for caution and concern. Fear of signing the wrong paper that could result in someone taking their children away. It often causes paralysis in the women as to how to make decisions regarding requests for things like signing a power of attorney or temporary guardianship. Fear of doing something that could be construed as giving away their parental rights.

Twenty-five years ago, the presence of women—especially mothers—was an aberration in the criminal justice system. That was before the war on drugs. Following federal and state adoption of mandatory sentencing in the mid 1980's, the number of women in prison skyrocketed, and black women are twice as likely to be incarcerated as white women. We are viewed as mothers who violated a basic maternal commitment to care for our children. Instead we engaged in wrongful criminal activities . . . but mothers' pathways to incarceration are complex, and often rooted in issues of sexual and physical violence.[1] The reality is, seventy-some percent of our female population are low-level, nonviolent offenders. Most of them would have gotten probation years ago.[2]

The women were in Danbury (Connecticut) for all kinds of things, mostly related to money or drugs. A woman I met had already been there for four years of an eight-year sentence for selling heroin. One day, just before Thanksgiving, she sat down next to me and picked up a conversation we had a few weeks earlier about her 15-year-old daughter being sexually active.

"Can you believe it?" she said. "Now my other daughter is smoking marijuana and they want me to sit here for another four years. I can't do nothing

to help my kids. My son thinks God is a liar because I keep telling him to have faith that I will be able to come home; but he doesn't believe it anymore. He says he doesn't believe in God anymore either. We got nothing to do here," she continued. "I sat here for four years doing nothing and they want me to sit for another four. For what? I can't do nothing to help my kids. What's the good in that?"

The role that mothers play as parents during their incarceration is minimal due to the nature of the correctional system. Given these constraints, it is not surprising that mothers express feelings of inadequacy, despondency, and fear of losing their children permanently. Furthermore because their own behavior has caused the separation, most mothers feel intense guilt and shame.[3]

Mother's Day 2010 was heavy with the emotions of women missing their families. One woman who received a visit that day had come to prison when her son was only three years old. He was now sixteen years old and came to see her for Mother's Day, alone, for the first time. Another young mother who had just started a 10-year mandatory minimum sentence for selling drugs was visited by her four sons, aged 14, 10, 6, and 17 months. This was the first time they had seen her since her incarceration. They were brought to the prison from their home in Washington D.C. by an organization called Our Place that brings children to visit their mothers in prison. Later that day the woman sat on the stairs outside the visiting room, weeping, because her 17-month-old wouldn't come to her during the visit. He cried the entire time. A father came to visit his daughter but was turned away because he didn't know that it wasn't her designated visiting day. Like all other weekends, some women got visits, most didn't. And some would remember this Mother's Day more than others.

The *New York Daily News* headline read, "Mom's Day Horror: 2 Teens Killed, Woman Wounded After Gunman Taunts Mother at Bronx Party." The article reported that two innocent teenagers were killed at a party when they tried to defend a friend's mom. One of them, Quanisha Wright, aged 16, was a student at the Bronx Leadership Academy. She was raised by her grandmother because her mother, Desiree Wright, is in prison.[4]

Every now and then Desiree would pull out the photo book and we would look at the pictures of Quanisha. A beautiful girl with two braids framing her smiling face. Sometimes Des would wear her hair with two pieces hanging down in the front and I would say, "Look at you lookin' like Quanisha." This would always make Des smile. Some days if you just looked at Desiree too long she would be overwhelmed with sadness.

No special consideration was provided to Desiree by the Federal Bureau of Prisons after her daughter's death, but after five years of being warehoused in federal prisons across the country she was finally transferred to Danbury where I met her, so that she could be closer to her remaining two sons in the Bronx.

The Federal Bureau of Prisons has the discretionary power of compassionate release, but it has only rarely been used to release prisoners who are terminally ill and in their final days. Desiree had served more than half of her 10-year mandatory minimum sentence, participated in rehabilitative programs, and worked for Unicor. She was designated to the lowest security level in the federal prison system where women drove vehicles and moved freely on the prison grounds. They went outside the grounds to help clean the town of Danbury and to speak to high school students about staying out of trouble. Despite all this, it was still deemed necessary to continue holding Desiree in a low-level prison camp. She could not go home to help rebuild the lives of her remaining children.

Not too long after Desiree's daughter's death, Nancy Flores heard about the death of her 17-year-old son. He had been shot multiple times. When Nancy and her sister Maricelis were informed of his death their screams and wails brought the prison to a standstill. At the time we others didn't know what had happened but we knew from the appearance of the chaplain and the women's screams that a family member had probably died.

I came to know Nancy because her sister, Maricelis, was a student in the English-as-a-Second-Language class I taught. Nancy spoke even less English than Maricelis but would stop me in the hallway everyday to ask whether her youngest sister was paying attention in class. Maricelis had arrived at Danbury with a 5-year sentence for selling crack cocaine. She was a young, 24-year-old mother from Puerto Rico. Her way of communicating to everyone was a smile. As co-defendants in the same drug case, Maricelis, Nancy, and six other brothers and sisters, and three nieces and nephews

were sentenced and dispersed from Puerto Rico to federal prisons throughout the country. Their elderly parents were left to care for the very young children of these siblings and were now dealing with the death of Nancy's son and trying to raise money for a funeral.

As a family their troubles had been ongoing for some time. In response to a writing assignment in class and with the help of her Spanish-English dictionary, Maricelis wrote about her life struggles and "a lot of sadness and pain." She was married at fifteen, divorced two years later, and started using and selling drugs and alcohol. When she was sixteen her niece was gunned down in front of her. Soon after that Maricelis gave birth to her daughter. Three weeks later, her daughter's father was murdered. Maricelis described this time as so traumatic that she thought of killing herself but didn't want to leave her daughter. Years after her involvement in drug selling had ended, she was prosecuted and sentenced to federal prison for five or more years, together with many other family members. She described this as something that destroyed her family but that God gave her the strength to keep moving.

Desiree was working down in the kitchen when she heard that Nancy's son had been killed and she went up to the chapel to console her. Des said she just wanted to give Nancy support because she knew what the woman was feeling. The prison administration didn't allow Nancy to attend her son's funeral in Puerto Rico. The stated reason was that his killing was determined to be gang related. We often experienced times when both Nancy and Des would be inconsolable as they continued to mourn for their children.

During my incarceration, I was deeply affected by the many women who would remain there long after I left. Most of them were serving long federal mandatory minimum or guideline sentences for participation in drug selling. Most were mothers. Their average sentence was ten years. They were provided very limited educational and employment training opportunities. Yet they managed to hold it together while enduring such long sentences. They tried to remain positive and hopeful amidst a torrent of regret, heartache, remorse, alienation, loneliness, and a host of other problems, mostly related to being in prison while their children struggled to survive.

Prison is the place where statistics come to life. There are more than two million children in this country with one or both parents incarcerated. Most of these parents are first time, nonviolent offenders serving drug related sentences. A large number of them have not seen their children since they were incarcerated. Many families are unable to visit due to a lack of resources to travel to faraway prisons. A majority of parents in state prisons (62 percent) and federal prison (84 percent) are held over 100 miles from their last residence. In federal prisons, about 43 percent of parents are held over 500 miles from home.[5]

Often multiple family members are incarcerated simultaneously for the same drug offense. For example, Desiree Wright is the cousin and co-defendant of my friend at Danbury, Monique Williams, who is also serving a ten-year mandatory minimum drug sentence. Like Des, Monique is the mother of two children and her husband is also incarcerated for the same drug case. There were many others with multiple members of the same family in prison. The effect of a mother's arrest and incarceration on a family is often even more disruptive than that of a father's arrest and incarceration.[6] That is because approximately two-thirds of incarcerated mothers are the primary caregivers for at least one child before their arrest.[7]

When I came to prison my son was six months old. During those early visits he didn't remember me. He cried and clung to my husband when I tried to hold him. I had to remind myself that I was very fortunate. My husband brought my children to see me every weekend. There were many women who hadn't seen their children and wouldn't see them for a very long time. Many women leave prison after being incarcerated for years and do not know where their children are. Some states extinguish parents' rights if the parent is "out of the child's life" for more than two years. Under the federal Adoption and Safe Families Act of 1997, parental rights can be terminated if a child has been in foster care for 15 of the previous 22 months.[8] Some of this "absence" is a direct result of the difficulty of navigating the logistics required to arrange visitation to correctional facilities.

Secure facilities, jails, and prisons all have elaborate and time-consuming procedures regarding visits to prisoners, and arranging visits are a caseworker's responsibility. Corrections officials must receive prior notification of a visit to insure the parent's presence in the visiting room, and caseworkers need to prepare children for what they will experience when entering a jail or prison. They need to schedule transportation, and arrange for someone—either a caseworker or other staff member—to accompany foster children during these visits. In sum, arranging all this is not an easy task.[9]

Because so many women are homeless on leaving prison with no money or access to resources, reuniting with their families becomes all that more difficult. One woman described her experience to me. "I've been locked up for twelve years. They kept me in prison and stupid, and now they tell me it's time for me to get out, find a job—with no skills. Find a place to live that I can afford. Find food and clothing. And I'm leaving here with nothing. I can't even remember how to pay a bill. The system didn't require me to do anything but stay in prison." Discharged women prisoners with drug convictions who do manage to reunite with their children face another set of challenges. Because they have been convicted of drug crimes, they are subject to federal bans on public housing, welfare and other social services.[10]

In addition to the many barriers to maintaining family ties, overcrowded conditions were also problematic for our visitors at Danbury. Our television room/chapel/occasional classroom became our weekend visiting room. Because of limited space, the visiting policy kept changing. The camp administrator told us to get together and make sure that everyone was able to have a visit. The "problem" was the family members who came every available visiting day and took up space in the visiting room, not that the prison crammed over two hundred women in a space built for less than a third that number. Husbands, children, mothers and fathers coming to visit their wives, mothers, daughters, and sisters, taking advantage of every opportunity they could to see their loved one. That was the problem, and if we didn't make it work the response would be to regulate visits even more. Without visitation, the government imposes a double punishment on convicted parents. In addition to loss of liberty, the lack of contact may further strain parent-child relationships. In the worst case, lengthy separation without visits leads to the permanent dissolution of the family.[11]

Another devastating impact of the separation of parent and child due to incarceration are the negative feelings often experienced by children left behind. The Osborne Association found that children of incarcerated parents were more likely to experience fear, anxiety, sadness, loneliness, and guilt. Their self-esteem was lower; they were more likely to be depressed, and to withdraw from remaining family and friends. This often led to greater likelihood of problems at school, as well as other antisocial behaviors.[12] In February 2010, while I was in Danbury, the *New Britain Herald* newspaper reported that, according to state officials, 70 percent of juvenile detainees in Connecticut had parents who were incarcerated.

Something I never thought about before being in prison is that the long mandatory minimum sentences take women's childbearing years and the ability to start a family. Many of the women at Danbury were relieved to find out that I had a child at age forty-four. I never told them about the miscarriages I endured for years before carrying my last child to full term and that the difficulties were directly related to my age. Many of them were just happy to know there was still a chance to experience pregnancy and motherhood. My son's name is Jon Romero Stanley Matthew James, but we call him Lucky.

My experience in prison allowed me to see through all the heavy labels—bad mother, inmate, convict, felon, junkie, crack whore, thief—to the real person underneath. It's the place where the simplest gesture of kindness can be a lifesaver at the right moment, even from the coldest, meanest person you thought you didn't want to know. Sisterhood in prison allowed me to understand and appreciate other women. I learned firsthand the true profile of who is in our country's prisons and how wrong it is to cage people up, particularly women with children.

NOTES

1. Malika Saada Saar, 2010. Alternative Sentencing to Maternal Incarceration Saves Money and Families, *Huff Post Politics* posted: May 17. www.huffingtonpost.com/sexual-justice/alternative-sentencing-to_b_528797.html

2. Kathleen Hawk-Sawyer, Director, Bureau of Prisons, testimony before House of Representatives, March 2, 2000.

3. García Coll, C.T., P. Buccio-Notaro, B. Molla, and J. L. Surrey. 1998. Incarcerated mothers: crimes and punishments. In *Mothering Against the Odds: Diverse Voices of Contemporary Mothers.* edited by C.T. García Coll, J. L. Surrey, and K. Weingarten. New York: Guilford Press.

4. *New York Daily News*, May 10, 2010.

5. Mumola, C. 2000. Incarcerated Parents and Their Children. Washington, D.C.: U.S. Department of Justice, Bureau of Justice Statistics (NCJ 182335).

6. Barbara Bloom. 1995. Imprisoned Mothers, In *Children of Incarcerated Parents*, edited by Katherine Gabel and Denise Johnston. New York: Lexington Books, p. 21.

7. U.S. GAO, *Women in Prison*, Washington, D.C., December 1999, p. 32.

8. Ibid.

9. Ross, T., A. Khashu, and M. Wamsley. 2004. *Hard Data on Hard Times: An Empirical Analysis of Maternal Incarceration, Foster Care, and Visitation.* New York: Vera Institute of Justice.

10. Perkinson, R. 2010. *Texas Tough: The Rise of America's Prison Empire.* New York: Metropolitan Books/Henry Holt, p.27.

11. Ross, Kahshu and Wamsley, 2004. *Hard Data on Hard Times.*

12. Gabel, S. 1992. Children of incarcerated and criminal parents: Adjustment, behavior, and prognosis, *Bulletin of the American Academy of Psychiatry and the Law*, 20 (1).

F I F T Y - T W O

◆◆◆

Barriers to Basic Care (2009)

Victoria Law

Victoria Law is a writer, photographer, and mother. She was arrested for armed robbery, aged 16, and sentenced to probation. Since then she has helped start Books Through Bars–New York City, a group that sends free books to prisoners nationwide. Her writings include *Resistance Behind Bars: The Struggles of Incarcerated Women; Tenacious: Art and Writings from Women in Prison;* and *Don't Leave Your Friends Behind: Concrete Ways to Support Families in Social Justice Movements and Communities* (with China Martens). She has been involved with ABC No Rio, a collectively run arts center on New York's Lower East Side, curating exhibits and coordinating photography classes for neighborhood youth.

In 1976, in *Estelle* v. *Gamble,* the Supreme Court ruled that deliberate indifference to a prisoner's serious medical needs violates the Eighth Amendment. Despite this ruling, prison health care continues to neglect, and even jeopardize, the health of its prisoners. Incarcerated women face the additional challenge of trying to obtain adequate care for specifically female health concerns within a system still designed with the violent male prisoner in mind.

Female Concerns

Pregnancy is one of the more common female health concerns. A 2003 report by the United States Department of Justice indicated that 6% of women entered local jails and 5% of women entered state prison pregnant.[1] However, despite these numbers, even prison wardens agree that several of the particular needs of pregnant women "have yet to be dealt with in any of the facilities." Most, if not all prisons, lack not only maternity clothing but also adequate resources to deal with false labors, premature births and miscarriages. In addition, many states require that pregnant prisoners wear belly chains when being transported to and from the hospital.[2]

. . .

Pregnancy is not the only specifically female medical concern ignored by prison officials. Prevention, screening, diagnosis, care, pain alleviation and rehabilitation for breast cancer are virtually nonexistent in prisons. In 1998, a study at an unnamed southern prison found that 70% of the women who should have had mammograms under standard medical protocol had not been tested. Although many of the women were at high risk because of family histories, they were not provided with a clinical breast exam, information or basic education on self-examination upon admittance.[3]

. . .

Similarly, cervical cancer and other female illnesses are commonly misdiagnosed and mistreated, sometimes with alarming consequences. At the Coffee Creek Correctional Facility in Oregon, Danielle Conatser's pap smear showed abnormalities. The prison's doctor informed her that she had cervical cancer. Conatser, who had had a baby six weeks earlier, requested a second opinion. She was told she would be put to sleep for a biopsy. When she awoke, she was told that the doctor who had originally diagnosed her had removed a good portion of her cervix, thus making it unlikely that she would be able to have children in the future. Conatser never received her second opinion, nor did she receive any follow-up care. She continues to live with the fear that she has cancer.[4]

General Medical Care

Not only are the particular health care needs of women ignored or dismissed, but medical care in general is often inadequate or life-threatening. This is all the more dangerous considering that women frequently enter prison in poor health already after years of poverty, poor nutrition, inadequate health care, and substance abuse. According to the U.S. Department of Justice, female prisoners also experience more severe health problems than their male counterparts."[5] However, the prison system does little, if anything, to meet their health needs.

. . . This past year, officials in Oregon ignored Michelle Everett's repeated requests for medical care. She was given medical attention only after turning yellow. After both hepatitis and cirrhosis of the liver were ruled out, she was told that a bile duct was obstructed, but that the prison could do nothing about it. Like Conatser, she was not given a biopsy and has received no further medical care.[6]

In addition, illiteracy and poor literacy can be an obstacle to obtaining medical care. As Ellen Richardson, a prisoner at Valley State Prison for Women (VSPW) in California, testified, "The medical staff triage [is] based on how the patient states her symptoms on paper." This procedure ignores the fact that the average literacy level at VSPW is less than ninth grade, that over 700 women have a below sixth-grade reading level and that approximately 100 are illiterate or speak English as a second language. "A woman may have extreme stomach pain and cramping, but only have the literacy level to write, 'I have a tummy ache.' That is not enough for medical staff to let her see a doctor."[7]

This practice is not limited to California. Jerrye Broomhall, a prisoner at the Mabel Bassett Correctional Center in Oklahoma (MBCC), states that women unable to articulate their ailments are often denied medical attention: "If a woman is not literate or articulate enough to convince staff that she needs medical attention, she will be in a lot of trouble if she is quiet and/or friendless."[8]

Lack of funds may also prohibit a woman from seeking medical attention. At FMC Carswell, where the average wage ranges between 17¢ and 24¢ per hour, women are charged a three-dollar fee for each visit to the medical staff. "I do feel that the fee actually pushed away the people who really needed the health care," recalled Kirsten, a former prisoner who was released in 2007 shortly after the fee was implemented.[9]

The climate of medical neglect has sometimes led to preventable deaths. In February 2000, Wisconsin prisoner Michelle Greer suffered an asthma attack and asked to go to the Health Services Unit (HSU). When the guard and captain on duty contacted the nurse in charge, he did not look at Greer's medical file and simply instructed her to use her inhaler (which was not working). Half an hour later, Greer's second request to go to HSU was also ignored. After another half hour, Greer was told to walk to HSU but collapsed en route. The nurse arrived without a medical emergency box or oxygen. A second nurse arrived with the needed emergency box, but again with no oxygen. Forty-five minutes after her collapse (and less than two hours after her initial plea for medical help), Greer died.[10]

Greer's case is far from unique. At Central California Women's Facility, nine women died within eight weeks. In the case of Pamela Coffey, her fellow prisoners called for medical assistance. Not only did Coffey suffer from abdominal pain and numbness in her legs, but "her tongue was so swollen she could hardly speak." An MTA (or Medical Technical Assistant—a guard with low-level medical training) arrived and, according to Coffey's fellow prisoners, "he was laughing. He said 'I can't understand a word she's saying—you can do more for her than I can.'" Coffey died that same night. An outside medical investigation revealed that abnormal blood tests had never been followed up, and concluded that "there were significant problems with her medical care that might have contributed to her death."[11]

State prison systems have also begun contracting for-profit corporations to provide health care.

These corporations promise quality care at a much lower cost than state governments can provide. What these corporations provide in actuality, however, is often little better and, because the main motive is profit rather than providing services, sometimes worse than prison-run health care.

Darlene Dixon recalled her visit to a private clinic contracted by the prison: "There was no disposable paper on the table to create a sanitary barrier between my body and the examination table. The room was basically in disarray; there were spilled liquids on the counter tops as well as debris on the floor." In the restroom was a sink filled with "soiled and bloody tubes, lids and bottles. Even more disturbing were the clean ones located on top of the toilet tank beside it. It rapidly became apparent to me that these items were being washed and reused."[12]

In New York State, Prison Health Services (PHS), a for-profit corporation, won hundreds of millions of dollars of jail and prison contracts. . . . A yearlong investigation by the *New York Times* found that the care provided by PHS was often deficient, flawed and/or lethal. According to the *Times*, state investigators scrutinizing ten prisoner deaths came to the same conclusion after finding the same circumstances in each case: to cut expenses, PHS trimmed medical staffs, hired under-qualified doctors, had nurses doing tasks beyond their training and withheld prescription drugs. The investigators also found that PHS allowed patient records to remain unread and employee misconduct to go unpunished.[13]

PHS is not alone. Correctional Medical Services (CMS) has been the nation's largest provider of prison health care, with nearly 300 sites in 19 states.[14] . . .

Since 2003, the Michigan Department of Corrections has contracted with CMS to provide health care throughout its prisons.[15] . . . An investigative article in *Harper's* revealed that CMS stymies those seeking treatment for hepatitis C, requiring them to fulfill a long list of conditions, known as "the protocol pathway," before they can receive any care.[16]

In 1999, CMS regional medical director Gary Campbell issued a memo to his fellow directors, stating, "I am not encouraging anyone to undergo therapy. However, if you have someone that is insistent, then this pathway is to be fulfilled."[17] Although the memo specifically referred to patients seeking treatment for hepatitis C, who make up approximately twenty to forty percent of the U.S. prison population, prisoners seeking care for other diseases, viruses and illnesses have also been frustrated when trying to receive care—or even information—about their medical conditions.[18]

In 2006, Stephanie Walters Searight entered the Scott Correctional Facility in Plymouth, Michigan. There she was tested and told that she had HIV. "The door [was] left wide open while I received the news. Prisoners walking by hearing the most devastating news of my life."

Lack of confidentiality was not all that Searight had to contend with: "I wait to see the doctor. I wait to ask questions. I wait to see if they will treat me. I start a medical journal to keep records of my health. I begin to request health care regarding my symptoms. I request mental health for counseling. I ask when I will see a doctor. They say don't worry. You will see him soon."

Searight waited three months before prison officials allowed her to see a doctor. However, once she arrived at the office, she found that her appointment was cancelled. "I still have questions that can't get answered. The nurses tell me that they don't specialize in HIV." When Searight finally did see the specialist, he prescribed her a multi-vitamin to boost her immune system. Upon her return to prison, Searight was told that the prison would not provide the vitamins free of charge; she needed to purchase them from the prison commissary.

In August 2007, Searight saw the doctor again. "I just saw the HIV specialist," she wrote. "I was just told that they will start medication in three to six weeks and that they want to run a few more tests first, but that is the same thing they told me six months ago."[19]

Organizing for Their Lives

Women have been active trying to change their sometimes life-threatening medical neglect. The most successful and well-known prisoner-initiated project organized around health care is ACE (AIDS Counseling and Education) at Bedford Hills. AIDS is the leading cause of death among U.S. prisoners,

being five to ten times more prevalent in prison than in the outside society.[20] . . .

This prevalence is not new: a 1988 study by the New York State Department of Health revealed that almost 20% of women entering the maximum-security Bedford Hills Correctional Center were HIV-positive.[21] By 1992, one of every five women entering the New York State prison system tested positive for the HIV virus. Despite these numbers, attitudes around HIV and AIDS were characterized by secrecy, denial, shame, ignorance and fear. Both prisoners and staff ostracized women who were believed to be HIV-positive.[22] In 1987, six women chose to act against the fear, ignorance and social ostracism around HIV and AIDS. They petitioned the administration to allow them to create a peer counseling and education group. ACE was the result.[23]

ACE founders recognized that changing attitudes toward the disease and those who had it required prisoners to play an active role in dealing with the crisis. Although representatives from the Department of Health and other state agencies did live presentations at Bedford, many women did not trust them because they were state officials. ACE founders hoped that having prisoners as peer educators would generate the cooperation, trust and support needed to change both attitudes toward and the care of women with HIV/AIDS.[24]

Although the prison superintendent Elaine Lord had originally approved the program, ACE continually faced staff harassment and administrative interference. For instance, because both Kathy Boudin and Judith Clark, alleged members of the Weather Underground, were active ACE members, the group was constantly monitored and sometimes prevented from officially meeting. Fears that the one-to-one peer counseling sessions would lead to organizing around other issues as well as the staff's own ignorance and fear of HIV/AIDS, led to staff harassment and interference. Educators from the Montefiore Hospital holding training sessions were banned from the facility for suggesting that the Department of Correctional Services lift its ban on dental dams and condoms.[25] A year after its formation, ACE members were prohibited from meeting at its regular time, using its meeting room, giving educational presentations or referring to themselves as "counselors."[26]

Despite these setbacks, ACE members not only managed to implement and continue their program, they helped women prepare for their medical examinations by working with them to define and articulate their main questions. They also accompanied women to consultations and worked to improve communication between patients and medical staff. ACE members also presented educational seminars to women throughout the facility, often using role-playing to break through barriers, generate discussion and examine the issues—both inside and outside the prison—that surround the disease.[27] "If you hear stigma now, there are five people who immediately go, 'Why did you have to say that?' It's not okay anymore. And I know that is a direct result of ACE and the education process," reported Vinice Walker, a peer educator.[28]

The program was also awarded a $250,000 grant from the AIDS Institute that allowed it to create several paid staff positions for prisoners as well as hire an outside coordinator. In 1998, ACE members wrote and published *Breaking the Walls of Silence*, a book detailing the group's history and its positive impact on women with AIDS as a guide for other prison AIDS programs.

Other women political prisoners have focused on the AIDS crisis behind bars. Linda Evans, for example, started the Pleasanton AIDS Education and Counseling program.[29] During her 14 year incarceration, Laura Whitehorn set up AIDS peer education programs in every federal prison where she was housed.[30]

Women who were not politically active before incarceration have also created programs to challenge the prison's unresponsiveness to their health. HIV-positive prisoners at Central California Women's Facility began a peer-education program encompassing not only HIV and AIDS, but also other sexually transmitted diseases, tuberculosis and Hepatitis C.[31] The women went from prison yard to prison yard talking to their peers about these diseases: "There has been a great response from the population and HIV/AIDS testing requests have gone up tremendously," wrote Joann Walker, one of the peer educators.[32]

Not all of their efforts have been as successful. In late 2003, the women started PRIDE, a prisoner-run HIV support group. The group's desire for confidentiality clashed with the prison's security protocol: "We didn't want a CO [correctional officer] or guard] sitting there listening to our medical information, so they shut us down after three weeks," recalled PRIDE cofounder Misty Rojo.[33]

However, with the exception of ACE at Bedford Hills, researchers and scholars have largely ignored these programs, overlooking the difficulties faced by those organizing around HIV/AIDS issues in prison. The reality of a prisoner-organized initiative, even one with the positive goal of educating women about HIV/AIDS, contradicts the concept of prison as a locale for punishment and control. "Once we, as prisoners, were given permission to become educated, to take initiative, and to organize our own community, many of us in ACE felt more motivated and empowered than we had ever before in our lives," wrote cofounders Kathy Boudin and Judith Clark.[34] Such empowerment runs counter to the premise of prisons and can be (and often is) seen as a threat to its security.

Women have also worked individually and without the auspices of administrative approval to change their health care, sometimes risking sanctions and retaliation. The California Department of Corrections and Rehabilitation (CDCR) expressly prohibits prisoner organizing, stating that all "inmate clubs, activity groups, associations, or other organizations within the facility are permissible only when specifically approved by the Warden."[35] Charisse Shumate, a prisoner at the Central California Women's Facility (CCWF), did not allow this policy to stop her from working with other women who had sickle-cell anemia. Until her death, she helped them understand the disease and the necessary treatments.[36] She also advocated the right to compassionate release for any prisoner with less than a year to live and was the lead plaintiff in *Shumate v. Wilson*, the class-action lawsuit filed by prisoners at CCWF and the California Institution for Women (CIW) against the state. Prisoners charged that those with cancer, heart disease and other serious illnesses were denied medical care and that the prisons' medical staff failed to protect the confidentiality of prisoners with HIV and AIDS. In 1997, the CDCR agreed to a settlement: untrained prison employees would be barred from making judgments about prisoners' medical care, prisons would ensure medicines without undue lapses or delays, and medical staff would offer preventive care, including pelvic and breast exams, pap smears and mammograms.[37]

Unfortunately Shumate herself died at CCWF. The Board of Prison Terms recommended clemency rather than compassionate release, which required the governor's approval. Because Shumate had been sentenced to life in prison for killing her abusive lover, then-governor Gray Davis refused to approve the Board's recommendation.[38] Shumate never expressed regret for her organizing work: "I took on [the battle] knowing the risk could mean my life in more ways than one . . . And yes, I would do it all over again. If I can save one life from the medical nightmare of CCWF Medical Department then it's well worth it."[39]

Shumate's work did not cease with her death. Women who had learned from her now continue the task of teaching others how "to understand their labwork and how to chart their results, keep a medical diary, hold 'these people' accountable to what they say and do to them."[40] Sherrie Chapman, one of the 26 women who testified in *Shumate* v. *Wilson*, became the primary plaintiff in a class-action suit over medical conditions in addition to filing a civil suit charging the CDC with cruel and unusual punishment after waiting over a decade for cancer treatment.[41]

. . .

In October 2000, women at CCWF, VSPW [Valley State Prison for Women] and CIW [California Institution for Women] testified about the inadequacy of prison medical care at legislative hearings. The women's testimony drew public attention to the chronic neglect and malpractice that they experienced on a daily basis. Their stories highlighted prison policy of not informing women that they had tested positive for Hepatitis C; many women accidentally discovered their status years later. The women also described the lack of counseling and information provided to women with chronic illnesses and the steps they took to fill these gaps. They testified about the administration's retaliatory actions against the women who participated in *Shumate v. Wilson*.[42] These women did so knowing that after the hearings they would return to prison where, out of public sight, they risked retaliation for their outspokenness.

Women prisoners in California are not the only ones who have organized and acted surreptitiously around health care. Former Pennsylvania prisoner Waheedah Shabazz-El stated that when she worked in the prison's gym, women who were HIV-positive gathered as an informal support group. "We knew each other from [the] clinic," she recalled. "We'd talk about the meds, the side effects, the people in denial."[43]

Retaliation

Women in prison face not only medical neglect and malpractice, but also retaliation from the prison administration should they advocate for themselves and demand adequate treatment. Even after the *Shumate* settlement, those who speak out about the prison's medical practices have been subject to reprisals. At CCWF, prison officials have punished prisoners seeking medical attention by upending their cells, confiscating medications and threatening to break up the living arrangements of those who ask for help in the middle of the night.[44]

In December 2001, prisoner Delores (Dee) Garcia began speaking out against the physical abuse, medical neglect and staff callousness at the Skilled Nursing Facility (SNF) at CCWF. Although the SNF is the only licensed medical facility for California's women prisoners, the staff has continually displayed callousness, neglect and incompetence. "Getting the wrong medication is excused because the nurse got me 'mixed up' with another patient," Garcia wrote. "Medical staff also asks me to explain my condition . . . Needing my linens changed is called a 'comfort not a necessity' after a week."[45]

In response, staff members have threatened her, placing the entire facility on lockdown after Garcia and others filed grievances about conditions. In May 2002, she was moved from the Skilled Nursing Facility, the only facility able to treat her Chronic Obstructive Pulmonary Disease, sleep apnea, hepatitis C and arthritis, to Valley State Prison for Women, which has only an unlicensed infirmary with a part-time staff. After a month of advocacy by outside support groups, Garcia was returned to CCWF where staff warned her that if she continued to file grievances and speak to advocates, she would be returned to VSPW. Garcia immediately filed a grievance against the staff and, on July 12, 2002, was transferred to Valley State Prison, where medical staff admitted that they cannot adequately treat her illnesses.[46]

The actions and continued works of ACE members, Linda Evans, Charisse Shumate and many other lesser-known women address crucial issues facing women in prison. They also contradict the notion that women do not and cannot network and organize to change their conditions.

NOTES

1. Barbara Bloom, Barbara Owen, and Stephanie Covington, *Gender-Responsive Strategies: Research, Practice, and Guiding Principles for Women Offenders* (National Institute of Corrections, 2003) 6, http://www.nicic.org/pubs/2003/018017.pdf.

2. James Boudouris, *Parents in Prison: Addressing the Needs of Families* (Lanham, MD: American Correctional Association, 1996), 11.

3. "Statement by Dr. William F. Schulz, Executive Director of Amnesty International USA," *National Jeff Dicks Medical Coalition Newsletter* (October 2002): 8.

4. "Deficient Diagnosis," *Tenacious: Writings from Women in Prison* 2 (Fall 2002): 13.

5. Bloom, Owen and Covington cite L. Acoca, "Defusing the Time Bomb: Understanding and Meeting the Growing Health Care Needs of Incarcerated Women in America," *Crime and Delinquency* 44, no. l: 49–70 and D. S. Young, "Contributing Factors to Poor Health Among Incarcerated Women: A Conceptual Model," *Affilia* 11, no. 4: 440-461.

6. "Deficient Diagnosis," *Tenacious: Writings from Women in Prison* 2 (Fall 2002): 13.

7. Ellen Richardson, "Medical Conditions at Valley State Prison for Women," *The Fire Inside* 17 (March 2001): 5, http://www.womenprisoners.org/fire/000209.html.

8. Jerrye Broomhall, letter to the author, June 13, 2008.

9. Kirsten, e-mail to the author, March 16, 2008.

10. Dan Pens, "Bag'm, Tag'm and Bury'm: Wisconsin Prisoners Dying for Health Care," *Prison Legal News* 12, no. 2 (2001): 1–2.

11. Donna Willmott, "'Am I Gonna Die in Here?' Medical Neglect in California Women's Prisons," *Sojourner: The Women's Forum* 26, no. 7 (March 2001): 22.

12. Darlene Dixon, "Private Health Care in Prisons: Take it or Leave It," *Sojourner: The Women's Forum* 27, no. 7 (2002): 15.

13. Paul von Zielbauer, "As Health Care in Jails Goes Private, Ten Days Can Be a Death Sentence," *New York Times*, February 27, 2005.

14. Correctional Medical Services, Locations, www.cmsstel.com/locations/index.asp.

15. Correctional Medical Services, Locations: Michigan, www.cmsstl.com/locations/state-locations-michigan.asp.

16. Wyl S. Hilton, "Sick on the Inside: Correctional HMOs and the Coming Prison Plague," *Prison Profiteers: Who Makes Money from Mass Incarceration*, ed. Tara Herivel and Paul Wright (New York: New Press, 2007), 186.

17. Hilton, "Sick on the Inside," 187.

18. Stephanie Walters, "Let My Voice Be Heard," *Tenacious: Art and Writings from Women in Prison* 11 (Spring 2007).

19. Stephanie Walters Searight, letter to the author, August 30, 2007.

20. Women of the ACE Program at the Bedford Hills Correctional Facility, *Breaking the Walls of Silence: AIDS and Women in a New York State Maximum Security Prison* (Woodstock, NY: Overlook Press, 1998), 23.

21. Kathy Boudin and Judith Clark, "A Community Of Women Organize Themselves To Cope With The AIDS Crisis: A Case Study From Bedford Hill Correctional Facility," *Columbia Journal of Gender and the Law* 1, no. 1, Jan 31, 1991. Cites New York State Department of Health, AIDS in New York State, 1989.

22. Ibid.

23. Women of the ACE Program at the Bedford Hills Correctional Facility, *Breaking the Walls of Silence: AIDS and Women in a New York State Maximum Security Prison* (Woodstock, NY: Overlook Press, 1998), 17.

24. Kathy Boudin and Judith Clark, "A Community Of Women Organize Themselves To Cope With The AIDS Crisis: A Case Study From Bedford Hill Correctional Facility," *Columbia Journal of Gender and the Law* 1, no. l, Jan 31, 1991.

25. Women of the ACE Program at the Bedford Hills Correctional Facility, *Breaking the Walls of Silence: AIDS and Women in a New York State Maximum Security Prison* (Woodstock, NY: Overlook Press, 1998), 54.

26. ACE, 66-7.

27. Kathy Boudin and Judith Clark, "A Community Of Women Organize Themselves To Cope With The AIDS Crisis: A Case Study From Bedford Hill Correctional Facility," *Columbia Journal of Gender and the Law* 1, no. l, Jan 31, 1991.

28. Michael Gruzuk, "Breaking the Walls of Silence," WNYC Arts and Community radio program, July 30, 1999. The stigma of HIV/AIDS is still prevalent in most prisons, sometimes even in those facilities with peer education programs. At Oklahoma's Mabel Bassett Correctional Center, the HIV peer education program is often disrupted for months by staff turnover, construction and other outside factors. Jerrye Broomhall, who acts as a peer educator when the program is functioning, reports, "the level of ignorance is shocking. Stuff like, 'I don't want to wash my clothes after her, what if her panties were bloody'. People don't want to share cells, meals, so most women just keep their status a secret." (Jerrye Broomhall, letter to the author, October 2, 2007.)

29. Resistance in Brooklyn, *Enemies of the State: A frank discussion of past political movements, victories and errors, and the current political climate for revolutionary struggle within the U.S.A. with european-American political prisoners Marilyn Buck, David Gilbert and Laura Whitehorn* (Brooklyn, NY: 1998).

30. Laura Whitehorn was charged and convicted of "conspiracy to oppose, protest and change the policies and practices of the United States government in domestic and international matters by violence and illegal means." She spent 14 years in prison and was released on parole on August 6th, 1999.

31. Beverly Henry, letter to the author, May 27, 2002.

32. Joann Walker, "Medical Treatment at Chowchilla," *Criminal Injustice: Confronting the Prison Crisis*, ed. Elihu Rosenblatt (Boston, MA: South End Press, 1996), 124. Walker died on July 13, 1994, two months after winning compassionate release from CCWF.

33. Tim Murphy, "Getting Out Alive," *POZ*, April 2004, http://www.poz.com/ articles/153_238.shtml.

34. Kathy Boudin and Judith Clark, "A Community Of Women Organize Themselves To Cope With The AIDS Crisis: A Case Study From Bedford Hill Correctional Facility," *Columbia Journal of Gender and the Law* 1, no. 1, Jan 31, 1991.

35. Cynthia Chandler, "Death and Dying in America: The Prison Industrial Complex's Impact on Women's Health," *Berkeley Women's Law Journal* 18 (January 31, 2003). See California Department of Corrections, Department Operations Manual, page 753:. http://www.cdcr.ca.gov/Regulations/Adult_Operations/docs/DOM/Ch_10_Final_DOM-rev.pdf.

36. "Dedication," *The Fire Inside* 4 (1997), http://www.womenprisoners.org/fire/000482.html.

37. "California Agrees to Settle Inmates' HIV Privacy Claims," *AIDS Policy and Law* 12, no. 17 (1997). On July 31, 2000, in light of evidence of tampering with medical files to prepare for the assessors' visits, the Department of Health Services' reports citing CCWF's failure to comply with regulations, and the CDC's failure to retest prisoners who had received fraudulent lab results, the plaintiffs' attorney submitted a motion to reopen discovery in the case. The motion was denied by Judge Shubb and the case was dismissed in August 2000. (See "Strategies for Change: Litigation," http://www.prisonerswithchildren.org/litigation.htm.)

38. Cassie M. Pierson, *Memorial for Charisse Shumate*, spoken at the First Unitarian Church, San Francisco, CA, September 23, 2001.

39. Charisse Shumate,"The Pros and Cons of Being a Lead Plaintiff," *The Fire Inside* 6 (December 1997), http://www.womenprisoners.org/fire/000464.html.

40. Prisoner from Central Correctional Women's Facility, letter to the author, March 3, 2002.

41. A. Clay Thompson, "Cancer in the Cells," *San Francisco Bay Guardian*, February 24, 1999. Sherrie Chapman died on December 12, 2002.

42. Judy Greenspan, Beverly Henry, Theresa Martinez, Judy Ricci, Charisse Shumate, and Jess West, "The State of Prison Healthcare Activism: Fighting the HIV and Hepatitis C Epidemics," in *States of Confinement: Policing, Detention and Prisons*, ed. Joy James (New York: Palgrave, 2002).

43. Tim Murphy, "Getting Out Alive," *POZ*, April 2004, http://www.poz.com/articles/153_238.shtml.

44. Donna Willmott, "'Am I Gonna Die in Here?' Medical Neglect in California Women's Prisons," *Sojourner: The Women's Forum* 26, no. 7 (March 2001): 23.

45. Delores Garcia, "The Out of Sight Out of Mind Skilled Nursing Facility." Article circulated by Judy Greenspan in an e-mail to the Prison Activist Resource Center listserv, July 18, 2002. Garcia has since been released from prison. She continues to speak out about conditions inside.

46. *National Jeff Dicks Medical Coalition newsletter*, "Women Prisoners Have the Right to Fight Medical Neglect: Stop the Retaliation Against Dee Garcia, Prisoner Organizer, " October 2002, 8–9.

F I F T Y - T H R E E

◆◆◆

Media Representations and the Criminalization of Arab Americans and Muslim Americans (2005)

Suad Joseph and Benjamin D'Harlingue

Suad Joseph is Director of the Middle East/South Asia Studies Program and Distinguished Professor of Anthropology and Women's Studies at the University of California, Davis. She is general editor of the *Encyclopedia of Women and Islamic Cultures*, editor of *Gender and Citizenship in the Middle East*, and coordinator of the Arab Families Working Group

Benjamin D'Harlingue earned his PhD in Cultural Studies at the University of California, Davis. He has taught Women and Gender Studies courses at U.C.-Davis, San Francisco State University, and St. Mary's College. His dissertation is entitled *Haunted Tourism: Sites of Violence in the United States.*

Arab Americans and Muslim Americans are heterogeneous peoples from all over the world. They come from different countries, have different histories, belong to different cultures, and use different languages. Arabs, for example, are highly diverse, and include large numbers of Christians and Jews who consider themselves Arab. The total world Arab population is over 300 million (Arab American Anti-Discrimination Committee 2004). By contrast, there are about 1.3 billion Muslims in the world. The majority of Muslims are neither Arab nor Middle Eastern. Over 50 percent of the world's Muslims are from South Asia—India, Pakistan, Bangladesh, and Afghanistan. From the nineteenth century to the middle of the twentieth century, the overwhelming majority of immigrants to the United States from the Arab region were Christian. It was not until the 1960s and 1970s that Muslim immigrants from the Arab world began to outnumber Christian Arab immigrants. The first Muslims in the United States were African slaves. Estimates indicate that 30 to 40 percent of Muslims in the United States are African American; 25 to 30 percent are South Asian Americans; and 12 to 15 percent are Arab American (Ibish 2002).

Despite this wide diversity, however, U.S. media and popular culture tend to portray Arab Americans and Muslim Americans as if they are all the same. This erasure of differences makes it easier for government and the wider society to treat them the same and to make them all, collectively, different from "us." The "us" is the West, the United States—that is, the imagined United States, a white Christian nation that does not include Arabs and Muslims. As Nadine Naber (2000) has argued, Islam has been essentialized and racialized in the U.S., particularly in the politics of citizenship. Persons from Muslim countries and U.S. citizens from Muslim regions are represented in terms of their religion before any of their other multiple identities. Their actions are invariably characterized as "Muslim" regardless of their nature and intent. By prioritizing Islam as their overriding identity, the popular media portray every act of violence or incivility committed by a Muslim as a Muslim act.

. . .

Yet, when a Christian person acts, their action is not represented as "Christian." Timothy McVey, who bombed the federal building in Oklahoma City, was not described in media reports as committing a Christian act, even though fundamentalist Christianity was part of his worldview. Immediately after the September 11, 2001, bombing of the World Trade Center, the Reverend Jerry Falwell commented that the attacks were the wrath of God brought upon us by gays, lesbians, and feminists. Newspaper reports did not refer to these comments as Christian statements even though Reverend Falwell presents himself as speaking in a Christian voice. The killings of the Ku Klux Klan are not described as Christian although the Christian cross is central to their symbolism. When domestic abuse occurs in Christian homes the media do not look to the Bible to explain domestic abuse. Historians do not try to analyze what it is about Christianity that gives rise to dictators and tyrants such as Hitler, Mussolini, or Franco. In the dominant discourse, however, Muslims are defined by their religion and constructed as "alien," while the normative "we" is defined by economics and politics.

The U.S. government, popular media, TV and radio news, and print journalism often represent Arab Americans and Muslim Americans as uncertain, problematic, or suspect citizens (Joseph 1999). This began long before 9/11/01 (Abraham and Abraham 1983, Aswad 1974, Leonard 2003, Suleiman 1999). In 1914, an immigrant by the name of George Dow was denied U.S. citizenship based on the 1790 statute, which defined citizens as "free white persons" (*Dow v. United States et al.*, No. 1345. 4th Cir. 1915). As a "Syrian of Asiatic birth," (probably a Lebanese Christian), George Dow was not considered to be a "free white person" and therefore ineligible for citizenship. The decision was later appealed and reversed on the basis that Syrians were Semitic, even part Jewish, and therefore white—a clear example of the social construction of race. This case is emblematic of the on-going ambivalence in U.S. citizenship laws and practices towards U.S. citizens of Arab or Muslim origin (Cainkar 1999, Naff 1985, Suleiman 1999). By definition, to be a U.S. citizen was to be white. But, as Mary Ramadan (1996) has pointed out, white was understood to mean not only European but also Christian. Arabs and Muslims are not only "not quite white" as Nadine Naber argued (2000), Muslims are not Christians, and the majority of Arabs are Muslims. Arabs and Muslims are not the same as each other, as argued above, nor with the imagined U.S. white, Christian citizen. Arab and Muslim U.S. citizens embody this contradiction; they continue to be seen as against the grain of the nation (Joseph 1999), as not quite white (Naber 2000, Saliba 1999, Samhan 1999), and, despite legal citizenship, not quite citizens.

. . .

Trinh Minh-ha (1989) has noted that colonialist strategy—through law, policy, military and police activity, and media representations—homogenizes the "other" as a way of creating an oppositional binary that defines the other as enemy. President George W. Bush relied on popularly held stereotypic binaries in his designation of an "axis of evil" which included two Muslim countries, Iraq and Iran, fostering further demonization of Muslims in the U.S. media and popular opinion. The United States is waging a war based on the construction of binary opposites. President Bush's statement, "You are either with us or you are with the terrorists," comes out of a history of control based on the construction of difference.

The impact of the targeting of Arabs and Muslims through media discourse and public policy has been to control both Arab and non-Arab, Muslim and non-Muslim U.S. citizens. Fear mongering has affected the majority of U.S. citizens, particularly people of color, as more repressive measures are implemented in the name of "national security." What is at stake for Arab and Muslim U.S. citizens in the aftermath of 9/11/01 is not simply their home, but the home of all U.S. citizens. The exclusions and inconsistencies of citizenship applied to Arab and Muslim Americans can be used to justify the abuse of the citizenship rights of others. Just as oppression against Native Americans, African Americans, Asian Americans, and Latino Americans laid the groundwork for discriminations toward Arab and Muslim Americans, so do the exclusions and inconsistencies practiced toward Arab and Muslim Americans add bricks to a house heated by fear. Moreover, stereotypical and negative portrayals of Arabs, Arab Americans, and Muslim Americans in the news media are integral to the construction of these diverse people as intrinsically suspect, a key step in the process of their criminalization.

REFERENCES

Abdelkarim, R.Z. 2002. American Muslims and 9/11: A Community Looks Back . . . and to the Future."

Washington Report on Middle East Affairs. Vol. XXI, No. 7, pp. 82 (Oct. 31).

Abraham, Sameer Y. and Nabeel Abraham, eds. 1983. *Arabs in the New World: Studies on Arab-American Communities.* Detroit: Wayne State University Center for Urban Studies.

Akram, S. M. and K. Johnson. 2002. Race, Civil Rights, and Immigration Law After September 11, 2001: The Targeting of Arabs and Muslims, *New York University Annual Survey of American Law*, Vol. 58.

American Arab Anti-Discrimination Committee. 2004. *Facts about Arabs and the Arab World.* http://www.adc.org/index.php?id5248 (accessed: 22 July 2004).

Aswad, Barbara C., ed. 1974. *Arabic Speaking Communities in American Cities.* New York: Center for Immigration Studies.

Cainkar, Louise. 1999. The Deteriorating Ethnic Safety Net Among Arab Immigrants in Chicago. In *Arabs in America: Building a New Future,* edited by Michael Suleiman. Philadelphia: Temple University Press, pp. 192–206.

———. 2002. No Longer Invisible: Arab and Muslim Exclusion After September 11, *Middle East Report* 224 (Fall).

Gonzaga, Russell Reza-Khaliq. 2002. One Nation Under Allah: Islam Is the Fastest Growing Religion in America, But It Still Fits the Profile of the "Other." *Colorlines.* Vol 5. No. 3, p. 27 (Oct 31).

Goodstein, Laurie. 2003. Seeing Islam as "Evil" Faith, Evangelicals Seek Converts, *The New York Times,* Section A, pp. 1, 22, May 27.

Ibish, Hussein. 2002. *Post 9/11 Anti-Arab Discrimination in American Immigration Policy and Practice.* Presented at the Middle East Studies Association Meeting, Washington, D.C., November.

Joseph, Suad. 1999. Against the Grain of the Nation—The Arab. In *Arabs in America: Building a New Future,* edited by Michael Suleiman. Philadelphia: Temple University Press, pp. 257–271.

Leonard, Karen Isaksen. 2003. *Muslims in the United States: The State of Research.* New York: Russell Sage.

Middle East Report. 2002. Arabs, Muslims and Race in America (Special Issue). No. 224. Fall.

Minh-ha, Trinh. 1989. *Woman, Native, Other: Writing Postcoloniality and Feminism.* Bloomington: Indiana University Press.

Naber, Nadine. 2000. Ambiguous Insiders: An Investigation of Arab American Invisibility, *Ethnic and Racial Studies.* Vol. 23. No. 1 (Jan.), pp. 37–61.

Naff, Alexa. 1985. *Becoming American: The Early Arab Immigrant Experience.* Carbondale, Il.: Southern Illinois University Press.

Ramadan, Mary. 1996. *Anti-Arab Racism and Arab-American Response.* Paper presented at the Association of Arab-American University Graduates Convention. Anaheim, CA, October.

Saliba, Therese. 1999. Resisting Invisibility: Arab Americans in Academia and Activism. In *Arabs in America: Building a New Future,* edited by Michael Suleiman. Philadelphia: Temple University Press, pp. 304–319.

Samhan, Helen Hatab. 1999. Not Quite White: Race Classification and the Arab-American Experience.

In *Arabs in America: Building a New Future,* edited by Michael Suleiman. Philadelphia: Temple University Press, pp. 209–226.

Suleiman, Michael, ed. 1999. *Arabs in America: Building a New Future.* Philadelphia: Temple University Press.

FIFTY-FOUR

Disappearing Parents
Summary Report on Immigration Enforcement and the Child Welfare System (2011)
Nina Rabin

Nina Rabin is Associate Clinical Professor of Law and Director of the Bacon Immigration Law and Policy Program at the University of Arizona, Tucson. She also directs the Border Research program for the Southwest Institute for Research on Women, which provides outreach, legal services, and advocacy on behalf of low-wage immigrant women workers, and also advocates for improvements and greater gender sensitivity in detention facilities housing immigrant women. Her publications include law journal articles on women in immigration detention.

Quiet, slow motion tragedies unfold every day in immigration detention centers throughout the country, as parents caught up in immigration enforcement are separated from their young children and disappear into the detention system. If no relative is identified who can take the children at the time of an immigrant parent's apprehension, the children may be placed in state custody and find themselves in foster homes, abruptly unable to communicate with their parents or even know where their parents are. If parents choose to accept their deportation, they risk being forever separated from their children, since their children will likely be unable to accompany them so long as they remain in state custody. If parents choose instead to fight their deportation, they often remain detained for months or even years, greatly complicating efforts to reunify as a family even if they are eventually successful in their case against deportation.

The story of Laura (a pseudonym), a mother recently detained in an immigration detention center in Arizona illustrates the problem:

Laura is a single mother of three children, ages 16, 11, and 5 years old, the youngest of whom is a U.S. citizen. Laura spent over ten years in a severely violent relationship with her husband, who was eventually deported last year. As the family worked towards recovery from this trauma, Laura's teenage son threw a rowdy party without her permission. The police were called, and when they arrived on the scene, they arrested Laura for serving alcohol to minors. They contacted CPS [Child Protective Services] and her children were taken into state custody.

Laura was taken into ICE custody, where she had no contact with her children, her juvenile court attorney, or the CPS case worker for over two months. Her repeated requests to ICE for release were denied and she could not afford to pay the $4,000 bond ordered by the Immigration Judge to secure her release. ICE finally released her after three months, when another immigration agency, Citizenship and Immigration Services, found her eligible for a visa based on her experience of severe domestic violence. During this time, her children were moved three times within the foster care system.

Laura now must make immediate progress on her CPS case plan for family reunification, as the clock is ticking before the state could move to terminate her parental rights based on her children's lengthy stays in out-of-home placements. She waits anxiously for a final determination on her application for a visa, since without it, her prospects of complying with the reunification case plan are dim.

This report provides data obtained from surveys and interviews with over 50 personnel in the child welfare system that reveal that Laura's story is far from unique or idiosyncratic. On the contrary, the child welfare system encounters families caught up in immigration enforcement with some frequency. Yet the data also reveal a striking absence of systemic mechanisms for addressing the challenges posed by these cases. With no policies or practices in place in either the immigration or the child welfare system to address the unique situation of immigrant parents in detention or deportation proceedings, stories like Laura's are unfolding with alarming frequency. The key findings of this research are listed below. . . .

Key Findings

1. Frequency of the Problem

   - Across the board, attorneys, judges, and case workers working in the child welfare system all had experience with cases involving parents in detention or deportation proceedings. While such cases do not dominate their caseloads, they arose frequently enough so that all the personnel interviewed were aware of the challenges posed by such cases. Yet no formal policies or mechanisms exist to address these cases.

2. Problems Created by Immigration Enforcement

   - Disappearing Parents: child welfare personnel all used strikingly similar language to describe their observation that parents "disappear" into the immigration enforcement system and are exceedingly difficult to track down once they are apprehended by ICE.

   - Better Off in Jail: parents struggle in detention facilities to participate in the "case plan" for reunification with their children. Many personnel in the child welfare system noted that, because immigration detention facilities lack the programming or services

available in some jails or prisons, these detained parents are actually worse off than incarcerated parents.

   - The Climate of Fear: the pervasive fear under which undocumented immigrants live has specific effects on families involved in the child welfare system. Parents are reluctant to provide information for kinship placements, so their children are more likely to wind up in the foster care system instead of with family members. In some cases, parents and children abscond from the child welfare system altogether due to fear.

   - Prolonged Detention and ICE's Failure to Exercise Prosecutorial Discretion: if an immigrant parent chooses to fight her deportation, she will likely face many months and potentially years in detention. Although in many cases ICE has the discretion to decide whether or not to initiate deportation proceedings and/or detain immigrants, it often fails to exercise its discretion in favor of immigrants, even those with young U.S. citizen children in state custody.

   - The Criminalization of Immigrants: the current immigration enforcement regime criminalizes immigrants, even those who are not criminal offenders. One impact of the criminalization of immigrants is that it encourages personnel in the child welfare system to "write off" parents in detention and/or deportation proceedings and assume that they will be unable to regain custody of their children.

3. Problems Created by the Child Welfare System

   - Ad Hoc Approach to Immigration Issues: Not a single one of the participants in the interviews and focus groups mentioned a policy or written guidance regarding work with families with undocumented family members. Instead, participants repeatedly described a process in which outcomes are highly dependent on the personnel involved, most significantly the CPS case worker and, to a lesser extent, attorneys and judges.

- Timelines for Dependency/Permanency: the state has detailed statutory timelines that must be met once a child is in state custody. These timelines are difficult to reconcile with the timeline of immigration cases, which tend to be long and unpredictable.

- Under-Utilization of Consular Offices: the consulate can play a critical role when parents are detained and/or deported and their children are in state custody. In particular, the consulate can assist in identifying, evaluating, and communicating with family placements in the parent's home country. Yet they are only incorporated into a small number of such cases.

Summary of Recommendations

The findings summarized above . . . demonstrate that any attempt to address these complex tragedies will require reforms of both the federal immigration enforcement system and the state child welfare system. A list of suggested reforms follows. . . .

1. For the Department of Homeland Security

    - Establish a mechanism for early identification of cases in which immigrant parents in detention and/or deportation proceedings have children in the child welfare system.

    - Increase the use of parole, prosecutorial discretion, and alternatives to detention for these cases.

    - Improve detention facilities' compliance with telephonic appearances and establish procedures for parents to appear in person in child welfare hearings.

    - Increase the availability of services in detention facilities, such as parenting classes, substance abuse rehabilitation programs, and access to psychiatric evaluations.

    - Establish a key liaison position in each detention facility that can be a point of contact for all child welfare personnel.

    - Train deportation officers and detention facility personnel to be familiar with the challenges facing detained parents with children in state custody.

    - Reform immigration enforcement measures that rely on local law enforcement agencies and create a climate of fear for immigrant families that chills their ability to interact with the child welfare system.

2. For the Child Welfare System

    - Establish mandatory and regular trainings for judges, attorneys, and CPS case workers regarding immigration detention and deportation proceedings.

    - Create a key liaison position in each CPS region for case workers to contact when immigration issues arise.

    - Increase utilization of the consulate in cases involving foreign nationals.

    - Establish statewide policies or practices to improve the provision of reunification services to immigrants in detention facilities.

3. For the Department of Justice

    - Establish a portion of the Legal Orientation Program devoted to educating immigrant detainees about defending their parental rights.

4. For Congress

    - Provide funding for attorneys specializing in representation of immigrant parents with U.S. citizen children. . . .

    - Increase funding for the Legal Orientation Program, which informs immigrant detainees of their legal rights, to allow for education on the dependency process for immigrant parents with children in state custody.

    - End mandatory detention. Establish judicial discretion to consider urgent circumstances including children in state custody in determining whether detention is warranted.

    - Increase judicial discretion in cases for relief from deportation involving parents with children in state custody.

NOTES

The full report of this research is available at www. detentionwatchnetwork.org/sites/detention-watchnetwork.org/files/06.09.2011_ DisappearingParents.pdf

Background to this study: Over the past few years, staff members of the Southwest Institute for Research on Women (SIROW) who provide social and legal services to women in immigration detention facilities have repeatedly come into contact with mothers experiencing extreme stress and anxiety about the custody of their children while they are detained. In several of these cases, the children have been in state custody and the mothers have encountered significant frustration attempting to participate in the juvenile court process while they are detained. In an effort to understand how often these cases arise and analyze how equipped the immigration and child welfare systems are to deal with these circumstances, SIROW and the Bacon Immigration Law and Policy Program of the James E. Rogers College of Law developed a research project to take an in-depth look at how often such cases arise in Pima county, Southern Arizona. The results of this study are summarized in this report.

Methodological Note: In the summer of 2010, SIROW conducted surveys and interviews with personnel in the Pima County Juvenile

Court system. This is a border county with a population of roughly one million and has a 120-mile border along the southern and central region of Arizona. It contains Tucson, the second largest city in the state. Also, Pima County is a "model court." The Model Courts consist of 25 juvenile and family courts nationwide that work with the National Council of Juvenile and Family Court Judges and use a best-practices bench book as a guide to systems reform.

Through the Juvenile Court's training center, which offers training opportunities to judges, attorneys, case workers, and other personnel in the county's child welfare system, SIROW offered a training on immigration issues in June 2010. Attendees were invited to fill out a survey at the training or complete it online. Those interested could volunteer to participate in a follow up interview to discuss the issues in more detail. SIROW received a total of 52 survey responses from a mix of attorneys, CPS case workers and other personnel, social service providers who work in partnerships with CPS, and juvenile court judges. The researchers then conducted a total of 20 interviews, some individually and some in focus groups. While the number of participants is modest, they clearly confirm that Laura's story is not an outlier, but rather taps into issues faced by many immigrant families caught in the intersecting systems of immigration and child welfare.

F I F T Y - F I V E

◆◆◆

Women of Color, Globalization, and the Politics of Incarceration (2003)

Julia Sudbury

Scholar and activist **Julia Sudbury** is Professor of Ethnic Studies at Mills College. Editor of *Global Lockdown: Race, Gender and the Prison-Industrial Complex*, her work focuses on women of color, women's activism, globalization and the transnational prison-industrial complex. Other books include *Activist Scholarship: Antiracism, Feminism and Social Change* (co-editor) and *Outsiders Within: Writings on Transracial Adoption* (co-editor).

In November 1999, 40,000 people came together in an explosion of street activism to protest the policies of the World Trade Organization and to highlight the impact of neoliberal globalization on the global south and poor communities in the global north. . . . Labor, environmental, human rights, housing, antiracist, and feminist activists came to Seattle out of a common understanding that problems such as sweatshop working conditions, toxic dumping in black neighborhoods, and cutbacks in welfare, housing, and health care are all rooted in a global capitalist system that values corporate interests and freedoms over human needs for decent wages, shelter, food, and health care. At the Seattle protests, . . . activists used puppets, banners, and flyers to link the struggle against global capital with opposition to the current criminal justice system. Activists challenged police brutality, racial profiling, the death penalty, and the prison industrial complex, arguing that dramatic increases in prison populations have occurred as a result of globalization.

While these connections are being made at the street level, feminist criminologists have had little to say about what connections, if any, may be made between women's imprisonment and the rise of global corporate capital that has occurred in the past two decades. Such an analysis would need to stray beyond the boundaries of what has traditionally been considered within the scope of criminology to examine the broader socioeconomic context of women's criminalization and incarceration. . . . [I] argue that the explosion in women's incarceration is the hidden face of globalization and cannot be understood without reference to three overlapping phenomena. The first is the restructuring of national economies and social welfare provision that has occurred as a result of the globalization of capital. The second . . . is the emergence and subsequent global expansion of what has been labeled a "prison industrial complex" made up of an intricate web of relations between criminal justice institutions, politicians, and . . . corporations. The third is the . . . U.S.-led war on drugs that has crossed national borders to become a global phenomenon.

The Boom in Women's Imprisonment

The past 25 years have witnessed dramatic increases in the use of incarceration in the United States, leading to a prison building boom as federal and state governments rush to keep up with demand for prison beds. Although there are more men in prison than women, the rate of women's imprisonment is spiraling upward at a greater rate than that of men. . . . Similar patterns have occurred in Canada, Europe, and Australasia. In Britain, for example,

the number of women in prison doubled between 1985 and 1998. . . .

Statistics that look at gender but not race under-represent the impact of the prison boom on women of color and indigenous women. In all the countries just mentioned, oppressed racialized groups are disproportionately targeted by the criminal justice system. For example, in the United States, Latinas and African American women make up 60 percent of the prison population. And despite their small numbers in the population, Native Americans are 10 times more likely than whites to be imprisoned.[1] In New South Wales, Australia, where all women's imprisonment increased by 40 percent in five years, aboriginal women's incarceration increased by 70 percent in only two years.[2] In Canada, aboriginal people comprise 3 percent of the general population and 12 percent of federal prisoners, a figure that increases to over 60 percent in . . . Saskatchewan and Alberta.[3] African Canadians are also disproportionately policed, prosecuted, and incarcerated.[4] Finally, 12 percent of women prisoners in England and Wales are British citizens of African Caribbean descent compared to 1 percent of the general population.[5] In addition, British prisons hold numerous women from West Africa, the Caribbean, and Latin America, either as immigration detainees or serving sentences for drug importation. The crisis of women's prisons can therefore be read as a crisis for women of color and indigenous women worldwide.

Explaining the Prison Boom

How can we explain this explosion in the population of women prisoners? In the 1970s, "emancipation theorists" put forward a possible explanation for an upward trend in women's incarceration. In her influential study, Freda Adler suggested that the women's liberation movement had opened up new opportunities for women, both in the legitimate and in the criminal worlds.[6] Thus women who were now working in white-collar jobs could commit crimes such as fraud and embezzlement, which previously would have been inaccessible to them. Women's liberation was also credited with giving women a more assertive stance and enabling them to engage in violence, burglary, and organized crime, acts that were previously the domain of men.

Subsequent studies challenged Adler's findings; they contested her claim that there had been a rise in women's offending and suggested that any increase could in fact be explained by social factors such as an increase in women's poverty.[7] Despite vigorous challenges to Adler's claims, subsequent work by feminist criminologists has failed to shift the debate around women and crime in two important ways. First, it perpetuates the commonsense equation between crime and punishment that is at the core of both Adler's work and mainstream criminology. This equation leads us to look to women's behavior for explanations of increases in women's incarceration. If more women are being arrested, prosecuted, and punished, this argument goes, it must be because they are committing more crimes. Sociologists working within a radical framework make a different argument. Rather than looking to women's behavior, we should look at the shifting actions of the state as it seeks to control poor communities and populations of color. Rather than women's criminality, the focus of study should be the role of the state in labeling, prosecuting, and punishing women—that is, women's criminalization. Our search for an explanation for the prison boom must therefore ask: Who benefits when more women are imprisoned? What are the processes by which certain actions are labeled criminal and others are not, and how are women channeled into these actions and thus into conflict with the criminal justice system?

The second limitation of feminist criminology is its unwillingness to engage meaningfully with the significance of race in the criminal justice system, choosing to view women first as gendered beings and only secondly as having a social class, national, or racialized identity. . . . Rather than talking about "woman" as a unitary category, as if all women's experiences were fundamentally the same, feminists of color argue that we must always be explicit about the ways that racism and racial privilege intersect with class location and gender to create unique experiences for diverse women. Intersectionality may produce unexpected outcomes. In some instances, for example, women of color may have as much in common with men of color as they do with middle-class white women. Deploying an intersectional approach to explain women's criminalization therefore requires us to pay as much attention to racial profiling and racialized discrepancies within the criminal justice system as we do to gender disparities. It also requires us to examine the feminization of poverty, the impoverishment and surveillance of communities of color, and global inequalities between third- and first-world nations as causal factors behind the growing criminalization of women.

1. Globalization and the Racialized Feminization of Poverty

. . .

Both urban "ghettos" and small rural towns have been hard hit by the downsizing of manufacturing since the 1970s, suffering high unemployment and a decline in tax revenues. For inner-city residents, especially African Americans and Latinos, these declines have meant underfunded schools, dirty streets, insufficient public housing, and poor health care facilities. Neighborhoods have been taken over by liquor stores, crack houses, and prostitution as supermarkets and department stores relocate to more profitable locations. Women bear the brunt of this social dislocation, because they tend to be the primary caretakers of children and elderly relatives and are responsible for providing adequate food, shelter, medicine, and clothing. For working-class women of color in the inner cities, the globalization of capital translates into few opportunities for a living wage, food and clothing that is expensive and of poor quality, and inadequate day care and schooling for their children.

Rural areas have also been affected by the radical restructuring signaled by globalization. Faced with global commodities markets that set the price for meat, milk, or grain according to the lowest price that can be obtained internationally, small farmers have been unable to compete and have been forced to sell their land or contract to sell their produce to large farming corporations.[8] The emergence of agribusiness as the primary supplier of the nation's food has led to a rise in rural poverty as farm workers, particularly immigrant workers, are forced to work for low wages in insecure, seasonal jobs. Small rural towns that relied on car, munitions, and other industries have also been hit as factories have relocated abroad or closed as a result of a decline in cold war–era military investment. . . .

This newfound mobility has given corporations the ability to pack up and move to a new location if they find that policies and legislation governing workers' rights, wages, and environmental protections are not to their liking. Thus, national governments within the global capitalist economy have seen their policy options narrowed if they wish to remain attractive to corporate capital. The 1990s, therefore, witnessed a shift toward neoliberal policies being pursued by conservative and liberal governments alike. These policies aim to create a liberal environment for corporate profit making and financial speculation. . . .

The global spread of neoliberal social and economic policies is underpinned by two international institutions. The World Trade Organization (WTO) was established as the global headquarters for the drafting and policing of international trading rules. In the past decade, the WTO has come under criticism by activists who claim that by enforcing rules that benefit corporate profit while ignoring the exploitation of child laborers, the use of sweatshops, and environmental destruction by those same corporations, it is complicit in these exploitative practices.[9] The International Monetary Fund (IMF) is an organization with 184 member countries that promotes international monetary exchange and trade and provides loans and economic guidance to impoverished countries. The IMF has been criticized for imposing economic policies on formerly colonized countries that generate immense poverty and suffering. Governments have been forced to cut back public expenditure. In Jamaica, for example, policies introduced since the mid-1980s by the Jamaican Labour Party working closely with the IMF have led to cuts in public-sector employment; the scaling back of local government services in health and education; increases in the cost of public utilities as state-owned companies are sold to the private sector; and a dramatic decline in real wages. Such cuts hit working-class Jamaican women particularly hard because they carry the burden of caring for children and sick or elderly relatives. This disproportionate impoverishment of third-world women is referred to as the racialized feminization of poverty.

At the same time that the Jamaican state has cut back its role in social welfare, it has stepped up its role in subsidizing foreign and domestic capital. Free trade zones established in Kingston, Montego Bay, and elsewhere offer foreign garment, electronic, and communications companies factory space and equipment, tax exemptions, a cheap female workforce, and for the busy foreign executive, weekends of sun, sea, and sand.[10] Foreign-owned agribusiness

and mining companies have also been encouraged, displacing traditional subsistence farming and causing migration from rural areas to the cities, which now account for 50 percent of the Jamaican population. As the economy has shifted, women working in the informal economy as farmers and higglers[11] find themselves unable to keep up with the rising costs of survival. Whereas younger women may find employment in the tourist industry as maids, entertainers, or prostitutes, or within the free trade zones assembling clothes or computers for Western markets, working-class women in their 30s and older have fewer options. Even where these women do find employment, low wages—driven down by multinational corporations in search of ever greater profit margins and kept low by governments unwilling to set a living minimum wage for fear of losing foreign investment—mean that women cannot earn a sufficient income to support their families. The failure of the legal economy to provide adequate means for women's survival then becomes a key incentive for Jamaican women who enter the drug trade as couriers and are subsequently incarcerated in British, Canadian, and U.S. prisons. . . .

2. The Prison Industrial Complex

Why has the racialized feminization of poverty under neoliberal globalization led to an explosion in the imprisonment of women? In other words, how can we explain the current state response to the increase in poverty among working-class women and women of color, a response that deploys criminalization and punishment rather than poverty relief or empowerment? Scholars, activists, and former prisoners seeking to explain this problem . . . [rely on] the concept of the prison industrial complex.[12] Joel Dyer argues that three components make up the "perpetual prisoner machine" that transforms criminalized populations in the United States into fodder for the prison system.[13] The first are the large media corporations, like CNN and NBC, that rely on violent and crime-oriented content to grab ratings. The disproportionate airtime dedicated to crime-related news, dramas such as *NYPD Blue* and *Law and Order*, and real-life shows such as *America's Most Wanted* and *Cops* have created a dramatic rise in the fear of crime in the U.S. population at large.[14] These shows provide stereotypical representations of communities of color, from the black drug dealer to the Latino "gangbanger," that fuel a racialized fear of crime. The second is the use of market research by politicians to align their platforms with popular views about policy areas. Since the voting population tends to believe that criminal penalties are too soft and that "criminals" are unlikely to serve adequate prison sentences, politicians can win votes by appearing to be "tough on crime." Although Republicans have traditionally positioned themselves as tougher on crime than Democrats, it is only by positioning themselves as equally punitive that liberals can achieve power. Thus the unfounded assumption that building more prisons and jails and incapacitating more people for longer periods will solve deep-rooted social problems, such as drug use, poverty, and violence, remains unchallenged by both major parties. . . .

The third component is the intervention of private prison corporations such as Wackenhut Corporation and Corrections Corporation of America, which have generated millions for their shareholders by designing, constructing, financing, and managing prisons, jails, and detention centers. The mutually profitable relationship between private corporations and public criminal justice systems enables politicians to mask the enormous cost of their tough-on-crime policies. Instead of allocating millions for new prison construction in their annual budgets, politicians can simply reallocate revenue funds from welfare, health, or education into contracts with privately run for-profit prisons. . . .

. . . Although the prison industrial complex emerged in the United States, the past 15 years have witnessed its transformation into a transnational phenomenon. . . . U.S.-based prison corporations and their subsidiaries now manage prisons in Britain, Canada, New Zealand, Puerto Rico, Australia, and South Africa; and in all these locations, prison populations are rising. The prison industrial complex incorporates diverse interest groups, all of which stand to profit from the global prison boom. State and national politicians, correctional officer unions, media and corporate executives, and shareholders all benefit in very direct ways from the growth in women's imprisonment.

3. The Global War on Drugs

The third factor implicated in the explosion in women's imprisonment is the global war on drugs.

The contemporary war on drugs was announced by U.S. president Ronald Reagan in the early 1980s and formalized in the 1986 Anti Drug Abuse Act. The act made a critical break with the concept of drug users as a medical population in need of treatment and instead targeted them as a criminal population. It also utilized the erroneous assumption that users would be deterred from their habit and dealers and traffickers incapacitated by extensive use of penal sanctions. It was assumed that by removing those involved in the criminalized drug trade from the streets for long periods of time, syndicates would be severely damaged in their ability to get drugs to the streets.[15] Since "liberal" judges could not be trusted to hand down sufficiently severe sentences to deter and incapacitate those involved in the drug trade, the act removed judicial discretion and imposed mandatory minimum sentences.

Thus, treatment programs and community service were effectively barred in cases involving drugs, and sentence length related not to the role of the defendant in the offense, but to the weight and purity of drugs involved. In the United States, African American women and Latinas are disproportionately affected by mandatory minimums for reasons that are both gendered and racialized. The only way a lesser sentence can be given is in cases in which the defendant provides "substantial assistance" in the prosecution of another person. However, women, who tend to be in subordinate positions within drug syndicates and thus have little access to information, are usually unable to make such a deal. The crack-cocaine disparity also feeds the disproportionate impact on women of color. The mandatory minimum sentence for cocaine is one hundred times harsher for crack than for powder cocaine. Thus, being caught with 500 grams of powder cocaine is equivalent to being caught with only 5 grams of crack, itself a derivative of powder cocaine. Since crack is cheaper and has flooded poor inner city neighborhoods, African Americans and Latinos and Latinas receive disproportionate sentences when compared with powder cocaine users and dealers, who are much more likely to be white.

Although the war on drugs has had a dramatic impact on U.S. communities of color, it has reached far beyond U.S. borders. From the mid-1980s, the war on drugs increasingly played a key role in U.S. foreign policy decisions as the Reagan and Bush administrations pushed a U.S. drug agenda on the global community. . . . Whereas the domestic war on drugs is fought primarily by the police, beyond the borders of the United States it has become a military war justifying U.S. military interventions throughout Latin America. By the mid-1990s, Canada, Australia, New Zealand, Taiwan, South and Central America, the Caribbean, and African countries including Nigeria and South Africa were full-fledged partners in the U.S.-driven global war on drugs.

Inside the Transnational Prison Industrial Complex: Three Women's Stories

Accounts of structural economic and political processes are important if we are to understand the reasons behind the boom in women's imprisonment. However, by putting these macrolevel processes in the foreground, we risk losing sight of women's agency. Indeed, in such accounts, women, especially women of color and third-world women, are often reduced to faceless victims while corporations, governments, and supranational bodies such as the IMF and World Bank take center stage. In order to move women of color from the margin to the center, I have chosen to highlight three women's stories. These stories reflect the lives of women incarcerated in three national locations: Britain, Canada, and the United States. Looking beyond the borders of the United States enables us to examine the ways in which globalization, the transnational prison industrial complex, and the global war on drugs lead to the criminalization and incarceration of women of color and third-world women.

Narrative One: Militarization, Displacement, and the War on Drugs

Teresa is a Colombian woman in her early 40s.[16] As a single mother, she struggled to support her three children. Carrying Class A drugs (cocaine) between Colombia and England enabled her to supplement her meager income. She was arrested at Heathrow airport in England and was given a five-year sentence. . . . She does not know what has become of her three children and has not been able to contact them since she was arrested. Her fear is that they

will be homeless since she did not leave any emergency funds for them. Teresa's story challenges us to rethink common sense ideas about dangerous Latin American "drug traffickers" flooding the United States and Europe with cocaine. In common with many drug "mules" from developing countries, Teresa was pushed into trafficking drugs by desperation. In her words:

> Cargamos drogas porque lo necessitamos; porque tenemos situations de financia. Somos de Colombia, de paises del tercer mundo, que son pobres. La situacion en lo que viven, por eso lo hicemos.

> We carry drugs because we need to, because we have financial difficulties. We come from Colombia, the third world, which are poor countries. The conditions we live in, that's what pushed us.

Colombia is a country shackled by foreign debt, political and social dislocation, violence, war, and kidnappings. As a leading harvester of the coca leaf, estimated to produce 80 percent of the world's cocaine, Colombia has been a key target of U.S. anti-drug interventions. Instead of alleviating horrendous social, political, and economic conditions for women in Latin America, U.S. financial assistance is targeted at building military forces that participate in the war on drugs. These forces have been used to carry out counterinsurgency wars against revolutionary groups like the FARC (Revolutionary Armed Forces of Colombia) and ELN (National Liberation Army) that have spearheaded the struggle for indigenous and poor people's rights. The U.S. military alleges that such groups have received millions of dollars per annum for protecting coca plantations, drug trafficking routes, and airstrips. By identifying these revolutionary groups as "narco-terrorists," the U.S. administration is able to justify providing military expertise and assistance to Colombia, despite its poor human rights record and evidence of collusion between the military and right-wing paramilitary death squads.[17] . . .

In tying aid to military gains against the FARC, the United States finances a four-decade-old civil war in which at least 35,000 people have died and two million have been internally displaced or forced to emigrate. The displacement of peasants and indigenous people is further exacerbated by the use of herbicides and organic toxins that affect large areas of rain forest and groundwater and create health problems for local people in addition to destroying the coca.[18] Women bear the brunt of this atmosphere of violence and instability as displaced landless peasants, as primary caretakers seeking to feed their children, and as spouses of men killed in the fighting. Ironically, the very conditions that pushed Teresa to risk importing Class A drugs are caused in part by the war on drugs. She, like many other foreign nationals in U.S. and European prisons, will be deported after serving a long sentence to a homeland where she has no house, no income, and no social security. In the meantime, she will be replaced by any of the millions of impoverished and desperate women in Latin America, the Caribbean, and Africa who become drug mules each year.

Narrative Two: Racialization, Labeling, and Exclusion

Camille is a 21-year-old African Canadian woman. Camille's mother, an immigrant from Jamaica, brought her up in public housing in the declining West End of Toronto. As a young girl, Camille was in constant conflict with her mother's expectations. She experienced difficulties at school, was labeled as having attention deficit hyperactive disorder (ADHD), and was sent to a school for children with special needs:

> They always told me I was bad, but you know kids. They said I had attention deficit disorder. I went to a couple of behavior schools, after that my mum switched us to Catholic school. I was going there for a while, then grade 2, me and the teacher got into something. I think I hit the teacher. They sent me to another behavior school for a couple of years.

At age 11, Camille was sent by her mother to a group home; this move started a pattern of disruption as she was shuttled between group homes and her mother's apartment. Raising two girls in the racist and often dangerous environment of the inner city, Camille's mother attempted to impress rigid gender roles on her daughters, encouraging them to limit themselves to the domestic sphere. African Caribbean women in Canada are located within a racially gendered capitalist economy in which black femininity

is constructed as simultaneously a sign of hard labor and sexual availability.[19] Fearing the racialized sexual subordination of their Canadian-born children, many immigrant women seek to enforce strict sexual mores and harsh discipline. Such attempts can lead to generational conflicts that are sometimes interpreted as a culture gap but in fact arise out of the survival strategies engendered by the experience of migration. Camille resisted her mother's attempts to "protect" her by curtailing her freedom:

> I was a tomboy. Me and my brother always used to do stuff. But then he got older, he didn't want to hang out with me no more. He always got to go outside, and she's always telling me I'm a girl and I can't do this and that. She was always beating me. But I always did my own thing.

On leaving school with few qualifications, Camille found herself unemployed and living with her mother with no source of income. When she was approached by a male friend who asked her if she was interested in earning $5,000 in a week by importing cocaine from Jamaica, she accepted. After being detained by customs at Toronto airport, she was sentenced to two years and four months . . .

Unlike Teresa, Camille did not have children to support, and her mother paid for her basic needs. However, her situation is indicative of the problems facing young black Canadians who have been failed by an underfunded educational system that is unwilling to deal with the diverse needs of a multiracial population. Rather than places of education, inner-city schools have become locations where young black people are warehoused and, increasingly, policed. Unfamiliar with the Canadian school system, immigrant parents are ill equipped to challenge the labeling of their children as educationally subnormal or suffering from ADHD. Rather than dealing with working-class black children's needs, schools and child psychiatrists treat difficult behavior as medical problems, thus justifying notions of inherent (racialized) mental incapacity. Camille emerged from the school system with few skills and qualifications into a racially and gender stratified labor market that offers, at best, minimum-wage jobs to young women of color. In the context of a North American youth culture that defines personal value via consumerism, Camille's lack of legitimate access to money, or routes to better earning power, is a significant motivation for her involvement in drug importation.

. . . When funding for prisons and additional policing is squeezed from the budget of a government committed to making tax cuts, further cuts in social spending become inevitable. Youth programs, shelters for women and teens, schools, black community projects, and social workers are all affected. As social workers are forced to raise minimum intervention levels, families with problems that are not considered urgent are left without support. Underfunded social programs are limited to crisis intervention rather than prevention. As schools are forced to operate on limited budgets, the incentive to exclude children who behave in difficult ways is increased. The pattern of Camille's life, dotted with family conflict and violence, school exclusions, and unemployment, is evidence of an absence of appropriate social support. By redirecting tax monies from social programs into the prison industrial complex and by promoting a low-wage, "flexible"[20] labor market, the state exacerbates this trend and ensures that there will be a pool of young women from Ontario's inner-city projects willing to risk their lives by importing drugs.

Narrative Three: Gender Entrapment and the Crack Cocaine Disparity

Kemba Smith was a middle-class African American student at Hampton College, a traditionally black college in Virginia. She became involved with a young man, Khalif Hall, who, unknown to her, was a key figure in a large drug operation. When Hall began to abuse Kemba and threatened to kill her, she did not leave him because she was afraid for her family and herself and because she had become pregnant. Shortly before the drug ring was apprehended, Hall was shot and killed. Kemba pleaded guilty to conspiracy to distribute crack cocaine, but hoped Hall's intimidation would be taken into account. Instead, she was held responsible for the full 255 kilos involved in the offense—although she personally was not found to have handled the drugs—and was sentenced to 24.5 years in prison. Kemba's case has been adopted by activists who oppose the war on drugs, including Families Against Mandatory Minimums, the Kemba Smith Justice Project, and the Million Woman March.[21] . . . The 24.5-year sentence Kemba received is not indicative of a

particularly unsympathetic judge but of a series of laws and policies introduced since the mid-1980s that have targeted users and street-level retail sales, highlighting crack cocaine as a particular threat. As Kemba argues:

> While laws should be designed to protect our communities from drug kingpins, instead, low level offenders with little or no involvement in the sale of drugs are being locked up for 15, 25, 30 [years], or 13 life sentences. In fact, I know a 30 year old Black woman, mother of two girls who was sentenced to 13 life sentences.[22]

Under the Anti Drug Abuse Act, Kemba's knowledge of her boyfriend's drug dealing was sufficient for her to receive a mandatory minimum sentence. However, her lack of involvement in the drug ring prevented her from providing information that might have reduced her sentence.

Kemba's case also illustrates what Beth Richie calls the "gender entrapment of battered black women": the high levels of male violence and abuse experienced by African American women entering the criminal justice system.[23] Many women are incarcerated as a direct result of a coercive and violent male figure. The woman's situation may have been caused by involvement in criminal activities, such as prostitution and drug dealing, in which the male is profiting from her; alternatively, her incarceration may be because of self-defense against a violent male partner. Feminist activists have organized around the cases of women incarcerated for killing their abusive partners, but there has been less awareness of the role of male violence—from early childhood sexual abuse to domestic violence—in the lives of women incarcerated for other types of offenses. In this sense, the psychological, physical, and sexual abuse that women are subjected to in prison is just one aspect of a continuum of violence in incarcerated women's lives. Women of color who live in emotionally and economically vulnerable positions in relation to men may be pressured by them to serve as free or cheap labor in the drug business. Although the women's movement has attempted to reduce women's dependence on men, welfare reforms and cutbacks in funding for women's shelters and day care under the Clinton and Bush administrations in the United States have further limited the choices of working-class women in particular. Kemba's case demonstrates that mandatory minimums and heightened police surveillance of communities of color, when combined with women's dependence on and coercion by male family members, create the conditions under which increasing numbers of women of color have been criminalized and turned into fodder for the prison industrial complex. As Kemba argues:

> With the entering of the New Year, I want to give you the gift of vision, to see this system of Modern Day Slavery for what it is. The government gets paid $25,000 a year by you (taxpayers) to house me (us). The more of us that they incarcerate, the more money they get from you to build more prisons. The building of more prisons create more jobs. The federal prison system is comprised of 61% drug offenders, so basically this war on drugs is the reason why the Prison Industrial Complex is a skyrocketing enterprise.[24]

Conclusions and Reflections on Abolitionism

This . . . [article] has described an exponential increase in women's imprisonment internationally and has suggested a new set of questions for feminist researchers and criminologists who wish to explain this phenomenon. . . .

. . .

At a time when increasing numbers of women are being incarcerated, families separated, and communities devastated, any discussion of women, crime, and punishment must end with proposals for change. There are three possible approaches for those wishing to challenge the status quo regarding women's imprisonment: reform, decarceration, and abolition. *Reformers* focus on producing suggestions for change that are practical within the existing system. Feminist reformers have proposed women-centered prison regimes, for example, that require female prison officers, introduce programs on domestic violence and rape, or provide therapists working within a framework of women's empowerment. Feminist reformers have also proposed reforms to the law, legalizing prostitution, for example, or removing status offenses from the criminal law.

There are three problems with reformism. First, . . . reform tends to be incorporated into the prison and used as justification for its expansion. For example, in Canada, demands for women-centered prison regimes led to the construction of five new federal prisons, thus increasing the number of women behind bars. In Britain, the provision of a mother and baby unit led judges to feel more comfortable with sentencing pregnant women to prison. Second, reformers tend to work with the system, thus enabling the stigmatization of those with more radical proposals as idealist and unrealistic. Finally, reformers frequently fail to question why and whether women should be imprisoned in the first place and instead focus on reducing the pains of imprisonment. They are therefore ill equipped to oppose the explosion in women's imprisonment.

The second possibility is *decarceration*. This strategy goes a step further than reform by pushing for laws that will lead to people being released from prison. For example, decarceration strategies emphasize alternative forms of punishment, including fines and community service, as well as rehabilitation and reeducation programs in the free world, such as sex offender training and anger management. . . . A first step toward decarceration is the establishment of a prison moratorium, whereby states are petitioned to pass a resolution preventing the construction of any new prisons. If no new prison beds are made available, the argument goes, officials will have to find other ways to deal with men and women in conflict with the law. Decarceration is an important political strategy that challenges the constant expansion of the prison industrial complex and seeks to reduce the profit motive in prison growth. However, decarceration policies are vulnerable to political swings, and a moratorium can swiftly be reversed.

The third possibility is *abolition*. Prison abolitionists use this term to identify the prison as a fundamentally unjust institution that, like slavery, cannot be reformed.[25] They argue that prisons do not work, fail to reduce crimes, and fail to make vulnerable populations—including women and people of color—safer. Abolitionists also argue that prisons are incapable of rehabilitating people; instead, they brutalize prisoners and return them to their communities ill equipped to survive by legitimate means. Abolitionists point out the huge economic costs of imprisonment, and they argue that public funds could more effectively be spent preventing social problems by creating jobs with a living wage, providing women's shelters, creating youth programs, and developing high-quality education. They also point out the social costs of incarcerating two million people in the United States, with a devastating impact on their families and communities, particularly communities of color.

Abolitionism is the only strategy that requires a fundamental rethinking of the way in which justice is delivered. It requires that we look for the *root causes* of antisocial acts, such as assault, burglary, or domestic violence, and look for alternatives that address these root causes. Abolitionism has not been viewed with great enthusiasm by many feminists, however. After spending years campaigning for the criminal justice system to take rape, domestic violence, and child abuse seriously, many feminists have seen abolitionism as a mechanism that will remove valuable legal protections from women. Feminist abolitionists have dealt with this problem in two ways. First, some have called for the abolition of women's prisons only, arguing that women are imprisoned for very different reasons than men and therefore need different treatment.[26] This argument is, however, unsustainable in the light of calls for equal treatment of women under the law. Second, others have challenged the idea that "the nonsolution of imprisonment" makes women safe and have argued that, in fact, an overreliance on punitive strategies prevents a more fundamental challenge to the patriarchal gender roles—and the institutions that support them—that are at the root of male violence against women.[27]

Reform *in isolation of a broader strategy for social change* serves to legitimize and even expand the prison industrial complex, and decarceration is only a stopgap measure. In contrast, abolitionism . . . offers a radical critique of the punitive approach to women's survival strategies. Abolitionism is the only strategy that removes the profit motive from the criminal justice system and the only approach that challenges the belief that prison works. Although it does not offer an immediate solution, it does provide a *critical framework* within which proposed legislation, campaigns, and activism can be assessed. By working together within an abolitionist framework, scholars, activists, prisoners, and their families are building a

movement for lasting social change and for a safe and just global community.[28]

NOTES

1. Patricia Macias Rojas. 1998. Complex Facts, *Colorlines,* Fall.

2. Parliament of New South Wales, Select Committee on the Increase in Prisoner Population, www.parliament .nsw.gov.au, accessed July 4, 2000.

3. Canadian Criminal Justice Association. 2000. *Aboriginal Peoples and the Criminal Justice System,* Ottawa.

4. Commission on System Racism in the Ontario Criminal Justice Sytem. 1994. *Racism Behind Bars,* Toronto: Queens Printers.

5. Mike Elkins, Carly Gray, and Keith Rogers. 2001. *Prison Population Brief: England and Wales April 2001.* London: Home Office Research Development Statistics.

6. Freda Adler, 1975. *Sisters in Crime: The Rise of the New Female Criminal.* New York: McGraw-Hill.

7. Carol Smart. 1979. The New Female Offender: Reality or Myth, *British Journal of Criminology* 19(1): 50–59.

8. William Grieder. 2000. "The Last Farm Crisis," *The Nation,* November 20.

9. Manning Marable. 2000. Seattle and Beyond: Making the Connection in the 21st Century, *Dialogue and Initiative,* Fall.

10. "As Jamaica gets ready to go global and sticks to liberal policies, international investors need look no further than this Caribbean island to find opportunities which they won't regret." Quoted from *Jamaica: Island of Opportunity,* www.vegamedia.com/jamaica/jamaica .html, accessed January 20, 2002.

11. Higglers are traders, often women, who buy and resell cheap clothing, food, and other low-cost products in Jamaica's informal economy.

12. Angela Y. Davis. 1998. Race and Criminalization: Black Americans and the Punishment Industry. In *The Angela Y. Davis Reader,* ed. Joy James. Malden, MA: Blackwell.

13. Joel Dyer. 2000. *The Perpetual Prisoner Machine: How America Profits from Crime.* Boulder, CO: Westview.

14. Mark Fishman and Gray Cavender, eds. 1998. *Entertaining Crime: Television Reality Programs.* New York: Aldine DeGruyter.

15. This has not been the case; instead, criminalization and targeting by law enforcement artificially inflate the price of drugs, so that manufacturing, trafficking, and selling them become immensely profitable and increasingly associated with violence. This mutually profitable relationship between law enforcement and the drug trade has been labeled the "international drug complex" (Hans Van Der Veen. 2000. *The International Drug Complex.* Amsterdam: Center for Drug Research, University of Amsterdam).

16. Pseudonyms have been used to protect the identities of the first two interviewees. The case of Kemba Smith has reached national prominence due to the clemency granted her by president Bill Clinton at the end of his term in office. I have therefore used her real name.

17. Human Rights Groups Criticize Clinton over Aid to Colombian Military. 2000. *San Francisco Chronicle,* August 29.

18. US Sprays Poison in Drug War. 2000. *Observer,* July 2.

19. Dionne Brand. 1999. Black Women and Work: The Impact of Racially Constructed Gender Roles on the Sexual Division of Labour. In *Scratching the Surface: Canadian Anti-Racist Feminist Thought.* ed. Enakshi Dua and Angela Robertson. 1999. Toronto: Women's Press.

20. Corporations prefer a workforce that can be hired and fired according to seasonal fluctuations in demand. This "flexible" workforce is thereby denied stable, permanent employment and adequate compensation for being laid off.

21. These groups were largely responsible for bringing about the pardoning of Kemba Smith in the last days of the Clinton administration in 2000. Kemba has continued to campaign on behalf of the thousands of low-level, drug-involved prisoners who remain incarcerated for obscenely long terms of imprisonment.

22. Kemba Smith, From the Desk of Kemba Smith, www.geocities.com/CapitolHill/Lobby/8899/pen.html, December 13, 1999.

23. Beth Richie. 1996. *Compelled to Crime: The Gender Entrapment of Battered Black Women.* London and New York: Routledge.

24. www.geocities.com/CapitolHill/Lobby/8899.

25. Jim Thomas and Sharon Boehlefeld. 1991. Rethinking Abolitionism: "What Do We Do with Henry?" *Social Justice* 18(3): 239–25.

26. Pat Carlen. 1998. *Sledgehammer: Women's Imprisonment at the Millennium.* Basingstoke and London: MacMillan.

27. Fay Honey Knopp. 1993. On Radical Feminism and Abolition. In *We Who Would Take No Prisoners: Selections from the Fifth International Conference on Penal Abolition,* ed. Brian D. MacLean and Harold E. Pepinsky, p. 55. Vancouver: Collective Press.

28. Organizations working within this framework include Critical Resistance http://www.criticalresistance.org and the International Conference on Penal Abolition (ICOPA) http://www.actionicopa.org.

10

◆◆◆

Women and the Military, War, and Peace

In the United States most people grow up with pride in this country, its wealth, its power, and its dominant position in the world. We learn the Pledge of Allegiance, a sense of patriotism, and that our way of life is worth fighting and perhaps dying for. Most families have at least one member who has served in the military. The United States is number one in the world in terms of military technology, military exports, and military expenditure. It accounts for 43 percent of world military spending (Perlo-Freeman et al. 2011). The largest proportion of our federal budget, $1,355 billion for fiscal year 2013 or 47 percent, supports current and past military operations, including the upkeep of over four hundred bases and installations at home and one thousand of those abroad, the development and maintenance of weapons systems, pensions for retired military personnel, veterans benefits, and interest on the national debt attributable to military spending (War Resisters League 2012). Major companies with household names like Westinghouse, Boeing, and General Electric research and develop weapons systems and military aircraft. War movies are a film industry staple, portraying images of manly heroes. "Full Spectrum Warrior," a video game set in an apparently Arab city, was developed with $4 million from the U.S. Army as a training tool for recruits (Ahn and Kirk 2005). The Army also has its own video game, America's Army, as a recruitment tool (www.americasarmy.com). Toy manufacturer Mattel markets a female colleague for G.I. Joe, a helicopter pilot dressed in a jumpsuit and helmet and armed with a 9mm Beretta. Even Barbie is in uniform. Political scientist Cynthia Enloe shows that many aspects of U.S. culture have become militarized and notes specific ways that culture is deployed in the service of **militarism** (Reading 56). There are "G.I. Jane Boot Camp" fitness programs. High-fashion designers are promoting the "military look" and camouflage chic. Backpacks, cell phone covers, baby clothes, and condoms all come in "camo."

The military shapes our notions of patriotism, heroism, honor, duty, adventure, and citizenship. Psychologist Stephen Ducat (2004) discussed the importance of "the wimp factor" in U.S. politics where the president is also commander-in-chief of the armed forces. In the 2008 race for Democratic party presidential candidate, neither Hillary Clinton nor Barack Obama, the main contenders, had military experience, and at times both presented themselves as tough candidates who would not be "soft on defense."

Politically, economically, and culturally, the military is a central U.S. institution. This has been more explicit since the attacks on the World Trade Center and Pentagon on September 11, 2001, and the Bush administration's declaration of an open-ended "war on terrorism," given the more bureaucratic-sounding title "overseas contingency operation" by President Obama. Under the banner of patriotism, young people enlisted in the military and parents were encouraged to support them. By the end of 2011, 4,486 U.S. troops had been killed in Iraq; thousands more had been seriously injured or were suffering from trauma. Some had gone AWOL (absent without leave) or sought conscientious objector status. Others had committed suicide. Military recruiters have been under pressure to sign up new recruits. The No Child Left Behind Act concerning education also requires high schools to provide the Department of Defense with a directory of all juniors and seniors (names, addresses, and phone numbers) or risk losing federal funding. Parents must be notified; if they object to having their child's information released to military recruiters, the onus is on them to write to the school administration and say so. Also, the Bush administration called on the Hollywood film industry to make more pro-war movies (see, e.g., Boggs and Pollard 2006; Robb 2004).

The Need for Women in the Military

Although the vast majority of U.S. military personnel have always been male, the military has needed and continues to need women's support and participation in many capacities. It needs mothers to believe in the concept of patriotic duty and to encourage their sons, and more recently their daughters, to enlist or at least to support their desire to do so. It needs women nurses to heal the wounded and the traumatized. It needs wives and girlfriends back home, the prize waiting at the end of war or a period of duty overseas, who live with veterans' trauma or who mourn loved ones killed in action (see, e.g., D'Amico and Weinstein 1999; Enloe 1983, 2000a; Isakson 1988; Weinstein and White 1997).

During World War II, women were needed for the war effort working in shipyards and munitions factories while men were drafted for active service overseas (Denman and Inniss 1999; Gluck 1987). Currently the military needs women to work in electronics and many other industries producing weapons components, machine parts, tools, uniforms, household supplies, and foodstuffs for military contracts. It needs women working in nightclubs, bars, and massage parlors near foreign bases and ports providing R and R, rest and relaxation, for military personnel, or, as it is sometimes called, I and I, intoxication and intercourse (Enloe 1993, 2000a; Sturdevant and Stoltzfus 1992; Reading 58). And the military needs women on active duty in all service branches.

Women's Participation in the Military

Having women in the military in significant numbers is a relatively new phenomenon. In 1972, near the end of the Vietnam War, women were only 1.2 percent of military personnel. The following year, after much debate, Congress ended the draft for men, though young men are still required to register for the draft when they turn 18. Many left the services as soon as they could, causing a manpower shortfall that has been made up by recruiting women, especially women of color. In 2010, women made up 14.6 percent of military personnel: 14 percent in enlisted ranks and 16 percent of commissioned officers. Fewer military women compared to men are serving in the Army (37 percent of military women compared to 40 percent of men); more women are in the Air Force (31 percent compared to 22 percent) and Navy (25 percent compared to 22 percent). The Marines is the most male-dominated service with 7 percent of military women compared to 16 percent of military men (Patten and Parker 2011). Black women are a crucial source of new recruits, especially for the Army and Air Force. They make up 31 percent of active-duty enlisted women, although they are only 15 percent of the civilian population, aged 18–44. Asian women enlist at roughly the same rate as their numbers in the civilian population (4 percent). Latinas are somewhat underrepresented at 13 percent of enlisted women compared to 16 percent in the population (Patten and Parker 2011). By contrast, the majority of women officers are white. In the military, as in the civilian job market, most enlisted women are doing "women's work," including support and administration (30 percent), health care (15 percent), service and supply (14 percent), and communications and intelligence (10 percent) (Patten and Parker 2011). As part of the long process of accommodating women, all service branches have had to design uniforms for them, including for pregnant soldiers, and to specify rules for hairstyles and makeup (see Box).

Army Regulations on Hair and Cosmetics

Military uniforms are the subject of detailed regulations and protocols. Uniform committees have long deliberated over appropriate dress for women—seeking to balance the soldier (read male) with the feminine. Nowadays women's uniforms emphasize practicality; they include pants, for example. Maternity uniforms have been introduced for pregnant servicewomen. The emphasis is on uniformity and professionalism, with precise rules governing all aspects of appearance, including fingernails and scrunchies, as shown in this excerpt from Army Regulation 670-1 (AR 670-1) Wear and Appearance of Army Uniforms and Insignia:

(3) Female haircuts will conform to the following standards.

(a) Females will ensure their hair is neatly groomed, that the length and bulk of the hair are not excessive, and that the hair does not present a ragged, unkempt, or extreme appearance. Likewise, trendy styles that result in shaved portions of the scalp (other than the neckline) or designs cut into the hair are prohibited. Females may wear braids and cornrows as long as the braided style is conservative, the braids and cornrows lie snugly on the head, and any hair-holding devices comply with the standards in 1-8a(3)(d) below. Dreadlocks (unkempt, twisted, matted individual parts of hair) are prohibited in uniform or in civilian clothes on duty. Hair will not fall over the eyebrows or extend below the bottom edge of the collar at any time during normal activity or when standing in formation. Long hair that falls naturally below the bottom edge of the collar, to include braids, will be neatly and inconspicuously fastened or pinned, so no free-hanging hair is visible. This includes styles worn with the physical fitness uniform/improved physical fitness uniform (PFU/IPFU).

(b) Styles that are lopsided or distinctly unbalanced are prohibited. Ponytails, pigtails, or braids that are not secured to the head (allowing hair to hang freely), widely spaced individual hanging locks, and other extreme styles that protrude from the head are prohibited. Extensions, weaves, wigs, and hairpieces are authorized; however, these additions must have the same general appearance as the individual's natural hair. Additionally, any wigs, extensions, hairpieces, or weaves must comply with the grooming policies set forth in this paragraph.

(c) Females will ensure that hairstyles do not interfere with proper wear of military headgear and protective masks or equipment at any time [see1-8a(1)(a), above]. When headgear is worn, the hair will not extend below the bottom edge of the front of the headgear, nor will it extend below the bottom edge of the collar.

(d) Hair-holding devices are authorized only for the purpose of securing the hair. Soldiers will not place hair-holding devices in the hair for decorative purposes. All hair-holding devices must be plain and of a color as close to the soldier's hair as is possible or clear. Authorized devices include, but are not limited to, small, plain scrunchies (elastic hair bands covered with material), barrettes, combs, pins, clips, rubber bands, and hair bands. Devices that are conspicuous, excessive, or decorative are prohibited. Some examples of prohibited devices include, but are not limited to, large, lacy scrunchies; beads, bows, or claw clips; clips, pins, or barrettes with butterflies, flowers, sparkles, gems, or scalloped edges; and bows made from hairpieces.

b. Cosmetics.

(1) General. As with hairstyles, the requirement for standards regarding cosmetics is necessary to maintain uniformity and to avoid an extreme or unmilitary appearance. Males are prohibited from wearing cosmetics, to include nail polish. Females are authorized to wear cosmetics with all uniforms, provided they are applied conservatively and in good taste and complement the uniform. Leaders at all levels must exercise good judgment in the enforcement of this policy.

(a) Females may wear cosmetics if they are conservative and complement the uniform and their complexion. Eccentric, exaggerated, or trendy cosmetic styles and colors, to include makeup designed to cover tattoos, are inappropriate with the uniform and are prohibited. Permanent makeup, such as eyebrow or eyeliner, is authorized as long as the makeup conforms to the standards outlined above.

(b) Females will not wear shades of lipstick and nail polish that distinctly contrast with their complexion, that detract from the uniform, or that are extreme. Some examples of extreme colors include, but are not limited to, purple, gold, blue, black, white, bright (fire-engine) red, khaki, camouflage colors, and fluorescent colors. Soldiers will not apply designs to nails or apply two-tone or multi-tone colors to nails.

For many of these women, the military offers much better opportunities than the wider society: jobs with better pay, health care, pensions, and other benefits, as well as the chance for education, travel, and escape from crisis-torn inner cities in the United States or economically depressed small towns and rural areas. It enhances women's self-esteem and confers the status of first-class citizenship attributed to those who serve their country. Some women who have been stationed in Iraq have commented that the physical and mental challenges of serving in a war zone and engaging in combat gave them a sense of agency and accomplishment. (see, e.g., Benedict 2009; Blair 2011; Bowden and Cain 2008; Crow 2012; Holmstedt 2007; Williams 2005). In Reading 57, Anuradha Kristina Bhagwati gives thumbnail sketches of her experiences. She suggests her intense sense of belonging to the military, or at least people she describes as "the good ones I used to know," despite deep contradictions.

As we argued in Chapter 7, the U.S. labor market has changed markedly over the past forty years through automation and the movement of jobs overseas. In addition to a loss of jobs, there are few sources of public funding for working-class women's (and men's) education. Government funding for education and many welfare programs has been cut back since the 1980s, but the military budget has been maintained at high levels. Similar to men, over 80 percent of military women who were interviewed by the Pew Research Trust joined the military to serve the country and to receive education benefits. Many more women said they joined because jobs were hard to find (42 percent of military women compared to 25 percent of military men) (Patten and Parker 2011). Women who enter the military are going where the money is. Their very presence, however, exposes serious dilemmas and contradictions for the institution, which we explore in the next section. Another contradiction of this situation is the fact that massive government spending on the military diverts funds that could otherwise be invested in civilian job programs, education, and community services.

Contradictions for Women in a Male-Dominated Military

Despite the military's need for women and their capabilities in military roles, military culture has remained overwhelmingly male (see, e.g., Burke 2004; D'Amico 1998; Dean 1997; Guenter-Schlesinger 1999; Morris 1999; Pershing 2003). Political scientists Francine D'Amico and Laurie Weinstein (1999) argued that the "military must camouflage its reliance on *woman* power in order to maintain its self-image as a quintessentially *masculine* institution" (p. 6). This contradiction has serious implications for women, who have been marginalized through professional disparagement, sexual harassment, and distinctions between combatant and noncombatant.

Women in Combat

Women served in the U.S. military during World War II, the Korean War, and the Vietnam War. They were generally designated as auxiliary, according to political scientist Mary Katzenstein (1993), despite the fact that they performed a wider range of tasks than is usually recognized—as transport pilots (Cole 1992), mechanics, drivers, underground reconnaissance, nurses (Camp 1997), and administrators. The influx of women into the military since the mid-1970s and the question of whether to train women for combat exposed a range of stereotypical attitudes toward women on the part of military commanders, Pentagon planners, and members of Congress, depending on the degree to which they believe that combat is male. Many argued that women are not physically strong enough, are too emotional, and lack discipline or stamina. They would be bad for men's morale, it was said, and would disrupt fighting units because men would be distracted if a woman buddy was hurt or captured. Many of these stereotypes

Are we willing to sacrifice one or two of the children for oil?

have been confounded by women's skills, professionalism, focus, endurance, strength, and loyalty to the services.

Media attention on women's participation in the 1991 Persian Gulf War showed that many performed combat roles similar to those of men, and this led to changes in laws and regulations that had previously kept women out of combat assignments (Peach 1997; Sadler 1997; Skaine 1998). In 1993, when the combat exclusion law was repealed, some women began to train for combat roles. In 2008, close to 90 percent of military jobs were open to women, to fly helicopters and fighter jets, work on combat ships, or command military police units. In 2010, a change in Navy policy allowed women to work on submarines, though they are still not permitted to engage in "direct ground combat." These changes open up the possibility of career advancement for women, as senior positions often require combat experience. Restricting women from combat roles was a way of limiting their military careers.

What counts as combat in modern warfare is not as simple as it might seem, however. Communications and supply, for example, defined as noncombat areas where women work, are both likely targets of attack. During the war against Iraq, "traditional front lines were virtually obliterated, and women were tasked to fill lethal combat roles more routinely than in any conflict in U.S. history" according to *Chicago Tribune* reporter

Kirsten Scharnberg (2005). She described a mission just south of Baghdad where

> a young soldier jumped into the gunner's turret of an armored Humvee and took control of the menacing .50-caliber machine gun. She was 19 years old, weighed barely 100 pounds and had a blond ponytail hanging out from under her Kevlar helmet.
>
> "This is what is different about this war," Lt. Col. Richard Rael, commander of the 515th Corps Support Battalion, said of the scene at the time. "Women are fighting it. Women under my command have confirmed kills. These little wisps of things are stronger than anyone could ever imagine and taking on more than most Americans could ever know."

Some women soldiers have played a special role in both Iraq and Afghanistan. Team Lioness, for example, included mechanics, supply clerks, and engineers who fought alongside the Marines in the Iraq War. They took part in offensive operations, raids, security patrols, and vehicle checkpoints, as shown in the film *Lioness*. In 2010, the Marine Corps established a Female Engagement Team (FET) in Afghanistan to engage with Afghan women, provide supplies to local schools, organize women's discussions, and seek out information concerning local conditions. NATO News (2011) quoted Second Lieutenant Melanie Piedra who said that the FETs are seen as a "third gender": Afghan men recognize that they have power and responsibility "on the same level as a male. Yet, FETs are still viewed as females, allowing the teams to have access . . . to Afghan females."

Returning women veterans face similar challenges in adjusting to civilian life as reported by male soldiers (Patten and Parker 2011). Fully half say they experienced strains in family relations, and 42 percent said that they suffered from posttraumatic stress disorder (PTSD). On the other hand, 97 percent felt proud of their service. Female veterans said their service experience helped them grow and mature as a person (93 percent) and built their self-confidence (87 percent).

Recognizing that many service women are not adequately cared for by Veterans Administration health programs, the Service Women's Action Network (SWAN) was founded in 2007 to create support for military service women, especially women of color, and to offer women veterans alternative options for the many-layered process of healing and transitioning back into the civilian world.

Soldier Mothers

In 1991, for the first time, significant numbers of military women were deployed to the Persian Gulf War. Saying goodbye to their families as they prepared to go overseas, they were portrayed in news reports as professional soldiers as well as mothers. Reporters noted the change in social attitudes this represented, and some questioned whether war was the right place for mothers.

Currently, almost half (48 percent) of all married women in the military are married to a fellow service member (Patten and Parker 2011). In 2008, the active-duty military included 73,000 single parents (E. Wilson 2010a): 12 percent of military women are single mothers, and 4 percent of military men are single fathers (Patten and Parker 2011). The military's mission and absolute priority at all times is "readiness" for war, but with more single women and dual-military couples in the services, the Department of Defense (DoD) has had to pay more attention to the needs of military families.

In 1991, hundreds of single parents and dual-military couples had no contingency plans for the care of their children, which necessitated rescheduling and delaying their deployment (Newsome 2011). The following year the military barred single parents from enlisting and made a Family Care Plan (FCP) mandatory for parents of dependent children. The FCP must name a short-term and long-term caregiver, detail the financial and logistical arrangements for transporting children to their caregiver, and designate a guardian in the event of death or incapacity (Newsome 2011). If a service member becomes a single parent while in the military—due to the death of a spouse, separation, divorce, or adoption—he or she must make adequate provisions for the care of the children. If a child care plan falls through, deployment may be deferred until the issue is resolved. Commanders have the option to terminate service if the service member cannot piece together adequate child care arrangements (E. Wilson 2010a).

Sexual Harassment and Rape

Many women in military academies, as well as enlisted women and officers, experience sexual harassment, even though the DoD has had a "zero tolerance" policy for over thirty years. *Time* magazine reporter Elizabeth Gleick (1996) argued that such abuse of power by superiors threatens "to undermine the thing that many in the military hold sacred: the chain of command" (p. 28).

Over the past twenty years, military women have reported several major incidents, which has opened up this issue to public awareness and official scrutiny. For example, in 1991, helicopter pilot Paula Coughlin went public with her experiences of sexual assault at the Tailhook naval aviators' convention at the Las Vegas Hilton, where women were subjected to sexual harassment, indecent assault, and indecent exposure. She testified that she resigned her commission as a Navy lieutenant under relentless harassment from colleagues afterward (Noble 1994). In 1996, women at the Aberdeen Proving Grounds Ordnance Center in Maryland complained of being sexually harassed and raped by drill sergeants during training. As part of its investigations into these allegations, the Army set up a toll-free hotline, which took four thousand calls in the first week relating to sexual harassment at many military facilities, and suggesting the broad scope of the problem (McKenna 1996/1997). In 2003, women cadets reported widespread sexual assault at the Air Force Academy. During the war against Iraq, Colonel Janis Karpinksi commented on the tragedy of several women who died of dehydration because they stopped drinking liquids after 3 or 4 PM. "They were afraid of being assaulted or even raped by male soldiers if they had to use the women's latrine after dark" (in Cohn 2006). Moreover, male colleagues have also sexually assaulted women working for military contractors in Iraq and Afghanistan (see, e.g., Snell 2011).

A growing outcry in response to such claims led the DoD to increase sensitivity training for military personnel, and Congress to require the DoD to make a report on sexual assault in the military each year. In 2007, of 2,212 service members investigated for sexual assault—including 1,259 reports of rape—only 181 individuals were referred to courts martial, the military equivalent of a criminal prosecution. Another 218 cases were handled by nonpunitive administrative action or discharge, and 201 offenders were disciplined through "nonjudicial punishment" (Department of Defense 2008, pp. 15–19). Congresswoman Jane Harman, then

Chair of the House Homeland Security Subcommittee on Intelligence, contended that nonjudicial punishment meant being confined to quarters, assigned extra duty, or "a similar slap on the wrist" (Harman 2008). In nearly half of the cases investigated, the chain of command took no action.

According to law professor Marjorie Cohn (2006), commands can reject complaints if they decide they are not credible, and women who come forward have limited protection against retaliation from perpetrators, colleagues, or superiors. Women who report sexual abuse often find themselves interrogated by skeptical officers. Some have been disciplined for drinking or wearing civilian clothes at the time of the assaults. Others have said that they were given a medical discharge or otherwise "hounded out" of the military (Cohn 2006; National Women's Law Center 2003; Shumway 2004; N. Wilson 2010).

According to a DoD survey, 71 percent of women did not report an incident of unwanted sexual contact (Department of Defense 2010). Their reasons were that they didn't want anyone to know (67 percent); felt uncomfortable making the report (65 percent); were worried about confidentiality (60 percent); were afraid of retaliation (54 percent); feared being labeled a troublemaker (52 percent); knew about negative experiences of other victims (47 percent); and believed nothing would be done (47 percent). The Government Accountability Office (2011) reported that the DoD office mandated to oversee investigations into military sexual assault does not appear to do so. The Holley Lynn James bill introduced in Congress in May 2011 would allow victims access to legal services, a chance to transfer jobs away from their attacker, and a promise that their private counseling sessions would not be used against them in court (Waddington 2011). However, the bill failed at the committee stage. Several military women and veterans have joined a class action lawsuit against the military for condoning sexual violence (N. Wilson 2010).

Sexual Orientation

A final area of limitation for women—and men—in the military concerned sexual orientation, though this policy was changed in December 2011. The Pentagon had long considered homosexuality incompatible with military service, and regulations precluded lesbians and gay men from serving openly, despite their presence as officers and enlisted personnel (Scott and Stanley 1994; Webber 1993). Army veteran and political scientist Jean Grossholtz (1998) pinpointed the contradiction implicit in this policy: The military is based on male bonding, yet homosexuality is banned. The Servicemembers Legal Defense Network (2002) argued that "forcing lesbian, gay and bisexual service members to hide, lie, evade and deceive their commanders, subordinates, peers, families and friends breaks the bonds of trust among service members essential to unit cohesion" (p. 6).

During his first presidential campaign, Bill Clinton promised to lift the ban on gays in the military when he came into office in 1992, but concerted opposition from the Pentagon and many politicians made this impossible. Some argued that the law enacted under Clinton, summed up as "Don't Ask, Don't Tell, Don't Pursue," was not much different than before. Reports of antigay harassment—including verbal abuse, beatings, death threats, and apparent killings—more than doubled in the late 1990s, even though military policy expressly forbade it. In August 1999, the Department of Defense issued an updated policy requiring mandatory training on antiharassment guidelines for all troops, beginning in boot camp. In March 2000, Pentagon officials conceded that there was a "disturbing" level of gay harassment in the military (Richter 2000).

Between 1998 and 2003, 6,300 people were discharged, including linguists, nuclear warfare experts, and those in other job specialties that require years of training and expertise (Fouhy 2004). Women were 30 percent of those discharged, though they made up only 15 percent of active duty personnel. The Army was responsible for 41 percent of these discharges, although it was down on its recruitment targets and had invoked a "stop loss" order to stop soldiers from retiring or leaving if they were deployed to Iraq or Afghanistan. The repeal of "Don't Ask, Don't Tell" is attributable to shifts in military culture, severe personnel shortages in a time of war, and the concerted efforts of service members, their allies, and organizations such as Gay, Lesbian, and Bisexual Vets of America, the National Gay and Lesbian Task Force, and Servicemembers Legal Defense Network.

Military Wives

The model military wife is a staunch supporter of her husband's career (e.g., Cline 2009; D'Amico and Weinstein 1999; Enloe 1983, 2000a; Weinstein and White 1997). She learns to manage the moves from base to base, the disruption of family life, and interruptions in her own work. Increasingly, she may be in the military herself. Kristin Henderson (2004, 2006), a writer who is married to a Navy chaplain, interviewed military wives whose husbands had been deployed to Iraq. She noted the strains on personal relationships and family life and the wide gaps in the military's family policy that wives attempt to fill on a voluntary basis as they also juggle paid employment and care for their children. In addition, they are a crucial source of emotional support, via phone and e-mail, for husbands thousands of miles away.

Wives and children of military families also suffer abuse at the hands of servicemen husbands and fathers. Anthropologist Catherine Lutz (2004) found that "the immediate pre- and post-deployment periods are the most dangerous for women: their partners fear losing control as they prepare to leave and attempt to reassert it when they return" (p. 17). She commented, "rates of domestic violence are 3 to 5 times higher in military couples than in comparable civilian ones." This finding was corroborated by Deborah Tucker, executive director of the National Center on Domestic and Sexual Violence, who also co-chaired the Department of Defense Task Force on Domestic Violence (Gettelman 2005; also see Houppert 2005a, 2005b). Women abused by military spouses are often fearful of reporting incidents because of a combination of lack of confidentiality; limited victim services; lack of training and assistance on the part of military commanders; and disruption caused by moving from base to base. As in civilian families, estimates of domestic violence in military families are undoubtedly underestimates.

A made-for-TV documentary, "The War at Home," which aired on *60 Minutes* in January 1999 and again in September 2002, helped to make this issue more public as has the work of the Miles Foundation (Waterbury, Conn.) and Survivors in Service United (Hansen 2001). In 2000, President Clinton appointed a Defense Task Force on Domestic Violence to assist in improving the military's response to it. In November 2001, then Deputy

Secretary of Defense Paul Wolfowitz issued an official memorandum stating that domestic violence would not be tolerated. This issue hit the headlines in the summer of 2002 when, within six weeks, the wives of three soldiers who had served in Afghanistan were killed at Fort Bragg (N.C.), allegedly by their husbands. Two of the soldiers killed themselves as well. Three of the four men were in the Special Forces, considered the toughest and most aggressive unit in the Army. The Special Operation command said it would study the stress wartime deployments may be adding to already-shaky marriages. Soldiers would be screened for psychological problems before they leave Afghanistan and commanders would watch out for symptoms of depression and anxiety among their troops. Also in 2002, a bipartisan effort by elected officials and activists was successful in getting increased funding for domestic violence services. Moreover, the 2002 Armed Forces Security Act provided for the enforcement of civilian court protective orders. These efforts, however, do not address systemic issues. Catherine Lutz (2004) argued that "there is no workplace more supportive of a masculine identity centered in power, control, and violence"; "there is little institutional incentive to rid the service of men who batter, since the military puts its war-making mission above all others" (pp. 17, 18).

The Impact of the U.S. Military on Women Overseas

The worldwide superiority of the United States—in political, economic, and military terms—is sustained by a global network of ships, submarines, aircraft, and around 1,000 overseas bases. This U.S. presence in other nations relies on agreements with "host" governments. In return the military may pay rent for the land it occupies. Some local people may be employed directly on the bases; many others work in nearby businesses patronized by U.S. troops. U.S. military policies and bases abroad affect women in several ways, for example, through militarized prostitution, crimes of violence committed by servicemen, and the direct effects of war. In her discussion of mixed-race identity, Patti Duncan refers to Amerasian children fathered by U.S. troops in Japan/Okinawa, Korea, and the Philippines,

another impact of U.S. military presence on women overseas (Reading 16).

Militarized Prostitution

As a way of keeping up the morale of their troops, military commanders have long tolerated, and sometimes actively encouraged, women to live outside military camps to support and sexually service the men. With U.S. bases positioned strategically around the globe, militarized prostitution has required explicit arrangements between the U.S. government and the governments of the Philippines, Japan (Okinawa), Thailand, and South Korea, for example, where women work in bars and massage parlors, "entertaining" U.S. troops (Enloe 1990, 1993, 2000a; Sturdevant and Stoltzfus 1992). As a way of protecting the men's health, women who work in bars must have regular medical exams, on the assumption that they are the source of sexually transmitted infections (Moon 1997). If the bar women fail such tests, they are quarantined until they pass. They usually earn better money than they can make in other ways, though this may be much harder as they grow older.

Occupational dangers for the women include psychological violence, rape, and beatings from some of their customers; health risks from abortions; HIV/AIDS and other sexually transmitted infections; drug use; and a general lack of respect associated with this stigmatized work. Currently, most women working in bars around U.S. bases in South Korea and Okinawa are recruited from the Philippines, due to a lack of jobs at home. Women displaced due to the collapse of the former Soviet Union and subsequent transition to a market economy also work in bars around U.S. bases overseas. Militarized prostitution is an integral part of the global sex trade, as mentioned by Ursula Biemann (see Reading 47).

Crimes of Violence Against Women

The behavior of U.S. troops in other countries is governed by agreements between the U.S. government and the host government, called Status of Forces Agreements (SOFAs). Usually U.S. military personnel who commit crimes against civilians are dealt with, if at all, through military channels rather than the local courts. In many cases, U.S. troops are not held responsible for crimes they commit. Sometimes they are simply moved to another posting. In Reading 58, Anne Lacsamana discusses the Subic rape case, in which U.S. Marine Daniel Smith was found guilty of raping a Philippine woman, referred to as "Nicole" to protect her identity. Smith was convicted by a Philippine court and sentenced to jail, but was transferred to the U.S. embassy in Manila and acquitted on appeal. Nicole apparently "recanted" her original testimony in return for the opportunity to live in the United States. Suzuyo Takazato (2000), cofounder of Okinawa Women Act Against Military Violence, has reported on the long history of crimes of violence committed by U.S. troops against women and girls in Okinawa (see also Fukumura and Matsuoka 2002).

The Effects of War

The many direct effects of wars on human beings include the killing of soldiers—mainly younger men—and of noncombatants—mainly women, children, and elders; the trauma of experiencing or witnessing destruction, torture, or rape; physical injuries and disabilities and posttraumatic stress disorders; the chaos of everyday life; and the trauma of being forced to flee from home and live as refugees. Other effects include contaminated water, broken sewers, power outages, environmental devastation, and the prevalence of weapons. Economic collapse resulting from war causes shortages of food, water, and basic supplies; exorbitant prices; destruction of farms and gardens, factories, and other workplaces; endless queuing for necessities; and having to go without. This situation impacts women severely as they try to care for children and sustain their families and communities. An Iraqi woman, who took the name Riverbend (2005, 2006), gave outsiders a rare window into the daily effects of war and occupation through her blog reports from Baghdad. She wove descriptions of her family's experiences—of raids, queuing, cuts in water and electricity services, the noise of helicopters, explosions at night—together with her analysis of news reports and current events (www.riverbendblog.blogspot.com; also see Al-Ali and Pratt 2009; Zangana 2007).

In Reading 59, Afghan human rights advocate Malalai Joya challenges the claim that the invasion of Afghanistan has helped Afghan women.

She details many ways that Afghan women are repressed, but contends that U.S. military operations have exacerbated not reduced this situation (also see Reading 11).

News reports of U.S. military women raped or sexually assaulted by U.S. troops or contract personnel trickled into the U.S. news during 2007 and 2008. There have been far fewer accounts of sexual abuse of Iraqi women by U.S. troops, whether in prison or in their homes and neighborhoods. Sexual abuse and torture committed by U.S. military personnel and contractors against Iraqi prisoners in Abu Ghraib prison shocked the world in 2004 and introduced a grim new twist on sexualized military violence, where race and nation "trumped" gender. White U.S. women were among the perpetrators (taking on the masculinist role); Iraqi men were violated (forced into the feminized role). Seeing women engaged in torture turned upside down "deeply gendered presumptions" (Enloe 2007, p. 100) of militarized sexual abuse as a crime against women by men. Some feminist scholars emphasized the process of feminization—"imposing allegedly feminine characteristics on a person . . . or a group or a kind of activity" often with the goal of lowering their status—at the heart of these atrocities (Enloe 2007, p. 95). U.S. women captors were deployed strategically to shame and humiliate Iraqi men. However, the power they wielded derived from their national affiliation as members of the United States military and from their whiteness as well as their gender (McKelvey 2007; Nussair 2008: Oliver 2010; Sjoberg and Gentry 2008).

As a weapon of war, rape of women involves a complex intertwining of gender and race/ethnicity and is a strategic and systematic way of dishonoring and attacking enemy men. In World War II, Korean, Philippine, Indonesian, and Chinese "comfort women" were forced to provide sexual services for the Japanese Imperial Army (Hicks 1997; Kim-Gibson 1999; Sajor 1998). In the 1990s, armies conducted systematic rapes in the Balkans (Cockburn 1998; Kesic 2000; Walsh 2000) and in Rwanda (Newbury and Baldwin 2001; Rehn and Sirleaf 2002). More recently, militias have raped women and girls in the Darfur region of Sudan (Kristof 2005; Lacey 2004) and in the Democratic Republic of the Congo (Whitman 2010). Rape is explicitly listed among crimes against humanity, which can occur in war or in peacetime (Leatherman 2011; Peterson and Runyan 1993; Rayner 1997; Tétreault 1997).

Health Effects of Environmental Contamination

Militaries create more pollution than other institutions, but unlike industry, military pollution is governed by fewer regulations, monitoring programs, and controls (Seager 1993). Routine military operations involve the use of highly carcinogenic materials, including fuels, oils, solvents, and heavy metals that are regularly released, affecting the land, water, air, and ocean, as well as the health of people living around U.S. bases or training areas (Institute for Policy Studies 2000; Kirk 2008; Zamora-Olib 2000). The U.S. nuclear weapons industry has caused long-term environmental destruction in this country and overseas (Birks and Erlich 1989; Lindsay-Poland 2003; Seager 1993; Shulman 1990), with serious effects on people's health. In the 1950s and early 1960s the United States military, as well as those of Britain and France, undertook a series of atomic tests in the Pacific that irradiated whole islands and contaminated soil and water for generations to come. Micronesian women gave birth to children with severe illnesses or disabilities caused by radiation, including some "jellyfish babies" without skeletons who lived only a few hours (de Ishtar 1994; Dibblin 1989). Pacific Island women and men have contracted several kinds of cancer as a result of their exposure to radioactive fallout. Given the long-lasting effects of atomic materials in the food chain and people's reproductive systems, these disabilities and illnesses are likely to last for generations. The environmental health effects of more recent wars against Afghanistan and Iraq are still to be assessed.

Women's Opposition to Militarism

Early U.S. Women's Peace Organizations

Although many women have supported and continue to support the military in various ways, there is a history of women's opposition to militarism and war with roots in Quakerism and the nineteenth-century suffrage and temperance movements (Alonso 1993; Plastas 2011; Washburn 1993).

Julia Ward Howe, for example, remembered as the author of the Civil War song "The Battle Hymn of the Republic," was involved in the suffrage movement as a way of organizing women for peace. In 1873 she initiated Mothers' Day for Peace on June 2, a day to honor mothers, who, she felt, best understood the suffering caused by war. Howe's *Mother's Day Proclamation*, written in 1870, calls on women to oppose war (Reading 60). Women's peace festivals were organized in several U.S. cities with women speakers who opposed war and military training in schools. During the 1890s many women's organizations had peace committees. The Philadelphia Peace Society was still organizing in this way as late as 1909 (Alonso 1993). In 1914 the Women's Peace Party was formed under the leadership of Carrie Chapman Catt and Jane Addams.

Despite difficulties of obtaining passports and wartime travel, over one thousand women from twelve countries, "cutting across national enmities," participated in a Congress of Women in the Hague, Holland, in 1915, calling for an end to World War I. The congress sent delegations of women to meet with heads of state in fourteen countries and influenced press and public opinion (Foster 1989). A second congress at the end of the war proposed an ongoing international organization: the Women's International League for Peace and Freedom (WILPF), which is active in thirty-seven countries today and maintains international offices at the United Nations and in Geneva, Switzerland. Among the participants at the second congress were Mary Church Terrell, a Black labor leader from the United States, and Jeanette Rankin, the first U.S. congresswoman and the only member of Congress to vote against U.S. involvement in both world wars. From World War I onward, U.S women's peace organizations opposed U.S. involvement in successive wars, especially the Vietnam War, and also opposed the nuclear arms race with the (then) Soviet Union (see, e.g., Adams 1991; Swerdlow 1993).

Feminist Antimilitarist Perspectives

Women's opposition to militarism draws on a range of theoretical perspectives, which we discuss briefly below. In any particular organization several of these perspectives may provide the basis for activism, but it is useful to look at them separately to clarify different and sometimes contradictory positions.

Women's Peaceful Nature Although some women —and men—believe that women are "naturally" more peaceful than men, there is no conclusive evidence for this. Differences in socialization, however, from infancy onward, lead to important differences in attitudes, behavior, and responsibilities in caring for others. Many who oppose the military see the current division of labor in society between men's and women's roles as a fundamental aspect of military systems, whereby men (and now a few women) "protect" women, children, and older people. They ask: Can we afford this dichotomy? Where does it lead? They argue that the abolition of war is dependent on changing this division of labor, with men becoming involved in what have been women's roles and caring for infants and small children, the elderly, and the sick (Dinnerstein 1989; Ruddick 1989).

Maternalism Some women see their opposition to war mainly in terms of their responsibility to protect and nurture their children; they want to save the lives of their own children and the children of "enemy" mothers. In the early 1980s, for example, when the U.S. and Soviet militaries were deploying nuclear weapons in Europe, Susan Lamb, who lived near USAF Greenham Common in England, a nuclear base, put it this way:

> I've got two young children, and I've taken responsibility for their passage into adulthood. Everyone tells me they are my responsibility. The government tells me this. It is my responsibility to create a world fit for them to grow up in. I can't say I'm responsible for my children not catching whooping cough and not responsible for doing anything about the threat of annihilation that hangs over them every minute of the day.
>
> *(Quoted in Cook and Kirk 1983, p. 27)*

Although this approach can sentimentalize motherhood, it is also powerful because mothers are behaving according to conventional roles and it is difficult for the state to suppress them. They expose contradictions: that the state, through militarism, does not let them get on with their job of mothering.

Diversion of Military Budgets to Socially Useful Programs Organizations like Women's Action for New Directions (WAND) and the Women's International League for Peace and Freedom (WILPF, U.S. section) have long argued for reductions in military expenditures and redistribution of funds to provide social programs that benefit women, their families, and communities. Cuts in funding for nuclear weapons, chemical and biological weapons, and U.S. troops, ships, and aircraft carriers around the world, they argue, could fund job-training programs, public housing, education, urban development, and environmental cleanup, for example. Former legislative and executive director for WILPF (U.S. section) Jane Midgley (2005) provided gender-sensitive ways of thinking about the bloated military budget and alternative people-centered budgets. A lack of civilian jobs is a key reason women enlist. However, the military is very capital intensive and generates fewer jobs than other forms of public spending. Researchers Robert Pollin and Heidi Garrett-Peltier (2009) found that spending on "clean energy, health care and education create a much larger number of jobs across all pay ranges" (p. 1) compared with spending the same amount of money on the military.

The Military as a Sexist and Racist Institution The armed services were officially integrated in 1948, many years before desegregation in the southern states; they take pride in being an "equal opportunity" employer with a much more diverse workforce than many civilian businesses. However, a 1994 House Armed Services Committee report found that service members of color perceived racial discrimination in opportunities for career-enhancing assignments, training, and promotions (Hall 1999). The report uncovered serious problems with institutionalized racism and warned about skinhead and other extremist activity on four military bases visited by investigators. During the late 1990s, high-ranking officials regularly included declarations against racial discrimination in speeches and news briefings on behalf of the DoD (e.g., Department of Defense 1996, 1997; Hamre 1998). More recently, racism in the military has been reported "alive and well" (Reuters 2012b). Like sexual assault, racist incidents are underreported. Often the DoD analyzes personnel data by race or by gender, which makes it difficult to track data concerning women of color. The overrepresentation of African American women in the enlisted ranks shows the institutionalized racism of the

Carrying large puppets symbolizing mourning, rage, empowerment, and defiance, women protested against militarism at the Pentagon, November 1980.

wider society (Hall 1999; Moore 1996). Currently, military recruiters "target" high school students of color, including Spanish language ads aimed at Latino youth and their parents.

Professor of sociology and activist Barbara Omolade (1989) noted the contradictions of militarism for people of color in the United States, many of whom support the military because it provides opportunities that are lacking in civilian society. At the same time, they fight for a country where they are oppressed. Since World War II, those they have fought against have been other people of color, for example, in Vietnam, Grenada, Libya, Panama, Afghanistan, and Iraq.

Opposition to the military also turns on the argument that, by its very nature, the military is profoundly anti-feminist and racist and based on the objectification of "others" as enemies. Its effectiveness depends on people's ability to see reality in oppositional categories: us and them, friends and enemies, kill or be killed (Reardon 1985). To this end it is organized on rigidly hierarchical lines, demanding unquestioning obedience to superiors. Although the military uses women's labor in many ways, it does so strictly on its own terms.

Militarism is a system of investments, institutions, values, and practices that is much broader than any specific war. The Women's Pentagon Action identified militarism as a cornerstone of the oppression of women and the destruction of the environment. Thousands of women surrounded the Pentagon in November 1980 and 1981. They protested massive military budgets; the fact that militaries cause more ecological destruction than any other institutions; the widespread, everyday culture of violence manifested in war toys, films, and video games; and so forth. This was no routine demonstration but a highly creative action organized in four stages: mourning, rage, empowerment, and defiance, culminating in the arrest of many women who chose to blockade the doors of the Pentagon (King 1983). These activists saw crucial connections between personal violence and international violence, both based on the objectification of others. Psychologist Stephen Ducat (2004) discussed the development of male identity "in a culture that disparages the feminine and insists that the boundaries between masculine and feminine remain unambiguous and impermeable" (p. 5). He argued that in most patriarchal cultures "the most important thing about being a man is *not being a woman*" (p. 6) and emphasized men's fear of feminization and the liability for men in public life of "the wimp factor." Political scientist Cynthia Enloe's (1990, 1993) concept of a constructed **militarized masculinity** fits in here, an ideal of manhood that involves individualistic heroism of physical strength, emotional detachment, the capacity for violence and killing, and an appearance of invulnerability. She also emphasized the role masculinity plays in national foreign policy making (Enloe 2000b). Other scholars have argued that the nation-state, which the military is designed to protect, is a patriarchal, heterosexist institution (Allen 2000; Peterson 2000; Plumwood 1993). Thus, women in combat roles, for example, threaten the manliness of war and the very nature of militarism as male.

Women who oppose militarism have very different perspectives from those who enter the military. They may also have different class positions and more opportunities for education and employment. Liberal feminists have criticized peace activists for opposing militarism when working women, especially women of color, have few employment options. While liberal feminists call for women's equality within the military, peace activists have argued against participation in the military by women or men.

Globalization and Militarism Colonial expansion and the quest for control of strategic locations and scarce resources have been a major justification and impetus for military intervention for centuries. In the war on Iraq, a key issue was access to oil

DO YOU HAVE A FEMALE *ACTION FIGURE* THAT SPEAKS OUT AGAINST *DISCRIMINATION AND WAR!?*

supplies. As Chair of the International Network on Disarmament and Globalization (Vancouver, Canada), Steven Staples argued that

> globalization and militarism should be seen as two sides of the same coin. On the one side, globalization promotes the conditions that lead to unrest, inequality, conflict, and, ultimately war. On the other side, globalization fuels the means to wage war by protecting and promoting the military industries needed to produce sophisticated weaponry. This weaponry, in turn, is used or is threatened to be used to protect the investments of transnational corporations and their shareholders.
>
> *(Staples 2000, p. 18)*

Nation-states, militaries, and corporations are increasingly intertwined as military functions are privatized and outsourced (Ferguson and Turnbull 2004). As far back as 1961, President Dwight Eisenhower warned against the power of the "military industrial complex" in a speech on leaving office. Political scientist Spike Peterson has used the term "military industrial congressional academic media complex" to refer to these institutional interconnections which include "revolving-door job opportunities" among the higher echelons of government, military, and corporations.

Former Secretary of State Condoleeza Rice is one of the few women in this loop—formerly a political science professor, administrator, and Provost of Stanford University, she was also on the board of Chevron oil company. Military contractors, like Lockheed Martin and Haliburton, provide substantial campaign contributions and receive government contracts valued in billions of dollars. Staples (2000, p. 19) argued that the large U.S. military budget "is for all practical purposes a corporate subsidy" siphoning public money into private hands and protected under Article XXI of the General Agreement on Tariffs and Trade (GATT), which allows "governments free reign for action taken for national security interests."

The international arms trade, especially trade in smaller arms, is a key part of the global economy because it is an earner of hard currency and a way for many countries to repay foreign debt. Major bombing and missile strikes function like giant bazaars for arms manufacturers as war-tested planes and munitions command a price double or triple that of weapons without such testing. Jostling for contracts to rebuild Iraq was well under way before the war was started, as reported on the business pages and in the financial press.

Redefining Security

Since the attacks of September 11, 2001, and the Bush administration's immediate decision to take military action, many people have questioned whether the military and the wider system of militarism can provide everyday human security or even national security. This open-ended war on terrorism has generated new feminist research and analysis (see, e.g., Riley, Mohanty and Pratt 2008; Sjoberg and Via 2010; Sutton, Morgen, and Novkov 2008) and new energy for established organizations like Women's International League for Peace and Freedom (Boston), Women's Action for New Directions (WAND, Arlington, Mass.), Women in Black (New York and other cities), and Women Against Military Madness (Minneapolis). It has also given rise to many new groups, including Code Pink (San Francisco and other cities), Mothers Acting Up (Boulder, Colo.), Gather the Women, the Lysistrata Project, Racial Justice 911, and Women United for Peace, with an emphasis on organizing in a decentralized way, often via the Internet. The Women of Color Resource Center (Oakland, Calif.) created an antimilitary fashion show, "Fashion Resistance to Militarism," in 2005, as a popular way to highlight and critique the militarization of daily life through "camouflage chic," and this has been taken up by other groups (see Ahn and Kirk 2009; Enloe, ch. 6). In Reading 72, members of the International Women's Network for Genuine Security discuss transnational feminist organizing on these issues.

Families for Peaceful Tomorrows came together in 2001 soon after the attacks of September 11 around their belief, "Our grief is not a cry for war." Military Families Speak Out formed in 2002 to oppose the war in Iraq. Gold Star Families for Peace came to prominence in the summer of 2005, when Cindy Sheehan and others who had lost loved ones in the war in Iraq camped outside the Bush family ranch in Crawford (Tex.), asking the president to explain why their sons had died. The G.I. Rights Hotline takes calls from military personnel who want to leave, and the Youth and Militarism project of the American Friends Service Committee provides information for young people considering enlistment.

On the international level, women have come together to articulate new perspectives on security (Reading 61). Global Women's Strike links groups in over thirty countries under the slogan "Invest in Caring, Not Killing." In 2005, one thousand women were recognized and honored for their peace-making work worldwide. This project had two components: nominating a group of outstanding women from over 150 countries for the 2005 Nobel Peace Prize and creating a permanent record of their work. Choosing a thousand women was symbolic—a way of saying that one cannot make peace alone. Although this remarkable group did not win the Nobel Prize, the documentation of their work through video, photography, and writing continues to spread knowledge of their contributions to peacemaking (1000 Women for the Nobel Peace Prize, 2005; see also Cockburn 2007; Porter 2007).

A significant tool for women's peace work was provided by the UN Security Council, which adopted Resolution 1325 on women, peace, and security in October 2000. The resolution addresses the disproportionate impact of armed conflict on women. It recognizes the undervalued contributions that women make to conflict prevention, conflict resolution, and peace building and stresses the importance of women's equal and full participation in peace negotiations. Although not binding on governments, Resolution 1325 sets a new standard of inclusiveness and gender sensitivity in peace negotiations and provides leverage for women's efforts to influence policy in postconflict reconstruction (Lynes and Torry 2005).

The UN Development Program identified four basic requirements for human security:

- The environment in which we live must be able to sustain human and natural life.

- People's basic survival needs for food, clothing, shelter, health care, and education must be met.

- People's fundamental human dignity, agency, and cultural identities must be honored.

- People and the natural environment must be protected from avoidable harm.

This view includes security for the individual—a major reason why women in the United States enlist in the military—but also involves security at the meso, macro, and global levels.

◆◆◆

Questions for Reflection

As you read and discuss this chapter, think about these questions:

1. What purposes does the military serve in this society?

2. Who joins the military? Why?

3. What types of agency do women have in armed conflict, as combatants or as civilians? What is this based on? How is it complicated by oppression and abuse of women in various forms?

4. What is your idea of security—at all levels of analysis? How do you know when you are secure?

5. What can you do to improve your sense of safety/security in different settings?

6. Based on your reading of this chapter, how well do you think militarism contributes to human security as defined by the UN Development Program?

◆◆◆

Finding Out More on the Web

1. Compare the proportion of the federal budget that is spent on education, social services, health, and foreign aid with that spent on the military. How much does your state contribute to the military budget? How much do you contribute? Use the following Web sites:

   National Priorities Project: **www.nationalpriorities.org**

   New Priorities Network: **http://newprioritiesnetwork.org**

   Stockholm International Peace Research Institute: **www.sipri.org**

   War Resisters League: **www.warresisters.org/federalpiechart**

2. Find out more about the organizations mentioned in this chapter. What are their strategies and activities?

   Additional websites for military women include:

   Military Spouse Resource Center: www.milspouse.org

   Military Woman: www.militarywoman.org

   Service Women's Action Network: www.servicewomen.org

Taking Action

1. Think about the ways you usually resolve conflicts or serious differences of opinion with your family, friends and peers, teachers, and employers. What are the dynamics involved in each case? Do you cave in without expressing your opinion? Do you insist that you are right? Does violence play a part in this process? If so, why? What, if anything, do you want to do differently about resolving conflicts in the future?

2. List all the kinds of service you can imagine, as an alternative to military service, that would improve people's security at micro, meso, macro, and global levels.

3. Keep a personal log for a week of the daily ways that militarism affects your life. Watch what makes you feel proud, what you find moving—are any of these things linked to militarization of our culture?

4. Analyze the representation of armed conflict and war in the news media or popular culture. Compare various U.S. news reports with those from other nations.

5. Create an antimilitary fashion show on campus or in your community (www.genuinesecurity.org/projects/fashionshow.html).

F I F T Y - S I X

Sneak Attack (2002)
The Militarization of U.S. Culture

Cynthia Enloe

Cynthia Enloe is Research Professor in International Development and Women's Studies at Clark University. Her many books include *Nimo's War, Emma's War: Making Feminist Sense of the Iraq War*; *Globalization and Militarization: Feminists Make the Links; The Curious Feminist: Searching for Women in the New Age of Empire*, and *Maneuvers: The International Politics of Militarizing Women's Lives.*

Things start to become militarized when their legitimacy depends on their associations with military goals. When something becomes militarized, it appears to rise in value. Militarization is seductive.

But it is really a process of loss. Even though something seems to gain value by adopting an association with military goals, it actually surrenders control and gives up the claim to its own worthiness.

Militarization is a sneaky sort of transformative process. Sometimes it is only in the pursuit of *de*militarization that we become aware of just how far down the road of complete militarization we've gone. Representative Barbara Lee (D.-Calif.) pulled back the curtain in the aftermath of the September 11 attacks when she cast the lone vote against giving George W. Bush carte blanche to wage war. The loneliness of her vote suggested how far the militarization of Congress—and its voters back home—has advanced. In fact, since September 11, publicly criticizing militarization has been widely viewed as an act of disloyalty.

Whole cultures can be militarized. It is a militarized U.S. culture that has made it easier for Bush to wage war without most Americans finding it dangerous to democracy. Our cultural militarization makes war-waging seem like a comforting reconfirmation of our collective security, identity and pride.

Other sectors of U.S. culture have also been militarized:

- **Education.** School board members accept Jr. ROTC programs for their teenagers, and social studies teachers play it safe by avoiding discussions of past sexual misconduct by U.S. soldiers overseas. Many university scientists pursue lucrative Defense Department weapons research contracts.

- **Soldiers' girlfriends and wives.** They've been persuaded that they are "good citizens" if they keep silent about problems in their relationships with male soldiers for the sake of their fighting effectiveness.

- **Beauty.** [In 2002] the Miss America Pageant organizers selected judges with military credentials, including a former Secretary of the Navy and an Air Force captain.

- **Cars.** The Humvee ranks among the more bovine vehicles to clog U.S. highways, yet civilians think they will be feared and admired if they drive them.

Then there is the conundrum of the flag. People who reject militarization may don a flag pin, unaware that doing so may convince those with a militarized view of the U.S. flag that their bias is universally shared, thus deepening the militarization of culture.

The events of post–September 11 have also shown that many Americans today may be militarizing non-U.S. women's lives. It was only after Bush declared "war on terrorists and those countries that harbor them" that the violation of Afghan women's human rights took center stage. Here's the test of whether Afghan women are being militarized: if their well-being is worthy of our concern only because their lack of well-being justifies the U.S.'s bombing of Afghanistan, then we are militarizing Afghan women—as well as our own compassion. We are thereby complicit in the notion that something has worth only if it allows militaries to achieve their missions.

It's important to remember that militarization has its rewards, such as new-found popular support for measures formerly contested. For example, will many Americans now be persuaded that drilling for oil in the Alaskan wilderness is acceptable because it will be framed in terms of "national security"? Will most U.S. citizens now accept government raids on the Social Security trust fund in the name of paying for the war on terrorism?

Women's rights in the U.S. and Afghanistan are in danger if they become mere by-products of some other cause. Militarization, in all its seductiveness and subtlety, deserves to be bedecked with flags wherever it thrives—fluorescent flags of warning.

FIFTY-SEVEN

◆◆◆

Belonging (2008)

Anuradha Kristina Bhagwati

Anuradha Bhagwati is a former captain in the Marine Corps and the second woman to complete the Marine Corps Martial Arts Program instructor training, earning a black belt in close combat techniques. She is the executive director of Service Women's Action Network, a nonprofit organization that advocates for and provides services to servicewomen, women veterans, and their families.

Unwrapped

The twelve of us are crawling on our hands and feet. I have long since stopped feeling my arms.

Not feeling helps me to keep inching my feet forward. My head down, I see a large pair of black boots in front of me. In seconds, I am hauled into the air like a ragdoll and tossed over a wide set of shoulders. Bristol has removed me from my squad and proceeds to parade me around them.

Straight out of a Marvel comic strip, Bristol is the size of Godzilla. His nose is still crooked from years of fighting. His skin is cracked, his voice smooth and deep but weathered. I am one-third of his mass.

Bristol is a master manipulator. I am wary of letting him in, this beast of a man. The first woman he ran through this course was hazed, several hours a day for six weeks, in the heat of summer. Bristol's minions told him it was dangerous and unfair. Bristol uses pepper spray and pain to reinforce one's desire to succeed. He gave her more of it, but finally let her pass. I am his second experiment. I am too proud for this shit. In what way will he penetrate my pride?

Bristol's war stories are private affairs, but he will reveal information if it serves his purpose. Bristol and I share many things in common, and he will use these details to draw me in and spit me out at will. Bristol lets me know he's a cultured man. He can get away with this because he knows it's true. Why waste his poetry on the likes of thugs? Bristol will wax poetic with me because he'll know I'm listening.

We've circled my squad three times now. For all I know, they have no idea I'm being strutted around them like some giant girl trophy. Bristol is concerned that the third woman in his experiment is failing miserably. It is my job to make sure she gets through. She's not in my squad, so what do I care? I am trying to breathe as his shoulder blade cuts into my gut. Upside down, I see them still inching forward. I can't stand that I'm getting a break now. I have to earn my respect. Goddamnit, put me down.

The last time he wanted to prove I was different, he grabbed my hair, hard. "See, this is what they'll do to you if they really get their hands on you." Never flinch before the master. Why don't you say it, sir, say what they'll really do to me. Or are you scared I might cry and call daddy.

My knee went on strike before I arrived here. Flew out of the socket because I was hauling packs filled with sand and people twice my size for three straight weeks. The damn thing still wobbles around in a pool of jelly and reminds me of my fallibility and pride with every movement I make. It reinforces my inferior size and strength and boils the essence of this fight down to will. At the end of each day, I can barely walk without going numb. I fall asleep on several tablets of Naproxyn and bags of ice melting in between my legs. I have to prove I can make it on my own. Every time someone says to take it easy, I want to stab them.

Two weeks later and these nights have turned into longer days. Bristol appears and disappears, without notice. I see him now in my sleep. I am armed, moving through woods with bayonet. His eyes are everywhere to reinforce my vulnerabilities. The woods have no exit. His voice has no bottom. I feel it will snap into insanity if I ever wake up. I must keep him calm.

Bristol calls me into his office this week to tell me I'm not cutting it. He says something is missing. I'm disappointing. I am lulled into his throat again. Bristol has found it, finally, the son of a bitch. Goddamn spooks and operatives think they're masters of the universe and all of its minds. Bristol's playing dad. On the inside I tell him to go fuck himself. I'd rather take another blown leg than this psychodrama bullshit. I won't let him do this again.

Boredom

We are stripped down to t-shirts and trousers. It's as far as we can go without breaking regulations. Everyone has something to sport: tattoos encircling bulging biceps and forearms, cut-up pecs, and by the end of the afternoon, chafed and sunburned skin.

In this business of making riflemen, the peanut gallery shows no mercy. Everyone uprange is a loser, a boot. When our man hits too low, the berm crackles into hundreds of particles of dirt that tumble down over our heads and cake against our soaked shirts. When he hits too high, someone echoes the sound of a plane crashing. And while the shooters shift windage and measure their breaths in time with the pull of the trigger, we get bored.

Sergeant Mac wants some action. He finds an unsuspecting bug walking along the concrete, among cigarette stubs and Wonder Bread crumbs. It's got long thread-like legs, long enough for Mac to easily snatch him up.

It's a preying mantis. *Mac, what the hell is that?* Mac doesn't hear anyone. Just surveys the curves of the insect's legs, fully admiring its anatomy.

We're changing targets from 200 to 300 yards. Mac is still stroking his trophy. The creature doesn't seem to mind its newfound attention. And then Mac has an idea. With one hand wrapped around the bug, he reaches for the stickers we use to mark up a bullet-ridden target. Black and white one-inch-by-one-inch squares. Mac pulls down the target and places the bug smack in the center of the bulls-eye. Taking six stickers, he tapes the bug down by each leg.

No one notices this. If they do, they're unimpressed.

The bug is squirming on its canvas. Immobilized, it is now detached from the hands that found it. The bug misses Mac.

Mac is proud. Without batting an eye, he proclaims, "If you make it out alive, I'll let you go." Mac is convinced his idea is utterly original. Directly addressing his trainee, and with the utmost confidence, Mac really doesn't need an audience to affirm his self-worth.

Thirty 556 rounds from 300 yards away is a hell of a lot of racket for a bug on a target. But he stands a chance. He's got those fine, spindly legs, which means there's less of him to hit. And our shooter's been having a rough day. Hitting black only gets harder the further back he goes. All bets are on Mac's bug.

On "targets up," Mac raises our target to the sky. There's always a five second pause before the first shooter gets his round off. When it comes crackling through that giant piece of paper, the bug starts flipping out. He's struggling to unpin himself as rounds streak by him on both sides. Ten seconds later, they subside, and we pull the target down. Mac checks for six legs, and before the thing has time to breathe, Mac sends him up again for a second round.

I lose count as I watch Mac and the bug in their game of Russian roulette. Like a proud trainer, Mac is delighted that the bug's made it so far.

And then it happens. *Pow!*

Faces glance over for only a second. Mac brings down the target. He counts five and a half legs. The bug is in hysterics.

"Not bad, little man." Generous in doling out praise when it is due, Mac has become this bug's ringside coach.

As Mac raises the target for the bug's last dance, he bets with pride that the bug won't crack. And then it starts, the rapid fire. A deafening hail of three or four shots on target, then down and up again for more thunder, so many times, up and down, that I wonder if this bug knows which way is heaven and which way is hell.

Finally, a way out. A man of honor, Mac keeps his word and releases the bug from the canvas. Numb again, Mac grabs a cigarette.

Camouflage

Camouflage has mutated over the years. In order to survive, it has adapted with the times. It used to be about wanting to be all that you can be. The mystery of the jungle: its vines and darkness, the unexpected bayonet. Today, it has taken on the character of its hosts. In the personality, it is harder to detect as its own species.

Sexy brown women with six packs and glistening skin sport camouflage bikinis, bandanas, and combat boots in hip hop videos. Teenagers on the street wear cammies baggy and low just to own the uniform. Others wear it ripped and washed too many times to state that they'll never be what the government wants them to be. Camouflage has taken on all the colors of the rainbow. Orange and green or blue and gray camouflage means you can be part of the system and against it. You can recognize its vices and virtues, or maybe you don't have to recognize it at all.

I find a rich white college kid in a coffee shop one evening talking about himself to his father. Recruit Tommy is sporting a light pink shirt with a solid black print of an Apache helicopter, over blue jeans.

Instant analysis of the weaponry: This version of the helicopter has been hand-crafted. Another mutation. No hellfire, no tanks, no napalm. Neither sound, nor fury. It's Apache Lite. But Tommy takes the game of softening the warrior too far. This pink is the one parents choose to make their little girls look like dolls. Real GQ men choose harder versions. Tommy will never survive.

Men in Uniform

It is October in Boston, Massachusetts, and there are 2,000 of us gathered on the Common. It has begun to snow lightly. I am about to never look back again.

Seven white kids in their twenties are holding signs that say "Support the Troops" and "Hippies Smell." I recognize these counter-protesters from an anti-war rally on campus. I approached them intent to understand why they were there. My favorite patriot told me she was there because she "loved America." I told her to sign up. Today she and her friends are barricaded by a stretch of riot police. She's being lectured by some of the older peace veterans, their fingers pointing through shields and helmets to drive home the point. Her red, white and blue balloons are no match for their words.

I find a couple of guys in camouflage jackets, and they take me to see Jose. He is standing by a small table with a picture of a tank in the desert. He's blowing air into his hands and slowly swaying from side to side. He is underdressed and out of camouflage.

Jose is 31 and speaks like an older man who knows the bottom of things. He reminds me of the good ones I used to know, but there is no instinct to impress left in him. Jose tells me that somewhere between meditation and education he determined he didn't want to kill anyone. Jose still worries about his buddies, but he will refuse to participate. Jose is a conscientious objector.

I'm listening to a series of activists from around the globe decry the administration's war. They are a haze of brown—Filipino, Haitian, Colombian, Liberian. The United States has screwed them all. None of them reach me till the thirty-something black man gets up to perform his verse. It is eerie to recall desert duty in this bitter cold. He's a Gulf War infantryman, who reenacts his fixation to kill Saddam in rhythmic repetition, like a prayer and a promise, like cadence. I feel the tingle again, the reminder that this man and I are linked by virtue of our understanding the permanent influence of the institution on our psyche. This performance art goes straight to the heart of our experience. I wonder if anyone else knows.

He is followed by families of the war dead. The Puerto Rican father who killed the Marine messenger and tried to burn himself alive after being told his son had died overseas, the sister who watched her brother tormented by memories of combat finally kill himself, and Cindy Sheehan, the mother I'd heard about who made everyone believe accountability counted for something.

We march through Boston, somewhere towards the end of the pack of socialists and anarchists and peaceniks and pissed-offniks.

Watching Jose I remember why that pull into proud immersion still lays there, deep in my gut. God, I miss it so. This Staff Sergeant I could have used. Even-tempered and in full control, seeing the whole field as he addresses each member of his society as if they were the one. Resting his hand on the shoulders of those who fought before, Jose invites the Vietnam generation to walk side by side with ours.

We pass a group of seven skinheads dressed mostly in black, protesting the rally with signs that say "AIDS cures Fags" and "Commies are Scum." All the vets start laughing, which jars the skinheads. Andy almost starts talking to the one with the pointy beard, but we tug him back. I feel the pull again to watch and protect. No one will touch these boys, or over my dead body.

Up ahead on our right we see the Park Street Armed Forces Recruiting Station. Outside the building are three Marine recruiters dressed in camouflage. GI Joe and his minority sidekicks: one white man, one black man, and one Latina—a picture of diversity for urban youth. I am reminded that Marines once took pride in not being allowed to wear camouflage utilities in the civilian world. Only the nasty Army could walk around off base in their utilities, as if they were no different than civilians. Regulations changed a few months ago, when the Commandant realized he'd have to switch tactics to get the teenagers to sign up for war. No more bling-bling and polished belt buckles for these Marines. It would be all about combat. Urban combat.

As we pass the station, no one speaks. There is a gulf between us and them as we observe one another watching. A few steps beyond, the conversation starts up again, but not about the recruiters. In the world of "been there, done that, so shut the fuck up," I wonder if these three give more thought to us than we do to them.

It begins to snow now, hard, and true to spirit, we get prouder. I waltz around gleefully documenting the throngs on the streets, the cops in riot gear and the endless parade of people too pissed off to be quiet ever again. When the band passes a riot squad in front of Macy's, we witness a cop on the sidewalk staring into the crowd.

Firmly nodding his head he says, "Goddamn right, bring the troops home."

♦♦♦

FIFTY-EIGHT

Empire On Trial:
The Subic Rape Case and the Struggle For
Philippine Women's Liberation (2011)

Anne E. Lacsamana

Anne E. Lacsamana is associate professor of Women's Studies at Hamilton College. Her publications include *Revolutionizing Feminism: The Philippine Women's Movement in the Age of Terror* (2011), *Women and Globalization* (co-editor, 2004), and articles in *Nature, Society and Thought, Socialist Review, Critical Asian Studies, and Amerasia*.

It wasn't easy for me to file a complaint against my rapists. And neither was the (legal) system kind to me after I decided to pursue the case. Instead of taking my side in the fight, our government took steps to make my situation much harder. I have not received a single message of support from our woman President, while the secretary of justice has even repeatedly defended my rapists.

—*Nicole, November 1, 2006*

My conscience continues to bother me realizing that I may have in fact been so friendly and intimate with Daniel Smith at the Neptune Club that he was led to believe that I was amenable to having sex or that we simply just got carried away. I would rather risk public outrage than do nothing to help the court in ensuring that justice is served.

—*Nicole, March 8, 2009*

By the time Philippine media outlets were alerted to the March 8, 2009 affidavit signaling that Nicole, the pseudonym of the woman at the center of the Subic rape case, had "recanted" her earlier testimony accusing U.S. Marine Daniel Smith of raping her almost four years earlier, she had already fired her lawyer, Evalyn Ursua, accepted a settlement from the accused, and departed for the United States where she planned to live

permanently. This was a stunning decision in an epic legal battle that, less than three years earlier, had resulted in the historic conviction of Smith for the rape of Nicole on November 1, 2005, marking the first time a member of the U.S. military had ever been tried, convicted, and sentenced for a crime on Philippine soil. For many Filipinos, the landmark "guilty" verdict and the sentencing of Smith to forty years in a Philippine penitentiary delivered by Makati Regional Trial Judge Benjamin Pozon on December 4, 2006 represented not only a victory for Nicole but for a nation that had grown accustomed to seeing its own interests subordinated to those of its former colonial ruler. The occasion, unfortunately, would be short lived: on the evening of December 29, 2006 Smith was secretly transferred from the Makati City Jail to the U.S. Embassy to await his appeal, once more throwing the issue of Philippine sovereignty starkly into question.

In addition to highlighting critical questions concerning violence against women and sexual assault, the Subic rape case has reignited protests over U.S. military intervention in the Philippines, specifically regarding the terms and conditions outlined in the controversial Visiting Forces Agreement (VFA). Seven years after a broad coalition of progressive forces successfully ousted the two major U.S. military installations, Subic Bay Naval Base (Olongapo City) and Clark Air Force Base (Angeles City), former President Joseph Estrada signed the Visiting Forces Agreement into law in 1998, granting the United States military *unlimited* access to twenty-two ports throughout the country to conduct "joint" training exercises with members of the Armed Forces of the Philippines. Deployments of U.S. troops have escalated since the 9/11 attacks and the subsequent declaration of the Philippines as the "second front" in the U.S. led "war on terror" in 2002, with the majority of soldiers being sent to the southern, predominately Muslim region of the country. Though the stated goal of their mission is to provide humanitarian aid to the war-torn area, most believe U.S. military personnel are involved in a "counter-terrorist" operation against the Abu-Sayyaf, an elusive bandit group comprised of roughly 100 members with alleged loose ties to al-Qaeda.

As well as enabling the United States military to re-establish a dominant presence throughout the archipelago, the VFA extends extraordinary privileges and protections to U.S. soldiers, effectively undermining Philippine sovereignty and, by extension, the safety and dignity of its citizens. For example, Article III "Entry and Departure" of the VFA states that members of the U.S. military are "exempt from passport and visa regulations upon entering and departing the Philippines" while Article IV, "Driving and Vehicle Registration," stipulates that Philippine officials will "accept as valid, without test or fee, a driving permit or license issued by the appropriate United States personnel for the operation of military or official vehicles" and that U.S. government vehicles "need not be registered, but shall have appropriate markings." Moreover, Article VII, "Importation and Exportation," excuses U.S. soldiers from paying taxes and duty fees on items purchased during their "temporary stay" in the Philippines. The most flagrant violation of Philippine sovereignty, however, is found under Article V "Criminal Jurisdiction." In the case of crimes committed by members of the U.S. armed forces, this section of the VFA expects that "Philippine authorities will, upon request by the United States, waive their primary right to exercise jurisdiction except in cases of particular importance to the Philippines." If the Philippine government decides not to waive their right, officials have twenty days, after receiving the United States request, to submit their communication to U.S. authorities. Should the Philippines be granted the right to prosecute a U.S. soldier for a criminal offense, Article V requires all legal proceedings to be completed within a one-year period, during which the accused will remain in the custody of the U.S. military. If a soldier is convicted, the United States government has an unspecified amount of time to appeal. In contrast, the complementary agreement governing the treatment of visiting Filipino soldiers to the United States, known as the VFA 2, requires that they be detained in a U.S. jail. Specifically, Article 9 states

that if a Filipino serviceman is accused of committing a crime in the U.S. "confinement imposed by a United States federal or state court upon a Republic of the Philippines personnel shall be served in penal institutions in the United States suitable for the custody level of the prisoners, chosen after consultation between the two governments, once more illustrating the inherent inequities underpinning the military arrangements (Uy and Guinto, 2009).

Long before Nicole brought charges against her accused rapists, the lopsided provisions contained within the VFA raised alarm for Filipino feminists. Days after [President] Ramos signed the treaty, GABRIELA, an umbrella federation of women's groups in the Philippines, argued the VFA, specifically Article V, provided U.S. military personnel with the "diplomatic license to violate our women and children" (GABRIELA Press Release, 1998). Their concerns were not unfounded; incidences of sexual assault perpetrated by U.S. servicemen against Filipino women had become routine around the military bases. During the Marcos dictatorship, for example, a U.S. soldier was allowed to leave the country after it was discovered he was responsible for organizing a prostitution ring in Olongapo involving twelve young girls, otherwise known as the "Olongapo Twelve," infected with a number of sexually transmitted diseases (San Juan, 1998). In another case, a U.S. soldier escaped prosecution for the rape and murder of Rosario Baluyot, a twelve-year-old girl who died after being poisoned by a vibrator that had been broken off and left inside her body. Though gruesome, both of these crimes belong to a much larger pattern of militarized violence, comprising approximately 2,000 reported cases in the post World War II period, that never reached Philippine courts (Rosca, 2007, p. 2). Susan R. McKay reminds us that these patterns of gendered violence are typically manifest indirectly, through macro forces, such as the global economy, or international law, and directly through interpersonal forms of violence, such as assault and rape. However, McKay claims "it is essential that both indirect and direct violence toward women are understood as fundamental phenomena that maintain inequality" (1998, p. 349). This is why, in the shadow of the U.S. military and the VFA, the Subic rape case takes on a special significance when connected to structural and micro forms of violence against women in militarized spaces.

After a night of drinking at the Neptune Club in Subic Freeport, home to the former naval base, a U.S. Marine raped Nicole inside a moving van as three of his friends cheered him on. Afterwards, Nicole was dumped, half-clothed on the side of the road as the van sped off. Court documents later identified the accused as Lance Corporals Daniel Smith, Keith Silkwood, Dominic Duplantis and Staff Sergeant Chad Carpentier. Members of the 31st Marine Expeditionary Force stationed in Okinawa, the four soldiers had just completed *Balikatan* exercises with members of the Philippine military. Adhering to the guidelines of the VFA, a one-year deadline was imposed for the trial, thus placing the prosecution team under enormous pressure to present their case with the necessary evidence. It quickly became clear that Nicole was not simply going to trial against four soldiers, but a military superpower prepared to flex its political and economic muscle to protect its personnel from prosecution.

During the proceedings, Duplantis, Carpentier, and Silkwood maintained their innocence by corroborating Smith's testimony that he and the victim engaged in "consensual sex." Although these three soldiers were eventually acquitted due to lack of evidence, the conviction of Smith rested on DNA evidence and Makati Regional Trial Court Judge Benjamin Pozon's interpretation of Republic Act No. 8353, otherwise known as the Anti-Rape Law of 1997. Testimony from medical experts, bar patrons and police investigators indicated that "Nicole" was too intoxicated to "consent" to sex with Smith. Agreeing with their findings, Pozon delivered the landmark "guilty" verdict, sentencing Smith to 40 years in the Makati City Jail and ordering him to pay "Nicole" P100,000 ($2000). In the lengthy decision Pozon argued the "court is morally convinced that Smith committed the crime charged. He admitted having sex with the complainant whom he knew was intoxicated . . . thus she could not have consented on the bestial acts of the accused" (Torres, 2006). According to the Anti-Rape Law, a rape is committed "when the offended party is deprived of reason or otherwise unconscious" (1997). After the verdict, Smith was escorted directly to the Makati City Jail to begin his sentence, despite appeals from his lawyers to have him remain in U.S. custody.

Outraged over the conviction, the United States threatened to cancel all future joint military exercises if Smith was not transferred back to the U.S. Embassy to appeal the decision. Considering that the Armed Forces of the Philippines "has received the most dramatic increase in foreign military funding from the U.S. since 2001" (Docena, 2006, p. 7) the prospect of losing a critical source of financial support proved too great for the Arroyo administration. Circumventing Pozon's decision, an agreement was signed between Foreign Affairs Secretary Alberto Romulo and U.S. Ambassador to the Philippines Kristie Kenney, enabling Smith's return to the U.S. Embassy after serving only twenty-five days of his sentence. Soon after, the resumption of *Balikatan* operations was announced, and the U.S. Marines issued a public statement promising that its members would commit "no more rape" during their stay in the Philippines (Orejas, 2007).

The diplomatic bullying and behind-the-scenes legal wrangling that U.S. officials used to secure Smith's custody underscore the iniquitous neocolonial relationship between the United States and the Philippines. This is most evident when compared to the way U.S. officials have recently handled other high profile military crimes in the region. For example, in 2007, the U.S. Army publicly apologized to S. Korean officials for the rape of a 67-year-old woman by a U.S. solider, claiming that the "vicious act is an affront to all soldiers" assuring the country that the United States military was "cooperating fully with Korean authorities" (Agence France-Presse, 2007). A similar situation occurred in 2008 after Japanese authorities detained a U.S. Marine for the abduction and alleged rape of a 14-year-old young woman. Although she dropped the charges a few days later, the U.S. Marine Corps conducted its own internal investigation and sentenced the man to four years in prison for "abusive sexual conduct with a Japanese teenager in Okinawa" (Wright, 2008, p. 3). Fearing the incident would endanger the important military alliance between the two countries, U.S. officials, including former Secretary of State Condoleeza Rice, issued formal apologies to Japanese Prime Minister Yasuo Fukuda and Foreign Minister Mashiko Komura (Wright, 2008, p. 2). Reminiscent of the widely publicized 1995 Okinawan rape case, involving the prosecution and sentencing of three U.S. soldiers to seven years in a Japanese penitentiary for the gang rape of a 12-year-old Okinawan school girl, the effort made by U.S. authorities to smooth over diplomatic relations stands in sharp contrast to their handling of the Subic rape case.

Highlighting these recent events, however, is not intended to imply that the United States is, or has always been, cooperative with governments hosting its military installations . . . Similar to Filipinos, S. Koreans and Okinawans have all seen their sovereignty jeopardized by Status of Forces Agreements (SOFA) that govern the behavior of U.S. military personnel during their tours of duty. Typically, SOFAs are negotiated in private, between the U.S. government and the specific country that will be "home" to its military base (Moon, 1997; Enloe, 2000). As a result, the U.S. frequently has invoked the shield of these military agreements to protect its troops from prosecution for crimes such as rape and/or murder. For example, in Okinawa "between 1972 and 1995, U.S. servicemen were implicated in 4,716 crimes, nearly one per day . . . and few indeed have suffered any inconvenience for their crimes" (Magdoff et al, 2002, p. 9). On the rare occasion that a serviceman is actually punished for a crime in the "host" country, it is largely due to organized anti-bases protests, particularly those spearheaded by grassroots women's organizations that draw explicit attention to the gendered and racialized dimensions of military violence.

Cynthia Enloe explains that during the 1970s, after a string of unsolved murders allegedly perpetrated by U.S. soldiers, S. Korean women located in and around the military camptowns began organizing and pressuring the local police and government officials to be more vigilant in tracking down the assailants (2000, p. 92). Similarly, in the aftermath of the 1995 gang rape in Okinawa, Japanese women forged broad coalitions with S. Korean and Filipino feminists to protest U.S. militarization throughout the Asia Pacific region. In the Philippines, the women's movement has a lengthy history of utilizing rallies, vigils, marches, and other forms of public protest to demonstrate their opposition to U.S. military aggression, acknowledging that the presence of U.S. troops is "more than a question of sovereignty [but] is in fact a question of national dignity, class inequalities, sexual politics, and racism" (Santos, 1992, p. 38). Expanding the anti-imperialist nationalist movement's analysis of militarization to include issues of gender and race, the Philippine women's movement makes explicit that national liberation is intimately tied to women's liberation. By directly assailing U.S. militarism, and by extension U.S. imperialism, Filipino women's grassroots activism

underscores the importance and necessity of a "nationalist feminist" perspective in a "Third World" formation. Despite the fact that "nationalism" has been maligned in much of western feminist theory due to its modernist and patriarchal moorings, Filipino feminists, through vigorous debate and dialogue with their male counterparts, have forged a unique and vibrant anti-imperialist women's liberation movement. As Filipino critic Delia Aguilar notes, many Filipino women strongly believe that "freedom from oppression as women can become possible only when the nation is liberated from U.S. domination and when the majority of the people can be released from poverty, illness, malnutrition, and other forms of deprivation rampant in a neocolony" (1998, p. 45). Thus, it makes sense that a focal point for women's organizing would center on the effects of U.S. militarism in the country, symbolic of both the suppression of Philippine sovereignty and the violation of Filipino women's dignity.

Prior to granting formal "independence" on July 4, 1946, the United States signed the Military Bases Agreement, and the Military Assistance Agreement enabling it to maintain two major military installations in the Philippines: Clark Air Force Base and Subic Naval Base along with 23 smaller facilities. Often praised by both U.S. and Philippine governments for providing an economic boost to the country, the military facilities became notorious for generating prostitution in their respective communities. According to the feminist NGO WEDPRO (Women's Education Development Productivity and Research Organization), 70 percent of women working around the bases "were in prostitution well before they turned 18" with 50 percent reporting they had "never worked in similar situations" prior to working in the "entertainment" or "red light" districts (Santos, Hoffman, and Bulawan, 1998, p. 3). The sheer magnitude of prostitution during this period resulted in its "normalization" whereby the sexual assault and exploitation of women became a routine, acceptable part of life in the cities of Angeles and Olongapo (Santos, Hoffman, and Bulawan, 1998, p. 3). Not surprisingly, the presence of the bases further inculcated a deep sense of racial and cultural inferiority among many Filipinos, particularly women, who often found themselves attempting to reconcile contradictory processes. . . . Indeed, the desire to improve one's status by marrying a white American man and having light-skinned, blue-eyed children became a dream for many women working as prostitutes, despite being surrounded by U.S. soldiers proudly wearing t-shirts depicting Filipinas as "Little Brown Fucking Machines Powered By Rice." More often than not, however, most women never achieved these dreams, left behind to care for the thousands of Amerasian children abandoned by servicemen once their stay in the Philippines had expired. According to feminist scholars Gwyn Kirk and Margo Okazawa-Rey, the situation for these children had become so acute that a lawsuit was filed in the United States in 1993 on their behalf, only to have it not be "considered in any serious way" by U.S. government officials (1998, p. 312).

Throughout the 1980s, various sectors of the Philippine women's movement, including GABRIELA, BUKLOD Center, Coalition Against Trafficking in Women Asia-Pacific (CATWAP), and WEDPRO, mobilized to respond to the crisis of militarized prostitution by creating women's shelters, providing health and counseling services, and offering educational seminars on HIV/AIDS, among other practical initiatives (Santos, Hoffman, and Bulawan, 1998; Kirk and Okazawa-Rey, 1998). Together, in conjunction with the broader anti-imperialist nationalist movement, Filipino feminists played an important role in convincing members of the Philippine Senate to reject the lease renewal on the bases in 1991. Preferring the term "prostituted" women to denote the larger socio-economic factors responsible for forcing many women into the industry, Filipino feminist activists have been vocal in their efforts to end the traffic in women and children.

This anti-trafficking position has, in certain feminist theoretical circles, provoked consternation among those who claim such efforts do more harm than good to the women involved. For example, in her analysis of Korean NGOs involved in anti-trafficking campaigns, Na Young Lee (2006) acknowledges the significant accomplishments various groups have achieved in bringing greater attention to issues of militarism and prostitution. However, she argues that they "cannot allow any other perspectives besides the anti-sex work feminist position which sees prostitution as a form of sexual exploitation or patriarchal crimes" (p. 465). By using terms such as "prostituted" women instead of "sex workers," Lee maintains that the diversity and complexity of women's individual lives become obscured when there is an "official frame or master narrative informing a particular analysis" (2006, p. 466). In many ways, Lee's work echoes that of Anne-Marie Hilsdon (1995) who argued that "prostitution at the former U.S. bases was a narrative of both exploitation and agency" since it allowed greater economic and sexual independence for Filipino women compared to those living in more rural areas (p. 106). The social costs of such independence, however, are rarely discussed in analytical formulations dedicated to recuperating women's "agency" at the expense of other pressing considerations. Indeed, this specific theoretical stance has grown in popularity over the recent years, as feminists have become increasingly more interested in examining women's subjectivity within the libidinal rather than the political economy.

. . .

[T]he anti-imperialist feminist perspective informing grassroots Filipino women's activism against U.S. militarism can serve as a necessary antidote to the recent spate of postmodern-inspired feminist theoretical production. By organizing mass campaigns against militarized sexual violence, the Philippine women's movement has helped raise the profile of a historically overlooked by-product of U.S.-Philippine relations, arguably paving the way for the historic conviction of Daniel Smith in 2005.

United under the slogan "Justice For Nicole, Justice For Our Nation," members of GABRIELA, Task Force Subic Rape (TFSR), and the Nicole Information Bureau worked collectively throughout the court proceedings to monitor the trial, provide support to Nicole and her family, and help educate the general public about the relationship of the case to the larger issue of Philippine sovereignty. With over 200 member organizations GABRIELA is the largest alliance of women's groups in the country. Founded in 1984, it has played a critical role during its history in advocating on behalf of women who have suffered under unjust military agreements. In the aftermath of the Subic rape, women affiliated with GABRIELA continued to pressure the Arroyo administration to nullify the VFA. . . . Other groups, such as Task Force Subic Rape, a women-led coalition of 17 member organizations working outside the purview of GABRIELA, was created to "support a fair trial for Nicole's case and to bring justice not only to Nicole, but also to the women and children violated by the U.S.-led wars of aggression all over the world" (2006, p.8). Members drafted and distributed a primer on the Anti-Rape Law of 1997 and the VFA and encouraged citizens to "always anchor the rape case on the issue of the legitimacy of the VFA and how this agreement violates the sovereignty of the Philippines as a duly recognized independent state" (2006, p. 7). Similarly, the Nicole Defense Campaign and its media relations arm, the Nicole Information Bureau, developed online resources to provide the public inside and outside the Philippines with accurate information concerning the trial. For example, a paper outlining the specific connections between the Subic rape case and the VFA is contained on their website, among various other documents. Specifically, it explains that while the VFA is a variation of the aforementioned Status of Forces Agreements that the United States has in place with other countries hosting its military installations, it is significantly different because it was negotiated in the absence of bases, therefore placing the *entire* country under the auspices of its terms and regulations (www.subicrapecase.wordpress.com). Since this formation essentially gives the U.S. military unchecked power over the whole territory of the Philippines, the vigorous, organized response of a diverse array of Filipino feminists is evidence of the tremendous importance placed on the outcome of the Subic rape case.

Given this context many of Nicole's supporters were shocked and saddened when her second affidavit emerged. Still, they urged the public not to blame Nicole for her decision, acknowledging the tremendous pressure and scrutiny she and her family had faced since 2005. Speaking on behalf of GABRIELA, Liza Maza characterized Nicole's sudden change of heart as "unfortunate," noting that it made her a "victim of three aspects: rape, the government, and the VFA" (Maragay, 2009). In a statement to the press, Nicole's former lawyer Evalyn Ursua explained that the family had grown "tired of the case" and that Nicole left the country because "there was no justice" in the Philippines (Jiminez-David, 2008). Women's groups were also quick to counter media reports that Nicole had "recanted," arguing that she never retracted her original claim that she was raped by Smith. On their website, members of Task Force Subic Rape reminded readers that there were "three other conditions for rape apart from sexual

coercion" that included the victim being "drugged or intoxicated." Arguing that her "affidavit was not a recantation," TSFR reiterated Pozon's decision that Nicole was too intoxicated to give consent to Smith (www.subicrapecase.wordpress.com). Moreover, feminist organizations stressed the document was completely irrelevant since the Anti-Rape Law of 1997 declared rape to be a *public*, rather than a private, crime. This meant that the trial, having already been determined, was no longer between Nicole and Smith, but rather the Republic of the Philippines and Smith. Still, many were left puzzled by both the timing of her decision and the surreptitious manner in which her affidavit was executed. For example, just a month earlier, on February 11, 2009, the Philippine Supreme Court ruled that Smith be returned immediately to Philippine custody. . . . Though the Supreme Court did not declare the VFA illegal, as many had hoped, their judgment remanding Smith to Philippine custody was, in light of the circumstances, a momentary victory for Nicole and her legal team.

Despite the ruling, however, the United States refused to hand Smith over to Philippine authorities. This blatant rejection of Philippine law only strengthened calls, among progressive nationalist organizations, to abrogate the VFA. By early March, with Smith continuing to languish in U.S. custody, newly elected U.S. President Obama made a "surprise" phone call to President Arroyo assuring her of his continued support for the VFA. Two days later, Nicole signed her "recantation" in the office of the law firm representing Smith and left for the United States. In response to suggestions that Nicole might have been pressured or bribed by U.S. officials to change her previous testimony, Nicole's mother asked the public to respect her decision, noting that the family had "fought long enough. We just want peace of mind, to live quietly" (Quismundo and Alipala, 2009, p. 2). She went on to explain that the protracted legal battle had taken a toll on her daughter, stating, "every time we went out and people recognized us, my daughter almost melted with shame. We couldn't have peace" (Quismundo and Alipala, 2009, p. 2). . . . Though it is futile to speculate what planted the seeds of doubt in Nicole's mind, the historic circumstances surrounding her trial must be tied forever to the collective memory of the thousands of Filipinas who have preceded her down the difficult and daunting task of seeking justice and accountability from the imperial hegemon.

Notwithstanding the presence of a well-organized women's movement, the Subic rape case exposed contradictions regarding traditional notions of Philippine womanhood and femininity, with some women rallying behind Smith while publicly chastising Nicole for her "reckless" behavior. In letters written to the *Philippine Daily Inquirer,* for example, some Filipinas expressed their willingness to join a "club or something in support of Smith" as others questioned Nicole's motives by asking "[w]hat kind of woman will get herself drunk in a bar, flirt with soldiers, go out with them, and expect not to get molested?" (Tulfo, 2006, p. 1–2). The release of two pornographic DVD's titled *Olongapo Scandal* and *Nicole,* both based on the events of November 1, 2005, only added to the public humiliation Nicole endured. Although it has been common in rape cases to "blame the victim," it is important to locate these responses to Nicole within the history of Spanish and U.S. colonialism.

One of the most enduring legacies of 350 years of Spanish colonial rule was the introduction of Catholicism that radically altered existing ideologies concerning gender and sexuality. Discussing this period, Elizabeth Eviota notes that "religion was to have different consequences for women and men" thus producing a sexual double-standard that circumscribed Filipino women's sexuality, relegating her to the domestic sphere (1992, p. 39). According to the teachings of the Catholic Church, "[d]aughters should be taught to fear God, to take care of their virginity and to be modest so as not to be taken advantage of by men. Women should be taught to keep house and to love the home because according to the Bible, the fortunes of the household lay on their shoulders" (Eviota, 1992, p. 60). Spanish colonialists justified the regulation of Filipino women's sexual behavior through religious doctrine because they felt most were "'licentious' and 'immoral' [who] did not know the meaning of 'love'" (Eviota, 1992, p.41). . . . By describing Filipino women as "erotically driven, sensually charged, and sexually precocious" the Spanish were able to further their colonial project through the religious disciplining of Filipino women's sexuality (Stoler 1995, p.115; Eviota 1992, p. 39). Women who were to step outside the traditional notions of respectable Philippine femininity were subject to censure and rebuke. Several centuries later, the Catholic Church continues to wield enormous influence in the social and political affairs of the Philippines. With over 90% of the population Catholic, divorce remains illegal in the country, abortion is prohibited as well as contraception, thereby limiting the availability of condoms and other methods of family planning to Filipino citizens. In this context, it is not difficult to see why Nicole and the Subic rape case stirred so many differing emotions.

Indeed, these cultural ideals governing Philippine womanhood manifested themselves a little more than a month after Nicole left the country, when the Philippine Court of Appeals (CA) acquitted Lance Corporal Daniel Smith. In their decision, the justices, comprised of three women, ruled that Smith and Nicole shared a "spontaneous, unplanned romantic episode" and were simply "carried away by their passions" (Torres, 2009). The judgment also indicted Nicole for her "audacity" to flirt with Smith with "reckless abandon," claiming that when their brief "romance" ended, Nicole became irritated and charged Smith with rape. Despite the mounds of medical testimony presented at the original trial indicating force had been used, the CA claimed they could find "no evidence" that this was the case. Within hours of his acquittal, Smith left the country for a "secret" location to be reunited with his family, ending a nearly three year legal battle that, if the conviction was upheld, would have been a momentous victory for Filipino women and Philippine sovereignty. Smith's acquittal has only strengthened the resolve of the Philippine women's movement, however, as mass protests demanding the abolition of the VFA continue at the time of this writing.

NOTE

The research and writing of this essay was generously supported by an American Association of University Women (AAUW) Post Doctoral Fellowship.

REFERENCES

Agence France-Presse. (2007). US military apologizes for South Korean rape case. *Philippine Daily Inquirer,* January 15.

Docena, Herbert. (2006). On the job training: Are U.S. soldiers engaged in actual combat in the Philippines? *Asia Times,* March 9.

Enloe, Cynthia. (2000). *Maneuvers: The international politics of militarizing women's lives.* Berkeley: University of California Press.

Eviota, Elizabeth. (1992). *The political economy of gender: Women and the sexual division of labour in the Philippines.* 1992. London: Zed Books.

GABRIELA. (1998). GABRIELA says no to VFA. GABRIELA press release. http://members.tripod.com/~gabriela_p/6-pressreles/980213_vfa.html (accessed April 30, 2007).

Hilsdon, Anne-Marie. (1995). *Madonnas and martyrs: Militarism and violence in the Philippines.* Quezon City: Ateneo de Manila University Press.

Jimenez-David, Rina. (2009). At Large: Confused about 'Nicole.' *Philippine Daily Inquirer,* March 20.

Kirk, Gwyn and Margo Okazawa-Rey. (1998). Making connections: Building an East Asia-U.S. women's network against U.S. militarism. In Lois Ann Lorentzen and Jennifer Turpin (Eds.), *The women and war reader* (pp. 308-322). New York: New York University Press.

Lee, Na Young. 2006. Gendered nationalism and otherization: transnational prostitutes in South Korea. *Inter-Asia Cultural Studies,* 7.

Magdoff, Harry, John Bellamy Foster, Robert W. McChesney, Paul Sweezy. (2002). U.S. military bases and empire. *Monthly Review,* March.

McKay, Susan. (1998). The psychology of societal reconstruction and peace: a gendered perspective. In Lois Ann Lorentzen and Jennifer Turpin (Eds.), *The women and war reader* (pp. 348-362). New York: New York University Press.

Moon, Katharine. (1997). *Sex among allies: Military prostitution in U.S.-Korea relations.* New York: Columbia University Press.

Orejas, Tonette. (2007). US marines promise no more rape in Luzon. *Philippine Daily Inquirer,* October 21.

Quismundo,Tarra and Julie Alipala. (2009). "Not Nicole's style, that's defense line." *Philippine Daily Inquirer,* March 19.

Rosca, Ninotchka. (2007). Rape case exposes U.S. domination of Philippine government. *Socialism and Liberation,* http://socialismandliberation.org/mag/index (accessed March 24, 2009).

San Juan, E. (1998). *Filipina insurgency.* Quezon City: Giraffe Books.

Santos, Aida, Cecilia T. Hofmann, and Alma Bulawan. (1998). Prostitution and the bases: a continuing saga of exploitation. *Coalition Against Trafficking in Women-Asia Pacific* (Speeches/Papers), May.

Santos, Aida. (1992). Gathering the dust: The bases issue in the Philippines. In Saundra Pollock Sturdevant and Brenda Stoltfzus (Eds.), *Let the good times roll: Prostitution and the U.S. military in Asia* (pp. 32–44). New York: The New Press.

Stoler, Ann Laura. (1995). *Race and the education of desire: Foucault's history of sexuality and the colonial order of things.* Durham: Duke University Press.

Task Force Subic Rape. (2006). Briefing paper: Rape and the VFA. 1–8. Manila: Philippines.

Torres, Tetch. (2006). U.S. Marine guilty of raping Filipina, 3 others acquitted. *Philippine Daily Inquirer,* December 4.

Torres, Tetch. (2009). U.S. Marine in Subic rape case acquitted. *Philippine Daily Inquirer,* April 23.

Tulfo, Ramon. (2006). Comments on "Nicole" case. *Philippine Daily Inquirer,* December 21.

Uy, Veronica and Joel Guinto. 2009. Palace: 'VFA 2' not a secret. *Philippine Daily Inquirer,* February 20.

Wright, Ann. 2008. Rape hobbles Bush administration policies. *Truthout,* May 26.

FIFTY-NINE

◆◆◆

A Bird with One Wing (2009)

Malalai Joya

Internationally respected women's rights activist **Malalai Joya** grew up in refugee camps in Iran and Pakistan. She returned to Afghanistan under the Taliban regime to teach girls in secret home-based classes. She was the youngest member elected to the Afghan parliament but was suspended in 2007 on the grounds that she had insulted fellow representatives during a television interview. She is a vocal critic of the Afghan government and the presence of US-NATO forces in Afghanistan. *Time* magazine named her one of the "Top 100 Most Influential People of 2010." Her memoir, *A Woman Among Warlords* (2009), is her first book (www.malalaijoya.com).

In June 2008, Laura Bush made her third and last visit to Afghanistan as first lady of the United States. As usual, her trip was brief and heavily guarded, and served mainly to expose her complete ignorance of the reality of life in Afghanistan.

She defended Hamid Karzai in her statements to the American media, insisting that he was a "popular" president. "It's really not that fair to blame him for a lot of the things that may or may not be his fault," she said. "He inherited, just by becoming president, a country that's been totally devastated."

During her nine-hour stopover, Mrs. Bush was flown by helicopter to visit some of that devastation in the town of Bamiyan, where the Taliban had famously demolished two enormous, ancient statues of Buddha because they were "un-Islamic."

"It's more important than ever for the international community to continue to support Afghanistan, certainly for the U.S. to continue to support Afghanistan," Mrs. Bush said as she surveyed the ruins. . . .

. . . Like so many other Western dignitaries, the first lady did not recognize that the devastation in our country was not caused by the Taliban alone—but by years of foreign interference. The Taliban is not the problem, it is a symptom of the disease of corruption, violence, and feudalism that has plagued my country since the United States, Pakistan, and Iran started funneling arms and money to fundamentalist terrorist groups and warlords. Instead of ridding Afghanistan of these criminals, Karzai has embraced them. The people hate the warlords, and so they have come to hate Karzai. He says he champions the rights of Afghan women—which was supposedly one of Laura Bush's main causes—but he supported as chief justice of the Supreme Court a hard-line fundamentalist who revived some of the Taliban's oppressive policies against women.

And for this reason, Afghanistan remains like a bird with one wing—women—clipped. As long as the subjugation of women persists, our society will not be able to take off and move forward. Not only are women still denied their rights in Afghanistan, but also, in a cruel irony, the cause of women has been used to justify and perpetuate a brutal occupation of my country.

A few weeks after the U.S. invasion in 2001, Laura Bush made an official White House radio address: "I hope Americans will join our family in working to ensure that dignity and opportunity will be secured for all the women and children of Afghanistan." The first lady's words of concern for Afghan women showed much more nuance and understanding than the crude rhetoric of her husband. Yet her sentiments have proved meaningless, more dust in the eyes of the world, considering the brutal policy they have helped justify. Just as the Bush administration's lies about "weapons of mass destruction" were used to rationalize its invasion and occupation of Iraq, the cause of "liberating women" was added to the list of reasons the United States invaded and remains in Afghanistan.

. . .

Western journalists rarely challenge the fables that are spun for them. Because of the laziness and complicity within the mainstream media, the United States and its allies have been able to perpetuate the myth that Afghanistan has always been an ungovernable state, and that the oppression of women is embedded in Afghan culture. The brutality of the Taliban, the myth goes, was only an extreme expression of an old problem. And so only foreign occupation can save Afghanistan from itself.

I want you to know that this is a lie. We are not a helpless country. We have been able to manage our own affairs, and women's rights have not always been in such a terrible state. It is the policies of the big powers intervening and backing the most extreme elements in Afghanistan that have rolled back the rights of women.

Afghanistan's first modern ruler, King Amanullah Khan, who won independence from the British in 1919, was a freedom-loving and democratic leader. He believed that Pashtuns, Tajiks, Hindus, Uzbeks, Hazaras, and people from other different tribes are simply Afghan. He strengthened national unity so that there was no racial, linguistic, or religious discrimination. He also advanced a modern constitution that incorporated equal rights and individual freedoms.

His wife, Queen Soraya, played a vital role in regard to his policy toward women. She made trips to European countries on behalf of women without wearing a scarf and in modern clothes. In 1920, she gave a public speech—a first for an Afghan queen—describing the benefits of women's rights. After that, many women volunteered to help her and established a number of organizations for the benefit of women.

The nation's first women's magazine, *Irshadul Naswan*, was published on March 17, 1921. Women workers were accepted by factories. The first women's hospital was established in Kabul, and for the first time women served as representatives in the Loya Jirga, in 1928.[1] In that Jirga, Amanullah Khan suggested abolishing polygamy and forced marriage. The legal age for marriage was established at eighteen. The king encouraged the building of roads, factories, and rail lines. He built libraries, cinemas, and theaters. Wageless labor, forced labor, and slavery were abolished.

During the time of Amanullah Khan, education became compulsory for every Afghan. The first girls' school was established in 1924. A group of girls was sent to Turkey for higher education, without having to wear the hijab, or Islamic covering, or be accompanied by a male relative, or mahram. Later, hundreds of girls went to school in foreign countries such as Germany, Russia, and France.

Unfortunately, some of the king's reform measures went too far, too fast. For example, he announced that no Afghan man could go out without a modern-style hat and trousers, and if they failed to do so they were fined. It was the same for women who went out wearing a burqa. He also changed the religious holiday from Friday to Sunday. The fundamentalists were in an uproar, and Amanullah Khan's enemies used this to their advantage.

The British were still angry at the loss of their colony and afraid of having a modern, independent country next to India, which was still under its control. Thus they maintained a network of their own puppets in Afghanistan among reactionary religious scholars and rival aristocrats. Through these people, the British quietly sowed rebellion against Amanullah Khan and his reforms. Since a majority of the Afghans were uneducated and deeply influenced by religious beliefs, the British were successful and the king lost the support of the people. He went into exile and, in 1929, was forced to give up the throne.

. . .

Amanullah Khan's overthrow is considered a disaster in the history of Afghanistan. Immediately after he was exiled, a strongman named Habibullah Kalakani became emir. He was a dark-minded and ignorant man backed by the British. His first official act was to close all the schools. Only months later,

Kalakani's forces were overcome by Mohammad Nadir Shah, a Pashtun aristocrat, who invaded from India with British help. Nadir Shah lured Kalakani to a peace conference and then had him executed. The brutal Nadir Shah immediately repealed most of Amanullah's reforms—he even brought back the women who had been sent to Turkey for higher education and made them stay at home. Nadir Shah was assassinated in 1933, and was succeeded by his son, Zahir Shah, who was only nineteen at his coronation.

King Zahir served as a passive figurehead for most of his rule. His paternal uncles, who were the real power holders, presided over a reign of terror for much of the next three decades. Non-Pashtun ethnic groups were particularly oppressed during this time. But constitutionalists continued to struggle against the repressive monarchy, and they eventually forced the government to accept some reforms in order to keep the people from open rebellion. By the middle of the twentieth century, King Zahir started to assert his authority and began experimenting with a limited democracy, if only to satisfy the people and put an end to mass movements. Zahir freed more than five hundred political prisoners and brought in other reforms. University students were allowed to form unions, and political parties that had been banned in previous years were given some freedom to regroup. But the government wouldn't tolerate too much opposition, and some were rounded up, jailed, and killed.

During these turbulent years, however, women's rights were gradually restored.

By the 1950s, women in Afghanistan were encouraged to work in many professions. By the end of the decade they were staging demonstrations and asking for their rights. The government even passed laws to ban the wearing of the burqa and to legalize the wearing of skirts and short sleeves. Here, for example, is how the *New York Times* reported on the condition of Afghan women half a century ago, on November 8, 1959: "Afghanistan's Women Lift the Veil" read the headline. "A new world of freedom, spiritual as well as sartorial, has been opened to the women of this Moslem nation after centuries of seclusion."

The freedoms achieved by women were not the result of some invasion from the West, but from the development of our own society, our own political process, and the struggle of democratic-minded forces of Afghanistan who risked death for their beliefs.

...

Although Zahir Shah tried to establish a constitutional monarchy, the people lost faith in him and took to the streets in demonstrations. In 1973, while King Zahir was out of the country for medical treatment, he was overthrown by his pro-Soviet cousin, Daud Khan. Afghanistan's "constitutional era" was over, replaced by a nominal republic, and, in 1979, Soviet invaders.

It was the women of Afghanistan who offered the first show of resistance against the Soviet puppet regime by staging a demonstration in Kabul. The police reacted with violence, and women such as Nahid Sahid and Wajeha were killed on the spot. It was during this era that RAWA—the Revolutionary Association of the Women of Afghanistan—was established by Meena and other women intellectuals in Kabul.

As recently as the 1970s, the extremists who now have so much power to implement anti-women policies—with their misinterpretations of Islam to justify them—were marginal figures. The notorious warlord Gulbuddin Hekmatyar, for example, was a totally discredited force in those days, known for having led attacks on unveiled women at the University of Kabul that included burning these women with acid. It was the United States, Pakistan, and Iran's arming of these forces during the 1980s—Hekmatyar was one of their favorites during this period—that helped unleash the religious fascism that has plagued Afghanistan for the past three decades.

It is hard to fathom the pivotal role the United States played in nourishing a violent, fundamentalist mentality in generations of young Afghans. But starting in the 1980s, the U.S. government spent more than $50 million to publish textbooks through the University of Nebraska that promoted a fanatic, militaristic agenda. In a March 2002 article, the *Washington Post* called it the "Jihad Schoolbook Scandal," describing the books as "filled with talk of jihad" and warlike images. It taught children to count using "illustrations of tanks, missiles and landmines." The books were shipped into Soviet-occupied Afghanistan to fuel a jihad against the Soviets, but, according to the *Post,* they made up the core curriculum in the Afghan school system

long after the Soviets had been defeated. "Even the Taliban used the American-produced books, though the radical movement scratched out human faces in keeping with its strict fundamentalist code." And after the Taliban was gone, USAID continued to send the textbooks into Afghanistan, where fundamentalists still use them to teach a violent brand of Islam.

These fundamentalist groups gained prominence and support, as I have said, partly because of the aggressive and criminal invasion of our country by a great power that claimed to be "bringing women's rights" to Afghanistan. All sectors of Afghan society fought against the Soviet invasion and the people's resistance was honorable and legitimate. Unfortunately, some of the mujahideen factions—the criminal mujahideen that I speak of—then turned their weapons and their violence against the Afghan people, especially women. Some of these groups even burned down girls' schools, much as the Taliban has done in more recent years.

It is important to remember that when the Taliban first swept into power in 1996, many Afghans, at first, welcomed this development because at least it put an end to the vicious killings that had taken up to eighty thousand lives in Kabul alone during the civil war of 1992 to 1996. Even the then so-called president, Burhanuddin Rabbani, called the Taliban "angels of peace," and Ahmad Shah Massoud, then the defense minister, went to meet the Taliban leaders and told them that they shared the same way of thinking.

...

The Taliban's denial of women's rights, including enforcing the use of the burqa, is common knowledge. These facts were well publicized in the United States, especially after 9/11 and in the run-up to the war that followed. . . . Because the Taliban regime had been so repressive, many of our people—even those who detest the very idea of foreign troops on Afghan soil—were hopeful that this incursion represented a chance for democracy. They hoped the United States had learned from its past mistakes. Some took Laura Bush at her word when she said the purpose of the American invasion was to restore women's rights. . . .

It is important to remember that the Taliban has never been the only force in Afghanistan that represses women. A number of the laws against women were actually first implemented during the civil war, and then maintained and enforced by the Taliban. For instance, the Ministry for the Promotion of Virtue and Prevention of Vice, which would become infamous under the Taliban, was actually set up in the civil war era. Not only are many of these laws still on the books, but what's more, many of the warlords that introduced these restrictions are still in power in the current NATO-backed government.

The crimes of the warlords during the 1990s are well documented in the book *Bleeding Afghanistan,* by Sonali Kolhatkar and James Ingalls, who are great supporters of mine and who work to raise money for Afghan women in the United States. In their book, they point out the U.S. government's lack of concern for the impact of their policy of encouraging extremists: "If Afghanistan ever deserved the label 'failed state,' it was most appropriate in the years 1992–1996, when U.S. eyes were averted while U.S. weapons were eliminating the buildings, institutions, and people required for the survival of the State of Afghanistan." If today Afghanistan is failing as a state it is because the warlords who had failed our country before were once again put in power, even though they had well earned the hatred of our people.

Those same warlords not only control Parliament and many of Karzai's cabinet posts, they also run the judiciary system. At the Loya Jirga in 2003, for instance, Abdul Sayyaf and other warlords used their influence to put a fundamentalist named Fazl Hadi Shinwari into the key position of chief justice of the Supreme Court, with Abdul Malik Kamawi as his deputy. In fact, all nine justices of the Supreme Court are dark-minded mullahs. . . .

. . . Shin-wari, Sayyaf, and other fundamentalists insisted at the Loya Jirga that the new constitution name the country the Islamic Republic of Afghanistan, and they have misused Islam through the courts to deny women's and human rights.

. . .

It does not seem that the legislature will deliver any higher degree of justice than the courts. In September 2008, the Wolesi Jirga prepared a draft law that, when approved, will ban obscene movies, female dances, and high-volume music at parties.[2] According to the proposed law, those behind professional dancing events and those coordinating such programs will face up to a year in jail. It will also be illegal for hotels to allow males and females from different families to get together. Organizers of sports events involving men and women participants will also be punished. The new bill forbids wearing shorts and skintight outfits. It also proposes different penalties for the practices that lead to a delay in marriage, while allowing girls to be given away to settle disputes and condoning forced marriages.

Another myth about Afghanistan is that women and girls are all free to go to school. It is true that in Kabul and some other cities, some girls are now able to go to school, and that certain jobs are available to women, but this is the situation of a fortunate minority. The conditions of schools outside Kabul are deplorable and in many remote areas there are neither teachers nor any buildings available to house these so-called schools. In many remote villages, girls learn their lessons while sitting in the dirt.

When Laura Bush made her last visit to Afghanistan she boasted that six million children are enrolled in school, a figure that is always trumpeted as an Afghan success story. But according to the United Nations, more than five million children are still not getting any education at all. In early December 2008, an Afghanistan Independent Human Rights Commission (AIHRC) survey showed that only 5 percent of girls and 11 percent of boys could pursue their education all the way to the twelfth grade.

According to the Ministry of Labor, Social Affairs, Martyrs, and Disabled, more than six million children in the country face problems such as smuggling, abduction, child labor, and lack of education. Due to severe poverty, many children have to leave school to work at hard labor to help their parents make a living. In a study released by AIHRC, 60 percent of families surveyed stated that almost half their children were involved in some kind of labor.

. . .

Going to school is becoming more and more dangerous for girls, with renewed attacks against teachers and students. In November 2008, eight girls were splashed with acid while on their way to school, in an attack by men on a motorcycle in Kandahar. Incidents like this are multiplying, and girls' attendance at school is declining. It was heartening to see one of the girls who was badly injured tell reporters that she was not afraid of such acts, and would finish her studies even if this would cause her to lose her life.

After many years of teaching in underground classrooms during the Taliban, it is painful for me to know that girls and women still have to be afraid to get an education.

Not only is it dangerous for women to go to school, in many regions of the country women cannot even leave the house unless accompanied by a male relative, or mahram. And women continue to wear the burqa, even in Kabul. For all intents and purposes, the position of women is the same now as it was under the Taliban. In some respects, the situation is worse, with higher rates of suicide and abduction, and total impunity in cases of rape.

. . .

According to the U.N. Population Fund (UNFPA), 25 percent of Afghan women face sexual violence. Some specific examples will suffice to illustrate the brutal treatment of women in Afghanistan today. These are disturbing stories, but they are the reality and, sadly, they represent only the tip of the iceberg of women's oppression.

In May 2007, in Takhar Province, an eight-year-old girl named Bibi Fatima was abducted, raped by several men, and then murdered. In this all-too-rare instance, authorities responded quickly and arrested five individuals. The case was reported on Ariana TV and the news was translated into English for RAWA's website, which has documented many of the horrific cases of violence against women.

In the Gulran district of Herat Province, Fatima, a twenty-two-year-old woman, checked herself into a hospital with multiple wounds. Fatima reported that her husband had carried out serial assaults against her, in addition to killing their newborn baby. He had pulled her hair out with his bare hands, and burned her with boiling water. Fatima is not the only woman to suffer mutilation by her husband's hands. Also in Herat, a woman named Nafisa reported that her opium-addicted husband broke her nose and cut off her ear with a knife.

Bashir Chahaabi, one of the warlords of Takhar, was assigned to be governor of the northern Sar-e-Pul Province. Since then, there have been reports of young girls being gang-raped there. In these cases, few of the victims have the courage to raise their voices and make it public because rape is regarded as a shame to the family. But a fourteen-year-old girl named Bashira and her father decided to speak out. Bashira was gang-raped while going to pick up supplies from an aid distribution center. One of the accused is the son of a member of Parliament. This MP intervened to help his son avoid real justice for his crime. So while I have been kicked out of Parliament for demanding the prosecution of war criminals, other MPs use their positions of power so that friends and family can avoid prosecution for their crimes against women.

I met Bashira and her father in Kabul in the presence of British journalist Glyn Strong, who later made a short documentary about the case. Bashira was so distraught after the rape that she tried to burn herself to death. Her hands still bore the scars when I met her. Her lovely young face was creased with worry as I held her against me and listened to her agonizing story. Everyone was weeping as she and her father described the assault and the horrors that followed. Her father said that his daughters' rapists tried to bribe him to drop the case, and when he refused, they had him beaten so badly he spent two weeks in the hospital. But despite his complaints, the authorities and the courts turned a deaf ear to his plea for justice.

. . .

. . . Many women who are raped or are forced into marriage lose all hope. In recent years, literally hundreds of women have committed suicide to escape abusive relationships, many of them by burning themselves to death.

In Laghman Province, twenty-five-year-old Puktana immolated herself in front of the local courthouse as a protest against this intolerable state of affairs—the *injustice* system in Afghanistan today. Keeping in mind that the real figures may be much higher, in the first half of 2007 a shocking 250 suicides were reported. IRIN humanitarian news documented these cases, but I am afraid they have received too little attention in the Western media. This terrible phenomenon is a result of the total failure of the courts and legal system in Afghanistan. Husbands can abandon their wives with ease, yet it is extremely difficult for a woman to legally obtain a divorce.

. . .

I can remember too many cases where women and girls came to me to unburden their hearts of their sorrows; I would try to comfort and help them, and to urge them not to choose suicide, but instead to choose to be part of the collective struggle to achieve justice for women in Afghanistan. The extent of misery of Afghan women was captured in a UNIFEM study that found 65 percent of the fifty thousand widows in Kabul felt that suicide was the only option to get rid of their desolation.

There are an estimated 1.5 million widows in Afghanistan, most of them living in terrible poverty. Some have even resorted to prostitution in order to survive. Although prostitution is nothing new in my country— and it even existed during the Taliban regime—it is now much more widespread. According to the *South China Morning Post,* "Afghan women's rights groups believe the number of sex workers in the country is increasing at a greater rate than before because the country has reached an unprecedented level of economic hardship and lawlessness."

. . .

Afghanistan, like other developing countries, has been feeling the disastrous outcome of globalization in the years following the U.S. occupation. The reliance on privatization and the unchecked market economy has had a terrible impact on the poorest people, and it has widened the gap between the rich and poor. Remember, with the worldwide increase in the price of staple foods, it is the poor in places like Afghanistan who suffer the most. And women and children suffer the most of all.

. . .

In the winter of 2007, more than one thousand people were estimated to have died due to exposure, because of poverty and poor housing. With the grinding poverty and a lack of health facilities, diseases such as tuberculosis also thrive and claim too many lives. Electricity is scarce and service unreliable, and many do not even have fuel for heating their homes or cooking. More than thirty-seven thousand children work and beg in the streets of Kabul alone, some 80 percent of them boys, 36 percent of whom are eight to ten years old. There are at least two hundred thousand children in Afghanistan living with a permanent disability (physical, sensory, and/or mental impairment), according to a 2005 survey by Handicap International.

Statistics put the rate of unemployment around 60 percent, but in reality it may be closer to 90 percent. Although some women in Kabul and a few other cities have access to education and jobs, life for women in rural areas is worse than ever. Infant and maternal mortality rates are among the highest in the world. . . . Badakhshan Province has the highest maternal mortality rate in the world—6,500 deaths out of 100,000 live births, 123 times higher than in the United States.

If the United States and its allies were serious about liberating Afghanistan's women, then it would not be protecting and promoting the warlords and fundamentalists who cause us such grief. And more important, women's rights can't be donated from abroad or forced at gunpoint. Equality is a value that should and will be achieved through the struggle of Afghan women and men. The fact is that women's rights were merely the pretext, and not the real motivation, for the war. . . .

To fight for women's rights in a besieged and benighted country like Afghanistan is to accept a big risk, with many challenges. It is like trying to swim against a strong current. But it is a proud struggle. It is a dream of mine that one day a democratic-minded woman will take the reins of power in Afghanistan. By shining a light on the real state of women's rights in Afghanistan today, we can teach even the most dark-minded misogynists that women are capable of changing the world when they move into action together.

Wherever I have traveled, I have met wonderful activists working for women's rights. It is very meaningful to me that women who face so many struggles in their own country take time to support the women of Afghanistan. This solidarity is a living example that as long as one of us is not free, none of us is free.

EDITOR'S NOTES

1. A Loya Jirga is a forum unique to Afghanistan in which male tribal leaders come together to discuss national issues. A Pashto term, it is translated as "Grand Council." Traditionally, a Loya Jirga may be called by the people, especially in times of national crisis, or by the ruler.
2. The Wolesi Jirga is the lower house of the Afghan National Assembly, comprising 249 delegates who serve for five years. The constitution guarantees that at least 64 delegates must be women. The first parliamentary elections were held in 2005.

SIXTY

Mother's Day Proclamation (1870)

Julia Ward Howe

Julia Ward Howe (1819–1910) is known for her Civil War poem, *The Battle Hymn of the Republic*, championing freedom for all men and women. She published poems, plays, and travel books and played a prominent role in several women's suffrage organizations. She saw the devastation of the Civil War through her work with widows and orphans on both sides, and called for women to oppose war in all its forms.

Arise then . . . women of this day!
Arise, all women who have hearts!
Whether your baptism be of water or of tears!
Say firmly:
"We will not have questions answered by
    irrelevant agencies,
Our husbands will not come to us, reeking with
    carnage,
For caresses and applause.
Our sons shall not be taken from us to unlearn
All that we have been able to teach them of charity,
    mercy and patience.
We, the women of one country,
Will be too tender of those of another country
To allow our sons to be trained to injure theirs."
From the voice of a devastated Earth a voice goes
    up with
Our own. It says: "Disarm! Disarm!
The sword of murder is not the balance of justice."

Blood does not wipe out dishonor,
Nor violence indicate possession.
As men have often forsaken the plough and the
    anvil
At the summons of war,
Let women now leave all that may be left of
    home
For a great and earnest day of counsel.
Let them meet first, as women, to bewail and
    commemorate the dead.
Let them solemnly take counsel with each other as
    to the means
Whereby the great human family can live in
    peace . . .
Each bearing after his own time the sacred
    impress, not of Caesar,
But of God—
In the name of womanhood and humanity,
    I earnestly ask
That a general congress of women without limit of
    nationality,
May be appointed and held at someplace deemed
    most convenient
And the earliest period consistent with its objects,
To promote the alliance of the different
    nationalities,
The amicable settlement of international questions,
The great and general interests of peace.

Gender and Human Security (1999)

The **Gender and Human Security Network** was an international group convened by peace educator Betty A. Reardon to articulate a gender perspective on human security at the Hague Appeal for Peace in 1999. Individual group members continue to be active on these issues in international organizations and in their home communities.

We are women from the Earth's five continents. We are moved by profound anger, fear, hope, determination, patience, impatience, stubborn conviction, common sense, the real possibility of change, a belief in the miracle of life and human community, and a commitment to justice. To realise justice, we must renounce the war system and adopt alternatives to it.

We believe that human security begins in the home and in our communities. A nation is secure only when its most vulnerable are secure. We want to create and share a new reality of a culture of peace where women have full participation in the decisions that affect our lives, our communities, and our relations with the world.

A culture of peace grows from full democratic participation of all members of society, replacing the top-down system of the present globalizing economic/military structure. These power relationships pervade all levels of our lives, from personal to global, bringing multiple forms of violence into all human relationships.

Women bear the most oppressive weight of the violence from the home to the war zone. Human security calls us to recognise the interconnectedness among all forms of violence and address them in a holistic and systematic way. For these forms of violence are the means by which both women and the natural environment are treated as resources to be controlled and exploited by these same male-dominated structures.

Our security is based on deep respect for life and the right to resist oppression. Our security involves an ongoing commitment to staying connected to each other, to nurturing bonds of trust and caring, and to constructive forms of contention and conflict. Our security is to live, to think, to love, to choose, to express, to decide, to move, to work, to relax, and to organise.

Human security is our ability to speak about the effects of violence on our bodies, minds, and hearts and those of our children. We cannot tolerate violence in the home, on the streets, in schools and communities.

Human security includes diversity, self-determination and freedom—freedom from deprivation, all forms of discrimination, and from injustice and oppression; freedom of expression and in establishing personal and social relationships. Security is about accountability and responsibility—of parents to children; teachers to students; of leaders, governments, and corporations to all people; and people to the chain of life that sustains us.

Our security requires the sharing of resources. It is daily violated by the unequal distribution of wealth, over-consumption and waste by countries of the North and elites in countries of the South, and by inequalities within and between families, communities, and countries.

Human security can be achieved through the wise and just use of the Earth's resources. We can craft ways to share these resources, drawing on people's caring attitudes, skills, knowledge, experience, and creativity, transcending the greed, consumerism, and pursuit of profit that characterise the present global system.

A culture of peace means we are respected and heard; we have education, health care, and a dependable source of livelihood. We have nourishing food, clean and accessible water, clean air, adequate shelter with a good place to sleep, clothing, and physical and psychological safety. We have love and a sense of belonging, and participate in all decisions that affect us. We have time, exercise, rest, peace of mind and spirit. We have music, dance, laughter, joy. To live in a culture of peace, we have a code of ethics that denounces all forms of violence. We have spiritual growth and fulfilment and bodily integrity.

Human security is based upon respect for human life as a foundational principle of politics and economics; just and effective international laws; people-to-people communication; a commitment to peaceful conflict-resolution; equitable distribution of resources (material and information); democratic control of economic institutions; and the health of the biosphere.

Human security in a culture of peace depends on all people from all countries and all walks of life being convinced that it is possible. It depends on us all working to bring this vision closer to reality, and to making choices that honour the sacredness of life.

We pledge to do all in our collective power and call upon our respective societies to foreswear militarised security, and to develop alternatives to violence as we struggle toward realising a culture of peace.

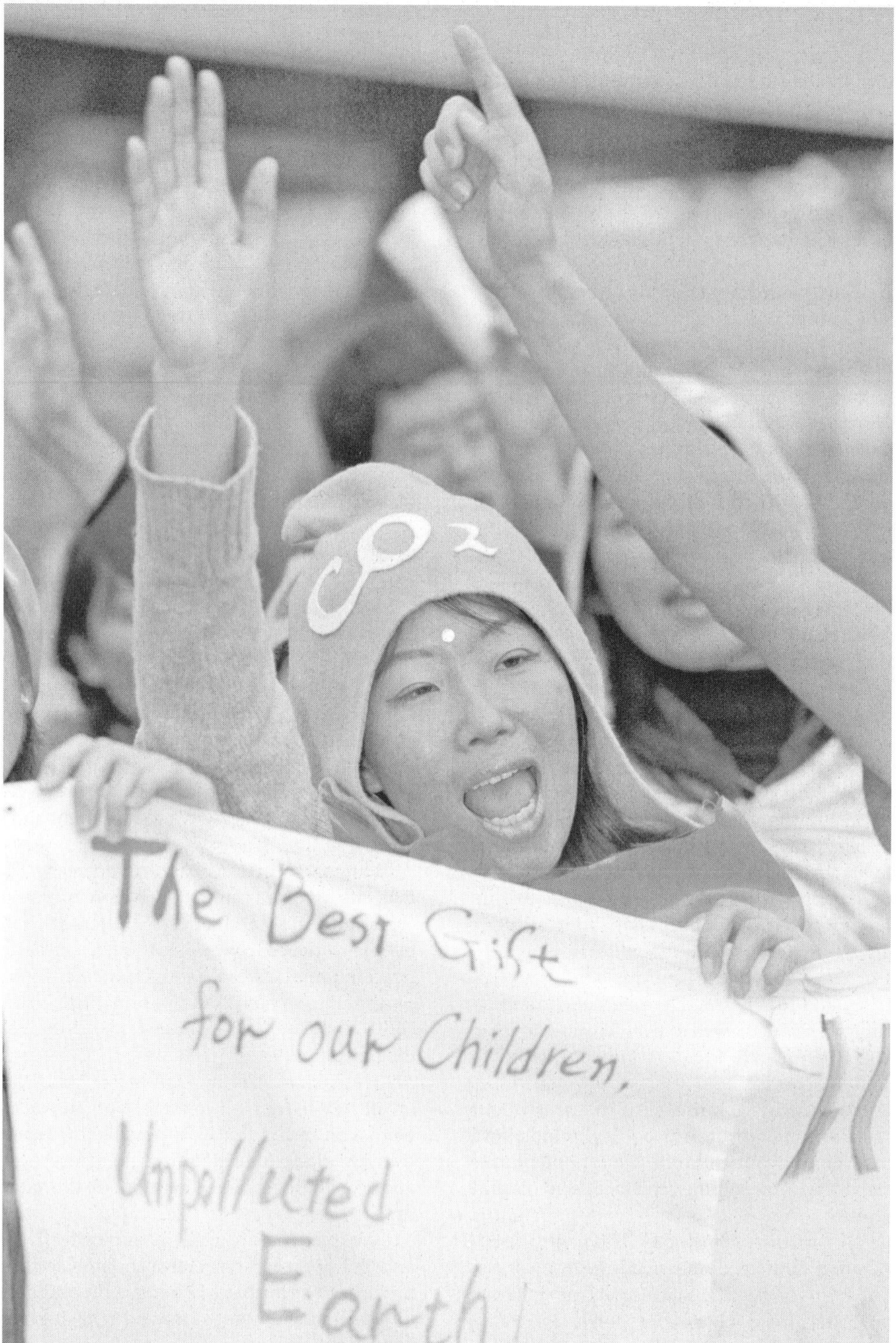
The Best Gift
for our Children,
Unpolluted
Earth!

11

♦♦♦

Women and the Environment

Place is fundamental in people's lives, whether we live in a leafy suburb, a vibrant downtown area, an inner-city neighborhood, or on a farm, ranch, or reservation (see, e.g., Anderson 1991; Barnhill 1999; Williams 1992). Cities change over time so that a formerly Polish American or Italian American community may now be home to African Americans or Vietnamese immigrants. A poorer neighborhood may become gentrified as middle-class people move in. In general, middle-class and upper-middle-class communities have better school buildings; more sports facilities, doctors' offices, and banks; more open space; and a wider range of stores, cafés, and restaurants than low-income neighborhoods. They are also farther from factories, oil refineries, power plants, sawmills, stockyards, railway terminals, highways, garbage dumps, waste incinerators, and other sources of pollution, bad smells, and noise.

This chapter is concerned with impacts of the physical environment on women's lives and with women's activism around environmental issues. As with other topics in this book, environmental issues are experienced at the micro and meso levels, but they also have macro- and global-level dimensions.

The Body, the First Environment

The environment is not something "out there" to be enjoyed on occasional hiking or camping trips; it is all around us all the time. The skin, the body's largest organ, is also a somewhat porous boundary. Everything we eat, drink, and breathe interacts with the "inside," in continuous interpenetrations between our body and the "outside" world.

Asthma in children, the incidence of cancer clusters, and illnesses involving chemicals are just a few environmental health issues. Toxic chemicals are widespread in beauty products (Malkan 2007). Industrial processes affect the health of workers and people who live near or downwind of industrial areas. Pollutants, chemical pesticides and fertilizers, and wastes from nuclear power plants and uranium mines are seeping into the groundwater in many parts of the country. Homes and schools have been built on land once used for toxic dumps (Gibbs 1995, 1998). Firms have tried to keep women of childbearing age out of the most noxious production processes—often the highest paid—or insist that they be sterilized, lest women sue them later for fetal damage (Gonen 2003; Stone 2000). Women who

work in computer manufacturing, chicken processing, the dairy industry, and housecleaning are all exposed to chemicals as part of their work, as are manicurists (Kang 2010). Contact with pesticides has led to poor health for many farmworkers and their children (Chavez 1993; Moses 1993; Reeves, Katten, and Guzman 2003; Thompson and Wiggins 2002). A significant number of babies without brains have been born to women on both sides of the Rio Grande, a river polluted by U.S.-controlled *maquiladora* industries located on the Mexican side of the border.

Environmental contamination affects men as well as women, but women and children show the effects earlier than men do, either because of low body weight or because women's bodies become what some have termed "unhealthy environments" for their babies (Kettel 1996; Nelson 1990; Steingraber 2001). In Reading 62, biologist Sandra Steingraber argues that even relatively low chemical levels may affect the development of an infant or a fetus. During the sixth month of her pregnancy, she studied fetal brain development. In the excerpt reprinted here, she discusses the effects of lead on this highly complex and delicate process. Steingraber (2001) also discussed breastfeeding as the best way to nurture infants. Environmental writer Florence Williams (2005) commented that an ingredients

label for human breast milk might read: "4 percent fat, vitamins A, C, E, and K, lactose, essential minerals, growth hormones, proteins, enzymes and antibodies." To this list, Steingraber added traces of chemicals like DDT, PCBs, dioxin, mercury, lead, benzene, arsenic, or flame-retardants that women who have been exposed to these toxins may pass to their babies through the placenta or their breast milk (see, e.g., Boswell-Penc 2006; LaDuke 1999, ch.1).

In Reading 63, Julie Sze, a professor of American Studies, examines the growing levels of asthma in children in the South Bronx and West Harlem, neighborhoods with high proportions of people of color in New York City. Some commentators have argued that asthma is caused by roaches and mold, and have blamed mothers for bad housekeeping. These pests have been around for a long time, however, and are common in rental housing that is poorly maintained by building owners. Rather, women working on this issue through West Harlem Environmental Action have focused on waste incinerators and other noxious facilities that have been sited in the neighborhood, spewing dust and chemical particles into the air.

The people most affected by poor physical environments in the United States are women and children, particularly in communities of color. Twenty years after the publication of *Toxic Wastes and Race in the United States* (Lee 1987), an updated study showed that "racial disparities in the distribution of hazardous wastes are greater than previously reported" (Bullard et al. 2007, p. x). The theory of **environmental racism** and the movement for **environmental justice** are based on the concept of civil rights, and claim that all citizens have a right to healthy living and working conditions. Many women of color and low-income white women are active in hundreds of local organizations working on this issue across the country (see, e.g., Adamson, Evans, and Stein 2002; Bullard 1990, 1993; Hofrichter 1993; LaDuke 1999; Quintero-Somaini and Quirindongo 2004; Spears 1998; Stein 2004; Szasz 1994).

Both Steingraber and Sze believe that current environmental policies and regulations do not protect people's health adequately. Moreover, the legal system requires victims to show specific harm caused by a specific facility or practice in order to claim legal remedies for environmental illness. This is a difficult standard of proof because people may be exposed to several sources of toxins at the same time. The onus is on victims to prove that products or activities harmed them, not on corporations to prove that what they do is safe. These writers argue for the **precautionary principle,** defined as follows:

> When an activity raises threats of harm to human health or the environment, precautionary measures should be taken even if some cause and effect relationships are not fully established scientifically. In this context the proponent of an activity, rather than the public, should bear the burden of proof.
> (*Rachel's Environment and Health Weekly* 1998, p. 1)

Or as the French philosopher Voltaire succinctly put it, "In ignorance, abstain" (quoted in Reading 62).

The Gendered Politics of Food

Food is a cornerstone of human health. Given the gendered division of household labor, women bear the major responsibility for providing food for their families: making menus, grocery shopping, cooking, preparing school lunches, and so on. They are also the majority of those working in the food industry, and at the forefront of grassroots efforts to improve access to healthy food. In Reading 65, rural sociologists Patricia Allen and Carolyn Sachs connect women's food work in the labor market, their responsibility for food-related work at home, and their relationship with eating and corporeality. They note the rich feminist literature on body politics (see Chapter 5), as well as substantial gaps in feminist theorizing about the food system, and a lack of attention to gender by agriculturalists.

In 2010, 14.5 percent of U.S. households were food insecure at some time during the year, the highest level ever recorded. This included 5.4 percent with very low food security, meaning that the eating patterns of one or more household members were disrupted and reduced at times during the year because the household lacked money or other resources for food (Coleman-Jensen et al. 2011). In the United States, access to nourishing food is linked to race and class. Low-income neighborhoods lack supermarkets that carry a full range of fresh fruit and vegetables, a factor in the increase in obesity as we noted in Chapter 5 (see, e.g., Gonzalez 2008; Shaffer and Gottlieb 2007). Fast food restaurants are more prevalent in low-income neighborhoods than in middle-class areas, and fast food is offered at a lower price compared to more healthy options (Morland et al. 2002). Government food stamps and the Women, Infants, and Children (WIC) Program provide limited support to buy food; in some states these can be exchanged at farmers' markets. Local government agencies and nonprofit organizations run food pantries and food banks, and these are well used, especially at the end of the month.

The Food Industry

The food industry is a for-profit business, increasingly dominated by a few transnational corporations including Monsanto and Cargill. Factory-farming methods require chemical pesticides and fertilizers, and focus on monoculture—growing large fields of one crop such as soybeans or corn. Experience has shown that chemically dependent agriculture is not sustainable over the long term (Kimbrell 2002; Kremen, Bacon, and Miles 2012; Pimentel et al. 2005). It requires increasing amounts of chemical "inputs" and results in declining yields and impoverished soils. Monoculture makes plants more vulnerable to pests and diseases that can wipe out

Women's environmental activism includes caring for home and community gardens or gathering herbs for medicinal uses.

a whole crop. Industrialized food production provides relatively "cheap" foods in the United States because the government subsidizes agribusiness under the Farm Bill. But these foods are not cheap if the costs to the environment, the cost of oil, and the costs to people's health are included.

As consumers, we have become accustomed to even-sized, waxed fruits selected as much for their long shelf life and ability to withstand being transported over long distances as for their flavor or nutritional value. Indeed, a major cost of food is transportation. Many U.S. and Canadian supermarket chains source fresh produce from Mexico, as described by Deborah Barndt (1999, 2002) in her studies of growers, truckers, food processors, and supermarket workers along this food chain. Fresh produce from Chile and New Zealand, countries in the southern hemisphere where summer coincides with the northern winter, is imported so we can eat apples year round. Tea, coffee, and tropical fruits are imported from countries of the global South, where they compete with subsistence farming for land, labor, and water. They earn hard currency; in addition, agricultural exports are required under World Bank and IMF structural adjustment programs to increase market profitability (see Chapter 8).

Trade agreements also affect the availability and price of food. Rice grown in the United States, subsidized under the U.S. Farm Bill, is sold in South Korea, a rice-producing country, at half the cost of Korean-grown rice. In 2008, a new phase of the North American Free Trade Agreement (NAFTA) came into effect, opening up the Mexican market for U.S.-grown corn. Further, the development of biofuels based on corn has sent corn prices skyrocketing as corporations buy up corn stocks for fuel and take them out of the food supply. Food riots in many poorer nations were in the news in 2008, sparked by increased oil prices, drought, crop failure, and competition from cash crops and biofuels (Magdoff and Tokar 2010).

A hazard of industrial food production in the United States is pesticide poisoning of farm workers, many of them Mexicans and Mexican Americans. Among an estimated two million agricultural workers, physicians diagnose ten to twenty thousand pesticide poisonings a year (National Institute for Occupational Safety and Health 2012). Contaminated produce is not good for consumers either. Middle-class mothers were very effective in getting the pesticide Alar—used to spray apples—banned in the United States in the late 1980s to safeguard children's health, but showed no apparent awareness of or concern for farmworkers exposed to it in the course of their work (see, e.g., Garland 1989; Mott and Snyder 1987). In many areas, mainly white middle-class consumers choose to buy organically grown fruits and vegetables, which are generally more expensive than those grown under industrialized farming methods. Although beneficial for the individual, this does not improve conditions for farmworkers. People need a livelihood as well as a sound environment, and the two are not mutually exclusive (see, e.g., Goodstein 1999; Pulido 1996; Schwab 1994; Alliance for Sustainable Jobs and the Environment, Portland, Ore.).

Sustainable Food Systems

Given the fact of hunger in many nations, including the United States, there is a need for more intensive food production to feed the growing world population. Much scientific literature focuses on yields and supports industrialized farming systems as more productive than sustainable farming practices that rely on biofertilizers and biopesticides. Biologist Jules Pretty (2009) argued that is possible to feed nine billion people with sustainable agriculture. Claire Kremen and Albie Miles (2012) pointed out that agro-ecological farming systems have additional benefits beyond yields. They conserve biodiversity, enhance natural pest control, increase pollination, improve soil quality, use water and energy more efficiently, reduce the potential for global warming, and increase resilience of farming systems to extreme weather events. Despite hunger, food is not scarce, as argued over twenty years ago by Frances Moore Lappé and Joseph Collins (1986, 1998), founders of Food First: Institute for Food and Development Policy. Hunger is not due to insufficient food production but to social, political, and economic factors that have dislocated people from the land and agricultural livelihoods, cut state subsidies for food as with structural adjustment programs, and limited access to affordable food supplies (McMichael 2009; Food and Agriculture Organization 2011; Rosset 2011).

In Reading 64, sociology professor Michelle R. Loyd-Paige discusses her decision to "eat like a vegan" on health grounds and to bring her eating habits into line with her ideas of social justice and equitable distribution of the earth's resources. She chose a mainly plant-based diet as part of living sustainably and asked: "Why do we commit so much of our land and water to growing grain to feed animals when we could grow grain that is a healthier source of protein" for people. Farmworker's health is also an integral part of a sustainable food system, as Patricia Allen and Carolyn Sachs (1991) argued over twenty years ago. Much more needs to be done to build alliances between farm workers and consumers, for example, by supporting farm workers' campaigns for better working conditions, shopping at local farmers' markets, and investing in community supported agriculture (see, e.g., Winne 2008). Various networks and organizations in many states link people involved in small-scale organic production, farmers' markets, schoolyard gardens, hospital food services, food banks, and food pantries. Eating locally produced food supports local growers, cuts down on transportation costs and the need for oil, and provides better nutrition because produce is fresher. Women play a key role in the movement for sustainable food systems as consumers, growers, organizers, administrators, researchers, and policy makers (Reading 65; also see Bollinger 2007; Costa 2010).

Population, Resources, and Climate Change

In 2011, the world's population topped seven billion, though as Betsy Hartmann and Elizabeth Barajas-Roman point out, the rate of population growth has slowed and in some industrialized countries population is declining (Reading 66). These authors note that arguments about population growth are being linked to concerns over climate change, immigration, and national security. For example, anti-immigration groups are using environmental arguments to oppose immigration into the United States on the grounds that additional people will overburden the country's resource base (see, e.g., Angus and Butler 2011; Lindsley 2004; Urban 2008). Typically, such arguments draw on ideologies of racism and national chauvinism and are cast in terms of "overpopulation" in the global South rather than focusing on the high levels of consumption in the global North.

Overpopulation, Overconsumption, or Both?

A simplistic emphasis on numbers masks the vast inequities in resource consumption among nations and within nations. Sustainability advocates use the concept of **ecological footprint** to calculate the

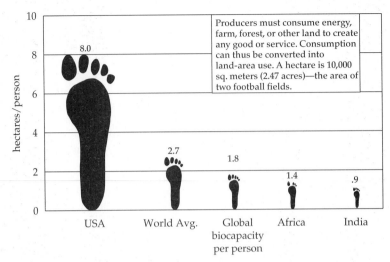

Producers must consume energy, farm, forest, or other land to create any good or service. Consumption can thus be converted into land-area use. A hectare is 10,000 sq. meters (2.47 acres)—the area of two football fields.

FIGURE 11.1 Comparative Consumption of Environmental Resources, 2003 (in hectares per person). (*Source:* Ewing et al. 2010.)

amount of energy, land, water, minerals, and other natural resources required by varying levels of consumption (see Figure 11.1). They estimate that currently there are 1.8 global hectares of biocapacity available per person worldwide. In 2007, the average footprint was 2.7 global hectares. This 50 percent "overshoot" means that humanity used the equivalent of 1.5 Earths to support its consumption in 2007, though rich nations had a much greater "overshoot" (Ewing et al. 2010, p. 18). The national footprint measures the amount of bioproductive space required to support the average individual of that country. This land may be outside the nation's borders as biocapacity is embodied in imported goods (p. 100).

This tool can be used to analyze and measure comparative levels of consumption at micro, meso, macro, and global levels, and to evaluate changes in consumption patterns. In the early 1990s, sociologist Maria Mies (1993) noted that for countries of the global South to follow the development model of the industrial North there would need to be two more Earths: one for natural resources and the other for the waste. Since then, this estimate has been revised drastically as consumption has continued to increase. Current estimates assume the need for between two and seven Earths for the South to consume at the same rate as the North.

In recent years the scramble to secure natural resources has become more overt. Access to adequate supplies of uncontaminated water, for example, has become a major issue worldwide, exacerbated by the fact that, increasingly, water supplies are owned and managed by transnational corporations (see Box). Vandana Shiva, Director of the Research Foundation on Science, Technology, and Ecology (Dehra Dun, India), commented, "Companies like Coca-Cola are fully aware that water is the real thirst quencher" (2002b, p. 99). Bottled water is a fast-growing business, consumed by many people in the global North as well as élites and middle classes in the South. Again, structural adjustment programs are implicated as indebted countries are pressured by international financial institutions to allow the privatization of publicly owned and managed water supplies.

Water has long been assumed to be part of the Commons—the wealth of natural resources available to all to fulfill our basic needs. People in many parts of the world—in India, Cochabamba (Bolivia), Europe, and the United States—are standing up to corporate control of water and working for what Shiva (2005) called "water democracy." Coca-Cola, Nestlé, and Pepsi have all been sued by local communities for excessive use of water supplies. A case in Plachimada

The Water Business

- Water is essential. There are no alternatives. We die without it.

- Most of the earth's surface is water, but almost all of it is salt water or glaciers. Less than 1 percent is freshwater that is potentially available for human use.

- The World Bank has estimated the potential water market at $1 trillion (Shiva 2002b).

- In Bolivia, the World Bank pressured the government to privatize water in the city of Cochabamba as a condition of receiving new development loans. The Bechtel corporation raised water prices there by 300 percent (Caplan 2004).

- Two French companies, Veolia Environnement and Suez Environnement, are the world's largest private water companies with operations in Europe, Africa, the Middle East, and the Americas. British conglomerates, Biwater and Thames, have operations in Asia, South Africa, and the Americas.

- Transnational corporations like Coca-Cola (Dasani) and Pepsi (Aquafina) are making massive profits out of bottled water.

- Other well-known brands include Perrier, Evian, and Poland Spring. Norway and Fiji export drinking water.

- Bottled water is marketed as pristine. Many people in the United States have assumed that it is safer than tap water. Research shows that this is not so; indeed, some bottled water is tap water (Morrison 2007; Natural Resources Defense Council 1999; Steingraber 2001). Big city tap water is tested at least 100 times a month, whereas the FDA requires bottlers to test only once a week (Morrison 2007).

- Annually, at least 1.5 million tons of plastics and 1.5 million barrels of oil go into the production of bottles. The manufacturing process releases toxics such as nickel, ethylbenzene, ethylene oxide, and benzene. Most bottles end up in landfills (Caplan 2004).

- It takes 174 gallons of water to produce 1 pound of wheat; 5,100 gallons for one pound of beef (Hiller et al. 2005).

- It takes 25 liters of water to manufacture 1 liter of Coca-Cola and 250 liters of water to irrigate the sugar cane that sweetens it (Glantz 2007).

(southern India) led to a court ruling against Coca-Cola (see Reading 49). In the United States, too, communities have organized to resist water privatization, as shown in the documentary film *Thirst*.

A second example concerns fossil fuels. The United States' energy plan is heavily dependent on fossil fuels, including going to war against Iraq to secure oil supplies, drilling for oil in the Arctic National Wildlife Refuge, and extracting coal through mountaintop removal in West Virginia (Barry 2012). Such macro- and global-level policies have a profound impact at local level. For example, communities along the Gulf of Mexico were hit hard—environmentally, economically, and socially—by the worst offshore oil spill in U.S. history, caused by the explosion of a BP drilling rig in 2010. Women working in small environmental organizations provided local leadership to communities that lost their livelihood as a result of this disaster (Juhasz 2010). In Reading 67, Sokari Ekine discusses women's resistance to environmental destruction and state violence related to the extraction of oil by Shell, Chevron/Texaco, and Elf in the Niger Delta region of Nigeria. The largest country in Africa with a population of two hundred million people, Nigeria has rich natural resources, but this wealth has benefited transnational corporations and Nigerian political élites rather than local communities. Oil extraction has destroyed the local economy and the local environment. Since the 1980s, there have been more than five hundred massive oil spills in the Niger Delta region. As well as being severely contaminated, the area has become highly militarized. Government forces have brutally suppressed local opposition to the oil companies, which employ their own security forces to safeguard oil rigs and piplelines. Local militias try to ensure some local control over natural resources (see Agbola and Alabi 2003). In the United States, gasoline prices at the pump have been rising, but they do not reflect the high human and environmental costs of oil.

Gender and Climate Change

Some U.S. elected officials still debate whether climate change is really happening despite consensus on this issue among scientists for more than a decade (Oreskes 2004). Climate skeptics work in the political arena, seeking to downplay the seriousness of global warming. Ignoring scientific findings, they function as ideologues rather than as scientists. Indeed, potentially severe, even catastrophic changes in climate are under way due to increased carbon emissions that affect the entire planet. This includes the melting of glaciers and ice caps, rising sea levels, changing rain patterns, and greater extremes of weather such as droughts and heavy storms.

So far, relatively little research has investigated the gendered impacts of global warming. Extremes of heat and cold are killing people, often women who are poor, elderly, and uninsured. Severe storms and flooding affect women differently than men. The Intergovernmental Panel on Climate Change (2007) acknowledged that gender roles affect people's vulnerability and capacity to adapt to climate change, especially rural women in the global South. Women are responsible for feeding their families and keeping them safe, including elderly parents and young children, the most vulnerable family members. Women also clean up the mud and debris, which may be contaminated by broken sewers or dead animals, and put what is left of their homes to rights after a disaster. Historian Barbara Ransby (2006) commented that women worked tirelessly in the aftermath of Hurricane Katrina at the grassroots level and in larger coalitions and community-based organizations such as the People's Hurricane Relief Fund and Oversight Coalition (PHRFOC). Beverly Wright, professor of Environmental Studies at Dillard University, initiated *A Safe Way Back Home*, a project to educate residents on what they could do about the toxins in their homes and

Diane "Momma D." Frenchcoat testifies on Capitol Hill before the House Select Bipartisan Committee to Investigate the Preparation for and Response to Hurricane Katrina (December 6, 2006).

in the soil after the flooding caused by Hurricane Katrina (also see Jones-DeWeever 2007; Pastor et al. 2006).

As colleagues at the Population and Development Program (Hampshire College), Betsy Hartmann and Elizabeth Barajas-Roman examined the political discourse on climate change, including arguments in favor of population control as a way to address global warming (Reading 66). They oppose this logic as blaming the world's poorest people, who, although they have the highest birthrates, are the least responsible for global warming due to their very low levels of consumption. Their perspective connects environmental factors, women's reproductive health, food security, military operations (which have a huge carbon footprint), and the disparities of disaster response based on gender, race, and class. Geraldine Terry (2009), a researcher and consultant on development issues, noted that the climate change discourse has been dominated by natural science approaches focused on elaborate technical solutions, large-scale economic instruments, and complex computer modeling, rather than paying attention to social issues. She argued for the following changes: "switching to renewable sources of energy and using fossil fuels more efficiently, curbing deforestation, adopting more efficient agricultural practices, and . . . transforming consumption patterns" (p. 9).

Recognizing the high U.S. carbon footprint, environmentalists urge us to use less electricity, recycle reusable materials, take public transportation, reduce travel by plane, cut down consumption, simplify our lifestyles, and so on. Important as they are, these micro-level efforts cannot keep up with the scale and pace of global warming, which require macro- and global-level policies and agreements to make a drastic and rapid cut in greenhouse-gas emissions (Terry 2009, p. 9). In the United States, macro-level factors such as the development of low-density suburbs, zoning laws, and inadequate public transportation all mean that many people have to drive on a regular basis, thus generating carbon emissions, unless meaningful alternatives are available. Patricia Hynes (1999), professor of environmental health, argued for meso-, macro-, and global-level changes that go beyond individual decisions to live more simply. She warned that "green consumerism" is *still* consumerism and involves the systematic promotion of "needs" as with any business venture. She asked: what insights and efforts can a woman-centered analysis bring to the issue of consumption in order to further the goals of redistributing and humanizing our use of natural resources?

Defining Sustainability

Many researchers and environmental organizations see environmental problems, including climate change, as rooted in unsustainable lifestyles in rich nations. "They argue that, rather than seeking technical and economic 'fixes,' we need to move away from consumerism as a way of life and reject globalisation in its current, big-business driven form, in order to avert environmental disaster" (Terry 2009, p. 9).

The term *sustainability* has become commonplace but means very different things to different people. For corporate economists, it means sustained economic growth that will yield ongoing profits; for ecologists it involves the maintenance of natural systems—wetlands, forests, wilderness, air and water quality; for environmentalists it means using only renewable resources and generating low or nonaccumulating levels of pollution (Pearce, Markandya, and Barbier 1990).

Ecological relationships are circular not linear, as with the water cycle, the oxygen cycle, and the decaying of organic matter that fertilizes the ground for new growth. Many concerned with environmental economics have pointed out the inherent contradiction between the linear expansionism of capitalist economies and long-term sustainability (see, e.g., Daly and Cobb 1989; Henderson 1991; O'Connor 1994). Advocate for a clean energy economy, Van Jones (2008) argued that a "green-collar economy" could solve two major problems at the same time: climate change and unemployment. He advocated renewable energy as U.S. national policy, including the education and training of millions of people to install renewable technologies like solar panels.

Environmental studies researcher Giovannna Di Chiro argued that a definition of sustainability must incorporate everything needed to reproduce everyday life, what feminists and Marxist scholars have termed **social reproduction**, much of which is unpaid work done by women. This includes biological reproduction, socializing and educating children, training workers, and caring for all members of society, as well as "the ability to produce healthy food, clean water, decent shelter, clothing and health care" (Di Chiro 2009 p. 2). Di Chiro emphasized that "*all* environmental issues are reproductive issues" and called for more effective political alliances between feminists and environmentalists based on this concept. Sociologist Mary Mellor (1992) noted that this caring work is geared to biological time. Children need feeding when they are hungry; sick people need care regardless of what time of day it is; gardens need planting in the right season. She argued that "women's responsibility for biological time means that men have been able to create a public world that largely ignores it," a world "no longer rooted in the physical reality of human existence" (pp. 258–59). A sustainable future must be based on biological time and will require the valuing of all caring work, emotional as well as physical and intellectual labor.

In the United States, sustainability implies support for local initiatives like community gardens, farmers' markets, credit unions, and small-scale, worker-owned businesses and markets, as mentioned in Chapter 7. It requires local control over transnational corporations, reduction of poor countries' foreign debt, and investments in development that is ecologically and culturally sound, as suggested in Chapter 8. Vandana Shiva (2002a) argued for **relocalization** as opposed to globalization, which places enormous economic and environmental burdens on countries of the global South. She maintained that "what can be grown and produced locally should be used locally" rather than exported, and further, that "relocalization everywhere—in the South and in the North—would conserve resources, generate meaningful work, fulfill basic needs and strengthen democracy" (p. 249).

Such major changes also involve changing definitions of wealth from the current emphasis on materialism and consumerism. This is not a philosophy of denial or a romanticization of poverty, though it does involve a fundamental **paradigm shift,** or change of worldview, in a country so dominated by material consumption and wealth. A broader notion of wealth includes everything that has the potential to enrich a person and a community, such as health, physical energy and strength, safety and security, time, skills, talents, wisdom, creativity, love, community support, a connection to one's history and cultural heritage, and a sense of belonging.

Theory and Practice

Feminist thought concerning environmental issues continues to develop. There are considerable gaps and inadequate attention to gender in theorizing and activism about sustainable food systems (Reading 65). Also, much environmental justice organizing does not focus on gender even though the majority of grassroots participants are women.

Theoretical Frameworks: Gender, Race, Class and Environmental Issues

Generally, women in the environmental justice movement ground their activism in experiences of race and class rather than gender. In October 1991, women were 60 percent of participants at the First National People of Color Environmental Leadership Summit. A decade later, women were credited as the major organizers of the Second Environmental Justice Summit, and several women were honored for their life work (Bullard 2002). But this women's work is not identified as feminist "in the sense of being strategically oriented toward improving gender relations" (Allen and Sachs 2007, p. 1).

The term **ecofeminism,** attributed to French feminists, addressed the connections they saw between masculinist social institutions and the destruction of the physical environment (d'Eaubonne 1994). This perspective was taken up by U.S. writers and scholars who pointed to the gendered ways in which Western thought and science have seen nonhuman nature as wild and hostile, so much matter to be mastered (Griffin 1978; Merchant 1980). Nature is often feminized and sexualized through imagery such as "the virgin forest," "the rape of the earth," and "penetrating" the wilderness. Shiva (1988) noted that in the Western model of development, *sources,* living things that can reproduce life—whether forests, seeds, or women's bodies—are turned into *resources* to be objectified, controlled, and used. The first ecofeminist gathering in the United States, titled "Women for Life on Earth," was held in Amherst (Massachusetts) in 1980 in response to the near-meltdown at the Three Mile Island nuclear power plant (Charman 2011; King 1983). A key concern was the effect of nuclear technology on people's health and the health of the planet. One outcome of the conference was the Women's Pentagon Action, a feminist network that organized major demonstrations against militarism in the early 1980s (see Chapter 10).

A key point in ecofeminist thought involves the concept of dualism, where various attributes are defined as oppositions: culture/nature, mind/body, male/female, civilized/primitive, sacred/profane, subject/object, self/other. Philosopher Val Plumwood (1993) argued that these dualisms are mutually reinforcing and should be thought of as an interlocking set. In each pair, one side is valued over the other. Culture, mind, male, civilized, for example, are valued over nature, body, female, primitive, which are thought of as "other" and inferior. Plumwood saw dualism as the logic of hierarchical systems like colonialism, racism, sexism, and militarism that rely on the idea of otherness and inferiority to justify superiority and domination.

Many ecofeminists included **speciesism** as an analytical category akin to sexism, racism, and classism, and argued strongly for the liberation of animals as part of ecofeminist practice (e.g., Adams 1999; Gaard 1993). In Reading 64, Michelle Loyd-Paige notes:

> The conditions under which many feed animals are raised are inhumane. . . . Animals are a part of creation, just as humans. Treating them so callously is symptomatic of a general disregard for anything our culture defines as inferior and expendable.

She goes on to comment that, "this is reminiscent of how people of color were treated." Some U.S. women of color critiqued ecofeminist approaches on the grounds that they emphasized gender over race and class or focused on abstract ideas about women and nature rather than everyday reality (e.g., Davis 1998; Smith 1997; Taylor 1997). Some academic feminists discredited ecofeminism on grounds of **essentialism**—that in their essence women are closer to nature than men. Although most ecofeminists did not hold this view, the term ecofeminism was tainted by this charge.

An intersectional analysis has the potential to link opposition to the systems identified by Plumwood—racism, economic exploitation, militarism, and colonialism—with opposition to the domination of women and nature (see, e.g., Hawthorne 2002; Kirk 1997, 1998; Mies and Shiva 1993; Shiva 1988). This means seeing women's liberation, antiracist principles, and economic justice as integral to a sustainable future. It also requires building relationships and alliances by working together on common issues such as environmental health, food production and consumption, and making cities liveable. Readings 65 and 66 provide examples of feminist intersectional analysis with a strong material basis.

Women's Environmental Activism

Many more women than men are involved in environmental issues at a grassroots level, though this is reversed at the national level (Mohai 1997). We see women's environmental activism as an extension of their roles as daughters, wives, and mothers, caring for families and communities. Women have a long history of community organizing and urban politics: protesting bad housing conditions, high rents, unsafe streets, lead in gasoline, toxic dumps, trash incinerators, and so on (e.g., Cockburn 1977; Gilkes 1988; Krauss 1993; McCourt 1977). Much environmental activism can be seen in this context. Women have been persistent in searching for explanations for environmental illnesses or tracing likely sources of pollution affecting their neighborhoods (e.g., Gibbs 1995, 1998; Kaplan 1997; Krauss 1993; Zeff, Love, and Stults 1989). They have been ridiculed as "hysterical housewives" by officials and reporters, and their research trivialized as emotional and unscholarly. By contrast, women's health advocate Lin Nelson (1990) honored this work as kitchen table science. Examples of local organizations include the Asia Pacific Environmental Network (Oakland, Calif.), the Mothers of East Los Angeles (Pardo 1990), the Newtown Florist Club (Gainesville, Ga.), and West Harlem Environmental Action (New York) mentioned in Reading 63. Sociologist Nancy Naples (1998) described such community work as "activist mothering." Ideally, taking care of children and other family members should be everyone's responsibility, including governments and corporations, and would involve safeguarding and restoring the environment.

Ecofeminist writers and researchers have worked with activist groups or contributed to national and international debates. Examples include the National Women's Health Network's research and organizing around industrial and environmental health, critiques of reproductive technology and genetic engineering by the Feminist Network of Resistance to Reproductive and Genetic Engineering (FINRRAGE), and the work of the Committee on Women, Population, and the Environment, which has critiqued overpopulation arguments that focus on the global South rather than addressing the overconsumption of the North (see Reading 66). Ecofeminist ideas have been circulated in newsletters and study groups, college courses, animal rights organizing, and long-term women's land projects (see, e.g., Adams 1999; Diamond and Orenstein 1990; Gaard 1993; King 1988, 1993b; Sturgeon 1997; Warren 1994, 2000).

Projects that intertwine ecological, economic, and cultural survival are a key part of a sustainable future. Examples include Tierra Wools (Los Ojos, New Mexico) where a workers' cooperative produces high-quality, handwoven rugs and clothing, and organically fed lamb from their sheep (Peña 1999; Pulido 1996; Sargent et al. 1991); the White Earth Land Recovery Project (Minnesota) which harvests wild rice, maple sugar, berries, and birch bark using traditional sustainable practices (LaDuke 1993, 1999); and Dudley Street Neighborhood Initiative, Boston, which entailed major environmental cleanup and the development of affordable housing for a low-income multicultural community (Layzer 2006; Tulloss 1996). Many community garden projects produce food for local consumption (e.g., Hynes 1996; Warner 1987). Elderly African American women are prominent among the gardeners (e.g., Bagby 1990), as are Latina and Asian immigrants who continue the gardening traditions of their homelands. In rural areas, some women are farmers; others work on garden plots, planting, harvesting, and processing fruits and vegetables for home use (Sachs 1996). Some know the woods or backcountry areas in great detail, as ethnobotanists; they go there in different seasons to gather herbs for medicinal purposes. Among Mexican Americans, for example, *curanderas*—traditional healers—continue to work with herbal remedies and acquire their knowledge from older women relatives (Perrone, Stockel, and Krueger 1989). Others attest to the healing and redemptive power of gardening and caring for plants. Catherine Sneed, for example, who founded the Garden Project for prisoners and former prisoners, wrote: "we're not just growing plants—we're growing people" (Sneed 2000, p. 27).

The widespread and profoundly serious nature of environmental devastation means that environmental issues have great potential to bring people together across lines of race, class, and gender, as well as transnationally. Implicitly or explicitly, writers in this chapter argue for a future in which human life and the life of the natural world are valued, cared for, and sustained. As Ynestra King (1983) wrote: "Ecofeminism is about connectedness and wholeness of theory and practice. It asserts the special strength and integrity of every living thing."

◆◆◆

Questions for Reflection

As you read and discuss this chapter, consider these questions:

1. What does the environment mean to you?
2. Who grew and prepared the food you eat and under what circumstances?
3. How far are you from farming—in geographical distance and generations of your family?
4. What is your relationship to animals and plants?
5. What would you like your parents' generation to leave to you? What does the older generation owe you, if anything? What do you want to leave to your children? What do you owe them?

◆◆◆

Finding Out More on the Web

1. Find out about pollution in your community at **www.scorecard.org.**

   Find the safety assessment of ingredients in personal care products at **www.ewg.org/ skindeep.**

2. What is the current situation regarding community control of water supplies in Plachimada (India), or environmental destruction caused by oil extraction in the Niger Delta?

3. Explore the work of organizations such as:

    Asian Pacific Environmental Network: **www.apen4ej.org**

    Center on Race, Poverty and the Environment: **www.crpe-ej.org**

    Center for Health, Environment, and Justice: **www.chej.org**

    Climate Justice Now: **www.climate-justice-now.org**

    Community Food Security Coalition: **www.foodsecurity.org/**Committee on Women, Population, and the Environment: **www.cwpe.org**

    Environmental Justice and Climate Change: **www.ejcc.org**

    Indigenous Environmental Network: **www.ienearth.org**

    National Healthy Nail and Beauty Salon Alliance: **http://nailsalonalliance.org**

    People's Grocery: **www.peoplesgrocery.org**

    Student Environmental Action Coalition: **www.seac.org**

    White Earth Land Recovery Project: **www.welrp.org**

    Women for Climate Justice: **www.gendercc.net**

    Women's Earth Alliance: **www.womensearthalliance.org**

    Women's Environment and Development Organization: **www.wedo.org**

    What are their theoretical frameworks and organizing practices? Who is their constituency?

◆◆◆

Taking Action

1. Write your personal environmental history. Use the theoretical lenses outlined in this book to analyze and reflect on your experiences.

2. Identify plants, birds, and animals; sources of food and water, sewage, and trash disposal for your campus or community. Are the plants introduced or native? How did Native Americans use them?

3. Find out what happened to the Native American people who live/lived where you live now. Are there other groups who used to live there? How did they support themselves? Why did they move? How are they living now?

4. Find out about sustainability efforts on your campus or in your community. How can you help/participate?

5. Create and plan an activity concerning the environment that would bring people together across lines of gender, race, and class.

6. Calculate your ecological footprint at these sites:

    http://myfootprint.org/en/
    www.footprintnetwork.org/en/index.php/GFN/page/calculators/

    What will it take to make it smaller? Think in terms of all levels of analysis.

SIXTY-TWO

Rose Moon (2001)—Excerpt

Sandra Steingraber

Sandra Steingraber is a biologist, an award-winning science writer, teacher, cancer survivor, and expert on environmental links between cancer and human health. Author of *Living Downstream: An Ecologist Looks at Cancer and the Environment*, *Having Faith: An Ecologist's Journey to Motherhood*, and *Post-Diagnosis*, a volume of poetry, her awards include *Ms* magazine's "Woman of the Year" and the Rachel Carson Leadership Award.

Editors' note: In *Having Faith,* Sandra Steingraber names the months of her pregnancy according to traditional names given to each month's full moon in the agricultural calendar. Rose moon is the sixth month. At the end of a semester as visiting professors in Illinois, Steingraber and her husband drive back to their home in Somerville, near Boston. This excerpt refers to their conversations and to Steingraber's ongoing research into fetal development.

. . . In its narration of life in the womb, the popular literature waxes eloquent over a completely different set of milestones than do the academic texts to which I'm more accustomed. The textbooks devote most of their pages to the complicated early events of organogenesis, with all their origami-like precision. The writing perks up again at the end with the avalanche of hormonal changes that triggers labor and delivery. But the discussion of fetal changes during the second and third trimesters is swift and almost dismissive: growth of body parts, fat deposition, refinement of features. . . .

By contrast, the popular media pass swiftly over the treacherous early months—except to mention morning sickness and symptoms of imminent miscarriage—and hit their rhetorical stride during the months of mid- and late pregnancy. These periodicals dote lovingly on such achievements as growth of the eyebrows (well developed by month six!), the secretion of waxy *vernix* (protects the skin from chapping), and the growth of *lanugo* (fine downy hair that holds the vernix in place). What

mother-to-be can resist these endearing details, this special language, which resembles the vocabulary of a Catholic Mass? ("Vernix" is Latin for varnish, "lanugo," for wool). From the popular books, I learn that a six-month-old fetus is about thirteen inches long and weighs a little more than a pound. I learn that the top of my uterus has risen above my belly button and that the fetus, now pressed directly against the wall of the uterus, is affected by the womb's various squeezings.

. . .

What the popular books and magazines do not talk much about are environmental issues. Even the March of Dimes publication, *Mama,* which is devoted to the prevention of birth defects, does not mention solvents or pesticides or toxic waste sites or Minamata or Vietnam. There is some kind of disconnect between what we know scientifically and what is presented to pregnant women seeking knowledge about prenatal life. At first, I assumed the silence around environmental threats to pregnancy might be explained by the emerging nature of the evidence. Perhaps the writers of public educational materials choose to present only the dangers for which the data are iron-clad and longstanding. All the books and periodicals include a standard discussion of rubella, for example, and urge pregnant smokers to quit.

But the more I read, the more I realize that scientific certainty is not a consistent criterion by which reproductive dangers are presented to pregnant mothers. For example, pregnant women are urged to drink no alcohol. The guidebooks and magazines are unanimous about this. While fetal alcohol syndrome is a well-described and incontrovertible phenomenon . . . no one knows if an occasional glass of wine is harmful. Nevertheless, caution dictates—and again I wholeheartedly agree—that in the absence of information to the contrary, one should assume no safe threshold level. One of the pregnancy books in my collection, *Life Before Birth,* even quotes Voltaire on this issue: "In ignorance, abstain."

Yet this same principle is not applied to nitrates in tap water. Here we assume we *can* set safe thresholds—in this case ten parts per million—even though these thresholds have never been established for fetuses and even though almost nothing is known about transplacental transfer of nitrates or about how nitrate-inactivated hemoglobin in the mother's blood might interfere with oxygen delivery to the fetus. What's more, we allow 4.5 million Americans to drink water with nitrate levels above this arbitrary limit. Four and a half million people surely includes a lot of pregnant women. We also presume we can set safe limits on pesticide residues, solvents, and chlorination byproducts in drinking water—and yet none of these thresholds has ever been demonstrated to protect against fetal damage. In fact, plenty of evidence exists to the contrary. When it comes to environmental hazards, not only do we dispense with the principle of "In ignorance, abstain," we fail to inform pregnant women that the hazards even exist. . . .

The more I read, the more contradictions I see. A recent scientific report summarizing the reproductive effects of chemical contaminants in food reaches a strong conclusion: "The evidence is overwhelming: certain persistent toxic substances impair intellectual capacity, change behavior . . . and compromise reproductive capacity. The people most at risk are children, pregnant women, women of childbearing age. . . . Particularly at risk are developing embryos and nursing infants."

By comparison one of the most popular guidebooks to pregnancy opens a discussion of this same topic with a complaint about that kind of bad news: "Reports of hazardous chemicals in just about every item in the American diet are enough to scare the appetite out of anyone. . . . Don't be fanatic. Though trying to avoid theoretical hazards in food is a commendable goal, making your life stressful in order to do so is not."

Of course, the don't-worry-be-happy approach does not apply to smoking and drinking; the authors take a very stern, absolutist position on these topics.

I look over at my [husband] who's been singing louder and louder.

"Hey, Jeff?"

"Mmm."

"I'm trying to figure something out."

"What's that?" He turns down the radio.

"Not a single one of these pregnancy magazines encourages mothers to find out what the Toxics Release Inventory shows for their own communities."

"You did it though, right?"

"Yeah, I looked it up on the Internet."

"And?"

"'And McLean County is one of the top counties in Illinois for airborne releases of reproductive poisons."

I detail for him the results of my research. The biggest emissions of fetal toxicants are hexane from the soybean processing plant and toluene from the auto plant. My list also includes glycol ethers and xylene. All are solvents.

"Jesus," says Jeff.

"I also found out that the university uses six different pesticides on their grounds and fields. So I looked up their toxicology profiles. Two of them are known to cause birth defects in animals." . . .

"So what are you trying to figure out?"

"Two things. One, why is there is no public conversation about environmental threats to pregnancy?"

"What's the other thing?"

I quote Voltaire: "In ignorance, abstain." "Why does abstinence in the face of uncertainty apply only to individual behavior? Why doesn't it apply equally to industry or agriculture?"

"Okay, let me think for a minute." Jeff turns the radio back on. And then turns it off again. "I think the questions overlap. Pregnancy and motherhood are private. We still act like pregnant women are not part of the public world. Their bodies look strange. They seem vulnerable. You are not supposed to upset them. If something is scary or stressful, you shouldn't talk about it."

"But pregnant women are constantly being told what to do. No coffee. No alcohol. No sushi. Stay away from cat feces."

"That's still private. Industry and agriculture are political, public. They exist outside one's own body, outside one's own house. You can't do something immediately about them within the time period of a pregnancy. So it seems unmanageable."

"It's pregnant women who have to live with the consequences of public decisions. We're the ones who will be raising the damaged children. If we don't talk about these things because it's too upsetting, how will it ever change?"

Jeff throws me a look.

"You're the writer. Can you find a language to manage it? Break the taboo?"

Now I have to think for a while.

. . .

Back in our Somerville neighborhood, with its views of Bunker Hill and low-lying, wealthier Cambridge, I forget the expanses of Illinois. Up in our third-floor apartment in this most densely populated city in North America (or so claims the Somerville newspaper on a regular basis), Jeff and I spend a few days bumping into each other and reacquainting ourselves with car alarms and Indian take-out food. In the evenings, we sit out on the balcony and wait for an ocean breeze. The neighbor who shares the balcony with us has planted morning glories and tomatoes, which are already twining up the latticework. In the mornings, I walk the dog to the park, sharing the sidewalk with caravans of strollers pushed by pouty teenagers and muttering grandmothers. I never noticed how many babies lived in my neighborhood. Up and down the block, rhododendrons are blooming in tiny cement yards, and vines of purple wisteria wrap the porches of shingled triple-deckers. Underwear flaps on a hundred clotheslines. From the park's old locust trees hang panicles of fragrant white flowers. It is Somerville's finest season.

With the public library only two blocks away, I resume my research. What interests me now is the sine qua non of pregnancy's sixth month: fetal brain development.

Trying to understand the embryological anatomy of the vertebrate brain nearly unhinged me two decades ago. It was some of the most difficult biology I had ever encountered—and the most beautiful. It was like watching a rose bloom in speeded-up time. Or like spelunking in an uncharted cave. My embryology professor, Dr. Bruce Criley, used to drill us by flashing slides of fetal brain sections on a huge screen while we sat in the darkened lab trying to keep our bearings. "Okay, where are we now?" he would demand, whacking a pointer against an unfamiliar structure. Prosencephalon, rhombencephalon, mesencephalon—ancient-sounding names identified rooms in a continuously morphing cavern.

Both the brain and the spinal cord are made up of the same three layers. The brain then adds a fourth layer when cells migrate from the inside out to form the cortex. It's what happens during and after this migration that is so dazzlingly disorienting. Indeed, in order to explain it all, the language of human brain development borrows its vocabulary from botany, architecture, and geography. There are lumens, islands, aqueducts, and isthmuses. There are ventricles, commissures, and hemispheres. There are roofs and floors, pyramids and pouches. There are furrows called sulci and elevations called gyri. Structures are said to balloon, undulate, condense, fuse, and swell. They pass by, flatten, overgrow, and bury each other. They turn, grow downward, turn again, grow upward.

Some structures are formed from tissues derived from two completely different locations. The pituitary gland, for example, is at the place where an upgrowth from a valley near the mouth meets a downgrowth from the forebrain. Meanwhile, the twelve cranial nerves go forth like apostles to make contact with the far-flung, newly developing eyes, ears, tongue, nose, etc. It was all enough to make us mild-mannered, high-achieving biology majors reel with panic. It also was enough to make us feel, once the lights went on again, that we had just emerged from a secret temple, the likes of which we had never seen before.

On a microscopic scale, the story is a bit simpler—although this may only be because we know so little about what actually goes on at the cellular level. All embryological structures are created through migration. But brain cells travel like spiders, trailing silken threads as they go.

There are two kinds of threads: dendrites and axons. Dendrites are fine and short. They receive messages from other nearby cells. Axons are ropy and long. They send out messages, often over great distances. Of the two, axons develop first. They grow out from the body of the brain cell along a specific pathway and in a specific direction. In this they are guided by proteins called cell adhesion molecules. The dendrites are spun out later. In fact, the peak period of dendrite growth doesn't even begin until late in the third trimester, and it continues until at least a year after birth.

Despite these differences, axons and dendrites have a lot in common. Both types of fibers branch after they elongate so that connections can be made with many other cells. These connecting points—the synapses—continue to increase in number throughout the first two years of life. Both axons and dendrites transmit messages by sending electrochemical signals down their lengths. Sometimes, these signals can also fly between fibers. But in most cases, in order to continue a message from one nerve cell to the next, chemicals have to diffuse across the synaptic space. These are the neurotransmitters, with their role call of familiar names: acetylcholine, dopamine, serotonin.

Fetal brain mysteries abound. Chief among them is the role of the neuroglia, whose name means nerve glue. These are brain cells that do not themselves conduct messages but that apparently exert control over the cells that do. They are far more than glue. In some cases they act as coaches to the neurons' athletes—wrapping their axons in ace-bandage layers of fat and thereby speeding the passage of electricity. They also appear to alter the neurons' diets, for example, by modulating the amount of glucose available. And they provide signals and pathways for migration. In this last capacity, they work in tandem with early-migrating neurons. That is to say, the brain cells that are the first to make the journey to the cortex provide essential cues—along with those of the neuroglia—that help later migrants find their way. But no one knows exactly how these trails are blazed, maps are drawn, and bread crumbs scattered.

Once you understand how the embryonic brain unfolds, chamber after hidden chamber, and how its webs of electricity all get connected up, you can easily see why neurological poisons have such profound effects in utero. Exposures that produce only transient effects in adult brains can lay waste to fetal ones. This happens through a variety of pathways. Neurotoxins can impede synapse formation, disrupt the release of neurotransmitters, or strip off the fatty layers wound around the axons. Neurotoxins can also slow the outward-bound trekking of migrating fetal brain cells. Because the earliest-maturing brain cells erect a kind of scaffolding to help their younger siblings find their way, a single exposure at the onset of migration can irretrievably alter the brain's architecture. A fetus also lacks the efficient detoxification systems that already-born human beings carry around within their livers, kidneys, and lungs. And, until they are six months old, fetuses and infants lack a blood-brain barrier, which prevents many blood-borne toxins from entering the brain's gray matter.

As if all this weren't enough, fetal brains are made even more vulnerable by lack of fat in the fetal body. The brain is 50 percent fat by dry weight, and after birth, body fat competes with the brain in attracting fat-soluble toxic chemicals. But throughout most of pregnancy, the fetus is lean, plumping up only during the last month or so. In fetuses, toxic chemicals that are fat-soluble—and many of them are—do not have other fat depots in which to be sequestered, and so they have disproportionately greater effects on the brains of fetuses than on the brains of the rest of us.

More than half of the top twenty chemicals reported in the 1997 Toxics Release Inventory are known or suspected neurotoxins. These include solvents, heavy metals, and pesticides. And yet our understanding of brain-damaging chemicals is vague and fragmentary. Part of the problem is that animal testing is of limited use in trying to figure out how a human baby might be affected by exposure to a particular neurotoxin. Humans are born at a much earlier stage of fetal brain development than, for example, monkeys. Rhesus monkeys' brains are closer to their final form when the monkeys are born, and the young are upright and walking before they are two months old, whereas the average age of human walking is thirteen months. Certain structures within rodent brains, on the other hand, are less well developed at birth than ours. For example, cells in the human hippocampus, the seat of memory, are finished being produced at the time of birth, whereas in rodents, they are not formed until well into postnatal life. These kinds of differences between species mean that extrapolating from animal studies to humans is tricky. The windows of vulnerability are different. And obviously, conducting controlled experiments on human embryos and fetuses is not permissible.

Unhappily, plenty of human fetuses have been exposed to brain-damaging chemicals anyway—not through controlled experiments but through unintended exposures. There is much we can learn by studying their various deficits. However, this kind of research did not begin in earnest until the last few decades. According to the old thinking, either a chemical killed the fetus or it didn't. Either a chemical could produce an obvious structural deformity like anencephaly (no brain) or it couldn't. Not until the 1960s and '70s did fetal toxicologists recognize that certain low-level exposures can elicit functional abnormalities in the brain. That is, the brain *looks* fine—it has all the necessary structures—but it doesn't *act* fine. Once researchers tested children who had had low-level exposures to toxicants on cognitive and motor performance, subtle problems became apparent. The same was true for animals. As soon as laboratory testing of neurotoxicants was expanded to include not just birth defects but also behavioral problems (learning, memory, reaction time, the ability to run a maze), myriad other problems became evident. In both cases, researchers began to see that toxicants can affect brain functioning at much lower levels of exposure than they had previously imagined.

Unfortunately, this epiphany in brain research happened long after the establishment of environmental regulations governing toxic chemicals. Many of these regulations are based on pre–World War II assumptions about neurological development, not on the findings of recent studies. When it comes to fetal neurotoxicants, instead of following the admonition "In ignorance, abstain," we adhere to the principle "In ignorance and disregarding emerging science, proceed recklessly."

The sixth month of pregnancy is a joyful one. My round belly elicits smiles and happy comments from postal workers, dog walkers, and fellow subway riders, who compete to be the first to surrender a seat to me.

Meanwhile, the random fetal movements of last month have evolved into a predictable and reassuring choreography. And as the weeks go by, I begin to notice something else about the baby's movements: they are often generated *in response* to something that I do. When I take a warm bath, she begins to squirm and shimmy, as if she were bathing as well. When I curl up to Jeff at night, my belly pressing against his back, she kicks—with enough force that Jeff can feel it, too. If I roll over in bed, she sometimes rolls over. If police cars or fire trucks suddenly blare down the street, she becomes very still, and I know I won't hear much from her for a while. I pat my belly and try to comfort her. "It's okay, baby; it's just a siren." In these moments, I realize that I am beginning to perceive her as a sentient being—as a child—and myself more and more as her mother.

. . .

A commonly held belief is that natural substances are less toxic to the human body than synthetic ones. Like a lot of folk biology, this idea is both true and misleading at the same time. It all depends on what you mean by "natural."

Consider lead, the element that occupies square number eighty-two in the periodic chart. It is indeed present in the earth's crust. But lead is not really part of nature in the sense that it has no function in the world of living organisms. While abundant in the geological world, it does not naturally inhabit the ecological one. A normal blood lead level in a human being—or any other animal—should be zero. And even in the inanimate world of rocks, the soft, dense, silvery substance we know as lead cannot really be said to exist. Elemental lead has to be roasted and smelted out of other minerals. In this sense, a lead fishing weight is as much a synthetic creation as polyester, plastic wrap, or DDT.

There is no doubt that lead is a remarkable material. Its Latin name *plumbum* (abbreviated Pb by chemists) hints at its usefulness. Think plumbing. Essentially uncorrodible, it has long been used to line water pipes. For the same reason, it has found a place in roofing. Lead salts make excellent pigments, thus lead paint. Tetraethyl lead stops engine knocking, thus leaded gasoline. Lead also has handy electrical properties. Its largest use now is in the manufacture of lead-acid storage batteries, especially the ones used in cars.

Lead is also a formidable destroyer of human brains. This property has been recognized for at least 2,000 years. Once called plumbism, lead poisoning causes capillaries in the brain to erode, resulting in hemorrhage and swelling. Its symptoms include irritability, abdominal spasms, headache, confusion, palsy, and the formation of a black line across the gums. Prenatal transfer of lead across the placenta is also old news. In 1911, women working in the white-lead factories of Newcastle noticed that pregnancy cured plumbism. They were right: by passing lead on to their fetuses, workers lowered their own body burdens and thereby alleviated their symptoms of lead poisoning. Of course, most of their babies died. We now know that lead, once it gains entry into the adult female body, settles into bones and teeth. During the sixth month of pregnancy, when the fetal skeleton hardens, placental hormones free up calcium from the mother's bones and direct it through the placenta. Whatever stores of lead lay in the bones are also mobilized and follow calcium into the fetal body. In this way, a developing baby receives from its mother *her* lifetime lead exposure.

Our understanding about lead's toxicity changed radically in the 1940s. Before then, victims of acute lead poisoning who escaped death were presumed to enjoy a complete recovery. But soon a few observant physicians began to notice that child survivors often suffered from persistent nervous disorders and were failing in school. In the 1960s, behavioral changes were noted in experimental animals exposed to low doses of lead. Then, in the early 1970s, children living near a lead smelter in El Paso, Texas, were found to have lower IQ scores than children living farther away. By the 1980s, studies from around the world documented problems in lead-exposed children who had never exhibited any physical symptoms of acute poisoning. These included short attention spans, aggression, poor language skills, hyperactivity, and delinquency. We now know that lead can decrease mental acuity at levels one sixth those required to trigger physical symptoms. The new thinking is that no safe threshold exists for lead exposure in children or fetuses.

Fetal neurologists have also shed new light on the various ways by which lead wrecks brain development. At levels far lower than required to swell the brain, lead alters the flow of calcium in the synapses, thereby altering neurotransmitter activity. It also prevents dendrites from branching, and it interferes with the wrapping of fat around axons. But it doesn't stop there. Lead affects the adhesion molecules that guide the growth of these axons, thereby altering the architecture of the entire electrical web. It also poisons the energy-generating organelles (mitochondria) within the neuronal bodies and so lowers overall brain metabolism. In laboratory rats, lead inhibits a receptor known to play a key role in learning and memory. The adult brain can fend off some of these problems, thanks both to its blood-brain barrier and to an ability to bind lead to protein and so keep it away from the mitochondria. Fetal brains lack these defenses. This is why early lead exposures have life-changing consequences.

On its surface, the story of lead seems like a story of science triumphing over ignorance. Lead paint was banned in the United States in 1977, the year I graduated from high school, and leaded gas was phased out soon after, finally banned in 1990. With paint and gasoline as the two biggest sources of human lead exposure, the decisions to prohibit—and not just regulate—these products is a shining victory for public health. In their wake, the average blood lead levels in American children have fallen dramatically—75 percent between 1976 and 1991.

But there is another story about lead, told by historians and toxicologists who fought long and hard to banish lead from the human economy. It's a story about the willful suppression of science by industry. It's a story that helps explain why one in twenty American children still suffers from lead poisoning in spite of everything we know. It helps explain why lead, never outlawed for use in cosmetics, can still be found in some lipsticks and hair dyes. And it helps explain why the soil in my neighborhood in Somerville is so full of lead that we are still advised not to grow vegetables in our gardens.

Consider lead paint. Its production was halted in this country in the late 1970s. But in 1925, an international covenant had already banned lead-based paints for interior use in much of the rest of the world. This agreement acknowledged that lead was a neurotoxin and that lead paint in the homes produced lead dust, which is easily ingested when crawling babies put their hands in their mouths or chew on toys. But the United States was not a signatory to this agreement. In fact, the same industry trade group that prevented the United States from adopting the covenant also succeeded in blocking restrictions on lead in plumbing. The lead industry—which owned at least one paint company outright—treated the emerging science on low-level lead poisoning as a public relations problem, dismissing objective research as "anti-lead propaganda."

As has been meticulously documented by two public health historians, Gerald Markowitz and David Rosner, the manufacturers of lead pigments went on the offensive after the 1925 agreement. They reassured the American public that lead fears were unfounded. They even promoted lead paint for use in schools and hospitals. Most wickedly, they employed images of children in advertising. The most famous of these was the Dutch Boy, a cartoon character dreamed up by the National Lead Company. With his requisite haircut, overalls, and wooden shoes, the little Dutch Boy cheerfully sloshed buckets of paint labeled "white lead" in ad campaigns throughout the midcentury. The implicit message was that lead paint was safe for children to handle. . . .

The industry also fought labeling requirements that would warn buyers not to use lead paint on children's toys, furniture, or rooms. Many a nursery was painted with lead by pregnant women eagerly awaiting the birth of their babies. Those questioning the safety of such practices were repeatedly reassured by Lead Industry Associates that a link between lead paint exposure and mental deficiencies has never been proved. And up until the 1970s, this was true—in no small part because the lead industry was the main source of funding for university research on the health effects of lead. Researchers with other opinions and other funding sources were condemned as hysterical and sometimes threatened with legal action. Only when the U.S. government became a major funder of lead research did the case against lead began to mount.

When the truth eventually became undeniable, the industry shifted tactics. Instead of denying lead's powers to damage children's brains, it blamed inner-city poverty and unscrupulous landlords who, the argument went, had allowed paint to peel in their tenement buildings. And the neglected children living there, with nothing better to do, ate it. At one point, recalls a leading toxicologist deeply involved in the lead wars, an industry representative actually suggested that the problem was not that eating lead paint chips made children stupid but rather that stupid children ate paint. All these arguments finally collapsed under the weight of emerging scientific evidence. But decades were wasted in denials, obfuscations, deflections of responsibility, counter-accusations, intimidation of scientists, and attempts to tranquilize a legitimate public concern. The result is that any home built and painted before 1978 probably contains lead paint, and all children and pregnant women living in such buildings continue to face risks from it. And since I live in a century-old building listed on Somerville's historical registry, I am now such a woman. It is a problem that continues to vex landlords and homeowners alike, as removing the lead is expensive and is itself a health menace. It is a problem that could have been solved in 1925.

Now consider leaded gas. In 1922, General Motors discovered that adding lead to gasoline helped alleviate its tendency to "knock," to burn explosively under high compression. Solving this problem meant that automobile engines could be made bigger, and cars could go faster. Ethanol, which can be distilled from corn, also worked well as an antiknock additive but could not be patented and was therefore not as profitable to the oil companies. In 1923 leaded gas went on sale for the first time. This development immediately attracted the attention of public health officials, who raised urgent questions about the effects of broadcasting lead-laced fumes into public air space. At about the same time, serious health problems began afflicting refinery workers whose jobs involved formulating the lead additive. Several died and many others suffered hallucinations. The tetraethyl lead building at one plant was even nicknamed the House of Butterflies because so many employees who worked in it saw imaginary insects crawling on their bodies.

Then a remarkable thing happened. In 1925, a meeting was convened by the U.S. Surgeon General to address the issue of lead dust. And a moratorium was declared. The sale of leaded gas was banned on the grounds that it might well pose a public health menace. It was a perfect expression of the principle "In ignorance, abstain"—what is now popularly called the precautionary principle. Unfortunately for us all, the moratorium did not hold. After the prohibition took effect, the lead industry funded a quick study that showed no problems with lead exposure. Over the objection that lead was a slow, cumulative poison and that such a study could not possibly reveal the kind of human damage researchers were worried about, the ban was subsequently lifted. The production of leaded gas resumed.

It continued for almost seventy years. By the time it was banned again, this time for good, more than 15.4 billion pounds of lead dust had been released into the environment. Much of this has sifted down into the topsoil. As a metal, lead is not biodegradable and is considered absolutely persistent. In other words, it is not going away anytime soon. It is tracked into homes on the bottoms of shoes. It is absorbed from soil into plant roots. This is why, in high-traffic urban areas such as my neighborhood in Somerville, we cannot grow and eat carrots.

The irony of our gardening situation is that lead in gasoline was finally removed on the basis of a landmark 1979 study showing significant IQ changes among first- and second-graders in response to environmental lead exposures. And the children investigated lived here in Somerville.

Should you ever find yourself in Boston, you may wish to pay a visit to the Old North Church in the North End. It's the one-if-by-land-two-if-by-sea church made famous by Paul Revere. If you go, take a look at the pale violet walls inside the sanctuary. Jeff painted them. Well, he and a crew of men that he supervised. Restoration work and decorative painting are specialties of his; these skills have helped to fund a lot of art projects over the years and paid a lot of rent. Elegant old homes up and down Beacon Hill and on Cambridge's Brattle Street contain his handiwork, as do buildings at Harvard University. Jeff is more at ease with a paintbrush and a sander in his hands than anyone else I have ever met, which is one reason (among others) I fell in love with him.

Now we lie awake on a summery night, reggae drifting into the window from the street below, and discuss whether or not he should continue this work. His blood lead levels are more than double that of the average American male. One physician actually congratulated him for this. Given that his line of work puts him in direct contact with old, lead-based paint, she expected they would be much higher. Jeff is very careful. But even when he changes clothes at the job site and leaves his work pants out on our fire escape, he still comes home covered in dust and paint. He's paying the price for reckless decisions made three generations ago.

But we would like to ensure that our daughter doesn't. Almost nothing is known about how lead exposures in fathers affect their unborn children. "Lower lead levels have not been well studied for their possible effects on the male reproductive system or on pregnancy in the partners of exposed males."

In ignorance, abstain. But can we afford to? With a baby coming? In the end, we decide that Jeff should fold his business. And as soon as the baby is crawling, we'll move out of our apartment. We know there is lead paint under the many layers of latex—our landlord has confirmed it—and we know that painting over lead paint is not considered a safe method of containment. We also know that our neighbors around the corner discovered very high lead levels in the soil in their back yard. Nevertheless, a home lead detector kit has revealed

no lead on the surface of our interior walls, in the cupboards, or in the dusty corners behind the radiators. For now, we'll stay put. . . .

"Don't grow our own root vegetables. Quit a job I like. How come we're always the ones that have to do the abstaining?" Jeff wants to know.

And that is my question exactly. . . .

NOTES

516 Quotation by Voltaire: P. W. Nathanielsz, *Life Before Birth: The Challenges of Fetal Development* (New York: W. H. Freeman, 1996), pp. 158. The literal translation of the original quotation is "Abstain from an action if in doubt as to whether it is right or not" (from "Le Philosophe Ignorant," in *Mélanges de Voltaire* [Paris: Bibliothèque de la Pléiade, Librairie Gallimard, 1961], p. 920). Thanks to Dr. James Matthews, a French scholar, of Illinois Wesleyan University for tracking down the original source.

517 Standards for nitrates in drinking water not shown safe for fetuses: Committee on Environmental Health, American Academy of Pediatrics, *Handbook of Pediatric Environmental Health* (Elk Grove Village, Ill.: AAP, 1999), p. 164; National Research Council, *Nitrate and Nitrite in Drinking Water* (Washington, D.C.: National Academy Press, 1995), p. 2.

517 4.5 million Americans drink water with elevated nitrate levels: AAP, *Handbook of Pediatric Environmental Health,* p. 164.

517 Quote from scientific report: International Joint Commission, *Ninth Biennial Report on Great Lakes Water Quality* (Ottawa, Ont.: International Joint Commission, 1998), p. 10.

517 Quote from popular guidebook: A. Eisenberg et al., *What to Expect When You're Expecting* (New York: Workman, 1996), pp. 129–32.

517 Toxic releases in McLean County: Data on toxic emissions are measured and sent by the industries in question to the U.S. Environmental Protection Agency. These are disseminated on the Internet in a user-friendly format by the Environmental Defense (www.scorecard.org).

517 University's use of pesticides: According to the director of the grounds crew, pesticides used in 1999 include mecoprop and bromoxynil. As of 2001 they are no longer used. Thanks to my student, Sarah Perry, for investigating this issue.

518 34 million pounds of reproductive toxicants released in Illinois in 1997: Toxics Release Inventory (www.scorecard.org).

518 Description of fetal brain development, gross anatomy: B. M. Carlson, *Human Embryology and Developmental Biology,* 2d ed. (St. Louis: Mosby, 1999) pp. 208–48; England, *Life Before Birth,* pp. 51–70.

518 Description of fetal brain development, cellular anatomy: D. Bellinger and H. L. Needleman, "The Neurotoxicity of Prenatal Exposure to Lead: Kinetics, Mechanisms, and Expressions," in H. L. Needleman and D. Bellinger, eds., *Prenatal Exposure to Toxicants: Developmental Consequences* (Baltimore: Johns Hopkins University Press, 1994), pp. 89–111; Carlson, *Human Embryology*, pp. 208–48; England, *Life Before Birth*, pp. 51–70; Victor Friedrich, "Wiring of the Growing Brain," presentation at the conference Environmental Issues on Children: Brain, Development, and Behavior, New York Academy of Medicine, New York City, 24 May 1999; Nathanielsz, *Life Before Birth*, pp. 38–42; T. Schettler et al., *In Harm's Way: Toxic Threats to Child Development* (Cambridge: Greater Boston Physicians for Social Responsibility, 2000), pp. 23–28.

519 Neuroglia modulate available glucose: Nathanielsz, *Life Before Birth*, p. 16.

519 Later brain cells follow early-migrating neurons: K. Suzuki and P. M. Martin, "Neurotoxicants and the Developing Brain," in G. J. Harry, ed., *Developmental Neurotoxicology* (Boca Raton: CRC Press, 1994), pp. 9–32.

519 Mechanisms of fetal neurotoxicity: G. J. Harry, "Introduction to Developmental Neurotoxicology," in Harry, *Developmental Neurotoxicology*, pp. 1–7.

519 More than half of TRI chemicals are neurotoxins: U.S. releases of neurotoxins into air, water, wells, and landfills totaled 1.2 billion pounds in 1997. These chemicals include heavy metals such as lead and mercury as well as methanol, ammonia, manganese compounds, chlorine, styrene, glycol ethers, and a variety of solvents, such as toluene and xylene (Schettler, *In Harm's Way*, pp. 103–5).

519 Interspecific differences in brain development: E. M. Faustman et al., "Mechanisms Underlying Children's Susceptibility to Environmental Toxicants," *EHP 108* (2000, sup. 1): 13–21; P. M. Rodier, "Comparative Postnatal Neurologic Development," in Needleman and Bellinger, *Prenatal Exposure to Toxicants*, pp. 3–23.

520 When testing expanded to include behavior: Harry, "Introduction to Developmental Neurotoxicology"; H. L. Needleman and P. J. Landrigan, *Raising Children Toxic Free: How to Keep Your Child Safe from Lead, Asbestos, Pesticides and Other Environmental Hazards* (New York: Farrar Straus & Giroux, 1994), pp. 11–15.

521 Historical awareness of lead poisoning: Bellinger and Needleman, "The Neurotoxicity of Prenatal Exposure to Lead: Kinetics, Mechanisms, and Expressions"; Suzuki and Martin, "Neurotoxicants and the Developing Brain."

520 Lead's migration into fetal body: Bellinger and Needleman, "The Neurotoxicity of Prenatal Exposure to Lead."

521 Awareness in the 1940s: AAP, *Handbook of Pediatric Environmental Health*, pp. 131–43; H. L. Needleman, "Childhood Lead Poisoning: The Promise and

Abandonment of Primary Prevention," *Am. J. of Public Health* 88(1998): 1871–77; Needleman and Landrigan, *Raising Children Toxic Free*, pp. 11–15.

521 Lowering of IQs in El Paso: Described in Needleman and Landrigan, *Raising Children Toxic Free*, pp. 11–15.

521 Studies from around the world: AAP, *Handbook of Pediatric Environmental Health*, pp. 131–43.

521 Lead levels required to affect mental acuity: Suzuki and Martin, "Neurotoxicants and the Developing Brain."

521 Mechanisms by which lead wrecks brain development: Bellinger and Needleman, "The Neurotoxicity of Prenatal Exposure to Lead"; M. K. Nihei et al., "*N*-Methyl-D-Aspartate Receptor Subunit Changes are Associated with Lead-Induced Deficits of Long-Term Potentiation and Spatial Learning," *Neuroscience* 99(2000): 233–42; Suzuki and Martin, "Neurotoxicants and the Developing Brain."

521 Vulnerability of fetus to lead: The elderly are also at risk. As bone demineralizes with age, blood lead levels can rise. In seniors, even slight elevations can have adverse cognitive effects (Bernard Weiss, University of Rochester, personal communication).

521 Life-changing consequences: New research suggests that these consequences include a propensity to violent behavior, as well as a lowered IQ. See, for example, R. Nevin, "How Lead Exposure Relates to Temporal Changes in I.Q., Violent Crime, and Unwed Pregnancy," *Environmental Research* 83(2000): 1–22.

521 Public health triumph of lead bans: AAP, *Handbook of Pediatric Environmental Health*, pp. 131–43.

521 75 percent decline: Nevin, "How Lead Exposure Relates to Temporal Changes."

521 One in twenty children: G. Markowitz and D. Rosner, "'Cater to the Children': The Role of the Lead Industry in a Public Health Tragedy, 1900–1955," *Am. J. of Public Health*, 90(2000): 36–46.

521 Lead not outlawed in cosmetics: T. Schettler et al., *Generations at Risk: Reproductive Health and the Environment* (Cambridge: MIT Press, 1999), p. 273.

521 Lead paint: Markowitz and Rosner, "'Cater to the Children'"; E. K. Silbergeld, "Protection of the Public Interest, Allegations of Scientific Misconduct, and the Needleman Case," *Am. J. of Public Health* 85(1995): 165–66; Schettler et al., *Generations at Risk*, pp. 52–57.

522 A leading toxicologist remembers: Herbert Needleman, "Environmental Neurotoxins and Attention Deficit Disorder," presentation at the conference Environmental Issues on Children: Brain, Development, and Behavior, New York Academy of Medicine, New York, N.Y., 24 May 1999.

522 Leaded gas: J. L. Kitman, "The Secret History of Lead," *The Nation* 270(20 March 2000): 11–41; Needleman, "Childhood Lead Poisoning"; H. L. Needleman, "Clamped in a Straitjacket: The Insertion of Lead into

Gasoline," *Environmental Research* 74(1997): 95–103; D. Rosner and G. Markowitz, "A 'Gift of God'?: The Public Health Controversy over Leaded Gasoline During the 1920s," *Am. J. of Public Health* 75(1985): 344–52; Silbergeld, "Protection of the Public Interest."

522, 523 1979 study of Somerville children: Needleman, J. Palca, "Lead Researcher Confronts Accusers in Public Hearing," *Science* 256(1992): 437–38.

524 Quote on lower lead levels in men: Schettler et al., *Generations at Risk*, p. 57.

S I X T Y - T H R E E

◆◆◆

Gender, Asthma Politics, and Urban Environmental Justice Activism (2004)

Julie Sze

I've got asthma but asthma doesn't have me!

—New York City Department of Health's Childhood Asthma Initiative Campaign

Julie Sze is Associate Professor of American Studies at University of California–Davis where she founded the Environmental Justice Project. Her prize-winning book, *Noxious New York: The Racial Politics of Urban Health and Environmental Justice*, concerns the culture, politics, and history of environmental justice activism in New York City. Her research investigates environmental justice, community health, and activism.

In the 1980s and 1990s, community concern over the problem of childhood asthma in minority communities in New York City reached a crescendo. At protests over controversial polluting facilities—incinerators, diesel bus depots, sewage and sludge treatment plants, solid waste transfer stations and power plants—in the South Bronx and West Harlem, groups of low-income African American and Latino children routinely protested with asthma pumps in hand. Many students attended rallies wearing gas and surgical masks, to dramatize how the air itself had become their enemy. "Fatigo," as asthma is known in Spanish, has become a way of life. A major advertisement campaign on bus shelters paid for by a community-based organization working to pressure the New York Metropolitan Transit Authority to convert its buses to natural gas read: "If you live Uptown breathe at your own risk. Diesel bus fumes can kill. Six out of seven of Manhattan's diesel bus depots are located Uptown. This puts the health of a

half million mostly African-Americans and Latinos at risk. Don't just breathe this all in. Do something. Because clean air is a right, not a privilege, even if you live above 96th St." The text accompanied a dramatic photograph of a grandfather and two children of color wearing large gas masks.

. . .

Asthma is not a female health problem, nor is it a race disease in the sense that it only strikes a particular group of people. It is a disease that strikes a wide array of populations. However, diseases are racialized and gendered in how certain diseases are "defined, characterized, and dramatized," which provide a window on social relations and social values (Wailoo 2001). Asthma is a racialized and gendered disease in the sense that the environmental justice movement activism around asthma is fundamentally shaped by larger debates on disease causation, the role of gender, and asthma management. Asthma activism is gendered insofar as parents in general (themselves a gendered constituency) and mothers in particular occupy a dominant discursive authority in child asthma issues. Historically, mothers of asthmatics were thought to be ambivalent, overprotective, and rejecting toward their children, thereby contributing to the development of childhood asthma. (Gabbay 1982; Guyer 2000). Although this notion of maternal causation has been largely discarded, asthma management remains gendered. Because childhood asthma is a chronic condition, parents and other caretakers of children are heavily involved with its management. And although asthma has become a major public health problem affecting Americans of all ages, races, and ethnic groups, children have been particularly severely affected, and the epidemic is most severe among lower-income and minority children. Children of color in low-income neighborhoods have shown the highest increase in rates of asthma in recent years. The racial disparity has grown steadily since 1980. This essay is focused on asthma activism in New York City, specifically in the South Bronx and West Harlem. These two neighborhoods have the highest hospitalization rates for asthma in New York City as well as a long and vibrant history of environmental justice activism.

I address two main questions in what I call asthma politics: the question posed by environmental justice activists, particularly low-income urban women of color, which is why so many urban kids have asthma; and the clinical literature on management interested in how best to treat it. . . . While the problem of high rates of childhood asthma in minority communities is understood in public health circles, the larger *social meanings* of this community-based activism in the context of the larger politics of asthma have been underexplored. . . . In focusing on outdoor air pollution as a primary factor in why their communities face high asthma rates, environmental justice activists are involved in larger public health debates about the nature of disease causation. A central theme of this essay is how environmental justice asthma activists seek to make the problem of childhood asthma a political and structural issue and to emphasize precaution in public health in response to countervailing pressures to individualize and personalize the problem, an approach that is not unique to asthma but also central to debates about cancer and other diseases (Hubbard and Wald 1993; Steingraber 1997).

Childhood Asthma: The Growing Epidemic

For the past fifteen years, an epidemic of asthma has been occurring in the United States as defined by the Centers for Disease Control and Prevention (CDC), medical and public health communities, and health activists. In particular, it is a disease that has risen in spectacular numbers for children. The CDC reports that more than 48 million children under eighteen in the United States, or approximately 6.9 percent, have asthma, making it one of the most common chronic health conditions of childhood. Its prevalence increased by 52 percent for those ages five to thirty-four between 1982 and 1996 (ALA 2003; Wilson et al. 1998). The costs for asthma are numerous and multidimensional, negatively affecting children and their caretakers in work issues (school and housework); social life and recreation; and emotional well-being, personal, and financial relationships (Nocon and Booth 1989–1990). It is the leading cause of childhood hospitalizations and absenteeism (school and work). In 1998, in the United States, the National Heart, Lung, and Blood Institute (NHLBI) estimated that the annual costs of asthma were $11.3 billion (President's Task Force on Environmental Health Risks and Safety Risks to Children 1999). Asthma is receiving a great deal of attention and public funds.

Asthma and Environmental Justice Politics in New York City

. . . The New York City Department of Health estimated recently that over 700,000 adults and 300,000 children in the city have been diagnosed with asthma at some time in their lives (2003). . . . Hospitalization rates are three times higher than the national average and low-income children have a rate 3.5 times greater than higher-income children (Stevenson and Leighton 2000). One recent study estimated that one in four children in Central Harlem has asthma, double the expected rate and among the highest rates ever recorded (Pérez-Peña 2003).

Asthma is also a growing political issue, especially in environmental justice campaigns in New York City. Childhood asthma was an extremely important organizing issue in the South Bronx Clean Air Coalition (SBCAC) campaign against the Bronx-Lebanon Medical Waste Incinerator and the West Harlem Environmental Action (WEACT) campaign against the North River Sewage Treatment Plant. In 1986, community outrage erupted in response to beginning of operations of a $1.3 billion North River Sewage Treatment plant located at 137th Street along the Hudson River in West Harlem. Residents persistently complained of rancid odors from hydrogen sulfide (which smells like rotten eggs) and grew increasingly concerned about air quality including higher-than-permitted levels of nitrogen oxide. In the 1980s, WEACT was founded to spearhead an organizing and legal campaign as well as to act as a community watchdog to monitor the operations of the plant, which was located near a densely populated housing development. The Bronx-Lebanon Medical Waste Incinerator opened in 1991, and immediately catalyzed a vibrant multiyear organizing campaign to shut it down. The incinerator was sited just blocks away from 2,300 units of public housing, three public schools, and several parochial schools in one of the poorest congressional districts in the nation. It was finally closed in 1998 at least in part due to the organizing against the facility. The smokestacks that released its fumes were torn down in 1999. The incinerator, which cost almost $20 million to build, was built to burn forty-eight tons of medical waste per day from fifteen hospitals throughout the region. By the time the incinerator closed, the facility had been cited for over five hundred violations of toxic releases.

Both SBCAC and WEACT actively believed and organized around the belief that there was a direct relationship between the high asthma rates and the polluting infrastructure in their communities. The campaigns asserted that their neighborhoods were already exposed to disproportionate levels of outdoor air pollution, and that the addition of another polluting facility was unjust and potentially racially discriminatory, especially since the siting of the incinerator and plant have a long, convoluted and corrupt history (Miller 1994). Under circumstances of oversaturation of polluting facilities, campaigning against a new polluter was a natural mobilizing step. . . .

Children's Urban Environmental Health Activism

Children with asthma are not generally activists, although they are the focal point of activist concern. Parents of asthmatics and administrators of schools with a large asthma problem tend to speak for the children . . . out of serious concern for their health. The concern for health moves from an individualized focus on single children to a politicized asthma activism when a controversial

noxious facility opens that exacerbates already poor environmental health conditions in a low-income neighborhood. The language and the discourse of the national environmental justice movement provide a politicized framework for childhood asthma. Consciousness of the role of outdoor air pollution in the disease tends to increase as a result of environmental justice asthma activism.

The centrality of childhood asthma as a political issue is simultaneously a response to increased incidences and an affirmation by environmental justice activists of the importance of the lives of poor urban children of color who have been historically marginalized. Asthma prevalence is higher in poorer populations and among urban as opposed to rural dwellers (Wilson et al. 1998). The racial disparity of rising asthma rates is a very real problem. According to the American Lung Association, asthma attack prevalence rates among African Americans are 32 percent higher than the rates in whites. Additionally, African Americans make up a disproportionate percentage of all asthma-related deaths. Black children are four times more likely to die from asthma than white children and three times as likely to be hospitalized for asthma. The prevalence of asthma among Hispanic children has also risen sharply (CDC 2000).

Suffering from poor health conditions as a result of substandard environmental conditions is an important part of the landscape of urban inequity—measurable and comparable to poor education, housing, income, and mobility. Additionally, this poor health is concentrated among people of color and the young and the old, who are already the most vulnerable to pollution exposures. Sociologists Cynthia Hamilton and Robert Bullard have suggested that the exposure of African Americans and other minorities in metropolitan areas to high levels of pollution is an outcome of racialized urban development. They argue that urban growth and development exist beside decay and blighted slums (Hamilton 1993). According to Bullard, "toxic time bombs" are not randomly scattered across the urban landscape, but in fact concentrated in communities that have a high percentage of poor, elderly, young, and minority residents (Bullard 1994). In addition to asthma rates, the communities of the South Bronx and West Harlem share racial and class demographics: they are primarily occupied by low-income people, racial minorities, and high numbers of young and old.[1] Along with demographics, the communities share a physical landscape of blight and despair. Both communities have an excess concentration of noxious facilities and a lack of environmental benefits, such as open space.[2] Harlem has six of the seven diesel bus depots in Manhattan. The South Bronx community is burdened with a punishing transportation and polluting infrastructure as a result of geography and a legacy of destructive urban planning. (As New York City's only borough linked to the mainland of the United States, it is bounded by the city's most concentrated transportation infrastructure: Bruckner Expressway, Major Deegan Expressway, the Sheridan Expressway, Cross Bronx Expressway, the Willis Ave. Bridge, and Third Ave. Bridge. That infrastructure translates into thousands of vehicles crossing through the community daily.) The South Bronx is also where 70 percent of the city's sludge is treated, at the New York Organic Fertilizer Company.

In both the SBCAC's campaign against the Bronx-Lebanon Medical Waste Incinerator and the WEACT's campaign against the North River Sewage Treatment Plant, the issue of childhood asthma became a central organizing theme. Environmental justice campaigns became largely movements for clean air and children's health. . . . The South Bronx Clean Air Coalition, comprised of sixty schools, churches, and community groups, successfully engaged large segments of the community, especially schools, through a culture of confrontation combined with a language of morality/religion/righteousness. The coalition, like the community overwhelmingly poor and nonwhite, relished its David versus corporate Goliath image. In naming the coalition the "Clean Air Coalition," the issues of air pollution, asthma, and health were pushed to the fore. The emphasis on clean air seemed obvious from the beginning, as community residents grew concerned about air emissions from the incinerator stacks. The campaign helped dramatize the human face behind alarming health statistics, particularly around asthma. Carlos Padilla, a former chair of the coalition, has a daughter who has asthma. According to Padilla, "[W]hat angers me is that some want to get the better of life at the expense of others, including their health. Profit at my children's expense makes me angry. These people from the incinerator are not from the community. They don't employ the community. But they take the resources and health of the community" (personal communication, April 15,1999). Another community

leader and member of the coalition, Yolanda Garcia, executive director of a community-based organization called Nos Quedamos (We Stay), had a son who died of an asthma attack. The principal of St. Luke's School connected the rising student absentee rate to the asthma epidemic, estimating that 40 percent of children in pre-K to eighth grade in her school have asthma (Nossiter 1995). Entire schools attended rallies against the incinerator, and buses were chartered to press conferences at City Hall to dramatize the human and social costs of the facility on the community, costs that hit their children particularly hard.

The Politics of Asthma Causation and Treatment

Asthma politics encompasses debates on disease causation. Environmental justice activists are deeply involved in these debates. Asthma does not have a single cause but results from a complex interaction of genetic and environmental factors. While there is no known biological reason for the greater prevalence of asthma among racial minorities, higher asthma rates may be a surrogate for lower quality of health care, limited health care access, lack of access to culturally appropriate medical care, and the higher number of minorities living in low-income neighborhoods with substandard housing, which exposes them to cockroaches, peeling paint and the resulting dust, and higher rates of exposure to smokers, all of which can trigger attacks among asthmatics.

Environmental justice activists in New York focus on the *outdoor air pollution* risks as exacerbating already poor health conditions in their communities. Children with asthma are sensitive to outdoor air pollution. Common air pollutants, such as ozone, sulfur dioxide, and particulate matter are respiratory irritants and can exacerbate asthma. . . .

In West Harlem and the South Bronx, supporters of each facility (either from the state or corporate sector) argued that there was no scientific proof that a particular facility contributed [to] exacerbating asthma rates.[3] This point was countered with another narrative. Community activists, often women of color, testified at public hearings and public events, often citing their asthma or their child's asthma. They countered that the increase of childhood asthma rates must have something to do with outdoor air pollution, and the science of risk assessment was inadequate to deal with the cumulative exposure that their residents faced . . . (as opposed to single sources in conventional risk assessment analysis). In essence, these activists argue that while it is difficult to scientifically prove the direct impact of a new facility (incinerator, solid waste transfer station, power plant, or sewage treatment plant) manifesting in increased asthma rates . . ., the extra burden that these neighborhoods already face due to the higher rates of pollution exposure, and (therefore) more fragile health status to (particularly of young and old), special protective precautions should be taken. This concept draws from the "Wingspread Statement on the Precautionary Principle" that is being advanced by public health and cancer activists (Steingraber 1997). This "principle of precautionary action" . . . calls for preventing harm to the environment and to human health. An international group of scientists, government officials, lawyers, and labor and grassroots environmental activists defined the principle as follows:

- The release and use of toxic substances, the exploitation of resources, and physical alterations of the environment have had substantial unintended consequences affecting human health and the environment. Some of these concerns are high rates of learning deficiencies, asthma, cancer, birth defects and species extinctions, along with global climate change, stratospheric ozone depletion and worldwide contamination with toxic substances and nuclear materials.

- We believe existing environmental regulations and other decisions, particularly those based on risk assessment, have failed to protect adequately human health and the environment—the larger system of which humans are but a part.

- We believe there is compelling evidence that damage to humans and the worldwide environment is of such magnitude and seriousness that new principles for conducting human activities are necessary.

- While we realize that human activities may involve hazards, people must proceed more carefully than has been the case in recent history. Corporations, government entities, organizations, communities, scientists and other individuals must adopt a precautionary approach to all human endeavors.

- Therefore, it is necessary to implement the Precautionary Principle: When an activity raises threats of harm to human health or the environment, precautionary measures should be taken even if some cause and effect relationships are not fully established scientifically. In this context the proponent of an activity, rather than the public, should bear the burden of proof. (Steingraber 1997, 284)

Significantly, asthma is identified as a key problem in the statement. The statements of New York City environmental justice advocates on the issue of causality, proof, and outdoor air pollution and its impact on asthma reflect the importance of the precautionary principle to their activism, although they did not phrase it as such.

Another major source of triggers for asthmatics is the indoor environment (Jones 1998). The home environment exposures include tobacco, mold, poor ventilation, water damage, heat irritants (electric, gas, oil, wood), chemical irritants (air fresheners, ammonia, and other chemicals), dust (carpet, cloth-covered furniture, drapes or curtains), pets, dust mites, and bed covers (comforters and wool, cotton, or acrylic blankets). The most controversial theory of indoor triggers involves cockroaches. The National Institute of Allergy and Infectious Diseases (NIAID) and the National Institute for Environmental Health Science (NIEHS) conducted the National Cooperative Inner City Asthma Study, a study of children with asthma in eight U.S. cities that tested the effects of interventions that reduce children's exposure to indoor allergens and that sought to improve communication with their primary care physicians. The study compared the effects of various allergens on asthmatic children living in poor urban areas. The results, published in 1997 in the *New England Journal of Medicine*, suggested that cockroaches may be the chief culprit in childhood asthma. Nearly 40 percent of the asthmatic children were found to be allergic to the insects' droppings and body parts.

However, community leaders in New York City questioned the emphasis on indoor air pollution, pointing out that dirt, dust mites, cockroaches, mice/rat urine, poor housing, or conditions of poverty are not new phenomena. The focus on indoor household triggers, particularly cockroaches, inspires particular ire by some environmental justice activists because of the racialized and gendered implications of dirty homes and substandard housekeeping as opposed to external outdoor pollution as the primary cause of high asthma rates. The focus on housekeeping rather than poor housing conditions (for example, mold in public housing, an endemic problem), represents this emphasis on individualized versus systemic approaches to the childhood asthma epidemic. As Marian Feinberg from the South Bronx Clean Air Coalition commented, "The problem with the National Inner City Asthma Study is how it was manipulated in the media. Two bad things happened: the emphasis on cockroaches implied that bad moms caused asthma, and it focused on cockroaches as the main factor" (personal communication, May 2002). She points out the ironic effects of this conclusion: after the media attention, pesticide companies started marketing their products on Spanish language and black radio stations in ads that portrayed a child gasping for air. These commercials ran despite the fact that pesticide sprays themselves can function as asthma triggers. Environmental justice activists, in contrast, have focused on a multidimensional approach to asthma causation and management, exemplified by the campaign slogan "Cleaner Air, Cleaner Housing, Cleaner Lungs."

The main aspects of asthma management are taking medication properly, taking care of the home, monitoring air flow, and reducing exposure to common indoor household triggers. Asthma medicines keep the air tubes in the lungs open. The main treatment regimen is the correct taking of preventative medication. This process has grown increasingly complex with the advent of more sophisticated medication, and some children take up to eight different medications a day. Taking care of the home environment means recognizing the indoor triggers for asthma and taking steps to remedy these conditions. Home inspection of household exposures is a common approach to asthma management programs. Typically in this approach, representatives of a "Healthy Homes" project inspect the home, measure the caregiver's knowledge about asthma triggers, and suggest steps to reduce exposures (Krieger et al. 2000). The homes chosen for inspection are usually poor households with asthmatic children. The question of how to choose what homes to visit is significant given that most homes in the developed world probably have at least one of the household exposures. An important question to consider, and

a key area for further research, is how the "correction" of the household environment is done without implying that poor women or women of color have bad housekeeping practices and blaming mothers for their children's asthma.

Some environmental justice activists have an ambivalent view of the home visits approach to asthma for this very reason of where the burden of blame ends up. As one SBCAC leader, Marian Feinberg, explained, the emphasis on indoor allergens and housekeeping practices tends to privilege an individualistic versus a systematic approach to the problem: "I understand that it can help some individuals, and that if it helps even one household or child, then it's valuable. But aren't we then accepting the basic conditions of poor housing and outdoor air pollution by this approach, instead of systemically trying to improve housing and the external environment?" (Feinberg, personal communication, May 2002).

The home visits can be a part of a balanced and fair asthma intervention approach. Also, community-based asthma education is increasingly being recognized as . . . an effective tool to deal with asthma in low-income and minority populations (Ford et al. 1996; Wilson et al. 1998). Another multidimensional approach to children's environmental health research is being advanced by WEACT, which is the community partner in a nationally recognized collaboration with Columbia University's School of Public Health through their Columbia Center for Children's Environmental Health (CCEH). WEACT has transformed its environmental justice activism into a vibrant and significant force in community-based public health research that is generating new knowledge about asthma. The CCEH was founded in 1998 as one of eight Centers for Children's Environmental Health and Disease Prevention established jointly by the National Institute of Environmental Health Sciences and the Environmental Protection Agency. The Columbia Research Project on Asthma is charting possible links between signs of asthma in very young children and exposure to allergens and pollutants in their homes and outdoor environment, the role of nutrition, as well as the impact of air pollution on birth weights. Preliminary findings from air quality tests in the homes of the first group of mothers suggest virtually universal exposure to two highly toxic pesticides during pregnancy, while biomarkers in maternal and cord blood show high rates of exposure to allergens, air pollutants, and secondhand tobacco smoke (Miller 1999). The study also found air pollutants are linked to lower birth weights and skills in African American babies. This study suggests that the problems that low-income urban children face and the health effects of pollution exposure begin before birth, and one potential implication is an incentive to reduce pollution exposures that negatively affect children's environmental health.

Conclusion

By demonstrating that the environmental justice movement's concern with asthma politics encompasses environmental policy as well as health debates about causation and management, I hope to recognize the contribution that the environmental justice movement has made to explicating complex debates about asthma in particular, and the politics of race and urban environmental health more generally. Asthma rates in New York City are finally starting to fall, at least in part because the sense of community crisis catalyzed an action and research agenda that forced bureaucracy into action.[4] The politicization of asthma as an environmental justice issue contributed at least in part to the success in chipping away at the racial disparity of the disease. The larger political contribution the environmental justice movement makes is in re-envisioning environmental policy making, reintegrating the health aspects of environmental policy and in engaging questions of risk assessment.

Asthma is a complex disease and a fascinating one for this complexity. . . . The politics of asthma causation, the answer to the problem of racial disparities in asthma rates, and the gender politics of asthma management are tremendously complex, and much more research needs to be done on the various questions and issues I have raised, especially as tremendous federal resources pour into asthma research.

NOTES

1. According to the New York City Department of City Planning based on 2000 census data, West Harlem is primarily African American, low income, and over 90 percent are renters. Almost 50 percent of the South Bronx is on public assistance. Approximately 92 percent of the population is renters, and 96 percent of this community is Hispanic or African American. The South Bronx is one of the poorest congressional districts in the nation and houses the largest concentration of New York City Housing Authority Projects in the Bronx (http://www.nyc.goc/html/dcp/html/lucds/cdstart.html).

2. Harlem and the South Bronx are severely underserved by public space and parks because of a legacy of neglect in open-space planning. For example, in Robert Moses' capacity as commissioner of the New York City Department of Parks and Recreation, from 1934 to 1959, he built 255 parks, only one of which was in Harlem. Riverbank State Park in West Harlem was built on top of the North River Sewage Treatment Plant as a concession to the community.

3. A vast literature on risk discusses the politics of proof. For example, Tesh argues that the lack of scientific corroboration of environmental activists' claims may be an artifact of the slow incorporation of environmentalism into science rather than a statement about the actual effect of pollution on health (2000). See also Davis 2002.

4. At the city level, the New York City Department of Health (DOH) began a Community Asthma Program and a New York City Childhood Asthma Initiative that sponsored the asthma education campaigns on the New York City train and bus system. The DOH also coordinates the New York City Asthma Partnership (NYCAP), a coalition of individuals and organizations who share an interest in reversing the asthma epidemic in New York City.

REFERENCES

American Lung Association, Epidemiology and Statistics Unit. 2003. "Trends in Asthma Morbidity and Mortality." (Mar.).

Bullard, Robert, ed. 1994. *Unequal Protection: Environmental Justice and Communities of Color.* San Francisco: Sierra Club.

Centers for Disease Control, *Morbidity and Mortality Weekly Report,* Oct. 13, 2000. "Measuring Childhood Asthma Prevalence Before and After the 1997 Redesign of the National Health Interview Survey—United States." 49, no. 40: 908–11.

Davis, Devra. 2002. *When Smoke Ran Like Water.* New York: Basic Books.

Ford, M., G. Edwards, J. Rodriguez, R. Gibson, and B. Tilley. 1996. "An Empowerment-Centered, Church-Based Asthma Education Program for African American Adults." *Health and Social Work* 21:1, 70–75.

Gabbay, John. 1982. "Asthma Attacked? Tactics for the Reconstruction of a Disease Concept." In *The Problem of Medical Knowledge: Examining the Social Construction of Medicine,* ed. Peter Wright and Andrew Treacher. Edinburgh: Edinburgh University Press.

Guyer, Ruth. 2000. "Breath of Life: Stories of Asthma from an Exhibition at the National Library of Medicine." *American Journal of Public Health* 90, no. 6: 874–79.

Hamilton, Cynthia. 1993. "Environmental Consequences on Urban Growth and Blight." In *Toxic Struggles: The Theory and Practice of Environmental Justice,* ed. Richard Hofrichter. Philadelphia: New Society.

Hubbard, Ruth, and Elijah Wald. 1993. *Exploding the Gene Myth: How Genetic Information is Produced and Manipulated by Scientists, Physicians, Employers, Insurance Companies, Educators, and Law Enforcers.* Boston: Beacon Press.

Jones, A. P. 1998. "Asthma and Domestic Air Quality." *Social Science and Medicine* 47, no. 6: 755–64.

Krieger, J., L. Song, T. Takaro, and J. Stout. 2000. "Asthma and the Home Environment of Low-Income Urban Children: Preliminary Findings from the Seattle–King County Health Homes Project." *Journal of Urban Health: Bulletin of the New York Academy of Medicine* 77, no. 1: 50–67.

Miller, R. L. 1999. "Breathing Freely: The Need for Asthma Research on Gene–Environment Interactions." *American Journal of Public Health* 89, no. 6: 819–22.

Miller, Vernice. 1994. "Planning, Power and Politics: A Case Study of the Land Use and Siting History of the North River Water Pollution Control Plant." *Fordham Urban Law Journal* 21, no. 3: 707–22.

New York City Department of Health. 2003. "NYC Vital Signs." *Community Health Survey* 2: 4.

Nocon, A., and Tim Booth. 1989–1990. "The Social Impact of Asthma: A Review of the Literature." *Social Work and Social Sciences Review* 1 no. 3:177–200.

Nossiter, Adam. 1995. "Asthma Common and on the Rise in the Crowded South Bronx." *New York Times,* Sept. 5, p. A1.

Pérez-Peña, Richard. 2003. "Study Finds Asthma in 25% of Children in Central Harlem." *New York Times,* Apr. 19, p. A1.

President's Task Force on Environmental Health Risks and Safety Risks to Children. 1999. "Asthma and the Environment: A Strategy to Protect Children." Revised. May 2000.

Steingraber, Sandra. 1997. *Living Downstream: An Ecologist Looks at Cancer and the Environment.* Reading, Mass: Addison-Wesley.

Stevenson, L, R. Garg, and J. Leighton. 2000. "Asthma Hospitalization in New York City 1988–1997." *Journal of Urban Health: Bulletin of the New York Academy of Medicine* 77:1,137–39.

Tesh, S. 2000. *Uncertain Hazards: Environmental Activists and Scientific Proof.* Ithaca: Cornell University Press.

Wailoo, Keith. 2001. *Dying in the City of the Blues: Sickle Cell Anemia and the Politics of Race and Health.* Chapel Hill: University of North Carolina Press.

Wilson, S., P. Scamagas, J. Grado, and L. Norgaard. 1998. "The Fresno Asthma Project: A Model Intervention to Control Asthma in Multi-Ethnic, Low-Income, Inner-City Communities." *Health Education and Behavior* 25, no. 1: 79–98.

SIXTY-FOUR

◆◆◆

Thinking and Eating at the Same Time (2010)
Reflections of a Sistah Vegan

Michelle R. Loyd-Paige

Michelle R. Loyd-Paige is Professor of Sociology and Dean of Multicultural Affairs at Calvin College, Grand Rapids, Michigan. Her research interests include the social worlds of African American clergywomen, the role of Afro-Christian worship, Christian responses to racism, and the religious roadblocks that hinder the elimination of domestic violence toward women. She is the founder of Preach Sistah! Inc. (www.PreachSista.com).

It was the Saturday after Thanksgiving in 2005. I was out shopping at the local mall when my husband called and asked me if I would pick up a six-piece chicken-wing snack for him on my way home because he was tired of the turkey leftovers. Soon after his call, I found myself at a fast-food chicken restaurant. I was standing in line trying to remember what type of sauce he said he wanted—*Was it the hot barbeque, the honey mustard, or the teriyaki? Was that with or without ranch dressing?*—when, from out of nowhere, I began wondering what happened to the rest of the bodies of the three chickens it took to create this snack for my husband that I was about to so casually order. Almost immediately, other questions popped into my head: *Just how many other people would stand in this same line in this restaurant to order chicken wings today? And how many other fast-food chicken restaurants are experiencing an increase in business today because people are out shopping and they are tired of leftover turkey from Thanksgiving? Just how many chickens were being grown so my husband, and three hundred million other Americans, could have chicken wings anytime they wanted—not to mention in the world?*

Little did I know that my questions about chicken wings on that day would lead to a radical change in the way I eat. Believe me, it's not that I have some great love for chickens as a part of God's creation and think that they should have the same sacred status as cows in India or humans in every part of the world. My thinking and eating habits changed as a result of what I call a *kairos* moment. *Kairos* is an ancient Greek word meaning the "right or opportune moment."[1] In my faith tradition it also means "the appointed time in the purpose of God." At this appointed time, four previously unassociated thoughts—the content of a lecture I had just presented four days prior on the global inequities in food distribution; a vague recollection of a statement from PETA [People for the Ethical Treatment of Animals] about the cruelties associated with chicken production; the remembrance of how surprisingly good I felt physically while on a forty-day spiritually motivated fast from meat and dairy at the beginning of the year; and my own desire to live an authentic life—yanked me into an uncomfortable realization that, when it came to food consumption, I was not living according to my beliefs.

I did purchase the chicken-wing snack for my husband, but with that sales transaction I began earnestly thinking about what I ate. I became conscious that what I ate was not merely a combination of taste preference, convenience, and cultural heritage. Before that moment in the chicken restaurant, I had given very little thought to how the food I enjoyed got to my table, and I certainly didn't think I was hurting anything or anyone. I am a socially aware college professor who challenges her students to think about how their social (and predominantly white) privilege supports the inequities that position people of color on the fault lines of life AND how their privilege allows them to be unconcerned about issues they do not think pertain to them. *How could I be guilty of the offense with which I indicted my students?*

As a middle-class citizen of the United States, I had been exercising status privilege every time I went to the grocery store or picked up a takeout dinner on my way home from work or shopping. It's a privilege to be able to eat what I want without ever having to think about how the food gets to my table. As I exercise this privilege, I am unconsciously participating in patterns of indifference and oppression. *I was guilty of the offense with which I indicted my students!* And here was truth in a Styrofoam box, which held six whole chicken wings covered in hot barbeque sauce with a side of ranch dressing. The truth is that no matter how good a person I was, my eating habits were contrary to what I believed. All of my actions either contribute to patterns of social inequities or to the solutions to the ills of our society. All social inequities are linked. Comprehensive systemic change will happen only if we are aware of these connections and work to bring an end to all inequalities—not just our favorites or the ones that most directly affect our part of the universe. No one is on the sidelines; by our actions or inactions, by our caring or our indifference, we are either part of the problem or part of the solution. I was beginning to see my lifestyle as it really was: a part of the problem and not part of the solution.

Not liking what I saw, I made a conscious decision to change my eating habits so that they would more closely represent my thinking on issues of social justice, the equitable use and distribution of global resources, and the health-diet-survival connection for African-Americans. Since my *kairos* moment in a chicken fast-food restaurant, I have chosen to eat like a vegan and have changed my shopping habits. I now buy fair trade tea and chocolate, and when possible, I purchase fresh and organic produce from local farmers. I do have a few nonvegan-friendly clothing items hanging in my closet from before my transformation, but none of my post-transformation clothing purchases contain animal skins or animal products.

My initiation into veganism actually occurred eleven months before that *kairos* moment in the fast-food chicken restaurant. I usually spend the first weekend of a new year on a personal spiritual retreat. In January 2005, I also participated in a month of fasting from meat, dairy, and sugar, facilitated by my church. The fast was voluntary and was supposed to *detoxify* the mind, body, and spirit. My church called it a "Daniel Fast." With the exception of the sugar restriction, the diet fit the vegan way of eating—soybean products became the main-stay of family and church dinners. (I'm sure the local health-food store was wondering what was going on with *all* these Black people buying up eve-rything soy during that month.)

Twenty of us stuck with the fast for the entire month without slipping back into old eating habits. We all saw improvements in our health. Not un-expectedly, we lost weight; I lost ten pounds. But to my surprise, by the end of the month I was also experiencing fewer hot flashes (associated with ap-proaching menopause) and was sleeping better at night. However, as soon as the fast was over, I added poultry, dairy, and sugar products back into my diet. Red meat was no longer on the menu in my home be-cause it was giving my daughter headaches and my husband had been told to change his diet in order to lower his cholesterol levels. A month after reintro-ducing these foods to my diet, the hot flashes began to return. Several months after the reintroduction of meat and dairy, right around the time of the chicken-restaurant moment, the hot flashes were becoming so bothersome that I actually began to think seri-ously about hormone replacement therapy. I spoke to my doctor, and he suggested that I first consider adding the soy back into my diet.

I now credit the end of my hot flashes to the elimination of all meat and dairy from my diet, the eating of organic produce (when possible), and the daily consumption of soy. January 2005 marked the beginning of my understanding of how food affects the functioning of my body. It was November 2005 that marked the beginning of my understanding of how the food I ate contributed to social inequalities, and it marked my transforma-tion to eating like a vegan; in late November I began thinking and eating at the same time.

Thinking about what I was eating led me on a search for the answer to the question I had raised to myself about chicken consumption in the U.S. I discovered that in 2005 the total number of broil-ers—chickens raised for their meat—produced in the U.S. for the year was 8.87 billion.[2] "Each week, Pilgrim's Pride (the number-two poultry producer) turns about 30 million chickens into nuggets, wings, drumsticks, and sundry other parts." According to the National Chicken Council, "American consumers are eating an unprecedented 81 pounds of chicken per person this year . . . and plan to purchase more in the months to come."[3] The U.S. appetite for chicken

has grown steadily since 1970 when the per-person average was 37 pounds.[4] Americans eat more chicken than beef (69 pounds) and pork (52 pounds). The amount of meat in a typical American diet far exceeds the daily allowances suggested by the U.S. Department of Agriculture's food pyramid.[5]

The sheer number of feed animals necessary to satisfy the American diet is staggering. In order to keep costs low and production high, animals and chickens are routinely crowded into small pens or cages, mutilated, and drugged with antibiot-ics and growth hormones. Crowded and stressful conditions have been associated with feed animals and chickens becoming ill. Because chickens in such conditions will turn on each other, chickens are de-beaked so they will not kill each other. Feed animals that do not grow fast enough or are too old or sick are sometimes killed and ground into animal feed. Cows, who are by nature herbivores, are routinely fed a protein mixture prepared from ground cows.[6] Laying chicks who are the wrong sex are discarded in garbage bags—sometimes still living.[7] The conditions under which many feed animals are raised are inhumane. While human-kind may have been granted dominion over ani-mals,[8] I don't believe we were also given the right to be cruel, brutal, and heartless in our treatment of them. Animals are a part of creation, just as hu-mans. Treating them so callously is symptomatic of a general disregard for anything our culture de-fines as inferior and expendable.

In the U.S., how we treat food animals is remi-niscent of how people of color were treated. Andrea Smith made such a connection with Native women and children and animals in her book *Conquest*:

> Native people often view their identities as in-separable from the rest of creation, and hence, creation requires care and respect, but colo-nizers viewed Indian identity as inseparably linked to animal and plant life, and deserving of destruction and mutilation. This equation between animals and Native people continues.[9]

Smith's statement was in the context of discuss-ing the U.S. government's practices of medical ex-perimentation on Native inhabitants in reservations. African-Americans have also been used as human guinea pigs for some of our government's medi-cal experiments: The Tuskegee syphilis studies are a well-known example. Africans were brought to this country in mass numbers as slaves. They were chained together and kept in the cramped holds of ships as they crossed the Atlantic. In order to justify the brutality of slavery, the oppressors deemed Africans as less-than-human and undeserving of decent housing, education, food, health care, justice, or respect. African women who were enslaved were often used as breeders for a new crop of slaves. It was not uncommon for Africans who were too sick, too old, or too rebellious to be killed if it was thought cheaper to replace them than to keep them. Prized animals were often treated better than slaves.

Seeing a connection between the treatment of feed animals, laying chickens, and people of color is a rather recent phenomenon for me. Two years ago, I wouldn't have believed there was such a connection. Today, I know better. The connection becomes clear with a careful reading of our history and an understanding of the true nature of food production in the United States. The connection, however, is also observable by a thorough analysis of today's headlines and an informed critique of social policy and community life. Understanding the connection strengthens my resolve to continue eating like a vegan. Choosing to eat this way is a reminder to myself and a demonstration to those around me that all of creation is worthy of respect and humane treatment, even chickens.

At the time I raised my questions about chicken consumption, I was simply curious about how many chickens Americans ate. As I searched to satisfy my curiosity of that day, I have changed from wondering about numbers of chickens to the costs of the American diet. *What are the health-related costs to the lives of people eating a typical American diet? Why does it cost more to eat healthy? Why is it "unusual" to have a meal without meat? Why do feed animals need so many growth hormones and antibiotics in their feed? What do these animal growth hormones and antibiotics do in our human bodies? Why do we commit so much of our land and water resources to growing feed for animals when we could grow grain that is a healthier source of protein? Can we really afford to not know where our food comes from and how it is produced?* I am convinced that eating a meat-based diet—not to mention dairy products, eggs, and fish— is not only hazardous to food animals and harmful to the land, but, more important to me, perilous to the health of my people.

The top five leading causes of death among African-Americans are: heart disease, cancer,

cerebrovascular disease, accidents, and diabetes.[10] Currently, 27 percent of deaths in the Black U.S. population are from heart disease, and the death rate from diabetes for Blacks is twice that of whites.[11] According to the American Heart Association, women of color are particularly vulnerable:

> African-American and Hispanic women have higher prevalence rates of high blood pressure, obesity, physical inactivity, diabetes and metabolic syndrome than white women. Yet they are less likely than white women to know that being overweight, smoking, physical inactivity, high cholesterol and a family history of heart disease increase their heart disease risk.[12]

The prevalence of being overweight (including obesity) in African-American women is 77 percent; the prevalence of obesity is 49 percent.[13] Obesity has a strong correlation to diabetes. The traditional African-American diet is loaded with deep-fried chicken; meats are smothered in cream-based gravies; vegetables are slow-cooked with pork and pork fat until the color of the vegetables is no longer bright; and desserts are loaded with butter and cream. Soul Food (a.k.a. Southern home-cooking or comfort food) is often jokingly referred to as a "heart-attack on plate."

For African-Americans, however, it's no laughing matter. We are literally killing ourselves and decreasing our quality of life by the way we eat. Of the leading causes of death for African-Americans, all but one, accidents, have a connection to diet and lifestyle. Heart disease, obesity, and diabetes do not have to be such a prominent part of the African-American experience. Switching to an all-plant or nearly all-plant diet is one of the most effective ways to stop the progress of heart disease,[14] reversing the tendency to obesity, and controlling the onset of diabetes.

Every now and then my husband will ask me, "How long are you going to eat like this?" He used to ask because he and the rest of my immediate family thought that I wasn't going to get enough protein in my diet. Through my sharing of nutrition facts with them, they no longer think that eating like a vegan is unhealthy—strange for a Black person, perhaps, but not unhealthy. In fact, my husband has switched to soy butter and eats several meatless meals a week with me. My mother has also declared that a vegan restaurant I introduced her to is now one of her favorites and has dined there several times without me. Now when my husband asks, "How long are you going to eat like this?" it's because he has noticed that I no longer have hot flashes and he wants me to stay hot-flash-free, because "if momma is happy, everybody is happy." Although he appreciates the improvement in my comfort level and disposition, he and I are reminded of just how challenging it can be to maintain this lifestyle every time we try to go out for dinner, attend a birthday party, or go to a church potluck.

I'm the only vegan in my household. I think I'm the only Black female in all of western Michigan who eats like a vegan; if I'm not, it sure seems like it. There are no true vegan restaurants within ninety miles of our home. The closest vegetarian restaurant is forty-eight miles away, in a trendy, white, college-student side of town. When we do go out to eat (which is not very often) I usually opt for a salad without meat or cheese. Family holiday dinners, church potlucks, and birthday parties call for several different strategies. There's the "I'll be happy to bring something" so I can be sure that there's at least one item I can eat; there's the "Really, I am full. I just ate, all I want is a glass of water" so I don't have to explain to sistah sistah why I'm not eating her prized chicken salad; and then there are the times when I feel up to being an educator and I share with people why I no longer eat meat.

How long will I continue to eat like this? I can't see returning to eating meat, eggs, or dairy products, even with the inconveniences associated with eating out, dinner parties, church potlucks, family holiday dinners, and birthday parties. I am healthier now. I know too much now. I am committed to living an authentic life and to working for the elimination of all forms of injustice. I am now thinking and eating at the same time. There is no turning back.

NOTES

1. Retrieved from en.wikipedia.org/wiki/Kairos.
2. National Agricultural Statistical Service, USDA, Washington D.C. Retrieved from www.slate.com/id/2112698.
3. Retrieved from www.spcnetwork.com/mii/2000/000508.htm.
4. Ibid.
5. Marilyn Hughes Gaston and Gayle Porter, *Prime Time: The African American Woman's Guide to Midlife Health and Wellness* (New York: One World Press, 2001), p. 174.
6. Erik Marcus, *Vegan: New Ethics of Eating* (Ithaca, N.Y.: McBooks Press, 2001).
7. Ibid.
8. Genesis 1:26 (Living Bible) reads, "Then God said, 'Let us make a man—someone like ourselves, to be the master of all life upon the earth and in the skies and in the seas.'" Many people interpret this passage of scripture as God's mandate for humans to dominate animals.
9. Andrea Smith, *Conquest: Sexual Violence and American Indian Genocide* (Cambridge, Mass.: South End Press, 2005), p. 117.
10. American Cancer Society, *Cancer Facts and Figures for African Americans 2005–2006* (Atlanta: author, 2005), p. 1.
11. Ibid.
12. Retrieved from www.americanheart.org/presenter.jhtml?identifier=3018809.
13. American Cancer Society, *Cancer Facts and Figures for African Americans 2005-2006*, p. 16.
14. Marcus, *Vegan: New Ethics of Eating*, p. 4.

S I X T Y - F I V E

◆◆◆

Women and Food Chain: The Gendered Politics of Food (2007)

Patricia Allen and Carolyn Sachs

Patricia Allen chairs the Department of Food Systems and Society at Marylhurst University, Oregon. She has published widely on the political ecology of agrifood systems, alternative agrifood institutions, and the environmental, social, and ethical aspects of sustainable agrifood systems.

Carolyn Sachs is Professor of Rural Sociology and head of the Women's Studies Department at Penn State University. Her many publications include *Invisible Farmers: Women in Agricultural Production and Gendered Fields: Rural Women, Agriculture, and Environment.* She serves on an expert panel to the UN on Gender, Water, and Sanitation, and provides hands-on training for the Pennsylvania Women's Agricultural Network (PAWAgN).

Introduction

Throughout history, the social relations of food have been organized along lines of gender. Today, in most societies women continue to carry the responsibility for the mental and manual labor of food provision—the most basic labor of care. Women's involvement with food constructs who they are in the world—as individuals, family members, and workers—in deep, complex, and often contradictory ways. Women perform the majority of food-related work, but they control few resources and hold little decision-making power in the food industry and food policy. And, although women bear responsibility for nourishing others, they often do not adequately nourish themselves. These long-standing contradictions are seemingly immune to the dynamism that characterizes nearly every other aspect of the agrifood system in this era of globalization and innovation.[1]

In this article we reflect on these contradictions, taking up three questions about gender relations in the contemporary agrifood system. First, we ask how the subordination of women and sublimation of feminist consciousness in relation to food has been engaged and explained in agrifood and feminist scholarship. We find a rich literature on body politics and gendered eating patterns, but substantial gaps in the areas of structural issues and social change. Second, we ask what are the configurations of food-connected gender relations? We discuss this within a framework of what we call food domains—material, socio-cultural, and corporeal—that define women's relationships to food. We find, unsurprisingly, that women are disadvantaged in each of these domains. This leads to our next question, what actions are being taken to change gender relations in the agrifood system? We look at the locations of women's agency in improving social and economic conditions in these three domains. While women are engaging in numerous important efforts to change the food system, these efforts are rarely coordinated. Neither are they generally identified as feminist projects, in the sense of being strategically oriented toward improving gender relations.

How can we work to better understand the complicated and contradictory connections between gender and food? Avakian and Haber (2006) have called for a new field of feminist food studies. For this field of study to emerge, the connections between women's food work in the labor market (material), their responsibility for food-related work in the home (socio-cultural), and their relationship with eating (corporeal) must be studied and adequately theorized. Until recently, these areas have been both understudied and unconnected. . . . We suggest that weaving the strands of feminist studies together with political economy and sociology can provide strong theoretical grounding for feminist food studies that would illuminate causes, conditions, and possibilities for change in gender relations in the agrifood system.

. . .

Resistance and Feminism

Feminist scholarship . . . provides complex understandings of resistance strategies. Resistance to neo-liberal globalization in the food system and gender relations with food comes in heterogeneous forms that are not necessarily connected to each other (Della Porta and Diani 2006). As with resistance to neo-liberal globalization in general, these activities include individual acts, workers' movements including organizing union activities, and organizing in the form of new social movements that focus on gender, environment, race, ethnicity, and consumer movements.

Women's efforts to resist and reshape the food system take multiple forms. . . . Women may act to meet their practical needs, such as access to healthy food, without altering gender power relations. These resistance efforts focus on helping women survive within the current structure. Women also act to meet their strategic needs—acts that involve altering gender power relations—such as equity in the workplace, shared responsibility for cooking, and healthy approaches to women's bodies. These efforts strive to change the core of the structure that subordinates women in the first place. Attempts at resistance to the food system occur in both production and consumption politics. In the USA, many of these efforts are often not explicitly feminist or part of the feminist movement.

How do we explain the perplexing absence of a feminist agenda in women's actions in food-system work? One key factor is agrarian ideology, which tends to support and reinforce the subordination of women. Fink (1992: 196) characterizes the

exclusionary nature of agrarian ideology stating
that it has been "a white male vision that has failed
to consider the full human integrity of other persons." She points out that agrarianism is a gendered
ideology that projects different ideals for men and
women. Women have been expected to support the
farm, men, and children ahead of their own needs
or aspirations. Focused on the nuclear family and
the male farmer, agrarian ideology embodies traditional gendered roles and can pose a roadblock to
raising issues of gender equality for both men and
women. . . . . Studies of masculinities and farming
also emphasize how gender constructs both men's
and women's identities on farms (Brandth 1999).
Hassanein (1999) points out that the limitations
women face in agricultural environments come not
only from overt discrimination or institutional barriers but also from their socialization in rural communities and unequal gender relations experienced
in daily life. Women farmers report that they are
often not taken seriously or treated respectfully by
other farmers, family members, and agricultural
professionals (Trauger and Sachs 2006).

Domains of Gendered Relations In Food

Here we examine gender relations in the food system in the material, sociocultural, and corporeal
domains. Beginning with the material domain, we
trace women's labor from field to table within the
agrifood system in the USA. Certainly these issues
of gender and food are global, cross-borders, and
are not confined to any one country. We focus principally on the USA to set boundaries to our study.
The USA is a particularly interesting case in terms
of the political economy of the food system since it
often wields control in terms of globalization of the
food system and has high levels of concentration in
production, processing, and retailing.

The Material Domain: Women's Paid Labor in the Agrifood System

Increasing concentration and globalization of food
production, processing, distribution, and retailing
characterize the food industry. These changes have
shifted the jobs in the food industry, the largest

industrial sector in the USA, from production and
manufacturing to service. In this section we document how material relations in the agrifood system
are highly gendered from field to table.

The dramatic restructuring and concentration of
production agriculture has resulted in fewer farms
and farmers in the USA. The size of farms has increased at the same time that smaller family farms
continue to go out of business. Despite, or maybe
because of, these trends, more women are farming
today than in the past. The percentage of women
farmers doubled from 5 percent in 1978 to 10 percent in 1997 to 12 percent in 2002 (U.S. Census of
Agriculture 2002). In addition, the Census of Agriculture began to count multiple operators on farms
in 2002 and reported that 27 percent of farmers were
women. Women farmers remain underrepresented
relative to their proportion in the population, however. In addition, women farmers typically own
smaller, less-capitalized farms and have lower farm
incomes and farm sales than men farmers (U.S.
Census of Agriculture 2002).

While women farmers face difficulty in terms
of gaining access to land, capital, credit, and
knowledge, women farm laborers are certainly
even more disadvantaged. Women farm laborers
earn extremely low wages and are often subject
to sexual harassment. Among U.S. farm workers,
women are more vulnerable to exploitation than
men, and they are paid even lower wages and
given fewer benefits than their male family members. Women farm workers median yearly earnings were between $2,500 and $5,000 compared to
men farm workers whose median yearly earnings
were between $5,000 and $7,500 (U.S. Department
of Labor 2005).

Gender divisions of labor also characterize food
processing and manufacturing. Global commodity
chains, especially in horticulture, rely on women as
disadvantaged workers in processing and packing-
houses (Dolan 2004; Collins 1995; Barndt 1999;
Barrientos 2001). Women are preferred workers in
vegetable and fruit production, which is seasonal,
part-time, and flexible. Increasingly, fresh fruits and
vegetables are tended and harvested by women in
Southern countries for export to the USA and Europe.
In the USA, women are the preferred workers in the
lower echelons of food processing, where they tend
to dominate low-level, high-intensity jobs, while men
dominate supervisor and driver jobs. According to

the U.S. Department of Labor and the U.S. Bureau of Labor Statistics (2005), women comprised 75 percent of graders and sorters of agricultural products, but only 20 percent of meat processing workers; in both cases their earnings were approximately three-fourths of men's earnings. . . .

With shifts in diet, farm-export policies, and retail stores demand for prepackaged meat, processors have deskilled jobs and shifted plants from unionized areas to rural areas with cheaper land and labor. The meat industry has changed with changes in diet—the shift from beef consumption to poultry consumption due to health concerns has resulted in poultry processing becoming the largest sector of the meat industry (Kandel 2006). Women, immigrants, and Hispanics have become preferred workers in these low-paying, difficult, and dangerous jobs.[2] These jobs fit the International Labor Organization's definition of 3D jobs: jobs that are dirty, dangerous, and degrading.

In food retailing, globalization has led to dramatic restructuring, with the 10 largest food companies now controlling 49 percent of food sales. Grocery stores ranked among the largest industries in the USA in 2002, providing 2.5 million jobs. Food retailers rely heavily on women workers. . . . In their efforts to be competitive, retailers' cost-cutting strategies often translate into low pay for the women workers on whom they rely. . . At the other end of the spectrum, management in the food retailing industry has been male dominated, so much so that one large grocery chain . . . instituted policies to increase the number of women in management.[3]

One of the major shifts in food labor results from increased dining outside the home—in restaurants and other institutions such as schools, hospitals, and prisons. The percent of food expenditures for food eaten outside the home increased from 33 percent in 1970 to 49 percent in 2005 (Economic Research Service 2006). This shift away from domestic food preparation is due in large part to the entry of more women into the labor force and their lack of time to prepare food at home. As more and more people eat out, the number of jobs in food service increases. Women hold most of the jobs in food service. The 2002 U.S. Census reports that women comprise 77 percent of the 6.5 million workers in food preparation and service. Sixty-eight percent of food servers and 78 percent of restaurant greeters are women (U.S. Bureau of Labor Statistics 2005b). . . . Many of these food service

workers are entry-level employees who often work long shifts in temporary positions and wield very little power in terms of their schedules or other terms of employment. Many of the jobs held by women in food service are part-time, flexible positions in which the workers earn relatively low wages with few benefits. Part-time work is more common among food and beverage serving workers than among workers in almost any other occupation. . . .

In the commercial kitchen, we might expect women to outnumber men as cooks. After all, cooking is almost universally coded as women's work in the home. Yet women are less likely than men to work as cooks in restaurants—whether McDonald's or five-star restaurants. Women comprise less than 40 percent of paid cooks and less than 20 percent of head cooks and chefs (U.S. Bureau of Labor Statistics 2005a). Wages of chefs and cooks vary significantly by type of eating establishment. In 2002, median hourly earnings of chefs and head cooks, jobs that men dominate, were $13.43 with the highest 10 percent earning more than $25.86 per hour. By contrast, women cooks often work in institutions and cafeterias earning an average of $8.72 per hour. Fast-food cooks earned the least—$6.90 per hour (U.S. Bureau of Labor Statistics 2005a). Not surprisingly, women in the cooking occupations predominate in places with lower earnings.

Women are not well represented in the leadership of agribusinesses. Even though the number of women-owned businesses in agriculture has almost doubled since 1980, only one business sector (the transportation, communication, and utilities sector), reported fewer women-owned businesses than agriculture. . . . In addition, of 11 major U.S. industries, agriculture has historically been the least likely to employ women as managers, executives, or administrators. . . .

Decisions related to agriculture and food often rely on science and scientific data about agricultural production and food that contain little input from women. Feminist critiques of agricultural science suggest that women's knowledge is often devalued (Feldman and Welsh 1995; Sachs 1996). Agricultural and food-related sciences are historically extremely gendered, with men predominating in agricultural science and women finding a place in nutrition or home economics. . . . While women have historically been excluded from scientific professions in general, their exclusion continues to be particularly glaring in the agricultural sciences.

In 1995, women comprised 13 percent of employed agricultural scientists compared to 28 percent of biological scientists (Buttel and Goldberger 2002). However, the under-representation of women in the agricultural sciences is shifting, with the percentage of women receiving their Ph.D. degrees in agricultural sciences increasing substantially in the past ten years from 23 percent in 1995 to 36 percent in 2005 (National Science Foundation 2006).

. . .

The Socio-Cultural Domain: Nourishing Others

Although women rarely work as chefs and head cooks in restaurants, they almost always hold the position of head cook in their homes. Regardless of culture, class, or ethnicity, the majority of women cook and serve food for their families. . . . Women go to the store, shop, unpack groceries, prepare food, cook meals, serve food, wash dishes, and clean the kitchen. Food work is not merely physical but involves relentless mental and caring labor—planning meals, worrying about nutrition, and arranging and serving meals (DeVault 1991). Women must know the food likes and dislikes of their family members, plan the timing and location of meals, and keep up with complicated and ever-changing news on nutrition and food safety. DeVault likens this work of feeding the family to solving a puzzle. DeVault addresses class differences between women. She suggests that in solving the puzzle of what's for dinner, middle-class women consult recipes and working-class women rely on tradition. However, she neglects to consider how race and ethnicity effect women's cooking efforts (Avakian and Haber 2006). Gullah women, African American women, and Jewish women also attempt to maintain their marginalized cultural traditions through food production (Betts 1995; Harris 1995; Kirshenblatt-Gimblett l997).

In solving the food-provision puzzle women typically select food that pleases other family members, especially their husbands. . . . Furthermore, since men's needs dominate the organization of cooking and eating in terms of the composition and timing of meals, many women face serious repercussions if food is not prepared correctly and on time (Bell and Valentine 1997). Women who fail to please their husband's food preferences often experience negative consequences ranging from small arguments to domestic violence. . . . As with other household work, women experience a fundamental ambivalence between the tedium and marginalizing aspects of their work and the love and caring they feel for their families. Such work can be pleasurable or onerous depending on circumstances such as time or financial pressure.

While women remain responsible for food provision in the home, the nature of this caring work of feeding others has shifted over time. Few families or individuals in households eat all of their meals together. Household members who work, go to school, or spend time outside the home often eat breakfast, lunch, and sometimes dinner away from home in restaurants, cafeterias, or other food establishments. Women who work outside the home have less time to prepare food for their families. Much of food processing and cooking activities for food eaten at home now takes place in the market. Convenience foods, such as pre-cooked meals, save women time preparing meals and bring increased profits to the processing, retailing and restaurant industries. But, convenience foods are expensive, stretching the budgets of low-income women. And as we discussed in the previous section, the labor to produce these convenience foods is often provided by women, often women of color, working for low wages in difficult working conditions (Julier 2006).

Still, despite the increasing entry of women into the labor force, women spend at least twice as much time as men doing domestic chores, an imbalance particularly marked in food labor. Even when men share more domestic labor in the home, they are only marginally involved with food provisioning activities. Studies show that mothers, still considered the experts on children, do the majority of work in taking care of children, including feeding them (Coltrane 1996; Zimmerman et al. 2001).

Another aspect of the entry of women into the labor force is that in upper-middle and middle-class U.S households employed women lack the time to do housework and child care. Male household members rarely step in. Women either work almost around the clock or, if they can afford it, hire domestic help. Affluent career women increasingly maintain the illusion of "doing it all" by hiring domestic workers and nannies to clean the house, feed the children, and magically disappear from sight (Ehrenreich and Hothschild 2002). While most women in U.S. households maintain responsibility for cooking and serving food, the dislocation of third-world women to the USA and other industrialized countries enables relatively affluent women to hire immigrant women to perform domestic work while they work outside the home (Mack-Canty 2004). . . .

The Corporeal Domain: Embodied Politics

While women have primary responsibility for feeding others, they often fail to take care of their own nutritional needs. Many women, regardless of their age or weight are dissatisfied with their bodies (Paquette and Raine 2004). Seventy-five percent of "normal" weight women consider themselves overweight, and 90 percent of women overestimate their body size. The average woman sees 400 to 600 advertisements per day and by the time a girl is 17 years old, she has received over 250,000 commercial messages. Most of these messages directly or indirectly promote physical attractiveness, including being thin. Nearly three-quarters of girls report that magazine models influence their concept of an ideal body shape, yet a woman between the ages of 18 and 34 has only a one percent chance of being as thin as a supermodel. Body discontent leads to dieting by normal weight women, unhealthy weight loss practices, restrained eating, eating disorders, depression, and poor self-esteem (Paquette and Raine 2004).

Within the agrifood system, the diet industry profits enormously from women's obsession with thinness and attempts to maintain unattainable body weights. The numbers of girls and women on diets has skyrocketed. . . . That the perfect body is, by definition, unattainable, traps many women and girls in a relentless cycle of failure. The proliferation of eating disorders, heavily gendered, is also class specific. Bordo (1998) claims that many women, who can afford to eat well, diet and go hungry most of the time. Girls and women, especially from the upper and upper-middle classes, deny themselves food as they tie their hopes for happiness on being thin.

On the other end of the weight continuum, the number of women who are overweight and obese is increasing. . . . Gender, class, ethnicity, and race intersect in defining who is likely to be overweight or obese. A negative correlation exists between income and weight; as incomes go down

weight goes up. People with low incomes find that foods high in sugar and fat are cheap and readily available, while "healthy" foods are relatively expensive and not necessarily available in their local stores (Morton et al. 2005). Obesity in women is also correlated with race and ethnicity. Obesity is most prevalent among non-Hispanic black women (49 percent) compared with Mexican-American women (38 percent) and non-Hispanic white women (31 percent) (National Center for Health Statistics 2004). For men, however, there is very little difference in obesity levels based on race/ethnicity (National Center for Health Statistics 2004). Obesity is connected to many health problems and the link between obesity and diabetes is particularly high in women. Obesity among children is also on the rise. Mothers often take the blame for their failure to provide their children with nutritious foods. Women with children are caught in a double bind as they are enjoined to make their children happy by feeding them junk food while they are simultaneously exhorted to be "good mothers" by ensuring the nutritional health of their children.

Eating disorders, whether resulting in being too thin or too fat, have been analyzed and treated principally as individual, psychological, and medical problems. Studies of obesity similarly focus the problem on individual eating behaviors rather than the food industry, limited access to nutritious food, or the increasing loss of public space for physical activity. Medicalization and individualization of public health and social problems obscure the food industry's role in constructing people's food desires and behaviors and blame the individual. . . .

Women cannot help but be caught up in some form of schizophrenic positioning with regard to food—eat more, eat less; eat well, eat badly—due to the contradictory and simultaneous marketing of thinness and food indulgence. . . . Despite, or maybe due to, their schizophrenic position, women are leading efforts to create change in the agrifood system. We highlight some of these efforts in the next section.

Working Against Homeostasis

Gender relations in the agrifood system have remained surprisingly static despite sea changes taking place in other dimensions of the agrifood system. One thing that has changed, however, is the extent of women-led initiatives. While women have always been involved in the food system, they now are playing expanded roles in changing material, socio-cultural, and corporeal conditions. Their efforts take multiple forms ranging from individual-level actions to collective resistance in the form of union organizing or involvement in agrifood social movements.

Women have taken the lead in resisting the repressive and exploitative conditions women face as hired labor in the food system. For example, women farm workers have organized for the rights of women farm workers, farm worker health, and day care and schools for migrant children. One group, Organización en California de Lideras Campesinas (Farm Worker Women's Leadership Network), organized in 1992, trains and organizes farm worker women on health issues, nutrition, pesticide issues, domestic violence, and economic development. Women have also taken the lead in the retail workers movement, beginning in 2000 when Betty Dukes filed a sex discrimination claim against Wal-Mart, her employer.[4] Wal-Mart is the largest food retailer in the United States as well as one of the largest employers in many regions of the country. . . .

In the public domain, women have worked to reshape the food system through organizing around livelihood issues and claims made on the state. Women were instrumental in establishing and managing federal food assistance programs to combat hunger and poor nutrition, and they continue to lead the fight to hold the line on cutbacks in public programs that provide assistance to impoverished families in the USA. For example, the National Council for Women's Organizations has a food security program that works to protect and expand the Food Stamp Program, the WIC Program (Women, Infants, and Children), and other supplemental food programs.

Women have also played central roles in shaping and furthering alternative agrifood movements and institutions. For example, women have led the National Campaign for Sustainable Agriculture, the California Campaign for Sustainable Agriculture, the California Food and Justice Coalition, the USDA Community Food Projects program, and the USDA SARE [Sustainable Agriculture Research and Education] program. Peter et al. (2000) found that women are better represented and more

prominent in sustainable agriculture organizations than they are in conventional agricultural organizations. Women often take the lead in urban agriculture, developing community gardens in diverse, low-income communities (Hynes 1996). For example, women have created Grow Pittsburgh, an organization that works to reclaim abandoned urban lots, build kitchen gardens to improve nutrition, and engage youth in food system work (Grow Pittsburgh 2006).

In Vermont, Maine, Iowa, and Pennsylvania women farmers have formed new types of networks for educational, social, and entrepreneurial support to empower women in sustainable agriculture and food-related businesses (Trauger 2005). For example, the Pennsylvania Agricultural Women's Network began in 2003 as a fledgling organization of women farmers and agricultural professionals with the goals of creating an empowering learning environment and network. The network's rapid growth surprised the organizers. As of 2006, more than 600 members participate in the network, the majority who work as farmers on small or medium-sized operations. Women farmers often lead the way for environmental sustainability and innovative entrepreneurship on farms. For example, in DeLind and Ferguson's (1999) study of community supported agriculture, they discovered that women were the primary workers on CSAs. Other women farmers, frustrated with working so hard to raise crops and livestock with very little return, form nonprofits or educational programs on their farms—one woman runs a farm camp for girls and several women involve at-risk children on their farms (Sachs 2006).

women also lead broad-scale efforts to create healthy, environmentally sustainable, and socially just food cultures and systems. For example, women are key leaders in pushing for changes in food and agriculture issues in the anti-globalization struggle (Mohanty 2003; Shiva 2002). While some organizing efforts engage the state, most fall into the domain of the consumer politics of food. Women are at the forefront of ethical buying, supporting fair trade, humane, organic, and local food. Some of these efforts are individual acts by consumers and business owners, others are collective actions, and some combine individual and collective actions. For example, Judy Wickes, owner of the White Dog Café in Philadelphia, works with her restaurant and her Fair Food Foundation to strengthen and connect locally owned businesses and farms committed to working in harmony with natural systems, providing meaningful living wage jobs, supporting healthy community life, and contributing to economic justice (White Dog Café 2006). Her efforts are tied more broadly to the fair trade, sustainable agriculture, and local food movements. One of their innovative projects, the Sister Restaurant Project develops "sister" relationships with African-American owned restaurants. They promote visits to their sister restaurants to encourage their customers to visit neighborhoods they otherwise might not go to in order to increase understanding, build city-wide community, and support minority businesses and cultural institutions.

In the corporeal realm, women's organizations combat the cultural impositions such as advertising that contribute to the destructive eating behaviors of many women and girls. The concern with eating disorders is the major food-related issue that has been taken up by the feminist movement. For example, the National Organization for Women organizes a "Love Your Body Day" to provide a forum for people to speak out against advertising and images of women that are harmful or offensive. . . .

Despite all of these women-led efforts in the agrifood system, there is a curious absence of feminism per se in women's efforts to create change in the agrifood system, with the exception of corporeal politics. This is true in three ways. First, while the efforts described above are by women, they are not necessarily consciously "feminist" in the sense of resisting the oppressive nature of gender relations. Second, some of the efforts may be counter to a feminist agenda. Third, the feminist movement rarely takes up issues relating to women and food in material and domestic realms.

Women's efforts to change the food system rarely take an explicitly feminist approach. The leader of the farm women's network studied by Hassanein (1999) emphasized that it was not a "feminist" organization. Luminary women such as Dolores Huerta played strong roles in the farm labor movement. While Huerta was herself a feminist, the farm labor movement, infused with a machismo culture, rarely addresses women's issues.[5] In some cases, women may be instigators, but still play support roles. For example, a study of women in the sustainable agriculture movement in California found that while women were active in

the movement, particularly at the grassroots level, men tended to hold the more visible leadership and decision-making positions (Sachs 1996). A Minnesota study found that men acted as teachers, leaders, and decision makers in the sustainable agriculture movement while women involved in the movement tended to occupy support roles such as providing food, working registration tables, and sending mailings (Meares 1996). Men are disproportionately represented in leadership roles in sustainable agriculture such as project directors, conference speakers, and authors just about everywhere. Women have been correspondingly overrepresented in social cohesion roles such as organizing conferences, coordinating community endeavors, and fostering networks among different groups. The "traditional" roles played by women in these movements may serve to reinscribe and normalize gendered relations.

Beyond this, agrifood women activists have also historically tended to overlook their needs or subordinate themselves. For example, rural women in the USA have tended to join organizations that support their families or farm organizations rather than participating in organizations dedicated to women's empowerment (Sachs 1996). . . .

In other ways, some of women's food-system efforts are contradictory—or at least ironic—in terms of a feminist agenda. For example, some practices advocated by alternative agrifood movements, such as farmers' markets and CSAs, can add both to the workload of farm women and to women's already overburdened workload in food procurement and preparation in the home (Allen 1999). Some of the women in Meares' (1997) study of the sustainable agriculture movement reported that their workloads had increased as a result of their partners' participation in the movement, but that the workloads of their male partners had not increased. And, the Slow Food movement, a shining light of contemporary food movements, promotes the leisurely consumption of elaborate, home-prepared meals without acknowledging that time pressures for the women who are the traditional preparers of food have tightened. On the other hand, a woman resisting domestic servitude in the kitchen might turn to fast foods to feed her children and then feel guilty. And, the body-acceptance movement rightly resists cultural stereotypes of thinness for women, but may lead women to accept obesity, a condition that negatively affects their health.

. . . Changing the division of labor in the home or kitchen has largely been a struggle for women at the individual level of negotiating with their partners and other family members, as opposed to an organized feminist struggle.

Conclusion

· · ·

. . . Feminist scholarship's focus on the connections between gendered divisions of labor in the home and in the labor market and distinctions between the private and public realms prove useful in understanding women's relationship to food. Women's work with food spans the formal economy, informal economy, and household economy. Thus, in studying women's connections to food, we have examined their work in both the formal economy and the household.

Barndt's (1999) Tomasita project is an example of this type of interaction that combines research and action. In the commodity chain tradition, the research traces women's work with tomatoes from the fields and processing plants in Mexico to the supermarkets and fast food restaurants in Canada. This research shows how labor practices of Maquilization and McDonaldization have resulted in the feminization of the workforce as deskilled, part-time, low-wage women workers replaced skilled, permanent, often male, workers. What makes Barndt's project particularly important is the way in which it went beyond research to bring Mexican and Canadian women workers and scholars together to discuss strategies for action and resistance.

Women's experiences in the food system also must be examined through feminist standpoint theory, which holds that feminist social science should be conducted from the standpoint of women in order to examine and understand the systematic oppressions of women in society. Sometimes a source of power, more often one of subordination, the fact remains that we need to understand much more about gender relations in the food system. We need to know much more about who women food activists are, their motivations, and their visions for the food system. We have much to learn about the possibilities for changing gender relations and the emerging field of feminist food studies can lead the

way through weaving together feminist studies of food and the body with feminist work in the sociology and political economy of agriculture.

ACKNOWLEDGMENTS

The authors would like to thank Hilary Melcarek for her invaluable research support and the anonymous reviewers for their insightful comments and suggestions.

NOTES

1. The agrifood system is the complex of institutions and organizations that define, regulate, and shape the organization of agriculture and food from field to table.

2. While in 1980, 74 percent of meat processing workers were white, by 2000, 49 percent of meat processing workers were Hispanic (Kandel and Parrado 2005).

3. Between 2000 and 2005, Safeway increased the number of women store managers by 40 percent, 34 percent for white women and 65 percent for women of color. During the same period of time, the number of women in vice-president positions increased from 12 percent to 25 percent (Catalyst 2006).

4. Specifically, Dukes claimed that despite her hard work and excellent performance, she was denied the training she needed to advance to higher, salaried position.

5. Huerta worked diligently with Cesar Chavez to organize farmworkers in the United Farm Workers of America, AFL-CIO (UFW) until his death in 1993. Huerta continues her work organizing farmworkers as Secretary-Treasurer Emeritus of the UFW and also organizes on feminist issues in her position as a board member of the Feminist Majority Foundation (www.doloreshuerta.org).

REFERENCES

Allen, Patricia. 1999. "Reweaving the Food Security Safety Net: Mediating Entitlement and Entrepreneurship." *Agriculture and Human Values* 16 (2): 117–129.

Avakian, Alrene Voski, and Barbara Haber. 2006. "Feminist Food Studies: A Brief History." Pp 1–26 in *From Betty Crocker to Feminist Food Studies: Critical Perspectives on Women and Food*, edited by A. V. Avakian and B. Haber. Amherst, MA: University of Massachusetts Press.

Barndt, Deborah, ed. 1999. *Women Working the NAFTA Food Chain: Women, Food and Globalization*. Toronto, ON: Sumach Press.

Barrientos, Stephanie. 2001. "Gender, Flexibility and Global Value Chains." *Institute of Development Studies Bulletin* 32(3): 83–94.

Bell, David and Gill Valentine. 1997. *Consuming Geographies*. London, UK: Routledge.

Beoku-Betts, Josephine. 1995. "We Got Our Way of Cooking Things: Women Food and Preservation of Cultural Identity among the Gullah." *Gender and Society* 9(5): 535–555.

Bordo, Susan. 1998. "Hunger as Ideology." Pp 11–35 in *Eating Culture*, edited by R. Scapp and B. Sietz. Albany, NY: State University of New York Press.

Brandth, Berit. 1999. "Modernity, Feminism and Farm Women." Unpublished paper given at Gender and Transformation in Rural Europe Wageningen, Netherlands, 14–17 October 1999.

Buttel, Frederick and Jessica Goldberger. 2002. "Gender and Agricultural Science: Evidence from Two Surveys of Land Grant Scientists." *Rural Sociology* 57 (10): 24–46.

Catalyst. 2006. "Safeway's Championing Change for Women: An Integrated Strategy." http://www. catalystwomen.org.

Collins, Jane. 1995. "Transnational Labor Process and Gender Relations: Women in Fruit and Vegetable Production in Chile, Brazil, and Mexico." *Journal of Latin American Anthropology* 1(1): 78–99.

Coltrane, Scott. 1996. *The Family Man: Fatherhood, Housework, and Gender Equality*. New York, NY: Oxford University Press.

Della Porta, Donatella and Mario Diani. 2006. *Social Movements: An Introduction*. London, UK: Blackwell.

DeLind, Laura and Anne Ferguson. 1999. "Is This a Woman's Movement?: The Relationship of Gender to Community-Supported Agriculture in Michigan." *Human Organization* 58: 190–200.

DeVault, Marjorie L. 1991. *Feeding the Family: The Social Organization of Caring as Gendered Work*. Chicago, IL: University of Chicago Press.

Dolan, Catherine. 2004. "On Farm and Packhouse: Employment at the Bottom of a Global Value Chain." *Rural Sociology* 69 (1): 99-126.

Economic Research Service. 2006. "Food Consumer Price Index, Prices, and Expenditures: Food Expenditure Tables." Washington, DC: United States Department of Agriculture, https://www. ers.usda.gov

Ehrenreich, Barbara and Arlie R. Hochschild. 2002. *Global Woman: Nannies, Maids and Sex Workers in the New Economy*. London, UK: Granta Books.

Feldman, Shelley and Rick Welsh. 1995. "Feminist Knowledge Claims, Local Knowledge and Gender Divisions of Agricultural Labor." *Rural Sociology* 60(1): 23–43.

Fink, Deborah. 1992. *Agrarian Women: Wives and Mothers in Rural Nebraska*. Chapel Hill, NC: University of North Carolina Press.

Grow Pittsburgh. 2006. http://www.growpittsburgh.org.

Harris, Jessica. 1995. *The Welcome Table: African American Heritage Cooking*. New York: Simon & Schuster.

Hassanein, Neva. 1999. *Changing the Way America Farms: Knowledge and Community in the Sustainable Agriculture Movement*. Lincoln, NE: University of Nebraska Press.

Hynes, H. Patricia. 1996. *A Patch of Eden: America's Inner City Gardeners*. Boston, MA: Chelsea Green.

Inness, Sherrie A. 2001. *Dinner Roles: American Women and Culinary Culture*. Iowa City, IA: University of Iowa Press.

Julier, Alice. 2006. "Hiding Gender and Race in the Discourse of Commercial Food Consumption." Pp 27–46 in From *Betty Crocker to Feminist Food Studies: Critical Perspectives on Women and Food*, edited by A. V. Avakian and B. Haber. Amherst, MA: University of Massachusetts Press.

Kandel, William. 2006. "Meat Processing Firms Attract Hispanic Workers to Rural America." Amber Waves, June. Washington, DC: United States Department of Agriculture, Economics Research Service.

Kirshenblatt-Gimblett, Barbara. 1997. "The Temple Emanuel Fair and Its Cookbook, Denver 1888." In *Recipes for Reading*. Anne Bower (ed). Amherst: University of Massachusetts Press.

Mack-Canty, Colleen. 2004. "Third-Wave Feminism and the Need to Reweave the Nature/Culture Duality." *NWSA Journal* 16 (3): 154–174.

Meares, A.C. 1997. "Making the Transition from Conventional to Sustainable Agriculture: Gender, Social Movement Participation, and Quality of Life on the Family Farm." *Rural Sociology* 62 (1): 21–47.

Mohanty, Chandra. 2003. *Feminism Without Borders: Decolonizing Theory, Practicing Solidarity*. Durham, NC: Duke University Press.

Morton, Lois Wright, Annette Bitto Ella, Mary Jane Oakland, and Mary Sand. 2005. "Solving the Problems of Iowa Food Deserts: Food Insecurity and Civic Structure." *Rural Sociology* 70(1): 94–112.

National Center for Health Statistics. 2004. "Obesity Still a Major Problem." Atlanta, GA: Center for Disease Control, http://www.cdc.gov/ nchs/pressroom/04facts/obesity

National Science Foundation. 2006. "Women, Minorities, and Persons with Disabilities in Science and Engineering." http://www.nsf.gov/statistics

Paquette, Marie-Claude and Kim Raine. 2004. "Sociocultural Context of Women's Body Image." *Social Science & Medicine* 59: 1047–1058.

Sachs, Carolyn E. 1996. *Gendered Fields: Rural Women, Agriculture, and Environment*. Boulder, CO: Westview Press.

Sachs, Carolyn E. 2006. "Going Public: Networking Globally and Locally." Presidential Address at Rural Sociological Society Annual Meeting, Louisville, KY, August, 2006.

Shiva, Vandana. 2002. *Sustainable Agriculture and Food Security: The Impact of Globalization*. Thousand Oaks, CA: Sage Publications.

Trauger, Amy K. 2005. Social, Economic, and Environmental Justice: a Network Analysis of Sustainable Agriculture in Pennsylvania. PhD dissertation, Department of Geography, Penn State University.

Trauger, Amy and Carolyn Sachs. 2006. "Understanding Effective Educational Programming for Women Farmers in the Pennsylvania Women's Agricultural Network." Paper presented at Rural Sociological Society Annual Meeting, Louisville, KY, August 2006.

U.S. Bureau of Labor Statistics. 2005a. *Occupational Outlook Handbook*. Washington, DC: U.S. Department of Labor. http://www.bls.gov

U.S. Bureau of Labor Statistics. 2005b. *Women in the Labor Force: A Data Book*. Report 95. Washington, DC: U.S. Department of Labor. http://www.bls.gov/cps/wlfdatabook-2005.pdf

U.S. Census of Agriculture. 2002. U.S. Census of Agriculture. Washington, DC: United States Department of Agriculture.

U.S. Department of Labor and U.S. Bureau of Labor Statistics. 2005. Highlights of Women's Earnings in 2004. Washington, DC: US Department of Labor. http://www.bls.gov/cps/cpswom2004. pdf# search=%22%22highlights%20 of%20 women's%20earnings%22%22

U.S. Department of Labor. 2005. "Income and Poverty," Chapter 3 in National Agricultural Workers Survey. http://www.dol.gov/asp/programs/agworker/report/ch3.htm

White Dog Café. 2006. http://www.whitedogcafe. com

Zimmerman, Toni Schindler, Shelly A. Haddock, Scott Ziemba, and Aimee Rust. 2001. "Family Organizational Labor: Who's Calling the Plays?" *Journal of Feminist Family Therapy* 13 (2–3), 65–90.

◆◆◆

SIXTY-SIX

Reproductive Justice, Not Population Control

Breaking the Wrong Links and Making the Right Ones in the Movement for Climate Justice (2009)

Betsy Hartmann and Elizabeth Barajas-Roman

Betsy Hartmann is Professor of Development Studies and Director of the Population and Development Program at Hampshire College. Her research and teaching focus on the intersections between population, migration, environment, and security issues. Her books include *Reproductive Rights and Wrongs: The Global Politics of Population Control* and *Making Threats: Biofears and Environmental Anxieties* (co-editor).

Elizabeth Barajas-Román is Director of Policy at the National Latina Institute for Reproductive Health. Previously she was Associate Director of the Population and Development Program at Hampshire College, where she developed strategies for a national and international agenda to challenge conventional thinking about population growth.

Climate change is clearly one of the most urgent environmental, economic and social issues of our time. . . . [It] is attracting the attention of multiple political constituencies, some operating out of genuine conviction, others out of a strategic calculus that it is pragmatic to link their particular policy focus to climate change in order to achieve higher visibility and support. This paper argues that we are presently witnessing the development of a population/immigration/national security nexus in the climate change arena. This nexus poses a serious threat to the advancement of climate justice both nationally and internationally. To counter this threat and to strengthen the climate justice movement, we need to clearly articulate an alternative vision based on progressive linkages between reproductive, environmental and climate justice.

Wrong Links: Population/Immigration/National Security

The past year has witnessed escalating rhetoric from mainstream population and environment organizations about how population growth is

a major cause of global warming. For example, the Washington, DC–based Population-Health-Environment Policy and Practice Group, a coalition of key NGOs and the U.S. Agency for International Development, recently issued a fact sheet on Human Population Growth and Greenhouse Gas Emissions. It argues that population growth threatens to offset progress in emission reductions and investments in family planning and reproductive health should be a key part of strategies to address climate change.[1]

There are a number of obvious and not-so-obvious problems with this approach. For one, it doesn't make demographic sense. Today most countries in the world are already moving to a smaller family size. While world population is projected to increase from 6.7 billion today to 9.2 billion in 2050, the rate of growth has slowed considerably. The average number of children per woman in the Global South is now 2.75, and the UN predicts this figure will drop to 2.05 by 2050. The future trend is towards population stabilization.[2]

Moreover, per capita carbon emission rates are low in countries where birth rates remain relatively high, as in sub-Saharan Africa. From 1950–2000, the entire continent of Africa was responsible for only 2.5 percent of greenhouse gas emissions. In Kenya the average per capita carbon emission in 2002 was 0.3 tons, compared to 20 in the U.S. Rapidly industrializing countries such as China will account for a higher percentage of emissions in the future, but it will be a long time before their accumulated emissions reach the level of today's already industrialized nations.[3] China already has a negative birth rate; the most effective approach to emissions reduction there is clearly investment in conservation, green technologies and alternative energy. Worldwide, reducing the population of cars makes a lot more sense than trying to drive down already decreasing birth rates.

Focusing on population growth as a major cause of climate change places the blame on the world's poorest people who are the least responsible for global warming and lets rich countries, corporations and consumers off the hook. It obscures the difference between survival and luxury emissions. It is part of a long tradition of eugenic environmentalism in which environmental and economic resource scarcities are attributed to "too many people"—usually meaning too many people of color—and not to highly inequitable and environmentally damaging capitalist processes of production and consumption.[4]

While most mainstream population and environment organizations insist that they oppose coercive family planning and support women's rights, viewing family planning as a means to an end (in this case the mitigation of climate change) rather than as a basic human right tends to undermine the quality of contraceptive delivery services and freedom of choice.[5] The fertility of poor women of color becomes a target of elitist social engineering.

Arguably, current rhetoric on population and climate change is based less on reality than on the decision of population and environment groups to hitch their horse to the global warming bandwagon. This strategy is seen as a way to build political support for international family planning after eight years of the Bush administration's anti-abortion, abstinence-only policies. Though understandable, this strategy is shortsighted. In trying to counter one segment of the Right, namely the anti-abortion movement, population and environment groups play into the hands of conservative anti-immigrant and national security forces that deploy overpopulation fears to further repressive agendas.

In the greening of hate, anti-immigrant groups masquerading as liberal environmentalists argue that immigrants are overpopulating the U.S. and causing everything from urban sprawl to traffic jams to water scarcity. For example, the headline of a recent ad in the *New York Times* by right-wing anti-immigrant groups reads, "Population, Immigration and the Foreseeable Limits of America's Capacity: A Conundrum of Epic Proportions for the Progressive Thinker."[6] Now they are adding climate change to the mix. In August 2008, the Center for Immigration Studies released a report blaming immigrants for rising carbon emissions and suggesting they remain in their home countries where they consume less energy. The message is that reducing immigration is a far more effective way to address global warming than investing in conservation and renewable energies![7] . . .

In the national security arena, narratives about climate conflict and climate refugees build on racialized fears of overpopulation in the Global South and encourage anti-immigrant sentiment. A 2003 Pentagon-sponsored study of the potential impacts of abrupt climate change paints a grim scenario of poor, starving, overpopulated communities overshooting the reduced carrying capacity of their lands, engaging in violent conflict over scarce resources, and storming en masse towards Western borders.[8] Such narratives provide a rationale for further militarization of immigration enforcement and the expansion of U.S. military intervention, especially into Africa.[9] Unfortunately, this kind of reasoning is not limited to national security and intelligence reports. A recent article on global warming and sea-level rise in Bangladesh in the Natural Resources Defense Council's *Onearth* magazine depicts millions of destitute Bangladeshi environmental refugees as potential Islamic terrorists.[10]

This is not to argue that climate change won't displace large numbers of people—it well could in many places. But to portray those people as a dark, dangerous, overpopulated mass of violent migrants instead of human beings with human rights is deeply problematic. During Hurricane Katrina, the media whipped up the same kind of fears about African Americans in New Orleans, with devastating effects on rescue, relief and recovery efforts. It is a tragic irony that the people who are likely to be the main victims of climate change are doubly victimized by these vicious stereotypes.

By normalizing the idea that population growth is a major cause of global warming and giving it a liberal, feminist gloss, mainstream population and environment organizations make these kinds of stereotypes more palatable to the general public and contribute to generating a negative climate of fear. They also reduce reproductive rights to an instrumental means to an end, rather than ends worthy of pursuit in and of themselves. Meanwhile, they obscure the real causes of the climate crisis, hindering action on realistic economic and political solutions. Going down the population road is a diversion we can ill afford in the movement for climate justice.

Right Links: Reproductive Justice/Environmental Justice/Climate Justice

Developed and advanced by women of color activists, the concept of reproductive justice strongly condemns population control, noting its long history of targeting the fertility of oppressed communities. At the same time it includes support for full access to safe, voluntary birth control, abortion and reproductive health services. But reproductive justice goes far beyond the need for adequate services. According to Asian Communities for Reproductive Justice (ACRJ), reproductive justice "will be achieved when women and girls have the economic, social and political power and resources to make healthy decisions about our bodies, sexuality and reproduction for ourselves, our families and our communities in all areas of our lives."[11] Reproductive justice refers not only to biological reproduction but to social reproduction.

Feminist scholar Giovanna Di Chiro argues that the concept of social reproduction is crucial to understanding the possibilities for linking struggles for women's rights and environmental justice. "Social reproduction is the intersecting complex of political-economic, socio-cultural, and material-environmental processes required to maintain everyday life and to sustain human cultures and communities on a daily basis and intergenerationally."[12] Whether or not individuals and communities can fulfill their basic needs and sustain themselves depends critically on the extent of race, class and gender inequalities in access to resources and power. Unlike the population framework with its focus on numbers, social reproduction focuses on social, economic and political *systems*. It helps us to look more deeply at the underlying power dynamics that determine who lives and who dies, who is healthy and who is sick, whose environment is polluted and whose is clean, who is responsible for global warming and who suffers most from its consequences.

Looking through this lens leads to a much more liberatory understanding of the convergences of reproductive and climate politics. It encourages us to consider:

Connections between the Local and the Global: Some of the same powerful forces that drive environmental injustice at the local level contribute to climate change on the global level. While marginalized communities all over the world experience environmental injustices at the hands of powerful corporate and political actors, their experiences and concerns are diverse. Local battles against environmental injustice include coal mining towns in rural Appalachia, indigenous communities of the Arctic and Subarctic, the oil fields of Nigeria and the oil refineries of the Gulf Coast. The task of confronting global climate change challenges us to build alliances, coalitions, and political solidarity across borders and among a wide range of communities. The global nature of climate change means our struggles are not in isolation from one another.[13]

Environmental Dimensions of Health: Communities subjected to environmental racism experience daily exposure to cancer-causing chemicals and other toxins that cause respiratory, reproductive, and skin disorders. Women experience this toxic burden twofold. They often must shoulder their own health concerns while taking on the role of caring for others in the community who have been harmed, particularly children and the elderly. Women are also physiologically more susceptible to the health effects of a number of common pollutants which can build up and be stored for long periods of time in the fatty tissue of their breasts. Women may then pass on concentrated doses of toxins to their infants during breastfeeding. Women have spearheaded many of the battles against environmental injustice. This stems largely from their roles as caretakers of their families and the fact that they are more often in a position to bear direct witness to the health impacts of toxic infrastructure on their community. The dialogue on climate change must open space for these women to contribute their knowledge and voice their concerns.

Food Security: Climate-related scarcities of food and other natural resources such as water and firewood are likely to create burdens that fall disproportionately on poor people, especially women and girls whose domestic responsibilities include the management of these resources. In some families and communities, gendered food hierarchies in the household can put women at greater risk of malnutrition in times of crisis.[14] Achieving food security for all people should be a high priority in national and international responses to climate change. This means challenging present corporate food systems that appropriate land from peasant producers (many of whom are women) for large-scale luxury export crop production; engage in environmentally unsustainable mono-cropping and chemical-intensive agriculture; and draw down water supplies through inappropriate irrigation technologies. It also means opposing the transformation of lands that grow food crops into plantations of commercial biofuels.

The Failure of Corporate Solutions to Climate Change: In the international arena, corporate needs outweigh human needs when it comes to official climate change agreements. Ironically, a number of the mechanisms put in place by the Kyoto Protocol are not only doing little to reduce carbon emissions, but are increasing poor people's vulnerability. Carbon trading schemes allow corporate energy guzzlers to maintain high levels of emissions if they invest in carbon sequestration projects in the Global South. Many of these projects are huge monoculture tree plantations (also corporately owned) that reduce biodiversity and take over lands and forests from indigenous peoples, preventing women from collecting plants and firewood. These projects effectively shut the door on small-scale, non-corporate solutions such as systems that encourage local control of existing forests and improvements in their ability to sequester carbon and produce sustainable fuelwood supplies for community needs.[15]

The Nature of Disaster Response: Early warning systems and disaster management schemes often neglect the needs of poor women and communities of color. In the U.S. Hurricane Katrina illustrated how race, class and gender intersect in shaping who is most at risk during a disaster and who has the right to return afterwards. Activists should work together to press for more socially just and effective disaster responses, including those that take into account women's increased vulnerability to sexual and domestic violence and their need for safe reproductive health services in periods of dislocation. For strategic reasons, the U.S. military presently wants to expand its role in disaster response in the U.S. and globally. We need to resist this development and insist that publicly accountable civilian institutions be strengthened to cope with climate-related natural disasters.

Saying No to Nuclear Power: The reproductive health effects of the release of radiation and toxic chemicals are a powerful reason to oppose the expansion of nuclear power as a solution to climate change. Plutonium, the most dangerous byproduct of nuclear energy, crosses the placenta in the developing embryo and can cause birth defects. Plutonium affects male reproductive health as well. Stored in the testicles, it can cause mutations in reproductive genes, increased incidence of genetic disease in future generations, and testicular cancer. Long ignored, the chemical byproducts of nuclear energy are also linked to genetic mutations, Down's syndrome, autism, and other serious health effects. The U.S. nuclear industry has no regulations to protect women workers from the risk of early miscarriages and fetal malformations or men from potential harm to their ability to reproduce. A resurgence of nuclear power would also bring increased uranium mining on indigenous lands, with consequent environmental pollution and negative health impacts.[16] Nuclear power threatens both biological and social reproduction.

Immigrant and Refugee Rights: In the U.S. reproductive justice advocates have been some of the most vocal supporters of immigrant rights and effective organizers in immigrant communities. They point out how policies restricting immigration and blocking access to social services prevent immigrant women from getting the reproductive and basic health care they need. They also work with poor immigrant communities who suffer disproportionately from environmental racism.[17] This support of immigrant and refugee rights helps counter the negative scapegoating of immigrants by the population/immigration/national security nexus. Climate justice must include immigrant rights high on the agenda. In the event that people are displaced by global warming, we need to ensure that they are welcomed—not further traumatized and stigmatized.

Ending Militarism: Militarism in all its forms, from the prison-industrial complex to the occupation of Iraq, is one of the most powerful obstacles to the achievement of reproductive, environmental and climate justice. Ending militarism is a point where our struggles can and should converge, where there are multiple overlaps. The list is long: Military toxins damage the environment and harm reproductive health. Militarism increases violence against women, racism and anti-immigration activity. Militarism robs resources from other social and environmental needs. War destroys ecosystems, livelihoods, and health and sanitation infrastructure; it is the biggest threat of all to sustainable social reproduction.[18]

Militarism also stands in the way of effective solutions to climate change. Not only is the U.S. military a major emitter of greenhouse gases—it burns the same amount of fossil fuel every day as the entire nation of Sweden—but it spends up to 30 percent of its annual budget on military actions to secure oil and gas reserves around the world. Imagine if those funds flowed instead to the development of renewable energy, green technologies, and programs to ensure that low-income people are not adversely affected by the transition to a new

energy regime. Meanwhile, military research into controlling the climate poses a potentially grave danger to the environment.[19]

. . .

Conclusion: Toward a Holistic Politics

While addressing climate change is clearly an urgent priority, a failure to consider how it is connected to a host of other social and environmental justice issues could lead to narrow technocratic proposals that take some steps to reduce carbon emissions but none to reduce inequality. With the escalating rhetoric about overpopulation and climate conflict and refugees, we could also witness a resurgence of population control programs and the increased militarization of the climate policy arena. This could dangerously shrink the space for open democratic participation and debate. Contextualizing climate change, and locating it within a progressive nexus of related concerns, is a way to challenge these developments and build a broader and more powerful movement for climate justice. The reproductive justice movement serves as a positive model for this kind of political thinking and organizing.

NOTES

1. Population-Health-Environment-Policy and Practice Group, *Human Population Growth and Greenhouse Gas Emissions,* January 2008. The members of this coalition are Conservation International, National Audubon Society, Population Action International, Population Reference Bureau, Sierra Club, US Agency for International Development, Woodrow Wilson Center, World Wildlife Fund, and Worldwatch Institute.

2. UN Population Division, *World Population Prospects: The 2006 Revision (Highlights),* accessed at http://www.un.org/esa/population/publications/wpp2006WPP2006_Highlights_rev.pdf on 5 January 2009. For a short critique of overpopulation, see the Population and Development Program, "Ten Reasons to Rethink 'Overpopulation,'" *DifferenTakes* 40 (Fall 2006), accessed at http://popdev.hampshire.edu/projects/dt/40 on 7 January 2009.

3. Kirsten Dow and Thomas E. Downing. *The Atlas of Climate Change.* (University of California Press, 2007): 40–41, 96,100.

4. For a history of population control, see Matthew Connelly. *Fatal Misconception: The Struggle to Control World Population.* (Harvard University Press, 2008). On the link between eugenics and environmentalism, see Alexandra Minna Stern. *Eugenic Nation: Faults and Frontiers of Better Breeding in Modern America.* (University of California Press, 2005).

5. For case studies of the negative impacts of population control on family planning, see Connelly, *Fatal Misconception;* Lisa Ann Richey. *Population Politics and Development: From the Policies to the Clinics.* (Palgrave Macmillan, 2008); M. Catherine Maternowska. *Reproducing Inequities: Poverty and the Politics of Population in Haiti.* (Rutgers University Press, 2006); and Betsy Hartmann. *Reproductive Rights and Wrongs: The Global Politics of Population Control* (South End Press, 1995).

6. *The New York Times,* 12 October 2008. (Page 33). Sponsors of the ad are the American Immigration Control Foundation, Californians for Population Stabilization, FAIR, Numbers USA and Social Contract Press.

7. Leon Kolankiewicz and Stephen A. Camarota. *Immigration to the United States and Worldwide Greenhouse Gas Emissions.* (Center for Immigration Studies, 2008). Accessed at http://www.cis.org/GreenhouseGasEmissions on 2 January 2009. For a critique, see Angela Kelley, "Voodoo Science Blames Climate Change on Immigrants," 18 August 2008, accessed at http://www.alternet.org/story/95493/ on 30 December 2008.

8. Peter Schwartz and Doug Randall. *An Abrupt Climate Change Scenario and its Implications for United States National Security.* 2003. Accessed at http://www.gbn.com/GBNDocumentDisplayServlet.srv?aid=26231&url=/UploadDocumentDisplayServlet.srv?id=28566 on 5 January 2009.

9. Betsy Hartmann, "Climate Refugees and Climate Conflict: Who's Taking the Heat for Global Warming?" (paper presented at the panel on climate change, 4S Annual Conference, Montreal, Canada; October 2007, available online at http://www.radixonline.org/ccm2.html. Also see Betsy Hartmann, "War Talk and Climate Change," *Truthout,* 26 November 2007, available at http://www.truthout.org/article/betsy-hartmann-war-talk-and-climate-change.

10. George Black,"The Gathering Storm: What Happens When Global Warming Turns Millions of Destitute Muslims into Environmental Refugees?" *Onearth,* Summer 2008:22–37.

11. Asian Communities for Reproductive Justice, *A New Vision for Advancing our Movement for Reproductive Health, Reproductive Rights and Reproductive Justice,* accessed at http://www.sistersong.net/documents/ACRJ_Reproductive_Justice_Paper.pdf on 7 January 2009. For a history of the reproductive justice movement and its opposition to population control, see Jael Silliman, Marlene Gerber Fried, Loretta Ross, and Elena R. Gutiérrez. *Undivided Rights: Women of Color Organize for Reproductive Justice.* (South End Press, 2004).

12. Giovanna Di Chiro, "Living Environmentalisms: Coalition Politics, Social Reproduction, and Environmental Justice," *Environmental Politics* 17 (April 2008): 281.

13. The following sections draw on Stephen Blake Figura, Betsy Hartmann, and Elizabeth Barajas-Roman, "Reproductive Justice, Climate Justice, Peace: A Call for Solidarity, Not Population Control," Working Paper of the Population and Development Program, (March 2008), accessed at http://popdev.hampshire.edu/blog/reproductive-justice-climate-justice-peace on 7 January 2009.

14. For more on gender and climate change, see Irene Dankelman, *Gender, Climate Change and Human Security,* Women's Environment and Development Organization (May 2008), accessed at http://www.wedo.org/files/HSN%20Study%20Final%20May%2020,%202008.pdf on 7 January 2009. Also see WEDO's gender action link, accessed at http://www.genderaction.org/images/Gender%20Action%20Link%20-%20Climate%20Change.pdf, on 7 January 2009.

15. See *Carbon Trading: A Critical Conversation on Climate Change, Privatization, and Power,* special issue of *Development Dialogue* 48 (September 2006), accessed at http://www.dhf.uu.se/pdffiler/DD2006_48_carbon_trading/carbon_trading_web.pdf on 7 January 2009.

16. Meredith Crafton, "Why a Nuclear Renaissance Threatens Our Bodies, the Environment and Our Future," *DifferenTakes* 56 (Winter 2009), available at http://popdev.hampshire.edu/projects/dt/56.

17. ACRJ, *A New Vision for Advancing our Movement for Reproductive Health, Reproductive Rights and Reproductive Justice,* accessed at http://www.sistersong.net/documents/ACRJ_Reproductive_Justice_Paper.pdf on 7 January 2009. See Reading 30 in this volume.

18. See Population and Development Program, "Ten Reasons Why Militarism is Bad for Reproductive Freedom," *DifferenTakes* 20 (Winter 2003), accessed at http://popdev.hampshire.edu/projects/dt/20 on 6 January 2009, and Simon Doolittle, "Ten Reasons Why Militarism is Bad for the Environment," *DifferenTakes* 22 (Spring 2003), accessed at http://popdev.hampshire.edu/projects/dt/22 on 6 January 2009.

19. On military consumption of oil, see Nick Turse, "The Military-Petroleum Complex," *Foreign Policy in Focus,* 24 March 2008, accessed at http://www.fpif.org/fpiftxt/5097/ on 7 January 2009; on military costs of securing oil supplies, see Anita Dancs, *The Military Cost of Securing Energy,* National Priorities Project (October 2008), accessed at http://www.nationalpriorities.org/auxiliary/energy_security/full_report.pdf on 7 January 2009; on military schemes of climate control, James R. Fleming, "The Climate Engineers," *The Wilson Quarterly* (Spring 2007), accessed at http://www.wilsoncenter.org/index.cfm?fuseaction=wq.essay&essay_id=231274 on 7 January 2009.

SIXTY-SEVEN

Women's Responses to Environmental Destruction and State Violence in the Niger Delta (2008)

Sokari Ekine

Sokari Ekine is a Nigerian feminist writer and activist who has undertaken documentation and advocacy work in Niger River Delta communities struggling against transnational corporations, military repression, and environmental destruction.

This paper will discuss the ways in which the women of the Niger Delta have responded to acts of violence by the Nigerian State and its allies, the multinational oil companies. I first briefly outline the background to the crises in the Niger Delta and then discuss the responses and resistance of the women.[1]

Introduction

Nigeria, for the past 39 years, has been a militarised state even when so-called civilian governments, including the present one, have been in power. Militarisation consists of the use of the threat of violence to settle political conflicts, the legitimization of state violence, the curtailment of freedom of opinion, the domination of military values over civilian life, the violation of human rights, extra judicial killings and the gross repression of the people (Chunakara, 1994). . . . The Niger Delta is a region of Nigeria that has been subjected to excessive militarisation for the past 13 years, where violence is used as an instrument of governance to force the people into total submission (Okonta & Douglas, 2001; Na'Allah, 1998). . . . This region has little or no development, no electricity, no water, no communications, no health facilities, little and poor education. In contrast, the region generated an estimated over US $30 billion in oil revenues, over a 38-year period, in the form of rents for the government and profit for the multinational oil companies (Rowell, 1996).

The multinational oil companies, mainly Shell, Chevron/Texaco, and Elf, have treated both the people and the environment with total disdain and hostility (Okonta & Douglas, 2001). They have worked hand in hand with a succession of brutal and corrupt regimes to protect their exploitation of the land and people by providing the Nigerian military and police with weapons, transport, logistical support and finance. In return the Nigerian government has allowed the oil companies a free hand to operate without any monitoring. In fact, the oil companies in the Niger Delta have one of the worst environmental records in the world.

Destruction of the Ecological System

The Niger Delta has become an ecological disaster zone, a place where rusty pipelines run through farms and in front of houses (Rowell, 1996). Day and night huge gas fires rage in massive pits and towers, spewing noxious gases and filth into people's homes and farms. Oil spills and fires are a regular occurrence, often causing the death of local people as well as the destruction of wildlife and property. . . .

Often, the spillages lead to raging fires as in the case of the Jesse fire (17th October, 1998[2]) when over a thousand people were killed and thousands more horrifically burned and left homeless. To date, not a single person has received compensation. Indeed, in a region where medical care is scarce and only available to the rich, it is easy to envision the fate of these people. Ponds, creeks, rivers and land are soaked with thick layers of oil. Terisa Turner, co-director of the United Nations NGO, International Oil Working Group (IOWG), describes one particular oil spill that she personally witnessed as follows:

> 150,000 residents of the community of Ogbodo battled a massive petroleum spill from a Shell pipeline, which burst on 24 June, churning crude into the surrounding waterways for 18 days until Shell clamped the pipe on 12 July. Severe environmental damage and threat to life by

Group discussion of strategies for women's peacebuilding initiatives in the Niger Delta

Shell's neglect is the other side of the 'corporate rule' coin of ever-expanding neo-liberal license. The dangers to human life, human rights and the environment were dramatically experienced by Ogbodo community members in Nigeria's 'Shell-Shocked' oil belt. (Turner, 2001: 11)

This scene is typical. The common response of the oil companies to such spills however, has been to blame the villagers for sabotage. The question is, why would the villagers commit acts of sabotage that will only worsen the environmental damage and pollution of their land and prevent them from engaging in their livelihoods, namely farming, fishing and trading? In this particular case, the pipeline in question was buried 6 feet deep (many pipelines in the region are built above ground, running through farm land and through villages), and split underneath the ground (Turner, 2001). In addition to air and water pollution and other kinds of environmental degradation, lands have been expropriated and personal property damaged. The people have received only very little compensation for the land taken or damages from oil spillage and fires. Indeed, efforts at compensation have been "case(s) of broken promises, development programmes that are abandoned

halfway, poor quality facilities that break down and simply rust away as soon as they are installed" (Okonta & Douglas, 2001: 106).

Militarisation

As the dispossessed communities demand corporate responsibility, environmental, economic and social justice and proper compensation, their protests have been met with violence including extrajudicial killings and mass murder, torture, rape, the burning of homes and property, and increased military presence. As such, the Niger Delta has become completely militarised and "secured" by unrestrained and unaccountable Nigerian military personnel. The report by Human Rights Watch, "No Democratic Dividend," notes that violence in the region continues despite the change from military to civilian rule (Human Rights Watch, 2002).

The Niger Delta is a particularly extreme example of a culture of violence that is woven into the fabric of a society ruled by military dictators. Former President Olusegun Obasanjo was a key player in no less than three successive military regimes. He was a senior officer under General Gowon and participated in the 1975 *coup d'etat* that overthrew General Gowon. He then served as the Deputy Supreme Commander under Brigadier General Murtala Mohammed until the latter's assassination in the 1976 coup. General Obasanjo then took over as Supreme Commander until he handed power to the second civilian government of Shehu Shagari in 1979. Four more military regimes followed this brief interregnum, including the particularly brutal regime of General Sani Abacha between 1993 and 1998. It was during this period that Ogoni activists, including Ken Saro-Wiwa, were murdered. Despite the fact that the Obasanjo government, which ruled from 1999 until 2007, was viewed as a transition to civilian rule, the level of violence in the region continued to escalate. . . .

The government of the newly elected President of Nigeria, Umaru Yar'Adua, continues the policy of militarisation of the region in response to the increased militancy of local people.

· · ·

Resistance and Responses to State-Sponsored Violence

One of the most common forms of violence is destruction of property: burning homes and shops, looting and stealing money. Communities often respond to these attacks by fleeing either to a nearby village or to a hiding place in the bush (forest). In Green's (1999) schema, escape is considered to be the most extreme form of resistance as it is usually ventured only in the direst circumstances.

During the invasion of Odi town in 1999, many townsfolk escaped, leaving behind their meagre possessions accumulated over a lifetime, often losing family members during the escape, and eventually returning to find other family members killed, their homes burnt to the ground, and property looted. For women, this was particularly difficult as the following interviewees explain:

> I left everything to run for my dear life and pleaded with people to let me in their canoe with my children. . . . I don't even know the destination they were, where they ran to. I started to trace my children. . . . As God would have it none of them died and at the end all of us came

here. When I saw my house I cried. . . . People were hugging me. We will survive this thing with God. (Charity, Odi Woman)

> When the soldiers came we were in our various houses, we only heard that soldiers have come and surrounded everywhere. Since the soldiers were coming we were all afraid. Everyone started packing and running away, we were not able to stand soldiers. We carried a few things and we left. When we came back we saw all our houses, food had been burned down, all burned down money that we left in our houses. Since then we have been trying to manage with nothing again. We are lying on the ground nothing to sleep on. (Amasin, primary school teacher, Odi).

> We ran to a nearby village called Odoni. We were crying our houses are finished. We also heard the gunshots and knew people were being killed. Others ran to the bush. Those who could not get boats ran to the bush. . . . Women, not men, only women, the men were dead. (Imegbele, school teacher, Odi Town).

· · ·

The testimonies in *Blood and Oil* (Ekine, 2000) and in other interviews conducted by activists and researchers in the region, are all examples of women speaking out about their personal and community experiences of violence. Women narrated their stories of rape, beatings, sexual harassment, burning of their property, arrest and murder of their husbands, sons, fathers and brothers. They spoke of the loss of their fishing ponds and farmlands to pollution, and the poverty of their lives. They also mentioned the lack of employment opportunities for the male family members, the harassment of their young sons by police and army personnel. Moreover, these women talked about both the support and, in most cases, the lack of support they received from their husbands and traditional elders in their activism. . . .

Silence as Resistance

Closely related to the act of speaking out is the act of silent resistance, by which I mean not speaking and choosing to do nothing. The question of whether silence constitutes resistance, an exercise of choice, is worth exploring.

Before undertaking fieldwork for *Blood and Oil*,[3] I had never considered silence as an act of resistance. However, during the interviews with groups of women, I observed that there would often be some women who did not speak or spoke very little. . . . I became aware of the power of these silent voices. I saw their silence as an act of defiance and strength and also a way to manage the pain in their lives. . . . In other words, what may appear as doing nothing is, in effect, making a choice not to do anything. In local parlance, this kind of deliberate inaction is referred to as "sitting on oneself."

One example of silent resistance took place in the small town of Kaiama in Western Ijaw. Here, on the 11th of December 1998, representatives of over 40 Ijaw clans issued a communiqué known as the Kaiama Declaration and created the Ijaw Youth Council (IYC) to administer the affairs of the Ijaw youth. The communiqué called for an end to 40 years of environmental damage and underdevelopment in the region and asserted the right to ownership of resources and land by the indigenous people. In response, the Nigerian government created a Naval Special Task Force and, on the 29th of December, sent 1500 federal troops to the nearby state capital at Yenagoa and occupied it and the surrounding area. Following a massacre, rape and burning of properties in Yenagoa on January 1st 1999, the army invaded the town of Kaiama on 2nd January. On the 4th January, using Chevron helicopters and boats, the army invaded seven other Ijaw towns.

During interviews with women, one woman stood out because she was not interested in speaking. We learned that her son had been killed on the day of the invasion. . . . Standing face to face with her silence was an overpowering experience which conveyed her profound grief and loss at least as effectively as speech. In this case, a woman had survived by a silence that allowed her to disengage herself from her surroundings and she continued to live and hold herself with a dignity that denied her violators any sense of victory. Given that Kaiama is still under occupation today, she lives a situation in which she has to face her son's murderers every day, possibly even having to sell them foodstuffs from the stall she runs in order to earn a living to support her surviving children. Her silence, her stance and her body language thus serve her well in an inescapable situation. . . .

Responses to Sexual Violence

. . .

In the Niger Delta, rape and other forms of sexual violence such as forced prostitution, have taken place repeatedly in communities that have been invaded by the Nigerian army, where paramilitary forces have been used to quell demonstrations, or simply to make a particular town or village an "example" of what would happen should the people assert their human rights.

Blessing, one of my interviewees, explained that the soldiers and police often forced girls to "befriend" them. If they refused, they were threatened with rape and beatings. She had managed to avoid being "befriended" by her lack of fear and sheer stubbornness. She explained that at first she had tried to make friends for protection and was bought drinks following which the soldiers attempted to force her into having sex with them. She said, "the pressure was terrible and most girls just gave in."[4] Another woman reported seeing a soldier walking into the bush with a girl of about 12 years. After the abuse (the woman did not know what actually took place) they came out and the soldier gave money to the child.

The responses to rape have varied from community to community. Several factors explain the varying responses of the women, the male members of their families, and their wider community. Using two different incidents of rape in two different ethnic groups, I will examine the different responses.

The town of Choba is an Ikwerre community in Rivers State and the headquarters of a pipeline construction company called Wilbros Nigeria Ltd. (a subsidiary of Wilbros Group, a US company). Community relations between Wilbros and the people of Choba were poor mainly because of two reasons. The company demonstrated disdain and disinterest in Choba and its people and they failed to employ local people, even at lower unskilled levels. This led to a number of demonstrations against Wilbros. In June 1999 the youth of Choba began a series of demonstrations and sit-ins outside the company gates. The youth demanded that Wilbros replace 600 of their employees with Choba residents. On the 28th of October, the mobile police—a paramilitary group—invaded Choba and once again, unleashed murder, destruction of property and rape on the people of the town. The rapes of women by soldiers were captured on film by a journalist and published in the Nigerian daily press.

President Obasanjo's response was to declare the photographs a fake, asserting that *his* soldiers would never do such a thing. The response of the women of Choba was one of insulation, turning inward towards their community. These women not only had to cope with the trauma of being publicly raped but also with the shame that they and their community felt when the photographs were published in the newspaper. Some months later, a local journalist spoke anonymously to some of the rape survivors.

> It is a taboo to rape a married woman. . . . (now) these women cannot sleep with their husbands and cannot cook for them. It is our tradition and we have to respect it, not just for the sake of respecting our custom but because there are grave implications for disobedience. . . .
>
> At the time, we rallied our women to protest to the wife of the governor so that she can help us to push the case but we were arrested and detained for four days. It took the intervention of well-meaning elders before we were released. . . . We, the women of Choba, appeal to those behind the ugly event to come and do the necessary things to appease the gods. . . . This is important to us because without this, these women are as good as divorced.

The community did not judge the women survivors totally negatively. On the contrary, they acknowledged the women's pain and suffering. The women supported each other and organised themselves according to traditional ways. They sought help from their village elders and the governor's wife. Their response was part of their healing process and, seemingly, of the community, so they could all move past the trauma to some kind of normalcy in their lives.

The responses of rape victims and their families in Ogoniland were very different from those of Choba. The Ogoni Bill of Rights (OBR) was launched on the 26th August 1990. The OBR, like the declarations and communiqués of other ethnic groups, articulated the basis of a struggle for ethnic autonomy and self-determination for the Ogoni peoples and challenged both the Nigerian government and Shell's legitimacy to determine the economic and political affairs of the Ogoni people and the entire Niger Delta communities (Ekine, 2000). The Move-

ment for the Survival of the Ogoni peoples (MOSOP) was to become the mechanism to carry out the objectives of OBR along with the Federation of Ogoni Women's Organisations (FOWA) (Turner, 2001).

The troubles in Ogoniland came to a head in November 1993 when the Nigerian military government began a three-year campaign of violence, murder, rape, burning, looting, beatings and torture, against the Ogoni people.[5] For the Ogoni women, resistance was a daily norm as they faced both the impact of Shell's destruction of their environment and the presence of the Nigerian army and mobile police every day. Women were harassed on the way to their farms, on the way to their markets, in their villages minding their homes, and at night when they were asleep.

In interviews with members of FOWA, woman after woman stood up, said their names, and described in graphic detail the rapes and other types of sexual violence they had been subjected to.

> They started beating the women, dragging them into the bush. And they started loosing their cloth and raping them...my mate was with pregnancy. One army man just used his leg and hit her stomach and she miscarry. That was the beginning of suffering in Nyo Khana.[6] (Comfort Aluzim)
>
> They started beating us; all that we were carrying to the market to sell, they took. They took our things, our bags. They asked us to raise our hands and jump like frogs. There was an old woman with us that could not jump. What the army man did was to use his double barrel gun to beat the old woman's back and she fell down. (Mercy Nkwagha)
>
> One day we were demonstrating. We sang as we moved from our town to Ken Khana. Singing near the main road we met face to face with the army. . . they asked us to lie down on the road. After using the koboko (whip) on us they started kicking us with their foot. They dragged some of the women into the bush. We were naked, our dresses were torn, our wrapper were being loosed by a man who is not your husband. They tore our pants and began raping us in the bush. The raping wasn't secret because about two people are raping you there.

They are raping you in front of your sister. They are raping your sister in front of your mother. It was like a market. (Mrs Kawayorko)

Unlike in Choba, the Ogoni women were able to stand up and publicly speak about the violence they had suffered. Through the actions of FOWA and MOSOP, the women became highly politicised and engaged actively with elders and youth in the struggle against Shell's activities and for the political autonomy of their land. . . . Thus, FOWA was able to use a strategy of collective action as an act of resistance in their struggle and coordinate their activities with men in the community. . . . Women were not ostracised or excluded because they had been raped, as explained by a FOWA member:

Our men just take it as what happen because they know their wives did not just go out like that but it was forceful. Also the other women took it the same way. (Ogoni woman)

. . .

FOWA's response to violence was a combination of collective action, individual courage and sheer defiance in the face of military aggression and environmental destruction. More recently, women of the Niger Delta have used both collective action and traditional methods in response to the complete neglect of their ecosystem: natural environment, health, education, infrastructure, employment and general underdevelopment by the government and multinationals.

Mass Protests

Between June and August 2002, thousands of women occupied no less than eight oil facilities belonging to Chevron/Texaco and Shell Petroleum including Chevron's main oil terminal at Escravos in Delta State. This series of direct actions by women in the Niger Delta was unprecedented for a number of reasons.

First, never before had so many women taken a series of actions against an oil company within such a short period of time. Second, the actions, in particular the initial occupation of Escravos oil terminal, were highly organised. The women divided themselves into seven groups, each occupying a different strategic area of the complex, including the main office building (Okon, 2001).

Third, because the actions taken by the women— all mothers and grandmothers whose age ranged from 30 to 90—had been organised collectively in the interest of the community at large, they had the complete support of their communities including their husbands, the youth, elders and chiefs. Finally, and most important, in the final occupation, for the first time women from three different ethnic nationalities, Ijaw, Itsekiri, and Ilaje, came together in a united action against corporate irresponsibility, putting aside previous inter-ethnic hostilities and grievances.

One of the strategies used by both the multinational oil companies and successive Nigerian governments has been to deliberately exploit existing tensions between the various ethnic nationalities in the region and also, to encourage antagonisms between youth and women, elders and youth, and elders and women in towns and villages. Therefore, the importance of the solidarity between women in this instance is indeed major. This solidarity across different ethnic divides was forged because the situation had become so desperate that many women realised that such cooperation was essential for their success. Their political awareness of the divide-and-rule tactics encouraged them to put aside previous hostilities and fight the common enemy together.

The women occupied the operational headquarters of Chevron/Texaco and Shell Petroleum, singing songs of solidarity to protest years of plunder of their rural environment by the oil companies (Okon, 2001). In this particular siege, about 800 women were injured during a particularly brutal encounter with security forces belonging to the oil companies. The . . . women speak of their coming together and their grievances:

The river they are polluting is our life and death. We depend on it for everything. . . . When this situation is unbearable, we decided to come together to protest, Ijaw, Itsekiri and Ilaje we are one, we are brothers and sisters, it is only people who do not understand that think we are fighting ourselves. Our common enemies are the oil companies and their backers. (Mrs Bmipe Ebi (Ilaje))

We don't want Shell, Chevron, Texaco or any other oil companies again. They should leave us alone. We don't have guns, and we don't have any weapon to fight them. Since they have treated us like this. We are prepared to die. (Mrs Rose Miebi (Ijaw))

If Chevron no keep the promises, next time I ready to go naked. (Mrs Funke Tunjor (Ilaje))

The women were relentless in their protest and demands. In a final act of defiance, they confronted the oil companies with one ingenious and powerful weapon: they threatened to remove all their clothes in what is known as "the curse of nakedness." The stripping off of clothes, particularly by married and elderly women, is a way of shaming men, some of whom believe that if they see the naked bodies they will go mad or suffer great harm.

. . .

Women in the Niger Delta resorted to using the "curse of nakedness" as a weapon after they had failed to have their demands met through more conventional protest actions. Though greatly feared and rarely used, nakedness as a form of protest is legitimate within the cultural context of the Niger Delta. In this instance, it was one of the few occasions when women were able to manoeuvre themselves into a position of power. Also, because it is used only under extreme provocation, it has remained a powerful weapon of women's collective resistance. It is also critical to note that while the scale of destruction and violence within the Delta is overwhelming, at a day to day level women continue not just to survive but also to put up resistance within the territories, using the means at their disposal: *If Chevron no keep the promises, next time I ready to go naked.*

NOTES

1. The testimonies used in this paper were gathered by members of the Niger Delta Women for Justice (NDWJ), the Ijaw Council for Human Rights (ICHR), and myself during fieldwork undertaken between 2000 and 2003. NDWJ works with other women's organisations across the Niger Delta; ICHR works alongside Environmental Rights Action, Oil Watch Nigeria, and NDWJ.

2. ERA field report 17. http://www.essentialaction. org/shell/era/eraField17.html

3. *Blood and Oil: Testimonies of Violence from Women of the Niger Delta*, is a collection of testimonies of women from seven different ethnic groups. The testimonies cover

the period from 1990–2000 of state and multinational violence against Niger Delta communities and the impact of the violence specifically on women's lives.

4. I have paraphrased Blessing's testimony because, due to her use of local English, the reader would find it very hard to understand.

5. When the brutal military dictator, General Sani Abacha, came to power in November 1993, one of the first things he did was to create the now notorious Rivers State Internal Security Task Force led by Lt Colonel Paul Okuntimo and to appoint a new military governor of the Rivers State, Lt Colonel Dauda Komo. These two together with Shell Oil spent the next three years terrorising the Ogoni people culminating in the judicial murder of Ken Saro-Wiwa and 8 other activists on 10th November, 1995. Following the execution of Ken Saro-Wiwa, the women of FOWA became prime targets of the RSISTF who in the words of a FOWA member "were looking for us the way children look for rats in the bush."

6. Nyo Khana—Ogoniland is divided into six kingdoms (or clans) of Babbe, Eleme, Gokana, Nyo-Khana, Ken-Khana and Tai.

REFERENCES

Chunakara, M. G. 1994. *The Militarisation of Politics and Society: Southern Asia Experience*. Hong Kong: Daga Press.

Ekine, S. 2000. *Blood and Oil: Testimonies of Violence from Women of the Niger Delta*. London: Centre for Democracy and Development.

Green, D. 1999. *Gender Violence in Africa: African Women's Responses*. New York: St Martin's Press.

Na'Allah, A. ed. 1998. *Ogoni's Agonies: Ken Saro-Wiwa and the Crisis in Nigeria*. Trenton, NJ: Africa World Press.

Niger Delta Women for Justice, http://www.ndwj/kabissa.org.

Okon, E. 2002, August. *Report of the Niger Delta Women for Justice (NDWJ) on the Delta Women's Seige on the American Oil Company, Chevron-Texaco in Delta State, Nigeria*. Available from Niger Delta Women for Justice: http://www.ndwj.kabissa.org.

Okonta, I. and Douglas, O. 2001. *Where Vultures Feast*. San Francisco: Sierra Club Books.

Rowell, A. 1996. *Green Backlash: Global Subversion of the Environment Movement*. New York: Routledge.

Turner, T. E. 1997. *Oil Workers and Oil Communities: Counterplanning from the Commons in Nigeria*. Available at: http://www.uoguelph.ca/~terisatu/ Counterplanning/c3.htm.

Turner, T. E. 2001. *The Land is Dead: Women's Rights as Human Rights: The Case of the Ogbodo Shell Petroleum Spill in Rivers State, Nigeria*. Paper published by T. Turner.

Activism is not issue-specific
It's a moral posture that, steady state, propels you
forward, from one hard hour to the next.
Believing that you can do something to make things
better, you do
Something, rather than nothing.
You assume responsibility for the privilege of your
abilities.
You do whatever you can.
You reach beyond yourself in your imagination, and
in your wish for
Understanding, and for change.
You admit the limitations of individual perspectives.
You trust somebody else.
You do not turn away.

June Jordan

12

◆◆◆

Creating Change
Theory, Vision, and Action

Although women in the United States have broken free from many earlier limitations, this book also shows how much still needs to be done. As we argue in previous chapters, many aspects of women's lives are subject to debate and controversy. These contentious issues include sexuality, reproductive freedom, the nature of marriage and family relationships, the right to independent livelihood, and the right to affordable health care. Gains have been made and also eroded, as conservative politicians aided by conservative religious leaders and media personalities have organized to limit or reverse women's progress.

It is easy to review the details of U.S. women's experiences of discrimination and to come away feeling angry, depressed, hopeless, and disempowered. The interlocking systems that keep women oppressed can seem monolithic and unchangeable. Major U.S. social movements of the past one hundred years—for the rights of working people; the civil rights of peoples of color; women's liberation; disability rights; gay, lesbian, bisexual, and transgender rights—have all made significant gains and also seen those gains challenged and attacked.

In this final chapter we consider what is needed to tackle the problems we have identified throughout

the book. How can this be done in ways that address underlying causes as well as visible manifestations? How can women and men build relationships, systems of work, local communities, and a wider world based on sustainability and real security?

We believe that each person needs to find meaning in his or her life. Knowing what matters to you means that you can begin to take charge of your life and direct change. This process involves examining your own life, as suggested through the questions included in each chapter. Unless you do this, you will be absent from your own system of knowledge. The article by Abra Fortune Chernik provides an excellent example of this (Reading 68). She reflects on her struggle with an eating disorder and the process of overcoming it. Moving beyond her own experience, she asks, "Why society would reward my starvation and encourage my vanishing?" She explores psychological, sociological, and feminist theories for answers to this question. Other writers in this collection also start by examining their own lives but go beyond micro-level explanations. Examples include articles by Dorothy Alison (Reading 13), Julia Serano (Reading 22), Surina Khan (Reading 25), Aurora Levins Morales (Reading 34), Ann Filemyr (Reading 38), and Michelle Loyd-Paige (Reading 64).

How Does Change Happen?

The process of creating change requires a combination of theoretical insights and understandings, visions of alternatives, and action. This involves using your head, heart, and hands in ways that reinforce one another. The readings in this chapter include a blend of these three aspects.

Using the Head: Theories for Social Change

As we pointed out in Chapter 2, doing something about an issue or a problem requires us to have a theory, an explanation, of what it is. The theory we create directly shapes what we think ought to be done. Thus *how* we theorize is a key first step in creating change. If we examine only certain aspects of an issue, look at issues separately, or use a limited analytical framework, we will end up with limited understandings of women's lives. For a fuller picture we need to analyze issues individually and together, looking for commonalities and patterns, recognizing differences, and using frameworks that illuminate as many parts as possible. Our theoretical ideas, which run through the previous chapters—sometimes explicit, sometimes implicit—are summarized here:

- A social-constructionist perspective allows us to see how social and political forces shape people's lives and our sense of ourselves. It encourages us to focus on the specificity of experience and also the diversity of people's experiences. It allows us to see that situations and structures are not fixed for all time but are changeable under the right circumstances.

- How an issue is defined and framed will affect how we think about the problem, where we look for probable causes, ideas about what ought to be done, and who is likely to become involved in working to change it.

- It is necessary to analyze social situations at micro, meso, macro, and global levels and to understand how these levels affect one another. Strategies for change need to address all of these levels.

- Using an intersectional framework and understanding the concept of social location enables us to see similarities, differences, and contradictions in women's lives.

- Many women's activist organizations and projects are working on the issues discussed in this book.

- Efforts to create equal opportunities for women and equal access to current institutions have made a difference for many women, but by themselves they cannot achieve a genuinely secure and sustainable world because these are not the goals of most institutions.

Using the Heart: Visions for Social Change

Vision is the second ingredient needed to create social change—some idea of a different way of doing things, a different future for humankind, framed by explicit principles around which human relations ought to be organized. Otherwise, as the saying goes, "If you don't know where you're headed, any road will get you there."

Visions are about values, drawing from inside ourselves everything we value and daring to think big. The many demands of our busy lives leave most people with little time or opportunity to envision alternatives. In school and college, for example, students are rarely asked to think deeply about their hopes and dreams for a more truly human world in which to live. Much of what we do is guided not by our own visions but in reaction to the expectations of others and outside pressures. Social issues, too, are framed in reactive and negative terms. People talk about "antiracism," for instance, not about what a truly multicultural society would be like.

Some people scorn this step as time-wasting and unrealistic. What matters, they say, is to come up with "realistic" ideas that people feel comfortable with, that businesses will want to invest in, or that fit government programs and guidelines. Tackle something specific, something winnable. Don't waste time on grandiose ideas.

Because most of us are not encouraged to envision change, it may take a while to free ourselves from seemingly practical ideas as we envision something new. Our imaginations are often limited to what we know, and that makes it difficult to break out of our cramped habits of thought. Envisioning something different also means putting on hold the voice inside your head that says: Are you *crazy*? This will never work! Who do you think you are? Where will you *ever* get the money?

Go ahead. Envision the multicultural society, the women's health project, the community play/ read/care program for elders and children, the Internet information business run by inner-city teenagers, the women's taxi service, the intimate relationship of your dreams, your blossoming sexuality. Envision it in as much detail as you can. Think it, see it, taste it, smell it, sing it, draw it, and write it down. Share it with others who you think will be sympathetic to it. This is where you're headed. Now all you need is to create the road. The projects we mention throughout this book, like this book itself, all started this way, as somebody's dream.

Using the Hands: Action for Social Change

The third ingredient for change is action. Through action, theories and visions are tested, sharpened, and refined to create even more useful theories and more dynamic visions. In Chapter 2 we referred to philosopher Alan Rosenberg's (1988) distinction between *knowing* and *understanding.* Rosenberg further argued that understanding compels us to action, even though we may not initially want to change our habitual ways of thinking and being. When you understand something, you

> find that [your] world becomes a different world and that [you] must generate a new way to be in the new world. Since each person's way of being in the world is relatively fixed— and serves as protection against the anxieties of the unknown—integration is extremely hard. To give up a world in which one's life makes sense means undergoing great loss. Yet without the readiness to risk that loss we cannot hope to pursue understanding.   *(p. 382)*

Here we suggest a range of avenues for trying to implement your visions. Some will be more appropriate than others, depending on your goals and theoretical perspectives. Some of the activities we list below may be difficult for students, who need to concentrate on getting degrees, to participate in. Progressive social change is a long-term project; there will be plenty more to do after you graduate (see Naples and Bojar 2002).

- Think of yourself as someone with something valuable to say, who can take the initiative and start something you think is important. Think

never give up

about what you want to do after college, how to live your values and ideals.

- Express your ideas: talk to others; write 'zines, poems, leaflets, speeches, letters to newspaper editors and politicians; put up flyers or posters; organize a film series; paint murals, dance, sing, or perform your ideas.

- Be a conscious shopper. Support fair-trade products. Buy directly from farmers' markets, local producers, or small businesses. Spend your money where it will uphold your values.

- Support women's organizations, environmental groups, antiracist organizations, or LGBTQQI groups by letting them know you appreciate their work, letting others know these groups exist, attending events, donating money or something the group needs, volunteering your time, proposing ideas for projects, working as an intern for college credit.

- Work for institutional change. Within your family you may want to stop others from telling sexist or racist jokes, or to develop more egalitarian relationships. At school you may want to set up study groups to work together, support teachers who help you, point out gaps in the curriculum or college services to teachers and administrators, challenge racism or sexual harassment.

- Participate in direct action. This may include interrupting, keeping silent, organizing groups of women to walk together at night, defending women's health services, participating in demonstrations and rallies, boycotts, picketing, rent strikes, tax resistance. Whatever the setting, take back the Nike slogan. Just Do It!

- Get involved in grassroots organizing. Meet with others and decide what you can do together to tackle some issue of shared concern.

- Participate in coalitions. Consider joining with other groups on an issue of shared concern so as to be more visible and effective by working together.

- Learn about local and national issues, and let your representatives at city, state, and congressional levels know your opinions. Urge them to pass appropriate laws and to speak out in public situations and to the media. Use your vote. Help to elect progressive candidates. Support them if they get into office, and hold them accountable to their election promises.

- Learn more about international networks and organizations working on issues that concern you. Consider participating in an international meeting and bringing the knowledge you gain there to your organizing work back home.

A range of factors help us in taking action: a sense of hope and conviction that women's lives can be improved, frustration and anger at current inequalities and injustices, reliable allies, well-thought-out strategies, and help from parents, partners, neighbors, friends, children, or total strangers who may make a crucial contribution, which allows us to be involved.

Overcoming Blocks to Effective Action

Political action does not always work; that is, a chosen course of action may not achieve your original goals. There are many possible reasons for this: in-adequate theoretical understandings and analysis of the issues; inappropriate or ineffective strategies; not following through on the course of action; not being able to get enough people involved for a particular strategy to be effective; wrong timing; the failure of the group to work together well enough; the failure of people whom you thought were allies to come through when needed; and so on. The other major reason, of course, is that the opposition—whether this is your sexist uncle, your boss, the university administration, the city school board, the opposing political party, or the U.S. Congress—was simply more powerful.

Feeling that an action has failed is disheartening and may lead people to give up, assuming that creating change is hopeless. But action *always* accomplishes something, and in this sense it always works. At the very least, activism that does not meet your goals teaches you something important. In hindsight, what may seem like mistakes are valuable ways to learn how to be more effective in the future. This is what we called "socially lived" theorizing in Chapter 2. Always evaluate what you did after some activity or event, personally and with the group. If it worked as you hoped, why did it work? What have you learned as a result? If it did not work, why? What will you do differently next time?

Personal blocks to activism may include practical factors like not having enough time or energy, or needing to focus on some other aspect of life. Emotional blocks include guilt—a paralyzing feeling that keeps us stuck—and cynicism—a frustrated idealism that has turned hopeless and bitter. Anger can be a very useful, high-octane fuel if you can channel it in a constructive direction. Overextending yourself is not a sign of commitment to your ideals, and trying to do more than you can is one sure way to burn out quickly. Activism for progressive social change is not the same as being anti-authoritarian. It needs patience, humor, creativity, a range of skills and resources, an ability to work with other people, a willingness to listen and to be reflective, refining your ideas and your visions.

We see a key role for individuals, as change agents, working with others to envision alternatives and bring them into being through identity-based politics, feminist organizing, electoral politics, framing public discourse, and broad-based coalitions and alliances. We explore these forms of activism in the next section.

Women and Political Activism

Politics involves the use of power. What is it? Who has it? How is it used? Who does it benefit, and who is disadvantaged? Sociologists and political scientists define **power** as the ability to influence others. This may be by persuasion, charisma, law, political activism, or violence (Andersen 2000). As we argue throughout this book, individuals and groups have power and influence based on a range of attributes, such as race, class, gender, age, and education, that are valued in this society. Many people focus on the ways in which others exert power over us or on the fact that they have more power than we have. We generally pay less attention to the ways in which we have more power than others. This is true especially for people in subordinated groups, such as women and men of color in the United States, where some fundamental aspect of our existence, if not our identity, is predicated on being "the power-less" in many settings.

Poet and essayist Audre Lorde writes of women's personal power (Reading 20, Chapter 4), and several writers in this book refer to the importance of personal empowerment. People exercise power through institutions such as education, religion, corporations, the media, the law, the military, and all aspects of government. Sometimes this happens regardless of individual intent or knowledge. Power is also expressed in the values and practices of institutions that compel people to think and behave in specific ways. For example, the heterosexist values embedded in our culture and its institutions define the family as a man and a woman, legally bound by marriage, and their children (Reading 41). The value and legitimacy attached to this institution is a powerful influence on everyone and is in itself a pressure to marry. Higher education operates out of values that are Eurocentric, middle class, and masculinist. These values uphold particular ways of learning, certain kinds of discourse, and the use of a specific language. To succeed in college, students must work within these parameters even if they do not subscribe to these values (Reading 69).

Political scientists have focused on formal political organizations, especially the U.S. Congress, where there are relatively few women. As a result, studies of women's political influence have seriously underestimated it. Feminist researchers have pointed out that women's political participation includes active membership in a wide range of local, state, and national organizations including community groups, religious groups, women's clubs, parent-teacher associations (PTAs), and labor unions. Women work in support of candidates for political office, organize fund-raising events, circulate petitions, participate in letter-writing, call-in, and e-mail campaigns, and they vote (see, e.g., Freeman 2008; Naples 1997, 1998; Swers 2001; West and Blumberg 1990). Several articles in this collection

give details of women's organizing (e.g., Readings 30, 36, 49, and 63). In this chapter, Edna Ishayik reflects on her work as a campaign manager, supporting women running for elected office (Reading 71). Amy Jo Goddard emphasizes cultural work as an effective form of activism and popular education (Reading 70). Other writers focus on organizing across national borders (Readings 72, 73, and 74).

Identity-Based Politics

Throughout this book many contributors write about identity. Some mention the difficulties of coming to terms with who they are, the complexities of their contradictory positions, or breaking the silence surrounding taboo subjects, thoughts, and feelings. They also comment that coming to new understandings about themselves and being able to speak from a place of self-knowledge is profoundly empowering.

Identity politics is, literally, a politics that puts identity at the center, based on, for example, gender, age, race, ethnicity, or sexual orientation. It usually involves the assumption that this particular characteristic is the most important in the lives of a specific identity group. Identity politics is concerned with wider opportunities—maybe greater visibility and recognition in society, equality, justice, even liberation for ourselves and our group. Our authoritativeness comes from some common ground of experience that allows a group to say "we." This is the foundation for many student organizations, community groups, national networks, and major social movements. Thus, identity can be a very effective springboard for action.

At the same time, identity politics has serious limitations. Groups tend to remain separate, focused on their own issues and concerns, sometimes competing with each other for recognition and resources. The language of identity politics gives voice to people's discrimination and oppression. It does not encourage us to think about identity in a more complex way, as a mix of privilege and disadvantage. In Chapter 3 we noted that most people occupy multiple positions and that salient aspects of identity may vary significantly depending on the context. An African American graduate student who is about to receive her PhD, for example, may be highly respected by her teachers and peers, regardless of their race or hers. A white

man walking past her in the street may insult her because she is Black.

Understanding this notion of multiple **positionality** helps us to see how our personal and group identities are political and how the various identity groups fit together in the wider society. The specific context is crucial. In U.S. public discourse about immigration, for example, there is a fear on the part of white people—usually hinted at rather than stated directly—of being "overrun" by Latinos or Asians. When the context shifts to a discussion of peoples of color in the United States, however, Asian immigrants and Asian Americans become the "model minority," the standard against which Latinos or African Americans are compared unfavorably. Understanding one's identity involves a recognition of the ways in which one is privileged as well as disadvantaged, and the contradictions that this raises. With this more nuanced perspective, one not only focuses on the circumstances and concerns of one's own group, but also can use the complexity of one's identity to make connections to other groups. Thus, a white, middle-class woman with a hearing disability can take all of these aspects of her identity and understand her social location in terms of privilege as well as disadvantage. This is important for building effective alliances with others, which

we discuss in more detail later. We make a distinction between a narrower identity politics, discussed above, and **identity-based politics,** which has a strong identity component and also a broader view that enables people to make connections to other groups and issues. Melanie Kaye/Kantrowitz (Reading 14), Combahee River Collective (Reading 3), Leslie Feinberg (Reading 19), Michelle Loyd-Paige (Reading 64), and Amy Jo Goddard (Reading 70) all exemplify this more connective, identity-based politics. Feminist movements have grown out of identity-based politics. Movements call forth the energies, passions, and visions of many people, often in ways that are life-changing for the participants, as we discussed in Chapter 1. They inspire and make space for groundbreaking projects and alternative institutions. Some women have created change through grassroots organizing, or by providing services that did not exist before. Others focused on the need for changes in laws and public policy and set their sights on elected office.

Women in Electoral Politics

Women who seek political office invariably do so because they want to make a difference in people's lives. Those who work hard to support women candidates argue that a critical mass of women in elected office will be able to change public policy and legislation to benefit women (see Reading 71). This includes local offices like parent-teacher associations (PTAs), city council seats, statewide offices, and the U.S. Congress. Together with male allies in Congress, women elected officials and their staffs have worked long and hard to pass legislation to ensure better opportunities for women, including, for example, Title IX of the 1972 Education Act, which requires schools and colleges that receive federal funding to provide equal opportunities for male and female students (see the Box on page 568), the Family and Medical Leave Act, and the Violence

Against Women Act. They have also worked for reproductive rights, health care, improvements in women's wages, the availability of affordable child care, the opening of military combat roles to women, and so forth.

In 1990 women were a mere 5.6 percent of congressional representatives. At the slow rate women's participation was growing, it would take at least another three hundred years before there were equal numbers of women and men in Congress. The proportion of women elected to political office has increased since then, though the United States has fewer women in office than many other countries (see Table 12.1). In 2012 women held

Table 12.1 Women's Representation in National Legislatures

COUNTRY	% WOMEN IN LOWER OR SINGLE HOUSE	COUNTRY	% WOMEN IN LOWER OR SINGLE HOUSE
Rwanda	56.3	Uzbekistan	22.0
Cuba	45.2	Peru	21.5
Sweden	44.7	China	21.3
South Africa	42.3	Lithuania	19.1
Nicaragua	40.2	France	18.9
Mozambique	39.2	Venezuela	17.0
Denmark	39.1	United States of America	16.8
Costa Rica	38.6	North Korea	15.6
Spain	36.0	Ireland	15.1
Germany	32.9	Republic of South Korea	14.7
Switzerland	28.5	Turkey	14.2
Tunisia	26.7	Dominican Republic	12.5
Mexico	26.2	India	11.0
Iraq	25.2	Japan	10.8
Canada	24.8	Malaysia	10.4
Australia	24.7	Panama	8.5
Vietnam	24.4	Ghana	8.3
Croatia	23.8	Algeria	8.0
Poland	23.7	Kuwait	7.7
Philippines	22.9	Iran (Islamic Republic of)	2.8
Pakistan	22.5	Saudi Arabia	0.0
United Kingdom	22.3		

Source: Inter-Parliamentary Union. Women in National Parliaments (31 December 2011) www.ipu.org/wmn-e/classif.htm.

Title IX

Title IX ("title nine") of the 1972 Education Act was a landmark piece of civil rights legislation requiring educational institutions that receive federal funding to provide equal opportunities for male and female students in academics, athletics, financial assistance, and resources like student health and housing. Indeed, Title IX is a key reason that girls and women have made such gains in higher education, particularly in sports. In 1971, 294,015 girls participated in high school athletics compared to over 2.7 million girls in 2001—an 847 percent increase (U.S. Department of Education, quoted in Nelson 2002, p. 33), and there are now many more opportunities and facilities at the college level also.

A college must meet one of the following three standards to comply with the law. It must have roughly the same proportion of women among its varsity athletes as it has in its undergraduate student body; it must have a "history and continuing practice" of expanding opportunities for women; or it must demonstrate that it is "fully and effectively accommodating the interests and abilities" of its women students (Suggs 2002). Detractors have argued that increased resources

for women have resulted in fewer opportunities for men, and some athletics departments have achieved parity by cutting opportunities for male students rather than increasing those for women. A General Accounting Office report released in March 2001, found a net gain in men's teams from 1982 to 1999, and many more opportunities for men than for women (Nelson 2002). Several Ivy League colleges and state universities have been forced to comply with the law, as women sued them for discrimination.

In March 2005, the U.S. Supreme Court decided that individuals who protest sex discrimination may sue to challenge retaliation if their schools punish them as a result (*Jackson v. Birmingham Board of Education*), a significant re-affirmation of rights provided under Title IX. Moreover, the Court held that for effective enforcement of Title IX, retaliation against those who come forward to report discrimination must be prohibited.

The Title IX Action Network provides information to help Title IX Coordinators understand and manage their functions as Title IX experts in their states, districts, and schools (www.titleix-action.net).

---

90 (16.8 percent) of the 535 seats in the U.S. Congress: 17 percent of the 100 seats in the Senate and 73 (16.8 percent) of the 435 seats in the House of Representatives. Of the 1,747 women state legislators nationwide, 20.1 percent were women of color (Center for American Women and Politics 2012). Sociologist Margaret Andersen (2000) noted the impediments that limit women who want to run for political office: voter and media prejudice against women candidates, lack of support from party leaders, lack of access to extensive political networks, and lack of money. At the same time, women seeking office and organizations like Emily's List, the Fund for a Feminist Majority, the National Women's Political Caucus, and the White House Project are working to overcome these limitations (e.g., Burrell 1994; Ford 2002; Norris 1997; Thomas and Wilcox 1998; Woods 2000).

More women are registered voters than men across all age and racial groups. In the 2008 presidential elections, 60.4 percent of women voted compared to 55.7 percent of men, a difference of ten million votes (Center for American Women and Politics 2011). Women are more likely than men to hold liberal views, with African American women the most progressive group. More women than men support a comprehensive national health care system, government funding for social programs, gun control, workplace equity, reproductive freedom, LGBT rights, and an end to wars. This gender gap can be significant in two ways: getting more progressive candidates—women and men—elected and giving greater focus to liberal issues once such candidates are in office (see, e.g., Adam and Derber 2008; Ducat 2004; Gallagher 1993; Norris 1997; Whittaker 2008).

Many elected women are on committees concerned with health, education, and social services. Political scientist Michele Swers (2001) found that at state and national levels women "bring different policy priorities to the legislative agenda, particularly in the area of women's issues" (also see Carroll 2001). However, at the highest level, electoral politics is ruthlessly competitive and constrained by the need to raise huge campaign funds. Most women run for office because they want to solve problems, and many do not want to embroil themselves in what they see as a "dirty" business. In addition, a Supreme Court ruling that "the government may not ban political spending by corporations in candidate elections" has allowed a more explicit corporate role in politics (Liptak 2010). Corporations have long been considered "persons" under the U.S. Constitution and entitled to First Amendment rights to free speech. Critics argued that the effect of the Court's 2010 decision would be to further distort the electoral process and drown out the voices of ordinary citizens in Washington.

Over the last decade, a worsening economy, changes in public policy, and skewed federal budget priorities have had disastrous effects on many people in this country. Restrictions on welfare payments, the steady erosion of reproductive rights and affirmative action policies, major tax cuts for the richest citizens, increasing levels of incarceration, and vast military budgets have all taken resources away from women and their communities. Individuals, organizations, and elected officials who seek to improve women's lives face a hard road ahead, where a hallmark of success will be holding onto previous gains as well as trying to move forward. This will require clear thinking, hard work, and acts of personal courage by elected representatives, with strong support from voters.

Framing Public Discourse

An important aspect of women's political work is to frame issues in ways that affect public discourse and change public opinion. In the late nineteenth and early twentieth century, feminists circulated ideas by giving public lectures, standing on picket lines, and participating in rallies and demonstrations. They published essays and pamphlets and staged performances to spread the word regarding women's rights. Over the years, feminist scholars,

writers, and activists have sought to influence dominant ideology by bringing issues into public debate that were once thought of as private matters, such as rape, intimate partner violence, child sexual abuse, women's sexuality, reproductive freedom, and so on.

Feminist scholarship and activism continue to do this. In this book, for example, articles on Muslim women (Reading 11), engaging men against violence (Reading 35), the privileging of marriage (Reading 40), economic insecurity (Reading 43), gender and human security (Reading 61), and perspectives on climate change (Reading 66) all frame these issues in ways that challenge the dominant discourse. As well as providing services, many of the organizations and projects we mention undertake research, define campaigns, and work to create a climate of opinion that will benefit women. For individuals and groups, creating independent media through Web sites, blogs, Facebook, and You Tube is crucial to widening debate beyond classrooms, lobbying efforts, and conversations in dorm rooms, coffee shops, or around kitchen tables (e.g., Bailey and Gumbs 2010; Breitbart and Nogueira 2004; Crabb 2006; Pozner 2006).

Organizations whose main goal is to change public policy constantly position themselves in relation to views expressed by elected officials, policy think tanks, and media reports. During the spring of 2012, feminist organizations coordinated a vital counterdiscourse to misogynist opinions underlying Republican candidates' campaign speeches, Right wing talk shows, and bills in Congress and state legislatures that sought to limit reproductive freedom and turn the clock back decades on this issue. Women's groups organized e-mail blasts, online articles and petitions, and rallies and demonstrations defining this discourse as nothing less than a "war on women" (Schuetz 2012).

A new movement to emerge since the Great Recession (2007–2009) was Occupy Wall Street, started in September 2011, to protest the vast inequalities of the economic and political system that, as they framed it, benefits 1 percent of the population at the expense of the 99 percent (see Box on p. 317). Whereas the business pages hailed an economic recovery for corporations and banks, the Occupy movement stressed that home foreclosures and high unemployment still continued, and that banks had been bailed out with billions of dollars in public money. Nationwide, people from diverse backgrounds gathered in public spaces to live, learn, and work together as the protest developed. The economy was the uniting factor, though groups within the movement brought many related issues, such as the colonization of Native Americans (who see the whole continent as occupied), high rates of incarceration and police brutality against communities of color, the demands of immigrant workers, as well as feminist concerns. Blogger Angi Becker Stevens (2011) stressed that "the various forms of oppression in our society are so interwoven that it would be impossible to truly fight one without fighting the others." A key issue for any broad-based movement is to define its goals so that they resonate with people of diverse backgrounds. Articulating connections among issues and forging links among activists are essential to building broader political alliances, as discussed next.

Building Alliances for the Twenty-First Century

The many inequalities among women, mentioned throughout this book, often separate us and make it difficult to work together effectively. Those with power over us know this and often exploit differences to pit one group against another. Progressive social change is a slow process that needs sustained action over the long haul. Effective alliances are necessary for long-term efforts, as well as coalition work where the important thing is to stand together on a specific issue regardless of other differences. We see alliances across lines of difference as both a means and an end. They provide both the process for moving toward, and some experience of, multicultural society. Melanie Kaye/Kantrowitz (Reading 14) and Ann Filemyr (Reading 38) offer insights for alliance building, especially across lines of race and class. In Reading 69, Kathleen Yep reflects on a course she taught in which Asian American college students and Asian immigrant women each contributed to a shared learning environment. Some of the skills the students learned through this process, such as careful listening, being open to others, and working with patience and empathy, are essential for creating alliances.

Some Principles for Alliance Building

Alliances may be personal, campus-wide, city-wide, national, or transnational in scope. Regardless of scale, some basic principles apply:

- Know who you are, what is important to you, what are your non-negotiables. Know your strengths and what you bring to a shared partnership or project.

- Decide whether you want to be allies with a particular person or group. What are their values? What are they interested in doing in terms of creating social change? Are they open to the alliance? What is the purpose for coming together? Are you coming together as equals? Or in solidarity with another group?

- Check out the person or the group as the acquaintance grows. Are they who they say they are? Do you have reason to trust them to be there for you? Judge them by their track records and what actually happens, not by your fears, hopes, or expectations based on previous experiences.

- Commit yourself to communicate. Listen, talk, and listen more. Be committed to the process of communication rather than overly attached to a specific position. Communication may be through conversations, reading, seeing films, attending events, or learning about one another's communities. Work together on projects and support one another's projects. Go into one another's settings as participants, observers, guests.

- Share your history. Talk about what has happened to you and to the people of your group.

- Be patient. Wanting to understand, to hear more, to stay connected requires patience from the inside. Allow one another room to explore ideas, make mistakes, be tentative. Hold judgment until you understand what's going on.

- Be honest and authentic and ask for authenticity from others. If this is not possible, what is the alliance worth?

- Keep the process "clean." Call one another on bad things if they happen. Don't try to disentangle difficulties when it is impossible to do so meaningfully, but don't use externals (too late, too tired, too busy, too many other items on the agenda) to avoid this.

- Be open to being called on your own mistakes, admitting when you're wrong, even if it is embarrassing or makes you feel vulnerable. Tell the other person when his or her opinions and experiences give you new insights and help you to see things differently.

- Do some people in the group take up a lot of time talking about their own concerns? Are they aware of it? How does privilege based on gender, race, class, nation, sexuality, disability, age, culture, or language play out in this relationship or alliance? Can you talk about it openly?

- What is the "culture" of your group or alliance? What kinds of meetings do you have? What is your decision-making style? If you eat together, what kind of food do you serve? What kind of music do you listen to? Where do you meet? What do you do when you are together? Does everyone in the group feel comfortable with these cultural aspects?

- Work out the boundaries of your responsibilities to one another. What do you want to do for yourself? What do you need others to help with? When? How?

- Look for the common ground. What are the perspectives, experiences, and insights we share?

Overcoming Impediments to Effective Alliances

Many sincere and committed attempts at building alliances have been thwarted, despite the best of intentions. Be aware of several common impediments to creating effective alliances, including the following beliefs and behaviors, which apply at meso, macro, and global levels of interaction and analysis.

Internalized Oppression   This is a learned mind-set of subservience and inferiority in oppressed peoples. It includes the acceptance of labels, characteristics, prejudices, and perceptions promoted by the dominant society. Specific behaviors include self-hatred and dislike, disrespect for, even hatred of others of the same group.

Internalized Domination   This is a mind-set of entitlement and superiority among members of dominant groups. Always speaking first in discussions, being unconscious of the large amount of physical and social space one takes up, and automatically assuming leadership roles are some of its manifestations.

Operating from a Politics of Scarcity   This results from a deeply held, sometimes unconscious, belief that there is not enough of anything—material things as well as nonmaterial things like power, positive regard, popularity, friendship, time—and, more important, that however much there is, it will not be shared equally. In this view, inequality is simply a given that cannot be changed. It also justifies individualism and competition.

Subscribing to a Hierarchy of Oppression   This involves the placement of one oppressed group in relation to another so that one group's experiences of discrimination, prejudice, and disadvantage are deemed to be worse or better than another's.

Not Knowing One Another's History   Ignorance about other persons' backgrounds often results in drawing incorrect conclusions about their experiences. This prevents us from recognizing the complexity of women's experiences and can hide the ways our experiences are both different and similar.

Transnational Women's Organizing

Alliances have been central to women's movements in the United States and around the world, as mentioned by Peggy Antrobus (Reading 74). Several readings in this collection focus on transnational feminist efforts, such as the International Community of Women Living with HIV/AIDS (Reading 31), the International Women's Network against Militarism (Reading 72), and Mobility International USA (Reading 73).

Transnational alliances are not new. Historian Bonnie Anderson (2000) found that in the mid-nineteenth century feminists from Britain, France, Germany, Italy, Sweden, and the United States shared tactics and ideas through letters, personal visits, and published writings. Nowadays feminist work across national boundaries, facilitated

U.N. Millennium Development Goals

The United Nations articulated eight Millennium Development Goals to be achieved by 2015. These goals were drawn from the Millennium Declaration adopted by 189 nations and signed by 147 heads of government during the U.N. Millennium Summit in September 2000. The Millennium Development Goals exemplify the constructive nature of United Nations' efforts that oppose global trends. They generate an alternative discourse that is hopeful and human centered.

- Goal 1: Eradicate extreme poverty and hunger
- Goal 2: Achieve universal primary education

- Goal 3: Promote gender equality and empower women
- Goal 4: Reduce child mortality
- Goal 5: Improve maternal health
- Goal 6: Combat HIV/AIDS, malaria, and other diseases
- Goal 7: Ensure environmental sustainability
- Goal 8: Develop a Global Partnership for Development

Source: United Nations, http://www.undp.org/mdg/basics.shtml

---

by e-mail, conference calls, and air travel, involves many coordinated campaigns and activities.

Conferences under the auspices of the United Nations have provided one avenue for international networking, consolidating shared understandings and solidarity as argued by Peggy Antrobus (Reading 74). Although the world headquarters of the United Nations is in New York City, it is a long way from most people's awareness in the United States. Many women's groups and organizations around the world, particularly outside the U.S., have come to see the U.N. as a potential ally in their struggles for women's rights and have been using its various instruments as tools for improving women's lives. One of the most widely known is CEDAW (Convention on the Elimination of All Forms of Discrimination against Women). Since its adoption by the U.N. General Assembly in 1979, CEDAW has been used to pressure individual countries to implement laws, policies, and services to advance women's economic, political, and social status in that society. Other examples of U.N. conventions include: the International Covenant on Economic, Social, and Cultural Rights; the Convention on Rights of the Child; and the Convention on the Elimination of All Forms of Racial Discrimination.

In September 1995, more than thirty thousand women from virtually every country in the world

gathered in Huairou, China, to discuss the many issues and problems faced by women and girls. This was an NGO forum with nearly five thousand workshops listed in the schedule and the largest meeting of women in history. A two-hour bus ride away at the official U.N. Fourth World Conference on Women in Beijing, some five thousand delegates discussed what their governments were doing to improve women's lives and negotiated an official U.N. document, the *Platform for Action*. The U.N. Fourth World Conference was the culmination of over twenty years of meetings, proposals, position papers, and discussions by women activists, government delegates to the U.N., and U.N. staff, starting with International Women's Year in 1975.

Individual governments must ratify United Nations conventions and resolutions for them to become accepted as national law and policy. Even if governments do not ratify them—and the U.S. has not ratified several U.N. conventions including CEDAW—they are still useful for activists in their attempts to hold governments accountable and to show what others have pledged to do for women and girls.

In March 2005, the U.N. Commission on the Status of Women affirmed the Beijing *Platform for Action*, adopted ten years earlier. Delegates reported on the progress—or in many cases, the lack of progress—governments had made to create opportunities for women and to safeguard their health, well-being, and overall security. In contrast to the congratulatory reports of many governments, the New York–based Women's Environment and Development Organization concluded that, in the main, "governments have failed to turn the platform into action, and that, despite well-meaning intentions, many women in all regions are actually worse off than they were ten years ago" (Lederer 2005; WEDO 2005).

Although feminists from many countries are engaged in U.N.-based efforts, they recognize the limitations and tensions inherent in this system. The United Nations was established after World War II and focuses on relations among nations. Its foundational document, the *Universal Declaration of Human Rights*, and its organizational structure assume equality among nations, which is not current reality. Some activists and commentators ask: Is it meaningful to talk of universal human rights? How can specific cultural values be respected and women protected in cases where cultural values and practices violate their rights and dignity? Our discussion of cultural relativism in Chapter 2 is relevant here. The chief deliberative body, the U.N. General Assembly, comprises 192 member nations, but the much smaller Security Council is the center of power. Its five permanent members are China, France, the Russian Federation, the United Kingdom, and the United States, with the United States dominating this body since the beginning.

Chandra Talpade Mohanty (2003) discusses challenges of transnational feminist organizing and critiques organizing efforts that reproduce similar inequalities to those that exist between rich and poor nations. As mentioned in Chapter 2, Mohanty embraces transnational multicultural feminism, by which she means a theory and practice that is "non-colonized," and anchored in equality and respect. This would avoid false universalisms and involve ethical and caring dialogue across differences, divisions, and conflicts. From their very different social locations, women would define "common contexts of struggle." These are laudable goals. They require good intentions, knowledge, and political awareness as well as determination, creativity, trust, and considerable patience to tackle, let alone surmount, structural inequalities between women from richer and poorer nations. These inequalities include the fact that most women do not have reliable

Internet access; interpretation and translation services are necessary to include women who do not speak a common language; there are disparities in fundraising opportunities; the unequal purchasing power of currencies is problematic; difficulties of travel must be solved, including the need for women to take time away from home and work responsibilities; women from poorer countries face difficulty securing visas to travel to meetings in the global North; organizational styles and cultures vary greatly; and last, but certainly not least, differences in political perspectives abound. In Reading 72, members of the International Women's Network against Militarism discuss such challenges in their work.

Providing services to women in the United States and reforming existing institutions to make them more responsive to those who are excluded are crucially important in the overall work of progressive social change and have made a difference to generations of women. The challenge for the future is to maintain and expand this work.

Given that corporations control more and more of the world and that women's rights are under serious attack in this country, we need to work together to address interconnected issues: economic survival, reproductive rights, all forms of violence including state violence, criminalization and incarceration, immigrant rights, and so on, as argued by Labaton and Martin (2004). These broadbased efforts draw on people's creativity, our emotions, our spirituality, and our sense of justice, strengthening connections between people and communities. There is great accumulated experience and insight about how to work on multi-issue politics, and also much to learn. Grace Lee Boggs, a long-time activist in Detroit, noted that this is both an exciting and a daunting time in human history (Boggs and Kurashige 2011). She urged: "For our own well-being, for the health and safety of our communities, our cities and our country, we need to accept the awesome responsibility of creating new ways of . . . living" (1994, p. 2).

This book is about U.S. women's lives and the kind of world we need to create for women's empowerment, development, and well-being. This world will be based on notions of genuine security and sustainability. The project of human development—for both women and men—has

been in process for a very long time. It is our challenge to take the next steps in this process. How can
we settle for anything less?

Activism is not issue-specific
It's a moral posture that, steady state, propels you
forward, from one hard hour to the next.
Believing that you can do something to make things
better, you do
Something, rather than nothing.

You assume responsibility for the privilege of your
abilities.
You do whatever you can.
You reach beyond yourself in your imagination, and
in your wish for
Understanding, and for change.
You admit the limitations of individual perspec-
tives.
You trust somebody else.
You do not turn away.   *(June Jordan)*

Questions for Reflection

As you read and discuss this chapter, think about these questions:

1. What are your assumptions about how people and societies change? What do you
   think needs changing, if anything? How is knowledge related to social change?
2. Have you ever been involved in a social-action project or electoral politics? What
   was your experience like? If you have not, why not?
3. Have you tried to establish and maintain an ongoing relationship, friendship, or
   working partnership with someone from a background very different from your
   own? What happened? What did you learn from that experience? What would you
   do differently another time, if anything?
4. If you have had such a relationship, why did you become involved? Was this a
   good enough reason? Why or why not? If you never have, why not?
5. What do you know about the history of the various groups you are a member of?
   What do you know about groups that are not your own? How does knowing this
   history help, and how does not knowing it hinder you in making alliances across
   lines of difference? How can you learn what you don't know?
6. What is your vision of a secure and sustainable personal relationship? Community?
   Society? World?
7. Assuming you had time, energy, resources, and support, what kind of an organization would you create to work for changes in women's lives, and why do you think
   it would be effective?

Finding Out More on the Web

1. Research the work of women's organizations cited in this chapter. What are their
   strategies and visions? Who do they speak to? These are additional resources:

   Guerilla Girls, a group of women intent on exposing patterns of sexism, racism, and
   censorship in the art world: www.guerillagirls.com

   African Women's Development and Communication Network: www.femnet.or.ke

   Articulacion Feminista Marcosur: www.mujeresdelsur-afm.org.uy/

   Isis International-Manila: www.isiswomen.org

Public Leadership Education Network (PLEN): www.plen.org

Women Against Violence Europe: www.wave-network.org/

Working Group on Girls: www.girlsrights.org

Women Living Under Muslim Laws: www.wluml.org/

2. Learn more about the Occupy movement: its theories, visions, and actions. Who identifies with this movement and why? What can you learn from this about building alliances?

◆◆◆

Taking Action

1. List all the ways you are an activist. Review the suggestions for taking action at the end of each chapter. Commit yourself to continuing to involve yourself in issues that matter to you.

2. Think about how aspects of your identity can help you to make alliances with others. Support campus or community groups that are working together on an issue of shared concern.

3. Where do your elected officials (at the city, state, and national levels) stand on issues that matter to you? What is their voting record on these issues? Write to thank them for supporting issues you care about (if they do), or urge them to change their positions. Present them with information from your course materials or other sources to make a strong case.

4. Many of the issues discussed in this book have implications at the global level. What can you do that will have an impact at that level?

S I X T Y - E I G H T

The Body Politic (1995)

Abra Fortune Chernik

Abra Fortune Chernik is a teacher, writer, and photographer based in Chapel Hill. She established the Chernik Group in 1999, a private tutoring practice for high school students. She also studies and teaches Vipassana meditation.

My body possesses solidness and curve, like the ocean. My weight mingles with Earth's pull, drawing me onto the sand. I have not always sent waves into the world. I flew off once, for five years, and swirled madly like a cracking brown leaf in the salty autumn wind. I wafted, dried out, apathetic.

I had no weight in the world during my years of anorexia. Curled up inside my thinness, a refugee in a cocoon of hunger, I lost the capacity to care about myself or others. I starved my body and twitched in place as those around me danced in the energy of shared existence and progressed in their lives. When I graduated from college crowned with academic honors, professors praised my potential. I wanted only to vanish.

It took three months of hospitalization and two years of outpatient psychotherapy for me to learn to nourish myself and to live in a body that expresses strength and honesty in its shape. I accepted my right and my obligation to take up room with my figure, voice and spirit. I remembered how to tumble forward and touch the world that holds me. I chose the ocean as my guide.

Who disputes the ocean's fullness?

Growing up in New York City, I did not care about the feminist movement. Although I attended an all-girls high school, we read mostly male authors and studied the history of men. Embracing mainstream culture without question, I learned about womanhood from fashion magazines, Madison Avenue and Hollywood. I dismissed feminist alternatives as foreign and offensive, swathed as they were in stereotypes that threatened my adolescent need for conformity.

Puberty hit late; I did not complain. I enjoyed living in the lanky body of a tall child and insisted on the title of "girl." If anyone referred to me as a "young woman," I would cry out, horrified, "Do not call me the *W* word!" But at sixteen years old, I could no longer deny my fate. My stomach and breasts rounded. Curly black hair sprouted in the most embarrassing places. Hips swelled from a once-flat plane. Interpreting maturation as an unacceptable lapse into fleshiness, I resolved to eradicate the physical symptoms of my impending womanhood.

Magazine articles, television commercials, lunchroom conversation, gymnastics coaches and write-ups on models had saturated me with diet savvy. Once I decided to lose weight, I quickly turned expert. I dropped hot chocolate from my regular breakfast order at the Skyline Diner. I replaced lunches of peanut butter and Marshmallow Fluff sandwiches with small platters of cottage cheese and cantaloupe. I eliminated dinner altogether and blunted my appetite with Tab, Camel Lights, and Carefree bubble gum. When furious craving overwhelmed my resolve and I swallowed an extra something, I would flee to the nearest bathroom to purge my mistake.

Within three months, I had returned my body to its preadolescent proportions and had manipulated my monthly period into drying up. Over the next five years, I devoted my life to losing my weight. I came to resent the body in which I lived, the body that threatened to develop, the body whose hunger I despised but could not extinguish. If I neglected a workout or added a pound or ate a bite too many, I would stare in the mirror and drown myself in a tidal wave of criticism. Hatred of my body generalized to hatred of myself as a person, and self-referential labels such as "pig," "failure" and "glutton" allowed me to believe that I deserved punishment.

My self-hatred became fuel for the self-mutilating behaviors of the eating disorder.

As my body shrank, so did my world. I starved away my power and vision, my energy and inclinations. Obsessed with dieting, I allowed relationships, passions and identity to wither. I pulled back from the world, off of the beach, out of the sand. The waves of my existence ceased to roll beyond the inside of my skin.

And society applauded my shrinking. Pound after pound the applause continued, like the pounding ocean outside the door of my beach house.

The word "anorexia" literally means "loss of appetite." But as an anorexic, I felt hunger thrashing inside my body. I denied my appetite, ignored it, but never lost it. Sometimes the pangs twisted so sharply, I feared they would consume the meat of my heart. On desperate nights I rose in a flannel nightgown and allowed myself to eat an unplanned something.

No matter how much I ate, I could not soothe the pangs. Standing in the kitchen at midnight, spotlighted by the blue-white light of the open refrigerator, I would frantically feed my neglected appetite: the Chinese food I had not touched at dinner; ice cream and whipped cream; microwaved bread; cereal and chocolate milk; doughnuts and bananas. Then, solid sadness inside my gut, swell-ing agitation, a too-big meal I would not digest. In the bathroom I would rip off my shirt, tie up my hair, and prepare to execute the desperate ritual, again. I would ram the back of my throat with a toothbrush handle, crying, impatient, until the food rushed up. I would vomit until the toilet filled and I emptied, until I forgave myself, until I felt ready to try my life again. Standing up from my position over the toilet, wiping my mouth, I would believe that I was safe. Looking in the mirror through puffy eyes in a tumescent face, I would promise to take care of myself. Kept awake by the fast, confused beating of my heart and the ache in my chest, I would swear I did not miss the world outside. Lost within myself, I almost died.

By the time I entered the hospital, a mess of protruding bones defined my body, and the bones of my emaciated life rattled me crazy. I carried a pillow around because it hurt to sit down, and I shivered with cold in sultry July. Clumps of brittle hair clogged the drain when I showered, and blackened eyes appeared to sink into my head. My vision of reality wrinkled and my disposition turned mercurial as I slipped into starvation psychosis, a condition associated with severe malnutrition. People told me that I resembled a concentration camp prisoner, a chemotherapy patient, a famine victim or a fashion model.

In the hospital, I examined my eating disorder under the lenses of various therapies. I dissected my childhood, my family structure, my intimate relationships, my belief systems. I participated in experiential therapies of movement, art and psychodrama. I learned to use words instead of eating patterns to communicate my feelings. And still I refused to gain more than a minimal amount of weight.

I felt powerful as an anorexic. Controlling my body yielded an illusion of control over my life; I received incessant praise for my figure despite my sickly mien, and my frailty manipulated family and friends into protecting me from conflict. I had reduced my world to a plate of steamed carrots, and over this tiny kingdom I proudly crowned myself queen.

I sat cross-legged on my hospital bed for nearly two months before I earned an afternoon pass to go to the mall with my mother. The privilege came just in time; I felt unbearably large and desperately wanted a new outfit under which to hide gained weight. At the mall, I searched for two hours before finally discovering, in the maternity section at Macy's, a shirt large enough to cover what I perceived as my enormous body.

With an hour left on my pass, I spotted a sign on a shop window: "Body Fat Testing, $3.00." I suggested to my mother that we split up for ten minutes; she headed to Barnes & Noble, and I snuck into the fitness store.

I sat down in front of a machine hooked up to a computer, and a burly young body builder fired questions at me:

"Age?"

"Twenty-one."

"Height?"

"Five nine."

"Weight?"

"Ninety-nine."

The young man punched my statistics into his keyboard and pinched my arm with clippers wired to the testing machine. In a moment, the computer spit out my results. "Only ten percent body fat!

Unbelievably healthy. The average for a woman your age is twenty-five percent. Fantastic! You're this week's blue ribbon winner."

I stared at him in disbelief. *Winner? Healthy? Fantastic?* I glanced around at the other customers in the store, some of whom had congregated to watch my testing, and I felt embarrassed by his praise. And then I felt furious. Furious at this man and at the society that programmed him for their ignorant approbation of my illness and my suffering.

"I am dying of anorexia," I whispered. "Don't congratulate me."

I spent my remaining month in the hospital supplementing psychotherapy with an independent examination of eating disorders from a social and political point of view. I needed to understand why society would reward my starvation and encourage my vanishing. In the bathroom, a mirror on the open door behind me reflected my backside in a mirror over the sink. Vertebrae poked at my skin, ribs hung like wings over chiseled hip bones, the two sides of my buttocks did not touch. I had not seen this view of myself before.

In writing, I recorded instances in which my eating disorder had tangled the progress of my life and thwarted my relationships. I filled three and a half Mead marble notebooks. Five years' worth of: *I wouldn't sit with Daddy when he was alone in the hospital because I needed to go jogging; I told Derek not to visit me because I couldn't throw up when he was there; I almost failed my comprehensive exams because I was so hungry; I spent my year at Oxford with my head in the toilet bowl; I wouldn't eat the dinner my friends cooked me for my nineteenth birthday because I knew they had used oil in the recipe; I told my family not to come to my college graduation because I didn't want to miss a day at the gym or have to eat a restaurant meal.* And on and on for hundreds of pages.

This honest account of my life dissolved the illusion of anorexic power. I saw myself naked in the truth of my pain, my loneliness, my obsessions, my craziness, my selfishness, my defeat. I also recognized the social and political implications of consuming myself with the trivialities of calories and weight. At college, I had watched as classmates involved themselves in extracurricular clubs, volunteer work, politics and applications for jobs and graduate schools. Obsessed with exercising and exhausted by starvation, I did not even consider joining in such pursuits. Despite my love of writing and painting and literature, despite ranking at the top of my class, I wanted only to teach aerobics. Despite my adolescent days as a loud-mouthed, rambunctious class leader, I had grown into a silent, hungry young woman.

And society preferred me this way: hungry, fragile, crazy. *Winner! Healthy! Fantastic!* I began reading feminist literature to further understand the disempowerment of women in our culture. I digested the connection between a nation of starving, self-obsessed women and the continued success of the patriarchy. I also cultivated an awareness of alternative models of womanhood. In the stillness of the hospital library, new voices in my life rose from printed pages to echo my rage and provide the conception of my feminist consciousness.

I had been willing to accept self-sabotage, but now I refused to sacrifice myself to a society that profited from my pain. I finally understood that my eating disorder symbolized more than "personal psychodynamic trauma." Gazing in the mirror at my emaciated body, I observed a woman held up by her culture as the physical ideal because she was starving, self-obsessed and powerless, a woman called beautiful because she threatened no one except herself. Despite my intelligence, my education, and my supposed Manhattan sophistication, I had believed all of the lies; I had almost given my life in order to achieve the sickly impotence that this culture aggressively links with female happiness, love and success. And everything I had to offer to the world, every tumbling wave, every thought and every passion, nearly died inside me.

As long as society resists female power, fashion will call healthy women physically flawed. As long as society accepts the physical, sexual and economic abuse of women, popular culture will prefer women who resemble little girls. Sitting in the hospital the summer after my college graduation, I grasped the absurdity of a nation of adult women dying to grow small.

Armed with this insight, I loosened the grip of the starvation disease on my body. I determined to re-create myself based on an image of a woman warrior. I remembered my ocean, and I took my first bite.

Gaining weight and getting my head out of the toilet bowl was the most political act I have ever committed.

I left the hospital and returned home to Fire Island. Living at the shore in those wintry days of my new life, I wrapped myself in feminism as I hunted seashells and role models. I wanted to feel proud of my womanhood. I longed to accept and honor my body's fullness.

During the process of my healing, I had hoped that I would be able to skip the memory of anorexia like a cold pebble into the dark winter sea. I had dreamed that in relinquishing my obsessive chase after a smaller body, I would be able to come home to rejoin those whom I had left in order to starve, rejoin them to live together as healthy, powerful women. But as my body has grown full, I have sensed a hollowness in the lives of women all around me that I had not noticed when I myself stood hollow. I have made it home only to find myself alone.

Out in the world again, I hear the furious thumping dance of body hatred echoing every place I go. Friends who once appeared wonderfully carefree in ordering late-night french fries turn out not to eat breakfast or lunch. Smart, talented, creative women talk about dieting and overeating and hating the beach because they look terrible in bathing suits. Famous women give interviews insulting their bodies and bragging about bicycling twenty-four miles the day they gave birth.

I had looked forward to rejoining society after my years of anorexic exile. Ironically, in order to preserve my health, my recovery has included the development of a consciousness that actively challenges the images and ideas that define this culture. Walking down Madison Avenue and passing emaciated women, I say to myself, *those women are sick.* When smacked with a diet commercial, I remind myself, *I don't do that anymòre.* I decline invitations to movies that feature anorexic actors, I will not participate in discussions about dieting, and I refuse to shop in stores that cater to women with eating-disordered figures.

Though I am critical of diet culture, I find it nearly impossible to escape. Eating disorders have woven their way into the fabric of my society. On television, in print, on food packaging, in casual conversation and in windows of clothing stores populated by ridiculously gaunt mannequins, messages to lose my weight and control my appetite challenge my recovered fullness. Finally at home in my body, I recognize myself as an island in a sea of eating disorder, a sea populated predominantly by young women.

A perversion of nature by society has resulted in a phenomenon whereby women feel safer when starving than when eating. Losing our weight boosts self-esteem, while nourishing our bodies evokes feelings of self-doubt and self-loathing.

When our bodies take up more space than a size eight (as most of our bodies do), we say, *too big*. When our appetites demand more than a Lean Cuisine, we say, *too much*. When we want a piece of a friend's birthday cake, we say, *too bad*. Don't eat too much, don't talk too loudly, don't take up too much space, don't take from the world. Be pleasant or crazy, but don't seem hungry. Remember, a new study shows that men prefer women who eat salad for dinner over women who eat burgers and fries.

So we keep on shrinking, starving away our wildness, our power, our truth.

Hiding our curves under long T-shirts at the beach, sitting silently and fidgeting while others eat dessert, sneaking back into the kitchen late at night to binge and hating ourselves the next day, skipping breakfast, existing on diet soda and cigarettes, adding up calories and subtracting everything else. We accept what is horribly wrong in our lives and fight what is beautiful and right.

Over the past three years, feminism has taught me to honor the fullness of my womanhood and the solidity of the body that hosts my life. In feminist circles I have found mentors, strong women who live with power, passion and purpose. And yet, even in groups of feminists, my love and acceptance of my body remains unusual.

Eating disorders affect us all on both a personal and a political level. The majority of my peers—including my feminist peers—still measure their beauty against anorexic ideals. Even among feminists, body hatred and chronic dieting continue to consume lives. Friends of anorexics beg them to please start eating; then these friends go home and continue their own diets. Who can deny that the millions of young women caught in the net of disordered eating will frustrate the potential of the next wave of feminism?

Sometimes my empathy dissolves into frustration and rage at our situation. For the first time in history, young women have the opportunity to create a world in our image. But many of us concentrate instead on re-creating the shape of our thighs.

As young feminists, we must place unconditional acceptance of our bodies at the top of our political agenda. We must claim our bodies as our own to love and honor in their infinite shapes and sizes. Fat, thin, soft, hard, puckered, smooth, our bodies are our homes. By nourishing our bodies, we care for and love ourselves on the most basic level. When we deny ourselves physical food, we go hungry emotionally, psychologically, spiritually and politically. We must challenge ourselves to eat and digest, and allow society to call us too big. We will understand their message to mean too powerful.

Time goes by quickly. One day we will blink and open our eyes as old women. If we spend all our energy keeping our bodies small, what will we have to show for our lives when we reach the end? I hope we have more than a group of fashionably skinny figures.

SIXTY-NINE

◆◆◆

The Power of Collective Expression (2012)
College Students and Immigrant Women Learning Together

Kathleen S. Yep

Kathleen S. Yep is Associate Professor of Asian American Studies at Pitzer College of the Claremont Colleges. She authored *Outside the Paint: When Basketball Ruled at the Chinese Playground*, which examines how working-class Chinese American women and men used basketball as a source of collective empowerment in the 1930s. Her work on integrating antiracist/feminist pedagogies in community-based learning is published in *Democratic Dilemmas of Service-Learning: Curricular Strategies for Success* and in the *Journal for Civic Commitment*.

On a warm April evening in Southern California, over seventy-five people crowded into a spacious room at a public library. Leaning against the wall, an older woman clutched her purse against her chest while raptly listening to the speaker. A young mother soothed her fussy baby as she craned her neck to hear the program in Mandarin and English. People clustered in front of tables, filling their plates with cookies and sesame *bau*. For the finale, a group of eight Asian and Asian American women of different ages filed out to form a row in front of the audience. One by one, each woman stepped forward and read one line of a poem. Their families and friends applauded, hooted, and hollered. The poets smiled, blushed, and clapped to this boisterous and joyful response.

The tone of this event reflected what had evolved over the course of the semester in a class that brought together college students and older immigrant women from a community-based literacy program: Literacy for All of Monterey Park (LAMP). Through our weekly sessions in the public library, Asian and Asian American women ranging in age from their early twenties to late seventies shared their knowledge and experiences, and gradually formed a small community. The students wrote group poems, created a web site, and produced an anthology that included biographies, photographs, graphics, individual written pieces, and collaborative writing.

With the support of the Community Engagement Center at Pitzer College and the Weingart Foundation, I started a partnership between the Asian American Studies department and LAMP in the fall of 2009. With a commitment to using education for creating change, we wanted to combine the resources of a liberal arts college with a community project. We intended for college students to learn not only from books and lectures but also by being engaged in the world. As feminist educators, we wanted to nourish all the students' sense that they could create knowledge, empower themselves, and enact change in the world. We were fortunate to have a variety of resources to make this combined class happen: flexible students, good communication, empathy, transportation, a college dean who supports community engagement, community engagement staff, promotion and tenure procedures for faculty

that value it, an institutional climate of growth rather than budget cuts, and co-facilitators—Traci Kato-Kiriyama and me—who were challenged, humbled, and inspired by the risk-taking and movement of the students.

One in eight residents in this country is an immigrant. More than half of them are women who play a key role in navigating the myriad barriers facing their families in the United States (New American Media 2009). Immigrants and refugees struggle with limited access to educational services, low wages, lack of secure jobs and safe affordable housing (Garrett 2006). Asians are the fastest growing of the major ethnic groups, with the largest number of people born outside the United States (Segal et. al. 2010).

Monterey Park is a small suburban community in the heart of San Gabriel Valley just east of Los Angeles; people of color are 81 percent of its population; 54 percent are born outside the United States; and 76 percent speak a language other than English at home. The adult and family literacy program, LAMP, supports a growing immigrant population from Burma, China, Hong Kong, Indonesia, Korea, the Philippines, Taiwan, and Vietnam. Due to the economic downturn and severe budget cuts, the shortage of adult-education classes has hindered immigrants' ability to learn English, find better jobs, and secure adequate housing. This scarcity of resources amplified the need for LAMP's programs and its partnership with the college.

Building a Community of Learners

The two different groups of students brought a range of skills and experiences to this class. The college students provided English-language practice and citizenship coaching for LAMP students, covering different aspects of the citizenship exam to prepare them for the naturalization interview. The college students also taught English as a Second Language (ESL) using movement, art, poetry, and other participatory methods. In the combined class, the two groups delved into their life stories and worked on collaborative creative writing projects. We used storytelling not just as a matter of individual identity but also as a way for students to explore broader social processes such as colonialism, diaspora, migration, racism, patriarchy, and poverty. In one session, everyone, including the facilitators, brought a photograph or object that meant a great deal to her and discussed it in front the class. While we used these treasures to learn about each other, they were also points of departure to map out broader themes of migrations, loss, transformation, and courage. Then we wrote pieces based on those themes.

Addressing Difference and Similarities

Initially, many of the college students operated from a "missionary" service-learning model, wanting to "give" to the immigrant learners as invisible "helpers." There were hiccups along the way as students began to learn together across differences of class background, age, and immigration status. One student wanted a "fun and easy" class where she "could help those less fortunate" than herself. In the beginning, she focused on the immigrant learners and did not offer much of herself. Rather than seeing the LAMP students as objects of college students' charity or pity, the focus of this class was on engaging with differences and relative privilege in order to co-create something new and possibly transformative.

The college students read academic journal articles about the differences between service learning and social justice service learning. They examined their social locations and explored ideas of empowerment. They undertook research on social issues facing immigrants. Moreover, they reflected on how their backgrounds were similar to and different from the LAMP students and how this might enhance or inhibit their work together.

The course emphasized the creation of a healing, respectful, and nourishing learning community as a central organizing principle. This recognizes the fact that education can reproduce social inequalities both in course content and classroom dynamics. Rather than focusing on a text or debate as the central mode of learning, our students learned about patriarchy, immigration, and racism through democratic and collaborative learning methods.

The students described the process this way:

(We) learned from each other's experiences and helped to maintain a supportive space in which each woman could express her voice through writing and dialogue. . . . The flow of our voices allowed us to grow out of a classroom-dynamic and into a family.

(Introduction to Anthology)

Place and (Dis)placements

A premise of this collaboration was to co-create a sense of place by naming the various forms of (dis)placement that both the Asian immigrant learners and college students confronted. Many of the immigrant women discussed feeling "useless" in the United States. Several described their frustrations with learning English and finding employment. One student, Yin, reflected on her downward mobility on leaving Asia:

It is much harder for older immigrants. I was an accountant in China. I apply, apply, apply for jobs. No one hire me. I am too old. I am an in-care worker. It is hard.

Others explained that daily life tasks were often daunting and exhausting due to racism and language barriers. Their stories reflected the difficulties of navigating new places while learning a new language. As they struggled to learn English and combated discrimination, they questioned their place in this country and also challenged the subordination of "knowing their place" as Asian immigrant women in the racialized and gendered logic of the United States. Many women described struggling with patriarchy. For example, Amy reflected on the unspoken double-shift for women: "I come home from work. I cook and clean for my husband and son. I have two jobs. No money for cooking and cleaning." The class was a place where the immigrant women felt welcome. One student, Yin, reflected on why she liked the combined class: "I work. I come home. Eat fast. Come here fast. I like it here. Everyone smiles. I am not scared."

The college students described feeling out of place and experiencing marginalization on the campus and in many of their classes. As Asian Americans in predominantly white colleges with a prevalent culture of class privilege, they often felt invisible and ostracized. They were inspired by the LAMP students and began to document and reflect on the struggles and coping strategies of their own grandmothers, mothers, and aunties. The students wrote about various themes of displacement and finding a sense of place in their own personal and family histories. Most of the college students engaged intensely because they were heartened and challenged by the LAMP learners. The LAMP students felt encouraged by the college students, sought them out as resources, and also pushed them to stretch farther. Together, the students described the common themes in their lives:

> All through our lives, we experience moments of vulnerability, weakness, and fragility. Inside each of us are fighters. Our courage fuels our determination to handle the curve balls that life throws at us.
>
> *(Introduction to Anthology)*

Giving and Receiving

Overall, the students experienced the power and strength that comes from being seen and seeing others through creative expression and participatory learning. However, it was quite a process to get to these positive outcomes. The college students struggled through some significant hurdles in this unconventional learning environment.

For example, Kelly worked closely with Amy, an immigrant woman in her sixties. Initially, Kelly was somewhat impatient with Amy—asking Amy to hurry up, and rushing her when she looked up English words in her Chinese dictionary. However, during the course of the semester Kelly learned that Amy battled with back pain and wrist pain due to her work as an in-home health care worker, and that she also struggled with her husband and son. Despite these challenges, Amy always came to class and powered through the assignments even as she wrestled with the language and the instructors speaking too fast. Through collaborative writing and peer editing, each learned about the other's stories, struggles, and transformations. As they worked together, they became curious about each other and their shared experiences as women under patriarchy. By the end of the semester, Kelly had become more open to comments and insights from Amy. Moreover, Kelly's poetry was deeper and more nuanced as she began to include life-changing events in her writing. At the same time, Amy developed a stronger and stronger voice in the classroom and in her writing. She started to question Kelly about her poems and statements. They ended the semester with appreciation for each other's perspectives, experiences, and skills. It became more reciprocal and dialogical rather than being one-way and hierarchical. Because of their investment in their developing partnership, Kelly and Amy were able to co-create the following poem together.

> It happened by chance, unknowing danger would strike—an uphill battle
> He came to the United States with wonderful dreams for the future
> Life was not as easy as they said it would be in stories

In the collaborative writing process each person wrote one line and passed the paper to her partner, rotating back and forth. Rather than waiting impatiently or rushing her partner, Kelly and Amy learned to work from a place of support, kindness, and empathy. Together, they were able to draw from their families' stories of immigration, highlighting themes of loss and hope.

Wholeness: Heart, Mind, and Soul

Because one of the main feminist principles of the class was to create a reciprocal and mutually beneficial learning community, we emphasized more democratic ways of learning than is typical in many college classrooms. Often, the college students compartmentalized their schoolwork from the rest of their lives in order to survive in an intensely competitive academic environment. One student, Carla, explained: "Usually in my classes, I just slip in. Get lectured at. Take notes. Pack up my things and go. Sometimes I don't talk to anyone and no one talks to me. It's about learning the material and demonstrating that I learned it the way the professor wanted it."

The joint class was much more than meeting together in the same room and writing individual stories in an atomized fashion. By shifting away from competitiveness and self-reliance, students learned about and nourished a sense of belonging and collectivity. This culture of mutual respect opened up the possibility for alternative viewpoints and constructive conflict. The feminist democratic pedagogies contributed to building a community that encouraged all the students to give voice to what is often buried or marginalized in the classroom and in society.

One college student, Carla, was proficient in completing the assignments. She was efficient, thorough, and precise. She never spoke in class unless called upon. At the beginning of the semester her poems focused on light-hearted, happy topics. Even if they dealt with a challenging social issue such as immigration, they tended to wrap up neatly by the end. The class compelled students like Carla to participate on cognitive and affective levels. Rather than interacting only with students' minds through abstract ideas and theories, we engaged with them as whole human beings with feelings, emotions, histories, ideas, and complex experiences. Initially, there was some push back from some college students who felt they were not learning much. Talking about their lives and their feelings made them feel vulnerable and as if they were not "serious" students. Moreover, they did not want other students to feel sorry for them. Some questioned the writing assignments as being too vague or wondered how they would be graded. As facilitators, our task was to invite the students to speak from the heart and soul as well as the head. Rather than being distant and alienated from the course content, students' lives and histories were at the center.

By learning alongside the immigrant women, the college students came to identify relevant analytical themes in their own lives and to see that their experiences mattered. They affirmed that the immigrant women's stories were personally and theoretically significant. Placing the students' stories at the center countered dominant norms about what is considered valid knowledge and scholarship. Typically, in a college classroom a book published by a university press on the topic of female immigrants is privileged over a poem written by a female immigrant. Immigrant women are seen as informants and subjects of study to be talked about by researchers rather than as co-producers of new knowledge. With a feminist approach to epistemology (i.e., how we know what we know), the course embodied the idea that everyone can produce knowledge, not just those within privileged, elite circles. Although feminist scholarship has discussed this democratizing of knowledge production extensively, creating contexts where this can happen is relatively rare.

One immigrant student, Emma, was confident in speaking English but less so about writing in English. A force to be reckoned with, she gradually found a way to integrate her powerful speaking voice with her writing voice. She wrote about her immigration experience, following a haiku format:

> Once a wanderer
> Suffering pain and sorrow
> Became a fighter.

For the college students, the LAMP women were the same generation as their grandmothers, mothers, and aunties. Inspired by the LAMP students, the college women began to explore and reflect on the struggles of their own family members. For example, the following was part of a poem written by Carla:

> Hearing the angry rumbles of a plane
> Her gut sank.
> Expecting bombs to fall
> And herself to die.
> Every day.

Carla made her grandma's experience central as a means to look at her own history. By making these experiences visible, she was able to examine how broader processes such as war had impacted her grandmother, her mother, and herself. Grounded in the multiple layers of her family's experiences, this poem differed dramatically from her earlier poems. Rather than glossing over such complexities, this work engaged with both suffering and determination.

Feminist Learning Communities and Redefining the Political

By knowing and naming their own stories, students came to better understand themselves in relation to the wider society. Speaking out about their experiences and the social contradictions in their lives meant being visible and engaged with the world. This paved the way for a deepening sense of political empowerment, which we defined as feeling whole, connected, and conscious in order to be active in a larger project of social change. Students learned that creating community, sharing resources—information, literacy skills, wisdom, and encouragement—and listening can be political acts. This opened the door to reimagining what is considered political and what their role might be as politically engaged women. At the end of the semester, Jill explained her idea of "political" like this:

> . . . there are ways to intervene in the system of structural and individual silencing. Intervention takes various forms. One can take English classes in order to learn to use the tool that is the language of oppression, essentially learning to work within the system. Sometimes individuals can learn to break away from using those tools and find their own ways of expressing themselves. For each individual, the best way to address silencing is different. But the possibilities really are infinite.

The students grappled with creating a learning community as active participants rather than as passive consumers. They wrestled with content that felt relevant, meaningful, and inspiring. Moreover, they created a deep sense of connection among the group by learning to give and take. This reciprocal relationship created a healing, restorative, and sacred space to learn and build confidence. The college students increased their sense of internal efficacy. One reflected on how this would affect her future actions: "I am not going to be a turtle anymore—hiding when I want to feel safe." By the end of the semester, all the students defined themselves as social change agents.

This combined class highlights the importance of feminist, community-based learning. First, it creates a relevant education by centering students' lives and perspectives as the foundation to examine broader social processes like immigration, poverty, colonialism, and patriarchy. When this is done, what is considered legitimate knowledge becomes democratized and students become deeply invested in learning and in the learning community. Second, a feminist, community-based classroom engages with students' social locations and differences among them. Working with the LAMP students, the college students learned to relate to differences based on age, citizenship, primary language, socioeconomic status, and political viewpoints. More than recognizing differences in interpersonal interactions, they learned to work across and beside different positions of relative privilege as essential for building coalitions and creating change. This feminist approach to learning fosters skills, knowledge, and motivation for students to think critically about themselves and their communities in order to transform society and, in the words of bell hooks, "to move forward, to change, to grow" (1994: 202).

NOTES

1. Much gratitude to LAMP (Norma Arvisu, Lilian Kawaratani, Jose Garcia, and Denise Tang), Traci Kato-Kiriyama, the students in Asian American Voices, the Community Engagement Center at Pitzer College (Susan Phillips, Tessa Hicks, Martha Barcenas-Mooradian, Tricia Morgan), the Weingart Foundation, Gwyn Kirk, Margo Okazawa-Rey, Ray Young, Lee Sun Ngan, Michael James, Kaela Wan, Carolyn Wan, Sefa Aina, and Karin Mak.

2. Aliases were used to preserve the confidentiality of the students.

REFERENCES

Darder, Antonia. 1991. *Culture and Power in the Classroom: A Critical Foundation for Bicultural Education.* Chicago: Greenwood Publishing.

Garrett, Katherine E., ed. 2006. *Living in America: Challenges Facing New Immigrants and Refugees.* Princeton, NJ: Robert Wood Johnson Foundation.

hooks, bell. 1994. *Teaching to Transgress: Education as the Practice of Freedom.* New York: Routledge.

New American Media. 2009. *Women Immigrants: Stewards of the 21st Century Family.* http://media.namx.org/images/communications/immwomenexecsummary.pdf. Accessed April 17, 2012.

Segal, Uma A., Doreen Elliott, and Nazneen S. Mayadas. eds. 2010. *Immigration Worldwide: Policies, Practices, and Trends.* New York: Oxford University Press.

SEVENTY

◆◆◆

Staging Activism: New York City Performing Artists as Cultural Workers (2008)

Amy Jo Goddard

Amy Jo Goddard is a writer, playwright, filmmaker, performing and visual artist, and professional sexuality educator and coach. She teaches about sexuality in schools, community-based organizations, and colleges and is an advocate for comprehensive sexuality education. She co-authored *Lesbian Sex Secrets for Men,* and directed the documentary film *At Your Cervix* (http://amyjogoddard.com).

. . .

Imani Henry, Susana Cook, and Diyaa MilDred Gerestant are performing artists based in New York City that produce original work addressing cultural themes related to sexual, gender, ethnic, and class identities. These three artists have been strongholds in many of New York City's alternative performance spaces, such as The Kitchen, La Mama, WOW Café Theater, Brooklyn Arts Exchange, and Dixon Place, to name a few. In these spaces, audiences can anticipate thought-provoking work that often challenges established theater norms. Audiences comprised of social activists, gender and sexual minorities, outsiders, and people with low or fixed income are, unsurprisingly, drawn to the work of these artists since it reflects their worlds. These worlds are different from the typical upwardly mobile status quo that many mainstream performing arts programs and Broadway theaters highlight in content and/or form. I will consider these three performing artists as activists and cultural workers who persistently create political work in an artistic environment where many cultural institutions and alternative arts spaces struggle to keep their leases and maintain low ticket prices.

The work of each artist/performer reveals their mulitiplicitous identities and explores and gives voice to racial, national, class, gender, and sexual identities that are not the dominant norm in the U.S. Such intersections of multiple identities make their bodies of work unique and allow audience members who share those identities to see images of themselves that rarely get front and center stage. Moreover, the artists' positions as cultural workers allow them to bridge activist movements and communities that might not otherwise form alliances. . . .

. . .

Trans, Butch, and King: The Gender Lens of Three Activist Artists

I conducted face-to-face, in-depth interviews about art and social change with Imani Henry, Susana Cook, and Diyaa MilDred Gerestant. . . . Each is nationally or internationally known for a distinctive artistic style in work that is seen as a catalyst for social change. As artists with varying levels of outsider status—that is, outside the North American mainstream—their perspectives on the dominant culture and the current state of affairs are valuable to understanding oppression, power, sexuality, and political structures where dominant privilege may be taken for granted. Additionally, all are educated, accomplished mid-career artists, and people of color who identify as queer or lesbian.

Since audience members commit at least an hour to listen to what an artist has to say, performance becomes fertile ground for activating social change. These interviews focus on art and social change through the following questions and expand into territory organically produced in the interview process: How do these artists define themselves? What is the role of the artist who works for social change? How do these artists use their performance to encourage, inspire, or incite activism for social change, and what effects have they observed? Why are sexuality, nationality, gender, class, and race important subject matter? How do working class, communities of color, gay and lesbian, and queer communities intersect? I also draw upon my own experiences as a performance artist in this context.

In 1999, Susana Cook regularly produced and directed shows at the WOW Café Theater. One of the best-established women's theaters in the world, it is collectively run and has ensemble casts of mostly people of color. Cook asked three performers with whom she had not previously worked, Diyaa MilDred Gerestant, Imani Henry, and myself, to perform in a second run of the highly successful play, *Hot Tamale.* I had known Gerestant before as Dred, a preeminent drag king in New York City, and a regular at Club Casanova, the first weekly drag king performance night in the country. Highly regarded as a performer, she was one of the kings who had inspired me to perform male drag myself. Imani Henry, in the midst of his own gender transition, had recently relocated to New York City and was eager to get involved with New York's downtown theater scene. Cook's play facilitated our first meeting.

As a playwright and performer who came out of the spoken word boom of the 1990s, I found drag kinging to be an important bridge between my work with text and work that incorporates the body. "Kinging" is a term Judith Halberstam (1998) uses to describe the performance of masculinity. Drag kings bring masculinity into the theater as a spectacle, particularly through humor, and challenge the idea that male masculinity is unquestionable, authentic, and non-performative. When masculine roles are parodied or disassembled in a drag king performance, the idea that masculinity belongs solely to men is destabilized, and the performance provides, for lesbians in particular, "the rare opportunity to expose the artificiality of all genders and all sexual orientations" (*Ibid.:* 240). The electric nature of spaces such as Club Casanova gave rise to subcultures within the lesbian community, creating more freedom around gender, especially to explore, play with, and make humorous masculine gender expression. This freedom grew not only in performance spaces where drag kings were central and lesbians were the primary audience, but also in terms of greater acceptance of queer masculine gender identities, such as bois and female-to-male transsexuals (transmen or FTMs).[1]

Gender identity is complex. Each artist identifies with gender differently, with each having a relationship to a masculine identity on some level. Diyaa MilDred Gerestant is a drag king and "gender illusionist" who aims to expose the artificiality and illusory nature of gender. Imani Henry identifies as a transman and is strongly connected to the transgender community. Susana Cook identifies as a butch lesbian, an often misunderstood or misrepresented identity. As a butch, she expresses her masculinity and is at the same time comfortable being a woman. As Halberstam (1998) has noted, butch—or what she calls "transgender butch"—is not a preamble to an FTM identity, but has a rich history within lesbian communities and is its own identity.

Since I am a white woman writing about three people of color with complex identities, throughout this article I am conscious of honoring their voices and words. . . . Each section on a given artist begins and ends with quotes from the artists to privilege their own words and thoughts about their work. During the article's development, each artist received a copy for feedback, dialogue, and inclusion in the process. The reader should gain a real sense of Henry, Cook, and Gerestant on their own terms. This format was used in an attempt to dismantle the traditional paradigm of a white, privileged researcher who writes about other cultural groups and may inappropriately represent their real experiences through a skewed lens of dominant cultural privilege.

Imani Henry

In the U.S. there needs to be a clear understanding that we are cultural workers—like in Cuba. This is our work and there needs to be health benefits. The "starving artist" thing is so capitalist. It is unbelievably damaging and disrespectful how racist and sexist the oppression of queer folks plays out as artists; how commercial marketability is valued under capitalism over the merit of someone's expression, craft, or point of view.

Imani Henry, a self-defined Caribbean, FTM transsexual activist, writer, and performer, promotes himself as a "cultural worker," knowing the importance of identifying his work as a meaningful societal contribution and, as such, deserving of support and economic compensation. Frustrated with the few and narrow roles that existed for him as an actor, he began to create his own work, knowing well the limitations for a queer actor of color who was often recruited to play thugs, prostitutes, and other stereotypical roles.

Henry made his "home" at the Brooklyn Arts Exchange, where he created and produced three plays during his artist residency from 2002 to 2004. He is a slam poet champion and is often featured as a performance poet or speaker at political rallies and events. Political activism and performance are intrinsically connected in his work. "Art can be a form of resistance under capitalism," he says, noting that when disenfranchised, multinational voices make art, it is an act of resistance because it disrupts and challenges the notion that art can be accessed only by the elite, as stories of people who do not have the same access as those with economic privilege, artistic training, and/or ethnic and gender privilege are told.

Henry expresses his work as an activist through his plays. Two of them actually feature a political demonstration. He brings his multiple personal identities into his work and says, "All of those identities mean something to me. To represent them is a big deal." Asked about the importance of visibility for identities that fall outside the dominant norm, he says that "visibility is everything." When Henry performs butch or other transgender characters, or when he travels and meets people who have never met a trans person, he gives visibility to those identities and the real life experiences that go with them. On and off stage representation allows him to do the thing he values most as "an out radical activist," which is to build coalitions and solidarity, since building solidarity requires working to understand the struggles of others.

B4T (Before Testosterone), Henry's first play, has functioned in this way. He calls it an "ode to butch blackness."

A woman looking like a man
looking for a woman
who likes women
who look like men.

Now, ain't that some shit?. . .

You ask me what it is to be Black, Butch and
*   Lesbian.*
Words, names, I have never claimed for myself. It
*   was given and now I can only remember before*

there was words, before there were names, before
I could, would, say it out loud. . .

I am only telling you because it needs to be said. I
am only saying it because it lays too heavy, cuts
too deep, runs like water bursting from a dam.

(Henry, 2002)

This passage from *B4T* (2002) speaks to the complex issues around identity: who has the right to name us, the power of words, and how having a word for something can give us comfort, or alternately, disturb us. The act of identifying oneself allows for the development of communities around common experience, and education across lines of difference.

In 1999, Henry began his gender transition, while participating as an activist within the antiwar and Millions for Mumia movements in New York City. The latter developed to support Mumia Abu-Jamal, a journalist accused of killing a police officer in Philadelphia in 1981. Abu-Jamal has since served 22 years as a political prisoner and is currently on death row. Henry, a leader in this movement, says: "People have gone through that [gender] transition process with me inside a larger political movement. I look different. People respected my pronoun changes." One of Henry's great achievements was spearheading Rainbow Flags for Mumia and connecting the struggles of the lesbian/gay/bisexual/transgender/queer (l/g/b/t/q) community with those of political prisoners like Mumia Abu-Jamal. He worked to build solidarity between these two movements and was instrumental in the large l/g/b/t/q turnout for Mumia demonstrations and events. Within these movements, he has seen the transformation of homophobia or transphobia on a personal level, as people have been able to see him as a brother in the struggle. Though he has had many positive experiences, he acknowledges that unlike other transgender individuals, such as transwomen or effeminate men, he has the ability to be more invisible because he more easily "passes" as a man.

Indeed, within a larger movement of people working publicly for change, another level of change happens among activists on an interpersonal level. At an antiracism or anti-police brutality demonstration, as people of color make the connection that queer people are fighting for the same issues, many are forced to think about the connections between racial, gender, and sexual justice. Research has shown that one way homophobia is healed is by knowing someone personally who is gay, lesbian, or bisexual. According to Poynter and Talbot (2006: 276), "personal contact is a significant event in the development as an ally to GLB people." Henry works hard to bridge connections and build coalitions across lines of difference, within his performances and as a cultural worker. Human connection is a fundamental component for coalition building within social justice movements. Henry speaks passionately on this issue:

> Social justice and change happens by the living, breathing struggle. You can't learn it in a book. Solidarity is what happens in the streets—you have to work with people. You can do trainings, but what is it to go to an anti-police brutality demonstration? What is it to stand in solidarity with a family whose house has been firebombed by the Klan? You can't learn solidarity any other way.

Henry echoes Bernice Johnson Reagon's (1983) statement that "coalition work is not work done in your home. Coalition work has to be done in the streets." Indeed, many activists enter political movements with high ideals about justice and human rights, but personal growth occurs when we learn to work effectively with people who speak different languages, have different customs, or look different. The difficult work of coalescing with others is the real work, especially in situations where the people involved experience different levels of dominant privilege, and in which privilege and oppression beg to be examined.

During his performances, coalescence happens as Henry intentionally breaks the fourth wall[2]—the accepted barrier between the actors onstage and the audience—exploiting the intimacy of theater and including his audience to the point where he actually makes the audience part of his pieces. In *B4T*, Henry stationed his co-actor in the audience; in his second show, *The Strong Go Crazy*, he created a living room out of the theater and had a TV party where the audience was encouraged to talk back to the television along with him in a group cultural critique, resulting in lines being added to his script that came directly from audience members. After he welcomed everybody and passed out popcorn, he would stand outside the theater, listening:

people are talking and making their own jokes or comments and just being together. And I love it. People who didn't know each other came for a night of theater, and they're just laughing with each other. I thought it was brilliant—beyond what I've ever seen in theater. People organically became connected to each other and became part of the show.

The structure for audience members encourages and supports connection and coalescence with one another, and to Henry as performer. Some of his characters are fictional and others are based on real people; at times he weaves his own stories into the fibers of his work. Whether audience members attribute those stories to him personally, they experience an intimacy with him onstage that functions as a connecting force.

Henry is a sought-after performer on U.S. college campuses and has seen his work affect thousands of students and university communities. Audience members may not necessarily attend a march for l/g/b/t/q equality or a demonstration against violence toward young people of color, but they will come to see a play. His work functions as activism in myriad ways, reaching students who would never decide to attend his show if it were not for the extra credit offered by professors. Many of his predominantly white, heterosexual, student audience members are compelled to write academic papers about race, gender, and sexual identity after seeing his show. Additionally, various student groups have built coalitions and worked together to raise money to bring Henry to their campus. . . .

Henry has a class-consciousness that pervades his approach to politics and artistic work. He attests that in a capitalist system, where making money is the primary goal, art that serves other purposes such as raising awareness, creating visibility for noncommercial stories, or activating people is not going to bring in big money. Rather, it becomes a form of resistance. Much of Henry's energy is spent supporting and engaging in such acts of resistance. He states:

> If art is political, it discusses issues meant to be silent. When we create art that is political in any shape or form, or when we as oppressed peoples stand up and talk about our truth or experience—if a woman talks about what it's

like to be sexually assaulted or abused, that's political. Capitalism would say "be silent, don't talk about that."

Susana Cook

I am your Hot Tamale baby.
Come sweet señorita, you know you can't resist our
full lips and curvaceous bodies . . .
Let's dance colonizer
I am for civilization and progress
I am your colonized stereotype of the
Latino-macho-catholic fatalism
I am an insatiable sex machine. . . . Market me baby
I love you my democratic enlightened post-modern
one
on the basis of this confrontation with this exotic
other
I am your significant other. . . . Do you want to
know what I signify?
Do you want to taste my exotic Passion. . . . with
beans. . . .
Chew my uncivilized, primitive, barbarian second-
class identity, while I drink your bold superior
fully shaped identity of the one. . . .
Let's walk half naked under the sun eating tortilla
and mango
I was recently brought into civilization
I could never fully overcome the fact of carrying
primitiveness in my blood
I arrived late to the capitalist fiesta. . . but I run
I am your Speedy Gonzales baby
I am your bandit. . . your papi chulo
Sit back, look pretty and let the immigrant do the
work (Cook, 1999)

In this classic Susana Cook opening monologue, all of the Argentine, butch, lesbian, . . . performing artist's signature elements are there: seducing the audience through clever poetics, using shameless humor that forces the audience into an uncomfortable place of self-reflection, pointedly poking fun at U.S. establishments and the privileged classes, and bringing her multiplicitous identities to center stage. Other elements from a Susana Cook performance . . . are unabashed butches and femmes, quick-fire dialogue with her ensemble cast made up of lesbian and queer women of color, music scored by her son Julian, and playful choreography. Cook's shows

are community in the making, a dynamic, at times disjointed cultural experience for audience members and performers alike, due to the often nonlinear structure.

Cook's life experience significantly affected her creative work and career moves. Since 1991, she has participated in the New York City performing arts scene and continues to write and direct all of her own work . . . At age 16, Cook joined a theater group run by political Jewish artists in Argentina. It was 1976, the year the Argentine dictatorship began. The Internet was not yet a tool of global connection and Las Madres de Plaza de Mayo (Mothers of the Disappeared) started what became a political movement in Buenos Aires. As the government abducted people, the Mothers of the Disappeared searched for their sons and daughters in hospitals, jails, police stations, and morgues, finding each other and organizing themselves. The Madres had a significant impact on Cook. "Somehow my theater and activism came together out of this," she explains. When I interviewed her . . ., she spoke with effusive pride about the Madres, whose images were depicted in large framed pictures on her walls.

For Cook, it is important to have images that represent her politics, images with which she, and others like her, can relate. This visibility is a central political force in her work and she becomes frustrated if the impact of her work is minimized because of what may be perceived as a limited audience of converts.

> I love preaching to the converted. The "norm" has a whole culture preaching to them—every magazine, movie, TV program is preaching to them and we have a couple of lesbian cultural events, and [critics say], 'Oh, they're preaching to the converted.' It's not enough to convert, you also need to create a culture we can identify with, to help us reflect on our communities.

As a teen, Cook did not see images of lesbians in Buenos Aires. When she came to New York City and discovered women's bookstores and women's theater, her life experience and her own struggles with hiding parts of herself were validated by knowing that there were other lesbians like her and community spaces where she could find them. She became involved with the WOW Café Theater, a (predominantly lesbian-run) women's theater, which has since changed its mission to include trans people, marking a challenging shift within the WOW collective. Learning of the disproportionately high suicide rates of l/g/b/t youth (Garofalo et al., 1998; D'Augelli et al., 2001), it became critical for Cook to place lesbian women and butch identities at the epicenter of her work.

"Masculinity is not the monopoly of men," she says about her identity in a time when butches are being eclipsed in queer communities by various transgender and gender-variant masculine identities, such as transmen, bois, and gender queer people. She echoes what has been called a "butch phobia" that impedes many women from identifying as butch (Halberstam, 1998: 244).

> Many women think the associations or the stereotype of a butch are so negative. It's a whole idea that butches are imitating men. Also, butches are identified with the working class, which is seen as a negative thing. That they were working class and supposedly imitating patriarchal values gave butches a bad rap.

Cook takes great pride in her butch identity and her own embodiment of masculinity. Because she has made it a central and positive place from which to create artistic work, exploring the butch/femme identities and "energy" in lesbian relationships, she has encouraged and made a space for many others to claim their butch identities. Since it is not tied to male privilege, she rejects the compulsory abnegation of butch identities that views them as dated or as a limited form of masculinity. Indeed, because she creates an affirming space and positively encourages butch identifications, many of her cast members have come out as butch after working on her plays.

Like Henry, Cook identifies herself as a "Creator of Culture" or "Worker of Culture." Having produced 16 plays between 1991 and 2006, she sees her role as a person who likes to read, develop political analysis, and cull it into something explored onstage through humor for people who do not read or follow the news. Given her subject matter of politics, war, class struggles, and homophobia, she often grapples with how to make her shows funny. She believes her cultural role as an artist is to "create culture that will support the values or countervalues that we think are important."

. . .

Currently, she is exploring how nationalism and religion have been used in the U.S. to promote homophobia. Her . . . show, *The Idiot King* (2006), mocks the stupid, vacuous monarch who kills in the name of religious nationalism . . . As the king, Cook (who dons a gold and red rubber crown from which her long hair steals out, and a tattered jacket adorned with gold braided rope and insignia on the shoulders) is surrounded onstage by the nurse, several advisors, and the queen. In a campy moment, the queen invites a gang comprised of gender queer people wearing pink bandanas to visit, thinking they will be reformed by seeing how royalty lives. Illuminating a blatant collapsing of the church with the nation-state, the king discusses parts of the Bible that should be modified or removed, and then addresses some homophobic concerns with his Christian God.

> King—Hi God. Yes, I called you. I wanted to talk to you about the pearly gates, the walls of alabaster, and the floors made of gold. Suddenly I realized that it might look pretty gay in heaven. Yes, of course it is up to you, the decoration. Yes, I want to go to heaven. I just had the disturbing thought of Saint Peter with a pearly keyholder. I can't stop thinking about the pearly, pearly gates. . . (2006).

Her political positions are evident in her work and in her choices about how and what to produce. Disturbed by what she calls the "worship" of the rich and celebrities, Cook aims to expose the economic and political forces that support such worship. Cook says she is not interested in being a part of U.S. corporations or Broadway. "I'm a butch. I have an accent. I didn't have what they wanted." And, she sees value in the aesthetic of the underground. In her casts, she highlights the experiences of the working class, women of color, and sexual minorities. She consciously brings her work to downtown audiences, where she can "preach to the converted," keep ticket prices low, and her art accessible. Cook carefully considers what to expose, and who and what to make visible in her work, knowing that each decision expresses her values and is part of her political practice.

> Even if you don't want to be political, you are being political. If you are not saying anything, then in a way you make a political choice of complying with the general discourse. The place where you choose to perform, the price

of tickets, the people you put in your show, everything is a choice where you are showing something onstage—the winners, the losers, the minorities—this whole system is based on a certain set of values.

Diyaa MilDred Gerestant

I, Diyaa MilDred Gerestant, aka Drag King/ Gender-Illusionist Dred, am a multi-spirited, Haitian-American, gender-illusioning, black, shaved, different, Goddess, anti-oppression, open, nontraditional, self-expressed, blessed, gender-bending, drag-kinging, fluid, ancestor-supported, and—after all that—non-labeling woman! (Gerestant, 2006)

Diyaa MilDred Gerestant describes her childhood self as shy, lonely, and sad, and as someone who had difficulty with self-expression. Like Henry, Gerestant grew up connected to the church and questioned the homophobic preachers who articulated hatred in their sermons as if it were God's word. She found this inauthentic, and her spiritual path has taken her to a very different and powerful spirituality that connects to her many genders and identities. "Performance is a spiritual tool. Everything I do is a spiritual tool. . . . My performance has definitely helped me open up to my spirit."

Her life transformation mirrored what she expresses in her drag king performances. For many years, Gerestant stormed stages from New York to London to Rio in sophisticated male cross-dressing performances as Drag King Dred, dancing and lip-syncing as she brought to life dynamic characters such as Shaft or Superfly, and paid homage to Marvin Gaye, Grace Jones, P. Diddy, and Busta Rhymes. She would shape-shift from one character into another with onstage costume and prop changes that allow her audiences to be insiders in her transformational process. Over the last few years, Gerestant has taken the stage as herself, merging those dynamic drag performances with her own personal voice to talk about the story behind Dred. Doing so brought her full-circle, with a new confidence and ability to celebrate her multifaceted self. She reflects on her life in a deeply honest way with her audiences, and her candor imbues her audience with the strength of feeling connected to someone's struggle. She says,

A lot of us are under a cloud or shadow of something keeping us from seeing who we really are. I can only share that from my own life experience, because most of my life was like that. I went through a lot of abuse and teasing; I didn't have any kind of self-worth. For a while, Dred was someone I was hiding behind. Dred was my male character. I had to really look at that and face those demons—like I wasn't worthy of just being myself as MilDred.

That spirit and her ability to "speak from a truthful place," she believes, contribute to social change; she hopes this will "inspire others to do the same for themselves."

Gerestant never thought she would be a performer. In 1995, though, she attended a drag king show at the Pyramid in the East Village, just as the pulse of the New York City drag king scene was starting to thump. Performances by soon-to-be notorious kings such as Busta Hymen and Mo B. Dick empowered her: "They were free of any particular gender box and I was like a little kid in a candy store." Gerestant's first transformation into what would become Dred preceded hundreds of women she would similarly inspire over the next 10 years. It was expressed in her first play in 2006,

Looking in the mirror, I couldn't believe my transformation. I wondered, "Where did that handsome man come from?" I couldn't believe that I was looking at another side of me, that this side existed. It's still incredible each time I do it.

Gerestant's life was transformed by her introduction to kinging in a way she never anticipated. Over the years, the style of her character Dred solidified into a performance of a medley of songs and characters, climaxing with Aretha Franklin's "Natural Woman," and stripping down from her final male drag king costume into a sexy red bikini top and miniskirt, full with a bulge, and her facial hair still intact. At the pinnacle of the medley, she reaches into her skirt in a typical male gesture, revealing a shiny red apple that she bites into, reflecting her power as a woman and referencing Eve's transgression in the Garden of Eden. She has been one of the most inspiring contemporary drag kings, claiming a trademark masculinity—a political flip of the stereotypical macho man into one who did not need to denigrate women to be powerful. This is part of the reason drag kinging can be so stalwart; the way a woman interprets masculinity need not rely on sexism, but rather, on exposing the gimmicks that create a sexist persona, revealing how gender, specifically, masculinity, is manufactured.

Gerestant's strength lies in her exploration of her gender before an audience. As a gender illusionist, she challenges the internalized belief systems of audiences regarding gender. To say her performances make people think differently is to put the power of her transformation delicately. They have pushed people's boundaries in over 20 countries, each with its own set of gender norms. One of the most well-known drag kings in the world, many people find themselves attracted to her and approach her after her shows. In the presence of a person with a womanly body and a goatee, the conflicted desire becomes wholly complex, as audience members are forced to think about what they are attracted to and why. A heterosexual man will be attracted to her "from the neck down" and struggle to rectify her hairy face; someone else's attraction may be based on the belief that she is transitioning from a male into a woman—that her facial hair is "real" and her breasts are implants. Each scenario forces a person to consider how desire can be bound to ideas or expressions of gender, rather than to a real person. She aims to break down all of these illusions and get people to question what makes a man or a woman, and at the core, the nature of what is "real." In those intimate exchanges between audience member and performer, how does her joy in her whole self, with all her levels of gender expression, affect those who watch her?

"I'm very much into opening people's eyes up to [the question], 'are they really living as who they want to be or is it just something they've been trained to do?'" she asserts. Now able to more fully have Dred and Diyaa MilDred co-exist onstage, she uses storytelling, singing, and drag to speak her truths and inspire her audiences.

> The man, or the yang in me, really empowered the woman, the yin. The male in me broadened and empowered the woman I was born as and integrated all that I am. . . . That's where true wholeness, I'm realizing, comes in, and accepting all of who you are.

In her first full-length play, she tells the story of competing in a "Superfly Look-Alike Competition"

sponsored by a mainstream hip-hop and R&B radio station in New York City, where,

> I wore a red velour suit, black ribbed turtleneck, thick black platforms, gold chains, a gold tooth engraved with the peace symbol, a fake black fur coat with a bright yellow lining draped over my shoulder, dark shades, and a big, sweet black hat with a feather glued to the top, tilted over my right eye.

She embodies that character, oozing confidence, as she pays homage to Superfly, the blaxploitation character, and honors her culture. At the Superfly competition, the women were crazy for her and she took second place, at which point she, wishing to express the full scope of her act, took the microphone. In her feminine voice, she told the audience she is a woman who performs as a drag king, at which point the crowd of 1,500 fell silent. For an audience she describes as "nowhere near queer," this jolt calls many assumptions into question and positions her in the middle of a bold activist move. Most people in such an audience have never seen a drag king and may have never heard of the concept. She thus simultaneously expresses her yin and yang, the flow of power between her genders in the context of her performance, and she undoubtedly sends many viewers home thinking in new ways about gender and desire.

Gerestant believes all of what we do is performance, and all of it is drag in one form or another. Social change through performance, for her, is summed up in one idea: acceptance.

> From all different cultures where I've been asked to perform, whether it's Germany, or Korea, or Croatia, Australia . . . the one thing everyone really got was wanting to be accepted for who they are—I think that's the base of everything whether it's dealing with race, religion, sexuality, spirituality, gender, whatever it is, people just want to be who they are. . . . All cultures get that.

Activist Performance Art Is Cultural Work

For each artist, creating connections across lines of difference is a critical aim, and their cultural work functions as activism on multiple levels. Henry,

Cook, and Gerestan use participatory processes of audience engagement. Connecting the collaborative process of activist artists to the process of public participation, Nina Felshin (1995:12) explains: "Such participation is a critical catalyst for change, a strategy with the potential to activate both individuals and communities, and takes many forms." The tactic of breaking the fourth wall makes audience members a constitutive part of a production; for example, Henry's *The Strong Go Crazy* (2003) dismantles the fabricated fissure between what is "real" and what is "just play." With that dismantling, the issues hit closer to home and there is less illusion that performance is something simply to watch and enjoy, then forget, as audience members quickly go back to their "real" lives. These artists' audiences are activated in classrooms and schoolwork, personal exploration of cross-dressing, community organizing, and decisions about claiming sexual identities, to name a few.

These artists have taken great risks in their work and by exposing their personal selves through performance to dispense their messages. From their own cultural perspectives, each addresses and analyzes issues of race and ethnicity. Cook and Henry depict masculine gender identities—butch and transman respectively—that they live every day, whereas Gerestant performs gender as drag, but does not identify in her daily life with a masculine gender identity. A critical component of their work is that each artist challenges a gender binary and gender roles. As descendents of the feminist artists of the 1970s "that made creative use of feminist methodologies to grapple with issues of self-representation, empowerment, and community identity" (Felshin, 1995: 19), these three artists continue to change the dialogue about social issues and assumptions about people's identities and place within communities. Claiming an identity makes possible communities based on common experience. Each performer appeals to queer or lesbian communities, artist communities of color, and many political communities; they create community within their shows, facilitating a deepening of the experience and connections made during a production.

Independent artists that connect and explore issues, invite audience involvement, and create community through theater productions perform the role of cultural workers and cultural activists. Brian Wallis (1990: 8) defines *cultural activism*

as "the use of cultural means to try to effect social change." For all three artists, the activist/performer nexus is built into their role as cultural workers or creators of culture through their performances, where ethnic, gender, and sexual identities, as well as conversations regarding identity, are invoked. If, as George and Trimbur (2004: 2) argue, culture includes "social institutions, patterns of behavior, systems of belief, and . . . popular entertainment that create the social world in which people live," then Cook, Henry, and Gerestant's work on and off the stage of translating, critiquing, and participating in these cultural elements for the public can be deemed cultural work. Henry writes for *Worker's World* and organizes protests and community events; Cook teaches theater and dreams of creating a "School for the Revolution"; and Gerestant plans to open an alternative healing center and teaches drag king workshops around the world. Each act creates culture, explores and expands belief systems, creates literary texts and art, culls current events into critical analysis, facilitates critical thought and dialogue, builds communities around common values, and generates community-based institutions and organizations.

Performance is, by nature, a political tool of visibility in which the artisan has the power to give voice to the stories and perspectives they wish to value. The manipulation of language and the creation of images manufacture power by establishing a presence. These artists put power into the hands of the underrepresented and the disenfranchised, making important those lesser-heard stories. The meaning of gender shifts as an audience gets to know a gender variant character's inner thoughts and struggles with his or her place in society, observes lesbians expressing the norms of their community, or watches a handsome man win a contest only to find out that he is a biological woman. For mainstream audiences unaccustomed to such gendered performances, or who do not typically question gender roles believed to be axiomatic, these performances may mean a shift in consciousness. Yet an audience of similarly disenfranchised individuals may experience empowerment by seeing stories with which they can relate.

Henry, Gerestant, and Cook cite many instances of the impact their work has had on individuals and communities. A young lesbian thanked Cook for validating or giving voice to her experience,

Gerestant's drag king workshops helped young women explore gender expression, while students on college campuses connected to these issues and to one another due to Henry's work. Gerestant brings it back to human connection, live performance's strength over non-live media:

> When you treat others as yourself, or when you realize we are all connected, you won't want to bomb someone in Iraq, you won't want to abuse somebody, you won't want rape to be happening, you won't want somebody homeless on the street. We're all connected and to me that's the basis of social change.

Engaging audiences "every single time" he performs, Henri leaves political literature on the theater seats and talks afterwards about what people can do next. In a mobilization effort, he educates people about little-known cases of injustice. Cook and Gerestant also engage audiences with question-and-answer periods following performances, so that conversation and critical analysis of issues raised in their work can continue dialogue with all in the room. These acts are ways of creating community and solidarity around issues and between people, both of which are necessary for effective activism.

Sociopolitical movements require consciousness-raising art. Because burnout is common, activist movements need to celebrate identities, laugh, and find humor in the dire issues they face. Political art and theater are creative outlets for activists, and the presence of a larger social movement allows artists such as Henry, Cook, and Gerestant to tell the stories people need to hear.

Interviews with these performing artists reveal a commitment to using the stage to involve and speak with audiences. Important aspects of Imani Henry's activism encompass the visibility of identities, including as a cultural worker, supporting acts of resistance, and coalition and solidarity building. Susana Cook's activist work cites issues of representation and visibility, creating images with which to identify, and her choices and political practice concerning her performance. Diyaa MilDred Gerestant's activism is based on challenging illusions surrounding gender and desire, and spotlighting transformational processes for growth as ways of creating wholeness and acceptance among people. Since performance can create contexts for new understanding through the dynamic relationship of these artists to their audiences, action is encouraged and the possibility for shifting consciousness is expanded. In New York and on their tours, they are making a meaningful contribution to activist movements working toward social change.

NOTES

1. Transmen, FTMs, and bois are individuals who may have been assigned a female gender at birth and socialized accordingly, but whose identity and gender expression become masculinized. This may or may not include taking testosterone to assist the development of male secondary sex characteristics or having surgery to alter the body to appear more masculine. Many people clearly distinguish between identifying as a transman or as a boi, and each is its own masculine gender identity. FTM has been widely used, but can be seen as offensive for a person of trans experience, and transman is more appropriate (Gender Identity Project, 2006). As ideas about the multiplicity of gender identities continue to develop, individual identities are expanding. *Gender queer* is a term some use to resist established gender norms and to challenge the traditional gender binary. I say this to give the reader who may be unfamiliar with these terms some understanding of what is being discussed, but do not wish to imply that it is at all simple. See the work of Judith Halberstam, Kate Bornstein, and Leslie Feinberg for more analysis of gender identity specifically in transgender individuals. Not much has been written on the identity boi, but a mainstream article was featured in *New York Magazine* in 2004 (Levy, 2004).

2. The ritual breaking of the fourth wall to address the audience directly is generally attributed to Bertolt Brecht's *epic theater;* however, Brecht's exploration of this method was based on his research of *the alienation effect* in Chinese theater (Brecht, 1992: 136; Brockett, 1991: 523). The alienation effect has been used onstage and in cinema as an intentional jolt for the viewer, reminding them that they are watching something unreal and to allow for more objective analysis of what they are watching.

REFERENCES

Brecht, B. 1992. *Brecht on Theater: The Development of an Aesthetic.* J. Willett (ed. and trans.). New York: Hill and Wang. (Original work published in 1957.)

Brockett, O. 1991. *History of the Theater* (sixth edition). Needham Heights, MA: Allyn and Bacon.

Cook, S. 2006. *The Idiot King.* Unpublished play.

——— 1999. *Hot Tamale.* Retrieved on June 28, 2006, from *http://susanacook.com/words2.htm#hot.*

D'Augelli, A.R., S.L. Hershberger, and N.W. Pilkington. 2001. "Suicidality Patterns and Sexual Orientation-Related Factors Among Lesbian, Gay, and Bisexual Youths." *Suicide and Life Threatening Behavior* 31: 250–264.

Felshin, Nina 1995. "Tailor-Made." *Art Journal* 54, 1, *Clothing as Subject* (Spring): 7–16.

————1995. *But Is It Art? The Spirit of Art As Activism.* Editor. Seattle: Bay Press.

Garofalo, R., R.C. Wolf, S. Kessel, J. Palfrey, and R.H. DuRant. 1998. "The Association Between Health Risk Behaviors and Sexual Orientation Among a School-Based Sample of Adolescents." *Pediatrics* 101:895–902.

Gender Identity Project. 2006. *Trans-Care.* Training presented at the Lesbian, Gay, Bisexual and Transgender Community Center Y.E.S. Program. New York, NY (November).

George, D. and J. Trimbur (eds.). 2004. *Reading Culture: Contexts for Critical Reading and Writing.* Fifth edition. New York: Pearson Longman.

Gerestant, M. 2006. "Exposures of a Multi-Spirited, Haitian-American, Gender-Harmonizing Woman." Robin Bernstein (ed.), *Cast Out: Queer Lives in Theater.* Michigan: University of Michigan Press.

Halberstam, J. 1998. *Female Masculinity.* Durham, NC: Duke University Press.

Hall, D. (ed.). 2003. *Queer Theories (Transitions).* United Kingdom: Palgrave Macmillan.

Henry, I. 2004. *Living in the Light.* Unpublished play.

————2003. *The Strong Go Crazy.* Unpublished play.

————2002. *B4T.* Unpublished play.

Levy, A. 2004. *Where the Bois Are.* Retrieved on November 12, 2006, from *http://nymag.com/nymetro/news/features/n_9709/index.html.*

Poynter, K. and D. Talbot. 2006. *Heterosexual Allies in Higher Education: The Development of a Model.* Retrieved July 5, 2006, from *www.duke.edu/~kpoynter/Heterosexual Allies%20(Jan06).doc.* Manuscript submitted for publication.

Reagon, B.J. 1983. "Coalition Politics: Turning the Century." Barbara Smith (ed.), *Home Girls: A Black Feminist Anthology.* New York: Kitchen Table Press: 356–368.

Wallis, B. (ed.). 1990. *Democracy: A Project by Group Material.* Seattle: Bay Press: 8.

Wikholm, A. 1999. *Words: A Glossary of the Words Unique to Modern Gay History.* Retrieved April 29, 2005, from *www.gayhistory.com/rev2/words/queer.htm.*

SEVENTY-ONE

◆◆◆

Changing the Face of Leadership (2010)
Legislators at Large for American Women

Edna Ishayik

Edna Ishayik is the communications director at the Institute for Policy Integrity, New York University School of Law. She worked on electoral campaigns all over the Northeast in fundraising, field operations, and campaign management. She was Deputy Political Director for Eliot Spitzer's gubernatorial campaign, and executive director of the New York State Democratic Party. As a student, she was an Eagleton Institute of Politics Undergraduate Fellow and a scholar at the Institute of Women's Leadership, Rutgers University.

. . .

Growing up, I was more interested in music, movies, and malls than I was in politics. I was not particularly concerned with women's status in society past a [2 words] "girls rule, boys drool" mentality. But through Douglass College and my participation in its organizations, I came to realize there was a world past the end of my own nose, and the women in it were not doing as well as they should. This startling realization and the questions it raised prompted me to take classes in women's studies, and classes about women in politics. . . .

I remember reading with deep sadness about welfare moms who struggled to feed their children who were then stereotyped as lazy and used as scapegoats every time there was a budget crunch. I was outraged at the fact that women earn less than men for doing the same work. I thought about what it might mean if access to reproductive health care were scaled back. I worried about all the messages about body image we are bombarded with every day and how these messages make young women see themselves. I was overwhelmed with all the problems that affected the female population in our courtry.

As the summer before my senior year approached, I began to think about careers I could pursue and paths I might follow. My question was, how could I use my life's work in a way that would begin to untangle the messy knot of women's place in the world? I wondered where my efforts to help would be most effective. With so many issues to be addressed, how could I choose just one?

Like so many things in life, my answer came by chance. I was recruited to take an internship with a Congressional campaign in a neighboring district. The candidate was a woman fighting in a fierce primary battle with a typical "gool ole' boy" from New Jersey's Democratic Party machine. I had never worked on a campaign before and was not sure what to expect. After this intense, hands-on experience, all my thoughts about women, leadership, and politics jelled. More women in elected office would mean more attention paid to the women's issues that concerned me. One of the best ways to ensure that these topics were on the national agenda was to campaign for progressive women running for office. So after graduation I continued working on campaigns for other female candidates. Political campaigns . . . and working to elect female legislators became . . . my way of changing the world for the better.

There are many challenges in this line of work, but I love it so much that the downside is insignificant in comparison to the rewards. Having found my path I ripped up my LSAT scores, canceled my appointment with career counseling, and did not worry about what color my parachute was. The long, grueling hours of campaigns did not faze me. Nor did the need to uproot my life and move every nine months to pick up a different race. I was unperturbed by the low pay or the lack of health care benefits—I was so swept up in the idea that I could have an impact on issues that were important to me that none of these factors seemed problematic.

When I was on a campaign, I worked twelve to eighteen hours a day, seven days a week, barely able to return a personal phone call. In between campaigns was the opposite: I would either take a few months off to travel or spend the time relaxing and deciding on my next move. To me, this was the most valuable "perk" of the job. I did not mind working my fingers to the bone for nine months partly because I knew I would have three months of free time afterward. Looking back, I wish I had

thought more about what it would mean to miss being with friends and family for months at a time—the death of a close friend brought that into focus and led me to work closer to home.

After eight years in campaigns, I have worked for a variety of candidates—women and men, gay and straight—always selecting individuals I believed would bring a fresh perspective to their elected offices. Up and down the ticket and across the Northeast, I supported candidates I thought were interesting, smart, and progressive, including Patti Morrissey for delegate in Virginia and Eliot Spitzer for governor in New York. After Spitzer's victory in November 2006, I became the executive director of New York State's Democratic Party. But the idea of building a career around electing more women continued to drive me.

Lessons from the Campaign Trail

From my experiences in political campaigns, I have learned that female candidates can face unique challenges. Take as an example the single working mom with two young daughters aged eight and ten. After six months on her campaign, it was clear to me why more young women weren't running for office. While working out of the candidate's basement, we encountered outrageous temper tantrums, loud sleepovers, and even the occasional head injury. Balancing work and parenting is difficult enough; adding the full-time stress of a campaign seemed next to impossible.

In addition to the rigors of the campaign, I found myself making peanut butter and jelly sandwiches, driving the girls to soccer practice, and making sure homework was done to free up the candidate for campaigning. I'll grant you that working in electoral politics tends to blur the lines between the personal and the professional to begin with, but when your candidate's child is screaming, "You're taking my mommy away from me" in front of a room full of donors, I would argue that the intermingling of work and family has gone too far. . . .

Sexism added to the burdens of juggling campaign, career, and family obligations: the comments about accessories (like the American flag–print scarf one candidate used to wear so often that it caught the attention of the local press), dresses versus pantsuits, and the ultimate negative attention getter—cleavage. There is the constant mistaking of a male staffer for the candidate or elected official. There are jokes about frizzy hair and the resulting weekly, ninety-minute blow outs. . . . In the world of politics where time is money *and* votes, these little annoyances can turn into death by one thousand paper cuts. And when publicized, these annoyances unfairly trivialize the woman's candidacy.

Usually sexism surfaces in subtle, insidious, arguably more dangerous ways, but occasionally it hits blatantly, such as the radio ads depicting one of my candidates as a "ditsy" game show contestant who was "confused" about the issues. Studies have shown that voters do not discriminate against women, but that does not stop opponents from doing their best to eke out a percentage point or two by making gender an issue.[1]

Even if we assume that the "iron my shirt" comment shouted out by a male audience member and its reverberations did not cost Democratic presidential candidate Hillary Clinton her nomination in 2008, we should not discount the effects that these kinds of low blows may have had. And although I agree with the opinion that Gov. Sarah Palin was not prepared to run for the vice presidency, calling her "Caribou Barbie" is still not appropriate. There is artifice in people (both men and women) laughing off these remarks. Attempts to categorize them as problematic are shot down as nit-picky or hair-splitting. So embedded and sewn-in is the tendency to want to play down these sexist sentiments that to call them out is characterized as a shrill, whiny, windmill-tilting endeavor. But it can take its toll on a candidate and on her campaign just as it seeps into the psyche of any woman striving to achieve big things in a male-dominated field.

Fundraising can also be more difficult for female candidates (although some of the best fundraisers I have seen have been women). First-time candidates in particular do not like the idea of it; they do not want to make the "asks," and it can become a struggle to get them on the phones. In their study of 3,700 professionals, Jennifer Lawless and Richard Fox found that women in more significant numbers than men find the idea of fundraising repulsive enough to deter them from running for office. Some of these negative feelings filter in even once women do decide to become candidates. When that happens, it can put a stress on the entire campaign that can be difficult to overcome.[2]

Expanding the Definition of Leadership

Despite these and other factors stacked against them, I believe women would run in larger numbers if they were simply asked. Anecdotally, I find it true that they are not encouraged as often as men are, and studies prove this is the case. Party officials and other "gatekeepers" are less likely to identify women as leaders who can win.[3] But "leadership" is one of those loosely defined terms, completely contextual; there can be almost as many definitions of the term as there are people defining it. Must a leader hold a formal position or title within an organization? Must leaders have a staff or a following? Must they produce something quantifiable such as money or laws? Must they be well known? Someone with a traditional conception of leadership might answer "yes" to these questions because, historically, definitions of "leader" conjure up images of military might, business boardrooms, or presidential speeches.

But women have had a difficult time fitting these characterizations. The arenas in which they have historically been allowed to take responsibility—the family, the community, and female-dominated occupations—are not incorporated in the narrow definition that is implied by the word "leadership." Traditional definitions of leadership trump a more inclusive version of the word. When scoping for candidates, for example, nurses and teachers are routinely passed over for lawyers and millionaires. Women have been constrained from participating in the military, their input has rarely been asked for when deciding strategy, they have been discouraged from working outside the home, and they have not been allowed to vote let alone participate in lawmaking until they have fought for it. Only in the most recent decades have women been able to break through to become leaders in some of the historically male roles that the public equates with leadership.

There is also a more nuanced view of what people think leadership looks like: it should not appear that you have studied too diligently for it, worked too hard to get it, or thought too much about it. Amanda Fortini wrote in *New York Magazine* during the heated Democratic primary campaign of 2008: "'Leadership' is more effortless, an *assumed* mantle of authority, confidence that doesn't need a PowerPoint presentation to back it up. But it's difficult to imagine this traditionally male archetype—embodied in [then-presidential candidate Barack] Obama's easy manner and unscripted, often overly general approach—working for a woman in the same way it does for a man."[4] In fact, Hillary Clinton was harangued for trying the same approach early in her campaign. Her tone was interpreted as disingenuous, too forced. She was the smarty-pants in the front row with her hand in the air waiting to be called on. But this may not be fair. Women often combat the subtle sexism (and sometimes the more obvious discrimination) they face by working harder, being better prepared, having all the answers. Traditional leadership looks different on us because women's practicing it is not the norm.

Enough time has passed since the days of strict gender roles that we should be expanding our conceptions and definitions of what it means to be a "leader." Leadership must include social roles that do not involve titles, money, or power. When thinking about women's leadership in particular, the definition must make room for the ways that mothers, sisters, grandmothers, and first ladies have been organizing their families and communities throughout history. We should be able to apply the term to teaching fifth grade classes, balancing the family checkbook, demanding a crosswalk at a dangerous school crossing, or increasing profit margins of a corporation. As our definition expands, maybe we will broaden the profile of who is encouraged to run for elective office and how we treat those that do.[5]

"If You Want Something Done . . ."

Women often approach leadership roles, particularly political ones, fueled by a desire for social change— by an obligation to help a community or solve a problem. By virtue of their powerful positions, politicians have the potential to be agents of social change. My hope is that legislatures and executive offices will fill with women committed to enacting social change in general and for women's issues specifically.

Although women candidates gained impressive ground in the 2008 elections, they are still underrepresented in our local and national governments. We are 51 percent of the population and less than 20 percent of the legislatures and executive positions of this nation. Currently 17 percent of the representatives and senators in the U.S. Congress are women. In 2009 there will be eight women

governors in our fifty states; women constitute about one-fourth (24.2 percent) of the membership of state legislators on average. We have never had a female president or vice president. . . .[6]

In the abstract, this imbalance seems incongruous at best and tragically flawed at worst. On its face it doesn't seem right, but how bad is the reality? Does the male majority in the public offices of the United States suffice to solve the problems that expressly face women? Furthermore, are their decisions better off, better informed, more balanced without the input of women?

A number of national studies reveal that the majority of women who serve in public office believe they have a special responsibility to represent women and their interests. These interests admittedly are broad but include women's health care, family policies, equal pay, children's well-being, gender equity laws, sexual harassment, and reproductive rights, among others. Women representatives from the 103rd and 104th Congresses who were interviewed about their commitment to "women's issues" produced "near universal agreement concerning their responsibility to represent women."[7]

Some examples in a representative's own words include Nydia Velázquez, a Democrat from New York's Lower East Side who said, "Before I came here, I worked for a congressman. And while I worked for him, I saw that women's issues were not part of the national agenda . . . and it is as true today. . . . If we don't force others to focus on women's issues, then it will not be part of the debate."[8]

We hear the same thoughts from the moderates on the Republican side of the aisle: women's issues are not part of the agenda and women representatives find themselves saying, "If you want something done, you've got to do it yourself." This is what former representative Nancy Johnson, a Republican from Connecticut, did when she stated "I know a lot more about the shape of women's lives and the patterns of women's lives, so I need to look and see: how will the public policy affect those patterns? How will they help or hurt?"[9]

These women's words are not just lip service. Ongoing research finds that women in office have a direct and significant effect "not only in the outcomes of the policy process, but in defining the legislative agenda and in framing issues to advance women's needs and interests." Since the mid-seventies, "the role of 'legislator at large for

America's women' is being embraced more and more by women in public office."[10]

Elected officials shouldering this responsibility should not be taken for granted—it is no easy task. Serving as a watchdog for America's women requires resources of time, energy, and money—three things that no politician has in abundance. But more women in public office, compared to their male cohorts, are willing to expend those resources. As Del. Eleanor Holmes Norton (D-DC) said, "The kind of concentrated, systematic focus that goes from bill to bill . . . is what I think women mean when they say, 'We represent women.' It means not just on this issue or that issue, but [that we] . . . in addition to everything else we do, keep a watch for women's issues."[11]

In 1964 Margaret Chase Smith demonstrated that one woman among one hundred senators can make historical differences that improve women's situation for generations. Smith was the first female senator in America. Hailing from the Republican state of Maine, she never embraced the term "feminist" or admitted that women's issues were a priority to her. Nevertheless, there were plenty of instances throughout her career as a public servant when she became a bastion for women's liberties and equality. The most impressive of these was her leadership in including gender in Title VII of the Civil Rights Act of 1964, the "closest approximation that women now have to legislation granting them equal rights." The phrase that would outlaw discrimination based on "race, creed, color, and national origin" was enhanced with the word "sex." When the minority leader moved to have that word removed from the bill during a committee meeting, Smith asked, "Do you mean to say that you are going to state on the floor of the Senate that the Republican Policy Committee voted to strike the word 'sex' and have it known around the country that the Republican Party is opposed to women?" The leader rethought his position, the phrase stood as it was, and the lone woman senator changed the course of history for women.[12]

In . . . the early nineties debate over funding for breast cancer prevention, the work of a few Democratic women legislators raised funding levels from 72.3 to 100 million dollars. This funding made it easier for low-income women to gain access to health care services to prevent the incidence of breast cancer. As one staff member close to the process observed, "without Rosa DeLauro and the other two [Democratic] women . . . that program would not have seen the increases it saw over the last two years. I don't think there is anyone who would question that."[13]

These examples of women acting on behalf of their gender prompt the question, would men have picked up the slack if those women were not leading the charge? A quote by former Rep. Marge Roukema (R-NJ) leads one to think not: "I didn't really want to be stereotyped as the woman legislator. . . . I wanted to deal with things like banking and finance. But I learned very quickly that if the women like me in Congress were not going to attend to some of these [women's issues] . . . then they weren't going to be attended to. So I quickly shed those biases that I had and said, 'Well nobody else is going to do it; I'm going to do it.'"[14]

Looking at the numbers behind Roukema's "on the ground" assessment, we see that even men in public office who say they support women's issues will rarely do the heavy lifting to work on them. A study conducted by the Center for American Women and Politics at Rutgers University examined the strength of state legislators' declarations of support for women's issues. They wanted to know how often those who say they care about women's issues actually work on relevant legislation. The study concluded that over one-half of women state representatives and nearly two-thirds of women state senators addressed women's issues, compared with just over one-third of their male colleagues.[15]

This same study found that in the upper houses of state legislatures across the nation, nearly 75 percent of Democratic women senators worked on women's rights bills, as did half of Republican women senators. In comparison, 45 percent of Democratic male senators contributed to legislation that would benefit women, as did 33 percent of male Republican senators."[16] The gap in these statistics raises the question, what issues would be ignored if women were not in office to work on them? More disturbingly, what issues continue to suffer because there are not more women around to do that legislative work?

. . .

In the eight years since that first campaign I worked on in 2000, the numbers of women politicians has inched forward at a snail's pace. Hopefully, their ranks will continue to swell and they will bring greater focus to how policy and legislation affect the female population of this country. Women in elected office act as watchdogs for women: they put the problems that affect us high on their lists of legislative priorities, they speak up on our behalf, and—dramatically more than men—they take on the political tasks of passing laws that will improve the quality of our lives in the family, community, workplace, and other social institutions. In the meantime, we will rely heavily on the minority of women sitting in seats of power to bring women's issues forward, to monitor the ways that policies affect women uniquely, and to expand the definition and "the face" of leadership.

Despite the difficulties, young women must take up the task of helping to increase the numbers of women in public office, both by running ourselves and by campaigning for those who do. Just as the women in the 103rd and 104th congresses found they had no one to rely on but themselves when it came to legislating for the female population, young women today have no choice but to shoulder the job of striving to balance the male-dominated halls of power in the U.S. government. If we want to see our issues championed and bring our own insights about leadership to the table, it is up to us. Leading the way in the twenty-first century means taking on this challenge.

NOTES

1. Jennifer Lawless and Richard L. Fox, "Why Are Women Still Not Running for Office?" *Brown Policy Report* (Department of Political Science, Brown University, March 2008), 2.

2. Ibid., 5.

3. Ibid., 6.

4. Amanda Fortini, "The Feminist Reawakening: Hillary Clinton and the Fourth Wave," *New York Magazine* April 13, 2008, http://nymag.com/news/features/46011/.

5. Mary S. Hartman, ed., *Talking Leadership: Conversations with Powerful Women* (New Brunswick, NJ: Rutgers University Press, 1999), 3.

6. Center for the American Women and Politics, Rutgers University, "Women Achieve Record Numbers in State Legislatures, Advance to Statewide Offices; Republican Women See Setbacks at Both Levels," CAWP Election Watch, November 11, 2008, http://www.cawp.rutgers.edu/press_room/news/documents/PressRelease_11-11-08.pdf; "Record Numbers of Women to Serve in Senate and House," http://www. cawp.rutgers.edu/press_room/news/documents/PressRelease_11-5-08updated.pdf.

7. Mary Hawkesworth, "Legislating By and For Women: A Comparison of the 103rd and 104th Congresses" (Center for American Women and Politics, Rutgers University, November 2001), 4–9; see also Institute for Women's Leadership, "Power For What? Women's Leadership: Why Should You Care?" National Dialogue on Educating Women for Leadership, no. 2 (New Brunswick, NJ: May 2002), 21–27.

8. Hawkesworth, "Legislating By and For Women," 9.

9. Ibid., 11.

10. Ibid., 5–6.

11. Ibid., 6.

12. Susan J. Carroll, *The Impact of Women in Public Office* (Bloomington: Indiana University Press, 2001), 109–110.

13. Hawkesworth, "Legislating By and For Women," 29.

14. Ibid., 6.

15. Carroll, *Impact of Women in Public Office*, 10.

16. Ibid., 12.

17. Hawkesworth, "Legislating By and For Women," 10; Hartman, *Talking Leadership*, 229.

SEVENTY-TWO

◆◆◆

Women Working across Borders for Peace and Genuine Security (2010)

Ellen-Rae Cachola, Gwyn Kirk, LisaLinda Natividad, and Maria Reinat Pumarejo

Ellen-Rae Cachola works with Women for Genuine Security (San Francisco Bay Area) and Women's Voices Women Speak (Hawai'i). **Gwyn Kirk** is a member of Women for Genuine Security. **LisaLinda Natividad** is president of the Guahan Coalition for Peace and Justice (Guam) and featured in the documentary *Living*

Along the Fenceline. **María Reinat Pumarejo** is a member of Colectivo Ilé: Organizadoras para la Conciencia-en-Acción (Puerto Rico) and a key organizer for the eighth meeting of the International Women's Network in Puerto Rico (February 2012). They work together in the International Women's Network against Militarism.

The International Women's Network against Militarism started in 1997 when some 40 women activists, organizers, policy-makers, teachers and students from South Korea, Okinawa, mainland Japan, the Philippines and the United States gathered to share information and to strategize together about the negative effects of U.S. military operations in all our countries.[1] Since then, women from Puerto Rico, Hawai'i and Guahan (Guam) have joined. The Network is organized in national groups, with Puerto Rico, Guahan, Hawai'i, and Okinawa recognized as sovereign nations. Country group representatives co-ordinate affairs at the international level.

Over the past 13 years, the Network has created a space where women can share strategies and inspiration, and encourage each other's efforts. This has included learning about histories of colonization, war, occupation, and the connections between our varied histories, as well as learning about culture—music, dance, food, stories, language, and different ways of organizing. Each country group has its own history with the Network and makes its own distinctive contributions to our collaboration.

The Network's pulse is felt in the relationships maintained by its members. From the start we realized that to stay connected over vast geographical distances and variations of culture, language, and history, strong heart connections would be necessary, beyond simply coming together around a list of issues. Members who have participated in past international meetings introduce others who they are working with at home, which has provided stability and continuity to our gatherings. Similarly, new country groups are invited to join through personal links and on the basis of compatible values and approaches to advocating for human rights and genuine security.

In all our communities, militarism jeopardizes people's opportunities to live in sustainable ways. Despite our very different locations, we face many similar issues: distorted national budget priorities due to high levels of military spending, military violence against women, health effects of environmental contamination caused by preparations for war, the challenges of base conversion to civilian use, and the everyday militarization of our societies. In the United States (including Guahan, Hawai'i, and Puerto Rico), low-income communities face aggressive military recruiting and inadequate local services due to inflated military budgets maintained at the expense of socially useful programs. Learning

from each other's situations, we analyze these issues using the lenses of gender, race, class and nation. Part of our work is to redefine security, especially for women, children, and the environment. Alongside our anti-military critiques, we also envision and seek to create sustainable communities.

The Network is not a membership organization but a collaboration of women active in our respective communities: mothers, grandmothers, young women, students, teachers, professors, social workers, religious workers, and community organizers. Activities vary from country to country and include the provision of services to victims/survivors, public education and protest, research, lobbying, litigation, promoting alternative economic development, and networking. The country groups all include experienced organizers working on the issues mentioned above. Many Network participants give talks and workshops, and write popular articles and more scholarly papers.[2] The Network includes visual artists, filmmakers, poets, dancers, and performers. We see a crucial connection between the arts and action for social change.

Network members have also participated in international gatherings such as the Hague Appeal for Peace (Netherlands, 1999), the Grassroots Military Toxics Conference (Washington DC, 1999), and the World Social Forum (India, 2004). At the national organizing conference on U.S. bases in Washington DC (2009), Network women conducted presentations on environmental issues and militarism, human trafficking, and organizing against U.S. bases in the Asia-Pacific region. We contributed to an opening ceremony at the Pentagon and walked the runway in an anti-military fashion show.[3]

As an international network we seek to:

- Promote solidarity and healing among the diversity of women affected by militarism and violence;

- Integrate our common understandings into our relationships in the Network and in our daily lives;

- Promote leadership and self-determination among all the sisters of the Network;

- Initiate and support local and international efforts against militarism; and

- Strengthen our work by exploring our diverse historical, social, political, and economic experiences in each nation.

Complex Inequalities

A key part of working together is recognizing the complex inequalities and unequal relationships among us as individuals and among our nations. For example, Japan colonized Okinawa (1879), Korea (1910–1945), Guahan (1941–1944), and the Philippines (1942–1945). Many Koreans were forcibly drafted to work for Japanese imperial expansion—as factory workers, miners, and "comfort" women. Filipinas and Chamoru women from Guahan/Guam were forced to be "comfort" women. Nowadays, Korea's post-war economic growth means that Korean companies are making money in the Philippines, alongside companies from Japan, Taiwan, Europe and the United States. Okinawa was used as a shield in World War II to protect mainland Japan from direct U.S. invasion. Hawai'i was annexed by the United States in 1898. Guahan, Puerto Rico, and the Philippines became U.S. colonies in the same year, following the U.S. defeat of Spain. Guahan was occupied by the Japanese Imperial Army during World War II as a result of being a territory and possession of the United States.

These histories and inequalities may make it difficult for women from different nations to sit down together, hear what each is saying, and trust that those with relative privilege will be their allies. Among ourselves, we do not want to reproduce the unequal relationships that obtain among our nations. Nonetheless, the economic and political structures that shape all our lives continually recreate these inequalities and overcoming them is an ongoing challenge that takes mindfulness, honest communication, and concerted effort.

These inequalities are reflected in various ways. One example is in something as mundane as access to visas. Attending a Network meeting in Okinawa, for example, is straightforward for those of us with European or U.S. passports, as we do not need a visa to enter Japan. Korean women must attend an interview at the Japanese embassy in Seoul and explain the purpose of their visit. Those with Philippine passports have to queue for hours at the Japanese embassy in Manila, which is open from 2–4 pm, 4 days a week. They must show a return ticket and an invitation letter from a Japanese organization. They must explain their circumstances and answer the many questions posed by embassy staff. If successful, they must return 3 working days later to collect the visa in person. Similarly, when Network meetings are held in the United States (including a U.S. territory like Guahan) women from the Philippines must apply for a visa in person. Currently, each U.S. visa application costs them $175. Over the years we have held three international meetings in the United States. Each time, one or more women from the Philippines had her visa application denied.

A second difference among us is the buying power of our currencies. U.S. dollars go a long way in the Philippines. In Japan, many everyday things are expensive, even for those from the United States. For Filipinas who have to change pesos into hard currency, Japanese prices are astronomical. This also affects our relative capacities regarding fundraising to cover ongoing expenses as well as to attend international gatherings.

A third difference concerns the social and political risks we take in our respective countries by speaking out on these issues. Under the National Security Law, it is still illegal for Koreans to publicly oppose U.S. military policy in South Korea. They risk being labeled communist or unpatriotic, a serious charge in a context where many social activists have served jail sentences for opposing the government. The Philippines also has a hostile political climate for activists, with even more human rights violations, "disappearances" and extra-judicial killings under President Gloria Macapalang Arroyo (2001–2010) than under the military dictatorship of Ferdinand Marcos (1965–1986). Following the Bush administration's declaration of a "global war on terror," all our governments passed new anti-terrorism laws that can be used against activists.

Decolonizing Solidarity

From the beginning we decided not to work only in English at international meetings as many women activists who are doing cutting edge work in member countries are not fluent in English. We did not want to limit participation to college-educated women able to participate in English. Currently, the Network uses five languages: English, Japanese, Korean, Spanish and Tagalog. We have a number of dedicated interpreters/translators who view interpretation as important political work.[4] They have compiled a Peace Activists dictionary of over 400 terms to allow for precise, systematic translation.

But working with interpretation is something we are still learning how to do well. This process can be slow and cumbersome, requiring time, patience, concentration, and skilled interpreters who not only know language but also understand nuances of culture and history. Despite our best intentions, English is still very dominant at our international gatherings.

In addition, practices of decolonizing solidarity come through sharing worldviews and building relationships. During international gatherings we discuss issues that our local communities are facing and talk about how colonialism and militarism have caused these effects both historically and currently. We visit bases, war memorials, and other military sites. We see these site visits to militarized localities as pilgrimages and acts of memory-making that serve to surface grief and repressed memories of colonialism and the traumas of war. The process of building solidarity is very important to us because it is an ongoing challenge not to reproduce both subtle and spectacular acts of discrimination in the process of resistance.

Due to the national, political, and economic inequalities among women in this Network, it has been important to explain the stratifications and complexities within our communities and locations in the world, in order to break through stereotypical assumptions that we may all have of partner countries, as well as of our own country. For example, knowledge of economic, political and social inequalities in the United States helps to explain why military recruitment occurs and how the socialization and training of recruits may manifest in communities abroad during war, preparations for war, and periods of "Rest and Recreation."

As well as making formal country reports and engaging in strategic planning sessions, the women of the Network also embody ways of knowing based on indigenous and postcolonial cultural and spiritual beliefs, such as storytelling, art, poetry, dance, ritual, land-based practices, and symbol making. Despite differences of language and culture that are not completely understood across a multilingual group, the power of expressive articulation and the intentions of such messages are part of our commitment to solidarity. The courage to say what one feels among Network women creates opportunities for individual and group-wide consciousness-raising that can begin to shift perspectives in order to undo the systematic ways that colonialism and militarism disconnect us.

We are proud that this Network has kept going—and growing—these past 13 years. At the same time, our ideas, dreams, and plans are so much bigger than we have been able to manifest in practice so far. We appreciate the support of families and friends, as well as modest grants from foundations, churches, colleges, and community groups. Special mention should be made of The Global Fund for Women (San Francisco), a major supporter of women's human rights work internationally, and the foundation that has supported us most consistently. As with any all-volunteer organization, our efforts tend to be uneven. Women are busy with paid work, home commitments, studying, and local projects, as well as national level organizing. Working at the international level can easily get squeezed out of our overfull schedules. It has taken time, commitment, respect, mindfulness, and love to maintain our connections. Together we have created a space for women and have worked hard to maintain that space. We are going against the grain of prevailing discourses and beliefs, dominant cultures and histories, including our histories of separation, inequality, suspicion, prejudice, ignorance, shame, silence and being silenced. However partial, fragile, and flawed our efforts, without a strong commitment to maintaining our connections that space would not exist.

Vision and Mission

We envision a world of genuine security based on justice, respect for others across national boundaries, and economic planning based on local people's needs, especially the needs of women and children. Our shared mission is to build and sustain a network of women to promote, model, and protect genuine security in the face of militarism. Our goals are to

- contribute to the creation of societies free of militarism, violence, and all forms of sexual exploitation in order to guarantee the rights of marginalized people, particularly women and children, and to ensure the safety, well-being, and long-term sustainability of all our communities; and

- strengthen our common consciousness and voice by sharing experiences and making connections among militarism, imperialism, and systems of oppression and exploitation based on gender race, class and nation.

Our activities include:

- International meetings,
- Facilitating links among country groups,
- Coordinating Network-wide activities,
- Supporting each others' activities and campaigns by writing letters of solidarity, signing petitions, providing financial support, and selling goods, and
- Educating people in our communities about how U.S. militarism impacts women, children, and the environment in other countries of the Network.

The Network came together across the ocean to meet in Guahan (Guam) from September 14–19, 2009, around the theme: "Resistance, Resilience, and Respect for Human Rights." Guahan Network sisters offered to host the meeting in light of the unprecedented military expansion planned for the island, which is known as the "Tip of the Spear" of U.S. military might. In attendance there were 62 delegates from 12 countries—including Australia, the Commonwealth of the Northern Mariana Islands, the Republic of Belau (Palau), and the Republic of the Marshall Islands—as well as women of Guahan and other Network country groups. Specific areas of conversation included: redefining concepts of security, human trafficking of women, alternatives to military economies, reclaiming physical environments, and promoting security for women and children. The week also showcased a round-the-island tour focused on history and culture, a Peace Walk protest, and a public forum at the University of Guam. We participated in a healing ritual at the beach where we burned the Treaty of Paris, which dates back to the end of the Spanish-American War in 1898, when the United States gained the territories of Guam, Puerto Rico, and the Philippines from Spain. This meeting provided a space for women to share their personal encounters with militarism as sisters seeking to create sustainable lives for our communities. It allowed us to examine our purpose and future directions, and share our joy in working together.

Future growth for the International Women's Network involves the following:

- More regular communication among our country groups,
- Deepening our understanding of the issues and how to address them,
- More country-to-country connections and activities,
- More Network-wide activities,
- Building relationships with other women's networks and communities grappling with related issues such as environmental injustice and aggressive development, and
- Being able to support a Network secretariat with paid staff time.

A U.S. Department of Defense web site described the Pentagon as the "oldest," "largest," "busiest," and "most successful" U.S. company, boasting a budget bigger than ExxonMobil, Ford, or General Motors, and with wider geographical reach (U.S. Department of Defense 2002). Indeed, the United States maintains around 1,000 military bases worldwide, on all continents, with the consent—sometimes through bribery, bullying, or coercion—of "host" governments.

However, it is clear to many people that neither capitalism nor militarism can guarantee true security for the majority of the world's population or for the planet itself. To challenge—and ultimately to end—U.S. military empire will require more strong networks of activists and scholars to develop shared analyses, and generate—or restore—alternative definitions of a genuinely secure and sustainable future, based on relationships between people and the land, and sturdy connections among people that both acknowledge and go beyond narrow identities and territories.

NOTES

1. See Cynthia Cockburn. 2007. *From where we stand: War, women's activism and feminist analysis*, London and New York: Zed Books, ch. 2.

2. See, e.g., Yoko Fukumura and Martha Matsuoka. 2002. "Redefining security: Okinawa women's resistance to U.S. militarism." In *Women's activism and globalization: Linking local struggles and transnational politics* edited by Nancy Naples & Manisha Desai. New York: Routledge, 239–263; Gwyn Kirk and Carolyn Bowen Francis. 2000.

"Redefining security: Women challenge U.S. military policy and practice in East Asia," *Berkeley Women's Law Journal.* (15) 229–271; LisaLinda Natividad and Victoria-Lola Leon Guerrero. 2010. "The explosive growth of U.S. military power on Guam confronts people power: Experiences of an island people under Spanish, Japanese and American colonial rule," *The Asia-Pacific Journal: Japan Focus:* www.japanfocus.org/-Victoria_Lola_Leon-Guerrero/3454; Aida F. Santos. 1992. "Gathering the dust: The bases issue in the Philippines." In *Let the good times roll: Prostitution and the U.S. military in Asia* edited by Saundra Sturdevant and Brenda Stolzfus. New Press: New York; Suzuyo Takazato. 2000. "Report from Okinawa: Long term military presence and violence against women," *Canadian Woman Studies*

(19) #4: 42–47; Ellen-Rae Cachola, Lizelle Festejo, Annie Fukushima, Gwyn Kirk, and Sabina Perez. 2008. "Gender and U.S. Bases in the Asia-Pacific Region," *Foreign Policy in Focus:* www.fpif.org/fpiftxt/5069

3. Christine Ahn and Gwyn Kirk. 2009. "Fashioning Resistance to Militarism," *Foreign Policy in Focus:* www.fpif.org/fpiftxt/5929

4. Don Mee Choi. 2007. *Interpretation is a political act,* statement available from Women for Genuine Security: www.genuinesecurity.org

A version of this article was published in *Peace Review: A Journal of Social Justice,* vol. 22 (2) special issue on military bases, edited by Joseph Gerson.

◆◆◆

SEVENTY-THREE

Meeting the Leadership Challenges of Women with Disabilities
Mobility International USA

Cindy Lewis

Director of Programs at Mobility International USA (MIUSA), **Cindy Lewis** specializes in the empowerment of women and girls with disabilities through international exchange and leadership training. She is co-author and producer of educational and organizing materials for MIUSA and also co-authored the ground-breaking resource, *Building an Inclusive Development Community: A Manual on Including People with Disabilities in International Development Programs,* sponsored by the U.S. Agency for International Development.

Since 1981, Mobility International USA (MIUSA) has collaborated with women with disabilities from every region of the world through international exchange programs emphasizing leadership training and disability rights. MIUSA specializes in leadership programs for women with disabilities, including the International Symposium on Issues of Women with Disabilities preceding the Fourth U.N. World Conference on Women in Beijing (1995), the International Symposium on Microcredit by and for Women with Disabilities (1998), Global Options for Women with Disabilities in Leadership and Employment (2000), and Loud, Proud, and Prosperous: Microcredit By and For Women with Disabilities in Southern Africa

(2000–2003). MIUSA's three International Women's Institutes on Leadership and Disability (1997, 2003, and 2006) included women from Albania, Argentina, Armenia, Australia, Belarus, Brazil, Canada, Cambodia, Chile, Colombia, Dominican Republic, Ecuador, Egypt, El Salvador, Fiji, France, Gambia, Georgia, Guatemala, Guyana, Haiti, Honduras, India, Indonesia, Jamaica, Kenya, Kosovo, Korea, Kyrgyzstan, Lebanon, Lesotho, Mali, Malaysia, Malawi, Mauritius, Mexico, Moldova, Nepal, Nicaragua, Nigeria, West Bank/Gaza, Pakistan, Panama, Palau, the Philippines, Peru, Romania, Russia, Rwanda, Somalia, Syria, Thailand, Turkey, Uganda, Uzbekistan, Vietnam, Zambia, Zimbabwe, and the U.S.

Mobility International USA's women's leadership programs are guided by lessons learned from women with disabilities over the past 25 years:

- Women and girls with disabilities experience challenges to leadership and leadership development based on gender and disability-based discrimination.

- In spite of obstacles, women with disabilities around the world are nevertheless taking leadership: directing organizations, running businesses, heading families, assuming political offices, and advocating for their rights.

- Hands-on experiences of inclusion and accessibility are powerful catalysts for strengthening leadership capacity of women with disabilities. New experiences create visions; visions spark ideas that become action for change and empowerment.

- Women with disabilities gain valuable insights by sharing the challenges and solutions lived by women from diverse circumstances. International, cross-disability, cross-cultural exchange programs offer a rich pool of resources for learning and creating solutions.

Women's Institutes on Leadership and Disability (WILD)

Mobility International USA's WILD programs are built around MIUSA's trademark curriculum, a combination of practical workshops with dynamic, hands-on activities. WILD participants share experiences, advice, and ideas in workshops on such issues as microenterprise, education and literacy, violence prevention, HIV/AIDS and reproductive health, and the development of skills such as proposal writing and use of the media. Challenge and cultural activities provide opportunities for risk taking, team building, leadership practice, and development of "disability pride." Each participant creates individual as well as collaborative action plans to address issues of women with disabilities in their home communities.

"When we began our women's programs, there were so few women with disabilities in leadership positions," said Susan Sygall, MIUSA CEO. "In 1997, WILD participants were just beginning to see the potential of women with disabilities, of themselves, as leaders. The discussions at that time were about how to start disabled women's groups, whether and how to break away from disability organizations that were completely controlled by men. We focused on basic leadership skills, looking for solutions and developing confidence and pride in ourselves as women with disabilities."

Over the years, the experience and leadership needs of the participants has shifted. "Now, WILD women already understand the importance of leadership and women's solidarity, and they are more confident in their skills. Their concerns today are practical: how to tap into the development programs that are working—but not including women with disabilities—in their communities, to address the survival issues of women with disabilities: poverty, lack of education, violence, disease," said Sygall.

Gender, Disability, and Development Institute

During WILD 2003 and WILD 2006, representatives of leading U.S.-based international development organizations joined WILD participants for a five-day Gender, Disability, and Development Institute (GDDI), coordinated by MIUSA. During this intensive "think tank," WILD women and international development professionals worked together to identify issues that impact participation of women with disabilities in development efforts, strategize solutions, and create collaborative plans to promote inclusion of women with disabilities in development programs. International development organizations at the 2003 and/or 2006 GDDI included American Friends Service Committee, the Association for the Rights of Women in Development (AWID), CBM, the Global Fund for Women, the Hesperian Foundation, Holt International, Mercy Corps, Trickle Up Program, Women Pushing Forward, and Whirlwind Wheelchair International.

Important outcomes of the Gender, Disability, and Development Institute activities include new avenues of communication and relationships between disabled women leaders and development professionals. All participants agreed that disabled women's organizations often do not have experience or information necessary to effectively approach development NGOs, while NGOs are not equipped with accurate information about the issues and capacity of disabled women to respond effectively. Formal GDDI activities provided opportunities for participants on both sides to identify common interests, to gain insight into different perspectives, and to more accurately understand the constraints, goals, and resources of women with disabilities and development program implementers.

Gender, Disability, and Development Institute participants met over the course of the Institute in sector-specific work groups, to articulate issues, identify obstacles, and generate strategies to ensure that women with disabilities are included and more effectively served in micro finance, health, education, civil society, and refugee assistance programs. In one particularly powerful exercise, WILD women were assigned the roles of development organization staff, while development professionals played leaders of disability organizations. Each side presented and deliberated requests from the other, for inclusion, funding, assistance with outreach, etc. WILD women and participants from development organizations each recounted valuable and often surprising insights gained from the exercise, including feedback on how they were perceived by the other side.

Sharing of unstructured time also gave all participants unprecedented opportunities to establish relationships and deepen the dialogues begun in structured seminars. Relaxed, informal settings, small group activities, and opportunities for individual consultations resulted in personalized advice and enabled delegates to make connections with people who hold potential for valuable information and resources. Simple adaptations made by the owners of the rustic retreat center where the GDDI took place, such as small homemade ramps, a bathroom door replaced by a curtain, and a mattress raised by boards, were also eye opening for all participants.

While discussion focused on how development organizations can reach out and make programs accessible to women with disabilities, Susan Sygall, MIUSA CEO, also urged women with disabilities to take initiative by reaching out to international development organizations in their communities. A brainstorming session on recommendations for disability-led organizations to approach development NGOs more effectively incorporated suggestions from development professionals and WILD women. These included:

- Do your homework. Know the goals and mission of the development organization, and be sure that your request is compatible with that mission. Be able to explain how your organization's goals fit with the overall mission of the development organization. Learn the development vocabulary used by the organization, and use it.

- Be prepared to explain the mission of your organization and the key points of your request as concisely as possible. Practice expressing your main idea in one sentence, then making a brief explanation of your idea.

- Be specific about exactly what your organization wants from the international development organization. For example, "we want women with disabilities to participate in your microcredit program" is more effective than "women with disabilities need economic empowerment."

- Be prepared to counter stereotypes about women with disabilities. Emphasize the capabilities of women with disabilities rather than focusing only on their problems. Emphasize that women with disabilities are not interested in handouts but want the opportunity to show what they are capable of.

- Be polite, positive, and persistent. If an international development organization is resistant on the first approach, try again (and again!).

- Make an offer. Ask how you can assist the organization, for example with recruitment efforts, ideas, and contacts for making adaptations, accessible meeting space, etc., or support the NGO in meeting its goals in some other way.

Results

The impact of Mobility International USA's women's leadership programs is clear. MIUSA's women's program alumni today include a government minister and an elected representative to national Parliament; founders, directors, and officers of national and international organizations; Fulbright scholars and Fellowship recipients. MIUSA's alumni have created opportunities for countless other women with disabilities, initiating microcredit programs, business training, health projects, accessible transportation systems, and empowerment programs for disabled girls. Our alumni from all over the world credit MIUSA women's leadership programs with giving them the skills, resources, and confidence to step up as leaders in their communities and countries.

Our development program partners have also been affected. One participant reports that her experience at the Institute has led her to change the focus of development projects involving people with disabilities from "provision of care services" to "services to promote rights and empowerment." Another organization reports that the experience of working side by side with blind women made her understand very concretely what had previously been an abstract concept: the need for accessible format materials. All NGO participants noted that the opportunity to spend time with disabled women as colleagues had brought home the importance of providing access, and all have incorporated accessibility considerations into the regular project planning process.

As an organization, MIUSA has also greatly benefited from the WILD trainings. By bringing women together, MIUSA learns from the experts about the critical, real life issues that affect women with disabilities, and so is better prepared to advocate and provide technical assistance and information to promote inclusive development practice. "WILD helps us learn concretely what we often talk about in theory," said Sygall. "We are able to speak more accurately about the issues that women face throughout the world. In the same way, listening to dialogues between women with disabilities and development practitioners has enabled us to understand more practically the kind of issues that development organizations face as they work to include women with disabilities."

The Women's Institutes on Leadership and Disability program can be adapted and replicated anywhere in the world, by bringing cross-disability groups of women together to build confidence and skills as leaders, facilitating discussions between disabled women and development organizations, and focusing on solutions. "We want other people to do this," said Sygall. "We encourage our WILD participants to take our framework and adapt it to work in their own community. Or make up something new—anything that works to tap into the power of women with disabilities to contribute to international development."

NOTES

For more information and resources by MIUSA, including *Loud, Proud and Passionate®: Including Women with Disabilities in International Development Programs; Loud, Proud and Passionate®* Video (available in open-captioned format and in English, Spanish, Arabic, Russian, and French); and *Loud, Proud and Prosperous®: A Video Documentary* (available in open-captioned format and in English, Spanish, French, and Arabic), as well as recommendations for women with disabilities and international development organizations for inclusive development programs, see MIUSA's website: www.miusa.org

A version of this article is available at http://www.miusa.org/publications/freeresources/mti/chapter3

SEVENTY-FOUR

The Global Women's Movement (2004)
Definitions and Origins

Peggy Antrobus

Peggy Antrobus is an economist whose work focuses on women in development. She set up the Women and Development Unit at the University of the West Indies. She was a founding member of both the Caribbean Association for Feminist Research and Action (CAFRA) and DAWN, the network of Third World women promoting Development Alternatives with Women for a New Era. She has published widely; served as a consultant for international agencies including CIDA, FAO, UNDP, and UNIFEM; and received awards and honors for her lifelong service.

. . . This [article] attempts to answer the questions: Is there a global women's movement? How can we understand such a movement? How can it be defined, and what are its characteristics? My conclusion is that there is a global women's movement . . . different from other social movements and . . . defined by diversity, its feminist politics and perspectives, its global reach and its methods of organizing.

Definitions

Many authors admit that this movement does not conform to conventional definitions of a "movement" lacking as it does common objectives, continuity, unity and coordination. Yet this should not surprise us, nor should it be taken as a sign of deficiency. . . . Only a few activists take the view that the objectives of the women's movement are similar to those of labor, human rights and student groups, which seek justice for their members. Many see the objectives of women's groups as broader, seeking changes in relationships that are more varied and complex. At the same time it is sometimes difficult to identify clear objectives; worse, the objectives articulated by some groups seem to contradict those of others. The following quotes from [a] Nigerian case study illustrate the problem:

> The Nigerian women's movement is an unarmed movement. It is non-confrontational. It is a movement for the progressive upliftment of women for motherhood, nationhood and development.[1]

And again:

> When African women demand equality, we are only asking for our rights not to be tampered with, and the removal of laws that oppress and dehumanize women. We are not asking for equality with our husbands. We accept them as the bosses and heads of the family.[2]

The confusion and contradictions captured in these statements reflect the complexity of a movement that is caught in the tension between what is possible and what is dreamed of, between short-term goals and long-term visions, between expediency and risk-taking, pragmatism and surrender, between the practical and the strategic. Most of all, there is understandable ambivalence surrounding challenging and confronting relationships that are intimate and deeply felt. But the confusion also reflects a lack of clarity about definitions of what groups might be considered part of a "women's movement."

Many activists, including Nigerian activists who identify themselves with a women's movement, would question definitions of the objectives of their movement in terms of the "upliftment of women for motherhood, nationhood and development." They would argue that this instrumentalizes women, while being in complete accord with patriarchal definitions of women's traditional role.

It seems to me that the continuing confusion about what defines women's movements relates not so much to the fact that this movement does not conform to a conventional definition of a movement, but rather to lack of clarity about objectives in contexts that differ widely.

One way of clarifying these apparent contradictions is to recognize two mutually reinforcing tendencies within women's movements—one focused on gender identity (identity politics) and the other concerned with a larger project for social transformation. There are two entry points to concerns about a larger social project. One is recognition of the centrality of the care and nurture of human beings to the large social project, and that to address this, given the primacy of women's gendered role in this area, requires addressing gender relations in all the complex interplay of their economic, social, political, cultural and personal dimensions. It also involves locating gender inequality within other forms of inequality that shape and often exacerbate it.

Another entry point is recognition that women cannot be separated from the larger context of their lived experience and that this includes considerations of class, race/ethnicity and geographic location, among other factors. This means that the struggle for women's agency must include engagement in struggles against sources of women's oppression that extend beyond gender.

The larger social project would therefore include transforming social institutions, practices and beliefs so that they address gender relations along with other oppressive relationships, not simply seeking a better place within existing institutions and structures. For this reason, women's movements in countries where the majority of women are marginalized by class, race or ethnicity must be concerned with the larger social project.

This is often a point of tension between women's movements in the context of North–South relations, as well as in the context of struggles against oppression on the basis of class, race and ethnicity.

I believe that confusion about definitions of women's movements is also caused by failure to make distinctions between women's organizations as part of a wide spectrum of non-governmental organizations (NGOs) or civil society organizations (CSOs), and those that might be better understood as part of a politically oriented social movement.

Similarly, the term "women's movements" is sometimes used interchangeably with "feminist movements," an error that confuses and misrepresents both feminism and the broad spectrum of women's organizations.

In the final analysis, it seems to me that the identification of feminist politics as the engine of women's movements may help to clarify some of the confusion around women's organizing . . . as well as to focus the answer to the central question: Can women's movements make a difference in the struggle for equity, democracy and sustainability in today's globalized economy? It is the combination of struggles for gender justice with those for economic justice and democracy that enables women's movements to make a difference to the larger social project for transformation of systems and relationships.

An important segment of women's movements is composed of the associations that work to incorporate a feminist perspective into their theoretical, analytical, professional and political work. In academia, most disciplines now have feminist associations—Anthropology, Economics, Political, Social and Natural Sciences and Theology, among others. Moreover, within these disciplines—whether women are organized into feminist associations or not—women in the academies are doing important theoretical and empirical work that deepens our understanding of women's realities and produces the analyses and insights that strengthen the work of activists.

In the professions there are also women's associations—doctors, nurses, midwives, social workers, teachers, lawyers, bankers, etc.—that are challenging patriarchal patterns and relationships, raising new questions and changing the practices and methods by which their professions operate.

Many women's organizations, even those that focus on traditional concerns of home and family, are nevertheless important participants in women's movements. Among these are grassroots women's organizations of various kinds—Women's Institutes, Federations of Women, the YWCA, and many worldwide organizations identified with strong advocacy on behalf of women's rights, although they may not describe themselves as feminist.[3]

Finally, a definition of a women's movement must include those individual women who would never join an organization, nor define themselves as feminists, but whose lives and actions nevertheless serve to advance the liberation of women in their community and beyond.

All of these women must be seen as part of, or at least contributing to, women's movements. They are all part of the diversity and richness of a movement that seeks change in the relationships of superiority and inferiority, domination and subordination between women and men in a patriarchal world.

The following statements summarize my own views on women's movements:

- A women's movement is a *political* movement—part of the broad array of social movements concerned with changing social conditions . . .

- A women's movement is grounded in an understanding of women's relations to *social conditions*—an understanding of gender as an important relationship within the broad structure of social relationships of class, race and ethnicity, age and location.

- A women's movement is a *process,* discontinuous, flexible, responding to specific conditions of perceived gender inequality or gender-related injustice. Its focal points may be in women's organizations, but it embraces individual women in various locations who identify with the goals of feminism at a particular point in time.

- Awareness and *rejection of patriarchal privilege* and control are central to the politics of women's movements.

- In most instances, the "movement" is born at the moments in which individual women become aware of *their separateness as women,* their alienation, marginalization, isolation or even abandonment within a broader movement for social justice or social change. In other words, women's struggle for agency within the broader struggle is the catalyst for women's movements.

bell hooks describes this process of *conscientization* thus:

> Our search leads us back to where it all began, to that moment when an individual woman . . . who may have thought she was all alone, began a feminist uprising, began to name her practice, indeed began to formulate theory from lived experience.[4]

Women from across the world who identify themselves as part of an international and global women's movement are to be found participating in international meetings organized by feminist associations, networks and organizations such as the International Inter-disciplinary Congress, the Association for Women's Rights and Development (AWID) and UN conferences.[5] They celebrate annual special "days" such as International Women's Day (IWD) on 8 March and International Day Against Violence Against Women on 25 November. They are in constant communication with each other through the Internet, where they sign petitions and statements in solidarity with women around the world, formulate strategies and organize campaigns and meetings.

The movement has important resources:

- resource centers such as the International Women's Tribune Centre (IWTC), set up following the 1975 International Women's Year (IWY) Conference in Mexico City;
- media, such as feminist radio stations like the Costa Rica–based FIRE (Feminist International Radio Endeavor); news services like WINGS (Women's International News Gathering Service) and Women's Feature Services (WFS) . . .
- websites;
- publishers and women's presses;
- artists . . . —filmmakers, musicians, dancers, painters, writers, poets and playwrights;
- women's funds started by individual philanthropists and organizations that support women's projects, organizations and networks.

Characteristics

Diversity

Experience of the past thirty years points to the pitfall of starting with an assumption of a "global sisterhood," especially when that "sisterhood" is defined by a privileged minority. The emergence of a global movement has indeed depended on the emergence of new and different voices challenging hegemonic tendencies and claiming their own voice and space, and the acceptance of differences within the movements.

Diversity is now recognized as perhaps the most important characteristic of women's movements. Nevertheless, many of the tensions among women in their movements can be related to differences of race/ethnicity, nationality/culture and class, although, as Audre Lorde points out:

> [I]t is not those differences between us that are separating us. It is rather our refusal to recognize [them] and to examine the distortions which result from our misnaming them and their effects upon human behaviour and expectation.[6]

She also reminds us, "There is no such thing as a single-issue struggle because we do not live single-issue lives."[7] Women understand that each of us has multiple identities and that at any point in time one or other may be more important than others. Insistence on focusing on gender in isolation from issues like race, ethnicity and class has often been more divisive than the inclusion of these issues in the agendas of the various movements. It is indeed impossible and even counterproductive to separate the varied forms of oppression because of the systemic links between them. Thus in many countries of the South women have had to confront colonialism, imperialism or racism before they could confront patriarchy.

Feminist Politics

It may be useful to identify feminism as a specific politics, grounded in a consciousness of all the sources of women's subordination, and with a commitment to challenge and change the relationships and structures which perpetuate women's subordinate position, in solidarity with other women.

The consciousness of sexism and sexist oppression is the essence of feminist politics, and it is this politics that energizes women's movements, whether or not the word "feminist" is used. It is possible then to identify feminist politics as a specific element within a broader universe of women's organizations, women's movements and other social movements.

Feminists have worked with and within other social movements—especially those on peace, racism, the environment, indigenous peoples and the poor. These initiatives have served both to broaden and redefine the issues of concern to women, as well as to refocus the agendas of these movements.

In addition, there are feminists within institutions and agencies who recognize the ways in which the ideology of patriarchy constrains and diminishes the achievement of laudable goals and objectives, and who engage in the struggle to challenge it.

Feminist politics can also be identified within bureaucratic initiatives and institutional arrangements established for the improvement of the condition and position of women, enabling them to contribute to the movement for gender justice. These include women's bureaus, desks, commissions, special units and gender focal points within mainstream institutions.

Global Reach

Our understanding of the diversity within women's movements that has led us to speak more often of a multiplicity of "movements" would lead many to question the concept of a single global women's movement. However, I would argue, as others have done, that despite the rich diversity of experience, grounded in specific local struggles, women have been able to transcend these to become a movement of global proportions, with a global agenda and perspective.

Here I want to distinguish between an international women's movement and a global women's movement.[8] Although, as Uta Ruppert has pointed out, local or national women's movements have never viewed their activities as "simply crossing the borders of nation states,"[9] I would conceptualize an "international" movement as one in which the national and cultural differences between women were recognizable and paramount. Indeed, this was characteristic of women's movements at the international level in the mid-1970s, at the launching of

the UN Decade for Women (1975–85), and to some extent throughout most of the Decade. However, as women established their separate identities along the prevailing axes of North–South, East–West, they discovered commonalities that moved them increasingly towards greater coherence and even common positions in the policy debates around issues of environment, poverty, violence and human rights. At the same time, as these issues became increasingly "global" (as reflected in the themes and agendas of the global conferences of the 1990s), women's movements converged in these global arenas to negotiate and articulate common agendas and positions. As Ruppert puts it:

> The political process of international women's movements has been shaped by the insight that international politics does not simply take place at the inter-nation-state level, but also encompasses multicentric and multilevel processes. Thus the movement's multidimensional political understanding, which is sensitive to differences, almost predestined it to become the most global of social movements of the 1990s.[10]

. . .

Methods of Organizing

It is widely understood that a characteristic of a global women's movement is the linking of local to global, the particularities of local experience and struggles to, as Ruppert says, "the political creation and establishment of global norms for world development and global ethics for industrial production, such as (social and gender) justice, sustainability and peace, based on the creation of globally valid fundamental human rights."[11] However, few have related this to the particular methods of feminist organizing.

Although . . . this practice has not been the subject of an explicit discourse, it has nevertheless been based on conscious decisions to involve women from different backgrounds and regions in the search for "globality." These decisions have been the result of an understanding of the ways in which global events, trends and policies impact on local experience, and in particular on the experiences of poor women in the global South.

While Ruppert and others cite women's organizing around the 1992 UN Conference on Environment and Development (UNCED) and the 1993 International Conference on Human Rights as the first signs of this kind of organizing, I would refer to the experience of the network of Third World women, DAWN,[12] in their preparations for the Forum of the 1985 Third World Conference on Women. It was here that a conscious attempt was made to bring together local and regional experiences as the beginning of a process for the preparation of a platform document for a global event.

. . . The starting point was a meeting at which women were invited to reflect on their experience of development over the course of the Decade for Women—from the perspective of poor women living in the economic South. In this way the final document reflected regional differences, even as it reached for a framework that revealed the linkages between these experiences. This process—which starts with testifying to local, regional, or even individual experiences ("telling our stories," "speaking our truths"), leading to the negotiation of differences and finally to the articulation of a position that attempts to generalize, synthesize or "globalize" the diversity of experience—was repeated in the processes leading to the global conferences on environment, human rights and population. . . .

This methodology, clearly related to that of feminist consciousness-raising and Freirian *conscientization*[13] (combining reflection on personal experience with socio-political analysis to construct and generate global advocacy) has been a powerful tool for the global women's movement. Like *conscientization,* which takes specific realities "on the ground" as the basis for social analysis that can lead to action, it is a *praxis* (process of reflection and action) that has helped to mobilize women to challenge neoliberal and fundamentalist state policies at national and global levels. This praxis has also been a powerful tool in feminist theorizing.

To drive home one of the differences between international women's movements and a global women's movement, I want to compare this feminist method of globalizing to the process of regional meetings and consultations used by the UN in the preparation of their international conferences. The documents that feed into and emerge from these processes have to be screened and sanctioned by governments and, by their very nature, are limited in the degree to which they are able to reflect the realities of women. While the plans and platforms of action that emerge from the conferences contain many recommendations and resolutions that accord with the advocacy of women's movements, they often lack the coherence and clarity of the platforms produced by a movement unrestrained by the conventions of international diplomacy. Moreover, without the vigilance and political activism of women's movements, especially at local or national, but also at global, levels, these recommendations are meaningless to women.

This brings me to another aspect of the links between global and local—the ways in which local actors organize to defend themselves against global threats. Recognizing the relationship between global trends and local realities, women are organizing around the defence of their bodies, their livelihoods and their communities. The word "glocality" has been coined to highlight the ways in which global trends affect local experience. This recognition of a "politics of place" poses new challenges to a global women's movement. While organizing in the defence of "place" has the potential to be the most powerful and effective form of organizing,[14] local groups clearly need information and analysis on the broader policy frameworks that are affecting their lives. A global women's movement also needs links to this level of organizing to retain its relevance and to legitimize its advocacy.

. . .

A second method of organizing . . . is networking. Some may say that women's movements invented networking! Networking is the method used to make the vertical (local-global) as well as the horizontal (inter-regional as well as issue-specific) links that generate the analysis and the organizing underlying global action.

A third is the linking of the personal to the political, the ways in which gender identification and recognition of common experience can short-circuit difference to create a sense of solidarity. This often makes it easier for women who are strangers to each other to work together.

Symbols and Images

In the final analysis, words may not be enough to enable us to understand the complexity of a global women's movement made up of such a diversity of movements. . . . I have often been struck by the ways in which images and symbols capture the shape and structure of a global women's movement. The images and symbols that come to mind are those of the spiral, the wheel, the pyramid, the web and the patchwork quilt.

A spiral is an open-ended circle. As an adjective it is a "winding about a centre in an enlarging or decreasing continuous cone." As a noun, "a plane or three-dimensional spiral curve" (*Concise Oxford Dictionary*, 1990). In both cases it captures images of continuity and change, depth and expansion— something that is identifiable yet varied.

. . . A spiral is open-ended, continuous, ever enlarging our understanding of events, our perspectives. The global women's movement can be thought of as a spiral, a process that starts at the centre (rather than at the beginning of a line) and works its way outwards, turning, arriving at what might appear to be the same point, but in reality at an expanded understanding of the same event.

A spiral is also dialectic, allowing for the organic growth of a movement of women organizing—a movement in a state of on-going evolution as consciousness expands in the process of exchanges between women, taking us backwards (to rethink and reevaluate old positions) and forwards (to new areas of awareness).

As a number of interlocking networks, a global women's movement might also be likened to pyramids, webs and wheels. In a study of two campaigns, the campaign against breast-milk substitutes in Ghana, and against child labor in the carpet industry in India, the New Economics Foundation (NEF) identified

> three structures for organizing constructive collaboration: the pyramid, the wheel, and the web. Pyramids have a coordinating secretariat who disseminates information through the campaign; wheels have one or more focal points for information exchange, but information also flows directly among the members; in the web, no focal point exist, so information flows to and from all the members in roughly equal quantities.[15]

The pyramid, the wheel and the web underline the fluidity of the global women's movement,

comprised as it is of interlocking networks that come together as appropriate, even as each continues to focus on its specific area of interest.

The movement can also be understood as a patchwork quilt, full of color and different patterns, discontinuous and defying description, but nonetheless an identifiable entity made up of units that have their own integrity. A quilt, an art form peculiarly developed by women, uses whatever material is available to make something both beautiful and functional. It represents ingenuity, creativity, caring and comfort. A global women's movement can have no better symbol as it seeks to create a world in which people might find beauty, comfort and security.

. . .

Conclusion

It is clear that, despite the lack of clear and common objectives, continuity, unity and coordination, . . . there is nevertheless an identifiable movement enriched by its diversity and complexity, sustained by the depth of its passions and enduring commitment to its causes, and strengthened by the apparent lack of coordination and spontaneity of its strategizing.

Varied experiences highlight the complexity of women's struggles, the interplay between race, class and gender and the need to distinguish between the material and the ideological relations of gender.

There are many roads to the awareness that manifests as involvement in a women's organization or identification as part of a women's movement. There are still more steps towards a feminist consciousness, which would transform involvement in a women's organization into a political struggle for gender equity and equality, often within a broader project for social transformation. Many of the women involved in women's organizations, or movements, were influenced by leftist politics, and discovered their own marginalization within the processes of these struggles. Others began the journey to feminist consciousness through personal experiences; still others through their work experience. A characteristic of many of those involved in women's movements is the process of personal transformation which they undergo as they become aware of gender subordination. At the same time, this essentially individualistic experience seems to engender a connection to the wider universe of injustice in a way that leads to a better understanding of the link between different forms of oppression and builds life-long commitments to the struggle against injustice.

Given these histories, there is no doubt that there is a global women's movement, recognizable in its understanding of how "common difference"[16] links us all in a political struggle for recognition and redistributive justice. Its difference from other social movements lies not only in the absence of homogeneity . . . but in the value it places on diversity, its commitment to solidarity with women everywhere, its feminist politics and its methods of organizing. . . . as an important global actor in the struggles for a more equitable, humane, sustainable and secure world.

NOTES

1. Interview with representatives of the National Commission for Women, Abuja, 2 February 1993, Amrita Basu (ed.) *The challenge of local feminism: Women's movements in global perspective.* Boulder: Westview Press. (1995), p. 211.

2. Interview with Obiageli Nwankwo, project coordinator, International Federation of Women Lawyers, Enugu, 1993, Basu (1995), p. 212.

3. However, there may be self-defined feminists among their members.

4. bell hooks, 1994. *Teaching to transgress.* New York: Routledge, p. 75.

5. Although UN conferences are also attended by women and organizations that are opposed to advances in women's human rights, as was seen at the Five-Year-Review of the Fourth World Conference on Women, when the call went out from right-wing religion-based organizations for women to come to New York to "defend" women against that "dangerous" document, the Beijing *Platform for Action.*

6. Audre Lorde, *Sister outsider: Essays and speeches by Audre Lorde.* Freedom, Calif.: Crossing Press. p. 115.

7. Ibid., p. 138.

8. In thinking about this distinction I have found Uta Ruppert's analysis extremely helpful in M. Braig and S. Wolte (eds.) 2002. *Common ground or mutual exclusion? Women's movements and international relations.* New York: Zed Books.

9. Ibid., p. 148.

10. Ibid., p. 149.

11. Ibid.

12. The Network of Third World women promoting Development Alternatives with Women for a New Era. see www.dawnnet.org/

13. The combination of consciousness and action, "praxis," introduced by Brazilian educator, Paolo Freire, to enable oppressed groups to gain an understanding of the forces impinging on their world, the sources of their oppression.

14. Examples abound. The work of the Chipko movements and of the Self-Employed Women's Association (India) come to mind because they are so well-documented; however, there are examples of this kind of organizing in every region.

15. Jennifer Chapman. 2001. What makes international campaigns effective? Lessons from India and Ghana. In *Global citizen action,* edited by M. Edwards and J. Gaventa, Boulder: Lynne Rienner Publishers, pp. 263–64.

16. Gloria Joseph and Jill Lewis. 1986. *Common differences: Conflicts in Black and White feminist perspectives.* Boston: South End Press.

Glossary

GLOSSARY OF TERMS IN COMMON USE

This glossary contains key concepts found in this book. The first time the concept is used in the text it is shown in **bold.** Refer to the definitions here to refresh your memory when you come across the terms again later.

able-bodyism—Attitudes, actions, and institutional practices that subordinate people with disabilities.

adultism—Attitudes, actions, and institutional practices that subordinate young people on the basis of their age.

ageism—Attitudes, actions, and institutional practices that subordinate elderly persons on the basis of their age.

analytical framework—A theoretical perspective that allows one to analyze the causes and implications of a particular issue, rather than simply describing it.

anti-Arabism—Attitudes, actions, and institutional practices that subordinate Arabs and Arab Americans.

anti-Semitism—Attitudes, actions, and institutional practices that subordinate Jewish people. (The term *Semite* is used also to refer to some Arabs.)

assimilation—The process by which a minority group adopts the customs, values, and attitudes of the dominant culture.

biological determinism—A general theory holding that a group's biological or genetic makeup shapes its social, political, and economic destiny. This view is used to justify women's subordination or the subordination of peoples of color on the argument that they are biologically or genetically different from, and usually inferior to, men or white people, respectively.

blame the victim—An analysis or recommended course of action that attributes responsibility for a problem to those who experience it. An example is to urge women not to be out alone at night, for their safety, rather than to curb male violence against women.

capitalism—An economic system in which most of the capital—property, raw materials, and the means of production (including people's labor)—and goods produced are owned or controlled by individuals or groups—capitalists. The goal of all production is to maximize profit making. Also referred to as free market system.

classism—Attitudes, actions, and institutional practices that subordinate working-class and poor people on the basis of their economic condition.

coalition—Usually a short-term collaboration of organizations in which the strategy is to stand together to achieve a specific goal or set of goals around a particular issue, regardless of other differences among the organizations.

commodification—The process of turning people into things, or commodities, for sale; an example is the commodification of women's bodies through advertising and media representations. Sometimes, a cultural group's sacred objects, such as Native American people's dream-catchers, are also commodified and sold.

comparable worth—A method of evaluating jobs that are traditionally defined as men's work or women's work—in terms of the knowledge and skills required for a particular job; the mental demands or decision making involved; the accountability or degree of supervision involved; and working conditions, such as how physically safe the job is—so as to eliminate inequities in pay based on gender.

conscientization—A methodology for understanding reality, or gaining a "critical consciousness," through group dialogue, critical analysis, and examination of people's experiences and conditions that face them, which leads to action to transform that reality (Freire 1989).

criminalization—The processes whereby people who do not fit dominant societal norms are labeled as criminals. Their circumstances and behaviors are defined as crimes, such as mothers with HIV/AIDS, homeless people, immigrants, and gender-nonconforming people.

cultural appropriation—Taking possession of specific aspects of another group's culture in a gratuitous, inauthentic way, as happens, for example, when white people wear their hair in "dreads" or when nonindigenous people use indigenous people's names and symbols or adopt indigenous people's spiritual practices without being taught by indigenous practitioners. A particularly egregious form of cultural appropriation involves using another group's culture to make money. This is routine in the tourist industry, and it also occurs in the "New Age" spirituality movement, for example.

culture—The values, symbols, means of expression, language, and interests of a group of people. The dominant culture includes the values, symbols, means of expression, language, and interests of people in power in this society.

discrimination—Differential treatment against less powerful groups (such as women, the elderly, or people of color) by those in positions of dominance.

ecofeminism—A philosophy that links the domination of women with the domination of nature.

ecological footprint—The amount of land and energy required by various lifestyles and levels of consumption; calculated by estimating the amount of productive land needed to provide food, housing, transport, and consumer goods and services, and to absorb the waste that results from these processes; expressed in hectares or acres.

emigrate—The process of leaving one's native country to settle in another.

environmental justice—A philosophy and movement based on the belief that all citizens have a right to healthy living and working conditions.

environmental racism—The strong correlation between the distribution of environmental pollution and race.

epistemology—A theory about knowledge, including its sources, structure, validity, and limits. This includes who can know, under what circumstances, as well as the researcher's values and choices about how to carry out her or his inquiry.

essentialism—The view that people have some inherent essence, or characteristics and qualities, that define them. Some people argue, for example, that women are essentially more caring and nurturing than men.

eugenics—The belief that the human race can be "improved" through selective breeding; linked to racism and able-bodyism.

feminization of poverty—Women and children constitute the majority of poor people in the United States and throughout the world, a result of structural inequalities and discriminatory policies.

first-wave feminism—Organizations and projects undertaken by suffragists and women's rights advocates from the 1830s to the 1920s.

First World—Countries grouped together according to political alliances and economic status: western Europe, Japan, Australia, New Zealand, Canada, and the United States. This is often contrasted with the Third World, which includes most of Asia, Latin America, Africa, and the Caribbean.

gendered division of labor—A division of duties between men and women under which women have the main responsibility for home and nurturing and men are mainly active in the public sphere. Also referred to as **gender roles.**

gender gap—A significant difference between the political attitudes and voting patterns of women and men.

gender roles—The roles and behaviors considered culturally appropriate for women or men.

gender socialization—The process of learning the attitudes and behaviors that are considered culturally appropriate for boys or girls.

glass ceiling—An unseen barrier to women's promotion to senior positions in the workplace. Women can see the senior positions in their company or field, but few women reach them because of negative attitudes toward senior women and low perceptions of their abilities and training. This barrier may also be based on race/ethnicity.

globalization—Contemporary form of cultural and economic integration facilitated by electronic media, international financial institutions, trade agreements, and national immigration policies.

global level—A term used to describe and analyze the connections among people, institutions, and issues as viewed from a worldwide perspective.

hegemony—A dominant organizing principle or the permeation throughout society of the ruling elite's values, attitudes, beliefs, and morality. To the extent that people internalize this prevailing consciousness, it appears natural.

heteronormativity—Portrayal of the institution of heterosexuality, its norms and practices, as natural and inevitable; also "compulsory heterosexuality" (Rich 1986a).

heterosexism—Attitudes, actions, and institutional practices that subordinate people on the basis of their gay, lesbian, bisexual, or transgender orientation and identification.

identity-based politics—Activism and politics that have a strong identity component but also a broader view that enables people to make connections to other groups and issues.

identity politics—Activism and politics that put identity at the center. This usually involves the assumption that a particular characteristic, such as race, ethnicity, or sexual orientation, is the most important in the lives of group members and that the group is not differentiated according to other characteristics in a significant way.

ideology—Ideas, attitudes, and values that represent the interests of a group of people. The dominant ideology comprises the ideas, attitudes, and values that represent the interests of the dominant group(s). The ideological role of the idealized nuclear family, for example, is to devalue other family forms.

imperialism—The process of domination of one nation over other nations that are deemed inferior for the purpose of exploiting their human and natural resources, to consolidate its power and wealth. An empire is able to draw resources from many nations and to use their institutions and territory in its interest. Examples include the Roman empire, the British empire, and the current U.S. empire.

internalized oppression—Attitudes and behavior of some oppressed people that reflect the negative, harmful, stereotypical beliefs of the dominant group directed at them. An example of internalized sexism is the view of some women that they and other women are inferior to men, which causes them to adopt attitudes and behaviors that reinforce the subordination of women.

international division of labor—A division of work between rich and poor countries under which low-waged workers in the global South do assembly, manufacturing, and office work on contract to companies based in the global North.

intersectionality—An integrative perspective and analytical framework that illuminates how gender, class, nation, sexuality, religion, and other categories of identity, power, privilege, and oppression interconnect to affect the lives of individuals and groups and social, economic, and political phenomena at community, societal, and global levels.

liberal feminism—A philosophy that sees the oppression of women as a denial of equal rights, representation, and access to opportunities.

liberalism—A political theory about individual rights, freedom, choice, and privacy with roots in seventeenth-century European ideas (e.g., the writings of political philosopher John Locke).

macro level—A term used to analyze the relationships among issues, individuals, and groups as viewed from a national institutional perspective.

marginality—The situation in which a person has a deep connection to more than one culture, community, or social group but is not completely able to identify with or be accepted by that group as an insider. For example, bisexual, mixed-race/mixed-culture, and immigrant peoples have connections with different groups and may find themselves caught between two or more social worlds.

marginalization—Attitudes and behaviors that relegate certain people to the social, political, and economic margins of society by branding them and their interests as inferior, unimportant, or both.

matrix of oppression, privilege, and resistance—The interconnections among various forms of oppression based on gender, race, class, nation, and so on. These social attributes can be sources of disadvantage or privilege. Negative ascriptions and experiences may be the source of people's resistance to oppression.

medicalization—The process of turning life processes, like childbirth or menopause, into medical issues. Thus, menopause becomes an illness to be treated by medical professionals with formal educational qualifications and accreditation. By the same token, experienced midwives are considered unqualified because they lack these credentials.

meso level—A term used to analyze the relationships among issues, individuals, and groups as viewed from a community, or local, perspective.

micro level—A term used to analyze the connections among people and issues as seen from a personal or individual perspective.

militarism—A system and worldview based on the objectification of "others" as enemies, a culture that prepares for, invests in, and celebrates war and killing. This worldview operates through specific political, economic, and military institutions, investments, and actions.

militarized masculinity—A masculinity constructed to support militarism, with an emphasis on heroism, physical strength, lack of emotion, and appearance of invulnerability (Enloe 1990, 1993).

misogyny—Woman-hating attitudes and behavior.

neocolonialism—Economic, political, and cultural domination by which a nation maintains or extends its control and influence over other nations, creating new forms of colonialism.

neoliberal/neoliberalism—Economic philosophy and policies that call for the freedom of business to operate with minimal interference from governments, international organizations, or labor unions. Basic tenets include the rule of the market, free trade, economic deregulation, privatization of government-owned industries, reduction of social welfare spending, and belief in individual responsibility rather than valuing community and the public good. Termed "neo" liberal because it calls for a revival of the free-market philosophy that prevailed in the United States through the 1800s and early 1900s prior to the enhanced role of government that gained legitimacy during the Depression (1930s), culminating in the "War on Poverty" and other "Great Society" programs of the 1960s.

objectification—Attitudes and behaviors by which people are treated as if they were "things." One example is the objectification of women through advertising images.

objectivity—A form of understanding in which knowledge and meaning are believed to come from outside oneself and are presumably not affected by personal opinion or bias.

oppression—Prejudice and discrimination directed toward whole social groups and promoted by the ideologies and practices of all social institutions. The critical elements differentiating oppression from simple prejudice and discrimination are that it is a group phenomenon and that institutional power and authority are used to support prejudices and enforce discriminatory behaviors in systematic ways. Everyone is socialized to participate in oppressive practices, either as direct and indirect perpetrators or passive beneficiaries, or—as with some oppressed peoples—by directing discriminatory behaviors at members of one's own group or another group deemed inferior. **See internalized oppression.**

paradigm shift—A complete change in one's view of the world.

patriarchy—A family, social group, or society in which men hold power and are dominant figures. Patriarchal power in the United States plays out in the family, the economy, the media, religion, law, and electoral politics.

positionality—How a person is situated or positioned in terms of gender, race, class, sexuality, age, ability, national origin etc.

positivism—A version of empirical science to be applied to social as well as physical phenomena. French philosopher August Comte believed that the only authentic knowledge is scientific knowledge and that such knowledge can only come from positive affirmation of theories through strict scientific method.

postcolonial feminism—A perspective that critiques Western imperialism and imperialist tendencies of Western feminism and emphasizes historically defined colonial power relations that provide a foundational context for women's lives and struggles for change.

poverty level—An income level for individuals and families that officially defines poverty.

power—The ability to influence others, whether through persuasion, charisma, law, political activism, or coercion. Power operates informally and through formal institutions and at all levels (micro, meso, macro, global).

praxis—The cycle of action and reflection upon the world in order to transform it; a key part of socially lived theorizing.

precautionary principle—The view that when an activity raises threats of harm to human health or the environment, precautionary measures should be taken even if some cause and effect relationships are not fully established scientifically. Those proposing the activity should bear the burden of proof rather than the public.

prejudice—A closed-minded prejudging of a person or group as negative or inferior, even without personal knowledge of that person or group and often contrary to reason or facts; unreasonable, unfair, and hostile attitudes toward people.

privilege—Benefits and power from institutional inequalities. Individuals and groups may be privileged without realizing, recognizing, or even wanting it.

productive economy—Characterized by monetary exchanges through trade, the organization of work, distribution and marketing of goods, contracts, negotiation of wages and salaries, and so forth.

public versus private dichotomy—The view that distinguishes between the private and personal (dating, marriage, sexual habits, who does the housework, relationships between parents and children) and the public (religion, law, business). Although these two spheres affect each other, according to this view they are governed by different rules, attitudes, and behavior.

racism—Racial prejudice and discrimination that are supported by institutional power and authority. In the United States, racism is based on the ideology of white (European) superiority and is used to the advantage of white people and the disadvantage of peoples of color.

radical feminism—A philosophy that sees the oppression of women in terms of patriarchy, a system of male power and authority, especially manifested in sexuality, personal relationships, and the family, and carried into the male-dominated world of work, government, religion, media, and law.

relativism—The view that all "authentic" experience is equally valid and cannot be challenged by others. For example, White Supremacist views of Ku Klux Klan members are seen to be equally as valid as those held by antiracist activists. There are no external standards or principles by which to judge people's attitudes and behaviors.

relocalization—Emphasis on local production and use of goods, crops, and media productions rather than on production for export. "Relocalization would conserve resources, generate meaningful work, fulfill basic needs, and strengthen democracy" (Shiva 2002a, p. 249).

reproductive economy—This domestic labor includes biological and social reproduction, mainly done by women, to maintain daily life, raise children, care for elders, and so on. It is often considered unproductive because it is unwaged, but it is fundamental to the ability to do waged work. See **social reproduction.**

reproductive justice—A perspective that links health and reproductive rights to broader issues of social and economic justice. It offers a view of wellness for individuals, communities, and the wider society based on the eradication of inequality, oppression, and injustice.

second shift—Responsibilities for household chores and child care mostly by women after having already done a full day's work outside the home.

second-wave feminism—Feminist projects and organizations from the late 1960s to the mid-1980s that campaigned for women's equality in all spheres of life and, in some cases, that argued for a complete transformation of patriarchal, capitalist structures. See liberal feminism, radical feminism, socialist feminism.

separatism—The process of creating a separate life-space, often for political purposes, such as white lesbian separatists in the 1970s who chose to live in community with other women, to work with women, and to support women's projects. Some people of color may also advocate separatism from white people, institutions, values, and culture and decide to put their energies only in support of other people of color.

sexism—Attitudes, actions, and institutional practices that subordinate individuals because of their gender.

situated knowledge—Knowledge and ways of knowing that are specific to a particular historical and cultural context and life experiences.

social constructionism—The view that concepts that appear to be immutable and often solely biological, such as gender, race, and sexual orientation, are defined by human beings and can vary, depending on cultural and historical contexts. On this view, for example, heterosexuality is something learned—socially constructed—not innate. The "normalcy" of heterosexuality is systematically transmitted, and appropriate attitudes and behaviors are learned through childhood socialization, life experiences, and reinforced through institutional norms, policies, and law.

social control—Attitudes, behaviors, and mechanisms that keep people in their place. Overt social controls include laws, fines, imprisonment, and violence. Subtle ones include ostracism and withdrawal of status, affection, and respect.

social institutions—Institutions such as the family, education, the media, organized religion, law, and government.

social reproduction—Everything needed to reproduce everyday life, much of which is unpaid work done by women. See **reproductive economy.**

socialist—Someone who believes that work should be organized for the collective benefit of workers rather than the profit of managers and corporate owners, and that the state should provide for human needs.

socialist feminism—A view that sees the oppression of women in terms of their subordinate position in a system defined as both patriarchal and capitalist.

social location—The social features of one's identity incorporating individual, community, societal, and global factors such as gender, class, ability, sexual orientation, age, and so on.

speciesism—Attitudes, actions, and institutional practices that subordinate nonhuman species; usually used in discussions of environmental and ecological issues.

standpoint theory—The view that different social and historical situations give rise to very different group and individual experiences and theories about those experiences. Standpoint shapes a person's view of the world and what she or he may or may not be able to comprehend about it. See **situated knowledge.**

state—Government institutions, authority, and control. This includes the machinery of electoral politics, lawmaking, government agencies that execute law and policy, law enforcement agencies, the prison system, and the military.

sticky floor—Structural limitations for women in low-paid, low-status jobs that block them from moving up. Also **glass ceiling.**

subjectivity—A form of understanding in which knowledge and meaning are grounded in people's lived experiences; also being the subject rather than an object of theorizing. Since powerless groups have historically been treated as objects of "objective" knowledge production, feminist assertions of subjectivity are also assertions of objectified groups' claims to the subject position (that of actor and agent of action), their ability to create knowledge, and, therefore, their agency in knowledge production.

subjugated knowledge—Knowledge generated from positions of subordination.

theory—An explanation of how things are and why they are the way they are; a theory is based on a set of assumptions, has a perspective, and serves a purpose.

third-wave feminism—Feminist perspectives adopted in the 1990s, often by younger women, with an emphasis on personal voice and multiple identities, intersectionality, ambiguity, and contradictions.

transnational—Relationships, organizations, or movements that connect individuals or groups across national boundaries. These boundaries are not erased but are greatly reduced as barriers. Emphasis is on activities that transcend national boundaries, such as transnational corporations or transnational feminist organizing.

transnational feminism—Feminism without borders that links scholars and activists in "noncolonized" dialogue across differences. This includes a commitment to avoid reproducing inequalities among feminists that parallel those among nations.

References

1000 Women for the Nobel Peace Prize. 2005. *1000 Peacewomen across the globe.* Zurich: Scalo.

Abbey, S., and A. O'Reilly, eds. 1998. *Redefining motherhood: Changing identities and patterns.* Toronto, ON: Second Story Press.

Abramovitz, M. 1996. *Regulating the lives of women.* Rev. ed. Boston: South End Press.

Abramson, W., E. Emanuel, V. Gaylord, and M. Hayden. 2000. Impact: Special issue on violence against women with developmental or other disabilities 13(3). Minneapolis: The Institute on Community Integration, University of Minnesota. Available online at http://ici.umn.edu/products/impact/133.

Adair, V. 2004. Reclaiming the promise of higher education: Poor single mothers in academe. *On Campus with Women* 33(3–4), Spring/Summer.

———, and S. Dahlberg. 2003. *Reclaiming class: Women, poverty, and the promise of higher education in America.* Philadelphia: Temple University Press.

Adam, K., and C. Derber. 2008. *The new feminized majority: How Democrats can change America with women's values.* Boulder, CO: Paradigm.

Adams, C. J. 1999. *The sexual politics of meat: A feminist-vegetarian critical theory.* 10th anniversary ed. New York: Continuum.

Adams, J. P. 1991. *Peacework: Oral histories of women peace activists.* New York: Twayne.

Adamson, J., M. M. Evans, and R. Stein, eds. 2002. *The environmental justice reader: Politics, poetics and pedagogy.* Tucson: Arizona University Press.

Adler, F. 1975. *Sisters in crime: The rise of the new female criminal.* New York: McGraw-Hill.

Agbola, T., and M. Alabi. 2003. Political economy of petroleum resources development, environmental justice and selective victimization: A case study of the Niger delta region of Nigeria. In *Just sustainabilities: Development in an unequal world*, eds. J. Agyeman, R. D. Bullard, and B. Evans. pp. 269–88. Cambridge, MA: MIT Press.

Agosín, Marjorie, ed. 2001. *Women, gender, and human rights: A global perspective.* New Brunswick, NJ: Rutgers University Press.

Agyeman, J., and A. H. Alkon, eds. 2011. *Cultivating food justice: Race, class and sustainability.* Cambridge, MA: MIT Press.

Ahn, C., and G. Kirk. 2005. Why war is all the rage. *San Francisco Chronicle*, May 29, p. D5.

Al-Ali, N., and N. Pratt. 2009. *What kind of liberation? Women and the occupation of Iraq.* Berkeley: University of California Press.

Albelda, R. 2009. Up with women in the downtown. *Ms.*, Spring, pp. 35–37.

Albelda, R., and C. Tilly. 1997. *Glass ceilings and bottomless pits: Women's work, women's poverty.* Boston: South End Press.

Albrecht, G. H. 2004. *Hitting home: Feminist ethics, women's work, and the betrayal of "family values."* New York: Continuum.

Alexander, J. M., and C. T. Mohanty, eds. 1997. *Feminist genealogies, colonial legacies, democratic futures.* New York: Routledge.

Alexander, M. 2012. *The new Jim Crow: Mass incarceration in the age of colorblindness.* Rev. ed. New York: New Press.

Allen, D., R. R. Rush, and S. J. Kaufman, eds. 1996. *Women transforming communications: Global intersections.* Thousand Oaks, CA: Sage.

Allen, H. 2000. Gender, sexuality and the military model of U.S. national community. In *Gender ironies of nationalism: Sexing the nation*, ed. Tamar Mayer, 306–27. New York: Routledge.

Allen, N. 2011. Arizona sheriff introduces all female chain gang. *The Telegraph*, Jan. 2. www.telegraph.co.uk/news/worldnews/northamerica/usa/8236125/Arizona-sheriff-introduces-all-female-chain-gang.html

Allen, P., and C. Sachs. 1991. The social side of sustainability: Class, gender and race. *Science as Culture* 2(pt. 4, no. 13).

———. 2007. Women and Food Chains: The gendered politics of food, *International Journal of Sociology of Food and Agriculture*, 15 (1): 1–23.

Allen, P. G. 1986. *The sacred hoop: Recovering the feminine in American Indian traditions.* Boston: Beacon Press.

Alonso, H. H. 1993. *Peace as a women's issue: A history of the U.S. movement for world peace and women's rights.* Syracuse, NY: Syracuse University Press.

Alterman, Eric. 2003. *What liberal media? The truth about bias and the news.* New York: Basic Books.

Amadeo, K. 2012. What exactly was the Bank Bailout Bill? http://useconomy.about.com/od/criticalissues/a/govt_bailout.htm

American Civil Liberties Union. 2002. *The USA Patriot Act.* Accessed online at http://www.aclu.org.

American Heritage Dictionary. 1993. 3rd ed. Boston: Houghton Mifflin.

Amnesty International USA. 2000. *United States of America: Breaking the chain. The human rights of women prisoners.* New York: Amnesty International USA.

———. n.d. Women in prison: A fact sheet. www.prisonpolicy.org/scans/women_prison.pdf

Anderlini-D'Onofrio, S., ed. 2003. *Women and bisexuality: A global perspective.* New York: Haworth Press.

Andersen, M. 2000. Women, power and politics. In *Thinking about women: Sociological perspectives on sex and gender*, 5th ed., 290–322. Boston: Allyn and Bacon.

Anderson, B. 2000. *Joyous greetings: The first international women's movement. 1830–60.* New York: Oxford University Press.

Andersen, M., and P. H. Collins. eds. 1998. *Race, Class and Gender: An anthology.* 3rd ed. Belmont, CA: Wadsworth.

Anderson, L., ed. 1991. *Sisters of the earth: Women's prose and poetry about nature.* New York: Vintage Books.

Andre, J. 1988. Stereotypes: Conceptual and normative considerations. In *Racism and sexism: An integrated study*, ed. P. S. Rothenberg. New York: St. Martin's Press.

Angus, I., and S. Butler. 2011. *Too many people? Population, immigration, and environmental crisis.* Chicago: Haymarket.

Angwin, J. 1996. Pounding on the glass ceiling. *San Francisco Chronicle*, November 24, p. C3.

Antrobus, P. 2004. *The global women's movement: Origins, issues and strategies.* New York: Zed Books.

Anzaldúa, G. 1987. *Borderlands la frontera: The new mestiza.* San Francisco: Spinsters/Aunt Lute.

———. 2002. Now let us shift . . . the path of conocimiento . . . inner work, and public acts. In *This bridge we call home,* ed. Gloria Anzaldúa and Analouise Keating, pp. 540–78. New York: Routledge.

Applebome, P. 1997. Citadel's president insists coeducation will succeed. *New York Times,* January 14, p. A1.

Arcana, J. 1994. Abortion is a motherhood issue. In *Mother journeys: Feminists write about mothering,* ed. M. Reddy, M. Roth, and A. Sheldon, pp. 159–63. Minneapolis: Spinsters Ink.

———. 2005. *What if your mother.* Goshen, CT: Chicory Blue Press.

Arditti, R., R. D. Klein, and S. Minden, eds. 1984. *Test-tube women: What future for motherhood?* Boston: Pandora Press.

———, and T. Schreiber. 1998. Breast cancer: The environmental connection—A 1998 update, in *Resist Newsletter.* May/June.

Arias E. 2011. United States life tables, 2007. *National Vital Statistics Reports* 59(9). Hyattsville, MD: National Center for Health Statistics.

Arredondo, G. F., A. Hurtado, N. Klahn, O. Nájera-Ramírez, and P. Zavella. eds. 2003. *Chicana feminism: A critical reader.* Chapel Hill, NC: Duke University Press.

Atkinson, T. 1974. *Amazon odyssey.* New York: Links Books.

Avery, B. 1990. Breathing life into ourselves: The evolution of the Black women's health project. In *The Black women's health book,* ed. E. White, pp. 4–10. Seattle, WA: Seal Press.

Azuma, A. 2007. Food access in Central and South Los Angeles: Mapping injustice, agenda for action. Urban and Environmental Policy Institute, Occidental College. www.uepi.oxy.edu

Bagby, R. 1990. Daughter of growing things. In *Reweaving the world: The emergence of ecofeminism,* ed. I. Diamond and G. Orenstein, pp. 231–48. San Francisco: Sierra Club.

Bailey, M. and A. P. Gumbs. 2010. We are the ones we've been waiting for, *Ms magazine.* Winter.

Bailey, M., P. Kandaswamy, and M. U. Richardson. 2004. Is gay marriage racist? In *That's revolting: Queer strategies for resisting assimilation,* ed. M.B . Sycamore. Brooklyn: Soft Skull Press.

Baird-Windle, P., and E. J. Bader. 2001. *Targets of hatred: Anti-abortion terrorism.* New York: Palgrave.

Baker, B. 1993. The women's convergence for national health care. *The Network News,* July/August, pp. 1, 3.

Baldwin, James. 1984. On being white and other lies, *Essence* (April).

Bandarage, A. 1997. *Women, population and global crisis: A political-economic analysis.* London and New Jersey: Zed Books.

Barndt, D., ed. 1999. *Women working the NAFTA food chain: Women, food and globalization.* Toronto, ON: Sumach Press.

———. 2002. *Tangled routes: Women, work and globalization on the tomato trail.* Lanham, MD: Rowman and Littlefield.

Barnett, E. 2002. Prison coffee and games: Starbucks and Nintendo admit their contractor uses prison labor. *Prison Legal News* 13(3): 12–13.

Barnett, R., and C. Rivers. 1996. *She works, he works: How two-income families are happier, healthier, and better-off.* New York: HarperSanFrancisco.

Barnhill, D. L., ed. 1999. *At home on the earth: Becoming native to our place.* Berkeley: University of California Press.

Barr, D. A. 2008. *Heath disparities in the United States: Social, class, race, ethnicity and health.* Baltimore: Johns Hopkins University Press.

Barry, J. 2012. *Standing our ground: Women, environmental justice, and the fight to end mountaintop removal.* Athens: Ohio University Press.

Bart, P., and P. O'Brien. 1993. *Stopping rape: Successful survival strategies.* New York: Teachers College Press.

Bartlett, J. 1994. *Will you be a mother? Women who choose to say no.* London: Virago.

Bass, E., and L. Davis. 1988. *The courage to heal.* New York: Harper & Row.

Baumgardner, J., and A. Richards. 2000. *Manifesta: Young women, feminism, and the future.* New York: Farrar, Straus and Giroux.

Baxandall, R., and L. Gordon, eds. 2000. *Dear sisters: Dispatches from the women's liberation movement.* New York: Basic Books.

Beasley, M., and D. Thomas. 1994. Violence as a human rights issue. In *The public nature of private violence: The discovery of domestic abuse,* ed. M. A. Fineman and R. Mykitiuk, pp. 323–46. New York: Routledge.

Beauboeuf-Lafontant, T. 2007. "You have to show strength": An exploration of gender, race, and depression. *Gender and Society.* 21(1): 28–51.

———. 2009. *Behind the mask of the strong black woman: Voice and the embodiment of a costly performance.* Philadelphia: Temple University Press.

Belenky, M. F., B. M. Clinchy, N. R. Goldberger, and J. M. Tarule. 1997. *Women's ways of knowing: The development of self, voice, and mind.* 10th anniversary ed. New York: Basic Books.

Belkin, L. 2007. The feminine critique. *New York Times.* November 1. www.nytimes.com/2007/11/01/fashion/01WORK.html?pagewanted=2&_r=1&ei=5070&en=91feaf95fabced83&ex=1194580800

Bell, D., and R. Klein, eds. 1996. *Radically speaking: Feminism reclaimed.* North Melbourne, Australia: Spinifex Press.

Benard, C., and E. Schlaffer. 1997. "The man in the street": Why he harasses. In *Feminist frontiers IV,* ed. L. Richardson, V. Taylor, and N. Whittier, pp. 395–98. New York: McGraw-Hill.

Benedict, H. 2009. *The lonely soldier: The private war of women serving in Iraq.* Boston: Beacon Press.

Bennett, K. 1992. Feminist bisexuality: A both/and option for an either/or world. In *Closer to home: Bisexuality and feminism,* ed. E. R. Weise, pp. 205–31. Seattle, WA: Seal Press.

Benston, M. 1969. The political economy of women's liberation. *Monthly Review* 21(4): 13–27.

Bernstein, R., and S. C. Silberman, eds. 1996. *Generation Q.* Los Angeles: Alyson.

Bianchi, S., M. Milkie, L. Sayer, and J. Robinson. 2002. Is anyone doing the housework? Trends in the gender division of household labor. In *Workplace/women's place,* 2nd ed., ed. P. Dubeck and D. Dunn, pp. 174–87. Los Angeles: Roxbury.

Bigelow, B., and B. Peterson, eds. 2002. *Rethinking globalization: Teaching for justice in an unjust world.* Milwaukee, WI: Rethinking Schools.

Bird, C. 1995. *Lives of ours: Secrets of salty old women.* New York: Houghton Mifflin.

Birks, J., and A. Erlich, eds. 1989. *Hidden dangers: The environmental consequences of preparing for war.* San Francisco: Sierra Club Books.

Black Women's Health Project. 1995. *Reproductive health and African American women. Issue brief.* Washington, DC: Black Women's Health Project.

Blair, Jane. 2011. *Hesitation kills: A female officer's combat experience in Iraq*. Lanham, MD: Rowman and Littlefield.

Blakely, M. K. 1994. *American mom: Motherhood, politics, and humble pie*. Chapel Hill, NC: Algonquin Books.

Blank, H., ed. 2001. *Zaftig: Well-rounded erotica*. San Francisco: Cleis Press.

Blauner, R. 1972. *Racial oppression in America*. New York: Harper & Row.

Bleier, R. 1984. *Science and gender: A critique of biology and its theories on women*. New York: Pergamon Press.

Bleyer, J. 2004. Cut-and-paste revolution: Notes from the girl zine explosion. In *The fire this time: Young activists and the new feminism*, ed. Vivien Labaton and Dawn Lundy Martin, pp. 42–60. New York: Anchor Books.

Bloom, S., J. Miller, J. Warner, and P. Winkler, eds. 1994. *Hidden casualties: Environmental, health and political consequences of the Persian Gulf War*. Berkeley: North Atlantic Books.

Boggs, C., and T. Pollard. 2006. *The Hollywood war machine: U.S. militarism and popular culture*. Boulder, CO: Paradigm.

Boggs, G. L. 1994. Fifty years on the left. *The Witness*, May, 8–12.

———, and S. Kurashige. 2011. *The next American revolution: Sustainable activism for the twenty-first century*. Berkeley: University of California Press.

Bogle, K. 2008. *Hooking up: Sex, dating and relationships on campus*. New York: New York University Press.

Bohmer, C., and A. Parrot. 1993. *Sexual assault on campus: The problem and the solution*. New York: Lexington Books/Macmillan.

Bollinger, H. 2007. *Women of the harvest: Inspiring stories of contemporary farmers*. Osceola, WI:Voyageur Press.

Bonsignore, A. 2011. The military's rape and sexual assault epidemic. *Truthout*, April 3. http://truthout.org/militarys-rape-and-sexual-assault-epidemic/1301554800

Boonstra, H. D. 2007. The case for a new approach to sex education mounts: Will policymakers heed the message? *Guttmacher Policy Review*, 10(2). www.guttmacher.org/pubs/gpr/10/2/gpr100202.html

Bordo, S. 1993. *Unbearable weight: Feminism, Western culture, and the body*. Berkeley: University of California Press.

Boris, E. 2010. Feminism's histories. In K. A. Laughlin et al. Is it time to jump ship? *Feminist Formations* 22(1): 90–97.

———, and R. S. Parennas, eds. 2010. *Intimate labors: Cultures, technologies, and the politics of care*. Palo Alto: Stanford University Press.

Borjesson, Kristina, ed. 2002. *Into the buzzsaw: Leading journalists expose the myth of a free press*. Amherst, NY: Prometheus Books.

Borkovitz, D. K. 1995. Same-sex battering and the backlash. *NCADV Voice*, Summer, 4.

Bornstein, K. 1995. *Gender outlaw: On men, women, and the rest of us*. New York: Vintage/Random House.

———. 1998. *My gender workbook: How to become a real man, a real woman, the real you, or something else entirely*. New York: Routledge.

Boston Women's Health Book Collective. 2005. *Our bodies ourselves: A new edition for a new era*. New York: Simon and Schuster.

Boswell, J. 1994. *Same-sex unions in premodern Europe*. New York: Villard Books.

Boswell-Penc, M. 2006. *Tainted milk: Breastmilk, feminisms, and the politics of environmental degradation*. Albany.: State University of New York Press.

Bousquet, S., and C. Edds. 2012. State purges 7,000 felons from voting rolls, *Miami Herald*, May 12. www.miamiherald. com/2012/05/22/2812435/state-purges-7000-felons-from.html#storylink=cpy

Bowden, L., and S. Cain. 2008. *Powder: Writing by women in the ranks from Vietnam to Iraq*. Tucson, AZ: Kore Press.

Bowman, R. 2009. VMI is subject of sexism probe. *Roanoke Times*, August 8. www.roanoke.com/news/roanoke/wb/214636

Boxer, M. 1998. *When women ask the questions: Creating women's studies in America*. Baltimore: Johns Hopkins University Press.

Boyd, S. C. 2004. *From witches to crack moms: Women, drug law, and policy*. Durham, NC: Carolina Academic Press.

Boylan, J. F. 2003. *She's not there: A life in two genders*. New York: Broadway Books.

Brandzel, A. 2005. Queering citizenship? Same-sex marriage and the state. *GLQ: A Journal of Lesbian and Gay Studies* 11(2).

Braveman, P. 2006. Health disparities and health equity: Concepts and measurements. *Annual Review of Public Health* 27: 167–194.

Breitbart, J, and A. Nogueira. 2004. An independent media center of one's own: A feminist alternative to corporate media. In *The fire this time: Young activists and the new feminism*, ed. Vivien Labaton and Dawn Lundy Martin, pp. 19–41. New York: Anchor Books.

Brennan, S., J. Winklepleck, and G. MacNee. 1994. *The resourceful woman*. Detroit: Visible Ink.

Brenner, J. 1996. The best of times, the worst of times: Feminism in the United States. In *Mapping the women's movement*, ed. M. Threlfall, pp. 17–72. London: Verso Books.

Brettschneider, M. 2006. *The family flamboyant: Race politics, queer families, Jewish lives*. Albany: State University of New York Press.

Brice, Carleen. 2003. *Age ain't nothing but a number: Black women explore midlife*. Boston: Beacon Press.

Bright, S. ed. 2000. *The best American erotica*. New York: Simon & Schuster.

Brown, T. M. 2011. *Raising Brooklyn: Nannies, childcare and Caribbeans creating communities*. New York: New York University Press.

Browne, C. 1998. *Women, feminism, and aging*. New York: Springer.

Browne, J. 1996. The labor of doing time. In *Criminal injustice: Confronting the prison crisis*, ed. E. Rosenblatt. Boston: South End Press.

Brownell, K. D., and K. B. Horgen. 2004. *Food fight: The inside story of the food industry, America's obesity crisis, and what we can do abut it*. Chicago: Contemporary Books.

Brownmiller, S. 1975. *Against our will: Men, women, and rape*. New York: Simon & Schuster.

Bruce, C., ed. 2001. *Best bisexual women's erotica*. San Francisco: Cleis Press.

Brumberg, J. J. 1997. *The body project: An intimate history of American girls*. New York: Random House.

Buchwald, E., P. Fletcher, and M. Roth, eds. 2005. *Transforming a rape culture, Rev. ed*. Minneapolis: Milkweed.

Buck, M. 2004. Women in prison and work. *Feminist Studies* 30(2): 451–455.

Bulhan, H. A. 1985. *Frantz Fanon and the psychology of oppression*. New York: Plenum Books.

Bullard, R. D. 1990. *Dumping in Dixie: Race, class, and environmental quality*. Boulder, CO: Westview Press.

———. ed. 1993. *Confronting environmental racism: Voices from the grassroots*. Boston: South End Press.

———. 2002. Crowning women of color and the real story behind the 2002 EJ Summit. www.ejrc.cau.edu/SummCrowning04.html

———, P. Mohai, R. Saha, and B. Wright. 2007. *Toxic waste and race at twenty 1987–2007: Grassroots struggles to dismantle environmental racism in the United States.* Cleveland, OH: United Church of Christ.

Bunch, C. 1987. *Passionate politics: Essays 1968–1986.* New York: St. Martin's Press.

———, and R. Carillo. 1991. *Gender violence: A human rights and development issue.* New Brunswick, NJ: Center for Women's Global Leadership, Rutgers University.

———, and N. Reilly. 1994. *Demanding accountability: The global campaign and Vienna Tribunal for women's human rights.* New Jersey: Center for Women's Global Leadership, Rutgers University; New York: UNIFEM.

Bureau of Justice Statistics. 1995. *Violence against women: Estimates from the redesigned survey.* Washington, DC: U.S. Department of Justice.

Bureau of Labor Statistics, 2010. Current population survey, Table 2. www.bls.gov/cps

———. 2011. Employment status of civilian population, Table A-6. www.bls.gov/news.release/empsit.t06.htm

Burke, C. 2004. *Camp all-American, Hanoi Jane, and the high-and-tight: Gender, folklore, and changing military culture.* Boston: Beacon Press.

Burnham, Linda. 2001. *The wellspring of Black feminist theory.* Oakland: Women of Color Resource Center. www.coloredgirls.org

Burrell, B. 1994. *A woman's place is in the House: Campaigning for Congress in the feminist era.* Ann Arbor: University of Michigan Press.

Burton, N. 1998. Resistance to prevention: Reconsidering feminist antiviolence rhetoric. In *Violence against women: Philosophical perspectives,* ed. S. French, W. Teays, and L. Purdy, pp. 182–200. Ithaca, NY: Cornell University Press.

Bush, Melanie E. L. 2004. *Breaking the code of good intentions: Everyday forms of whiteness.* Lanham, MD: Rowman and Littlefield.

Butler, J. 1990. *Gender trouble: Feminism and the subversion of identity.* New York: Routledge, Chapman, & Hall.

Byerly, C. M., and K. Ross. 2006. *Women and media: A critical introduction.* Malden, MA: Blackwell.

Calasanti, T. M., and K. F. Slevin, eds. 2006. *Age matters: Realigning feminist thinking.* New York: Taylor and Francis.

Califia. P. 2000. *Public sex: The culture of radical sex.* San Francisco: Cleis Press.

Camp, L. T. 1997. *Lingering fever: A World War II nurse's memoir.* Jefferson, NC: McFarland and Co.

Campbell, D., with F. D'Amico. 1999. Lessons on gender integration from the military academies. In *Gender camouflage: Women and the U.S. military,* ed. F. D'Amico and L. Weinstein, pp. 67–79. New York: New York University Press.

Cancian, F. M., D. Kurz, A. S. London, R. Reviere, and M. C. Tuominen. 2002. *Child care and inequality: Rethinking carework for children and youth.* New York: Routledge.

Caplan, P., ed. 1987. *The cultural construction of sexuality.* London: Tavistock.

Caplan, R. 2004. *Thirst: A guide to the film for teachers and discussion leaders.* San Francisco: Sierra Club Water Privatization Task Force.

Caputi, J., and D. E. H. Russell. 1990. "Femicide": Speaking the unspeakable. *Ms.,* September/October, pp. 34–37.

Carilli, T., and J. Campbell, eds. 2005. *Women and the media: Diverse perspectives.* Lanham, MD: University Press of America.

Carlen, P. 1989. Feminist jurisprudence, or womenwise penology. *Probation Journal* 36(3): 110–14.

Carroll, S. J., ed., 2001. *The impact of women in public office.* Bloomington: Indiana University Press.

Carson, R. 1962. *Silent spring.* Boston: Houghton Mifflin.

Catalano, S. 2008. *Intimate partner violence in the United States.* Bureau of Justice Statistics. Washington, DC: U.S. Department of Justice. www.ojp.usdoj.gov/bjs/homicide/intimates.htm#intimates

Catalyst. 2010. Fortune 500 women executive officers and top earners. www.catalyst.org/publication/459/2010-catalyst-census-fortune-500-women-executive-officers-and-top-earners

Cavin, S. 1985. *Lesbian origins.* San Francisco: Ism Press.

Center for American Women and Politics. 2011. Gender differences in voter turn out: Fact sheet. www.cawp.rutgers.edu/fast_facts/voters/documents/genderdiff.pdf

———. 2012. Women of color in elective office 2012. www.cawp.rutgers.edu/fast_facts/levels_of_office/StateLeg-CurrentFacts.php

Center for Arms Control and Non-Proliferation. 2008. *Total Iraq and Afghanistan supplemental war funding to date.* Washington DC: CACNP. www.armscontrolcenter.org/policy/securityspending/articles/supplemental_war_funding/

Centers for Disease Control and Prevention. 2008a. Prevalence of overweight, obesity and extreme obesity among adults: U.S. trends. www.cdc.gov/nchs/fastats/overwt.htm

———. 2008b. Sexual violence and intimate partner violence. www.cdc.gov/injury/ResearchAgenda/pdf/Sexual Violence-a.pdf

———. 2009. Births: Final data for 2009. www.cdc.gov/nchs/fastats/teenbrth.htm

Chalker, R. 1995. Sexual pleasure unscripted. *Ms.,* November/December, pp. 49–52.

Chang, G. 2000. *Disposable domestics: Immigrant women workers in the global economy.* Cambridge, MA: South End Press.

———, and K. Kim. 2007. Reconceptualizing approaches to human trafficking: New directions and perspectives from the field(s). *Stanford Journal of Civil Rights and Civil Liberties,* III(2): 317–344.

Charman, K. 2011. Nuclear revival? Lessons for women from the Three Mile Island accident. *On the Issues,* Spring. www.ontheissuesmagazine.com/2011spring/2011spring_Charman.php

Chavez, C. 1993. Farm workers at risk. In *Toxic struggles: The theory and practice of environmental justice,* ed. R. Hofrichter, pp. 163–70. Philadelphia and Gabriola Island, BC: New Society.

Chernin, K. 1994. *The obsession: Reflections on the tyranny of slenderness.* New York: Harper Perennial.

Chesler, P. 1972. *Women and madness.* New York: Avon.

Chesney-Lind, M. 1995. Rethinking women's imprisonment: A critical examination of trends in female incarceration. In *Women, crime, and criminal justice,* ed. B. R. Price and N. Sokoloff. New York: McGraw-Hill.

———, and K. Irwin. 2008. *Beyond bad girls: Gender, violence and hype.* New York: Routledge.

———, and L. Pasko. 2004. *The female offender: Girls, women and crime.* 2nd ed. Thousand Oaks, CA: Sage.

———. eds. 2003. *Girls, women and crime: Selected readings.* Thousand Oaks, CA: Sage.

———, and R. G. Shelden. 1992. *Girls, delinquency and juvenile justice.* Pacific Grove, CA: Brooks/Cole.

Chiawei O'Hearn, Claudine, ed. 1998. *Half and half: Writers on growing up biracial and bicultural.* New York: Pantheon.

Children's Defense Fund. 2010. The state of America's children. www.childrensdefense.org/child-research-data-publications/data/state-of-americas-children.pdf

Chodorow, N. 1978. *Reproduction and mothering: Psychoanalysis and the sociology of gender.* Berkeley: University of California Press.

Clare, E. 2009. *Exile and pride: Disability, queerness and liberation.* Cambridge, MA: South End Press.

Cline, L. S. 2009. *Toda s military wife: Meeting the challenges of service life.* 6th ed echanicsburg, PA: Stackpole Books.

Cobble, D. S., ed. 200 *The sex of class: Women transforming American labor.* Itl ca: Cornell University Press.

Cockburn, C. 1977. Women get involved in community action. In *Women in the Community,* ed. M. Mayo. London: Routledge and Kegan Paul.

———. 1998. *The space between us: Negotiating gender and national identities in conflict.* London and New Jersey: Zed Books.

———. 2007. *From where we stand: War, women's activism and feminist analysis.* London: Zed Press.

Cofer, J. O. 1993. The story of my body. In *The Latin Deli: Prose and poetry.* Athens: University of Georgia Press.

Cohen, Elliot D., ed. 2005. *News incorporated: Corporate media ownership and its threat to democracy.* Amherst, NY: Prometheus Books.

Cohn, M. 2006. Military hides cause of women's soldiers deaths. *Truthout.* January 30. www .truthout.org/cgi-bin/artman/exec/view.cgi/57/17327/printer

Cole, J., and B. Guy-Sheftall. 2003. *Gender talk: The struggle for women's equality in African American communities.* New York: Ballantine.

Cole, J. H. 1992. *Women pilots of World War II.* Salt Lake City: University of Utah Press.

Coleman-Jensen, A., M. Nord, M. Andrews, and S. Carison. 2011. Household food security in the United States in 2010. *Economic Research Report 125.* www.ers.usda.gov/Publications/err125/

Colligan, S. 2004. Why the intersexed shouldn't be fixed: Insights from queer theory and disability studies. In *Gendering Disability,* ed. B. G. Smith and B. Hutchinson, pp. 45–60. New Brunswick, NJ: Rutgers University Press.

Collins, J. 2003. *Threads: Gender, labor, and power in the global apparel industry.* Chicago: University of Chicago Press.

Collins, L. 2008. Pixel perfect: Pascal Dangin's virtual reality. *The New Yorker.* May 12. www.newyorker.com/reporting/2008/05/12/080512fa_fact_collins

Collins, P. H. 1990. *Black feminist thought: Knowledge, consciousness, and the politics of empowerment.* Boston: Unwin Hyman.

———. 1997. Comment on Hekman's 'Truth and method: feminist standpoint revisited': Where's the Power? *Signs: Journal of Women in Culture and Society* 22(2): 375–81.

———. 2004. *Black sexual politics: African Americans, gender, and the new racism.* New York: Routledge.

Condry, I. 2006. *Hip-hop Japan: Rap and the paths of cultural globalization.* Durham: Duke University Press.

Connell, R. W. 1990. The state, gender, and sexual politics: Theory and appraisal. *Theory and Society* 19(4): 507–44.

Cook, A., and G. Kirk. 1983. *Greenham women everywhere: Dreams, ideas, and actions from the women's peace movement.* Boston: South End Press.

Coontz, S. 1997. *The way we really are: Coming to terms with America's changing families.* New York: Basic Books.

Cooper, F., and A.L. Stoler, eds. 1997. *Tensions of empire: Colonial cultures in a bourgeois world.* Berkeley: University of California Press.

Corea, G. 1985. *The mother machine: Reproductive technologies from artificial insemination to artificial wombs.* New York: Harper & Row.

———. 1987. *Man-made women: How reproductive technologies affect women.* Bloomington: Indiana University Press.

Cornell. A, 2004. We do? Queers question the politics of gay marriage, *Clamor,* July/August, pp. 21–23.

Cornell, D., ed. 2000. *Feminism and pornography.* New York: Oxford University Press.

Costa, T. 2010. *Farmer Jane: Women changing the way we eat.* Layton, UT: Gibbs Smith.

Costantini, C. 2011. Undocumented women forced to give birth while shackled and in police custody. *Huffington Post,* September 20. www.huffingtonpost.com/2011/09/20/undocumented-pregnant-woman-gives-birth-in-shackles_n_971955.html

Cox, T. 1999. *Hot sex: How to do it.* New York: Bantam Books.

Crabb, C. 2006. The chain reaction of unsilencing. In *We don't need another wave: Dispatches from the next generation of feminists,* ed. M. Berger, pp. 193–99. Emeryville, CA: Seal Press.

Craviotto, N. 2010. The impact of the global economic crisis on women and women's human rights across regions. *Association for Women's Rights in Development.* www.awid.org/Library/2010-Updates-Impacts-of-the-Crisis-on-Women-s-Rights-Sub-regional-perspectives

Crenshaw, K. 1993. The marginalization of sexual violence against Black women. Speech to the National Coalition Against Sexual Assault, 1993 Conference, Chicago. http://www.ncasa.org/marginalization.html

Critical Resistance. 2005. *Instead of prisons: A handbook for abolitionists.* Oakland, CA: AK Press.

Croteau, D., and W. Hoynes. 1997. *Media/society: Industries, images, and audiences.* Thousand Oaks, CA: Pine Forge Press.

Crow, T. 2012. *Eyes right: Confessions from a woman Marine.* Lincoln: University of Nebraska Press.

Cruickshank, M. 2003. *Learning to be old: Gender, culture, and aging.* Lanham, MD: Rowman and Littlefield.

———. 2008. *Learning to be old: Gender, culture, and aging,* 2nd ed. Lanham, MD: Rowman and Littlefield.

Daly, H. E., and J. B. Cobb Jr. 1989. *For the common good: Redirecting the economy toward community, the environment, and a sustainable future.* Boston: Beacon Press.

Daly, M. 1976. *Gyn/ecology: The metaethics of radical feminism.* Boston: Beacon Press.

D'Amico, F. 1998. Feminist perspectives on women warriors. In *The women and war reader,* ed. L. A. Lorentzen and J. Turpin, pp. 119–25. New York: New York University Press.

D'Amico, F., and L. Weinstein, eds. 1999. *Gender camouflage: Women and the U.S. military.* New York: New York University Press.

Daniels, R., S. C. Taylor, and H. H. L. Kitano, eds. 1991. *Japanese Americans from relocation to redress.* Seattle: University of Washington Press.

Danquah, M. 1998. *Willow weep for me: A Black women's journey through depression.* New York: W. W. Norton.

Darling, M., and J. Tyson. 1999. The state: Friend or foe? Distributive justice issues and African American women. In *Dangerous intersections: Feminist perspectives on population, environment, and development,* ed. J. Silliman and Y. King, pp. 214–41. Cambridge, MA: South End Press.

das Dasgupta, S., and S. DasGupta. 1996. Public face, private space: Asian Indian women and sexuality. In *"Bad girls"/"good girls": Women, sex, and power in the nineties,* ed. N. Bauer Maglin and D. Perry, pp. 226–43. New Brunswick, NJ: Rutgers University Press.

Davis, Angela. 1983. Racism, birth control, and reproductive rights. In *Women, race, and class.* New York: Vintage Books.

———. 1997. A plenary address. Paper presented at conference, Frontline Feminisms: Women, War, and Resistance, January 16, at University of California, Riverside.

———. 1998. Masked racism: Reflections on the prison industrial complex. *Color Lines,* Fall.

———. 2001. The color of violence against women. *Sojourner: The Women's Forum,* October, pp. 12–13.

———. 2003. *Are prisons obsolete?* New York: Seven Stories Press.

Davis, A. 2008. Interpersonal and physical dating violence among teens. *The National Council on Crime and Delinquency Focus.* http://www.nccd-crc.org/nccd/pubs/2008_focus_teen_dating_violence.pdf

Davis, B. 2004. Will debt move backfire on Argentina? *Asian Wall Street Journal,* November 29, A6.

Davis, D. 2009. *Genetic dilemmas: Reproductive technology, parental choices, and children's futures.* New York: Oxford University Press.

Davis, F. 1991. *Moving the mountain: The women's movement in America since 1960.* New York: Simon & Schuster.

Davis, K. 2007. *The making of* Our Bodies, Ourselves: *How feminist knowledge travels across borders.* Durham, NC: Duke University Press.

Davis, S. W. 2011. Inside-out: The reaches and limits of a prison program. In *Razor Wire Women,* ed. J. M. Lawston and A. E. Lucas. Albany, NY: State University of New York Press.

Dean, D. 1997. *Warriors without weapons: The victimization of military women.* Pasadena, MD: The Minerva Center.

d'Eaubonne, F. 1994. The time for ecofeminism. In *Ecology,* ed. C. Merchant. Atlantic Highlands, NJ: Humanities Press.

Deech, R., and A. Smajdor. 2007. *From IVF to immortality: Controversy in the era of reproductive technology.* New York: Oxford University Press.

de Ishtar, Z. 1994. *Daughters of the Pacific.* Melbourne, Australia: Spinifex Press.

De León, G., and R. Griswold del Castillo. 2006. *North to Aztlán: A history of Mexican Americans in the United States,* 2nd ed. Wheeling, IL: Harlan Davidson.

de Vise, D. 2012. Female VMI cadets offended by sexist online posts. *Washington Post,* February 7. www.washingtonpost.com/blogs/college-inc/post/female-vmi-cadets-offended-by-sexist-online-posts/2012/02/07/gIQAC57wwQ_blog.html

D'Emilio, J. 1984. Capitalism and gay identity. In *Powers of desire: The politics of sexuality,* ed. A. Snitow et al., pp. 100–13. New York: Monthly Review Press.

———, and E. Freedman. 1997. *Intimate matters: A history of sexuality in America.* 2nd ed. Chicago: University of Chicago Press.

Denman, J. E., and L. B. Inniss. 1999. No war without women: Defense industries. In *Gender camouflage: Women and the U.S. military,* ed. F. D'Amico and L. Weinstein, pp. 187–99. New York: New York University Press.

Department of Defense. 1996. *DoD news briefing: Mr. Kenneth H. Bacon.* www.defenselink.mil/transcripts/transcript.aspx?transcriptid=571

———. 1997. *DoD news briefing: Secretary of Defense William S. Cohen.* www.defenselink.mil/transcripts/transcript.aspx?transcriptid=419

———. 2008. *FY07 report on sexual assault in the military.* Washington, DC: Author.

———. 2010. *Department of Defense annual report on sexual assault in the military, FY 2010.* www.sapr.mil/media/pdf/reports/DoD_Fiscal_Year_2010_Annual_Report_on_Sexual_Assault_in_the_Military.pdf

Dermody, E. 2002. *Convicted survivors: The imprisonment of battered women who kill.* Albany: State University of New York Press.

Detention Watch Network. 2011. Securely insecure: The real costs, consequences and human face of immigration detention. www.detentionwatchnetwork.org/sites/detentionwatchnetwork.org/files/1.14.11_Fact%20Sheet%20FINAL_0.pdf.

Diamond, I., and G. F. Orenstein, eds. 1990. *Reweaving the world: The emergence of ecofeminism.* San Francisco: Sierra Club Books.

Diamond, L. M. 2008. *Sexual fluidity: Understanding women's love and desire.* Cambridge, MA: Harvard University Press.

Dibblin, J. 1989. *The day of two suns: U.S. nuclear testing and the Pacific Islands.* New York: New Amsterdam Books.

Di Chiro, G. 2009. Sustaining everyday life: Bringing together environmental, climate and reproductive justice. *Climate Change Series, no. 58.* Population and Development Program. http://popdev.hampshire.edu/projects/dt/58

Dicker, R., and A. Piepmeier, eds. 2003. *Catching a wave: Reclaiming feminism for the 21st century.* Boston: Northeastern University Press.

Digby, T., ed. 1998. *Men doing feminism.* New York: Routledge.

Dines, G. 2010. *PornLand: How pornography has hijacked our sexuality.* Boston: Beacon Press.

Dinnerstein, D. 1976. *Sexual arrangements and the human malaise.* New York: Harper & Row.

———. 1989. Surviving on earth: Meaning of feminism. In *Healing the wounds,* ed. J. Plant. Philadelphia: New Society.

Díaz-Cotto, J. 2006. *Chicana lives and criminal justice: Voice from el barrio.* Austin: University of Texas Press.

Domhoff, G. W. 2011. Wealth, income and power. www2.ucsc.edu/whorulesamerica/power/wealth.html

Donchin, A., and L. M. Purdy. 1999. *Embodying bioethics: Recent feminist advances.* Lanham, MD: Rowman and Littlefield.

Doress-Worters, P., and D. L. Siegal. 1994. *The new ourselves, growing older.* New York: Simon & Schuster.

Dorsey, E., and M. Thormodsgard. 2003. Rachel Carson warned us. *Ms.,* December 2002/January 2003, pp. 43–45.

Dougherty, A. 2007. No media, no progress, *Women's Review of Books,* 24(6): 25.

Douglas, S. 2010. *Enlightened sexism: The seductive message that feminism's work is done.* New York: Henry Holt.

Douglas, S. J., and M. W. Michaels. 2004. *The mommy myth: The idealization of motherhood and how it has undermined women.* New York: Free Press.

Drucker, J. L. 1998. *Lesbian and gay families speak out: Understanding the joys and challenges of diverse family life.* Cambridge, MA: Perseus.

Duberman M. B., M. Vicinus, and G. Chauncey Jr. 1989. *Hidden from history: Reclaiming the gay and lesbian past.* New York: New American Library.

Dubinsky, K. 2010. *Babies without borders: Adoption and migration across the Americas.* New York: New York University Press.

Ducat, S. J. 2004. *The wimp factor: Gender gaps, holy wars, and the politics of anxious masculinity.* Boston: Beacon Press.

Duff, K. 1993. *The alchemy of illness.* New York: Pantheon.

Duggan, L., and N. Hunter. 1995. *Sex wars: Sexual dissent and political culture.* New York: Routledge.

Duhigg, C., and D. Barboza. 2012. In China, human costs are built into an iPad, *New York Times*, January 25. www.nytimes.com/2012/01/26/business/ieconomy-apples-ipad-and-the-human-costs-for-workers-in-china.html?pagewanted=all

Dujon, D., and A. Withorn, eds. 1996. *For crying out loud: Women's poverty in the United States.* Boston: South End Press.

Dula, A. 1996. An African American perspective on reproductive freedoms. Panel on Reproduction, Race, and Class at the Third World Congress of Bioethics, Feminist Approaches to Bioethics, November, San Francisco.

DuPlessis, R. B., and A. Snitow, eds. 1998. *The Feminist Memoir Project: Voices from women's liberation.* New York: Three Rivers Press.

Duran, J. 1998. *Philosophies of science/feminist theories.* Boulder, CO: Westview Press.

Dworkin, A. 1987. *Intercourse.* New York: Free Press.

———. 1993. *Letters from a war zone.* Chicago: Chicago Review Press.

Echols, A. 1989. *Daring to be bad: Radical feminism in America 1967–1975.* Minneapolis: University of Minnesota Press.

Edison, L. T., and D. Notkin. 1994. *Women en large: Images of fat nudes.* San Francisco: Books in Focus.

Ehrenreich, B. 2001. *Nickel and dimed: On (not) getting by in America.* New York: Henry Holt/Metropolitan Books.

———, and D. English. 2010. *Witches, midwives, and nurses: A history of women healers,* 2nd ed. Old Westbury, NY: Feminist Press.

———, and A. R. Hochschild, eds. 2003. *Global woman: Nannies, maids, and sex workers in the new economy.* New York: Henry Holt.

Ehrenreich, B., E. Hess, and G. Jacobs. 1986. *Remaking love: The feminization of sex.* New York: Anchor/Doubleday.

Eisenstein, Z. R. 1979. *Capitalism, patriarchy, and the case for socialist feminism.* New York: Monthly Review Press.

———. 1981. *The radical future of liberal feminism.* New York: Longman.

———. 1998. Socialist feminism. In *The reader's companion to U.S. women's history,* ed. W. Mankiller, G. Mink, M. Navarro, B. Smith, and G. Steinem, pp. 218–19. Boston: Houghton Mifflin.

Eisler, R. 2007. *The real wealth of nations: Creating a caring economics.* San Francisco: BK.

Elam, H., and K. Jackson, eds. 2005. *Black cultural traffic: Crossroads in global performance and popular culture.* Ann Arbor: University of Michigan Press.

Emmet, B. 2009. Paying the price for the economic crisis. Oxfam International Discussion paper. www.oxfam.org/en/policy/women-workers-pay-price-global-economic-crisis

Eng, D., and A. Y. Hom, eds. 1998. *Q & A: Queer in Asian America.* Philadelphia: Temple University.

Enloe, C. 1983. *Does khaki become you? The militarization of women's lives.* Boston: South End Press.

———. 1990. *Bananas, beaches and bases: Making feminist sense of international politics.* Berkeley: University of California Press.

———. 1993. *The morning after: Sexual politics at the end of the cold war.* Berkeley: University of California Press.

———. 1995. The globetrotting sneaker, *Ms.*, March/April, pp. 10–15.

———. 2000a. *Maneuvers: The international politics of militarizing women's lives.* Berkeley: University of California Press.

———. 2000b. Masculinity as foreign policy issue. *Foreign Policy in Focus* 5(36). www.fpif.org/briefs/vol5/v5n36masculinity_body.html

———. 2007. *Globalization and militarism: feminists make the links.* Lanham, MD: Rowman and Littlefield.

Enos, S. 2001. *Mothering from the inside: Parenting in a women's prison.* Albany: State University of New York Press.

Ensler, E. 1998. *The vagina monologues.* New York: Villard/Random House.

Epstein, B. 1993. Ecofeminism and grassroots environmentalism in the United States. In *Toxic struggles: The theory and practice of environmental justice,* ed. R. Hofrichter, pp. 144–52. Philadelphia and Gabriola Island, BC: New Society.

Eridani. 1992. Is sexual orientation a secondary sex characteristic? In *Closer to home: Bisexuality and feminism,* ed. E. R. Weise. Seattle, WA: Seal Press.

Ettelbrick, P. 1989. Since when is marriage a path to liberation? *Out/Look: National Gay and Lesbian Quarterly,* no. 6 (Fall).

Evans, S. 1980. *Personal politics.* New York: Vintage Books.

Ewing, B., D. Moore, S. Goldfinger, A. Oursler, A. Reed, and M. Wackernagel. 2010. *The ecological footprint atlas.* Oakland: Global Footprint Network.

Facts on the global sweatshop. 1997. *Rethinking Schools: An Urban Education Journal* 11(4): 16.

Faderman, L. 1981. *Surpassing the love of men: Romantic friendship and love between women from the Renaissance to the present.* New York: William Morrow.

Falcón, S. 2006. "National security" and the violation of women: Militarized border rape at the US-Mexico border. In *Color of violence: The Incite! anthology,* ed. Incite! Women of Color Against Violence, pp. 119–129. Cambridge, MA: South End Press.

Falk, J. 2003. Fiscal lockdown, *Dollars and Sense,* July/August, pp. 19–23, 45.

Faludi, S. 1991. *Backlash: The undeclared war against women.* New York: Crown.

Family Equality Coalition. 2011. LGBT families: Facts at a glance. http://action.familyequality.org/site/DocServer/AllChildrenMatterFactsFinal10192011.pdf?docID=2404

Fausto-Sterling, A. 1993. The five sexes: Why male and female are not enough. *The Sciences,* March/April, pp. 20–24.

———. 2000. The five sexes, revisited. *Sciences,* July/August 40(4):18. www.neiu.edu/lsfuller/5sexesrevisited.htm

FBI Crime Report. 2009. Crime rates continue to decline. December 21. www.fbi.gov/news/stories/2009/december/crimestats_122109

Featherstone, L. 2002. *Students against sweatshops: The making of a movement.* New York: Verso.

———. 2004. Will labor take the Wal-Mart challenge? *The Nation,* June 28.

Feinberg, L. 1996. *Transgender warriors: Making history from Joan of Arc to RuPaul.* Boston: Beacon Press.

———. 1998. *Trans liberation: Beyond pink or blue.* Boston: Beacon Press.

Feldt, G. 2004. *The war on choice: The right wing attack on women's rights and how to fight back.* New York: Bantam.

Feminist Anti-Censorship Task Force. 1992. *Caught looking: Feminism, pornography, and censorship.* East Haven, CT: Long River Books.

Ferguson, K., and P. Turnbull. 2004. Globalizing militaries. In *Rethinking globalism,* ed. M. B. Steger, pp. 79–91. Lanham, MD: Rowman and Littlefield.

Fernández-Kelly, M. P. 1983. *For we are sold, I and my people: Women and industry in Mexico's frontier.* Albany: State University of New York Press.

Fiduccia, B. W., and M. Saxton. 1997. Disability feminism: A manifesto. *New Mobility: Disability Culture and Life-style* 8(49): 60–61.

Findlen, B., ed. 1995. *Listen up: Voices from the next feminist generation.* Seattle, WA: Seal Press.

Fine, M., and A. Asch, eds. 1988. *Women with disabilities: Essays in psychology, culture and politics.* Philadelphia: Temple University Press.

Fineman, M. A., and R. Mykitiuk, eds. 1994. *The public nature of private violence: The discovery of domestic abuse.* New York: Routledge.

Finger, A. 1990. *Past due: A story of disability, pregnancy, and birth.* Seattle, WA: Seal Press.

Firestone, S. 1970. *The dialectics of sex: The case for feminist revolution.* New York: Morrow.

Fisher. B., F. Cullen, and M. Turner. 2000. *The sexual victimization of college women.* Washington, DC: U.S. Department of Justice and the National Institute of Justice.

Flax, J. 1986. Gender as a social problem: In and for feminist theory. *Amerikastudien/American Studies* 31: 193–213.

Folbre, N. 2001. *The invisible heart: Economics and family values.* New York: New Press.

Foo, L.J., G. Villareal, and N. Timbang. 2007. The Trafficking of Asian Women. In *Asian American Women: Issues, concerns, and responsive human and civil rights advocacy,* eds. L. J. Foo. 2nd ed. New York: National Asian American Women's Forum, iUniverse.

Food and Agriculture Organization. 2011. The state of food insecurity in the world. www.fao.org/docrep/014/i2330e/i2381e00.pdf

Ford, L. E. 2002. *Women and politics: The pursuit of equality.* Boston: Houghton Mifflin.

Foster, C. 1989. *Women for all seasons: The story of W.I.L.P.F.* Athens: University of Georgia Press.

Fouhy, B. 2004. Gay, patriotic and banished. *San Francisco Examiner,* June 21, p. 1.

Fox-Genovese, E. 1994. Beyond individualism: The new Puritanism, feminism, and women. *Salmagundi* 101(2): 79–95.

Fraden, R. 2001. *Imagining medea: Rhodessa Jones and theater for incarcerated women.* Chapel Hill: University of North Carolina Press.

Frankenberg, R. 1993. *White women, race matters: The social construction of whiteness.* Minneapolis: University of Minnesota Press.

Freeman, C. 2000. *High tech and high heels in the global economy: Women, work and pink-collar identities in the Caribbean.* Durham, NC: Duke University Press.

Freeman, J. 2008. *We will be heard: Women's struggles for political power in the United States.* Lanham, MD: Rowman and Littlefield.

Fregoso, R-L., and C. Bejarano, eds. 2010. *Terrorizing women: Feminicide in the Americas.* Durham, NC: Duke University Press.

Freire, P. 1989. *Pedagogy of the oppressed.* New York: Continuum.

Friedan, B. 1963. *The feminine mystique.* New York: W. W. Norton.

Friedman, M., and S. L. Calixte. 2009. *Mothering and blogging: The radical act of the mommyblog.* Toronto, ON: Demeter Press.

Frye, M. 1992. *Willful virgin: Essays in feminism 1976–1992.* Freedom, CA: The Crossing Press.

Fuchs, L. 1990. The reaction of Black Americans to immigration. In *Immigration reconsidered,* ed. V. Yans-McLaughlin. New York: Oxford University Press.

Fukumura, Y., and M. Matsuoka. 2002. Redefining security: Okinawa women's resistance to U.S. militarism. In *Women's activism and globalization: Linking local struggles and transnational politics,* ed. Nancy Naples and Manisha Desai, pp. 239–263. New York: Routledge.

Gaard, G., ed. 1993. *Ecofeminism: Women, animals, nature.* Philadelphia: Temple University Press.

Gage, S., L. Richards, and H. Wilmot. 2002. *Queer.* New York: Thunder's Mouth Press.

Gaines, P. 1994. *Laughing in the dark: From colored girl to woman of color—a journey from prison to power.* New York: Anchor Books.

Gallagher, N. W. 1993. The gender gap in popular attitudes toward the use of force. In *Women and the use of military force,* ed. R. Howes and M. Stevenson, pp. 23–37. Boulder, CO: Lynne Rienner.

Garcia, C. A., and J. Lane. 2009. What a girl wants, what a girl needs. Findings from a gender-specific focus group study. *Crime and Delinquency.* doi: 10.1177/0011128709331790

Garland, A. W. 1989. *For our kids' sake: How to protect your children against pesticides in food.* New York: Natural Resources Defense Council.

Garside, J. 2012. Apple's factories in China are breaking employment laws, audit finds, *The Guardian,* March 29. www.guardian.co.uk/technology/2012/mar/30/apple-factories-china-foxconn-audit

Gaspar de Alba, A., and Guzmán, G., eds. 2010. *Making a killing. Femicide, free trade, and la frontera.* Austin: University of Texas Press.

Gavey, N., K. McPhillips, and M. Doherty. 2001. "If it's not on, it's not on"—or is it? Discursive constraints on women's condom use. *Gender and Society* 15(6): 917–34.

Geller, J. 2001. *Here comes the bride: Women, weddings, and the marriage mystique.* New York: Four Walls Eight Windows.

George, S. 1988. Getting your own back: Solving the Third World debt crisis. *New Statesman & Society,* July 15, p. 20.

Gettelman, E. 2005. The Pentagon v. abuse: An interview with Deborah Tucker. *Mother Jones,* June 28.

Gibbs, L. 1995. *Dying from dioxin: A citizens' guide to reclaiming our health and rebuilding democracy.* Boston: South End Press.

———. 1998. *Love canal: The story continues.* Gabriola Island, BC: New Society.

Gilkes, C.T. 1988. Building in many places: Multiple commitments and ideologies in Black women's community work.

In *Women and the politics of empowerment,* eds. A. Bookman and S. Morgen. Philadeplia: Temple University Press.

Ginsburg, F. D., and R. Rapp. 1995. *Conceiving the new world order: The global politics of reproduction.* Berkeley: University of California Press.

Giordano, P., S. Kerbel, and S. Dudley. 1981. The economics of female criminality. In *Women and crime in America,* ed. L. Bowker, pp. 15–82. New York: Macmillan.

Girshick, L. B. 2002. *Women-to-women sexual violence.* Boston: Northeastern University Press.

Girshick, L. 2008. *Transgender voices; Beyond women and men.* Lebanon, NH: University Press of New England.

Glantz, A. 2007. Coke faces new charges in India, including "greenwashing." *One World,* June 7. http://us.oneworld.net/section/us/current

Glaze, L. E., and T. P. Bonczar. 2011. Probation and parole in the United States, 2010. Bureau of Justice Statistics. http://bjs.ojp.usdoj.gov/content/pub/pdf/ppus10.pdf
———, and L. M. Maruschak. 2008. Parents in prison and their minor children. Bureau of Justice Statistics special report, revised 3/30/2010. http://bjs.ojp.usdoj.gov/content/pub/pdf/pptmc.html

Gleick, E. 1996. Scandal in the military. *Time,* 25 November, 28–31.

Gluck, S. 1976. *From parlor to prison: Five American suffragists talk about their lives.* New York: Vintage Books.

Gluck, S. B. 1987. *Rosie the riveter revisited: Women, war and social change.* Boston: Twayne.

Gold, J., and S. Villari, eds. 2000. *Just sex: Students rewrite the rules on sex, violence, activism, and equality.* Lanham, MD: Rowman and Littlefield.

Gold, S. S. 2011. *Food: The good girl's drug. How to stop using food to control your feelings.* New York: Berkley Books.

Golden, R. 2005. *War on the family: Mothers in prison and the families they leave behind.* New York: Routledge.

Gonen, J. S. 2003. *Litigation as lobbying: Reproductive hazards and interest aggregation.* Columbus: Ohio State University Press.

Gonzalez, D. 2008. The lost supermarket: A breed in need of replenishment. *New York Times.* May 5. www.nytimes.com/2008/05/05/nyregion/05citywide.html?_r=1&oref=slogin

Goodstein, E. 1999. *The trade-off myth: Fact and fiction about jobs and the environment.* Washington, DC: Island Press.

Goodstein, L. 2012. Bishops reject White House's new plan on contraception. *New York Times,* February 11. www.nytimes.com/2012/02/12/us/catholic-bishops-criticize-new-contraception-proposal.html

Gordon, L. 1988. *Heroes of their own lives: The politics and history of family violence, Boston 1880–1960.* New York: Viking.
———. 1997. Killing in self-defense. *The Nation,* March 24, pp. 25–28.

Gore, A. 2004. *The essential* Hip Mama: *Writing from the cutting edge of parenting.* Seattle, WA: Seal Press.

Gore, A., and B. Lavendar. 2001. *Breeder: Real life stories from the new generation of mothers.* Seattle, WA: Seal Press.

Goss R., and A. S. Strongheart, eds. 1997. *Our families, our values: Snapshots of queer kinship.* New York: Harrington Park Press.

Gottschalk, M. 2006. *The prison and the gallows: The politics of mass incarceration in America.* New York: Cambridge University Press.

Gottlieb, R., and A. Joshi. 2010. *Food justice.* Cambridge: Massachusetts Institute of Technology.

Government Accountability Office. 2011. Military justice: Oversight and better collaboration needed for sexual assault investigations and adjudications. GAO-11-579, June 22. www.gao.gov/products/GAO-11-579?source=ra

Gozemba, P., K. Kahn, and M. Humphries. 2007. *Courting equality: A documentary history of America's first legal same-sex marriages.* Boston: Beacon Press.

Grady, D. 2000. Study backs hormone link to cancer for women. *New York Times,* January 27, p. A17.

Grahn, J. 1984. *Another mother tongue: Gay words, gay worlds.* Boston: Beacon Press.

Grail, T. 2009. Custodial mothers and fathers and their child support: 2007. U. S. Census Department. www.census.gov/prod/2009pubs/p60-237.pdf

Green, J., ed. 2007. *Making space for indigenous feminism.* New York: Zed Books.

Greider, W. 1997. *One world ready or not: The manic logic of global capitalism.* New York: Simon & Schuster.

Griffin, S. 1971. Rape: The all-American crime. *Ramparts* 10(3): 26–35.
———. 1978. *Woman and nature: The roaring inside her.* San Francisco: Harper Colophon.
———. 1999. *What her body thought: A journey into the shadows.* San Francisco: Harper San Francisco.

Gross, J. 1992. A jail garden's harvest: Hope and redemption, *New York Times,* September 3.

Grossholtz, J. 1998. The search for peace and justice: Notes toward an autobiography. In *Women's Lives: Multicultural perpectives,* 1st ed. New York: McGraw-Hill.

Grossman, R. 1998a. Can corporations be accountable? (Part 1). *Rachel's Environment and Health Weekly,* July 30, pp. 1–2.
———. 1998b. Can corporations be accountable? (Part 2). *Rachel's Environment and Health Weekly,* August 6, pp. 1–2.

Guenter-Schlesinger, S. 1999. Persistence of sexual harassment: The impact of military culture on policy implementation. In *Beyond zero tolerance,* ed. M. Katzenstein and J. Reppy, pp. 195–212. Lanham, MD: Rowman and Littlefield.

Guerino, P., P. M. Harrison, and W. J. Sabol. 2011. Prisoners in 2010. Bureau of Justice Statistics. http://bjs.gov/index.cfm?ty=pbdetail&iid=2230

Gullette, M. M. 2004. *Aged by culture.* Chicago: University of Chicago Press.
———. 2011. *Agewise: Fighting the new ageism in America.* Chicago: University of Chicago Press.

Gupta, V., and L. Graybill. 2009. Justice denied: Immigrant families detained at Hutto. *ACLU of Texas.* www.udhr60.org/justice_denied.pdf

Gustafson, K. 2005. *To punish the poor: Criminalizing trends in the welfare system.* Oakland: Women of Color Resource Center.

Guthman, J. 2011. *Weighing in: Obesity, food justice, and the limits of capitalism.* Berkeley: University of California Press.

Guttmacher Institute. 2011. An overview of abortion in the United States. www.guttmacher.org/presentations/abort_slides.pdf
———. 2012. *An overview of abortion laws.* www.guttmacher.org/statecenter/spibs/spib_OAL.pdf

Guy-Sheftall, Beverly, ed. 1995. *Words of fire: An anthology of African-American feminist thought.* New York: The New Press.

Haines, S. 1999. *The survivor's guide to sex: How to have an empowered sex life after childhood sexual abuse.* San Francisco: Cleis Press.

Halberstam, J. 1998. *Female masculinity.* Durham, NC: Duke University Press.

———. 2005. *In a queer time and place.* New York: New York University Press.

Hall, G. M. 1999. Intersectionality: A necessary consideration for women of color in the military? In *Beyond zero tolerance,* ed. M. Katzenstein and J. Reppy, pp. 143–61. Lanham, MD: Rowman and Littlefield.

Hall, K. Q., 2011. Feminist disability studies. Bloomington: Indiana University Press.

Halva-Neubauer, G. A., and S. L. Zeigler. 2010. Promoting fetal personhood: The rhetorical and legislative strategies of the pro-life movement after *Planned Parenthood v. Casey. Feminist Formations* 22(2): 101–23.

Hamer, D., and B. Budge. 1994. *The good, the bad and the gorgeous: Popular culture's romance with lesbianism.* London: Pandora.

Hamilton, B. E., J. A. Martin, and S. J. Ventura. 2011. *Births: Preliminary data for 2010. National Vital Statistics Report* 60(2). www.cdc.gov/nchs/data/nvsr/nvsr60/nvsr60_02.pdf

———. 2007. Births: Preliminary data for 2006. *National Vital Statistics Reports* 56(7). Washington, DC: Centers for Disease Control and Prevention.

Hamilton, C. 1993. Coping with industrial exploitation. In *Confronting environmental racism: Voices from the grassroots,* ed. R. Bullard. Boston: South End Press.

Hamilton, J. T. 2004. *All the news that's fit to sell: How the market transforms information into news.* Princeton, NJ: Princeton University Press.

Hammonds, E. 1995. Missing persons: African American women, AIDS, and the history of disease. In *Words of fire: An anthology of African-American feminist thought,* ed. B. Guy-Sheftall, pp. 443–49. New York: New Press.

Hamre, J. 1998. *Racial, gender bias will not be tolerated.* Speech to World-Wide Equal Opportunity Conference, July 26. www.defenselink.mil/speeches/speech.aspx?speechid5722

Hans, J. D., M. Gillen, and K. Akande. 2010. Sex redefined: The reclassification of oral-genital contact. *Perspectives on Sexual and Reproductive Health* 42(2): 74–78.

Hansen, C. 2001. A considerable service: An advocate's introduction to domestic violence and the military. *Domestic Violence Report* 6(4): 49, 50, 60–64.

Harding, K. 2009. Is there a next generation of abortion providers? *Salon,* June 15. www.salon.com/2009/06/15/abortion_providers_2/

Harding, S. 1987. *Feminism and methodology: Social science issues.* Bloomington: University of Indiana Press.

———. 1998. *Is science multicultural? Postcolonialisms, feminisms, and epistemologies.* Bloomington: Indiana University Press.

———, ed. 2004. *The feminist standpoint theory reader: Intellectual and political controversies.* New York: Routledge.

Harman, B. 1996. Happy ending. In *"Women in the trees": U.S. women's short stories about battering and resistance, 1839–1994,* ed. S. Koppelman, pp. 286–90. Boston: Beacon Press.

Harman. J. 2008. Rapists in the ranks: Sexual assaults are frequent, and frequently ignored, in the armed services. *Los Angeles Times.* March 31. www.latimes.com/news/opinion/commentary/la-oe- harman31mar31,0,5399612.story

Harne, L., and E. Miller, eds. 1996. *All the rage: Reasserting radical lesbian feminism.* New York: Teachers College Press.

Harper, A. B. 2010. *Sistah vegan: Food, identity, health and society: Black female vegans speak.* Brooklyn: Lantern Books.

Hartmann, B. 1995. Dangerous intersections. *Political Environments,* no. 2 (summer): 1–7. Publication of the Committee on Women, Population and the Environment, Hampshire College, Amherst, MA.

Hartmann, H. 1981. The unhappy marriage of Marxism and feminism: Towards a more progressive union. In *Women and revolution: A discussion of the unhappy marriage of Marxism and feminism,* ed. L. Sargent. Boston: South End Press.

———. 2012. *Can boomer women afford to retire?* Washington, DC: Institute for Women's Policy Research. www.iwpr.org/publications/pubs/can-boomer-women-afford-to-retire

Hartsock, N. 1983. *Money, sex, and power: Toward a feminist historical materialism.* New York: Longman.

Hawthorne, S. 2002. *Wild politics: Feminism, globalization, bio/diversity.* Melbourne, Australia: Spinifex.

Hays, S. 1996. *The cultural contradictions of motherhood.* New Haven, CT: Yale University Press.

———. 2004. *Flat broke with children: Women in the age of welfare reform.* New York: Oxford University Press.

Healey, S. 1997. Confronting ageism: A MUST for mental health. In *In our own words: Readings on the psychology of women and gender,* ed. M. Crawford and R. Unger, pp. 368–76. New York: McGraw-Hill.

Heath, J., and A. Zahedi. 2011. *Land of the unconquerable: The lives of contemporary Afghan women.* Berkeley: University of California Press.

Heidenreich, L. 2011. Transgender women, sexual violence, and the rule of law: An argument in favor of restorative and transformative justice. In *Razor wire women,* ed. J. M. Lawston and A. E. Lucas. Albany: State University of New York Press.

Heise, J. Pitanguy, and A. Germain. 1994. *Violence against women: The hidden health burden.* World Bank Discussion Papers #255. Washington, DC: The World Bank.

Hemmings, C. 2002. *Bisexual spaces: A geography of sexuality and gender.* New York: Routledge.

Henderson, H. 1991. *Paradigms in progress: Life beyond economics.* Indianapolis: Knowledge Systems.

Henderson, K. 2004. The siege. *Washington Post,* October 10.

———. 2006. *While they're at war: The true story of American families on the homefront.* New York: Houghton Mifflin.

Hennessy, R., and C. Ingraham, eds. 1997. *Materialist feminism: A reader in class, difference, and women's lives.* New York: Routledge.

Herivel, T., and P. Wright, eds. 2003. *Prison nation: The warehousing of America's poor.* New York: Routledge.

———, eds. 2007. *Prison profiteers. Who makes money from mass incarceration.* New York: New Press.

Herman, J. 1992. *Trauma and recovery.* New York: Basic Books.

Hernández, A. 1975. *Equal Opportunity Commission and the women's movement (1965–1975).* Unpublished paper for the Symposium on the Tenth Anniversary of the U.S. EEOC, sponsored by Rutgers University Law School, November 28–29.

———. 2002. *In pursuit of equality: The ups and downs in the struggle for inclusion.* Available from Aileen C. Hernández Associates, 818 47th Ave., San Francisco, CA 94121.

Hernandez, J., 2011. On visual politics and poetics: Incarcerated girls and women artists. In *Razor wire women,* ed. J. M. Lawston and A. E Lucas. Albany: State University of New York Press.

Hernández, R., and B. Flory. 2005. The label is Justicia! *Quaker Action,* 86(1): 7.

Hesse-Biber, S. J. 1996. *Am I thin enough yet?* New York: Oxford University Press.

Heymann, J. 2006. *Forgotten families: Ending the growing crisis confronting children and working parents in the global economy.* New York: Oxford University Press.

Heywood, L., and J. Drake. 1997. *Third wave agenda: Being feminist, doing feminism.* Minneapolis: University of Minnesota Press.

Hicks, G. 1997. *The Comfort Women; Japan's brutal regime of enforced prostitution in the Second World War.* New York: W. W. Norton.

Hill, F., and M. Aboitiz. 2002. Women are opening doors: Security Council Resolution 1325 in Afghanistan. In *Women for Afghan women: Shattering myths and claiming the future,* ed. Sunita Mehta, pp. 156–165. New York: Palgrave/Macmillan.

Hiller, L., L. Gates, N. Munger, N. Douttiel, E. Ehrlich-Walsh, and M. Zepernick. 2005. *Save the water: A curriculum study guide.* Philadelphia: Women's International League for Peace and Freedom.

History Project. 1998. *Improper Bostonians: Lesbian and gay history from the Puritans to Playland.* Boston: Beacon Press.

Hite, S. 1994. *Women as revolutionary agents of change: The Hite Report and beyond.* Madison: University of Wisconsin Press.

Hochschild, A. R. 1989. *The second shift: Working parents and the revolution at home.* New York: Viking.

———. 1997. *The time bind: When work becomes home and home becomes work.* New York: Henry Holt.

Hofrichter, R., ed. 1993. *Toxic struggles: The theory and practice of environmental justice.* Philadelphia and Gabriola Island, BC: New Society.

Holmstedt, K. 2007. *Band of sisters: American women at war in Iraq.* Mechanicsburg, PA: Stackpole Books.

Hondagneu-Sotelo, P. 2001. *Doméstica: Immigrant workers cleaning and caring in the shadows of affluence.* Berkeley: University of California Press.

Honderich, K. 2003. *The real cost of prison for women and their children.* Washington, DC: The Real Cost of Prisons Project/The Sentencing Project.

hooks, b. 1984a. *Feminist theory: From margin to center.* Boston: South End Press.

———. 1984b. Feminist movement to end violence. In *Feminist theory: From margin to center,* ed. b. hooks, pp. 117–31. Boston: South End Press.

———. 1993. *Sisters of the yam: Black women and self recovery.* Boston: South End Press.

———. 1994. Seduced by violence no more. In *Outlaw culture: Resisting representations,* ed. b. hooks, pp. 109–13. New York: Routledge.

———. 2000. *Feminism is for everybody: Passionate politics.* Cambridge, MA: South End Press.

Hoon, S. 2010. *Dreaming a world: Korean birthmothers tell their stories.* St. Paul, MN: Yeong and Yeong.

Houppert, K. 2005a. Base crime. *Mother Jones,* July/August.

———. 2005b. *Home fires burning: Married to the military—for better or worse.* New York: Ballantine.

Howe, F., ed. 2000. *The politics of women's studies: Testimony from 30 founding mothers.* New York: The Feminist Press at the City University of New York.

Howey, N., and E. Samuels, eds. 2000. *Out of the ordinary: Essays on growing up with gay, lesbian, and transgender parents.* New York: St. Martin's Press.

Hubbard, R. 1989. Science, facts, and feminism. In *Feminism and science,* ed. N. Tuana. Bloomington: Indiana University Press.

———. 1990. *The politics of women's biology.* New Brunswick, NJ: Rutgers University Press.

Hübinette, T. 2006. From orphan trains to babylifts: Colonial trafficking, empire building, and social engineering. In *Outsiders within: Writing on transracial adoption,* ed. Jane Jeong Trenka, Julia Chinyere Oparah, and Sun Yung Shin, pp. 139–149. Cambridge, MA: South End Press.

Human Rights Watch. 2011. US: Protect against rape in immigration detention. June 24. www.hrw.org/news/2011/06/24/us-protect-against-rape-immigration-detention

Humphrey, S., and A. Kahn. 2000. Fraternities, athletic teams and rape: Importance of identification with a risky group. *Journal of Interpersonal Violence,* 15(12): 1313–22.

Hutchins, L., and L. Ka'ahumanu. 1991. *Bi any other name: Bisexual people speak out.* Boston: Alyson.

Hynes, H. P. 1989. *The recurring silent spring.* New York: Pergamon Press.

———. 1996. *A patch of Eden.* White River Junction, VT: Chelsea Green.

———. 1999. Consumption: North American perspectives. In *Dangerous intersections: Feminist perspectives on population, environment, and development,* ed. J. Silliman and Y. King. Cambridge, MA: South End Press.

Indigo, Susannah. 2000. *Blow jobs and other boring stuff: Teens have casually redefined what used to be called sex.* http://www.salon.com/sex/feature/2000/12/14/teens/print.html

Ingraham, C. 2004. *Thinking straight: The power, promise, and paradox of heterosexuality.* New York: Routledge.

In Phoenix chain gangs for women. 1996. *New York Times,* 28 August, p. C1.

Institute for Policy Studies. 2000. *International grassroots summit on military base cleanup conference report.* Washington, DC: Institute for Policy Studies.

Institute for Women's Policy Research. 2011. Social Security helps older women, especially Black women and Latinas, stay out of poverty. www.iwpr.org/press-room/press-releases/new-research-social-security-helps-older-women-especially-black-women-and-latinas-stay-out-of-poverty

Intergovernmental Panel on Climate Change. 2007. Fourth Assessment Report: Climate Change Synthesis Report. Available at HYPERLINK "http://www.ipcc.ch/publications_and_data/ar4/syr/en/contents.html" www.ipcc.ch/publications_and_data/ar4/syr/en/contents.html. Accessed May 12, 2012.

International Organization for Migration. 2007. *About migration.* www.iom.int/jahia/Jahia/lang/en/pid/3

Isakson, E., ed. 1988. *Women and the military system.* New York: St. Martin's Press.

Iwamura, J. M. 2007. Critical faith: Japanese Americans and the birth of a new civil religion. *American Quarterly* 59(3): 937–968.

Jacob, K. 2002. *Our choices, our lives: Unapologetic writings on abortion.* Minneapolis: Writers Advantage.

Jacobsen, C. 2008. Creative politics and women's criminalization in the United States. *Signs* 33(2).

Jaggar, A. M. ed. 1994. *Living with contradictions: Controversies in feminist social ethics.* Boulder, CO: Westview Press.

Jaimes, A., and T. Halsey. 1986. American Indian women at the center of indigenous resistance in contemporary North America. In *The state of Native America: Genocide, colonization, and resistance,* ed. A. Jaimes, pp. 311–44. Boston: South End Press.

Jamall, D. 2010a. Rape rampant in U.S. military. *Al Jazeera.* December 21. http://english.aljazeera.net/indepth/features/2010/12/2010122182546344551.html

―――. 2010b. Military sexual abuse "staggering." *Al Jazeera.* December 23. http://english.aljazeera.net/indepth/2010/12/20101223113859171112.html

Jefferis, J. L. 2011. *Armed for life: The Army of God and anti-abortion terror in the United States.* Santa Barbara, CA: Praeger.

Jeffreys, Sheila. 1997. *The idea of prostitution.* North Melbourne, Australia: Spinifex.

Jetter, A., A. Orleck, and D. Taylor, eds. 1997. *The politics of motherhood: Activist voices from left to right.* Hanover, NH: University Press of New England.

Joffe, C. 1995. *Doctors of conscience: The struggle to provide abortion before and after* Roe v. Wade. Boston: Beacon Press.

―――. 2009. *Dispatches from the abortion wars: The costs of fanaticism to doctors, patients, and the rest of us.* Boston: Beacon Press.

Johnson, A. G. 2005. *The gender knot: Unraveling our patriarchal legacy.* Philadelphia: Temple University Press.

Johnson, M. L. 2002. *Jane sexes it up: True confessions of feminist desire.* New York: Four Walls, Eight Windows.

Johnson, P. C. 2002. *Inner lives: Voices of African American women in prison.* New York: New York University Press.

Jones, A. 1980. *Women who kill.* New York: Holt, Rinehart, and Winston.

―――. 1994. *Next time, she'll be dead: Battering and how to stop it.* Boston: Beacon Press.

Jones-DeWeever, A. A. 2007. *Women in the wake of the storm: Examining the post-Katrina realities of the women of New Orleans and the Gulf coast.* Washington, DC: Institute for Women's Policy Research.

Jones, V. 2008. *The Green Collar Economy: How one solution can fix our two biggest problems.* New York: HarperOne.

Jong, E. 1998. Ally McBeal and *Time* magazine can't keep the good women down. *New York Observer,* July 13, p. 19.

Jordan, J. 1985. Report from the Bahamas. In *On call: Political essays.* Boston: South End Press.

―――. 1992. A new politics of sexuality. In *Technical difficulties: African american notes on the state of the union.* New York: Pantheon Books.

Josefowitz, N. 1980. *Paths to Power: A woman's guide from first job to top executive.* Reading, Mass.: Addison Wesley.

Juhasz, A. 2010. Man-made, women-saved. *Ms.,* Summer, pp. 48–49.

Just Detention. 2012. Vulnerable inmates. www.justdetention.org/en/vulnerable.aspx

Justice Policy Institute. 2002. *Cell blocks or classrooms?* Washington, DC: Justice Policy Institute. www.justicepolicy.org/article.php?id=3

―――. 2011. Crime, incarceration down in 2010. www.justicepolicy.org/uploads/justicepolicy/documents/fbi_ucr_2010_factsheet_final.pdf

Kadi, J. 1996. *Thinking class: Sketches from a cultural worker.* Boston: South End Press.

Kaiser Family Foundation. 2012. Fact sheet: Women and HIV/AIDs in the United States. www.kff.org/hivaids/upload/6092-10.pdf.

Kamel, R. 1990. *The global factory: Analysis and action for a new economic era.* Philadelphia: American Friends Service Committee.

Kamen, P. 2000. *Her way: Young women make the sexual revolution.* New York: New York University Press.

Kandaswamy, P. 2008. State austerity and the racial politics of same sex marriage in the United States. *Sexualities: Studies in Culture and Society* 11(6): 707–26.

Kang, M. 2010. *The managed hand: Race, gender and the body in beauty service work.* Berkeley: University of California Press.

Kaplan, L. 1995. *The story of Jane: The legendary underground feminist abortion service.* New York: Pantheon Books.

Kaplan, T. 1997. *Crazy for democracy: Women in grassroots movements.* New York: Routledge.

Kaschak, E., ed. 2002. *Intimate betrayal: Domestic violence in lesbian relationships.* New York: Haworth Press.

Kates, E., and P. Ransford, with Carol Cardozo. 2005. *Women in prison in Massachusetts: Maintaining family connections—A research report.* Boston: Center for Women in Politics and Public Policy, McCormack Graduate School of Public Policy, University of Massachusetts.

Katz, J. N. 1995. *The invention of heterosexuality.* New York: Plume.

Katz Rothman, B. 1986. *Tentative pregnancy: Prenatal diagnosis and the future of motherhood.* New York: Viking.

Katzenstein, M. F. 1993. The right to fight. *Women's Review of Books* 11(2): 30–31.

Kaufman, M., and M. Kimmel. 2011. *The guy's guide to feminism.* Emeryville, CA: Seal Press.

Kaufman, M., C. Silverberg, and F. Odette. 2003. *The ultimate guide to sex and disability: For all of us with disabilities, chronic pain and illness.* San Francisco: Cleis Press.

Kawachi, I., N. Daniels, and D. Robinson. 2005. Health disparities by race and class: Why both matter, *Health Affairs,* 24(2): 343–352.

Kaye/Kantrowitz, M. 1992. *The issue is power: Essays on women, Jews, violence, and resistance.* San Franciso: Aunt Lute Books.

Kaysen, S. 1994. *Girl interrupted.* New York: Vintage Books.

Kearney, M. C. 2006. *Girls make media.* New York: Routledge.

Kellner, D., and J. Share. 2005. Toward critical media literacy: Core concepts, debates, organizations, and policy. *Discourse: Studies in the Cultural Politics of Education* 26(3): 369–86.

Kempadoo, K., and J. Doezema, eds. 1998. *Global sex workers: Rights, resistance and redefinition.* New York: Routledge.

Kerr, J., ed. 1993. *Ours by right: Women's rights as human rights.* London: Zed Books.

Kesic, V. 2000. From reverence to rape: An anthropology of ethnic and genderized violence. In *Frontline feminisms: Women, war, and resistance,* ed, Marguerite Waller and Jennifer Rycenga. New York: Garland Publishing.

Kettel, B. 1996. Women, health and the environment. *Social Science Medicine* 42(10): 1367–79.

Kich, G. K. 1992. The developmental process of asserting a biracial, bicultural identity. In *Racially mixed people in America,* ed. M. P. Root, pp. 304–17. Newbury Park, CA: Sage.

Kilbourne, J. 1999. *Deadly persuasion: Why women and girls must fight the addictive power of advertising.* New York: Free Press.

Kim, E. 2010. *Adopted territory: Transnational Korean adoptees and the politics of belonging.* Durham, NC: Duke University Press.

Kimbrell, A., ed. 2002. *Fatal harvest: The tragedy of industrial agriculture.* Washington, DC: Island Press.

Kim-Gibson, D. S. 1999. *Silence broken: Korean comfort women.* Parkersburg, IA: Mid Prairie Books.

Kimmel, M. 1993. Clarence, William, Iron Mike, Tailhook, Senator Packwood, Spur Posse, Magic . . . and us. In *Transforming a rape culture,* ed. E. Buchwald, R. Fletcher, and M. Roth, pp. 119–38. Minneapolis: Milkweed Editions.

———. 2000. *The gendered society.* New York: Oxford University Press.

———, and M. Messner. 1998. *Men's lives.* 3rd ed. Boston: Allyn & Bacon.

———, and T. Mosmiller, eds. 1992. *Against the tide: Pro-feminist men in the United States, 1776–1990.* Boston: Beacon Press.

Kincaid, J. 1988. *A small place.* New York: Penguin/Plume.

King, R., and C. Sweetman. 2010. Gender perspectives on the global economic crisis. *Oxfam International Discussion Paper.* www.oxfam.org.uk/resources/policy/economic_crisis/downloads/dp_gender_perspectives_gec_020210.pdf

King, Y. 1983. All is connectedness: Notes from the Women's Pentagon Action, USA. In *Keeping the peace,* ed. L. Jones. London: The Women's Press.

———. 1988. Ecological feminism, *Z Magazine,* July/August, pp. 124–27.

———. 1993a. The other body. *Ms.,* March/April, pp. 72–75.

———. 1993b. Feminism and ecology. In *Toxic struggles: The theory and practice of environmental justice,* ed. R. Hofrichter, pp. 76–84. Philadelphia and Gabriola Island, BC: New Society.

Kinser, A, 2010. *Motherhood and feminism.* Emeryville, CA: Seal Press.

Kirk, G. 1997. Standing on solid ground: Towards a materialist ecological feminism. In *Materialist feminism: A reader in class, difference, and women's lives,* ed. Rosemary Hennessy and Chrys Ingraham, pp. 345–63. New York: Routledge.

———. 1998. Ecofeminism and Chicano environmental struggles: Bridges across gender and race. In *Chicano culture, ecology, politics: Subversive kin,* ed. D. G. Peña, pp. 177–200. Tucson: University of Arizona Press.

———. 2008. Environmental effects of U.S. military security: Gendered experiences from the Philippines, South Korea, and Japan. In *Gender and globalization in Asia and the Pacific: Method, practice, theory,* edited by K. E. Ferguson and M. Mironesco. Honolulu: University of Hawaii Press.

Kline, C. B., ed. 1997 *Child of mine: Writers talk about the first year of motherhood.* New York: Hyperion.

Koedt, A. 1973. The myth of the vaginal orgasm. In *Radical feminism,* ed. A. Koedt, E. Levine, and A. Rapone. New York: Times Books.

———, E. Levine, and A. Rapone, eds. 1973. *Radical feminism.* New York: Quadrangle Books.

Kohl, H. 1992. *From archetype to zeitgeist: Powerful ideas for powerful thinking.* Boston: Little Brown.

Kolmar, W. K., and F. Bartowski. 2010. *Feminist theory: A reader.* 3rd ed. New York: McGraw-Hill.

Koppleman, S. ed. 2004. *"Women in the trees": U.S. Women's short stories about battering and resistance, 1839–2000.* New York: Feminist Press at CUNY.

Koss, M. P., L. Goodman, A. Browne, L. Fitzgerald, G. P. Keita, and N. F. Russo. 1994. *No safe haven: Male violence against women at home, at work, and in the community.* Washington, DC: American Psychological Association.

———, C. A. Gidycz, and N. Wisiewski. 1987. The scope of rape: Incidence and prevalence of sexual aggression and victimization in a national sample of higher education students. *Journal of Consulting and Clinical Psychology* 55(2): 162–70.

Koyama. E. 2003.The transfeminist manifesto. In *Catching a wave: Reclaiming feminism for the 21*st century, ed. Rory Dicker and Alison Piepmeier, pp. 244–259. Boston; Northeastern University Press.

Kraemer, K. L., G. Linden, and J. Dedrick. 2011. *Capturing value in global networks: Apple's iPad and iPhone.* Berkeley, CA: University of California-Irvine, University of California-Berkeley, and Syracuse University.

Krauss, C. 1993. Blue-collar women and toxic-waste protests: The process of politicization. In *Toxic struggles: The theory and practice of environmental justice,* ed. R. Hofrichter, pp. 107–17. Philadelphia and Gabriola Island, BC: New Society.

Kremen, C., C. Bacon, and A. Iles. 2012. Diversified farming systems: An agro-ecological, systems-based alternative to modern industrial agriculture, *Ecology and Society* (in press).

Kremen, C., and A. Miles. 2012. Ecosystem services and diversified farming systems: Analysis of costs, benefits and tradeoffs for food production, resilience and biodiversity, *Ecology and Society* (in press).

Kristof, N. D. 2005. *A policy of rape,* New York Times, June 5. HYPERLINK "http://www.nytimes.com/2005/06/05/opinion/05kristof.html" www.nytimes.com/2005/06/05/opinion/05kristof.html. Accessed on April 20, 2012.

Kuhn, T. 1962. *The structure of scientific revolutions.* Chicago: University of Chicago Press.

Kulwicki, C. 2008. Real sex education. In *Yes means yes: Visions of female sexual power and a world without rape,* ed. Jaclyn Friedman and Jessica Valenti. Emeryville, CA: Seal Press.

Kurshan, Nancy. 1996. Behind the walls: The history and current reality of women's imprisonment. In *Criminal injustice: Confronting the prison crisis,* ed. E. Rosenblatt. Cambridge, MA: South End Press.

Kwan, S. 2010. Navigating public spaces: Gender, race, and body privilege in everyday life. *Feminist Formations* 22(2): 144–66.

Labaton, V., and D. Lundy Martin, eds. 2004. *The fire this time: Young activists and the new feminism.* New York: Anchor/Random House.

Labelle, D., and Kubiak, S. P. 2004. Balancing gender equity for women prisoners. *Feminist Studies* 30(2): 416–26.

Lacey, M. 2004. *Amnesty says Sudan militias use rape as a weapon,* New York Times. July 19. HYPERLINK "http://www.nytimes.com/2004/07/19/world/amnesty-says-sudan-militias-use-rape-as-weapon.html" www.nytimes.com/2004/07/19/world/amnesty-says-sudan-militias-use-rape-as-weapon.html. Accessed on April 20, 2012.

LaDuke, W. 1993. A society based on conquest cannot be sustained: Native peoples and the environmental crisis. In *Toxic struggles: The theory and practice of environmental justice,* ed. R. Hofrichter. Philadelphia and Gabriola Island, BC: New Society.

———. 1999. *All our relations: Native struggles for land and life.* Cambridge, MA: South End Press.

Lagarde y de los Rios, M. 2010. Feminist keys for understanding feminicide: Theoretical, political and legal constructions. In *Terrorizing women: Feminicide in the Americas,* ed. Rosa-Linda Fregoso and Cynthia Bejarano, pp. xi–xxvi. Durham, NC: Duke University Press.

Lake, C. 2005. The polls speak: Americans support abortion. *Ms.* XV(2), Summer: 37, 39.

Lamb, W., and the Women of York Correctional Facility. 2003. *Couldn't keep it to myself: Testimony from our imprisoned sisters.* New York: ReganBooks.

———. ed. 2007. *I'll fly away: Further testimonies from the women of York Prison.* New York: HarperCollins.

Lamm, N. 1995. It's a big, fat revolution. In *Listen up: Voices from the next feminist generation,* ed. Barbara Findlen, pp. 85–94. Seattle, WA: Seal Press.

Lancaster, R. N., and M. di Leonardo, eds. 1997. *The gender/sexuality reader: Culture, history, political economy.* New York: Routledge.

Lappé, F. M., and J. Collins. 1986. *World Hunger: Twelve Myths.* New York: Grove Press.

Lappé, F. M., Collins, J., Rosset, P., and Esparza, L. 1998. *World Hunger: Twelve Myths.* New York: Grove Press.

Larkin, J., and K. Popaleni. 1997. Heterosexual courtship violence and sexual harassment: The private and public control of young women. In *In our own words: Readings on the psychology of women and gender,* ed. M. Crawford and R. Unger, pp. 313–26. New York: McGraw-Hill.

Lasch, C. 1977. *Haven in a heartless world: The family besieged.* New York: Basic Books.

Latty, E. 2006. The silence that surrounds: Queer sexual violence and why we're not talking. In *We don't need another wave: Dispatches from the next generation of feminists,* ed. Melody Berger. Emeryville, CA: Seal Press.

Laughlin, K. A., J. Gallaher, D. S. Cobble, E. Boris, P. Nadasen, S. Gilmore, and L. Zarnow. 2010. Is it time to jump ship? Historians rethink the waves metaphor. *Feminist Formations* 22(1): 76–135.

LaVeist, T. A. 2005. *Minority population and health: An introduction to health disparities in the U.S.* San Francisco: Jossey-Bass.

Law, V. 2009. *Resistance behind bars: The struggles of incarcerated women.* Oakland, CA: PM Press.

Lawston, J. M., and A. E. Lucas, eds. 2011. *Razor wire women: Prisoners, activists, scholars, and artists.* Albany: State University of New York Press.

Layzer, J. A. 2006 Community Activism and Environmental Justice: The Dudley Street Neighborhood Initiative. In *The environmental case: Translating values into policy,* 2nd ed. Washington, DC: CQ Pres.

Leatherman, J. 2011. *Sexual violence and armed conflict.* Boston: Polity Press.

Lederer, E. 2005. Women said worse off now than 10 years ago. *Associated Press,* March 4.

Lee, C. 1987. *Toxic wastes and race in the United States.* New York: New York Commission for Racial Justice United Church of Christ.

Lefkowitz, B. 1997. *Our guys: The Glen Ridge rape and the secret life of the perfect suburb.* Berkeley: University of California Press.

Leidholdt, D., and J. Raymond. 1990. *The sexual liberals and the attack on feminism.* New York: Pergamon.

Leong, L. C. P. 2004. Virulent virginity: "Abstinence-only" sex ed programs are putting youth at risk. *Color Lines* 7(4): 36–37.

Leong, R., ed. 1996. *Asian American sexualities: Dimensions of the gay and lesbian experience.* New York: Routledge.

Lerman, H. 1996. *Pigeonholing women's misery: A history and critical analysis of the psychodiagnosis of women in the twentieth century.* New York: Basic Books.

Le Sueur, M. 1982. *Ripening: Selected work.* 2nd ed. New York: Feminist Press at the City University of New York.

Levister, C. 2006. *A sweatshop behind bars.* www.alternet.org/story/41481/ Accessed May 2, 2008.

Levy, A. 2005. *Female chauvinist pigs: Women and the rise of raunch culture.* New York: Free Press.

———. 2009. Either/or: Sports, sex, and the case of Caster Semenya. *The New Yorker,* November 30.

Lichtenstein, A. C., and M. A. Kroll. 1996. The fortress economy: The economic role of the U.S. prison system. In *Criminal injustice: Confronting the prison crisis,* ed. E. Rosenblatt. Boston: South End Press.

Lindsay-Poland, J. 2003. *Emperors in the jungle: The hidden history of the U.S. in Panama.* Durham: Duke University Press.

Lindsley, S. 2004. Bearing the blame: Gender, immigration, reproduction, and the environment. In *The fire this time: Young activists and the new feminism,* ed. Vivien Labaton and Dawn Lundy Martin, pp. 220–253. New York: Anchor/Random House.

Linton, S. 1999. *Claiming disability: Knowledge and identity.* New York: New York University Press.

Liptak, A. 2006. Prisons often shackle pregnant inmates in labor. *New York Times.* March 2. www.nytimes.com/2006/03/02/national/02shackles.html?_r=3&oref=slogin&oref=slogin&oref=slogin

———. 2008. Inmate count in U.S. dwarfs other nations'. *New York Times.* April 23. www.nytimes.com/2008/04/23/us/23prison.html? pagewanted=3&_r=2&hp

———. 2010. Justices, 5-4, reject corporate spending limit. *New York Times,* January 21. www.nytimes.com/2010/01/22/us/politics/22scotus.html?pagewanted=all

Litt, J. S., and M. K. Zimmerman. 2003. Global perspectives on gender and carework: An introduction. *Gender and Society* 17(2): 156–65.

Lopez, I. 1997. Agency and constraint: Sterilization and reproductive freedom among Puerto Rican women in New York City. In *Situated lives: Gender and culture in everyday lives,* ed. L. Lamphere, H. Ragone, and P. Zavella, pp. 157–74. New York: Routledge.

Lorber, J. 1994. *Paradoxes of gender.* New Haven, CT: Yale University Press.

Lorde, A. 1996. *The cancer journals.* San Francisco: Aunt Lute Books.

Lovejoy, M. 2001. Disturbances in the social body: Differences in body image and eating problems among African American and White women. *Gender and Society* 15(2): 239–61.

Lowy, J. 1999. Gay adoption backlash growing. *San Francisco Examiner,* 7 March, p. A20.

Lublin, N. 1998. *Pandora's box: Feminism confronts reproductive technology.* Lanham, MD: Rowman and Littlefield.

Luebke, B. F., and M. E. Reilly. 1995. *Women's studies graduates: The first generation.* New York: Teachers College Press.

Lutz, C. 2004. Living room terrorists. *Women's Review of Books* 21(5): 17–18.

Lynes, K. and G. Torry. 2005. *From local to global: Making peace work for women. Security Council Resolution 1325 five years on.* New York: NGO Working Group on Peace and Security.

Macdonald, C. L. 2010. *Shadow mothers: Nannies, au pairs, and the micropolitics of mothering.* Berkeley: University of California Press.

MacDorman, M. F., and T. J. Mathews. 2008. Recent trends in infant mortality. Centers for Disease Control and Prevention. www.cdc.gov/nchs/data/databriefs/db09.htm

MacGregor, S. 2006. *Beyond mothering earth: Ecological citizenship and the politics of care.* Vancouver: University of British Columbia Press.

Mack-Canty, C. 2004. Third-wave feminism and the need to reweave the nature/culture duality. *NWSA Journal* (16)83, Fall: 154–79.

Mackinnon, C. 1991. From practice to theory, or what is a white woman anyway? *Yale Journal of Law and Feminism* 4(13–22): 1281–1328.

Magdoff, F., and B. Tokar. 2010. *Agriculture and food in crisis: Conflict, resistance and renewal.* New York: Monthly Review Press.

Magnani, L. and H. L. Wray. 2006. *Beyond prisons: A new interfaith paradigm for our failed prison system.* Minneapolis: Fortress Press.

Maher, F. A., and M. K. T. Tétreault. 1994. *The feminist classroom.* New York: Basic Books.

Mahoney, M. 1994. Victimization or oppression? Women's lives, violence, and agency. In *The public nature of private violence: The discovery of domestic abuse,* ed. M. A. Fineman and R. Mykitiuk, pp. 59–92. New York: Routledge.

Mainardi, P. 1992. The politics of housework. *Ms.,* May/June, pp. 40–41.

Malkan, S. 2007. *Not just a pretty face: The ugly side of the beauty industry.* Gabriola Island, BC: New Society.

Mallicoat, S. L. 2012. *Women and crime: A text/reader.* Los Angeles: Sage.

Mairs, N. 1996. *Waist-high in the world: A life among the nondisabled.* Boston: Beacon Press.

Mamo, L. 2007. *Queering reproduction: Achieving pregnancy in the age of technoscience.* Durham, NC: Duke University Press.

Marcus, S. 2005. Queer theory for everyone: A review essay. *Signs: Journal of Women in Culture and Society* 31(1): 191–218.

Markle, G. 2008. "Can women have sex like a man?": Sexual scripts in *Sex and the City. Sexuality and Culture* 12: 45–57.

Marre, D., and L. Briggs, eds. 2009. *International adoption: Global inequalities and the circulation of children.* New York: New York University Press.

Martin, C. E. 2007. *Perfect girls, starving daughters: The frightening new normalcy of hating your body.* New York: Simon and Schuster.

Martinez, E. 1998. *De colores means all of us: Latina views for a multi-colored century.* Boston: South End Press.

Martinson, K., and J. Strawn. 2003. *Built to last: Why skills matter for long-run success in welfare reform.* Washington, DC: Center for Law and Social Policy.

Martone, C. 2005. *Loving through bars: Children of parents in prison.* Santa Monica, CA: Santa Monica Press.

Marx, F. 2002. Grassroots to graduation: Low-income women accessing higher education. *Final Report: Evaluation of the Women in Community Development Program, Women's Institute for Housing and Economic Development.* Boston: Center for Research on Women, Wellesley College.

Mason, M. G. 2004. *Working against odds: Stories of disabled women's work lives.* Boston: Northeastern University Press.

Mauer, M., and M. Chesney-Lind, eds. 2002. *Invisible punishment: The collateral consequences of mass imprisonment.* New York: The New Press.

May, L. 2005. *Transgenders and intersexuals: Everything you ever wanted to know but couldn't think of the question.* Bowden, South Australia: Fast Lane.

McChesney, R. W. 2004. *The problem of the media: US communications politics in the 21st century.* New York: Monthly Review Press.

McClintock, A. 1995. *Imperial leather: Race, gender, and sexuality in the colonial context.* New York: Routledge.

McCormick, S. 2010. *No family history: The environmental links to breast cancer.* Lanham, MD: Rowman and Littlefield.

McCourt, K. 1977. *Working class women and grassroots politics.* Bloomington: Indiana University Press.

McIntosh, P. 1988. *White privilege and male privilege: A personal account of coming to see correspondences through work in women's studies.* Wellesley, MA: Center for Research on Women, Wellesley College.

McKelvey, T., ed. 2007. *One of the guys: Women as aggressors and torturers.* Emeryville, CA: Seal Press.

McKenna, T. 1996/1997. Military culture breeds misogyny. *Women Against Military Madness,* December/January, 1.

McMichael, P. 2009. A food regime analysis of the "world food crisis." *Agriculture and Human Values* 26(4): 281–95.

McQuirter, T. Y. 2010. *By any greens necessary: A revolutionary guide for Black women who want to eat great, get heathy, lose weight, and look phat.* Chicago: Lawrence Hill Books.

Meckler, L., and D. Crowe. 2012. U.S. drug policy faces Latin dissent. *Wall Street Journal,* April 14–15, p. A12.

Mello, F. V. 1996. Population and international security in the new world order. *Political Environments,* 3(Winter/Spring): 25–26. Publication of the Committee on Women, Population and the Environment, Hampshire College, Amherst, MA.

Mellor, M. 1992. *Breaking the boundaries: Towards a feminist green socialism.* London: Virago Press.

Members of the AIDS Counseling and Education Program of the Bedford Hills Correctional Facility. 1998. *Breaking the walls of silence: AIDS and women in a New York State maximum security prison.* Woodstock, NY: Overlook Press.

Mendez, J. B. 2002. Creating alternatives from a gender perspective: Transnational organizing for maquila workers' rights in Central America. In *Women's activism and globalization: Linking local struggles and transnational politics,* ed. Nancy A. Naples and Manisha Desai, pp. 121–141. New York: Routledge.

Merchant, C. 1980. *The death of nature: Ecology and the scientific revolution.* San Francisco: Harper & Row.

Messerschmidt, J. W. 1986. *Capitalism, patriarchy, and crime: Toward a socialist feminist criminology.* Totowa, NJ: Rowman and Littlefield.

Messner, M. 1992. *Power at play: Sports and the problem of masculinity.* Boston: Beacon Press.

MetLife Mature Market Institute. 2011. *Double jeopardy for baby boomers caring for their parents.* Westport, CT: MetLife. www.metlife.com/assets/cao/mmi/publications/studies/2011/mmi-caregiving-costs-working-caregivers.pdf

Meyers, D. T. 2001. The rush to motherhood—pronatalist discourse and women's autonomy. *Signs: Journal of Women in Culture and Society* 26(3): 735–73.

Midgley, J. 2005. *Women and the U.S. budget: Where the money goes and what you can do about it.* Gabriola, BC: New Society Publishers.

Mies, M. 1993. The need for a new vision: The subsistence perspective. In *Ecofeminism,* ed. M. Mies and V. Shiva. London: Zed Books.

———, and V. Shiva, eds. 1993. *Ecofeminism.* London: Zed Books.

Miller, P. 1993. *The worst of times: Illegal abortion—survivors, practitioners, coroners, cops, and children of women who died talk about its horrors.* New York: HarperCollins.

Miller, S. 2005. California prison boom ends, signaling a shift in priorities. *Christian Science Monitor,* June 20.

Millett, Kate. 1990. *The loony bin trip.* New York: Simon & Schuster.

Mink, G. 1998. Feminists, welfare reform, and welfare justice. *Social Justice* 25(1): 146–57.

———. 2002. Violating women: Rights abuses in the welfare police state. In *Lost ground: Welfare, poverty, and beyond*, ed. R. Albelda and A. Withorn, pp. 95–112. Cambridge, MA: South End Press.

Minton, T. D. 2011. Jail inmates at mid-year 2010. *Bureau of Justice Statistics.* http://bjs.gov/content/pub/pdf/jim10st.pdf

Mitchell, T. ed. 2001. *Global noise: Rap and hip hop outside the USA.* Middletown, CT: Weslyan University Press.

Mohai, P. 1997. Men, women, and the environment: An examination of the gender gap in environmental concern and activism. In *Women working in the environment*, ed. C. Sachs, pp. 215–39. New York: Taylor and Francis.

Mohanty, C. T. 2003. *Feminism without borders: Decolonizing theory, practicing solidarity.* Durham, NC: Duke University Press.

Moon, K. 1997. *Sex between allies: Military prostitution in U.S.–Korea relations.* New York: Columbia University Press.

Moore, B. 1996. From underrepresentation to overrepresentation: African American women. In *It's our military too! Women and the U.S. military*, ed. J. H. Stiehm, pp. 115–35. Philadelphia: Temple University Press.

Moraga, C. 1997. *Waiting in the wings: Portrait of a queer motherhood.* Ithaca, NY: Firebrand.

———, and G. Anzaldua. 1981. *This bridge called my back: Writings by radical women of color.* New York: Kitchen Table/Women of Color Press.

Morell, C. M. 1994. *Unwomanly conduct: The challenge of intentional childlessness.* New York: Routledge.

Morgan, L. M., and M. Michaels. 1999. *Fetal subjects: Feminist positions.* Philadelphia: University of Pennsylvania Press.

Morgan, R. 1996. Dispatch from Beijing, *Ms.* January/February, pp. 12–15.

Morgen, S. 2002. *Into our own hands: The women's health movement in the United States, 1969–1990.* Piscataway, NJ: Rutgers University Press.

Morland, K., S. Wing, A. D. Roux, and C. Poole. 2002. Neighborhood characteristics associated with the location of food stores and food service places. *American Journal of Preventive Medicine* 22(1): 23–29.

Morris, M. 1999. In war and peace: Incidence and implications of rape by military personnel. In *Beyond zero tolerance: Discrimination in military culture*, ed. M. F. Katzenstein and J. Reppy, pp. 163–94. Lanham, MD: Rowman and Littlefield.

Morrison, A., R. White, E. Van Velsor, and the Center for Creative Leadership. 1992. *Breaking the glass ceiling: Can women reach the top of America's largest corporations?* Reading, MA: Addison-Wesley.

Morrison, P. 2007. Hey, why not try the tap sometime? *San Francisco Examiner,* August 6, p. 11.

Morrison, T., ed. 1992. *Race-ing, justice, en-gendering power: Essays on Anita Hill, Clarence Thomas, and the construction of reality.* New York: Pantheon.

Morrone, L. 2009. *Overcoming overeating: It's not what you eat, it's what's eating you!* Eugene, OR: Harvest House.

Morrow, L. 1999. Folklore in a box. In *Readings in mass communication: Media literacy and culture*, ed. K. B. Massey, pp. 22–26. Mountain View, CA: Mayfield.

Moses, M. 1993. Farmworkers and pesticides. In *Confronting environmental racism: Voices from the grassroots*, ed. R. Bullard, pp. 161–78. Boston: South End Press.

Mott, L., and K. Snyder. 1987. *Pesticide alert: A guide to pesticides in fruit and vegetables.* San Francisco: Sierra Club Books.

Movement for a New Society. 1983. *Off their backs . . . and on our own two feet.* Philadelphia: New Society.

Müller, A. R. 2010. Does fair trade coffee eliminate poverty? www.lab.org.uk/index.php/news/57-focus/701-central-america-does-fair-trade-coffee-eliminate-poverty

Mullings, L. 1997. *On our own: Race, class, and gender in the lives of African American women.* New York: Routledge.

Mundy, L. 2007. *Everything conceivable: How assisted reproduction is changing men, women, and the world.* New York: Knopf.

Muscio, I. 1999. *Cunt: A declaration of independence.* Seattle, WA: Seal Press.

Nacos, B. L., and O. Torres-Reyna. 2007. *Fueling our fears. Stereotyping, media coverage, and public opinion of Muslim Americans.* Lanham, MD: Rowman and Littlefield.

Nadasen, P. 2005. *Welfare warriors: The welfare rights movement in the United States.* New York: Routledge.

Naffine, N. 1987. *Female crime: The construction of women in criminology.* Boston: Allen & Unwin.

Nagel, J. 1997. *Whores and other feminists.* New York: Routledge.

Naidus, B. 1993. *One size does not fit all.* Littleton, CO: Aigis.

Namaste, V. K. 2000. *Invisible lives: The erasure of transsexual and transgendered people.* Chicago: University of Chicago Press.

Naples, N., ed. 1997. *Community activism and feminist politics: Organizing across race, class, and gender.* New York: Routledge.

———. 1998. *Grassroots warriors: Activist mothering, community work, and the war on poverty.* New York: Routledge.

———, and K. Bojar, eds. 2002. *Teaching feminist activism: Strategies from the field.* New York: Routledge.

National Council for Research on Women. 2004. *Missing: Information about women's lives.* New York: NCRW.

National Immigration Forum. 2011. The math of immigration detention. www.immigrationforum.org/images/uploads/MathofImmigrationDetention.pdf

National Institute for Occupational Safety and Health. 2012. A story of impact. www.cdc.gov/niosh/docs/2012-108/pdfs/2012-108.pdf

National Institute of Justice. 2003. Correctional boot camps: Lessons from a decade of research. U.S. Department of Justice. www.ncjrs.gov/pdffiles1/nij/197018.pdf

National Women's Law Center. 2003. *Air Force must face systemic problems to address sexual assaults at Academy*, press release, February 28. www.nwlc.org/details.cfm?id=1331&section=newsroom

———. 2004. *Slip-sliding away: The erosion of hard-won gains for women under the Bush administration and an agenda for moving forward.* Washington, DC: National Women's Law Center.

NATO News. 2011. Engaging women on the frontline. July 18. www.nato.int/cps/en/natolive/news_76542.htm

Nelson, J. 2003. *Women of color and the reproductive rights movement.* New York: New York University Press.

Nelson, K. P. 2006. Shopping for children in the international marketplace. In *Outsiders within: Writing on transracial adoption*, ed. Jane Jeong Trenka, Julia Chinyere Oparah, and Sun Yung Shin, pp. 89–104. Cambridge, MA: South End Press.

Nelson, L. 1990. The place of women in polluted places. In *Reweaving the world: The emergence of ecofeminism*, ed. I. Diamond and G. Orenstein. San Francisco: Sierra Club Books.

Nelson, M. B. 2002. And now they tell us women don't really like sports? *Ms.*, December 2002/January 2003, pp. 32–36.

Nestle, J., C. Howell, and R. Wilchins. 2002. *Genderqueer: Voices from beyond the sexual binary.* Los Angeles: Alyson.

Neumann, C. E. 2007. United Kingdom lifts ban on gays and lesbians in the military. In *Gay, lesbian, bisexual, transgender events 1848–2006*, vol 2, ed. Lillian Faderman, Horacio Roque Ramírez, Yolanda Retter, Stuart Timmons, and Eric C. Wat, pp. 669–71. Pasadena, CA: Salem Press.

Newbury, C. and H. Baldwin. 2001. Confronting the aftermath of conflict: Women's organizations in post-genocide Rwanda. In *Women and civil war: Impact, organizations, and action*, ed. K. Kumar. Boulder, CO: Lynne Reinner.

Newsome, M. 2011. The military family care plan: What you need to know. www.care.com/child-care-the-military-family-care-plan-what-you-need-to-know-p1017-q6466718.html

Nguyen, T. 2005. *We are all suspects now.* Boston: Beacon Press.

NiCarthy, G. 1987. *The ones who got away: Women who left abusive partners.* Seattle, WA: Seal Press.

———. 2004. *Getting free: You can end abuse and take back your life.* Expanded ed. Seattle, WA: Seal Press.

Nicholson, L. J., ed. 1990. *Feminism/postmodernism.* New York: Routledge.

Nimoy, L. 2007. *The full body project.* Brooklyn, NY: Five Ties.

Noble, K. 1994. Woman tells of retaliation for complaint on Tailhook. *New York Times*, 5 October, p. A10.

Norris, P., ed. 1997. *Women, media, and politics.* New York: Oxford University Press.

Norsigian, J. 1996. The women's health movement in the United States. In *Man-made medicine: Women's health, public policy, and reform*, ed. K. L. Moss, pp. 79–97. Durham, NC: Duke University Press.

Nowrojee, S., and J. Silliman. 1997. Asian women's health: Organizing a movement. In *Dragon ladies: Asian American feminists breathe fire*, ed. S. Shah, pp. 73–89. Boston: South End Press.

Nussair, I. 2008. Gendered, racialized and sexualized torture at Abu Ghraib. In *Feminism and war: Confronting U.S. imperialism*, ed. R. L. Riley, C. T. Mohanty, and M. B. Pratt, pp. 179–93. New York: Zed Books.

NWSAction. 2004. Feminist uses of science and technology. College Park, MD: National Women's Studies Association.

Ochs, Robyn, and Sarah F. Rowley, eds. 2005. *Getting bi: Voices of bisexuals around the world.* Boston: Bisexual Resource Center.

O'Connor, M., ed. 1994. *Is capitalism sustainable? Political economy and the politics of ecology.* New York: Guilford Press.

Office on Women's Health. 2009. Sexually transmitted infections fact sheet. http://womenshealth.gov/publications/our-publications/fact-sheet/sexually-transmitted-infections.cfm#a

Ogden, S. 2006. Pomo woman, ex-prisoner, speaks out. In *The color of violence*, ed. Incite! Women of Color Against Violence, pp. 164–169. Cambridge, MA: South End Press.

Ogur, B. 1996. Smothering in stereotypes: HIV-positive women. In *Talking gender: Public images, personal journeys, and political critiques*, ed. N. Hewitt, J. O'Barr, and N. Rosebaugh. Chapel Hill: University of North Carolina Press.

Okazawa-Rey, M. 1994. Racial identity development of mixed race persons: An overview. In *Diversity and human service education*, ed. J. Silver-Jones, S. Kerstein, and D. Osher. Council of Standards in Human Service Education Monograph Series, No. 4.

Oliver, K. 2010. *Women as weapons of war: Iraq, sex, and the media.* New York: Columbia University Press.

Olson, E.D. 1999. *Bottled Water: Pure drink or pure hype?* San Francisco: Natural Resources Defense Council.

Olson, R. 2008. *This is who i am: Our beauty is all shapes and sizes.* New York: Artisan/Workman.

Omolade, B. 1983. Hearts of darkness. In *Powers of desire*, eds. A. Snitow, C. Stansell, and S. Thompson. New York: Monthly Review Press.

———. 1986. *It's a family affair: The real lives of Black single mothers.* New York: Kitchen Table: Women of Color Press.

———. 1989. We speak for the planet. In *Rocking the ship of state: Toward a feminist peace politics*, ed. A. Harris and Y. King. Boulder, CO: Westview Press.

———. 1994. Ella's daughters. In *The rising song of African American women.* New York: Routledge.

O'Reilly, A, 2006. *Rocking the cradle: Thoughts on feminism, motherhood, and the possibility of empowered mothering.* Toronto, ON: Demeter Press.

———, ed. 2010. *Twenty-first century motherhood: Experience, identity, policy, agency.* New York: Columbia University Press.

O'Reilly, B. 1991. Cooling down the world debt bomb. *Fortune*, May 20, p. 123.

Oreskes, N. 2004. The scientific consensus on climate change. *Science* 36(3): 1686.

Orlando, L. 1991. Loving whom we choose. In *Bi any other name: Bisexual people speak out*, ed. L. Hutchins and L. Ka'ahumanu, pp. 223–32. Boston: Alyson.

Orleck, A. 2005. *Storming Caesar's Palace: How black mothers fought their own war on poverty.* Boston: Beacon Press.

O'Shea, K. 1998. *Women and the death penalty in the United States, 1900–1998.* Westport, CT: Praeger.

Owen, B., and B. Bloom. 1995. Profiling women prisoners. *The Prison Journal* 75(2): 165–85.

Oxfam International. 2004. *Trading away our rights: Women working in global supply chains.* Oxford, UK: Oxfam.

Paasonen, S., K. Nikunen, and L. Saarenmaa, eds. 2008. *Pornification: Sex and sexuality in media culture.* Oxford, UK: Berg.

Page, S. 1988. *If I'm so wonderful, why am I still single? Ten strategies that will change your love life forever.* New York: Viking.

Paglia, C. 1990. *Sexual personae: Art and decadence from Nefertiti to Emily Dickinson.* New Haven, CT: Yale University Press.

Paley, G. 1998. The illegal days. In *Just as I thought*, pp. 13–20. New York: Farrar, Straus, Giroux.

Pardo, M. 1990. Mexican American women grassroots community activists: "Mothers of East Los Angeles." *Frontiers: A Journal of Women's Studies* 11(1): 1–7.

Parenti, C. 1999, September. The prison industrial complex: Crisis and control. *Corporate Watch.* San Francisco: Transnational Resource and Action Center.

Parks, S. 2010. *Fierce angels: The strong black woman in American life and culture.* New York: Random House.

Parreñas, R. S. 2001. *Servants of globalization: Women, migration, and domestic work.* Stanford, CA: Stanford University Press.

Pastor, M., R. Bullard, J. Boyce, A. Fothergill, R. Morello-Frosch, and B. Wright. 2006. *In the wake of the storm: Environment, disaster, and race after Katrina.* New York: Russell Sage Foundation.

Patten, E., and K. Parker. 2011. Women in the U.S. military: Growing share, distinctive profile. Pew Research Center. www.pewsocialtrends.org/2011/12/22/women-in-the-u-s-military-growing-share-distinctive-profile/

Peach, L. J. 1997. Behind the front lines: Feminist battles over combat. In *Wives and warriors: Women and the military in the United States and Canada*, ed. L. Weinstein and C. White, pp. 99–135. Westport, CT: Bergin & Garvey.

Pearce, D., A. Markandya, and E. B. Barbier. 1990. *Blueprint for a green economy*. London: Earthscan.

Peña, D. 1997. *The terror of the machine: Technology, work, gender, and ecology of the U.S.-Mexico border*. Austin: University of Texas Press.

Peña, D.G. 1999. Cultural landscapes and biodiversity: The ethnoecology of an Upper Rio Grande watershed commons. In *Ethnoecology: Situated knowledge/Located lives*, ed. Virginia D. Nazarea. Tucson: University of Arizona Press.

Perlo-Freeman, O. Ismail, N. Kelly, E. Sköns, and C. Solmirano. 2011. *SIPRI Yearbook 2011*. Stockholm International Peace Research Institute.

Perrone, B., H. H. Stockel, and V. Krueger. 1989. *Medicine women, curanderas, and women doctors*. Norman: University of Oklahoma Press.

Pershing, J. 2003. Why women don't report sexual harassment: A case study of an elite military institution. *Gender Issues* 21(4): 3–30.

Petchesky, R. 1990. *Abortion and woman's choice: The state, sexuality, and reproductive freedom*. Rev. ed. Boston: Northeastern University Press.

———. 1997. Fetal images: The power of visual culture in the politics of reproduction. In *The gender/sexuality reader*, ed. R. Lancaster and M. di Leonardo, pp. 134–50. New York: Routledge.

Petersen, B. 1991. *Dancing with Daddy: A childhood lost and a life regained*. New York: Bantam Books.

Peterson, V. S. 2000. Sexing political identity/Nationalism as heterosexism. In *At home in the nation? Gender, states and nationalism*, edited by Sita Ranchod-Nilson and Mary Ann Tétreault. pp. 54–80. New York: Routledge.

Peterson, S. 2003. *A critical rewriting of global political economy: Integrating reproductive, productive, and virtual economies*. New York: Routledge.

Peterson, V. S., and A. S. Runyan. 1993. *Global gender issues*. Boulder, CO: Westview Press.

Pharr, S. 1988. *Homophobia: A weapon of sexism*. Inverness, CA: Chardon Press.

Phifer, R. 2011. Giving the voiceless a voice. In *Razor wire women*, ed. J. M. Lawston and A. E Lucas. Albany: State University of New York Press.

Phillips, L. 2000. *Flirting with danger: Young women reflect on sexuality and domination*. New York: New York University Press.

Pilkington, E. 2011. Sexual abuse of immigrant detainees rampant across US, lawyers warn. *Guardian* (U.K.), October 19. www.guardian.co.uk/world/2011/oct/19/sexual-abuse-immigration-detention-aclu

Pimentel, D., P. Hepperly, J. Hanson, D. Douds, and R. Seidel. 2005. Environmental, energetic, and economic comparisons of organic and conventional farming systems. *Bioscience* 55(7), 573–82.

Plastas, M. 2011. *A band of noble women: Racial politics in the women's peace movement. Syracuse*, NY: Syracuse University Press.

Plath, S. 1971. *The bell jar*. New York: Harper and Row.

Plumwood, V. 1993. *Feminism and the mastery of nature*. New York: Routledge.

Polikoff, N. 2008. *Beyond (straight and gay) marriage: Valuing all families under the law*. Boston: Beacon Press.

Pollin, R., and H. Garrett-Peltier. 2009. *The U.S. employment effects of military and domestic spending priorities: An updated analysis*. Amherst: University of Massachusetts, Political Economy Research Institute.

Porter, E. 2007. *Peacebuilding: Women's international perspectives*. Routledge: New York.

Portes, Alejandro. 1997. *Los Angeles in the context of the new immigration*. Los Angeles: UCLA, Lewis Center for Regional Policy Studies, Working Paper, no. 18.

Poverty Guidelines. 2005. *Federal Register*, February 18, 70(33): 8373–75.

Pozner, J. L. 2006. Reclaiming the media for a progressive feminist future. In *We don't need another wave: Dispatches from the next generation of feminists*, ed. M. Berger, pp. 287–306. Emeryville, CA: Seal Press.

Prann, E. 2011. States spend almost four times more per capita on incarcerating prisoners than educating students, studies say. *Fox News*, March 4. www.foxnews.com/politics/2011/03/14/states-spend-times-incarcerating-educating-studies-say-464156987/

Pratt, M. B. 1984. Identity: Skin blood heart. In *Yours in struggle: Three feminist perspectives on anti-semitism and racism*, E. Bulkin, M. B. Pratt, and B. Smith, 9–63. Brooklyn, NY: Long Haul Press.

Pretty, J. 2009. Can ecological agriculture feed nine billion people? *Monthly Review*, November, pp. 46–58.

Prilleltensky, O. 2003. A ramp to motherhood: The experience of mothers with physical disabilities. *Sexuality and Disability*, 21: 21–47.

Project for Excellence in Journalism. 2005. *The gender gap: Women are still missing as sources for journalists*. www.journalism.org/resources/research/reports/gender/default.asp

Prokosch, M., and L. Raymond, eds. 2002. *The global activist's manual: Local ways to change the world*. New York: Thunder's Mouth Press/Nation Books.

Pulido, L. 1993. Sustainable development at Ganados del Valle. In *Confronting environmental racism: Voices from the grassroots*, ed. R. Bullard. Boston: South End Press.

———. 1996. *Environmentalism and economic justice: Two Chicano struggles in the Southwest*. Tucson: University of Arizona Press.

Queen, C. 2002. *Real live nude girl: Chronicle of sex positive culture*. San Francisco: Cleis Press.

Quintero-Somaini, A., and M. Quirindongo. 2004. *Hidden danger: environmental health threats to the Latino community*. New York: Natural Resources Defense Council.

Rabin, N. 2011. *Disappearing parents: A report on immigration enforcement and the child welfare system*. Tucson, AZ: Southwest Institute for Research on Women and Bacon Immigration Law and Policy Program, University of Arizona. www.detentionwatchnetwork.org/sites/detentionwatchnetwork.org/files/06.09.2011_DisappearingParents.pdf

Rachel's Environment and Health Weekly. 1998. *The precautionary principle*. February 19, p. 586. www.monitor.net/rachel/r586.html

Radical Women. 2001. *The radical women manifesto: Socialist feminism theory, program, and organizational structure*. Seattle, WA: Red Letter Press.

Rafter, N. 1990. *Partial justice: Women, prisons and social control.* New Brunswick, NJ: Transaction.

Ragone, H., and F. W. Twine, eds. 2000. *Ideologies and technologies of motherhood: Race, class, sexuality and nationalism.* New York: Routledge.

Randall, M. 2011. The women of Juárez. *Women's Review of Books* 28(4): 12–13.

Ransby, B. 2006. Katrina, Black women, and the deadly discourse on Black poverty in America. *Du Bois Review* 3(1): 215–22.

Raphael, J., and R. Tolman. 1997. *Trapped in poverty, trapped by abuse: New evidence documenting the relationship between domestic violence and welfare.* Project for Research on Welfare, Work, and Domestic Violence. A collaboration between Taylor Institute and University of Michigan Development Center on Poverty, Risk, and Mental Health.

Rasmussen, V. 1998. Rethinking the corporation. *Food and Water Journal*, Fall, 17–21.

Rathbone, C. 2006. *A world apart: Women, prison, and life behind bars.* New York: Random House.

Raymond, D. 2003. Popular culture and queer representation. In *Gender, race, and class in media: A text-reader*, ed. Gail Dines and Jean M. Humez, pp. 98–110. Thousand Oaks, CA: Sage.

Rayner, R. 1997. Women in the warrior culture. *New York Times Magazine*, June 22, pp. 24–29, 40, 49, 53, 55–56.

Reagan, L. J. 1997. *When abortion was a crime: Women, medicine, and law in the United States 1867–1973.* Berkeley: University of California Press.

Reardon, B. A. 1985. *Sexism and the war system.* New York: Teachers College Press.

Reaves, S., J. B. Hitchon, S.-Y. Park, and G. W. Yun. 2004. If looks could kill: Digital manipulation of fashion models. *Journal of Mass Media Ethics* 19(1): 56–71.

Reese, E. 2005. *Backlash against welfare mothers: Past and present.* Berkeley: University of California Press.

Reeves, M., A. Katten, and M. Guzman. 2003. *Fields of poison: Califonria farmworkers and pesticides.* Darby, PA: Diane.

Reger, J. 2010. *Everywhere and nowhere: Contemporary feminism in the United States.* New York: Oxford University Press.

Rehn, E., and E. J. Sirleaf. 2002. *Women, war, peace: The independent experts' assessment.* New York: UNIFEM.

Rennison, C. M. 2002. *Rape and sexual assault: Reporting to police and medical attention, 1992–2000.* Bureau of Justice Statistics, selected findings. Washington, DC: U.S. Department of Justice.

———. 2003. *Intimate partner violence, 1993–2001.* Bureau of Justice Statistics, Crime Data Brief. Washington, DC: U.S. Department of Justice.

Rentz, C. 2011. *New documents detail sex abuse of detained immigrants.* American University School of Communication Investigative Reporting Workshop, October 19. http://investigativereportingworkshop.org/investigations/immigration-detention/story/new-documents-detail-sex-abuse-detained-immigrants/

Renzetti, C. M. 1992. *Violent betrayal: Partner abuse in lesbian relationships.* Newbury Park, CA: Sage.

Resnick, B. 2011. One year of prison costs more than one year at Princeton. *The Atlantic*, November 1. www.theatlantic.com/national/archive/2011/11/chart-one-year-of-prison-costs-more-than-one-year-at-princeton/247629/

Reti, I., ed. 1992. *Childless by choice: A feminist anthology.* Santa Cruz, CA: Her Books.

Reuters. 2012a. Apple iPad maker gives China workers a raise. www.msnbc.msn.com/id/46427617/ns/business-world_business/t/apple-ipad-maker-gives-china-workers-raise/#.T3NMzJhOGS0

———. 2012b. Racism in US military 'alive and well.' *United States Military News Aggregator*, February 20. http://militaryfeed.com/racism-in-us-military-alive-and-well/

Rhodes, J. 2005. *Radical feminist writing and critical agency: From manifesto to modern.* Albany, NY: SUNY Press.

Rich, A. 1986a. Compulsory heterosexuality and lesbian existence. In *Blood, bread, and poetry.* New York: W. W. Norton.

———. 1986b. *Of woman born: Motherhood as experience and institution.* 10th anniversary ed. New York: W. W. Norton.

———. 1986c. Notes towards a politics of location. In *Blood, bread, and poetry*, pp. 210–31. New York: W. W. Norton.

Richie, B. 1996. *Compelled to crime: The gender entrapment of battered Black women.* New York: Routledge.

Richter, P. 2000. Armed forces find "disturbing" level of gay harassment. *Los Angeles Times*, March 25, p. A1.

Rierden, A. 1997. *The farm: Inside a women's prison.* Amherst: University of Massachusetts Press.

Riley, R., C. T. Mohanty, and M. B. Pratt, eds. 2008. *Feminism and war: Confronting U.S. imperialism.* New York: Zed Books.

Risman, B. J. 1998. *Gender vertigo: American families in transition.* New Haven, CT: Yale University Press.

Ristock, J. 2002. *No more secrets: Violence in lesbian relationships.* New York: Routledge.

———. 2009. ed. *Intimate partner violence in LGBTQ lives.* Routledge: New York.

Ritchie, A. 2006. Law enforcement violence against women of color. In *Color of violence: The Incite! anthology*, ed. Incite! Women of Color Against Violence. Cambridge, MA: South End Press.

Ritz, D., ed. 2001. *Defying corporations, defining democracy.* New York: Apex Press.

Ritzer, G. 1993. The *McDonaldization of society: An investigation into the changing character of contemporary social life.* Thousand Oaks, CA: Pine Forge Press.

Riverbend. 2005. *Baghdad burning: Girl blog from Iraq.* New York: Feminist Press of the City University of New york.

———. 2006. *Baghdad burning II: More girl blog from Iraq.* New York: Feminist Press of the City University of New York.

Rivers, C. 2007. *Selling anxiety: How the news media scare women.* Hanover and London: University Press of New England.

Robb, A. 2010. Not a lone wolf. *Ms.* 20(2), pp. 26–31.

Robb, D.L. 2004. *Operation Hollywood: How the Pentagon shapes and censors the movies.* Amherst, N.Y.: Prometheus Books.

Roberts, D. 1997. *Killing the Black body: Race, reproduction, and the meaning of liberty.* New York: Pantheon.

Roberts, M. M., and T. Mizuta, eds. 1993. *The reformers: Socialist feminism.* London: Routledge/Thoemmes Press.

Rodríguez, J. M. 2003. *Queer latinidad: Identity practices, discursive spaces.* New York: New York University Press.

Roediger, D. R. 1991. *The wages of whiteness: Race and the making of the American working class.* New York: Verso.

Roiphe, K. 1993. *The morning after: Sex, fear, and feminism.* Boston: Little Brown.

Rojas, M. 2009. *Women of color and feminism.* Emeryville, CA: Seal Press.

Root, M. P., ed. 1996. *The multiracial experience: Racial borders as the new frontier.* Thousand Oaks, CA: Sage.

Rose, Tricia. 2003. *Longing to tell: Black women talk about sexuality and intimacy.* New York: Farrar, Straus & Giroux.

Rosen, R. 2000. *The world split open: How the modern women's movement changed America.* New York: Viking.

Rosenberg, A. 1988. The crisis in knowing and understanding the Holocaust. In *Echoes from the Holocaust: Philosophical reflections on a dark time,* ed. A. Rosenberg and G. E. Meyers. Philadelphia: Temple University Press.

Rosenberg, H. H. 1998. *How to get married after thirty-five: The game plan for love.* New York: HarperCollins.

Rosenblum, B. 1997. Living in an unstable body. In *Staring back: The disability experiences from the inside out,* ed. K. Fries, pp. 93–104. New York: Penguin/Plume.

Ross, A., ed. 1997. *No sweat: Fashion, free trade, and the rights of garment workers.* New York: Verso.

Ross, L. J. 1993. African-American women and abortion: 1800–1970. In *Theorizing black feminisms: The visionary pragmatism of black women,* ed. S. M. James and A. P. A. Busia, pp. 141–59. New York: Routledge.

———, S. L. Brownlee, D. D. Diallo, L. Rodriquez, and the SisterSong Women of Color Reproductive Health Project. 2002. Just choices: Women of color, reproductive health and human rights. In *Policing the national body: Race, gender, and criminalization,* ed. J. Silliman and A. Bhattacharjee, pp. 147–74. Cambridge, MA: South End Press.

Rosset, P. 2011. Preventing hunger: Change economic policy. *Nature* 479(73/74): 472–73.

Roth, B. 2003. *Separate roads to feminism: Black, Chicana and white feminist movements in America's second wave.* New York: Cambridge University Press.

Rothblum, E., and S. Solovay, eds. 2009. *The fat studies reader.* New York: New York University Press.

Rousso, H. 2001. *Strong proud sisters: Girls and young women with disabilities.* Washington, DC: Center for Women Policy Studies.

Roychouduri, O. 2007. Constructing news, creating worldviews. In *Women's Lives: Multicultural Persectives,* 4th ed., eds. Gwyn Kirk and Margo Okazawa-Rey. New York: McGraw-Hill.

Rubin, G. 1984. Thinking sex: Notes for a radical theory of the politics of sexuality. In *Pleasure and danger: Exploring female sexuality,* ed. C. S. Vance, pp. 267–319. Boston: Routledge and Kegan Paul.

Ruddick, S. 1989. *Maternal thinking: Toward a politics of peace.* Boston: Beacon Press.

Russell, B. 1935. *In praise of idleness and other essays.* New York: W. W. Norton.

Russell, D. 1995. *Women, madness, and medicine.* Cambridge, England: Polity Press.

Russell, D. E. H. 1975. *The politics of rape: The victim's perspective.* New York: Stein and Day.

———. 1990. *Rape in marriage.* Rev. ed. Bloomington: Indiana University Press.

———. 1993. *Making violence sexy: Feminist views on pornography.* New York: Teachers College Press.

Saad, L. 2011. Americans still split along "pro-choice," "pro-life" lines. *Gallup politics.* www.gallup.com/poll/147734/americans-split-along-pro-choice-pro-life-lines.aspx

Sachs, C. 1996. *Gendered fields: Rural women, agriculture, and environment.* Boulder, CO: Westview Press.

Sachs, S. 2000. Sexual abuse reported at an immigration center. *New York Times,* October 5, p. A20.

Sacks, K. B. 1976. The class roots of feminism. *Monthly Review* 27(9).

Sadler, G. C. 1997. Women in combat: The U.S. military and the impact of the Persian Gulf War. In *Wives and warriors: Women and the military in the United States and Canada,* ed. L. Weinstein and C. White, pp. 79–97. Westport, Conn.: Bergin and Garvey.

Sajor, I., ed. 1998. *Common grounds: Violence against women in war and armed conflict.* Quezon City, Philippines: ASCENT.

Samath, F. 2011. Now for "Millennium Consumption Goals." *Inter Press Service News Agency,* January 24. http://ipsnews.net/newsTVE.asp?idnews=54211

Sampson, R. 2002. *Acquaintance rape of college students.* Washington, DC: U.S. Department of Justice, Office of Community Oriented Policing Services.

Sanger, M. 1920. *Women and the new race.* New York: Brentano's.

Sarah, R. 2006. *Single mom seeking: Playdates, blindates, and other dispatches from the dating world.* Emeryville, CA: Seal Press.

Sargent, F. O., P. Lusk, J. Rivera and M. Varela. 1991. *Rural Environmental Planning for Sustainable Communities.* Washington, DC: Island Press.

Saxton, M. 1995. Reproductive rights: A disability rights issue, *Sojourner.* July.

Scharnberg, K. 2005. Female GIs hard hit by war syndrome. *Chicago Tribune,* March 24.

Schneir, M. 1994. *Feminism: The essential historical writings.* New York: Vintage Books.

Scholinski, D. 1997. *The last time I wore a dress.* New York: Riverhead Books.

Schuetz, K. 2012. Stand up, fight back!: Unite against the war on women. *Ms.blog,* May 3. http://msmagazine.com/blog/blog/2012/05/03/stand-up-fight-back-unite-against-the-war-on-women/

Schultz, A. J. and L. Mullings. 2005. *Gender, race, class and health: Intersectional approaches.* San Francisco: Jossey-Bass.

Schur, L. 2004. Is there still a "double handicap"? Economic, social and political disparities experienced by women with disabilities. In *Gendering disability,* ed. B. G. Smith and B. Hutchison, pp. 253–71. New Brunswick: Rutgers University Press.

Schwab, J. 1994. *Deeper shades of green: The rise of blue-collar and minority environmentalism in America.* San Francisco: Sierra Club Books.

Schwartz, P. 1994. *Love between equals: How peer marriage really works.* New York: Free Press.

Scott, J. W. 1988. Deconstructing equality-versus-difference: Or, the uses of poststructuralist theory for feminism. *Feminist Studies* 14(1): 33–50.

———. 1993. The evidence of experience. In *The lesbian and gay studies reader,* ed. Henry Abelove, Michele Aina Barale and David M. Halperin, pp. 397–415. New York: Routledge.

Scott, W. J., and S. C. Stanley. 1994. *Gays and lesbians in the military: Issues, concerns, and contrasts.* Hawthorne, NY: Aldine de Gruyter.

Scott-Dixon, K., ed. 2006. *Trans/forming feminisms: Transfeminist voices speak out.* Toronto, ON: Sumach Press.

Seager, J. 1992. Operation desert disaster: Environmental costs of the war. In *collateral damage: The 'new world order' at home and abroad,* ed. Cynthia Peters. Boston: South End Press.

Segal, L. 1994. *Straight sex: Rethinking the politics of pleasure.* Berkeley: University of California Press.

Segrest, M. 1994. *Memoir of a race traitor.* Boston: South End Press.

Sentencing Project. 2007. *Women in the criminal justice system: Barriers to re-entering the community.* www.sentencingproject.org/PublicationDetails.aspx?PublicationID5586

Serano, J. 2007. *Whipping girl: A transsexual woman on sexism and the scapegoating of femininity.* Emeryville, CA: Seal Press.

Servicemembers Legal Defense Network. 1999. *Conduct unbecoming. Fifth annual report on "Don't ask, don't tell, don't pursue."* http://www.sldn.org/scripts/sldn.ixe?page?pr_03_15_99.

———. 2002. *Conduct unbecoming: The eighth annual report on "Don't ask, Don't tell, Don't pursue, Don't harass."* Washington, DC: SLDN.

Shaffer, A., and R. Gottlieb. 2007. Filling in 'food deserts.' *Los Angeles Times,* November 5. www.latimes.com/news/opinion/la-oe-gottlieb5nov05,0,7040113.story?coll=la-opinion-rightrail

Shah, S. 2012. Family detention center halted in Texas. *Detention Watch Network,* February 8. http://detentionwatchnetwork.wordpress.com/2012/02/08/family-detention-centers-halted-in-texas/

Shanley, M. ed. 2004. *Just marriage.* New York: Oxford University Press.

Shannonhouse, R. 2003. *Out of her mind: Women writing on madness,* Expanded ed. New York: Modern Library.

Shashahani, A. 2012. The 'sunk costs' of a profit-driven prison system, *Huffington Post,* May 30. www.huffingtonpost.com/azadeh-shahshahani/the-sunk-costs-of-a-profi_b_1554603.html

She, P. and G. A. Livermore. 2006. *Long-term poverty and disability among working-age adults.* Washington, DC: Cornell University Institute for Policy Research.

Sherrill, R. 1997. A year in corporate crime. *The Nation,* April 7, pp. 11–20.

Shih, E. 2007. Spirits in traffic: Transient community formation in opposition to forced victimization. In *Shout out: Women of color respond to violence,* ed. María Ochoa and Barbara K. Ige, pp. 86–100. Emeryville, CA: Seal Press.

Shih, J. 2006. Circumventing discrimination: Gender and ethnic strategies in Silicon valley. *Gender and Society* 20(2): 177–206.

Shin, A. 1999. Testing Title IX. *Ms.,* April/May, pp. 32–33.

Shiva, V. 1988. *Staying alive: Women, ecology and development.* London: Zed Books.

———. 2002a. Relocalization not globalization. In *Rethinking globalization: Teaching for justice in an unjust world,* ed. B. Bigelow and B. Peterson, pp. 248–49. Milwaukee, WI: Rethinking Schools.

———. 2002b. *Water wars: Privatization, pollution, and profit.* Cambridge, MA: South End Press.

———. 2005. *Earth democracy: Justice, sustainability, and peace.* Cambridge, MA: South End Press.

Showalter, E. 1987. *The female malady: Women, madness, and English culture, 1830–1980.* London: Virago.

Shugar, D. R. 1995. *Separatism and women's community.* Lincoln: University of Nebraska Press.

Shulman, S. 1990. Toxic travels: Inside the military's environmental nightmare. *Nuclear Times,* Autumn, pp. 20–32.

Shumway, C. 2004. Violence against female soldiers ignored. *The New Standard,* June 16.

Sidel, R. 1996. *Keeping women and children last: America's war on the poor.* New York: Penguin Books.

Siegal, N. 1998. Women in prison. *Ms.,* September/October, pp. 64–73.

Sigler, H., S. Love, and J. Yood. 1999. *Hollis Sigler's breast cancer journal.* New York: Hudson Hills Press.

Silliman, J., and A. Bhattacharjee, eds. 2002. *Policing the national body: Sex, race, and criminalization.* Cambridge, MA: South End Press.

———, M. G. Fried, L. Ross, and E. R. Gutiérrez. 2004. *Undivided rights: Women of color organize for reproductive justice.* Cambridge, MA: South End Press.

———, and Y. King, eds. 1999. *Dangerous intersections: Feminist perspectives on population, environment, and development.* Cambridge, MA: South End Press.

Simon, R. 1975. *Women and crime.* Lexington, MA: Lexington Books.

Simon, R. J., and R. M. Roorda. 2000. *In their own words: Transracial adoptees tell their stories.* New York: Columbia University Press.

Sirimanne, S. 2009. *The gender perspectives of the financial crisis.* For United Nations Commission on the Status of Women, 2009. www.un.org/womenwatch/daw/csw/csw53/panels/financial_crisis/Sirimanne.formatted.pdf

Sivard, R. L. 1996. *World military and social expenditures 1996.* 16th ed. Washington, DC: World Priorities.

Sjoberg, L., and C. Gentry. 2008. *Mothers, monsters, whores: Women's violence in global politics.* New York: Zed Books.

———, and S. Via, eds. 2010. *Gender, war, and militarism: Feminist perspectives.* Santa Barbara, CA: Praeger Security International.

Skaine, R. 1998. *Women at war: Gender issues of Americans in combat.* Jefferson, NC: McFarland and Co.

Skover, S. 2012. *The continuous appetite: Understanding your cravings, ending your overeating!* Bloomington, IN: Balboa Press.

Slater, L. 1998. *Prozac diary.* New York: Random House.

Slugocki, L. A., and E. C. Wilson. 2000. *The erotica project.* San Francisco: Cleis Press.

Smith, A. 1991. To all those who were Indian in a former life. *Ms.,* November/December, pp. 44–45.

———. 2002. Better dead than pregnant: The colonization of Native women's reproductive health. In *Policing the national body: Race, gender, and criminalization,* ed. J. Silliman and A. Bhattacharjee, pp. 123–46. Cambridge, MA: South End Press.

———. 2005a. Beyond pro-choice versus pro-life: Women of color and reproductive justice. *NWSA Journal* 17(1): 119–40.

———. 2005b. *Conquest: Sexual violence and American Indian genocide.* Cambridge, MA: South End Press.

Smith, B. ed. 1983. *Home girls: A Black feminist anthology.* New York: Kitchen Table/Women of Color Press.

———. 1998. *The truth that never hurts: Writings on race, gender, freedom.* New Brunswick, NJ: Rutgers University Press.

Smith, B. G., and B. Hutchison, eds. 2004. *Gendering disability.* New Brunswick, NJ: Rutgers University Press.

Smith, E. S. 2010. *The evolution of coffee markets for sustainable development: A Honduran cooperative's experience with fair trade.* MA thesis in anthropology, California State University-Chico.

Smith, M. 1997. When violence strikes home. *The Nation,* June 30, pp. 23–24.

Smith, S. 2005. *Women and socialism: Essays on women's liberation.* Chicago: Haymarket Books.

Sneed, C. 2000. Seeds of change, *Yes: A journal of positive futures,* Fall, no. 15.

Snell, A. 2011. The absence of justice: Private military contractors, sexual assault, and the U.S. government's policy of indifference. *University of Illinois Law Review* (3): 1125–64.

Snitow, A., C. Stansell, and S. Thompson, eds. 1983. *Powers of desire: The politics of sexuality.* New York: Monthly Review Press.

Solinger, R. 1994. *The abortionist: A woman against the law.* New York: Routledge.

———. 1998. *Abortion wars; A half century of struggle, 1950–2000,* Berkeley: University of California Press.

———. 2000. *Wake up little Susie: Single pregnancy and race before Roe v. Wade.* New York: Routledge.

———. 2005. *Pregnancy and power: A short history of reproductive politics in America.* New York: New York University Press.

Solinger, R., P. C. Johnson, M. L. Raimon, T. Reynolds, and R. C. Tapia, eds. 2010. *Interrupted life: Experiences of incarcerated women in the United States.* Berkeley: University of California Press.

Spears, E. G. 1998. *The Newtown story: One community's fight for environmental justice.* Gainesville, GA: Center for Democratic Renewal and Newtown Florist Club.

Spelman, E. V. 1988. *Inessential woman: Problems of exclusion in feminist thought.* Boston: Beacon Press.

Spivak, G. C. 1988. *In other worlds: Essays in cultural politics.* New York: Routledge.

Sprague, J. 2005. *Feminist methodologies for critical researchers: Bridging differences.* Walnut Creek, CA: AltaMira Press.

Springer, K. 2005. *Living for the revolution: Black feminist organizing, 1968–1980.* Durham, NC: Duke University Press.

Stacey, Jackie. 1993. Untangling feminist theory. In *Thinking feminist: Key concepts in women's studies,* ed. D. Richardson and V. Robinson, pp. 49–73. New York: Guilford Press.

Stacey, Judith. 1996. *In the name of the family: Rethinking values in the postmodern age.* Boston: Beacon Press.

Stan, A. 1995. *Debating sexual correctness.* New York: Delta.

Staples, S. 2000. The relationship between globalization and militarism. *Social Justice: A Journal of Conflict and World Change* 27(4): 18–22.

Starhawk. 2002. *Webs of power: Notes from the global uprising.* Gabriola Island, BC: New Society.

Stark, E. 2007. *Coercive control: The entrapment of women in personal life.* New York: Oxford University Press.

Stefan, S. 1994. The protection racket: Rape trauma syndrome, psychiatric labeling, and law. *Northwestern Law Review* 88(4): 1271–1345.

Stein, R., ed. 2004. *New perspectives on environmental justice: Gender, sexuality, and activism,* New Brunswick, NJ: Rutgers University Press.

Steinem, G. 1983. *Outrageous acts and everyday rebellions.* New York: Holt, Rinehart, & Winston.

Steingraber, S. 2001. *Having faith: An ecologist's journey to motherhood.* Cambridge, MA: Perseus.

Stevens, A. B. 2011. We are the 99% too: Creating a feminist space within Occupy Wall Street. *Ms. blog,* October 11. http://msmagazine.com/blog/blog/2011/10/11/we-are-the-99-too-creating-a-feminist-space-within-occupy-wall-street/

Stewart, N. A. 2007. Transform the world: What you can do with a degree in women's studies, *Ms.* Spring, pp. 65–66.

Stites, J., 2010. What the health care bill means for women. *Ms. blog,* March 24. http://msmagazine.com/blog/ blog/2010/03/24/what-the-health-care-bill-means-for-women/

Stockholm International Peace Research Institute. 2006. *The fifteen major spenders in 2006.* www.sipri.org/contents/milap/milex/mex_trends.html

Stoller, E. P., and R. C. Gibson, eds. 1994. *Worlds of difference: Inequality in the aging experience.* Thousand Oaks, CA: Pine Forge.

Stone, D. 2000. Fetal risks, women's rights: Showdown at Johnson Controls. *The American Prospect,* December 4. http://prospect.org/article/fetal-risks-womens-rights-showdown-johnson-controls

Stone, P. 2007 *Opting out? Why women really quit careers and head home.* Berkeley: University of California Press.

Stonequist, E. V. 1961. *The marginal man: A study in personality and cultural conflict.* New York: Scribner & Sons.

Storr, M., ed. 1999. *Bisexuality: A critical reader.* New York: Routledge.

St. Paige, E. 1999. *Zaftig: The case for curves.* Seattle, WA: Darling and Co.

Strossen, N. 2000. *Defending pornography: Free speech, sex, and the fight for women's rights.* New York: New York University Press.

Stryker, S. 2008. *Transgender history.* Emeryville, CA: Seal Press.

Stryker, S., and S. Whittle, eds. 2006. *The transgender reader.* New York: Routledge.

Sturdevant, S., and B. Stoltzfus. 1992. *Let the good times roll: Prostitution and the U.S. military in Asia.* New York: New Press.

Sturgeon, N. 1997. *Ecofeminist nature: Race, gender, feminist theory and political action.* New York: Routledge.

Sudbury, J. 2011. From women prisoners to people in women's prisons: Challenging the gender binary in antiprison work. In *Razor wire women,* ed. J. M. Lawston and Ashley E. Lucas. Albany, NY: State University of New York Press.

Suggs, W. 2002. Title IX at 30. *Chronicle of Higher Education,* June 21, pp. A38–41.

Sutton, B., S. Morgen, and J. Novkov, eds. 2008. *Security disarmed: Critical perspectives on gender, race, and militarization.* New Brunswick , NJ: Rutgers University Press.

Suzack, C., S. M. Huhndorf, and J. Perreault, eds. 2011. *Indigenous women and feminism: Politics, activism, culture.* Seattle: University of Washington Press.

Swerdlow, A. 1993. *Women strike for peace: Traditional motherhood and radical politics in the 1960s.* Chicago: University of Chicago Press.

Swern, A. J. 2008. *Drug treatment alternative-to-prison, seventeenth annual report.* Kings County District Attorney's Office. www.BrooklynDA.org

Swers, M. 2001. Research on women in legislatures: What have we learned, Where are we going? *Women and Politics* 23: 167–85.

Swiss, S., and J. Giller. 1993. Rape as a crime of war: A medical perspective. *Journal of the American Medical Association* 27: 612–15.

Szasz, A. 1994. *Ecopopulism, toxic waste and the movement for environmental justice.* Minneapolis: University of Minnesota Press.

Tadiar. N. 2003. *Fantasy production: Sexual encounters and other Philippine consequences for the new world order.* Hong Kong: Hong Kong University Press.

Takahashi, R. 1998. U.S. concentration camps and exclusion policies. In *Women's lives: Multicultural perspectives,* ed. Gwyn Kirk and Margo Okazawa-Rey, pp. 362–68. Mountain View, CA: Mayfield.

Takaki, R. 1987. *Strangers from a different shore: Perspectives on race and ethnicity in America.* New York: Oxford University Press.

Takazato, S. 2000. Report from Okinawa: Long-term U.S. military presence and violence against women, *Canadian Women's Studies,* 19 (4): 42–47.

Tanenbaum, L. 2000. *Growing up female with a bad reputation.* New York: HarperCollins.

Tarrant, S., ed. 2007. *Men speak out: Views on gender, sex and power.* New York: Routledge.

Tashiro, Akira. 2001. *Discounted casualties: The human cost of depleted uranium.* Hiroshima, Japan: Chugoku Shimbun.

Tateishi, J. 1984. *And justice for all: An oral history of the Japanese American detention camps.* New York: Random House.

Taylor, D. E. 1997. Women of color, environmental justice, and ecofeminism. In *Ecofeminism: Women, culture, nature,* ed. K. Warren, pp. 38–81. Bloomington: Indiana University Press.

Teays, W., and L. Purdy. 2001. *Bioethics, justice, and health care.* Belmont, CA: Wadsworth.

Tenenbein, S. 1998. Power, beauty, and dykes. In *Looking queer,* ed. D. Atkins, pp. 155–60. Binghamton, NY: Harrington Park Press.

Terry, G. 2009. No climate justice without gender justice: An overview of the issues, *Gender and Development* 17 (1): 5–18.

Tetlow, T. 2009. Discriminatory acquittal. *William & Mary Bill of Rights Journal* 18(1): 75–129. http://scholarship.law.wm.edu/wmborj/vol18/iss1/4

Tétreault, M. A. 1997. Accountability or justice? Rape as a war crime. In *Feminist frontiers IV,* ed. L. Richardson, V. Taylor, and N. Whittier, pp. 427–39. New York: McGraw-Hill.

Thomas, S., and C. Wilcox, eds. 1998. *Women and elective office: Past, present, and future.* New York: Oxford University Press.

Thompson, B. W. 1994. *A hunger so wide and so deep.* Minneapolis: University of Minnesota Press.

Thompson, C., and M. Wiggins, eds. 2002. *The human cost of food: Farmworkers' lives, labor and advocacy.* Austin: University of Texas Press.

Thornhill, R., and C. T. Palmer. 2000. *A natural history of rape: Biological bases of sexual coercion.* Cambridge, MA: MIT Press.

Toman, E. and T. Jolls. 2005. *Literacy for the 21st century: An overview and orientation guide to media literacy education.* Santa Monica, CA.: Center for Media Literacy. Accessed on August 24, 2012 at http://www.medialit.org/sites/default/files/mlk/01_MLKorientation.pdf.

Trask, H-K. 1999. *From a native daughter: Colonialism and sovereignty in Hawai'i.* Honolulu: University of Hawaii Press.

Trask, M. 1992. Native Hawaiian historical and cultural perspectives on environmental justice. *Race, Poverty and the Environment* 3(1).

Trenka, J. J., J. C. Oparah, and S. Y. Shin, eds. 2006. *Outsiders within: Writing on transracial adoption.* Cambridge, MA: South End Press.

Trigg, M., ed. 2010. *Leading the way: Young women's activism for social change.* New Brunswick, NJ: Rutgers University Press.

Troustine, J. 2001. *Shakespeare behind bars: The power of drama in a women's prison.* New York: St. Martin's Press.

Trujillo, C., ed. 1991. *Chicana lesbians: The girls our mothers warned us about.* Berkeley, CA: Third Women Press.

Tuana, N., ed. 1989. *Feminism and science.* Bloomington: Indiana University Press.

Tucker, S., and E. Cadora. 2003. *Justice reinvestment, Ideas for an Open Society,* vol. 3, no. 3, November. Available at HYPERLINK "http://www.soros.org/sites/default/files/ideas_reinvestment.pdf" www.soros.org/sites/default/files/ideas_reinvestment.pdf.

Tuloss, J.K. 1996. Transforming Urban Regimes-A grassroots approach to comprehensive community development: The Dudley Street Neighborhood Initiative. Available at http://comm-rg.wisc.edu/papers98/tulloss.htm. Accessed May 18, 2012.

Tuominen, M. C. 2003. *We are not babysitters: Family care providers redefine work and care.* Piscataway, NJ: Rutgers University Press.

U.N. High Commissioner for Refugees. 2002. Refugee Women. http://www.worldrefugeeday.info/men2.html

UNICEF. 2007. *The state of the world's children 2008: Child survival.* New York: UNICEF. www.unicef.org/publications/index_42623.html

U.N. Interagency Group on Child Mortality Estimation. 2011. *Levels and trends in child mortality 2011.* www.unicef.org/media/files/Child_Mortality_Report_2011_Final.pdf

University of Maryland. 2007. *J-school administrators overwhelmingly white and male, survey finds.* Press release, August 14. www.journalism.umd.edu/newrel/07newsrel/jmcsurvey07.html

Urban, J. L. 2008. *Nation, immigration, and environmental security.* New York: Palgrave MacMillan.

U.S. Department of Justice. 1997. *Violence-related injuries treated in hospital emergency departments.* Michael R. Rand. Washington, DC: Bureau of Justice Statistics.

———. 2008. *National teen dating violence awareness and prevention week,* February 4–8, 2008 www.ovw.usdoj.gov

———. 2011. *Criminal victimization in the United States, 2008.* Bureau of Justice Statistics, Table 29. http://bjs.ojp.usdoj.gov/content/pub/pdf/cvus0802.pdf

U.S. Department of Labor, Bureau of Labor Statistics, 2011. *Women at work.* www.bls.gov/spotlight/2011/women/pdf/women_bls_spotlight.pdf

———. 2012. *Union members summary,* Table 2. www.bls.gov/news.release/union2.nr0.htm

Ussher, J. 1991. *Women's madness.* Hemel Hempstead, England: Harvester Wheatsheaf.

Uttal, L. 2002. *Making care work: Employed mothers in the new childcare market.* New Brunswick, NJ: Rutgers University Press.

Vance, C., ed. 1984. *Pleasure and danger: Exploring female sexuality.* Boston: Routledge and Kegan Paul.

Van Sommer, A. and S. M. Zwemer, 1907. *Our Moslem Sisters: A Cry of Need from the Lands of Darkness Interpreted by Those Who Heard It.* New York: F.H. Revell Company.

Waddington, L. 2011. Braley hopes to end sexual and domestic violence against women in the military. *The Iowa Independent,* May 3. http://iowaindependent.com/55497/braley-hopes-to-end-sexual-and-domestic-violence-against-women-in-the-military

Wade-Gayles, G. 1993. *Pushed back to strength: A Black woman's journey home.* Boston: Beacon Press.

Walby, S. 2011. *The future of feminism.* Malden, MA: Polity Press.

Walker, J. 1996. The prison industrial complex. *RESIST Newsletter* 5(9): 4–6.

Walker, L. 1979. *The battered woman.* New York: Harper & Row.

———. 1984. *The battered woman syndrome.* New York: Springer.

Walker, R. 1995a. Lusting for freedom. In *Listen up: Voices of the next generation,* ed. Barbara Findlen, pp. 95–101. Seattle, WA: Seal Press.

———. 1995b. *To be real: Telling the truth and changing the face of feminism.* New York: Anchor/Doubleday.

———. 2001. *Black, white, and Jewish: Autobiography of a shifting self.* New York: Riverhead Books.

Wal-Mart. 2012. Walmart corporate: FAQs. http://investors. walmartstores.com/phoenix.zhtml?c=112761&p=irol-faq

Walsh, M. 2000. *Aftermath: The impact of conflict on women in Bosnia and Herzegovina.* Working paper no. 302. Washington, DC: Center for Development Information and Evaluation, U.S. Agency for International Development. http://pdf.usaid.gov/pdf_docs/PNACJ322.pdf. Accessed on April 19, 2012.

Walters, B., and H. Downs. 1996. *20/20,* November 15. New York: American Broadcasting Company.

Walters, S. D. 2001. *All the rage: The story of gay visibility in America.* Chicago: Chicago University Press.

Wann, M. 1998. *Fat! So? Because you don't have to apologize for your size.* New York: Ten Speed Press.

Waring, M. 1988. *If women counted: A new feminist economics.* New York: Harper & Row.

Warner, S. 2011. Restorytive justice: Theater as a redressive mechanism for incarcerated women. In *Razor wire women,* ed. J. M. Lawston and A. E Lucas. Albany, NY: State University of New York Press.

Warner, S. B. 1987. *To dwell is to garden: A history of Boston's community gardens.* Boston: Northeastern University Press.

War Resisters League. 2012. *Where your income tax money really goes.* www.warresisters.org/sites/default/files/ FY2013piechart-english-color_0.pdf

Warren, K. J., ed. 1994. *Ecological feminism.* New York: Routledge.

———. 2000. *Ecofeminist philosophy: A western perspective on what it is and why it matters.* Lanham, MD: Rowman and Littlefield.

Washburn, P. 1993. Women and the peace movement. In *Women and the use of military force,* ed. R. Howes and M. Stevenson, pp. 135–48. Boulder, CO: Lynne Rienner.

Wasserman, C. 1992. FMS: The backlash against survivors. *Sojourner: The Women's Forum,* November, pp. 18–20.

Watterson, K. 1996. *Women in prison.* Rev. ed. Boston: Northeastern University Press.

Webber, W. S. 1993. *Lesbians in the military speak out.* Northboro, MA: Madwoman Press.

WEDO, 2005. Beijing Betrayed. Available at www.wedo.org/ themes/global-governance/beijing-betrayed-2005

Weedon, C. 1987. *Feminist practice and poststructuralist theory.* New York: Blackwell.

Weeks, J. 2010. *Sexuality.* New York: Routledge.

Weinstein, L., and C. White, eds. 1997. *Wives and warriors: Women and the military in the United States and Canada.* Westport, CT: Greenwood Press.

Weise, E. R., ed. 1992. *Closer to home: Bisexuality and feminism.* Seattle, WA: Seal Press.

Wendell, S. 1996. *The rejected body.* New York: Routledge.

Werner International. 2009. *International comparison of the hourly labor cost in the primary textile industry.* www .werner-newtwist.com/en/newsl-vol-006/index.htm

Wessler, S. F. 2011. Thousands of kids lost from parents in U.S. deportation system. *ColorLines,* November 2. http:// colorlines.com/archives/2011/11/thousands_of_kids_ lost_in_foster_homes_after_parents_deportation.html

West, G., and R. L. Blumberg, eds. 1990. *Women and social protest.* New York: Oxford University Press.

Whisnant, R., and C. Stark. 2004. *Not for sale: Feminists resisting prostitution and pornography.* North Melbourne, Australia: Spinifex.

Whitaker, L. D., ed. 2008. *Voting the gender gap.* Urbana: University of Illinois Press.

White, A. M. 2010. *African Americans doing feminism: Putting theory into everyday practice.* Albany, NY: SUNY Press.

White, E. 2002. *Fast girls: Teenage tribes and the myth of the slut.* New York: Penguin.

White, E. C. 1985. *Chain, chain, change: For Black women dealing with physical and emotional abuse.* Seattle, WA: Seal Press.

———, ed. 1990. *The Black women's health book: Speaking for ourselves.* Seattle, WA: Seal Press.

———. 1991. Unhealthy appetites: Large is lovely, unless you're unhappy overeating and unable to lose weight. *Essence,* September, p. 28.

White House Council on Women and Girls. 2011. *Women in America: Indicators of social and economic wellbeing.* www .whitehouse.gov/sites/default/files/rss_viewer/ Women_in_America.pdf

Whitman, S. 2010. Sexual violence, coltan and the Democratic Republic of Congo. In *Critical environmental security: Rethinking the links between natural resources and political violence,* ed. M. A. Schnurr and L. A. Swatuk. Halifax, Nova Scotia: Dalhousie University, Center for Foreign Policy Studies.

White, L. 1988. *The obsidian mirror: An adult healing from incest.* Seattle, WA: Seal Press.

Wilchins, R. A. 1997. *Read my lips: Sexual subversion and the end of gender.* Ithaca, NY: Firebrand.

Wilkerson, A. 2011. Disability, sex radicalism, and political agency. In *Feminist disability studies,* ed. Kim Q. Hall, pp. 193–217. Bloomington: Indiana University Press.

Williams, F. 2005. Toxic breast milk? *New York Times Magazine,* January 9.

Williams, J. 2000. *Unbending gender: Why family and work conflict and what to do about it.* New York: Oxford University Press.

Williams, K., with M. E. Straub. 2005. *Love my rifle more than you: Young and female in the U.S. army.* New York: Norton.

Williams, T. T. 1992. *Refuge: An unnatural history of family and place.* New York: Vintage.

Wilson, E. 2010. Single parents juggle military, home demands. *American Forces Press Service,* May 20. www.af.mil/news/story.asp?id=123205583

———. 2010a. *Care plan to encompass more military families.* American Forces Press Service. HYPERLINK "http:// www.defense.gov/news/newsarticle.aspx?id=58339" www.defense.gov/news/newsarticle.aspx?id=58339. Accessed April 15, 2012.

Wilson, M. 1993. *Crossing the boundary: Black women survive incest.* Seattle, WA: Seal Press.

Wilson, N. 2010. Culture of rape. *Ms.,* 20(2), pp. 32–35.

Wingspan Domestic Violence Project. 1998. *Abuse and violence in same-gender relationships: A resource for lesbian, gay, bi, and transgendered communities.* Tucson, AZ: Wingspan Domestic Violence Project.

Winne, M. 2008. *Closing the food gap: Resetting the table in the land of plenty.* Boston: Beacon Press.

Winterich, J. A. 2007. Review of "age matters" edited by T. M. Calasanti and K. F. Slevin. *Gender and Society* 21(5): 783–86.

Withorn, A. 1999. Temp work: "A devil's bargain" for women. *Sojourner: The Women's Forum,* October, 9.

Wittig, M. 1978. *The straight mind.* Boston: Beacon Press.

Woelfle-Erskine, C., J. O. Cole, L. Allen, and A. Danger. 2007. *Dam nation: Dispatches from the water underground.* Brooklyn, NY: Soft Skull Press.

Wolf, N. 1991. *The beauty myth.* New York: Doubleday.

———. 1997. *Promiscuities: The secret struggle for womanhood.* New York: Ballantine.

Women and Environments. 2007. special issue on Gender and Climate Change. no. 74/75.

Women of Color Policy Network. 2011. *Wage disparities and women of color.* New York University Wagner School of Public Service. http://wagner.nyu.edu/wocpn/publications/files/Pay_Equity_Policy_Brief.pdf

Women's Foundation. 2002. *Failing to make ends meet: The economic status of women in California.* San Francisco: The Women's Foundation.

Women's Refugee Commission. 2010. *Torn apart by immigration enforcement: Parental rights and immigration detention.* http://womensrefugeecommission.org/programs/detention/parental-rights

Women's Research and Education Institute. 2002. *Women in the military.* Washington, DC: WREI. http://www.wrei.org/projects/wiu/wim/index.htm

Women's Prison Association. 2009. *Women's voices: Advocacy by criminal justice involved women.* http://66.29.139.159/pdf/Womens Voices March 2009.pdf

Woods, H. 2000. *Stepping up to power: The political journey of American women.* Boulder, CO: Westview Press.

Worcester, N. 2004. Hormone replacement therapy: Getting to the heart of the politics of women's health? *NWSA Journal* 16(3): 56–69.

Working Group on the WTO. 1999. *A citizens' guide to the World Trade Organization.* New York: Apex Press.

World Bank. 2004. *Global debt finance.* Washington, DC: World Bank.

World Health Organization. 1946. *Preamble to the constitution of the World Health Organization,* adopted by the International Health Conference, New York, June 19–22.

Yancey, A. K., J. Leslie, and E. K. Abel. 2006. Obesity at the crossroads: Feminist and public health perspectives. *Signs: Journal of Women in Culture and Society* 31(2): 425–43.

Yans-McLaughlin, V., ed. 1990. *Immigration reconsidered.* New York: Oxford University Press.

Yeates, N. 2009. *Globalizing care economies and migrant workers: Exploration in global care chains.* New York: Palgrave/Macmillan.

Yen, M. 1989. Refusal to jail immigrant who killed wife stirs outrage. *Washington Post,* April 10, p. A3.

Yoder, J. 1989. Women at West Point: Lessons for token women in male-dominated occupations. In *Women: A feminist perspective,* ed. J. Freeman. Mountain View, CA: Mayfield.

Yoo, D. K. 2000. *Growing up Nisei: Race, generation and culture among Japanese Americans of California, 1924–1949.* Urbana-Champagne: University of Illinois Press.

Young, M. E., M. A. Nosek, C. A. Howland, G. Chanpong, and D. H. Rintala. 1997. Prevalence of abuse of women with physical disabilities. *Archives of Physical Medicine and Rehabilitation* 78: S34–S38.

Young, W. A. 1997. Women and immigration. Unpublished manuscript produced for Women's Commission for Refugee Women and Children, Washington, DC.

Zahn, M. A., S. R. Hawkins, J. Chiancone, and A. Whitworth. 2008. *The Girls Study Group: Charting the way to delinquency prevention for girls.* Office of Juvenile Justice and Delinquency Prevention, www.ncjrs.gov/pdffiles1/ojjdp/223434.pdf

Zakaria, F. 2102. Incarcerated nation. *Time Magazine,* April 2. www.time.com/time/magazine/article/0,9171,2109777-2,00.html

Zambrano, M. Z. 1985. *Mejor sola que mal accompanda: For the Latina in an abusive relationship.* Seattle, WA: Seal Press.

Zamora-Olib, O. A., ed. 2000. *Inheritors of the earth: The human face of the U.S. military contamination at Clarke Air Base, Pampanga, Philippines.* Quezon City, Philippines: People's Task Force for Bases Cleanup.

Zangana, H. 2007. *City of widows: An Iraqi woman's account of war and resistance.* New York: Seven Stories Press.

Zeff, R., M. Love, and K. Stults, eds. 1989. *Empowering ourselves: Women and toxics organizing.* Falls Church, VA: Citizens Clearinghouse for Hazardous Wastes.

Zepernick, M. 1998a. The sovereign people are stirring. *The Cape Cod Times,* November 27, p. A15.

———. 1998b. A lesson in democracy. *The Cape Cod Times,* December 11, p. A15.

Zimmerman, L. 2003. Where are the women? The strange case of the missing feminists. When was the last time you saw one on TV? *The Women's Review of Books* 21(1): 5–6.

Zimmerman, M., J. Litt, and C. Bose. 2006. *Gender and care work in global perspective.* Palo Alto, CA: Stanford University Press.

Zinn, H. 1995. *People's history of the United States: 1492–present.* Rev. and updated ed. New York: HarperPerennial.

Zita, J., ed. 1997. Special issue: Third wave feminism. *Hypatia: A Journal of Feminist Philosophy* 12(3) (Summer).

Credits

Page 227 "The Black Beauty Myth" by Sirena J. Riley from COLONIZE THIS! Young Women of Color on Today's Feminism, edited by Daisy Hernandez and Bushra Rehman, pp. 357–369. Copyright © 2002. Used by permission of Perseus Books Group. **Page 232** "Feminist Theory, the Body and the Disabled Figure" by Rosemarie Garland-Thomson from DISABILITY STUDIES READER, edited by Lennard Davis, pp. 279–292. Reprinted by permission of Routledge/Taylor & Francis Group, LLC and Rosemarie Garland-Thomson. **Page 238** "Three Generations of Native American Women's Birth Experience" by Joy Harjo from MS. Magazine, 1991. Reprinted by permission of Joy Harjo. **Page 241** "Young Women's Eggs: Elite and Ordinary" by Elizabeth Reis, from BIOPOLITICAL TIMES, September 15, 2011. Used by permission of the author. **Page 243** "Reproductive Justice: Vision, Analysis, and Action for a Stronger Movement" reprinted by permission. **Page 245** "Reproductive Justice: Vision, Analysis, and Action for a Stronger Movement" reprinted by permission. **Page 246** "Reproductive Justice: Vision, Analysis, and Action for a Stronger Movement" reprinted by permission. **Page 247** "Understanding Positive Women's Realities" by Emma Bell and Luisa Orza from EXCHANGE ON HIV/AIDS, SEXUALITY AND GENDER, Autumn 2006, pp. 1–4. Reprinted by permission of the authors. **Page 250** "Living to Love" by bell hooks from SISTERS OF THE YAM, pp. 97–111. Copyright © 1993. Reprinted by permission of South End Press.

Chapter 6: Page 261 Source: Asian Women's Shelter, adapted from Domestic Abuse Intervention Project, Duluth, MN. Used with permission. **Page 263** With kind permission of Jacky Fleming. **Page 274** "Sexual Violence and American Indian Genocide" by Andrea Smith. Reprinted by permission of the author. **Page 283** "Radical Pleasure: Sex and the End of Victimhood" by Aurora Levins Morales from MEDICINE STORIES, pp. 117–119. Reprinted by permission of South End Press. **Page 284** "Engaging Men Against Violence" by Jonathan Grove. Used by permission of the author. **Page 290** "Alternative Interventions to Violence: Creative Interventions." Used by permission of Creative Interventions, www.creative-interventions.org. **Page 297** "Territory, Sovereignty, and Crimes of the Second State: The Writing on the Body of Murdered Women" by Rita Laura Segato from TERRORIZING WOMEN: Feminicide in the Americas, edited by Rosa-Linda Fregoso and Cynthia Bejarano, pp. 70–92. Copyright © 2010. Used by permission of Duke University Press.

Chapter 7: Page 309 By Kirk as appeared in MS Magazine, May/June 1997, p. 5. Copyright © 1994 by Kirk. **Page 314** Baby Blues Partnership. King Features Syndicate. Used by permission. **Page 322** "Loving Across the Boundary." Copyright © 1995 Ann Filemyr. Reprinted by permission of the author. **Page 330** "Shattering Two Molds, Feminist Parents with Disabilities" by Carol J. Gill and Larry A. Voss, 1994. Used by permission of the authors. **Page 333** "Why Privilege Marriage?" from "Breaking Vows: Marriage Promotion, The New Patriarchy, and the retreat from Egalitarianism" by Kaaryn Gustafson from STANFORD JOURNAL OF CIVIL RIGHTS AND CIVIL LIBERTIES, 5(2), October 2009. Used by permission of Kaaryn Gustafson. **Page 342** "The Mommy Tax" from THE PRICE OF MOTHERHOOD by Ann Crittenden, © 2001 by Ann Crittenden, pp. 87–109. Reprinted by permission of Henry Holt and Company, LLC and Ann Crittenden. **Page 343** Copyright Nicole Hollander. Reprinted by permission. **Page 350** "To Whom Much Is Given, Much Is Expected: Successful Women, Family, and Responsibility" from HAVING IT ALL? Black Women and Success by Veronica Chambers, copyright © 2003 by Veronica Chambers. Used by permission of Doubleday, a division of Random House, Inc. **Page 358** "Women and Men Living on the Edge: Economic Insecurity After the Great Recession" 2011, by Jeff Hayes and Heidi Hartman.

Chapter 8: Page 364 From CAFRA NEWS, March-May 1990, p. 9. Reprinted by permission. **Page 376** Herri/Mujeres en Accion. **Page 370** "Supply Chain Pressures Create Precarious Employment" from OXFAM INTERNATIONAL (2004, 5). Reprinted by permission. **Page 382** "The Homeland, Aztlan," from BORDERLANDS/LA FRONTERA: The New Mestiza. Copyright © 1987, 1999 by Gloria Anzaldúa. Reprinted by permission of Aunt Lute Books. **Page 388** "Shilling Love" by Shailja Patel. Reprinted by permission. **Page 390** "The Care Crisis in the Philippines: Children and Transnational Families in the New Global Economy" by Rhacel Salazar Parreñas from GLOBAL WOMAN: Nannies, Maids and Sex Workers in the New Economy, edited by Barbara Ehrenreich and Arlie Hochschild, pp. 39–54. Reprinted by permission of Rhacel Salazar Parreñas. **Page 399** "Remotely Sensed: A Topography of the Global Sex Trade" by Ursula Biemann from FEMINIST REVIEW (70) 2002, pp. 75–88. Reprinted by permission of Palgrave Macmillan. **Page 403** From MADE IN CHINA by Pun Ngai. Copyright © 2005. Durham, NC: Duke University Press. Used by permission. **Page 411** "Building Water Democracy: People's Victory Against Coca-Cola in Plachimada" by Vandana Shiva from ZNet Commentary, May 13, 2004.

Chapter 9: Page 423 "The Funnel of Injustice" by Kiaran Honderich 2003, p. 10. Reprinted by permission of the author. **Page 432** "Women in Prison and Work" by Marilyn Buck, originally published in FEMINIST STUDIES, 30(2), Summer 2004: 451–455, by permission of the publisher, Feminist Studies, Inc. **Page 435** "A Mother's Love" by Andrea C. James, 2012. Used by permission of the author. **Page 439** "Barriers to Basic Care" from RESISTANCE BEHIND BARS: The Struggles of Incarcerated Women, by Victoria Law. Copyright © 2009. Oakland, CA: PM Press. **Page 446** "Media Representations and the Criminalization of Arab Americans and Muslim Americans" by Suad Joseph and Benjamin D'Harlingue. Reprinted by permission. **Page 449** "Disappearing Parents: Immigration Enforcement and the Child Welfare System" by Nina Rabin from CONNECTICUT LAW REVIEW, 44(1), 2011. Used by permission. **Page 452** Excerpts from "Women of Color, Globalization and the Politics of Incarceration" by Julia Sudbury from THE CRIMINAL JUSTICE SYSTEM AND WOMEN, edited by Barbara Raffel Price and Natalie Sokoloff, pp. 219–234. Reprinted by permission of The McGraw-Hill Companies.

Chapter 10: Page 469 © 2005 P.S. Mueller. Used by permission. **Page 478** Cartoon by bulbul-www.bulbul.com, P.O. Box 4100, Mountain View, CA 94040. Reprinted by permission. **Page 481** "Sneak Attack: The Militarization of U.S. Culture" by Cynthia Enloe, from MS Magazine, December/January 2002. Reprinted by permission of MS Magazine, © 2002. **Page 482** "Belonging" by Anuradha Kristina Bhagwati. Reprinted by permission of the author. **Page 486** "Empire on Trial: The Subic Rape Case and The Struggle for Philippine Women's Liberation" by Anne E. Lacsamana from WORK AND DAYS, 57/58, Vol. 29, 2011, pp. 203–215. Used by permission of the author. **Page 493** "A Bird with One Wing" from A WOMAN AMONG WARLORDS by Malalai Joya. Copyright © 2009. NY: Scribner, Simon & Schuster. **Page 500** "Mother's Day Proclamation—1870" by Julia Ward Howe.

Chapter 11: Page 504 © M. Wuerker **Figure 11.1. p. 508** Source: Bill Bigelow and Bob Peterson, editors, RETHINKING

GLOBALIZATION, Rethinking Schools Press, Milwaukee, WI, 2002. Reprinted by permission of Rethinking Schools Press. **Page 516** Excerpt from "Rose Moon" from HAVING FAITH by Sandra Steingraber. Copyright © 2001 by Sandra Steingraber. Reprinted by permission of Da Capo Press, a member of Perseus Books, LLC. **Page 563** "Gender, Asthma Politics, and Urban Environmental Justice Activism" by Julie Sze, from NEW PERSPECTIVES ON ENVIRONMENTAL JUSTICE: Gender, Sexuality and Activism, edited by Rachel Stein, pp. 177–190. Copyright © 2004. NJ: Rutgers University Press. Used by permission. **Page 532** "Thinking and Eating at the Same Time" by Michele Loyd Paige from SISTAH VEGAN, edited by A. Breeze Harper. Copyright © 2010. NY: Lantern Books. **Page 536** "Women and Food Chains: The Gendered Politics of Food" by Patricia Allen and Carolyn Sacks, from INTERNATIONAL JOURNAL OF SOCIOLOGY OF FOOD AND AGRICULTURE 15(1): 1–23, © 2007. **Page 546** "Reproductive Justice, Not Population Control: Breaking the Wrong Links and Making the Right Ones in the Movement for Climate Justice" by Betsy Hartmann and Elizabeth Barajas-Roman, 2009. Reprinted by permission of Stephanie McMillan. **Page 553** "Women's Responses to Environmental Destruction and State Violence in the Niger Delta, by Sokari Ekin, from FEMINIST AFRICA #10. Copyright © 2008. Used by permission of the author.

Chapter 12: Page 563 With kind permission of Jacky Fleming. **Page 566** By Yang as appeared in MS Magazine, January/February 1993, p. 30. **Page 567** Source: http://www.ipu.org/wmn-e-classif.htm.

Reprinted by permission of Inter-Parliamentary Union. **Page 572** UN Millenium Development Goals from www.undp.org. Reprinted by permission. **Page 575** "The Body Politic" by Abra Fortune Chernik from LISTEN UP: Voices From the Next Feminist Generation, edited by Barbara Findlen. Copyright © 1995 by Barbara Findlen. Reprinted by permission of Seal Press, a member of Perseus Books Group. **Page 579** "The Power of Collective Expression: College Students and Immigrant Women Learning Together" by Kathleen S. Yep. Copyright © 2012. Used by permission of the author. **Page 585** "Staging Activism: New York City Performing Artists as Cultural Workers" by Amy Jo Goddard from SOCIAL JUSTICE, 34(1), 2007. Reprinted by permission. **Page 595** "Changing the Face of Leadership: Legislators at Large for American Women" by Edna Ishayik from LEADING THE WAY: Young Women's Activism for Social Change, edited by Mary K. Trigg. Copyright © 2010. NJ: Rutgers University Press. Used by permission. **Page 600** "Women Working Across Borders for Peace and Genuine Security" by Ellen-Rae Cachola, Gwyn Kirk, Lisa Linda Natividad, and Maria Reinat Pumarejo, from PEACE REVIEW: A Journal for Social Justice #22, pp 164–170. Copyright © 2010. NY: Routledge/Taylor & Francis. **Page 605** "Meeting the Leadership Challenges of Women with Disabilities: Mobility International USA," by Cindy Lewis. Reprinted by permission of the author. **Page 608** Excerpts from "The Global Women's Movement: Definitions and Origins" by Peggy Antrobus from THE GLOBAL WOMEN'S MOVEMENT: Origins, Issues and Strategies, © 2004, pp. 9–25. Reprinted by permission of Zed Books Ltd.

Photo Credits

Chapter 1: **Page 2** © Bettmann/Corbis Chapter Copyright W.W. Gustin/Library of Congress. **Page 28** © Tia Cross.

Chapter 2: **Page 50** Doug Menuez/PhotoDisc/Getty Images. **Page 90** AP Photo/Adam Butler.

Chapter 3: **Page 100** Maria Teijeiro/Getty Images. **Page 100** © Royalty-Free/Corbis. **Page 100** Hoby Finn/PhotoDisc/Getty Images. **Page 100** © Rick Reinhard. **Page 108** © Rick Reinhard. **Page 113** Gary Kazanijan/Associated Press.

Chapter 4: **Page 172** © Bettmann/Corbis. **Page 172** © Underwood & Underwood/Corbis. **Page 172** © Albert Ferreira/Corbis. **Page 172** Philippe Petit-Mars/Corbis. **Page 181** © JupiterImages/ThinkStock.

Chapter 5: **Page 208** © David Sherman/NBAE/Getty Images. **Page 212** © Reuters NewMedia Inc/Corbis. **Page 235** © Brenda Prager.

Chapter 6: **Page 258** Created by Southpaw (www.southpaw.org) for the Commission on the Status of Women in San Francisco.

Page 289 Courtesy Seth Bynum. **Page 298** Marco Ugarte/ Associated Press.

Chapter 7: **Page 306** © Andersen Ross/PhotoDisc/Getty Images. **Page 306** © Geoff Manasse/PhotoDisc/Getty Images. **Page 306** © Studio M/Jupiter Images. **Page 306** Geoff Manasse/PhotoDisc/Getty Images. **Page 308** Jose Luis Pelaez Inc./Getty Images. **Page 310** © Barbara Seyda. **Page 311** © Owen Seumptewa.

Chapter 8: **Page 362** Wang wei cd-Imaginechina. **Page 368** "Remote Sensing" © Ursula Biemann. **Page 371** © Reuters NewMedia, Inc./ Corbis.

Chapter 9: **Page 416** Scott Braley (www.scottbraley.com). **Page 425** AP/World Wide Photos.

Chapter 10: **Page 464** AP/World Wide Photos. **Page 477** Courtesy of the War Resisters League.

Chapter 11: **Page 502** © Thierry Orban/Sygma/Corbis. **Page 506** © Jim Cummins/Corbis. **Page 510** AP/World Wide Photos. **Page 554** Inyene Benedicta Okon.

Name Index

Subject Index

About the Authors

Gwyn Kirk (right) has taught courses in women's studies, environmental studies, political science, and sociology at several U.S. academic institutions, most recently at the University of Oregon. She received a Rockefeller Fellowship at the University of Hawaii (2002) and was a Visiting Scholar at the Women's Leadership Institute, Mills College (2001–2003). She shared the Jane Watson Irwin Chair in Women's Studies at Hamilton College with Margo Okazawa-Rey (1999–2001). Her articles on feminism, ecology, militarism, and transnational feminist organizing have appeared in various anthologies and journals including *Asia-Pacific Journal, Berkeley Women's Law Journal, Foreign Policy in Focus, Frontiers, Peace Review,* and *Social Justice*. She writes for popular audiences through activist publications and op ed pieces. As an editor, Dr. Kirk has contributed to materials published by Asian Communities for Reproductive Justice, California Wellness Foundation, Dasi Hammke Center, and Women's Center for Legal Aid and Counseling. She is a founding member of the International Women's Network Against Militarism, started in 1997 by academics and activists concerned about the negative effects of U.S. military operations on local communities. She co-directed the 2011 documentary, *Living Along the Fenceline*, featuring seven women in this network. Other major publications include *Greenham Women Everywhere: Dreams, Ideas, and Actions from the Women's Peace Movement* (1983) co-authored with Alice Cook, and *Urban Planning in a Capitalist Society* (1980). Gwyn Kirk holds a PhD in political sociology from the London School of Economics.

Margo Okazawa-Rey (left) is a professor in the School of Human and Organizational Development at Fielding Graduate University and Professor Emerita at San Francisco State University. She was Barbara Lee Chair in Women's Leadership and Visiting Professor of Ethnic Studies at Mills College (2010–2011), and Feminist Activist Scholar in Residence at Scripps College (Fall 2006). Professor Okazawa-Rey's current work focuses on teaching feminist activist research methodology to African women activists in postconflict and highly militarized zones. She is on the editorial boards of *Social Justice* and *Feminist Africa* and has published in *Affilia, Asian Journal of Women's Studies, Feminist Review,* and *Peace Studies*. In the 1970s, she was a member of the Combahee River Collective, a Black feminist group that developed the theory of intersectionality as a basis for feminist praxis. She is a cofounder of the International Women's Network Against Militarism, a transnational project that generates feminist analyses and resistance to militarism and militarization. She is on the board of Peace Women Across the Globe, which grew out of the international campaign that nominated 1,000 women collectively for the Nobel Peace Prize 2005. She has been Feminist Research Consultant at the Women's Centre for Legal Aid and Counseling in Palestine since 2005. Margo Okazawa-Rey received her doctorate from the Harvard Graduate School of Education in 1987.